PLUNKETT'S E-COMMERCE & INTERNET BUSINESS ALMANAC

The only complete guide to the E-Commerce & Internet Industry

Jack W. Plunkett

Published by:
Plunkett Research, Ltd.
Houston, Texas
www.plunkettresearch.com

3 9902 00051 2360

Copyright © 2000 by Plunkett Research, Ltd.
All rights reserved. No part of this book may be reproduced or transmitted in any form by any means, electronic or mechanical, including by photocopying or by any information storage or retrieval system, without the written permission of the publisher.

Published by:

Plunkett Research, Ltd.
P. O. Drawer 541737
Houston, Texas 77254-1737

Phone: 713.932.0000
Fax: 713.932.7080
Internet: www.plunkettresearch.com

ISBN # 1-891775-11-1

Disclaimer of liability for use and results of use:

The editors and publishers assume no responsibility for your own success making an investment or business decision, in seeking or keeping any job, in succeeding at any firm, or in obtaining any amount or type of benefits or wages. Your own results and the job stability or financial stability of any company depend on influences outside of our control. All risks are assumed by the reader. Investigate any potential employer or business relation carefully, and carefully verify past and present finances, present business conditions and the level of compensation and benefits currently paid. Each company's details are taken from sources deemed reliable; however, their accuracy is not guaranteed. The editors and publishers assume no liability, beyond the actual payment received from a reader, for any direct, indirect, incidental or consequential, special or exemplary damages, and they do not guarantee, warrant, nor make any representation regarding the use of this material. Trademarks or tradenames are used without symbols and only in a descriptive sense to the benefit of their owners, with no intention of infringement. Ratings are presented as an introductory and general glance at corporations based on our research and our knowledge of businesses and the industries in which they operate. The reader should use caution.

PLUNKETT'S E-COMMERCE & INTERNET BUSINESS ALMANAC

Editor and Publisher:
Jack W. Plunkett

Contributing Senior Writer:
Joan Hiller
Senior Editors and Researchers:
Crystal Jackson
Macy McBeth
Emma Tsai
Editors, Researchers and Assistants:
Lam Hoang
Mclissa A. Ibanez
Melanie E. Fox Kean
Melissa Lonchambon
Robert Lopes
Nik A. Meurer
Neeran Pathak
Tonya Steckbeck
Suzanne Zarosky

Database Consultant:
Martha M. Burgher
Senior Customer Support Manager:
Nancy Brown
Customer Support Specialist:
Bronwyn Bowser
CD-ROM Programming and Design:
Shyh-Huei (Sherri) Jang
Cover Design:
Kim Paxson, Just Graphics
Boerne, TX

Special Thanks to:
U.S. Department of Commerce
Economics & Statistics Administration
eMARKETER
www.emarketer.com
Georgia Institute of Technology
Graphics, Visualization & Usability Center
www.cc.gatech.edu

Plunkett Research, Ltd.
P. O. Drawer 541737, Houston, Texas 77254
Phone: 713.932.0000 Fax: 713.932.7080
www.plunkettresearch.com

PLUNKETT'S
E-COMMERCE & INTERNET
BUSINESS
ALMANAC

CONTENTS

List of Major Tables

A Short E-Commerce & Internet Business Glossary

Access Network: The network that connects a user's telephone equipment to the telephone exchange.

Active Server Pages: This term refers to a specification for a web page with an ASP extension containing Java Script or Visual Basic code. (See "ASP" and "JAVA" below.)

Active X: Active X is a set of technologies developed by Microsoft Corporation for sharing information across different applications.

ADN: Stands for "Advanced Digital Network."

ADSL (Asymmetrical Digital Subscriber Line): High-speed technology that enables the transfer of data over existing copper phone lines, allowing more bandwidth downstream than upstream.

Analog IC: A semiconductor that processes a continuous wave of electrical signals based on real-world analog quantities such as speed, pressure, temperature, light, sound and voltage.

Applets: Small applications that Net browsers may download from the Internet on an as-needed basis. These may be software, accessories (such as spell checkers or calculators), information-packed databases or other items. Applets are object-based. (See "Object Technology" below.)

Appliance: See "Internet Appliance" below.

Archie: This software tool can be used to find files stored on anonymous FTP sites, as long as the user knows the file name or a substring of the file name that is being searched for. (See "FTP" below.)

ARPANet: This term, standing for "Advanced Research Projects Agency Network," was developed during the latter part of the 1960's by the United States Department of Defense and was the forefather of the Internet.

ASCII: An acronym meaning "American Standard Code for Information Exchange." 128 standard ASCII codes exist that represent all Latin letters, numbers and punctuation. Each ASCII code is represented by a seven-digit binary number, such as 0000000 or 0000111. This code is accepted as a standard throughout the world.

ASP: "Application Service Provider." A web site that enables utilization of software and databases that reside permanently on the web site rather than downloading them to the user's computer. Advantages include the fact that multiple remote users may access the same tools over the Internet, and the fact that the ASP provider is responsible for developing and maintaining the software.

Asynchronous Transfer Mode (ATM): A digital switching and transmission technology based on high speed. ATM allows voice, video and data signals to be sent over a single telephone line at speeds from 25 <u>million</u> to 1 <u>billion</u> bits per second (bps). This digital ATM speed is an immense advantage over the slow speeds of traditional analog phone lines, which allow no more than 2 million bps. (See "Broadband" below.)

B to B: See "Business-to-Business" below.

Bandwidth: The data transmission capacity of a network.

Baud: Refers to how many times the carrier signal in a modem switches value per second, or how many bits a modem can send and receive in a second.

BBS (Bulletin Board System): A BBS is a computer-accessible system that enables people to upload and download files, discuss issues and make announcements without actually being connected to other computers at concurrent times. Several million of such systems exist.

Beams: The coverage and geographic service area offered by a satellite transponder. A global beam effectively covers one-third of the earth's surface. A spot beam provides a very specific high-powered downlink pattern that is limited to a particular geographical area to which it may be steered or pointed.

Binhex: This is a means of changing non-ASCII (or non-text) files into text/ASCII files so that they can be used, for example, as Internet e-mail.

Bit: This is a single digit number, either a one or a zero, that is the smallest unit of computerized data.

Bookmark: Nearly all browsers support this feature. Users can bookmark a site by saving its URL for future retrieval.

BPS: An acronym for "bits per second." This is an indicator of the speed of data movement.

Bridge (networking): A device that links two local area networks together so they can share files and e-mail.

Broadband: This is the high-speed transmission range for telecommunications and computer data. Broadband means any transmission at 2 million bps (bits per second) or higher (higher than analog speed). A broadband network is so sophisticated and so fast that it can carry voice, video and data all at the same time.

Browse: A term referring to the viewing of computerized data. Several Internet browsers support a browse mode that allows users to sort through data quickly. (See "Browser" below.)

Browser: A program that allows a user to read (on the Internet) text or graphics and to navigate from one page to another. The most popular browsers are Microsoft Internet Explorer and Netscape Navigator.

Business-to-Business: A rapidly growing category of Internet sites aimed at selling products, services or data to commercial customers rather than consumers. The opposite of "Business-to-Consumer."

Byte: There are eight bits in a byte, and this set then stands for a single character.

CAD: An acronym for "computer-aided design." CAD software generally runs on workstations and is a tool used to provide three-dimensional, on-screen design for everything from buildings to automobiles to clothing. (See "CAM" and "CAE" below.)

CAE: An acronym for "computer-aided engineering."

CAM: An acronym for "computer-aided manufacturing."

Call Automation: Call automation is part of the telephone equipment revolution, which includes voice mail, automated sending and receiving of faxes and the ability for customers to place orders and gather information by using a touch-tone telephone to access sophisticated databases. (See "Voice Mail" below.)

Cell: Geographic unit of a wireless phone system, from whence came the term "cellular." Regions are divided into small cells, each equipped with a low-powered radio transmitter. When a mobile phone moves from one cell to another, phone calls are handed off.

CGI: Stands for "Common Gateway Interface." This is a set of guidelines that determines the manner in which a web server receives and sends information to and from software on the same machine.

CGI-BIN: This is a frequently used name of a directory on a web server where CGI programs exist.

Client/Server (networking): A way of running a large computer setup. The "Server" is a host computer that acts as the central holding ground for files, databases and application software. The "Clients" are all of the PCs connected to the network that share data with the Server. This is a vast change from the networks of the past that were connected to expensive, complicated "mainframe" computers.

Coaxial cable: A type of cable widely used to transmit telephone and broadcast traffic. The distinguishing feature is an inner strand of wires carrying a signal surrounded by an insulator that in turn is surrounded by another conductor that serves as the ground.

Co-location: Refers to having a server belonging to one group that is physically located on a network belonging to another group. Co-location is usually practiced for security reasons.

Compression: A technology in which a communications signal is squeezed so that it uses less bandwidth (or capacity) than it normally would. This saves storage space and shortens transfer time. The original data is decompressed when read back into memory.

Cookie: A piece of information sent to a web browser from a web server that the browser software saves and then sends back to the server upon request. Cookies are used by web site operators to track the actions of users returning to the site.

Cyber: This term is commonly used as a prefix to things and ideas that are being made more prevalent in society through the spread of computers and technology.

Cyberspace: This term refers to the entire realm of information available through computer networks.

Datanets: Datanets are generally private networks of land-based telephone lines, satellites or wireless networks that allow corporate users to send data at high speeds to remote locations while bypassing the speed and cost constraints of traditional telephone lines.

Dial-Up Access: This term refers to the connection of a computer or other device to a network through a modem and a public telephone network. The only difference between dial-up access and a telephone connection is that computers are at each end of the connection rather than people. Dial-up access is slower than DSL, ISDN and other advanced connections.

Digital: Transmission of a signal reducing all of its information to ones and zeros and then regrouping them at the reception end. Digital transmission vastly improves the carrying capacity of the spectrum while reducing noise and distortion of the transmission.

Digital Local Telephone Switch: A computer that interprets signals (dialed numbers) from a telephone caller and routes calls to their proper destinations. A digital switch also provides a variety of calling features not available in older analog switches, such as call waiting.

Digital Signal Processor: Chip that converts analog signals such as sound and light into digital signals.

Digital Subscriber Line (DSL): A set of technologies that increases the rate at which information can be delivered across a copper subscriber line. This provides much faster Internet access.

Disaster Recovery: A set of rules and procedures that allow a computer site to be put back in operation after a disaster has occurred. The concept of moving backups off-site constitutes the minimum basic precaution for disaster recovery. The remote copy is used to recover data when the local storage is inaccessible after a disaster.

Discrete Semiconductor: Chip with one diode or transistor.

Disk Mirroring: A data redundancy technique in which data is recorded identically on multiple separate disk drives at the same time. When the primary disk is off-line, the alternate takes over, providing continuous access to data. Disk Mirroring is sometimes referred to as "RAID."

Domain: A domain is a "domain name" that has server records associated with it.

Domain Name: This name identifies an individual site on the Internet and is always comprised of at least two parts, separated by dots, such as IBM.com.

Domain (Top-Level): Either an ISO country code or a common domain name such as .com, .org or .net.

DS-1: A digital transmission format that transmits and receives information at a rate of 1,544,000 bits every second.

DSL: See "Digital Subscriber Line" above.

Duplicate Host: A duplicate host is a single host name that maps to duplicate IP addresses.

Dynamic HTML: This term refers to web content that changes with each individual viewing. The same site, for example, could appear different to the viewer depending on conditions such as the geographic location of the reader, the time of day, previous pages viewed by the reader and the user's profile.

Electronic Data Interchange (EDI): This is an accepted standard format for the exchange of data between various companies' networks. EDI allows for the transfer of e-mail as well as orders, invoices and other files from one company to another.

Electronic Funds Transfer (EFT): A method of moving money from one account to another via computer. Withdrawing funds from your account using an automatic teller machine (ATM) is a good example. Likewise, paying bills using Quicken software from your PC is an electronic funds transfer.

E-Mail: E-mail is the use of software that allows the posting of messages (text, audio or video) over a network. E-mail may be used on a LAN, a WAN or on the Internet. It also may be used via on-line services such as America Online. E-mail can be used to send a message to a single recipient or may be broadcast to a large group of people at once.

Ethernet (networking): This is the standard format on which local area network equipment works. Abiding by Ethernet standards allows equipment from various manufacturers to work together.

Extensible Markup Language: See "XML."

Extranet: A computer network that is accessible in part to authorized outside persons instead of operating like an Intranet, which uses a firewall to limit accessibility.

FAQ: An acronym for "frequently asked questions," this kind of document answers inquiries about a given topic. Generally, FAQs come in the form of a help file or as a hypertext document.

Fiber Distributed Data Interface (FDDI): This is a standard for data transmission on optical-fiber cables. This type of connection is faster than both Ethernet and T-3 connections.

Fiber-optics: Fiber-optic is a type of telephone cable made from glass that can handle vast amounts of voice, data and video at once by carrying them along on beams of light.

Firewall: Hardware and software that keep unauthorized users from accessing a network.

Frame Relay: This is an accepted standard for sending large amounts of data over phone lines and private datanets. Frame Relay refers to the fact that data is broken down into standard size "frames" prior to transmission.

Frequency Band: A term for designating a range of frequencies in the electromagnetic spectrum.

FTP (File Transfer Protocol): This is a widely used method of transferring data and files between two Internet sites.

Fuzzy Logic: Used in artificial intelligence, fuzzy logic recognizes that statements are not only just "true" or "false"–but also "more or less certain" or "very unlikely."

Gateway: A device connecting two or more networks that may use different protocols and media. Gateways translate between the different networks and can connect locally or over wide area networks.

Gigabyte: This is a group of bytes and is generally defined as either 1,000 or 1,024 megabytes.

Gopher: A way of making menus of material available over the Internet. This is a client-and-server form of program, meaning that the user must have a gopher client program in order to utilize it.

Graphic Interchange Format (GIF): A widely used format for image files.

Groupware: This is an emerging type of software that is gaining immense popularity. Groupware enables various people on a network to contribute to one document at the same time, sharing ideas, molding the final product and monitoring its progress along the way. It's a new way of group "thinking" without physical meetings. Lotus Notes pioneered this market.

Hertz: A measure of frequency equal to one cycle per second. Most radio signals operate in ranges of megahertz or gigahertz.

Hit: A single request from a web browser for something from a web server; i.e. a request for text or graphics.

Home Page: This term refers to the main page of a web site. Usually, the home page features links to other pages within the site.

Host: A host computer is any machine on a network that is responsible for services received by other machines on that network.

Host Name (or Firstname): The first portion of a host's domain name.

HotJava: This set of products, developed by Sun Microsystems, utilizes Java technology. A set of libraries intended for building applications and a Java-enabled web browser are among existing HotJava products.

HTML (Hypertext Markup Language): A language for coding text for viewing on the World Wide Web. It is unique because it enables the use of hyperlinks from one site to another. Such hyperlinks create a web, the World Wide Web.

HTTP (Hypertext Transfer Protocol): The protocol used most frequently on the World Wide Web to move hypertext files between clients and servers on the Internet.

Hub (networking): A centralized switch box, or a common connection point, for devices in a network. Hubs contain multiple ports which can intertransmit information in order to maximize the viewing of data. Several types of hubs exist, such as passive hubs (data conduits), intelligent or manageable hubs (hubs with additional traffic-monitoring features) and switching hubs. Switching hubs read the destination address of each packet of information and then forwards the packet to the correct location.

Hub (Internet): A comprehensive Internet site dedicated to one category of user or one niche of interest.

Hyperlink: A hyperlink is an element in an electronic document that links to another document or to another place in the same document. Generally, the user clicks on the hyperlink in order to follow it.

ICANN: The Internet Corporation for Assigned Names and Numbers. It acts as the central coordinator for the Internet's technical operations.

Information Superhighway: This common term refers to the Internet, bulletin board services, on-line services and other types of connective, telecommunication-like services.

Infrastructure: The telecommunications infrastructure is comprised of all of the cable and equipment installed in the worldwide telecommunications market. Most of today's telecommunications infrastructure is connected by copper and fiber optic cable, which represents a huge capital investment that telephone companies would like to continue to utilize in as many ways as possible.

Integrated Circuit (IC): Another name for a semiconductor, an IC is a piece of silicon on which thousands (or millions) of transistors have been combined.

Integrated Services Digital Networks (ISDN): Advanced telecommunications services offered at higher speeds over standard copper phone lines. While slower than fiber-optic cable, ISDN is a big step up from traditional copper wire speeds.

Interexchange Carrier (IXC or IEC): Any company providing long distance phone service between LECs and LATAs. (See "LEC" and "LATAs" below.)

Internet: The Internet (the "Net") is a global computer network that provides a unique (and currently cost-free) way for millions of users to access each other by e-mail. Additionally, users may access thousands of databases at sites that are open to the Internet. Access is generally through HTML-enabled sites on the World Wide Web.

Internet Appliance: A non-PC device that connects users to the Internet for specific or general purposes. A good example is a cellular mobile telephone with a small screen and Internet capabilities.

Internet Telephony: This category of hardware and software enables users to utilize the Internet to make telephone calls.

InterNIC: This collaboration between AT&T and Network Solutions, Inc. offers directory and database services, registration services, support services and net scout services to the public. Through InterNIC, one can gain access to white pages, domain name and IP address management services, education and information services and Internet-related publications.

Intranet: A network protected by a firewall for sharing data and e-mail within an organization or company. Usually Intranets are used by organizations for internal communication.

IP Number/IP Address: "IP" stands for "Internet Protocol," a number or address with four parts that are separated by dots. Each machine on the Internet has its own IP number, which serves as an identifier.

ISDN: See "Integrated Services Digital Networks" above.

ISO 9001: Standards set by the International Organization for Standardization for quality procedures. ISO 9001 is the quality certification for manufacturing.

ISP (Internet Service Provider): A company that sells access to the Internet to individual subscribers.

ITU-T (International Telecommunications Union for Telephony): The international body responsible for telephone and computer communications standards describing interface techniques and practices. These standards include those that define how a nation's telephone and data systems connect to the worldwide communications network.

Java: A programming language developed by Sun Microsystems that spices up World Wide Web pages on the Internet with interactive graphics. Java can be read by people using any type of computer or operating system. Netscape Communications (a hot developer of Internet software) and other leading firms have licensed Java for use in new browsing tools.

JPEG: A JPEG, or "Joint Photographic Experts Group," is a widely used format for image files.

Kilobyte: This is a measure for 1,000 or 1,024 bytes.

Leased Line: This kind of connection is a phone line that is rented for use for continuous, long-term data connections.

LINUX: An open, free operating system that is shared readily with millions of users worldwide. These users continuously improve and add to the software's code. It can be used to operate computer networks and Internet appliances as well as PCs.

Local Access and Transport Areas (LATAs): Operational service areas established after the breakup of AT&T to distinguish local from long-distance service. The U.S.A. is divided into 161 LATAs.

Local Area Network (LAN): This is a computer network that is generally within one office or one building. The LAN can be very inexpensive and efficient to set up when small numbers of computers are involved. It may require a network administrator and a serious investment if hundreds of computers are hooked up to the LAN. A LAN enables all computers within the office to share files and printers, to access common databases and to send e-mail to others on the network.

Local Exchange Carrier (LEC): Any local telephone company, i.e., a carrier that provides ordinary phone service under regulation within a service area.

Megabytes: A measure of one million bytes, or 1,024 kilobytes.

Microprocessor (aka Central Processing Unit or CPU): Computer on a digital semiconductor chip. It performs math and logic operations and executes instructions from memory.

MIME: This term, short for "Multipurpose Internet Mail Extentions," is a widely used method for attaching non-text files to e-mails.

Modem: This device allows a computer to be connected to a phone line, which in turn enables the computer to receive and exchange data with other machines.

Network: A network is created when two or more computers are connected.

Network Numbers: The first portion of an IP address that identifies the network on which hosts in the rest of the address are connected.

Node: Any single computer connected to a network.

Object Technology: By merging data and software into "objects," a programming system becomes "object-oriented." For example, an object called "weekly inventory sold" would have the data and programming needed to construct a flow chart. Some new programming systems–including Java–contain this feature. Object Technology is also feature in many Microsoft products. (See "Java" above.)

On-Line: When a device is on-line, it is turned on and connected, whether to the Internet or to another device. When printers are ready to receive data from a computer, they are considered on-line.

OS (Operating System): This is the software that allows applications like word processors or web browsers to run on a computer. For example, Windows 2000 is an operating system.

Packet Switching: This is a higher-speed way to move data through a network. Files are broken down into smaller "packets" that are reassembled electronically after transmission.

PBX: A PBX is a central telephone system within one large business office used to route incoming and outgoing calls to various employees and onto long-distance networks. PBX functions are being revolutionized by the application of computer functions, such as voice mail. (See "Voice Mail" below.)

PC: "PC" stands for personal computer, an affordable, efficient computer meant to be used by one person and frequently connected to a network as a "client."

Perl: An acronym for "practical extraction and report language," this programming language is geared towards text processing and was developed by Larry Wall.

Personal Communication Service (PCS): This is a new type of cellular mobile phone service that works on shorter range.

Plug-in: Any small piece of software that adds extra functions to a larger piece of software.

POP: This term is an acronym for both "Point of Presence" and "Post Office Protocol." Point of presence refers to a location that a network can be connected to, while post office protocol refers to the way in which e-mail software obtains mail from a mail server.

Port: An interface (connector) between the computer and the outside world. The number of ports on a communications controller or front-end processor determines the number of communications channels that can be connected to it. The number of ports on a computer determines the number of peripheral devices that can be attached to it.

Portal: Refers to a comprehensive web site that is designed to be the first site seen when a computer logs on to the web. Portal sites often have links to e-mail usage, a search engine or other features. Yahoo! and MSN.com are portals. Portals are aimed at broad audiences with common interests. (Also see "Hub.")

PPP: This term, short for "Point to Point Protocol," refers to protocol that enables a computer to use the combination of a standard telephone line and modem to make TCP/IP connections.

PTSN: A term meaning "Public Switched Telephone Network" that represents the traditional telephone system.

Protocol: A set of rules for communicating between computers. The use of standard protocols allows products from different vendors to communicate on a common network.

RAM (Random Access Memory): Computer memory used to temporarily hold programs and data.

Real Time: A real-time system or software is one specially designed to acquire, process, store and display large amounts of rapidly changing information almost instantaneously with microsecond responses as changes occur.

Router (networking): This is an electronic link that enables two different local area networks to talk to each other, even though each network may be based on a different standard.

Scalable: A scalable network is one that can grow and adapt as customer needs increase and change. Scalable networks can easily manage increasing numbers of workstations, servers, user workloads and added functionality.

SCSI (Small Computer System Interface): A dominant, international standard interface used by UNIX servers and many desktop computers to connect to storage devices; a physical connection between devices.

Semiconductor: Generic term for a device that controls electronic signals. It specifically refers to a material (such as silicon, germanium, or gallium arsenide) that can be altered to either conduct electrical current or block its passage.

Server: A computer that performs and manages specific duties for a network.

Shareware: Software that is available for users to download for free from the Internet, usually with the expectation that they will register or pay for the software if they continue to use it. Many shareware programs are set to expire after a period of time.

SLIP: This term, short for "Serial Line Internet Protocol," refers to the connection of a traditional telephone line, or serial line, and modem to connect a computer to an Internet site.

SMDS: Acronym for "Switched Multimegabit Data Service," which is a method of extremely high-speed transference of data.

SMTP: Short for "Simple Mail Transfer Protocol," or the primary form of protocol used in transference of e-mail.

SNMP: Short for "Simple Network Management Protocol," or a set of communication standards for use between computers connected to TCP/IP networks.

SONET (Synchronous Optical Network Technology): This is a mode of high-speed transmission meant to take full advantage of the wide bandwidth in fiber optic cables.

Spam: A term used to refer to generally unwanted, generally solicitous, bulk-sent e-mail.

SRDF (Symmetrix Remote Data Facility): A high-performance, host-independent business solution that enables users to maintain a duplicate copy of all or some of their data at a remote site.

Switch (networking): A network device that directs packets of data between multiple ports, often filtering the data so that it travels more quickly.

T1: This is a standard for digital transmission over phone lines. Generally, it can transmit at least 24 voice channels at once over copper wires–at a reasonably high speed of 1.5 million bps.

T3: This type of transmission over phone lines supports data rates of 43 Mbps. T3 lines consist of 672 channels, and such lines are generally used by Internet service providers. These lines are also referred to as DS3 lines.

Telnet: The Telnet program, which is a terminal emulation program for TCP/IP networks like the Internet, runs on a computer and connects to a particular network. Directions entered on a computer that is connected using Telnet will be read and followed just as if they had been entered on the server itself. Through Telnet, users are able to control a server and communicate with other servers on the same network at the same time. Telnet is commonly used to remotely control web servers.

Time Division Multiple Access (TDMA): A digital service for relatively large users of international public-switched telephony, data, facsimile and telex. TDMA also refers to a method of multiplexing digital signals that combines a number of signals passing through a common point by transmitting them sequentially, with each signal sent in bursts at different times.

Transistor: Device used for amplification or switching of electrical current.

UNIX: A multi-user, multitasking operating system that runs on a wide variety of computer systems from PCs to mainframes.

URL (Uniform Resource Locator): The "address" that allows an Internet browser to locate a homepage or web site. For example: *http:\\www.aol.com* is the URL for America Online.

Very Small Aperture Terminal (VSAT): A small Earth station terminal, generally 0.6-2.4 meters in size, that is often portable and primarily designed to handle data transmission and private-line voice and video communications.

Voice Mail: Voice mail is a sophisticated electronic telephone answering service that utilizes a computer. Voice mail enables users to receive faxes and phone messages and to access those messages from remote sites.

Webcasting: Webcasting is the act of using the Internet (the World Wide Web, usually) to broadcast information or entertainment.

Webmaster: This term refers to any individual who runs a web site. Webmasters generally perform maintenance and upkeep.

Web Page: This term refers to a document on the World Wide Web that is identified by a URL.

Web Site: This term refers to a specific domain name location on the World Wide Web. Each site, which contains a home page, usually consists of additional documents.

Wide Area Network (WAN): This is a regional or global network that provides links between all local area networks within a company. For example, Ford Motor Company might use a WAN to enable its factory in Detroit to talk to its sales offices in New York and Chicago, its plants in England and its buying offices in Taiwan. A WAN refers to the primary, globe-spanning networks linked together for one organization.

Workstation: Simply put, a workstation is a high-powered desktop computer, usually used by engineers.

World Wide Web: The "Web." This is a computer system that provides enhanced access to various sites on the Internet through the use of hyperlinks. Click your mouse on a link that is displayed in one document and it will take you to another, related document.

XML (Extensible Markup Language): This programming language enables designers to add extra functionality to documents that could not otherwise be utilized with standard HTML coding. XML was developed by the World Wide Web Consortium. It can communicate, to various software programs, the actual meanings contained in HTML documents. For example, it can enable the gathering and use of information from a large number of databases at once, and place that information into one web site window.

INTRODUCTION

PLUNKETT'S E-COMMERCE & INTERNET BUSINESS ALMANAC is the first edition of our guide to the exploding Internet & World Wide Web business, designed to be used as a general source for researchers of all types.

The data and areas of interest covered are intentionally broad, ranging from the various aspects of the Internet & World Wide Web industry, to emerging technology, to an in-depth look at the major for-profit firms within the many industries that make up the Internet and the World Wide Web.

Because of the exploding nature of the Internet industry, we were obviously not capable of including every Internet firm or supplier. Nonetheless, we did accomplish a significant and unique feat with this book: we identified, researched and profiled over 330 major companies that were operating at significant levels of revenues and services provided, as of the end of the third quarter of 1999. In addition, we were able to provide full 1998 and 1999 financial results for most of the firms (see Chapter 6 for more details).

In addition, this book presents a general overview of the Internet & World Wide Web business (see "How To Use This Book"). For example, the soaring use of Internet sites to boost business, deal in e-commerce and publish data of all types is covered in exacting detail, along with easy-to-use tables on all facets of the Internet & World Wide Web in general.

THE E-COMMERCE & INTERNET 300 is our unique grouping of the biggest, most successful corporations in all segments of the E-Commerce & Internet Business. Tens of thousands of pieces of information, gathered from a wide variety of sources, have been researched and are presented in a unique form that can be easily understood. This section includes thorough indexes to THE E-COMMERCE & INTERNET 300, by geography, industry, brand names, subsidiary names and other topics.

Especially helpful is the way in which PLUNKETT'S E-COMMERCE & INTERNET BUSINESS ALMANAC readily enables readers who have no business background to compare the financial records and growth plans of large Internet & World Wide Web companies and major industry groups. You will see the mid-term financial record of each firm along with the impact of earnings, sales and strategic plans on each company's potential to fuel growth, to create new technologies and to provide investment and employment opportunities.

No other source provides this book's easy-to-understand comparisons of growth, expenditures, technologies, corporations, research and many other items of great importance to people of all types who may be studying the Internet & the World Wide Web, undoubtedly the most exciting and fastest-growing industry in the world today.

By scanning the data groups and the unique indexes, you can find the best information to fit your personal research needs. The best, major growth companies in the E-Commerce & Internet Business are ranked and described, using different groups of specific criteria.

In addition to individual company profiles, an overview of technology and its trends is provided. This book's job is to help you sort through easy-to-understand summaries of today's Internet & World Wide Web products, services and trends in a quick and effective manner.

Whatever your purpose for researching E-Commerce and the Internet business, you will find this book to be a valuable guide. Nonetheless, as is true with all resources, this volume has limitations that the reader should be aware of:

- Financial data and other corporate information can change quickly. A book of this type can be no more current than the data that was available as of the time of editing. Consequently, the financial picture, management and ownership of the firm(s) you are studying may have changed since the date of this book. For example, this almanac includes the most up-to-date sales figures and profits available to the editors as of early 2000. That means that we have typically used financial data for fiscal year 1999.

- Corporate mergers and acquisitions are occurring at a very rapid rate. Such events may have created significant change, subsequent to the publishing of this book, within a company you are studying.

- Some of the companies profiled are so large in scope and in variety of business endeavors conducted within a parent organization that we have been unable to completely list all subsidiaries, affiliations, divisions and activities within a firm's corporate structure.

- This volume is intended to be a general guide. That means that researchers should look to this book for an overview and, when conducting in-depth research, should contact the specific corporations or industry associations in question for the very latest changes and data. Where possible, we have listed contact names, toll-free telephone numbers and World Wide Web site addresses for the companies, government agencies and industry associations involved so that the reader may get further details without unnecessary delay.

- We have used exhaustive efforts to locate and fairly present accurate and complete data. However, when using this book or any other source for business and industry information, the reader should use caution and due diligence by conducting further research where it seems appropriate. We wish you success in your endeavors, and we trust that your experience with this book will be both satisfactory and productive.

Jack W. Plunkett
Houston, Texas
February 2000

HOW TO USE THIS BOOK

The two primary sections of this book are devoted first to the E-Commerce & Internet industry as a whole and then to the "Individual Data Listings" for THE E-COMMERCE & INTERNET 300. If time permits, you should begin your research in the front chapters of this book. Also, you will find lengthy indexes in Chapter 6 and in the back of the book.

THE E-COMMERCE & INTERNET BUSINESS

Glossary: A short list of E-Commerce & Internet Industry terms.

Chapter 1: On-Line Retailing (Business-to-Consumer)

Chapter 2: Business-to-Business

Chapter 3: On-Line Financial Services

Chapter 4: Trends in Personal Computers, Internet Access and Internet Domains

Chapter 5: E-Commerce & Internet Business Contacts -- Addresses, Telephone Numbers and World Wide Web Sites. This chapter covers contacts for important government agencies, E-Commerce & Internet organizations and trade groups.

THE E-COMMERCE & INTERNET 300

Chapter 6: The E-Commerce & Internet 300: Who They Are and How They Were Chosen. The companies compared in this book were carefully selected from all E-Commerce & Internet industries on a nationwide basis. (The actual count is 333 companies.) For a complete description, see Chapter 6: THE E-COMMERCE & INTERNET 300.

Individual Data Listings --
Look at one of the companies in The E-Commerce & Internet 300's Individual Data Listings. You'll find the following information fields:

Company Name:
The company profiles are in alphabetical order by company name. If you don't find the company you are seeking, it may be a subsidiary or division of one of the firms covered in this book. Try looking it up in the Index by Store Names, Subsidiaries, Brand Names and Selected Affiliations in the back of the book.

Ranks:
Industry Group Code: A unique code used within this book in order to group companies within like segments. (See Chapter 6 for a list of codes.)

Ranks Within This Company's Industry Group: Ranks, within this firm's segment only, for annual sales and annual profits.

Business Activities:

A grid divided into six categories. A complete index by industry is in Chapter 6.

Types of Business:

A listing of descriptions of the types of business specialties conducted by the firm.

Brands/Divisions/Affiliations:

Major brand names, operating divisions or subsidiaries of the firm, as well as major corporate affiliations, such as another firm that owns a significant portion of the stock. A complete Index of Subsidiaries, Brand Names and Selected Affiliations is in the back of the book.

Contacts:

The names and titles of top officers of the company are listed.

Address:

The firm's full headquarters address, the headquarters telephone, plus toll-free and fax numbers where available. (Also provided are World Wide Web site addresses at the top of the page.)

Financials:

Annual Sales (1999 or the latest fiscal year available to the editors, plus up to four previous years): These are stated in thousands of dollars; add three zeros for the full number. This figure represents consolidated worldwide sales from all operations. 1999 figures may be estimates. (Also, you may want to see the Rankings Within Industry Table in Chapter 6.)

Annual Profits (1999 or the latest fiscal year available to the editors, plus up to four previous years): These are stated in thousands of dollars; add three zeros for the full number. This figure represents consolidated, after-tax net profit from all operations, generally before non-recurring items. 1999 figures may be estimates.

Total Number of Employees: The approximate total number of employees, worldwide, as of the end of 1999 (or the latest data available to the editors).

Apparent Salaries/Benefits:

Due to wide variations in the manner in which corporations report benefits to the U.S. Government's regulatory bodies, not all plans will have been uncovered during our effort to research this data. Also, the availability of such plans to employees will vary according to the qualifications that employees must meet to become eligible. For example, some benefit plans may be available only to salaried workers, while others are only for employees who work more than 1,000 hours yearly. Benefits that are available to employees of the main or parent company may not be available to employees of subsidiaries.

A "Y" in appropriate fields indicates "Yes."

NOTE: Generally, employees covered by wealth-building benefit plans do not fully own ("vest in") funds contributed on their behalf by the employer until five years of service with that employer have passed.

Pension Plan: The firm offers a pension plan to qualified employees. The type and generosity of these plans varies widely from firm to firm.

ESOP Stock Plan (Employees' Stock Ownership Plan): This plan is gaining in popularity. Typically, the plan borrows money from a bank and uses those funds to purchase a large block of the corporation's stock. The corporation makes contributions to the plan over a period of time, and the stock purchase loan is eventually paid off. The value of the plan grows significantly as long as the market price of the stock holds up. Qualified employees are allocated a share of the plan based on their length of service and their level of salary.

Savings Plan, 401(k): Under this type of plan, employees make a tax-deferred deposit into an account. In the best plans, the company makes annual matching donations to the employees' accounts, typically in some proportion to deposits made by the employees themselves. A good plan will match one-half of employee deposits of up to 6% of wages. In other words, an employee earning $30,000 yearly might deposit $1,800 (6%) into the plan. The company might match one-half of the employee's deposit, or $900. The plan grows on a tax-deferred basis, similar to an IRA. A very generous plan will match 100% of employee deposits. However, some plans do not call for the employer to make a matching deposit at all. Actual terms of these plans vary widely from firm to firm. Generally, these savings plans will allow employees to deposit as much as 15% of salary into the plan on a tax-deferred basis. However, the portion that the company uses to calculate its matching deposit is limited to a maximum of 6% of salary.

Stock Purchase Plan: Qualified employees may purchase the company's common stock at a price below its market value under a specific plan. Typically, the employee is limited to investing a small percentage of wages in this plan. These plans usually offer a 15% discount, but the discount may range from 5% to 15%.

Profit Sharing: Qualified employees are awarded an annual amount equal to some portion of a company's profits. In a very generous plan, the pool of money awarded to employees would be 15% of profits. Typically, this money is deposited into a long-term retirement account.

Highest Executive Salary: The highest executive salary paid, typically a 1998 amount (or the latest year available to the editors) and typically paid to the Chief Executive Officer.

Highest Executive Bonus: The apparent bonus, if any, paid to the above person.

Second Highest Executive Salary: The next-highest executive salary paid, typically a 1998 amount (or the latest year available to the editors) and typically paid to the President or Chief Operating Officer.

Second Highest Executive Bonus: The apparent bonus, if any, paid to the above person.

Competitive Advantage:

A brief statement regarding an outstanding feature that gives the firm an edge in the marketplace.

Other Thoughts:

A "Y" in appropriate fields indicates "Yes."

Stock Ticker: When available, the unique stock market symbol used to identify a firm's common stock for trading and tracking purposes.

Apparent Women Officers or Directors: It's difficult to obtain this information on an exact basis, and employers are not required to disclose the data in a public way. (Equal Employment Opportunity Commission records are not entirely subject to the Freedom of Information Act.) However, we have indicated what our best efforts reveal to be the apparent number of women who are either in the posts of corporate officers or who sit on the board of directors. There is a wide variance from company to company.

Apparent Minority Officers or Directors: As noted above, it's difficult to obtain this information on an exact basis, and employers are not required to disclose the data in a public way. However, we have indicated what our best efforts reveal to be the apparent number of minorities who are either in the posts of corporate officers or who sit on the board

of directors. If a woman who is a minority is involved in the top ranks of the company, she is counted twice: once in the Apparent Women number and once in the Apparent Minorities number.

Hot Spot for Advancement for Women/Minorities: These are firms who either have posted a far-above-average number of women and/or minorities to high posts or who have a good record of going out of their way to recruit, train, promote and retain women or minorities in top jobs. (See the Index of Hot Spots For Women and Minorities in the back of the book.)

Growth Plans/Special Features:

Listed here are observations regarding the firm's reputation, hiring plans and plans for growth and product development, along with general information regarding a company's business and prospects.

Locations:

Primary locations outside of the headquarters, categorized by regions of the United States and by "International" locations. A "Y" in the appropriate field indicates "Yes." A complete index by locations is in Chapter 6.

Chapter 1
Business-to-Consumer
(On-line Retailing)

Overview:

Significant Trends to Watch:

A. Service and Security:
Privacy, delivery, service, transaction security and honesty are the biggest concerns of Internet consumers. *(See item G. below.)*

Service and follow-through that will retain customers (once they have responded to the costly process of advertising and promotion) will be the benchmark of successful on-line retailers.

Large numbers of consumers continue to be frustrated by breakdowns or complications in the on-line ordering process.

Fulfillment and shipping remain immense challenges to most on-line retailers, particularly during holiday periods.

Analysts at BizRate.com state that nearly one-fourth of the 34 million on-line 1999 holiday season orders were not delivered in a timely manner.

B. Business Models:
A growing number of well-established "bricks-and-mortar" retailers are integrating comprehensive Internet sites into their business models, creating a "clicks and mortar" environment with synergistic advantages.

In general, on-line business-to-consumer sites continue to lose vast quantities of money in their quest to build customer bases and beat the competition. The most profitable business model on-line may turn out to be the auction. Many auction or name-your-own-price sites such as e-Bay are scoring significant levels of success.

C. Early Entry Continues to Mean Market Dominance:
Despite the fame of traditional retail names, early Internet-only companies continue to dominate their categories. For example, Amazon.com continues to get vastly more traffic than Barnesandnoble.com, and eToys receives greater traffic than better known Toys "R" Us.

Amazon was the top shopping destination for consumers during the Christmas 1999 season. Amazon received 5.7 million unique visits during the holiday season, and, according to Media Metrix, eBay received 4.1 million, eToys 1.6 million, Barnesandnoble.com 1.5 million and Toysrus 1.5 million.

D. Personal Items and Consumables are Rapidly Growing Categories:
Pet products, personal hygiene items and groceries are enjoying booming Internet sales. In particular, book retailing magnate Louis Borders has set the standard with the most aggressive Internet startup in history, Webvan. The site, which sells groceries on-line, will eventually be backed up by home delivery in 26 major U.S. markets and will provide home delivery of a long list of consumer items.

E. On-line Shoppers Deliver High Purchase Amounts:

Ernst & Young reports that consumers spent big bucks while shopping on-line in 1999, including an average amount of $233 spent at Best Buy's site, $167 at Wal-Mart's dotcom, $134 at Toysrus.com and $138 at L.L.Bean's site.

F. Acquiring the Customer, at any Cost, Remains a Primary Strategy:

Amazon.com, using aggressive methods that include affiliate marketing, heavy advertising and cutthroat pricing, continues to build its customer list while losing vast sums. Amazon added an astonishing 2 million customers during the fourth quarter of 1999, bringing its total customer base to 16.9 million.

Likewise, Buy.com has acquired over 20 million customers by selling leading brand-name electronic goods, books, videos and more at near-wholesale prices. In fact, some of its items are sold at prices that are below cost. Needless to say, the company is losing buckets full of cash. As the site's popularity builds and its customer base grows, the company is slowly raising prices.

A business-to-consumer site's ratio of stock market capitalization to the total number of customers on its list is an interesting way to gauge stock price. According to *Business 2.0* magazine, in February 2000 Amazon measured $2,746 in this manner, drugstore.com $4,487 and eToys $11,102.

G. Highly Sophisticated Cyberpsychographics Profile and Track Millions of Individual Users:

Internet marketing consulting firms have developed complicated methods, including collaborative filtering, cookies and clickstream analysis, to profile individual customers' web site viewing behavior, personal interests and shopping habits. For example, Engage Technologies has built behavior profiles on more than 40 million web users.

Consumers will become increasingly uncomfortable with this surreptitious gathering of data. Government regulation may follow. One result will be growing success of opt-in lists where consumers agree to receive targeted direct marketing via e-mail. Another result will be the rapidly growing importance of free ISPs (Internet service providers), where consumers receive Internet access free-of-charge in exchange for supplying data about their interests and households.

Making retail purchases over the Internet is growing in popularity among consumers for a variety of reasons, including:

- Concerns about the security of consumers' credit card numbers have been successfully addressed by technology, including "secure transaction" systems, the SET standards adopted by Mastercard and VISA and the e-cash systems invented for facilitating payments on the web. Another advance, "SSL" (Secure Socket Layer) technology, digitally encrypts sensitive consumer information that can be decoded only by the server that receives the information using digital "keys" or certificates.

- Web site responses can be customized to a consumer's tastes and shopping habits, resulting in "one-to-one" marketing. Many sites use complex algorithms to make recommendations that match consumer preferences based on their shopping histories. Amazon.com is a trendsetting site in this regard. The technology used to measure and monitor the behavior of the cyber consumer is astonishing. A customer's previous clickstreams, purchases and stated preferences are all taken into consideration when suggesting a product match. For example, at The Sharper Image's site, customers can enter a detailed personal profile that will enable the site to show them the specific types of merchandise in which they are interested. Web sites can combine video, music, animation, graphics, photos and words in a manner that printed catalogs will never achieve. Some sites even allow the consumer to directly influence product research and development.

- Millions of households have purchased advanced personal computers that include relatively high-speed modems. Higher bandwidth telecommunication lines, such as DSL, ISDN lines and cable modems, are becoming widespread. (See *Plunkett's InfoTech Industry Almanac*.) The number of homes wired for on-line use has already reached critical mass. By the end of 1999, roughly 221 million people used the Internet worldwide. Of those, 118.4 million Internet users were in America, according to

Nielsen/NetRatings data in their November 1999 study. According to Media Metrix, the number of unique weekly Internet users over the age of 12 in the U.S. grew to 47.8 million at the beginning of 2000.

- <u>Internet site developers have learned to use powerful databases to enable consumers to conduct customized searches for products. For instance, the more than 1.5 million book titles available at Amazon.com. can be searched by author, title or subject.</u>

- <u>Items the consumer need not touch and feel prior to buying are ideal for purchase over the Net.</u> These items include books, CDs, personal computers, software and tickets to concerts and other events (as sold on sites operated by Ticketmaster). CDNow, **www.cdnow.com**, offers over 250,000 CD music titles on its web site. 1-800-Flowers, **www.flowers.com,** sells millions of dollars in delivered floral arrangements via the Internet each year. Items subject to bids or negotiated prices are also very suitable for purchase over the Net. That's why auction sites and sites that allow consumers to post their needs to automobile dealers, who then send bids back to the car-buyer, are doing well. This allows the customer to be in control. (See "Internet auctions" below.)

Selected High Traffic Sites, U.S.

General:	Retailers:
Yahoo!	Amazon.com
AOL	eBay
MSN	eToys
NBC	barnesandnoble
About	Buy.com
Microsoft	CDNow
Go Network	Toysrus
Lycos	
Excite@home	

Source: Media Metrix, Forrester Research, Plunkett Research

- <u>Ideally, a site on the web shouldn't be just another place to buy something; it should offer a better way to make that purchase.</u> For

excellent examples of sites that make shopping a better experience, click through **www.buy.com** and **www.dell.com**. On well-designed sites such as these, consumers find broader selections of merchandise, more choices and options, more product information and other advantages that they will never receive in a physical retail store. On the other hand, cyber shoppers lack the ability to touch and see the merchandise first hand. One company that is taking direct selling to a new level is Gateway. Its Gateway Country stores are being opened across the nation. Here, a consumer can actually see and use Gateway computers before placing an order for a computer to be built and delivered to the customer's home or business. These showroom-type stores supplement Gateway's catalogs and web site. Traditional merchants know that information gathered by consumers over the Net about stores and merchandise will also lead to additional store sales by walk-in, telephone and fax methods, as well as direct purchases made on-line.

- <u>Internet consumers can also participate in virtual auctions on sites like eBay.com.</u> The auctions are real-time and last a few hours or more. The virtual auctions function in a manner very similar to real auctions, with bidders competing for products like jewelry, clothing, golf clubs and collectibles. The bidding is done in set increments. PriceLine.com allows cyber-shoppers to bid for airline tickets and hotel rooms. Amazon.com and Sharper Image also recently rolled out auction formats, and mortgage companies are entering into the auction fray as well. IMX Mortgage Exchange posts brokers' loan requests, and participating lenders bid on them. Virtual auctions are expected to account for nearly 30% of all e-commerce by 2002.

- <u>Retailers may save costs by selling over the Net because they don't have to rent or build expensive retail store space, print and mail catalogs, pay commissions to salespersons or endure other front-end costs.</u> Many carry only small amounts of merchandise and order on a just-in-time basis from their vendors. The low operating costs of web-based vendors is passed along to consumers as competition mounts (something that has rarely happened in the printed catalog business). Traditional retailers will be forced to adapt to these rapidly changing business conditions in the same way they were forced to adapt by the roaring success of Wal-Mart and other discount center operators. In fact, Wal-Mart, Target and Kmart are entering the Internet arena with major sites of their own.

- According to Media Metrix, over 25 of the 50 most-visited sites on the Internet during the five weeks leading up to Christmas 1999 are supplements to pre-existing corporations, such as Toys "R" Us. Although incredible amounts of advertising dollars are spent on launching and promoting start-up Internet companies, very few newcomers were in the top 50 during that critical retail period. According to the study, Amazon.com, Inc. and eBay, Inc. continued their reign as the most-visited retail sites on the Internet worldwide. Sites with high visitation didn't necessarily achieve the highest growth in visits. On-line toy stores such as KBkids.com and Toys "R" Us demonstrated the largest increases in traffic during the period studied. During the 1999 period of November 14 through December 26, Toysrus.com received 1.5 million unique visitors, and eToys, which experienced much less of a traffic increase than its competitors, ranked as the third most-visited site in the study at 1.6 million. Other on-line retailers like Wal-Mart, Target and Nordstrom experienced significant traffic increases as well.

- Analysts at BizRate.com state that entertainment products received the highest sales of any consumer category during holiday 1999, followed by gifts, computer products, food and wine, consumer goods, apparel and home and garden.

- Scarborough Research, which divides American consumers into three groups, "E-shoppers," "wired but wary" or "non-wired," reported in December 1999 that two-thirds of those in the E-shopper category are college educated with white-collar jobs. Over one-third of all E-shoppers have an annual income of over $75,000. Those in the "wired but wary" segment generally use the Internet for

e-mail, and "non-wired" persons tend to be females over 55. Almost three-quarters of those in the non-wired category have incomes below $55,000.

Major Trends in On-line Business-to-Consumer Selling

Internet selling is going to continue to move forward at a soaring rate, partly due to advances in technology. Methods of providing forgery-proof identification for on-line consumers have improved greatly in recent years, thanks to developments by GTE in Stamford, Connecticut and by VeriSign in Mountain View, California. Technology for making purchases over the Net, even small purchases that total only a few cents, has improved due to payment systems initiated by CyberCash of Reston, Virginia.

Amazon.com and IBM have launched their own major programs to help retailers establish web-based selling sites. America Online continues to sell hundreds of thousands of dollars in merchandise daily via its on-line service that now reaches more than 22 million members. In fact, AOL has repeatedly earned fees in excess of $100 million each for pushing a particular company or service on the AOL site.

Internet Marketing Consulting Firms with Customer Profiling Expertise

Andromedia	*andromedia.com*
BroadVision	*broadvision.com*
DoubleClick	*doubleclick.net*
Engage Technologies	*engage.com*
Net Perceptions	*netperceptions.com*
Personify	personify.com
Younology	*younology.com*

Leading brick and mortar corporations are increasingly working toward becoming Internet giants as well.

Major, traditional retail merchants, even those dominant in their store segments, are investing heavily in new web sites, including such department stores as Nordstrom and Sears. Selling on-line is no longer a unique or futuristic thought -- it's a vibrant mode of alternative selling that is rocketing ahead at a rate so fast that no one pundit can keep up with it.

Wal-Mart's web site received over one million visitors in November 1999 and is expected to produce over $50 million in sales by the end of fiscal 2000. The company recently redesigned and expanded its site to attract even more visitors, due to an alliance with America Online. (Soon, Wal-Mart will begin providing its own Internet services through AOL.) The improved Wal-Mart site features over 600,000 products from all 25 categories found in traditional Wal-Mart stores, as well as services including car-rentals, airline tickets and hotel booking. Customers can compile a list of products and then reorder that same list with one click. Products ordered on-line can be returned to any physical Wal-Mart location, a practice that is growing among Internet retailers with brick-and-mortar establishments.

In August 1999, Nordstrom, Inc., a leading high-end brick-and-mortar department store chain, created a partnership with venture capital firms Madrona Investment Group and Benchmark Capital. Even though brick-and-mortar retailers that launch e-business ventures generally experience results that are less promising than their Internet-only counterparts, Nordstrom isn't alone in jumping on the cyber bandwagon. Nordstrom has followed the trend of creating a gimmick in order to differentiate its site. The company spent an amazing $17 million on a five-week-long promotion, its single biggest ad campaign ever. Nordstrom decided to offer its customers a very deep selection of shoes on-line for the 1999 holiday season.

Mainstay retailers Gap, Inc. and Macy's, Inc. are also using the Internet as an alternate channel to reach customers. Twice monthly, Gap sends its on-line customers tailored e-mails advertising sales, deals and new products. The company's on-line sales have more than tripled since 1998. Gap executives frequently use the term "clicks and mortar" to refer to the success of both types of retailing that exist in its infrastructure. The company has reached new heights in this type of integration, installing "web lounges" in several stores. If a customer is unable to find the appropriate size or a particular item, that customer is referred to the web site, which offers a much broader selection. In-store clerks are trained to direct customers webward as well. In addition, Gap, Inc. is in the process of launching sites for its subsidiaries Old Navy, Inc. and Banana Republic.

The pairing of both an Internet and a brick-and-mortar presence is becoming a winning combination. Although under one-half of all Internet retail visits result in on-line sales, a great portion of visits do result in sales at physical locations. Retail web sites, then, have proven that they serve a certain advertising function on top of serving as selling portals. J.C. Penney's on-line venture boasts a selection of 200,000 items, including its entire catalog line. The site will be heavily promoted in its catalogs and stores.

On-line apparel sales were estimated at $1.4 billion in 1999, up from $460 million in 1998.

Among Internet users, only 8% purchased items on-line during the holiday season in 1998, as opposed to an impressive 33% in 1999. From November 1 through December 31, 1999, on-line shopping totaled approximately $7 to $10 billion in the U.S. A nationwide survey by PeopleSupport.com found that 1999's Internet shoppers bought an average of six gifts on-line, with an average price of $134 per gift. A similar study by Ernst & Young confirmed high average purchases by Internet shoppers.

Recommended sources for on-line consumer buying pattern data and market analysis:

Cyber Dialogue www.cyberdialogue.com
Dataquest www.dataquest.com
Forrester Research www.forrester.com
Jupiter Communications http://jup.com
Shop.org/BCG www.shop.org
BizRate.com www.bizrate.com
Ernst & Young www.ey.com

One of the fiercest battles in on-line retailing is occurring in the toy market.

A slew of on-line retailers have cropped up, all striving to get a piece of the $250 million in Internet toy sales generated in fiscal 1999. Plaything giant Toys "R" Us, Inc. has launched an $80 million on-line campaign, and several companies such as eToys and Amazon.com are competing in this field. In fact, eToys brought in an estimated $100 million during 1999's holiday season. In mid-1999, K.B. Toys bought Brainplay.com, and subsequently spent $50 million on advertising its beefed-up Internet ventures. Mattel, Inc. has spent $90 million launching its own site, while Walt Disney Co. invested $45 million in Internet toy retailer toysmart.com.

```
┌─────────────────────────────────────────────┐
│        Common On-line Consumer Activities:    │
│                                               │
│   Automobile Purchase                         │
│   Chat                                        │
│   Check on/Trade in Stock Portfolios          │
│   E-Mail                                       │
│   Job Search                                   │
│   Mortgages                                    │
│   Participate in Auctions                      │
│   Play Games                                   │
│   Read News Items and Magazines                │
│   Read Product or Entertainment Reviews        │
│   Research Consumer Health Issues              │
│   Shop/Check Product Prices and Features        │
│   Travel Reservations                          │
│   Visit Pornographic Sites                     │
└─────────────────────────────────────────────┘
```

Internet giant Amazon.com has grown beyond its traditional offerings.

In September 1999, the company launched an offer of over 500,000 products through a flock of smaller merchants. These merchants are charged a fee and a small percentage of sales in exchange for being a part of one of the hottest retail sites on the web. Amazon, with its throng of almost 17 million customers, offers important exposure opportunities to small businesses. Also in 1999, Amazon added new categories of toys, electronics, auctions, software and home improvement to its own lineup of merchandise.

Internet auctions are rapidly becoming the most popular form of on-line purchase.

The most prominent of these on-line auction sites, eBay, had over 5.6 million registered users in October 1999. Over 2 million items are up for grabs on the site during any given day, and the company is one of the few large-scale Internet endeavors turning a sizable profit. It is estimated that $2.7 billion worth of items will have been bought through the site in 1999.

According to Forrester Research, an additional 11 million people will engage in on-line auctioning by 2003, bringing $19 billion into the Internet economy. Forrester Research also estimates that 35% of on-line purchases are made through auctions. The United States Postal Service has experienced a 5% increase in parcel delivery due directly to eBay.

In March 1999, Amazon.com and PriceLine.com launched merchandise auctions. Retailers such as Sharper Image and Cyberian Outpost have jumped on the auction wagon as well, and some analysts insist that it is only a matter of time before every retailer has its own form of on-line auction.

Auction retailing is predicted to change traditional retailing in several ways. When consumers begin to view prices of items as mere starting points and become increasingly accustomed to haggling, other retailers may be forced to make changes in the ways they do business.

The trend of creating one person's treasure out of another person's garbage changes things in the consumer mindset and in the economy as well. Since goods auctioned off on eBay are frequently items that have been sitting in the garage for some time, the re-flow contribution to the economy as a result of the sale of those items may be greater than a contribution from a newly produced item. Since eBay items entail little or no production costs, the total gain in national revenue production is immense.

Additionally, the creation of an "aftermarket" makes it much easier than before to sell previously owned goods, therefore creating somewhat less risk on the part of the consumer purchasing an item that he or she may want to sell later.

```
┌─────────────────────────────────────────────┐
│        Interesting On-line Auction Figures     │
└─────────────────────────────────────────────┘
```

- Auctions are moving toward becoming business-to-consumer transactions instead of consumer-to-consumer transactions. This form of auctioning is expected to account for 66% of on-line auction activity by 2003.
- By 2003, analysts expect $2.1 billion worth of airline tickets and hotel rooms to be sold on-line at auction.
- That same year, $1.7 billion worth of car sales will be derived from on-line auctions.
- $1.2 billion of sales in apparel will come from on-line auctions in 2003, analysts say.
- Industrial auction businesses such as FreeMarkets Online, Inc. are expected to grow from 1998's $8.7 billion to $52.6 billion in 2002, according to Forrester analysts.

Despite rapid growth, on-line retailers commonly lose money.

Even though on-line merchants revel in their newfound ability to operate businesses without having to deal with the expense of building stores, many are finding it difficult to convert dreams to profits. Even at giant Amazon, where sales more than doubled to $676 million in the fourth quarter of 1999, losses are massive, totaling $323 million in the same period.

For a better understanding of the losses incurred in today's on-line retailing scene, it is highly instructive to analyze Amazon's cost of sales structure:

Amazon.com
Breakdown of Revenues/Costs
Per Year on a Per Customer Basis

Revenue	$160.00
Cost of Goods Sold	$139.72
Marketing/Advertising	$ 42.47
Warehousing/Shipping/Operating	$ 19.83
Profit (Loss)	$ (21.68)

Source: Fortune Magazine

Some on-line sellers that originally planned on skirting brick and mortar costs now have to invest in warehouses and distribution centers. Moreover, companies are spending an incredible amount of money on marketing in order to differentiate themselves from the thousands of like sites. Companies are suddenly confronted with web-savvy consumers who can bargain shop with the click of a button. Worse still, on-line retailers have to drive prices down in order to keep sales up.

Additionally, on-line retailers have to learn how to ship millions of individual packages to customers around the globe.

Finally, retailers face problems from wholesalers that now desire to sell directly to the consumer on-line, bypassing the retailer.

Most Visited Consumer Health Sites

Drkoop.com
NIH.gov
OnHealth.com
HealthShop.com

Source: Media Metrix

Without a doubt, computer software and hardware are the most profitable products on the Internet.

On-line purchases of personal computers and peripherals may top $3 billion in year 2000, plus an additional $500 million in on-line sales of software.

Personal computers that are sold directly have made phenomenal successes out of Gateway and Dell. Both companies allow consumers to configure their own PCs by selecting from a wide range of device and software options such as operating systems, sound and video cards and RAM capacity. Dell has taken it a step further by providing customized, private ordering sites for its largest commercial customers, allowing them direct access to order tracking and special discounts.

Dell's Internet site is ringing up millions of dollars in daily sales. Compaq, one of Dell's biggest rivals, is building up its own direct-sales effort. Meanwhile, competitor Gateway is using a unique combination of the Internet, retail showrooms and print advertising to drive business.

One of the most intriguing goals of some entrepreneurs is to convince grocery shoppers to order over the Net.

Food retailing inherently deals in highly perishable, low-margin goods, which is why this sector of on-line retailing faces great risks. However, analysts say that the on-line grocery market could become bigger than on-line book, CD and apparel retailing, although on-line groceries are popular almost exclusively with affluent Americans. Americans spend over $500 billion on food annually. The average American household spends 9% of its weekly income on food and visits the local grocery store twice a week. All of this food consumption makes the prospect of adding convenience services such as on-line ordering and home grocery delivery look like an extremely lucrative endeavor. In 1998, the direct grocery industry brought in approximately $456 million in gross revenues.

Another factor leaning in favor of the on-line grocery industry is demographics. Since women tend to make most food buying decisions, the growing number of women on the Internet helps the industry. Analysts from Forrester Research estimate that about 1.1 million households purchased groceries through the Internet in 1999. Of those households, most opted for ordering specialty items from specialty companies, and only about 235,000 selected companies such as Peapod and Hannaford's HomeRuns to handle general grocery needs.

Peapod, an aggressive home delivery service that began business in 1989, has been building a base of shoppers slowly-but-surely. It operates through major retail grocery chains in Boston, Chicago, San Francisco, Ohio, Houston and other cities. Customers order on-line via Peapod and then receive home delivery of groceries that are packed at the participating supermarkets. The retail customer pays a fee for this service.

Several other on-line grocers are competing against Peapod, including Streamline and ShopLink. The most ambitious effort is the rapidly growing Webvan Group, Inc. Webvan began selling groceries to Internet customers in the San Francisco Bay area during mid-1999. It has accumulated more than $120 million in venture fund capital, made a highly successful IPO and plans to raise additional capital, much of which may be in the form of a junk bond offering. Webvan plans to rapidly gain nationwide market share by building highly automated warehouses in 26 major markets across the U.S. It currently has a state-of-the-art warehouse in Oakland, totaling 330,000 square feet, to serve its first market area. A second warehouse is already under construction in Atlanta. Webvan believes that high volume and highly efficient warehouses will enable it to profitably offer free delivery, as Webvan will not have to build and operate costly neighborhood stores.

Like other e-commerce ventures, most on-line grocers have yet to see a profit. They believe, however, that companies such as Amazon.com are setting a model that should be followed. Analysts at Andersen Consulting foresee 8% of all grocery sales in 2007 happening through the Internet, creating $60 billion in e-commerce.

One of the largest problems that the on-line grocery industry faces lies in the complexity of the task at hand.

While books, CDs and socks are not perishable and are not easily broken, eggs, milk, bread and round steak are delicate and easily spoiled. Storage problems both in warehouses and during the delivery process are common.

Some companies, such as Streamline, are working hard to offer solutions to these dilemmas. Streamline issues special keypad locks in order for drivers to be able to deliver goods to customers' garages in their absence. This is a major perk to customers who don't have to spend time waiting for

the delivery truck to arrive. Additionally, the company installs special refrigerators in these customers' garages, and delivers the goods in custom Tupperware-like tubs, ensuring freshness.

The e-commerce industry is a hotbed of mergers.

In fact, nearly 200 e-commerce and Internet-related companies were acquired in the first six months of 1999 alone. Major business-to-consumer or advertising services acquisitions include:
* EToys acquired BabyCenter in April 1999 for $652 million.
* Excite@Home acquired iMall in July 1999 for $427.5 million.
* Amazon.com bought Alexa Internet in April 1999 for $297.2 million and subsequently purchased Exchange.com for $248 million during the same month. Also in April, it gained Accept.com for $183.5 million.
* Getty Images snatched up art.com in May 1999 for $201.8 million.
* Beyond.com acquired BuyDirect for $133.7 million in February 1999.
* DoubleClick purchased NetGravity for $512 million in July 1999.
* Onsale purchased Egghead.com in July 1999 for $328.3 million.

Government-to-Consumer Internet activity is growing at an extremely rapid rate.

Throughout the nation, government agencies of all types are realizing that the Internet offers innovative new ways to create convenience for consumers, taxpayers and voters. Typical usage of the Internet includes enabling consumers to update car registrations and license plates on-line. The State of Maryland is enabling dozens of types of professionals to renew their business licenses on-line. The Federal Government is supplying an unprecedented amount of data via its multitude of Internet sites, from Bureau of Labor statistics to economic reports from the Governors of the Federal Reserve Board. Meanwhile, several private sector web sites have sprung up that intend to foster grass roots movements, provide links to representatives in Congress and act as a conduit to government services. The Atlanta, Georgia firm of egov.com assists on-line consumers with licenses and permits of many types. Watch for extremely rapid growth of additional government-to-consumer activity on the Internet over the next 36 months.

Chapter 2

Business-to-Business
Trends

Trends to Watch:

ASPs: Application Service Providers will rapidly gain a large market share of business software budgets by renting out software applications, via the Internet, on a monthly fee basis.

Vertical Portals: The number of "vertical" Internet portals catering to specific industries' needs will continue to blossom. The number may increase to 10,000 over the mid-term, from about 1,000 today.

On-line Purchasing: Well-funded, industry-specific business exchanges will enable nearly 100% of U.S. businesses to view catalogs and place orders or request and receive bids for components, products and services on-line.

Business Revenues vs. Consumer Revenues: Total Business-to-Business revenues will greatly overshadow the revenues generated by Business-to-Consumer, as businesses of all types take advantage of the efficiencies offered by the Internet.

Business Information: Well-designed and easy-to-use sites operated by Hoovers Online, *The Wall Street Journal* and other leaders will continue to build their audiences very quickly and will become the preferred method of receipt of day-to-day business news and information.

Shortly after the business-to-consumer segment of the Internet industry gained early ground, the framework was laid for rapid growth in the business-to-business end. In fact, business-to-business total revenues from e-commerce will vastly exceed e-commerce revenues from consumer transactions, because businesses, by their nature, engage in massive purchases and financial transactions in order to achieve economies of scale—transactions that can easily average in the hundreds of thousands of dollars—while consumer transactions will average much less.

Just as railroads, the automobile and the telephone created a swifter economy in days of yore, the Internet has increased the speed of worldly cash flows today. Companies can order a freight train load of products vital to their operations with the touch of a button. Computers can now automatically detect inventory shortages that could have caused chaos, had they gone unnoticed, and then post replenishment orders instantly via the Internet.

Perhaps the most important enablers in business e-commerce are "vertical hubs," niche industry sites that allow purchasers in need of components, products and services to post requests for proposals, while allowing suppliers to answer with firm bids.

Selected Business Exchange Software Development and Design Firms:

Ariba-software designer
Commerce One-software designer
Computer Sciences-software designer
Harbinger-software designer
Manugistics-software designer
Oracle-software designer
Sterling Commerce-software designer
ViaLink-software designer

Selected Business Exchange Sites:

Aerospace Online*-aerospace portal
AutoCentral.com*-auto industry portal
AutoXchange.com-auto industry portal
Bidworx.com (startup)-bids and proposals portal
Buzzsaw.com-construction industry portal
Chemdex-life sciences industry portal
Chemical Online*-chemical industry portal
Enron-trading of energy and broadband units
Food Online*-food industry portal
Intraware-IT professionals portal
MachineToolsOnline*-machining industry portal
TestandMeasurement.com*-portal
Ubarter.com-business services portal
VerticalNet-operates over 40 exchanges
WorldOil.com-petroluem industry portal

Part of Vertical Net

Global efficiency has been dramatically boosted by business-to-business e-commerce. Savings through business usage of the Internet are expected to rise from $17 billion in 1998, to $114 billion in 1999 and to $1.25 trillion in 2002 (source: *Giga Information Group, Inc and Goldman Sachs*).

Deloitte Consulting LLC estimated at the beginning of 2000 that 31% of U.S. companies currently do part of their purchasing via on-line methods, and 91% will purchase on-line by the end of 2001. Deloitte further predicts that business e-commerce revenues will be six times as great as consumer e-commerce revenues by the end of 2003.

Consider this: industry leader Cisco, a provider of state-of-the-art computer networking equipment, receives the majority of its business through its web-based ordering system, and software giant Oracle has put systems in place that will enable it to do likewise. *(See section I. below.)*

Companies based in the United States are estimated to enjoy over one-half of the current long-term benefits from this boom. Furthermore, the global community that the Internet creates will continue to dramatically increase the rate of trade between countries, thus speeding up e-communications among businesses the world over.

Key Words:

Vertical Hubs/Portals

These hub sites on the Internet are referred to as "vertical" because they attempt serve nearly all facets of one niche industry, such as the energy industry, the paper industry, etc. They bring together widely dispersed professionals, buyers and sellers in one convenient fully-featured portal. Advantages may include master catalogs of industry-specific components and services, as well as the enabling of bids and requests for proposals. They may include features from several different "functional hubs."

Functional or Horizontal Hubs/Portals

These Internet sites are called "functional" because they serve a specific function (or series of niche functions), as opposed to serving the entire needs of a specific industry. They may "horizontally" cross several different vertical hubs, while providing vital services. Examples include information and news sources, logistics management, calendar or scheduling applications, human resources applications or auction applications.

These vertical portals/purchasing centers tend both intermediaries and infomediaries (sites where a large amount of industry-specific data can be obtained on a regular basis), as well as centers for posting requests for bids.

In another category of service, major business-to-business Internet portals have emerged as pure business news and information plays. For example, Hoover's Online receives immense amounts of traffic for its business news and company profiles offerings, *The Wall Street Journal* has an extremely active on-line news site and other niche players providing day-to-day needs are rapidly gaining traffic. For instance, Houston-based MSDSOnline provides manufacturers' safety data sheets via its web site.

I.   From the Beginning of the Internet, Innovative Firms have Created an Immense Amount of e-Business.

Of all the major corporations that have utilized the Internet's powers to streamline business, Cisco Systems is a standout. Cisco harnessed e-commerce in a way that has resulted in great advancements in efficiency and profits. Cisco sells nearly 80% of all the networking equipment and routers that power the Internet. With 1998 profits of $1.4 billion and a $172 billion market value, the company is a major influence in global business practices.

Cisco's equipment, which is regarded as among the very best, is usually customized as needed. This customization means that, more often than not, special network configurations have to be implemented in order for the applications to function in a way that best fills the needs of the end user. With such complexity comes the need for constant customer support, which, in many cases, can be effectively supplied via the Internet.

The sheer volume of customer support questions coming into Cisco on a daily basis warrants the need for a powerful answering force. The natural solution for Cisco was a complete immersion in e-commerce. The company is able to service a tremendous amount of its customer support workload via on-line methods. As a result, an enviable amount of time and energy was freed up and re-routed towards other endeavors. Currently, over 80% of customers' questions are answered on-line. Although sales have risen dramatically, the company's customer support staff population has remained largely unchanged, thanks to the Internet.

Going beyond customer support, Cisco's entire ordering, contract manufacturing, payment and fulfillment branches are automated. In fact, most of the orders that come through Cisco are processed without the aid of a flesh-and-blood employee, significantly cutting down the company's payroll costs and speeding up handling and delivery for customers. The company's web site, which also acts as an on-line catalog, is where 80% of Cisco's orders originate. Here, customers can initiate and then track the progress of their orders from the comfort of their own desktops. E-business, in short, has helped a mega-company like Cisco maintain a level of personalized customer service and efficiency that would not otherwise be attainable.

Cisco's employees are constantly in contact with each other through the Internet, from all over the globe. Even Cisco's hiring process begins and is supported on the web in innovative ways that are the envy of other technological firms. Prospective employees can investigate the company, job openings and benefit plans via the Internet and may ask to be placed with a cyber mentor who can inform them about actual work conditions.

Dell Computers has also taken e-business to a new level. In fact, the computer manufacturing giant sells upwards of $15 million in computers and computer equipment from its web site every day. Through the company's corporate extranet, internal systems are able to easily serve the large number of customer orders. Furthermore, production and delivery processes are streamlined in order to ensure the completion of a nearly seamless process.

Chemdex Corporation is a leader in integrating e-commerce with regular business as well. The company, which is a shopping haven for pharmaceutical and biotechnology businesses, is one of the world's largest suppliers of biological equipment (chemicals, reagents, etc.). The company's huge offering of over 460,000 products and its army of over 170 suppliers places it at the top of its industry.

Such a giant corporation invariably faces problems due to the sheer size and complexity of its operations. Chemdex, which handles over 2,500 orders a day, predicts that the number of daily transactions it handles will skyrocket. Although growth is a wonderful thing, the company knew that it needed to make drastic operational improvements in order to prepare itself for the coming influx of business. For Chemdex, e-business solutions were the obvious choice.

Prior to the implementation of these solutions, customers such as researchers and scientists were forced to spend valuable research time thumbing through countless printed catalogs, searching for hard-to-find items.

Chemdex solved that sourcing problem by building a powerful and effective web site. It is now able to serve clients through chemdex.com, an informative on-line catalog and search engine. Here, prospective buyers can learn all they wish to know about a product and are able to quickly and efficiently place an order on-line. The company's suppliers are well served too, now that Chemdex has implemented a type of software that acts as a supply-chain automating system. Customer support is also available for these suppliers through a system that offers product information. For the company's business customers, the web site can be used in accompaniment with procurement and integration software.

Other leaders in business e-commerce include General Electric, an early leader in purchasing via on-line methods, and W.W. Grainger, a nationwide supplier of industrial and maintenance supplies that now has one of the most active business-to-business sites on the entire Internet.

II.   There has been an Immense Increase in the Quantity and Variety of Advertising Services Sold On-line.

Logically, a rapidly growing on-line viewer base will lead to a soaring number of advertisements placed on-line.

According to Forrester Research, on-line advertising spending will more than triple by the year 2004. By then, analysts say, the Internet will create revenues similar to that of broadcast radio as one of the four largest advertising mediums in the United States. Already, on-line advertising far surpasses the amount spent on outdoor billboard advertising. Analysts report that, by 2004, 8% of all American marketing budgets will be dedicated to on-line advertising. Currently, about 1.3% of all United States advertising is on-line, accounting for $2.8 billion annually.

Forrester Research surveyed approximately 50 Internet-based companies. Almost all of those companies reported that they expect on-line advertising budgets to swell dramatically by 2004, bypassing the amount spent on magazine and yellow pages advertising.

This influx of attention on Internet ads is changing the fundamental structure of the on-line advertising agency. For instance, advertisers are most likely to pay fees to web sites and ad agencies based on the amount of traffic a particular ad receives. Payment plans may spring up that are based on how much of a product or service is sold as a direct result of the advertising campaign. Already, the Internet advertising industry generally charges a rate for every 1,000 banner ads clicked through by users on a particular site (a cost per thousand or "CPM" basis).

While Forrester reports that only 15% of on-line advertisers are currently charging on the basis of sales produced, analysts expect that about one-half of all advertisers will use that method by 2003. Although advertisers are enthusiastic about the move towards performance-based payment methods, companies that provide the ad content may be less

pleased. This raising of stakes may create a more competitive atmosphere for advertising media everywhere.

III.   Application Service Providers (ASPs) will Rapidly Gain Immense Market Share in Business Software and Services.

ASPs, businesses that rent software applications for use over the Internet, are ideally positioned to serve small to mid-size businesses that can't administrate or install lengthy, involved software applications. Whether these applications would be difficult to install because of a lack of budget or a lack of technical staff in-house, ASPs come to the rescue. A business can simply log on to an ASP's site to access programs immediately that might otherwise take months of work and hundreds of thousands of dollars to implement.

For example, the standard-setting human resources software PeopleSoft is now available on a rental basis on-line via ASPs, as is the salesforce automation software of Siebel.

In fact, virtually all makers of business software will likely begin delivery through ASP methods eventually, because of the convenience, ease of maintenance, access to customization by experts and the advantages of a monthly fee or user-based fee system.

Even Microsoft's standard office applications in the Microsoft Office suite are now available on an ASP basis. In November 1999, Microsoft announced the launch of Office On Line, which is an ASP version of its Office applications. On sites such as bCentral.com, small businesses can rent the applications for a fee. Although Microsoft is still betting that the majority of its customers will prefer owning Microsoft Office applications in the traditional manner, it believes that many small businesses without technical staff will greatly appreciate the convenience of Office On-Line.

Microsoft's arch rival, Sun Microsystems, has long been advocating the use of business software on servers, rather than the installation of such software on each individual desktop in a network. Sun's new Star Office product is uniquely positioned to operate in this manner, easily filling the majority of the daily word processing, spreadsheet and data management needs of a typical office worker without local installation of the software.

Contact.com, a new ASP, offers a product that allows users to create and manage extensive contact lists through use of a browser and downloaded or remotely-hosted files.

IBM Net.Commerce Start Now enables customers to create an automated storefront for their web sites, while remotely providing back office applications that can be used for inventory and shipment tracking. Another ASP, OpenMarket, offers e-commerce software over the Internet. Combined with Shop Site, an on-line catalog template, OpenMarket's customers can operate on-line businesses that deal with a large variety of merchandise at a relatively low operating overhead.

Bitlocker.com, another ASP, offers a database application through its site. The company's customers can enter data into a template that can be easily shaped to fit the needs of a specific use. The fact that databases made through Bitlocker.com are hosted on Bitlocker's remote web server is an advantage to customers who won't need to worry about backing up information. Furthermore, authorized users can easily access, update or view information from remote locations, since it's on the web.

By opting for on-line software, companies are finding it increasingly easy to upgrade as well. Whereas store-bought software generally gets updated in an office every year or year and a half, software rented from Internet ASPs is upgraded continuously.

Schools are a good example of institutions that can benefit from ASP service. Several schools teach children through software run by an ASP called Learningstation.com. School children can use inexpensive, low-technology "thin client" PCs to access ASPs, since significant hard drive space and processing power may not be needed. Some school districts are able to save upwards of $100,000 per year on new computer and software costs, thanks to ASP systems like these.

ASP Summary:

- ASPs have the ability to deliver state-of-the-art software applications for immediate, cost-effective use.
- Users pay a reasonable monthly or per-use fee.
- The costs of developing, maintaining and upgrading software are borne by the ASP.
- Authorized users at remote locations are able to access users' files with great convenience.
- As Internet access becomes faster for small- and mid-size businesses that upgrade to DSL or T-1 connections, use of ASPs for day-to-day needs such as bookkeeping, inventory management and sales contact management will become commonplace.

Selected Major ASPs:

Concur.com   eWorkplace applications rented on a monthly basis.

Corio.com   Rents PeopleSoft, Siebel and other powerful business applications.

Digex.com   Hosts e-commerce applications for Internet transactions.

eAlity.com   Nearly four dozen rentable business applications.

HotOffice.com   Applications designed to fill the day-to-day needs of small- to mid-sized businesses.

Interliant.com   Provides sales automation, e-commerce, groupware and other business applications.

USInternetworking.com   Offers several customized, web-based applications, including human resources, Microsoft e-commerce and Sagent data analysis.

CHAPTER 3

On-Line Financial Services:
Banking, Mortgages, Insurance, Trading, etc.

CONTENTS

I.   **Day Trading/On-Line Trading**

II.   **International Finance**

III.   **On-Line Banking**

IV.   **New Technology**

V.   **Mortgages and the Internet**

VI.   **Insurance and the Internet**

I.   Day Trading/On-Line Trading

Without a doubt, the Internet is creating sweeping changes in the stock brokerage and trading landscape. To begin with, the cost of making a trade has plummeted. Many on-line brokers offer trades for less than $10, and even stalwart traditional brokers like Merrill Lynch and Morgan Stanley Dean Witter Discover & Co. have found themselves forced to announce on-line trading services for as little as $29.95.

As solid proof that the cost of creating an additional on-line line trade is next to nothing and in support of the theory that on-line trading fees will continue to plummet, American Express has announced that customers keeping at least $100,000 in their brokerage accounts will be able to execute trades on-line for free via Amex's on-line brokerage. At the same time, American Express' aggressive new reach into no-cost trading proves another irrefutable trend: the most viable way for stock brokerage firms to make money is through the control of substantial assets in their customers' accounts, not through fees charged for executing trades.

While there has always been a somewhat limited number of individual investors who trade stocks over the very short-term, buying and selling a security in the same day or even in the same hour, the Internet has created an entirely new category of investors who attempt to make their fortunes through extremely rapid buying and selling: The daytraders. This has not only increased the total volume of stocks traded on U.S. exchanges, it has also vastly decreased the average amount of time that a typical common stock is held by an investor. Over 75% of the shares of the average U.S.-based firm listed on the NYSE changed hands last year. That is, if a company had 10 million shares outstanding, 7.5 million of them were bought and sold last year alone, on average. That percentage has soared from 46% in 1990 and 12% in 1960. While the average time that a share of stock is owned in traditional old-line companies remains relatively long, the time line for the average ownership of a new Internet company is amazingly short. For example, the average investment in General Electric, Exxon or Johnson & Johnson is held for about 30 to 33 months. The average investment in Wal-Mart is held about 18 months. In contrast, the average investment in Microsoft is held only 6 months, and the average investment in Yahoo, Amazon.com, Doubleclick or Priceline.com is held for eight days or less.

Simply put, the Internet is an absolutely revolutionary catalyst in the financial services arena. It lowers the cost of saving, borrowing and processing funds transfers. It enables individuals working at their PCs at home to act like global financiers. The Internet has put so much money into action from so many new players that it is directly responsible for an immense increase in the pool of investment capital and the availability of venture capital. That venture capital is fueling the creation of new products, new services and new technologies that further fuel the investment fire. The Internet provides near-perfect, real-time market data and research to those willing to go to the trouble to dig it out of the hundreds of millions of web pages posted on the World Wide Web. The Internet is rapidly making markets of all types much more liquid and efficient.

On-line investors are using the Internet to their advantage, and the entire structure of Wall Street is changing as a result. The cost of trading stocks on-line has plummeted since the practice's inception, thanks to the low overhead achieved when an Internet-enabled brokerage cuts the amount of costly office space and support staff required to execute trades. Most on-line investors are not seeking personal investment advice — they know what they want, when they want it and how much of it they want. Consequently, they do not need to interact with

an individual stock broker. Furthermore, an increasing number of investors are turning to the Internet to make an entrance into the investment community. Advisory material is readily available and easily located on the Internet (see Chapter 2 for useful sites).

One in every three individual investors' equity trades is now being made on-line, and nearly 15% of all individual investor brokerage accounts are Internet-based. By 2005, nearly all investors with access to personal computers will use the Internet for their stock and mutual fund investments — if not to enter trades and orders, then at least to gather information about the status of their accounts. As the Internet becomes a required distribution channel, the distinction between "on-line" and "regular" trading will disappear. Analysts at Jupiter Communications expect on-line trading at home to grow from fewer than 5 million U.S. households to 20 million households with $3 trillion in assets by 2003.

Like any revolutionary practice, on-line trading's rapidly growing popularity requires the industry to constantly implement change. Firms must consistently upgrade computer systems in order to prevent catastrophic crashes.

Virtually all stock industry sectors are sharpening their technology as the market-sector competition intensifies. For example, for the first time in history, the New York Stock Exchange is considering trading NASDAQ stocks due to frustration with its inability to nab high-tech monsters such as Microsoft, Intel and Dell. The growth of technology stocks on the NASDAQ has taken a large bite out of the NYSE's market share.

Enhanced Technology and Extended Trading Hours: Due to increasing trade volume and investor demand, NASDAQ and the NYSE are completely changing the way they operate in several essential ways. For example, 24-hour trading is approaching quickly as on-line capabilities become increasingly ready to facilitate it. Already, some companies are building systems to allow investors to indulge in after-hours trading, and others are utilizing wireless devices to let customers trade at any time, from any place. Individual investors will continue to demand enhanced services. The ability to make trades after normal market hours is a logical way to serve the needs of individuals who can best make time to manage their portfolios after normal working hours.

However, existing technology has to be upgraded before promised services get too far ahead of systems. In early 1999, several of the largest on-line firms experienced difficulties when tidal waves of trades were unleashed by the heady stock market. Among firms whose systems floundered were Charles Schwab Corporation, E*Trade Group, Inc. and Toronto-Dominion Bank's Waterhouse Securities, Inc. Ameritrade hired a technology expert as its co-chief executive in an attempt to forestall systemic computer breakdowns.

Along with technical problems and changes, organizations in charge of regulatory practices have been forced to pick up the pace. Securities regulators are taking long, hard looks at day trading firms and those who promote rapid-fire trading designed to capture minuscule stock price differentials, as opposed to long-term securities holdings. Firms offering investors a pie-in-the-sky picture of quick wealth gained through rapid trading are being thoroughly scrutinized by state and federal officials.

Television commercials aired by such firms often feature what are supposed to be average people getting rich quickly through Internet trading. These ads are being eyed by regulators, as the distinction between humorous irony and false advertising blurs. Regulators may decide to target these messages, subjecting firms to fines or pre-airing clearance. In a June 1999 speech by Securities and Exchange Commission Chairman Arthur Levitt, allusions were made to the potential danger of humorous ads such as one of Morgan Stanley Dean Witter Discover & Co.'s. In the ad, a truck driving on-line trader accumulates enough wealth to buy his own private island. Levitt apparently didn't find it funny.

Crack-downs on stock fraud are intensifying as well, with the implementation of cyber-cops and Internet patrollers. On-line message boards and newsletters shouldn't be a safe place for those engaging in fraudulent behavior. Newsletters that tout stocks but fail to give supportive data and proper disclosures are a target for regulators, as are hucksters who promote stocks on-line to boost prices and then quickly liquidate their positions.

Trading via Electronic Communications Networks (ECN's): One of the most remarkable developments to spring from the on-line movement is the Electronic Communications Network, or ECN. These privately organized networks of investors allow buyers and sellers of securities to post notice of their desire to trade directly to each other, via the network, completely bypassing stockbrokers and traditional stock exchanges. These ECNs create highly-efficient markets that lower transaction costs for participating investors. The cost of trading on an ECN may run

from a fraction of one cent up to four cents per share, which may be as much as 99% lower than the cost of trading through a traditional market maker. While these networks are a relatively new development, there are already at least eight ECNs. The leaders include Instinet, The Island, MarketXT, REDIBook, Archipelago, Bloomberg Tradebook and The Brass Utility. These firms made a September 1999 announcement that they intend to create a joint, transparent network to make trading data and buy or sell orders available to members for extended hours and with enhanced accessibility. However, both the NYSE and the NASDAQ must be keenly aware of the competition from ECNs. Extended hours, enhanced services and even direct connection services identical to those offered by upstart ECNs could easily be offered by the major, traditional exchanges, rendering ECNs essentially superfluous. But that would only happen if the major exchanges created systems that could make trades at the vastly reduced costs offered by ECNs. Otherwise, the market share of these ECNs will continue to climb rapidly.

ECNs
Archipelago
Attain
BRUT
Instinet
Island
NexTrade
REDIBook
Strike
Tradebook
ALTERNATIVE TRADING SYSTEMS
Bernard Madoff
Knight/Trimark
OptiMark

II.   International Finance

The Internet is creating a more truly global economy than has ever existed. For example, if a company wishes to conduct a business meeting among its American, Japanese and German subsidiaries, it can now do so instantly via on-line video conferencing. International finance, arbitrage, trading and currency exchange can now be practiced 24-hours-a-day from any location on the planet.

Equally as important, the web provides a seemingly endless plethora of the latest global financial news, with a great deal more expedience than the morning paper (though you can usually read that on-line as well).

Several sites have surfaced that place an increased emphasis on international, as opposed to domestic, finance. For example, Worldlyinvestor.com focuses on international investing for individual investors. Original content from columnists and correspondents peppers the site, which has its own rankings that enable country and sector-divided individual screenings.

III.   On-Line Banking

Two types of banking institutions are now competing fiercely for on-line customers:
1. Internet-based, or "virtual," banks that have no traditional storefronts, lobbies or ATMs.
2. Traditional banks that offer Internet access to accounts and services as an additional convenience.

On-line-only banking firms are giving traditional brick-and-mortar establishments a run for their money. Throngs of technology firms have developed payment and payment processing software that easily runs over communication networks, creating the opportunity to cut out traditional brick-and-mortar offices as the economy's primary payment processors. Since commerce is clearly becoming more electronic and will continue to do so at an increasing rate, traditional banks are teaming up with technological firms in order to compete with slick on-line-only financial institutions.

On-line banks are simply more cost-effective to operate than traditional institutions. When the traditional expenditures associated with brick-and-mortar banks are eliminated and several new customer-friendly features are accessible to the user, the Internet bank arises as a viable competitor. The customer is often offered a much simpler, faster and direct banking experience on-line. Account information can be accessed with the click of a mouse at any time, and inter-account transfers can be seamlessly executed. Additionally, Internet banks are able to offer higher interest rates to depositors and often charge lower fees.

Internet banks' net interest margins are usually thinner than at traditional banks due to the payment of high interest rates. Internet banks' "efficiency ratios," measures of banks' operating economies, are hurt during the implementation of this strategy and

tend to be significantly lower than that of the average bank.

Internet banks are currently focused more on long-term growth than on accumulating fee business. Since Internet banks are regulated and must meet certain regulatory capital requirements, they must continuously tap equity markets so that growth does not outrun their capital-generating potential. This means that entrepreneurial on-line banks must consider an entirely different set of conditions for growth compared to other types of Internet businesses.

Traditional banks such as Wells Fargo and Citibank are determined to compete on-line. These establishments offer the same sets of customer-friendly services through web sites as do their Internet-based competitors and are able to offer free, traditional ATM services and lobby services as well. Since Internet banks are virtual by nature and cash is tangible by nature, banks with an established base of branches may be able to offer considerable competitive advantages.

In most instances, on-line account holders at Internet-only banks pay user fees at other banks' ATM machines each and every time actual cash is desired. Though direct deposit services can usually be arranged for paycheck transfer through the account-holder's place of business, other check deposits have to be snail-mailed to the Internet bank. Though some on-line account holders insist that lower user fees more than make up for inconvenience and ATM costs, others assert that the inconvenience associated with slow check processing negatively outweighs the benefits that Internet-only banking can offer.

Still, the "virtual vs. tangible" issue is one that analysts and critics believe will be bridged as technology further alters the public's view of financial services. Ideally, the ultimate e-bank will offer one-click access to complete financial services, such as loans and mortgages, checking, bill payment, securities trading and insurance. This banking ideal is not that far off, and new Internet banks, traditional banks and legislative forces alike are making progress toward all-inclusive on-line banking.

According to Gartner Group, Inc., existing Internet-only banks have currently accumulated approximately 2% of the estimated 9.5 million customers who choose to manage accounts on-line or through Internet banking sites. Analysts at Jupiter Communications expect that number to grow to 28 million by 2003. Only about 225,000 persons currently bank solely through Internet-only institutions, but that number is predicted to grow steadily.

During the summer of 1999, the U.S. Senate initiated work on bills that will further deregulate the financial services industry. Legislation is constantly loosening and changing as technological progression dictates the need for new guidelines, and proposed legislation is another outgrowth of that need.

Financial reform issues being debated include community reinvestment and operating subsidiaries. The House bill currently proposes extensive consumer privacy protection, an issue that plagues those considering handling their finances on-line. Customers would have a chance to block their banks from sharing financial information with third-party marketing establishments under the House's bill, garnering it much support. Additionally, several Democrats have proposed that new legislation should prevent banks from sharing information with affiliated companies. The bill has been called "the greatest expansion of privacy rights in modern finance" by House Banking Committee Chairman Jim Leach. The Senate bill, on the other hand, has no limits on information sharing, as the Senate proposes tackling those issues through separate pieces of legislation.

Over the mid-term, Internet-only banks will suffer from growth constraints due to a lack of physical facilities. The result will be a flurry of mergers and acquisitions as established, traditional financial services firms acquire Internet-based banking firms.

IV.   New Technology

Smarter Cards and Cyber Cash

Called the "first true Internet Visa" by its creators, Internet Access Financial, the NextCard serves as a pioneering model for credit cards of the future. Though there are several similarities between the operatory regimens of standard cards and the NextCard, a number of differences set it apart—and perhaps ahead—of the crowd.

To begin with, applicants go on-line to apply for the NextCard and get accepted or rejected in approximately two minutes. Customers are drawn towards NextCard not only because of an expedient application process but also because of unusually low introductory interest rates. After step one of the application process, NextCard automatically shows the customer's other credit card balances on the screen, without asking for the numbers, so that he/she

can specify what amount he/she wishes to transfer to the new NextCard balance.

NextCard has completely integrated its own computer systems with the national credit card processing system, allowing for these real-time credit and balance transfer approvals. All card-related business can be conducted through the card's web site. The customer can review statements, transfer balances, upgrade the card and obtain general services. Though the card seems fairly standard (with the exception of the application process), its creators are currently working on building a bank underneath the credit card company.

Jeremy Lent, CEO of Internet Access Financial, plans to attack Internet banking's principal dilemma: tangible cash vs. virtual or conceptual funds. Lent proposes that this dilemma will eventually be solved by the "smart card," a proposed relative of the NextCard. The smart card digitally represents cash by way of a small chip embedded in the card. Theoretically, every establishment will eventually accept smart cards instead of cash -- people will use these cards to complete transactions once requiring cash. Several analysts agree with Lent's money-evolution theory. According to Lent, just as customers can no longer present wheels of cheese or live chickens as barter at their favorite stores, cumbersome coins and flimsy paper slips may be on the road to extinction as well. On the other hand, such smart cards would require that transaction fees be paid, while the costs of cash transactions are currently borne by the U.S. Federal Reserve Bank system.

Electronic Billing and Payments

Though it may be at the expense of banks, e-billing may certainly benefit both the customer and a portion of the business world — it could save paper and some of the estimated $17 billion that businesses spent on postage in 1998 alone.

Businesses can send bills electronically, either through a customer's e-mail or via his/her bank's web site. When the customer is ready to pay, one simple click will automatically send the e-bill to an e-bill clearinghouse. There, the payment is deducted from the customer's account and the vendor's account is credited.

In June 1999, the Exchange clearinghouse was created by First Union, Wells Fargo and Chase Manhattan banks. Currently, Citibank is collaborating with Transpoint to offer e-billing services, and Bank One is teaming up with computer services giant EDS.

A few sites such as Bellserve.com and Paymybill.com already exist that enable businesses to send e-bills to individual e-mail accounts. Also, customers of Intuit's Quicken.com and Microsoft's Money software have electronic bill payment options. However, it is noteworthy that some firms have been trying to popularize electronic funds transfer (EFT) in the U.S. for decades with little success. EFT has been popular in France for business-to-business payments. As far back as the mid-1970s, the Bank of France established a subsidiary office in Dallas, Texas, in hopes of selling EFT services to Americans. However, acceptance was very limited.

V.   Mortgages and the Internet

For those seeking home financing, either for the purchase of a home or to refinance an existing mortgage, the Internet is a great place to start. Just type the word "mortgage" in your favorite search engine and you'll be sifting through thousands of search results. Try to get local companies first. You will get better service from a company with a branch office near you, since it is better equipped to handle any problems that arise. Furthermore, many companies with Internet services reduce or even eliminate the standard 1% origination fee, which will save you a great deal of money.

The automation that the Internet brings to many mortgage processes is a great benefit both to consumers and businesses. The time it takes to originate, process and underwrite a mortgage application can be whittled down to hours and days instead of weeks and months. The Internet is also a vast source of information on all aspects of the mortgage industry, resulting in empowered, better-informed customers. Jupiter Communications estimates that up to 16% of all mortgage applications will be originated on-line in 2003, for a total of one million mortgages representing $155 billion. Some loan portals, such as E-Loan, iOwn and Loan Works, are spending fortunes on radio, print and television advertising in an effort to build brand recognition. While these sites offer competitive rates and on-line applications, they still don't have the ability to process or close a loan electronically; consequently, total automation is not yet a fact. Some consumers still demand personal service when it comes to such an important business transaction. While much of the legwork can be done over the Internet with on-line mortgage companies, actually closing a loan electronically is still a few years down the road.

VI.   Insurance and the Internet

Insurance is one of the slowest sectors of financial services to move the selling process to the Internet. In the same way that very few companies have converted to direct mail to sell insurance, many companies are resisting using the Internet for direct selling. Insurance remains an agent-to-customer relationship industry. However, the purchase of some types of insurance via the Internet can offer the customer tremendous cost advantages. For example, life insurance lends itself to cost/features comparison, and the Internet is both an ideal way to receive such information and an excellent medium for making the purchase. Likewise, automobile insurance is already being sold directly via the Internet to a rapidly-growing degree. In fact, this growth is leading to the use of links to automobile insurance sites (and auto financing sites) that are being used by a large number of cyber customers.

In the near future, watch for leading edge insurance marketers to capture an excellent market share by selling homeowners' insurance and business insurance (including fire, extended coverage and liability insurance) at extremely competitive rates over the Internet.

If you are considering buying insurance via the Internet as a consumer or as a business owner, you should weigh the advantages and disadvantages. As with any financially-related venture, it's always wise to explore your options when it comes to insurance. It is easier than ever before to gather information and shop around for the best deal. This relatively new wave of information availability is creating an increasingly competitive market and is making it much more difficult for insurers to charge uncompetitive rates. It has never been more important — or easier — to do your insurance homework.

A number of insurance information portals have recently surfaced, enabling the customer to make informed decisions. One such site, Insure.com, informs its visitors on how to interpret misleading insurance sales pitches, how to file a complaint against an agent or insurer and what steps to take to collect a claim that an insurer won't pay. Like several of its contemporaries, the site features an extensive list of research links. It additionally offers free access to Standard & Poors and Duff & Phelps ratings of each insurance company's financial stability.

Reliaquote Insurance at www.insureclick.com offers well-organized information on life insurance basics and quotes from over 1,000 different insurers. The site asks the user to complete a short questionnaire regarding his or her needs and then offers several policies on-screen. The visitor can then apply for whichever policy is desired on-line, an impressively easy process. The site was listed as a favorite by *Forbes* magazine, and several similar quoting sites exist on the Internet.

Like any other financial services-related industry, the insurance segment will continue to undergo major changes as e-commerce and the Internet affect it. The Internet and the development of e-commerce promise to deliver more expedient operations and cost efficiency to the insurance industry, though they also raise many new questions.

According to consultants at Booze, Allen and Hamilton, insurers selling over the Internet have a substantial cost advantage over the lifetime of a customer, relative to non-Internet based insurers. Additionally, reports done by Datamonitor indicate that Internet insurers have a 23% expense advantage over agency insurers and a 5% advantage over direct response writers. Reduced sales costs, lower customer service expenses and more advanced information-gathering capacities fuel these efficiencies. Meanwhile, electronic commerce's progression is prompting the integration of insurers' information systems.

The role of insurance intermediaries/agents and the overall structure of the insurance market are changing dramatically as a result of Internet and e-commerce influences. Insurance portals now exist that can generate a number of competing insurance quotes within seconds. Since information transmission and the facilitation of transactions have been the primary function of insurance agents, electronic markets that can perform these tasks more efficiently and with fewer costs threaten these agents. Several agent functions are currently being disintermediated or simply replaced. Today, according to the Insurance Information Institute, there are approximately 1.8 million insurance agents in the U.S., taking an average commission of 11.3% of insurance policy premiums. The Center for Risk Management and Insurance Research at Georgia State University found that the furthering of electronic commerce will decrease the use of the independent agency system relative to exclusive agent and direct-response distribution systems that have grown since the 1970s. The future role of the insurance agent may be geared more toward customer

service and general advising roles. Nonetheless, most of today's on-line insurance sites require the services of a traditional agent to finalize the sale. This will change quickly as more new sites follow the lead of Ecoverage.com, a new firm that sells directly via on-line methods without the use of insurance agents.

The concept that the network becomes more valuable as more people are connected to it is also affecting the insurance industry. Hundreds of millions of people on the Internet translate into an increase in the value of Internet-based insurance services.

With the increased value of on-line connection comes decreased distribution costs. For example, products such as travel, credit or burial insurance have relatively high fixed costs and low value and are relatively expensive to produce. Customers purchasing these products generally pay a high price per dollar of coverage. The Internet allows the disintermediation of this high overhead for low face-value products, meaning that prices can be lowered and more insurance sold by reducing the transaction cost. Increased access through electronic commerce is also influencing some consumers to purchase broader, high-value insurance products, such as liability umbrellas, to manage their risk.

The sheer competitive edge that the Internet provides prompts firms to offer more unique and complex insurance and reinsurance products. Transactions involving many products rely heavily on information and communication, areas where the Internet proves to have a considerable competitive advantage. At the same time, the sale and servicing of complex insurance products will require different kinds of networks appropriate for individualized transactions. Security will be an important consideration, given the large amount of proprietary information at stake.

The Internet is currently prompting many insurers to restructure and repackage insurance services. In order to take advantage of advanced Internet technology, many companies are reengineering, outsourcing and/or streamlining their management functions or marketing and distribution arms. Some insurers will be able to reduce their investments in physical facilities and certain personnel as a result of the Internet's ability to more efficiently deliver their services. For example, mammoth firm Allstate Insurance announced in 1999 that it will layoff about 10% of its workforce and begin selling insurance over the Internet as part of its new plan to streamline the firm.

Electronic commerce may also enable independent agency insurers to more easily adapt their distribution mechanisms to market competition and expedite their transactions with intermediaries.

Several different strategies will be used as the insurance industry becomes more Internet-oriented. For example, on-line insurance sellers that rely heavily on information technology for many functions are rapidly emerging, while other insurers are simply using electronic commerce and the Internet (via wide area computer networks) to significantly increase the productivity of their human and physical resources. Some aggressive insurers will grow significantly through the effective use of the Internet and electronic commerce, while others will wane due to market changes. For example, consulting firm Forrester Research forecasts that sales of insurance to consumers via on-line methods will amount to about $250 million in 1999 (a tiny portion of the total insurance market) but will leap to $2.1 billion by 2001. Meanwhile, integration between the insurance industry and other financial services industries will become a more seamless and common process.

The inclusion of the Internet and e-commerce into the insurance industry changes the way that customers interact with their insurers. Customers can obtain quick quotes from a number of companies and can see ratings and evaluations of insurers on the Internet. Additionally, they can receive better customer service and enjoy cost savings provided by outsourcing. Price comparisons are easily obtained on-line, and customers can also have access to internal records in order to see where their claims are in terms of payment, when an annuity payment is due and how a mutual fund is performing. Technology brings customers closer to the basic insurance contract through eliminating inefficiencies.

Major Insurance-Selling Sites on the Internet

Ebix.com
www.ebix.com enables consumers to solicit bids from 170 agents in 46 states.

Ecoverage
www.ecoverage.com sells only its own brand of insurance, created with an underwriting partner. No agents are utilized.

Insweb
www.insweb.com enables consumers to compare quotes from 46 different insurance companies.

Quicken Insurance
www.insuremarket.com is part of the Intuit family and provides quotes from 21 different insurance carriers.

Quotesmith.com
www.quotesmith.com enables consumers to compare quotes from an array of insurers. Quotesmith has over 300 insurance companies in all 50 states within its database.

Chapter 4

Trends in Personal Computers, Internet Access and Internet Domains

Contents:
I. **Trends in the Personal Computer Market**
II. **Exponential Growth in use of the Internet**
III. **Internet Service and Access Trends**
IV. **The Battle for Internet Software Dominance**
V. **Internet Appliances and Evolutionary Changes in Personal Computers**
VI. **Host, Domain and Server Data**

Overview:

Worldwide PC Market: 110 million+ units, 1999.
Leading U.S. PC Makers: Compaq, Dell, IBM, Hewlett-Packard, Gateway.
PC Trends to Watch: Free or discounted PCs to consumers who enter into Internet service contracts; Extremely rapid growth of the under-$1,000 PC market.
Worldwide Annual Semiconductor Market: $150 billion+, 1999.
Leading U.S. Semiconductor Makers: Intel, AMD.
Percentage of U.S. Homes with PCs: 50%.
Internet Access Trends to Watch: 1) Growth of free or discounted Internet services that attempt to earn most of their profits through advertising; 2) Use of "Internet Appliances," including highly advanced video game consoles and cable TV modems; 3) Use of wireless devices to access the Net, including advanced cellular mobile phones.
Total Number of Domains: 56+ million.
Leading Domain Types: .com 19+ million, .net 13+million, .edu 5+million

I.   Trends in the Personal Computer Market

Today, about one-half of U.S. homes contain a PC, and many homes contain more than one. By 2002, the percentage will climb to about 60%, thanks to the rapidly declining retail price of high-power PCs and the growing usefulness of the Internet. In 1999, analysts at Strategy Analytics released a report predicting that 91% of U.S. homes will be on-line by 2005. Of these, 90% will be using an Internet browser on a PC, and 73% will also have interactive TVs or other Internet appliances (such as wireless phones or personal organizers with Internet abilities).

The annual production of all computers, peripherals and equipment (including large computers and PCs) in the U.S. is about $100 to $120 billion. Meanwhile, America imports about $80 billion in computer equipment of all types yearly. In the PC market in particular, International Data Corp. estimates total 1999 revenues worldwide for makers of PCs, portables and servers at $189 billion. Eventually, as the relative price of PCs continues to decline and the amount of entertainment and information delivered over the PC continues to expand, virtually every member of the household will have his or her own individual PC or Internet device. Soon after, the number of PCs per home will reach or exceed the number of automobiles per home.

However, not all Americans will be willing or able to participate in the InfoTech Revolution, and a growing gap will appear between those who are technically literate and those who are not. (A charitable foundation founded by Microsoft founder Bill Gates is making a serious effort to bring Internet access to lower income students and public library patrons.)

The PC is rapidly becoming the focus of home entertainment/home information. A well-equipped PC now functions as a CD player for music, a DVD player for movies, a video game machine, a storage and viewing device for family photos, a multi-media entertainment player, an e-mail enabler, a voice mail/fax machine and a gateway to the Internet. By the way, it still serves the old-fashioned roles of word processing, helping with homework and storing the family's favorite recipes. Today, the burden of paying bills and keeping the family's checkbook is made easy by electronic means. Color monitors, high-speed modems and affordable color printers have made the computer too cool for any young member of the family to ignore.

Meanwhile, the power of the PC has grown at a rocketing rate, while the cost of PCs and their accessories is falling rapidly. For the past seven years, the price of computers and office machinery has been falling at about a 15% yearly rate, because miniaturization and increased competition have driven down prices on many systems and accessories. Today, PCs that access the Internet are so cost effective that hundreds of millions of businesses and consumers around the globe are acquiring them for the first time.

New technological developments are occurring rapidly. For example, watch for 3-D computing to become common in a few years, with tremendous implications for engineering/design, medical applications and scientific use. At the same time, much of tomorrow's electronic entertainment may go 3-D.

Jupiter Communications projects that 30 million U.S. homes will have cable modems connecting interactive TVs to the Internet by 2004.

By far, the biggest trend to watch is Wireless Access to the Internet.

Wireless devices that access the Internet will become widespread, starting with new cell phones from Nokia and others and the latest Palm Pilots.

While many significant technological breakthroughs are taking place at once in the on-line world, the most significant development will be the explosive use of wireless devices (particularly cellular telephones) as a means of accessing the Internet. In fact, thanks to achievements in WAP (wireless access protocol) and state-of-the-art telephone sets, cellular telephones will become the <u>primary</u> way for many consumers to use the Net, once full-featured telephones and services are available.

As usual, the United States is way behind Japan and Western Europe in cell phone technology. For example, look at what is already happening in Japan, where subscribers to cell phones from NTT DoCoMo can use their phones for booking entertainment and travel, e-mail, on-line shopping, investments and news or information services of a vast variety. Why should consumers use a desktop for Internet access when cell phones will give them most of the services they want while on the go? For a European example of such advanced services, look at Telenor in Norway. Also, take a hard look at features under development for upcoming phones from Nokia.

Within five years (2005), about one-half of e-commerce transactions by consumers will be made via wireless methods.

Over 1 billion Internet-enabled cellular phones will exist worldwide within five years, and 80 million of those will be in use in the U.S.

Major changes in the Personal Computer market.

A revolution has taken place in the personal computer market due to 1) the introduction of the low-cost, full-featured PC and 2) the popularity of buying PCs directly from the manufacturer. Dell Computer and Gateway are leaders in selling top-quality computers at competitive prices via the web. Meanwhile, massive companies that previously acted only as wholesale distributors for name brand machines are now building and selling their own lines of clones at very competitive prices.

A few companies are giving free PCs to customers who agree to sign a long-term contract for Internet access service because: 1) The cost to produce an entry-level PC is falling dramatically, and may well reach $200 to $300 in the near future and 2) The long-term profit potential lies not in selling PCs, but in providing monthly services, such as those provided by America Online. The home PC industry is becoming much like the cellular telephone industry, where you get a high quality cell phone for little or no money as long as you agree to become a service subscriber.

More recently, the typical retail price of a very good quality PC for the home from Compaq, IBM, Dell and others, has plunged to the under-$1,000 level. Most major computer makers are offering $400 rebates to purchasers who sign three-year Internet service contracts. The inexpensive PC market is where the real growth in consumer PCs lies. These are very well-equipped machines, with stereo speakers, CD-ROM players, high-speed modems and many other features.

The PC manufacturing business is extremely competitive, and leadership in the marketplace has shifted dramatically, away from early leaders such as IBM, to today's top brands of Dell, Compaq and Gateway.

A future revolution in the personal computer market will occur due to the rapidly growing use of intranets within households. Easy to install and use systems by such suppliers as Intel will make it very simple and affordable for homes to connect every member of the household with a PC or Internet appliance in every room. A wide range of new uses for both the PC and the Internet will result.

II.   Exponential Growth in use of the Internet

In late 1999, the total number of Americans using the Net was placed at more than 118 million, more than double the 51 million users of only a few months before in mid-1998. Soon, the total number of users worldwide will approach 500 million.

---

eMARKETER'S (www.emarketer.com) 1999 "eUSER & USAGE REPORT" HIGHLIGHTS:

- The median income for on-line households is 57% higher than that of the average American household, $58,000 vs. $37,005.
- The number of teens on-line will grow 38%, from 11.1 million to 15.3 million by 2002.
- Teens average 8.5 hours on-line per week -- 27% more than average Net users.
- 87% of college students are currently on-line, representing the most active single group on the Net.

Think of the potential of consumer use of the Internet in these terms: Standard local telephone service has become so affordable and so accessible that over 95% of all U.S. households have a telephone. In comparison, only a little more than one-half of households have a personal computer, and only slightly more than one-half of those home computers have a modem. A much lower percent have high-speed access via DSL or cable modem. Only when Internet devices and access become as widespread as the telephone or the television (particularly when broadband access is as widespread) can the Internet reach its true potential as a business-to-consumer medium and as an entertainment/communication device.

Users are giving up their old habits to spend their free time on the Net. Sixty-four percent of Net users claim to be watching less television these days. Internet users initially tended to be white males from affluent households. However, as each year of the Net's existence passes and the use of the Internet becomes more widespread, the profile of the average Internet user starts to more closely match the profile of the average American. For example, early studies found that 80% of Internet users were male, while recent studies show that only 54% are male. Interestingly, the Georgia Tech Research Corporation's 1998 survey (one of the best surveys regarding web demographics) found more females than males using the Net in the 16 to 20 age group. (A 1999 survey has not been released by GVU.)

Despite rapid growth in use of the Internet, it probably delivers much less than 5% of the information used in the world today. The potential for development is unlimited, and vast fortunes will be made here, both by start-ups and by large, established firms.

Improvements that will allow the Internet's continued growth include:
- Better Net browsing software has made access easier.
- Search engines, such as Yahoo!, have become more powerful, more user-friendly and much more comprehensive.
- Day-to-day needs are fulfilled better. For example, the steps required to book travel reservations, save money when purchasing items such as automobiles, transmit e-mail, look up reference materials, order from catalogs and purchase staples such as groceries have become fairly simple.
- Better, faster modems have made data transmission vastly more efficient.
- Improved telephone lines, such as DSL and ISDN, and the use of cable TV modems make hookup and downloading faster and more satisfying for many users.
- Leisure activities, such as interactive electronic games and real-time gambling, are available on-line.
- Vital business and investment information is readily available.
- The latest news is becoming faster and easier to find via the Internet than through any other medium.
- Job openings are posted and resumes are accepted through major corporations' web sites and links.
- Secure software makes consumers more comfortable with making purchases on the Net.

III.   Internet Access and Service Trends

Mergers, consolidation, aggressive marketing, re-positioning and new business models characterize today's Internet access and service market.

The largest factor in Internet access is the continued dominance of the early leader, America Online (AOL). No one has come remotely close to touching AOL's lead. In fact, AOL continues to grow at an astonishing rate and now boasts about 24 million subscribers to its AOL brand and to Compuserve, which it acquired along with 2 million subscribers.

Even software giant Microsoft has not been able to shrink AOL's lead in a significant way. After an early stumble, Microsoft's MSN service has grown rapidly in recent months, and now has something close to 4 million subscribers (MSN and WebTV combined), which leaves it positioned miles behind AOL. Ironically, Microsoft's own corporate web site is one of the busiest sites on the Internet. With 500,000 pages, Microsoft.com enjoys five million viewers daily-- users who are interested in Microsoft's software and its features but not necessarily in its Internet access service.

Meanwhile, the major independent firms of Earthlink and Mindspring have merged, creating a giant 2.5 million subscriber firm.

The trend to watch keenly is the growing use of Internet service provided on a free-of-charge basis. Aggressive ISPs (Internet service providers) are able to offer free service to millions of users for two highly diverse reasons: First, the cost of providing telephone access has plummeted, thanks to fierce competition among local and long distance telephone carriers. Next, the free-of-charge ISPs have based their business models on revenue from advertising. These free access services collect a significant amount of demographic and psychographic data from their subscribers as a condition of joining the service. Then, these ISPs are able to offer carefully targeted advertising opportunities to various types of firms that wish to advertise effectively via the Internet. Free ISP service is usually delivered on a page that continuously displays a high number of ads. AltaVista signed up 1.5 million users for its free Internet service in its first five months of operation. Other leading free ISPs include 1st UP.com, Gay.com, thesimpsons.com (Fox Entertainment), Nettaxi.com and CollegeClub.com (Spin Media Network, Inc.) and BlueLight.com (Kmart Corp.).

Free ISPs will become a definite threat to for-fee services, including AOL. However, AOL's strong content offerings, particularly now that it will acquire Time Warner, will assist it in keeping a vast customer base willing to pay $21.95 for monthly service. Another strong factor in AOL's favor is the amount of time that its subscribers spend at the AOL site (averaging as much as 88% of their on-line time), as opposed to cruising the rest of the Internet. Finally, AOL will acquire a vast new customer base in the merger with Time Warner, including 48 million HBO and cable TV viewers and 25.4 million magazine subscribers. In addition, AOL can market to a total of 87 million ICQ and AOL Instant Messenger registrants and 20 million Netscape Netcenter registrants.

Leading U.S. Internet Service Providers (ISPs), as of late 1999.

Company:	Subscribers:
American Online (AOL)	24 million*
Microsoft	4 million**
NetZero (free-of-charge)	3 million
Mindspring/Earthlink	2.5 million
AltaVista (free-of-charge)	1.5 million

*AOL subscriber count includes 2 million Compuserve customers
**Microsoft count includes MSN and WebTV

Nonetheless, budget-conscious consumers and consumers who do not resist on-line advertising will continue to switch to free service in droves. Also, slightly altered business models or unique new services may enable free ISPs and other alternative services to steal market share and hurt the profits of the fee-based companies. For example, millions of mobile, affluent Internet users are now acquiring wireless access, via cellular phone and Palm Pilot type devices, here again using a non-traditional means to access the Internet.

Marketing will become more intense and more aggressive as the large ISPs attempt to emulate AOL's success in blanketing the nation with service offers. For example, Microsoft plans a $100 million campaign to attract subscribers beginning in the spring of 2000.

IV.   The Battle for Internet Software Dominance

Programming languages and access software for the Internet/World Wide Web are a hot field, and major companies are competing fiercely to see who sets the standards.

Sun Microsystems and Netscape Communications (recently acquired by America Online) are big players, but they have not been able to supercede the capabilities of Microsoft. These firms and others are mounting an intense effort to influence the underlying software used on the Internet and thereby control much of the Net's future. Microsoft's ability to greatly influence the Internet software market has made it the subject of intense investigation by federal antitrust regulators.

Netscape sells the Netscape Internet browser software, and Microsoft sells the Internet Explorer browser, creating intense competition.

Sun Microsystems is a world leader in the manufacture of the powerful "server" computers used for much of the advanced work done in network and Internet environments. More importantly, Sun is the owner of Java and Javascript, a powerful application language that lets software developers make extremely exciting multimedia and interactive applications for the World Wide Web portion of the Net. Java enables software designers to use sophisticated, pre-written groups of code to assemble new applications. This saves vast amounts of time and effort. Sun has been distributing Javascript at no cost in order to get users excited about its potential.

The HTML language allows the author of a web document to create links to other related documents, no matter where they may be located. In that way, a Net browser reading a product brochure touting a brand of personal computer might click on such a link to be taken directly to a computer magazine's review of that particular computer.

A new, advanced language called XML (Extensive Markup Language) promises to supersede HTML and make web pages a much more useful means of delivering data. (see www.w3.org.XML)

Also, Java and similar software packages are taking the Web and HTML to a higher level. Java, based on a revolutionary type of programming known as "object technology" enables a web document to contain software programs known as "applets" or "objects." A web browser that contains Java can access these applets instantly. Applets can bring web pages to life – with animated cartoons, spreadsheets, charts and tables that update themselves automatically from information in Internet databases. They can also contain bits of application software that a browser can access on an as-needed basis. For example, a user might access an applet that contains a spreadsheet program in order to calculate data found on the Net.

Internet sites with the latest information on worldwide markets in computing/telecommunications/InfoTech:

Dataquest -- www.dataquest.com
Forrester Research -- www.forrester.com
Morgan Stanley Dean Witter -- www.msdw.com
Cowles/Simba Information Services -- www.simbanet.com
Cyber Dialogue -- www.cyberdialogue.com
International Data Corporation -- www.idc.com
Jupiter Communications -- www.jup.com
O'Reilly & Assoc. -- www.ora.com

Internet sites with the latest statistics on Internet usage:

EMarketer -- www.emarketer.com
Georgia Institute of Technology--Graphics, Visualization & Usability Center -- www.cc.gatech.edu (see the GVU section)
Cyber Atlas -- www.cyberatlas.com
NUA Internet Survey -- www.nua.net/surveys/index.cgi

Stock investors might use a web page that contains applets to keep track of their own portfolios of stocks, getting an update on their value and their change since the last time the web page was opened. Potential applications for object technology, HTML and XML are unlimited and include everything from basic business computing needs to entertainment to personal computer-based advertising and shopping. To best conceptualize the use of applets, think of the Internet as a massive, virtual hard disk drive, where essentially all of the software you will ever need might reside. The software would be continuously added to and updated so that you might never again have to buy an upgrade or make a software installation, as in an ASP-provided service. Meanwhile, this virtual drive will contain billions and billions of pieces of information of every conceivable type, in the nature of the millions of databases and sites you can access over the Net.

Microsoft has counter-attacked the Java movement by offering several outstanding new software development tools, including "VB Script," a web software programming tool based on Microsoft's powerful and popular Visual Basic language. This has pre-empted much of Java's appeal.

V. Internet Appliances and Evolutionary Changes in Personal Computers

According to industry analysts, the number of computer-related consumer devices (such as Internet access appliances) sold in the United States will surpass the number of PCs in use. While 18.5 million computer-related devices are expected to sell in 2001, about 15.7 million home PCs will be sold that year. The public's perception of the PC is expected to change. After the number of computer-related consumer devices in the average American home rises, the public is expected to view the PC as an everyday piece of machinery. Microsoft was an early leader in non-PC Internet appliances when it introduced its "WebTV" product, enabling Internet viewing via a television set.

The PC has neared the end of its evolutionary journey. Although the machine has done wonders for the business world and is definitely a device capable of extensive multitasking, the range of its ability to diversify jobs is limited. Computer-related devices or "appliances" often outshine the PC itself when it comes to performing mundane tasks. Additionally, the size of a regular desktop PC places constraints on its usage away from a desk.

Even video game-playing consoles are classified as computer-like devices. Indeed, modems, processors, memory chips and other computer-like features grace many of these computer-toys. Their setup even mimics that of the PC. The design is no accident; video game device manufacturers are going to offer more and more computer-like products to the consumer.

Computer-related "appliance" devices will become more of an accepted and assimilated part of daily life and culture. For example, nearly 40% of American households own a video game console. Sony's PlayStation 2 is to be equipped with more computing capability than some PCs. For around $400, the PlayStation 2 will play DVDs and CDs, connect to the Internet, perform e-mail and video e-mail tasks, act as a word processor and serve as a cable television set-top box. This combination of tasks makes the device more than a mere supplement to personal computing. In fact, it performs many of the most popular computer applications for a lot less money than your average iMac. Forrester Research reports that of those who buy a home PC, 58% use it for playing video games in addition to such uses as Internet browsing and word processing. Intel plans an extensive line of non-PC Internet appliances that will use Linux software and will attach to telephone lines.

Panasonic will create a wireless home telephone appliance with a special button that will hook-up to Net2Phone, Inc.'s Internet-based long distance phone call service.

Internet Connection Options

Conventional Dial-up	0.056 kbps
ISDN Phone Line	0.112 kbps
DSL/SDSL Phone Line	0.8 Mbps
Cable TV Modem	1.0 Mbps
Satellite	0.4+ Mbps*
Microwave	1.4 Mbps

*Satellite dish speed is for download only until the next generation of service is available. Uploads move at a slower speed because they must travel by other means, such as phone lines.

VI. Host, Domain and Server Data

Copyright 1998 Georgia Tech Research Corporation. All rights reserved.
Source: GVU's WWW 10th User Survey (October 1998). Note: 1999 survey has not been completed.
www.gvu.gatech.edu/user_surveys

Browsers Internet Users Expect to Utilize in the Next 12 Months

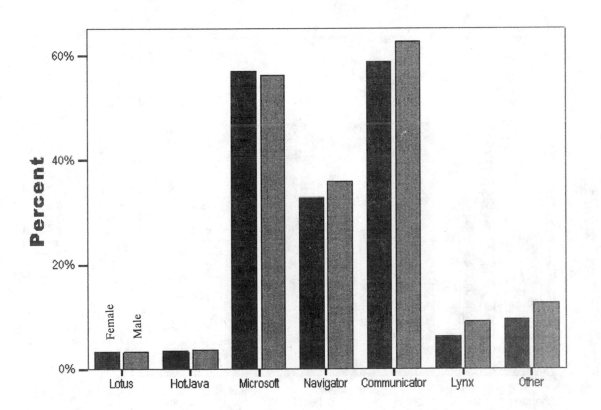

Copyright 1998 Georgia Tech Research Corporation. All rights reserved.
Source: GVU's WWW 10th User Survey (October 1998). Note: 1999 survey has not been completed.
www.gvu.gatech.edu/user_surveys

Primary Uses of the Internet

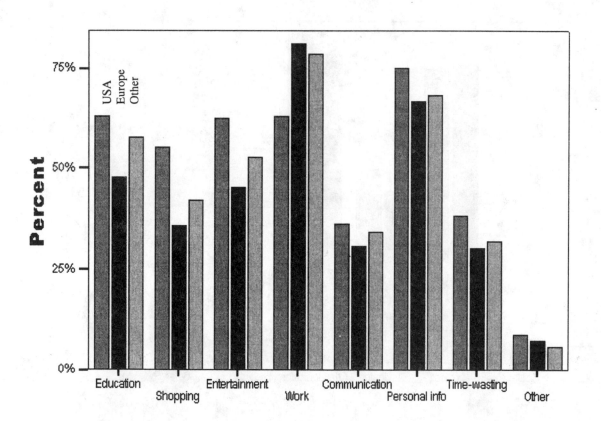

Copyright 1998 Georgia Tech Research Corporation. All rights reserved.
Source: GVU's WWW 10th User Survey (October 1998). Note: 1999 survey has not been completed.
www.gvu.gatech.edu/user_surveys

Frequency of Internet Use

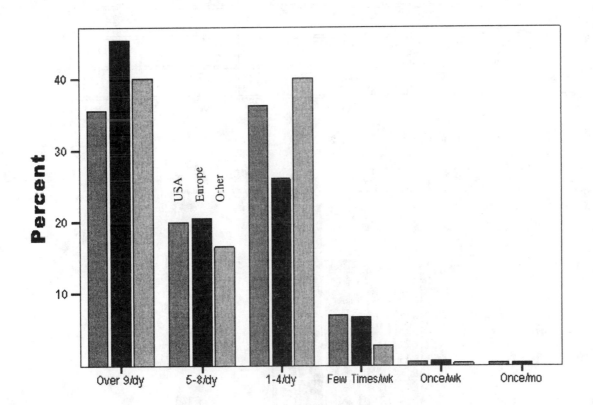

Copyright 1998 Georgia Tech Research Corporation. All rights reserved.
Source: GVU's WWW 10th User Survey (October 1998). Note: 1999 survey has not been completed.
www.gvu.gatech.edu/user_surveys

Years on Internet

		Frequency	Percent	Valid Percent	Cumulative Percent
Valid	Under 6 mo	273	5.4	5.4	5.4
	6-12 mo	380	7.6	7.6	13.0
	1-3 yr	1736	34.6	34.6	47.6
	4-6 yr	1861	37.1	37.1	84.6
	Over 7 yr	772	15.4	15.4	100.0
	Total	5022	100.0	100.0	

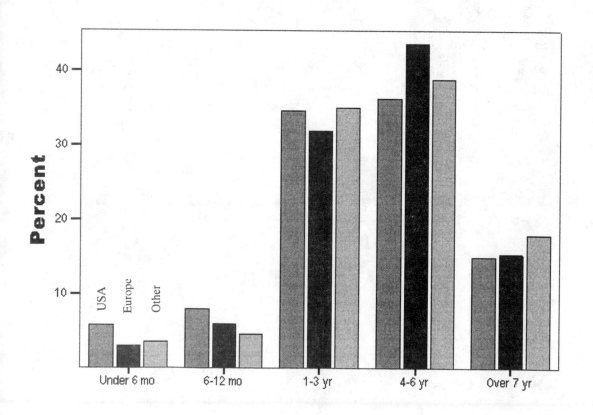

Copyright 1998 Georgia Tech Research Corporation. All rights reserved.
Source: GVU's WWW 10th User Survey (October 1998). Note: 1999 survey has not been completed.
www.gvu.gatech.edu/user_surveys

Primary Industry in Which Internet Users Work

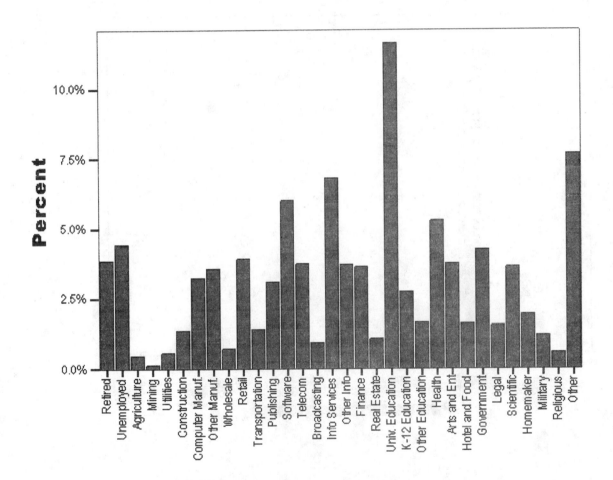

Copyright 1998 Georgia Tech Research Corporation. All rights reserved.
Source: GVU's WWW 10th User Survey (October 1998). Note: 1999 survey has not been completed.
www.gvu.gatech.edu/user_surveys

Primary Language of Internet Users

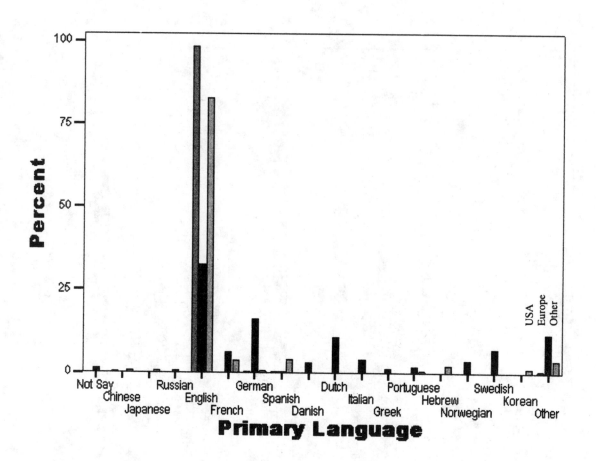

Copyright 1998 Georgia Tech Research Corporation. All rights reserved.
Source: GVU's WWW 10th User Survey (October 1998). Note: 1999 survey has not been completed.
www.gvu.gatech.edu/user_surveys

Household Income of Internet Users

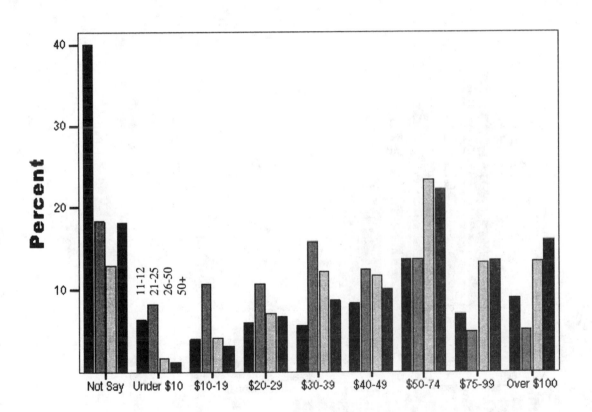

Copyright 1998 Georgia Tech Research Corporation. All rights reserved.
Source: GVU's WWW 10th User Survey (October 1998). Note: 1999 survey has not been completed.
www.gvu.gatech.edu/user_surveys

Education Attainment of Internet Users

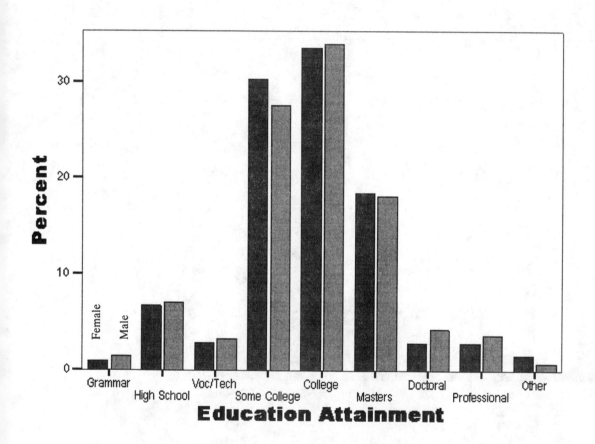

Copyright 1998 Georgia Tech Research Corporation. All rights reserved.
Source: GVU's WWW 10th User Survey (October 1998). Note: 1999 survey has not been completed.
www.gvu.gatech.edu/user_surveys

Kind of Area Internet Users Live In

		Frequency	Percent	Valid Percent	Cumulative Percent
Valid	Urban	1873	37.3	37.3	37.3
	Suburban	2455	48.9	48.9	86.2
	Rural	694	13.8	13.8	100.0
	Total	5022	100.0	100.0	

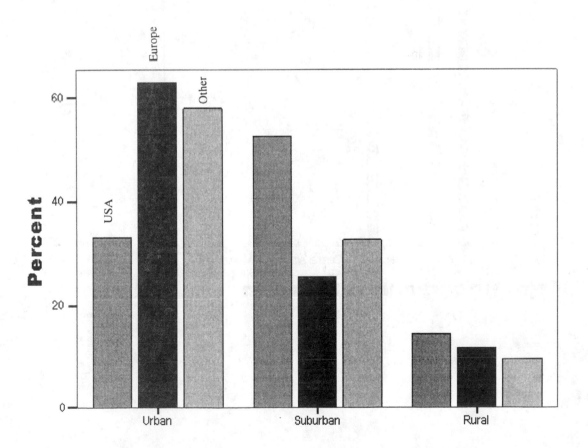

Copyright 1998 Georgia Tech Research Corporation. All rights reserved.
Source: GVU's WWW 10th User Survey (October 1998). Note: 1999 survey has not been completed.
www.gvu.gatech.edu/user_surveys

Major Geographic Location of Internet Users

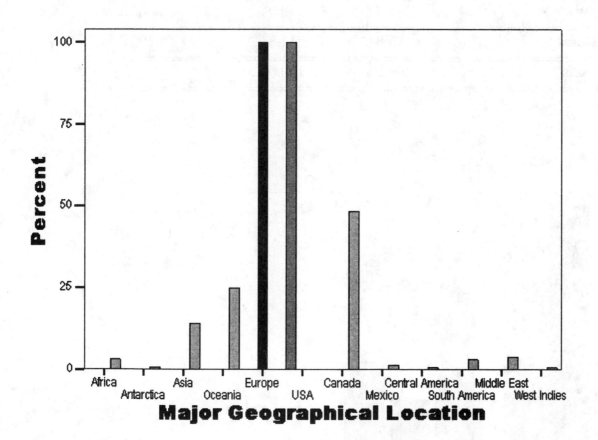

Copyright 1998 Georgia Tech Research Corporation. All rights reserved.
Source: GVU's WWW 10th User Survey (October 1998). Note: 1999 survey has not been completed.
www.gvu.gatech.edu/user_surveys

Ethnicity of Internet Users

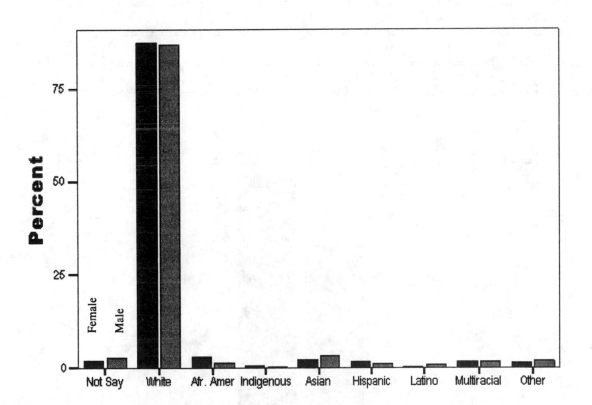

Copyright 1998 Georgia Tech Research Corporation. All rights reserved.
Source: GVU's WWW 10th User Survey (October 1998). Note: 1999 survey has not been completed.
www.gvu.gatech.edu/user_surveys

Gender of Internet Users

Gender

		Frequency	Percent	Valid Percent	Cumulative Percent
	Female	1685	33.6	33.6	33.6
Valid	Male	3337	66.4	66.4	100.0
	Total	5022	100.0	100.0	

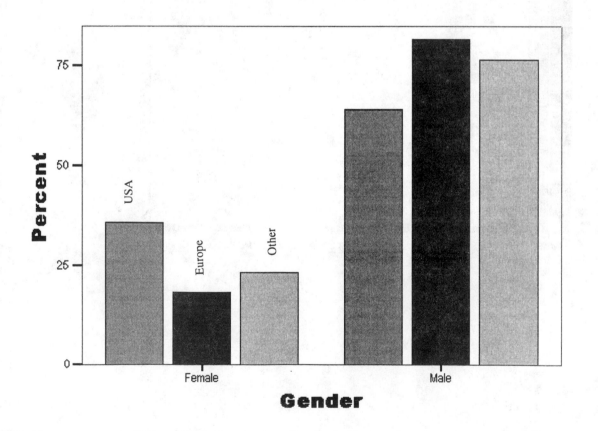

Copyright 1998 Georgia Tech Research Corporation. All rights reserved.
Source: GVU's WWW 10th User Survey (October 1998). Note: 1999 survey has not been completed.
www.gvu.gatech.edu/user_surveys

Age of Internet Users

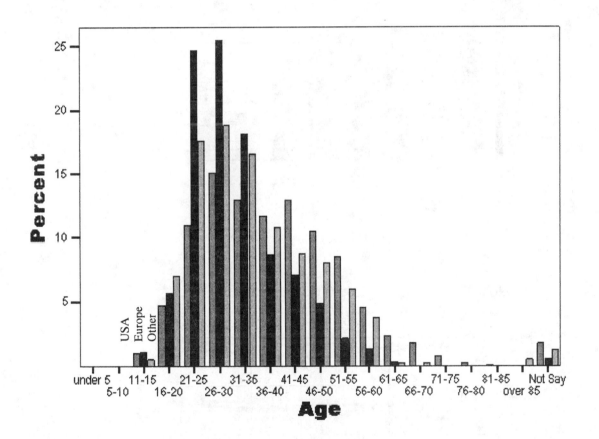

Copyright 1998 Georgia Tech Research Corporation. All rights reserved.
Source: GVU's WWW 10th User Survey (October 1998). Note: 1999 survey has not been completed.
www.gvu.gatech.edu/user_surveys

Search Engine Data
(collected from Oct.10-Dec. 15, 1998)

KEY: YH=Yahoo, AV=AltaVista, EX=Excite, LY=Lycos, Go=Go/Infoseek,
HB=HotBot, WC=WebCrawler, G2N=Go2Net/MetaCrawler, AOL=AOL NetFind.

Search Services Used

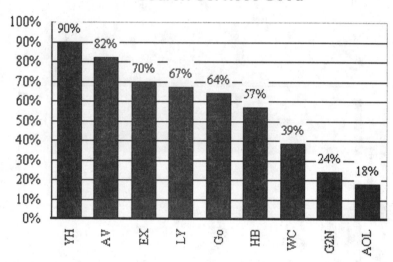

How Do You Find New Web Pages/Sites?

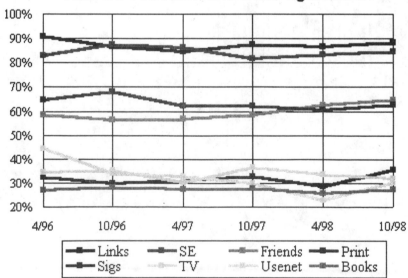

Copyright 1998 Georgia Tech Research Corporation. All rights reserved.
Source: GVU's WWW 10th User Survey (October 1998). Note: 1999 survey has not been completed.
www.gvu.gatech.edu/user_surveys

E-mail Packages Used

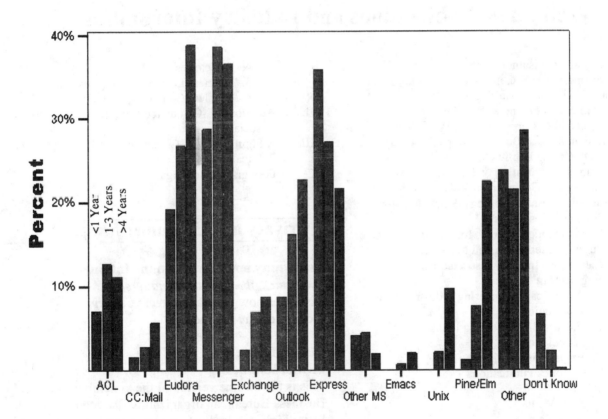

Chapter 5

E-COMMERCE & INTERNET CONTACTS

Web Sites, Publications and Industry Information

I.   Privacy and Consumer Matters
II. Major Internet & E-Commerce Consultants (and major firms with consulting arms)
III. Recommended Financial Data Sites
   A. Financial & Corporate Data Web Sites
   B. Recommended Business Magazines
   C. IPOS (Initial Public Offerings)
IV. E-Commerce Education & Training
V.   Recommended Government-Related Web Sites
VI. Internet Business/Technology-Related Contacts
   A. Business Resources
   B. Recommended Sources for On-line Consumer Buying Pattern Data and Market Analysis
   C. Electronics Industry Associations
   D. Engineering
      1. Acoustical Engineering Industry Associations
      2. Electrical Engineering Industry Associations
      3. Engineering Indices
   E. Fiber Optics Publications
   F. Media
      1. New Media
      2. Multimedia
   G. Microelectronics Industry
      1. Associations/Consortia
      2. Manufacturers/Suppliers
      3. Microelectronics Trade Associations
   H. Search Assistance
   I. Semiconductors
   J. Telecommunications
      1. Telecommunications Organizations
      2. Telecom Publications
      3. Regional

      4. Directories
      5. Wireless Local Loop Reports
      6. Wireless Communications Publications
VII. Additional E-Commerce and Internet Industry Associations
VIII. A Short List of E-Commerce and Internet Related Publications
IX.   Foreign Internet Organizations

I. Privacy and Consumer Matters

Anonymity and Privacy on the Internet
www.stack.nl/~galactus/remailers/
Discusses how you can protect your privacy and security on the Internet.

BBBOnLine
www.bbbonline.org
This is the on-line version of the venerable Better Business Bureau, an organization that attempts to foster high standards of customer service and on-line privacy.

Electronic Frontier Foundation
www.eff.org
EFF is a protector of civil liberties on the Internet. This non-profit, non-partisan organization strives to protect free speech while protecting children from potentially offensive materials, to protect privacy while allowing recovery for damages and to find ways

to legislate something that is everywhere and nowhere all at once.

Electronic Privacy Information

www.epic.org
EPIC, a public interest research center, examines emerging civil liberties issues, the First Amendment and constitutional values. Using the Freedom of Information Act and litigation, EPIC offers the public information about what its government is doing, ensuring oversight and accountability. This group works in tandem with Privacy International, a human rights group in the UK.

Federal Trade Commission

www.ftc.gov/privacy
This department of the Federal Government is responsible for many aspects of business-to-consumer and business-to-business trade and regulation.

MyPrivacy.org

www.myprivacy.org
A privacy service organized by PrivaSeek, MyPrivacy.org allows the Internet user to set specific preferences for on-line identification that will be honored by all web sites participating in the program.

Privacy International

www.privacyinternational.org
Privacy International is a government and business watchdog, alerting individuals to wiretapping and national security activities, medical privacy infringement, police information systems and the use of ID cards, video surveillance and data matching.

Privacy Journal

www.townonline.com/privacyjournal
The Privacy Journal is a monthly report on the impact of new technology on individual privacy.

Privacy Times

www.privacytimes.com
This site is for attorneys and professionals wishing to follow legislation and developments in the information privacy arena, including the Freedom of Information Act, direct marketing, Caller ID and credit reports.

PrivaSeek

www.privaseek.com
A for-profit company specializing in Internet privacy, PrivaSeek's Persona technology lets the user decide just what information is given and received while on-line.

TRUSTe

www.truste.org
TRUSTe, a non-profit agency, formed an alliance with all major portal sites to launch the Privacy Partnership campaign, a consumer education program designed to raise the awareness of Internet privacy issues. The organization works to meet the needs of business web sites while protecting user privacy.

To get names removed from most mailing lists, write to:

Mail Preference Service
Direct Marketing Association
P. O. Box 9008
Farmingdale, NY 11735-9008

II. Major Internet & E-Commerce Consultants (and major firms with consulting arms)

CPS Direct

www.cpsdirect.com
Woburn, MA

Computer Sciences Corp.

www.csc.com
El Segundo, CA

Deloitte Consulting

www.dc.com
New York, NY

EDS

www.eds.com
Plano, TX

Ernst & Young

www.ey.com
New York, NY

Euro RSCG Worldwide Interactive

www.eurorscg.com
New York, NY

Grey New Technologies

www.grey.com
New York, NY

Hewlett-Packard
www.hp.com
Palo Alto, CA

Hill, Holiday Interactive
www.hhcc.com
Boston, MA

IBM
www.ibm.com
Armonk, NY

IllusionFusion
www.illusionfusion.com
New York

iXL
www.ixl.com
Atlanta, GA

KPMG Consulting
www.kpmgconsulting.com
Mountain View, CA

Luminant Worldwide
www.luminant.com
Dallas, TX

Modem Media Poppe Tyson
www.modemmedia.com
Norwalk, CT

Netscape
www.iplanet.com
Mountain View, CA

Novo Interactive
www.novointeractive.com
San Francisco, CA

Periscope
www.periscope.com
Minneapolis, MN

PricewaterhouseCoopers
www.pwcglobal.com
London and New York

Proxicom
www.proxicom.com
Reston, VA

Publicis Technology
www.ptglobal.com
San Francisco, CA

Risdall Linnihan Interactive
www.risdall.com
New Brighton, MN

Sapient
www.sapient.com
Cambridge, MA

Silicon Graphics
www.sgi.com
Mountain View, CA

Stein Rogan and Partners
www.srpadv.com
New York, NY

Strategic Interactive Group
www.sig.bsh.com
Boston, MA

Sun Microsystems
www.sun.com
Palo Alto, CA

Targetbase Marketing
www.targetbase.com
Dallas, TX

Think New Ideas
www.thinkinc.com
New York, NY

Transaction Information Systems
www.tisny.com
New York, NY

US Interactive
www.usinteractive.com
New York, NY

USWeb/CKS
www.uswebcks.com
San Francisco, CA

Viant
www.viant.com
Boston

Xceed

www.xceed.com

New York, NY

III. Recommended Financial Data Sites

A. Financial & Corporate Data Web Sites

CBS Marketwatch

www.cbsmarketwatch.com

In addition to financial news, CBS Marketwatch offers multiple personal portfolios, market and company research, interday and technical charting, mutual and money market fund data, direct brokerage access and reliable delayed quotes. All services are offered free of charge.

CNNfn Home Page

www.CNNfn.com

The same in-depth financial information that this cable television financial news unit provides to television viewers can be found on this web site.

Companylink

www.companylink.com

Current news, contacts and web site links for 85,000 private and public companies are available here.

Corporate Information Online

www.corporateinformation.com

This site contains a list of other sites that offer information about companies and is organized by country. This useful site's wealth of corporate links can both enhance and ease any researcher's work.

Hoover's Online

www.hoovers.com

Austin, Texas-based Hoover's provides business information on-line through its superior web site. This comprehensive site features links to news, lists, stock quotes and other products such as Hoover's Industry Snapshots. This site offers over 50,000 company capsules (brief company descriptions and financials), and thousands of in-depth company profiles (company histories, strategies, market positions, major events and other information). The profiles cover U.S. and foreign public and nonpublic companies and are written in an engaging style. These snapshots are provided free-of-charge.

Internet Stock Reporter

www.internetnews.com/stocks/

This site offers Steve Harmon's insights on Internet stocks and allows users to receive free e-mail reports each morning before the market opens.

InvesterTech

www.easystock.com

Here, users can find powerful, easy-to-use technical analysis tools. Easy Chart Live, included in these tools, has an interactive intraday Java applet. Charts are updated every minute, and users can analyze up to eight different data periods. InvesterTech features a custom outlook tool that enable multiple stocks to be viewed through one chart window.

Market Guide

www.marketguide.com

For over 15 years, Market Guide has provided the professional investment community with investment information. New companies are added and updated continually to make Market Guide's database extremely timely and comprehensive. Over 12,000 companies can be researched here.

MSN Money Central

http://moneycentral.msn.com

This site features daily announcements, special reports, highlights from financial providers and a wealth of links and other financial information.

Nasdaq-Amex.com

www.amex.com

In November 1998, the National Association of Securities Dealers, Inc. (NASD) and the American Stock Exchange (Amex) officially joined forces. As a result of this merger, The Nasdaq-Amex Market Group has been formed, creating one of the most advanced, efficient and globally competitive markets in the world.

Silicon Valley.com

www.siliconvalley.com

This site offers an excellent summary of current news in the field of technology, including six daily updates. Silicon Valley additionally offers useful information on Asian and Israeli markets.

Silicon Investor

www.siliconinvestor.com

Silicon Investor is focused on investments in technology companies. The site serves as a financial discussion forum and additionally offers quotes, profiles and charts.

B. RECOMMENDED BUSINESS MAGAZINES

Business 2.0
www.business2.com
Business 2.0 takes a look at business in the information age. A well-rounded and focused magazine for e-commerce entrepreneurs and investors.

Business Week Online
www.businessweek.com
This informative and useful on-line version of Business Week magazine offers an investor service, global business advice, technology news, small business guides, career information, a retirement guide, daily news briefs and more.

Computerworld E-Commerce
www.computerworld.com/home/ecommerce.nsf/all/index
Bi-weekly on-line companion to ComputerWorld covering e-commerce trends and developments.

E Business Magazine
http://hpcc920.external.hp.com
Monthly magazine from Hewlett Packard covering electronic commerce, e-trends, and more.

EC.com
www.ecmedia.com
Monthly publication written for technical and corporate managers that covers who technical issues and business strategies relating to the converging technologies of Electronic Commerce.

eCommerce Guidebook
www.online-commerce.com
A step-by-step guide to the process of becoming eCommerce enabled, a listing of all the known Online Transaction Providers, and a condensed comparison of the prices and services they offer.

eCommerce Info Center
www.ecommerceinfocenter.com
Informative Web site covering all aspects of e-commerce. Contains over 3000 links in a variety of categories.

E-Commerce Tax News
www.ecommercetax.com
Weekly newsletter covering taxation of electronic commerce.

Electronic Commerce World
www.ecomworld.com
Monthly magazine covering electronic commerce implementation, financial EDI, electronic messaging, workflow automation and imaging.

EMarketer
www.emarketer.com
eMarketer is a comprehensive, objective and easy to use resource for anyone or any business interested in the Internet. The site offers news articles, market projections and analytical commentaries.

Forbes Online
www.forbes.com
This top-quality financial and business magazine maintains a fascinating web site. The toolbox contains calculators, a financial calendar, current economic information, Forbes lists and surveys. A mortgage center, a career center, a small business center and a mutual funds buyer's guide are available. Archives, Forbes global information, e-business information, technology news and company files can be accessed through this comprehensive site as well.

Fortune
www.fortune.com
One of the world's best business magazines, Fortune contains comprehensive information about all facets of U.S. and international business.

IBM's Think Leadership Magazine
www.ibm.com/thinkmag/index1.html
Includes in-depth articles related to management, e-commerce and IT issues.

Industry Standard
www.thestandard.net
The Industry Standard features industry news and information on commerce, media, politics and policy, technology and health. Its focus is on e-business. The web site is chock full of up-to-the-minute information. The Standard also hosts numerous conferences, including The Internet Summit, iB2B, Net 21 Honors and iDeals.

Internet World

www.internetworld.com

This magazine focuses on the business and technology segments of the Internet. Past issues have focused on such topics as Globalization, Web Host and ISP rankings, Metamodels and The Most Influential Internet Services and Products.

MIT Sloan eBusiness Awards

www.mit.awards.org

The MIT Sloan eBusiness Awards recognize and reward successful innovation in eBusiness in such categories as Global Reach, Industry Transformation and International Power Player.

Net Market Makers

www.netmarketers.com

Covers developments, trends, and issues for intermediate, or vertical markets bringing together business to business transactions on the Internet.

Red Herring

www.redherring.com

Red Herring "covers the business of technology and all the business that technology touches." The magazine looks at companies and industries, analyzing the impact of technology and its position as an asset to business.

Upside

www.upside.com

This magazine examines industries that are involved with the Internet and technology, including media, telecommunications and entertainment. Each issue offers editorial comment, company profiles, market analysis and profiles of the people making things happen in the industry, as well as articles that look at the way technology is influencing our lives on a daily basis.

VentureWire

www.venturewire.com

(on-line only, published by Technologic Partners)

A daily electronic newsletter with the latest information on venture capital, mergers, acquisitions, startups and management changes in the e-commerce business.

The Wall Street Journal Online

www.wsj.com

The outstanding resources of The Wall Street Journal are now available on-line for a nominal fee.

C. IPOS (INITIAL PUBLIC OFFERINGS)

Alert IPO

www.ostman.com/alert-ipo

This site provides subscribers with e-mail alerts about IPO-related SEC filings.

Inter@ctive Investor

www.zdii.com/thedayahead.asp

This site's stock commentary focuses on IPOs and tech stocks. With quick and easy analysis and outlook capabilities, this site's can assist the beginner and the experienced investor. A mutual funds research feature adds to this site.

IPO Central

www.hoovers.com

The IPO-specific section within the respected Hoover's Online business and financial information site.

IPO Data Systems

www.ipodata.com

In-depth data on recent initial public offerings is provided here.

IPO Maven

www.ipomaven.com

This site features both historical and current information on initial public offerings for investors.

Open IPO

www.openipo.com

This site, run by W.R. Hambrecht, focuses on ferreting out new and emerging companies. This site features information on research methods and capabilities, IPOs, an investor center and more.

Wit Capital

www.witcapital.com

Wit Capital is an investment banking and brokerage firm that develops relationships with substantial numbers of on-line individual investors.

IV. E-Commerce Education & Training
UNIVERSITY RESEARCH | UNIVERSITY
COURSES | ONLINE COURSES/TUTORIALS

ECRC E-business Education Seminars
www.online-commerce.com
The Department of Defense offers free e-business education seminars through the Electronic Commerce Resource Center program, with 17 outlets around the country.

UCLA
www.unex.ucla.edu/ecommerce
UCLA DCE (Division of Continuing Education) is offering a unique, hands-on, six module program through Extension. The program lasts twelve weeks and there are two sections: Friday-Saturday all day; Tuesday-Thursday evenings, Sunday all day session.

Electronic Commerce Resources at Berkeley
www.sims.berkley.edu/resources.ecommerce
The University of California Berkeley has a number of new courses, research projects, and special programs for e-commerce study. Last year, IBM was a major sponsor of this activity at the Haas School of Business, donating hardware, software, and staff time to design and run a new e-commerce course for undergraduate business students.

The ABC's of E-Commerce
www.virtualpromote.com/guest5.html
A Guide to Setting up a Profitable Web Site, By George DeCourcy, Anacom Communications, Inc.

How To Set Up Your E-Business
www.ibm.com/e-business/what/how/index.html
From IBM. Everything from identifying your target customers to technical issues. Focuses on unsing IBM's e-commerce products as solutions.

Wharton Forum on Electronic Commerce
http:// ecom.wharton.upenn.edu
From the Wharton School of the University of Pennsylvania: the Wharton Forum on Electronic Commerce is pursuing a research agenda to examine critical issues related to electronic commerce.

Introduction to Electronic Commerce
http://cism.bus.utexas.edu
Offered at University of Texas at Austin.

Information Technology & Electronic Commerce
www.dcb.du.edu/eccenter/center.htm
Offered at Daniels College of Business, University of Denver.

Electronic Commerce
www.heinz.cmu.edu/project/ec/hb/index.html
Offered at Carnegie Mellon University.

Electronic Commerce
www2.smeal.psu.edu/courses/mktg597d.rangaswamy
Offered at Penn State University.

Electronic Commerce
www.lehigh.edu/~mmg0/BIS331.html
Offered at Lehigh University.

Electronic Commerce
http://ecommerce.ncs.edu
Offered at NC State.

University of Texas at Arlington, The Art and Science of E-Commerce
www.uta.edu/infosys/e_comm
Offered at University of Texas at Arlington, The Art and Science of Electronic Commerce will explore the use of electronic media as an innovative approach for effective marketing. In this course the highly dynamic and rapidly expanding area of electronic commerce shall be viewed from multiple perspectives.

The Center for Research in Electronic Commerce
http://cism.bus.utexas.edu
The CREC, at the University of Texas is the leading research institution in generating critical knowledge and understanding in the fields of Information Systems and Management, Electronic Commerce and the Digital Economy.

Agent Mediated E-Commerce
http://ecommerce.media.mit.edu
From MIT Media Lab. Investigates how software agent technologies can expedite the electronic commerce revolution.

International Center for Electronic Commerce
http://icec.net
Based in Korea. Objectives include development of the next generation electronic commerce technologies and management schemes and establish an international research consortium of electronic commerce related companies.

Electronic Commerce Research Project
www.ecrp.org/english/ecrp_e.html
Located at the Keio Business School, Keio University, Japan. The Laboratory conducts research on the effects of the introduction of information technology on management processes within and between companies.

Center For Managing in Electronic Environments
http://130.207.57.82
Research center devoted to the study of how organizations and managers make use of information technology to manage in electronic environments.

Center for the Study of Electronic Commerce
www.dcb.du.edu/eccenter/center.htm
Daniels College of Business, University of Denver.

WebSite 101
www.website101.com
Weekly tips and suggestions to help improve your on-line store.

V. Recommended Government-Related Web Sites

Access to Federal Implementation Conventions
http://snad.ncsl.nist.gov/dartg/edi/fededi.html
The National Institute of Standards and Technology.

Advisory Commission on Electronic Commerce
www.ecommercecommission.org
The Advisory Commission on Electronic Commerce (ACEC) was created by Congress to study federal, state, local and international taxation and tariffs on transactions using the Internet and Internet access.

Board of Governors of the Federal Reserve System
Phone: 202-452-3684
www.bog.frb.fed.us
This free site offers extensive background on the Federal Reserve System, as well as congressional testimony, economic indicator analyses and specific consumer information.

Bureau of Economic Analysis
Phone: 202-606-9600
www.bea.doc.gov
BEA, an agency of the U.S. Department of Commerce, is the nation's economic accountant, preparing estimates that illuminate key national, international and regional aspects of the United States economy.

Bureau of Labor Statistics
Phone: 202-606-5886
http://stats.bls.gov
The BLS is the principal fact-finding agency for the Federal Government in the broad field of labor economics and statistics. The BLS is an independent national statistical agency that collects, processes, analyzes and disseminates essential statistical data to the American public, the U.S. Congress, other Federal agencies, state and local governments, business and labor. The BLS also serves as a statistical resource to the Department of Labor.

Federal Electronic Commerce Program Office
http://ec.fed.gov
Official web site of the office, whose mission is to develop a policy framework to support EC, help government agencies find and use the best EC tools, and spread the most promising ideas across government.

National Electronic Commerce Resource Center
www.ecrc.ctc.com
The ECRC Program assists industrial and government organizations to enter the world of electronic commerce.

STAT-USA Internet
www.stat-usa.gov
STAT-USA delivers vital economic, business and international trade information produced by the U.S. Government to persons that may then use that information to make important decisions affecting business, community and personal finances. This site scours the government information vaults, assembles information in one location and delivers it to the public.

U.S. Census Bureau
www.census.gov
The Census Bureau web site is designed to enable intuitive use of the bureau's Internet offerings. Designed with user-friendliness, visitors do not need much familiarity with the bureau's internal organizational structure to utilize this site.

U.S. Department of Commerce
www.doc.gov
The Department of Commerce promotes job creation, economic growth, sustainable development and improved living standards for all Americans by working in partnership with businesses, universities, communities and workers to build for the future and to

promote U.S. competitiveness in the global marketplace.

U.S. Government Policy on Electronic Commerce
www.ecommerce.gov
Outline of the U.S. Government's official policy regarding electronic commerce and its involvement with the Internet.

U.S. Securities and Exchange Commission
www.sec.com
The SEC is a nonpartisan, quasi-judicial regulatory agency responsible for administering federal securities laws. These laws are to protect investors in securities markets and ensure they have access to disclosure of all material information concerning publicly-traded securities.

White House
www.whitehouse.gov/WH/Welcome.html
This site was designed for communication between the Federal Government and the American people. It provides access to all government information and services that are available on the Internet.

VI. Internet Business/Technology-Related Contacts

A. Business Resources

AT&T Business Network
www.att.com/business/
Offers powerful business services such as CNN, Dow Jones, the Thomas Register and TRW databases.

Commercial Internet eXchange
www.cix.org
Tel.: 703-709-8200
1041 Sterling Rd.
Herndon, VA 20170

Emerging E-Commerce Regulation
www.techweb.com
Articles about e-commerce and Information Technology.

InterNIC
www.internic.net
Provides public information regarding Internet domain name registration services.

Intercat
www.intercat.com/
Ph: 562-961-0103
Fax: 800-634-9524
3399 East 19th Street
Long Beach, CA 90804
Publishes catalogs or other information to the web. Links to catalogs and other services.

Internet Providers' Consortium
www.ispc.org
Fax: 603-372-1539
221 14th St.
San Francisco, CA 94103

Internet Society
www.isoc.org
Tel.: 703-326-9880
Fax: 703-326-9881
11150 Sunset Hills Rd., Ste. 100
Reston, VA 20190

List, The
http://thelist.internet.com
Tel.: 203-662-2800
Internet Service Providers. Find ISPs by entering an area code or country.

B. Recommended sources for on-line consumer buying pattern data and market analysis:

Cyber Dialogue
www.cyberdialogue.com

Dataquest
www.dataquest.com

Forrester Research
www.forrester.com

Jupiter Communications
http://jup.com

Shop.org/BCG
www.Shop.org

BizRate.com
www.bizrate.com

Ernst & Young
www.ey.com

C. Electronics Industry Associations

American Electronics Association
www.aeanet.org
Toll-free: 800-284-4232
5201 Great American Pkwy., Ste. 520
Santa Clara, CA 95054

The Electronic Industries Association
www.eia.org
Tel.: 703-907-7500
2500 Wilson Blvd.
Arlington, VA 22201

Electronics Technicians Association
www.eta-sda.com
Tel.: 765-653-8262
602 North Jackson
Greencastle, IN 46135

Institute for Electrical and Electronics Engineers Employment Service
www.ieee.org/jobs.html
1828 L Street, NW, Ste. 1202
Washington, DC 20036-5104
Job listings by geographic area, a resume bank and links to employment services are featured among other items of interest.

D. Engineering

1. ACOUSTICAL ENGINEERING INDUSTRY ASSOCIATIONS

Audio Engineering Society
www.aes.org
Tel.: 212-661-8528
Fax: 212-682-0477
60 East 42nd Street, Room 2520
New York, NY 10165
Information on educational and career opportunities in audio engineering.

2. ELECTRICAL ENGINEERING INDUSTRY ASSOCIATIONS

ASEE Clearinghouse for Engineering Education
www.asee.org/
Tel.: 202-331-3500
Fax: 202-265-8504
1818 N Street N.W., Ste. 600
Washington, DC 20036

Includes databases of engineering associations and education programs, as well as links to electrical engineering resources.

Electrical Engineering on the World Wide Web
www.e2w3.com/
E2W3 provides a searchable index of links to companies that manufacture semiconductors, computer hardware and software, including links to publications and information on conferences, educational programs and associations.

EXACT
http://exact.fmv.se/
Access to reports and a directory of test equipment.

Institute of Electrical and Electronics Societies
www.ieee.org/society.html
Directory of technical societies from the Institute of Electrical and Electronics Engineers.

International Electrotechnical Commission
www.hike.te.chiba-u.ac.jp/ikeda/IEC/home.html
Site of the Switzerland-based IEC, which promotes international cooperation on all questions of standardization and related matters in electrical and electronic engineering.

Professional Organizations and Government Labs for Electrical Engineers
www.ee.umr.edu/orgs/
Links to professional organizations and government labs.

3. ENGINEERING INDICES

Applied Research Laboratories
http://gopher.arlut.utexas.edu
Tel.: 512-835-3200
Fax: 512-835-3259
P.O. Box 8029
Austin, TX 78713
Applied Research Laboratories at the University of Texas provides organizational directories and electronic resources.

Engineer's Club, The
www.engineers.com/
Tel.: 408-445-2902
Fax: 408-265-2410
1737 Silverwood Dr.
San Jose, CA 95124

Internet Connections for Engineering Index
www.englib.cornell.edu/ice
A comprehensive catalog of engineering resources.

E. Fiber Optics Publications

Fiber Optics News
Phillips International, Inc.
www.phillips.com
Tel: 301-340-2100
1201 Seven Locks Road
Potomac, MD 20854

IEEE LCS (The Magazine of Lightwave Communications Systems)
IEEE Communications Society
www.comsoc.org
Tel: 212-705-8900
Fax: 212-705-8999
345 East 47th Street
New York, NY 10017-2394

Laser Focus World: Global Electro-Optic Technology and Markets
PennWell Publishing Co.
www.pennwell.com
Tel: 918-835-3161
1421 S. Sheridan
Tulsa, OK 74112

Lightwave
PennWell Publishing Co.
www.pennwell.com
Tel: 918-835-3161
1421 S. Sheridan
Tulsa, OK 74112

Photonics Spectra
Laurin Publishing Co., Inc.
www.photonics.com
Tel: 413-499-0514
Berkshire Common
P.O. Box 4949
Pittsfield, MA 01202

F. Media

1. NEW MEDIA

Association for Interactive Media
www.interactivehq.org
Tel.: 202-408-0008
Fax: 202-408-0111

1301 Connecticut Ave. NW, 5th Fl.
Washington, DC 20036
Non-profit trade association for business users of the Internet.

2. MULTIMEDIA

MMWIRE WEB
www.mmwire.com/
On-line magazine about multimedia and design

G. Microelectronics Industry

The following list is of various private web sites that provide microelectronics industry information provided by the Department of Commerce.

1. ASSOCIATIONS/CONSORTIA

American Electronics Association
www.aeanet.com

Electronic Industries Association
www.eia.org
Tel.: 703-907-7500
2500 Wilson Blvd.
Arlington, VA 22201

Institute for Interconnecting and Packaging Electronic Circuits
www.ipc.org/
Tel.: 847-509-9700
Fax: 847-509-9798
2215 Sanders Rd.
Northbrook, IL 60062

Interconnection Technology Research Institute
www.itri.org/
Tel.: 512-833-9930
11801 Stonehollow Drive, Ste. 400
Austin, TX 78758

International Microelectronics and Packaging Society
www.ishm.ee.vt.edu
Toll-free: 888-464-6277
1850 Centennial Park Drive, Ste. 105
Reston, VA 20191

National Consortia of Manufacturing Sciences
www.ncms.org

Semiconductor Equipment Material International
www.semi.org
Tel.: 650-964-5111
805 East Middlefield Rd.
Mountain View, CA 94043

Semiconductor Industry Association
www.semichips.org
Tel.: 408-436-6600
181 Metro Drive, Ste. 450
San Jose, CA 95110

Virginia Center for Innovative Technology
www.cit.org

2. MANUFACTURERS/SUPPLIERS

DataGalaxy
www.datagalaxy.com

Hearst's Electronic Engineers Master On-line Catalog
www.hearstelectroweb.com

Interconnect Information Resource Directory
www.eenet.com/intc

Interactive Component Sourcing Directory
www.ace-quote.com

Semiconductor Online
www.semiconductoronline.com

3. MICROELECTRONICS TRADE ASSOCIATIONS

American Electronics Association
www.aeanet.com
Tel.: 408-987-4200
AEA represents thousands of U.S. electronics firms including electronic systems and component manufacturers, suppliers and end-users. Publishes annual AEA Directory with geographic and product indexes.

Electronic Industries Alliance
www.eia.org
Tel.: 703-907-7500
2500 Wilson Blvd.
Arlington, VA 22201

EIA, formerly known as the Electronics Industries Association, represents thousands of electronics firms, including electronic components (especially passive components manufacturers and end user) and consumer electronics manufacturers. Publishes annual Electronic Market Data Book and Trade Directory and Membership List. Hosts domestic Trade Shows and Conferences.

Institute for Interconnecting and Packaging Electronic Circuits
www.ipc.org
Tel.: 847-509-9700
2215 Sanders Rd.
Northbrook, IL 60062
IPC represents companies whose products relate to: printed circuit boards (PCBs), materials or equipment used in PCB production processes and the assembly of board products (including OEMs, independent producers and contract manufacturers/assembly-houses). Publishes the semi-annual report from Technology Market Forecast Committee and numerous standards publications and organizes numerous semi-annual conferences on technology and marketing issues. Hosts domestic Trade Show–IPC EXPO.

International Microelectronics and Packaging Society
www.imaps.org
Tel.: 703-758-1060
1850 Centennial Park Dr., Ste. 105
Reston, VA 20191
IMAPS represents manufacturers of hybrid microcircuits and electronic packaging products. Publishes the International Journal of Microcircuits and Electronic Packaging among other publications. They host the semi-annual technology and market research conference.

Semiconductor Industry Association
www.semichips.org/
Tel.: 408-436-6600
181 Metro Dr., Ste. 450
San Jose, CA 95110
SIA represents U.S. semiconductor manufacturers. Publishes annual Status Report & Industry Directory, and World Semiconductor Trade Statistics, which tracks semiconductor shipments by regional market and by product.

Semiconductor Equipment and Materials International
www.semi.org/
Tel.: 650-964-5111
805 E. Middlefield Rd.
Mountain View, CA 94043
SEMI represents international manufacturers production and test equipment and electronic materials. Publishes CHANNEL magazine and hosts domestic and international trade events.

Surface Mount Technology Association
www.smta.org
Tel: 612-920-7682
Fax: 612-926-1819
5200 Willson Rd., Ste. 215
Edina, MN 55424
SMTA represents manufacturers of products utilizing SMT applications. Involved in technical conference and seminar organization.

H. Search Assistance

Business Directions International
www.business.com.au/
Search directory to find business sites on the Internet.

Index
www.library.vanderbilt.edu/law/acqs/pubr.htm
Search for vendors or publishers by name, subject, e-mail address or geographic location.

Starting Points for Internet
www.ncsa.uiuc.edu/SDG/Software/Mosaic/StartingPoi nts/NetworkStartingPoints.html
Links to Internet resources. Including Gopher, Veronica, Finger, Usenet, WAIS.

I. Semiconductors

Semiconductor Business Association
www.semiconductor.org

Semiconductor Equipment and Materials International (SEMI)
www.semi.org
Tel.: 650-964-5111
805 East Middlefield Rd.
Mountain View, CA 94043

Semiconductor Manufacturing Technology (SEMATECH)
www.sematech.org/public/home.htm

Semiconductor Online
www.semiconductoronline.com
News and analysis of semiconductor business.

SPECNet
www.smartlink.net/~bmcd/semi/cat.html
Tel.: 805-254-7543
23535 Avenida Rotella
Valencia, CA 91355
Home of Semiconductor Process Equipment and Materials Network. News briefs and press releases.

SuperSite.Net
http://semiconductor.supersites.net

J. Telecommunications

1. TELECOMMUNICATIONS ORGANIZATIONS

American Communication Association
www.americancomm.org

Communications Workers of America
www.cwa-union.org

Federal Communications Commission, The
www.fcc.gov
Tel.: 202-418-0190
445 12th St. SW
Washington, D.C. 20554

Institute of Telecommunication Sciences
its.bldrdoc.gov.
325 Broadway
Boulder, CO 80303-3328
Tel.: 303-497-5216
ITS is the research and engineering branch of the National Telecommunications and Information Administration.

International Brotherhood of Electrical Workers
www.ibew.org
Tel.: 202-833-7000
Fax: 202-728-6056
1125 15th St. NW
Washington, D.C. 20005

National Exchange Carrier Association
www.neca.org/
Toll-free: 800-228-8597
80 South Jefferson Rd.
Whippany, NJ 07981

National Electrical Manufacturers Association
www.nema.org
Tel.: 703-841-3200
1300 North 17th St., Ste. 1847
Roslyn, VA 22209

Telecommunications Industry Association (TIA)
www.tiaonline.org
Tel.: 703-907-7700
Fax. 703-907-7727
2500 Wilson Boulevard, Ste. 300
Arlington, VA 22201
Represents small and large communications and
information technology providers.

Telecom Insight, Ltd.
www.telecominsight.com
Tel.: 303-683-3268
9457 S. University Blvd., #352
Highlands Ranch, CO 80162
Job matching service of professionals with
telecommunications and/or information technology
experience with companies.

TeleCom Resources
www.telecomresources.com
Toll-free: 800-800-6577
1824 N.E. Division, Ste. B
Bend, OR 97701
Search and placement services for the
telecommunications industry.

United States Telecom Association
www.usta.org
Tel.: 202-326-7300
1401 H St. NW, Ste. 600
Washington, DC 20005

World of Wireless Communications, The
www.wow-com.com
Tel.: 202-785-0081
1250 Connecticut Ave. NW, Ste. 800
Washington, D.C. 20035

2. TELECOM PUBLICATIONS

The Office of Telecommunications provides the
following list of publications as a convenient reference

for people seeking information on the
telecommunications industry, some of which are
endorsed by the U.S. Government.

America's Network
www.americasnetwork.com
Tel.: 714-513-8400
201 East Sandpointe Ave., Ste. 600
Santa Ana, CA 92707

Communications Week International
CMP Publications, Inc.
www.commweek.com
Tel: 516-562-5000
600 Community Drive
Manhasset, NY 11030

Discount Long Distance Digest
www.thedigest.com/current/index.html
Long-distance industry webzine.

Phone+Magazine
www.phoneplusmag.com
Telecommunications webzine.

Telecommunications Reports
www.tr.com
Tel: 202-842-3006
1333 H Street NW, Ste. 100 East
Washington, DC 20005

X-change Magazine
www.x-changemag.com/
Telecommunications webzine.

3. REGIONAL

AsiaCom
EuroCom
LatinCom
Pan-Asian Telecom
Baskerville Communications Corp.
www.baskervilleonline.com
Toll-free: 800-533-5909
15165 Ventura Blvd., Ste. 310
Sherman Oaks, CA 91403

Telecom Asia
Edgell Communications Co.
www.edgellcommunications.com
1 East First Street
Duluth, MN 55802

Brazil Telecom
European Telecom
India Telecom
Japan Telecom
Mexico Telecom
Russian Telecom
South American Telecom
Information Gatekeepers, Inc.
www.igigroup.com
214 Harvard Avenue
Boston, MA 02134
Tel: 617-232-3111
Fax: 617-734-8562

Middle East Communications
ICOM Publications
www.icompub.com

Telecom Market Report: China, India & Pacific Rim
Telecom Market Report: Latin America & the Caribbean
Telecom Market Report: Russia, Central Europe & Central Asia
International Technology Consultants
www.intl-tech.com
Tel: 301-907-0060
Fax: 301-907-6555
4340 East-West Highway, Ste. 1020
Bethesda, MD 20814-4411

4. DIRECTORIES

Allied Wireless Directory
Allied Business Intelligence, Inc.
www.alliedworld.com
Tel: 516-624-3113
Fax: 516-624-3115
202 Townsend Square
Oyster Bay, NY 11771

America's Network Directory (annual)
Advanstar Communications
www.advanstar.com
Tel.: 440-891-2766
Toll-free: 1-800-598-2839
Fax: (216) 891-2726
7500 Old Oak Boulevard
Cleveland, OH 44130

Global Mobile Directory & Yearbook
Baskerville Communications Corp.
Tel: 818-461-9660
Fax: 818-461-9661
15165 Ventura Blvd., Ste. 310
Sherman Oaks, CA 91403

Industry Basics,
Telecommunications Market Review and Forecast,
Telecommunications Export Guide,
Annual Telecommunications Source Book,
Newton's Telecom Dictionary
Multimedia Telecommunications Association
www.mmta.org
Tel.: 703-907-7470
2500 Wilson Blvd.
Arlington, VA 22201

ITU Global Directory
Statistical Yearbook
World Telecommunications Development Report
International Telecommunication Union
www.itu.int/home/
Tel: 011-41-22-730-51-11
General Secretariat - Sales Section
Place des Nations, CH-1211
Geneva 20, Switzerland

Official TIA Directory & Desk Reference (annual)
Telecommunications Industry Association
www.tiaonline.org
Tel: 703-907-7700
Fax: 703-907-7727
2500 Wilson Boulevard, Ste. 300
Arlington, VA 22201

Tarifica
Telephone Industry Directory (annual)
Wireless Industry Directory (annual)
Phillips Business Information, Inc.
www.phillips.com
Tel: 301-424-3338
1201 Seven Locks Road
Potomac, MD 20854

5. WIRELESS LOCAL LOOP REPORTS

Global Wireless Local Loop Markets
Northern Business Information
Tel: 212-512-2900
Fax: 212-512-2859
1221 Avenue of the Americas, 37th Floor
New York, NY 10020

Daily On-line News Services Competition NOW ($400)
Paging NOW ($450)
Wireless Net NOW ($450)
Wireless NOW ($400)
The Strategis Group
www.strategisgroup.com
Tel: 202-530-7500
Fax: 202-530-7550
1130 Connecticut Avenue, NW, Ste. 325
Washington, DC 20036-3915

Wireless Access Solutions to Local Loop Telephony: Emerging Markets & Competitive Analysis
Allied Business Intelligence
www.alliedworld.com
Tel: 516-624-3113
Fax: 516-624-3115
202 Townsend Square
Oyster Bay, NY 11771

World Demand for Wireless Local Loop Systems: A Country-By-Country Forecast Through Year 2002 ($4,995)
Herschel Shosteck Associates, Ltd.
www.shosteck.com
Tel: 301-589-2259
Fax: 301-588-3311
11160 Veirs Mill Road, Ste. 709
Wheaton, MD 20902-2538

6. WIRELESS COMMUNICATIONS PUBLICATIONS

The Office of Telecommunications provides the following list of publications as a convenient reference for people seeking information on the wireless communications industry, and inclusion does constitute U.S. Government endorsement of the publications listed below.

America's Network
www.americasnetwork.com
Tel: 714-513-8400
201 E. Sandpointe, Ste. 600
Santa Ana, CA 92707

Billing World
Telestrategies
www.telestrategies.com
Tel: 703-734-7050
1355 Beverly Road
McLean, VA 22101

Cellular Networking Perspectives
www.cnp-wireless.com
Toll-free: 800-633-5514
2636 Toronto Crescent NW
Calgary, Alberta Canada T2N3W1

Global Mobile Daily
Baskerville Communications Corp.
www.baskervilleonline.com
Tel: 818-461-9660
Fax: 818-461-9661
15165 Ventura Blvd., Ste. 310
Sherman Oaks, CA 91403

Global Telephony
Intertec Publishing
www.intertec.com
Tel: 913-341-1300
Fax: 913-967-1904
9800 Metcalf Ave.
Overland Park, KS 66212-2215

Microcell News
Probe Research, Inc
www.probersearch.com
Tel.: 973-285-1500
Three Wing Drive, Ste. 240
Cedar Knolls, NJ 07927-1097

Mobile Europe
Nexus Media Limited
www.commsjobsearch.com/nexusIT.html
Tel.: 44-1322-660070
Fax: 44-1322-661257
Nexus House
Swanley, Kent BR8 8HY
United Kingdom

Mobile Phone News
Phillips Business Information, Inc.
www.phillips.com
Tel: 301-340-1520
Fax: 301-424-4297
1201 Seven Locks Road
Potomac, MD 20854

Mobile Radio Technology
Intertec Publishing
www.intertec.com
Tel: 913-341-1300
Fax: 913-967-1904
9800 Metcalf Avenue
Overland Park, KS 66212-2215

Navigator
Imagination Publications
www.imaginepub.com
Tel: 312-627-1020
820 W. Jackson Blvd., Ste. 450
Chicago, IL 60607

PCS Week
Phillips Business Information, Inc.
www.phillips.com
Tel: 301-340-1520
Fax: 301-424-4297
1201 Seven Locks Road
Potomac, MD 20854

RCR (Radio Communications Report) (weekly)
Crain Communications Inc.
www.rcrnews.com
Toll-free: 800-678-9595
777 East Speer Boulevard
Denver, CO 80203

RF Design
Intertec Publishing
www.intertec.com
Tel: 913-341-1300
Fax: 913-967-1904
9800 Metcalf Avenue
Overland Park, KS 66212-2215

TR Wireless News
Telecommunications Reports International, Inc.
Toll-free: 800-822-6338
1333 H Street, NW, Ste. 100 E
Washington, DC 20005

Wideband
www.widebandmag.com
Tel.: 212-951-6600
270 Madison Ave.
New York, NY 10016

Wireless Access & Personal Communications Networks
Communications & Marketing Systems
Tel.: 301-975-9700
P.O. Box 1479
Bethesda, MD 20827

Wireless Business & Finance
Phillips Business Information, Inc.
www.phillips.com
Tel: 301-340-1520
Fax: 301-424-4297
1201 Seven Locks Road
Potomac, MD 20854

Wireless Business & Technology
Phillips Business Information, Inc.
www.phillips.com
Tel: 301-340-1520
Fax: 301-424-4297
1201 Seven Locks Road
Potomac, MD 20854

Wireless Data News
Phillips Business Information, Inc.
www.phillips.com
Tel: 301-340-1520
1201 Seven Locks Road
Potomac, MD 20854

Wireless Review
Intertec Publishing
www.intertec.com
Tel: 913-341-1300
Fax: 913-967-1904
9800 Metcalf Avenue
Overland Park, KS 66212-2215

Wireless Systems Design
Penton Media, Inc.
www.penton.com
Tel: 201-393-6286
Fax: 201-393-6297
611 Route 46 West
Hasbrouck Heights, NJ 07604

Wireless Telecommunications
Information Gatekeepers, Inc.
www.igigroup.com
Tel: 617-232-3111
214 Harvard Avenue
Boston, MA 02134

Wireless Today (electronic newsletter)
Phillips Business Information, Inc.
www.phillips.com
Tel: 301-340-1520
1201 Seven Locks Road
Potomac, MD 20854

Wireless Week
www.wirelessweek.com
Tel.: 303-470-4800
P.O. Box 266008
Highlands Ranch, CO 80163

VII. Additional E-Commerce and Internet Industry Associations

Advanced Network & Services
www.advanced.org
This organization strives to advance education through the increased use of computer network applications and technology.

American Registry for Internet Numbers
www.arin.net
ARIN is a non-profit organization that administers and registers Internet Protocol (IP) numbers.

Association for Interactive Media (AIM)
www.interactivehq.org/
This non-profit association is geared toward persons using the Internet for business purposes.

Association for Local Telecommunications Services
www.alts.org
ALTS is the trade association that represents the builders of high-speed local communications – CLECs that are "facilities-based." ALTS was founded to harness the shared energy and vitality of the new local competitors and to help ensure regulations for robust competition (spawned by the 1996 Act) are implemented and enforced.

Berkman Center for Internet & Society
http://cyber.harvard.edu/
This research center focuses on the exploration of the development, inner-workings of and laws pertaining to the Internet. The center offers Internet courses, conferences and more.

Better Ethics Online
http://actionsites.com/beo/index.html
Better Ethics Online provides information concerning protecting on-line copyrights and detecting unauthorized web site use.

Chatabox
www.chatabox.com
Chatabox is a non-profit organization that strives to create and maintain communities on the World Wide Web in Australia.

CIX Association
www.cix.org
This association is geared toward entities that offer TCP/IP or OSI public data internetworking services.

Commerce Net
http://www.commerce.net
The premier industry consortium for companies using, promoting and building electronic commerce solutions on the Internet.

Cooperative Association for Internet Data Analysis (CAIDA)
www.caida.org
CAIDA works to promote an atmosphere of greater cohesion on the Internet.

CSPACE
http://cspace.unb.ca/
This non-profit organization focuses on maintaining and developing educational resources on the Internet.

Cyber District Association
www.cyberdistrict.org
This association is dedicated to improving and creating interactive media.

CyberSkills Association, The
www.cyberskills.org
This association's program serves to provide the skills, knowledge and training needed to compete and thrive in today's changing Internet industry.

Data Interchange Standards Association (DISA)
http://www.disa.org
DISA is the leading provider of educational and networking forums on e-business. They provide technical and management services to standards and specification development organizations, including OTA, the IFX Forum, MBA's MISMO, and ASC X12. DISA's affiliation with EC user groups and emerging initiatives around the world facilitates an interchange of e-commerce topics hitting the marketplace.

Dual-Use Marketplace
http://www.crimson.com/market
A marketplace for technologies and partnering ideas.

Financial Services Technology Consortium
http://www.fstc.org
FSTC sponsors project-oriented collaborative research and development on interbank technical projects affecting the entire financial services industry. Particular emphasis is placed on payment systems and services, and leveraging new technologies that help banks cement customer relationships, boost operational efficiency, and expand their market reach.

Florida FastNet Now Coalition
www.floridafastnetnow.org/
Florida FastNet Now is a coalition bringing together Florida citizens, organizations and companies to support public policy encouraging competition in the fast-growing marketplace for high-speed Internet access.

Florida Internet Service Providers Association
www.fispa.org
FISPA encourages discussion and education concerning the Internet industry.

Global Business Dialogue on Electronic Commerce
http://www.gbd.org
GBDe is a company-led response to the need for strengthened international coordination with regard to worldwide electronic commerce. Steering Committee includes CEOs from 24 international companies, including IBM, AOL, Bertelsmann, Fujitsu, HP, and Time Warner.

Global Internet Liberty Campaign (GILC)
www.gilc.org
This association stands up and takes action when it comes to free speech and privacy protection.

Hands Off the Internet
www.handsofftheinternet.org
This association opposes government regulation of entrepreneurial ventures.

Hudson Valley New Media Association
www.quickpages.com/hvnma
This organization focuses on artistic and creative talent in electronic communications.

iAdvance
www.iadvance.org
iAdvance advocates the implementation of affordable high-speed Internet access across the United States.

Information Insfrastructure Technology and Applications
http://iita.nasa.gov/
This organization, funded by NASA, is funding over 50 different programs intended to increase the understanding and use of the Internet.

Information Systems Security Association
www.uhsa.uh.edu/issa
ISSA is geared towards those in the information security industry.

International Academy of Digital Arts and Sciences
www.iadas.net
IADAS is dedicated to the progress of new media worldwide.

International Center for Electronic Commerce
http://icec.net
Based in Korea. Objectives include development of the next generation electronic commerce technologies and management schemes and establish an international research consortium of electronic commerce related companies.

International Society for Mental Health Online
www.ismho.org
This society strives to promote on-line communication, information and technology for the mental health community.

Internet Alliance, The
www.internetalliance.org
Strives to assist the Internet industry in becoming the most important mass market medium of the 21st century.

Internet and Computer Law Association

http://grove.ufl.edu/~cmplaw
This site offers information concerning the Internet and its surrounding laws.

InterNet Assigned Numbers Authority (IANA)

www.iana.org
This association serves as the central coordinator for the assignment of parameter values for Internet Protocols.

Internet Commerce Association

www.whew.com/ICA/index/shtml
This association advocates use of the Internet for advertising.

Internet Content Coalition

www.netcontent.org
The ICC is a non-profit organization for producers and distributors of original content on the Internet.

Internet Developers Users Group

www.envisiondev.com/internetdev/
This organization keeps Internet developers in touch with the latest technology and news.

Internet Education Foundation

www.neted.org
The Internet Education Foundation is a non-profit organization dedicated to educating the public and policymakers about the potential of a decentralized global Internet.

Internet International Ad Hoc Committee (IAHC)

www.iahc.org
The IAHC is a coalition of participants from the broad Internet community working to satisfy the requirement for enhancements to the Internet's global Domain Name System (DNS).

Internet Public Policy Network

www.internetpublicpolicy.com
The Internet Public Policy Network (IPPN) is a virtual company. It connects organizations to writers, speakers and experts on issues such as electronic commerce, telecommunications and community technology.

Internet Service Providers' Consortium

www.ispc.org
The goal of the ISP/C is to function as the lead international trade association of ISPs, representing all of its ISP members.

Internet Software Consortium

www.isc.org
This non-profit organization has extensive expertise in the development, management, maintenance and implementation of Internet technologies.

ISP Consortium

www.ispc.net
The ISP Consortium was created mainly to supply Internet Bandwidth via leased-lines using a superb frame-relay network spanning the UK.

MIT - Intelligent Information Infrastructure Project

www.ai.mit.edu/projects/iiip/home-page.html
The Intelligent Information Infrastructure Project seeks to develop an extremely general system for distributing and retrieving information that will work over major Internet protocols.

National Industrial Information Infrastructure Protocols (NIIIP) Consortium

http://www.niiip.org
A team of organizations that has entered into a cooperative development agreement with the U.S. Government to develop open industry software protocols that will make it possible for manufacturers and their suppliers to effectively interoperate.

NetCoalition

www.netcoalition.com
Some of the most innovative Internet companies in the world belong to this organization, which serves as a discussion forum for exchanging ideas about the Internet.

New Media Association of New Jersey

www.nmanj.com
The New Media Association of New Jersey is a regional organization made for and of users of the new media industry, where members can strengthen their skills, expand their networks and learn from each other.

New York New Media Association

www.nynma.org
NYNMA is a not-for-profit industry association founded in 1994 to support and promote the new media industry in New York.

Nogatekeepers.Org
www.nogatekeepers.org
This site is dedicated to educating the public, local and federal policy makers, advocates and the press about the importance of open broadband networks and the need to preserve competition in the Internet access market in order to protect consumer choice, privacy and freedom of speech.

OASIS
http://www.sgmlopen.org
Organization for the Advancement of Structured Information Standards, is a nonprofit, international consortium dedicated to accelerating the adoption of product-independent formats based on public standards, including SGML, XML, and HTML.

OpenNET Coalition
www.opennetcoalition.org
The openNet Coalition strives to promote the rights of all consumers to obtain affordable, high-speed Internet access.

People For Internet Responsibility
www.pfir.org
PFIR is a global, grassroots, ad hoc network of individuals who are concerned about the current and future operations, development, management and regulation of the Internet in responsible manners.

RosettaNet
http://www.rosettanet.org
A consortium of computer makers, resellers, and users creating e-commerce standards for transaction-centered data exchanges using a standardized set of terms for product, partner, and transaction properties.

Smart Card Industry Association (SCIA)
http://www.scia.org
SCIA is a global trade association which strives to stimulate the use and understanding of smart card technology in the marketplace.

Texas Internet Service Providers Association
www.tispa.org
This organization is one of the nation's strongest state ISP organizations and operates on a non-profit basis.

U.S. Congress Internet Caucus
www.netcaucus.org
The Congressional Internet Caucus is a bi-partisan group of over 100 members of the House and Senate working to educate their colleagues about the promise and potential of the Internet.

Voice On the Net Coalition (VON)
www.von.org
The VON Coalition's mission is twofold: actively advocate the viewpoint that the IP Telephony industry should remain as free of governmental regulations as possible and to educate consumers and the media on Internet communications technologies.

WWW Consortium Electronic Commerce Interest Group
http://www.w3.org/ecommerce
Describes the various activities of the W3C Electronic Commerce Interest Group.

VIII. A Short List of E-Commerce and Internet-Related Publications

A. On-line Publications

Access Online's Weekly Newsletter
http://accessonline.listbot.com
This publication fills members' mailboxes with code snippets, articles and visual basic resources every Saturday night.

Alistapart
www.alistapart.com
This publication is a weekly 'zine and daily digest for people who make web sites and covers everything from pixels to prose, coding to content.

Automatic I.D. News
www.autoidnews.com
Bar codes, RF/DC and other automatic data capture technologies are the focus via product listings, case studies, trade show lists and more.

Card Technology Magazine
http://cardtech.faulknergrey.com
This magazine examines issues and developments in smart cards and other advanced card technologies in banking, transportation, government and university settings.

Cascade News
www.cascadestudios.com
This publication features Web News, Web Books to order, a Chat Room, a Question of the Week, Resource

Sites, Web Courses and more. Cascade w3 is a useful site for web designers, web graphic designers and HTML coders.

Caught in the Net
http://sos-conect.com/caught
This site features previously published columns and current rants concerning the Internet.

CyberClub, The
http://members.xoom.com/thecyberclub/
The CyberClub is a weekly newsletter containing reviews of sites, software, desktop themes, screen savers and fonts, helpful tips/tricks, breaking news and a Q & A section where readers can ask Internet/computer-related questions.

Diverge Dot Org
www.diverge.org
This publication contains a collection of periodic documents about technology such as architectures and software engineering.

DWAHL
www.vaxxine.com/dwahl/index.html
This publication focuses on on-line security issues.

ECMgt.com
www.ecmgt.com
ECMgt.com is designed to keep the visitor up to speed with EC developments by highlighting eCommerce strategy, trends and news.

E-Commerce Times
www.ecommercetimes.com
This magazine offers news, features and special reports.

ENYC.Com - Silicon Alley's Definitive Resource
www.enyc.com
Here, readers can find out what's going on with Silicon Alley's small Internet businesses.

FlamingoLingo Webmaster Resources
www.flamingolingo.com
This useful webmaster resource offers tutorials on HTML, DHTML, CSS, JavaScript and more.

HotWired_ Webmonkey
www.hotwired.com/webmonkey/frontdoor/index.html
This publication serves as a how-to guide for web developers.

MagNet Interactive
www.magnet-i.com
Computers, community and commerce are among topics discussed here.

Net Link Times
wwwnetlinktimes.com
This site is very helpful to newbies and experts alike; there is a great wealth of informative information.

.net Magazine
www.futurenet.com/net/
This webzine focuses on Internet issues pertaining to the United Kingdom.

Net Market Makers
www.netmarketmakers.com
Net Market Makers covers developments, trends and issues for intermediate or vertical markets bringing together business to business transactions on the Internet.

NetReview Email Newsletter
www.geocities.com/siliconvalley/circuit/2701
This publication features news covering the latest Internet and software developments.

NetSlaves
www.disobey.com/netslaves/
NetSlaves is a new e-zine and listserv devoted to persons working in the Internet/computer industries.

Personalization.com
www.personalization.com
This publication offers news, information and analysis on web personalization for on-line marketers and e-businesses.

Sell It on the Web
www.sellitontheweb.com
Sell It on the Web is designed to help small businesses learn how to sell their products on-line. It includes shopping cart reviews, industry news and marketing tips.

Swag.com
www.swagmag.com
This magazine contains building and branding for web geeks—log, commentary and discussion.

Tri-State Computer Chronicle
http://3aweb.com/tscc
This publication provides answers to questions about the Internet for people in Iowa, Minnesota and South Dakota.

Virtual Book Of Knowledge (VBOK)
www.biogate.com/vbok
The Virtual Book Of Knowledge (VBOK) is a monthly newsletter for Internet newcomers, as well as for experienced users. In the publication are articles that explain how the Internet and computers work, as well as helpful tips/tricks to ease using a computer.

VZINE The Cyberspace Portal
www.vzine.com
This publication is an EZINE portal for web beginners to webmasters covering all things Internet. Web Design, Graphics, HTML, Javascript Domains, Email, Hardware and Software are among the topics discussed here.

Web Developer's Journal
www.webdevelopersjournal.com
This publication features news and reviews of the latest web tools and techniques, product reviews, tutorials and discussion groups. HTML, Java, CGI, E-commerce and Web Multimedia are among the topics covered here.

WebReference Update Newsletter
www.webreference.com/new/
This publication, updated weekly, highlights what's new on the web.

Web World E-Zine
http://lost12.hypermart.net
This publication is a free promotional E-Zine based on member submitted topics. Each topic is reviewed and then followed by opinionated member posts. Topics include web design, site promotion and more.

WindoWatch
www.windowatch.com
Here readers can find a full range of in-depth articles covering all flavors of Windows that are written by computer professionals.

WWWiz
www.wwwiz.com
This publication features Internet and web news.

IX.   Foreign Internet Organizations

Argentine Chamber of Databases and Online Services
www.cabase.org.ar/
This organization focuses on forming ethical codes in the Argentine on-line industry, among serving other cohesive industry functions.

CORDIS, the Community Research and Development Information
http://www.cordis.lu
Provides information about Research and Development sponsored and supported by the European Union.

Electronic Commerce and the European Union
http://bscw2.ispa.cec.be/ecommerce.welcome.html
Encourages the vigorous growth of electronic commerce in Europe.

Electronic Commerce Europe
http://www.ec-europe.org/
Main objective of the association is to promote, co-ordinate and assist in the development of Electronic Commerce in Europe.

European Community Programmes related to the Information Market (Index)
http://www.echo.lu/promgrammes/en/programmesindex.html
Centrum voor Wiskunde en Informatica (Netherlands) European Community ESPRIT project to develop a secure electronic payment system which protects the privacy of the user.

Internet Association of Cyprus (IAC)
www.spidernet.net/web/~iacinfo/
This association strives to promote Internet use in Cyprus.

Irish Internet Association (IIA)
www.iia.ie/
The IIA site is a resource of information on events and happenings in the internet world, as well as reviewed and catalogued links for topics to research.

Hong Kong Internet Service Providers Association
www.hkispa.org.hk/
HKISPA serves as a forum for consideration of issues or topics that may affect the development and deployment of the Internet in Hong Kong.

Chapter 6
The E-COMMERCE & INTERNET 300
Who they are and how they were chosen

Note: financial data given for each of the E-COMMERCE & INTERNET 300 firms is for the year ended December 31, 1999, or for the latest date available to the editors. Telephone numbers, addresses, contact names, Internet addresses and other vital facts were collected in late 1999 to early 2000.

The E-COMMERCE & INTERNET 300 is a unique list of companies. (The actual count is 333 firms.) These firms were chosen specifically for their prominence in E-Commerce & Internet fields and in related support industries. A complete list of these industries follows. Complete information about each firm can be found in the "Individual Data Listings" at the end of this chapter.

The E-COMMERCE & INTERNET 300 Firms are among the largest, most successful companies in the E-Commerce & Internet industry. To be included in our list, the firms had to meet the following criteria:

1) Generally, these are U.S.-based, private-sector corporations. However, a handful of foreign-based companies of great interest have been added, and firms that were recently acquired by foreign corporations may be included.

2) Publicly-held companies where stocks or bonds issued by the firm have been sold to the public (except for a very small number of firms that are privately-held that we have added in order to round-out certain niche sets of companies).

3) Prominence, or a significant presence, in E-Commerce & Internet or supporting fields as of mid to late 1999. Obviously, in a field that is exploding as quickly as the Internet industry, new companies are being launched and new IPOs are occurring at blinding speed. Because of this extremely rapid growth, it was impossible for all potential companies to be included in this study. (See the following Industry Codes section for a complete list of types of businesses that are covered).

4) The companies in The E-COMMERCE & INTERNET 300 do not have to be exclusively in the E-Commerce & Internet field.

5) Financial data and vital statistics must have been reasonably available to the editors of this book, either directly from the company being written about, or from outside sources deemed reliable and accurate by the editors.

The companies were chosen in this manner for the following reasons:
...333 COMPANIES so there is a broad base among which to make comparisons.
...COMPANIES WITH STOCKS THAT ARE OR HAVE BEEN PUBLICLY TRADED because publicly-held firms can be compared fairly since they are required by law to meet federal government standards in their methods of reporting, and accounting for, their vital statistics.

INDEXES TO THE E-COMMERCE & INTERNET 300, AS FOUND IN THIS CHAPTER AND IN THE BACK OF THIS BOOK:

INDUSTRY LIST, WITH CODES

The E-COMMERCE & INTERNET 300 contains companies from the following industries. (The code that follows each industry will be useful when looking at certain of the indexes both in this chapter and in the back of the book.)

Code	Industry
54189	ADVERTISING SERVICES
54189A	ADVERTISING/MARKETING-INTERNET FOCUSED
4541B	AUCTIONS ON-LINE
522A	BANKING/ON-LINE
522	BANKING/SAVINGS ASSOCIATIONS
51312	BROADCAST TELEVISION
5132	CABLE TV NETWORKS
3344	CHIPS (SEMICONDUCTORS)/CIRCUITS/ COMPONENTS MANUFACTURER
3341B	COMPUTER ACCESSORIES MANUFACTURING
3341D	COMPUTER DRIVES AND MISC PARTS MANUFACTURER
42143	COMPUTER EQUIPMENT-WHOLESALE DISTRIBUTION
3341A	COMPUTER HARDWARE MANUFACTURER
3341C	COMPUTER NETWORKING EQUIPMENT MANUFACTURER
5112	COMPUTER SOFTWARE DESIGN AND MANUFACTURER
54151	CONSULTING SERVICES-COMPUTER & INTERNET
52221	CREDIT CARD ISSUING
4541	DIRECT SELLING-ON-LINE
42292	DISTRIBUTORS (WHOLESALE) OF BOOKS OR MAGAZINES
443	ELECTRONICS, AUDIO AND APPLIANCE STORES-RETAIL
5141	FINANCIAL DATA PUBLISHING
5133C	HIGH SPEED ACCESS PROVIDER (DSL, CABLE, ETC.)
52421	INSURANCE BROKERAGE AND MANAGEMENT
51339A	INTERNET BUSINESS-TO-BUSINESS OR TO-CONSUMER INTERMEDIARY
51339	INTERNET SERVICE HOSTS AND PROVIDERS
51311B	INTERNET-BASED BROADCASTING
5133A	LOCAL TELEPHONE SERVICE
5133B	LONG DISTANCE TELEPHONE SERVICE
51112	MAGAZINE PUBLISHING
5511	MANAGEMENT OF COMPANIES AND ENTERPRISES
52231	MORTGAGES
514191	ON-LINE INFORMATION SERVICE, ON-LINE PUBLISHING AND NICHE PORTALS
52252A	PAYMENT PROCESSING SERVICE
5133E	PRIVATE NETWORKS/CORPORATE TELECOMMUNICATIONS & NETWORK SERVICES
5133D	SPECIALTY AND INTERNET TELECOMMUNICATIONS SERVICES
5611	STAFFING AND OUTSOURCING SERVICES-INFOTECH RELATED
5231	STOCK BROKERAGE/INVESTMENT BANKING
33421	TELECOMMUNICATIONS EQUIPMENT MANUFACTURER/TELECOMMUNICATIONS INDUSTRY SERVICES
7131	THEME PARKS/RIDES/GAME CENTERS

COMPANY	Industry Code	Sales 1998 $ thousands	Sales Rank	Profits 1998 $ thousands	Profits Rank
ADVERTISING SERVICES					
TMP WORLDWIDE INC	54189	406,800	1	4,300	1
ADVERTISING/MARKETING-INTERNET FOCUSED					
@PLAN.INC	54189A	3,100	15	-1,900	5
24/7 MEDIA INC	54189A	19,900	7	-24,700	19
ADFORCE INC	54189A	4,300	13	-15,000	16
AGENCY.COM LTD	54189A	26,500	5	-1,800	3
AUTOBYTEL.COM INC	54189A	23,800	6	-19,400	18
AUTOWEB.COM INC	54189A	13,000	9	-11,500	13
BAMBOO.COM INC	54189A	100	20	-1,800	4
COBALT GROUP (THE)	54189A	6,200	12	-5,100	8
DOUBLECLICK INC	54189A	80,200	2	-18,200	17
ENGAGE TECHNOLOGIES INC	54189A	2,200	17	-13,800	74
EXACTIS.COM INC	54189A	2,800	16	-7,900	10
FLYCAST COMMUNICATIONS CORP	54189A	8,000	10	-9,300	11
GENESISINTERMEDIA.COM	54189A	14,900	8	1,400	1
LEAPNET INC	54189A	30,660	4	-9,390	12
MEDIA METRIX INC	54189A	6,300	11	-7,200	9
MODEM MEDIA.POPPE TYSON INC	54189A	42,500	3	-3,200	6
NETCENTIVES	54189A	600	19	-14,100	15
NETCREATIONS	54189A	3,400	14	600	2
USWEB/CKS	54189A	228,600	1	-188,300	20
VISUAL DATA	54189A	1,900	18	-3,400	13
AUCTIONS, INTERNET-BASED					
EBAY INC	4541B	47,400	2	2,400	1
PRICELINE.COM	4541B	35,200	3	-112,200	3
UBID INC	4541B	48,200	1	-10,200	2
BANKING/SAVINGS ASSOCIATIONS					
BANK ONE CORP	522	17,524,000	1	3,108,000	1
BANKING/ON-LINE					
NET.B@NK	522A	18,800	1	4,500	1
BROADCAST TELEVISION					
CBS ENTERPRISES	51312	5,363,000	1	549,000	1
BROADCASTING, INTERNET-BASED					
AUDIOHIGHWAY.COM	51311B	100	7	-5,800	3
CNET INC	51311B	56,400	2	2,600	1
INTERVU INC	51311B	1,700	5	-15,700	6

COMPANY	Industry Code	Sales 1998 $ thousands	Sales Rank	Profits 1998 $ thousands	Profits Rank
LAUNCH MEDIA INC	51311B	5,000	4	-13,400	5
MEDIUM4.COM INC	51311B				
MP3.COM INC	51311B	1,200	6	-400	2
NEWSEDGE	51311B	79,500	1	-17,200	7
QUOKKA SPORTS	51311B	8,600	3	-9,500	4
CABLE TV NETWORKS					
COMCAST CORP	5132	4,912,600	3	-238,700	3
TIME WARNER INC	5132	14,582,000	1	168,000	1
VIACOM INC	5132	12,096,100	2	-122,400	2
CHIPS (SEMICONDUCTORS/CIRCUITS/COMPONENTS) MANUFACTURER					
BROADCOM CORP	3344	203,100	2	36,400	2
INTEL CORP	3344	26,273,000	1	6,068,000	1
COMPUTER ACCESSORIES MANUFACTURER					
FVC.COM INC	3341B	37,300	1	-8,000	1
COMPUTER DRIVES AND MISC PARTS MANUFACTURER					
EMC CORP	3341D	3,973,700	1	793,400	1
NETWORK APPLIANCE INC	3341D	166,200	2	21,000	2
COMPUTER EQUIPMENT-WHOLESALE DISTRIBUTION					
TECH DATA CORP	42143	7,056,600	1	89,500	1
COMPUTER HARDWARE MANUFACTURER					
APPLE COMPUTER INC	3341A	5,941,000	7	309,000	6
COMPAQ COMPUTER CORP	3341A	31,169,000	3	-2,743,000	8
DELL COMPUTER CORPORATION	3341A	12,327,000	4	944,000	3
GATEWAY INC	3341A	7,467,900	6	346,400	5
HEWLETT-PACKARD CO	3341A	47,061,000	2	2,945,000	2
INTERNATIONAL BUSINESS MACHINES CORP	3341A	81,667,000	1	6,328,000	1
SILICON GRAPHICS INC	3341A	3,100,600	8	-459,600	7
SUN MICROSYSTEMS INC	3341A	9,790,800	5	762,900	4
COMPUTER NETWORKING EQUIPMENT MANUFACTURER					
3COM CORP	3341C	5,420,400	2	30,200	2
CISCO SYSTEMS INC	3341C	8,458,800	1	1,350,100	1
CYBERGUARD CORP	3341C	14,200	5	-15,500	4
JUNIPER NETWORKS INC	3341C	3,800	8	-31,000	7
NOVELL INC	3341C	1,007,311	3	-78,296	8
RAMP NETWORKS	3341C	9,900	7	-13,400	3
TERAYON COMMUNICATION SYSTEMS	3341C	31,700	4	-23,200	6
TUT SYSTEMS	3341C	10,600	6	-16,300	5

COMPUTER SOFTWARE DESIGNER AND MANUFACTURER

COMPANY	Industry Code	Sales 1998 $ thousands	Sales Rank	Profits 1998 $ thousands	Profits Rank
ACCRUE SOFTWARE INC	5112	1,100	76	-3,900	29
AGILE SOFTWARE CORP	5112	8,000	52	-8,900	49
ALLAIRE CORP	5112	20,500	37	-10,800	55
APPNET INC	5112	17,700	40	-14,400	66
ARIBA INC	5112	8,400	51	-10,900	56
ART TECHNOLOGY GROUP INC	5112	12,100	44	-2,900	25
AXENT TECHNOLOGIES INC	5112	101,000	10	7,700	9
BOTTOMLINE TECHNOLOGIES INC	5112	29,000	29	1,600	16
BROADVISION INC	5112	50,900	17	4,000	12
BUSINESS OBJECTS S A	5112	166,900	8	10,300	7
CITRIX SYSTEMS INC	5112	248,600	5	61,100	3
COMMTOUCH SOFTWARE LTD	5112	400	78	-4,400	32
CONNECTINC.COM	5112	6,500	59	-7,900	43
CYLINK CORP	5112	42,800	21	5,100	11
DIGITAL LAVA INC	5112	1,500	75	-3,700	27
DIGITAL RIVER INC	5112	20,911	36	-13,798	65
EDIFY CORP	5112	70,900	12	-6,700	40
ENTRUST TECHNOLOGIES INC	5112	49,000	18	-23,800	75
F5 NETWORKS INC	5112	4,800	63	-3,700	27
FOREFRONT DIRECT	5112	22,300	35		
FUNDTECH LTD	5112	23,100	34	-11,400	57
HOMECOM COMMUNICATIONS INC	5112	3,300	66	-1,200	24
INKTOMI CORP	5112	20,400	39	-22,400	72
INPRISE CORPORATION	5112	189,100	6	8,300	8
INTERNET PICTURES CORP	5112	3,000	68	-13,200	63
INTUIT INC	5112	592,700	4	-12,200	60
ISS GROUP INC	5112	35,900	26	-4,100	30
LIBERATE TECHNOLOGIES	5112	10,300	47	-94,400	78
LIQUID AUDIO INC	5112	2,800	69	-8,500	47
LITRONIC INC	5112	6,600	58	900	18
MACROMEDIA INC	5112	113,086	9	-6,200	38
MARIMBA INC	5112	17,100	41	-5,700	35
METACREATIONS CORP	5112	42,800	22	-19,800	70
MICROSOFT CORP	5112	14,484,000	1	4,490,000	1
NEON SYSTEMS	5112	12,000	45	1,100	17
NET PERCEPTIONS	5112	300	79	-5,000	34

COMPANY	Industry Code	Sales 1998 $ thousands	Sales Rank	Profits 1998 $ thousands	Profits Rank
NETMANAGE INC	5112	71,700	11	-10,000	51
NETOBJECTS INC	5112	15,300	43	20,900	6
NETSCOUT SYSTEMS	5112	42,800	22	5,400	10
NETSPEAK	5112	7,700	55	-12,100	59
NETWORK ASSOCIATES INC	5112	990,000	3	36,400	4
NETWORK-1 SECURITY SOLUTIONS	5112	1,800	73	-5,800	36
NFRONT.COM	5112	1,100	76	-500	21
ONDISPLAY INC	5112	3,300	66	-8,300	45
ONLINE RESOURCES & COMMUNICATIONS	5112	4,300	64	-11,600	58
OPEN MARKET INC	5112	62,100	14	-30,500	76
OPEN TEXT	5112	45,600	19	-23,500	74
ORACLE CORP	5112	7,143,900	2	813,700	2
PACIFIC SOFTWORKS	5112	2,800	69	-500	21
PACKETEER	5112	7,200	56	-8,800	48
PERSISTENCE SOFTWARE	5112	10,200	48	-4,100	30
PHONE.COM	5112	2,200	71	-10,600	52
PORTAL SOFTWARE	5112	9,400	49	-7,600	42
PRIMUS KNOWLEDGE SOLUTIONS	5112	8,600	50	-10,600	52
QUEST SOFTWARE	5112	34,800	27	2,300	13
REALNETWORKS INC	5112	64,800	13	-16,400	67
RED HAT	5112	5,200	62	0	20
ROGUE WAVE SOFTWARE	5112	44,400	20	2,200	15
RSA SECURITY INC	5112	171,300	7	29,400	5
S1 CORPORATION	5112	24,200	32	-30,800	77
SAGENT TECHNOLOGY	5112	17,000	42	-13,700	64
SECURE COMPUTING CORP	5112	61,400	15	-3,300	26
SILKNET SOFTWARE	5112	3,600	65	-6,000	37
SILVERSTREAM SOFTWARE	5112	6,800	57	-12,900	61
SOFTWARE.COM	5112	25,600	30	-7,400	41
SPYGLASS	5112	20,500	37	-8,000	44
TANNING TECHNOLOGY	5112	33,300	28	2,300	14
TIBCO SOFTWARE	5112	52,800	16	-13,000	62
TUMBLEWEED COMMUNICATIONS	5112	2,000	72	-6,600	39
VASCO DATA SECURITY	5112	10,432	46	-648	23
VERISIGN	5112	38,900	24	-19,700	69
VERITY	5112	38,900	24	-16,500	68
VERSANT CORP	5112	23,200	33	-19,900	71

COMPANY	Industry Code	Sales 1998 $ thousands	Sales Rank	Profits 1998 $ thousands	Profits Rank
VOCALTEC	5112	24,700	31	-23,200	73
V-ONE	5112	6,300	60	-9,200	50
VOXWARE	5112	5,900	61	-4,700	33
WEBB INTERACTIVE	5112	1,600	74	-10,600	52
WEBTRENDS CORP	5112	8,000	52	200	19
WHITE PINE SOFTWARE	5112	7,800	54	-8,400	46
CONSULTING SERVICES-COMPUTER & INTERNET					
BRAUN CONSULTING INC	54151	27,900	8	800	3
CAMBRIDGE TECHNOLOGY PARTNERS INC	54151	612,000	1	51,900	1
CONVERGENT COMMUNICATIONS INC	54151	61,600	4	-50,600	16
FINE.COM INTERNATIONAL CORP	54151	3,400	14	100	4
IXL ENTERPRISES INC	54151	64,800	3	-48,900	15
LION-BRIDGE TECHNOLOGIES INC	54151	38,400	7	-4,300	10
NAVIDEC	54151	8,600	12	-3,900	8
PERFICIENT	54151	826	15	68	5
PRIMIX SOLUTIONS INC	54151	4,800	13	-4,200	9
PROXICOM INC	54151	42,400	6	-20,600	13
RAZORFISH	54151	13,800	10	0	6
SCIENT CORP	54151	200	16	-1,200	7
THINK NEW IDEAS	54151	42,600	5	-27,600	14
U S INTERACTIVE	54151	13,600	11	-8,400	12
VIANT	54151	20,000	18	-6,500	11
WHITTMAN-HART INC	54151	307,600	2	18,800	2
CREDIT CARD ISSUING					
NEXTCARD	52221	1,200	1	-16,100	1
DIRECT SELLING-ON-LINE					
1-800-FLOWERS.COM INC	4541	220,600	4	5,100	3
AMAZON.COM INC	4541	610,000	2	-124,500	33
AMERICANGREETINGS.COM INC	4541	3,900	22	-1,200	8
ASHFORD.COM INC	4541				
AUDIBLE INC	4541	400	29	-8,100	19
BARNESANDNOBLE.COM INC	4541	61,800	13	-83,100	32
BEYOND.COM CORP	4541	36,700	16	-31,100	27
BIGSTAR ENTERTAINMENT INC	4541	800	26	-3,200	12
BLUEFLY INC	4541	200	30	-3,700	14
BUY.COM INC	4541	125,300	9	-17,800	25
CDNOW INC	4541	56,400	14	-43,800	29

COMPANY	Industry Code	Sales 1998 $ thousands	Sales Rank	Profits 1998 $ thousands	Profits Rank
CHEAP TICKETS INC	4541	171,100	8	1,100	4
CREATIVE COMPUTERS INC	4541	6,400	20	-600	7
CYBERIAN OUTPOST INC	4541	22,681	18	-7,092	16
CYBERSHOP.COM INC	4541	4,814	21	-7,888	17
DRUGSTORE.COM INC	4541	100	31	-8,000	18
EGGHEAD.COM INC	4541	207,800	5	-14,700	23
ETOYS INC	4541	700	27	-2,300	10
FASHIONMALL.COM INC	4541	2,100	24		
FATBRAIN.COM INC	4541	10,900	19	-3,190	11
GETTY IMAGES INC	4541	185,100	7	-36,400	28
GLOBAL MEDIA CORPORATION	4541	0	34	-305	6
IMALL INC	4541	1,600	25	13,200	2
INSIGHT ENTERPRISES INC	4541	1,002,800	1	20,500	1
MOTHERNATURE.COM INC	4541	500	28	-6,600	15
MULTIPLE ZONES INTERNATIONAL INC	4541	501,400	3	-8,300	20
MUSICMAKER.COM	4541	100	31	-2,100	9
ONSALE INC	4541	207,751	6	-14,666	22
PEAPOD INC	4541	69,300	12	-21,565	26
PHOTOWORKS INC	4541	96,700	11	7,600	5
PROTEAM.COM INC	4541	107,200	10	-76,200	31
TICKETMASTER ONLINE-CITYSEARCH INC	4541	27,900	17	-17,200	24
VALUE AMERICA INC	4541	41,500	15	-53,600	30
VITAMINSHOPPE	4541	2,900	23	-3,200	12
WEBVAN GROUP INC	4541	100	31	-12,000	21
DISTRIBUTORS (WHOLESALE) OF BOOKS OR MAGAZINES					
ROWECOM	42292	19,100	1	-7,600	1
ELECTRONICS, AUDIO AND APPLIANCE STORES-RETAIL					
TANDY CORP	443	4,787,900	1	61,300	1
FINANCIAL DATA PUBLISHING					
EDGAR ONLINE INC	5141	2,000	4	-2,200	1
MARKETWATCH.COM INC	5141	7,000	2	-12,400	3
MULTEX.COM	5141	13,200	1	-9,700	2
THESTREET.COM	5141	4,600	3	-16,400	4
HIGH SPEED ACCESS PROVIDER (DSL, CABLE ETC.)					
CAIS INTERNET INC	5133C	5,300	1	-12,900	2
COVAD COMMUNICATIONS GROUP INC	5133C	5,300	1	-48,200	5
HIGH SPEED ACCESS CORP	5133C	300	5	-10,000	1

COMPANY	Industry Code	Sales 1998 $ thousands	Sales Rank	Profits 1998 $ thousands	Profits Rank
RHYTHMS NETCONNECTIONS	5133C	500	4	-36,300	4
WORLDGATE COMMUNICATIONS	5133C	1,000	3	-27,000	3
INSURANCE BROKERAGE, MANAGEMENT OR DATA					
INSWEB CORP	52421	4,300	2	-22,500	2
QUOTESMITH.COM INC	52421	5,600	1	-200	1
INTERNET BUSINESS-TO-BUSINESS OR BUSINESS-TO-CONSUMER INTERMEDIARY					
ADSTAR.COM INC	51339A	1,600	11	100	4
CHEMDEX CORPORATION	51339A	100	15	-8,500	7
COMMERCE ONE INC	51339A	2,600	10	-24,600	13
CYBER MERCHANTS EXCHANGE INC	51339A	66	16		16
CYBERSOURCE.COM CORP	51339A	3,400	7	-10,100	10
E-STAMP CORP	51339A	100	14	-10,700	11
GETTHERE.COM INC	51339A	3,000	9	-6,400	6
HEALTHEON/WEBMD CORP	51339A	48,800	3	-54,000	15
IMAGEX.COM INC	51339A	1,000	12	-8,600	8
INTRAWARE INC	51339A	10,400	6	-4,000	5
NETWORK SOLUTIONS INC	51339A	93,700	2	11,200	2
PCORDER.COM	51339A	21,700	4	-9,600	9
PREVIEW TRAVEL INC	51339A	14,000	5	-27,000	14
SABRE INC	51339A	2,306,400	1	231,900	1
STAMPS.COM	51339A	100	13	4,200	3
VERTICALNET	51339A	3,100	8	-13,600	12
INTERNET SERVICE SITE HOSTS AND ACCESS PROVIDERS					
ABOVENET COMMUNICATIONS INC	51339	3,400	21	-5,400	9
APPLIEDTHEORY CORP	51339	22,600	11	-6,900	12
BIZNESS ONLINE.COM INC	51339	6,200	19	-2,600	6
DIGITAL ISLAND INC	51339	2,300	22	-16,800	17
EARTHLINK NETWORK INC	51339	175,900	2	-59,800	20
EXODUS COMMUNICATIONS INC	51339	52,700	9	-66,400	22
FLASHNET COMMUNICATIONS INC	51339	26,900	10	-5,200	8
FREESERVE PLC	51339				
FRONTLINE COMMUNICATIONS CORP	51339	600	24	-1,700	5
INTERLIANT INC	51339	4,900	20	-9,700	15
INTERNET AMERICA INC	51339	10,600	15	1,000	2
INTERNET INITIATIVE JAPAN INC	51339	92,600	6	-2,700	7
JUNO ONLINE SERVICES INC	51339	21,700	12	-31,600	18
LOG ON AMERICA INC	51339	800	23	-400	4

COMPANY	Industry Code	Sales 1998 $ thousands	Sales Rank	Profits 1998 $ thousands	Profits Rank
MINDSPRING ENTERPRISES INC	51339	114,700	5	10,500	1
NETZERO	51339	0	25	0	3
ONEMAIN.COM	51339	56,700	8	-67,600	23
PILOT NETWORK SERVICES	51339	11,300	13	-6,700	10
PRODIGY COMMUNICATIONS	51339	136,100	3	-65,100	21
PSINET INC	51339	259,600	1	-261,900	25
RMI.NET	51339	10,100	16	-10,700	16
SPLITROCK SERVICES	51339	63,600	7	-57,800	19
US SEARCH CORP.COM	51339	9,200	17	-6,800	11
VERIO INC	51339	120,700	4	-122,000	24
VOYAGER.NET	51339	10,700	14	-7,300	13
ZIPLINK INC	51339	7,100	18	-8,400	14
LOCAL TELEPHONE SERVICE					
GTE CORPORATION	5133A	25,473,000	1	2,172,000	1
LONG DISTANCE TELEPHONE SERVICE					
AT&T CORP	5133B	53,223,000	1	5,450,000	1
GLOBAL CROSSING LTD	5133B	424,100	5	-87,900	4
IDT CORPORATION	5133B	335,400	6	-6,400	3
MCI WORLDCOM INC	5133B	17,678,000	2	-2,669,000	6
NETCOM	5133B	736,600	4	8,200	2
QWEST COMMUNICATIONS INTERNATIONAL INC	5133B	2,242,700	3	-844,000	5
MAGAZINE PUBLISHING					
ADVANCE PUBLICATIONS INC	51112	3,859,100	1		1
DOW JONES & COMPANY INC	51112	2,158,106	2	8,362	2
MANAGEMENT OF COMPANIES AND ENTERPRISES					
CMGI INC	5511	91,500	1	16,600	1
INTERNET CAPITAL GROUP INC	5511	3,100	2	13,900	2
MORTGAGES					
E-LOAN INC	52231	55,500	2	-11,200	2
MORTGAGE.COM INC	52231	193,400	1	-6,100	1
ON-LINE INFORMATION SERVICE, ON-LINE PUBLISHING AND NICHE PORTALS					
ABOUT.COM INC	514191	3,700	25	-15,600	36
ALLOY ONLINE INC	514191	1,800	32	-1,900	11
AMERICA ONLINE INC	514191	2,600,000	1	92,000	1
ASK JEEVES INC	514191	600	38	-4,300	21
CAREERBUILDER INC	514191	7,000	19	-12,000	31
CHINADOTCOM CORP	514191	3,500	28	-11,000	30

COMPANY	Industry Code	Sales 1998 $ thousands	Sales Rank	Profits 1998 $ thousands	Profits Rank
COMPS.COM INC	514191	12,900	14	-1,700	9
CROSSWALK.COM INC	514191	1,100	36	-3,500	18
DIALOG CORPORATION PLC (THE)	514191	283,400	2	7,400	3
DRKOOP.COM INC	514191	100	41	-9,100	27
EARTHWEB INC	514191	3,300	29	-9,000	26
EXCITE@HOME	514191	48,000	7	-144,200	44
GO.COM	514191	50,700	6	-5,700	23
GO2NET INC	514191	4,800	23	-2,400	14
GOTO.COM INC	514191	800	37	-14,000	34
HEADHUNTER.NET INC	514191	1,100	35	-4,300	20
HEARME.COM	514191	8,000	18	-12,000	31
HOMESTORE.COM INC	514191	0	44	0	5
HOOVER'S INC	514191	5,200	22	-1,800	10
HOTJOBS.COM LTD	514191	4,200	24	-1,600	8
ILIFE.COM	514191	3,500	26	-2,100	12
INFONAUTICS INC	514191	14,900	13	-17,400	39
INFOSPACE.COM INC	514191	9,400	15	-9,100	27
INTERNET.COM	514191	3,500	27	-2,700	16
ITURF INC	514191	134	40	-49	6
IVILLAGE INC	514191	15,000	12	-43,700	41
LOOKSMART LTD	514191	8,800	16	-12,900	33
LYCOS INC	514191	56,100	4	-96,900	43
MAPQUEST.COM INC	514191	24,700	10	-3,200	17
N2H2	514191	3,100	30	-2,600	15
NETIVATION.COM INC	514191	100	43	-2,300	13
ONESOURCE INFORMATION SERVICES	514191	30,400	9	5,600	4
QUEPASA.COM	514191	100	42	-6,500	24
SALON.COM	514191	1,200	34	-3,800	19
SPORTSLINE USA	514191	30,600	8	-35,500	40
STARMEDIA NETWORK	514191	5,300	21	-45,900	42
STUDENT ADVANTAGE	514191	17,400	11	-5,100	22
TALK CITY	514191	1,500	33	-15,700	37
THEGLOBE.COM	514191	5,500	20	-16,000	38
TOWN PAGES NET.COM	514191	1,900	31	-1,500	7
WINK COMMUNICATIONS	514191	500	39	-14,000	34
XOOM.COM	514191	8,318	17	-10,798	29
YAHOO! INC	514191	203,300	3	25,600	2

COMPANY	Industry Code	Sales 1998 $ thousands	Sales Rank	Profits 1998 $ thousands	Profits Rank
ZDNET GROUP	514191	56,100	5	-7,900	25
PAYMENT PROCESSING SERVICE					
CHECKFREE HOLDINGS CORP	52252A	233,864	1	-3,703	2
CLAIMSNET.COM INC	52252A	200	4	-4,700	3
CYBERCASH INC	52252A	12,600	3	-30,900	4
PEGASUS SYSTEMS	52252A	29,100	2	5,400	1
PRIVATE NETWORKS/CORPORATE TELECOMMUNICATIONS AND NETWORK SERVICES					
CONCENTRIC NETWORK CORPORATION	5133E	82,800	1	-82,100	3
DIGEX INC	5133E	22,600	3	700	1
IXNET INC	5133E	35,900	2	-27,600	2
SPECIALTY AND INTERNET TELECOMMUNICATIONS SERVICES					
CLARENT CORP	5133D	14,600	2	-5,800	3
CRITICAL PATH INC	5133D	900	6	-11,500	4
EFAX INC	5133D	30,200	1	-1,500	1
JFAX.COM INC	5133D	3,500	4	-17,200	6
MAIL.COM INC	5133D	1,500	5	-12,500	5
NET2PHONE	5133D	12,000	3	-3,500	2
STAFFING OR OUTSOURCING SERVICES-INFOTECH RELATED					
NAVISITE	5611	4,000	2	-9,200	2
USINTERNETWORKING INC	5611	4,100	1	-32,500	1
STOCK BROKERAGE/INVESTMENT BANKING					
A B WATLEY GROUP INC	5231	9,200	8	-600	7
AMERITRADE HOLDING CORP	5231	164,100	5	210	5
CHARLES SCHWAB CORP (THE)	5231	3,388,100	2	348,500	2
DATEK ONLINE HOLDING CORP	5231	75,000	7		
DLJDIRECT INC	5231	117,900	6	1,500	4
E*TRADE GROUP INC	5231	285,000	3	-700	8
MORGAN STANLEY DEAN WITTER DISCOVER & CO	5231	31,131,000	1	3,276,000	1
NATIONAL DISCOUNT BROKERS	5231	164,500	4	12,000	3
ONLINETRADINGINC.COM	5231	3,549	9	-20	6
WIT CAPITAL GROUP	5231	1,900	10	-8,800	9
TELECOMMUNICATIONS EQUIPMENT MANUFACTURER/TELECOMMUNICATIONS INDUSTRY SERVICES					
LUCENT TECHNOLOGIES INC	33421	30,147,000	1	970,000	1
METRICOM INC	33421	15,900	3	-84,200	3
QUALCOMM INC	33421	3,347,900	2	108,500	2
STARTRONIX	33421				

COMPANY	Industry Code	Sales 1998 $ thousands	Sales Rank	Profits 1998 $ thousands	Profits Rank
THEME PARKS/RIDES/GAME CENTERS					
WALT DISNEY COMPANY (THE)	7131	22,976,000	1	1,850,000	1

ALPHABETICAL INDEX

If you are seeking a company by name and you do not find it on this list, please turn to the back of the book to the Index by Subsidiaries, Brand Names and Selected Affiliations. You may find your target firm there.

FINE.COM INTERNATIONAL CORP	54151	LOG ON AMERICA INC	51339
FLASHNET COMMUNICATIONS INC	51339	LOOKSMART LTD	514191
FLYCAST COMMUNICATIONS CORP	54189A	LUCENT TECHNOLOGIES INC	33421
FOREFRONT DIRECT	5112	LYCOS INC	514191
FREESERVE PLC	51339	MACROMEDIA INC	5112
FRONTLINE COMMUNICATIONS CORP	51339	MAIL.COM INC	5133D
FUNDTECH LTD	5112	MAPQUEST.COM INC	514191
FVC.COM INC	3341B	MARIMBA INC	5112
GATEWAY INC	3341A	MARKETWATCH.COM INC	5141
GENESISINTERMEDIA.COM	54189A	MCI WORLDCOM INC	5133B
GETTHERE.COM INC	51339A	MEDIA METRIX INC	54189A
GETTY IMAGES INC	4541	MEDIUM4.COM INC	51311B
GLOBAL CROSSING LTD	5133B	METACREATIONS CORP	5112
GLOBAL MEDIA CORPORATION	4541	METRICOM INC	33421
GO.COM	514191	MICROSOFT CORP	5112
GO2NET INC	514191	MINDSPRING ENTERPRISES INC	51339
GOTO.COM INC	514191	MODEM MEDIA.POPPE TYSON INC	54189A
GTE CORPORATION	5133A	MORGAN STANLEY DEAN WITTER	5231
HEADHUNTER.NET INC	514191	MORTGAGE.COM INC	52231
HEALTHEON/WEBMD CORP	51339A	MOTHERNATURE.COM INC	4541
HEARME.COM	514191	MP3.COM INC	51311B
HEWLETT-PACKARD CO	3341A	MULTEX.COM	5141
HIGH SPEED ACCESS CORP	5133C	MULTIPLE ZONES INTERNATIONAL INC	4541
HOMECOM COMMUNICATIONS INC	5112	MUSICMAKER.COM	4541
HOMESTORE.COM INC	514191	N2H2	514191
HOOVER'S INC	514191	NATIONAL DISCOUNT BROKERS	5231
HOTJOBS.COM LTD	514191	NAVIDEC	54151
IDT CORPORATION	5133B	NAVISITE	5611
ILIFE.COM	514191	NEON SYSTEMS	5112
IMAGEX.COM INC	51339A	NET PERCEPTIONS	5112
IMALL INC	4541	NET.B@NK	522A
INFONAUTICS INC	514191	NET2PHONE	5133D
INFOSPACE.COM INC	514191	NETCENTIVES	54189A
INKTOMI CORP	5112	NETCOM	5133B
INPRISE CORPORATION	5112	NETCREATIONS	54189A
INSIGHT ENTERPRISES INC	4541	NETIVATION.COM INC	514191
INSWEB CORP	52421	NETMANAGE INC	5112
INTEL CORP	3344	NETOBJECTS INC	5112
INTERLIANT INC	51339	NETSCOUT SYSTEMS	5112
INTERNATIONAL BUSINESS MACHINES	3341A	NETSPEAK	5112
INTERNET AMERICA INC	51339	NETWORK APPLIANCE INC	3341D
INTERNET CAPITAL GROUP INC	5511	NETWORK ASSOCIATES INC	5112
INTERNET INITIATIVE JAPAN INC	51339	NETWORK SOLUTIONS INC	51339A
INTERNET PICTURES CORP	5112	NETWORK-1 SECURITY SOLUTIONS	5112
INTERNET.COM	514191	NETZERO	51339
INTERVU INC	51311B	NEWSEDGE	51311B
INTRAWARE INC	51339A	NEXTCARD	52221
INTUIT INC	5112	NFRONT.COM	5112
ISS GROUP INC	5112	NOVELL INC	3341C
ITURF INC	514191	ONDISPLAY INC	5112
IVILLAGE INC	514191	ONEMAIN.COM	51339
IXL ENTERPRISES INC	54151	ONESOURCE INFORMATION SERVICES	514191
IXNET INC	5133E	ONLINE RESOURCES &	5112
JFAX.COM INC	5133D	ONLINETRADINGINC.COM	5231
JUNIPER NETWORKS INC	3341C	ONSALE INC	4541
JUNO ONLINE SERVICES INC	51339	OPEN MARKET INC	5112
LAUNCH MEDIA INC	51311B	OPEN TEXT	5112
LEAPNET INC	54189A	ORACLE CORP	5112
LIBERATE TECHNOLOGIES	5112	PACIFIC SOFTWORKS	5112
LIONBRIDGE TECHNOLOGIES INC	54151	PACKETEER	5112
LIQUID AUDIO INC	5112	PCORDER.COM	51339A
LITRONIC INC	5112	PEAPOD INC	4541

PEGASUS SYSTEMS	52252A	TUT SYSTEMS	3341C
PERFICIENT	54151	U S INTERACTIVE	54151
PERSISTENCE SOFTWARE	5112	UBID INC	4541B
PHONE.COM	5112	US SEARCH CORP.COM	51339
PHOTOWORKS INC	4541	USINTERNETWORKING INC	5611
PILOT NETWORK SERVICES	51339	USWEB/CKS	54189A
PORTAL SOFTWARE	5112	V-ONE	5112
PREVIEW TRAVEL INC	51339A	VALUE AMERICA INC	4541
PRICELINE.COM	5141B	VASCO DATA SECURITY	5112
PRIMIX SOLUTIONS INC	54151	VERIO INC	51339
PRIMUS KNOWLEDGE SOLUTIONS	5112	VERISIGN	5112
PRODIGY COMMUNICATIONS	51339	VERITY	5112
PROTEAM.COM INC	4541	VERSANT CORP	5112
PROXICOM INC	54151	VERTICALNET	51339A
PSINET INC	51339	VIACOM INC	5132
QUALCOMM INC	33421	VIANT	54151
QUEPASA.COM	514191	VISUAL DATA	54189A
QUEST SOFTWARE	5112	VITAMINSHOPPE	4541
QUOKKA SPORTS	51311B	VOCALTEC	5112
QUOTESMITH.COM INC	52421	VOXWARE	5112
QWEST COMMUNICATIONS	5133B	VOYAGER.NET	51339
RAMP NETWORKS	3341C	WALT DISNEY COMPANY (THE)	7131
RAZORFISH	54151	WEBB INTERACTIVE	5112
REALNETWORKS INC	5112	WEBTRENDS CORP	5112
RED HAT	5112	WEBVAN GROUP INC	4541
RHYTHMS NETCONNECTIONS	5133C	WHITE PINE SOFTWARE	5112
RMI.NET	51339	WHITTMAN-HART INC	54151
ROGUE WAVE SOFTWARE	5112	WINK COMMUNICATIONS	514191
ROWECOM	42292	WIT CAPITAL GROUP	5231
RSA SECURITY INC	5112	WORLDGATE COMMUNICATIONS	5133C
S1 CORPORATION	5112	XOOM.COM	514191
SABRE INC	51339A	YAHOO! INC	514191
SAGENT TECHNOLOGY	5112	ZDNET GROUP	514191
SALON.COM	514191	ZIPLINK INC	51339
SCIENT CORP	54151		
SECURE COMPUTING CORP	5112		
SILICON GRAPHICS INC	3341A		
SILKNET SOFTWARE	5112		
SILVERSTREAM SOFTWARE	5112		
SOFTWARE.COM	5112		
SPLITROCK SERVICES	51339		
SPORTSLINE USA	514191		
SPYGLASS	5112		
STAMPS.COM	51339A		
STARMEDIA NETWORK	514191		
STARTRONIX	33421		
STUDENT ADVANTAGE	514191		
SUN MICROSYSTEMS INC	3341A		
TALK CITY	514191		
TANDY CORP	443		
TANNING TECHNOLOGY	5112		
TECH DATA CORP	42143		
TERAYON COMMUNICATION SYSTEMS	3341C		
THEGLOBE.COM	514191		
THESTREET.COM	5141		
THINK NEW IDEAS	54151		
TIBCO SOFTWARE	5112		
TICKETMASTER ONLINE-CITYSEARCH	4541		
TIME WARNER INC	5132		
TMP WORLDWIDE INC	54189		
TOWN PAGES NET.COM	514191		
TUMBLEWEED COMMUNICATIONS	5112		

GEOGRAPHICAL INDEXES

1) **Company headquarters locations by state**
2) **Locations and subsidiaries by regions of the U.S.**
3) **Firms with international operations**

The headquarters locations of each company are on the following indexes to help you locate members of THE E-COMMERCE AND INTERNET 300 within the part of the country, or the world, of interest. However, companies are constantly opening and closing various locations. You should consider contacting companies that particularly interest you, to see whether they have locations in your area. You can also try looking for companies in on-line telephone and address directories (such as infousa.com), to see which cities have locations of the firms that interest you.

HEADQUARTERS LOCATION, BY STATE

ARIZONA
INSIGHT ENTERPRISES INC;Tempe
QUEPASA.COM;Phoenix

CALIFORNIA
3COM CORP;Santa Clara
ABOVENET COMMUNICATIONS INC;San Jose
ACCRUE SOFTWARE INC;Fremont
ADFORCE INC;Cupertino
ADSTAR.COM INC;Marina Del Rey
AGILE SOFTWARE CORP;San Jose
APPLE COMPUTER INC;Cupertino
ARIBA INC;Sunnyvale
ASK JEEVES INC;Berkeley
AUDIOHIGHWAY.COM;Cupertino
AUTOBYTEL.COM INC;Irvine
AUTOWEB.COM INC;Santa Clara
BAMBOO.COM INC;Palo Alto
BEYOND.COM CORP;Sunnyvale
BROADCOM CORP;Irvine
BROADVISION INC;Redwood City
BUY.COM INC;Aliso Viejo
CHARLES SCHWAB CORP (THE);San Francisco
CHEMDEX CORPORATION;Palo Alto
CISCO SYSTEMS INC;San Jose
CLARENT CORP;Redwood City
CNET INC;San Francisco

COMMERCE ONE INC;Walnut Creek
COMMTOUCH SOFTWARE LTD;Santa Clara
COMPS.COM INC;San Diego
CONCENTRIC NETWORK CORPORATION;San Jose
CONNECTINC.COM;Mountain View
COVAD COMMUNICATIONS GROUP;Santa Clara
CREATIVE COMPUTERS INC;Torrance
CRITICAL PATH INC;San Francisco
CYBER MERCHANTS EXCHANGE INC;Pasadena
CYBERSOURCE.COM CORP;San Jose
CYLINK CORP;Sunnyvale
DIGITAL ISLAND INC;San Francisco
DIGITAL LAVA INC;Los Angeles
E*TRADE GROUP INC;Palo Alto
EARTHLINK NETWORK INC;Pasadena
EBAY INC;San Jose
EDIFY CORP;Santa Clara
EFAX INC;Menlo Park
E-LOAN INC;Dublin
E-STAMP CORP;San Mateo
ETOYS INC;Santa Monica
EXCITE@HOME;Redwood City
EXODUS COMMUNICATIONS INC;Santa Clara
FATBRAIN.COM INC;Sunnyvale
FLYCAST COMMUNICATIONS CORP;San Francisco
FVC.COM INC;Santa Clara
GATEWAY INC;San Diego
GENESISINTERMEDIA.COM;Van Nuys
GETTHERE.COM INC;Menlo Park
GLOBAL CROSSING LTD;Beverly Hills
GO.COM;Sunnyvale
GOTO.COM INC;Pasadena
HEARME.COM;Mountain View
HEWLETT-PACKARD CO;Palo Alto
HOMESTORE.COM INC;Thousand Oaks
IMALL INC;Santa Monica
INKTOMI CORP;San Mateo
INPRISE CORPORATION;Scotts Valley
INSWEB CORP;Redwood City
INTEL CORP;Santa Clara
INTERVU INC;San Diego
INTRAWARE INC;Orinda
INTUIT INC;Mountain View
JFAX.COM INC;Los Angeles
JUNIPER NETWORKS INC;Mountain View
LAUNCH MEDIA INC;Santa Monica
LIBERATE TECHNOLOGIES;San Carlos
LIQUID AUDIO INC;Redwood City
LITRONIC INC;Irvine
LOOKSMART LTD;San Francisco
MACROMEDIA INC;San Francisco
MARIMBA INC;Mountain View
MARKETWATCH.COM INC;San Francisco
METACREATIONS CORP;Carpinteria
METRICOM INC;Los Gatos
MP3.COM INC;San Diego
NETCENTIVES;San Francisco
NETMANAGE INC;Cupertino

NETOBJECTS INC;Redwood City
NETWORK APPLIANCE INC;Sunnyvale
NETWORK ASSOCIATES INC;Santa Clara
NETZERO;Westlake Village
NEXTCARD;San Francisco
ONDISPLAY INC;San Ramon
ONSALE INC;Menlo Park
ORACLE CORP;Redwood City
PACIFIC SOFTWORKS;Newbury Park
PACKETEER;Cupertino
PERSISTENCE SOFTWARE;San Mateo
PHONE.COM;Redwood City
PILOT NETWORK SERVICES;Alameda
PORTAL SOFTWARE;Cupertino
PREVIEW TRAVEL INC;San Francisco
QUALCOMM INC;San Diego
QUEST SOFTWARE;Newport Beach
QUOKKA SPORTS;San Francisco
RAMP NETWORKS;Santa Clara
SAGENT TECHNOLOGY;Mountain View
SALON.COM;San Francisco
SCIENT CORP;San Francisco
SECURE COMPUTING CORP;San Jose
SILICON GRAPHICS INC;Mountain View
SOFTWARE.COM;Santa Barbara
STAMPS.COM;Santa Monica
STARTRONIX;Irvine
SUN MICROSYSTEMS INC;Palo Alto
TALK CITY;Campbell
TERAYON COMMUNICATION SYSTEMS;Santa Clara
TIBCO SOFTWARE;Palo Alto
TICKETMASTER ONLINE-CITYSEARCH;Pasadena
TUMBLEWEED COMMUNICATIONS;Redwood City
TUT SYSTEMS;Pleasant Hill
US SEARCH CORP.COM;Beverly Hills
USWEB/CKS;Santa Clara
VERISIGN;Mountainview
VERITY;Sunnyvale
VERSANT CORP;Fremont
WALT DISNEY COMPANY (THE);Burbank
WEBVAN GROUP INC;Foster City
WINK COMMUNICATIONS;Alameda
XOOM.COM;San Francisco
YAHOO! INC;Santa Clara
ZDNET GROUP;San Francisco

COLORADO
CONVERGENT COMMUNICATIONS INC;Englewood
EXACTIS.COM INC;Denver
HIGH SPEED ACCESS CORP;Denver
NAVIDEC;Englewood
QWEST COMMUNICATIONS
INTERNATIONAL;Denver
RHYTHMS NETCONNECTIONS;Englewood
RMI.NET;Denver
ROGUE WAVE SOFTWARE;Boulder
TANNING TECHNOLOGY;Denver
VERIO INC;Englewood

WEBB INTERACTIVE;Denver

CONNECTICUT
@PLAN.INC;Stamford
CYBERIAN OUTPOST INC;Kent
EDGAR ONLINE INC;Norwalk
GTE CORPORATION;Stamford
INTERNET.COM;Darien
MODEM MEDIA.POPPE TYSON INC;Norwalk
PRICELINE.COM;Stamford

DISTRICT OF COLUMBIA
CAIS INTERNET INC;Washington

FLORIDA
CITRIX SYSTEMS INC;Fort Lauderdale
CYBERGUARD CORP;Fort Lauderdale
FOREFRONT DIRECT;Clearwater
ILIFE.COM;North Palm Beach
MORTGAGE.COM INC;Plantation
NETSPEAK;Boca Raton
ONLINETRADINGINC.COM;Boca Raton
SPORTSLINE USA;Fort Lauderdale
TECH DATA CORP;Clearwater
VISUAL DATA;Pompano Beach

GEORGIA
CHECKFREE HOLDINGS CORP;Norcross
HEADHUNTER.NET INC;Norcross
HEALTHEON/WEBMD CORP;Atlanta
HOMECOM COMMUNICATIONS INC;Atlanta
ISS GROUP INC;Atlanta
IXL ENTERPRISES INC;Atlanta
MINDSPRING ENTERPRISES INC;Atlanta
NET.B@NK;Alpharetta
NFRONT.COM;Norcross
S1 CORPORATION;Atlanta

HAWAII
CHEAP TICKETS INC;Honolulu

IDAHO
NETIVATION.COM INC;Coeur d' Alene

ILLINOIS
BANK ONE CORP;Chicago
BRAUN CONSULTING INC;Chicago
LEAPNET INC;Chicago
PEAPOD INC;Skokie
QUOTESMITH.COM INC;Darien
SPYGLASS;Naperville
UBID INC;Elk Grove Village
VASCO DATA SECURITY;Oakbrook Terrace
WHITTMAN-HART INC;Chicago

MASSACHUSETTS
ALLAIRE CORP;Cambridge

ART TECHNOLOGY GROUP INC;Cambridge
CAMBRIDGE TECHNOLOGY PARTNERS;Cambridge
CMGI INC;Andover
EMC CORP;Hopkinton
ENGAGE TECHNOLOGIES INC;Andover
INTERLIANT INC;Cambridge
LIONBRIDGE TECHNOLOGIES INC;Waltham
LYCOS INC;Waltham
MOTHERNATURE.COM INC;Concord
NAVISITE;Andover
NETSCOUT SYSTEMS;Westford
NETWORK-1 SECURITY SOLUTIONS;Waltham
NEWSEDGE;Burlington
ONESOURCE INFORMATION SERVICES;Concord
OPEN MARKET INC;Burlington
PRIMIX SOLUTIONS INC;Watertown
ROWECOM;Cambridge
RSA SECURITY INC;Bedford
SILVERSTREAM SOFTWARE;Burlington
STUDENT ADVANTAGE;Boston
VIANT;Boston
ZIPLINK INC;Lowell

MARYLAND
APPNET INC;Bethesda
AXENT TECHNOLOGIES INC;Rockville
DIGEX INC;Beltsville
USINTERNETWORKING INC;Annapolis
V-ONE;Germantown

MICHIGAN
VOYAGER.NET;East Lansing

MINNESOTA
DIGITAL RIVER INC;Eden Prairie
NET PERCEPTIONS;Minneapolis

MISSISSIPPI
MCI WORLDCOM INC;Clinton

NEBRASKA
AMERITRADE HOLDING CORP;Omaha

NEW JERSEY
AUDIBLE INC;Wayne
BIZNESS ONLINE.COM INC;Wall
CYBERSHOP.COM INC;Jersey City
DATEK ONLINE HOLDING CORP;Iselin
IDT CORPORATION;Hackensack
LUCENT TECHNOLOGIES INC;Murray Hill
NATIONAL DISCOUNT BROKERS;Jersey City
NET2PHONE;Hackensack
PROTEAM.COM INC;Secaucus
VOCALTEC;Fort Lee
VOXWARE;Princeton

NEW YORK
1-800-FLOWERS.COM INC;Westbury
24/7 MEDIA INC;New York
A B WATLEY GROUP INC;New York
ABOUT.COM INC;New York
ADVANCE PUBLICATIONS INC;Staten Island
AGENCY.COM LTD;New York
ALLOY ONLINE INC;New York
APPLIEDTHEORY CORP;Great Neck
AT&T CORP;New York
BARNESANDNOBLE.COM INC;New York
BIGSTAR ENTERTAINMENT INC;New York
BLUEFLY INC;New York
CBS ENTERPRISES;New York
CDNOW INC;New York
DLJDIRECT INC;New York
DOUBLECLICK INC;New York
DOW JONES & COMPANY INC;New York
EARTHWEB INC;New York
FASHIONMALL.COM INC;New York
FRONTLINE COMMUNICATIONS CORP;Pearl River
HOTJOBS.COM LTD;New York
INTERNATIONAL BUSINESS MACHINES;Armonk
ITURF INC;New York
IVILLAGE INC;New York
IXNET INC;New York
JUNO ONLINE SERVICES INC;New York
MAIL.COM INC;New York
MAPQUEST.COM INC;New York
MEDIA METRIX INC;New York
MEDIUM4.COM INC;New York
MORGAN STANLEY DEAN WITTER DISCOVER & CO;New York
MULTEX.COM;New York
NETCREATIONS;New York
PRODIGY COMMUNICATIONS;White Plains
RAZORFISH;New York
STARMEDIA NETWORK;New York
THEGLOBE.COM;New York
THESTREET.COM;New York
THINK NEW IDEAS;New York
TIME WARNER INC;New York
TMP WORLDWIDE INC;New York
VIACOM INC;New York
VITAMINSHOPPE;New York
WIT CAPITAL GROUP;New York

NORTH CAROLINA
RED HAT;Durham

OHIO
AMERICANGREETINGS.COM INC;Cleveland

OREGON
WEBTRENDS CORP;Portland

PENNSYLVANIA
COMCAST CORP;Philadelphia
INFONAUTICS INC;Wayne
INTERNET CAPITAL GROUP INC;Wayne
U S INTERACTIVE;King of Prussia
VERTICALNET;Horsham
WORLDGATE COMMUNICATIONS;Benasalem

RHODE ISLAND
LOG ON AMERICA INC;Providence

TENNESSEE
INTERNET PICTURES CORP;Oak Ridge

TEXAS
ASHFORD.COM INC;Houston
CLAIMSNET.COM INC;Dallas
COMPAQ COMPUTER CORP;Houston
DELL COMPUTER CORPORATION;Round Rock
DRKOOP.COM INC;Austin
ENTRUST TECHNOLOGIES INC;Plano
FLASHNET COMMUNICATIONS INC;Fort Worth
HOOVER'S INC;Austin
INTERNET AMERICA INC;Dallas
NEON SYSTEMS;Sugar Land
PCORDER.COM;Austin
PEGASUS SYSTEMS;Dallas
PERFICIENT;Austin
SABRE INC;Fort Worth
SPLITROCK SERVICES;The Woodlands
TANDY CORP;Fort Worth

UTAH
NOVELL INC;Provo

VIRGINIA
AMERICA ONLINE INC;Dulles
CAREERBUILDER INC;Reston
CROSSWALK.COM INC;Chantilly
CYBERCASH INC;Reston
MUSICMAKER.COM;Reston
NETWORK SOLUTIONS INC;Herndon
ONEMAIN.COM;Reston
ONLINE RESOURCES &
COMMUNICATIONS;McLean
PROXICOM INC;Reston
PSINET INC;Herndon
VALUE AMERICA INC;Charlottesville

WASHINGTON
AMAZON.COM INC;Seattle
COBALT GROUP (THE);Seattle
DRUGSTORE.COM INC;Bellevue
EGGHEAD.COM INC;Liberty Lake
F5 NETWORKS INC;Seattle
FINE.COM INTERNATIONAL CORP;Seattle
GETTY IMAGES INC;Seattle

GO2NET INC;Seattle
IMAGEX.COM INC;Bellevue
INFOSPACE.COM INC;Redmond
MICROSOFT CORP;Redmond
MULTIPLE ZONES INTERNATIONAL INC;Renton
N2H2;Seattle
PHOTOWORKS INC;Seattle
PRIMUS KNOWLEDGE SOLUTIONS;Seattle
REALNETWORKS INC;Seattle

INDEX BY REGIONS OF THE NATION WHERE THE E-COMMERCE & INTERNET 300 FIRMS HAVE LOCATIONS

WEST

1-800-FLOWERS.COM INC
24/7 MEDIA INC
3COM CORP
ABOVENET COMMUNICATIONS INC
ACCRUE SOFTWARE INC
ADFORCE INC
ADSTAR.COM INC
ADVANCE PUBLICATIONS INC
AGENCY.COM LTD
AGILE SOFTWARE CORP
AMAZON.COM INC
AMERICA ONLINE INC
APPLE COMPUTER INC
APPNET INC
ARIBA INC
ASK JEEVES INC
AT&T CORP
AUDIOHIGHWAY.COM
AUTOBYTEL.COM INC
AUTOWEB.COM INC
BAMBOO.COM INC
BANK ONE CORP
BEYOND.COM CORP
BROADCOM CORP
BROADVISION INC
BUSINESS OBJECTS S A
BUY.COM INC
CAMBRIDGE TECHNOLOGY PARTNERS
CAREERBUILDER INC
CBS ENTERPRISES
CHARLES SCHWAB CORP (THE)
CHEAP TICKETS INC
CHECKFREE HOLDINGS CORP
CHEMDEX CORPORATION
CISCO SYSTEMS INC
CLARENT CORP
CMGI INC
CNET INC
COBALT GROUP (THE)
COMCAST CORP
COMMERCE ONE INC
COMMTOUCH SOFTWARE LTD
COMPS.COM INC
CONCENTRIC NETWORK CORPORATION

CONNECTINC.COM
CONVERGENT COMMUNICATIONS
COVAD COMMUNICATIONS GROUP
CREATIVE COMPUTERS INC
CRITICAL PATH INC
CYBER MERCHANTS EXCHANGE
CYBERSOURCE.COM CORP
CYLINK CORP
DELL COMPUTER CORPORATION
DIALOG CORPORATION PLC (THE)
DIGEX INC
DIGITAL ISLAND INC
DIGITAL LAVA INC
DOUBLECLICK INC
DOW JONES & COMPANY INC
E*TRADE GROUP INC
E-LOAN INC
E-STAMP CORP
EARTHLINK NETWORK INC
EBAY INC
EDIFY CORP
EFAX INC
EGGHEAD.COM INC
EMC CORP
ETOYS INC
EXACTIS.COM INC
EXCITE@HOME
EXODUS COMMUNICATIONS INC
F5 NETWORKS INC
FATBRAIN.COM INC
FINE.COM INTERNATIONAL CORP
FLASHNET COMMUNICATIONS INC
FLYCAST COMMUNICATIONS CORP
FOREFRONT DIRECT
FUNDTECH LTD
FVC.COM INC
GATEWAY INC
GENESISINTERMEDIA.COM
GETTHERE.COM INC
GETTY IMAGES INC
GLOBAL CROSSING LTD
GO.COM
GOTO.COM INC
GTE CORPORATION
HEARME.COM
HEWLETT-PACKARD CO
HOMESTORE.COM INC
HOTJOBS.COM LTD
IMALL INC
INKTOMI CORP
INPRISE CORPORATION
INSWEB CORP
INTEL CORP

INTERNATIONAL BUSINESS
MACHINES CORP
INTERNET.COM
INTERVU INC
INTRAWARE INC
INTUIT INC
IXL ENTERPRISES INC
JFAX.COM INC
JUNIPER NETWORKS INC
LAUNCH MEDIA INC
LEAPNET INC
LIBERATE TECHNOLOGIES
LIONBRIDGE TECHNOLOGIES INC
LIQUID AUDIO INC
LITRONIC INC
LOOKSMART LTD
LUCENT TECHNOLOGIES INC
LYCOS INC
MACROMEDIA INC
MAIL.COM INC
MAPQUEST.COM INC
MARIMBA INC
MARKETWATCH.COM INC
MCI WORLDCOM INC
MEDIA METRIX INC
METACREATIONS CORP
METRICOM INC
MICROSOFT CORP
MINDSPRING ENTERPRISES INC
MODEM MEDIA.POPPE TYSON INC
MORGAN STANLEY DEAN WITTER
DISCOVER & CO
MORTGAGE.COM INC
MP3.COM INC
MULTEX.COM
MULTIPLE ZONES INTERNATIONAL
N2H2
NAVIDEC
NEON SYSTEMS
NETCENTIVES
NETIVATION.COM INC
NETMANAGE INC
NETOBJECTS INC
NETWORK APPLIANCE INC
NETWORK ASSOCIATES INC
NETZERO
NEWSEDGE
NEXTCARD
NOVELL INC
ONDISPLAY INC
ONESOURCE INFORMATION
SERVICES
ONSALE INC

OPEN MARKET INC
ORACLE CORP
PACIFIC SOFTWORKS
PACKETEER
PEAPOD INC
PERSISTENCE SOFTWARE
PHONE.COM
PHOTOWORKS INC
PILOT NETWORK SERVICES
PORTAL SOFTWARE
PREVIEW TRAVEL INC
PRIMUS KNOWLEDGE SOLUTIONS
PROTEAM.COM INC
PROXICOM INC
PSINET INC
QUALCOMM INC
QUEST SOFTWARE
QUOKKA SPORTS
QWEST COMMUNICATIONS
INTERNATIONAL INC
RAMP NETWORKS
RAZORFISH
REALNETWORKS INC
RED HAT
RHYTHMS NETCONNECTIONS
RMI.NET
ROGUE WAVE SOFTWARE
ROWECOM
RSA SECURITY INC
S1 CORPORATION
SABRE INC
SAGENT TECHNOLOGY
SALON.COM
SCIENT CORP
SECURE COMPUTING CORP
SILICON GRAPHICS INC
SILKNET SOFTWARE
SILVERSTREAM SOFTWARE
SOFTWARE.COM
SPORTSLINE USA
SPYGLASS
STAMPS.COM
STARTRONIX
STUDENT ADVANTAGE
SUN MICROSYSTEMS INC
TALK CITY
TANDY CORP
TANNING TECHNOLOGY
TECH DATA CORP
TERAYON COMMUNICATION
SYSTEMS
THINK NEW IDEAS
TIBCO SOFTWARE

TICKETMASTER ONLINE-
CITYSEARCH INC
TIME WARNER INC
TMP WORLDWIDE INC
TUMBLEWEED COMMUNICATIONS
TUT SYSTEMS
U S INTERACTIVE
US SEARCH CORP.COM
USINTERNETWORKING INC
USWEB/CKS
V-ONE
VERIO INC
VERISIGN
VERITY
VERSANT CORP
VIACOM INC
VIANT
VOXWARE
WALT DISNEY COMPANY (THE)
WEBB INTERACTIVE
WEBTRENDS CORP
WEBVAN GROUP INC
WHITE PINE SOFTWARE
WHITTMAN-HART INC
WINK COMMUNICATIONS
WIT CAPITAL GROUP
XOOM.COM
YAHOO! INC
ZDNET GROUP

SOUTHWEST
ABOVENET COMMUNICATIONS INC
ADVANCE PUBLICATIONS INC
AGENCY.COM LTD
AMERICA ONLINE INC
APPLE COMPUTER INC
ASHFORD.COM INC
AT&T CORP
BANK ONE CORP
BUSINESS OBJECTS S A
CAMBRIDGE TECHNOLOGY
PARTNERS INC
CAREERBUILDER INC
CBS ENTERPRISES
CHARLES SCHWAB CORP (THE)
CHECKFREE HOLDINGS CORP
CISCO SYSTEMS INC
CLAIMSNET.COM INC
COMCAST CORP
COMPAQ COMPUTER CORP
CONVERGENT COMMUNICATIONS
COVAD COMMUNICATIONS GROUP
CYBERGUARD CORP

DELL COMPUTER CORPORATION
DIALOG CORPORATION PLC (THE)
DIGEX INC
DOUBLECLICK INC
DOW JONES & COMPANY INC
DRKOOP.COM INC
EMC CORP
ENTRUST TECHNOLOGIES INC
EXCITE@HOME
EXODUS COMMUNICATIONS INC
FLASHNET COMMUNICATIONS INC
GATEWAY INC
GLOBAL CROSSING LTD
GTE CORPORATION
HEWLETT-PACKARD CO
HOMECOM COMMUNICATIONS INC
HOOVER'S INC
INPRISE CORPORATION
INSIGHT ENTERPRISES INC
INTEL CORP
INTERNATIONAL BUSINESS
MACHINES CORP
INTERNET AMERICA INC
INTUIT INC
IXL ENTERPRISES INC
LUCENT TECHNOLOGIES INC
LYCOS INC
MACROMEDIA INC
MARIMBA INC
MCI WORLDCOM INC
METRICOM INC
MICROSOFT CORP
MINDSPRING ENTERPRISES INC
MORGAN STANLEY DEAN WITTER
DISCOVER & CO
NEON SYSTEMS
NETWORK ASSOCIATES INC
NEWSEDGE
NOVELL INC
OPEN MARKET INC
ORACLE CORP
PCORDER.COM
PEAPOD INC
PEGASUS SYSTEMS
PERFICIENT
PRIMUS KNOWLEDGE SOLUTIONS
PROXICOM INC
PSINET INC
QUALCOMM INC
QUEPASA.COM
QWEST COMMUNICATIONS
INTERNATIONAL INC
REALNETWORKS INC

RHYTHMS NETCONNECTIONS
RMI.NET
RSA SECURITY INC
S1 CORPORATION
SABRE INC
SAGENT TECHNOLOGY
SCIENT CORP
SILICON GRAPHICS INC
SILKNET SOFTWARE
SILVERSTREAM SOFTWARE
SPLITROCK SERVICES
STAMPS.COM
SUN MICROSYSTEMS INC
TANDY CORP
TANNING TECHNOLOGY
TECH DATA CORP
THINK NEW IDEAS
TIBCO SOFTWARE
TICKETMASTER ONLINE-
CITYSEARCH INC
TIME WARNER INC
TMP WORLDWIDE INC
USWEB/CKS
V-ONE
VERIO INC
VIACOM INC
VIANT
WALT DISNEY COMPANY (THE)
WHITTMAN-HART INC
YAHOO! INC
ZDNET GROUP

MIDWEST

24/7 MEDIA INC
3COM CORP
ABOVENET COMMUNICATIONS INC
ADVANCE PUBLICATIONS INC
AGENCY.COM LTD
AMERICA ONLINE INC
AMERICANGREETINGS.COM INC
AMERITRADE HOLDING CORP
APPLE COMPUTER INC
APPNET INC
AT&T CORP
BANK ONE CORP
BRAUN CONSULTING INC
BROADVISION INC
BUSINESS OBJECTS S A
CAMBRIDGE TECHNOLOGY
PARTNERS INC
CAREERBUILDER INC
CBS ENTERPRISES
CHARLES SCHWAB CORP (THE)

CHECKFREE HOLDINGS CORP
CISCO SYSTEMS INC
CLARENT CORP
CMGI INC
CNET INC
COMCAST CORP
COMMERCE ONE INC
CONCENTRIC NETWORK
CONVERGENT COMMUNICATIONS
COVAD COMMUNICATIONS GROUP
DELL COMPUTER CORPORATION
DIALOG CORPORATION PLC (THE)
DIGEX INC
DIGITAL RIVER INC
DOUBLECLICK INC
DOW JONES & COMPANY INC
EGGHEAD.COM INC
EMC CORP
EXODUS COMMUNICATIONS INC
F5 NETWORKS INC
FLASHNET COMMUNICATIONS INC
GATEWAY INC
GLOBAL CROSSING LTD
GO.COM
GTE CORPORATION
HEWLETT-PACKARD CO
HIGH SPEED ACCESS CORP
HOMECOM COMMUNICATIONS INC
HOTJOBS.COM LTD
INPRISE CORPORATION
INTEL CORP
INTERNATIONAL BUSINESS
MACHINES CORP
INTERNET.COM
INTERVU INC
INTUIT INC
IXL ENTERPRISES INC
LEAPNET INC
LUCENT TECHNOLOGIES INC
LYCOS INC
MARIMBA INC
MCI WORLDCOM INC
MICROSOFT CORP
MINDSPRING ENTERPRISES INC
MODEM MEDIA.POPPE TYSON INC
MORGAN STANLEY DEAN WITTER
DISCOVER & CO
MULTIPLE ZONES INTERNATIONAL
NEON SYSTEMS
NET PERCEPTIONS
NETWORK ASSOCIATES INC
NEWSEDGE
NOVELL INC

ONESOURCE INFORMATION
SERVICES
ONLINETRADINGINC.COM
OPEN MARKET INC
OPEN TEXT
ORACLE CORP
PEAPOD INC
PILOT NETWORK SERVICES
PRIMUS KNOWLEDGE SOLUTIONS
PROXICOM INC
PSINET INC
QUALCOMM INC
QUOTESMITH.COM INC
QWEST COMMUNICATIONS
INTERNATIONAL INC
RHYTHMS NETCONNECTIONS
ROWECOM
RSA SECURITY INC
SABRE INC
SCIENT CORP
SECURE COMPUTING CORP
SILICON GRAPHICS INC
SILKNET SOFTWARE
SILVERSTREAM SOFTWARE
SPORTSLINE USA
STUDENT ADVANTAGE
SUN MICROSYSTEMS INC
TALK CITY
TANDY CORP
TECH DATA CORP
THINK NEW IDEAS
TIBCO SOFTWARE
TICKETMASTER ONLINE-
CITYSEARCH INC
TIME WARNER INC
TMP WORLDWIDE INC
UBID INC
USWEB/CKS
V-ONE
VASCO DATA SECURITY
VERIO INC
VIACOM INC
VOYAGER.NET
WALT DISNEY COMPANY (THE)
WHITTMAN-HART INC
YAHOO! INC
ZDNET GROUP

NORTHEAST
@PLAN.INC
1-800-FLOWERS.COM INC
24/7 MEDIA INC
3COM CORP

A B WATLEY GROUP INC
ABOUT.COM INC
ABOVENET COMMUNICATIONS INC
ADVANCE PUBLICATIONS INC
AGENCY.COM LTD
ALLAIRE CORP
ALLOY ONLINE INC
AMAZON.COM INC
AMERICA ONLINE INC
AMERICANGREETINGS.COM INC
APPLE COMPUTER INC
APPLIEDTHEORY CORP
APPNET INC
ART TECHNOLOGY GROUP INC
AT&T CORP
AUDIBLE INC
AXENT TECHNOLOGIES INC
BANK ONE CORP
BARNESANDNOBLE.COM INC
BIGSTAR ENTERTAINMENT INC
BIZNESS ONLINE.COM INC
BLUEFLY INC
BOTTOMLINE TECHNOLOGIES INC
BROADVISION INC
BUSINESS OBJECTS S A
CAIS INTERNET INC
CAMBRIDGE TECHNOLOGY PARTNERS
CAREERBUILDER INC
CBS ENTERPRISES
CDNOW INC
CHARLES SCHWAB CORP (THE)
CHECKFREE HOLDINGS CORP
CISCO SYSTEMS INC
CMGI INC
CNET INC
COMCAST CORP
COMMERCE ONE INC
COMMTOUCH SOFTWARE LTD
CONVERGENT COMMUNICATIONS INC
COVAD COMMUNICATIONS GROUP
CROSSWALK.COM INC
CYBERCASH INC
CYBERGUARD CORP
CYBERIAN OUTPOST INC
CYBERSHOP.COM INC
CYLINK CORP
DATEK ONLINE HOLDING CORP
DELL COMPUTER CORPORATION
DIALOG CORPORATION PLC (THE)
DIGEX INC
DLJDIRECT INC
DOUBLECLICK INC
DOW JONES & COMPANY INC

DRUGSTORE.COM INC
EARTHWEB INC
EDGAR ONLINE INC
EMC CORP
ENGAGE TECHNOLOGIES INC
EXCITE@HOME
EXODUS COMMUNICATIONS INC
F5 NETWORKS INC
FASHIONMALL.COM INC
FINE.COM INTERNATIONAL CORP
FLASHNET COMMUNICATIONS INC
FRONTLINE COMMUNICATIONS CORP
FUNDTECH LTD
GATEWAY INC
GLOBAL CROSSING LTD
GO2NET INC
GTE CORPORATION
HEWLETT-PACKARD CO
HOMECOM COMMUNICATIONS INC
HOOVER'S INC
HOTJOBS.COM LTD
IDT CORPORATION
IMAGEX.COM INC
INFONAUTICS INC
INFOSPACE.COM INC
INPRISE CORPORATION
INTEL CORP
INTERLIANT INC
INTERNATIONAL BUSINESS
MACHINES CORP
INTERNET CAPITAL GROUP INC
INTERNET.COM
INTERVU INC
INTUIT INC
ISS GROUP INC
ITURF INC
IVILLAGE INC
IXL ENTERPRISES INC
IXNET INC
JUNIPER NETWORKS INC
JUNO ONLINE SERVICES INC
LEAPNET INC
LIONBRIDGE TECHNOLOGIES INC
LOG ON AMERICA INC
LUCENT TECHNOLOGIES INC
LYCOS INC
MAIL.COM INC
MARIMBA INC
MARKETWATCH.COM INC
MCI WORLDCOM INC
MEDIA METRIX INC
MEDIUM4.COM INC
METACREATIONS CORP

METRICOM INC
MICROSOFT CORP
MINDSPRING ENTERPRISES INC
MODEM MEDIA.POPPE TYSON INC
MORGAN STANLEY DEAN WITTER
DISCOVER & CO
MORTGAGE.COM INC
MOTHERNATURE.COM INC
MULTEX.COM
MUSICMAKER.COM
NATIONAL DISCOUNT BROKERS
NAVIDEC
NAVISITE
NEON SYSTEMS
NET2PHONE
NETCREATIONS
NETIVATION.COM INC
NETMANAGE INC
NETSCOUT SYSTEMS
NETWORK ASSOCIATES INC
NETWORK SOLUTIONS INC
NETWORK-1 SECURITY SOLUTIONS
NEWSEDGE
NOVELL INC
ONEMAIN.COM
ONESOURCE INFORMATION SERVICES
ONLINE RESOURCES &
COMMUNICATIONS
ONLINETRADINGINC.COM
OPEN MARKET INC
ORACLE CORP
PEAPOD INC
PERFICIENT
PILOT NETWORK SERVICES
PRICELINE.COM
PRIMIX SOLUTIONS INC
PRIMUS KNOWLEDGE SOLUTIONS
PRODIGY COMMUNICATIONS
PROTEAM.COM INC
PROXICOM INC
PSINET INC
QUALCOMM INC
QWEST COMMUNICATIONS
INTERNATIONAL INC
RAZORFISH
RED HAT
RHYTHMS NETCONNECTIONS
ROGUE WAVE SOFTWARE
ROWECOM
RSA SECURITY INC
S1 CORPORATION
SABRE INC
SAGENT TECHNOLOGY

SCIENT CORP
SECURE COMPUTING CORP
SILICON GRAPHICS INC
SILKNET SOFTWARE
SILVERSTREAM SOFTWARE
SOFTWARE.COM
SPORTSLINE USA
SPYGLASS
STARMEDIA NETWORK
STUDENT ADVANTAGE
SUN MICROSYSTEMS INC
TALK CITY
TANDY CORP
TANNING TECHNOLOGY
TECH DATA CORP
THEGLOBE.COM
THESTREET.COM
THINK NEW IDEAS
TIBCO SOFTWARE
TICKETMASTER ONLINE-CITYSEARCH
TIME WARNER INC
TMP WORLDWIDE INC
TUMBLEWEED COMMUNICATIONS
U S INTERACTIVE
USINTERNETWORKING INC
USWEB/CKS
V-ONE
VERIO INC
VERISIGN
VERTICALNET
VIACOM INC
VIANT
VITAMINSHOPPE
VOCALTEC
VOXWARE
WALT DISNEY COMPANY (THE)
WHITE PINE SOFTWARE
WHITTMAN-HART INC
WIT CAPITAL GROUP
WORLDGATE COMMUNICATIONS
XOOM.COM
YAHOO! INC
ZDNET GROUP
ZIPLINK INC

SOUTHEAST

1-800-FLOWERS.COM INC
24/7 MEDIA INC
ABOVENET COMMUNICATIONS INC
ADVANCE PUBLICATIONS INC
AGENCY.COM LTD
AMERICA ONLINE INC
AMERICANGREETINGS.COM INC

APPLE COMPUTER INC
AT&T CORP
BANK ONE CORP
BUSINESS OBJECTS S A
CAMBRIDGE TECHNOLOGY
PARTNERS INC
CAREERBUILDER INC
CBS ENTERPRISES
CHARLES SCHWAB CORP (THE)
CHECKFREE HOLDINGS CORP
CISCO SYSTEMS INC
CITRIX SYSTEMS INC
CMGI INC
COMCAST CORP
COMMERCE ONE INC
CONVERGENT COMMUNICATIONS
COVAD COMMUNICATIONS GROUP
CREATIVE COMPUTERS INC
CYBERCASH INC
CYBERGUARD CORP
DELL COMPUTER CORPORATION
DIALOG CORPORATION PLC (THE)
DIGEX INC
DOUBLECLICK INC
DOW JONES & COMPANY INC
EMC CORP
EXCITE@HOME
EXODUS COMMUNICATIONS INC
FATBRAIN.COM INC
FLASHNET COMMUNICATIONS INC
FOREFRONT DIRECT
FUNDTECH LTD
GATEWAY INC
GLOBAL CROSSING LTD
GO.COM
GTE CORPORATION
HEADHUNTER.NET INC
HEALTHEON/WEBMD CORP
HEWLETT-PACKARD CO
ILIFE.COM
INPRISE CORPORATION
INTEL CORP
INTERNATIONAL BUSINESS
MACHINES CORP
INTERNET PICTURES CORP
INTERNET.COM
INTERVU INC
ISS GROUP INC
IXL ENTERPRISES INC
LUCENT TECHNOLOGIES INC
MARIMBA INC
MCI WORLDCOM INC
MEDIA METRIX INC

MICROSOFT CORP
MINDSPRING ENTERPRISES INC
MODEM MEDIA.POPPE TYSON INC
MORGAN STANLEY DEAN WITTER
DISCOVER & CO
MORTGAGE.COM INC
NEON SYSTEMS
NET.B@NK
NETSPEAK
NEWSEDGE
NFRONT.COM
NOVELL INC
ONLINETRADINGINC.COM
OPEN MARKET INC
ORACLE CORP
PEAPOD INC
PRIMUS KNOWLEDGE SOLUTIONS
PROTEAM.COM INC
PSINET INC
QUALCOMM INC
QWEST COMMUNICATIONS
INTERNATIONAL INC
RHYTHMS NETCONNECTIONS
ROGUE WAVE SOFTWARE
RSA SECURITY INC
S1 CORPORATION
SABRE INC
SAGENT TECHNOLOGY
SILICON GRAPHICS INC
SILKNET SOFTWARE
SILVERSTREAM SOFTWARE
SPORTSLINE USA
STARTRONIX
STUDENT ADVANTAGE
SUN MICROSYSTEMS INC
TANDY CORP
TECH DATA CORP
THINK NEW IDEAS
TIBCO SOFTWARE
TICKETMASTER ONLINE-
CITYSEARCH INC
TIME WARNER INC
TMP WORLDWIDE INC
USWEB/CKS
V-ONE
VALUE AMERICA INC
VERIO INC
VIACOM INC
VISUAL DATA
VOXWARE
WALT DISNEY COMPANY (THE)
WEBVAN GROUP INC
WHITTMAN-HART INC

YAHOO! INC
ZDNET GROUP

INDEX BY FIRMS WITH INTERNATIONAL OPERATIONS

PILOT NETWORK SERVICES
PORTAL SOFTWARE
PRIMUS KNOWLEDGE SOLUTIONS
PROTEAM.COM INC
PROXICOM INC
PSINET INC
QUALCOMM INC
QUEST SOFTWARE
QWEST COMMUNICATIONS
INTERNATIONAL INC
RAZORFISH
REALNETWORKS INC
RED HAT
ROWECOM
RSA SECURITY INC
S1 CORPORATION
SABRE INC
SAGENT TECHNOLOGY
SCIENT CORP
SECURE COMPUTING CORP
SILICON GRAPHICS INC
SILKNET SOFTWARE
SILVERSTREAM SOFTWARE
SOFTWARE.COM
SPORTSLINE USA
SPYGLASS
STAMPS.COM
SUN MICROSYSTEMS INC
TANNING TECHNOLOGY
TECH DATA CORP
THESTREET.COM
THINK NEW IDEAS
TIBCO SOFTWARE
TICKETMASTER ONLINE-
CITYSEARCH INC
TIME WARNER INC
TMP WORLDWIDE INC
TOWN PAGES NET.COM
TUMBLEWEED
COMMUNICATIONS
U S INTERACTIVE
USINTERNETWORKING INC
USWEB/CKS
V-ONE
VASCO DATA SECURITY
VERIO INC
VERITY
VERSANT CORP
VIACOM INC
VIANT
VOCALTEC
VOXWARE
WALT DISNEY COMPANY (THE)

WHITE PINE SOFTWARE
WHITTMAN-HART INC
WINK COMMUNICATIONS
XOOM.COM
YAHOO! INC
ZDNET GROUP

INDIVIDUAL PROFILES

ON EACH OF

THE E-COMMERCE & INTERNET 300

@PLAN.INC   www.webplan.net

Industry Group Code: 54189A
Ranks within this company's industry group: Sales: 15   Profits: 5

BUSINESS ACTIVITIES ("Y" = Yes)

Financial Services:	Information/Publ.:	Technology:	Services:		Retailing:	Telecommunications:
Stock Brokerage	Portal/Hub/News	Computer Manuf.	Payments/Transfers		Retailer	Internet Serv. Provider
Mortgages/Loans	On-Line Community	Networking Equip.	Consulting		Auctions	Web Site Host
Banking	Search Engine	Software Manuf.	Advertising/Marketing	Y	Mall	Server Farm
Insurance	Financial Data Publ.	Specialty Equipment	Outsourcing		Tickets/Travel	Specialty Telecom.
Credit Cards	Broadcasting/Music				Price Comparisons	High Speed Access

TYPES OF BUSINESS:
Advertising-Market Research

BRANDS/DIVISIONS/AFFILIATES:

GROWTH PLANS/SPECIAL FEATURES:

@plan provides market research decision planning and support services for Internet advertisers, advertising agencies and web publishers. @plan also has developed a system that caters to on-line retailers and consumer brand marketers. The company maintains databases of consumer lifestyles, demographic data and product preferences that clients can access through @plan's web site. @plan helps its clients analyze the role the Internet plays in their particular business, make comparisons of the costs of reaching target audiences on a large number of web sites and obtain a clearer understanding of its customers' lifestyles and interests. @plan recently conducted an Internet poll to examine the trends in Internet retail purchases made by consumers and its relation to store and catalogue shopping. The poll also assessed the on-line consumer's degree of concern for credit card security when making purchases. @plan's client base has shown very rapid growth. Some of the company's newest clients are AOL.com, Best Buy, iVillage, Mayo Clinic Health Oasis and Office Max. Other notable clients include eBay.com, E*TRADE, Eddie Bauer, Excite, Microsoft and Yahoo!.

CONTACTS: *Note: Officers with more than one job title may be intentionally listed here more than once.*
Mark K. Wright, CEO
Karl A. Spangenberg, Pres./COO
Nancy A. Lazaros, Sr. VP/CFO
Susan C. Russo, Executive VP
Nancy Lazaros, Sr., Chief Acc. Officer

Phone: 203-961-0340	Fax: 203-964-0136
Toll-Free:	
Address: 3 Landmark Sq., Ste. 400, Stamford, CT, 06901	

FINANCIALS: Sales and profits are in thousands of dollars—add 000 to get the full amount.
Notes regarding 1999: *(1999 sales and profits were not available for all companies at press time.)*

1999 Sales: $7,356	1999 Profits: $-2,085	Stock Ticker: **APLN**
1998 Sales: $3,100	1998 Profits: $-1,900	Employees: 19
1997 Sales: $ 400	1997 Profits: $-2,800	Fiscal Year Ends: 12/31
1996 Sales: $	1996 Profits: $- 700	
1995 Sales: $	1995 Profits: $	

SALARIES/BENEFITS:

Pension Plan:	ESOP Stock Plan:	Profit Sharing:	Top Exec. Salary: $	Bonus: $
Savings Plan:	Stock Purch. Plan:		Second Exec. Salary: $	Bonus: $

COMPETITIVE ADVANTAGE: Focus on market intelligence.

OTHER THOUGHTS:
Apparent Women Officers or Directors: 1
Apparent Minority Officers or Directors: 2
Hot Spot for Advancement for Women/Minorities: Y

LOCATIONS: ("Y" = Yes)

West:	Southwest:	Midwest:	Southeast:	Northeast:	International:
				Y	

1-800-FLOWERS.COM INC   www.1800flowers.com

Industry Group Code: 4541
Ranks within this company's industry group: Sales: 4   Profits: 3

BUSINESS ACTIVITIES ("Y" = Yes)

Financial Services:	Information/Publ.:	Technology:	Services:	Retailing:		Telecommunications:
Stock Brokerage	Portal/Hub/News	Computer Manuf.	Payments/Transfers	Retailer	Y	Internet Serv. Provider
Mortgages/Loans	On-Line Community	Networking Equip.	Consulting	Auctions		Web Site Host
Banking	Search Engine	Software Manuf.	Advertising/Marketing	Mall		Server Farm
Insurance	Financial Data Publ.	Specialty Equipment	Outsourcing	Tickets/Travel		Specialty Telecom.
Credit Cards	Broadcasting/Music			Price Comparisons		High Speed Access

TYPES OF BUSINESS:

Retail-Flowers
Gifts
Home Decor
Gardening Accessories
Gourmet Foods

BRANDS/DIVISIONS/AFFILIATES:

Conroy's Flowers
Bloomlink
BloomNet
Floraminder
800-CANDIES
800-BASKETS
800-GOODIES
Flora Plenty

CONTACTS: *Note: Officers with more than one job title may be intentionally listed here more than once.*

James F. McCann, CEO
Peter G. Rice, Pres., Plow & Hearth
John W. Smolak, Sr. VP-Finance
Jerry Noonan, Sr. VP/Chief Mktg. Officer
Jim Donovan, VP-Human Resources
Jeff Borror, CTO
Guru P. Ghosh, VP-Info.Tech.
Kenneth J. Mesnik, VP-Merch.
Gerald Gallagher, Sr. VP/General Counsel
John W.Smolak, VP-Admin.
T. Guy Minetti, Sr. VP- Corp. Dev.
Donna M. Iucolano, VP-Interactive Services
Joseph D.Pititto, VP-Investor Relations
William E. Shea, Treasurer & VP-Finance
Chris Mcann, Sr. VP
Julie McCann-Mulligan, Creative Director

Phone: 516-237-6000	Fax: 516-237-6060
Toll-Free: 1-800-Flowers	
Address: 1600 Stewart Ave., Westbury, NY, 11590	

GROWTH PLANS/SPECIAL FEATURES:

1-800-FLOWERS.COM provides flower bouquets and delivery, gift baskets, candles, gourmet food, home decorating accents, garden tools and other accessories. The company markets and sells its products through its web site, has strategic on-line relationships with Internet service providers such as Microsoft Network, Excite and AOL and has over 100 subsidiary locations throughout California, Arkansas, Arizona and New York. The company also educates its customers about flowers in an area of its web site called Fresh Ideas & Info, as well as through lectures and design classes at its stores. The orders placed through 1-800-FLOWERS.COM are fulfilled by a group of flower shops known as BloomNet. Plow & Hearth, a subsidiary of 1-800-FLOWERS.COM that does its business through a national mail order catalogue, specializes in home and garden merchandise and publishes many seasonal catalogs. In recent news, the company announced a multi-year contract with Snap.com, the fastest growing Internet portal from NBC and CNET. The agreement includes a media campaign to be run on the Internet and broadcast television that will promote shopping on Snap.com, spotlighting 1-800-FLOWERS.COM. The company also signed a one-year contract to be a floral and gift provider for PeoplePC, a new personal computing company.

FINANCIALS: Sales and profits are in thousands of dollars—add 000 to get the full amount.

Notes regarding 1999: *(1999 sales and profits were not available for all companies at press time.)*

1999 Sales: $295,900	1999 Profits: $-6,800	Stock Ticker: **FLWS**
1998 Sales: $220,600	1998 Profits: $5,100	Employees: 2,100
1997 Sales: $186,400	1997 Profits: $2,900	Fiscal Year Ends: 6/30
1996 Sales: $153,100	1996 Profits: $ 300	
1995 Sales: $116,800	1995 Profits: $ 800	

SALARIES/BENEFITS:

Pension Plan:	ESOP Stock Plan:	Profit Sharing:	Top Exec. Salary: $1,229,930	Bonus: $
Savings Plan:	Stock Purch. Plan:		Second Exec. Salary: $191,667	Bonus: $426,000

COMPETITIVE ADVANTAGE: Owns excellent 800 telephone numbers.

OTHER THOUGHTS:

	LOCATIONS: ("Y" = Yes)					
	West:	Southwest:	Midwest:	Southeast:	Northeast:	International:
Apparent Women Officers or Directors: 1	Y			Y	Y	
Apparent Minority Officers or Directors: 1						
Hot Spot for Advancement for Women/Minorities:						

Note: Financial information, benefits and other data can change quickly and may vary from those stated here.

24/7 MEDIA INC   www.247media.com

Industry Group Code: 54189A
Ranks within this company's industry group: Sales: 7   Profits: 19

BUSINESS ACTIVITIES ("Y" = Yes)

Financial Services:	Information/Publ.:	Technology:	Services:		Retailing:	Telecommunications:
Stock Brokerage	Portal/Hub/News	Computer Manuf.	Payments/Transfers		Retailer	Internet Serv. Provider
Mortgages/Loans	On-Line Community	Networking Equip.	Consulting		Auctions	Web Site Host
Banking	Search Engine	Software Manuf.	Advertising/Marketing	Y	Mall	Server Farm
Insurance	Financial Data Publ.	Specialty Equipment	Outsourcing		Tickets/Travel	Specialty Telecom.
Credit Cards	Broadcasting/Music				Price Comparisons	High Speed Access

TYPES OF BUSINESS:

Internet Advertising

BRANDS/DIVISIONS/AFFILIATES:

Intelligent Interacting Corp.
CLIQNOW! Sales Group
Sift, Inc.
InterAd Holdings, Ltd.
TechWave Inc.
China.com
The Sporting News Online

CONTACTS: Note: Officers with more than one job title may be intentionally listed here more than once.

David J. Moore, CEO
David J. Moore, Pres.
C. Andrew Johns, Exec. VP/CFO
Jacob I. Friesel, Exec. VP-Sales and Mktg.
Audrey Blauner, Dir.-Human Resources
Ron Johnson, Sr. VP/CIO
Megan M. Hurley, VP/General Counsel
Stuart D. Shaw, Sr. VP-Admin.
Joseph Apprendi, Sr. VP-Strategic Sales
Garrett P. Cecchini, Sr. VP-E-commerce
Joel Herskovits, Director of Investor Relations

Phone: 212-231-7100	Fax: 212-760-1774
Toll-Free:	
Address: 1250 Broadway, New York, NY, 10001-3701	

GROWTH PLANS/SPECIAL FEATURES:

24/7 Media offers a full suite of on-line media sales services to web publishers and advertisers and is one of the largest Internet media companies. It also provides worldwide Internet advertising sales and representation. The company reaches over half of all on-line users in the United States and maintains several databases, including one with demographic information on 100 million U.S. households. Recently, 24/7 Media acquired many companies, including Intelligent Interactions Corp., CLIQNOW! Sales Group and Sift, Inc. The company also has investment interests in InterAd Holdings Ltd., TechWave Inc. and China.com. In recent news, 24/7 Media launched its 24/7 Latino on-line ad sales company, making 24/7 the first to open a network for the entire Latin American market. 24/7 Media expects this growing market to supply the company with about $59 million in revenues the first year, with Brazil accounting for 40% to 45% of the market. The company has new offices in Mexico City, Sao Paulo, Buenos Aires and Lima. 24/7 Media recently announced that The Sporting News Online, a heavily trafficked site, will become one of its new web properties.

FINANCIALS: Sales and profits are in thousands of dollars—add 000 to get the full amount.

Notes regarding 1999: Through 9 months (1999 sales and profits were not available for all companies at press time.)

1999 Sales: $52,918	1999 Profits: $-26,075	Stock Ticker: **TFSM**
1998 Sales: $19,900	1998 Profits: $-24,700	Employees: 200
1997 Sales: $3,100	1997 Profits: $-5,300	Fiscal Year Ends: 12/31
1996 Sales: $1,500	1996 Profits: $-6,800	
1995 Sales: $ 200	1995 Profits: $-1,200	

SALARIES/BENEFITS:

Pension Plan:	ESOP Stock Plan: Y	Profit Sharing:	Top Exec. Salary: $259,137	Bonus: $343,750
Savings Plan:	Stock Purch. Plan:		Second Exec. Salary: $255,202	Bonus: $13,923

COMPETITIVE ADVANTAGE: Growth into foreign markets.

OTHER THOUGHTS:

Apparent Women Officers or Directors: 3
Apparent Minority Officers or Directors:
Hot Spot for Advancement for Women/Minorities: Y

LOCATIONS: ("Y" = Yes)

West:	Southwest:	Midwest:	Southeast:	Northeast:	International:
Y		Y	Y	Y	Y

3COM CORP   www.3com.com

Industry Group Code: 3341C
Ranks within this company's industry group: Sales: 2   Profits: 2

BUSINESS ACTIVITIES ("Y" = Yes)

Financial Services:	Information/Publ.:	Technology:		Services:	Retailing:	Telecommunications:
Stock Brokerage	Portal/Hub/News	Computer Manuf.		Payments/Transfers	Retailer	Internet Serv. Provider
Mortgages/Loans	On-Line Community	Networking Equip.	Y	Consulting	Auctions	Web Site Host
Banking	Search Engine	Software Manuf.		Advertising/Marketing	Mall	Server Farm
Insurance	Financial Data Publ.	Specialty Equipment	Y	Outsourcing	Tickets/Travel	Specialty Telecom.
Credit Cards	Broadcasting/Music				Price Comparisons	High Speed Access

TYPES OF BUSINESS:

Computer Networking Equipment

BRANDS/DIVISIONS/AFFILIATES:

Palm Computing
3Com Technologies
Primary Access Corporation
AccessWorks Communications, Inc.
NiceCom, Ltd.
Transcend Network Software
Chipcom Corporation
U S Robotics

CONTACTS: *Note: Officers with more than one job title may be intentionally listed here more than once.*

Eric A. Benhamou, CEO
Bruce L. Claflin, Pres./COO
Christopher B. Paisley, Sr. VP/CFO
Janice M. Roberts, Sr. VP-Mktg. And Business Dev.
John H. Hart, Sr. VP-Chief Tech. Officer
David H. Starr, Sr. VP/CIO
Randy R. Heffner, Sr. VP-Mfg. Oper.
Mark D. Michael, Sr. VP/Corp. Sec.
Mark D. Michael, Sr. VP/General Counsel
Janice M. Robers, Sr. VP-Mktg./Business Dev.
Ralph B. Godfrey, Sr. VP-e-commerce

Phone: 408-326-5000	Fax: 408-326-5001
Toll-Free: 800-638-3266	
Address: 5400 Bayfront Plaza, Santa Clara, CA, 95052	

GROWTH PLANS/SPECIAL FEATURES:

3Com is involved in the business of computer networking and is the leading industry provider of Ethernet, Fast Ethernet and Gigabit Ethernet connectivity. Its clients span from businesses to government and educational organizations. Out of the top 10 North American Internet service providers, 9 implement 3Com's Total Control multi-service access platform, which links subscribers to the Internet. The company is a leading supplier of network interface cards, mobile PC cards, hand-held computers and modems. 3Com has been acquiring companies recently. Among its acquisitions are NBX Corporation, ICS Networking, Smartcode Technologie, Euphonics and Lanwork Technologies. 3Com has spun off its subsidiary, Palm Computing, to make it an independent, publicly traded company. Palm Computing has become the world's leading hand held computing platform, with over five million customers and a market share of 68%. Palm Computing has strategic partnerships, including IBM, Qualcomm, Oracle, Lotus, AOL and Symbol Technologies.

Beyond salary, 3Com offers performance-based incentives, including a special bonus program, Kadoos. After four years of continuous service, employees are offered a paid sabbatical. Employees at 3Com can schedule their own hours as long as their schedule meets the needs of their position and responds to the advice of their managers. Many 3Com campuses offer fitness centers, cafeterias, coffee bars and stores. 3Com has two women sitting on its ten-person executive committee and has a 26% female managerial workforce.

FINANCIALS: Sales and profits are in thousands of dollars—add 000 to get the full amount.

Notes regarding 1999: *(1999 sales and profits were not available for all companies at press time.)*

1999 Sales: $5,800,000	1999 Profits: $403,900	Stock Ticker: **COMS**
1998 Sales: $5,420,400	1998 Profits: $30,200	Employees: 13,027
1997 Sales: $3,147,100	1997 Profits: $374,000	Fiscal Year Ends: 5/31
1996 Sales: $2,327,100	1996 Profits: $177,900	
1995 Sales: $1,295,300	1995 Profits: $125,700	

SALARIES/BENEFITS:

Pension Plan:	ESOP Stock Plan: Y	Profit Sharing:	Top Exec. Salary: $742,500	Bonus: $75,008
Savings Plan: Y	Stock Purch. Plan:		Second Exec. Salary: $395,833	Bonus: $29,673

COMPETITIVE ADVANTAGE: Superior quality of network adapters that are competitive on an international level/1997 acquisition of U S Robotics, a leading modem maker.

OTHER THOUGHTS:

Apparent Women Officers or Directors: 2
Apparent Minority Officers or Directors: 1
Hot Spot for Advancement for Women/Minorities:

LOCATIONS: ("Y" = Yes)

West:	Southwest:	Midwest:	Southeast:	Northeast:	International:
Y		Y		Y	Y

Note: Financial information, benefits and other data can change quickly and may vary from those stated here.

A B WATLEY GROUP INC   www.abwatley.com

Industry Group Code: 5231
Ranks within this company's industry group: Sales: 8   Profits: 7

BUSINESS ACTIVITIES ("Y" = Yes)

Financial Services:		Information/Publ.:	Technology:	Services:	Retailing:	Telecommunications:
Stock Brokerage	Y	Portal/Hub/News	Computer Manuf.	Payments/Transfers	Retailer	Internet Serv. Provider
Mortgages/Loans		On-Line Community	Networking Equip.	Consulting	Auctions	Web Site Host
Banking		Search Engine	Software Manuf.	Advertising/Marketing	Mall	Server Farm
Insurance		Financial Data Publ.	Specialty Equipment	Outsourcing	Tickets/Travel	Specialty Telecom.
Credit Cards		Broadcasting/Music			Price Comparisons	High Speed Access

TYPES OF BUSINESS:

On-line Financial Services

GROWTH PLANS/SPECIAL FEATURES:

A.B. Watley Group, Inc., formerly Internet Financial Services Inc., is the parent company of A.B. Watley, Inc., a multifaceted, technological and service-oriented brokerage firm. A.B. Watley provides large block institutional transactions with real-time data feed and instantaneous execution. The company offers two proprietary on-line trading systems: Ultimate Trader and Watley Trader. Ultimate Trader enables the self-directed active user in need of real-time information and quick order execution to access NASDAQ Level II data, market maker screens with time and sales, real-time charts and the ability to place orders into various exchanges and electronic communications networks (ECNs). Watley Trader provides 24/7 trading services, pre-market open and post-market close trading, free real-time quotes, automated telephone service trading and research, easy account administration, multiple test portfolio tracking and multipurpose quote, analytics and mutual fund services. Users can trade on the Internet for $9.95 per transaction. Orders are entered, processed and confirmed electronically. Founded in 1958, A.B. Watley, Inc. is a member of the National Association of Securities Dealers and the Securities Investment Protection Corporation. A.B. Watley works in partnership with Edgar Online, Cooper Trading, Wall Street on Demand, PC Quote, Market Gems and Briefing.Com in order to bring products and services to its clients.

BRANDS/DIVISIONS/AFFILIATES:

A.B. Watley, Inc.
Ultimate Trader
Watley Trader
Internet Financial Services, Inc.

CONTACTS: Note: Officers with more than one job title may be intentionally listed here more than once.

Steve Malin, CEO
Harry Simpson, COO/Pres.
Michael Fielman, VP-Finance
Jonathan Priddle, Sr. VP-Sales
Brett Vernick, Sr.VP-MIS
Eric Steinberg, Exec.VP-Admin.
Anthony G. Huston, Exec.VP- Strategic Planning
Leon Ferguson, Sr.VP-CIO

Phone: 212-422-1664	Fax: 212-634-9924
Toll-Free:	
Address: 40 Wall St., New York, NY, 10005	

FINANCIALS: Sales and profits are in thousands of dollars—add 000 to get the full amount.

Notes regarding 1999: (1999 sales and profits were not available for all companies at press time.)

1999 Sales: $21,000	1999 Profits: $- 800	Stock Ticker: ABWG
1998 Sales: $9,200	1998 Profits: $- 600	Employees: 45
1997 Sales: $4,500	1997 Profits: $-1,100	Fiscal Year Ends: 9/30
1996 Sales: $	1996 Profits: $	
1995 Sales: $	1995 Profits: $	

SALARIES/BENEFITS:

Pension Plan:	ESOP Stock Plan:	Profit Sharing:	Top Exec. Salary: $70,000	Bonus: $
Savings Plan:	Stock Purch. Plan:		Second Exec. Salary: $	Bonus: $

COMPETITIVE ADVANTAGE: Low transaction fees.

OTHER THOUGHTS:

Apparent Women Officers or Directors:
Apparent Minority Officers or Directors:
Hot Spot for Advancement for Women/Minorities:

LOCATIONS: ("Y" = Yes)

West:	Southwest:	Midwest:	Southeast:	Northeast:	International:
				Y	

Note: Financial information, benefits and other data can change quickly and may vary from those stated here.

ABOUT.COM INC   www.about.com

Industry Group Code: 514191
Ranks within this company's industry group: Sales: 25   Profits: 36

BUSINESS ACTIVITIES ("Y" = Yes)

Financial Services:	Information/Publ.:		Technology:	Services:	Retailing:	Telecommunications:
Stock Brokerage	Portal/Hub/News	Y	Computer Manuf.	Payments/Transfers	Retailer	Internet Serv. Provider
Mortgages/Loans	On-Line Community	Y	Networking Equip.	Consulting	Auctions	Web Site Host
Banking	Search Engine	Y	Software Manuf.	Advertising/Marketing	Mall	Server Farm
Insurance	Financial Data Publ.		Specialty Equipment	Outsourcing	Tickets/Travel	Specialty Telecom.
Credit Cards	Broadcasting/Music				Price Comparisons	High Speed Access

TYPES OF BUSINESS:

Search Portal
Niche On-line Communities

BRANDS/DIVISIONS/AFFILIATES:

GuideSites
MiningCo.com

CONTACTS:
Note: Officers with more than one job title may be intentionally listed here more than once.

Scott P. Kurnit, Pres./CEO
William C. Day, COO
Todd Sloan, CFO
John R. Kaplan, VP-Mktg.
Kenneth H. Appleman, VP/Chief Tech. Officer
Alan Blaustein, Sr. VP/General Counsel
Robert W. Harris, VP-Finance and Admin.
A. Jeffrey Radov, VP-Business Dev.
Barbara Manley, Financial Relations Board
Eric W. Bingham, VP-Business Oper.

Phone: 212-849-2000	Fax:
Toll-Free:	
Address: 220 E. 42nd St., 24th Fl., New York, NY, 10017	

GROWTH PLANS/SPECIAL FEATURES:

About.com, Inc. is an Internet directory that operates more than 650 GuideSites. The sites are grouped into one of eighteen categories, including such titles as Arts and Literature, Hobbies and Sports. What makes About.com unique from other web site aggregators is that, instead of using search engines to scan sites for key words, the company employs human guides to manage its sites. These guides create original content (such as e-mail newsletters), oversee chat rooms and respond to e-mail questions and requests. The company's editorial staff oversees the guides' sites to make sure quality and up-to-date information are maintained. About.com obtains most of its sales from advertising. In a move supported by a major advertising campaign, the company went public and changed its name from MiningCo.com to About.com in a push to position itself as an original content provider and not just a search engine. The firm also began a membership drive, with the expectation of creating communities of people who share similar interests. About.com now claims to be one of the top 25 most visited web sites.

FINANCIALS: Sales and profits are in thousands of dollars—add 000 to get the full amount.
Notes regarding 1999: Through 9 months *(1999 sales and profits were not available for all companies at press time.)*

1999 Sales: $13,958	1999 Profits: $-45,790	Stock Ticker: **BOUT**
1998 Sales: $3,700	1998 Profits: $-15,600	Employees: 113
1997 Sales: $ 400	1997 Profits: $-8,600	Fiscal Year Ends: 12/31
1996 Sales: $	1996 Profits: $-2,400	
1995 Sales: $	1995 Profits: $	

SALARIES/BENEFITS:

Pension Plan:	ESOP Stock Plan: Y	Profit Sharing:	Top Exec. Salary: $270,750	Bonus: $
Savings Plan:	Stock Purch. Plan:		Second Exec. Salary: $150,625	Bonus: $

COMPETITIVE ADVANTAGE: Unique search portal positioning.

OTHER THOUGHTS:

Apparent Women Officers or Directors: 2
Apparent Minority Officers or Directors:
Hot Spot for Advancement for Women/Minorities:

LOCATIONS: ("Y" = Yes)

West:	Southwest:	Midwest:	Southeast:	Northeast:	International:
				Y	

Note: Financial information, benefits and other data can change quickly and may vary from those stated here.

ABOVENET COMMUNICATIONS INC   www.abovenet.com

Industry Group Code: 51339
Ranks within this company's industry group: Sales: 21   Profits: 9

BUSINESS ACTIVITIES ("Y" = Yes)

Financial Services:	Information/Publ.:	Technology:	Services:	Retailing:	Telecommunications:	
Stock Brokerage	Portal/Hub/News	Computer Manuf.	Payments/Transfers	Retailer	Internet Serv. Provider	Y
Mortgages/Loans	On-Line Community	Networking Equip.	Consulting	Auctions	Web Site Host	Y
Banking	Search Engine	Software Manuf.	Advertising/Marketing	Mall	Server Farm	Y
Insurance	Financial Data Publ.	Specialty Equipment	Outsourcing	Tickets/Travel	Specialty Telecom.	
Credit Cards	Broadcasting/Music			Price Comparisons	High Speed Access	

TYPES OF BUSINESS:

Internet Service Provider
Server Farm
Web Site Host

BRANDS/DIVISIONS/AFFILIATES:

Metromedia Fiber Network

CONTACTS: Note: Officers with more than one job title may be intentionally listed here more than once.

Sherman Tuan, CEO
Warren J. Kaplan, Pres./COO
Dave Larson, Sr.VP/CFO
David Dembitz, Sr. VP-Sales and Mktg.
Barbara Meese, Dir.-Human Resources
David Rand, Chief Tech. Officer
Kevin Hourigan, Controller
Avi Freedman, VP-Engineering
Wayne Sanders, VP-Corp.Dev.
Rusty Walther, VP-Client Services

Phone: 408-367-6666	Fax: 408-367-6688
Toll-Free:	
Address: 50 W. Fernando St., Ste. 1010, San Jose, CA, 95113	

GROWTH PLANS/SPECIAL FEATURES:

AboveNet Communications, recently acquired by Metromedia Fiber Network, is an Internet hosting and connectivity services company. The company boasts one of the largest aggregated bandwidth networks in the world. AboveNet is a leading provider of Internet connectivity and co-location for Internet Service Providers (ISPs). By hosting their servers at AboveNet's facilities, ISPs reduce their operating costs and deliver enhanced Internet performance to end users. AboveNet offers many different types of facilities for companies desiring different levels of security. Private vaults are available with 24-hour supervised access. The company also offers security cameras, dedicated router ports for network security and biometric hand and iris scanners for verifying identity. Stringent physical security is also available, including multiple cement walls and RF shielding for protection against electromagnetic pulses. The company has the distinction of receiving an ISO 9002 certification. Recently, the company announced the opening of its New York facility, located in the Chelsea district where the financial and telecommunications sectors meet. Many financial companies, including Fortune 500 companies, will take advantage of AboveNet's new location. AboveNet also operates facilities in London, Frankfurt and Vienna.

FINANCIALS: Sales and profits are in thousands of dollars—add 000 to get the full amount.

Notes regarding 1999: (1999 sales and profits were not available for all companies at press time.)

1999 Sales: $14,000	1999 Profits: $-26,600	Stock Ticker: **ABOV**
1998 Sales: $3,400	1998 Profits: $-5,400	Employees: 71
1997 Sales: $ 600	1997 Profits: $-1,800	Fiscal Year Ends: 6/30
1996 Sales: $ 100	1996 Profits: $ 100	
1995 Sales: $	1995 Profits: $	

SALARIES/BENEFITS:

Pension Plan:	ESOP Stock Plan:	Profit Sharing:	Top Exec. Salary: $132,500	Bonus: $
Savings Plan:	Stock Purch. Plan:		Second Exec. Salary: $	Bonus: $

COMPETITIVE ADVANTAGE: Rapidly became one of the leading server farms.

OTHER THOUGHTS:

Apparent Women Officers or Directors: 3
Apparent Minority Officers or Directors: 1
Hot Spot for Advancement for Women/Minorities: Y

LOCATIONS: ("Y" = Yes)

West:	Southwest:	Midwest:	Southeast:	Northeast:	International:
Y	Y	Y	Y	Y	Y

ACCRUE SOFTWARE INC   www.accrue.com

Industry Group Code: 5112
Ranks within this company's industry group: Sales: 76   Profits: 29

BUSINESS ACTIVITIES ("Y" = Yes)

Financial Services:	Information/Publ.:	Technology:		Services:		Retailing:		Telecommunications:
Stock Brokerage	Portal/Hub/News	Computer Manuf.		Payments/Transfers		Retailer		Internet Serv. Provider
Mortgages/Loans	On-Line Community	Networking Equip.		Consulting	Y	Auctions		Web Site Host
Banking	Search Engine	Software Manuf.	Y	Advertising/Marketing	Y	Mall		Server Farm
Insurance	Financial Data Publ.	Specialty Equipment		Outsourcing	Y	Tickets/Travel		Specialty Telecom.
Credit Cards	Broadcasting/Music					Price Comparisons		High Speed Access

TYPES OF BUSINESS:

Software-Web Site Usage
Consulting
Marketing Analysis and Data

BRANDS/DIVISIONS/AFFILIATES:

DoubleClick
Accrue Insight
Accrue Vista
Accrue Hit List
Quickbridges

CONTACTS: Note: Officers with more than one job title may be intentionally listed here more than once.

Richard D. Kreysar, CEO
Richard D. Kreysar, Pres.
Gregory C. Walker, VP/CFO
Vito Salvaggio, VP-Mktg.
Bob Page, VP-Chief Tech. Officer
Giao Vu, Dir.-Server Engineering
Keith Thesing, Dir.-Int'l Sales/Business Dev.

Phone: 510-580-4500	Fax: 510-580-4501
Toll-Free:	
Address: 48634 Milmont Dr., Fremont, CA, 94538-7353	

GROWTH PLANS/SPECIAL FEATURES:

Accrue Software provides services for determining the effectiveness of business web sites. Accrue monitors visits to particular web sites and pages, determines who is visiting the sites, their visit frequency and duration and how much business a particular page generates. Accrue also offers on-site training and consulting. The company provides its services to many large firms, including Apple Computer, Eastman Kodak, Motorola, Bank of America, Compaq, IBM, Los Angeles Times, Viacom/MTV and Ford. Accrue offers many different products, including Accrue Insight, Accrue Vista, Accrue Hit List and Quickbridges. Accrue Insight assesses web site effectiveness by analyzing and reporting web site traffic information. Web managers and marketers can utilize this information to attract new customers and increase revenue. Recently, Accrue entered into an agreement with DoubleClick, the leading Internet advertising solutions company, to jointly market and sell a product to on-line businesses. It will combine Accrue's site-specific data savvy with DoubleClick's advertising data and analysis. Recently, Accrue opened a European office in the United Kingdom. The company also expanded into Japan's market by establishing a new alliance with Sumisho Electronics in Tokyo.

FINANCIALS: Sales and profits are in thousands of dollars—add 000 to get the full amount.

Notes regarding 1999: *(1999 sales and profits were not available for all companies at press time.)*

1999 Sales: $3,000	1999 Profits: $-6,600	Stock Ticker: **ACRU**
1998 Sales: $1,100	1998 Profits: $-3,900	Employees: 62
1997 Sales: $ 200	1997 Profits: $-1,900	Fiscal Year Ends: 3/31
1996 Sales: $	1996 Profits: $	
1995 Sales: $	1995 Profits: $	

SALARIES/BENEFITS:

Pension Plan:	ESOP Stock Plan:	Profit Sharing:	Top Exec. Salary: $	Bonus: $
Savings Plan:	Stock Purch. Plan:		Second Exec. Salary: $	Bonus: $

COMPETITIVE ADVANTAGE: Rapid expansion overseas/Relationship with DoubleClick.

OTHER THOUGHTS:

Apparent Women Officers or Directors: 2
Apparent Minority Officers or Directors: 2
Hot Spot for Advancement for Women/Minorities: Y

LOCATIONS: ("Y" = Yes)

West:	Southwest:	Midwest:	Southeast:	Northeast:	International:
Y					Y

Note: Financial information, benefits and other data can change quickly and may vary from those stated here.

ADFORCE INC   www.adforce.org

Industry Group Code: 54189A
Ranks within this company's industry group: Sales: 13   Profits: 16

BUSINESS ACTIVITIES ("Y" = Yes)

Financial Services:	Information/Publ.:	Technology:	Services:		Retailing:	Telecommunications:
Stock Brokerage	Portal/Hub/News	Computer Manuf.	Payments/Transfers		Retailer	Internet Serv. Provider
Mortgages/Loans	On-Line Community	Networking Equip.	Consulting		Auctions	Web Site Host
Banking	Search Engine	Software Manuf.	Advertising/Marketing	Y	Mall	Server Farm
Insurance	Financial Data Publ.	Specialty Equipment	Outsourcing		Tickets/Travel	Specialty Telecom.
Credit Cards	Broadcasting/Music				Price Comparisons	High Speed Access

TYPES OF BUSINESS:

Advertising-On-line Network

BRANDS/DIVISIONS/AFFILIATES:

GROWTH PLANS/SPECIAL FEATURES:

AdForce provides centralized ad servicing that allows web publishers and advertisers to run ad campaigns across several web sites. Adforce makes it possible for clients to plan and manage Internet advertising for maximum effectiveness. Agencies can schedule their campaigns using AdForce's software and, as the campaign is running, clients can analyze reports on targeting customers and ad rotation. AdForce's customers include Arthur Frommer's, Netscape, PointCast, adsm@rt, adauction.com and Virtual Vegas. The company's strategic partners include AOL and Euroserve. The company continues to grow aggressively and has expanded its presence in the market by adding over 45 domestic and international customers. In recent news, AdForce announced it will provide and manage electronic advertising for DigitalSquare, a company engaged in developing a worldwide network of retail software distribution outlets that will be placed on the hard drives of millions of new PCs.

CONTACTS:
Note: Officers with more than one job title may be intentionally listed here more than once.

Charles W. Berger, CEO
Charles W. Berger, Pres.
John A. Tanner, Exec. VP/CFO
A. Dee Cravens, VP-Worldwide Mktg.
Dawn Thompson, VP-Human Resources
Richard E. Theige, VP-Engineering Services
Rex S. Jackson, Sec.
Rex S. Jackson, General Counsel
Harish S. Rao, Exec. VP-Oper.
Anthony P. Glaves, VP-Worldwide Sales and Business Dev.
Stephanie Santa, Investor Relations Admin.

Phone: 408-873-3680	Fax: 408-873-3693
Toll-Free:	
Address: 10590 N. Tantau Ave., Cupertino, CA, 95014	

FINANCIALS: Sales and profits are in thousands of dollars—add 000 to get the full amount.

Notes regarding 1999: Through 9 months *(1999 sales and profits were not available for all companies at press time.)*

1999 Sales: $12,487	1999 Profits: $-16,691	Stock Ticker: **ADFC**
1998 Sales: $4,300	1998 Profits: $-15,000	Employees: 97
1997 Sales: $ 300	1997 Profits: $-5,700	Fiscal Year Ends: 12/31
1996 Sales: $	1996 Profits: $-3,500	
1995 Sales: $	1995 Profits: $	

SALARIES/BENEFITS:

Pension Plan:	ESOP Stock Plan:	Profit Sharing:	Top Exec. Salary: $	Bonus: $
Savings Plan:	Stock Purch. Plan:		Second Exec. Salary: $	Bonus: $

COMPETITIVE ADVANTAGE: Strong alliances.

OTHER THOUGHTS:

Apparent Women Officers or Directors: 2
Apparent Minority Officers or Directors: 1
Hot Spot for Advancement for Women/Minorities:

LOCATIONS: ("Y" = Yes)

West:	Southwest:	Midwest:	Southeast:	Northeast:	International:
Y					

Note: Financial information, benefits and other data can change quickly and may vary from those stated here.

ADSTAR.COM INC   www.adstar.com

Industry Group Code: 51339A
Ranks within this company's industry group: Sales: 11   Profits: 4

BUSINESS ACTIVITIES ("Y" = Yes)

Financial Services:	Information/Publ.:	Technology:	Services:		Retailing:	Telecommunications:
Stock Brokerage	Portal/Hub/News	Computer Manuf.	Payments/Transfers		Retailer	Internet Serv. Provider
Mortgages/Loans	On-Line Community	Networking Equip.	Consulting		Auctions	Web Site Host
Banking	Search Engine	Software Manuf.	Advertising/Marketing	Y	Mall	Server Farm
Insurance	Financial Data Publ.	Specialty Equipment	Outsourcing		Tickets/Travel	Specialty Telecom.
Credit Cards	Broadcasting/Music				Price Comparisons	High Speed Access

TYPES OF BUSINESS:
On-line Classifieds

BRANDS/DIVISIONS/AFFILIATES:
Advertise123
Ad-Star Services, Inc.

CONTACTS: *Note: Officers with more than one job title may be intentionally listed here more than once.*
Leslie Bernhard, CEO
Leslie Bernhard, Pres.
Benjamin J. Douek, Sr.VP/CFO
Richard Bassler, Human Resources
Eli Rousso, Exec. VP-Chief Tech. Officer
Richard Bassler, VP-Oper.
Michael Kline, Sr.VP-Strategy
Adam Leff, Sr.VP-Business Dev. and Corp. Comm.

Phone: 310-577-8255	Fax: 310-577-8266
Toll-Free:	
Address: 4553 Glencoe Ave., Ste. 325, Marina Del Rey, CA, 90292	

GROWTH PLANS/SPECIAL FEATURES:

AdStar.com, formerly Ad-Star Services, Inc., is a provider of remote ad entry software for newspapers and advertisers. AdStar's software allows 24-hour access for customers to place classified ads, which promotes the profitability of the advertisements. The company currently provides services for over 43 major metropolitan newspapers and over 1,400 professional journals. Its newspaper clients include the Chicago Tribune, Washington Post, Los Angeles Times, Miami Herald, New York Daily News and the Atlanta Journal & Constitution. AdStar's software saves newspapers time and money by reducing costs associated with errors from re-entering ads onto their computer systems. The company recently partnered with CareerPath.com to launch a new on-line job posting service. The new service allows employers to create, schedule and pay for their recruitment ads on the CareerPath.com web site and is implemented through AdStar's new remote ad entry network, Advertise123. The company has partnerships with AdOne, L.L.C. and PowerAdz.com, where it acts as a technology and production partner.

FINANCIALS: Sales and profits are in thousands of dollars—add 000 to get the full amount.
Notes regarding 1999: *(1999 sales and profits were not available for all companies at press time.)*

1999 Sales: $	1999 Profits: $	Stock Ticker: **ASCU**
1998 Sales: $1,600	1998 Profits: $ 100	Employees: 16
1997 Sales: $1,100	1997 Profits: $ 100	Fiscal Year Ends: 12/31
1996 Sales: $	1996 Profits: $	
1995 Sales: $	1995 Profits: $	

SALARIES/BENEFITS:

Pension Plan:	ESOP Stock Plan:	Profit Sharing:	Top Exec. Salary: $	Bonus: $
Savings Plan:	Stock Purch. Plan:		Second Exec. Salary: $	Bonus: $

COMPETITIVE ADVANTAGE: Unique technology provides vital services to both advertisers and publications.

OTHER THOUGHTS:
Apparent Women Officers or Directors: 1
Apparent Minority Officers or Directors:
Hot Spot for Advancement for Women/Minorities:

LOCATIONS: ("Y" = Yes)

West:	Southwest:	Midwest:	Southeast:	Northeast:	International:
Y					

ADVANCE PUBLICATIONS INC   www.advance.net

Industry Group Code: 51112
Ranks within this company's industry group: Sales: 1   Profits:

BUSINESS ACTIVITIES ("Y" = Yes)

Financial Services:	Information/Publ.:		Technology:	Services:		Retailing:	Telecommunications:	
Stock Brokerage	Portal/Hub/News	Y	Computer Manuf.	Payments/Transfers		Retailer	Internet Serv. Provider	
Mortgages/Loans	On-Line Community	Y	Networking Equip.	Consulting		Auctions	Web Site Host	Y
Banking	Search Engine		Software Manuf.	Advertising/Marketing	Y	Mall	Server Farm	
Insurance	Financial Data Publ.		Specialty Equipment	Outsourcing		Tickets/Travel	Specialty Telecom.	
Credit Cards	Broadcasting/Music					Price Comparisons	High Speed Access	

TYPES OF BUSINESS:
Portal-Media

BRANDS/DIVISIONS/AFFILIATES:
Conde Nast Publications
American City Business Journals
Architectural Digest
Advance Internet
Conde Net
GQ
Mademoiselle
The New Yorker

CONTACTS: Note: Officers with more than one job title may be intentionally listed here more than once.
Samuel I. Newhouse Jr., CEO
Donald E. Newhouse, Pres.
Jill H. Bright, Sr.VP-Human Resources
Arthur Silverstein, Comptroller

Phone: 718-981-1234	Fax: 718-981-1456
Toll-Free:	
Address: 950 Fingerboard Rd., Staten Island, NY, 10305	

GROWTH PLANS/SPECIAL FEATURES:

Advance Publications is primarily engaged in publishing a variety of magazines, newspapers and business weeklies. Its main titles include Conde Nast, Glamour, Vogue, GQ, The New Yorker, Wired and Vanity Fair. Advance has established a new media unit called Conde Net to build Internet presence. Advance Internet, a subsidiary of Advance Publications, is responsible for the development and management of 10 local web sites that are affiliated with newspapers owned by its parent company. On the Internet, Advance features on-line versions of its newspapers and other sites, including a children's educational site called The Yuckiest Site on the Internet. Recently, Advance partnered with Donrey Media Group, E.W. Scripps, Hearst Corporation and MediaNews Group to purchase AdOne Classified Network. The company is also a partner in Time Warner's Road Runner high-speed Internet access service. Advance Internet recently signed an agreement with Cassiopeia, Europe's leading chat and community software company, to help create a new version of its services for the American market.

FINANCIALS: Sales and profits are in thousands of dollars—add 000 to get the full amount.
Notes regarding 1999: (1999 sales and profits were not available for all companies at press time.)

1999 Sales: $	1999 Profits: $	Stock Ticker: private
1998 Sales: $3,859,100	1998 Profits: $	Employees: 24,000
1997 Sales: $	1997 Profits: $	Fiscal Year Ends: 12/31
1996 Sales: $	1996 Profits: $	
1995 Sales: $	1995 Profits: $	

SALARIES/BENEFITS:

Pension Plan:	ESOP Stock Plan:	Profit Sharing:	Top Exec. Salary: $	Bonus: $
Savings Plan:	Stock Purch. Plan:		Second Exec. Salary: $	Bonus: $

COMPETITIVE ADVANTAGE: Advance's affluent and highly-educated magazine subscriber base contains exactly the type of people most likely to utilize business-to-consumer services and products.

OTHER THOUGHTS:

Apparent Women Officers or Directors: 6
Apparent Minority Officers or Directors:
Hot Spot for Advancement for Women/Minorities: Y

LOCATIONS: ("Y" = Yes)

West:	Southwest:	Midwest:	Southeast:	Northeast:	International:
Y	Y	Y	Y	Y	

AGENCY.COM LTD   www.agency.com

Industry Group Code: 54189A
Ranks within this company's industry group: Sales: 5   Profits: 3

BUSINESS ACTIVITIES ("Y" = Yes)

Financial Services:	Information/Publ.:	Technology:	Services:		Retailing:		Telecommunications:
Stock Brokerage	Portal/Hub/News	Computer Manuf.	Payments/Transfers		Retailer		Internet Serv. Provider
Mortgages/Loans	On-Line Community	Networking Equip.	Consulting	Y	Auctions		Web Site Host
Banking	Search Engine	Software Manuf.	Advertising/Marketing	Y	Mall		Server Farm
Insurance	Financial Data Publ.	Specialty Equipment	Outsourcing		Tickets/Travel		Specialty Telecom.
Credit Cards	Broadcasting/Music				Price Comparisons		High Speed Access

TYPES OF BUSINESS:

Internet-Focused Marketing Services
Branding Consultancy

BRANDS/DIVISIONS/AFFILIATES:

i-traffic
Spiral Media
Online Magic
Ketchum Interactive
Interactive Solutions
Quadris
EDGE Consultants

CONTACTS: *Note: Officers with more than one job title may be intentionally listed here more than once.*

Chan Suh, CEO
Chan Suh, Pres.
Kenneth Trush, CFO/Treas.
Steven Smith, Human Resources
Larry Krakauer, Chief Tech. Officer
Janet Ambrosi Wertman, Exec. VP/General Counsel/Sec.
Mylene Dane, VP-Business Dev., Central Region
Kyle Shannon, Chief Creative Officer
Kevin Rowe, Pres.-North America

Phone: 212-358-8220	Fax: 212-358-8257
Toll-Free:	
Address: 665 Broadway, 9th Fl., New York, NY, 10012	

GROWTH PLANS/SPECIAL FEATURES:

Agency.com is an international Internet professional services firm. The company takes its clients from concept to launch to operation of their Internet businesses. The recent acquisition of i-traffic has allowed Agency.com to offer a range of interactive direct marketing services, including media planning and tracking, on-line advertising, on-line affiliate programs and on-line marketing alliance management. Interactive Relationship Management (IRM) is a discipline designed by Agency.com to deepen customer relationships on-line in four areas: branding (making a product come alive), content (providing a client with the ability to update its site regularly), transactions (ease of access for customers) and customer service (an e-business must keep its customers happy or they will move on to another site). Agency.com has offices across the U.S. and in Europe. The company acquired Spiral Media in New York, Online Magic in London, Ketchum Interactive in San Francisco, Interactive Solutions and Quadris in Boston, Twinspark Interactive in Amsterdam, Visionik in Denmark and Digital Vision and Eagle River Interactive in Chicago, as well as a 30% share of The EDGE Consultants in Singapore. Clients of Agency.com include Bank of America, British Airways, Compaq Computer, Gucci, Motorola and Texaco.

FINANCIALS: Sales and profits are in thousands of dollars—add 000 to get the full amount.

Notes regarding 1999: *(1999 sales and profits were not available for all companies at press time.)*

1999 Sales: $	1999 Profits: $	Stock Ticker: **ACOM**
1998 Sales: $26,500	1998 Profits: $-1,800	Employees: 748
1997 Sales: $13,000	1997 Profits: $1,200	Fiscal Year Ends: 12/31
1996 Sales: $6,100	1996 Profits: $1,500	
1995 Sales: $	1995 Profits: $	

SALARIES/BENEFITS:

Pension Plan:	ESOP Stock Plan: Y	Profit Sharing:	Top Exec. Salary: $250,000	Bonus: $320,000
Savings Plan:	Stock Purch. Plan:		Second Exec. Salary: $150,000	Bonus: $2,000

COMPETITIVE ADVANTAGE: Growth and extension of services through acquisitions.

OTHER THOUGHTS:

Apparent Women Officers or Directors: 2
Apparent Minority Officers or Directors: 2
Hot Spot for Advancement for Women/Minorities: Y

LOCATIONS: ("Y" = Yes)

West:	Southwest:	Midwest:	Southeast:	Northeast:	International:
Y	Y	Y	Y	Y	Y

AGILE SOFTWARE CORP   www.agilesoft.com

Industry Group Code: 5112
Ranks within this company's industry group: Sales: 52   Profits: 49

BUSINESS ACTIVITIES ("Y" = Yes)

Financial Services:	Information/Publ.:	Technology:		Services:	Retailing:	Telecommunications:
Stock Brokerage	Portal/Hub/News	Computer Manuf.		Payments/Transfers	Retailer	Internet Serv. Provider
Mortgages/Loans	On-Line Community	Networking Equip.		Consulting	Auctions	Web Site Host
Banking	Search Engine	Software Manuf.	Y	Advertising/Marketing	Mall	Server Farm
Insurance	Financial Data Publ.	Specialty Equipment		Outsourcing	Tickets/Travel	Specialty Telecom.
Credit Cards	Broadcasting/Music				Price Comparisons	High Speed Access

TYPES OF BUSINESS:

Software-Corporate

BRANDS/DIVISIONS/AFFILIATES:

Agile Anywhere
Agile eXpress Viewer
Digital Market, Inc.

CONTACTS: *Note: Officers with more than one job title may be intentionally listed here more than once.*

Bryan D. Stolle, CEO
Bryan D. Stolle, Pres.
Thomas P. Shanahan, Exec.VP/CFO
Carol B. Schrader, VP-Mktg.
Thomas P. Shanahan, Sec.
Mark C. Irvine, VP-North America Field Oper.
Gregory G. Schott, VP-Business Dev.
D. Kenneth Coulter, Sr. VP-Worldwide Sales

Phone: 408-975-3900	Fax: 408-271-4862
Toll-Free:	
Address: 1 Almaden Blvd., San Jose, CA, 95113-2211	

GROWTH PLANS/SPECIAL FEATURES:

Agile Software develops and markets Internet-based product content management software for businesses in a manufacturing electronic supply chain. Its Agile Anywhere products improve communications between members of a supply chain. It allows customers to manage product content information, publish that information to other companies in their supply chain and communicate with those companies on the Internet in real-time. Agile also has software called Agile eXpress Viewer in the Agile Anywhere suite that allows companies that do not have Agile software to view information in the chain. In recent news, Agile signed an agreement to acquire Digital Market, Inc., a company engaged in providing Internet-based solutions for procuring and sourcing materials. This agreement will significantly enhance Agile's business position and increase its product base. Agile anywhere is also being offered through Oracle Business Online, a leading Internet application hosting service. Agile Software was recognized by Start magazine, a leading publication for readers in the engineering and manufacturing industries, as one of the Hottest Companies two years in a row.

FINANCIALS: Sales and profits are in thousands of dollars—add 000 to get the full amount.
Notes regarding 1999: *(1999 sales and profits were not available for all companies at press time.)*

1999 Sales: $16,800	1999 Profits: $-11,400	Stock Ticker: **AGIL**
1998 Sales: $8,000	1998 Profits: $-8,900	Employees: 156
1997 Sales: $1,400	1997 Profits: $-4,800	Fiscal Year Ends: 4/30
1996 Sales: $	1996 Profits: $-1,300	
1995 Sales: $	1995 Profits: $	

SALARIES/BENEFITS:

Pension Plan:	ESOP Stock Plan: Y	Profit Sharing:	Top Exec. Salary: $	Bonus: $
Savings Plan:	Stock Purch. Plan:		Second Exec. Salary: $	Bonus: $

COMPETITIVE ADVANTAGE: Focus on supply chain management/Relationship with Oracle.

OTHER THOUGHTS:

Apparent Women Officers or Directors: 2
Apparent Minority Officers or Directors:
Hot Spot for Advancement for Women/Minorities:

LOCATIONS: ("Y" = Yes)

West:	Southwest:	Midwest:	Southeast:	Northeast:	International:
Y					

ALLAIRE CORP   www.allaire.com

Industry Group Code: 5112
Ranks within this company's industry group: Sales: 37   Profits: 55

BUSINESS ACTIVITIES ("Y" = Yes)

Financial Services:	Information/Publ.:	Technology:		Services:	Retailing:	Telecommunications:
Stock Brokerage	Portal/Hub/News	Computer Manuf.		Payments/Transfers	Retailer	Internet Serv. Provider
Mortgages/Loans	On-Line Community	Networking Equip.		Consulting	Auctions	Web Site Host
Banking	Search Engine	Software Manuf.	Y	Advertising/Marketing	Mall	Server Farm
Insurance	Financial Data Publ.	Specialty Equipment		Outsourcing	Tickets/Travel	Specialty Telecom.
Credit Cards	Broadcasting/Music				Price Comparisons	High Speed Access

TYPES OF BUSINESS:

Sofware-Web Site Design

BRANDS/DIVISIONS/AFFILIATES:

ColdFusion
HomeSite
Jrun
Spectra

CONTACTS: Note: Officers with more than one job title may be intentionally listed here more than once.

David J. Orfao, CEO
David J. Orfao, Pres.
David A. Gerth, CFO
Stephen F. Clark, VP-Mktg.
Victoria Reiff, Sr. Dir.-Human Resources
Jeremy Allaire, VP-Tech. Strategy
Jack P. Lull, VP-Dev.

Phone: 617-761-2000	Fax: 617-761-2001
Toll-Free: 888-939-2545	
Address: 1 Alewife Center, Cambridge, MA, 02140	

GROWTH PLANS/SPECIAL FEATURES:

Allaire Corporation is one of the industry's leading independent web application platform software makers. Its products include ColdFusion, HomeSite, JRun and Allaire Spectra. ColdFusion is the company's most successful product, and more than 3,500 companies have used it to integrate their businesses onto the Internet. VISA International, Eastman Kodak, Williams Sonoma, Reebok, Boeing and Autobytel.com are some of Allaire's customers that have implemented ColdFusion. Allaire provides integrated web application development internationally and has a network of over 1,500 partners, including consultants, Internet service providers, independent software vendors, interactive agencies and system integrators. In recent news, Allaire was chosen by Ableauctions.com to launch a new e-commerce system with ColdFusion software. The new web presence will allow Ableauctions to broadcast live auctions via the Internet and host live auctions, charity auctions and an on-line retail store. Chicago Mercantile Exchange, one of the world's premier futures and options exchanges, announced its plans to use Allaire Spectra to enhance its web site. Allaire Spectra is designed to provide content management, e-commerce and personalization solutions to web sites.

FINANCIALS: Sales and profits are in thousands of dollars—add 000 to get the full amount.

Notes regarding 1999: (1999 sales and profits were not available for all companies at press time.)

1999 Sales: $55,200	1999 Profits: $-5,500	Stock Ticker: ALLR
1998 Sales: $20,500	1998 Profits: $-10,800	Employees: 165
1997 Sales: $7,700	1997 Profits: $-7,400	Fiscal Year Ends: 12/31
1996 Sales: $2,400	1996 Profits: $-1,700	
1995 Sales: $	1995 Profits: $- 200	

SALARIES/BENEFITS:

Pension Plan:	ESOP Stock Plan:	Profit Sharing:	Top Exec. Salary: $167,355	Bonus: $58,000
Savings Plan:	Stock Purch. Plan:		Second Exec. Salary: $	Bonus: $

COMPETITIVE ADVANTAGE: ColdFusion is one of the most respected applications for major e-commerce site development.

OTHER THOUGHTS:

Apparent Women Officers or Directors: 3
Apparent Minority Officers or Directors:
Hot Spot for Advancement for Women/Minorities: Y

LOCATIONS: ("Y" = Yes)

West:	Southwest:	Midwest:	Southeast:	Northeast:	International:
				Y	Y

ALLOY ONLINE INC   www.alloyonline.com

Industry Group Code: 514191
Ranks within this company's industry group: Sales: 32   Profits: 11

BUSINESS ACTIVITIES ("Y" = Yes)

Financial Services:	Information/Publ.:		Technology:	Services:	Retailing:		Telecommunications:
Stock Brokerage	Portal/Hub/News	Y	Computer Manuf.	Payments/Transfers	Retailer	Y	Internet Serv. Provider
Mortgages/Loans	On-Line Community	Y	Networking Equip.	Consulting	Auctions		Web Site Host
Banking	Search Engine		Software Manuf.	Advertising/Marketing	Mall		Server Farm
Insurance	Financial Data Publ.		Specialty Equipment	Outsourcing	Tickets/Travel		Specialty Telecom.
Credit Cards	Broadcasting/Music				Price Comparisons		High Speed Access

TYPES OF BUSINESS:
Youth Portal

BRANDS/DIVISIONS/AFFILIATES:
Yahoo!
SonicNet

GROWTH PLANS/SPECIAL FEATURES:

Alloy Online specializes in clothing and compact discs sales through its web site and mail order catalogue. The company is concerned with targeting the market of Generation Y, or 10- to 24-year-olds. Alloy's web site offers free e-mail, chat rooms, home pages and information on relationships, fashion trends and music. Alloy is currently attempting to diversify its revenue sources through advertising and sponsorship agreements. The company has partnered with SonicNet, an Internet music company, to feature music reviews and news on its web site. Alloy signed an agreement with Yahoo! to co-brand a version of Alloy's on-line store. The company has a new agreement with Hotmail, in which Hotmail will distribute an Alloy e-zine for teenagers. New subscribers to Hotmail have the option of receiving the e-zine in their inboxes. This will greatly increase traffic to the Alloy web site.

CONTACTS: *Note: Officers with more than one job title may be intentionally listed here more than once.*
Matthew C. Diamond, CEO
James K. Johnson Jr., COO/Pres.
Samuel A. Gradess, CFO
Joan D. Rosenstock, Dir.-Mktg.
Samuel A. Gradess, Sec.
J. Scott Caldwell, Dir.-Catalog Oper.
Andrew A Roberts, VP-Business Dev.
Susan K. Kaplow, Dir.-Internet Development

Phone: 212-244-4307	Fax: 212-244-4311
Toll-Free:	
Address: 115 W. 30th St., #201, New York, NY, 10001	

FINANCIALS: Sales and profits are in thousands of dollars—add 000 to get the full amount.
Notes regarding 1999: *(1999 sales and profits were not available for all companies at press time.)*

1999 Sales: $10,200	1999 Profits: $-6,400	Stock Ticker: **ALOY**
1998 Sales: $1,800	1998 Profits: $-1,900	Employees: 25
1997 Sales: $	1997 Profits: $- 100	Fiscal Year Ends: 1/31
1996 Sales: $	1996 Profits: $	
1995 Sales: $	1995 Profits: $	

SALARIES/BENEFITS:

Pension Plan:	ESOP Stock Plan: Y	Profit Sharing:	Top Exec. Salary: $	Bonus: $
Savings Plan:	Stock Purch. Plan:		Second Exec. Salary: $	Bonus: $

COMPETITIVE ADVANTAGE: Focus on attracting 10-to 24-year-old users.

OTHER THOUGHTS:
Apparent Women Officers or Directors: 3
Apparent Minority Officers or Directors: 1
Hot Spot for Advancement for Women/Minorities: Y

LOCATIONS: ("Y" = Yes)

West:	Southwest:	Midwest:	Southeast:	Northeast:	International:
				Y	

AMAZON.COM INC   www.amazon.com

Industry Group Code: 4541
Ranks within this company's industry group: Sales: 2   Profits: 33

BUSINESS ACTIVITIES ("Y" = Yes)

Financial Services:	Information/Publ.:	Technology:	Services:	Retailing:	Telecommunications:	
Stock Brokerage	Portal/Hub/News	Computer Manuf.	Payments/Transfers	Retailer	Internet Serv. Provider	Y
Mortgages/Loans	On-Line Community	Networking Equip.	Consulting	Auctions	Web Site Host	Y
Banking	Search Engine	Software Manuf.	Advertising/Marketing	Mall	Server Farm	
Insurance	Financial Data Publ.	Specialty Equipment	Outsourcing	Tickets/Travel	Specialty Telecom.	
Credit Cards	Broadcasting/Music			Price Comparisons	High Speed Access	

TYPES OF BUSINESS:

Retail-Books, Music, Auctions, Toys
On-line Recorded Music Retailing
On-line Video Retailing
On-line Auctions
Internet Business Investments
On-line Electronics Sales
On-line Toy Sales

BRANDS/DIVISIONS/AFFILIATES:

Homegrocer.com
Editors service
MatchMaker collaborative filtering
Drugstore.com
Gear.com
Planetall.com
LiveBid.com
Pets.com

CONTACTS: *Note: Officers with more than one job title may be intentionally listed here more than once.*

Jeffrey P. Bezos, CEO
Joseph Galli, Pres./COO
Warren Jenson, CFO/VP-Finance and Admin.
Mark L. Breier, VP-Mktg.
Shel Kaphan, Chief Tech. Officer
Richard L. Datzell, VP/CIO
Oswaldo F. Duenas, VP-Oper.
Joy Covey, Chief Strategy Officer
David Risher, Sr. VP Product Dev.
Jimmy Wright, Chief Logistics Officer

Phone: 206-622-2335	Fax: 206-622-2405
Toll-Free:	
Address: 1516 Second Avenue, 4th Floor, Seattle, WA, 98101	

GROWTH PLANS/SPECIAL FEATURES:

Amazon.com is a leading on-line retailer of books and is one of the most widely known, used and cited commerce sites on the Internet. The company offers more than 2.5 million titles, including most of the estimated 1.5 million English-language books believed to be in print, more than one million out-of-print titles believed likely to be in circulation and a vast selection of CDs, videotapes and audiotapes. The company has customer accounts from over 100 countries. Amazon.com recently obtained a highly-mechanized distribution facility in Fernley, Nevada that will reduce standard shipping times to key markets in the western U.S. by a full day. In addition, Amazon.de and Amazon.co.uk recently opened their virtual doors on the World Wide Web. For the first time on a local basis, the sites make available to Europeans a vast selection, guaranteed safety of transactions, convenience and electronic gift certificates Amazon launched an on-line auction business to compete with eBay. The company recently launched toy sales on its site. It made major investments in sites selling drugstore items, groceries, pet supplies and outdoor gear. Revenues per customer are falling, from about $47 in 1997 to $29 in 1999. Early 1999, Amazon issued $1.25 billion in convertible bonds to pay for its expansion. Until those bonds are converted to equity, the company's yearly interest expense is $93 million. It also spends more than $300 million a year on sales and marketing. Overall, net losses for the company in 1999 topped $600 million. Meanwhile, the company is gaining new customers at a soaring rate. In the final quarter of 1999, Amazon added 2 million new customers, bringing its total to 15 million.

FINANCIALS: Sales and profits are in thousands of dollars—add 000 to get the full amount.

Notes regarding 1999: *(1999 sales and profits were not available for all companies at press time.)*

1999 Sales: $1,369,000	1999 Profits: $-719,000	Stock Ticker: **AMZN**
1998 Sales: $610,000	1998 Profits: $-124,500	Employees: 2,100
1997 Sales: $147,800	1997 Profits: $-27,600	Fiscal Year Ends: 12/31
1996 Sales: $15,700	1996 Profits: $-5,800	
1995 Sales: $ 500	1995 Profits: $- 300	

SALARIES/BENEFITS:

Pension Plan:	ESOP Stock Plan: Y	Profit Sharing:	Top Exec. Salary: $201,512	Bonus: $
Savings Plan: Y	Stock Purch. Plan:		Second Exec. Salary: $142,083	Bonus: $

COMPETITIVE ADVANTAGE: Got an early lead in on-line bookselling/Highly interactive site/Entry into the on-line auction business/Expansion into additional lines of retailing.

OTHER THOUGHTS:

Apparent Women Officers or Directors: 3
Apparent Minority Officers or Directors:
Hot Spot for Advancement for Women/Minorities: Y

LOCATIONS: ("Y" = Yes)

West:	Southwest:	Midwest:	Southeast:	Northeast:	International:
Y				Y	Y

Note: Financial information, benefits and other data can change quickly and may vary from those stated here.

AMERICA ONLINE INC   www.aol.com

Industry Group Code: 514191
Ranks within this company's industry group: Sales: 1   Profits: 1

BUSINESS ACTIVITIES ("Y" = Yes)

Financial Services:	Information/Publ.:		Technology:		Services:	Retailing:		Telecommunications:	
Stock Brokerage	Portal/Hub/News	Y	Computer Manuf.		Payments/Transfers	Retailer	Y	Internet Serv. Provider	Y
Mortgages/Loans	On-Line Community	Y	Networking Equip.		Consulting	Auctions	Y	Web Site Host	Y
Banking	Search Engine	Y	Software Manuf.	Y	Advertising/Marketing	Mall	Y	Server Farm	
Insurance	Financial Data Publ.	Y	Specialty Equipment		Outsourcing	Tickets/Travel	Y	Specialty Telecom.	
Credit Cards	Broadcasting/Music					Price Comparisons		High Speed Access	Y

TYPES OF BUSINESS:

On-line Portal-Media and Retail
E-Commerce Support
On-line Search, Games and Other Consumer Services
E-mail Services
On-line Chat
Computer and Internet Browser Software
On-line Retailing and Auctions
Travel, Finance and Other Specialties

BRANDS/DIVISIONS/AFFILIATES:

Netscape
Time Warner
Electra
Real Fans Sport Network
NaviSoft, inc.
Advanced Network and Servicers, Inc.
Medior, Inc.
CompuServe

CONTACTS: *Note: Officers with more than one job title may be intentionally listed here more than once.*

Stephen M. Case, CEO
Robert W. Pittman, Pres./COO
J. Michael Kelly, Sr. VP/CFO/Chief Acc. Officer
Jan Brandt, Pres.-Mktg.
Mark Stavish, VP-Human Resources
William Raduchel, Chief Tech. Officer
Miles R. Gilburne, Sr. VP-Corp. Dev.
Kathryn A. Bushkin, Sr. VP/Chief Comm. Officer
J. Michael Kelly, Treas.

Phone: 703-448-8700	Fax: 703-918-1400

Toll-Free:

Address: 22000 AOL Way, Dulles, VA, 20166-9323

GROWTH PLANS/SPECIAL FEATURES:

America Online, Inc. is a leading provider of on-line communication, information, retailing and entertainment services. The company operates two worldwide Internet on-line services. America Online appeals to those seeking entertainment and has 22 million members. CompuServe, geared toward professionals and small-business owners, has approximately two million members. The company was an early leader in offering a graphical user interface and now offers subscribers an advanced multimedia user interface. AOL generates revenues from membership and usage fees. In addition, it is increasingly generating income from other sources. Advertising and e-commerce retailing brought AOL nearly $1 billion in 1999 and will grow at a soaring rate over the mid-term. The AOLnet is the company's data communications network, which AOL continues to expand in order to increase its network capacity, provide its members with higher speed access and reduce data network costs on a per-hour basis. AOL recently acquired Netscape, giving it a huge boost in browser software and in the corporate software market. The company is launching an interactive TV service (AOL TV) via the DIRECTV satellite service. The biggest news is AOL's January 2000 announcement that it intends to merge with media giant Time Warner.

Nearly half of America Online's workforce is under the age of 30. Each employee recieves two free AOL accounts, and nearly each company member is a shareholder. AOL employees recieve about 24 hours of training every year.

FINANCIALS: Sales and profits are in thousands of dollars—add 000 to get the full amount.

Notes regarding 1999: *(1999 sales and profits were not available for all companies at press time.)*

1999 Sales: $4,800,000	1999 Profits: $396,000	Stock Ticker: **AOL**
1998 Sales: $2,600,000	1998 Profits: $92,000	Employees: 12,100
1997 Sales: $1,685,200	1997 Profits: $-499,300	Fiscal Year Ends: 6/30
1996 Sales: $1,093,900	1996 Profits: $29,800	
1995 Sales: $394,300	1995 Profits: $-33,600	

SALARIES/BENEFITS:

Pension Plan:	ESOP Stock Plan:	Profit Sharing:	Top Exec. Salary: $541,665	Bonus: $750,000
Savings Plan: Y	Stock Purch. Plan: Y		Second Exec. Salary: $426,667	Bonus: $750,000

COMPETITIVE ADVANTAGE:

Largest provider of consumer on-line services/Strategic alliances with major media, retail and technology companies/Strong on-line entertainment/Acquisition of Netscape/Merger with Time Warner.

OTHER THOUGHTS:

Apparent Women Officers or Directors: 3
Apparent Minority Officers or Directors:
Hot Spot for Advancement for Women/Minorities: Y

LOCATIONS: ("Y" = Yes)

West:	Southwest:	Midwest:	Southeast:	Northeast:	International:
Y	Y	Y	Y	Y	Y

Note: Financial information, benefits and other data can change quickly and may vary from those stated here.

AMERICANGREETINGS.COM INC
www.americangreetings.com

Industry Group Code: 4541
Ranks within this company's industry group: Sales: 22   Profits: 8

BUSINESS ACTIVITIES ("Y" = Yes)

Financial Services:	Information/Publ.:		Technology:	Services:	Retailing:		Telecommunications:
Stock Brokerage	Portal/Hub/News	Y	Computer Manuf.	Payments/Transfers	Retailer	Y	Internet Serv. Provider
Mortgages/Loans	On-Line Community		Networking Equip.	Consulting	Auctions		Web Site Host
Banking	Search Engine		Software Manuf.	Advertising/Marketing	Mall		Server Farm
Insurance	Financial Data Publ.		Specialty Equipment	Outsourcing	Tickets/Travel		Specialty Telecom.
Credit Cards	Broadcasting/Music				Price Comparisons		High Speed Access

TYPES OF BUSINESS:

Retail-Electronic Greetings

BRANDS/DIVISIONS/AFFILIATES:

American Greetings Corp. Subsidiary
Plus Mark, Inc.
Carlton Cards Retail, Inc.
Interactive Marketing, Inc.
Gibson Greetings
Camden Graphics Group
Hanson White Ltd.
John Sands Ltd.

CONTACTS: Note: Officers with more than one job title may be intentionally listed here more than once.

John M. Klipfell, CEO
John M. Klipfell, Pres.
Maureen M. Spooner, CFO
Anne C. Everhart, Sr. VP-Consumer Mktg.
Carol Shaull, Dir.-Human Resources
Andrew R. Cohen, Sr VP-Chief Tech. Officer
Josef A. Mandelbaum, Sr.VP-Business Dev. & Strategic Plan.
Ralph E. Shaffer, Sr.VP-Chief Creative Officer

Phone: 216-252-7300	Fax: 216-252-6726
Toll-Free: 800-711-4471	
Address: One American Rd., Cleveland, OH, 44144-2398	

GROWTH PLANS/SPECIAL FEATURES:

American Greetings Corporation and its subsidiaries operate predominantly in the design, manufacture and sale of everyday and seasonal greeting cards and other social expression products. Greeting cards, gift wrap, paper party goods, candles, balloons, stationery and giftware are manufactured and sold in the United States by numerous domestic and international subsidiaries, including Plus Mark, Carlton Cards Retail, Inc. and Quality Greeting Card Distributing Company. American Greetings manufactures and sells its products in the United States, Australia, France, Mexico, Canada, the United Kingdom and New Zealand. Interactive Marketing, Inc. markets e-mail greetings, personalized greeting cards and other social expression products through the company's web site. American Greetings formerly sold cards through CreataCard machines, but that business was discontinued in the fourth quarter of 1999. Recently, American Greetings announced plans to acquire Gibson Greetings Inc. American Greetings also completed the acquisition of Contempo Colours Inc., a party goods company based in Michigan. American Greetings has reported 93 consecutive years of increased sales.

FINANCIALS: Sales and profits are in thousands of dollars—add 000 to get the full amount.

Notes regarding 1999: *(1999 sales and profits were not available for all companies at press time.)*

1999 Sales: $12,300	1999 Profits: $1,700	Stock Ticker: **AM**
1998 Sales: $3,900	1998 Profits: $-1,200	Employees: 180
1997 Sales: $1,000	1997 Profits: $-2,400	Fiscal Year Ends: 2/28
1996 Sales: $	1996 Profits: $	
1995 Sales: $	1995 Profits: $	

SALARIES/BENEFITS:

Pension Plan:	ESOP Stock Plan:	Profit Sharing:	Top Exec. Salary: $572,000	Bonus: $464,835
Savings Plan:	Stock Purch. Plan:		Second Exec. Salary: $455,000	Bonus: $643,673

COMPETITIVE ADVANTAGE:

Must compete effectively against giant .com Blue Mountain Arts. However, American Greetings has tremendous resources to draw from.

OTHER THOUGHTS:

Apparent Women Officers or Directors: 3
Apparent Minority Officers or Directors:
Hot Spot for Advancement for Women/Minorities: Y

LOCATIONS: ("Y" = Yes)

West:	Southwest:	Midwest:	Southeast:	Northeast:	International:
		Y	Y	Y	Y

Note: Financial information, benefits and other data can change quickly and may vary from those stated here.

AMERITRADE HOLDING CORP
www.amertradeholding.com

Industry Group Code: **5231**
Ranks within this company's industry group: Sales: 5   Profits: 5

BUSINESS ACTIVITIES ("Y" = Yes)

Financial Services:		Information/Publ.:	Technology:	Services:	Retailing:	Telecommunications:
Stock Brokerage	Y	Portal/Hub/News	Computer Manuf.	Payments/Transfers	Retailer	Internet Serv. Provider
Mortgages/Loans		On-Line Community	Networking Equip.	Consulting	Auctions	Web Site Host
Banking		Search Engine	Software Manuf.	Advertising/Marketing	Mall	Server Farm
Insurance		Financial Data Publ.	Specialty Equipment	Outsourcing	Tickets/Travel	Specialty Telecom.
Credit Cards		Broadcasting/Music			Price Comparisons	High Speed Access

TYPES OF BUSINESS:

On-line Stock Brokerage/Investment Banking
Clearing Services
Investment Advice
Financial Planning

BRANDS/DIVISIONS/AFFILIATES:

Accutrade, Inc.
Ameritrade, Inc.
Advanced Clearing, Inc.
OnMoney
AmeriVest, Inc.
Televest
BankVest

CONTACTS: *Note: Officers with more than one job title may be intentionally listed here more than once.*

J. Joe Ricketts, Co-CEO
Robert T. Slezak, VP/CFO
Peter D. Horst, VP-Mktg.
David D. Jones, VP-Human Resources
Ronald K. Hill, CIO
Robert H. Fowler, Controller
Curt A. Conklin, Dir.-Internet Services
Brenda J. Pool, Investor Relations Mgr.
Robert T. Slezak, Treas.

Phone: 402-331-7856	Fax: 402-597-7789
Toll-Free:	
Address: 4211 South 102nd Street, Omaha, NE, 68127	

GROWTH PLANS/SPECIAL FEATURES:

Ameritrade Holding Corporation and its subsidiaries provide discount securities brokerage and clearing execution services to a wide variety of customers. The company's primary focus is in providing products and services at prices that are significantly less than traditional full-commission securities brokers. Ameritrade Holding offers its brokerage customers a variety of means to trade securities, including buying and selling by touchtone phone, fax, personal digital assistant (PDA) and the Internet. The company also has options for customers who prefer to purchase securities through a live broker. The company has five subsidiaries. Ameritrade, Inc. is a popular Internet brokerage firm. Advanced Clearing, Inc. provides clearing services for the investment advisory and banking industries and investment professionals. AmeriVest, Inc. provides brokerage services for banks, savings & loans and credit unions. Accutrade, Inc. is a value-added provider of Internet brokerage. Ameritrade Holding's fifth subsidiary, in its development phase, is OnMoney, which will seek to offer comprehensive access to consumers' personal finance needs through an Internet-based financial management system. The Ameritrade and Accutrade services make up a majority of the company's business, with 306,000 accounts and 24,000 trades per day.

FINANCIALS: Sales and profits are in thousands of dollars—add 000 to get the full amount.

Notes regarding 1999: *(1999 sales and profits were not available for all companies at press time.)*

1999 Sales: $315,300	1999 Profits: $11,500	Stock Ticker: **AMTD**
1998 Sales: $164,100	1998 Profits: $ 210	Employees: 2,379
1997 Sales: $95,600	1997 Profits: $13,822	Fiscal Year Ends: 09/25
1996 Sales: $65,400	1996 Profits: $11,158	
1995 Sales: $42,900	1995 Profits: $7,031	

SALARIES/BENEFITS:

Pension Plan:	ESOP Stock Plan:	Profit Sharing: Y	Top Exec. Salary: $435,000	Bonus: $
Savings Plan: Y	Stock Purch. Plan:		Second Exec. Salary: $300,000	Bonus: $

COMPETITIVE ADVANTAGE: Aggressive growth/Complete pricing and services.

OTHER THOUGHTS:

Apparent Women Officers or Directors: 3
Apparent Minority Officers or Directors:
Hot Spot for Advancement for Women/Minorities: Y

LOCATIONS: ("Y" = Yes)

West:	Southwest:	Midwest:	Southeast:	Northeast:	International:
		Y			

APPLE COMPUTER INC   www.apple.com

Industry Group Code: 3341A
Ranks within this company's industry group: Sales: 7   Profits: 6

BUSINESS ACTIVITIES ("Y" = Yes)

Financial Services:	Information/Publ.:	Technology:		Services:	Retailing:	Telecommunications:	
Stock Brokerage	Portal/Hub/News	Computer Manuf.	Y	Payments/Transfers	Retailer	Internet Serv. Provider	Y
Mortgages/Loans	On-Line Community	Networking Equip.	Y	Consulting	Auctions	Web Site Host	
Banking	Search Engine	Software Manuf.	Y	Advertising/Marketing	Mall	Server Farm	
Insurance	Financial Data Publ.	Specialty Equipment	Y	Outsourcing	Tickets/Travel	Specialty Telecom.	
Credit Cards	Broadcasting/Music				Price Comparisons	High Speed Access	

TYPES OF BUSINESS:

Personal Computer Manufacturer
Software
On-line Service for Consumers
Personal Information Managers
Printers
Computer Accessories

BRANDS/DIVISIONS/AFFILIATES:

Apple
MacIntosh
FileMaker
PowerBook G3
iMac
Power Macintosh G4

GROWTH PLANS/SPECIAL FEATURES:

Apple Computer, Inc. designs and manufactures microprocessor-based personal computers and related hardware and software for personal computers. Apple's products are primarily used for education and creative, home, business and government computing needs. The company offers a wide range of personal computing products, including personal computers, related peripherals, software and networking and connectivity products. Apple Computer is focusing on low-cost personal computing needs, primarily aimed towards Internet solutions. The company continues to develop new products and technologies to enhance existing hardware, peripherals, software, networking and Internet access. Apple is moving forward at a rapid pace with record sales of the iMac personal computer and new hardware and software products such as a new operating system and a high performance personal computer, the Power Mac G4.

Employees enjoy numerous perks, such as the Apple Health & Fitness Program which promotes positive lifestyle changes.

CONTACTS: *Note: Officers with more than one job title may be intentionally listed here more than once.*

Steve Jobs, Interim CEO
Fred D. Anderson, CFO
Eileen Schloss, VP-Human Resources
Jonathan Rubinstein, Sr. VP-Hardware Engineering
Nancy R. Heinen, Sr. VP/Sec./General Counsel
Timothy D. Cook, Sr. VP-Worldwide Oper.
Steve White, VP-Mktg. Comm.

Phone: 408-996-1010	Fax: 408-974-2113
Toll-Free: 1-800-937-2775	
Address: 1 Infinite Loop, Cupertino, CA, 95014	

FINANCIALS: Sales and profits are in thousands of dollars—add 000 to get the full amount.

Notes regarding 1999: *(1999 sales and profits were not available for all companies at press time.)*

1999 Sales: $6,134,000	1999 Profits: $601,000	Stock Ticker: **AAPL**
1998 Sales: $5,941,000	1998 Profits: $309,000	Employees: 9,736
1997 Sales: $7,081,000	1997 Profits: $-1,045,000	Fiscal Year Ends: 09/30
1996 Sales: $9,833,000	1996 Profits: $-816,000	
1995 Sales: $11,062,000	1995 Profits: $424,000	

SALARIES/BENEFITS:

Pension Plan:	ESOP Stock Plan: Y	Profit Sharing: Y	Top Exec. Salary: $604,283	Bonus: $
Savings Plan: Y	Stock Purch. Plan:		Second Exec. Salary: $402,253	Bonus: $

COMPETITIVE ADVANTAGE: Excellent new MacIntosh technology/Leading edge notebook computers/Outstanding styling/Cult-like following, particularly among professional graphic artists.

OTHER THOUGHTS:

Apparent Women Officers or Directors: 2
Apparent Minority Officers or Directors: 1
Hot Spot for Advancement for Women/Minorities: Y

LOCATIONS: ("Y" = Yes)

West:	Southwest:	Midwest:	Southeast:	Northeast:	International:
Y	Y	Y	Y	Y	Y

Note: Financial information, benefits and other data can change quickly and may vary from those stated here.

APPLIEDTHEORY CORP   www.appliedtheory.com

Industry Group Code: 51339
Ranks within this company's industry group: Sales: 11   Profits: 12

BUSINESS ACTIVITIES ("Y" = Yes)

Financial Services:	Information/Publ.:	Technology:		Services:		Retailing:	Telecommunications:	
Stock Brokerage	Portal/Hub/News	Computer Manuf.		Payments/Transfers		Retailer	Internet Serv. Provider	Y
Mortgages/Loans	On-Line Community	Networking Equip.		Consulting	Y	Auctions	Web Site Host	Y
Banking	Search Engine	Software Manuf.	Y	Advertising/Marketing		Mall	Server Farm	
Insurance	Financial Data Publ.	Specialty Equipment		Outsourcing	Y	Tickets/Travel	Specialty Telecom.	
Credit Cards	Broadcasting/Music					Price Comparisons	High Speed Access	Y

TYPES OF BUSINESS:

Internet Service Provider
Web Hosting
Application Development
Virtual Private Networks
Security

BRANDS/DIVISIONS/AFFILIATES:

NYSERNet
Gemini 2000

CONTACTS: Note: Officers with more than one job title may be intentionally listed here more than once.

Richard Mandelbaum, CEO
Lawrence B. Helft, Pres/COO
David A. Buckel, VP/CFO
Karen Lantier, VP-Mktg.
Debbie Newman, Head-Human Resources
Mark A. Oros, VP/Chief Tech. Officer
Dennis J. Martin, VP/Chief Software Engineer
John A. Wingert, VP-Oper.
Karen Lantier, VP-Strategic Planning

Phone: 516-466-8422	Fax: 516-466-8650
Toll-Free:	
Address: 40 Cutter Mill Rd., Ste. 405, Great Neck, NY, 11021	

GROWTH PLANS/SPECIAL FEATURES:

AppliedTheory was established in 1985 as NYSERNet to provide Internet services to New York universities. AppliedTheory offers high performance Internet solutions to midsize companies, midsize departments of larger corporations and public institutions. The company provides five main Internet-based products and services: Internet access, web hosting, application development, VPN's (virtual private networks) and security. The Internet is AppliedTheory's only business, so its expertise is focused only on providing state-of-the-art Internet solutions. The company's Internet availability rate is consistently 99.97%. This assures customers continuous, reliable, consistent, clear Internet access. AppliedTheory's end-to-end commitment provides customized applications tailored to meet customer needs from the development phase through implementation and beyond. The firm's extensive approach to customer support helps its customers with any problems, including those not originated in its server. Based in New York, AppliedTheory is expanding with its Gemini 2000 system to provide service to the entire country. The company will also be adding a DSL (digital subscriber line) to the current line of Internet access options. AppliedTheory is looking to the future by pioneering a CIO (chief information officer) Internet training program in Shanghai, China to train and certify current and future CIOs of Chinese corporations to serve as e-visionaries in China's Internet Revolution.

FINANCIALS: Sales and profits are in thousands of dollars—add 000 to get the full amount.

Notes regarding 1999: *(1999 sales and profits were not available for all companies at press time.)*

1999 Sales: $	1999 Profits: $	Stock Ticker: **ATHY**
1998 Sales: $22,600	1998 Profits: $-6,900	Employees: 151
1997 Sales: $15,200	1997 Profits: $-5,800	Fiscal Year Ends: 12/31
1996 Sales: $9,300	1996 Profits: $-5,700	
1995 Sales: $	1995 Profits: $	

SALARIES/BENEFITS:

Pension Plan:	ESOP Stock Plan:	Profit Sharing:	Top Exec. Salary: $327,823	Bonus: $
Savings Plan:	Stock Purch. Plan:		Second Exec. Salary: $204,177	Bonus: $

COMPETITIVE ADVANTAGE: High reliability rate/Full range of services.

OTHER THOUGHTS:

Apparent Women Officers or Directors: 2
Apparent Minority Officers or Directors:
Hot Spot for Advancement for Women/Minorities:

LOCATIONS: ("Y" = Yes)

West:	Southwest:	Midwest:	Southeast:	Northeast:	International:
				Y	

Note: Financial information, benefits and other data can change quickly and may vary from those stated here.

APPNET INC   www.appnet.com

Industry Group Code: 5112
Ranks within this company's industry group: Sales: 40   Profits: 66

BUSINESS ACTIVITIES ("Y" = Yes)

Financial Services:	Information/Publ.:	Technology:	Services:		Retailing:		Telecommunications:
Stock Brokerage	Portal/Hub/News	Computer Manuf.	Payments/Transfers		Retailer		Internet Serv. Provider
Mortgages/Loans	On-Line Community	Networking Equip.	Consulting	Y	Auctions		Web Site Host
Banking	Search Engine	Software Manuf.	Advertising/Marketing	Y	Mall		Server Farm
Insurance	Financial Data Publ.	Specialty Equipment	Outsourcing	Y	Tickets/Travel		Specialty Telecom.
Credit Cards	Broadcasting/Music				Price Comparisons		High Speed Access

TYPES OF BUSINESS:

Software-E-Commerce
Space Exploration Technology

BRANDS/DIVISIONS/AFFILIATES:

CONTACTS: Note: Officers with more than one job title may be intentionally listed here more than once.

Ken S. Bajaj, CEO
Ken S. Bajaj, Pres.
Jack Pearlstein, Sr.VP-CFO
Tom Rauh, Sr. VP-Sales
Bob Boehn, VP-Human Resources
John Cross, Exec. VP-Strategic & Tech. Consulting
Tom Rauh, Sr.VP-Business Dev.

Phone: 301-493-8900	Fax: 301-581-2488
Toll-Free:	
Address: 6707 Democracy Blvd., Bethesda, MD, 20817	

GROWTH PLANS/SPECIAL FEATURES:

AppNet is a premier provider of end-to-end e-business solutions, from interactive marketing to back-office integration. For companies transforming themselves for the new Internet economy, the firm offers a unique mix of Internet strategy, marketing and technology services. According to Ad Age, AppNet is the fourth largest interactive marketing agency. It is also one of the 50 largest pure Internet companies, according to Internet World. AppNet helps companies develop an Internet strategy that ties together marketing and technology. AppNet was recently awarded a multi-year contract to develop, build and maintain what it hopes will become the world's largest Internet marketplace for executing business-to-business (B2B) transactions. The multi-year contract was awarded by UCCnet, a subsidiary of the Uniform Code Council, Inc. (UCC), which administers the Universal Product Code. UCCnet and AppNet will develop the electronic marketplace to enable all item information to be synchronized and updated in real-time between manufacturers and retailers worldwide over the Internet. Since UCCnet's primary goal is to create an open environment for business of all sizes, industries and markets, UCCnet will create an open, standards-based marketplace for connecting global businesses on-line based on XML (extensible Markup Language). AppNet maintains strategic alliances with some of the leading providers of Internet-based hardware and software, including Allaire, Compaq, EMC, Hewlett Packard, IBM, Microsoft, NetScape, Oracle, SAP in Germany and Sun.

FINANCIALS: Sales and profits are in thousands of dollars—add 000 to get the full amount.

Notes regarding 1999: *(1999 sales and profits were not available for all companies at press time.)*

1999 Sales: $	1999 Profits: $	Stock Ticker: **APNT**
1998 Sales: $17,700	1998 Profits: $-14,400	Employees: 750
1997 Sales: $	1997 Profits: $	Fiscal Year Ends: 12/31
1996 Sales: $	1996 Profits: $	
1995 Sales: $	1995 Profits: $	

SALARIES/BENEFITS:

Pension Plan:	ESOP Stock Plan: Y	Profit Sharing:	Top Exec. Salary: $	Bonus: $
Savings Plan:	Stock Purch. Plan:		Second Exec. Salary: $	Bonus: $

COMPETITIVE ADVANTAGE: Tremendous list of strategic alliances.

OTHER THOUGHTS:

Apparent Women Officers or Directors:
Apparent Minority Officers or Directors:
Hot Spot for Advancement for Women/Minorities:

LOCATIONS: ("Y" = Yes)

West:	Southwest:	Midwest:	Southeast:	Northeast:	International:
Y		Y		Y	Y

ARIBA INC
www.ariba.com

Industry Group Code: 5112
Ranks within this company's industry group: Sales: 51   Profits: 56

BUSINESS ACTIVITIES ("Y" = Yes)

Financial Services:	Information/Publ.:	Technology:		Services:	Retailing:	Telecommunications:
Stock Brokerage	Portal/Hub/News	Computer Manuf.		Payments/Transfers	Retailer	Internet Serv. Provider
Mortgages/Loans	On-Line Community	Networking Equip.		Consulting	Auctions	Web Site Host
Banking	Search Engine	Software Manuf.	Y	Advertising/Marketing	Mall	Server Farm
Insurance	Financial Data Publ.	Specialty Equipment		Outsourcing	Tickets/Travel	Specialty Telecom.
Credit Cards	Broadcasting/Music				Price Comparisons	High Speed Access

TYPES OF BUSINESS:

Software-Transaction Processing

BRANDS/DIVISIONS/AFFILIATES:

Operating Resource Management System
Ariba Network

CONTACTS: *Note: Officers with more than one job title may be intentionally listed here more than once.*

Keith J. Krach, CEO/Pres.
Larry Mueller, COO
Edward P. Kinsey, CFO/VP-Finance
David L. Rome, VP-Mktg.
Shelley Brown, VP-Human Resources
K. Charly Kleissner, VP-Engineering
Edward P. Kinsey, Sec.
Paul L. Melchiorre, VP-North American Oper.
Robert D. Lent, VP-Business Dev.

Phone: 408-543-3800	Fax: 408-543-3900
Toll-Free:	
Address: 1314 Chesapeake Terrace, Sunnyvale, CA, 94089	

GROWTH PLANS/SPECIAL FEATURES:

Ariba is one of the world's leading providers of intranet and Internet-based business-to-business (B2B) electronic commerce solutions for operating resources. The company's products help requestors, suppliers, approvers and buyers communicate more effectively through the supply chain. Ariba's Operating Resource Management System allows organizations to automate procurement and lower the costs of managing and acquiring operating resources. Ariba Network also lowers the cost of transactions between buyers and suppliers by automating them on the Internet. Ariba has implemented its software and services in a variety of industries, including the consumer products, energy, financial services, high technology, pharmaceutical and telecommunications industries. Some of Ariba's clients include notable businesses such as Chevron, DOW, Earthgrains, FedEx, Visa International, Honda, Lucent Technologies, Motorola, Nestle, Charles Schwab, General Motors and Merck. Recently, MCI WorldCom chose Ariba to install its Operating Resource Management procurement system. The company also announced that Compaq will sell its products through the Ariba Network e-commerce platform. Ariba is active in the community as well; recently, employees donated $50,000 to the United Way of Santa Clara.

FINANCIALS: Sales and profits are in thousands of dollars—add 000 to get the full amount.

Notes regarding 1999: *(1999 sales and profits were not available for all companies at press time.)*

1999 Sales: $45,400	1999 Profits: $-29,300	Stock Ticker: **ARBA**
1998 Sales: $8,400	1998 Profits: $-10,900	Employees: 386
1997 Sales: $ 800	1997 Profits: $-4,700	Fiscal Year Ends: 9/30
1996 Sales: $	1996 Profits: $	
1995 Sales: $	1995 Profits: $	

SALARIES/BENEFITS:

Pension Plan:	ESOP Stock Plan: Y	Profit Sharing:	Top Exec. Salary: $106,667	Bonus: $76,605
Savings Plan:	Stock Purch. Plan:		Second Exec. Salary: $	Bonus: $

COMPETITIVE ADVANTAGE: One of the hottest names in e-commerce/Excellent buzz/Highly successful IPO.

OTHER THOUGHTS:

Apparent Women Officers or Directors: 1
Apparent Minority Officers or Directors: 1
Hot Spot for Advancement for Women/Minorities:

LOCATIONS: ("Y" = Yes)

West:	Southwest:	Midwest:	Southeast:	Northeast:	International:
Y					Y

ART TECHNOLOGY GROUP INC   www.atg.com

Industry Group Code: 5112
Ranks within this company's industry group: Sales: 44   Profits: 25

BUSINESS ACTIVITIES ("Y" = Yes)

Financial Services:	Information/Publ.:	Technology:		Services:		Retailing:		Telecommunications:
Stock Brokerage	Portal/Hub/News	Computer Manuf.		Payments/Transfers	Y	Retailer	Y	Internet Serv. Provider
Mortgages/Loans	On-Line Community	Networking Equip.		Consulting	Y	Auctions	Y	Web Site Host
Banking	Search Engine	Software Manuf.	Y	Advertising/Marketing	Y	Mall	Y	Server Farm
Insurance	Financial Data Publ.	Specialty Equipment		Outsourcing	Y	Tickets/Travel		Specialty Telecom.
Credit Cards	Broadcasting/Music					Price Comparisons		High Speed Access

TYPES OF BUSINESS:
Software-E-Commerce

BRANDS/DIVISIONS/AFFILIATES:
Dynamo

CONTACTS: Note: Officers with more than one job title may be intentionally listed here more than once.
Jeet Singh, CEO
Jeet Singh, Pres.
Ann C. Brady, VP/CFO
Lauren J. Kelley, VP-Sales
Barry Hartunian, Dir.-Human Resources
Joseph T. Chung, Chief Tech. Officer
William Wittenberg, Sr. VP-Product Dev.
Joseph T. Chung, Treas.
Brenda Sullivan, VP-Organizational Dev.

Phone: 617-386-1000	Fax: 617-386-1111
Toll-Free:	
Address: 25 1st Street, Cambridge, MA, 02141	

GROWTH PLANS/SPECIAL FEATURES:

Art Technology Group, ATG, helps companies manage and build personalized web environments and manage on-line storefronts, billing and advertising. Its main product, Dynamo, is designed to integrate with popular third-party products (like transaction management systems). Some of ATG's clients include BMG Direct, Eastman Kodak, John Hancock Funds, Sony and Sun Microsystems. ATG recently announced that it is launching an Internet Customer Relationship Management initiative across Europe that will enable web content to be displayed in multiple languages. This is in an effort to harness some of the upcoming talent and resources in the e-commerce industry that are appearing in Europe. ATG was recognized by Deloitte & Touche and Hale and Dorr LLP, in association with Mass High Tech, as one of the New England Fast 50, a list of the fastest growing technology companies in the New England area. ATG's Dynamo also received the Crossroads 2000 A-List Award from Open Systems Advisors, Inc. for the third year, an award that recognizes the best newly-proven products and services that improve the customer process for the quickly growing e-commerce industry.

FINANCIALS: Sales and profits are in thousands of dollars—add 000 to get the full amount.
Notes regarding 1999: *(1999 sales and profits were not available for all companies at press time.)*

1999 Sales: $32,100	1999 Profits: $-9,500	Stock Ticker: **ARTG**
1998 Sales: $12,100	1998 Profits: $-2,900	Employees: 165
1997 Sales: $6,500	1997 Profits: $-4,200	Fiscal Year Ends: 12/31
1996 Sales: $3,900	1996 Profits: $-1,400	
1995 Sales: $ 800	1995 Profits: $- 500	

SALARIES/BENEFITS:

Pension Plan:	ESOP Stock Plan: Y	Profit Sharing:	Top Exec. Salary: $	Bonus: $
Savings Plan:	Stock Purch. Plan:		Second Exec. Salary: $	Bonus: $

COMPETITIVE ADVANTAGE: Move into the European market.

OTHER THOUGHTS:
Apparent Women Officers or Directors: 1
Apparent Minority Officers or Directors: 1
Hot Spot for Advancement for Women/Minorities:

LOCATIONS: ("Y" = Yes)

West:	Southwest:	Midwest:	Southeast:	Northeast:	International:
				Y	Y

Note: Financial information, benefits and other data can change quickly and may vary from those stated here.

ASHFORD.COM INC   www.ashford.com

Industry Group Code: 4541
Ranks within this company's industry group: Sales: Profits:

BUSINESS ACTIVITIES ("Y" = Yes)

Financial Services:	Information/Publ.:		Technology:	Services:	Retailing:		Telecommunications:
Stock Brokerage	Portal/Hub/News	Y	Computer Manuf.	Payments/Transfers	Retailer	Y	Internet Serv. Provider
Mortgages/Loans	On-Line Community	Y	Networking Equip.	Consulting	Auctions		Web Site Host
Banking	Search Engine		Software Manuf.	Advertising/Marketing	Mall		Server Farm
Insurance	Financial Data Publ.		Specialty Equipment	Outsourcing	Tickets/Travel		Specialty Telecom.
Credit Cards	Broadcasting/Music				Price Comparisons		High Speed Access

TYPES OF BUSINESS:
Retail-Luxury Products

BRANDS/DIVISIONS/AFFILIATES:
TimeZone.com

CONTACTS: *Note: Officers with more than one job title may be intentionally listed here more than once.*
Kenneth E. Kurtzman, CEO
James H. Whitcomb Jr., Pres./COO
David F. Gow, VP/CFO
William M. Stewart, VP-Mktg.
Elizabeth A. Greenfield, VP-Merch.
James M. Gerber, VP-Business Dev.

Phone: 713-369-1300	Fax: 713-629-5631
Toll-Free:	
Address: 3355 W. Alabama, Ste. 175, Houston, TX, 77098	

GROWTH PLANS/SPECIAL FEATURES:

Ashford.com is an on-line retailer selling premium items such as vintage watches, writing instruments, diamonds, fragrances, sunglasses, jewelry and leather accessories. It boasts over 270 leading designer brands, including Bulova, Borghese, Montblanc, Rolex and Dooney and Burke, and also showcases over 10,000 styles of watches. The company's web site, in addition to displaying various luxury goods for sale, features a boutique section that was created to showcase one particular designer's line of fine accessories at one convenient site. Ashford carries products from Clever Carriage Company, Judith Jack, Adrienne Vittadini, Bettina Duncan, Franchi, Mandala, Nir Saban and a few others. Ashford recently announced the acquisition of TimeZone.com, a community site devoted to watches and the watch industry. With the completion of this acquisition, patrons of Ashford will be able to access community forums, discussion groups and in-depth technical articles and watch reviews on the site. Ashford also offers its customers an industry-leading customer protection policy on new watches. The policy offers a two-year warranty beyond the manufacturer's warranty, a 60-day money-back guarantee and a certificate verifying the authenticity of every watch.

FINANCIALS: Sales and profits are in thousands of dollars—add 000 to get the full amount.
Notes regarding 1999: *(1999 sales and profits were not available for all companies at press time.)*

1999 Sales: $5,900	1999 Profits: $-1,300	Stock Ticker: **ASFD**
1998 Sales: $	1998 Profits: $	Employees: 67
1997 Sales: $	1997 Profits: $	Fiscal Year Ends: 3/31
1996 Sales: $	1996 Profits: $	
1995 Sales: $	1995 Profits: $	

SALARIES/BENEFITS:

Pension Plan:	ESOP Stock Plan:	Profit Sharing:	Top Exec. Salary: $	Bonus: $
Savings Plan:	Stock Purch. Plan:		Second Exec. Salary: $	Bonus: $

COMPETITIVE ADVANTAGE: Focus on fine watches/Marketing arrangement with Hoovers.com.

OTHER THOUGHTS:
Apparent Women Officers or Directors: 1
Apparent Minority Officers or Directors: 1
Hot Spot for Advancement for Women/Minorities:

LOCATIONS: ("Y" = Yes)

West:	Southwest:	Midwest:	Southeast:	Northeast:	International:
	Y				

ASK JEEVES INC   www.ask.com

Industry Group Code: 514191
Ranks within this company's industry group: Sales: 38   Profits: 21

BUSINESS ACTIVITIES ("Y" = Yes)

Financial Services:	Information/Publ.:		Technology:		Services:		Retailing:	Telecommunications:
Stock Brokerage	Portal/Hub/News	Y	Computer Manuf.		Payments/Transfers		Retailer	Internet Serv. Provider
Mortgages/Loans	On-Line Community		Networking Equip.		Consulting		Auctions	Web Site Host
Banking	Search Engine	Y	Software Manuf.	Y	Advertising/Marketing		Mall	Server Farm
Insurance	Financial Data Publ.		Specialty Equipment		Outsourcing	Y	Tickets/Travel	Specialty Telecom.
Credit Cards	Broadcasting/Music						Price Comparisons	High Speed Access

TYPES OF BUSINESS:

Search Portal
Children-Specific Searches
Plain Language Searches
Back-End Search Engines for Corporate Clients

BRANDS/DIVISIONS/AFFILIATES:

Powered by Jeeves

CONTACTS: *Note: Officers with more than one job title may be intentionally listed here more than once.*

Robert W. Wrubel, CEO
Robert W. Wrubel, Pres.
Bruce Nakao, CFO
Cathy Hasenpflug, Dir.-Human Resources
David C. Warren, Chief Tech. Officer
Christine M. Davis, Controller
Amy Slater, Sec.
Amy Slater, General Counsel
Laurence G. Fishkin, Sr.VP-Business Dev.

Phone: 510-649-8685	Fax: 510-649-8633
Toll-Free:	
Address: 918 Parker St.,Ste. 12, Berkeley, CA, 94710	

GROWTH PLANS/SPECIAL FEATURES:

Ask Jeeves designs search engines that operate by a question and answer format in plain English rather than using keywords and Boolean language. Ask Jeeves also features a separate kids' site that conducts searches appropriate for the age of the user. The company designs search engines for corporate web sites. Over four million Internet users each month use Ask Jeeves. In recent news, the company announced a strategic alliance with Lynx Technology Group, LLC, which is aimed to broaden the reach of the Ask Jeeves brand name by additional media attention through print, digital media, broadcast, animation and live appearance vehicles. Artists Television Group, Artist Management Group and AMG Animation will create programs to spread the company's media presence and advertise its licensing, merchandising and on-line programming. Ask Jeeves continues to expand its client base, recently adding Hewlett-Packard Company, American Express, MyPoints.com, adam.com and F5 Networks. These clients will join the ranks of other highly notable Ask Jeeves clients, including Microsoft Corporation, Dell, E-Trade, Office Depot and Williams Sonoma. Martha Stewart Living Omnimedia, Inc. recently implemented Ask Jeeves' Corporate Question Answering Service for its wedding channel on marthastewart.com. This service enables corporate networks and Internet sites to incorporate Ask Jeeves' unique plain language search engine.

FINANCIALS: Sales and profits are in thousands of dollars—add 000 to get the full amount.
Notes regarding 1999: *(1999 sales and profits were not available for all companies at press time.)*

1999 Sales: $22,000	1999 Profits: $-52,900	Stock Ticker: **ASKJ**
1998 Sales: $ 600	1998 Profits: $-4,300	Employees: 200
1997 Sales: $	1997 Profits: $- 400	Fiscal Year Ends: 12/31
1996 Sales: $	1996 Profits: $- 100	
1995 Sales: $	1995 Profits: $	

SALARIES/BENEFITS:

Pension Plan:	ESOP Stock Plan: Y	Profit Sharing:	Top Exec. Salary: $	Bonus: $
Savings Plan:	Stock Purch. Plan:		Second Exec. Salary: $	Bonus: $

COMPETITIVE ADVANTAGE: Plain language search engine is extremely popular as an add-on to corporate networks.

OTHER THOUGHTS:

Apparent Women Officers or Directors: 3
Apparent Minority Officers or Directors: 1
Hot Spot for Advancement for Women/Minorities: Y

LOCATIONS: ("Y" = Yes)

West:	Southwest:	Midwest:	Southeast:	Northeast:	International:
Y					

AT&T CORP   www.att.com

Industry Group Code: 5133B
Ranks within this company's industry group: Sales: 1   Profits: 1

BUSINESS ACTIVITIES ("Y" = Yes)

Financial Services:	Information/Publ.:	Technology:		Services:		Retailing:	Telecommunications:	
Stock Brokerage	Portal/Hub/News	Computer Manuf.		Payments/Transfers		Retailer	Internet Serv. Provider	Y
Mortgages/Loans	On-Line Community	Networking Equip.		Consulting		Auctions	Web Site Host	Y
Banking	Search Engine	Software Manuf.	Y	Advertising/Marketing		Mall	Server Farm	
Insurance	Financial Data Publ.	Specialty Equipment	Y	Outsourcing	Y	Tickets/Travel	Specialty Telecom.	Y
Credit Cards	Broadcasting/Music					Price Comparisons	High Speed Access	Y

TYPES OF BUSINESS:

Long Distance Telephone Service
Wireless Services
Directory Publishing
Internet Access Service
Outsourcing, Consulting and Networking Integration
Cable Television Service
Voice and Data Communications Services
Local and Long Distance Telephone Service

BRANDS/DIVISIONS/AFFILIATES:

Teleport Communications Group
Media One
TCI (Telecommunications, Inc.)
AT&T Broadband & Internet Services
Network System Group
AT&T Bell Laboratories
ImagiNation Network
AT&T Wireless

CONTACTS: Note: Officers with more than one job title may be intentionally listed here more than once.

C. Michael Armstrong, CEO
John Zeglis, Pres.
Charles Noski, CFO/Sr. Exec. VP
Marilyn Laurie, Exec. VP-Brand Strategy and Mktg. Comm.
Mirian M. Graddick, Exec.VP-Human Resources
David Nagel, Chief Tech. Officer
Nicholas S. Cyprus, VP/Controller
Marilyn J. Wasser, VP-Sec.
James W. Cicconi, Exec. VP-General Counsel
John C. Petrillo, Exec.VP-Corp. Strategy and Business Dev.
Curt Hockemeir, COO AT&T Broadband & Internet Services

Phone: 212-387-5400	Fax: 212-841-4715
Toll-Free: 800-348-8288	
Address: 32 Avenue of the Americas, New York, NY, 10013-2412	

GROWTH PLANS/SPECIAL FEATURES:

AT&T Corporation provides voice, data and video telecommunications services to large and small businesses, consumers and government entities. AT&T and its subsidiaries furnish regional, domestic, international and local communication services. The firm has become extremely competitive and aggressive in its nationwide wireless telephone service. AT&T also provides billing, directory and calling card services to support its communications business. The company, through AT&T Solutions, Inc., recently entered the business segment of outsourcing, consulting, networking integration and multimedia call center services. AT&T Solutions provides clients with customized information technology solutions to operate and manage voice, data and video services, including local and wide area networks, PBXs, voice-processing systems and voice and data terminals. The company has also begun to provide a variety of on-line and Internet access services, which includes AT&T Worldwide Services. AT&T recently announced its plan to invest $1.25 million in four programs that will allow urban, at-risk youths to chart their careers and obtain training in the technology industry. AT&T plans to form a new public company, to be named AT&T Latin America, that will merge FirstCom (with operations in Chile, Columbia and Peru) and Netstream, a local exchange company that AT&T is acquiring in Brazil. Also, AT&T scheduled a public offering of stock in its wireless unit for April 2000.

Of the company's officials and managers, 21.4% are minorities, and 27.5% of the employees in the entire work force are minorities. The company offers a Work and Family Program designed to help employees balance personal commitments and job responsibilities.

FINANCIALS: Sales and profits are in thousands of dollars—add 000 to get the full amount.

Notes regarding 1999: (1999 sales and profits were not available for all companies at press time.)

1999 Sales: $62,391,000	1999 Profits: $5,450,000	Stock Ticker: T
1998 Sales: $53,223,000	1998 Profits: $5,450,000	Employees: 107,800
1997 Sales: $51,319,000	1997 Profits: $4,638,000	Fiscal Year Ends: 12/31
1996 Sales: $52,184,000	1996 Profits: $5,908,000	
1995 Sales: $79,609,000	1995 Profits: $139,000	

SALARIES/BENEFITS:

Pension Plan: Y	ESOP Stock Plan:	Profit Sharing:	Top Exec. Salary: $1,400,000	Bonus: $1,900,000
Savings Plan: Y	Stock Purch. Plan: Y		Second Exec. Salary: $700,000	Bonus: $950,100

COMPETITIVE ADVANTAGE: Universal name recognition/Large research and development budget/World's largest telephone system.

OTHER THOUGHTS:

Apparent Women Officers or Directors: 2
Apparent Minority Officers or Directors: 1
Hot Spot for Advancement for Women/Minorities: Y

LOCATIONS: ("Y" = Yes)

West:	Southwest:	Midwest:	Southeast:	Northeast:	International:
Y	Y	Y	Y	Y	Y

Note: Financial information, benefits and other data can change quickly and may vary from those stated here.

AUDIBLE INC   www.audible.com

Industry Group Code: 4541
Ranks within this company's industry group: Sales: 29   Profits: 19

BUSINESS ACTIVITIES ("Y" = Yes)

Financial Services:	Information/Publ.:	Technology:	Services:	Retailing:		Telecommunications:
Stock Brokerage	Portal/Hub/News	Computer Manuf.	Payments/Transfers	Retailer	Y	Internet Serv. Provider
Mortgages/Loans	On-Line Community	Networking Equip.	Consulting	Auctions		Web Site Host
Banking	Search Engine	Software Manuf.	Advertising/Marketing	Mall		Server Farm
Insurance	Financial Data Publ.	Specialty Equipment	Outsourcing	Tickets/Travel		Specialty Telecom.
Credit Cards	Broadcasting/Music Y			Price Comparisons		High Speed Access

TYPES OF BUSINESS:
Retail-On-line Audio Store

BRANDS/DIVISIONS/AFFILIATES:
AudiblePlayer
AudibleManagement
Audible.com
David Isay

CONTACTS: *Note: Officers with more than one job title may be intentionally listed here more than once.*
Donald R. Katz, Acting CEO
Andrew Kaplan, VP-Finance/CFO
Foy C. Sperring Jr., VP-Mktg.
Guy Story Jr., VP-Tech.
Brian M. Fielding, VP-Business and Legal Affairs
J. Travis Millman, VP-Business Dev.
Daniel C. Scheffey, VP-Comm.
David Simpson, Dir.-Business Dev.

Phone: 973-890-4070	Fax: 973-890-2442
Toll-Free:	
Address: 65 Willowbrook Blvd., Wayne, NJ, 07470	

GROWTH PLANS/SPECIAL FEATURES:

Audible, Inc. is a leading provider of Internet-delivered premium spoken audio content for playback on personal computers and mobile devices. The company offers a variety of software systems and audio programming software designed to download, store and play between 2 and 28 hours of content from its on-line store, Audible.com. Audible sells a wide array of audio content, including educational materials, humor, periodicals, fiction, non-fiction and time-shifted radio programming. The company also has partnerships with more than 100 leading audiobook, magazine and newspaper publishers, broadcasters, business information providers and educational and cultural institutions. The company recently announced a multi-year partnership with David Isay, an audio documentarian who has received the Peabody Award. The agreement will bring original programming to Audible and will also make Isay's public radio documentaries available for sale over the Internet. In other news, Audible, in conjunction with Motorola, demonstrated the ability for the Motorola i1000plus digital handset to download and play audio content from Audible's web site at the Personal Communications Showcase.

FINANCIALS: Sales and profits are in thousands of dollars—add 000 to get the full amount.
Notes regarding 1999: *(1999 sales and profits were not available for all companies at press time.)*

1999 Sales: $1,742	1999 Profits: $-13,476	Stock Ticker: **ADBL**
1998 Sales: $ 400	1998 Profits: $-8,100	Employees: 39
1997 Sales: $ 100	1997 Profits: $-8,000	Fiscal Year Ends: 12/31
1996 Sales: $	1996 Profits: $-3,500	
1995 Sales: $	1995 Profits: $	

SALARIES/BENEFITS:

Pension Plan:	ESOP Stock Plan:	Profit Sharing:	Top Exec. Salary: $	Bonus: $
Savings Plan:	Stock Purch. Plan:		Second Exec. Salary: $	Bonus: $

COMPETITIVE ADVANTAGE: Special digital audio technology and a wide range of content.

OTHER THOUGHTS:

| **Apparent Women Officers or Directors:** |
| **Apparent Minority Officers or Directors:** |
| **Hot Spot for Advancement for Women/Minorities:** |

LOCATIONS: ("Y" = Yes)

West:	Southwest:	Midwest:	Southeast:	Northeast:	International:
				Y	

AUDIOHIGHWAY.COM   www.audiohighway.com

Industry Group Code: 51311B
Ranks within this company's industry group: Sales: 7   Profits: 3

BUSINESS ACTIVITIES ("Y" = Yes)

Financial Services:	Information/Publ.:		Technology:	Services:	Retailing:		Telecommunications:
Stock Brokerage	Portal/Hub/News	Y	Computer Manuf.	Payments/Transfers	Retailer	Y	Internet Serv. Provider
Mortgages/Loans	On-Line Community		Networking Equip.	Consulting	Auctions		Web Site Host
Banking	Search Engine		Software Manuf.	Advertising/Marketing	Mall		Server Farm
Insurance	Financial Data Publ.		Specialty Equipment	Outsourcing	Tickets/Travel		Specialty Telecom.
Credit Cards	Broadcasting/Music	Y			Price Comparisons		High Speed Access

TYPES OF BUSINESS:

Portal-Audio Files
On-line Music Sales
On-line Music Delivery

BRANDS/DIVISIONS/AFFILIATES:

Mass Music

CONTACTS: *Note: Officers with more than one job title may be intentionally listed here more than once.*

Nathan M. Schulhof, Pres./CEO
Grant Jasmin, Exec. VP-Finance/COO
Gregory Sutyak, CFO
Hedi Payne, Human Resources
Grant Jasmin, Sec.
Marc Baum, VP-Product Dev.

Phone: 408-861-4000	Fax: 408-8614001

Toll-Free: 800-775-4783

Address: 20300 Stevens Creek Blvd. Suite 100A, Cupertino, CA, 95014

GROWTH PLANS/SPECIAL FEATURES:

Audiohighway.com is an entertainment and information Internet company that has one of the largest and most diverse libraries of free audio content for consumers on the Internet. Audiohighway's web site offers audiobooks, music, news, entertainment, education and information selections in many audio formats, including MP3, RealPlayer and Windows Media Player. The company's web site also features an on-line music store called Mass Music, which sells technology and digital products and music and video selections. Audiohighway also offers free web-based e-mail accounts, which allow three to five times the normal amount of mailbox storage than the industry standard. This enables users to store, send and receive up to 10 megabytes of text, graphic, audio and video files. Recently, Audiohighway announced that consumers can create their own personal Internet radio shows on its web site, based off the diverse programming available on the site. Unique consumer programming can consist of a variety of information and music, including breaking news, sports updates, feature newscasts, celebrity interviews, a wide variety of musical genres, financial news, television show updates and more. The company entered into an agreement with Microsoft to provide audio content to Microsoft's Web Events web site.

FINANCIALS: Sales and profits are in thousands of dollars—add 000 to get the full amount.

Notes regarding 1999: Through 9 months *(1999 sales and profits were not available for all companies at press time.)*

1999 Sales: $1,000	1999 Profits: $-6,800	Stock Ticker: **AHWY**
1998 Sales: $ 100	1998 Profits: $-5,800	Employees: 24
1997 Sales: $ 100	1997 Profits: $-3,800	Fiscal Year Ends: 12/31/
1996 Sales: $	1996 Profits: $-1,600	
1995 Sales: $	1995 Profits: $	

SALARIES/BENEFITS:

Pension Plan:	ESOP Stock Plan:	Profit Sharing: Y	Top Exec. Salary: $170,000	Bonus: $75,000
Savings Plan:	Stock Purch. Plan:		Second Exec. Salary: $140,000	Bonus: $37,500

COMPETITIVE ADVANTAGE: Unique e-mail system enables users to store and send large music files.

OTHER THOUGHTS:

Apparent Women Officers or Directors:	
Apparent Minority Officers or Directors:	
Hot Spot for Advancement for Women/Minorities:	

LOCATIONS: ("Y" = Yes)

West:	Southwest:	Midwest:	Southeast:	Northeast:	International:
Y					

AUTOBYTEL.COM INC   www.autobytel.com

Industry Group Code: 54189A
Ranks within this company's industry group: Sales: 6   Profits: 18

BUSINESS ACTIVITIES ("Y" = Yes)

Financial Services:	Information/Publ.:		Technology:	Services:		Retailing:		Telecommunications:
Stock Brokerage	Portal/Hub/News	Y	Computer Manuf.	Payments/Transfers		Retailer		Internet Serv. Provider
Mortgages/Loans	On-Line Community		Networking Equip.	Consulting		Auctions		Web Site Host
Banking	Search Engine		Software Manuf.	Advertising/Marketing	Y	Mall		Server Farm
Insurance	Financial Data Publ.		Specialty Equipment	Outsourcing		Tickets/Travel		Specialty Telecom.
Credit Cards	Broadcasting/Music					Price Comparisons		High Speed Access

TYPES OF BUSINESS:

On-line Automobile Buyers' Site
Internet-Based Advertising/Marketing Services

BRANDS/DIVISIONS/AFFILIATES:

A.I.N. Corporation
CarSmart.com

CONTACTS: Note: Officers with more than one job title may be intentionally listed here more than once.

Mark W. Lorimer, Pres./CEO
Ann Marie Delligatta, Exec. VP/COO
Robert S. Grimes, Sr.VP/CFO
Anne Benevenuto, Sr. VP-Mktg.
Karen Peterson-Kort, Dir.-Human Resources
David S. Grant, Chief Tech. Officer
Ariel Amir, VP-Sec.
Michael J. Lowell, VP-Oper.
Joshua Carter, VP-Strategic Business Dev.

Phone: 949-225-4500	Fax: 949-225-4541
Toll-Free:	
Address: 18872 MacArthur Blvd.,Ste. 200, Irvine, CA, 92612-1400	

GROWTH PLANS/SPECIAL FEATURES:

Autobytel.com plans to revolutionize the manner in which consumers buy automobiles. Autobytel is a global leader in automotive e-commerce that provides a wealth of information about new and pre-owned vehicles with a vast array of makes and models. It allows the customer to pick from a variety of options, such as accessories and method of payment. The site then searches all dealerships within a chosen radius from the users' home for a car that matches the customer's specifications. Dealerships pay a fee to receive inquiries from the site, but the customer is not charged. Autobytel helps over a million customers annually. The company is currently generating about one million dollars of car sales per hour. Recently, Autobytel executed an agreement to acquire A.I.N. Corporation, which owns CarSmart.com, the third-most visited on-line buying site for new vehicles. CarSmart has strategic marketing alliances with seven of the top 20 Internet portals. Autobytel also partnered with Toyota to mark the first time an e-commerce company and a manufacturer have developed a strategic venture to market factory-backed extended service contracts on-line. Autobytel has used depth of content, additional services and aggressive marketing to create a rapidly growing and highly successful site. It covers both new and used cars and small trucks.

FINANCIALS: Sales and profits are in thousands of dollars—add 000 to get the full amount.

Notes regarding 1999: *(1999 sales and profits were not available for all companies at press time.)*

1999 Sales: $40,300	1999 Profits: $-23,300	Stock Ticker: **ABTL**
1998 Sales: $23,800	1998 Profits: $-19,400	Employees: 177
1997 Sales: $15,300	1997 Profits: $-16,800	Fiscal Year Ends: 12/31
1996 Sales: $5,000	1996 Profits: $-6,000	
1995 Sales: $ 300	1995 Profits: $-1,000	

SALARIES/BENEFITS:

Pension Plan:	ESOP Stock Plan: Y	Profit Sharing:	Top Exec. Salary: $316,000	Bonus: $
Savings Plan:	Stock Purch. Plan:		Second Exec. Salary: $220,000	Bonus: $75,000

COMPETITIVE ADVANTAGE: An early leader in the on-line business/One of the best known brand names.

OTHER THOUGHTS:

Apparent Women Officers or Directors: 5
Apparent Minority Officers or Directors: 4
Hot Spot for Advancement for Women/Minorities: Y

LOCATIONS: ("Y" = Yes)

West:	Southwest:	Midwest:	Southeast:	Northeast:	International:
Y					

AUTOWEB.COM INC   www.autoweb.com

Industry Group Code: 54189A
Ranks within this company's industry group: Sales: 9   Profits: 13

BUSINESS ACTIVITIES ("Y" = Yes)

Financial Services:	Information/Publ.:		Technology:	Services:	Retailing:	Telecommunications:
Stock Brokerage	Portal/Hub/News	Y	Computer Manuf.	Payments/Transfers	Retailer	Internet Serv. Provider
Mortgages/Loans	On-Line Community		Networking Equip.	Consulting	Auctions	Web Site Host
Banking	Search Engine		Software Manuf.	Advertising/Marketing Y	Mall	Server Farm
Insurance	Financial Data Publ.		Specialty Equipment	Outsourcing	Tickets/Travel	Specialty Telecom.
Credit Cards	Broadcasting/Music				Price Comparisons	High Speed Access

TYPES OF BUSINESS:

On-line Automobile Buyers' Site
On-line Advertising/Marketing Services

BRANDS/DIVISIONS/AFFILIATES:

Automotive Information Center (AIC)
AutoSite Database

GROWTH PLANS/SPECIAL FEATURES:

Autoweb.com lets new or used car buyers outline specifications of the car they wish to buy. Registered car dealers respond within 24 hours with offers. Autoweb eliminates haggling over final purchase prices. The web site receives more than two million unique visits every month. It includes information on less common, older and foreign autos made by companies such as Hudson, MG, Lotus, Peugoet and Citroen. In recent news, Autoweb completed the acquisition of Automotive Information Center (AIC). This acquisition brings even more enhanced automotive content to the web site with the integration of AIC's AutoSite Database. Autoweb also announced a partnering agreement with Infiniti, the luxury division of Nissan North America, Inc., to execute a joint sales and marketing program. Autoweb implemented the use of alphanumeric pagers and PCS phones to enable dealers to respond more quickly to customers interested in purchasing cars.

CONTACTS: *Note: Officers with more than one job title may be intentionally listed here more than once.*

Dean A. DeBiase, Pres./CEO
Samuel M. Hedgpath III, VP/CFO
Michele Hickford, VP-Mktg.
Nancy Tingstrom, Dir.-Human Resources
Gordon Kass, Chief Tech. Officer
Smauel M. Hedgpath III, VP-Admin.
Robert M. Shapiro, VP-Business Dev.

Phone: 408-554-9552	Fax: 408-588-9772
Toll-Free:	
Address: 3270 Jay St., Bldg.6, Santa Clara, CA, 95054	

FINANCIALS: Sales and profits are in thousands of dollars—add 000 to get the full amount.

Notes regarding 1999: *(1999 sales and profits were not available for all companies at press time.)*

1999 Sales: $32,800	1999 Profits: $-18,200	Stock Ticker: **AWEB**
1998 Sales: $13,000	1998 Profits: $-11,500	Employees: 81
1997 Sales: $3,500	1997 Profits: $-2,900	Fiscal Year Ends: 12/31
1996 Sales: $ 300	1996 Profits: $- 800	
1995 Sales: $	1995 Profits: $- 100	

SALARIES/BENEFITS:

Pension Plan:	ESOP Stock Plan: Y	Profit Sharing:	Top Exec. Salary: $	Bonus: $
Savings Plan:	Stock Purch. Plan:		Second Exec. Salary: $	Bonus: $

COMPETITIVE ADVANTAGE: Great depth of database content/Relationship with Infiniti.

OTHER THOUGHTS:

Apparent Women Officers or Directors: 4
Apparent Minority Officers or Directors: 1
Hot Spot for Advancement for Women/Minorities: Y

LOCATIONS: ("Y" = Yes)

West:	Southwest:	Midwest:	Southeast:	Northeast:	International:
Y					

AXENT TECHNOLOGIES INC

www.axent.com

Industry Group Code: 5112
Ranks within this company's industry group: Sales: 10   Profits: 9

BUSINESS ACTIVITIES ("Y" = Yes)

Financial Services:	Information/Publ.:	Technology:		Services:		Retailing:	Telecommunications:
Stock Brokerage	Portal/Hub/News	Computer Manuf.		Payments/Transfers		Retailer	Internet Serv. Provider
Mortgages/Loans	On-Line Community	Networking Equip.		Consulting	Y	Auctions	Web Site Host
Banking	Search Engine	Software Manuf.	Y	Advertising/Marketing		Mall	Server Farm
Insurance	Financial Data Publ.	Specialty Equipment		Outsourcing		Tickets/Travel	Specialty Telecom.
Credit Cards	Broadcasting/Music					Price Comparisons	High Speed Access

TYPES OF BUSINESS:

Software-Security
Firewall Software

BRANDS/DIVISIONS/AFFILIATES:

Secure Network Consulting, Inc.
Lifecycle Security Model

CONTACTS: Note: Officers with more than one job title may be intentionally listed here more than once.

John C. Becker, CEO
Brett M. Jackson, Pres./COO
Bob Edwards Jr., CFO
Wayne Swann, Dir.-Human Resources
James R. Bowerman, VP-Engineering
Gary M. Ford, VP-Corp.Sec.
Gary M. Ford, VP-General Counsel
Joshua Carter, VP-Strategic Business Dev.

Phone: 301-258-5043	Fax: 301-330-5756
Toll-Free:	
Address: 2400 Research Blvd.,Ste. 200, Rockville, MD, 20850	

GROWTH PLANS/SPECIAL FEATURES:

Axent Technologies is a global leader in information security, providing Internet security solutions that optimize its clients' business advantages. Axent uses its Lifecycle Security Model to assess, protect, enable and manage different business and information processes. More than 5,000 companies and government agencies, including 45 of the top Fortune 50 U.S. companies, use Axent's products and services. The company has won a long list of awards for its suite of products, such as DataComm Magazine's Tester's Choice, Deloitte & Touche's Technology Fast 500 and the Info Security News Reader Trust Awards. Axent's subsidiary, Secure Network Consulting, Inc., boasts 115 years of consulting experience. Axent offers product training on-site or at one of its many locations, 24/7. Axent has expanded its security alliance with Compaq Computer to deliver the next versions of the AltaVista Firewall and Tunnel products. Axent will become Compaq's preferred multi-operating system partner. Axent recently won acclaim in Windows NT magazine for its intrusion detection and assessment e-security solutions. The Raptor Firewall is integrated with other AXENT and third-party solutions under AXENT's Smart Security Architecture, which builds smart and appropriate integration between products and services to deliver real value for customers. Integration includes standard IPSec VPN technology, International Computer Security Association (ICSA) certification, a Microsoft Management Console (MMC) interface, Entrust-Ready public key Infrastructure (PKI) encryption support and integration with other AXENT authentication and e-security solutions.

FINANCIALS: Sales and profits are in thousands of dollars—add 000 to get the full amount.

Notes regarding 1999: *(1999 sales and profits were not available for all companies at press time.)*

		Stock Ticker: **AXNT**
1999 Sales: $112,800	1999 Profits: $ 997	Employees: 527
1998 Sales: $101,000	1998 Profits: $7,700	Fiscal Year Ends: 12/31
1997 Sales: $41,700	1997 Profits: $-19,400	
1996 Sales: $22,100	1996 Profits: $5,700	
1995 Sales: $14,700	1995 Profits: $2,400	

SALARIES/BENEFITS:

Pension Plan:	ESOP Stock Plan: Y	Profit Sharing:	Top Exec. Salary: $220,000	Bonus: $62,400
Savings Plan:	Stock Purch. Plan:		Second Exec. Salary: $200,000	Bonus: $33,600

COMPETITIVE ADVANTAGE: Highly-regarded technology.

OTHER THOUGHTS:

Apparent Women Officers or Directors:
Apparent Minority Officers or Directors: 1
Hot Spot for Advancement for Women/Minorities:

LOCATIONS: ("Y" = Yes)

West:	Southwest:	Midwest:	Southeast:	Northeast:	International:
				Y	

BAMBOO.COM INC   www.bamboo.com

Industry Group Code: 54189A
Ranks within this company's industry group: Sales: 20   Profits: 4

BUSINESS ACTIVITIES ("Y" = Yes)

Financial Services:	Information/Publ.:	Technology:	Services:		Retailing:	Telecommunications:
Stock Brokerage	Portal/Hub/News	Computer Manuf.	Payments/Transfers		Retailer	Internet Serv. Provider
Mortgages/Loans	On-Line Community	Networking Equip.	Consulting		Auctions	Web Site Host
Banking	Search Engine	Software Manuf.	Advertising/Marketing	Y	Mall	Server Farm
Insurance	Financial Data Publ.	Specialty Equipment	Outsourcing		Tickets/Travel	Specialty Telecom.
Credit Cards	Broadcasting/Music				Price Comparisons	High Speed Access

TYPES OF BUSINESS:

Virtual Real Estate Tours
On-line Video Image Technology
On-Line Advertising/Marketing Services

BRANDS/DIVISIONS/AFFILIATES:

Jutvision
Interactive Pictures

CONTACTS: *Note: Officers with more than one job title may be intentionally listed here more than once.*

Leonard B. McCurdy, CEO
Mark R. Searle, COO
Randall I. Bresee, CFO
John Assaraf, Sr.VP-Sales
Diane Rigatuso, Dir.-Human Resources
Andrew P. Laszlo, Sr.VP-Business Dev.

Phone: 650-325-6787	Fax: 650-325-9337
Toll-Free:	
Address: 124 University Ave., Palo Alto, CA, 94301	

GROWTH PLANS/SPECIAL FEATURES:

Bamboo.com is a premier producer of virtual tours for the real estate industry. Real estate companies can pay a fee to have their properties videotaped on the inside and outside - then bamboo.com converts the video into a form that can be accessed on the Internet. While taking a virtual tour of the property, users can zoom in and out, pan back and forth and perform a variety of other viewing options. The web site offers virtual tours with no need for plug-ins, downloads or installations. The tours feature a 360-degree range of view and eliminate the need to drive around with a sales agent on previewing trips. The service also allows homebuyers and renters to view properties that are far from their locations. Realtors can choose to send a virtual tour as an attachment to an e-mail. Bamboo recently announced an agreement with Coldwell Banker/Ellison Realty to market all of Ellison's homes for sale on the Internet. Bamboo also announced the signing of an agreement to merge with Interactive Pictures, a world leader in imaging for the Internet. The new company will serve the real estate, travel and hospitality, e-commerce, electronic publishing, government and entertainment markets.

FINANCIALS: Sales and profits are in thousands of dollars—add 000 to get the full amount.

Notes regarding 1999: *(1999 sales and profits were not available for all companies at press time.)*

1999 Sales: $12,500	1999 Profits: $-56,900	**Stock Ticker: BAMB**
1998 Sales: $ 100	1998 Profits: $-1,800	Employees: 142
1997 Sales: $	1997 Profits: $- 100	Fiscal Year Ends: 12/31
1996 Sales: $	1996 Profits: $- 900	
1995 Sales: $	1995 Profits: $	

SALARIES/BENEFITS:

Pension Plan:	ESOP Stock Plan: Y	Profit Sharing:	Top Exec. Salary: $	Bonus: $
Savings Plan:	Stock Purch. Plan:		Second Exec. Salary: $	Bonus: $

COMPETITIVE ADVANTAGE: Merger with Interactive Pictures.

OTHER THOUGHTS:

Apparent Women Officers or Directors: 1
Apparent Minority Officers or Directors: 1
Hot Spot for Advancement for Women/Minorities:

LOCATIONS: ("Y" = Yes)

West:	Southwest:	Midwest:	Southeast:	Northeast:	International:
Y					

Note: Financial information, benefits and other data can change quickly and may vary from those stated here.

BANK ONE CORP

www.bankone.com
www.wingspan.com

Industry Group Code: 522
Ranks within this company's industry group: Sales: 1   Profits: 1

BUSINESS ACTIVITIES ("Y" = Yes)

Financial Services:		Information/Publ.:	Technology:	Services:		Retailing:	Telecommunications:
Stock Brokerage	Y	Portal/Hub/News	Computer Manuf.	Payments/Transfers	Y	Retailer	Internet Serv. Provider
Mortgages/Loans	Y	On-Line Community	Networking Equip.	Consulting		Auctions	Web Site Host
Banking	Y	Search Engine	Software Manuf.	Advertising/Marketing		Mall	Server Farm
Insurance	Y	Financial Data Publ.	Specialty Equipment	Outsourcing		Tickets/Travel	Specialty Telecom.
Credit Cards	Y	Broadcasting/Music				Price Comparisons	High Speed Access

TYPES OF BUSINESS:

Banking
Credit Card/Merchant Processing
Consumer Finance
Mortgage Banking
Insurance
Trust and Investment Management

BRANDS/DIVISIONS/AFFILIATES:

First USA
Wingspan.com
Banc One Community Development Corporation
Banc One Credit Card Services Company
Banc One Financial Card Services Corporation
Banc One Financial Services Corporation
Banc One Funds Management Company
Banc One Insurance Services Corporation

CONTACTS: Note: Officers with more than one job title may be intentionally listed here more than once.

John B. McCoy, CEO
Verne G. Istock, Pres./COO
Robert Rosholt, Exec.VP/CFO
Sherman I. Goldberg, Corp. Sec.
Sherman I. Goldberg, Exec. VP/General Counsel
William P. Boardman, Sr. Exec. VP/Head-Acquisitions

Phone: 312-732-4000	Fax: 312-732-3366
Toll-Free:	
Address: 1 First National Plaza, Chicago, IL, 60670	

GROWTH PLANS/SPECIAL FEATURES:

Bank One Corporation, formed by the 1998 merger of First Chicago NBD Corporation and Banc One Corporation, is the nation's fifth largest bank holding company, with assets of more than $256 billion.   With over 2,000 branches, the company provides financial services to commercial and business customers and consumers. Bank One is the world's largest Visa issuer and the third largest bank lender to small businesses.   Bank One recently announced the launch of a co-branded Bank One/Excite Personal Front Page that enables users to customize a start page with such items as news, stock quotes, sports and traveling tips. It will highlight special offers and provide a direct link to Bank One's web site. Bank One established a strategic alliance with GMAC Commercial Mortgage Corp. that will bring significant benefits to Bank One customers. The company also has an alliance with AT&T and IBM that provides the Bank with a world-class networking and computing services infrastructure to support its aggressive e-business and growth strategy.   Of most significance is Bank One's new Wingspan.com, operated by the First USA division. This is an independent, Internet-only bank that will compete directly against Bank One's traditional banks, as well as with the banking industry in general.

In 1998, the company established the Working Woman Entrepreneurial Excellence Awards in conjunction with Working Woman Magazine. In July 1999, Bank One, with the support of Chicago's mayor and the city, implemented its Wings to Work program, which offered training to 336 individuals on welfare as part of its commitment to strengthen its community.   Those who successfully complete the program are provided regular employment with benefits.

FINANCIALS: Sales and profits are in thousands of dollars—add 000 to get the full amount.

Notes regarding 1999: Through 9 months *(1999 sales and profits were not available for all companies at press time.)*

1999 Sales: $12,739,000	1999 Profits: $3,068,000	Stock Ticker: **ONE**
1998 Sales: $17,524,000	1998 Profits: $3,108,000	Employees: 91,310
1997 Sales: $115,901,300	1997 Profits: $1,305,700	Fiscal Year Ends: 12/31
1996 Sales: $101,848,100	1996 Profits: $1,426,500	
1995 Sales: $90,454,000	1995 Profits: $1,277,900	

SALARIES/BENEFITS:

Pension Plan: Y	ESOP Stock Plan:	Profit Sharing:	Top Exec. Salary: $995,000	Bonus: $1,500,000
Savings Plan: Y	Stock Purch. Plan:		Second Exec. Salary: $995,000	Bonus: $1,250,000

COMPETITIVE ADVANTAGE: Affiliate banks total over 1,300 nationwide/Ranks seventh among the nation's largest 50 publicly-owned banks in net income/Aggressive Internet banking programs.

OTHER THOUGHTS:

Apparent Women Officers or Directors: 1
Apparent Minority Officers or Directors:
Hot Spot for Advancement for Women/Minorities: Y

LOCATIONS: ("Y" = Yes)

West:	Southwest:	Midwest:	Southeast:	Northeast:	International:
Y	Y	Y	Y	Y	

Note: Financial information, benefits and other data can change quickly and may vary from those stated here.

BARNESANDNOBLE.COM INC   www.bn.com

Industry Group Code: 4541
Ranks within this company's industry group: Sales: 13   Profits: 32

BUSINESS ACTIVITIES ("Y" = Yes)

Financial Services:	Information/Publ.:		Technology:	Services:	Retailing:		Telecommunications:
Stock Brokerage	Portal/Hub/News		Computer Manuf.	Payments/Transfers	Retailer	Y	Internet Serv. Provider
Mortgages/Loans	On-Line Community		Networking Equip.	Consulting	Auctions		Web Site Host
Banking	Search Engine		Software Manuf.	Advertising/Marketing	Mall		Server Farm
Insurance	Financial Data Publ.		Specialty Equipment	Outsourcing	Tickets/Travel		Specialty Telecom.
Credit Cards	Broadcasting/Music	Y			Price Comparisons		High Speed Access

TYPES OF BUSINESS:
Retail-On-line Bookseller

GROWTH PLANS/SPECIAL FEATURES:

Barnesandnoble.com is an on-line retailer of books, magazines, software, videos, music and other items. It is the fifth-largest e-commerce site and is among the 25 largest sites overall on the Internet, according to Media Metrix. Barnesandnoble.com is also the exclusive bookseller on America Online. Its database offers books from the latest bestsellers, diverse titles from small presses and university publishers and millions of out-of-print, used and rare books. Barnesandnoble.com boasts 750,000 titles that are ready for delivery. The web site also contains many extra features such as book descriptions, reviews and excerpts and recommendations from other readers. Recently, barnesandnoble.com entered an agreement with Netmarket.com to feature its books and products on Netmarket web sites like AutoVantage.com, TravelersAdvantage.com, PrivacyGuard.com and FareAgent.com. Barnesandnoble also signed an agreement to purchase the URL www.books.com and the Books.com trademark from Cendant Corporation. Barnesandnoble.com has developed marketing relationships with other Cendant-related web sites, including ShoppersAdvantage.com and DaysInn.com. While this is a separate company from Barnes & Noble, it is able to use the Barnes & Noble retail stores as a method of increasing its branding and customer recognition.

BRANDS/DIVISIONS/AFFILIATES:
Barnes and Noble, Inc.
Books.com

CONTACTS: Note: Officers with more than one job title may be intentionally listed here more than once.
Stephen Riggio, Acting CEO
Alan Kahn, COO
Marie Toulantis, CFO
Carl Rosendorf, VP-Mktg. and Sales
Donna Telesca, Dir.-Human Resources
Gary King, Chief Info. Officer
Brenda Marsh, VP-Merch.
Michael N. Rosen, Sec.
William F. Duffy, VP-Oper.
Carl Rosendorf, VP-Business Dev.

Phone: 212-414-6000	Fax: 212-414-6140
Toll-Free:	
Address: 76 Ninth Ave.,11th Floor, New York, NY, 10011	

FINANCIALS: Sales and profits are in thousands of dollars—add 000 to get the full amount.
Notes regarding 1999: *(1999 sales and profits were not available for all companies at press time.)*

1999 Sales: $	1999 Profits: $	Stock Ticker: **BNBN**
1998 Sales: $61,800	1998 Profits: $-83,100	Employees: 654
1997 Sales: $11,900	1997 Profits: $-13,600	Fiscal Year Ends: 12/31
1996 Sales: $	1996 Profits: $	
1995 Sales: $	1995 Profits: $	

SALARIES/BENEFITS:

Pension Plan:	ESOP Stock Plan: Y	Profit Sharing:	Top Exec. Salary: $900,000	Bonus: $540,000
Savings Plan:	Stock Purch. Plan:		Second Exec. Salary: $460,000	Bonus: $276,000

COMPETITIVE ADVANTAGE:
Alliance with AOL as sole book seller on that site/Major boost from relationship with the retail stores of Barnes & Noble.

OTHER THOUGHTS:
Apparent Women Officers or Directors: 4
Apparent Minority Officers or Directors:
Hot Spot for Advancement for Women/Minorities: Y

LOCATIONS: ("Y" = Yes)

West:	Southwest:	Midwest:	Southeast:	Northeast:	International:
				Y	

BEYOND.COM CORP   www.beyond.com

Industry Group Code: 4541
Ranks within this company's industry group: Sales: 16   Profits: 27

BUSINESS ACTIVITIES ("Y" = Yes)

Financial Services:	Information/Publ.:	Technology:	Services:	Retailing:		Telecommunications:
Stock Brokerage	Portal/Hub/News	Computer Manuf.	Payments/Transfers	Retailer	Y	Internet Serv. Provider
Mortgages/Loans	On-Line Community	Networking Equip.	Consulting	Auctions		Web Site Host
Banking	Search Engine	Software Manuf.	Advertising/Marketing	Mall		Server Farm
Insurance	Financial Data Publ.	Specialty Equipment	Outsourcing	Tickets/Travel		Specialty Telecom.
Credit Cards	Broadcasting/Music			Price Comparisons		High Speed Access

TYPES OF BUSINESS:

Retail-On-line Software Seller

BRANDS/DIVISIONS/AFFILIATES:

TechShopper Software Store
Computer Currents Interactive Software Shop
BuyDirect

GROWTH PLANS/SPECIAL FEATURES:

Beyond.com offers over 50,000 software titles that can be shipped directly to its customers and, through its relationships with about 350 software publishers, it offers more than 6,000 that can be downloaded from the Internet. Downloadable software represents about half of sales. Though it receives over a quarter of its business from the United States government, the company has also made marketing alliances with America Online, Excite and Netscape. Beyond.com operates several co-branded sites as well, such as CMP's TechShopper Software Store and Computer Currents Interactive Software Shop. Beyond.com has developed technology for secure Internet transactions. Recently, the company bought BuyDirect, a rival, for $134 million. Beyond.com has an exclusive multi-year marketing and promotional agreement with NextCard, the creator of the first true Internet Visa, which will give Beyond.com customers exclusive NextCard privileges.

CONTACTS: Note: Officers with more than one job title may be intentionally listed here more than once.

Mark L. Breier, CEO/Pres.
James Lussler, VP-Business Oper.
C. Richard Neely, Jr., VP-Finance/CFO
Brian Sroub, VP-Mktg.
John P. Pettit, Exec. VP/Chief Tech. Officer
Gordon F. Jones, CIO
Mala Anand, VP-Engineering
Michael J. Praisner, VP-Admin.
John D. Vigouroux, VP-Business Dev.
William Headapohl, VP-Software and Digital Delivery
Laura Fulda, VP-Investor Relations
Alan C. DeClerck, VP-Sales
William C. Holtzman, VP-Site Mktg.

Phone: 408-616-4200	Fax: 408-530-0800
Toll-Free:	
Address: 1195 W. Fremont Avenue, Sunnyvale, CA, 94087	

FINANCIALS: Sales and profits are in thousands of dollars—add 000 to get the full amount.

Notes regarding 1999: (1999 sales and profits were not available for all companies at press time.)

1999 Sales: $117,300	1999 Profits: $-124,800	Stock Ticker: **BYND**
1998 Sales: $36,700	1998 Profits: $-31,100	Employees: 137
1997 Sales: $16,800	1997 Profits: $-5,300	Fiscal Year Ends: 12/31
1996 Sales: $5,900	1996 Profits: $-1,500	
1995 Sales: $1,000	1995 Profits: $- 500	

SALARIES/BENEFITS:

Pension Plan:	ESOP Stock Plan:	Profit Sharing:	Top Exec. Salary: $150,000	Bonus: $37,500
Savings Plan:	Stock Purch. Plan:		Second Exec. Salary: $141,000	Bonus: $

COMPETITIVE ADVANTAGE: One of the first to offer software over the Internet.

OTHER THOUGHTS:

| Apparent Women Officers or Directors: 1 |
| Apparent Minority Officers or Directors: |
| Hot Spot for Advancement for Women/Minorities: |

LOCATIONS: ("Y" = Yes)

West:	Southwest:	Midwest:	Southeast:	Northeast:	International:
Y					

Note: Financial information, benefits and other data can change quickly and may vary from those stated here.

BIGSTAR ENTERTAINMENT INC   www.bigstar.com

Industry Group Code: 4541
Ranks within this company's industry group: Sales: 26   Profits: 12

BUSINESS ACTIVITIES ("Y" = Yes)

Financial Services:	Information/Publ.:		Technology:	Services:	Retailing:		Telecommunications:
Stock Brokerage	Portal/Hub/News	Y	Computer Manuf.	Payments/Transfers	Retailer	Y	Internet Serv. Provider
Mortgages/Loans	On-Line Community		Networking Equip.	Consulting	Auctions		Web Site Host
Banking	Search Engine		Software Manuf.	Advertising/Marketing	Mall		Server Farm
Insurance	Financial Data Publ.		Specialty Equipment	Outsourcing	Tickets/Travel		Specialty Telecom.
Credit Cards	Broadcasting/Music				Price Comparisons		High Speed Access

TYPES OF BUSINESS:

Retail-On-line Video Store

BRANDS/DIVISIONS/AFFILIATES:

Astrophile.com

CONTACTS: *Note: Officers with more than one job title may be intentionally listed here more than once.*

David Friedensohn, CEO
Robert S. Yingling, CFO/VP-Finance
Donna M. Williams, VP-Mktg.
Eugene Mondrus, VP-Tech.
Anthony Witek, VP-Oper.
Brooke Bessert, VP-Site Dev.

Phone: 212-981-6300	Fax: 212-571-9284
Toll-Free:	
Address: 19 Fulton St., 5th Floor, New York, NY, 10038	

GROWTH PLANS/SPECIAL FEATURES:

BigStar Entertainment is an on-line store that offers more than 70,000 filmed entertainment products. The company sells films, educational and instructional videos, TV series and fitness shows. The products can be purchased in a variety of formats, including DVD, laserdisc and videocassette formats. The company's web site also features reviews, chats with famous individuals, celebrity biographies and daily movie news. BigStar Entertainment runs an information web site called Astrophile.com that holds over 4,400 biographies, 240 interviews, 2,000 movie stills and 150 transcripts of interviews with famous actors. PC Data, a company that tracks web purchases among U.S. households, recently ranked BigStar as number 17 out of all on-line retailers and number one of on-line movie retailers. BigStar Entertainment recently announced a strategic content and commerce agreement with MyWay.com that will allow BigStar to be the exclusive video and DVD retailer present on the myWay.com ports. BigStar also has similar agreements with Spree.com, America Online and Gay.com.

FINANCIALS: Sales and profits are in thousands of dollars—add 000 to get the full amount.
Notes regarding 1999: *(1999 sales and profits were not available for all companies at press time.)*

1999 Sales: $13,352	1999 Profits: $-20,857	Stock Ticker: **BGST**
1998 Sales: $ 800	1998 Profits: $-3,200	Employees: 50
1997 Sales: $	1997 Profits: $	Fiscal Year Ends: 12/31
1996 Sales: $	1996 Profits: $	
1995 Sales: $	1995 Profits: $	

SALARIES/BENEFITS:

Pension Plan:	ESOP Stock Plan:	Profit Sharing:	Top Exec. Salary: $	Bonus: $
Savings Plan:	Stock Purch. Plan:		Second Exec. Salary: $	Bonus: $

COMPETITIVE ADVANTAGE: Excellent partnerships assist Bigstar with marketing.

OTHER THOUGHTS:

Apparent Women Officers or Directors: 2
Apparent Minority Officers or Directors:
Hot Spot for Advancement for Women/Minorities:

LOCATIONS: ("Y" = Yes)

West:	Southwest:	Midwest:	Southeast:	Northeast:	International:
				Y	

Note: Financial information, benefits and other data can change quickly and may vary from those stated here.

BIZNESS ONLINE.COM INC   www.biznessonline.com

Industry Group Code: 51339
Ranks within this company's industry group: Sales: 19   Profits: 6

BUSINESS ACTIVITIES ("Y" = Yes)

Financial Services:	Information/Publ.:	Technology:	Services:		Retailing:	Telecommunications:	
Stock Brokerage	Portal/Hub/News	Computer Manuf.	Payments/Transfers		Retailer	Internet Serv. Provider	Y
Mortgages/Loans	On-Line Community	Networking Equip.	Consulting	Y	Auctions	Web Site Host	Y
Banking	Search Engine	Software Manuf.	Advertising/Marketing		Mall	Server Farm	
Insurance	Financial Data Publ.	Specialty Equipment	Outsourcing		Tickets/Travel	Specialty Telecom.	
Credit Cards	Broadcasting/Music				Price Comparisons	High Speed Access	Y

TYPES OF BUSINESS:

Internet Service Provider
ASP
Web Design and Enhancement Services

BRANDS/DIVISIONS/AFFILIATES:

Borg Internet Service
ICONN, L.L.C.
SuperNet
WebWay L.L.C.
Infoboard, Inc.

CONTACTS: Note: Officers with more than one job title may be intentionally listed here more than once.

Mark E. Munro, CEO
Mark E. Munro, Pres.
Daniel J. Sullivan, CFO
Lorin Beller, VP-Mktg.
Adam D. Wills, VP-Network Oper.
Keith S. London, Exec. VP-Business Dev.

Phone: 732-280-6408	Fax: 732-280-6409
Toll-Free:	
Address: 1720 Rte. 34, Wall, NJ, 07719	

GROWTH PLANS/SPECIAL FEATURES:

Bizness Online.com provides a wide array of services to small and medium-sized northeastern U.S. businesses that perform on the Internet. Bizness provides high speed Internet access, a custom-designed web site, ways to attract more net traffic and e-commerce solutions. Bizness also offers the advice of teams of marketing specialists, designers and programmers. In recent news, Bizness announced an agreement to acquire SuperNet, ICONN, L.L.C., WebWay L.L.C. and NECAnet, all regional providers of high speed Internet access and web hosting services. Bizness also acquired Infoboard, Inc., a web application service provider and host to more than 3,000 web domains. Infoboard currently serves customers such as American Honda Motor Company, Micron PC Partners, Simons Company and BioWhittaker Molecular Applications. Bizness designed and provided programming and hosting for the world's first web-based public radio station, which can be found at ThePublicRadioStation.com. Bizness also recently developed database applications, together with technology developers of WRGB Channel 6, to use information on the television company's web site to display during live news broadcasts.

FINANCIALS: Sales and profits are in thousands of dollars—add 000 to get the full amount.

Notes regarding 1999: *(1999 sales and profits were not available for all companies at press time.)*

1999 Sales: $	1999 Profits: $	Stock Ticker: **BIZZ**
1998 Sales: $6,200	1998 Profits: $-2,600	Employees: 60
1997 Sales: $	1997 Profits: $	Fiscal Year Ends: 12/31
1996 Sales: $	1996 Profits: $	
1995 Sales: $	1995 Profits: $	

SALARIES/BENEFITS:

Pension Plan:	ESOP Stock Plan:	Profit Sharing:	Top Exec. Salary: $	Bonus: $
Savings Plan:	Stock Purch. Plan:		Second Exec. Salary: $	Bonus: $

COMPETITIVE ADVANTAGE: Rapid growth through acquistions has led to a wide range of products and services.

OTHER THOUGHTS:

Apparent Women Officers or Directors: 1
Apparent Minority Officers or Directors:
Hot Spot for Advancement for Women/Minorities:

LOCATIONS: ("Y" = Yes)

West:	Southwest:	Midwest:	Southeast:	Northeast:	International:
				Y	

BLUEFLY INC   www.bluefly.com

Industry Group Code: 4541
Ranks within this company's industry group: Sales: 30   Profits: 14

BUSINESS ACTIVITIES ("Y" = Yes)

Financial Services:	Information/Publ.:		Technology:	Services:	Retailing:		Telecommunications:
Stock Brokerage	Portal/Hub/News		Computer Manuf.	Payments/Transfers	Retailer	Y	Internet Serv. Provider
Mortgages/Loans	On-Line Community	Y	Networking Equip.	Consulting	Auctions		Web Site Host
Banking	Search Engine		Software Manuf.	Advertising/Marketing	Mall		Server Farm
Insurance	Financial Data Publ.		Specialty Equipment	Outsourcing	Tickets/Travel		Specialty Telecom.
Credit Cards	Broadcasting/Music				Price Comparisons		High Speed Access

TYPES OF BUSINESS:

On-line Fashion Retailer
Home Furnishings
Fashion News and Opinions

BRANDS/DIVISIONS/AFFILIATES:

Pivot Rules

CONTACTS: *Note: Officers with more than one job title may be intentionally listed here more than once.*

E. Kenneth Seiff, CEO
E. Kenneth Seiff, Pres.
Patrick C. Barry, CFO
Sara Nott, Buyer
Andy Hilford, Dir.-MIS
Nicole Kule, Merchandise Mgr.
Patrick C. Barry, Exec.VP-Oper.
Margaret McCann, VP-Comm.
E. Kenneth Seiff, Treas.
Andy Hilford, VP-Creative Services
Sarah Dordel, Studio Supervisor

Phone: 212-944-8000	Fax: 212-354-3400
Toll-Free:	
Address: 42 W. 39th St., New York, NY, 10018	

GROWTH PLANS/SPECIAL FEATURES:

Bluefly, formerly Pivot Rules, sells discounted designer and name brand clothing for men, women and children via its web site, Bluefly.com. Bluefly offers 25%-75% off retail prices on names such as Polo Ralph Lauren and Tommy Hilfiger. The web site allows customers to make a personalized catalogue. In addition to clothes, Bluefly offers home furnishings. In recent news, Bluefly announced it is going to expand its off-line market campaign to radio advertising. The company has strategic alliances with important portals such as America Online, Excite, Go Network, Lycos, MSN, Netcenter, Women.com and Yahoo!. The company has partnered with Elle Magazine to conduct a cyber poll on the Internet that consists of questions about fashion and Internet related subjects. The results of the poll will be published in an issue of Elle magazine. Bluefly and Elle are also developing a monthly chat called Fashion Speak that will be on Bluefly's web site, featuring beauty experts and designers. Bluefly established a co-branded Visa and MasterCard with a subsidiary of First USA bank. Since the inception of the new card, Bluefly has become one of the most heavily trafficked clothing stores on the Internet.

FINANCIALS: Sales and profits are in thousands of dollars—add 000 to get the full amount.

Notes regarding 1999: *(1999 sales and profits were not available for all companies at press time.)*

1999 Sales: $	1999 Profits: $	**Stock Ticker: BFLY**
1998 Sales: $ 200	1998 Profits: $-3,700	Employees: 29
1997 Sales: $10,300	1997 Profits: $- 400	Fiscal Year Ends: 12/31
1996 Sales: $8,600	1996 Profits: $ 100	
1995 Sales: $7,100	1995 Profits: $	

SALARIES/BENEFITS:

Pension Plan:	ESOP Stock Plan:	Profit Sharing:	Top Exec. Salary: $165,000	Bonus: $25,000
Savings Plan:	Stock Purch. Plan:		Second Exec. Salary: $	Bonus: $

COMPETITIVE ADVANTAGE:
Name brand fashion at discount prices. Clever and aggressive marketing.

OTHER THOUGHTS:

Apparent Women Officers or Directors: 5
Apparent Minority Officers or Directors: 1
Hot Spot for Advancement for Women/Minorities: Y

LOCATIONS: ("Y" = Yes)

West:	Southwest:	Midwest:	Southeast:	Northeast:	International:
				Y	

BOTTOMLINE TECHNOLOGIES INC
www.bottomline.com
Industry Group Code: 5112
Ranks within this company's industry group: Sales: 29 Profits: 16

BUSINESS ACTIVITIES ("Y" = Yes)

Financial Services:	Information/Publ.:	Technology:		Services:	Retailing:	Telecommunications:
Stock Brokerage	Portal/Hub/News	Computer Manuf.		Payments/Transfers	Retailer	Internet Serv. Provider
Mortgages/Loans	On-Line Community	Networking Equip.		Consulting	Auctions	Web Site Host
Banking	Search Engine	Software Manuf.	Y	Advertising/Marketing	Mall	Server Farm
Insurance	Financial Data Publ.	Specialty Equipment		Outsourcing	Tickets/Travel	Specialty Telecom.
Credit Cards	Broadcasting/Music				Price Comparisons	High Speed Access

TYPES OF BUSINESS:
Software-Electronic Data Interchange

BRANDS/DIVISIONS/AFFILIATES:
Integrated Cash Management Services, Inc.

CONTACTS: *Note: Officers with more than one job title may be intentionally listed here more than once.*
Daniel M. McGurl, CEO
Daneil M. McGurl, Pres.
Robert A. Eberle, CFO
Leonard J. Diluro Jr., Exec. VP-Sales
Lisa Kolosey, Mgr. Human Resources
Joseph L. Mullen, Exec. Oper.
Cleo A. O'Donnell III, VP-Research and Dev.
John C. Insko, VP-e-Commerce and Finance Div.
Robert A. Eberle, Treas.
Philip P. Grannan, VP-Mktg.
Tom Daniels, VP-Customer Service and Support

Phone: 603-436-0700	Fax: 603-436-0300
Toll-Free:	
Address: 155 Fleet St., Portsmouth, NH, 03801	

GROWTH PLANS/SPECIAL FEATURES:
Bottomline Technologies provides services that allow organizations to control, manage and issue payments electronically to facilitate e-commerce. Bottomline Technologies' software integrates into existing corporate payment applications such as accounts payable and payroll. Over 2,500 customers from a wide array of industries have implemented the software. Industry leaders such as Wells Fargo Bank, Microsoft Corporation, Lockheed Martin, Johnson & Johnson, Proctor & Gamble and Nissan Motor Acceptance Corporation use Bottomline's products. The software presents a cost-effective and secure alternative to printing paper checks and also allows companies to do business more effectively over the Internet. In recent news, Bottomline named Dianne Gregg, formerly Vice President of Microsoft Corporation's eastern U.S. region, to a position on its Board of Directors. Bottomline also acquired Integrated Cash Management Services, Inc., a leading software development company specializing in web access to complex applications. The company acquired an electronic billing solution from The Northern Trust Company and integrated it into its electronic payment software to develop a payment solution solely for the business-to-business (B2B) market.

FINANCIALS: Sales and profits are in thousands of dollars—add 000 to get the full amount.
Notes regarding 1999: *(1999 sales and profits were not available for all companies at press time.)*

1999 Sales: $39,300	1999 Profits: $4,100	**Stock Ticker: EPAY**
1998 Sales: $29,000	1998 Profits: $1,600	Employees: 271
1997 Sales: $22,100	1997 Profits: $-1,300	Fiscal Year Ends: 6/31
1996 Sales: $18,100	1996 Profits: $ 900	
1995 Sales: $15,100	1995 Profits: $ 800	

SALARIES/BENEFITS:

Pension Plan:	ESOP Stock Plan:	Profit Sharing:	Top Exec. Salary: $172,333	Bonus: $50,000
Savings Plan:	Stock Purch. Plan:		Second Exec. Salary: $144,375	Bonus: $62,966

COMPETITIVE ADVANTAGE: Large customer base/Ability to integrate a variety of vital financial functions.

OTHER THOUGHTS:
Apparent Women Officers or Directors: 2
Apparent Minority Officers or Directors: 1
Hot Spot for Advancement for Women/Minorities:

LOCATIONS: ("Y" = Yes)

West:	Southwest:	Midwest:	Southeast:	Northeast:	International:
				Y	

Note: Financial information, benefits and other data can change quickly and may vary from those stated here.

BRAUN CONSULTING INC   www.braunconsult.com

Industry Group Code: 54151
Ranks within this company's industry group: Sales: 8   Profits: 3

BUSINESS ACTIVITIES ("Y" = Yes)

Financial Services:	Information/Publ.:	Technology:	Services:		Retailing:	Telecommunications:
Stock Brokerage	Portal/Hub/News	Computer Manuf.	Payments/Transfers		Retailer	Internet Serv. Provider
Mortgages/Loans	On-Line Community	Networking Equip.	Consulting	Y	Auctions	Web Site Host
Banking	Search Engine	Software Manuf.	Advertising/Marketing		Mall	Server Farm
Insurance	Financial Data Publ.	Specialty Equipment	Outsourcing		Tickets/Travel	Specialty Telecom.
Credit Cards	Broadcasting/Music				Price Comparisons	High Speed Access

TYPES OF BUSINESS:

Consulting Services-Internet Business
Software Implementation

BRANDS/DIVISIONS/AFFILIATES:

Vertex Partners

CONTACTS: Note: Officers with more than one job title may be intentionally listed here more than once.

Steven J. Braun, CEO/Pres.
Thomas J. Duvall, Exec. VP/COO
John C. Burke, CFO
Greg Matthews, Dir.-Human Resources
Gregory A. Ostendorf, Corp. Sec.
Gregory A. Ostendorf, General Counsel
John C. Burke, Treas.
Michael J. Evanisko, Exec.VP
James M. Kalustian, Exec.VP

Phone: 312-984-7000	Fax: 312-984-7033
Toll-Free:	
Address: 30 W. Monroe, Ste. 300, Chicago, IL, 60603	

GROWTH PLANS/SPECIAL FEATURES:

Chicago-based Braun Consulting, Inc. provides strategic solutions for Internet businesses. Braun focuses on helping businesses become more successful by using better strategies, data, information and knowledge. The company offers its services specifically to customers involved in e-commerce, and most of its clients are Fortune 500 and middle market businesses. Braun acquired Vertex Partners, a Boston consulting firm specializing in customer-oriented, growth- focused businesses that have presence on the Internet. Recently, Braun was named a Microsoft Certified Solution Provider. Hyperion Solutions, the leading provider of analytic application software for reporting, analysis, modeling and planning, named Braun a Gold Consulting Partner. This recognizes Braun as a successful consulting service that deploys many applications built on Hyperion Essbase OLAP (on-line analytical processing) Server, the leading cross-platform enterprise OLAP server. The company was also chosen to be in the Business Partner Program formed by SAS Institute, the market leader in integrated data warehousing and decision support software. The program aims at promoting long-term, mutually beneficial relationships with organizations that offer their customers SAS software solutions and services.

FINANCIALS: Sales and profits are in thousands of dollars—add 000 to get the full amount.

Notes regarding 1999: Proforma *(1999 sales and profits were not available for all companies at press time.)*

1999 Sales: $47,300	1999 Profits: $3,500	Stock Ticker: **BRNC**
1998 Sales: $27,900	1998 Profits: $ 800	Employees: 283
1997 Sales: $19,500	1997 Profits: $1,600	Fiscal Year Ends: 12/31
1996 Sales: $11,300	1996 Profits: $1,700	
1995 Sales: $8,400	1995 Profits: $ 600	

SALARIES/BENEFITS:

Pension Plan:	ESOP Stock Plan:	Profit Sharing:	Top Exec. Salary: $333,333	Bonus: $65,000
Savings Plan: Y	Stock Purch. Plan:		Second Exec. Salary: $200,000	Bonus: $24,000

COMPETITIVE ADVANTAGE: Relationships with Hyperion and Microsoft.

OTHER THOUGHTS:

Apparent Women Officers or Directors:
Apparent Minority Officers or Directors:
Hot Spot for Advancement for Women/Minorities:

LOCATIONS: ("Y" = Yes)

West:	Southwest:	Midwest:	Southeast:	Northeast:	International:
		Y			

BROADCOM CORP   www.broadcom.com

Industry Group Code: 3344
Ranks within this company's industry group: Sales: 2   Profits: 2

BUSINESS ACTIVITIES ("Y" = Yes)

Financial Services:	Information/Publ.:	Technology:		Services:	Retailing:	Telecommunications:	
Stock Brokerage	Portal/Hub/News	Computer Manuf.		Payments/Transfers	Retailer	Internet Serv. Provider	
Mortgages/Loans	On-Line Community	Networking Equip.	Y	Consulting	Auctions	Web Site Host	
Banking	Search Engine	Software Manuf.	Y	Advertising/Marketing	Mall	Server Farm	
Insurance	Financial Data Publ.	Specialty Equipment		Outsourcing	Tickets/Travel	Specialty Telecom.	
Credit Cards	Broadcasting/Music				Price Comparisons	High Speed Access	Y

TYPES OF BUSINESS:

Integrated Circuits
Circuits for Cable Modems
Circuits for DSL Devices

BRANDS/DIVISIONS/AFFILIATES:

Broadband Interactive Group Inc. (B.I.G.)
CablexChange

CONTACTS: Note: Officers with more than one job title may be intentionally listed here more than once.

Henry T. Nicholas III, CEO
Henry T. Nicholas III, Pres.
William J. Ruehle, VP/CFO
Tim M. Lindenfelser, VP-Mktg.
Nancy Tullos, VP-Human Resources
Henry Samueli, Chief Tech. Officer
Martin J. Colombatto, VP/General Mgr.-Networking Business
David A. Dull, Corp. Sec.
David A. Dull, General Counsel
Vahid Manian, VP-Mfg. Oper.
David A. Dull, VP-Business Affairs
Aurelio E. Fernandez, VP-Worldwide Sales

Phone: 949-450-8700	Fax: 949-450-8710
Toll-Free:	
Address: 16251 Alton Pkwy., Irvine, CA, 92618-3616	

GROWTH PLANS/SPECIAL FEATURES:

Broadcom Corporation provides highly integrated silicon solutions that enable broadband digital transmission of voice, data and video content to and throughout the home and within the business enterprise. Broadcom has products that enable digital data to be transmitted at high speeds over existing communications infrastructures that were not made to support this kind of transmission. The company also designs, develops and supplies integrated circuits for communications markets, including cable set-top boxes, cable modems, high speed office networks, direct broadcast satellite and terrestrial digital broadcast, home networking and DSL (digital subscriber lines). Recently, Broadcom launched its CablexChange software solution for voice-over Internet Protocol applications. The company also announced the industry's first four-channel voice modem reference design that will accelerate the deployment of devices that will enable the transmission of digital voice, fax and data packets over data networks and the Internet. Broadcom partnered with Gotcha International, a well-known surfwear and media company, to create Broadband Interactive Group, Inc., (B.I.G.) to target the creation of interactive content for the 10- to 24-year-old age group.

FINANCIALS: Sales and profits are in thousands of dollars—add 000 to get the full amount.

Notes regarding 1999: *(1999 sales and profits were not available for all companies at press time.)*

1999 Sales: $518,200	1999 Profits: $83,300	Stock Ticker: **BRCM**
1998 Sales: $203,100	1998 Profits: $36,400	Employees: 436
1997 Sales: $37,000	1997 Profits: $-1,200	Fiscal Year Ends: 12/31
1996 Sales: $21,400	1996 Profits: $3,000	
1995 Sales: $6,100	1995 Profits: $	

SALARIES/BENEFITS:

Pension Plan:	ESOP Stock Plan:	Profit Sharing:	Top Exec. Salary: $160,000	Bonus: $
Savings Plan:	Stock Purch. Plan: Y		Second Exec. Salary: $112,115	Bonus: $

COMPETITIVE ADVANTAGE: Chip designs to enable state-of-the-art broadband communications.

OTHER THOUGHTS:

Apparent Women Officers or Directors: 1
Apparent Minority Officers or Directors: 3
Hot Spot for Advancement for Women/Minorities: Y

LOCATIONS: ("Y" = Yes)

West:	Southwest:	Midwest:	Southeast:	Northeast:	International:
Y					

BROADVISION INC   www.broadvision.com

Industry Group Code: 5112
Ranks within this company's industry group: Sales: 17   Profits: 12

BUSINESS ACTIVITIES ("Y" = Yes)

Financial Services:	Information/Publ.:	Technology:	Services:	Retailing:	Telecommunications:
Stock Brokerage	Portal/Hub/News	Computer Manuf.	Payments/Transfers	Retailer	Internet Serv. Provider
Mortgages/Loans	On-Line Community	Networking Equip.	Consulting Y	Auctions	Web Site Host
Banking	Search Engine	Software Manuf. Y	Advertising/Marketing	Mall	Server Farm
Insurance	Financial Data Publ.	Specialty Equipment	Outsourcing	Tickets/Travel	Specialty Telecom.
Credit Cards	Broadcasting/Music			Price Comparisons	High Speed Access Y

TYPES OF BUSINESS:

Software-Web Site Tools

BRANDS/DIVISIONS/AFFILIATES:

BroadVision One-to-One
BroadVision One-to-One Visual Development Center
BroadVision One-to-One Application Center
Dynamic Command Center
BroadVision One-to-One Webapps

CONTACTS: Note: Officers with more than one job title may be intentionally listed here more than once.

Pehong Chen, CEO
Pehong Chen, Pres.
Randall Bolten, CFO
Sandra Vaughn, VP-Mktg.
Sharon Haag, Mgr.-Human Resources
Eric J. Golin, Chief Tech. Officer
Clark W. Catelain, VP-Engineering
Perry W. Thorndyke, VP-Business Dev.
Michael A. Kennedy, VP-Global Strategic Alliances
Gino Padua, VP/General Mgr.-Worldwide Channels

Phone: 650-261-5100	Fax: 650-261-5900
Toll-Free:	
Address: 585 Broadway, Redwood City, CA, 94063	

GROWTH PLANS/SPECIAL FEATURES:

BroadVision, Inc. provides industrial-strength software application solutions for personalized, one-to-one business systems on the global Internet, intranets and extranets. These solutions enable rapid and cost-effective prototyping, development and on-going operation of electronic commerce, customer service, interactive publishing and knowledge management applications over the Internet. The company's products and services are targeted at businesses developing web site applications for consumers, business customers and employees. The BroadVision One-to-One application system provides businesses with end-to-end solutions for developing, implementing, operating and maintaining web site applications tailored to the needs and interests of individual web site visitors. A principal feature of BroadVision One-to-One is a set of building blocks called dynamic objects and application templates that implement capabilities required to build industrial-strength web applications. The company also offers consulting, professional, education and client support services. BroadVision markets its products primarily through a direct sales organization with operations in North America, Europe and the Pacific Rim. Broadvision recently announced a strategic alliance with Seibel Systems, Inc., the world's leading supplier of web-based customer relationship management solutions. The company has entered into alliances with a variety of other businesses such as New Era of Networks, Inc., cozone.com and Shop at Home Network.

FINANCIALS: Sales and profits are in thousands of dollars—add 000 to get the full amount.

Notes regarding 1999: (1999 sales and profits were not available for all companies at press time.)

1999 Sales: $115,500	1999 Profits: $18,800	Stock Ticker: BVSN
1998 Sales: $50,900	1998 Profits: $4,000	Employees: 271
1997 Sales: $27,100	1997 Profits: $-7,400	Fiscal Year Ends: 12/31
1996 Sales: $10,900	1996 Profits: $-10,100	
1995 Sales: $ 500	1995 Profits: $-4,300	

SALARIES/BENEFITS:

Pension Plan:	ESOP Stock Plan:	Profit Sharing:	Top Exec. Salary: $200,000	Bonus: $75,000
Savings Plan:	Stock Purch. Plan:		Second Exec. Salary: $187,333	Bonus: $16,000

COMPETITIVE ADVANTAGE: Focus on software that assists specific industries

OTHER THOUGHTS:

Apparent Women Officers or Directors: 3
Apparent Minority Officers or Directors: 1
Hot Spot for Advancement for Women/Minorities: Y

LOCATIONS: ("Y" = Yes)

West:	Southwest:	Midwest:	Southeast:	Northeast:	International:
Y		Y		Y	Y

BUSINESS OBJECTS S A   www.businessobjects.com

Industry Group Code: 5112
Ranks within this company's industry group: Sales: 8   Profits: 7

BUSINESS ACTIVITIES ("Y" = Yes)

Financial Services:	Information/Publ.:	Technology:		Services:	Retailing:	Telecommunications:
Stock Brokerage	Portal/Hub/News	Computer Manuf.		Payments/Transfers	Retailer	Internet Serv. Provider
Mortgages/Loans	On-Line Community	Networking Equip.		Consulting	Auctions	Web Site Host
Banking	Search Engine	Software Manuf.	Y	Advertising/Marketing	Mall	Server Farm
Insurance	Financial Data Publ.	Specialty Equipment		Outsourcing	Tickets/Travel	Specialty Telecom.
Credit Cards	Broadcasting/Music				Price Comparisons	High Speed Access

TYPES OF BUSINESS:

Software-Corporate Data

BRANDS/DIVISIONS/AFFILIATES:

Next Action Technology
BUSINESSOBJECTS

CONTACTS: *Note: Officers with more than one job title may be intentionally listed here more than once.*

Bernard Liautaud, CEO
Bernard Liautaud, Pres.
Clifton T. Weatherfold Jr., CFO
David Kellogg, Group Sr. VP-Mktg.
Jean Marc Morawski, Dir.-Human Resource
Lawrence Lieberman, Group VP-Corp. Dev.
Terrie Ramsey, Group VP-Worldwide Customer Support
Mark Tice, VP-Global Alliances
Eric Bregand, VP-Enterprise Product Dev.

Phone: 33-1-41-25-21-21	Fax: 33-1-41-25-31-00
Toll-Free: 800-527-0580	
Address: 1 Square Capital, 92300 Levallois-Perret, France,	

GROWTH PLANS/SPECIAL FEATURES:

Business Objects S.A. develops, markets and supports integrated enterprise decision support software. Decision support software allows users to access, analyze and share information derived from a variety of sources and enhances the decision making process of a business by providing key information and analyses. The software also enables users to direct queries to databases using representations of information that are understandable by non-technical end users. Data retrieved by these queries can then be analyzed using various tools and reports can be produced to present the results of the analysis. The company's principal product, BUSINESSOBJECTS, is an integrated query, reporting and on-line analytical processing tool that operates on Windows 95, Windows NT and UNIX Motif client/server operating systems and is interoperable with most major databases. Business Objects S A has over 1,300,000 users at over 8,600 companies such as Peugeot, Shell Oil and British Telecom. Recently, Business Objects acquired Next Action Technology, a UK-based developer of customer selection and segmentation applications, for about $8 million.

FINANCIALS: Sales and profits are in thousands of dollars—add 000 to get the full amount.

Notes regarding 1999: *(1999 sales and profits were not available for all companies at press time.)*

1999 Sales: $153,700	1999 Profits: $23,800	Stock Ticker: **BOBJ**
1998 Sales: $166,900	1998 Profits: $10,300	Employees: 977
1997 Sales: $114,300	1997 Profits: $2,900	Fiscal Year Ends: 12/31
1996 Sales: $85,100	1996 Profits: $5,200	
1995 Sales: $60,600	1995 Profits: $8,000	

SALARIES/BENEFITS:

Pension Plan:	ESOP Stock Plan: Y	Profit Sharing:	Top Exec. Salary: $319,958	Bonus: $249,500
Savings Plan:	Stock Purch. Plan: Y		Second Exec. Salary: $	Bonus: $

COMPETITIVE ADVANTAGE: Growth through acquisition.

OTHER THOUGHTS:

Apparent Women Officers or Directors: 2
Apparent Minority Officers or Directors:
Hot Spot for Advancement for Women/Minorities:

LOCATIONS: ("Y" = Yes)

West:	Southwest:	Midwest:	Southeast:	Northeast:	International:
Y	Y	Y	Y	Y	Y

BUY.COM INC   www.buy.com

Industry Group Code: 4541
Ranks within this company's industry group: Sales: 9   Profits: 25

BUSINESS ACTIVITIES ("Y" = Yes)

Financial Services:	Information/Publ.:	Technology:	Services:	Retailing:		Telecommunications:
Stock Brokerage	Portal/Hub/News	Computer Manuf.	Payments/Transfers	Retailer	Y	Internet Serv. Provider
Mortgages/Loans	On-Line Community	Networking Equip.	Consulting	Auctions		Web Site Host
Banking	Search Engine	Software Manuf.	Advertising/Marketing	Mall		Server Farm
Insurance	Financial Data Publ.	Specialty Equipment	Outsourcing	Tickets/Travel		Specialty Telecom.
Credit Cards	Broadcasting/Music			Price Comparisons		High Speed Access

TYPES OF BUSINESS:

On-line Retailer

BRANDS/DIVISIONS/AFFILIATES:

BUYGOLF.com, Inc.
BUYCLEARANCE.com, Inc.
BUYCARS.com, Inc.
TENPERCENTOFFWALMART.com, Inc.

GROWTH PLANS/SPECIAL FEATURES:

Buy.com, Inc. is an on-line retailer that sells a wide variety of items, including computers, games, books, software, music and videos. The company became prominent through a strategy of pricing its goods at less than what it paid for them. As its popularity has grown, the company has raised its prices and increased its higher-margin offerings. Buy.com now provides golf gear at its new website BuyGolf.com and has bought the rights to over 4,000 Web addresses, many of which begin with the word buy, including BuyCars.com and BuyClearance.com. Since its introduction, the company has sold products to more than 1.3 million customers. To further its business even more, Buy.com recently formed an alliance with SoftBank America, Inc. to form an international joint venture in the United Kingdom, Australia, New Zealand and India. In addition, the firm established a relationship with UAL Corp. affiliate United Airlines.

CONTACTS: Note: Officers with more than one job title may be intentionally listed here more than once.

Gregory J. Hawkins, CEO
Mitch C. Hill, CFO
John C. Herr, VP-Sales and Mktg.
Lourdes Ramboa, Mgr. Human Resources
Robb Brock, VP-Tech.
Anthony A. McAlister, VP-Info. Services
Brent Rusick, VP-Sales and Oper.
Murray H. Williams, VP-Finance

Phone: 949-425-5200	**Fax:** 949-425-5300
Toll-Free: 888-880-1030	
Address: 21 Brookline, Aliso Viejo, CA, 92656	

FINANCIALS: Sales and profits are in thousands of dollars—add 000 to get the full amount.

Notes regarding 1999: *(1999 sales and profits were not available for all companies at press time.)*

1999 Sales: $	1999 Profits: $	**Stock Ticker: BUYX**
1998 Sales: $125,300	1998 Profits: $-17,800	Employees: 196
1997 Sales: $ 900	1997 Profits: $- 400	Fiscal Year Ends: 12/31
1996 Sales: $	1996 Profits: $	
1995 Sales: $	1995 Profits: $	

SALARIES/BENEFITS:

Pension Plan:	ESOP Stock Plan:	Profit Sharing:	Top Exec. Salary: $	Bonus: $
Savings Plan:	Stock Purch. Plan:		Second Exec. Salary: $	Bonus: $

COMPETITIVE ADVANTAGE: Extremely competitive prices.

OTHER THOUGHTS:

Apparent Women Officers or Directors: 1
Apparent Minority Officers or Directors: 1
Hot Spot for Advancement for Women/Minorities:

LOCATIONS: ("Y" = Yes)

West:	Southwest:	Midwest:	Southeast:	Northeast:	International:
Y					Y

CAIS INTERNET INC   www.cais.com

Industry Group Code: 5133C
Ranks within this company's industry group: Sales: 1   Profits: 2

BUSINESS ACTIVITIES ("Y" = Yes)

Financial Services:	Information/Publ.:	Technology:	Services:	Retailing:	Telecommunications:	
Stock Brokerage	Portal/Hub/News	Computer Manuf.	Payments/Transfers	Retailer	Internet Serv. Provider	Y
Mortgages/Loans	On-Line Community	Networking Equip.	Consulting	Auctions	Web Site Host	Y
Banking	Search Engine	Software Manuf.	Advertising/Marketing	Mall	Server Farm	
Insurance	Financial Data Publ.	Specialty Equipment	Outsourcing	Tickets/Travel	Specialty Telecom.	
Credit Cards	Broadcasting/Music			Price Comparisons	High Speed Access	Y

TYPES OF BUSINESS:

Mobile Internet Connection Services
Fixed Internet Service Provider

BRANDS/DIVISIONS/AFFILIATES:

OverVoice
CAIS Software Solutions
Business Anywhere

CONTACTS: Note: Officers with more than one job title may be intentionally listed here more than once.

Ulysses G. Auger II, CEO
Evans K. Anderson, COO
Barton R. Groh, CFO
Evans K. Anderson, Exec.VP-Sales and Mktg.
Frank R. Kent, VP- Human Resources
Richard W. Durkee, VP-Info. Tech.
Michael G. Plantamura, VP/Corp. Sec.
Michael G. Plantamura, VP/General Counsel
Richard W. Durkee, VP-Oper.
Stephen Rice, VP-Business Dev.
William M. Caldwell IV, Pres.
Gary H. Rabin, Exec.VP-Finance and Strategic Planning

Phone: 202-715-1300	Fax: 202-463-7190
Toll-Free:	
Address: 1255 22nd St. NW, 4th Fl., Washington, DC, 20037	

GROWTH PLANS/SPECIAL FEATURES:

CAIS Internet, Inc., headquartered in Washington, D.C., is a leading broadband access solutions provider that delivers the latest in end-to-end solutions to new and emerging Internet markets. CAIS specializes in giving customers Internet connection capabilities while traveling and staying in hotels, cruise ships, airports and public areas. The company also provides its services for businesses, apartment complexes and single-family homes. CAIS and its subsidiaries, CAIS Software Solutions and Business Anywhere, offer broadband connectivity solutions to markets where there was no previously existing Internet access. The company's offers a variety of DSL services, dedicated access products powered by Cisco and customized web packages. CAIS recently signed an agreement to provide United Dominion Realty Trust with high speed Internet access to over 80,000 of its apartments in 21 states. The company was awarded a contract to provide 400,000 guest rooms and 2,700 properties worldwide for Bass Hotels. Some of the popular hotels that will receive the services are Holiday Inn, Holiday Inn Express, Crown Plaza and Intercontinental Hotels and Resorts. CAIS was chosen to be the official Internet service provider for the 1999 Business Week CEO Summit in New York.

FINANCIALS: Sales and profits are in thousands of dollars—add 000 to get the full amount.

Notes regarding 1999: Through 9 months *(1999 sales and profits were not available for all companies at press time.)*

1999 Sales: $6,100	1999 Profits: $-28,800	Stock Ticker: **CAIS**
1998 Sales: $5,300	1998 Profits: $-12,900	Employees: 109
1997 Sales: $4,600	1997 Profits: $-4,600	Fiscal Year Ends: 12/31
1996 Sales: $3,700	1996 Profits: $1,700	
1995 Sales: $2,200	1995 Profits: $ 900	

SALARIES/BENEFITS:

Pension Plan:	ESOP Stock Plan:	Profit Sharing:	Top Exec. Salary: $280,140	Bonus: $28,000
Savings Plan:	Stock Purch. Plan:		Second Exec. Salary: $237,498	Bonus: $

COMPETITIVE ADVANTAGE: Unique focus on serving travelers who need Internet access.

OTHER THOUGHTS:

Apparent Women Officers or Directors: 2
Apparent Minority Officers or Directors:
Hot Spot for Advancement for Women/Minorities:

LOCATIONS: ("Y" = Yes)

West:	Southwest:	Midwest:	Southeast:	Northeast:	International:
				Y	

Note: Financial information, benefits and other data can change quickly and may vary from those stated here.

CAMBRIDGE TECHNOLOGY PARTNERS INC
www.ctp.com
Industry Group Code: 54151
Ranks within this company's industry group: Sales: 1 Profits: 1

BUSINESS ACTIVITIES ("Y" = Yes)

Financial Services:	Information/Publ.:	Technology:	Services:		Retailing:	Telecommunications:
Stock Brokerage	Portal/Hub/News	Computer Manuf.	Payments/Transfers		Retailer	Internet Serv. Provider
Mortgages/Loans	On-Line Community	Networking Equip.	Consulting	Y	Auctions	Web Site Host
Banking	Search Engine	Software Manuf.	Advertising/Marketing		Mall	Server Farm
Insurance	Financial Data Publ.	Specialty Equipment	Outsourcing	Y	Tickets/Travel	Specialty Telecom.
Credit Cards	Broadcasting/Music				Price Comparisons	High Speed Access

TYPES OF BUSINESS:
Consulting Services-Computer & Internet
Software Development Services
Training

BRANDS/DIVISIONS/AFFILIATES:
Cambridge Enterprise Resource
Cambridge Management Consulting
Excell Data Corporation

CONTACTS: *Note: Officers with more than one job title may be intentionally listed here more than once.*
Jack L. Messman, CEO/Pres.
Gerard Van Kemmel, COO
Arthur M. Toscanini, CFO/Exec. VP-Finance
Laura Zak, Sr.VP-Human Resources
Bruce Culbert, VP-Interactive Solutions
James P. O'Hare, Sr.VP/Sec.
James P. O'Hare, Sr.VP/General Counsel
I. Allen Shaheen, Exec.VP-Int'l Oper.
Arthur M. Toscanini, Treas.
Chester A. Ciccarelli, Sr.VP-North American Business Unit
Theo Schnitfink, Sr.VP-Europe

Phone: 617-374-9800   **Fax:** 617-914-8300
Toll-Free:
Address: 8 Cambridge Center, Cambridge, MA, 02142

GROWTH PLANS/SPECIAL FEATURES:
Cambridge Technology Partners, Inc. is an international management consulting and systems integration firm that combines Internet solutions, custom and packaged software deployment, network services and training to deliver end-to-end business solutions for Global 1000 organizations worldwide. The company's management consulting and information technology services are offered enterprise-wide. At the beginning of 2000, Cambridge developed a web site for Wal-Mart that incorporated photo-processing services, a travel agency and the ability to create a personal My Wal-Mart page with wish lists and e-mail reminders of birthdays and other important dates. Cambridge worked with over eight technology providers to create this web experience, including Hewlett-Packard and Grey Interactive, to select the proper hardware and software and to create a user-friendly front-end design. Cambridge's customers include Bahamas Ministry of Tourism, British Petroleum, Microsoft Marketing, Cisco, Nasdaq, SwissAir and Lockheed. Recently, Cambridge Technology was named to the FORTUNE e-50 list and was chosen as one of Industry Standard magazine's 100 Most Important Companies in the Internet Economy. The company has more than 4,500 employees and 55 offices worldwide.

FINANCIALS: Sales and profits are in thousands of dollars—add 000 to get the full amount.
Notes regarding 1999: Through 9 months *(1999 sales and profits were not available for all companies at press time.)*

1999 Sales: $483,000	1999 Profits: $19,384	Stock Ticker: **CATP**
1998 Sales: $612,000	1998 Profits: $51,900	Employees: 4,444
1997 Sales: $406,700	1997 Profits: $32,900	Fiscal Year Ends: 12/31
1996 Sales: $236,600	1996 Profits: $21,100	
1995 Sales: $132,400	1995 Profits: $12,700	

SALARIES/BENEFITS:
Pension Plan:	ESOP Stock Plan:	Profit Sharing:	Top Exec. Salary: $575,000	Bonus: $
Savings Plan: Y	Stock Purch. Plan: Y		Second Exec. Salary: $382,250	Bonus: $166,279

COMPETITIVE ADVANTAGE: Comphrensive suite of services.

OTHER THOUGHTS:
Apparent Women Officers or Directors: 1
Apparent Minority Officers or Directors: 1
Hot Spot for Advancement for Women/Minorities: Y

LOCATIONS: ("Y" = Yes)
West:	Southwest:	Midwest:	Southeast:	Northeast:	International:
Y	Y	Y	Y	Y	Y

CAREERBUILDER INC   www.careerbuilder.com

Industry Group Code: 514191
Ranks within this company's industry group: Sales: 19   Profits: 31

BUSINESS ACTIVITIES ("Y" = Yes)

Financial Services:	Information/Publ.:		Technology:	Services:		Retailing:	Telecommunications:
Stock Brokerage	Portal/Hub/News	Y	Computer Manuf.	Payments/Transfers		Retailer	Internet Serv. Provider
Mortgages/Loans	On-Line Community		Networking Equip.	Consulting		Auctions	Web Site Host
Banking	Search Engine		Software Manuf.	Advertising/Marketing		Mall	Server Farm
Insurance	Financial Data Publ.		Specialty Equipment	Outsourcing	Y	Tickets/Travel	Specialty Telecom.
Credit Cards	Broadcasting/Music					Price Comparisons	High Speed Access

TYPES OF BUSINESS:
Portal-Careers

BRANDS/DIVISIONS/AFFILIATES:
Mega Job Search

GROWTH PLANS/SPECIAL FEATURES:

Careerbuilder is the leading provider of targeted interactive recruiting on the Internet. The company has syndicated its technology and content to create a network that includes private-label careers sites for affiliates such as Microsoft Network, Ticketmaster Online-City Search, CNET, Business Week, USA Today, NBC Interactive and Bloomberg. Careerbuilder's Mega Job Search has the capability to provide access to over two million job postings. The web site also allows employers and human resource managers to access a broad reach of qualified candidates. This reduces their costs and allows them to select the individual most tailored to the position. Careerbuilder recently launched its first national branding campaign, which appeared on television, radio, print and Internet media. The company boasts a total of more than one million unique visitors each day. It has experienced rapid growth and rose from the number 10 ranking of career-oriented web sites to the number three ranking over a period of a few months.

CONTACTS: Note: Officers with more than one job title may be intentionally listed here more than once.

Robert J. McGovern, CEO
Robert J. McGovern, Pres.
James A. Tholen, Sr.VP/CFO
Partho Choudhury, VP-Mktg.
James A. Winchester Jr., Sr.VP/Chief Tech. Officer
Pete Kuzma, Network Systems Mgr.
Rich Wathen, Controller
James A. Winchester Jr., Sr.VP-Engineering
James A. Tholen, Corp. Sec.
Julie Chapman, Dir.-Business Dev.
Randy Potts, VP-Sales
Stephen Abel, CareerBuilder.com Product Mgr.

Phone: 703-709-1001	Fax: 703-709-1004
Toll-Free:	
Address: 11495 Sunset Hills Rd.,Ste. 210, Reston, VA, 20190	

FINANCIALS: Sales and profits are in thousands of dollars—add 000 to get the full amount.
Notes regarding 1999: *(1999 sales and profits were not available for all companies at press time.)*

1999 Sales: $14,900	1999 Profits: $-8,619	Stock Ticker: **CBDR**
1998 Sales: $7,000	1998 Profits: $-12,000	Employees: 120
1997 Sales: $1,900	1997 Profits: $-7,300	Fiscal Year Ends: 12/31
1996 Sales: $ 100	1996 Profits: $-2,400	
1995 Sales: $	1995 Profits: $- 100	

SALARIES/BENEFITS:

Pension Plan:	ESOP Stock Plan:	Profit Sharing:	Top Exec. Salary: $145,000	Bonus: $2,902
Savings Plan:	Stock Purch. Plan:		Second Exec. Salary: $130,000	Bonus: $5,804

COMPETITIVE ADVANTAGE: Over 2 million jobs posted.

OTHER THOUGHTS:

Apparent Women Officers or Directors: 5
Apparent Minority Officers or Directors: 2
Hot Spot for Advancement for Women/Minorities: Y

LOCATIONS: ("Y" = Yes)

West:	Southwest:	Midwest:	Southeast:	Northeast:	International:
Y	Y	Y	Y	Y	

CBS ENTERPRISES   www.cbs.com

Industry Group Code: 51312
Ranks within this company's industry group: Sales: 1 Profits: 1

BUSINESS ACTIVITIES ("Y" = Yes)

Financial Services:	Information/Publ.:		Technology:	Services:	Retailing:	Telecommunications:
Stock Brokerage	Portal/Hub/News		Computer Manuf.	Payments/Transfers	Retailer	Internet Serv. Provider
Mortgages/Loans	On-Line Community		Networking Equip.	Consulting	Auctions	Web Site Host
Banking	Search Engine		Software Manuf.	Advertising/Marketing	Mall	Server Farm
Insurance	Financial Data Publ.		Specialty Equipment	Outsourcing	Tickets/Travel	Specialty Telecom.
Credit Cards	Broadcasting/Music	Y			Price Comparisons	High Speed Access

TYPES OF BUSINESS:

Televison and Radio Broadcasting
Cable Progamming
Out-of-home Media

BRANDS/DIVISIONS/AFFILIATES:

CBS Cable Group
CBS Television Networks Group
Infinity Broadcasting Corporation
CBS Television Station Group
TDI-Transportation Displays
CBS Cable
Viacom, Inc.
CBS News Inc.

CONTACTS: *Note: Officers with more than one job title may be intentionally listed here more than once.*

Mel Karmazin, CEO
Mel Karmazin, Pres.
Frederic G. Reynolds, Exec. VP/CFO
David Zemelman, Exec.VP-Human Resources
Robert G. Freedline, VP-Controller
Angeline C. Straka, Corp. Sec.
Louis J. Briskman, Exec.VP/General Counsel
Russ Pillar, Pres./CEO-CBS Internet Group
Gil Schwartz, Sr.VP-Comm.
Chris Ender, Sr.VP-Comm., CBS Entertainment

Phone: 212-975-4321	Fax: 212-975-4516
Toll-Free:	
Address: 51 W. 52nd St., New York, NY, 10019	

GROWTH PLANS/SPECIAL FEATURES:

CBS Enterprises, formerly CBS Corporation, is one of the largest radio and television broadcasters in the United States. The corporation operates its businesses primarily in the U.S. through its Radio and Outdoor Advertising and Television business segments. The Radio segment consists of 160 AM and FM radio stations and the Television segment consists of 14 owned and operated television stations, the television network and the cable business. CBS is most recognized for its long-running programs such as CBS Evening News with Dan Rather, 60 Minutes, Face the Nation, The Late Show with David Letterman and 48 Hours. Recently, CBS took on a new organizational structure for its international distribution operation. The new structure is reflected in CBS's new name and unites King World Productions, Inc., EYEMARK Entertainment and CBS Broadcast International. Also, the shareholders of CBS and Viacom, Inc. recently approved a merger between the two companies. CBS closed a $105 million alliance with Hollywood.com that will span over seven years. The partnership is part of a plan to promote and brand Hollywood.com by applying CBS's advertising strength.

FINANCIALS: Sales and profits are in thousands of dollars—add 000 to get the full amount.

Notes regarding 1999: *(1999 sales and profits were not available for all companies at press time.)*

1999 Sales: $	1999 Profits: $	**Stock Ticker: CBS**
1998 Sales: $5,363,000	1998 Profits: $549,000	Employees: 46,189
1997 Sales: $4,143,000	1997 Profits: $95,000	Fiscal Year Ends: 12/31
1996 Sales: $1,074,000	1996 Profits: $-10,000	
1995 Sales: $	1995 Profits: $	

SALARIES/BENEFITS:

Pension Plan: Y	ESOP Stock Plan:	Profit Sharing:	Top Exec. Salary: $2,500,000	Bonus: $1,500,000
Savings Plan:	Stock Purch. Plan:		Second Exec. Salary: $1,000,000	Bonus: $3,000,000

COMPETITIVE ADVANTAGE: Recently refocused on the broadcasting business.

OTHER THOUGHTS:

Apparent Women Officers or Directors: 1
Apparent Minority Officers or Directors: 1
Hot Spot for Advancement for Women/Minorities:

LOCATIONS: ("Y" = Yes)

West:	Southwest:	Midwest:	Southeast:	Northeast:	International:
Y	Y	Y	Y	Y	Y

CDNOW INC   www.cdnow.com

Industry Group Code: 4541
Ranks within this company's industry group: Sales: 14   Profits: 29

BUSINESS ACTIVITIES ("Y" = Yes)

Financial Services:	Information/Publ.:	Technology:	Services:	Retailing:		Telecommunications:
Stock Brokerage	Portal/Hub/News	Computer Manuf.	Payments/Transfers	Retailer	Y	Internet Serv. Provider
Mortgages/Loans	On-Line Community	Networking Equip.	Consulting	Auctions		Web Site Host
Banking	Search Engine	Software Manuf.	Advertising/Marketing	Mall		Server Farm
Insurance	Financial Data Publ.	Specialty Equipment	Outsourcing	Tickets/Travel		Specialty Telecom.
Credit Cards	Broadcasting/Music			Price Comparisons		High Speed Access

TYPES OF BUSINESS:

Retail-Music
Videos
DVDs
Apparel
Music News/Articles

BRANDS/DIVISIONS/AFFILIATES:

N2K

GROWTH PLANS/SPECIAL FEATURES:

CDnow is a leading on-line retailer of CDs and other music-related products. The company's on-line store, cdnow.com, offers a broad selection, informative content, easy-to-use navigation and search capabilities, a high level of customer service, competitive pricing and personalized merchandising and recommendations. A number of characteristics of on-line music retailing make the sale of pre-recorded music via the Internet particularly attractive relative to traditional retail stores. The Internet offers many data management and multimedia features which enable consumers to listen to sound samples, search for music by genre, title or artist and access a wealth of information and events, including reviews, related articles, music history and news. In addition, the company seeks to enter into strategic alliances with major Internet content and service providers in order to enhance its new customer acquisition efforts, increase purchases by current customers and expand brand recognition. Recently, the company broadened its strategic alliance with Yahoo! to include Yahoo! Mail and Yahoo!'s music chat space. The company has also entered into new strategic alliances with Lycos, Tripod, JAMtv and Straight Arrow Publishers. Recently, the firm merged with Internet giant N2K, doubling CDNOW's overall size and increasing its competitive edge against rival Amazon.com.

CONTACTS: Note: Officers with more than one job title may be intentionally listed here more than once.

Jason Olim, CEO
Jason Olim, Pres.
Joel Sussman, VP/CFO
Rod Parker, Sr. VP-Product Mgmt. and Mktg.
Charlotte Caminos, Sr. VP-Human Resources
Matthew Olim, Tech. Lead
Matthew Olim, Principle Software Engineer
David Capozzi, VP/General Counsel
Steve Dong, VP-Oper.
Robert Salzman, VP-Strategic Business Dev.
Matthew Olim, Treas.
Anthony DeCurtis, Exec. Editor
Robert Salzman, VP-Corp. Sales and Advertising

Phone: 212-378-5555	Fax: 212-742-1755
Toll-Free:	
Address: 55 Broad Street, 26th Fl., New York, NY, 10004	

FINANCIALS: Sales and profits are in thousands of dollars—add 000 to get the full amount.
Notes regarding 1999: *(1999 sales and profits were not available for all companies at press time.)*

1999 Sales: $147,200	1999 Profits: $-119,200	Stock Ticker: **CDNW**
1998 Sales: $56,400	1998 Profits: $-43,800	Employees: 211
1997 Sales: $17,400	1997 Profits: $-10,700	Fiscal Year Ends: 12/31
1996 Sales: $6,300	1996 Profits: $-1,800	
1995 Sales: $2,200	1995 Profits: $- 200	

SALARIES/BENEFITS:

Pension Plan:	ESOP Stock Plan:	Profit Sharing:	Top Exec. Salary: $212,412	Bonus: $55,000
Savings Plan: Y	Stock Purch. Plan:		Second Exec. Salary: $149,327	Bonus: $

COMPETITIVE ADVANTAGE: Best-known CD seller on the Internet/Merged with N2K.

OTHER THOUGHTS:

Apparent Women Officers or Directors:
Apparent Minority Officers or Directors: 1
Hot Spot for Advancement for Women/Minorities: Y

LOCATIONS: ("Y" = Yes)

West:	Southwest:	Midwest:	Southeast:	Northeast:	International:
				Y	

CHARLES SCHWAB CORP (THE)
www.schwab.com

Industry Group Code: 5231
Ranks within this company's industry group: Sales: 2 Profits: 2

BUSINESS ACTIVITIES ("Y" = Yes)

Financial Services:		Information/Publ.:	Technology:	Services:	Retailing:	Telecommunications:
Stock Brokerage	Y	Portal/Hub/News	Computer Manuf.	Payments/Transfers	Retailer	Internet Serv. Provider
Mortgages/Loans		On-Line Community	Networking Equip.	Consulting	Auctions	Web Site Host
Banking		Search Engine	Software Manuf.	Advertising/Marketing	Mall	Server Farm
Insurance		Financial Data Publ.	Specialty Equipment	Outsourcing	Tickets/Travel	Specialty Telecom.
Credit Cards		Broadcasting/Music			Price Comparisons	High Speed Access

TYPES OF BUSINESS:

Stock Brokerage, On-line and Discount
Investment Services
Financial Services
Mutual Funds

BRANDS/DIVISIONS/AFFILIATES:

Charles Schwab & Co.
Charles Schwab Investment Management, Inc.
SchwabFunds
Mayer & Schweitzer, Inc.
TrustMark
Charles Schwab Trust Company
Performance Technologies Inc.

CONTACTS: *Note: Officers with more than one job title may be intentionally listed here more than once.*

Charles R. Schwab, Co-CEO
David S. Pottruck, Pres.
Christopher V. Dodds, CFO
Susanne D. Lyons, Exec. VP-Retail Mktg.
George A. Rich, Exec. VP-Human Resources
Frederick E. Matteson, Exec. VP-Tech. Services
Dawn G. Lepore, CIO
Carrie E. Dwyer, Exec.VP-Corp. Oversight/Gen. Coun.
Wayne W. Fieldsa, Exec.VP-Brokerage Oper.
Daniel O. Leemon, Exec.VP/Chief Stategy Officer
James M. Hackley, Exec.VP-Retail Branch Network

Phone: 415-627-7000	Fax: 415-627-8840
Toll-Free: 800-435-4000	
Address: 101 Montgomery Street, San Francisco, CA, 94104	

GROWTH PLANS/SPECIAL FEATURES:

The Charles Schwab Corporation is primarily a discount brokerage designed for investors who do not want individual advice. In an effort to broaden its service, Schwab recently started offering investors asset allocation advice and now refers clients to independent financial advisors. Schwab has 290 offices in Canada, the Cayman Islands, Hong Kong, Puerto Rico, the UK, the U.S. and the Virgin Islands. Its on-line trading system ranks number one in volume. Its web site accounts for over half of the firm's trades. Schwab OneSource is the company's mutual fund distributor, which sells more than 1,600 mutual funds from about 260 families of funds. The company also offers telephone-based trading, futures and commodities trading, access to initial public offerings and investment educational material. The company established Charles Schwab Canada and started a joint venture in Japan with companies led by Tokyo Marine & Fire Insurance. The company plans to allow customers to trade most NASDAQ and some NYSE listed stocks after-hours. Schwab introduced Velocity, a new trading system, to meet the needs of active investors with $100,000 in household equity, or over 12 commissionable trades per year.

Schwab is one of the most interesting business stories in the nation and one of the most aggressive marketers ever to hit the U.S. business scene. Brokers here will not make as much money as high-commission earners in traditional, full-service firms like Merrill Lynch. Schwab leads the nation in innovative uses of technology to interact with customers. Over the 12 years through the end of 1998, Schwab contributed an average of 8,109 shares of its stock to each of its employees' ESOP plans, worth more than $1 million each. Schwab has made millionaires out of about 2,000 of its employees. The firm is also known for providing employees with massages during busy periods.

FINANCIALS: Sales and profits are in thousands of dollars—add 000 to get the full amount.

Notes regarding 1999: *(1999 sales and profits were not available for all companies at press time.)*

1999 Sales: $3,944,800	1999 Profits: $588,900	Stock Ticker: **SCH**
1998 Sales: $3,388,100	1998 Profits: $348,500	Employees: 13,300
1997 Sales: $2,845,200	1997 Profits: $270,300	Fiscal Year Ends: 12/31
1996 Sales: $2,276,800	1996 Profits: $233,800	
1995 Sales: $1,777,100	1995 Profits: $172,600	

SALARIES/BENEFITS:

Pension Plan:	ESOP Stock Plan: Y	Profit Sharing: Y	Top Exec. Salary: $800,004	Bonus: $6,145,225
Savings Plan: Y	Stock Purch. Plan:		Second Exec. Salary: $800,004	Bonus: $6,145,225

COMPETITIVE ADVANTAGE: Excellent software technology/Well-positioned as the leader in discount brokerage.

OTHER THOUGHTS:

Apparent Women Officers or Directors: 4
Apparent Minority Officers or Directors:
Hot Spot for Advancement for Women/Minorities: Y

LOCATIONS: ("Y" = Yes)

West:	Southwest:	Midwest:	Southeast:	Northeast:	International:
Y	Y	Y	Y	Y	Y

CHEAP TICKETS INC   www.cheaptickets.com

Industry Group Code: 4541
Ranks within this company's industry group: Sales: 8   Profits: 4

BUSINESS ACTIVITIES ("Y" = Yes)

Financial Services:	Information/Publ.:	Technology:	Services:	Retailing:		Telecommunications:
Stock Brokerage	Portal/Hub/News	Computer Manuf.	Payments/Transfers	Retailer	Y	Internet Serv. Provider
Mortgages/Loans	On-Line Community	Networking Equip.	Consulting	Auctions		Web Site Host
Banking	Search Engine	Software Manuf.	Advertising/Marketing	Mall		Server Farm
Insurance	Financial Data Publ.	Specialty Equipment	Outsourcing	Tickets/Travel	Y	Specialty Telecom.
Credit Cards	Broadcasting/Music			Price Comparisons		High Speed Access

TYPES OF BUSINESS:

Retail-On-line Travel

BRANDS/DIVISIONS/AFFILIATES:

GROWTH PLANS/SPECIAL FEATURES:

Cheap Tickets specializes in offering low fare and discount airline tickets via the Internet. The company sells mainly non-published airfares through contracts with more than 25 airline carriers. The tickets are for regularly scheduled flights and domestic and international destinations. Cheap Tickets also offers discounted cruise ship tickets, hotel rooms and auto rental. Cheap Tickets emphasizes that its web site is for serious customers, not casual shoppers, and requires users to complete a standard profile for their records. This enables Cheap Tickets to service the customers quickly, and users do not have to enter their preferences repeatedly. The web site does, however, let non-registered shoppers see some featured special deals in order to preview a few examples of the types of deals that are available. Cheap Tickets recently launched its first sweepstakes, which offered leisure travelers the opportunity to win free plane tickets, hotel accommodations and car rentals.

CONTACTS: Note: Officers with more than one job title may be intentionally listed here more than once.

Michael J. Hartley, CFO
Sam Galeotos, COO/Pres.
Dale K. Jorgenson, CFO/VP-Finance
Lester R. Stiefel, Dir.-Human Resources
Donald K. Klabunde, VP-Systems and Tech.
Ronald L. McElfresh, VP-On-line Services
LaMont C. Brewer, Dir.-Call Centers
Tammy A. Ishibashi, Exec.VP-Ticket Distribution

Phone: 808-945-7439	Fax: 808-946-3844
Toll-Free:	
Address: 1440 Kapiolani Blvd., Honolulu, HI, 96814	

FINANCIALS: Sales and profits are in thousands of dollars—add 000 to get the full amount.

Notes regarding 1999: Through 9 months (1999 sales and profits were not available for all companies at press time.)

1999 Sales: $273,300	1999 Profits: $6,100	Stock Ticker: CTIX
1998 Sales: $171,100	1998 Profits: $1,100	Employees: 590
1997 Sales: $102,800	1997 Profits: $-1,000	Fiscal Year Ends: 12/31
1996 Sales: $64,600	1996 Profits: $ 700	
1995 Sales: $69,100	1995 Profits: $	

SALARIES/BENEFITS:

Pension Plan:	ESOP Stock Plan:	Profit Sharing:	Top Exec. Salary: $243,783	Bonus: $50,000
Savings Plan: Y	Stock Purch. Plan:		Second Exec. Salary: $201,923	Bonus: $

COMPETITIVE ADVANTAGE: Contracts with a long list of major airlines.

OTHER THOUGHTS:

Apparent Women Officers or Directors: 2
Apparent Minority Officers or Directors: 3
Hot Spot for Advancement for Women/Minorities: Y

LOCATIONS: ("Y" = Yes)

West:	Southwest:	Midwest:	Southeast:	Northeast:	International:
Y					

CHECKFREE HOLDINGS CORP   www.checkfree.com

Industry Group Code: 52252A
Ranks within this company's industry group: Sales: 1   Profits: 2

BUSINESS ACTIVITIES ("Y" = Yes)

Financial Services:		Information/Publ.:	Technology:	Services:		Retailing:	Telecommunications:
Stock Brokerage		Portal/Hub/News	Computer Manuf.	Payments/Transfers	Y	Retailer	Internet Serv. Provider
Mortgages/Loans		On-Line Community	Networking Equip.	Consulting		Auctions	Web Site Host
Banking	Y	Search Engine	Software Manuf.	Advertising/Marketing		Mall	Server Farm
Insurance		Financial Data Publ.	Specialty Equipment	Outsourcing		Tickets/Travel	Specialty Telecom.
Credit Cards		Broadcasting/Music				Price Comparisons	High Speed Access

TYPES OF BUSINESS:

Transaction Processing
Electronic Payment Systems and Services

GROWTH PLANS/SPECIAL FEATURES:

CheckFree Holdings Corporation, a Georgia-based company, provides electronic banking, bill payment and presentment and business payment services to some 2.5 million consumers, as well as 23 of the top 25 U.S. banks. CheckFree also produces software for financial applications and provides institutional investment services. Currently, the company provides service for nearly three million consumers through over 350 financial institutions and Internet financial sites like Quicken.com and Managing Your Money. In the late 1990s, CheckFree refocused on providing services to its commercial clients (including Bank One and First Union) and sold its credit card and recovery management operations and the majority of its software business. The company began providing AT&T with on-line billing and payment services. CheckFree also offers software products and services in safe box accounting and compliance with certain IRS regulations.

BRANDS/DIVISIONS/AFFILIATES:

CheckFree Corporation
CheckFree Investment Corporation
RCM Systems, Inc.

CONTACTS: Note: Officers with more than one job title may be intentionally listed here more than once.

Peter J. Kight, CEO
Peter F. Sinisgalli, COO/Pres.
Allen L. Shulman, CFO
Mark A. Johnson, Dir.-Corp. Mktg.
Dean C. Collins, VP-Human Resources
Ravi Ganesan, Exec.VP/Chief Tech. Officer
Stephen Olsen, CIO
Gary A. Luoma Jr., VP/Chief Acc. Officer
Curtis A. Loveland, Sec.
John J. Limbert, Exec.VP/EC Customer Oper.
James S. Douglass, Exec.VP-Corp.Dev.
Terrie O'Hanlon, Sr.VP-Comm. and Media Relations
Tina Moore, Investor Relations Mgr.
Keven M. Madsen, Treas.
Glen Sarvady, VP-Oper. Strategy and Planning

Phone: 770-441-3387	Fax: 770-840-1494
Toll-Free: 800-882-5280	
Address: 4411 East Jones Bridge Road, Norcross, GA, 30092	

FINANCIALS: Sales and profits are in thousands of dollars—add 000 to get the full amount.
Notes regarding 1999: (1999 sales and profits were not available for all companies at press time.)

1999 Sales: $250,100	1999 Profits: $10,500	Stock Ticker: CKFR
1998 Sales: $233,864	1998 Profits: $-3,703	Employees: 1,850
1997 Sales: $176,445	1997 Profits: $-161,813	Fiscal Year Ends: 6/30
1996 Sales: $51,040	1996 Profits: $-138,567	
1995 Sales: $49,330	1995 Profits: $- 215	

SALARIES/BENEFITS:

Pension Plan: Y	ESOP Stock Plan:	Profit Sharing:	Top Exec. Salary: $375,000	Bonus: $182,813
Savings Plan: Y	Stock Purch. Plan:		Second Exec. Salary: $260,417	Bonus: $103,125

COMPETITIVE ADVANTAGE: Experiencing tremendous growth/Continues to introduce new products for electronic commerce.

OTHER THOUGHTS:

Apparent Women Officers or Directors: 1
Apparent Minority Officers or Directors: 1
Hot Spot for Advancement for Women/Minorities:

LOCATIONS: ("Y" = Yes)

West:	Southwest:	Midwest:	Southeast:	Northeast:	International:
Y	Y	Y	Y	Y	

Note: Financial information, benefits and other data can change quickly and may vary from those stated here.

CHEMDEX CORPORATION

www.chemdex.com

Industry Group Code: 51339A
Ranks within this company's industry group: Sales: 15   Profits: 7

BUSINESS ACTIVITIES ("Y" = Yes)

Financial Services:	Information/Publ.:		Technology:	Services:		Retailing:	Telecommunications:
Stock Brokerage	Portal/Hub/News	Y	Computer Manuf.	Payments/Transfers		Retailer	Internet Serv. Provider
Mortgages/Loans	On-Line Community		Networking Equip.	Consulting		Auctions	Web Site Host
Banking	Search Engine		Software Manuf.	Advertising/Marketing		Mall	Server Farm
Insurance	Financial Data Publ.		Specialty Equipment	Outsourcing	Y	Tickets/Travel	Specialty Telecom.
Credit Cards	Broadcasting/Music					Price Comparisons	High Speed Access

TYPES OF BUSINESS:

Portal-Life Science
ASP-Ordering and Purchasing

BRANDS/DIVISIONS/AFFILIATES:

LabPoint

CONTACTS: Note: Officers with more than one job title may be intentionally listed here more than once.

David P. Perry, CEO/Pres.
Robin Abrams, COO
James G. Stewart, CFO
Martha D. Greer, VP-Mktg.
Michael Assad, VP-Human Resources
Jeff Leane, Chief Tech. Officer
Pierre V. Samec, CIO
Thomas P. Kudrycki, VP-Engineering
Derek McCall, VP-Special Projects
Robert W. Perreault, VP-Professional Services

Phone: 650-813-0300	Fax: 650-813-0304
Toll-Free:	
Address: 3950 Fabian Way, Palo Alto, CA, 94303	

GROWTH PLANS/SPECIAL FEATURES:

Chemdex Corporation is a leading provider of business-to-business e-commerce solutions for the life sciences industry. Chemdex brings researchers and suppliers together to efficiently buy and sell products. This allows businesses to reduce costs and streamline enterprise procurement processes. Chemdex's web site gives users the ability to customize their ordering process by using its configuration and customization services. Customers also receive the help and advice of an account development team to facilitate the adoption and streamlining of day-to-day ordering. The company markets its products principally to commercial and academic research institutions and programs such as Genentech, Harvard University, University of Illinois and Elan. Chemdex offers approximately 240,000 products from 100 different suppliers and plans to expand its catalogue, through a deal with VWR Scientific Products, to over one million products. The company launched an e-commerce solution called LabPoint that combines Chemdex's e-commerce expertise and technology with the robust distribution services of VWR. Recently, Roche Molecular Systems, one of the world's leading research-oriented healthcare groups in pharmaceuticals, diagnostics, vitamins, fragrances and flavors, chose the LabPoint solution as its supplier of products and services.

FINANCIALS: Sales and profits are in thousands of dollars—add 000 to get the full amount.

Notes regarding 1999: Through 9 months *(1999 sales and profits were not available for all companies at press time.)*

1999 Sales: $11,600	1999 Profits: $-33,300	Stock Ticker: **CMDX**
1998 Sales: $ 100	1998 Profits: $-8,500	Employees: 87
1997 Sales: $	1997 Profits: $- 400	Fiscal Year Ends: 12/31
1996 Sales: $	1996 Profits: $	
1995 Sales: $	1995 Profits: $	

SALARIES/BENEFITS:

Pension Plan:	ESOP Stock Plan: Y	Profit Sharing:	Top Exec. Salary: $150,070	Bonus: $27,237
Savings Plan:	Stock Purch. Plan:		Second Exec. Salary: $98,375	Bonus: $20,000

COMPETITIVE ADVANTAGE: Growing list of major clients.

OTHER THOUGHTS:

Apparent Women Officers or Directors: 1
Apparent Minority Officers or Directors:
Hot Spot for Advancement for Women/Minorities:

LOCATIONS: ("Y" = Yes)

West:	Southwest:	Midwest:	Southeast:	Northeast:	International:
Y					

CHINADOTCOM CORP   www.corp.china.com

Industry Group Code: 514191
Ranks within this company's industry group: Sales: 28   Profits: 30

BUSINESS ACTIVITIES ("Y" = Yes)

Financial Services:	Information/Publ.:		Technology:	Services:	Retailing:	Telecommunications:
Stock Brokerage	Portal/Hub/News	Y	Computer Manuf.	Payments/Transfers	Retailer	Internet Serv. Provider
Mortgages/Loans	On-Line Community		Networking Equip.	Consulting	Auctions	Web Site Host
Banking	Search Engine		Software Manuf.	Advertising/Marketing	Mall	Server Farm
Insurance	Financial Data Publ.		Specialty Equipment	Outsourcing	Tickets/Travel	Specialty Telecom.
Credit Cards	Broadcasting/Music				Price Comparisons	High Speed Access

TYPES OF BUSINESS:

Portal-Chinese Language

BRANDS/DIVISIONS/AFFILIATES:

taiwan.com
hongkong.com
cww.com
AOL Hong Kong
24/7 Media
The Web Connection

GROWTH PLANS/SPECIAL FEATURES:

China.com Corporation operates a web portal with four sites: china.com, taiwan.com, hongkong.com and cww.com. Chinese and English-language news and business information is offered on the company's sites as well as e-mail services, city guides and chat rooms. China.com currently boasts nearly two million registered users. The company originated as a spin-off of China Internet, set up by Xinhua, China's official news agency. China.com operates America Online's AOL Hong Kong for the United States-based giant. Additionally, the company owns the majority of Yes!Net, a Taiwanese Internet firm, provides Internet advertising services with 24/7 media and Internet consulting through The Web Connection.

CONTACTS: Note: Officers with more than one job title may be intentionally listed here more than once.

Peter Yip, CEO
Peter Hamilton, COO
Peter Hamilton, Interim CFO
Vicky Hung, Sr. VP-Mktg./Product Dev.
Aaron Cheung, Dir.-Network Tech.
Sammy Cheng, Group Financial Controller
Ian Henry, SVP-Strategy
Chueng Fai, Dir.-Web Publishing
Stephen McKay, Dir.-Web Solutions
Tanbir Rahman, Dir.-Software Tech.

Phone: +852-2691-2776	Fax: +852-2893-5245
Toll-Free:	
Address: 20/F Citicorp Centre,18 Whitfield Rd., Causeway Bay, Hong Kong,	

FINANCIALS: Sales and profits are in thousands of dollars—add 000 to get the full amount.

Notes regarding 1999: *(1999 sales and profits were not available for all companies at press time.)*

1999 Sales: $	1999 Profits: $	Stock Ticker: **CHINA**
1998 Sales: $3,500	1998 Profits: $-11,000	Employees: 285
1997 Sales: $ 500	1997 Profits: $-3,100	Fiscal Year Ends: 12/31
1996 Sales: $	1996 Profits: $	
1995 Sales: $	1995 Profits: $	

SALARIES/BENEFITS:

Pension Plan:	ESOP Stock Plan:	Profit Sharing:	Top Exec. Salary: $	Bonus: $
Savings Plan:	Stock Purch. Plan:		Second Exec. Salary: $	Bonus: $

COMPETITIVE ADVANTAGE: Internet use in China will grow at a soaring rate.

OTHER THOUGHTS:

Apparent Women Officers or Directors: 1
Apparent Minority Officers or Directors:
Hot Spot for Advancement for Women/Minorities:

LOCATIONS: ("Y" = Yes)

West:	Southwest:	Midwest:	Southeast:	Northeast:	International: Y

CISCO SYSTEMS INC　　www.cisco.com

Industry Group Code: 3341C
Ranks within this company's industry group: Sales: 1　Profits: 1

BUSINESS ACTIVITIES ("Y" = Yes)

Financial Services:	Information/Publ.:	Technology:		Services:	Retailing:	Telecommunications:
Stock Brokerage	Portal/Hub/News	Computer Manuf.		Payments/Transfers	Retailer	Internet Serv. Provider
Mortgages/Loans	On-Line Community	Networking Equip.	Y	Consulting	Auctions	Web Site Host
Banking	Search Engine	Software Manuf.	Y	Advertising/Marketing	Mall	Server Farm
Insurance	Financial Data Publ.	Specialty Equipment		Outsourcing	Tickets/Travel	Specialty Telecom.
Credit Cards	Broadcasting/Music				Price Comparisons	High Speed Access

TYPES OF BUSINESS:

Computer Networking Equipment
Backbone Routers
ATM and IP Switches
Access Routers
Adapters and Hubs
Router Management Software

BRANDS/DIVISIONS/AFFILIATES:

Cerent
Internet Commerce Solution
Catalyst LAN switch
ATM HyperSwitch
CLASS Data Systems
Cisco Service Management
NetSpeed, Inc.
Crescendo Communications, Inc.

CONTACTS: Note: Officers with more than one job title may be intentionally listed here more than once.

John T. Chambers, CEO
John T. Chambers, Pres.
Larry R. Carter, CFO/Sr.VP-Finance
Barbara Beck, Sr.VP-Human Resources
Judith Estrin, Sr.VP/Chief Tech. Officer
Carl Redfield, VP-Mfg.
Larry R. Carter, Sr.VP/Sec.
Larry R. Carter, Sr.VP-Finance and Admin.
Michelangelo Volpi, Sr.VP-Business Dev.
Edward R. Kozel, Sr.VP-Corp. Dev.
Gary J. Daichendt, Exec.VP-Worlwide Oper.

Phone: 408-526-4000	**Fax:** 408-526-4100
Toll-Free: 800-553-6387	
Address: 170 West Tasman Drive, San Jose, CA, 95134-1706	

GROWTH PLANS/SPECIAL FEATURES:

Cisco Systems Inc. was incorporated in California in December 1984 and is currently headquartered in San Jose. Cisco's products comprise the broadest range of networking solutions available from any single supplier. These solutions include routers, LAN and WAN switches, dial and other access solutions, SNA-to-LAN integration solutions, web site management tools, Internet appliances and network management software. These products, integrated by the Cisco IOS software, link geographically dispersed LANs, WANs and IBM networks, thus providing easy access to information without regard to differences in time, place or type of computer system. The company markets its products through its direct sales force, distributors, re-sellers, service providers and system integrators, thus covering a broad range of worldwide markets. Cisco Systems, Inc. recently announced that Pacific Gateway's wholly owned IP subsidiary, Onyx Networks, Inc., is teaming with Cisco to provide leading IP data services world-wide as a Cisco Powered Network (CPN). The company also announced that it will co-develop technologies with Citrix Systems, Inc. as part of the Cisco Hosted Applications Initiative to better address the needs of Application Service Providers (ASPs). The company also acquired privately-held Cerent, a leading developer of next-generation optical transport products.

Of the company's officials and managers, 21.2% are minorities, and 35.7% of the employees in the work force are minorities. The company offers flexible spending accounts, training courses, an on-site carwash, a Fitness Center and an Employee Assistance Program. Recently, the average gain on stock options for non-executives was calcualted to be $150,000. The company generally trains its employees for 80 hours out of the year, and added nearly 5,000 new employees in 1999. Cisco offers stock options to all of its employees, and has been known to grant on-the-spot bonuses of up to $2,000 for exceptional performance.

FINANCIALS: Sales and profits are in thousands of dollars—add 000 to get the full amount.

Notes regarding 1999: *(1999 sales and profits were not available for all companies at press time.)*

1999 Sales: $12,154,000	1999 Profits: $2,096,000	Stock Ticker: **CSCO**
1998 Sales: $8,458,800	1998 Profits: $1,350,100	Employees: 21,000
1997 Sales: $6,440,200	1997 Profits: $1,048,700	Fiscal Year Ends: 7/31
1996 Sales: $4,096,000	1996 Profits: $913,300	
1995 Sales: $1,978,900	1995 Profits: $421,000	

SALARIES/BENEFITS:

Pension Plan:	ESOP Stock Plan:	Profit Sharing:	Top Exec. Salary: $285,622	Bonus: $604,895
Savings Plan: Y	Stock Purch. Plan: Y		Second Exec. Salary: $326,439	Bonus: $555,152

COMPETITIVE ADVANTAGE: Broadened product offering to be able to include a complete enterprise solution from a single vendor/Focus on expertise in Internet Protocol (IP) switches.

OTHER THOUGHTS:

Apparent Women Officers or Directors: 1
Apparent Minority Officers or Directors: 3
Hot Spot for Advancement for Women/Minorities: Y

LOCATIONS: ("Y" = Yes)

West:	Southwest:	Midwest:	Southeast:	Northeast:	International:
Y	Y	Y	Y	Y	Y

Note: Financial information, benefits and other data can change quickly and may vary from those stated here.

CITRIX SYSTEMS INC   www.citrix.com

Industry Group Code: 5112
Ranks within this company's industry group: Sales: 5   Profits: 3

BUSINESS ACTIVITIES ("Y" = Yes)

Financial Services:	Information/Publ.:	Technology:		Services:	Retailing:	Telecommunications:
Stock Brokerage	Portal/Hub/News	Computer Manuf.		Payments/Transfers	Retailer	Internet Serv. Provider
Mortgages/Loans	On-Line Community	Networking Equip.		Consulting	Auctions	Web Site Host
Banking	Search Engine	Software Manuf.	Y	Advertising/Marketing	Mall	Server Farm
Insurance	Financial Data Publ.	Specialty Equipment		Outsourcing	Tickets/Travel	Specialty Telecom.
Credit Cards	Broadcasting/Music				Price Comparisons	High Speed Access

TYPES OF BUSINESS:
Software-Application Server

BRANDS/DIVISIONS/AFFILIATES:
Digital Independence
MetaFrame
Independent Computing Architecture

CONTACTS: *Note: Officers with more than one job title may be intentionally listed here more than once.*
Mark B. Templeton, CEO
Mark B. Templeton, Pres.
James J. Felcyn, CFO/VP-Finance and Admin.
Douglas Wheeler, Sr. VP-Mktg.
Leslie Pendergrast, VP-Human Resources
Edward E. Iacobucci, Chief Tech. Off./VP-Strategy & Tech.
Marc-Andre Boisseau, Controller/Principal Acct Officer
Bruce C. Chittenden, VP-Engineering
Daniel P. Roy, Sec.
Daniel P. Roy, General Counsel
Chris Phoenix, VP-Citrix iBusiness Unit
Michael Wendl, Managing Dir.-Europe, Middle East, Africa
Michael F. Passaro, VP-Worldwide Sales

Phone: 954-267-3000	Fax: 954-267-9319
Toll-Free:	
Address: 6400 NW 6th Way, Fort Lauderdale, FL, 33309	

GROWTH PLANS/SPECIAL FEATURES:

Citrix Systems, Inc. is an application-server software and services company. Citrix System's Digital Independence product allows organizations to run applications on servers that can be accessed from a variety of client devices. The company's products also include MetaFrame software and Independent Computing Architecture. The applications are installed and updated on servers instead of on each client, so local and remote users can access the latest applications over the Internet. This reduces the complexity, time and resources required to manage the applications. Citrix has more than 100,000 customers worldwide, including 99 of the Fortune 100 firms. Citrix Systems was recently included in the Standard & Poor's 500 Index. Citrix's achievements, which have been honored by publications, analyst organizations and the financial community, include financial success, rapid growth, leadership in the web arena and product excellence. Fortune magazine ranked Citrix in the top five fastest growing companies and included the company in the magazine's inaugural e-50 index, which tracks the impact of the Internet on the global economy. Business Week Magazine named Citrix a Hot Growth Company and Inter@ctive Week Magazine placed Citrix in the Fast 50 ranking.

FINANCIALS: Sales and profits are in thousands of dollars—add 000 to get the full amount.
Notes regarding 1999: *(1999 sales and profits were not available for all companies at press time.)*

1999 Sales: $403,000	1999 Profits: $116,900	Stock Ticker: **CTXS**
1998 Sales: $248,600	1998 Profits: $61,100	Employees: 620
1997 Sales: $123,900	1997 Profits: $41,400	Fiscal Year Ends: 12/31
1996 Sales: $44,500	1996 Profits: $18,700	
1995 Sales: $14,600	1995 Profits: $1,900	

SALARIES/BENEFITS:

Pension Plan:	ESOP Stock Plan: Y	Profit Sharing:	Top Exec. Salary: $230,000	Bonus: $154,590
Savings Plan:	Stock Purch. Plan:		Second Exec. Salary: $205,000	Bonus: $137,128

COMPETITIVE ADVANTAGE: Very rapid growth/Focus on products that serve Internet firms.

OTHER THOUGHTS:

Apparent Women Officers or Directors:
Apparent Minority Officers or Directors: 2
Hot Spot for Advancement for Women/Minorities: Y

LOCATIONS: ("Y" = Yes)

West:	Southwest:	Midwest:	Southeast:	Northeast:	International:
			Y		

Note: Financial information, benefits and other data can change quickly and may vary from those stated here.

CLAIMSNET.COM INC   www.claimsnet.com

Industry Group Code: 52252A
Ranks within this company's industry group: Sales: 4   Profits: 3

BUSINESS ACTIVITIES ("Y" = Yes)

Financial Services:	Information/Publ.:	Technology:	Services:		Retailing:	Telecommunications:
Stock Brokerage	Portal/Hub/News	Computer Manuf.	Payments/Transfers	Y	Retailer	Internet Serv. Provider
Mortgages/Loans	On-Line Community	Networking Equip.	Consulting		Auctions	Web Site Host
Banking	Search Engine	Software Manuf.	Advertising/Marketing		Mall	Server Farm
Insurance	Financial Data Publ.	Specialty Equipment	Outsourcing	Y	Tickets/Travel	Specialty Telecom.
Credit Cards	Broadcasting/Music				Price Comparisons	High Speed Access

TYPES OF BUSINESS:

Financial Services Outsourcing-On-line Claims Filing System
ASP

BRANDS/DIVISIONS/AFFILIATES:

Claims.now

CONTACTS: *Note: Officers with more than one job title may be intentionally listed here more than once.*

Bo W. Lycke, CEO
Bo W. Lycke, Pres.
Paul W. Miller, VP/CFO
Terry A. Lee, Exec.VP-Mktg. And Tech.
Randall S. Lindner, VP-Tech.
Abbas R. Kafi, VP-Info. Systems
C. Kelly Campbell, VP-Corp. Controller
C. Kelly Campbell, VP/Sec.
Cheryl L. Corless, VP-Customer Oper.
Ward L. Bensen, Treas.
William C. Guynup, VP-Sales and Mktg.

Phone: 972-458-1701	Fax: 972-458-1737
Toll-Free:	
Address: 12801 N. Central Expwy., Dallas, TX, 75243	

GROWTH PLANS/SPECIAL FEATURES:

Claimsnet.com is a leading applications services provider for electronic healthcare transaction processing for physicians and dentists. Claimsnet greatly reduces healthcare provider costs by as much as 90% by enabling medical offices to make insurance claims and post transactions via the Internet without any special software or networking. Customers can use their Internet browsers to access Claims.now on the company's web site where they can enter, edit and process claims. Users may also send out statements and provide patient eligibility and referrals via the Internet. Claimsnet recently announced a three-year master licensing agreement with McKessonHBOC, Inc., a leading provider of information technology services for the world healthcare market. The new agreement will integrate Claimsnet's claims processing technology with McKessonHBOC's e-commerce solutions. Claimsnet also recently began offering transaction-processing advice for physicians through its web site. Another new addition to the web site is a section entitled Officestaff.com, which is a web-based practice management system and communication tool for physicians, their staffs and patients. Also, Claimsnet entered into an agreement with Physicians Online, Inc. (POL), a leading Internet service for physicians, in which Claimsnet's services will be made directly available to physicians and their administrative staff on the POL network. Over 200,000 registered physicians use the POL network.

FINANCIALS: Sales and profits are in thousands of dollars—add 000 to get the full amount.

Notes regarding 1999: *(1999 sales and profits were not available for all companies at press time.)*

1999 Sales: $ 213	1999 Profits: $-6,469	Stock Ticker: **CLAI**
1998 Sales: $ 200	1998 Profits: $-4,700	Employees: 45
1997 Sales: $ 100	1997 Profits: $-2,800	Fiscal Year Ends: 12/31
1996 Sales: $	1996 Profits: $- 300	
1995 Sales: $	1995 Profits: $	

SALARIES/BENEFITS:

Pension Plan:	ESOP Stock Plan:	Profit Sharing:	Top Exec. Salary: $125,000	Bonus: $
Savings Plan:	Stock Purch. Plan:		Second Exec. Salary: $108,333	Bonus: $

COMPETITIVE ADVANTAGE: The company is gaining rapid growth in distribution through alliances with physician-focused portals.

OTHER THOUGHTS:

Apparent Women Officers or Directors: 1
Apparent Minority Officers or Directors: 1
Hot Spot for Advancement for Women/Minorities:

LOCATIONS: ("Y" = Yes)

West:	Southwest:	Midwest:	Southeast:	Northeast:	International:
	Y				

CLARENT CORP   www.clarent.com

Industry Group Code: 5133D
Ranks within this company's industry group: Sales: 2 Profits: 3

BUSINESS ACTIVITIES ("Y" = Yes)

Financial Services:	Information/Publ.:	Technology:	Services:		Retailing:	Telecommunications:	
Stock Brokerage	Portal/Hub/News	Computer Manuf.	Payments/Transfers		Retailer	Internet Serv. Provider	
Mortgages/Loans	On-Line Community	Networking Equip.	Consulting	Y	Auctions	Web Site Host	
Banking	Search Engine	Software Manuf.	Advertising/Marketing		Mall	Server Farm	
Insurance	Financial Data Publ.	Specialty Equipment	Outsourcing		Tickets/Travel	Specialty Telecom.	Y
Credit Cards	Broadcasting/Music				Price Comparisons	High Speed Access	

TYPES OF BUSINESS:

Internet-based Telephony
Training
Consulting

BRANDS/DIVISIONS/AFFILIATES:

ClarentONE

GROWTH PLANS/SPECIAL FEATURES:

Clarent engages in designing Internet-based telephony systems that transfer data, faxes and voice. It is a leading IP telephony technology supplier to mainstream service providers and carriers. Clarent has provided services for 30 of the world's largest long distance carriers; its customers include highly notable names such as AT&T, Sprint, Telia, KDD and Korea Telecom. Clarent has a wide array of services, including Clarent 3.0, Clarent Gateway, ODBC Relational Database, Clarent Connect and Clarent Roaming Server. Clarent also has a university that offers a variety of classes for engineers and administrators that give them technical training experience. Certified instructors who have in-depth expertise teach students how to tailor Clarent products to meet requirements for business needs. Recently, Clarent announced the release of a new product called ClarentONE (Open Network Environment). ClarentONE is designed to provide a standards-based multiprotocol service management and delivery platform for large-scale carrier networks.

CONTACTS: Note: Officers with more than one job title may be intentionally listed here more than once.

Jerry Shaw-Yau Chang, Pres./CEO
Richard J. Heaps, COO
Richard J. Heaps, CFO
Toma Kershaw, VP-Mktg. and Product Strategy
Joanne Webster, VP-Human Resources
Michael F. Vargo, Sr.VP-Chief Tech. Officer
Albert Mu, VP-Engineering
Ricahrd J. Heaps, Corp. Sec.
Richard J. Heaps, General Counsel
Heidi H. Bersin, Sr.VP-Corp. Mktg.and Comm.
Daniel Fung, VP-Professional Services
Mark E. McIlvane, Sr.VP-Worldwide Sales

Phone: 650-306-7511	Fax: 650-306-7512
Toll-Free:	
Address: 700 Chesapeake Dr., Redwood City, CA, 94063	

FINANCIALS: Sales and profits are in thousands of dollars—add 000 to get the full amount.

Notes regarding 1999: (1999 sales and profits were not available for all companies at press time.)

1999 Sales: $47,800	1999 Profits: $-30,800	Stock Ticker: **CLRN**
1998 Sales: $14,600	1998 Profits: $-5,800	Employees: 155
1997 Sales: $3,400	1997 Profits: $-2,100	Fiscal Year Ends: 12/31
1996 Sales: $	1996 Profits: $- 300	
1995 Sales: $	1995 Profits: $	

SALARIES/BENEFITS:

Pension Plan:	ESOP Stock Plan:	Profit Sharing:	Top Exec. Salary: $202,717	Bonus: $20,000
Savings Plan: Y	Stock Purch. Plan:		Second Exec. Salary: $131,875	Bonus: $7,500

COMPETITIVE ADVANTAGE: Exceptional growth/Global client base.

OTHER THOUGHTS:

Apparent Women Officers or Directors: 1
Apparent Minority Officers or Directors: 4
Hot Spot for Advancement for Women/Minorities: Y

LOCATIONS: ("Y" = Yes)

West:	Southwest:	Midwest:	Southeast:	Northeast:	International:
Y		Y			Y

CMGI INC   www.cmgi.com

Industry Group Code: 5511
Ranks within this company's industry group: Sales: 1   Profits: 1

BUSINESS ACTIVITIES ("Y" = Yes)

Financial Services:	Information/Publ.:	Technology:	Services:		Retailing:	Telecommunications:
Stock Brokerage	Portal/Hub/News	Computer Manuf.	Payments/Transfers		Retailer	Internet Serv. Provider
Mortgages/Loans	On-Line Community	Networking Equip.	Consulting	Y	Auctions	Web Site Host
Banking	Search Engine	Software Manuf.	Advertising/Marketing	Y	Mall	Server Farm
Insurance	Financial Data Publ.	Specialty Equipment	Outsourcing		Tickets/Travel	Specialty Telecom.
Credit Cards	Broadcasting/Music				Price Comparisons	High Speed Access

TYPES OF BUSINESS:

Investing-Internet Companies
Venture Capital

BRANDS/DIVISIONS/AFFILIATES:

@Ventures
AdSmart
AltaVista
iCast
MyWay.com
NaviNet
NaviSite
Engage Technologies

CONTACTS: *Note: Officers with more than one job title may be intentionally listed here more than once.*

David S. Wetherell, CEO
David S. Wetherell, Pres.
Andrew J. Hajducky III, Exec.VP/CFO
William White, Pres.-Mktg.
Susan E. Priestley, VP-Human Resources
David Andonian, Pres.-Corp. Dev.
William J. Hawkins, Pres.-Internet Tech.
William White, Exec.VP-Corp. Comm.
Andrew J. Hajducky III, Treas.
Hans Hawrysz, Exec.VP-Corp. Strategy
Robert Alperin, Sr.VP-Business Dev. And Integration

Phone: 978-684-3600	Fax: 978-684-3814
Toll-Free: 888-622-2244	
Address: 100 Brickstone Sq., Andover, MA, 01810	

GROWTH PLANS/SPECIAL FEATURES:

CMGI, Inc. represents the largest and most diverse network of Internet companies in the world. CMGI has a collection of over 50 operating companiesas well as companies with which it owns a majority interest. Some of its operating companies include Adsmart, AltaVista, iCAST, MyWay.com, NaviNet and NaviSite. CMGI also works with @Ventures, a private venture capital firm that takes strategic positions in potentially synergistic Internet companies. @Ventures has funded companies such as Buyingedge.com, CarParts.com, Chemdex, FindLaw, Furniture.com, GeoCities, Raging Bull and a long list of other firms. MyWay.com moved its entire affiliate network, including 800 local and national Internet service providers, to its personalized platform. MyWay.com provides Internet service providers, enterprises and affinity groups with customized co-branded start pages. CMGI has acquired Flycast Communications Corporation, AdKnowledge, AdForce, Signatures Network and 1stUp.com. Recently, the company announced $4 billion in acquisitions and 15 venture investments. CMGI also announced the launch of the CMGI @Ventures B2B Fund, a new venture that is focused on business-to-business Internet capital investments. CMGI expects the fund to reach up to one billion dollars.

FINANCIALS: Sales and profits are in thousands of dollars—add 000 to get the full amount.
Notes regarding 1999: *(1999 sales and profits were not available for all companies at press time.)*

1999 Sales: $175,700	1999 Profits: $476,200	Stock Ticker: **CMGI**
1998 Sales: $91,500	1998 Profits: $16,600	Employees: 1,594
1997 Sales: $70,600	1997 Profits: $-22,000	Fiscal Year Ends: 7/31
1996 Sales: $28,500	1996 Profits: $14,300	
1995 Sales: $11,200	1995 Profits: $27,200	

SALARIES/BENEFITS:

Pension Plan:	ESOP Stock Plan:	Profit Sharing:	Top Exec. Salary: $180,250	Bonus: $75,000
Savings Plan:	Stock Purch. Plan:		Second Exec. Salary: $154,976	Bonus: $50,000

COMPETITIVE ADVANTAGE: One of the most successful investment groups in the Internet field.

OTHER THOUGHTS:

Apparent Women Officers or Directors: 2
Apparent Minority Officers or Directors: 2
Hot Spot for Advancement for Women/Minorities: Y

LOCATIONS: ("Y" = Yes)

West:	Southwest:	Midwest:	Southeast:	Northeast:	International:
Y		Y	Y	Y	

CNET INC   www.cnet.com

Industry Group Code: 51311B
Ranks within this company's industry group: Sales: 2   Profits: 1

BUSINESS ACTIVITIES ("Y" = Yes)

Financial Services:	Information/Publ.:		Technology:	Services:	Retailing:	Telecommunications:	
Stock Brokerage	Portal/Hub/News	Y	Computer Manuf.	Payments/Transfers	Retailer	Internet Serv. Provider	
Mortgages/Loans	On-Line Community		Networking Equip.	Consulting	Auctions	Web Site Host	
Banking	Search Engine	Y	Software Manuf.	Advertising/Marketing	Mall	Server Farm	
Insurance	Financial Data Publ.		Specialty Equipment	Outsourcing	Tickets/Travel	Specialty Telecom.	Y
Credit Cards	Broadcasting/Music	Y			Price Comparisons	High Speed Access	

TYPES OF BUSINESS:

On-line Media Broadcasting
Internet Television Programming

BRANDS/DIVISIONS/AFFILIATES:

Builder.com
Snap.com
Computers.com
Gamecenter.com
Download.com
SavvySearch.com
Shopper.com
NBC Interactive

CONTACTS: *Note: Officers with more than one job title may be intentionally listed here more than once.*

Halsey M. Minor, CEO
Richard J. Marino, Pres.
Douglas N. Woodrum, Exec.VP/CFO
Annie Williams, Sr.VP-Mktg.
Heather McGaughy, VP-Human Resources
Ted Cahall, CIO
Tom Melcher, Exec.VP-Strategic Dev.
Matthew Barzun, Sr.VP-CNET On-line
Karen Wood, VP-Public Relations
Robin P. Wolaner, Exec.VP-CNET On-line
Cotton Coulson, VP/Exec. Producer

Phone: 415-395-7800	Fax: 415-395-9205
Toll-Free:	
Address: 150 Chestnut Street, San Francisco, CA, 94111	

GROWTH PLANS/SPECIAL FEATURES:

CNET, Inc. is a leading media company that produces a branded Internet network and television programming for both targeted and general audiences. On-line and on television, CNET is one of the leading authorities on computers, the Internet and digital technologies. The company's television programming airs on CNBC, USA Network, the Sci-Fi Channel and in national syndication, as well as in 61 foreign countries. CNET, in conjunction with NBC, is also the publisher of Snap.com, the free Internet directory, search and navigation service that offers a powerful way to find anything on the Internet. CNET currently has investments in cash and marketable securities that are valued at over $700 million, including its 13% stake in NBC Interactive. The company uses editorial, technical, product database and programming expertise to engage consumers and attract advertisers. Recently, CNET acquired SavvySearch Limited, a leading provider of metasearch technology in a combination of cash and stock totaling $22 million. SavvySearch will be incorporated into the CNET network, with the objective of bringing CNET users access to more comprehensive product information and tech-focused resources from around the Web.

FINANCIALS: Sales and profits are in thousands of dollars—add 000 to get the full amount.

Notes regarding 1999: Through 9 months *(1999 sales and profits were not available for all companies at press time.)*

1999 Sales: $74,036	1999 Profits: $60,334	Stock Ticker: **CNET**
1998 Sales: $56,400	1998 Profits: $2,600	Employees: 491
1997 Sales: $33,600	1997 Profits: $-24,700	Fiscal Year Ends: 12/31
1996 Sales: $14,800	1996 Profits: $-16,900	
1995 Sales: $3,500	1995 Profits: $-8,600	

SALARIES/BENEFITS:

Pension Plan:	ESOP Stock Plan: Y	Profit Sharing:	Top Exec. Salary: $194,000	Bonus: $
Savings Plan: Y	Stock Purch. Plan:		Second Exec. Salary: $160,000	Bonus: $

COMPETITIVE ADVANTAGE: Growing list of Internet investments.

OTHER THOUGHTS:

Apparent Women Officers or Directors:	
Apparent Minority Officers or Directors:	
Hot Spot for Advancement for Women/Minorities:	

LOCATIONS: ("Y" = Yes)

West:	Southwest:	Midwest:	Southeast:	Northeast:	International:
Y		Y		Y	

COBALT GROUP (THE)
www.cobaltgroup.com

Industry Group Code: 54189A
Ranks within this company's industry group: Sales: 12   Profits: 8

BUSINESS ACTIVITIES ("Y" = Yes)

Financial Services:	Information/Publ.:	Technology:	Services:		Retailing:	Telecommunications:
Stock Brokerage	Portal/Hub/News	Computer Manuf.	Payments/Transfers		Retailer	Internet Serv. Provider
Mortgages/Loans	On-Line Community	Networking Equip.	Consulting	Y	Auctions	Web Site Host
Banking	Search Engine	Software Manuf.	Advertising/Marketing	Y	Mall	Server Farm
Insurance	Financial Data Publ.	Specialty Equipment	Outsourcing	Y	Tickets/Travel	Specialty Telecom.
Credit Cards	Broadcasting/Music				Price Comparisons	High Speed Access

TYPES OF BUSINESS:

Internet Advertising-Autmotive Dealerships & Manufacturers

BRANDS/DIVISIONS/AFFILIATES:

Finance Solution 2-1-1
AutoVantage.com
Dealernet
PartsVoice

CONTACTS: *Note: Officers with more than one job title may be intentionally listed here more than once.*

Geoffrey T. Barker, Co-CEO
John W. P. Holt, Co-CEO
David M. Douglass, CFO
Diance R. Wetherington, VP-Mktg.
Rajan Krishnamurty, Exec.VP/Chief Tech. Officer
David M. Douglass, Corp. Sec.
David M. Douglass, VP-Oper.
David L. Potts, VP-Business Dev.
Jackie L. Davidson, VP Finance
Jeffrey B. Lissack, VP-Business Integration

Phone: 206-269-6363	Fax: 206-269-6350
Toll-Free:	
Address: 2030 First Ave., Ste. 300, Seattle, WA, 98121	

GROWTH PLANS/SPECIAL FEATURES:

The Cobalt Group is a leading provider of Internet marketing solutions for auto dealerships and manufacturers. Cobalt's services offer custom web sites, on-line media planning, software development, data collection and training and technical support. Cobalt has endorsements from 11 auto manufacturers, including Toyota, Lexus, Acura, Jaguar, Saab, Nissan, Mitsubishi and Infiniti. The company's media services offer dealers campaign strategy and rationale, full media research, site selection traffic monitoring, advertising effectiveness and result reports and analysis. Cobalt operates some of the best-known automotive destination sites on the Internet, including Dealernet and PartsVoice, a leading auto parts locating and data management service. Cobalt sponsored Cindi Lux and her car for the Women's Global GT Series race at the Las Vegas Motor Speedway (she won first place). Cobalt also announced an agreement with AutoVantage.com that will give AutoVantage customers access to Cobalt's used car listings. Cobalt's used car listing has a base of more than 4,500 dealer client sites. Cobalt recently introduced a new Internet services package called Finance Solution 2-1-1. Finance Solution 2-1-1 combines Kelley Blue Book used car-pricing information with a car-financing calculator that allows users to calculate variations of the financing of a possible car purchase.

FINANCIALS: Sales and profits are in thousands of dollars—add 000 to get the full amount.

Notes regarding 1999: *(1999 sales and profits were not available for all companies at press time.)*

1999 Sales: $23,300	1999 Profits: $-16,500	Stock Ticker: **CBLT**
1998 Sales: $6,200	1998 Profits: $-5,100	Employees: 264
1997 Sales: $1,700	1997 Profits: $-2,400	Fiscal Year Ends: 12/31
1996 Sales: $ 300	1996 Profits: $- 800	
1995 Sales: $ 100	1995 Profits: $- 400	

SALARIES/BENEFITS:

Pension Plan:	ESOP Stock Plan:	Profit Sharing:	Top Exec. Salary: $	Bonus: $
Savings Plan:	Stock Purch. Plan:		Second Exec. Salary: $	Bonus: $

COMPETITIVE ADVANTAGE: Growing range of automobile related content.

OTHER THOUGHTS:

Apparent Women Officers or Directors: 2
Apparent Minority Officers or Directors: 2
Hot Spot for Advancement for Women/Minorities: Y

LOCATIONS: ("Y" = Yes)

West:	Southwest:	Midwest:	Southeast:	Northeast:	International:
Y					

Note: Financial information, benefits and other data can change quickly and may vary from those stated here.

COMCAST CORP

www.comcast.com

Industry Group Code: 5132
Ranks within this company's industry group: Sales: 3   Profits: 3

BUSINESS ACTIVITIES ("Y" = Yes)

Financial Services:	Information/Publ.:		Technology:	Services:	Retailing:	Telecommunications:	
Stock Brokerage	Portal/Hub/News		Computer Manuf.	Payments/Transfers	Retailer	Internet Serv. Provider	Y
Mortgages/Loans	On-Line Community		Networking Equip.	Consulting	Auctions	Web Site Host	
Banking	Search Engine		Software Manuf.	Advertising/Marketing	Mall	Server Farm	
Insurance	Financial Data Publ.		Specialty Equipment	Outsourcing	Tickets/Travel	Specialty Telecom.	
Credit Cards	Broadcasting/Music	Y			Price Comparisons	High Speed Access	Y

TYPES OF BUSINESS:

Cable Television
Wireless Telecommunications
Programming Content
Internet Access
On-line Services

BRANDS/DIVISIONS/AFFILIATES:

QVC
C3-Comcast Content & Communications
Lenfest Communications
E! Entertainment
Comcast Telecommunications
First Union Complex
Hebenstreit Communications
Microsoft Corporation

CONTACTS: *Note: Officers with more than one job title may be intentionally listed here more than once.*

Brian L. Roberts, Pres.
David N. Watson, Exec. VP-Mktg. and Customer Service
Richard A. Petrino, VP-Human Resources
Stanley L. Wang, Sr.VP-Corp. Sec.
Stanley L. Wang, Sr.VP-General Counsel
Richard A. Petrino, VP-Planning and Development
John R. Alchin, Exec.VP-Treas.

Phone: 215-665-1700	Fax: 215-981-7790
Toll-Free:	
Address: 1500 Market St., Philadelphia, PA, 19102-2148	

GROWTH PLANS/SPECIAL FEATURES:

Comcast Corporation is principally engaged in both developing, managing and operating hybrid fiber-coaxial broadband cable communications networks and in providing programming content, primarily through QVC, the company's electronic retailing subsidiary. Comcast is currently the third-largest cable communications system operator in the United States. The company is in the process of implementing high-speed Internet access service and digital video applications to enhance the products available on its cable networks. Comcast recently completed the acquisition of Lenfest Communications, Inc., the nation's ninth largest cable television operator with approximately 1.25 million cable subscribers. Recently, the company celebrated the installation of its free high-speed Internet service using Comcast @Home cable modem technology to the 500th K-12 school and 50th public library in its national service area. Comcast and Lucent Technologies are involved in a cable telephony over Internet Protocol technical trial that delivers high-quality service to trial participants. The service is soon to be the first cable system in the world to comply with PacketCable 1.0, a new industry-wide specification for delivering real-time services over two-way cable networks. Microsoft is a major investor in Comcast.

FINANCIALS: Sales and profits are in thousands of dollars—add 000 to get the full amount.

Notes regarding 1999: Through 9 months *(1999 sales and profits were not available for all companies at press time.)*

1999 Sales: $4,378,000	1999 Profits: $1,257,000	Stock Ticker: **CMCSA**
1998 Sales: $4,912,600	1998 Profits: $-238,700	Employees: 17,000
1997 Sales: $4,038,400	1997 Profits: $-53,500	Fiscal Year Ends: 12/31
1996 Sales: $3,362,900	1996 Profits: $-43,900	
1995 Sales: $	1995 Profits: $	

SALARIES/BENEFITS:

Pension Plan:	ESOP Stock Plan:	Profit Sharing: Y	Top Exec. Salary: $1,000,000	Bonus: $500,000
Savings Plan: Y	Stock Purch. Plan:		Second Exec. Salary: $689,063	Bonus: $344,532

COMPETITIVE ADVANTAGE: Value-added services, such as cable modems/Microsoft is a major investor in this firm.

OTHER THOUGHTS:

Apparent Women Officers or Directors: 2
Apparent Minority Officers or Directors: 1
Hot Spot for Advancement for Women/Minorities: Y

LOCATIONS: ("Y" = Yes)

West:	Southwest:	Midwest:	Southeast:	Northeast:	International:
Y	Y	Y	Y	Y	Y

COMMERCE ONE INC   www.commerceone.com

Industry Group Code: 51339A
Ranks within this company's industry group: Sales: 10   Profits: 13

BUSINESS ACTIVITIES ("Y" = Yes)

Financial Services:	Information/Publ.:	Technology:		Services:		Retailing:	Telecommunications:
Stock Brokerage	Portal/Hub/News	Computer Manuf.		Payments/Transfers		Retailer	Internet Serv. Provider
Mortgages/Loans	On-Line Community	Networking Equip.		Consulting		Auctions	Web Site Host
Banking	Search Engine	Software Manuf.	Y	Advertising/Marketing		Mall	Server Farm
Insurance	Financial Data Publ.	Specialty Equipment		Outsourcing	Y	Tickets/Travel	Specialty Telecom.
Credit Cards	Broadcasting/Music					Price Comparisons	High Speed Access

TYPES OF BUSINESS:

Business-to-Business Intermediary
ASP

BRANDS/DIVISIONS/AFFILIATES:

MarketSite.net
BuySite
Commerce Chain Solution
CommerceBid.com

CONTACTS: *Note: Officers with more than one job title may be intentionally listed here more than once.*

Mark B. Hoffman, CEO
Mark B. Hoffman, Pres.
Peter F. Pervere, CFO
Charles Donchess, VP-Mktg.
Thomas J. Gonzales, VP-Chief Tech. Officer
Samuel C. Prather, VP-Engineering
Robert M. Tarkoff, VP-Corp. Sec.
Robert M. Tarkoff, VP-General Counsel
Kirby Coryell, VP-Oper.
Robert M. Tarkoff, VP-Corp. Dev.
Kit Robinson, Dir.-Corp. Comm.
Charles Donchess, VP-Business Dev.
Mark S. Biestman, VP-Worldwide Sales

Phone: 925-941-6000	Fax: 925-941-6060
Toll-Free:	
Address: 1600 Riviera Ave., Walnut Creek, CA, 94596	

GROWTH PLANS/SPECIAL FEATURES:

Commerce One is a leader in business-to-business electronic procurement solutions. The company links buying and supplying organizations into real-time trading communities, which significantly reduces costs throughout the supply chain. This solution, named Commerce Chain Solution, includes Commerce One BuySite, an automated internal procurement process solution that takes care of transactions from order to payment. Commerce One has a variety of partners that enhance the implementation of the Commerce Chain Solution. Some of its partners include American Express, General Electric, Microsoft, MasterCard, PriceWaterHouseCoopers, Compaq, Ernst & Young and UPS. In recent news, ImageX.com, Inc., a leading provider of e-commerce print solutions, announced a strategic agreement with Commerce One MarketSite to offer document modification, proofing and ordering of its printed business materials over the Internet. Commerce One was chosen by Microsoft Corp. to be one of only three independent software vendors to be named a Windows 2000 Global Launch Partner. Commerce One's products will support the Microsoft Windows 2000 operating system. This will significantly improve efficiency within e-commerce businesses. Commerce One is in the process of acquiring CommerceBid.com, a leading developer of business-to-business auction and reverse auction service solutions. This acquisition will give Commerce One customers more options when choosing suppliers of new goods and services and allow them to find better prices for currently purchased items.

FINANCIALS: Sales and profits are in thousands of dollars—add 000 to get the full amount.

Notes regarding 1999: *(1999 sales and profits were not available for all companies at press time.)*

1999 Sales: $33,600	1999 Profits: $-63,300	Stock Ticker: **CMRC**
1998 Sales: $2,600	1998 Profits: $-24,600	Employees: 209
1997 Sales: $1,700	1997 Profits: $-11,200	Fiscal Year Ends: 12/31
1996 Sales: $ 800	1996 Profits: $-1,800	
1995 Sales: $	1995 Profits: $	

SALARIES/BENEFITS:

Pension Plan:	ESOP Stock Plan:	Profit Sharing:	Top Exec. Salary: $175,000	Bonus: $162,829
Savings Plan: Y	Stock Purch. Plan:		Second Exec. Salary: $164,333	Bonus: $

COMPETITIVE ADVANTAGE: Extremely successful IPO/well positioned for the future with excellent partners and services.

OTHER THOUGHTS:

Apparent Women Officers or Directors: 1
Apparent Minority Officers or Directors: 1
Hot Spot for Advancement for Women/Minorities:

LOCATIONS: ("Y" = Yes)

West:	Southwest:	Midwest:	Southeast:	Northeast:	International:
Y		Y	Y	Y	Y

COMMTOUCH SOFTWARE LTD

www.commtouch.com

Industry Group Code: 5112
Ranks within this company's industry group: Sales: 78   Profits: 32

BUSINESS ACTIVITIES ("Y" = Yes)

Financial Services:	Information/Publ.:	Technology:		Services:	Retailing:	Telecommunications:
Stock Brokerage	Portal/Hub/News	Computer Manuf.		Payments/Transfers	Retailer	Internet Serv. Provider
Mortgages/Loans	On-Line Community	Networking Equip.		Consulting	Auctions	Web Site Host
Banking	Search Engine	Software Manuf.	Y	Advertising/Marketing	Mall	Server Farm
Insurance	Financial Data Publ.	Specialty Equipment		Outsourcing	Tickets/Travel	Specialty Telecom.
Credit Cards	Broadcasting/Music				Price Comparisons	High Speed Access

TYPES OF BUSINESS:
Software-Web Based E-Mail

BRANDS/DIVISIONS/AFFILIATES:

CONTACTS: *Note: Officers with more than one job title may be intentionally listed here more than once.*
Gideon Mantel, CEO
Isabel Maxwell, Pres.
James Collins, CFO
Robert Gerber, VP-Mktg.
Catherine Dowley, Dir.-Human Resources
Amir Lev, Chief Tech. Officer
James Collins, Sec.
Avner Amram, VP-Oper.
Yael Elish, VP-Strategic Dev.
Igor Gusak, VP-Sales
Ronen Rosenblatt, VP-Research and Dev.

Phone: 408-653-4330	**Fax:** 408-653-4331
Toll-Free:	
Address: 3945 Freedom Circle, Suite 730, Santa Clara, CA, 95054	

GROWTH PLANS/SPECIAL FEATURES:

Commtouch Software, Ltd. is a leading global provider of branded e-mail and on-line communications, serving more than six million individual subscribers through its 70,000 partner web sites. The company's software is now operating in 16 languages in over 150 countries around the world. Commtouch on-line messaging solutions enable partner web sites to proactively acquire and retain affinity relationships with their customers and viewers and to create revenue opportunities through advertising, direct marketing and premium services. Commtouch has been at the forefront of e-mail application development in the U.S. and abroad as the first web-based e-mail provider to offer multiple communication products from within a completely integrated and unified user interface and address book. These include e-mail-to-pager, e-mail-to-fax and e-mail-to-voicemail services. Commtouch has received several industry awards for its commercial and consumer e-mail applications, including international recognition for its small site solution, The ZapZone Network service. Among the company's customers are Excite@Home, LookSmart and NTT. Its business partners include Excite, Go2Net, FortuneCity, Talk City and Nippon Telephone and Telegraph. Through its business partners' sites, it now serves approximately 5.7 million e-mailboxes.

FINANCIALS: Sales and profits are in thousands of dollars—add 000 to get the full amount.
Notes regarding 1999: *(1999 sales and profits were not available for all companies at press time.)*

1999 Sales: $4,300	1999 Profits: $-19,900	
1998 Sales: $ 400	1998 Profits: $-4,400	**Stock Ticker: CTCH**
1997 Sales: $ 900	1997 Profits: $-3,500	**Employees:** 45
1996 Sales: $3,100	1996 Profits: $-1,300	**Fiscal Year Ends:** 12/31
1995 Sales: $	1995 Profits: $	

SALARIES/BENEFITS:

Pension Plan:	ESOP Stock Plan: Y	Profit Sharing:	Top Exec. Salary: $	Bonus: $
Savings Plan: Y	Stock Purch. Plan:		Second Exec. Salary: $	Bonus: $

COMPETITIVE ADVANTAGE: Almost 6 million subscribers/Focus on being one of the world's best e-mail enablers.

OTHER THOUGHTS:

Apparent Women Officers or Directors: 3
Apparent Minority Officers or Directors: 7
Hot Spot for Advancement for Women/Minorities: Y

LOCATIONS: ("Y" = Yes)

West:	Southwest:	Midwest:	Southeast:	Northeast:	International:
Y				Y	Y

Note: Financial information, benefits and other data can change quickly and may vary from those stated here.

COMPAQ COMPUTER CORP www.compaq.com

Industry Group Code: 3341A
Ranks within this company's industry group: Sales: 3   Profits: 8

BUSINESS ACTIVITIES ("Y" = Yes)

Financial Services:	Information/Publ.:	Technology:		Services:		Retailing:		Telecommunications:
Stock Brokerage	Portal/Hub/News	Computer Manuf.	Y	Payments/Transfers		Retailer	Y	Internet Serv. Provider
Mortgages/Loans	On-Line Community	Networking Equip.	Y	Consulting		Auctions		Web Site Host
Banking	Search Engine	Software Manuf.	Y	Advertising/Marketing		Mall		Server Farm
Insurance	Financial Data Publ.	Specialty Equipment	Y	Outsourcing		Tickets/Travel		Specialty Telecom.
Credit Cards	Broadcasting/Music					Price Comparisons		High Speed Access

TYPES OF BUSINESS:

Personal Computer Manufacturer
Handheld Portable Systems
Corporate Servers
Monitors and Accessories
Technology Services
Venture Capital/Technology Investments

BRANDS/DIVISIONS/AFFILIATES:

Compaq Works
Deskpro
ProLinea
LTE Elite
Rack-Mountable ProLiant
Digital Equipment Corp.
Presario

CONTACTS: *Note: Officers with more than one job title may be intentionally listed here more than once.*

Michael D. Capellas, CEO
Michael D. Capellas, Pres.
Ben Wells, Sr. VP/CFO
Richard N. Snyder, Sr. VP-Worldwide Sales and Mktg.
Yvonne Jackson, Sr. VP-Human Resources
William D. Strecker, Sr. VP-Tech.
Robert V. Napier, Sr.VP-Info. Mgmt./CIO
Gregory E. Petsch, Sr. VP-Mfg. and Quality
Thomas C. Siekman, Sr.VP/ Sec.
Thomas C. Siekman, Sr.VP/General Counsel
William D. Strecker, Sr. VP-Corp. Dev.
Flint J. Brenton, VP-eCommerce
Ben Wells, Treas.
William B. McBee III, VP-Quality and Customer Satisfaction

Phone: 281-370-0670	Fax: 281-374-1740
Toll-Free: 800-231-0900	
Address: 20555 State Highway 249, Houston, TX, 77070	

GROWTH PLANS/SPECIAL FEATURES:

Compaq is one of the leading computer makers in the world, with an enviable market share in corporate PCs. In addition to PCs, the company offers a variety of related products, including hand-held portable systems, corporate servers to assist company operations and a slew of technology services. Compaq acquired Digital Equipment to expand its presence in the high-end computer market. 1998's financial results were disappointing. However, the company is re-positioning itself and slashing costs under a new CEO. Late 1999 profits looked good. Also, the firm is making significant gains on its investments in other technology companies. The company derives the majority of its revenues from sales to business customers, but additionally markets products to home users, governments, schools and students. Compaq Computer Corporation acquired the AltaVista Internet search engine business when it bought Digital Equipment, but it sold off AltaVista in mid 1999. Meanwhile, Compaq has faced many challenges as a result of both the Digital acquisition and the intense competition that continues to proliferate throughout the PC business. Important trends include the fact that many Internet portals are now giving away either free PCs, or coupons good for huge discounts on PCs, to consumers who sign long-term contracts for Internet service. Meanwhile, there is a fast-growing market for PCs that sell for much less than $1,000, and in some cases less than $500. At the same time, competitors like Gateway and Dell that sell direct to the customer are stealing huge chunks of market share from the stores that traditionally sell Compaq's merchandise. Compaq is fighting back with its own catalog, mail-order and on-line businesses. Compaq also operates a retail outlet store in Houston, Texas.

FINANCIALS: Sales and profits are in thousands of dollars—add 000 to get the full amount.

Notes regarding 1999: *(1999 sales and profits were not available for all companies at press time.)*

1999 Sales: $38,525,000	1999 Profits: $569,000	Stock Ticker: **CPQ**
1998 Sales: $31,169,000	1998 Profits: $-2,743,000	Employees: 71,000
1997 Sales: $24,584,000	1997 Profits: $1,855,000	Fiscal Year Ends: 12/31
1996 Sales: $18,109,000	1996 Profits: $1,313,000	
1995 Sales: $14,755,000	1995 Profits: $789,000	

SALARIES/BENEFITS:

Pension Plan:	ESOP Stock Plan:	Profit Sharing:	Top Exec. Salary: $1,479,167	Bonus: $3,000,000
Savings Plan: Y	Stock Purch. Plan:		Second Exec. Salary: $520,830	Bonus: $625,000

COMPETITIVE ADVANTAGE: A leading global supplier of personal computers/New features to make Internet access more user-friendly.

OTHER THOUGHTS:

Apparent Women Officers or Directors: 2
Apparent Minority Officers or Directors:
Hot Spot for Advancement for Women/Minorities:

LOCATIONS: ("Y" = Yes)

West:	Southwest:	Midwest:	Southeast:	Northeast:	International:
	Y				Y

COMPS.COM INC　　　www.comps.com

Industry Group Code: 514191
Ranks within this company's industry group: Sales: 14　Profits: 9

BUSINESS ACTIVITIES ("Y" = Yes)

Financial Services:	Information/Publ.:		Technology:	Services:	Retailing:	Telecommunications:
Stock Brokerage	Portal/Hub/News	Y	Computer Manuf.	Payments/Transfers	Retailer	Internet Serv. Provider
Mortgages/Loans	On-Line Community		Networking Equip.	Consulting	Auctions	Web Site Host
Banking	Search Engine		Software Manuf.	Advertising/Marketing	Mall	Server Farm
Insurance	Financial Data Publ.		Specialty Equipment	Outsourcing	Tickets/Travel	Specialty Telecom.
Credit Cards	Broadcasting/Music				Price Comparisons	High Speed Access

TYPES OF BUSINESS:

On-line Commercial Real Estate Information

BRANDS/DIVISIONS/AFFILIATES:

ReaLBid
E-COMPS
DealPoint
CoStar Group

CONTACTS: *Note: Officers with more than one job title may be intentionally listed here more than once.*

Christopher A. Crane, CEO
Christopher A. Crane, Pres.
Karen Goodrum, CFO/VP-Finance
Craig S. Farrington, VP-Product Mktg. And Dev.
Candice Jenkins, Dir.-Human Resources
Karen Goodrum, Sec.
Joseph A. Mannina, VP-Oper.
Craig S. Farrington, VP-Dev.
Moira Conlon, Analyst Contact
Mary Tokita, Media Contact
Tim Kent, General Information Mgr.
Michael Arabe, Sr.VP-Sales
Karen Goodrum, VP-Admin.

Phone: 858-578-3000	Fax: 858-684-3288

Toll-Free:

Address: 9888 Carroll Centre Rd., Ste. 100, San Diego, CA, 92126-4581

GROWTH PLANS/SPECIAL FEATURES:

COMPS.com is a leading national provider of comprehensive commercial real estate sales information both on and off the Internet. COMPS has a highly-developed data collection system that includes sales prices, income and expenses, capitalization rates, loan data, property photographs, buyers, sellers, brokers and other key details. COMPS offers many search tools on its web site such as E-COMPS, RealBid and DealPoint. DealPoint is a search engine that offers remote data entry, the ability to search for properties based on geographic radius, photos and company logos for brokers to utilize. RealBid is a disposition marketing tool that quickly identifies, contacts, informs and captures potential investors and organizes competitive and efficient sales by using communication technologies. The web site also has a custom market research tool that identifies market trends and performance. COMPS recently released RealBid 1.1, an improved version that has new features such as a properties for sale page and a property brochures option. COMPS has signed a definitive agreement to merge with CoStar Group, a leading business-to-business provider of information services to the U.S. commercial real estate industry.

FINANCIALS: Sales and profits are in thousands of dollars—add 000 to get the full amount.

Notes regarding 1999: Through 9 months *(1999 sales and profits were not available for all companies at press time.)*

1999 Sales: $11,800	1999 Profits: $-7,500	
1998 Sales: $12,900	1998 Profits: $-1,700	Stock Ticker: **CDOT**
1997 Sales: $10,400	1997 Profits: $-1,600	Employees:　296
1996 Sales: $8,100	1996 Profits: $-2,300	Fiscal Year Ends: 12/31
1995 Sales: $6,700	1995 Profits: $-1,400	

SALARIES/BENEFITS:

Pension Plan:	ESOP Stock Plan:	Profit Sharing:	Top Exec. Salary: $150,000	Bonus: $65,000
Savings Plan:	Stock Purch. Plan:		Second Exec. Salary: $150,000	Bonus: $22,653

COMPETITIVE ADVANTAGE:　Focus on in-depth real estate sales data.

OTHER THOUGHTS:

Apparent Women Officers or Directors: 2
Apparent Minority Officers or Directors: 1
Hot Spot for Advancement for Women/Minorities:

LOCATIONS: ("Y" = Yes)

West:	Southwest:	Midwest:	Southeast:	Northeast:	International:
Y					

CONCENTRIC NETWORK CORPORATION
www.concentric.com

Industry Group Code: 5133E
Ranks within this company's industry group: Sales: 1   Profits: 3

BUSINESS ACTIVITIES ("Y" = Yes)

Financial Services:	Information/Publ.:	Technology:	Services:	Retailing:	Telecommunications:	
Stock Brokerage	Portal/Hub/News	Computer Manuf.	Payments/Transfers	Retailer	Internet Serv. Provider	Y
Mortgages/Loans	On-Line Community	Networking Equip.	Consulting	Auctions	Web Site Host	Y
Banking	Search Engine	Software Manuf.	Advertising/Marketing	Mall	Server Farm	
Insurance	Financial Data Publ.	Specialty Equipment	Outsourcing	Tickets/Travel	Specialty Telecom.	
Credit Cards	Broadcasting/Music			Price Comparisons	High Speed Access	Y

TYPES OF BUSINESS:

Internet Access and Services for Businesses
Web Site Hosting
Intranet Services
Co-Location
Commercial Networking Services
Virtual Private Networks

BRANDS/DIVISIONS/AFFILIATES:

Concentric CustomLink
Enterprise VPN
Concentric RemoteLink

CONTACTS: Note: Officers with more than one job title may be intentionally listed here more than once.

Henry R. Nothhaft, CEO
Henry R. Nothhaft, Pres.
Michael F. Anthofer, Sr. VP/CFO
Mark W. Fisher, VP-Corp. Mktg.
Frederick J. Schreiber, VP-Human Resources
Donn Dobkin, VP-CIO
Dave R. Schairer, VP-Controller
Les Hamilton, Sr.VP-Engineering
Les Hamilton, Sr.VP-Oper.
James L. Isaacs, VP-Business Dev.
Martin J. Levy, VP-Internet and Data Center Engineering
Robert Grosso, VP-Business Dev.
George D. Carr, VP-Sales and Strategic Accounts

Phone: 408-817-2800	Fax: 408-817-2810
Toll-Free:	
Address: 1400 Parkmoor Ave., San Jose, CA, 95126-3429	

GROWTH PLANS/SPECIAL FEATURES:

Concentric Network Corporation provides tailored, value-added Internet Protocol (IP) based network services for businesses and consumers. To provide these services, the company utilizes its low or fixed latency, high-throughput network, employing its advanced network architecture and the Internet. Concentric's service offerings for enterprises include virtual private networks (VPNs), dedicated access facilities (DAFs), remote access services and web hosting. These services enable enterprises to take advantage of standard Internet tools, such as web browsers and high-performance servers for customized data communications, both within an enterprise and between an enterprise and its suppliers, partners and customers. These services combine cost advantages, nationwide access and standard protocols of public networks with the customization, high performance, reliability and security of private networks. Among Concentric's strategic partners are Covad Communications, CyberCash, Inc., Microsoft Corporation, Nortel Networks, Register.com, Williams Communications Group and SBC Communications. Recently, Concentric teamed with SonicWALL Inc., a provider of Internet security for broadband access customers in the small- to medium-size company and branch office and education markets, to provide a firewall solution to Concentric's digital subscriber line customers. Concentric also has a partnership with Trellix Corporation to pair its web hosting platform with TrellixWeb, a PC-based application that allows users to create, publish and enhance their own web sites without knowledge of HTML, FTP or graphic design.

FINANCIALS: Sales and profits are in thousands of dollars—add 000 to get the full amount

Notes regarding 1999: (1999 sales and profits were not available for all companies at press time.)

1999 Sales: $147,800	1999 Profits: $85,100	Stock Ticker: CNCX
1998 Sales: $82,800	1998 Profits: $-82,100	Employees: 569
1997 Sales: $45,500	1997 Profits: $-55,600	Fiscal Year Ends: 12/31
1996 Sales: $15,600	1996 Profits: $-66,400	
1995 Sales: $2,500	1995 Profits: $-22,000	

SALARIES/BENEFITS:

Pension Plan:	ESOP Stock Plan:	Profit Sharing:	Top Exec. Salary: $288,942	Bonus: $2,296
Savings Plan: Y	Stock Purch. Plan:		Second Exec. Salary: $248,631	Bonus: $

COMPETITIVE ADVANTAGE: Rapidly growing private network services.

OTHER THOUGHTS:

Apparent Women Officers or Directors: 1
Apparent Minority Officers or Directors:
Hot Spot for Advancement for Women/Minorities:

LOCATIONS: ("Y" = Yes)

West:	Southwest:	Midwest:	Southeast:	Northeast:	International:
Y		Y			

Note: Financial information, benefits and other data can change quickly and may vary from those stated here.

CONNECTINC.COM   www.connectinc.com

Industry Group Code: 5112
Ranks within this company's Industry group: Sales: 59   Profits: 43

BUSINESS ACTIVITIES ("Y" = Yes)

Financial Services:	Information/Publ.:	Technology:		Services:		Retailing:		Telecommunications:
Stock Brokerage	Portal/Hub/News	Computer Manuf.		Payments/Transfers		Retailer		Internet Serv. Provider
Mortgages/Loans	On-Line Community	Networking Equip.		Consulting	Y	Auctions		Web Site Host
Banking	Search Engine	Software Manuf.	Y	Advertising/Marketing		Mall		Server Farm
Insurance	Financial Data Publ.	Specialty Equipment		Outsourcing	Y	Tickets/Travel		Specialty Telecom.
Credit Cards	Broadcasting/Music					Price Comparisons		High Speed Access

TYPES OF BUSINESS:

Software-Internet Business
Startup Assistance
On-line Marketplaces

BRANDS/DIVISIONS/AFFILIATES:

MarketStream
Calico Commerce
URLe2Market.com

CONTACTS: *Note: Officers with more than one job title may be intentionally listed here more than once.*

Craig D. Norris, CEO/Pres.
Lucille Hoger, COO
Kevin J. Berry, VP-Finance/CFO
David J. Wippich, Exec. VP-Mktg. and Sales
Vimal Goel, VP-Engineering
Ron Ibarra, Dir.-Admin.
Joseph E. Bentzel, VP-eServices
Joseph E. Bentzel, VP-Mktg.
Ron Ibarra, Dir.-Business Services

Phone: 650-254-4000	Fax: 650-254-4800
Toll-Free: 800-262-2638	
Address: 515 Ellis St., Mountain View, CA, 94043-2242	

GROWTH PLANS/SPECIAL FEATURES:

ConnectInc.com is a leading provider of technology and services that connect buying and selling companies through the Internet. ConnectInc.com implements its MarketStream 2.0 e-commerce software with URLe2Market.com to launch and host early stage Internet start up companies. URLe2Market consulting builds a customized e-business marketplace linking multiple buyers and sellers quickly for new e-businesses. Since time-to-market is critical for new Internet companies, ConnectInc.com specializes in providing support and easy application configuration and administration in as little as six to eight weeks. Some of ConnectInc.com's partners include Hewlett Packard, IBM, Object Design, Cognos and Sun Microsystems. Calico Commerce recently acquired ConnectInc.com. Calico Commerce's integrated suite of applications, called eSales, enables companies to sell complex products over the Internet and to unify marketing content and product data to guide buyers through a personalized purchasing process. The merger is part of Calico Commerce's plan to expand its services and to offer its customers a complete e-commerce solutions package. Also in recent news, Exclaim Technologies, Inc. chose the MarketStream e-commerce software to power its new vertical Internet marketplace for manufacturers and retailers.

FINANCIALS: Sales and profits are in thousands of dollars—add 000 to get the full amount.

Notes regarding 1999: Through 9 months *(1999 sales and profits were not available for all companies at press time.)*

1999 Sales: $4,900	1999 Profits: $-1,100	Stock Ticker: **CNKT**
1998 Sales: $6,500	1998 Profits: $-7,900	Employees: 35
1997 Sales: $9,400	1997 Profits: $-14,600	Fiscal Year Ends: 12/31
1996 Sales: $10,200	1996 Profits: $-16,100	
1995 Sales: $8,600	1995 Profits: $-14,100	

SALARIES/BENEFITS:

Pension Plan:	ESOP Stock Plan:	Profit Sharing:	Top Exec. Salary: $208,750	Bonus: $42,891
Savings Plan:	Stock Purch. Plan:		Second Exec. Salary: $151,422	Bonus: $35,892

COMPETITIVE ADVANTAGE: Rapid deployment for clients launching new sites.

OTHER THOUGHTS:

Apparent Women Officers or Directors: 1
Apparent Minority Officers or Directors: 2
Hot Spot for Advancement for Women/Minorities: Y

LOCATIONS: ("Y" = Yes)

West:	Southwest:	Midwest:	Southeast:	Northeast:	International:
Y					

CONVERGENT COMMUNICATIONS INC
www.converg.com

Industry Group Code: 54151
Ranks within this company's industry group: Sales: 4 Profits: 16

BUSINESS ACTIVITIES ("Y" = Yes)

Financial Services:	Information/Publ.:	Technology:	Services:		Retailing:		Telecommunications:	
Stock Brokerage	Portal/Hub/News	Computer Manuf.	Payments/Transfers		Retailer		Internet Serv. Provider	
Mortgages/Loans	On-Line Community	Networking Equip.	Consulting	Y	Auctions		Web Site Host	
Banking	Search Engine	Software Manuf.	Advertising/Marketing		Mall		Server Farm	
Insurance	Financial Data Publ.	Specialty Equipment	Outsourcing	Y	Tickets/Travel		Specialty Telecom.	Y
Credit Cards	Broadcasting/Music				Price Comparisons		High Speed Access	Y

TYPES OF BUSINESS:

Datanet Telecommunications Services-Data and Voice Transmission
Network Connectivity
Telecom Needs Outsourcing
Data Integration
Professional Services

BRANDS/DIVISIONS/AFFILIATES:

Entre Business Technology Group
ENS Connect

CONTACTS: Note: Officers with more than one job title may be intentionally listed here more than once.

John R. Evans, CEO
Keith V. Burge, COO/Pres.
John J. Phibbs, Exec.VP-CFO
Murray R. Smith, Exec.VP-Sales and Mktg.
D. Randall Hake, Exec. VP-Human Resources and Training
Brian J. McManus, Exec.VP/CIO
Michael P. Dykstra, Sr.VP-IT and CIO
Phillip G. Allen, Exec. VP/Corp. Sec.
Martin E. Freidel, Exec. VP/General Counsel
Brian J. McManus, Exec.VP-Internal Oper.
John C. Herbers, Sr. VP-Internet Services
John J. Phibbs, Treas.
Michael R. Dozier, Exec.VP-Market Oper.
W. Wood Alberts, VP-Enterprise Network Services

Phone: 303-749-3000	Fax: 303-749-3111
Toll-Free:	
Address: 400 Inverness Dr. South, Ste. 400, Englewood, CO, 80112	

GROWTH PLANS/SPECIAL FEATURES:

Convergent Communications, an Enterprise Network Carrier, delivers comprehensive, single-source communications solutions that capitalize on today's converging voice, data and multimedia technologies. Convergent provides a wide array of services, including the design of communications systems specifically for businesses, an integrated turnkey system of components, communications systems management, existing equipment purchases and updated systems. The Association for Local Telecommunications Services and X-Change magazine recognized Convergent as the Most Innovative Business Strategy. Convergent also recently launched a network connectivity service, called ENS Connect, for small and medium-sized businesses. The service includes high-speed Internet access, dedicated long distance service and frame relay service. All of these services are also monitored and pro-actively managed through Convergence's Central Technical Assistance Center. The company acquired Entre Business Technology Group, a privately-held provider of data integration and professional services to more than 500 active customers in Atlanta. Entre has installed more than 5,000 networks throughout the country.

FINANCIALS: Sales and profits are in thousands of dollars—add 000 to get the full amount.

Notes regarding 1999: (1999 sales and profits were not available for all companies at press time.)

1999 Sales: $	1999 Profits: $	Stock Ticker: CONV
1998 Sales: $61,600	1998 Profits: $-50,600	Employees: 1,080
1997 Sales: $10,200	1997 Profits: $-9,700	Fiscal Year Ends: 12/31
1996 Sales: $1,600	1996 Profits: $- 800	
1995 Sales: $1,400	1995 Profits: $- 100	

SALARIES/BENEFITS:

Pension Plan:	ESOP Stock Plan:	Profit Sharing:	Top Exec. Salary: $200,000	Bonus: $
Savings Plan:	Stock Purch. Plan:		Second Exec. Salary: $	Bonus: $

COMPETITIVE ADVANTAGE: Focus on comprehensive Internet service packages.

OTHER THOUGHTS:

	LOCATIONS: ("Y" = Yes)					
	West:	Southwest:	Midwest:	Southeast:	Northeast:	International:
Apparent Women Officers or Directors:	Y	Y	Y	Y	Y	
Apparent Minority Officers or Directors:						
Hot Spot for Advancement for Women/Minorities:						

Note: Financial information, benefits and other data can change quickly and may vary from those stated here.

COVAD COMMUNICATIONS GROUP INC   www.covad.com

Industry Group Code: 5133C
Ranks within this company's industry group: Sales: 1   Profits: 5

BUSINESS ACTIVITIES ("Y" = Yes)

Financial Services:	Information/Publ.:	Technology:	Services:	Retailing:	Telecommunications:	
Stock Brokerage	Portal/Hub/News	Computer Manuf.	Payments/Transfers	Retailer	Internet Serv. Provider	Y
Mortgages/Loans	On-Line Community	Networking Equip.	Consulting	Auctions	Web Site Host	
Banking	Search Engine	Software Manuf.	Advertising/Marketing	Mall	Server Farm	
Insurance	Financial Data Publ.	Specialty Equipment	Outsourcing	Tickets/Travel	Specialty Telecom.	
Credit Cards	Broadcasting/Music			Price Comparisons	High Speed Access	Y

TYPES OF BUSINESS:
High-Speed Internet Access
DSL Services

BRANDS/DIVISIONS/AFFILIATES:

GROWTH PLANS/SPECIAL FEATURES:

Covad Communications is a leading packet-based competitive local exchange carrier that provides dedicated high-speed digital communication services. The company provides high-speed Internet access through technology such as digital subscriber line (DSL) services that connect corporations to their employees at home. Covad has launched its services in the San Francisco Bay Area, Los Angeles, New York and Boston, and plans to implement its services in 22 regions across the nation. Covad has more than 350 partners, including equipment manufacturers and software developers that offer Covad's products. Some of its partners include Turnstone, Efficient Networks, Inc., Cisco Systems and Nokia. Covad was awarded The Peak award by X-Change and PHONE+ magazines for its innovation in local service. Covad also recently announced a joint marketing agreement that is targeted at the residential and business sectors and is designed to encourage the adoption of broadband services. The agreement calls for a co-branded My Yahoo!'s start page service through Covad's distribution channels and features Yahoo! free services and a Covad broadband sign-up section. That section will offer facts about broadband services and allow users to order the service. Covad's three founders are all former employees of Intel.

CONTACTS: *Note: Officers with more than one job title may be intentionally listed here more than once.*
Robert Knowling Jr., CEO
Robert Knowling Jr., Pres.
Timothy P. Laehy, CFO/VP-Finance
Robert A. Roblin, Exec. VP-Mktg.
Jane Marvin, VP-Human Resources
Rex Cardinale, Chief Tech. Officer
Rex Cardinale, VP-Engineering
Dhruv Khanna, Exec.VP/Corp. Sec.
Dhruv Khanna, Exec.VP/General Counsel
Catherine Hemmer, Pres.-Oper.
Robert Davenport III, Exec.VP-Business Dev.
Nick Kormeluk, VP-Investor Relations
Charles Haas, Exec.VP-Sales

Phone: 408-844-7500	Fax: 408-844-7501
Toll-Free: 888-462-6823	
Address: 2330 Central Expwy., Santa Clara, CA, 95050-2516	

FINANCIALS: Sales and profits are in thousands of dollars—add 000 to get the full amount.
Notes regarding 1999: *(1999 sales and profits were not available for all companies at press time.)*

1999 Sales: $66,500	1999 Profits: $-195,400	Stock Ticker: **COVD**
1998 Sales: $5,300	1998 Profits: $-48,200	Employees: 335
1997 Sales: $	1997 Profits: $-2,600	Fiscal Year Ends: 12/31
1996 Sales: $	1996 Profits: $	
1995 Sales: $	1995 Profits: $	

SALARIES/BENEFITS:

Pension Plan:	ESOP Stock Plan:	Profit Sharing:	Top Exec. Salary: $180,768	Bonus: $750,000
Savings Plan:	Stock Purch. Plan:		Second Exec. Salary: $	Bonus: $

COMPETITIVE ADVANTAGE: Aggressive marketing and advertising.

OTHER THOUGHTS:

Apparent Women Officers or Directors: 2
Apparent Minority Officers or Directors: 1
Hot Spot for Advancement for Women/Minorities:

LOCATIONS: ("Y" = Yes)

West:	Southwest:	Midwest:	Southeast:	Northeast:	International:
Y	Y	Y	Y	Y	

CREATIVE COMPUTERS INC   www.creativecomputers.com

Industry Group Code: 4541
Ranks within this company's industry group: Sales: 20   Profits: 7

BUSINESS ACTIVITIES ("Y" = Yes)

Financial Services:	Information/Publ.:	Technology:	Services:	Retailing:		Telecommunications:	
Stock Brokerage	Portal/Hub/News	Computer Manuf.	Payments/Transfers	Retailer	Y	Internet Serv. Provider	
Mortgages/Loans	On-Line Community	Networking Equip.	Consulting	Auctions	Y	Web Site Host	
Banking	Search Engine	Software Manuf.	Advertising/Marketing	Mall		Server Farm	
Insurance	Financial Data Publ.	Specialty Equipment	Outsourcing	Tickets/Travel		Specialty Telecom.	
Credit Cards	Broadcasting/Music			Price Comparisons		High Speed Access	

TYPES OF BUSINESS:

Retail-Computers
On-line Auction
Catalog Sales

BRANDS/DIVISIONS/AFFILIATES:

MacMall
PC Mall
DataCom Mall
uBID

CONTACTS: *Note: Officers with more than one job title may be intentionally listed here more than once.*

Frank F. Khulusi, CEO
Scott W. Klein, Pres.
Ted Sanders, CFO
Daniel J. De Vries, Exec. VP-Mktg. and Sales
Kathy Ressler, Personnel Admin.
David R. Burcham, Exec. VP-Oper.
Gregory K. Jones, Pres./CEO, uBID
S. Keating Rhodes, COO

Phone: 310-354-5600	Fax: 310353-7475
Toll-Free: 800-222-2808	
Address: 2555 W. 190th Street, Torrance, CA, 90504	

GROWTH PLANS/SPECIAL FEATURES:

Founded in 1987, Creative Computers, Inc. is a direct marketer of personal computer hardware, software and peripheral products. The company's catalogs include PC Mall, DataCom Mall, Mac Mall and ComputAbility, and generate over 85% of the company's sales. In addition, Creative Computers, Inc. sells products via telemarketing and Internet advertising. The firm's uBID website, set in an auction format, is taking off so quickly that the company has closed seven of its eight showrooms to concentrate on selling via the Internet and catalogs. The uBID web site offers computer-related products and consumer electronics to individual consumers, home offices, small businesses and large corporations. Creative Computers believes that its knowledgeable sales force and colorful catalogs are instrumental in placing the company in a leading position in its industry. Technical support, along with a high level of customer service, results in the company's earning of a broad, loyal consumer base. Creative Computers is focusing on the WINTEL (Windows/Intel) market through its PC Mall catalog.

FINANCIALS: Sales and profits are in thousands of dollars—add 000 to get the full amount.

Notes regarding 1999: *(1999 sales and profits were not available for all companies at press time.)*

1999 Sales: $8,900	1999 Profits: $ 700	Stock Ticker: **CAP**
1998 Sales: $6,400	1998 Profits: $- 600	Employees: 72
1997 Sales: $7,119	1997 Profits: $ 891	Fiscal Year Ends: 08/31
1996 Sales: $6,200	1996 Profits: $1,000	
1995 Sales: $5,900	1995 Profits: $	

SALARIES/BENEFITS:

Pension Plan:	ESOP Stock Plan:	Profit Sharing:	Top Exec. Salary: $400,000	Bonus: $
Savings Plan: Y	Stock Purch. Plan:		Second Exec. Salary: $	Bonus: $

COMPETITIVE ADVANTAGE: Offers more than 14,500 products/Continues to increase its line.

OTHER THOUGHTS:

Apparent Women Officers or Directors:
Apparent Minority Officers or Directors:
Hot Spot for Advancement for Women/Minorities:

LOCATIONS: ("Y" = Yes)

West:	Southwest:	Midwest:	Southeast:	Northeast:	International:
Y			Y		

CRITICAL PATH INC   www.cp.net

Industry Group Code: 5133D
Ranks within this company's industry group: Sales: 6   Profits: 4

BUSINESS ACTIVITIES ("Y" = Yes)

Financial Services:	Information/Publ.:	Technology:	Services:		Retailing:	Telecommunications:
Stock Brokerage	Portal/Hub/News	Computer Manuf.	Payments/Transfers		Retailer	Internet Serv. Provider
Mortgages/Loans	On-Line Community	Networking Equip.	Consulting		Auctions	Web Site Host
Banking	Search Engine	Software Manuf.	Advertising/Marketing		Mall	Server Farm
Insurance	Financial Data Publ.	Specialty Equipment	Outsourcing	Y	Tickets/Travel	Specialty Telecom.
Credit Cards	Broadcasting/Music				Price Comparisons	High Speed Access

TYPES OF BUSINESS:

Outsourcing Services-E-Mail Solutions
Messaging Solutions
Calendar Systems
Public Key Infrastructure

BRANDS/DIVISIONS/AFFILIATES:

Amplitude Software
XETI, Inc.

CONTACTS: Note: Officers with more than one job title may be intentionally listed here more than once.

Douglas T. Hickey, CEO
Paul R. Gigg, COO
David A. Thatcher, Exec.VP/CFO
Sharon Wienbar, VP-Mktg.
Helen Pass, Dir.-Human Resources
Joseph Duncan, CIO
Marcy Swenson, VP-Software Engineering
Carolyn J. Patterson, VP-Oper.
Mari E. Tangredi, VP-Business Dev.
Judie A. Hayes, VP-Corp. Comm.

Phone: 415-808-8800   **Fax:** 415-808-8882
Toll-Free:
Address: 320 1st St., San Francisco, CA, 94105

GROWTH PLANS/SPECIAL FEATURES:

Critical Path supplies full-service e-mail and messaging solutions to corporations, Internet service providers, web hosting companies and web portals. Critical Path's services allow companies to outsource certain aspects and functions of e-mail service, or the entire e-mail service. This reduces the costs of administration and support and enhances the performance of the e-mail system. Critical Path also offers web-based calendar solutions that can be integrated with e-mail. The calendar system is widely used by large corporations, universities and government agencies to help with enterprise communication. Critical Path's subsidiary, Amplitude Software, provides most of the company's calendar and resource-scheduling applications. Some of Critical Path's customers include corporations such as E*Trade, CompuServe, Network Solutions, Sprint and U.S. West. Critical Path recently acquired XETI, Inc., a leading developer of standards-based public key infrastructure (PKI) solutions. This acquisition was executed to improve Critical Path's guaranteed delivery service offerings with the PKI technology. Critical Path also recently announced a strategic partnership with Global TeleSystems Group, Inc. (GTS), one of the leading providers of borderless broadband communications services across Europe. GTS will offer Critical Path's messaging services under the GTS brand name to its customers through the company's sales and distribution network in more than 70 European cities.

FINANCIALS: Sales and profits are in thousands of dollars—add 000 to get the full amount.
Notes regarding 1999: *(1999 sales and profits were not available for all companies at press time.)*

1999 Sales: $16,200	1999 Profits: $-115,500	Stock Ticker: **CPTH**
1998 Sales: $ 900	1998 Profits: $-11,500	Employees: 106
1997 Sales: $	1997 Profits: $-1,100	Fiscal Year Ends: 12/31
1996 Sales: $	1996 Profits: $	
1995 Sales: $	1995 Profits: $	

SALARIES/BENEFITS:

Pension Plan:	ESOP Stock Plan:	Profit Sharing:	Top Exec. Salary: $	Bonus: $
Savings Plan:	Stock Purch. Plan:		Second Exec. Salary: $	Bonus: $

COMPETITIVE ADVANTAGE: Rapid expansion into new markets.

OTHER THOUGHTS:

Apparent Women Officers or Directors: 7
Apparent Minority Officers or Directors:
Hot Spot for Advancement for Women/Minorities: Y

LOCATIONS: ("Y" = Yes)

West:	Southwest:	Midwest:	Southeast:	Northeast:	International:
Y					Y

CROSSWALK.COM INC   www.crosswalk.com

Industry Group Code: 514191
Ranks within this company's industry group: Sales: 36   Profits: 18

BUSINESS ACTIVITIES ("Y" = Yes)

Financial Services:	Information/Publ.:		Technology:	Services:	Retailing:		Telecommunications:
Stock Brokerage	Portal/Hub/News	Y	Computer Manuf.	Payments/Transfers	Retailer	Y	Internet Serv. Provider
Mortgages/Loans	On-Line Community		Networking Equip.	Consulting	Auctions		Web Site Host
Banking	Search Engine	Y	Software Manuf.	Advertising/Marketing	Mall		Server Farm
Insurance	Financial Data Publ.		Specialty Equipment	Outsourcing	Tickets/Travel		Specialty Telecom.
Credit Cards	Broadcasting/Music				Price Comparisons		High Speed Access

TYPES OF BUSINESS:

Portal-Christianity
Acceptable Content Delivery Software

BRANDS/DIVISIONS/AFFILIATES:

DIDAX
Christian Community Network
CrossingGuard

CONTACTS: Note: Officers with more than one job title may be intentionally listed here more than once.

William M. Parker, CEO
William M. Parker, Pres.
Gary A. Struzik, CFO
Dane B. West, Sr. VP-Sales
Date Quo, Human Resources
William H. Bowers, Chief Tech. Officer
Rogers Hellman, Sr.VP/Dir.-Engineering
Gary A. Struzik, Corp. Sec.
Dane B. West, VP-Business Dev.
Robert E. Steele, eCommerce Mgr.

Phone: 703-968-4808	Fax: 703-968-4818
Toll-Free: 888-283-4329	
Address: 4206F Technology Ct., Chantilly, VA, 20151-1214	

GROWTH PLANS/SPECIAL FEATURES:

Crosswalk.com, formerly DIDAX, is a web site that offers Christian news, chat, advice and products tailored for the Christian community, including the sale of music and books. The site also offers free e-mail, a search engine and links to a wide variety of other subjects such as entertainment, health and news. The company formerly engaged in web site development and hosting, as well as Internet access. Crosswalk.com derives about 80% of its revenue from advertising, sponsorships and retail sales. A unique feature of this site is its free offering of CrossingGuard software, a comprehensive filtering solution to protect family members from viewing inappropriate material on the Internet. Crosswalk.com has more than 600,000 members and has received the Christian Web Site of the Year award two years in a row. Recently, Crosswalk.com announced its plan to market a co-branded PlatinumVisa credit card with First USA. Crosswalk.com also announced the launch of a Family Channel on its web site. FamilyLife, a division of Campus Crusade for Christ, sponsors the Family Channel. The channel features a broad range of content and RealAudio streaming broadcasts of the daily FamilyLife Today radio program.

FINANCIALS: Sales and profits are in thousands of dollars—add 000 to get the full amount.

Notes regarding 1999: Through 9 months *(1999 sales and profits were not available for all companies at press time.)*

1999 Sales: $4,900	1999 Profits: $5,200	Stock Ticker: **AMEN**
1998 Sales: $1,100	1998 Profits: $-3,500	Employees: 37
1997 Sales: $ 300	1997 Profits: $-4,100	Fiscal Year Ends: 12/31
1996 Sales: $ 200	1996 Profits: $-2,500	
1995 Sales: $	1995 Profits: $ 700	

SALARIES/BENEFITS:

Pension Plan:	ESOP Stock Plan:	Profit Sharing:	Top Exec. Salary: $80,177	Bonus: $
Savings Plan:	Stock Purch. Plan:		Second Exec. Salary: $23,077	Bonus: $

COMPETITIVE ADVANTAGE: Over 600,000 members.

OTHER THOUGHTS:

Apparent Women Officers or Directors: 1
Apparent Minority Officers or Directors: 1
Hot Spot for Advancement for Women/Minorities:

LOCATIONS: ("Y" = Yes)

West:	Southwest:	Midwest:	Southeast:	Northeast:	International:
				Y	

CYBER MERCHANTS EXCHANGE INC

www.c-me.com

Industry Group Code: 51339A
Ranks within this company's industry group: Sales: 16　Profits: 16

BUSINESS ACTIVITIES ("Y" = Yes)

Financial Services:	Information/Publ.:	Technology:	Services:	Retailing:	Telecommunications:
Stock Brokerage	Portal/Hub/News	Computer Manuf.	Payments/Transfers	Retailer	Internet Serv. Provider
Mortgages/Loans	On-Line Community	Networking Equip.	Consulting	Auctions	Web Site Host　Y
Banking	Search Engine	Software Manuf.	Advertising/Marketing　Y	Mall	Server Farm
Insurance	Financial Data Publ.	Specialty Equipment	Outsourcing	Tickets/Travel	Specialty Telecom.
Credit Cards	Broadcasting/Music			Price Comparisons	High Speed Access

TYPES OF BUSINESS:

Business-to-Business Intermediary
Internet Sourcing Networks

BRANDS/DIVISIONS/AFFILIATES:

Internet Sourcing Network
Wholesale Auction Center
Factory Outlet Mall
World Wide Magic Net

GROWTH PLANS/SPECIAL FEATURES:

Cyber Merchants Exchange, formerly Worldwide Magic Net, connects retailers with vendors via private Internet Sourcing Networks (ISNs) and other Internet technology to allow them to communicate and conduct business more effectively. ISNs also provide vendors with a way to showcase their products to major retailers. This interactive product display is more effective than merely sending a paper catalog. C-ME also hosts an on-line virtual trade show that features footwear, clothing, consumer electronics, baby goods, home furnishings and other categories of merchandise. In addition to these lines of business, C-ME also provides custom web design and hosting for vendors. The company plans to gain additional vendors from the Pacific Rim countries to partner with its U.S.-based retail partners.

CONTACTS: Note: Officers with more than one job title may be intentionally listed here more than once.

Frank S. Yuan, CEO
Frank S. Yuan, Pres.
David Rau, CFO
Luz Jimenez, Human Resources
James Zheng, Chief Tech. Officer
Elissa Kuykendall, Company Contact

Phone: 626-793-5000	Fax: 626-793-5096
Toll-Free:	
Address: 600 South Lake Ave., Ste. 405, Pasadena, CA, 91106	

FINANCIALS: Sales and profits are in thousands of dollars—add 000 to get the full amount.

Notes regarding 1999: (1999 sales and profits were not available for all companies at press time.)

1999 Sales: $	1999 Profits: $- 700	Stock Ticker: **CMEE**
1998 Sales: $ 66	1998 Profits: $	Employees:　6
1997 Sales: $	1997 Profits: $- 600	Fiscal Year Ends: 6/30
1996 Sales: $	1996 Profits: $	
1995 Sales: $	1995 Profits: $	

SALARIES/BENEFITS:

Pension Plan:	ESOP Stock Plan:	Profit Sharing:	Top Exec. Salary: $25,818	Bonus: $
Savings Plan:	Stock Purch. Plan:		Second Exec. Salary: $	Bonus: $

COMPETITIVE ADVANTAGE:　Moving to aggresively add new vendor relationships.

OTHER THOUGHTS:

Apparent Women Officers or Directors:
Apparent Minority Officers or Directors: 3
Hot Spot for Advancement for Women/Minorities: Y

LOCATIONS: ("Y" = Yes)

West:	Southwest:	Midwest:	Southeast:	Northeast:	International:
Y					

Note: Financial information, benefits and other data can change quickly and may vary from those stated here.

CYBERCASH INC   www.cybercash.com

Industry Group Code: 52252A
Ranks within this company's industry group: Sales: 3   Profits: 4

BUSINESS ACTIVITIES ("Y" = Yes)

Financial Services:	Information/Publ.:	Technology:	Services:		Retailing:	Telecommunications:
Stock Brokerage	Portal/Hub/News	Computer Manuf.	Payments/Transfers	Y	Retailer	Internet Serv. Provider
Mortgages/Loans	On-Line Community	Networking Equip.	Consulting		Auctions	Web Site Host
Banking	Search Engine	Software Manuf. Y	Advertising/Marketing		Mall	Server Farm
Insurance	Financial Data Publ.	Specialty Equipment	Outsourcing		Tickets/Travel	Specialty Telecom.
Credit Cards	Broadcasting/Music				Price Comparisons	High Speed Access

TYPES OF BUSINESS:

Transaction Processing

BRANDS/DIVISIONS/AFFILIATES:

ICVerify, Inc.
CyberCoin
PayNow
InstaBuy

CONTACTS: *Note: Officers with more than one job title may be intentionally listed here more than once.*

James Condon, CEO
James Condon, Pres.
Denis N. Cavender, CFO
Ken Perez, Sr. VP-Mktg.
George Pappas, Exec. VP-Tech. & Strategic Dev.
Russell B. Stevenson, Jr., Sec.
Russell B. Stevenson, Jr., Sr. VP/General Counsel
Bruce G. Wilson, Exec. VP-Int'l Oper.
Thomas P. Costello, Sr. VP-Dev.
Thomas F. Calcagni, Dir.-Corp. Comm.
Thomas P. Costello, Sr.VP-Dev.
Maria Izurieta, VP-Finance

Phone: 703-620-4200	Fax: 703-620-4215
Toll-Free:	
Address: 2100 Reston Parkway, 3rd Fl., Reston, VA, 20191	

GROWTH PLANS/SPECIAL FEATURES:

CyberCash, Inc. is a provider of payment software and services, enabling electronic commerce for merchants operating either through physical stores or through the virtual world of the Internet. The company has developed marketing technologies and services that provide a secure, convenient means of making and accepting payments over the Internet, making on-line shopping safe and simple for consumers. With CyberCash's CyberCoin, customers can pay with cash that is transferred from their bank accounts, while PayNow allows customers to pay in the form of electronic checks. CyberCash recently established joint ventures in Japan and Germany and a strategic licensing arrangement in the United Kingdom to commercialize some of its payment solutions in these countries. The company recently acquired ICVerify, Inc., whose products include point-of-sale credit card processing software. CyberCash introduced its new InstaBuy service, based on its Agile Wallet technology, which it offers to merchants, on-line communities and financial institutions to simplify the way consumers make payments on-line. CyberCash has entered a partnership with NetGravity, a creator of on-line advertising software, in order to produce e-commerce software that will let consumers buy products by clicking on advertisements.

FINANCIALS: Sales and profits are in thousands of dollars—add 000 to get the full amount.

Notes regarding 1999: *(1999 sales and profits were not available for all companies at press time.)*

1999 Sales: $20,300	1999 Profits: $-43,100	Stock Ticker: **CYCH**
1998 Sales: $12,600	1998 Profits: $-30,900	Employees: 337
1997 Sales: $4,500	1997 Profits: $-26,200	Fiscal Year Ends: 12/31
1996 Sales: $ 100	1996 Profits: $-26,600	
1995 Sales: $ 100	1995 Profits: $-10,000	

SALARIES/BENEFITS:

Pension Plan:	ESOP Stock Plan:	Profit Sharing:	Top Exec. Salary: $220,000	Bonus: $
Savings Plan:	Stock Purch. Plan: Y		Second Exec. Salary: $209,160	Bonus: $

COMPETITIVE ADVANTAGE: The ability to simplify and enable on-line payments.

OTHER THOUGHTS:

Apparent Women Officers or Directors: 2
Apparent Minority Officers or Directors: 2
Hot Spot for Advancement for Women/Minorities: Y

LOCATIONS: ("Y" = Yes)

West:	Southwest:	Midwest:	Southeast:	Northeast:	International:
			Y	Y	Y

Note: Financial information, benefits and other data can change quickly and may vary from those stated here.

CYBERGUARD CORP　　　www.cyberguardcorp.com

Industry Group Code: 3341C
Ranks within this company's industry group: Sales: 5　Profits: 4

BUSINESS ACTIVITIES ("Y" = Yes)

Financial Services:	Information/Publ.:	Technology:		Services:	Retailing:	Telecommunications:
Stock Brokerage	Portal/Hub/News	Computer Manuf.		Payments/Transfers	Retailer	Internet Serv. Provider
Mortgages/Loans	On-Line Community	Networking Equip.	Y	Consulting	Auctions	Web Site Host
Banking	Search Engine	Software Manuf.	Y	Advertising/Marketing	Mall	Server Farm
Insurance	Financial Data Publ.	Specialty Equipment	Y	Outsourcing	Tickets/Travel	Specialty Telecom.
Credit Cards	Broadcasting/Music				Price Comparisons	High Speed Access

TYPES OF BUSINESS:
Software-Internet Security (Firewalls)

BRANDS/DIVISIONS/AFFILIATES:
CyberGuard Firewall
TradeWave
KnightSTAR Applicance

CONTACTS: *Note: Officers with more than one job title may be intentionally listed here more than once.*
David Proctor, CEO
Tommy D. Steele, Pres./COO
Terrence Zielinski, CFO
Karen E. Bowling, VP-Mktg.
Michael Wittig, VP-Chief Tech. Officer
Brian Foremny, Corp. Sec.
Brian Foremny, General Counsel
Fred Hawkes, VP-Oper.
Michael Wittig, VP-Worldwide Dev.
Robert E. Gelinas, VP-Sales
Robert F. Perks, VP-Worldwide Support Oper. And Int'l Oper.

Phone: 954-958-3900	Fax: 954-958-3901
Toll-Free:	
Address: 2000 W. Commercial Blvd., Ste. 200, Fort Lauderdale, FL, 33309	

GROWTH PLANS/SPECIAL FEATURES:
CyberGuard develops network security solutions that protect data and networks from unauthorized access. It provides its services to Fortune 1000 companies and governments all over the world. CyberGuard's most notable product is the CyberGuard Firewall, which is certified by U.S. and European government and commercial testing authorities. CyberGuard Firewall has won awards from a wide array of magazines and societies, including BYTE magazine, Federal Computer Week, Network Computing, InfoWorld and the National Software Testing Laboratory. Current customers of CyberGuard include the Chicago Stock Exchange, AT&T, Motorola Cellular, Southwest Airlines, VISA International, the British Ministry of Defense, the U.S. Department of Defense and the National Aeronautics and Space Administration. CyberGuard partners have access to full account management resources as part of a new customer support program via the Internet. CyberGuard's products were recently chosen by the National Basketball Association's Miami HEAT to secure their enterprise networks and the networks of the new American Airlines Arena in Miami. CyberGuard also received a certification from West Coast Labs (called Checkmark) that is a new, internationally recognized standard for firewall solutions. The KnightSTAR Appliance is CyberGuard's new fully-functional hardware/software firewall appliance for network administrators.

FINANCIALS: Sales and profits are in thousands of dollars—add 000 to get the full amount.
Notes regarding 1999: *(1999 sales and profits were not available for all companies at press time.)*

1999 Sales: $112,800	1999 Profits: $-8,115	Stock Ticker: **CYBG**
1998 Sales: $14,200	1998 Profits: $-15,500	Employees: 86
1997 Sales: $15,600	1997 Profits: $-12,500	Fiscal Year Ends: 6/30
1996 Sales: $45,100	1996 Profits: $-11,100	
1995 Sales: $45,100	1995 Profits: $-11,100	

SALARIES/BENEFITS:
Pension Plan:	ESOP Stock Plan:	Profit Sharing:	Top Exec. Salary: $235,594	Bonus: $
Savings Plan: Y	Stock Purch. Plan:		Second Exec. Salary: $123,077	Bonus: $25,000

COMPETITIVE ADVANTAGE: Excellent technology/First class client list.

OTHER THOUGHTS:
Apparent Women Officers or Directors:
Apparent Minority Officers or Directors:
Hot Spot for Advancement for Women/Minorities:

LOCATIONS: ("Y" = Yes)
West:	Southwest:	Midwest:	Southeast:	Northeast:	International:
	Y		Y	Y	

CYBERIAN OUTPOST INC www.outpost.com

Industry Group Code: 4541
Ranks within this company's industry group: Sales: 18   Profits: 16

BUSINESS ACTIVITIES ("Y" = Yes)

Financial Services:	Information/Publ.:	Technology:	Services:	Retailing:		Telecommunications:
Stock Brokerage	Portal/Hub/News	Computer Manuf.	Payments/Transfers	Retailer	Y	Internet Serv. Provider
Mortgages/Loans	On-Line Community	Networking Equip.	Consulting	Auctions		Web Site Host
Banking	Search Engine	Software Manuf.	Advertising/Marketing	Mall		Server Farm
Insurance	Financial Data Publ.	Specialty Equipment	Outsourcing	Tickets/Travel		Specialty Telecom.
Credit Cards	Broadcasting/Music			Price Comparisons		High Speed Access

TYPES OF BUSINESS:

Retail-Computers and Software
E-commerce
Internet Superstore

BRANDS/DIVISIONS/AFFILIATES:

Internet Shopping Network's Computer Superstore
ShopperConnection
Outpost.com

CONTACTS: *Note: Officers with more than one job title may be intentionally listed here more than once.*

Darryl Peck, CEO
Darryl Peck, Pres.
Katherine N. Vick, Exec. VP/CFO
Louise R. Cooper, VP-Worldwide Mktg.
Nancy O'DeaWyrick, Dir.-Human Resources
Michael R. Starkenburg, Chief Tech. Officer
Bruce C. Schellinkhout, VP-Oper.
Katherine N. Vick, Exec.VP-Business Dev.
Brett Lauter, Dir.-Customer Retention and Loyalty
Derek Holding, Exec.Dir.-Customer Experience

Phone: 860-927-2050	Fax: 860-927-8372
Toll-Free:	
Address: P.O. Box 636, Kent, CT, 06757	

GROWTH PLANS/SPECIAL FEATURES:

A leader in global e-commerce since 1995, Cyberian Outpost, Inc. operates an Internet-only superstore for computer products 24-hours a day, seven days a week. Outpost.com provides consumer and small office purchasers of computer products a superior selection, quick and easy search capabilities and product information on over 140,000 hardware, software and peripheral products. The company recently announced an exclusive strategic partnership with the Pan-Nordic on-line service. Cyberian Outpost acquired over 160,000 customers with its acquisition of the Internet Shopping Network's Computer Superstore customer base. The company and three other well-known Internet brands formed a groundbreaking network, ShopperConnection, to connect the Internet's leading specialty retailers. The company is featured on Amazon.com's Shop the Web shopping referral service.

FINANCIALS: Sales and profits are in thousands of dollars—add 000 to get the full amount.

Notes regarding 1999: *(1999 sales and profits were not available for all companies at press time.)*

1999 Sales: $85,203	1999 Profits: $-25,220	Stock Ticker: **COOL**
1998 Sales: $22,681	1998 Profits: $-7,092	Employees: 164
1997 Sales: $10,790	1997 Profits: $-1,338	Fiscal Year Ends: 2/28
1996 Sales: $1,900	1996 Profits: $- 400	
1995 Sales: $	1995 Profits: $	

SALARIES/BENEFITS:

Pension Plan:	ESOP Stock Plan:	Profit Sharing:	Top Exec. Salary: $139,385	Bonus: $11,000
Savings Plan:	Stock Purch. Plan:		Second Exec. Salary: $	Bonus: $

COMPETITIVE ADVANTAGE: Offers wide variety of items/Connected with other Internet retailers.

OTHER THOUGHTS:

Apparent Women Officers or Directors: 2
Apparent Minority Officers or Directors:
Hot Spot for Advancement for Women/Minorities:

LOCATIONS: ("Y" = Yes)

West:	Southwest:	Midwest:	Southeast:	Northeast:	International:
				Y	

CYBERSHOP.COM INC   www.cybershop.com

Industry Group Code: 4541
Ranks within this company's industry group: Sales: 21   Profits: 17

BUSINESS ACTIVITIES ("Y" = Yes)

Financial Services:	Information/Publ.:	Technology:	Services:	Retailing:		Telecommunications:
Stock Brokerage	Portal/Hub/News	Computer Manuf.	Payments/Transfers	Retailer	Y	Internet Serv. Provider
Mortgages/Loans	On-Line Community	Networking Equip.	Consulting	Auctions		Web Site Host
Banking	Search Engine	Software Manuf.	Advertising/Marketing	Mall		Server Farm
Insurance	Financial Data Publ.	Specialty Equipment	Outsourcing	Tickets/Travel		Specialty Telecom.
Credit Cards	Broadcasting/Music			Price Comparisons		High Speed Access

TYPES OF BUSINESS:
On-line Retailer

BRANDS/DIVISIONS/AFFILIATES:
electronics.net

GROWTH PLANS/SPECIAL FEATURES:

CyberShop International, Inc., an on-line retailer, offers over 40,000 different products to consumers. Included in these items are over 500 brands of electronics, beauty and fashion accessories, bedding and bath items, furniture, appliances, toys, sports and fitness items, housewares and gourmet foods. CyberShop is currently an anchor tenant in the department store area of America Online's shopping channel. The company also offers corporate gift services and gift certificates through its web site. A frequent-buyer program operates within cybershop.com; points are awarded to customers that can then be redeemed during future purchases.   In recent news, CyberShop announced an agreement with e-centives, Inc., a leading Internet-based direct marketing company.   The agreement enables CyberShop to deliver special offers that are targeted to consumers based on their personal profiles.

CONTACTS: *Note: Officers with more than one job title may be intentionally listed here more than once.*
Jeffrey S. Tauber, CEO/Pres.
Jeffrey Liest, COO
Jeffery Liest, CFO
John Signorello, VP/CIO
Linda Wiatrowski, VP-General Merchandise Mgr.
Jill Markus, VP/Sec.
Tomas Montgomery, VP-Oper.
Jill Markus, VP-Business Dev.
Jill Markus, VP-Store Dev.
Richard D.Gilbert, VP-Planning and Dev.

Phone: 201-234-5000	Fax: 201-234-5099
Toll-Free:	
Address: 116 Newark Ave., Jersey City, NJ, 07302	

FINANCIALS: Sales and profits are in thousands of dollars—add 000 to get the full amount.
Notes regarding 1999: *(1999 sales and profits were not available for all companies at press time.)*

1999 Sales: $12,500	1999 Profits: $-56,900	Stock Ticker: **CYSP**
1998 Sales: $4,814	1998 Profits: $-7,888	Employees: 42
1997 Sales: $1,495	1997 Profits: $-1,806	Fiscal Year Ends: 12/31
1996 Sales: $ 513	1996 Profits: $- 650	
1995 Sales: $	1995 Profits: $	

SALARIES/BENEFITS:

Pension Plan:	ESOP Stock Plan:	Profit Sharing:	Top Exec. Salary: $190,000	Bonus: $
Savings Plan:	Stock Purch. Plan:		Second Exec. Salary: $129,888	Bonus: $

COMPETITIVE ADVANTAGE: Over 40,000 products to choose from/Relationship with AOL.

OTHER THOUGHTS:
Apparent Women Officers or Directors: 1
Apparent Minority Officers or Directors:
Hot Spot for Advancement for Women/Minorities:

LOCATIONS: ("Y" = Yes)

West:	Southwest:	Midwest:	Southeast:	Northeast:	International:
				Y	

CYBERSOURCE.COM CORP   www.cybersource.com

Industry Group Code: 51339A
Ranks within this company's industry group: Sales: 7   Profits: 10

BUSINESS ACTIVITIES ("Y" = Yes)

Financial Services:	Information/Publ.:	Technology:		Services:		Retailing:	Telecommunications:	
Stock Brokerage	Portal/Hub/News	Computer Manuf.		Payments/Transfers	Y	Retailer	Internet Serv. Provider	
Mortgages/Loans	On-Line Community	Networking Equip.		Consulting	Y	Auctions	Web Site Host	
Banking	Search Engine	Software Manuf.	Y	Advertising/Marketing	Y	Mall	Server Farm	
Insurance	Financial Data Publ.	Specialty Equipment		Outsourcing	Y	Tickets/Travel	Specialty Telecom.	Y
Credit Cards	Broadcasting/Music					Price Comparisons	High Speed Access	

TYPES OF BUSINESS:

E-Commerce Processing Services and Systems
ASP-E-Commerce
E-Commerce Solutions

BRANDS/DIVISIONS/AFFILIATES:

Beyond.com

CONTACTS: *Note: Officers with more than one job title may be intentionally listed here more than once.*

William S. McKiernan, CEO
I. Evan Ellis Jr., Pres./COO
Charles E. Noreen Jr., CFO/VP-Finance and Admin.
William E. Donahoo, VP-Mktg.
Suzan Brown, Mgr.-Human Resources
Thomas A. Arnold, Chief Tech. Officer
Anthony F. Quilici, VP-Merchant Support
Robert Ford, VP-Engineering
Richard Scudellari, Corp. Sec.
Eric M. Wun, VP-Oper.
Steven W. Klebe, VP-Strategic Alliances
David Daetz, VP-Corp. Business Dev., Worldwide

Phone: 408-556-9100	Fax: 408-241-8270
Toll-Free:	
Address: 550 S. Winchester, Ste. 301, San Jose, CA, 95128	

GROWTH PLANS/SPECIAL FEATURES:

CyberSource Corporation is a provider of Internet commerce services that enable the secure sale and distribution of products and services. CyberSource's Internet Commerce Suite allows businesses to automate transactions that can be accessed through a commerce server or URL link from a web page. Most of CyberSource's customers sell digital products such as software, music and documents, as well as on-line content, games, subscription sites, pay-per-use and broadcasts. Some of the company's services include credit card processing, tax calculation, Internet fraud screening, export compliance, policy compliance, digital delivery and delivery address verification. Beyond.com, Buy.com, Compaq Computer, Egghead.com, MarketWatch.com and Shopping.com are a few of CyberSource's notable customers. CyberSource recently announced a strategic relationship with eCredit.com to provide on-line merchants the ability to offer credit, financing and credit card payment options to businesses and consumers. This partnership will allow consumers to benefit from a variety of payment options, while businesses will have the opportunity to increase their sales and lower implementation costs.

FINANCIALS: Sales and profits are in thousands of dollars—add 000 to get the full amount.

Notes regarding 1999: *(1999 sales and profits were not available for all companies at press time.)*

1999 Sales: $12,900	1999 Profits: $-24,100	Stock Ticker: **CYBS**
1998 Sales: $3,400	1998 Profits: $-10,100	Employees: 146
1997 Sales: $1,000	1997 Profits: $-4,300	Fiscal Year Ends: 12/31
1996 Sales: $ 100	1996 Profits: $-1,100	
1995 Sales: $	1995 Profits: $	

SALARIES/BENEFITS:

Pension Plan:	ESOP Stock Plan:	Profit Sharing:	Top Exec. Salary: $144,375	Bonus: $
Savings Plan:	Stock Purch. Plan:		Second Exec. Salary: $137,500	Bonus: $36,500

COMPETITIVE ADVANTAGE: Makes it easy for on-line sites to enable payment options and reduce fraud.

OTHER THOUGHTS:

Apparent Women Officers or Directors: 3
Apparent Minority Officers or Directors: 1
Hot Spot for Advancement for Women/Minorities: Y

LOCATIONS: ("Y" = Yes)

West:	Southwest:	Midwest:	Southeast:	Northeast:	International:
Y					

Note: Financial information, benefits and other data can change quickly and may vary from those stated here.

CYLINK CORP   www.cylink.com

Industry Group Code: 5112
Ranks within this company's industry group: Sales: 21   Profits: 11

BUSINESS ACTIVITIES ("Y" = Yes)

Financial Services:	Information/Publ.:	Technology:		Services:		Retailing:	Telecommunications:
Stock Brokerage	Portal/Hub/News	Computer Manuf.		Payments/Transfers	Y	Retailer	Internet Serv. Provider
Mortgages/Loans	On-Line Community	Networking Equip.		Consulting		Auctions	Web Site Host
Banking	Search Engine	Software Manuf.	Y	Advertising/Marketing		Mall	Server Farm
Insurance	Financial Data Publ.	Specialty Equipment		Outsourcing		Tickets/Travel	Specialty Telecom.
Credit Cards	Broadcasting/Music					Price Comparisons	High Speed Access

TYPES OF BUSINESS:

Software-Security
Wireless Communications Products

BRANDS/DIVISIONS/AFFILIATES:

Security Design International Inc.
PrivateWire

CONTACTS: Note: Officers with more than one job title may be intentionally listed here more than once.

William P. Crowell, CEO
William P. Crowell, Pres.
Roger Barnes, VP/CFO
Theresa Marcroft, VP-Worldwide Mktg.
Paul Massie, VP/CIO
Peter J. Slocum, VP-Engineering
Robert B. Fougner, General Counsel
Beverlea Smith Kerner, Investor Relations Mgr.
Sarah L. Engel, VP-Professional Services

Phone: 408-735-5800	Fax: 408-774-2530
Toll-Free:	
Address: 910 Hermosa Court, Sunnyvale, CA, 94088-3759	

GROWTH PLANS/SPECIAL FEATURES:

Cylink develops, markets and supports a family of secure e-commerce and communications solutions that protect and manage the access, privacy and integrity of transmitted information. Cylink primarily serves Fortune 500 companies, multinational financial institutions and government agencies all over the world. Cylink's technology incorporates American National Standards Institute and National Institute of Standards and Technology protocols. Some of Cylink's customers include Cisco Systems, IBM, Bank of America, the United States Treasury Department, the United States Department of Justice and the U.S. Postal Service. Cylink recently announced that it would be offering security consulting services to customers across Europe through its subsidiary, Security Design International, Inc., a product-independent security company that specializes in assessing network vulnerability. Cylink's PrivateWire software enabled more than six million Brazilian citizens to file their tax returns efficiently and securely over the Internet. The software significantly reduced costs, and its efficiency improved the public's perception of Receita Federal, Brazil's internal revenue service. The software allows approximately one million forms to be processed the day before the deadline, and about 100,000 forms an hour can be processed during peak times.

FINANCIALS: Sales and profits are in thousands of dollars—add 000 to get the full amount.

Notes regarding 1999: Through 9 months *(1999 sales and profits were not available for all companies at press time.)*

1999 Sales: $42,200	1999 Profits: $8,100	**Stock Ticker: CYLK**
1998 Sales: $42,800	1998 Profits: $5,100	Employees: 325
1997 Sales: $49,300	1997 Profits: $-58,800	Fiscal Year Ends: 12/31
1996 Sales: $52,000	1996 Profits: $1,200	
1995 Sales: $34,900	1995 Profits: $-1,100	

SALARIES/BENEFITS:

Pension Plan:	ESOP Stock Plan:	Profit Sharing:	Top Exec. Salary: $214,369	Bonus: $82,800
Savings Plan:	Stock Purch. Plan:		Second Exec. Salary: $185,000	Bonus: $80,000

COMPETITIVE ADVANTAGE: Solutions for critical security issues/International growth.

OTHER THOUGHTS:

Apparent Women Officers or Directors: 2
Apparent Minority Officers or Directors: 1
Hot Spot for Advancement for Women/Minorities:

LOCATIONS: ("Y" = Yes)

West:	Southwest:	Midwest:	Southeast:	Northeast:	International:
Y				Y	Y

DATEK ONLINE HOLDING CORP   www.datek.com

Industry Group Code: 5231
Ranks within this company's industry group: Sales: 7   Profits:

BUSINESS ACTIVITIES ("Y" = Yes)

Financial Services:		Information/Publ.:		Technology:	Services:	Retailing:	Telecommunications:
Stock Brokerage	Y	Portal/Hub/News		Computer Manuf.	Payments/Transfers	Retailer	Internet Serv. Provider
Mortgages/Loans		On-Line Community		Networking Equip.	Consulting	Auctions	Web Site Host
Banking		Search Engine		Software Manuf.	Advertising/Marketing	Mall	Server Farm
Insurance		Financial Data Publ.	Y	Specialty Equipment	Outsourcing	Tickets/Travel	Specialty Telecom.
Credit Cards		Broadcasting/Music				Price Comparisons	High Speed Access

TYPES OF BUSINESS:

On-line Stock Brokerage/Investment Banking
ECNs

BRANDS/DIVISIONS/AFFILIATES:

Datek Online Brokerage Services
Island ECN
Datek Online Clearing Corp.
Big Think

CONTACTS: *Note: Officers with more than one job title may be intentionally listed here more than once.*

Edward J. Nicoll, CEO
John Grifonetti, COO/Pres.
John Grifonetti, CFO
Robert Bethge, Chief Mktg. Officer
Dana Gershgorn, Human Resources Rep.
Peter Stern, Chief Tech. Officer
John Mullin, Pres.-Datek On-line Brokerage Services
Ralph Sorrentino, Pres.-Datek On-line Clearing

Phone: 732-516-8000	Fax: 732-548-7668
Toll-Free:	
Address: 100 Wood Ave. South, Iselin, NJ, 08830-2716	

GROWTH PLANS/SPECIAL FEATURES:

Datek Online Holding is one of the top five on-line brokerages ranked according to market share. The site is known for speedy execution of orders and real-time portfolio updates. Datek offers its customers free and unlimited real-time quotes, as well as free access to charts, news, stocks and fund reports and Smart Money University. Datek was also the first major on-line brokerage to extend its trading hours for Nasdaq stocks for individual investors. The Smart Money University page offers a vast array of information and advice on topics such as college planning, debt management, strategic investing and retirement planning. Datek recently upgraded several areas of its personalized customer pages. The pages now offer display preferences for users and a new, redesigned portfolio summary page that gives customers important details concerning their portfolios. Datek offers a 12 hour on-line trading day through Island ECN, a subsidiary, and has reported a substantial response to this feature. Approximately 30% of Datek's customers have enabled their accounts for the extended hours trading session.

FINANCIALS: Sales and profits are in thousands of dollars—add 000 to get the full amount.

Notes regarding 1999: *(1999 sales and profits were not available for all companies at press time.)*

1999 Sales: $	1999 Profits: $	**Stock Ticker: private**
1998 Sales: $75,000	1998 Profits: $	Employees: 377
1997 Sales: $	1997 Profits: $	Fiscal Year Ends: 12/31
1996 Sales: $	1996 Profits: $	
1995 Sales: $	1995 Profits: $	

SALARIES/BENEFITS:

Pension Plan:	ESOP Stock Plan:	Profit Sharing:	Top Exec. Salary: $	Bonus: $
Savings Plan:	Stock Purch. Plan:		Second Exec. Salary: $	Bonus: $

COMPETITIVE ADVANTAGE: One of the best on-line trading sites/Includes comprehensive features and services.

OTHER THOUGHTS:

Apparent Women Officers or Directors: 1
Apparent Minority Officers or Directors:
Hot Spot for Advancement for Women/Minorities:

LOCATIONS: ("Y" = Yes)

West:	Southwest:	Midwest:	Southeast:	Northeast:	International:
				Y	

DELL COMPUTER CORPORATION   www.dell.com

Industry Group Code: 3341A
Ranks within this company's industry group: Sales: 4   Profits: 3

BUSINESS ACTIVITIES ("Y" = Yes)

Financial Services:	Information/Publ.:	Technology:		Services:		Retailing:		Telecommunications:	
Stock Brokerage	Portal/Hub/News	Computer Manuf.	Y	Payments/Transfers		Retailer	Y	Internet Serv. Provider	
Mortgages/Loans	On-Line Community	Networking Equip.	Y	Consulting		Auctions		Web Site Host	
Banking	Search Engine	Software Manuf.	Y	Advertising/Marketing		Mall		Server Farm	
Insurance	Financial Data Publ.	Specialty Equipment	Y	Outsourcing		Tickets/Travel		Specialty Telecom.	
Credit Cards	Broadcasting/Music					Price Comparisons		High Speed Access	

TYPES OF BUSINESS:

Personal Computer Manufacturer
On-line Sales
Peripherals
Support Programs
Catalog and Mail-order Sales

BRANDS/DIVISIONS/AFFILIATES:

Latitude
Latitude XP
OptiPlex
Dimension XPS
PowerEdge
PowerVault
Precision Workstation

CONTACTS: *Note: Officers with more than one job title may be intentionally listed here more than once.*

Michael Dell, CEO
Charles H. Saunders, VP/Pres., Dell Japan
Thomas J. Meredith, Sr. VP/CFO
Klee Kleber, Consumer Mktg. Director
Robert Selinger, VP/Chief Tech. Officer
Jerome Norman Gregoire, Sr. VP/CIO
Thomas B. Green, Sr.VP/Secretary
Thomas B. Green, Sr. VP-Law and Admin.
David Allen, VP-Worldwide Oper.
Richard Owen, VP-Dell On-line Worldwide
Elizabeth Heller Allen, VP-Corp. Communications
Alex C. Smith, VP/Treas.
Michael Clifford, VP/CIO Global Services
David Forsyth, VP-Sales

Phone: 512-338-4400	Fax: 512-728-3653
Toll-Free: 800-288-5627	
Address: One Dell Way, Round Rock, TX, 78682	

GROWTH PLANS/SPECIAL FEATURES:

Dell Computer Corporation was founded in 1984 by Michael Dell and is headquartered in Round Rock, Texas, near Austin. The company is the world's largest direct computer systems seller, with revenues of $18.2 billion for the fiscal year ended January 29, 1999. The company manufactures and markets a full range of computer systems, including desktop computers, notebook computers, workstations and network server and storage products, as well as an extended selection of peripheral hardware and computing software. The company offers in-person relationships with corporate and institutional customers, as well as telephone and Internet purchasing, build-to-order computer systems, telephone and on-line technical support and next-day, on-site product service. The company sells its products and services to large corporate, government, medical and education customers, small-to-medium businesses and individuals. Dell is one of the fastest-growing among all major computer systems companies worldwide, with more than 29,300 employees around the globe. The Dell line of high-performance computer systems includes Dimension and OptiPlex desktop computers, Latitude and Inspiron notebook computers, PowerEdge network servers, Dell Precision workstation products and PowerVault storage products. Dell recently acquired ConvergeNet, the creator of storage domain management technology for enterprise storage area networks (SAN).

Dell hires large numbers of people to work in telephone support and sales. The firm recently built a major corporate campus at Round Rock, north of Austin, Texas and has announced a major new facility to be built in Nashville, Tennessee. Employees recieve stock options, profit sharing, 12 paid holidays, 10 paid personal business days and a week off during christmas. The company's workforce is trained for 38 hours out of the year.

FINANCIALS: Sales and profits are in thousands of dollars—add 000 to get the full amount.

Notes regarding 1999: *(1999 sales and profits were not available for all companies at press time.)*

1999 Sales: $18,243,000	1999 Profits: $1,460,000	**Stock Ticker: DELL**
1998 Sales: $12,327,000	1998 Profits: $944,000	Employees: 24,400
1997 Sales: $7,759,000	1997 Profits: $518,000	Fiscal Year Ends: 1/31
1996 Sales: $5,296,000	1996 Profits: $272,000	
1995 Sales: $3,475,300	1995 Profits: $149,200	

SALARIES/BENEFITS:

Pension Plan:	ESOP Stock Plan:	Profit Sharing:	Top Exec. Salary: $788,462	Bonus: $2,000,000
Savings Plan: Y	Stock Purch. Plan: Y		Second Exec. Salary: $616,346	Bonus: $2,000,000

COMPETITIVE ADVANTAGE:
The number one computer retailer on the Internet/custom-tailored web sites enable large customers to configure and order new computers and obtain negotiated discount pricing while on-line.

OTHER THOUGHTS:

Apparent Women Officers or Directors:
Apparent Minority Officers or Directors: 2
Hot Spot for Advancement for Women/Minorities: Y

LOCATIONS: ("Y" = Yes)

West:	Southwest:	Midwest:	Southeast:	Northeast:	International:
Y	Y	Y	Y	Y	Y

Note: Financial information, benefits and other data can change quickly and may vary from those stated here.

DIALOG CORPORATION PLC (THE)   www.dialog.com

Industry Group Code: 514191
Ranks within this company's industry group: Sales: 2   Profits: 3

BUSINESS ACTIVITIES ("Y" = Yes)

Financial Services:	Information/Publ.:		Technology:	Services:	Retailing:	Telecommunications:
Stock Brokerage	Portal/Hub/News	Y	Computer Manuf.	Payments/Transfers	Retailer	Internet Serv. Provider
Mortgages/Loans	On-Line Community		Networking Equip.	Consulting	Auctions	Web Site Host
Banking	Search Engine		Software Manuf.	Advertising/Marketing	Mall	Server Farm
Insurance	Financial Data Publ.	Y	Specialty Equipment	Outsourcing	Tickets/Travel	Specialty Telecom.
Credit Cards	Broadcasting/Music				Price Comparisons	High Speed Access

TYPES OF BUSINESS:
On-line Business Information

BRANDS/DIVISIONS/AFFILIATES:
WebTop.com
InfoSort
OfficeShopper

CONTACTS: *Note: Officers with more than one job title may be intentionally listed here more than once.*
Daniel M. Wagner, CEO
Patrick Sommers, COO
David Mattey, CFO
Frank Reid, Sr. VP-Human Resources, N. Amer.
Stephen Maller, Chief Tech. Officer
Marck Shipley, Dir.-Info. Tech., USA
Angus J. Carroll, Exec. VP-Worldwide Mktg. And Strategy
Andre Brown, CEO-eCommerce Div.
Kristian Talvitie, Head-US Investor Relations
Jason Molle, Pres.-the Americas
Ciaran Morton, Pres.-Europe, Middle East, Africa and Asia

Phone: 44-171-930-6900	Fax: 44-171-930-6006

Toll-Free:

Address: The Communications Bldg., 48 Leicester Sq., London, UK, WC2H7DB

GROWTH PLANS/SPECIAL FEATURES:

The Dialog Corporation plc, created by the merger of M.A.I.D. plc and Knight-Ridder Information Inc., is a provider of Internet-based information, technology and eCommerce solutions to the corporate market. The company recently unveiled WebTop.com, a new search engine that gives users three different search options. The Type and Search method allows the user to search in full sentences or multiple keywords. Copy and Paste allows the ability to copy and paste text from a document into the search query box. Drag and Drop, available through the company's k-check desktop application, enables the user to check a document to find related information on the Web. Dialog Corporation plc consists of three divisions: Information Services, Web Solutions and Internet Software and eCommerce. The company's Information Services Division serves over 20,000 corporate customers in 120 countries and provides instantaneous access to more than six billion pages of professional on-line information collected over nearly three decades. The Web Solutions and Software Division markets and delivers the technology in the company's on-line information division, including Muscat's intelligent search and retrieval technologies and InfoSort, the company's indexing system. The company's eCommerce Division's OfficeShopper service allows corporations the ability to purchase office supplies on-line. Headquartered in London, the Dialog Corporation also has offices in California, North Carolina and Switzerland.

FINANCIALS: Sales and profits are in thousands of dollars—add 000 to get the full amount.
Notes regarding 1999: *(1999 sales and profits were not available for all companies at press time.)*

1999 Sales: $	1999 Profits: $	Stock Ticker: **DIAL**
1998 Sales: $283,400	1998 Profits: $7,400	Employees: 904
1997 Sales: $76,100	1997 Profits: $-34,300	Fiscal Year Ends: 12/31
1996 Sales: $36,700	1996 Profits: $-12,400	
1995 Sales: $21,100	1995 Profits: $-5,600	

SALARIES/BENEFITS:

Pension Plan:	ESOP Stock Plan: Y	Profit Sharing:	Top Exec. Salary: $165,250	Bonus: $2,828
Savings Plan:	Stock Purch. Plan:		Second Exec. Salary: $141,586	Bonus: $2,794

COMPETITIVE ADVANTAGE: Six billion pages of data delivered to customers in 120 nations.

OTHER THOUGHTS:

	LOCATIONS: ("Y" = Yes)					
	West:	Southwest:	Midwest:	Southeast:	Northeast:	International:
Apparent Women Officers or Directors:	Y	Y	Y	Y	Y	Y
Apparent Minority Officers or Directors: 1						
Hot Spot for Advancement for Women/Minorities:						

DIGEX INC   www.digex.com

Industry Group Code: 5133E
Ranks within this company's industry group: Sales: 3   Profits: 1

BUSINESS ACTIVITIES ("Y" = Yes)

Financial Services:	Information/Publ.:	Technology:	Services:		Retailing:	Telecommunications:	
Stock Brokerage	Portal/Hub/News	Computer Manuf.	Payments/Transfers		Retailer	Internet Serv. Provider	Y
Mortgages/Loans	On-Line Community	Networking Equip.	Consulting		Auctions	Web Site Host	Y
Banking	Search Engine	Software Manuf.	Advertising/Marketing		Mall	Server Farm	Y
Insurance	Financial Data Publ.	Specialty Equipment	Outsourcing	Y	Tickets/Travel	Specialty Telecom.	
Credit Cards	Broadcasting/Music				Price Comparisons	High Speed Access	

TYPES OF BUSINESS:

Internet Host
Web Site Management
Private Network Solutions
E-Commerce Solutions
Co-Location of Servers
ASP Hosting

BRANDS/DIVISIONS/AFFILIATES:

Intermedia Communications
LDS Communications
Electronic Press Services Group

CONTACTS:
Note: Officers with more than one job title may be intentionally listed here more than once.

Mark Shull, CEO
Mark Shull, Pres.
Bradley Sparks, CFO
Robert B. Patrick, VP-Mktg.
Marthe S. Lattinville-Pace, VP-Human Resources
Ed Kern, VP/Chief Network Engineer
Dale May, VP-Technical Oper.
John F. Scott, VP-Business Planning
Robert E. London, VP-Mktg. Comm.
Nancy G. Faigen, Pres.-Sales and Service Delivery Group
Bryan T. Gernert, Sr. VP-Sales, Distribution, Client Services

Phone: 301-847-5000	Fax: 301-847-5215
Toll-Free:	
Address: One Digex Plaza, Beltsville, MD, 20705	

GROWTH PLANS/SPECIAL FEATURES:

Digex, Inc. is a leading independent national Internet carrier that focuses exclusively on businesses, government agencies and other institutional customers. The company offers its Internet solutions through three separate and highly-focused business units. The Business Internet Connectivity Group offers dedicated high-bandwidth Internet connectivity and security solutions for commercial Internet and Intranet communication applications. The Web Site Management Group provides fault-tolerant web site management and electronic commerce integration services to companies seeking to outsource the management of mission-critical World Wide Web presences. The Private Network Solutions Group seeks to create customized private label solutions for businesses seeking to provide Internet services without incurring the cost of building and managing their own facilities. Digex currently maintains technology partnerships with Intel, Cisco Systems and Sun Microsystems. Digex operates two data centers that contain more than 1,300 company-owned and managed servers, and the company provides network connectivity through an agreement with Intermedia Communications. The company recently acquired Electronic Press Services Group, a prominent integrator of electronic commerce solutions. Recently, Digex announced the launch of its app-Link Partner Program, which will allow Application Service Providers to use Digex's managed hosting infrastructure and services, enabling them to more rapidly and cost effectively deploy customer applications on the Internet.

FINANCIALS:
Sales and profits are in thousands of dollars—add 000 to get the full amount.
Notes regarding 1999: *(1999 sales and profits were not available for all companies at press time.)*

1999 Sales: $59,786	1999 Profits: $-64,999	
1998 Sales: $22,600	1998 Profits: $ 700	**Stock Ticker: DIGX**
1997 Sales: $11,600	1997 Profits: $2,300	Employees: 436
1996 Sales: $2,800	1996 Profits: $ 100	Fiscal Year Ends: 12/31
1995 Sales: $	1995 Profits: $	

SALARIES/BENEFITS:

Pension Plan: Y	ESOP Stock Plan:	Profit Sharing:	Top Exec. Salary: $	Bonus: $
Savings Plan:	Stock Purch. Plan:		Second Exec. Salary: $	Bonus: $

COMPETITIVE ADVANTAGE: Focus on serving the business and government market.

OTHER THOUGHTS:

Apparent Women Officers or Directors: 3
Apparent Minority Officers or Directors:
Hot Spot for Advancement for Women/Minorities: Y

LOCATIONS: ("Y" = Yes)

West:	Southwest:	Midwest:	Southeast:	Northeast:	International:
Y	Y	Y	Y	Y	

DIGITAL ISLAND INC   www.digisle.com

Industry Group Code: 51339
Ranks within this company's industry group: Sales: 22   Profits: 17

BUSINESS ACTIVITIES ("Y" = Yes)

Financial Services:	Information/Publ.:	Technology:	Services:	Retailing:	Telecommunications:	
Stock Brokerage	Portal/Hub/News	Computer Manuf.	Payments/Transfers	Retailer	Internet Serv. Provider	Y
Mortgages/Loans	On-Line Community	Networking Equip.	Consulting	Auctions	Web Site Host	Y
Banking	Search Engine	Software Manuf.	Advertising/Marketing	Mall	Server Farm	Y
Insurance	Financial Data Publ.	Specialty Equipment	Outsourcing	Tickets/Travel	Specialty Telecom.	
Credit Cards	Broadcasting/Music			Price Comparisons	High Speed Access	

TYPES OF BUSINESS:

Internet Host
Co-Location of Servers
Network Management
Customized Operating Services

BRANDS/DIVISIONS/AFFILIATES:

AristaSoft
VIEWonTV

CONTACTS: Note: Officers with more than one job title may be intentionally listed here more than once.

Ruann F. Ernst, CEO
Leo S. Spiegel, Pres.
Tom L. Thompson, CFO
Tim Wilson, VP-Mktg. and Int'l Sales
Peter Ekman, Dir. Human Resources
Allan Leinwand, VP/Chief Tech. Officer
Bruce Pinsky, VP-Solutions Engineering/CIO
Allan Leinwand, VP-Engineering
Paul Everson, VP-Oper.
Christopher J. Albinson, VP-Corp. Dev.
Sanne Higgins, VP-Corp. Comm.
Michael T. Sullivan, VP-Finance
Larry Levinson, VP-Merger Integration and Strategic Dev.

Phone: 415-228-4100	Fax: 415-228-4141
Toll-Free:	
Address: 353 Sacramento St., Ste. 1520, San Francisco, CA, 94111	

GROWTH PLANS/SPECIAL FEATURES:

Digital Island, Inc. offers a leading global e-business network for companies that are using the Internet for worldwide deployment of business-critical applications. The company has developed a private global Internet protocol applications network to avoid congestion points common on the public Internet and to allocate bandwidth and storage to maximize the performance and structure of its customers' applications. The firm provides a complete range of applications hosting, server management and co-location services in its four state-of-the-art data centers, and network management expertise in connection with its customers own data centers. The company also offers service level guarantees, customized billing, security services, network management and other application services.   Digital Island mainly targets multinational corporations.   Its customers, which include Cisco Systems and E*TRADE Group, use its services to facilitate e-commerce, on-line customer service, software and multimedia document distribution, sales force automation and distance learning.   Digital Island is currently initiating many innovations. Recently, the company announced a partnership with AristaSoft to deliver e-business applications worldwide and announced a partnership with VIEWonTV to expand its reach of global streaming media services. Digital Island was named one of 100 emerging companies to watch in 2000 by ComputerWorld magazine.

FINANCIALS: Sales and profits are in thousands of dollars—add 000 to get the full amount.

Notes regarding 1999: (1999 sales and profits were not available for all companies at press time.)

1999 Sales: $12,400	1999 Profits: $-50,900	Stock Ticker: ISLD
1998 Sales: $2,300	1998 Profits: $-16,800	Employees: 267
1997 Sales: $ 200	1997 Profits: $-5,400	Fiscal Year Ends: 9/30
1996 Sales: $	1996 Profits: $	
1995 Sales: $	1995 Profits: $	

SALARIES/BENEFITS:

Pension Plan:	ESOP Stock Plan:	Profit Sharing:	Top Exec. Salary: $165,167	Bonus: $
Savings Plan:	Stock Purch. Plan: Y		Second Exec. Salary: $162,000	Bonus: $

COMPETITIVE ADVANTAGE: Ability to facilitate broadband Internet service.

OTHER THOUGHTS:

OTHER THOUGHTS:	LOCATIONS: ("Y" = Yes)					
Apparent Women Officers or Directors: 1	West	Southwest:	Midwest:	Southeast:	Northeast:	International:
Apparent Minority Officers or Directors: 3	Y					
Hot Spot for Advancement for Women/Minorities: Y						

Note: Financial information, benefits and other data can change quickly and may vary from those stated here.

DIGITAL LAVA INC   www.digitallava.com

Industry Group Code: 5112
Ranks within this company's industry group: Sales: 75   Profits: 27

BUSINESS ACTIVITIES ("Y" = Yes)

Financial Services:	Information/Publ.:	Technology:		Services:	Retailing:	Telecommunications:
Stock Brokerage	Portal/Hub/News	Computer Manuf.		Payments/Transfers	Retailer	Internet Serv. Provider
Mortgages/Loans	On-Line Community	Networking Equip.		Consulting	Auctions	Web Site Host
Banking	Search Engine	Software Manuf.	Y	Advertising/Marketing	Mall	Server Farm
Insurance	Financial Data Publ.	Specialty Equipment		Outsourcing	Tickets/Travel	Specialty Telecom.
Credit Cards	Broadcasting/Music				Price Comparisons	High Speed Access

TYPES OF BUSINESS:
Software-Interactive Videos

BRANDS/DIVISIONS/AFFILIATES:
vPrism
VideoCapsule
VideoVisor

CONTACTS: *Note: Officers with more than one job title may be intentionally listed here more than once.*
Robert F. Greene, CEO
Joshua D.J. Sharfman, Pres.
Dan Gampe, CFO
Kipley L. Bruketa, VP-Mktg.
Michael Goodell, VP-Consulting and Services
Peter J. Webb, VP-Sales

Phone: 310-470-1149	Fax: 310-470-1769
Toll-Free: 800-934-2826	
Address: 10850 Wilshire Blvd., Ste. 1260, Los Angeles, CA, 90024	

GROWTH PLANS/SPECIAL FEATURES:

Digital Lava is a provider of software products and services related to the use of video for corporate training, communications, research and other applications. Digital Lava's product line includes vPrism, which allows users to organize and manage video and perform other video applications via the Internet, and VideoVisor, which allows users to access Digital Lava's VideoCapsule files and manage, manipulate and integrate video with other information on their desktop computers. VideoVisor has won several awards, including the Best New Streaming Product award at the Desktop Video Communications conference. In order to grow and remain competitive for the future, Digital Lava plans to expand the features and breadth of its publishing and desktop video software by implementing the ability to support the synchronized deployment of additional types of data and enhancing the manipulation of digital video. The company also offers consulting and support services. Shell Chemical, Vantive and Cisco selected Digital Lava's Internet software for e-learning solutions and communications. Digital Lava also has alliances with such firms as RealNetworks and Microsoft.

FINANCIALS: Sales and profits are in thousands of dollars—add 000 to get the full amount.
Notes regarding 1999: *(1999 sales and profits were not available for all companies at press time.)*

1999 Sales: $1,488	1999 Profits: $-10,086	**Stock Ticker: DGV**
1998 Sales: $1,500	1998 Profits: $-3,700	Employees: 21
1997 Sales: $ 600	1997 Profits: $-4,200	Fiscal Year Ends: 12/31
1996 Sales: $	1996 Profits: $-2,400	
1995 Sales: $	1995 Profits: $	

SALARIES/BENEFITS:

Pension Plan:	ESOP Stock Plan:	Profit Sharing:	Top Exec. Salary: $230,000	Bonus: $
Savings Plan:	Stock Purch. Plan:		Second Exec. Salary: $195,000	Bonus: $

COMPETITIVE ADVANTAGE: Focus on on-line video technologies.

OTHER THOUGHTS:

	LOCATIONS: ("Y" = Yes)					
Apparent Women Officers or Directors:	West:	Southwest:	Midwest:	Southeast:	Northeast:	International:
Apparent Minority Officers or Directors:	Y					
Hot Spot for Advancement for Women/Minorities:						

DIGITAL RIVER INC   www.digitalriver.com

Industry Group Code: 5112
Ranks within this company's industry group: Sales: 36   Profits: 65

BUSINESS ACTIVITIES ("Y" = Yes)

Financial Services:	Information/Publ.:	Technology:		Services:		Retailing:	Telecommunications:
Stock Brokerage	Portal/Hub/News	Computer Manuf.		Payments/Transfers		Retailer	Internet Serv. Provider
Mortgages/Loans	On-Line Community	Networking Equip.		Consulting		Auctions	Web Site Host
Banking	Search Engine	Software Manuf.	Y	Advertising/Marketing		Mall	Server Farm
Insurance	Financial Data Publ.	Specialty Equipment		Outsourcing	Y	Tickets/Travel	Specialty Telecom.
Credit Cards	Broadcasting/Music					Price Comparisons	High Speed Access

TYPES OF BUSINESS:

Electronic Software Delivery Technology
Outsourcing
On-line Processing

BRANDS/DIVISIONS/AFFILIATES:

www.digitalriver.com

GROWTH PLANS/SPECIAL FEATURES:

Digital River, Inc. developed a technology pattern that has allowed the company to become a leading provider of comprehensive electronic commerce outsourcing solutions to software publishers and on-line retailers. The company utilizes ESD, or Electronic Software Delivery, to provide these services to its customers, which include Lotus Development Corporation, Wal-Mart Stores, Inc., CompUSA, Inc., Micro Warehouse, Inc., Kmart Corporation and many others. The company has contracts with over 1,600 software product clients and 1,170 on-line retailer clients. Digital River achieves a unique edge by providing an outsourcing solution that allows its clients to promote their own brands while leveraging the company's technological and infrastructural investments. Though the company uses ESD, its primary technology is its proprietary commerce network server, or CNS, technology. This incorporates custom software applications that enable ESD, web store authorizing, fraud prevention, export control, merchandising programs and on-line registration. The majority of the company's sales come from software publisher clients.

CONTACTS: Note: Officers with more than one job title may be intentionally listed here more than once.

Joel A. Ronning, CEO
Perry W. Steiner, Pres.
Robert E. Strawman, CFO
Terrence M. Strom, VP-Mktg.
Nancy Brown, Human Resources
Kelly J. Wical, Chief Tech. Officer
Randy J. Womack, CIO
Gregory R.L. Smith, Controller
Gregory R.L. Smith, Sec.
Draper M. Jaffray, VP-Business Dev.
Robert E. Strawman, Treas.

Phone: 612-253-1234	Fax: 612-253-8497
Toll-Free:	
Address: 9625 W. 76th Street, Suite 150, Eden Prairie, MN, 55344	

FINANCIALS: Sales and profits are in thousands of dollars—add 000 to get the full amount.

Notes regarding 1999: *(1999 sales and profits were not available for all companies at press time.)*

1999 Sales: $75,100	1999 Profits: $27,700	Stock Ticker: **DRIV**
1998 Sales: $20,911	1998 Profits: $-13,798	Employees: 148
1997 Sales: $2,472	1997 Profits: $-3,485	Fiscal Year Ends: 12/31
1996 Sales: $ 111	1996 Profits: $- 689	
1995 Sales: $	1995 Profits: $- 100	

SALARIES/BENEFITS:

Pension Plan:	ESOP Stock Plan:	Profit Sharing:	Top Exec. Salary: $171,875	Bonus: $225,000
Savings Plan:	Stock Purch. Plan:		Second Exec. Salary: $63,718	Bonus: $100,000

COMPETITIVE ADVANTAGE: Operates in the booming e-retail industry/Excellent client base.

OTHER THOUGHTS:

Apparent Women Officers or Directors:	
Apparent Minority Officers or Directors:	
Hot Spot for Advancement for Women/Minorities:	

LOCATIONS: ("Y" = Yes)

West:	Southwest:	Midwest:	Southeast:	Northeast:	International:
		Y			

DLJDIRECT INC   www.dljdirect.com

Industry Group Code: 5231
Ranks within this company's industry group: Sales: 6   Profits: 4

BUSINESS ACTIVITIES ("Y" = Yes)

Financial Services:		Information/Publ.:		Technology:	Services:	Retailing:	Telecommunications:
Stock Brokerage	Y	Portal/Hub/News		Computer Manuf.	Payments/Transfers	Retailer	Internet Serv. Provider
Mortgages/Loans		On-Line Community		Networking Equip.	Consulting	Auctions	Web Site Host
Banking		Search Engine		Software Manuf.	Advertising/Marketing	Mall	Server Farm
Insurance		Financial Data Publ.	Y	Specialty Equipment	Outsourcing	Tickets/Travel	Specialty Telecom.
Credit Cards		Broadcasting/Music				Price Comparisons	High Speed Access

TYPES OF BUSINESS:

On-line Stock Brokerage/Investment Banking

BRANDS/DIVISIONS/AFFILIATES:

Donaldson, Lufkin and Jenrette (DLJ)
iNautix Technologies Inc.
MarketSpeed

CONTACTS: *Note: Officers with more than one job title may be intentionally listed here more than once.*

K. Blake Darcy, CEO
Glenn Tongue, Pres.
Kenneth J. Olshansky, Dir.-Finance and Strategic Projects
Denise Benou Stires, Dir.-Mktg.
Nicholas J. Tortorella, Dir.-Human Resources
Suresh Kumar, CIO
Michael Hogan, Sr.VP/General Counsel
Anthony P. Festa, Dir.-Compliance and Oper.
Rosemary T. McFadden, Dir.-International Business Dev.
Barry B. Mione, Dir.-Investor Services

Phone: 212-892-3000	Fax:
Toll-Free: 800-825-5723	
Address: 277 Ave., New York, NY, 10172	

GROWTH PLANS/SPECIAL FEATURES:

DLJdirect is a leading provider of on-line brokerage and investment services, offering automated securities order placement and research capabilities on the Internet. DLJdirect offers a customized software package for on-line trading and investment management called MarketSpeed. It allows investors to trade stocks, options, fixed income securities and mutual funds on-line and provides real-time quotes and news. The web site also offers TheStreet.com for members, which features an industry-leading editorial team that publishes about 40 original news stories daily. Market research on the site highlights a wide array of subjects, including mergers and acquisitions, most active stocks, comments on the week ahead, IPO information and economic indicators and discussions. In recent news, DLJdirect entered into a strategic alliance with Scudder Kemper Investments' subsidiary, Scudder Investments. Scudder customers will be converted and serviced by DLJdirect under the name DLJdirect for Scudder Investments. Recently, DLJdirect's Japanese subsidiary, DLJdirect SFG Securities Inc., started real-time on-line trading of 100 selected U.S. stocks. The company also announced two new no-load mutual funds, the DLJdirect Strategic Growth Fund and the DLJdirect Choice Technology Fund.

FINANCIALS: Sales and profits are in thousands of dollars—add 000 to get the full amount.

Notes regarding 1999: *(1999 sales and profits were not available for all companies at press time.)*

1999 Sales: $	1999 Profits: $	Stock Ticker: **DIR**
1998 Sales: $117,900	1998 Profits: $1,500	Employees: 374
1997 Sales: $67,200	1997 Profits: $-3,600	Fiscal Year Ends: 12/31
1996 Sales: $63,200	1996 Profits: $7,900	
1995 Sales: $47,300	1995 Profits: $6,900	

SALARIES/BENEFITS:

Pension Plan:	ESOP Stock Plan:	Profit Sharing:	Top Exec. Salary: $	Bonus: $
Savings Plan:	Stock Purch. Plan:		Second Exec. Salary: $	Bonus: $

COMPETITIVE ADVANTAGE: DLJ was an early leader in providing extensive content and full services to on-line customers.

OTHER THOUGHTS:

Apparent Women Officers or Directors: 3
Apparent Minority Officers or Directors: 1
Hot Spot for Advancement for Women/Minorities: Y

LOCATIONS: ("Y" = Yes)

West:	Southwest:	Midwest:	Southeast:	Northeast:	International:
				Y	

DOUBLECLICK INC　　www.doubleclick.net

Industry Group Code: 54189A
Ranks within this company's industry group: Sales: 2　Profits: 17

BUSINESS ACTIVITIES ("Y" = Yes)

Financial Services:	Information/Publ.:	Technology:		Services:		Retailing:	Telecommunications:
Stock Brokerage	Portal/Hub/News	Computer Manuf.		Payments/Transfers		Retailer	Internet Serv. Provider
Mortgages/Loans	On-Line Community	Networking Equip.		Consulting	Y	Auctions	Web Site Host
Banking	Search Engine	Software Manuf.	Y	Advertising/Marketing	Y	Mall	Server Farm
Insurance	Financial Data Publ.	Specialty Equipment		Outsourcing		Tickets/Travel	Specialty Telecom.
Credit Cards	Broadcasting/Music					Price Comparisons	High Speed Access

TYPES OF BUSINESS:

Internet Advertising Services

BRANDS/DIVISIONS/AFFILIATES:

DoubleClick Network
DoubleClick DART
DoubleClick Direct
DoubleClick AdServer
DoubleClick Local
DoubleClick International
Abacus Direct
NetGravity

CONTACTS: Note: Officers with more than one job title may be intentionally listed here more than once.

Kevin J. O'Connor, CEO
Kevin P. Ryan, COO/Pres.
Stephen Collins, CFO
Wenda Harris Millard, Exec. VP-Mktg. & Sales
Laura Ianuly, VP-Human Resources
Dwight A. Merriman, Chief Tech. Officer
Robert Linsky, VP-MIS
Thomas Etergino, Controller
John Sabella, VP-Engineering
Robert Linsky, VP-Oper.
Jeffrey E. Epstein, Exec.VP-Business Dev. and Acquisitions
Jonathon Shapiro, VP-Business Dev.

Phone: 212-683-0001	Fax: 212-889-0062
Toll-Free:	
Address: 41 Madison Ave., 32nd Floor, New York, NY, 10010	

GROWTH PLANS/SPECIAL FEATURES:

DoubleClick is a leading provider of comprehensive Internet advertising solutions for advertisers and web publishers. The company's technology and media expertise enable it to dynamically deliver highly-targeted, measurable and cost-effective Internet advertising for advertisers and to increase ad sales and improve ad space inventory management for web publishers. DoubleClick AdServer is a complete ad management software solution and DoubleClick DART matches advertiser target profiles with user profiles and delivers a specifically designed ad. In addition to these products, the company offers an advertising solution, DoubleClick Local, which targets users in a specific geographic region. DoubleClick also contributes greatly to community action by running public service announcement campaigns for a myriad of causes, from education to the environment. The company has delivered over 225 million public service announcement impressions and has run ads for organizations such as Partnership for a Drug Free America, The League Treatment Center, The Jimmy Fund and United Cerebral Palsy Association. In addition, DoubleClick recently announced the completion of a merger with Abacus Direct and NetGravity. DoubleClick has begun providing 35 domestic and 16 international clients with its Closed-Loop Marketing Solutions products that aim to close the loop between sales and advertising. Some of these new clients include such notable names as hotjobs.com, WeddingChannel.com, Irish Times and Webcity.

FINANCIALS: Sales and profits are in thousands of dollars—add 000 to get the full amount.

Notes regarding 1999: *(1999 sales and profits were not available for all companies at press time.)*

1999 Sales: $258,300	1999 Profits: $55,800	Stock Ticker: **DCLK**
1998 Sales: $80,200	1998 Profits: $-18,200	Employees:　482
1997 Sales: $30,600	1997 Profits: $-8,400	Fiscal Year Ends: 12/31
1996 Sales: $6,500	1996 Profits: $-3,200	
1995 Sales: $	1995 Profits: $	

SALARIES/BENEFITS:

Pension Plan:	ESOP Stock Plan:	Profit Sharing:	Top Exec. Salary: $180,000	Bonus: $27,000
Savings Plan:	Stock Purch. Plan:		Second Exec. Salary: $175,000	Bonus: $70,000

COMPETITIVE ADVANTAGE: Leading on-line advertising company/Superior software technology.

OTHER THOUGHTS:

Apparent Women Officers or Directors: 2
Apparent Minority Officers or Directors: 1
Hot Spot for Advancement for Women/Minorities:

LOCATIONS: ("Y" = Yes)

West:	Southwest:	Midwest:	Southeast:	Northeast:	International:
Y	Y	Y	Y	Y	Y

Note: Financial information, benefits and other data can change quickly and may vary from those stated here.

DOW JONES & COMPANY INC   www.dowjones.com

Industry Group Code: 51112
Ranks within this company's industry group: Sales: 2   Profits: 1

BUSINESS ACTIVITIES ("Y" = Yes)

Financial Services:	Information/Publ.:		Technology:	Services:	Retailing:	Telecommunications:
Stock Brokerage	Portal/Hub/News	Y	Computer Manuf.	Payments/Transfers	Retailer	Internet Serv. Provider
Mortgages/Loans	On-Line Community		Networking Equip.	Consulting	Auctions	Web Site Host
Banking	Search Engine	Y	Software Manuf.	Advertising/Marketing	Mall	Server Farm
Insurance	Financial Data Publ.	Y	Specialty Equipment	Outsourcing	Tickets/Travel	Specialty Telecom.
Credit Cards	Broadcasting/Music				Price Comparisons	High Speed Access

TYPES OF BUSINESS:

Financial Data Publishing
Business Publishing
General Interest Community Newspapers
On-Line Services

BRANDS/DIVISIONS/AFFILIATES:

Dow Jones Telerate
Dow Jones News Service
Dow Jones Capital Markets Report
Bridge International
Dow Jones Asian Equities Report
National Business Employment Weekly
The Wall Street Journal
Indepth Data, Inc.

CONTACTS: *Note: Officers with more than one job title may be intentionally listed here more than once.*

Peter R. Kahn, CEO
Jerome H. Bailey, Exec. VP/CFO
Ann Marks, VP/Chief Corp. Mktg. Officer
William A. Godfrey III, Chief Tech. Officer
Peter G. Skinner, Sec.
Peter G. Skinner, General Counsel
Scott D. Schulman, VP-Strategic Planning and Dev.
Richard J. Tofel, VP-Corp. Comm.
James A. Scaduto, VP-Employee Relations
Thomas W. McGuirl, Treas.
Karen Elliott House, Pres.- Dow Jones Int'l
Paul J. Ingrassia, Pres., Dow Jones Newswires

Phone: 212-416-2000	Fax: 212-732-8356
Toll-Free:	
Address: 200 Liberty Street, New York, NY, 10281	

GROWTH PLANS/SPECIAL FEATURES:

As the publisher of The Wall Street Journal, Dow Jones & Company is a leading global provider of business news and information. Its operations are divided into three segments: print publishing, electronic publishing and general-interest community newspapers. Dow Jones' position as the pre-eminent publisher of business and financial news and information extends well beyond the printed page, as the company also excels in electronically-delivered real-time news. Subscribers to the Dow Jones Newswires have access to the company's worldwide network of editors and reporters who gather the most comprehensive real-time news available. For those seeking an on-line business news and research tool, Dow Jones offers Dow Jones Interactive, a service that provides access to news and information from more than 6,000 sources, a custom news-tracking tool that automatically filters news and information based on an individual's needs and a financial center that covers more than 10 million public and private companies worldwide. Recently, Dow Jones & Company and Reuters Group plc announced they would combine Dow Jones Interactive and Reuters Business Briefing. The new joint venture, Dow Jones Reuters Business Interactive LLC, will be a leading global service provider of proprietary and third-party business information to corporate and professional markets.

The company offers employees a Family Resource Service, a Dependent Care Program, and unpaid Child Care Leave.

FINANCIALS: Sales and profits are in thousands of dollars—add 000 to get the full amount.

Notes regarding 1999: *(1999 sales and profits were not available for all companies at press time.)*

1999 Sales: $2,001,800	1999 Profits: $272,400	**Stock Ticker: DJ**
1998 Sales: $2,158,106	1998 Profits: $8,362	Employees: 8,300
1997 Sales: $2,572,518	1997 Profits: $-802,132	Fiscal Year Ends: 12/31
1996 Sales: $2,481,592	1996 Profits: $189,969	
1995 Sales: $2,283,761	1995 Profits: $189,572	

SALARIES/BENEFITS:

Pension Plan: Y	ESOP Stock Plan:	Profit Sharing: Y	Top Exec. Salary: $750,000	Bonus: $402,885
Savings Plan: Y	Stock Purch. Plan: Y		Second Exec. Salary: $600,000	Bonus: $271,110

COMPETITIVE ADVANTAGE: Name recognition/Worldwide services/Powerful customer base.

OTHER THOUGHTS:

Apparent Women Officers or Directors: 2
Apparent Minority Officers or Directors: 1
Hot Spot for Advancement for Women/Minorities: Y

LOCATIONS: ("Y" = Yes)

West:	Southwest:	Midwest:	Southeast:	Northeast:	International:
Y	Y	Y	Y	Y	Y

Note: Financial information, benefits and other data can change quickly and may vary from those stated here.

DRKOOP.COM INC   www.drkoop.com

Industry Group Code: 514191
Ranks within this company's industry group: Sales: 41   Profits: 27

BUSINESS ACTIVITIES ("Y" = Yes)

Financial Services:	Information/Publ.:		Technology:	Services:	Retailing:	Telecommunications:
Stock Brokerage	Portal/Hub/News	Y	Computer Manuf.	Payments/Transfers	Retailer	Internet Serv. Provider
Mortgages/Loans	On-Line Community	Y	Networking Equip.	Consulting	Auctions	Web Site Host
Banking	Search Engine		Software Manuf.	Advertising/Marketing	Mall	Server Farm
Insurance	Financial Data Publ.		Specialty Equipment	Outsourcing	Tickets/Travel	Specialty Telecom.
Credit Cards	Broadcasting/Music				Price Comparisons	High Speed Access

TYPES OF BUSINESS:

Portal-Healthcare

BRANDS/DIVISIONS/AFFILIATES:

GROWTH PLANS/SPECIAL FEATURES:

Based on the vision of Dr. C. Everett Koop, the former U.S. Surgeon General, Drkoop.com is committed to informing the public on medical conditions and health. Visitors to the web site gain access to medical databases, real-time medical news and interactive communities, and can purchase health care-related products and services on-line. Interactive tools on the web site allow consumers to quickly search for drug information and check for interactions with other prescription and over-the-counter drugs. The company generates its revenues from selling vitamins and supplements, filling prescriptions, comparing health insurance options and selling insurance on-line. Drkoop.com recently added a comprehensive library of mental health information, a weight loss center and a breast cancer awareness center. Drkoop.com received two Gold and two Silver awards at the eHealthcare World Awards, honoring the site for its trusted content and health care information for users. These awards were for the Best Site for Women, Best Interactive Assessment Tool, Best Branding Campaign and Best Managed Care Site.

CONTACTS:
Note: Officers with more than one job title may be intentionally listed here more than once.

Donald W. Hackett, CEO/Pres.
Dennis J. Upah, COO
Susan M. Georgen-Saad, CFO
Guy D. MacNeill, VP-Product Mktg.
Roy A. Smith, Chief Tech. Officer
Elizabeth Fischer, VP-Medical Informatics
David Dow, VP-Technical Oper.
Robert C. Hackett Jr., Exec. VP-Business Dev.
Neal Longwill, Sr.VP-Corp.Dev.

Phone: 512-583-5667	Fax: 512-583-5727
Toll-Free:	
Address: 7000 N. Mopac Ste. 400, Austin, TX, 78731	

FINANCIALS: Sales and profits are in thousands of dollars—add 000 to get the full amount.
Notes regarding 1999: *(1999 sales and profits were not available for all companies at press time.)*

1999 Sales: $	1999 Profits: $	Stock Ticker: **KOOP**
1998 Sales: $ 100	1998 Profits: $-9,100	Employees: 63
1997 Sales: $	1997 Profits: $- 600	Fiscal Year Ends: 12/31
1996 Sales: $	1996 Profits: $	
1995 Sales: $	1995 Profits: $	

SALARIES/BENEFITS:

Pension Plan:	ESOP Stock Plan:	Profit Sharing:	Top Exec. Salary: $146,250	Bonus: $
Savings Plan:	Stock Purch. Plan:		Second Exec. Salary: $144,750	Bonus: $

COMPETITIVE ADVANTAGE: Very hot company with a successful IPO/Strong name brand recognition.

OTHER THOUGHTS:

Apparent Women Officers or Directors: 1
Apparent Minority Officers or Directors:
Hot Spot for Advancement for Women/Minorities:

LOCATIONS: ("Y" = Yes)

West:	Southwest:	Midwest:	Southeast:	Northeast:	International:
	Y				

Note: Financial information, benefits and other data can change quickly and may vary from those stated here.

DRUGSTORE.COM INC   www.drugstore.com

Industry Group Code: 4541
Ranks within this company's industry group: Sales: 31   Profits: 18

BUSINESS ACTIVITIES ("Y" = Yes)

Financial Services:	Information/Publ.:	Technology:	Services:	Retailing:		Telecommunications:
Stock Brokerage	Portal/Hub/News	Computer Manuf.	Payments/Transfers	Retailer	Y	Internet Serv. Provider
Mortgages/Loans	On-Line Community	Networking Equip.	Consulting	Auctions		Web Site Host
Banking	Search Engine	Software Manuf.	Advertising/Marketing	Mall		Server Farm
Insurance	Financial Data Publ.	Specialty Equipment	Outsourcing	Tickets/Travel		Specialty Telecom.
Credit Cards	Broadcasting/Music			Price Comparisons		High Speed Access

TYPES OF BUSINESS:
Retail-On-line Drug Store

BRANDS/DIVISIONS/AFFILIATES:
RxAmerica
Rite Aid
General Nutrition Companies (GNC)

CONTACTS: *Note: Officers with more than one job title may be intentionally listed here more than once.*
Peter M. Neupert, CEO
Peter M. Neupert, Pres.
David E. Rostov, VP/CFO
Suzan F. DelBene, VP-Mktg./Store Dev.
Molly Fitch, Human Resources Mgr.
Kal Raman, VP/CIO
Chris McClain, Dir.-Merchandising
Mike Concannon, Dir.-Manufacturer Relations
Mark L. Silverman, Corp. Sec.
Mark L. Silverman, General Counsel
John Williams, Dir.-Business Dev.
Debby Fry Wilson, Dir.-Public and Gov't Relations

Phone: 425-372-3200	Fax: 425-372-3800
Toll-Free:	
Address: 13920 SE Eastgate Way, Ste. 300, Bellevue, WA, 98005	

GROWTH PLANS/SPECIAL FEATURES:

Drugstore.com is a leading on-line drugstore that offers health, beauty, wellness, personal care and pharmaceutical products and information. The company started its operations in February 1999 and has made sales to hundreds of thousands of customers. The web site offers thousands of brand-name products and sends e-mail messages to remind customers to purchase frequently used products. Drugstore.com recently formed strategic relationships with General Nutrition Companies (GNC) and Rite Aid Corporation. The alliance with Rite Aid allows customers to order prescription drugs on-line for pick-up at Rite Aid stores the same day the order was made. Amazon.com provides advertisement on its web site for Drugstore.com and is also the company's largest shareholder. Drugstore.com has developed a strong marketing plan to increase customer traffic, maximize repeat purchases and build brand recognition. Some of the web sites that Drugstore.com advertises on are America Online, Excite, Yahoo!, Netscape NetCenter, OnHealth, MedScape and Women.com. ProVantage, a leading healthcare knowledge company, announced a strategic alliance with Drugstore.com that will actively promote the company's Internet prescription filling services.

FINANCIALS: Sales and profits are in thousands of dollars—add 000 to get the full amount.
Notes regarding 1999: *(1999 sales and profits were not available for all companies at press time.)*

1999 Sales: $	1999 Profits: $	Stock Ticker: **DSCM**
1998 Sales: $ 100	1998 Profits: $-8,000	Employees:
1997 Sales: $	1997 Profits: $	Fiscal Year Ends: 12/31
1996 Sales: $	1996 Profits: $	
1995 Sales: $	1995 Profits: $	

SALARIES/BENEFITS:

Pension Plan:	ESOP Stock Plan:	Profit Sharing:	Top Exec. Salary: $	Bonus: $
Savings Plan:	Stock Purch. Plan:		Second Exec. Salary: $	Bonus: $

COMPETITIVE ADVANTAGE: New alliance with Amazon.com will lead Amazon's customers to Drugstore.com.

OTHER THOUGHTS:

Apparent Women Officers or Directors: 1
Apparent Minority Officers or Directors: 1
Hot Spot for Advancement for Women/Minorities:

LOCATIONS: ("Y" = Yes)

West:	Southwest:	Midwest:	Southeast:	Northeast:	International:
				Y	

E*TRADE GROUP INC   www.etrade.com

Industry Group Code: 5231
Ranks within this company's industry group: Sales: 3   Profits: 8

BUSINESS ACTIVITIES ("Y" = Yes)

Financial Services:		Information/Publ.:		Technology:	Services:	Retailing:	Telecommunications:
Stock Brokerage	Y	Portal/Hub/News		Computer Manuf.	Payments/Transfers	Retailer	Internet Serv. Provider
Mortgages/Loans		On-Line Community	Y	Networking Equip.	Consulting	Auctions	Web Site Host
Banking		Search Engine		Software Manuf.	Advertising/Marketing	Mall	Server Farm
Insurance		Financial Data Publ.	Y	Specialty Equipment	Outsourcing	Tickets/Travel	Specialty Telecom.
Credit Cards		Broadcasting/Music				Price Comparisons	High Speed Access

TYPES OF BUSINESS:

On-line Stock Brokerage/Investment Banking
Account Security
Portfolio Tracking and Records Management
Cash Management Services
Venture Capital

BRANDS/DIVISIONS/AFFILIATES:

E*TRADE Capital, Inc.
E*TRADE Online Ventures, Inc.
E*TRADE Securities, Inc.
Share Data, Inc.

CONTACTS: Note: Officers with more than one job title may be intentionally listed here more than once.

Christos M. Cotsakos, CEO
Kathy Levinson, Pres./COO
Leonard C. Purkis, CFO
Jerry D. Gramaglia, Sr. VP-Mktg. and Sales
Jerry A. Dark, VP-Human Resources
Brigitte VanBaelen, Sec.
Tom Bevilacqua, Exec.VP/General Counsel
Leonard C. Purkis, Exec.VP-Admin.
Stephen C. Richards, Sr. VP-Corp. Dev.
Jerry D. Gramaglia, Sr. VP-Comm.
Susan Wolfrom, Dir.-Investor Relations
Connie M. Dotson, Sr. VP-Service Quality
Brigitte VanBaelen, VP-Exec. Services and Community Dev.

Phone: 650-842-2500	Fax: 650-842-2552
Toll-Free:	
Address: Four Embarcadero Place, 2400 Geng Rd., Palo Alto, CA, 94303	

GROWTH PLANS/SPECIAL FEATURES:

E*TRADE Group, Inc. is a leading provider of on-line investing services and has established a popular, branded destination web site for self-directed investors. The company offers automated order placement and execution, along with a suite of products and services that can be personalized, including portfolio tracking, Java-based charting and quote applications, real-time market commentary and analysis, news and other information services. The company provides these services 24 hours a day, seven days a week by means of the Internet and touch-tone telephone, including interactive voice recognition, on-line service providers and direct modem access. E*TRADE's proprietary transaction-enabling technology supports highly-automated, easy-to-use and cost-effective services that empower its customers to take greater control of their investment decisions and financial transactions. Free resources available to the public on E*TRADE's web site include breaking financial news, real-time stock and option price quotes, corporate financial information and news announcements, live market commentary, personalized investment portfolios, investor community areas and search and filtering tools for mutual fund and fixed income products. The company's web site services three levels of investors/visitors, members and customers, with each successive group gaining access to additional value-added products and services.

FINANCIALS: Sales and profits are in thousands of dollars—add 000 to get the full amount.

Notes regarding 1999: *(1999 sales and profits were not available for all companies at press time.)*

1999 Sales: $662,300	1999 Profits: $-54,400	Stock Ticker: **EGRP**
1998 Sales: $285,000	1998 Profits: $- 700	Employees: 1,735
1997 Sales: $157,600	1997 Profits: $13,900	Fiscal Year Ends: 9/30
1996 Sales: $53,800	1996 Profits: $- 800	
1995 Sales: $23,400	1995 Profits: $2,600	

SALARIES/BENEFITS:

Pension Plan:	ESOP Stock Plan: Y	Profit Sharing:	Top Exec. Salary: $476,862	Bonus: $160,236
Savings Plan: Y	Stock Purch. Plan:		Second Exec. Salary: $292,100	Bonus: $67,561

COMPETITIVE ADVANTAGE: Popular, branded destination web site for self-directed investors.

OTHER THOUGHTS:

Apparent Women Officers or Directors: 6
Apparent Minority Officers or Directors: 1
Hot Spot for Advancement for Women/Minorities: Y

LOCATIONS: ("Y" = Yes)

West:	Southwest:	Midwest:	Southeast:	Northeast:	International:
Y					

E-LOAN INC   www.eloan.com

Industry Group Code: 52231
Ranks within this company's industry group: Sales: 2 Profits: 2

BUSINESS ACTIVITIES ("Y" = Yes)

Financial Services:		Information/Publ.:	Technology:	Services:	Retailing:	Telecommunications:
Stock Brokerage		Portal/Hub/News	Computer Manuf.	Payments/Transfers	Retailer	Internet Serv. Provider
Mortgages/Loans	Y	On-Line Community	Networking Equip.	Consulting	Auctions	Web Site Host
Banking		Search Engine	Software Manuf.	Advertising/Marketing	Mall	Server Farm
Insurance		Financial Data Publ.	Specialty Equipment	Outsourcing	Tickets/Travel	Specialty Telecom.
Credit Cards	Y	Broadcasting/Music			Price Comparisons	High Speed Access

TYPES OF BUSINESS:

On-line Mortgage Broker

BRANDS/DIVISIONS/AFFILIATES:

Benchmark Capital
eVentures
flexemortgage.com

CONTACTS: Note: Officers with more than one job title may be intentionally listed here more than once.

Chris Larsen, CEO
Janina Pawlowski, Pres./COO
Frank Siskowski, CFO
Joseph Kennedy, Sr. VP-Mktg.
Ro Carbone, Mgr.-Human Resources
Cameron King, Sr.VP-Integrated Tech.
William Crane, Sr.VP-Engineering
Harold Bonnikson, Sr.VP-Oper.
Joseph Kennedy, Sr.VP-Business Dev.

Phone: 925-241-2400	Fax: 925-556-2178
Toll-Free: 888-356-2622	
Address: 5875 Arnold Road, Dublin, CA, 94568	

GROWTH PLANS/SPECIAL FEATURES:

E-loan is an on-line provider of mortgages, auto loans, credit cards and small business loans. The E-loan web site offers a variety of services for borrowers, including comparisons of loans from the nation's leading lenders, tools for managing debt, E-Track's exclusive 24-hour loan status access, automatic notification regarding new products that meet specific customer needs and a host of other useful services. E-loan has strategic partnerships with such companies as Yahoo!, CBS Market Watch, Kelley Blue Book, telebank, iNSWEB, USATODAY.com, financecenter.com, SmartMoney.com, GoTo.com, NewRealty.com and Homes.com. E-loan was awarded the Privacy in Commerce Award by Junkbusters, a leading consumer resource on privacy and marketing. E-loan established regular independent audits of compliance with its strict control over personal data and was one of only four for-profit companies that was nominated for a pro-consumer privacy protection award. Recently, a joint venture between E-loan and eVentures acquired flexemortgage.com, the leading central on-line source of information for flexible mortgages in the United Kingdom. Recently, Gomez Advisors, a leading provider of e-commerce research and analysis for consumers and businesses, rated E-loan the number one on-line mortgage site. It was honored for its outstanding web tools and dedicated personal loan consultants.

FINANCIALS: Sales and profits are in thousands of dollars—add 000 to get the full amount.

Notes regarding 1999: Proforma *(1999 sales and profits were not available for all companies at press time.)*

1999 Sales: $22,100	1999 Profits: $-39,900	Stock Ticker: EELN
1998 Sales: $55,500	1998 Profits: $-11,200	Employees: 228
1997 Sales: $4,700	1997 Profits: $-1,400	Fiscal Year Ends: 12/31
1996 Sales: $	1996 Profits: $	
1995 Sales: $	1995 Profits: $	

SALARIES/BENEFITS:

Pension Plan:	ESOP Stock Plan:	Profit Sharing:	Top Exec. Salary: $	Bonus: $
Savings Plan:	Stock Purch. Plan:		Second Exec. Salary: $	Bonus: $

COMPETITIVE ADVANTAGE: Excellent technology that serves an immense market.

OTHER THOUGHTS:

Apparent Women Officers or Directors: 4
Apparent Minority Officers or Directors:
Hot Spot for Advancement for Women/Minorities: Y

LOCATIONS: ("Y" = Yes)

West:	Southwest:	Midwest:	Southeast:	Northeast:	International:
Y					Y

Note: Financial information, benefits and other data can change quickly and may vary from those stated here.

E-STAMP CORP   www.e-stamp.com

Industry Group Code: 51339A
Ranks within this company's industry group: Sales: 14   Profits: 11

BUSINESS ACTIVITIES ("Y" = Yes)

Financial Services:	Information/Publ.:	Technology:	Services:	Retailing:		Telecommunications:
Stock Brokerage	Portal/Hub/News	Computer Manuf.	Payments/Transfers	Retailer	Y	Internet Serv. Provider
Mortgages/Loans	On-Line Community	Networking Equip.	Consulting	Auctions		Web Site Host
Banking	Search Engine	Software Manuf.	Advertising/Marketing	Mall		Server Farm
Insurance	Financial Data Publ.	Specialty Equipment	Outsourcing	Tickets/Travel		Specialty Telecom.
Credit Cards	Broadcasting/Music			Price Comparisons		High Speed Access

TYPES OF BUSINESS:
On-line Postage Stamps

BRANDS/DIVISIONS/AFFILIATES:
SmartStamp

CONTACTS: *Note: Officers with more than one job title may be intentionally listed here more than once.*
Robert H. Ewald, CEO
Robert H. Ewald, Pres.
Anthony H. Lewis Jr., CFO
Nicole Eagan, Sr. VP-Mktg. and Sales
Carolyn E. Carder, VP-Human Resources
Martin Pagel, Chief Tech. Officer
Daniel Sagalowicz, VP-Engineering
Edward F. Malysz, VP/General Counsel/Sec.
Gwen Morris, VP Oper.
Roderick Witmond, VP-Strategic Dev. and Oper.

Phone: 650-554-8454	Fax: 650-843-8078
Toll-Free:	
Address: 2855 Campus Dr., Ste. 100, San Mateo, CA, 94403	

GROWTH PLANS/SPECIAL FEATURES:

E-Stamp Internet Postage provides small office and home office customers with a post office inside their PCs. The company pioneered on-line postage technology using the Internet and was the first to market a secure Internet-based software solution that generates PC postage. Users purchase postage on-line by credit card, transferring funds electronically or by pre-paid check. The postage is then downloaded and secured in the E-Stamp Security Device, an electronic vault that connects to a PC's printer port. When users print out envelopes in standard word processing or business applications, E-Stamp Internet Postage verifies the address and prints a SmartStamp with the correct postage. The amount is then deducted from the electronic vault. SmartStamps also may be printed on mailing labels or on the piece of mail itself. SmartStamp is the first new postage approved by the Postal Service in almost 80 years. E-Stamp maintains its competitive edge with a strong patent position. America Online, Beyond.com, Micro Center and Office Max are just a few of the retail stores, catalogues and e-commerce sites that distribute the E-Stamp Internet postage solution. Microsoft and AT&T recently invested in E-Stamp.

FINANCIALS: Sales and profits are in thousands of dollars—add 000 to get the full amount.
Notes regarding 1999: *(1999 sales and profits were not available for all companies at press time.)*

1999 Sales: $1,300	1999 Profits: $-27,800	Stock Ticker: **ESTM**
1998 Sales: $ 100	1998 Profits: $-10,700	Employees: 75
1997 Sales: $	1997 Profits: $-7,900	Fiscal Year Ends: 12/31
1996 Sales: $	1996 Profits: $-6,300	
1995 Sales: $	1995 Profits: $-1,300	

SALARIES/BENEFITS:

Pension Plan:	ESOP Stock Plan:	Profit Sharing:	Top Exec. Salary: $163,750	Bonus: $
Savings Plan: Y	Stock Purch. Plan:		Second Exec. Salary: $158,750	Bonus: $

COMPETITIVE ADVANTAGE: E-Stamp offers an innovative product, but it faces stiff competition, including new product introduced by industriy leader Pitney Bowes.

OTHER THOUGHTS:
Apparent Women Officers or Directors: 2
Apparent Minority Officers or Directors:
Hot Spot for Advancement for Women/Minorities:

LOCATIONS: ("Y" = Yes)

West:	Southwest:	Midwest:	Southeast:	Northeast:	International:
Y					

EARTHLINK NETWORK INC   www.earthlink.net

Industry Group Code: 51339
Ranks within this company's industry group: Sales: 2   Profits: 20

BUSINESS ACTIVITIES ("Y" = Yes)

Financial Services:	Information/Publ.:	Technology:	Services:	Retailing:	Telecommunications:	
Stock Brokerage	Portal/Hub/News	Computer Manuf.	Payments/Transfers	Retailer	Internet Serv. Provider	Y
Mortgages/Loans	On-Line Community	Networking Equip.	Consulting	Auctions	Web Site Host	Y
Banking	Search Engine	Software Manuf.	Advertising/Marketing	Mall Y	Server Farm	
Insurance	Financial Data Publ.	Specialty Equipment	Outsourcing	Tickets/Travel	Specialty Telecom.	
Credit Cards	Broadcasting/Music			Price Comparisons	High Speed Access	Y

TYPES OF BUSINESS:

Internet Service Provider
Web Site Host
Domain Registration

BRANDS/DIVISIONS/AFFILIATES:

MindSpring
Sprint
The Mall

CONTACTS: *Note: Officers with more than one job title may be intentionally listed here more than once.*

Charles G. Betty, CEO
Charles G. Betty, Pres.
Grayson L. Hoberg, Sr.VP-Finance/CFO
Brinton O.C. Young, Sr. VP-Mktg.
Michael Ihde, VP-Human Resources
David Beckemeyer, Chief Tech. Officer
Michael L. Mushet, VP-MIS
Richard A. Quiroga, VP-Corp. Controller
David R. Tommela, Sr.VP-Oper.
Howard Lefkowitz, VP-Business Dev. & Internet Mktg.
Kirsten Kappos, VP-Corp. Comm.

Phone: 626-296-2400	Fax: 626-296-2470
Toll-Free:	
Address: 3100 New York Dr., Pasadena, CA, 91107	

GROWTH PLANS/SPECIAL FEATURES:

EarthLink Network provides homes and businesses with reliable, unlimited Internet access, web hosting services and technical support. EarthLink has more than one million customers throughout the U.S. and Canada and, after merging with MindSpring, will be one of the top five U.S. Internet service providers, with a combined total of about 2.5 million subscribers. The company is partially owned by Sprint, and its services are co-branded as EarthLink Sprint Internet. EarthLink provides its members with a personalized start page, Click-n-Build home page builder, six megabytes of web space and free software. The company also offers domain registration, corporate e-mail, the ability to print postage from a desktop computer and technical support for businesses. EarthLink recently announced that it received A+ ratings in four categories of the Internet Benchmark tests performed by the Visual Networks company, Inverse. EarthLink has sustained high growth since its start in 1998 and has managed to keep one of the industry's lowest ratios of lost accounts. EarthLink recently selected MaMaMedia Inc., the leading provider of creativity-powered, web-based products for children, to provide children's content for the EarthLink web site.

FINANCIALS: Sales and profits are in thousands of dollars—add 000 to get the full amount.

Notes regarding 1999: *(1999 sales and profits were not available for all companies at press time.)*

1999 Sales: $670,400	1999 Profits: $-25,400	**Stock Ticker: ELNK**
1998 Sales: $175,900	1998 Profits: $-59,800	Employees: 1,343
1997 Sales: $79,200	1997 Profits: $-29,900	Fiscal Year Ends: 12/31
1996 Sales: $32,500	1996 Profits: $-31,100	
1995 Sales: $3,000	1995 Profits: $-6,100	

SALARIES/BENEFITS:

Pension Plan:	ESOP Stock Plan:	Profit Sharing:	Top Exec. Salary: $312,000	Bonus: $60,142
Savings Plan:	Stock Purch. Plan:		Second Exec. Salary: $210,025	Bonus: $45,042

COMPETITIVE ADVANTAGE: Merger with MindSpring created one of the largest ISP subscriber bases in the U.S.

OTHER THOUGHTS:

Apparent Women Officers or Directors: 3
Apparent Minority Officers or Directors: 1
Hot Spot for Advancement for Women/Minorities: Y

LOCATIONS: ("Y" = Yes)

West:	Southwest:	Midwest:	Southeast:	Northeast:	International:
Y					

EARTHWEB INC   www.earthweb.com

Industry Group Code: 514191
Ranks within this company's industry group: Sales: 29   Profits: 26

BUSINESS ACTIVITIES ("Y" = Yes)

Financial Services:	Information/Publ.:		Technology:	Services:		Retailing:	Telecommunications:
Stock Brokerage	Portal/Hub/News	Y	Computer Manuf.	Payments/Transfers		Retailer	Internet Serv. Provider
Mortgages/Loans	On-Line Community		Networking Equip.	Consulting		Auctions	Web Site Host
Banking	Search Engine		Software Manuf.	Advertising/Marketing	Y	Mall	Server Farm
Insurance	Financial Data Publ.		Specialty Equipment	Outsourcing		Tickets/Travel	Specialty Telecom.
Credit Cards	Broadcasting/Music					Price Comparisons	High Speed Access

TYPES OF BUSINESS:

Portal-Information Technology

BRANDS/DIVISIONS/AFFILIATES:

Developer.com
Datamation.com
HTMLGoodies.com
Dice.com

CONTACTS: Note: Officers with more than one job title may be intentionally listed here more than once.

Jack D. Hidary, CEO
Jack D. Hidary, Pres.
Irene Math, VP-Finance
Lou Weiss, VP-Mktg. Alliances
Rebecca Haralabatos, Dir.-Human Resources
John Kleine, VP-Systems and Oper.
Murray Hidary, Corp. Sec.
Steve Walter, VP-Business Dev.
Murray Hidary, Treas.

Phone: 212-725-6550	Fax: 212-725-6559
Toll-Free:	
Address: Three Park Ave., New York, NY, 10016	

GROWTH PLANS/SPECIAL FEATURES:

EarthWeb is a leading provider of business-to-business on-line services for the global information technology industry. EarthWeb focuses on a series of vertical markets such as networking and telecommunications, software development and Internet technologies. EarthWeb offers approximately 150 reference manuals, links to over 17,000 other resources and 375 tutorials on its web sites. The company operates many web sites, including Developer.com, HTMLGoodies.com and Datamation.com. The EarthWeb Internet site offers useful information on the marketplace and careers, along with expert advice and news in the information technology industry. In recent news, Apple Computer, Bear Stearns, Cisco, 3Com, General Motors and Charles Schwab announced agreements to post their information technology job openings on EarthWeb's site, dice.com. Dice.com is a web site specifically designed to list jobs for a wide array of information technology professionals, such as software development engineers. It currently lists over 130,000 jobs. The company recently secured 40 new advertisers for its web site. This marked a significant expansion of its advertiser base and included industry-leading companies such as Gateway, Ericcson, Hitachi and Office Max.

FINANCIALS: Sales and profits are in thousands of dollars—add 000 to get the full amount.

Notes regarding 1999: Proforma *(1999 sales and profits were not available for all companies at press time.)*

1999 Sales: $31,100	1999 Profits: $-22,600	Stock Ticker: **EWBX**
1998 Sales: $3,300	1998 Profits: $-9,000	Employees: 121
1997 Sales: $1,100	1997 Profits: $-7,800	Fiscal Year Ends: 12/31
1996 Sales: $ 500	1996 Profits: $-2,000	
1995 Sales: $	1995 Profits: $- 600	

SALARIES/BENEFITS:

Pension Plan:	ESOP Stock Plan:	Profit Sharing:	Top Exec. Salary: $160,000	Bonus: $41,000
Savings Plan: Y	Stock Purch. Plan:		Second Exec. Salary: $151,000	Bonus: $37,000

COMPETITIVE ADVANTAGE: Focus on full services for the IT community.

OTHER THOUGHTS:

Apparent Women Officers or Directors: 6
Apparent Minority Officers or Directors: 1
Hot Spot for Advancement for Women/Minorities: Y

LOCATIONS: ("Y" = Yes)

West:	Southwest:	Midwest:	Southeast:	Northeast:	International:
				Y	

Note: Financial information, benefits and other data can change quickly and may vary from those stated here.

EBAY INC   www.ebay.com

Industry Group Code: 4541B
Ranks within this company's industry group: Sales: 2   Profits: 1

BUSINESS ACTIVITIES ("Y" = Yes)

Financial Services:	Information/Publ.:	Technology:	Services:	Retailing:		Telecommunications:
Stock Brokerage	Portal/Hub/News	Computer Manuf.	Payments/Transfers	Retailer	Y	Internet Serv. Provider
Mortgages/Loans	On-Line Community	Networking Equip.	Consulting	Auctions	Y	Web Site Host
Banking	Search Engine	Software Manuf.	Advertising/Marketing	Mall		Server Farm
Insurance	Financial Data Publ.	Specialty Equipment	Outsourcing	Tickets/Travel		Specialty Telecom.
Credit Cards	Broadcasting/Music			Price Comparisons		High Speed Access

TYPES OF BUSINESS:

On-line Auctions
Magazine

BRANDS/DIVISIONS/AFFILIATES:

ebay.com
Jump, Inc.
Up4sale
Butterfield & Butterfield
eBay Magazine
Kruse International
Billpoint

CONTACTS: *Note: Officers with more than one job title may be intentionally listed here more than once.*

Margaret C. Whitman, CEO
Margaret C. Whitman, Pres.
Gary F. Bengier, CFO
Patrick Meade, SVP-Mktg.
Michael R. Jacobson, General Counsel
Gary Bengier, VP-Oper.
Jefery S. Skoll, VP-Strategic Planning, Analysis
Matt Bannick, VP-Community

Phone: 408-369-4830	Fax: 408-369-4855
Toll-Free:	
Address: 2005 Hamilton Ave., Ste. 350, San Jose, CA, 95125	

GROWTH PLANS/SPECIAL FEATURES:

If you want it, you can most likely find it at eBay.com, the premier Internet auction site run by eBay, Inc. eBay offers a solution to trust issues raised on other auction-based sites. Buyers and sellers are able to rate each other's performances. Any participant who racks up four negative responses is kicked out of the auction pool and can no longer participate in eBay trading. This rating system, along with a seemingly endless list of items to bid on, has helped the site become the largest of its kind. Categories of items traded include jewelry, stamps, coins, antiques, computers, dolls, trading cards, toys, memorabilia and collectibles. The company's revenue comes from collecting a small percentage of the final trading price. With about 4 million users, and over 20 million auctions taking place each fiscal quarter, eBay, Inc. is collecting more profits by the minute. The company is currently the only publicly-traded Internet retailer, and is expected to triple earnings in the year 2000. In 1999, the number of registered eBay users soared. Nearly 65,000 items are added to the auction block daily, from Pokey in Space figures and Star Wars toys to Tiffany glass pieces. The company is currently expanding through acquisitions and eyeing an international presence. Recently, eBay aquired Jump, Inc., and later made a $75 million, four-year promotion deal with America Online. Plans are currently underway to purchase Kruse International and Billpoint, Inc.

FINANCIALS: Sales and profits are in thousands of dollars—add 000 to get the full amount.

Notes regarding 1999: *(1999 sales and profits were not available for all companies at press time.)*

1999 Sales: $224,700	1999 Profits: $10,800	Stock Ticker: **EBAY**
1998 Sales: $47,400	1998 Profits: $2,400	Employees: 138
1997 Sales: $5,700	1997 Profits: $ 900	Fiscal Year Ends: 12/31
1996 Sales: $ 400	1996 Profits: $ 100	
1995 Sales: $	1995 Profits: $	

SALARIES/BENEFITS:

Pension Plan:	ESOP Stock Plan:	Profit Sharing:	Top Exec. Salary: $145,833	Bonus: $100,000
Savings Plan:	Stock Purch. Plan:		Second Exec. Salary: $125,000	Bonus: $25,000

COMPETITIVE ADVANTAGE:

Offers anything and everything/Ratings system allows sellers and buyers to trust each other. By being first-to-market, the firm captured an overwhelming lead in buyer and seller count.

OTHER THOUGHTS:

Apparent Women Officers or Directors: 1
Apparent Minority Officers or Directors:
Hot Spot for Advancement for Women/Minorities:

LOCATIONS: ("Y" = Yes)

West:	Southwest:	Midwest:	Southeast:	Northeast:	International:
Y					

Note: Financial information, benefits and other data can change quickly and may vary from those stated here.

EDGAR ONLINE INC   www.edgar-online.com

Industry Group Code: 5141
Ranks within this company's industry group: Sales: 4   Profits: 1

BUSINESS ACTIVITIES ("Y" = Yes)

Financial Services:	Information/Publ.:		Technology:	Services:	Retailing:	Telecommunications:
Stock Brokerage	Portal/Hub/News		Computer Manuf.	Payments/Transfers	Retailer	Internet Serv. Provider
Mortgages/Loans	On-Line Community		Networking Equip.	Consulting	Auctions	Web Site Host
Banking	Search Engine		Software Manuf.	Advertising/Marketing	Mall	Server Farm
Insurance	Financial Data Publ.	Y	Specialty Equipment	Outsourcing	Tickets/Travel	Specialty Telecom.
Credit Cards	Broadcasting/Music				Price Comparisons	High Speed Access

TYPES OF BUSINESS:
On-line Financial Data

BRANDS/DIVISIONS/AFFILIATES:
FreeEDGAR.com
The IPO Profiler

CONTACTS: *Note: Officers with more than one job title may be intentionally listed here more than once.*
Susan Strausberg, CEO
Tom Vos, COO/Pres.
Greg D. Adams, CFO
Jay Sears, VP-Mktg.
Kim Paterson, Human Resources
Marc Strausberg, CIO
David Trenck, VP-Oper.
Jay Gaines, Mgr.-Business Dev.

Phone: 203-852-5666	Fax: 203-852-5667
Toll-Free:	
Address: 50 Washington St., 9th Fl., Norwalk, CT, 06854	

GROWTH PLANS/SPECIAL FEATURES:

Connecticut-based EDGAR Online is a leading provider of business, financial and competitive information derived from U.S. Securities and Exchange Commission data. EDGAR Online has strategic relationships with numerous portals and business and financial information sites. Some of its partners include Lycos, PointCast, SmartMoney.com, CBS MarketWatch, MSNBC, Business Wire, Quote.com, Hoover's, Raging Bull, AltaVista and SNAP. The company recently introduced a new business plan analysis and development tool, IPO Profiler, that combines EDGAR Online's IPO Express, a feature that contains information about initial public offerings of stock, with DR-LINK, a high-powered information retrieval system with natural language search technology. The IPO Profiler technology allows writers and analysts of business plans to instantly compare the plan to companies that have previously filed for IPOs. EDGAR Online recently acquired the privately-held Partes Corporation and its web site, FreeEDGAR.com. FreeEDGAR specializes in developing products that automatically structure and deliver financial data by transforming flat text and HTML formats into interactive interpretation tools. EDGAR Online's Chairman and Chief Information Officer, Marc Stausberg, was awarded the Wootergaard Broadcasting Network.com's Kjakan Award for his demonstration of and commitment to the entrepreneurial spirit.

FINANCIALS: Sales and profits are in thousands of dollars—add 000 to get the full amount.
Notes regarding 1999: *(1999 sales and profits were not available for all companies at press time.)*

1999 Sales: $5,200	1999 Profits: $-4,200	Stock Ticker: **EDGR**
1998 Sales: $2,000	1998 Profits: $-2,200	Employees: 16
1997 Sales: $1,000	1997 Profits: $-1,500	Fiscal Year Ends: 12/31
1996 Sales: $ 200	1996 Profits: $- 800	
1995 Sales: $	1995 Profits: $- 200	

SALARIES/BENEFITS:

Pension Plan:	ESOP Stock Plan:	Profit Sharing:	Top Exec. Salary: $150,000	Bonus: $
Savings Plan:	Stock Purch. Plan:		Second Exec. Salary: $150,000	Bonus: $

COMPETITIVE ADVANTAGE: Leading site for investors seeking corporate disclosure documents.

OTHER THOUGHTS:
Apparent Women Officers or Directors: 4
Apparent Minority Officers or Directors:
Hot Spot for Advancement for Women/Minorities: Y

LOCATIONS: ("Y" = Yes)

West:	Southwest:	Midwest:	Southeast:	Northeast:	International:
				Y	

EDIFY CORP   www.edify.com

Industry Group Code: 5112
Ranks within this company's industry group: Sales: 12   Profits: 40

BUSINESS ACTIVITIES ("Y" = Yes)

Financial Services:	Information/Publ.:	Technology:		Services:	Retailing:	Telecommunications:
Stock Brokerage	Portal/Hub/News	Computer Manuf.		Payments/Transfers	Retailer	Internet Serv. Provider
Mortgages/Loans	On-Line Community	Networking Equip.		Consulting	Auctions	Web Site Host
Banking	Search Engine	Software Manuf.	Y	Advertising/Marketing	Mall	Server Farm
Insurance	Financial Data Publ.	Specialty Equipment		Outsourcing	Tickets/Travel	Specialty Telecom.
Credit Cards	Broadcasting/Music				Price Comparisons	High Speed Access

TYPES OF BUSINESS:

Software-E-Commerce Enablers
Voice Management Software

BRANDS/DIVISIONS/AFFILIATES:

S1
SMART Options
Electronic Workforce

CONTACTS: *Note: Officers with more than one job title may be intentionally listed here more than once.*

Jeffrey M. Crowe, CEO
Jeffrey M. Crowe, Pres.
James D. Pangborn, Dir.-Finance
Thomas M. Glassanos, VP-Mktg.
Patricia A. Tomlinson, VP-Human Resources
Charles H. Jolissaint, VP/Chief Tech. Officer
Jim Sutton, VP-Engineering
William A. Soward, VP-Business Dev.

Phone: 408-982-2000	Fax: 408-982-0777
Toll-Free: 800-944-0056	
Address: 2840 San Tomas Expwy., Santa Clara, CA, 95051	

GROWTH PLANS/SPECIAL FEATURES:

Edify, recently acquired by S1 Corporation, is a provider of Internet and voice e-commerce solutions that help companies manage customer relationships and make them more profitable. Edify's solutions allow companies to automate, personalize and integrate interactions with customers on the Internet, phone, fax, kiosk and call center. The company's SMART Options, or Smart Marketing and Relationship Management Options, offers a solution for developing, targeting, executing and evaluating real-time marketing campaigns for web sites, call centers, fax, e-mail, ATM and direct sales channels. Some of Edify's strategic partners include Microsoft, CheckFree, Intuit, Compaq, Price Waterhouse, LLP, Hewlett Packard and NEC. Edify recently announced its membership in the Wireless Application Protocol Forum (WAP). WAP is an industry association consisting of more than 225 companies interested in the growth of the mobile Internet market and interoperability of digital phones and wireless terminals. Edify's Electronic Workforce application platform will power the Nordstrom National Credit Bank, a financial subsidiary of Nordstrom, Inc.

FINANCIALS: Sales and profits are in thousands of dollars—add 000 to get the full amount.

Notes regarding 1999: *(1999 sales and profits were not available for all companies at press time.)*

1999 Sales: $	1999 Profits: $	Stock Ticker: **EDFY**
1998 Sales: $70,900	1998 Profits: $-6,700	Employees: 442
1997 Sales: $57,100	1997 Profits: $4,000	Fiscal Year Ends: 12/31
1996 Sales: $33,000	1996 Profits: $- 800	
1995 Sales: $16,000	1995 Profits: $- 100	

SALARIES/BENEFITS:

Pension Plan:	ESOP Stock Plan:	Profit Sharing:	Top Exec. Salary: $280,000	Bonus: $61,250
Savings Plan:	Stock Purch. Plan:		Second Exec. Salary: $175,000	Bonus: $40,775

COMPETITIVE ADVANTAGE: Enables customer interaction and support in critical areas.

OTHER THOUGHTS:

Apparent Women Officers or Directors: 1
Apparent Minority Officers or Directors:
Hot Spot for Advancement for Women/Minorities:

LOCATIONS: ("Y" = Yes)

West:	Southwest:	Midwest:	Southeast:	Northeast:	International:
Y					

Note: Financial information, benefits and other data can change quickly and may vary from those stated here.

EFAX INC   www.efax.com

Industry Group Code: 5133D
Ranks within this company's industry group: Sales: 1   Profits: 1

BUSINESS ACTIVITIES ("Y" = Yes)

Financial Services:	Information/Publ.:	Technology:		Services:	Retailing:	Telecommunications:	
Stock Brokerage	Portal/Hub/News	Computer Manuf.		Payments/Transfers	Retailer	Internet Serv. Provider	
Mortgages/Loans	On-Line Community	Networking Equip.		Consulting	Auctions	Web Site Host	
Banking	Search Engine	Software Manuf.	Y	Advertising/Marketing	Mall	Server Farm	
Insurance	Financial Data Publ.	Specialty Equipment		Outsourcing	Tickets/Travel	Specialty Telecom.	Y
Credit Cards	Broadcasting/Music				Price Comparisons	High Speed Access	

TYPES OF BUSINESS:

On-line Fax Services
Fax-to-E-mail Service

BRANDS/DIVISIONS/AFFILIATES:

JetFax
JetSuite
HotSend
PaperMaster

CONTACTS: *Note: Officers with more than one job title may be intentionally listed here more than once.*

Edward Prince, CEO
Ronald P. Brown, Pres.
Todd J. Kenck, VP-Finance/CFO
Ronald P. Brown, VP-Mktg.
Bonnie Vranes, Dir.-Human Resources
Michael Crandell, Exec. VP-Tech.
Lon B. Radin, VP-Engineering
Josh Mailman, VP-Oper.
Michael Tonneson, VP-Business Dev.

Phone: 650-324-0600	Fax: 650-327-6003
Toll-Free:	
Address: 1378 Willow Rd., Menlo Park, CA, 94025	

GROWTH PLANS/SPECIAL FEATURES:

eFax is a leading provider of Internet unified messaging solutions and is the dominant provider of Internet Telephony messaging. eFax provides a unique telephone number to all of its subscribers. The company is known for offering the world's first free fax-to-email service. Since its inception in February 1999, eFax has accumulated over 1.4 million clients. Some of eFax's affiliates include XOOM.com, Phone.com, WebTV, fortunecity.com, eGroups, FindLaw and AllBusiness.com. The company develops and licenses its telecommunications and document communications to many partners, including Hewlett-Packard, Xerox and Konica. eFax also packages its software, HotSend, JetSuite and PaperMaster, with millions of scanners, CD-writers and other computer peripherals. The company recently took the first step in its plans of global expansion by launching its unified messaging services in the United Kingdom. eFax was chosen to power a Comdex demonstration for Ricoh Corporation, a leading provider of digital imaging systems. Ricoh released a new product at the demonstration called eCabinet that uses the eFax fax-to-email technology. PC Magazine chose eFax as one of 100 Top Web Sites.

FINANCIALS: Sales and profits are in thousands of dollars—add 000 to get the full amount.

Notes regarding 1999: *(1999 sales and profits were not available for all companies at press time.)*

1999 Sales: $33,600	1999 Profits: $-63,300	Stock Ticker: **EFAX**
1998 Sales: $30,200	1998 Profits: $-1,500	Employees: 116
1997 Sales: $23,000	1997 Profits: $-6,200	Fiscal Year Ends: 12/31
1996 Sales: $12,900	1996 Profits: $-1,000	
1995 Sales: $13,200	1995 Profits: $-2,900	

SALARIES/BENEFITS:

Pension Plan:	ESOP Stock Plan:	Profit Sharing:	Top Exec. Salary: $180,000	Bonus: $
Savings Plan:	Stock Purch. Plan:		Second Exec. Salary: $150,000	Bonus: $

COMPETITIVE ADVANTAGE: 1.4 million subscribers.

OTHER THOUGHTS:

	LOCATIONS: ("Y" = Yes)					
	West:	Southwest:	Midwest:	Southeast:	Northeast:	International:
Apparent Women Officers or Directors:	Y					Y
Apparent Minority Officers or Directors:						
Hot Spot for Advancement for Women/Minorities:						

EGGHEAD.COM INC　　www.egghead.com

Industry Group Code: 4541
Ranks within this company's industry group: Sales: 5　Profits: 23

BUSINESS ACTIVITIES ("Y" = Yes)

Financial Services:	Information/Publ.:	Technology:	Services:	Retailing:		Telecommunications:
Stock Brokerage	Portal/Hub/News	Computer Manuf.	Payments/Transfers	Retailer	Y	Internet Serv. Provider
Mortgages/Loans	On-Line Community	Networking Equip.	Consulting	Auctions	Y	Web Site Host
Banking	Search Engine	Software Manuf.	Advertising/Marketing	Mall		Server Farm
Insurance	Financial Data Publ.	Specialty Equipment	Outsourcing	Tickets/Travel		Specialty Telecom.
Credit Cards	Broadcasting/Music			Price Comparisons		High Speed Access

TYPES OF BUSINESS:

On-line Software Sales
On-line Computers and Peripherals
Auctions

BRANDS/DIVISIONS/AFFILIATES:

Surplusdirect.com
Surplusauction.com
Surplus Software, Inc.

CONTACTS: Note: Officers with more than one job title may be intentionally listed here more than once.

Jerry Kaplan, CEO
Jeffery F. Sheahan, COO
John E. Labbett, CFO
Bari M. Abdul, Sr. VP-Mktg.
William A. Skinner, VP-Human Resources
Barry L. Hills, Chief Tech. Officer
Merle W. McIntosh, VP-Merch. Acquisition
Norman F. Hullinger, Sr. VP-Oper.
Jonathan W. Brodeur, Sr. VP-Business Dev.

GROWTH PLANS/SPECIAL FEATURES:

Egghead.com, Inc. is one of the leading on-line resellers of personal computer hardware, software, peripherals and accessories to consumers and businesses. The company sells a broad selection of PC hardware and software products, as well as other consumer merchandise, through three Internet web sites: Egghead.com, Surplusdirect.com and Surplusauction.com. Egghead offers products consisting of current and off-price merchandise, including excess, closeout, refurbished and reconditioned goods. The company recently enhanced its Internet presence by acquiring Surplus Software, Inc., which is based in Oregon. Egghead has completely shifted its business emphasis to Internet commerce by closing its former 80-store retail network. Egghead plans to become profitable, taking advantage of the projected growth in Internet commerce through marketing agreements with other high-traffic web sites, increased brand recognition and unique and compelling merchandise offers. In addition, Egghead has developed direct-ship programs with some of its suppliers through the use of electronic data interchange links, allowing it to further expand its product offerings without increasing its inventory and handling costs or exposure to inventory risk.

Phone: 509-922-7031	**Fax:** 509-921-9729	
Toll-Free:		
Address: 22705 East Mission Avenue, Liberty Lake, WA, 99019		

FINANCIALS: Sales and profits are in thousands of dollars—add 000 to get the full amount.

Notes regarding 1999: *(1999 sales and profits were not available for all companies at press time.)*

1999 Sales: $	1999 Profits: $-34,400	**Stock Ticker: EGGS**
1998 Sales: $207,800	1998 Profits: $-14,700	Employees: 200
1997 Sales: $89,000	1997 Profits: $-2,500	Fiscal Year Ends: 3/28
1996 Sales: $14,300	1996 Profits: $ 400	
1995 Sales: $ 100	1995 Profits: $- 400	

SALARIES/BENEFITS:

Pension Plan:	ESOP Stock Plan: Y	Profit Sharing:	Top Exec. Salary: $175,000	Bonus: $
Savings Plan: Y	Stock Purch. Plan:		Second Exec. Salary: $	Bonus: $

COMPETITIVE ADVANTAGE:　Has developed direct ship relationships with suppliers/Well known brand name.

OTHER THOUGHTS:

Apparent Women Officers or Directors:	
Apparent Minority Officers or Directors:	
Hot Spot for Advancement for Women/Minorities:	

LOCATIONS: ("Y" = Yes)

West:	Southwest:	Midwest:	Southeast:	Northeast:	International:
Y		Y			

Note: Financial information, benefits and other data can change quickly and may vary from those stated here.

EMC CORP   www.emc.com

Industry Group Code: 3341D
Ranks within this company's industry group: Sales: 1   Profits: 1

BUSINESS ACTIVITIES ("Y" = Yes)

Financial Services:	Information/Publ.:	Technology:		Services:		Retailing:	Telecommunications:
Stock Brokerage	Portal/Hub/News	Computer Manuf.	Y	Payments/Transfers		Retailer	Internet Serv. Provider
Mortgages/Loans	On-Line Community	Networking Equip.		Consulting		Auctions	Web Site Host
Banking	Search Engine	Software Manuf.	Y	Advertising/Marketing		Mall	Server Farm
Insurance	Financial Data Publ.	Specialty Equipment	Y	Outsourcing	Y	Tickets/Travel	Specialty Telecom.
Credit Cards	Broadcasting/Music					Price Comparisons	High Speed Access

TYPES OF BUSINESS:

Information Storage and Retrieval Technology
Solid-State Disk Drives (SSD)
Main Memory Products
Tape Backup Systems

BRANDS/DIVISIONS/AFFILIATES:

Symmetrix
Harmonix
Champion
MOSAIC:2000
McDATA Corporation
McDATA Holdings Corporation

CONTACTS: *Note: Officers with more than one job title may be intentionally listed here more than once.*

Michael C. Ruettgers, CEO
Michael C. Ruettgers, Pres.
William J. Teuber, Jr., VP/CFO
Cosmo Santullo, Sr. VP-Global Mktg.
Paul T. Dacier, VP/General Counsel
Charles J. Cavallaro, Sr.VP-Channel oper.
David A. Donatelli, Sr. VP-New Business Dev.
Colin G. Patteson, Sr. VP-Chief Admin. Officer/Treas.
Harold R. Dixon, Sr. VP Global Sales and Services
Charles J. Cavallaro, Sr. VP-Markets and Channel Oper.

Phone: 508-435-1000	Fax: 508-497-6961

Toll-Free: 800-424-3622 x362

Address: 35 Parkwood Drive, Hopkinton, MA, 01748-9103

GROWTH PLANS/SPECIAL FEATURES:

EMC Corporation and its subsidiaries design, manufacture, market and support a wide range of storage-related hardware, software and service products for the open systems, mainframe and network attached information storage and retrieval system market. EMC introduced its first Symmetrix Integrated Cached Disk array in 1991. Since then, EMC has become the leading supplier of intelligent information storage and retrieval technology for enterprise computing environments. These products are sold as integrated storage solutions for customers utilizing a variety of the world's most popular computer system platforms, including those of the company's resellers and a variety of other open systems and mainframe platforms. The company's common hardware architecture on which its principal products are based, MOSAIC:2000, Is based on interfaces and a modular design that allows new technologies to be incorporated more rapidly than with traditional architectures. This hardware architecture enables EMC to deliver advanced technologies to market quickly, while maintaining a consistent platform upon which its customers can expand capacity, performance, connectivity and intelligent functionality. The company owns McDATA Corporation, which designs, develops and markets fiber channel solutions for switched enterprise environments. McDATA also performs services under the ESCON original manufacturer agreement with IBM on behalf of McDATA Holdings Corporation, another of EMC's subsidiaries.

EMC is highly dedicated to diversity in its workplace.

FINANCIALS: Sales and profits are in thousands of dollars—add 000 to get the full amount.

Notes regarding 1999: *(1999 sales and profits were not available for all companies at press time.)*

1999 Sales: $	1999 Profits: $	Stock Ticker: **EMC**
1998 Sales: $3,973,700	1998 Profits: $793,400	Employees: 9,700
1997 Sales: $2,937,900	1997 Profits: $538,500	Fiscal Year Ends: 12/31
1996 Sales: $2,273,700	1996 Profits: $386,200	
1995 Sales: $1,921,300	1995 Profits: $326,800	

SALARIES/BENEFITS:

Pension Plan:	ESOP Stock Plan:	Profit Sharing:	Top Exec. Salary: $673,462	Bonus: $1,089,100
Savings Plan: Y	Stock Purch. Plan: Y		Second Exec. Salary: $519,226	Bonus: $710,176

COMPETITIVE ADVANTAGE: World leader in strategic intelligent data storage solutions/Fastest growing supplier of intelligent disk arrays for IBM-compatible mainframe storage.

OTHER THOUGHTS:

OTHER THOUGHTS:		LOCATIONS: ("Y" = Yes)					
Apparent Women Officers or Directors: 3		West:	Southwest:	Midwest:	Southeast:	Northeast:	International:
Apparent Minority Officers or Directors: 1		Y	Y	Y	Y	Y	Y
Hot Spot for Advancement for Women/Minorities: Y							

ENGAGE TECHNOLOGIES INC   www.engage.com

Industry Group Code: 54189A
Ranks within this company's industry group: Sales: 17   Profits: 74

BUSINESS ACTIVITIES ("Y" = Yes)

Financial Services:	Information/Publ.:	Technology:		Services:		Retailing:	Telecommunications:
Stock Brokerage	Portal/Hub/News	Computer Manuf.		Payments/Transfers		Retailer	Internet Serv. Provider
Mortgages/Loans	On-Line Community	Networking Equip.		Consulting		Auctions	Web Site Host
Banking	Search Engine	Software Manuf.	Y	Advertising/Marketing	Y	Mall	Server Farm
Insurance	Financial Data Publ.	Specialty Equipment		Outsourcing		Tickets/Travel	Specialty Telecom.
Credit Cards	Broadcasting/Music					Price Comparisons	High Speed Access

TYPES OF BUSINESS:

Internet-Focused Advertising/Marketing
Software-Internet Marketing

BRANDS/DIVISIONS/AFFILIATES:

AdKnowledge
Engage AudienceNet
Engage AdManager
Flycast Communications
CMGI, Inc.
I/PRO

CONTACTS: Note: Officers with more than one job title may be intentionally listed here more than once.

Paul L. Schaut, CEO/Pres.
David A. Fish, COO
Stephen A. Royal, CFO
Betsy Zikakis, VP-Mktg.
Paul Silver, Dir.-Employment
Daniel J. Jaye, Chief Tech. Officer
John McNamara, VP-Engineering
Michael K. Baker, VP-General Counsel
Dennis Ford, VP-Business Dev.
Stephen A. Royal, Treas.
Michael K. Baker, VP-Business Affairs

Phone: 978-684-3884	Fax: 978-684-3636
Toll-Free:	
Address: 100 Brickstone Sq., 1st Floor, Andover, MA, 01810	

GROWTH PLANS/SPECIAL FEATURES:

Engage Technologies, a majority-owned operating company of CMGI, Inc., provides profile-driven Internet marketing solutions. The company offers publishers, advertisers and merchants a wide array of software products, services and data that are designed to target and deliver advertisements and e-commerce offerings to specific audiences. Engage's main product is Engage AudienceNet, which is a global database containing 35 million anonymous consumer profiles. Engage AdManager is an on-line advertisement management system that automates the scheduling, targeting and delivery of ads on the Internet and reports the results. I/PRO, an Engage subsidiary, specializes in web traffic verification, measurement and analysis. Using Engage AudienceNet, the company has the capability to insert targeted streaming media into streaming media content. Engage has partnered with Microsoft to try to make streaming media more commonplace on the Internet and to make it more affordable for Internet content publishers. The company recently signed an agreement with Flycast Communications, a leading provider of Internet direct response advertising solutions, to use Engage's profiling technology throughout the Flycast Network. This partnership is designed to enhance the value of both companies' services and to optimize the response and return on investment for their clients.

FINANCIALS: Sales and profits are in thousands of dollars—add 000 to get the full amount.

Notes regarding 1999: (1999 sales and profits were not available for all companies at press time.)

1999 Sales: $16,000	1999 Profits: $-3,200	Stock Ticker: ENGA
1998 Sales: $2,200	1998 Profits: $-13,800	Employees: 331
1997 Sales: $	1997 Profits: $-10,300	Fiscal Year Ends: 7/31
1996 Sales: $	1996 Profits: $-2,400	
1995 Sales: $	1995 Profits: $	

SALARIES/BENEFITS:

Pension Plan:	ESOP Stock Plan:	Profit Sharing:	Top Exec. Salary: $118,295	Bonus: $115,500
Savings Plan:	Stock Purch. Plan:		Second Exec. Salary: $109,375	Bonus: $37,500

COMPETITIVE ADVANTAGE: Unique profiting technology/Focus on leading-edge streaming media solutions.

OTHER THOUGHTS:

Apparent Women Officers or Directors: 2
Apparent Minority Officers or Directors: 2
Hot Spot for Advancement for Women/Minorities: Y

LOCATIONS: ("Y" = Yes)

West:	Southwest:	Midwest:	Southeast:	Northeast:	International:
				Y	

Note: Financial information, benefits and other data can change quickly and may vary from those stated here.

ENTRUST TECHNOLOGIES INC   www.entrust.com

Industry Group Code: 5112
Ranks within this company's industry group: Sales: 18   Profits: 75

BUSINESS ACTIVITIES ("Y" = Yes)

Financial Services:	Information/Publ.:	Technology:		Services:	Retailing:	Telecommunications:
Stock Brokerage	Portal/Hub/News	Computer Manuf.		Payments/Transfers	Retailer	Internet Serv. Provider
Mortgages/Loans	On-Line Community	Networking Equip.		Consulting	Auctions	Web Site Host
Banking	Search Engine	Software Manuf.	Y	Advertising/Marketing	Mall	Server Farm
Insurance	Financial Data Publ.	Specialty Equipment		Outsourcing	Tickets/Travel	Specialty Telecom.
Credit Cards	Broadcasting/Music				Price Comparisons	High Speed Access

TYPES OF BUSINESS:

Software-Security
Digital Certificates

BRANDS/DIVISIONS/AFFILIATES:

Entrust/PKI 5.0
Entrust/Roaming
Entrust/Toolkit
Entrust/AutoRA

CONTACTS: *Note: Officers with more than one job title may be intentionally listed here more than once.*

John A. Ryan, CEO
John A. Ryan, Pres.
David L. Thompson, Sr. VP-Finance/CFO
Richard D. Spurr, Sr. VP-Sales and Mktg.
Brian O'Higgins, Exec.VP/Chief Tech. Officer
Bradley N. Ross, Pres.-European Oper.
Ian Curry, VP-Investor Relations
Robert Heard, Sr. VP-Mktg.
Hansen Downer, VP-Professional Services

Phone: 972-943-7300	**Fax:** 972-943-7305
Toll-Free:	
Address: 4975 Preston Park Blvd., Ste. 400, Plano, TX, 75093	

GROWTH PLANS/SPECIAL FEATURES:

Entrust Technologies Inc. develops, markets and sells products and services that allow enterprises to manage trusted, secure electronic communications and transactions over the Internet, extranets and intranets. Entrust automates the management of digital certificates, similar to electronic passports, which are a more secure and manageable authentication technology versus usernames and passwords. This security allows for multiple protected uses such as on-line banking or safe access to a company's computers for telecommuters, as well as applications for monitoring remote access and e-mail. Entrust/PKI manages digital certificates that allow users access to information. Entrust/PKI includes a certificate repository, certificate revocation (for when an employee leaves), key backup and recovery (if user forgets password) and support for non-repudiation of digital signatures. Entrust's more than 1,100 customers have issued four million digital certificates. Clients include J.P. Morgan, Salomon Smith Barney, FedEx, the U.S. Postal Service and the Government of Canada. Red Herring magazine chose Entrust as one of the top 100 public developers of business-to-business electronic commerce, and Network Magazine chose Entrust/PKI as product of the year.

FINANCIALS: Sales and profits are in thousands of dollars—add 000 to get the full amount.

Notes regarding 1999: *(1999 sales and profits were not available for all companies at press time.)*

1999 Sales: $85,200	1999 Profits: $5,900	**Stock Ticker: ENTU**
1998 Sales: $49,000	1998 Profits: $-23,800	Employees: 456
1997 Sales: $25,000	1997 Profits: $ 500	Fiscal Year Ends: 12/31
1996 Sales: $12,800	1996 Profits: $ 400	
1995 Sales: $4,000	1995 Profits: $-2,100	

SALARIES/BENEFITS:

Pension Plan:	ESOP Stock Plan: Y	Profit Sharing:	Top Exec. Salary: $180,874	Bonus: $79,800
Savings Plan:	Stock Purch. Plan:		Second Exec. Salary: $94,319	Bonus: $46,123

COMPETITIVE ADVANTAGE: Operates in one of the fastest-growing fields in e-commerce.

OTHER THOUGHTS:

Apparent Women Officers or Directors:
Apparent Minority Officers or Directors:
Hot Spot for Advancement for Women/Minorities:

LOCATIONS: ("Y" = Yes)

West:	Southwest:	Midwest:	Southeast:	Northeast:	International:
	Y				Y

ETOYS INC   www.etoys.com

Industry Group Code: 4541
Ranks within this company's industry group: Sales: 27   Profits: 10

BUSINESS ACTIVITIES ("Y" = Yes)

Financial Services:	Information/Publ.:		Technology:	Services:	Retailing:		Telecommunications:
Stock Brokerage	Portal/Hub/News	Y	Computer Manuf.	Payments/Transfers	Retailer	Y	Internet Serv. Provider
Mortgages/Loans	On-Line Community		Networking Equip.	Consulting	Auctions		Web Site Host
Banking	Search Engine		Software Manuf.	Advertising/Marketing	Mall		Server Farm
Insurance	Financial Data Publ.		Specialty Equipment	Outsourcing	Tickets/Travel		Specialty Telecom.
Credit Cards	Broadcasting/Music				Price Comparisons		High Speed Access

TYPES OF BUSINESS:

Retail-On-line Toy Store
Retail-On-line Baby Products

BRANDS/DIVISIONS/AFFILIATES:

BabyCenter, Inc.
Toys.com
BabyCenter.com

CONTACTS: Note: Officers with more than one job title may be intentionally listed here more than once.

Edward C. Lenk, CEO
Edward C. Lenk, Pres.
Steven J. Schoch, Sr. VP/CFO
Janine Bosquette, Sr. VP-Mktg.
Celia Hall, Dir.-Human Resources
John R. Hnanicek, Sr. VP/CIO
Jane Saltzman, VP-Merch.
Louis V. Zambello III, Sr. VP-Oper.
Stephen Paul, VP-Business Dev.
Frank C. Han, Sr.VP/Product Dev.
Jordan Posell, VP-Finance and Admin.

Phone: 310-664-8100	Fax: 310-664-8101
Toll-Free:	
Address: 2850 Ocean Park Blvd., Ste. 225, Santa Monica, CA, 90405	

GROWTH PLANS/SPECIAL FEATURES:

Etoys, Inc. is an on-line retailer that gives parents an easy, on-line shopping alternative to big toy stores. Through its web site, Etoys.com, the company offers numerous toys, books, videos, educational software and other software products, music and video games. The company draws its stock from more than 750 brands, including popular labels like Fisher-Price, LEGO and Mattel, to hard-to-find brands such as Ambi and Wild Goose. In addition, the web site provides consumers with toy recommendations, gift wrap and even a birthday reminder service. Etoys launched its site in October 1997 with an inventory of 1,000 toys from 100 manufacturers and has since expanded rapidly, to over 100,000 items. Recently, it bought Toys.com, its closest competitor, increasing Etoys' customer base by 35%. The company also grew through the addition of music, software, video and video game departments and the inception of its first non-Internet advertising campaign. Through the acquisition of BabyCenter, Inc., the operator of BabyCenter.com, Etoys now provides a source for parenthood information and baby products and supplies. Etoys just launched its web site in the U.K.

FINANCIALS: Sales and profits are in thousands of dollars—add 000 to get the full amount.

Notes regarding 1999: (1999 sales and profits were not available for all companies at press time.)

1999 Sales: $30,000	1999 Profits: $-28,600	Stock Ticker: **ETYS**
1998 Sales: $ 700	1998 Profits: $-2,300	Employees: 306
1997 Sales: $	1997 Profits: $	Fiscal Year Ends: 3/31
1996 Sales: $	1996 Profits: $	
1995 Sales: $	1995 Profits: $	

SALARIES/BENEFITS:

Pension Plan:	ESOP Stock Plan:	Profit Sharing:	Top Exec. Salary: $200,000	Bonus: $115,000
Savings Plan:	Stock Purch. Plan:		Second Exec. Salary: $150,000	Bonus: $60,000

COMPETITIVE ADVANTAGE: Has a better record of follow-through than competing sites. However, it faces tough competitors, including Amazon.com.

OTHER THOUGHTS:

Apparent Women Officers or Directors: 3
Apparent Minority Officers or Directors: 2
Hot Spot for Advancement for Women/Minorities: Y

LOCATIONS: ("Y" = Yes)

West:	Southwest:	Midwest:	Southeast:	Northeast:	International:
Y					

Note: Financial information, benefits and other data can change quickly and may vary from those stated here.

EXACTIS.COM INC   www.exactis.com

Industry Group Code: 54189A
Ranks within this company's industry group: Sales: 16   Profits: 10

BUSINESS ACTIVITIES ("Y" = Yes)

Financial Services:	Information/Publ.:	Technology:	Services:		Retailing:	Telecommunications:
Stock Brokerage	Portal/Hub/News	Computer Manuf.	Payments/Transfers		Retailer	Internet Serv. Provider
Mortgages/Loans	On-Line Community	Networking Equip.	Consulting		Auctions	Web Site Host
Banking	Search Engine	Software Manuf.	Advertising/Marketing	Y	Mall	Server Farm
Insurance	Financial Data Publ.	Specialty Equipment	Outsourcing	Y	Tickets/Travel	Specialty Telecom.
Credit Cards	Broadcasting/Music				Price Comparisons	High Speed Access

TYPES OF BUSINESS:

Advertising-E-Mail Marketing Services
E-mail Based Marketing

BRANDS/DIVISIONS/AFFILIATES:

SchwabAlerts
InfoBeat, Inc.

CONTACTS: *Note: Officers with more than one job title may be intentionally listed here more than once.*

E. Thomas Detmer, Jr., CEO
E. Thomas Detmer, Jr., Pres.
Kenneth W. Edwards, CFO
Michael J. Rosol, VP-Sales
Cindy Boyles, Human Resources Dir.
Cynthia L. Brown, VP-Engineering
Kenneth W. Edwards, Sec.
Gregory B. Schneider, VP-Mktg. and Business Dev.
Kenneth W. Edwards, Treas.

Phone: 303-675-2300	Fax: 303-675-2399
Toll-Free:	
Address: 707 17th St., Ste. 2850, Denver, CO, 80202	

GROWTH PLANS/SPECIAL FEATURES:

Exactis.com, Inc., formerly InfoBeat, Inc., is a provider of permission-based outsourced e-mail marketing and communications solutions primarily to companies in the media, e-commerce and financial services industries. The company principally operates through its e-mail newsletter service and its order and trade confirmation delivery service, sending approximately 10 million e-mails each day on behalf of clients such as MSNBC and Sony Music. Exactis launched its e-mail services business in 1998 and sold its publishing business to Sony Music, entering into an agreement to manage the production and delivery of these publishing products for Sony. The company has landed many new, prominent clients for which it outsources e-mail communications. These include Standard & Poor's, Spinner.com, First Union Bank and The Economist magazine. Exactis announced a groundbreaking e-mail notification program called SchwabAlerts for Charles Schwab's 2.2 million on-line customers, the first of its kind in the financial services industry.

FINANCIALS: Sales and profits are in thousands of dollars—add 000 to get the full amount.

Notes regarding 1999: *(1999 sales and profits were not available for all companies at press time.)*

1999 Sales: $	1999 Profits: $	Stock Ticker: **XACT**
1998 Sales: $2,800	1998 Profits: $-7,900	Employees: 135
1997 Sales: $ 400	1997 Profits: $-7,700	Fiscal Year Ends: 12/31
1996 Sales: $	1996 Profits: $	
1995 Sales: $	1995 Profits: $	

SALARIES/BENEFITS:

Pension Plan:	ESOP Stock Plan:	Profit Sharing:	Top Exec. Salary: $213,360	Bonus: $
Savings Plan: Y	Stock Purch. Plan: Y		Second Exec. Salary: $159,712	Bonus: $

COMPETITIVE ADVANTAGE: Sends 10 million e-mails monthly.

OTHER THOUGHTS:

Apparent Women Officers or Directors: 2
Apparent Minority Officers or Directors:
Hot Spot for Advancement for Women/Minorities:

LOCATIONS: ("Y" = Yes)

West:	Southwest:	Midwest:	Southeast:	Northeast:	International:
Y					

EXCITE@HOME   www.home.com

Industry Group Code: 514191
Ranks within this company's industry group: Sales: 7   Profits: 44

BUSINESS ACTIVITIES ("Y" = Yes)

Financial Services:	Information/Publ.:		Technology:	Services:	Retailing:	Telecommunications:	
Stock Brokerage	Portal/Hub/News	Y	Computer Manuf.	Payments/Transfers	Retailer	Internet Serv. Provider	Y
Mortgages/Loans	On-Line Community		Networking Equip.	Consulting	Auctions	Web Site Host	
Banking	Search Engine		Software Manuf.	Advertising/Marketing	Mall	Server Farm	
Insurance	Financial Data Publ.		Specialty Equipment	Outsourcing	Tickets/Travel	Specialty Telecom.	
Credit Cards	Broadcasting/Music				Price Comparisons	High Speed Access	Y

TYPES OF BUSINESS:

Portal for use by Cable Modem Viewers
Search Portal
News and Entertainment Portal

GROWTH PLANS/SPECIAL FEATURES:

Excite@Home is a global media company focused on combining leading brands and media with powerful distribution. The company is the result of the recent merger between Excite, Inc. and @Home Network. Since the merger, @Home Network has reached affiliate agreements with 15 leading cable companies across North America, including AT&T Broadband and Internet Services and Bresnan Communications. This allows the company to have access to approximately 58.7 million homes, which includes exclusive access to over 50% of the households in the United States and Canada. Excite@Home aims at providing home and business customers with 24-hour access to advanced, personalized services at different speeds over numerous communications devices, including PCs, pagers, cellular phones and television sets. Excite@Home and AT&T recently agreed to give AT&T PocketNet subscribers wireless access to Excite personalized content delivered over the AT&T Wireless IP Network. Excite@Home also completed the acquisition of iMall, Inc. Under the terms of the acquisition, iMALL will operate within the company's @Work division as the E-Business Services Group.

BRANDS/DIVISIONS/AFFILIATES:

Excite Boards
Excite, Inc.
Excite Shopping Channel
Excite email
Excite Search
iMall
Excite, Inc.
@Home Network

CONTACTS: *Note: Officers with more than one job title may be intentionally listed here more than once.*

Thomas A. Jermoluk, CEO
George Bell, Pres.
Kenneth A. Goldman, CFO
Leilani T Gayles, VP- Human Resources
Adam Grosser, VP -Engineering and Oper.

Phone: 650-556-5000	Fax: 650-556-5100
Toll-Free:	
Address: 450 Broadway St., Redwood City, CA, 94063	

FINANCIALS: Sales and profits are in thousands of dollars—add 000 to get the full amount.

Notes regarding 1999: Proforma *(1999 sales and profits were not available for all companies at press time.)*

1999 Sales: $420,500	1999 Profits: $-14,600	Stock Ticker: **ATHM**
1998 Sales: $48,000	1998 Profits: $-144,200	Employees: 570
1997 Sales: $7,400	1997 Profits: $-219,100	Fiscal Year Ends: 12/31
1996 Sales: $ 700	1996 Profits: $-24,500	
1995 Sales: $	1995 Profits: $-2,800	

SALARIES/BENEFITS:

Pension Plan:	ESOP Stock Plan:	Profit Sharing:	Top Exec. Salary: $	Bonus: $
Savings Plan:	Stock Purch. Plan:		Second Exec. Salary: $	Bonus: $

COMPETITIVE ADVANTAGE: Access to over 50% of the homes in America and Canada.

OTHER THOUGHTS:

Apparent Women Officers or Directors:
Apparent Minority Officers or Directors:
Hot Spot for Advancement for Women/Minorities:

LOCATIONS: ("Y" = Yes)

West:	Southwest:	Midwest:	Southeast:	Northeast:	International:
Y	Y		Y	Y	Y

EXODUS COMMUNICATIONS INC   www.exodus.net

Industry Group Code: 51339
Ranks within this company's industry group: Sales: 9   Profits: 22

BUSINESS ACTIVITIES ("Y" = Yes)

Financial Services:	Information/Publ.:	Technology:	Services:	Retailing:	Telecommunications:
Stock Brokerage	Portal/Hub/News	Computer Manuf.	Payments/Transfers	Retailer	Internet Serv. Provider
Mortgages/Loans	On-Line Community	Networking Equip.	Consulting	Auctions	Web Site Host
Banking	Search Engine	Software Manuf. Y	Advertising/Marketing	Mall	Server Farm Y
Insurance	Financial Data Publ.	Specialty Equipment	Outsourcing Y	Tickets/Travel	Specialty Telecom. Y
Credit Cards	Broadcasting/Music			Price Comparisons	High Speed Access

TYPES OF BUSINESS:

On-line Telecommunication Services
Co-Location of Servers
Management Services
Web Site Performance Software

BRANDS/DIVISIONS/AFFILIATES:

Service Metrics, Inc.

GROWTH PLANS/SPECIAL FEATURES:

Exodus Communications, Inc. provides businesses with services that allow them to outsource the management of their Internet sites. Clients store their servers in secure vaults at one of Exodus' 22 Internet Data Centers located around the nation. Besides storage space, the company offers such services to these businesses as server hosting, Internet connectivity, maintenance and network connections. Exodus' clients include prominent names like eBay, Lycos, Nordstrom and CBS Sports. The company is currently undergoing rapid growth through the addition of numerous clients and business acquisitions, reporting an expansion of 40% per quarter. It is increasing its geographic penetration and security service offerings in an attempt to remain competitive in the hosting industry, which is becoming increasingly crowded and high-powered with such big names as Intel and AT&T joining the market. Exodus currently stands as the number three company in web hosting. Recently, Exodus announced the acquisition of Service Metrics, Inc., which adds web site performance software to its portfolio.

CONTACTS: Note: Officers with more than one job title may be intentionally listed here more than once.

Ellen M. Hancock, CEO/Pres.
Richard S. Stoltz, COO
Richard S. Stoltz, CFO/Exec. VP-Finance
Beverly Brown, Exec. VP/Chief Mktg. Officer
Robert Helms, Dir.-Human Resources
B. V. Jagadeesh, Chief Tech. Officer
Michael E. Healy, Corp. Controller
James J. McInerney, Exec. VP-Engineering
Adam Wegner, Sec./VP
Adam Wegner, General Counsel

Phone: 408-346-2200	Fax: 408-346-2201
Toll-Free:	
Address: 2831 Mission College Blvd., Santa Clara, CA, 95054	

FINANCIALS: Sales and profits are in thousands of dollars—add 000 to get the full amount.

Notes regarding 1999: *(1999 sales and profits were not available for all companies at press time.)*

1999 Sales: $242,140	1999 Profits: $-130,323	Stock Ticker: **EXDS**
1998 Sales: $52,700	1998 Profits: $-66,400	Employees: 472
1997 Sales: $12,400	1997 Profits: $-25,300	Fiscal Year Ends: 12/31
1996 Sales: $3,100	1996 Profits: $-4,100	
1995 Sales: $1,400	1995 Profits: $-1,300	

SALARIES/BENEFITS:

Pension Plan:	ESOP Stock Plan:	Profit Sharing:	Top Exec. Salary: $381,546	Bonus: $
Savings Plan:	Stock Purch. Plan:		Second Exec. Salary: $211,101	Bonus: $75,000

COMPETITIVE ADVANTAGE: The leading server farm to the nation's top e-commerce companies/Faces much competition, including that of Intel.

OTHER THOUGHTS:

Apparent Women Officers or Directors: 3
Apparent Minority Officers or Directors: 3
Hot Spot for Advancement for Women/Minorities: Y

LOCATIONS: ("Y" = Yes)

West:	Southwest:	Midwest:	Southeast:	Northeast:	International:
Y	Y	Y	Y	Y	

F5 NETWORKS INC   www.f5.com

Industry Group Code: 5112
Ranks within this company's industry group: Sales: 63   Profits: 27

BUSINESS ACTIVITIES ("Y" = Yes)

Financial Services:	Information/Publ.:	Technology:		Services:	Retailing:	Telecommunications:
Stock Brokerage	Portal/Hub/News	Computer Manuf.		Payments/Transfers	Retailer	Internet Serv. Provider
Mortgages/Loans	On-Line Community	Networking Equip.		Consulting	Auctions	Web Site Host
Banking	Search Engine	Software Manuf.	Y	Advertising/Marketing	Mall	Server Farm
Insurance	Financial Data Publ.	Specialty Equipment		Outsourcing	Tickets/Travel	Specialty Telecom.
Credit Cards	Broadcasting/Music				Price Comparisons	High Speed Access

TYPES OF BUSINESS:

Software-Server

BRANDS/DIVISIONS/AFFILIATES:

3DNS Load balancing controller
See/IT Network management console
BIG/ip Server monitor/request router
Global/SITE controller

GROWTH PLANS/SPECIAL FEATURES:

F5 Networks, Inc. is a leading provider of integrated Internet traffic management solutions designed to improve the availability and performance of mission-critical Internet-based servers and applications. Since the release of the BIG/ip Controller, the company has increased its investment in research and development, marketing programs, domestic and international sales channels, customer support and services and general and administrative infrastructure. F5 has engaged sales representatives in the European and Asia Pacific markets and established distributor relationships with two international re-sellers. Approximately 73% of its revenue is derived from sales of BIG/ip. F5 received a Best of Show award for its global/SITE controller at Fall Internet World. global/SITE is an operating system-independent appliance that manages the publishing, distribution, synchronization and replication of file-based content and applications to local and geographically distributed Internet sites.

CONTACTS: Note: Officers with more than one job title may be intentionally listed here more than once.

Jeffrey S. Hussey, CEO
Jeffrey S. Hussey, Pres.
Robert J. Chamberlain, CFO/VP-Finance
Steven Goldman, VP-Mktg. and Sales
Brian R. Dixon, VP-Oper.
Robert J. Chamberlain, Treas.

Phone: 206-505-0800	Fax: 206-505-0801
Toll-Free:	
Address: 200 1st Ave. West, Ste. 500, Seattle, WA, 98119	

FINANCIALS: Sales and profits are in thousands of dollars—add 000 to get the full amount.

Notes regarding 1999: *(1999 sales and profits were not available for all companies at press time.)*

1999 Sales: $27,800	1999 Profits: $-4,300	**Stock Ticker: FFIV**
1998 Sales: $4,800	1998 Profits: $-3,700	Employees: 187
1997 Sales: $ 200	1997 Profits: $-1,500	Fiscal Year Ends: 9/30
1996 Sales: $	1996 Profits: $- 300	
1995 Sales: $	1995 Profits: $	

SALARIES/BENEFITS:

Pension Plan:	ESOP Stock Plan: Y	Profit Sharing:	Top Exec. Salary: $131,945	Bonus: $
Savings Plan: Y	Stock Purch. Plan:		Second Exec. Salary: $125,000	Bonus: $

COMPETITIVE ADVANTAGE: Award-winning technology.

OTHER THOUGHTS:

Apparent Women Officers or Directors: 2
Apparent Minority Officers or Directors: 1
Hot Spot for Advancement for Women/Minorities:

LOCATIONS: ("Y" = Yes)

West:	Southwest:	Midwest:	Southeast:	Northeast:	International:
Y		Y		Y	

FASHIONMALL.COM INC   www.fashionmall.com

Industry Group Code: 4541
Ranks within this company's industry group: Sales: 24   Profits:

BUSINESS ACTIVITIES ("Y" = Yes)

Financial Services:	Information/Publ.:	Technology:	Services:	Retailing:		Telecommunications:
Stock Brokerage	Portal/Hub/News	Computer Manuf.	Payments/Transfers	Retailer	Y	Internet Serv. Provider
Mortgages/Loans	On-Line Community	Networking Equip.	Consulting	Auctions		Web Site Host
Banking	Search Engine	Software Manuf.	Advertising/Marketing	Mall	Y	Server Farm
Insurance	Financial Data Publ.	Specialty Equipment	Outsourcing	Tickets/Travel		Specialty Telecom.
Credit Cards	Broadcasting/Music			Price Comparisons		High Speed Access

TYPES OF BUSINESS:

On-line Retailer

BRANDS/DIVISIONS/AFFILIATES:

Outletmall.com, Inc.

CONTACTS: *Note: Officers with more than one job title may be intentionally listed here more than once.*

Benjamin Narasin, CEO/Pres.
Ronald Forehand, COO
Anne-Marie Forehand, VP, Outletmall.com

Phone: 212-891-6064	**Fax:** 212-891-6033
Toll-Free:	
Address: 575 Madison Ave., New York, NY, 10022	

GROWTH PLANS/SPECIAL FEATURES:

Fashionmall.com is an on-line retailer that sells such items as shoes, clothes, accessories and beauty products. The web site offers products from over 100 fashion retailers, magazines and manufacturers, including big names like Tommy Hilfiger, dELIA's, Liz Claiborne, Steve Madden and Brooks Brothers. These companies, called tenants, pay either a flat-rate fee or a fee based on site traffic in order to be featured on the site. Customers see the companies' advertisements and can then be linked to the retailers' own web sites. Fashionmall.com sells an average of $100 per purchase. The company also owns Outletmall.com, a discount on-line retailer. Fashionmall is currently focused on growth and innovation. Recently, the company announced a deal with Microsoft to offer Outletmall.com shoppers the use of the newly-created Microsoft Passport electronic wallet, which will give users a single sign-in service through which they can order products from more than 50 leading web merchants. The company has tripled its sales team's size. The new staff will focus on increasing tenants in the sportswear, footwear, beauty, accessory and bridal areas.

FINANCIALS: Sales and profits are in thousands of dollars—add 000 to get the full amount.

Notes regarding 1999: *(1999 sales and profits were not available for all companies at press time.)*

1999 Sales: $	1999 Profits: $	Stock Ticker: **FASH**
1998 Sales: $2,100	1998 Profits: $	Employees: 16
1997 Sales: $1,300	1997 Profits: $	Fiscal Year Ends: 12/31
1996 Sales: $	1996 Profits: $	
1995 Sales: $	1995 Profits: $	

SALARIES/BENEFITS:

Pension Plan:	ESOP Stock Plan:	Profit Sharing:	Top Exec. Salary: $	Bonus: $
Savings Plan:	Stock Purch. Plan:		Second Exec. Salary: $	Bonus: $

COMPETITIVE ADVANTAGE: Fee-based business model.

OTHER THOUGHTS:

Apparent Women Officers or Directors: 1
Apparent Minority Officers or Directors:
Hot Spot for Advancement for Women/Minorities:

LOCATIONS: ("Y" = Yes)

West:	Southwest:	Midwest:	Southeast:	Northeast:	International:
				Y	

FATBRAIN.COM INC   www.fatbrain.com

Industry Group Code: 4541
Ranks within this company's industry group: Sales: 19   Profits: 11

BUSINESS ACTIVITIES ("Y" = Yes)

Financial Services:	Information/Publ.:		Technology:	Services:	Retailing:		Telecommunications:
Stock Brokerage	Portal/Hub/News	Y	Computer Manuf.	Payments/Transfers	Retailer	Y	Internet Serv. Provider
Mortgages/Loans	On-Line Community		Networking Equip.	Consulting	Auctions		Web Site Host
Banking	Search Engine		Software Manuf.	Advertising/Marketing	Mall		Server Farm
Insurance	Financial Data Publ.		Specialty Equipment	Outsourcing	Tickets/Travel		Specialty Telecom.
Credit Cards	Broadcasting/Music				Price Comparisons		High Speed Access

TYPES OF BUSINESS:

Retail-On-line Book Store
Retail Stores
Technology-based Training Solutions
Product Manuals
Research Reports
Technical and Professional Books
On-line Book Publishing

BRANDS/DIVISIONS/AFFILIATES:

Computer Literacy Bookshops, Inc.

CONTACTS: *Note: Officers with more than one job title may be intentionally listed here more than once.*

Chris McAskill, CEO
Chris McAskill, Pres.
Donald P. Alvarez, CFO/VP-Finance
Dennis F. Capovilla, VP-Sales
Kim Orumchian, VP-Engineering
Dennis F.Capovilla, VP-Business Dev.

Phone: 408-541-2020	**Fax:** 408-752-9919
Toll-Free:	
Address: 1308 Orleans Dr., Sunnyvale, CA, 94089	

GROWTH PLANS/SPECIAL FEATURES:

Fatbrain.com, Inc., formerly Computer Literacy, Inc., is a growing on-line retailer of information sources. With a broad selection of hundreds of thousands of books and other information resource titles, visitors to Fatbrain.com's web site can plump up their cerebellums through technical and professional books, technology-based training solutions, product manuals and research reports. The company's materials are competitively priced, the web site is easily navigated and a number of value-added services are available. Fatbrain utilizes cross-traffic between its on-line and retail operations to acquire new customers. The company's strategic alliances include a number of publishers and suppliers, including CBT Group plc, Microsoft, Sun Microsystems, Cisco Systems, Hewlett-Packard Company, 3Com and Hughes. Since launching its on-line operations, Fatbrain has experienced continued rapid growth. The company focuses on enhancing the customer experience and expanding product offerings. Fatbrain differentiates itself from competitors like Amazon.com by focusing on books for business executives, professionals and technical customers. Its most exciting development is a new on-line book publishing system that holds thousands of books in its database in digitized form, enabling customers to download complete, unabridged books instantly via the Internet. Well known techie Paul Allen is an investor in Fatbrain.

FINANCIALS: Sales and profits are in thousands of dollars—add 000 to get the full amount.
Notes regarding 1999: *(1999 sales and profits were not available for all companies at press time.)*

1999 Sales: $19,780	1999 Profits: $-9,892	**Stock Ticker: FATB**
1998 Sales: $10,900	1998 Profits: $-3,190	Employees: 141
1997 Sales: $ 180	1997 Profits: $- 567	Fiscal Year Ends: 1/31
1996 Sales: $	1996 Profits: $	
1995 Sales: $	1995 Profits: $	

SALARIES/BENEFITS:

Pension Plan:	ESOP Stock Plan:	Profit Sharing:	Top Exec. Salary: $	Bonus: $
Savings Plan: Y	Stock Purch. Plan:		Second Exec. Salary: $	Bonus: $

COMPETITIVE ADVANTAGE: Focused on books for business and professional people.

OTHER THOUGHTS:

Apparent Women Officers or Directors:
Apparent Minority Officers or Directors:
Hot Spot for Advancement for Women/Minorities:

LOCATIONS: ("Y" = Yes)

West:	Southwest:	Midwest:	Southeast:	Northeast:	International:
Y			Y		

Note: Financial information, benefits and other data can change quickly and may vary from those stated here.

FINE.COM INTERNATIONAL CORP   www.fine.com

Industry Group Code: 54151
Ranks within this company's industry group: Sales: 14   Profits: 4

BUSINESS ACTIVITIES ("Y" = Yes)

Financial Services:	Information/Publ.:	Technology:	Services:		Retailing:		Telecommunications:
Stock Brokerage	Portal/Hub/News	Computer Manuf.	Payments/Transfers		Retailer		Internet Serv. Provider
Mortgages/Loans	On-Line Community	Networking Equip.	Consulting	Y	Auctions		Web Site Host
Banking	Search Engine	Software Manuf.	Advertising/Marketing	Y	Mall		Server Farm
Insurance	Financial Data Publ.	Specialty Equipment	Outsourcing	Y	Tickets/Travel		Specialty Telecom.
Credit Cards	Broadcasting/Music				Price Comparisons		High Speed Access

TYPES OF BUSINESS:

Web Site Development
E-Commerce Consulting

BRANDS/DIVISIONS/AFFILIATES:

ARIS
Pacific Analysis & Computing
Meta4 Digital Designs

CONTACTS: *Note: Officers with more than one job title may be intentionally listed here more than once.*

Daniel M. Fine, CEO
Tim Carroll, Exec.VP-Finance
Mark Herbold, Dir.-Human Resources
Bill Flowers, Chief Tech. Officer
Trevor Brannon, Sr.VP-Corp. Counsel
Tim Carrol, Exec. VP-Oper.
Keith Brandt, VP-Business Dev.

Phone: 206-292-2888	Fax: 206-292-2889
Toll-Free:	
Address: 1525 Fourth Ave., Ste. 800, Seattle, WA, 98101	

GROWTH PLANS/SPECIAL FEATURES:

Fine.com, a subsidiary of information technology services provider ARIS, develops Internet and intranet web sites for corporations and offers maintenance and analytical services. The company has designed web sites for highly notable companies such as FTD, Amway Corporation, Intel Corporation, Marriott International, Microsoft Corporation, Nasdaq Stock Exchange, 20th Century Fox Home Entertainment, Kellogg's and McDonald's Corporation. Fine.com's solutions are designed to help clients maximize return on investment, increase user response and provide increased opportunity for sales.   Dan Fine, the CEO, received the 1999 Northwest Internet Services Entrepreneur of the Year award from Ernst and Young, LLP. In other recent news, Fine.com signed a definitive agreement to acquire privately-owned Meta4 Digital Designs Inc., which specializes in providing full-service interactive marketing services and is strategically located in New Jersey to provide services to the large concentration of Fortune 1000 companies in the northeast.   The company was named the fourth fastest growing public company in Washington state by Puget Sound Business Journal. The company plans to expand its business further into the international marketplace and has the ability to address localization, culturalization, user interface differences, import or export taxes and legislation and currency differences on a country-by-country basis.

FINANCIALS: Sales and profits are in thousands of dollars—add 000 to get the full amount.

Notes regarding 1999: *(1999 sales and profits were not available for all companies at press time.)*

1999 Sales: $6,100	1999 Profits: $-3,600	Stock Ticker: **subsidiary**
1998 Sales: $3,400	1998 Profits: $ 100	Employees: 69
1997 Sales: $1,500	1997 Profits: $ 100	Fiscal Year Ends: 1/31
1996 Sales: $ 500	1996 Profits: $	
1995 Sales: $	1995 Profits: $	

SALARIES/BENEFITS:

Pension Plan:	ESOP Stock Plan:	Profit Sharing:	Top Exec. Salary: $86,750	Bonus: $
Savings Plan:	Stock Purch. Plan:		Second Exec. Salary: $	Bonus: $

COMPETITIVE ADVANTAGE: Impressive client list/Growth through acquisition.

OTHER THOUGHTS:

	LOCATIONS: ("Y" = Yes)					
	West:	Southwest:	Midwest:	Southeast:	Northeast:	International:
Apparent Women Officers or Directors:	Y				Y	Y
Apparent Minority Officers or Directors:						
Hot Spot for Advancement for Women/Minorities:						

FLASHNET COMMUNICATIONS INC

www.flash.net

Industry Group Code: 51339
Ranks within this company's industry group: Sales: 10   Profits: 8

BUSINESS ACTIVITIES ("Y" = Yes)

Financial Services:	Information/Publ.:	Technology:	Services:	Retailing:	Telecommunications:	
Stock Brokerage	Portal/Hub/News	Computer Manuf.	Payments/Transfers	Retailer	Internet Serv. Provider	Y
Mortgages/Loans	On-Line Community	Networking Equip.	Consulting	Auctions	Web Site Host	
Banking	Search Engine	Software Manuf.	Advertising/Marketing	Mall	Server Farm	
Insurance	Financial Data Publ.	Specialty Equipment	Outsourcing	Tickets/Travel	Specialty Telecom.	
Credit Cards	Broadcasting/Music			Price Comparisons	High Speed Access	

TYPES OF BUSINESS:

Internet Service Provider

BRANDS/DIVISIONS/AFFILIATES:

GROWTH PLANS/SPECIAL FEATURES:

FlashNet Communications, Inc. is a nationwide provider of business and consumer Internet access. The company initially served as an Internet access provider for consumers located primarily in the Dallas/Fort Worth area. Today, FlashNet serves markets containing more than 90% of the U.S. population. Recently, the company signed a national network access agreement with PSINet that provides access to PSINet's POPs. This agreement, combined with FlashNet's agreement with Level 3 Communications, has transformed the company into a national Internet service provider with 1,475 total POPs across 804 cities throughout the United States. The company has accumulated a subscriber base of approximately 244,000 users, including approximately 3,100 customers for its business services. FlashNet contracted with several vendors for the purchase of both new and refurbished PCs and began reselling them through a service offering combining Internet access with a computer in exchange for a two- or three-year contractual commitment.

CONTACTS: *Note: Officers with more than one job title may be intentionally listed here more than once.*

Albert Lee Thurburn, CEO
Michael Scott Leslie, COO/Pres.
Andrew N. Jent, CFO/Exec. VP
Theresa G. Frey, Pres.-Mktg.

Phone: 817-332-8883	Fax: 817-332-3934
Toll-Free:	
Address: 1812 N. Forest Park Blvd., Fort Worth, TX, 76102	

FINANCIALS: Sales and profits are in thousands of dollars—add 000 to get the full amount.

Notes regarding 1999: Through 9 months *(1999 sales and profits were not available for all companies at press time.)*

1999 Sales: $30,200	1999 Profits: $-19,000	Stock Ticker: **FLAS**
1998 Sales: $26,900	1998 Profits: $-5,200	Employees: 248
1997 Sales: $18,300	1997 Profits: $- 100	Fiscal Year Ends: 12/31
1996 Sales: $4,500	1996 Profits: $	
1995 Sales: $	1995 Profits: $	

SALARIES/BENEFITS:

Pension Plan:	ESOP Stock Plan: Y	Profit Sharing:	Top Exec. Salary: $128,000	Bonus: $
Savings Plan: Y	Stock Purch. Plan:		Second Exec. Salary: $128,000	Bonus: $

COMPETITIVE ADVANTAGE: Strategic alliances provide nationwide presence.

OTHER THOUGHTS:

Apparent Women Officers or Directors: 1
Apparent Minority Officers or Directors:
Hot Spot for Advancement for Women/Minorities:

LOCATIONS: ("Y" = Yes)

West:	Southwest:	Midwest:	Southeast:	Northeast:	International:
Y	Y	Y	Y	Y	

Note: Financial information, benefits and other data can change quickly and may vary from those stated here.

FLYCAST COMMUNICATIONS CORP   www.flycast.com

Industry Group Code: 54189A
Ranks within this company's industry group: Sales: 10   Profits: 11

BUSINESS ACTIVITIES ("Y" = Yes)

Financial Services:	Information/Publ.:	Technology:	Services:		Retailing:	Telecommunications:
Stock Brokerage	Portal/Hub/News	Computer Manuf.	Payments/Transfers		Retailer	Internet Serv. Provider
Mortgages/Loans	On-Line Community	Networking Equip.	Consulting		Auctions	Web Site Host
Banking	Search Engine	Software Manuf.	Advertising/Marketing	Y	Mall	Server Farm
Insurance	Financial Data Publ.	Specialty Equipment	Outsourcing		Tickets/Travel	Specialty Telecom.
Credit Cards	Broadcasting/Music				Price Comparisons	High Speed Access

TYPES OF BUSINESS:

Advertising-Web Ad Campaigns

BRANDS/DIVISIONS/AFFILIATES:

Network
eDispatch
Digital DM
MediaNet
AdLab
Response Point

CONTACTS: Note: Officers with more than one job title may be intentionally listed here more than once.

George R. Garrick, CEO
George R. Garrick, Pres.
Ralph J. Harms, CFO
Lyn Chitow Oakes, VP-Mktg.
Laura Whitt, Mgr. Human Resources
Frederick J. Ciaramaglia, VP-Engineering
Lawrence G. Braitman, VP-Business Dev.
Richard L. Thompson, VP-Client Services
Jeff J. Lehman, VP-Media Sales

Phone: 415-977-1000	Fax:
Toll-Free:	
Address: 181 Fremont Street, Ste 120, San Francisco, CA, 94105	

GROWTH PLANS/SPECIAL FEATURES:

San Francisco-based Flycast Communications is a leading provider of Internet direct response advertising solutions. The company focuses on return on investment (ROI) for advertisers, direct marketers and e-commerce companies by delivering ROI-effective audience response results. The company's flagship offering, the Flycast Network, reaches nearly 20 million people monthly. Flycast's advertisers include e-commerce companies, direct response marketers and interactive agencies that are interested in generating site traffic and increasing web-based sales through ROI-focused advertising. BellSouth Intelliventures and Flycast Communications Corp. formed an exclusive arrangement allowing BellSouth's local business customers to expand advertising on the web. The agreement also launched Flycast's Local Partner Program, which enables results-focused marketers to better target prospective customers and businesses in specific geographic areas. The program enables local advertisers and e-commerce sites to reach their target audiences and maximize the return on investment for their web advertising campaigns. Flycast's multiple divisions target specific areas of web advertising. They include eDispatch, an e-mail program; Digital DM, for direct marketing; MediaNet, for end to end ad campaigns across the entire web; AdLab, a testing program for on-line advertisers; and Response Point, for web ads using the interactive features of rich media.

FINANCIALS: Sales and profits are in thousands of dollars—add 000 to get the full amount.

Notes regarding 1999: *(1999 sales and profits were not available for all companies at press time.)*

1999 Sales: $	1999 Profits: $	Stock Ticker: **FCST**
1998 Sales: $8,000	1998 Profits: $-9,300	Employees: 70
1997 Sales: $ 600	1997 Profits: $-3,400	Fiscal Year Ends: 12/31
1996 Sales: $	1996 Profits: $- 400	
1995 Sales: $	1995 Profits: $	

SALARIES/BENEFITS:

Pension Plan:	ESOP Stock Plan:	Profit Sharing:	Top Exec. Salary: $182,981	Bonus: $
Savings Plan:	Stock Purch. Plan:		Second Exec. Salary: $157,500	Bonus: $

COMPETITIVE ADVANTAGE: Excellent selection of services/Ability to offer geographically-focused campaigns.

OTHER THOUGHTS:

Apparent Women Officers or Directors: 2
Apparent Minority Officers or Directors:
Hot Spot for Advancement for Women/Minorities:

LOCATIONS: ("Y" = Yes)

West:	Southwest:	Midwest:	Southeast:	Northeast:	International:
Y					

FOREFRONT DIRECT   www.ffg.com

Industry Group Code: 5112
Ranks within this company's industry group: Sales: 35   Profits:

BUSINESS ACTIVITIES ("Y" = Yes)

Financial Services:	Information/Publ.:	Technology:		Services:		Retailing:	Telecommunications:
Stock Brokerage	Portal/Hub/News	Computer Manuf.		Payments/Transfers		Retailer	Internet Serv. Provider
Mortgages/Loans	On-Line Community	Networking Equip.		Consulting		Auctions	Web Site Host
Banking	Search Engine	Software Manuf.	Y	Advertising/Marketing		Mall	Server Farm
Insurance	Financial Data Publ.	Specialty Equipment		Outsourcing	Y	Tickets/Travel	Specialty Telecom.
Credit Cards	Broadcasting/Music					Price Comparisons	High Speed Access

TYPES OF BUSINESS:

Software-Training
PC-related Educated
PC-Diagnosis Software

BRANDS/DIVISIONS/AFFILIATES:

SmartForce
The ForeFront Group

CONTACTS: *Note: Officers with more than one job title may be intentionally listed here more than once.*

Jerry Dyas, Gen. Mgr.
Ira J. Friedman, Sr. VP-Sales
Mary Heldt, Dir.- Human Resources
Kim Carvella, VP-Oper.
Bob Scott, VP- Oper., Ireland Office
Jamie Sene, VP-Mktg.

Phone: 727-724-8994	Fax: 727-726-6922
Toll-Free: 800-475-5831	
Address: 25400 US Hwy. 19 North, #285, Clearwater, FL, 33763	

GROWTH PLANS/SPECIAL FEATURES:

Forefront Direct (formerly The ForeFront Group), a subsidiary of SmartForce, is a provider of interactive software designed to meet the information technology (IT) education and training needs of network professionals, PC technicians, web masters/managers and other IT professionals. The company sells its computer-based training products on CD-ROMs. Products from the company's ClassWare and Test Prep provide training for different technical certifications, as well as on-line and telephone mentoring. If the needed training is not available in those two categories, Forefront also has access to the almost 1,000-title library in the CBT Courseware catalogue. Rather than having to attend classes for instructor-based training, the IT professional can study on the computer with hands-on simulations providing actual working experience. The company also publishes and markets a line of PC/Network utilities that allow the user to diagnose problems, manage systems and enhance the performance of networks and PCs. The self-study programs were developed in partnership with Novell, Cisco Systems and IBM. The company has offices in California, Florida, France, Germany and Ireland. Forefront Direct sells its products to IT professionals through telesales marketing.

FINANCIALS: Sales and profits are in thousands of dollars—add 000 to get the full amount.

Notes regarding 1999: *(1999 sales and profits were not available for all companies at press time.)*

1999 Sales: $	1999 Profits: $	**Stock Ticker: subsidiary**
1998 Sales: $22,300	1998 Profits: $	Employees:
1997 Sales: $18,400	1997 Profits: $-4,100	Fiscal Year Ends: 12/31
1996 Sales: $13,800	1996 Profits: $-7,300	
1995 Sales: $ 300	1995 Profits: $-1,500	

SALARIES/BENEFITS:

Pension Plan:	ESOP Stock Plan:	Profit Sharing:	Top Exec. Salary: $	Bonus: $
Savings Plan:	Stock Purch. Plan:		Second Exec. Salary: $	Bonus: $

COMPETITIVE ADVANTAGE: Large library of training titles/Telemarketing System.

OTHER THOUGHTS:

Apparent Women Officers or Directors:
Apparent Minority Officers or Directors:
Hot Spot for Advancement for Women/Minorities:

LOCATIONS: ("Y" = Yes)

West:	Southwest:	Midwest:	Southeast:	Northeast:	International:
Y			Y		Y

FREESERVE PLC   www.freeserve.net

Industry Group Code: 51339
Ranks within this company's industry group: Sales: Profits:

BUSINESS ACTIVITIES ("Y" = Yes)

Financial Services:		Information/Publ.:	Technology:	Services:	Retailing:	Telecommunications:	
Stock Brokerage		Portal/Hub/News	Computer Manuf.	Payments/Transfers	Retailer	Internet Serv. Provider	Y
Mortgages/Loans	Y	On-Line Community	Networking Equip.	Consulting	Auctions	Web Site Host	Y
Banking	Y	Search Engine	Software Manuf.	Advertising/Marketing	Mall	Server Farm	
Insurance		Financial Data Publ.	Specialty Equipment	Outsourcing	Tickets/Travel	Specialty Telecom.	
Credit Cards		Broadcasting/Music			Price Comparisons	High Speed Access	

TYPES OF BUSINESS:

Internet Service Provider-No Fee

BRANDS/DIVISIONS/AFFILIATES:

GROWTH PLANS/SPECIAL FEATURES:

Freeserve offers free Internet service in the United Kingdom. There are no registration or set-up fees and no monthly subscription charges. The user pays for a local phone call to access the service. Together with BT Cellnet, owner of the UK's first mobile ISP and portal (Genie Internet), Freeserve provides customers with interactive services via its Short Message Service. A new service provided by the company is e-mail notification service on mobile phones, including the first 140 characters of an e-mail. Freeserve's customers are able to use Genie Internet capabilities to type a message on their PC and send the message straight to any digital mobile phone user. In the first half of 2000, these services will be enhanced further when BT Cellnet offers its high speed Internet access providing mobile Internet services to a large and growing customer base. Users get 15MB of web space, unlimited e-mail access, on line e mail support and free sign-up and registration. Freeserve offers multiple channels that provide banking information, entertainment and shopping. Users must go on-line at least once every 90 days to keep their accounts active.

CONTACTS: *Note: Officers with more than one job title may be intentionally listed here more than once.*

John Pluthero, CEO
Mark James Danby, COO
Nicholas Paul Backhouse, CFO
Neil Sansom, Dir.-Mktg.
Sarah Carpenter, VP-Strategy and New Business
Robert Wilmot, Media Dev. Dir.
Ajaz Ahmed, Business Dev. Dir.

Phone: 44-1442-353-000	Fax: 44-1442-233-218
Toll-Free:	
Address: Maylands Ave., Hemel Hempstead, Hertfordshire, UK, HP2 7 TG	

FINANCIALS: Sales and profits are in thousands of dollars—add 000 to get the full amount.

Notes regarding 1999: *(1999 sales and profits were not available for all companies at press time.)*

1999 Sales: $4,400	1999 Profits: $-1,700	Stock Ticker: **FREE**
1998 Sales: $	1998 Profits: $	Employees: 16
1997 Sales: $	1997 Profits: $	Fiscal Year Ends: 4/30
1996 Sales: $	1996 Profits: $	
1995 Sales: $	1995 Profits: $	

SALARIES/BENEFITS:

Pension Plan:	ESOP Stock Plan: Y	Profit Sharing:	Top Exec. Salary: $	Bonus: $
Savings Plan:	Stock Purch. Plan:		Second Exec. Salary: $	Bonus: $

COMPETITIVE ADVANTAGE: Utilizing free service to attract and retain customers.

OTHER THOUGHTS:

Apparent Women Officers or Directors: 1
Apparent Minority Officers or Directors: 1
Hot Spot for Advancement for Women/Minorities:

LOCATIONS: ("Y" = Yes)

West:	Southwest:	Midwest:	Southeast:	Northeast:	International:
					Y

FRONTLINE COMMUNICATIONS CORP
www.frontline.net

Industry Group Code: 51339
Ranks within this company's industry group: Sales: 24   Profits: 5

BUSINESS ACTIVITIES ("Y" = Yes)

Financial Services:	Information/Publ.:	Technology:	Services:	Retailing:	Telecommunications:	
Stock Brokerage	Portal/Hub/News	Computer Manuf.	Payments/Transfers	Retailer	Internet Serv. Provider	Y
Mortgages/Loans	On-Line Community	Networking Equip.	Consulting	Auctions	Web Site Host	
Banking	Search Engine	Software Manuf.	Advertising/Marketing	Mall	Server Farm	
Insurance	Financial Data Publ.	Specialty Equipment	Outsourcing	Tickets/Travel	Specialty Telecom.	
Credit Cards	Broadcasting/Music			Price Comparisons	High Speed Access	

TYPES OF BUSINESS:

Internet Service Provider

BRANDS/DIVISIONS/AFFILIATES:

Web Prime
WOWfactor
ChanneliShop

CONTACTS: Note: Officers with more than one job title may be intentionally listed here more than once.

Stephen J. Cole-Hatchard, CEO
Michael Olbermann, COO
Vasan Thatham, CFO
Richard Byrne, Dir.-Mktg.
Lauren Diamond, VP-Business Dev./Corp. Counsel

Phone: 914-623-8553	Fax: 914-623-8669
Toll-Free:	
Address: One Blue Hill Plaza, Pearl River, NY, 10965	

GROWTH PLANS/SPECIAL FEATURES:

Frontline Communications, founded in 1995 as a privately held Internet Service Provider (ISP), offers dial-up Internet access in the Northeast United States. The company has grown quickly through a complement of technical depth, comprehensive creative resources, strategic acquisitions and partnerships and a niche-marketing strategy that no other Internet company employs. Frontline is poised to be a top choice for Internet services for small businesses nationwide. The company has been building e-commerce brands that target segments of the small business market. Frontline acquired WOWFactor, a web-based marketplace that provides e-commerce information and services to women, and channeliShop, an e-commerce company that provides retailers with the technology and security to sell goods and services over the web. During its history, Frontline has remained committed to the growth of its technical capabilities and its network infrastructure. The company has rapidly expanded its services geographically by establishing five POPs (points of presence). Recently, Frontline was granted competitive local exchange carrier (CLEC) status in New York State. The company is focused on building customer loyalty in target market segments for its suite of e-commerce solutions that will result in gaining a national presence at a fraction of the cost of a traditional national branding campaign.

FINANCIALS: Sales and profits are in thousands of dollars—add 000 to get the full amount.

Notes regarding 1999: (1999 sales and profits were not available for all companies at press time.)

1999 Sales: $	1999 Profits: $	Stock Ticker: FCCN
1998 Sales: $ 600	1998 Profits: $-1,700	Employees: 46
1997 Sales: $ 300	1997 Profits: $-2,000	Fiscal Year Ends: 12/31
1996 Sales: $ 100	1996 Profits: $- 100	
1995 Sales: $	1995 Profits: $	

SALARIES/BENEFITS:

Pension Plan:	ESOP Stock Plan:	Profit Sharing:	Top Exec. Salary: $34,486	Bonus: $
Savings Plan:	Stock Purch. Plan:		Second Exec. Salary: $	Bonus: $

COMPETITIVE ADVANTAGE: Unique marketing plan.

OTHER THOUGHTS:

Apparent Women Officers or Directors:
Apparent Minority Officers or Directors:
Hot Spot for Advancement for Women/Minorities:

LOCATIONS: ("Y" = Yes)

West:	Southwest:	Midwest:	Southeast:	Northeast:	International:
				Y	

Note: Financial information, benefits and other data can change quickly and may vary from those stated here.

FUNDTECH LTD   www.fundtech.com

Industry Group Code: 5112
Ranks within this company's industry group: Sales: 34   Profits: 57

BUSINESS ACTIVITIES ("Y" = Yes)

Financial Services:	Information/Publ.:	Technology:	Services:	Retailing:	Telecommunications:
Stock Brokerage	Portal/Hub/News	Computer Manuf.	Payments/Transfers	Retailer	Internet Serv. Provider
Mortgages/Loans	On-Line Community	Networking Equip.	Consulting	Auctions	Web Site Host
Banking	Search Engine	Software Manuf. Y	Advertising/Marketing	Mall	Server Farm
Insurance	Financial Data Publ.	Specialty Equipment	Outsourcing	Tickets/Travel	Specialty Telecom.
Credit Cards	Broadcasting/Music			Price Comparisons	High Speed Access

TYPES OF BUSINESS:

Software-Financial Services
Cash and Treasury Management Software

BRANDS/DIVISIONS/AFFILIATES:

FEDplu$
Global CASHstar

CONTACTS: *Note: Officers with more than one job title may be intentionally listed here more than once.*

Reuven Ben Menachen, CEO
Ariu Levi, Pres.
Michael Carus, CFO
Joseph Mazzetti, Exec. VP-Sales and Mktg.
Gil Gadot, Exec. VP-Tech.
Gil Gadot, Exec. VP-Oper.

Phone: +972-3-575-2750	**Fax:** +972-3-575-1725
Toll-Free:	

Address: Beit Habonim, 2 Habonim St., Ramat Gan, Israel, 52462

GROWTH PLANS/SPECIAL FEATURES:

Fundtech is a leading provider of software solutions that facilitate e-commerce and e-banking by enabling businesses and their banks to electronically manage cash, process payments and transfer funds. The company's client/server and Internet software products automate the process of transferring funds among corporations, banks and clearance systems and enable businesses to manage their global cash positions efficiently in real-time. Fundtech's proprietary innovative software architecture, based on the Windows NT and UNIX operating systems, provides modular, scalable and secure solutions. Its solutions have been sold to more than 220 financial institutions around the globe. As the only company offering a solution that integrates treasury management, cash management and funds transfer, the company's goal is to become a critical partner for companies pursuing success in the electronic transactions-based economy. The company recently introduced Global CASHstar, developed in cooperation with Merrill Lynch. This Internet/intranet-based solution provides real-time global treasury management for large multinational companies. In addition, Global CASHstar enables companies to electronically link their internal treasury management to integrated cash management systems at their banks worldwide, significantly improving their ability to conduct e-commerce on a global basis. Fundtech also recently acquired the wire transfer and cash management businesses of CheckFree Holdings Corporation.

FINANCIALS: Sales and profits are in thousands of dollars—add 000 to get the full amount.

Notes regarding 1999: *(1999 sales and profits were not available for all companies at press time.)*

1999 Sales: $31,700	1999 Profits: $-1,700	**Stock Ticker: FNDT**
1998 Sales: $23,100	1998 Profits: $-11,400	Employees: 226
1997 Sales: $8,000	1997 Profits: $ 600	Fiscal Year Ends: 12/31
1996 Sales: $3,600	1996 Profits: $-1,500	
1995 Sales: $	1995 Profits: $	

SALARIES/BENEFITS:

Pension Plan:	ESOP Stock Plan: Y	Profit Sharing:	Top Exec. Salary: $165,417	Bonus: $140,000
Savings Plan:	Stock Purch. Plan:		Second Exec. Salary: $146,875	Bonus: $25,000

COMPETITIVE ADVANTAGE: Fully-featured EFT, treasury and cash management suite.

OTHER THOUGHTS:

	LOCATIONS: ("Y" = Yes)					
	West:	Southwest:	Midwest:	Southeast:	Northeast:	International:
Apparent Women Officers or Directors:	Y			Y	Y	Y
Apparent Minority Officers or Directors: 1						
Hot Spot for Advancement for Women/Minorities:						

FVC.COM INC   www.fvc.com

Industry Group Code: 3341B
Ranks within this company's industry group: Sales: 1   Profits: 1

BUSINESS ACTIVITIES ("Y" = Yes)

Financial Services:	Information/Publ.:	Technology:		Services:	Retailing:	Telecommunications:	
Stock Brokerage	Portal/Hub/News	Computer Manuf.		Payments/Transfers	Retailer	Internet Serv. Provider	
Mortgages/Loans	On-Line Community	Networking Equip.		Consulting	Auctions	Web Site Host	
Banking	Search Engine	Software Manuf.	Y	Advertising/Marketing	Mall	Server Farm	
Insurance	Financial Data Publ.	Specialty Equipment	Y	Outsourcing	Tickets/Travel	Specialty Telecom.	Y
Credit Cards	Broadcasting/Music				Price Comparisons	High Speed Access	

TYPES OF BUSINESS:

Computer Networking Equipment-Video Networking
Viceo Conferencing Solutions

BRANDS/DIVISIONS/AFFILIATES:

ICAST
Video Services

CONTACTS: *Note: Officers with more than one job title may be intentionally listed here more than once.*

Richard M. Beyer, CEO
Richard M. Beyer, Pres.
Truman Cole, CFO
Allwyn Sequeira, Chief Tech. Officer
Allwyn Sequeira, VP-Engineering
Robin Ann Richards, VP-Oper.

Phone: 408-567-7200	Fax: 408-988-7077
Toll-Free: 800-351-8539	
Address: 3393 Octavius Dr., Santa Clara, CA, 95054	

GROWTH PLANS/SPECIAL FEATURES:

FVC.com provides high quality, cost-effective video networking solutions that integrate video with voice and data over existing and Next Generation Internet (NGI) network infrastructures. The company combines its expertise in real-time network systems and video technology to extend the capabilities of Quality of Service (QoS) across existing network architectures, including Internet Protocol (IP), Asynchronous Transfer Mode (ATM) and Ethernet. Designed for high-quality video delivery integrated with voice and data, these products enable applications such as distance learning, corporate communications, virtual meetings and telemedicine. FVC.COM's OEM, distribution and system integration partners include Bell Atlantic Network Integration, British Telecommunications plc, EDS, France Telecom, IBM, Lucent Technologies, NEC, Nortel Networks, PictureTel and other leading companies. In recent news, Polycom (a global leader in multimedia communication solutions) and FVC.COM announced an agreement that will reduce the cost of entry for ATM videoconferencing and expand ATM endpoint choice. Under this agreement, Polycom will offer an FVC-integrated ATM videoconferencing package through its extensive global channel network. FVC.COM will market similar product bundles through its established relationships in the broadband videoconferencing market.

FINANCIALS: Sales and profits are in thousands of dollars—add 000 to get the full amount.
Notes regarding 1999: *(1999 sales and profits were not available for all companies at press time.)*

1999 Sales: $45,700	1999 Profits: $-14,300	Stock Ticker: **FVCX**
1998 Sales: $37,300	1998 Profits: $-8,000	Employees: 100
1997 Sales: $18,800	1997 Profits: $-4,300	Fiscal Year Ends: 12/31
1996 Sales: $12,100	1996 Profits: $-2,200	
1995 Sales: $3,700	1995 Profits: $-5,300	

SALARIES/BENEFITS:

Pension Plan:	ESOP Stock Plan: Y	Profit Sharing:	Top Exec. Salary: $175,000	Bonus: $72,840
Savings Plan:	Stock Purch. Plan:		Second Exec. Salary: $156,250	Bonus: $73,700

COMPETITIVE ADVANTAGE: Innovative technology/Relationship with Polycom.

OTHER THOUGHTS:

Apparent Women Officers or Directors: 1
Apparent Minority Officers or Directors:
Hot Spot for Advancement for Women/Minorities:

LOCATIONS: ("Y" = Yes)

West:	Southwest:	Midwest:	Southeast:	Northeast:	International:
Y					

GATEWAY INC   www.gateway.com

Industry Group Code: 3341A
Ranks within this company's industry group: Sales: 6   Profits: 5

BUSINESS ACTIVITIES ("Y" = Yes)

Financial Services:	Information/Publ.:	Technology:		Services:		Retailing:	Telecommunications:
Stock Brokerage	Portal/Hub/News	Computer Manuf.	Y	Payments/Transfers		Retailer	Internet Serv. Provider
Mortgages/Loans	On-Line Community	Networking Equip.	Y	Consulting		Auctions	Web Site Host
Banking	Search Engine	Software Manuf.	Y	Advertising/Marketing		Mall	Server Farm
Insurance	Financial Data Publ.	Specialty Equipment	Y	Outsourcing		Tickets/Travel	Specialty Telecom.
Credit Cards	Broadcasting/Music					Price Comparisons	High Speed Access

TYPES OF BUSINESS:

Personal Computer Manufacturer
PCTVs
Retail Showrooms
On-line and Catalog Sales
Servers
Service and Support Programs
Internet Access
Computer Training

BRANDS/DIVISIONS/AFFILIATES:

GATEWAY 2000
Advanced Logic Research, Inc.
Gateway Country Stores
Gateway Solo
Gateway Gear
Gateway Partners
E-Series
NS-Series

CONTACTS: *Note: Officers with more than one job title may be intentionally listed here more than once.*

Theodore W. Waitt, CEO
Jeffrey Weitzen, Exec VP/COO
John J Todd, Sr. VP/CFO
Anil Arora, Sr.VP/Chief Mktg. Officer
Gary Glandon, VP-Human Resources
James Pollard, CIO
Joseph J. Burke, Sr. VP-Global Business Dev.

Phone: 619-799-3401	Fax: 605-232-2023
Toll-Free: 800-846-2000	
Address: 4545 Towne Centre Court, San Diego, CA, 92121	

GROWTH PLANS/SPECIAL FEATURES:

Gateway, Inc. is a leading direct marketer of personal computers, related products and services. The company offers desktop and portable personal computers, digital media personal computers, servers, workstations, Internet access, peripheral products, third party software and service and support of programs. Gateway's personal computers include a choice of varying clock-speed microprocessors, memory and storage capacities and other options, all specified by the customer. Gateway's products are used by individuals, families, businesses, government agencies and educational institutions. The company works directly with a broad range of suppliers to evaluate and implement the latest developments in personal computer technology. Gateway believes that these relationships have enabled it to bring products with broad market demand to the customer in a timely manner. The company recently announced the relocation of its executive offices from Sioux City, South Dakota to San Diego, California, though manufacturing and support services will remain in South Dakota. It also announced the development of an extremely successful chain of retail showrooms across the nation. Currently numbering over 200, the store count will grow to about 400 over the next two years. These locations generated about $2 billion in sales in 1999. Showrooms enable consumers to see the Gateway line of computers in person, to ask questions of well-trained staff members and to place made-to-order requests for PCs. Gateway is committed to providing new services, such as Internet access at Gateway.net and computer training. Gateway is now even offering Gateway Gear, a line of fun accessories and clothing with the well-known Gateway cow print graphic theme.

FINANCIALS: Sales and profits are in thousands of dollars—add 000 to get the full amount.
Notes regarding 1999: *(1999 sales and profits were not available for all companies at press time.)*

1999 Sales: $8,646,000	1999 Profits: $428,000	Stock Ticker: **GTW**
1998 Sales: $7,467,900	1998 Profits: $346,400	Employees: 19,300
1997 Sales: $6,293,680	1997 Profits: $109,800	Fiscal Year Ends: 12/31
1996 Sales: $5,035,228	1996 Profits: $250,700	
1995 Sales: $3,676,300	1995 Profits: $173,000	

SALARIES/BENEFITS:

Pension Plan:	ESOP Stock Plan:	Profit Sharing:	Top Exec. Salary: $1,000,000	Bonus: $800,000
Savings Plan: Y	Stock Purch. Plan: Y		Second Exec. Salary: $707,692	Bonus: $600,000

COMPETITIVE ADVANTAGE: Competitive pricing and superior customer service in a well-managed catalog sales effort/New retail stores.

OTHER THOUGHTS:

Apparent Women Officers or Directors:
Apparent Minority Officers or Directors: 1
Hot Spot for Advancement for Women/Minorities: Y

LOCATIONS: ("Y" = Yes)

West:	Southwest:	Midwest:	Southeast:	Northeast:	International:
Y	Y	Y	Y	Y	Y

GENESISINTERMEDIA.COM

www.genesisintermedia.com

Industry Group Code: 54189A
Ranks within this company's industry group: Sales: 8   Profits: 1

BUSINESS ACTIVITIES ("Y" = Yes)

Financial Services:	Information/Publ.:	Technology:	Services:	Retailing:	Telecommunications:
Stock Brokerage	Portal/Hub/News	Computer Manuf.	Payments/Transfers	Retailer	Internet Serv. Provider
Mortgages/Loans	On-Line Community	Networking Equip.	Consulting Y	Auctions	Web Site Host
Banking	Search Engine	Software Manuf. Y	Advertising/Marketing Y	Mall	Server Farm
Insurance	Financial Data Publ.	Specialty Equipment	Outsourcing	Tickets/Travel	Specialty Telecom.
Credit Cards	Broadcasting/Music			Price Comparisons	High Speed Access

TYPES OF BUSINESS:

Advertising-Internet and CD-ROM Marketing
Interactive Kiosks
Travel Industry Software

BRANDS/DIVISIONS/AFFILIATES:

Genesis Media Group
CENTERLINQ System
Contour System

CONTACTS: Note: Officers with more than one job title may be intentionally listed here more than once.

Ramy El-Batrawi, CEO
Craig T. Dinkel, COO
Douglas E. Jacobson, CFO
Sharise Russell, Dir.-Human Resources

Phone: 902-902-4100	Fax: 902-902-4101
Toll-Free:	
Address: 5805 Sepulveda Blvd., Van Nuys, CA, 91411	

GROWTH PLANS/SPECIAL FEATURES:

GenesisIntermedia is an integrated marketing and business solutions provider utilizing conventional, emerging and interactive multimedia technologies. The company has recently focused on providing innovative multimedia solutions. These solutions are delivered through a variety of platforms, including the Internet, interactive kiosks, CD-ROM, DVD-ROM and e-commerce enabled businesses. The company also markets and sells products through more conventional channels, such as network television, cable television, newspapers, magazines and radio. GenesisIntermedia has provided its services to well-known companies such as Apple Computer, Disney, Castle Rock, Epson, 20th Century Fox, Hallmark, Lexus, Microsoft, McDonnell Douglas and Warner Brothers. The company was awarded the Microsoft Retail Application Developer Award and was named one of the Top 100 Multimedia Producers in the United States. Its CENTERLINQ System is an interactive communications network consisting of Internet-based kiosks combined with video screen monitors that are strategically placed in highly-trafficked mall areas. The company's Contour System product provides centralized management information systems, accounting functions and research, analysis, booking, invoicing and collection functions for the travel industry and its agents. Recently, the company signed numerous agreements to install CENTERLINQ interactive kiosks in malls across the country and has also agreed to form a joint venture with Urmet S.p.A., one of Europe's largest telecommunications companies, to expand its CENTERLINQ network into some of Europe's most populated metropolitan areas.

FINANCIALS: Sales and profits are in thousands of dollars—add 000 to get the full amount.

Notes regarding 1999: (1999 sales and profits were not available for all companies at press time.)

1999 Sales: $	1999 Profits: $	Stock Ticker: GENI
1998 Sales: $14,900	1998 Profits: $1,400	Employees: 147
1997 Sales: $18,200	1997 Profits: $2,400	Fiscal Year Ends: 12/31
1996 Sales: $14,300	1996 Profits: $ 400	
1995 Sales: $8,700	1995 Profits: $ 100	

SALARIES/BENEFITS:

Pension Plan:	ESOP Stock Plan:	Profit Sharing:	Top Exec. Salary: $	Bonus: $
Savings Plan:	Stock Purch. Plan:		Second Exec. Salary: $	Bonus: $

COMPETITIVE ADVANTAGE: Unique kiosk technology.

OTHER THOUGHTS:

Apparent Women Officers or Directors: 1
Apparent Minority Officers or Directors: 1
Hot Spot for Advancement for Women/Minorities:

LOCATIONS: ("Y" = Yes)

West:	Southwest:	Midwest:	Southeast:	Northeast:	International:
Y					Y

GETTHERE.COM INC   www.getthere.com

Industry Group Code: 51339A
Ranks within this company's industry group: Sales: 9   Profits: 6

BUSINESS ACTIVITIES ("Y" = Yes)

Financial Services:	Information/Publ.:	Technology:	Services:		Retailing:		Telecommunications:
Stock Brokerage	Portal/Hub/News	Computer Manuf.	Payments/Transfers		Retailer		Internet Serv. Provider
Mortgages/Loans	On-Line Community	Networking Equip.	Consulting		Auctions		Web Site Host
Banking	Search Engine	Software Manuf.	Advertising/Marketing		Mall		Server Farm
Insurance	Financial Data Publ.	Specialty Equipment	Outsourcing	Y	Tickets/Travel	Y	Specialty Telecom.
Credit Cards	Broadcasting/Music				Price Comparisons		High Speed Access

TYPES OF BUSINESS:

On-line Travel Services
Travel Application Service Provider (ASP)

BRANDS/DIVISIONS/AFFILIATES:

Internet Travel Network

CONTACTS: *Note: Officers with more than one job title may be intentionally listed here more than once.*

Gadi Maier, CEO/Pres.
Kenneth R. Pelowski, COO
Kenneth R. Pelowski, CFO
John Metcalfe, VP-Mktg.
John Anderson, VP-Human Resources
Daniel Whaley, Chief Tech. Officer
Eric Sirkin, VP-Engineering
Christopher Andrews, VP-Sales
William Kohrs, VP-Services

Phone: 650-752-1500	Fax: 650-752-1515
Toll-Free:	
Address: 4045 Campbell Ave., Menlo Park, CA, 94025	

GROWTH PLANS/SPECIAL FEATURES:

GetThere.com, formerly Internet Travel Network, provides business-to-business e-commerce solutions to the travel management industry. Using secure, high-speed connections, users of a corporate intranet or web site can link directly to GetThere.com with no need for hardware, software, system upgrades or training. Low fare search tools help users save money and time with no log-in required to quickly check fares. Flight Status Info gives gate information and arrival/departure times for more than 15 domestic and international carriers. The site also books car rentals, hotels and vacation tours. GetThere.com brings travel booking capabilities to more than 150 companies such as Nike, Texas Instruments, Procter & Gamble, CNN Interactive and Diners Club. Travel agencies and third-party public Internet sites can create customized on-line reservation systems with their own look and feel. GetThere.com also works with airlines such as United Airlines and All Nippon Airways to build advanced, on-line reservations systems for their public Internet sites. GetThere.com provides on-line booking services for portals like iVillage, Mindspring and Rand McNally.The Technologic Partners Internet Outlook Conference in San Francisco rated the company as one of 10 e-commerce Investors Choice companies.

FINANCIALS: Sales and profits are in thousands of dollars—add 000 to get the full amount.

Notes regarding 1999: *(1999 sales and profits were not available for all companies at press time.)*

1999 Sales: $6,400	1999 Profits: $-15,600	Stock Ticker: **GTHR**
1998 Sales: $3,000	1998 Profits: $-6,400	Employees:
1997 Sales: $ 600	1997 Profits: $-3,400	Fiscal Year Ends: 1/31
1996 Sales: $	1996 Profits: $	
1995 Sales: $	1995 Profits: $	

SALARIES/BENEFITS:

Pension Plan:	ESOP Stock Plan: Y	Profit Sharing:	Top Exec. Salary: $237,827	Bonus: $
Savings Plan:	Stock Purch. Plan: Y		Second Exec. Salary: $233,358	Bonus: $15,000

COMPETITIVE ADVANTAGE:

Ability to enable other web sites to create travel pages using GetThere.com's content, booking and technology.

OTHER THOUGHTS:

Apparent Women Officers or Directors:
Apparent Minority Officers or Directors: 1
Hot Spot for Advancement for Women/Minorities:

LOCATIONS: ("Y" = Yes)

West:	Southwest:	Midwest:	Southeast:	Northeast:	International:
Y					

Note: Financial information, benefits and other data can change quickly and may vary from those stated here.

GETTY IMAGES INC   www.getty-images.com

Industry Group Code: 4541
Ranks within this company's industry group: Sales: 7   Profits: 28

BUSINESS ACTIVITIES ("Y" = Yes)

Financial Services:	Information/Publ.:	Technology:	Services:	Retailing:		Telecommunications:
Stock Brokerage	Portal/Hub/News	Computer Manuf.	Payments/Transfers	Retailer	Y	Internet Serv. Provider
Mortgages/Loans	On-Line Community	Networking Equip.	Consulting	Auctions		Web Site Host
Banking	Search Engine	Software Manuf.	Advertising/Marketing	Mall		Server Farm
Insurance	Financial Data Publ.	Specialty Equipment	Outsourcing	Tickets/Travel		Specialty Telecom.
Credit Cards	Broadcasting/Music			Price Comparisons		High Speed Access

TYPES OF BUSINESS:
Retail-Stock Photography

BRANDS/DIVISIONS/AFFILIATES:
Tony Stone Images
PhotoDisc
Allsport
Liason Agency

GROWTH PLANS/SPECIAL FEATURES:

A leading provider of stock photography images, Getty Images, Inc. offers over 30 million images and 13,000 hours of stock film footage to its customers. Getty Images recently completed a number of acquisitions that netted the company several branches. Among these are Tony Stone Images and PhotoDisc (providers of contemporary stock photos), Allsport (providers of sports photos) and Liason Agency (providers of news photos). The company's customers are largely comprised of ad agencies, print media and production companies. Getty Images' distribution occurs through e-commerce, a route that the company is currently emphasizing. Print and CD-ROM catalogs are also available. The company is 30% family-owned.

CONTACTS: Note: Officers with more than one job title may be intentionally listed here more than once.
Johnathan D. Klein, CEO
Christopher J. Roling, Sr. VP-Finance/CFO
Rebecca Clements, Sr. VP-Human Resources
Nicholas Evans-Lombe, Sr. VP-Strategy and Corp. Dev.
Warwick Woodhouse, Sr. VP-Planning
John Gonzales, VP-Strategic Relations

Phone: 206-695-3401	Fax: 206-695-3401
Toll-Free:	
Address: 2101 Fourth Avenue, Suite 500, Seattle, WA, 98121	

FINANCIALS: Sales and profits are in thousands of dollars—add 000 to get the full amount.
Notes regarding 1999: *(1999 sales and profits were not available for all companies at press time.)*

1999 Sales: $247,800	1999 Profits: $	Stock Ticker: **GETY**
1998 Sales: $185,100	1998 Profits: $-36,400	Employees: 1,345
1997 Sales: $100,800	1997 Profits: $4,000	Fiscal Year Ends: 12/31
1996 Sales: $85,000	1996 Profits: $2,700	
1995 Sales: $63,000	1995 Profits: $1,300	

SALARIES/BENEFITS:

Pension Plan:	ESOP Stock Plan:	Profit Sharing:	Top Exec. Salary: $520,000	Bonus: $
Savings Plan: Y	Stock Purch. Plan:		Second Exec. Salary: $337.804	Bonus: $

COMPETITIVE ADVANTAGE: Number one provider of stock photography images in the United States.

OTHER THOUGHTS:
Apparent Women Officers or Directors: 4
Apparent Minority Officers or Directors: 1
Hot Spot for Advancement for Women/Minorities: Y

LOCATIONS: ("Y" = Yes)

West:	Southwest:	Midwest:	Southeast:	Northeast:	International:
Y					

GLOBAL CROSSING LTD   www.globalcrossing.com

Industry Group Code: 5133B
Ranks within this company's industry group: Sales: 5   Profits: 4

BUSINESS ACTIVITIES ("Y" = Yes)

Financial Services:	Information/Publ.:	Technology:	Services:	Retailing:	Telecommunications:	
Stock Brokerage	Portal/Hub/News	Computer Manuf.	Payments/Transfers	Retailer	Internet Serv. Provider	
Mortgages/Loans	On-Line Community	Networking Equip.	Consulting	Auctions	Web Site Host	
Banking	Search Engine	Software Manuf.	Advertising/Marketing	Mall	Server Farm	
Insurance	Financial Data Publ.	Specialty Equipment	Outsourcing	Tickets/Travel	Specialty Telecom.	Y
Credit Cards	Broadcasting/Music			Price Comparisons	High Speed Access	Y

TYPES OF BUSINESS:

Local and Long Distance Telephone Service
Undersea Cable Systems
High Speed Access
Voice Mail Systems
Paging

BRANDS/DIVISIONS/AFFILIATES:

Pacific Capital Group
Frontier Corporation
TravelReach Paging
uCommand
Passport Solutions

CONTACTS: Note: Officers with more than one job title may be intentionally listed here more than once.

Robert Annunziata, CEO
David L. Lee, Pres./COO
Dan J. Cohrs, CFO
Elizabeth Greenwood, VP-Human Resources
James C. Gorton, Sr. VP-General Counsel
William B. Carter, Jr., Pres.-Global Crossing Dev.
David Millroy, Sr. VP-Network Dev.

Phone: 310-385-5200	Fax: 310-281-4942
Toll-Free:	
Address: 150 El Camino Dr., Ste. 204, Beverly Hills, CA, 90212	

GROWTH PLANS/SPECIAL FEATURES:

Global Crossing, a provider of long distance telecommunications facilities and services, offers tiered pricing and segmented products to licensed providers of international telecommunications services. The company utilizes a network of undersea digital fiber-optic cable systems that allow access to multiple worldwide destinations. Global Crossing's recent merger with Frontier Corporation put Global Crossing in the Standard and Poor's 500 Index and the NASDAQ 100. After the merger, Global Crossing acquired an end-to-end fiber-optic network that connects 88,000 route miles and 1.25 million fiber miles, offering ultra-high bandwidth to 170 major cities in 24 countries and 5 continents. This system now addresses 80% of the world's international communications traffic. The company's TravelReach Paging allows the business traveler to remain in touch anywhere in the U.S., Puerto Rico and the U.S. Virgin Islands. Its uCommand is a service that offers secure access to a user's account information via the Internet, eliminating manual paperwork and simplifying bill payment. PassPort Solutions, a service for companies too busy to answer all incoming calls, incorporates Interactive Voice Response technology without the necessity of purchasing or operating any equipment. Global Crossing is headquartered in Bermuda and has offices in California, Texas, New Jersey, Florida, South America and England.

FINANCIALS: Sales and profits are in thousands of dollars—add 000 to get the full amount.

Notes regarding 1999: Through 9 months/Pro forma *(1999 sales and profits were not available for all companies at press time.)*

1999 Sales: $2,972,600	1999 Profits: $-55,400	Stock Ticker: **GBLX**
1998 Sales: $424,100	1998 Profits: $-87,900	Employees: 148
1997 Sales: $	1997 Profits: $- 200	Fiscal Year Ends: 12/31
1996 Sales: $	1996 Profits: $	
1995 Sales: $	1995 Profits: $	

SALARIES/BENEFITS:

Pension Plan:	ESOP Stock Plan: Y	Profit Sharing:	Top Exec. Salary: $600,000	Bonus: $1,050,000
Savings Plan: Y	Stock Purch. Plan:		Second Exec. Salary: $450,000	Bonus: $480,000

COMPETITIVE ADVANTAGE: Rapid growth through acquisitions.

OTHER THOUGHTS:

Apparent Women Officers or Directors: 1
Apparent Minority Officers or Directors: 1
Hot Spot for Advancement for Women/Minorities:

LOCATIONS: ("Y" = Yes)

West:	Southwest:	Midwest:	Southeast:	Northeast:	International:
Y	Y	Y	Y	Y	Y

Note: Financial information, benefits and other data can change quickly and may vary from those stated here.

GLOBAL MEDIA CORPORATION   www.gmcorp.com

Industry Group Code: 4541
Ranks within this company's industry group: Sales: 34   Profits: 6

BUSINESS ACTIVITIES ("Y" = Yes)

Financial Services:	Information/Publ.:	Technology:	Services:	Retailing:		Telecommunications:
Stock Brokerage	Portal/Hub/News	Computer Manuf.	Payments/Transfers	Retailer	Y	Internet Serv. Provider
Mortgages/Loans	On-Line Community	Networking Equip.	Consulting	Auctions		Web Site Host
Banking	Search Engine	Software Manuf. Y	Advertising/Marketing	Mall		Server Farm
Insurance	Financial Data Publ.	Specialty Equipment	Outsourcing	Tickets/Travel		Specialty Telecom.
Credit Cards	Broadcasting/Music Y			Price Comparisons		High Speed Access

TYPES OF BUSINESS:

Retail-Entertainment Products
Internet Radio Station
On-line Sales of Recorded Music

BRANDS/DIVISIONS/AFFILIATES:

www.indieaudio.com

CONTACTS: *Note: Officers with more than one job title may be intentionally listed here more than once.*

Robert Fuller, CEO
Michael Metcalfe, Pres.

Phone: 250-716-9949	Fax: 250-716-0502
Toll-Free:	
Address: 83 Victoria Crescent, Nanaimo, BC, Canada, V9R 5B9	

GROWTH PLANS/SPECIAL FEATURES:

Global Media Corp. sells music CDs, videocassettes, DVDs, books, magazine subscriptions and other entertainment products through a series of web sites. The company is also a major participant in the newest methods of music and video distribution via direct Internet downloading. The company penetrates the market through the licensing of its back end infrastructure, allowing any Internet business to have its own store front and to be able to sell all of Global Media's products through a customized front end. Licensees are responsible for marketing, while Global Media manages all catalog and inventory database integration, packaging, shipping and secure transaction processing. The company has developed an on-line community and entertainment destination that consumers can visit for convenience, informative news and the purchase of downloadable music. Global Media launched a new on-line information center for its media distribution web site and is now accepting on-line licensing applications. This makes it easier for retailers to enter into the world of entertainment e-commerce. Global Media recently launched an on-line Independent Radio Station at www.indieaudio.com. In preparation for the station, the company launched its on-line Registration Center where independent artists may register to have their music heard and distributed on a global scale.

FINANCIALS: Sales and profits are in thousands of dollars—add 000 to get the full amount.

Notes regarding 1999: *(1999 sales and profits were not available for all companies at press time.)*

1999 Sales: $ 84	1999 Profits: $-2,229	**Stock Ticker: GLMC**
1998 Sales: $	1998 Profits: $- 305	Employees:
1997 Sales: $	1997 Profits: $- 70	Fiscal Year Ends: 7/31
1996 Sales: $	1996 Profits: $	
1995 Sales: $	1995 Profits: $	

SALARIES/BENEFITS:

Pension Plan:	ESOP Stock Plan:	Profit Sharing:	Top Exec. Salary: $	Bonus: $
Savings Plan:	Stock Purch. Plan:		Second Exec. Salary: $	Bonus: $

COMPETITIVE ADVANTAGE: Unique software and back-end abilities allow it to service multiple sites that want to deliver music on-line.

OTHER THOUGHTS:

Apparent Women Officers or Directors:
Apparent Minority Officers or Directors:
Hot Spot for Advancement for Women/Minorities:

LOCATIONS: ("Y" = Yes)

West:	Southwest:	Midwest:	Southeast:	Northeast:	International:
					Y

GO.COM   http://infoseek.go.com

Industry Group Code: 514191
Ranks within this company's industry group: Sales: 6   Profits: 23

BUSINESS ACTIVITIES ("Y" = Yes)

Financial Services:	Information/Publ.:		Technology:	Services:	Retailing:	Telecommunications:
Stock Brokerage	Portal/Hub/News	Y	Computer Manuf.	Payments/Transfers	Retailer	Internet Serv. Provider
Mortgages/Loans	On-Line Community		Networking Equip.	Consulting	Auctions	Web Site Host
Banking	Search Engine	Y	Software Manuf.	Advertising/Marketing	Mall	Server Farm
Insurance	Financial Data Publ.		Specialty Equipment	Outsourcing	Tickets/Travel	Specialty Telecom.
Credit Cards	Broadcasting/Music				Price Comparisons	High Speed Access

TYPES OF BUSINESS:

Search Portal
On-line Communities
Diversified On-line Entertainment
Search Engine Software

BRANDS/DIVISIONS/AFFILIATES:

ABC.com
Walt Disney Co.
ESPN.com
Family.com
Wall of Sound
Mr. Showbiz
ABCNEWS.com
Infoseek, Inc.

CONTACTS: Note: Officers with more than one job title may be intentionally listed here more than once.

Cynthia Stephens, CFO
Beth A. Haggerty, Sr. VP-Sales
Patty Bustos, Dir-Human Resources
Bhagwan D Geol, Sr. VP-e-commerce

Phone: 408-53-6000	Fax: 408 734-9350
Toll-Free:	
Address: 1399 Moffett Park Dr., Sunnyvale, CA, 94089	

GROWTH PLANS/SPECIAL FEATURES:

Go.com is a newly formed company with a long history in terms of Internet time. Walt Disney, which previously purchased a 100% interest in Infoseek, Inc., combined the Disney Internet assets with Infoseek to create a new, separate company named Go.com. Today, the company is a leading provider of Internet services and software products, including Infoseek's search engine, commerce connections to over two million customers and original programming content from leading consumer brands like ABC, Disney, ESPN and ZDNet. Initially, the company marketed Ultraseek Server software products. After the acquisition of WebChat Communications, Inc., the technology was utilized to enhance the Go Network. Go.com produces leading Internet sites such as ABCNEWS.com and ESPN.com in partnership with Disney affiliates. Recently, the company acquired Quando, Inc., a creator of constantly-updated directories of information obtained from the Internet, including shopping guides, event guides, contact directories and web site rating guides. While Go.com was initially positioned as a search portal to compete with Yahoo! and similar sites, the firm announced in early 2000 that it will change direction to become more of an entertainment and leisure destination.

FINANCIALS: Sales and profits are in thousands of dollars—add 000 to get the full amount.

Notes regarding 1999: *(1999 sales and profits were not available for all companies at press time.)*

1999 Sales: $137,200	1999 Profits: $-265,200	Stock Ticker: **GO**
1998 Sales: $50,700	1998 Profits: $-5,700	Employees: 319
1997 Sales: $34,600	1997 Profits: $-24,600	Fiscal Year Ends: 9/30
1996 Sales: $15,100	1996 Profits: $-15,900	
1995 Sales: $1,000	1995 Profits: $-3,100	

SALARIES/BENEFITS:

Pension Plan:	ESOP Stock Plan:	Profit Sharing:	Top Exec. Salary: $187,000	Bonus: $
Savings Plan:	Stock Purch. Plan:		Second Exec. Salary: $183,617	Bonus: $

COMPETITIVE ADVANTAGE: One of the leading portals to the web/Business and content ties to Disney.

OTHER THOUGHTS:

Apparent Women Officers or Directors: 2
Apparent Minority Officers or Directors: 1
Hot Spot for Advancement for Women/Minorities:

LOCATIONS: ("Y" = Yes)

West:	Southwest:	Midwest:	Southeast:	Northeast:	International:
Y		Y	Y		Y

Note: Financial information, benefits and other data can change quickly and may vary from those stated here.

GO2NET INC   www.go2net.com

Industry Group Code: 514191
Ranks within this company's industry group: Sales: 23   Profits: 14

BUSINESS ACTIVITIES ("Y" = Yes)

Financial Services:	Information/Publ.:		Technology:		Services:	Retailing:	Telecommunications:
Stock Brokerage	Portal/Hub/News	Y	Computer Manuf.		Payments/Transfers	Retailer	Internet Serv. Provider
Mortgages/Loans	On-Line Community		Networking Equip.		Consulting	Auctions	Web Site Host
Banking	Search Engine	Y	Software Manuf.	Y	Advertising/Marketing	Mall	Server Farm
Insurance	Financial Data Publ.		Specialty Equipment		Outsourcing	Tickets/Travel	Specialty Telecom.
Credit Cards	Broadcasting/Music					Price Comparisons	High Speed Access

TYPES OF BUSINESS:

Search Portals
Software
Business and Consumer Portals

BRANDS/DIVISIONS/AFFILIATES:

MetaCrawler
Haggie Online
HyperMart
100hot
Dogpile
PlaySite
Silicon Investor
StockSite

CONTACTS: *Note: Officers with more than one job title may be intentionally listed here more than once.*

Russell C. Horowitz, CEO/Pres.
Michael J. Riccio Jr., COO
Russell C. Horowitz, CFO
Laurie Likai, Dir.-Human Resources
Paul S. Phillips, Dir.-Research and Dev.

Phone: 206-447-1595	Fax: 206-447-1625
Toll-Free:	
Address: 999 Third Avenue, Suite 4700, Seattle, WA, 98104	

GROWTH PLANS/SPECIAL FEATURES:

Go2Net, Inc. offers a network of branded, technology-driven and community-driven web sites focused on various categories, including personal finance, search and directory, commerce, business services and games. The company also develops web-related software. Go2Net's properties include Silicon Investor, MetaCrawler, HyperMart, Virtual Avenue, WebMarket, PlaySite, 100hot, Haggle Online and IQ Charts. Go2Net depends on advertising and subscription and transaction fees from its Internet sites to generate revenues. The company is trying to effectively establish, develop and maintain relationships with advertising customers, advertising agencies and other third parties; enter into distribution relationships and strategic alliances to drive traffic to its web sites; provide original and compelling products and services to Internet users; develop and upgrade its technology; respond to competitive developments; attract new personnel and retain existing qualified personnel. It currently intends to substantially increase its operating expenses for expansion and improvement of its Internet operations and Internet user support capabilities, fund increased advertising and marketing efforts and develop new Internet technologies, applications and other products and services.

FINANCIALS: Sales and profits are in thousands of dollars—add 000 to get the full amount.

Notes regarding 1999: *(1999 sales and profits were not available for all companies at press time.)*

1999 Sales: $22,400	1999 Profits: $-10,800	Stock Ticker: **GNET**
1998 Sales: $4,800	1998 Profits: $-2,400	Employees: 69
1997 Sales: $ 300	1997 Profits: $-1,700	Fiscal Year Ends: 9/30
1996 Sales: $ 100	1996 Profits: $- 400	
1995 Sales: $	1995 Profits: $	

SALARIES/BENEFITS:

Pension Plan:	ESOP Stock Plan:	Profit Sharing:	Top Exec. Salary: $72,000	Bonus: $
Savings Plan:	Stock Purch. Plan:		Second Exec. Salary: $36,000	Bonus: $

COMPETITIVE ADVANTAGE: Excellent collection of popular portals.

OTHER THOUGHTS:

Apparent Women Officers or Directors: 2
Apparent Minority Officers or Directors: 2
Hot Spot for Advancement for Women/Minorities: Y

LOCATIONS: ("Y" = Yes)

West:	Southwest:	Midwest:	Southeast:	Northeast:	International:
				Y	

GOTO.COM INC   www.goto.com

Industry Group Code: 514191
Ranks within this company's industry group: Sales: 37   Profits: 34

BUSINESS ACTIVITIES ("Y" = Yes)

Financial Services:	Information/Publ.:		Technology:	Services:	Retailing:	Telecommunications:
Stock Brokerage	Portal/Hub/News	Y	Computer Manuf.	Payments/Transfers	Retailer	Internet Serv. Provider
Mortgages/Loans	On-Line Community		Networking Equip.	Consulting	Auctions	Web Site Host
Banking	Search Engine	Y	Software Manuf.	Advertising/Marketing	Mall	Server Farm
Insurance	Financial Data Publ.		Specialty Equipment	Outsourcing	Tickets/Travel	Specialty Telecom.
Credit Cards	Broadcasting/Music				Price Comparisons	High Speed Access

TYPES OF BUSINESS:
Search Portal

BRANDS/DIVISIONS/AFFILIATES:

GROWTH PLANS/SPECIAL FEATURES:

GoTo.com, Inc. operates an on-line marketplace that introduces consumers, who search the Internet using keyword terms, to advertisers who bid in an ongoing auction for priority placement in the search results for those keywords. Each advertiser pays GoTo.com the amount of its bid whenever a consumer clicks on the advertiser's listings in the search results. Advertisers must pay for each click-through, so they bid only on keywords relevant to their offerings. A search on the GoTo.com service leads directly to a list of 40 results per page. The search result pages avoid advertising banners, allowing them to load quickly. Recently, GoTo.com signed a contract with Netscape Communications, a subsidiary of America Online, agreeing to become a leading search provider for the Netscape Net Search program. GoTo.com filed a law suit against the Go Network, an Internet service created by an alliance between The Walt Disney Company and Infoseek Corporation, claiming the striking similarity between GoTo.com's logo and the Go Network logo is likely to cause confusion.

CONTACTS:
Note: Officers with more than one job title may be intentionally listed here more than once.

Jeffrey S. Brewer, CEO/Pres.
Ted Meisel, COO
Todd Tappin, CFO
Stephanie A. Sarka, Sr. VP-Mktg.
Manuel Nunez, Dir.-Human Resources

Phone: 626-685-5600	Fax: 626-685-5601
Toll-Free:	
Address: 140 W. Union St., Pasadena, CA, 91103	

FINANCIALS: Sales and profits are in thousands of dollars—add 000 to get the full amount.
Notes regarding 1999: *(1999 sales and profits were not available for all companies at press time.)*

1999 Sales: $	1999 Profits: $	Stock Ticker: **GOTO**
1998 Sales: $ 800	1998 Profits: $-14,000	Employees: 75
1997 Sales: $	1997 Profits: $- 100	Fiscal Year Ends: 12/31
1996 Sales: $	1996 Profits: $	
1995 Sales: $	1995 Profits: $	

SALARIES/BENEFITS:

Pension Plan:	ESOP Stock Plan: Y	Profit Sharing:	Top Exec. Salary: $70,833	Bonus: $
Savings Plan:	Stock Purch. Plan:		Second Exec. Salary: $	Bonus: $

COMPETITIVE ADVANTAGE: Alliances with Netscape and other leading companies.

OTHER THOUGHTS:

Apparent Women Officers or Directors: 1
Apparent Minority Officers or Directors: 1
Hot Spot for Advancement for Women/Minorities:

LOCATIONS: ("Y" = Yes)

West:	Southwest:	Midwest:	Southeast:	Northeast:	International:
Y					

GTE CORPORATION   www.gte.com

Industry Group Code: 5133A
Ranks within this company's industry group: Sales: 1   Profits: 1

BUSINESS ACTIVITIES ("Y" = Yes)

Financial Services:	Information/Publ.:	Technology:		Services:		Retailing:	Telecommunications:	
Stock Brokerage	Portal/Hub/News	Computer Manuf.		Payments/Transfers		Retailer	Internet Serv. Provider	Y
Mortgages/Loans	On-Line Community	Networking Equip.	Y	Consulting	Y	Auctions	Web Site Host	Y
Banking	Search Engine	Software Manuf.	Y	Advertising/Marketing		Mall	Server Farm	
Insurance	Financial Data Publ.	Specialty Equipment	Y	Outsourcing		Tickets/Travel	Specialty Telecom.	Y
Credit Cards	Broadcasting/Music					Price Comparisons	High Speed Access	Y

TYPES OF BUSINESS:

Telecommunications Products and Services
Local Telephone Service
Financing
Internet Service Provider
Cellular Mobile Telephone Service
Telecommunications Consulting
Telecommunications Switches
Internet Backbone

BRANDS/DIVISIONS/AFFILIATES:

GTE Service Corporation
GTE Data Services, Inc.
GTE Supply
GTE Card Services
GTE Long Distance
GTE Internetworking
GTE Wireless
Bell Atlantic

CONTACTS: *Note: Officers with more than one job title may be intentionally listed here more than once.*

Charles R. Lee, CEO
Kent B. Foster, Pres.
J. Michael Kelly, Exec. VP-Finance
Thomas W. White, Sr. Exec. VP-Mktg. Oper.
J. Randall MacDonald, Exec. VP-Human Resources
Armen Der Marderosian, Exec. VP-Tech. and Systems
J. Michael Kelly, Exec. VP-Planning
George H. Conrades, Pres.-GTE Internetworking

Phone: 203-965-2000	Fax: 203-965-2277
Toll-Free:	
Address: One Stamford Forum, Stamford, CT, 06904	

GROWTH PLANS/SPECIAL FEATURES:

GTE Corporation is one of the largest telecommunications companies in the world. GTE's domestic and international operations serve 27.7 million access lines through subsidiaries in the U.S., Canada, the Dominican Republic and Venezuela. The company provides internetworking services, ranging from dial-up Internet access for residential and small business consumers to web-based applications for Fortune 500 companies. GTE is also a leader in government and defense communications systems and equipment, aircraft-passenger telecommunications, directories and telecommunications-based information services and systems. The company's wireless services include 800 MHz cellular telephone and wireless data transmission services and 1.8 GHz Personal Communications Services (PCS). GTE Wireless provides cellular services and products to approximately 6 million subscribers through its 800 MHz operations and PCS services. GTE Wireless has employed Code Division Multiple Access digital technology in many of its markets and will continue to deploy CDMA over the next several years. CDMA technology allows for clearer calls, enhanced security, greater functionality and additional capacity to process more calls. GTE is an aggressive marketer of new services, especially in the wireless and Internet service markets. The company plans to merge with Bell Atlantic and may spin off its Internet backbone business and other key units as part of the merger.

FINANCIALS: Sales and profits are in thousands of dollars—add 000 to get the full amount.

Notes regarding 1999: *(1999 sales and profits were not available for all companies at press time.)*

1999 Sales: $25,336,000	1999 Profits: $4,033,000	**Stock Ticker: GTE**
1998 Sales: $25,473,000	1998 Profits: $2,172,000	Employees: 120,000
1997 Sales: $23,260,000	1997 Profits: $2,794,000	Fiscal Year Ends: 12/31
1996 Sales: $21,339,000	1996 Profits: $2,798,000	
1995 Sales: $19,957,000	1995 Profits: $-2,144,000	

SALARIES/BENEFITS:

Pension Plan: Y	ESOP Stock Plan: Y	Profit Sharing:	Top Exec. Salary: $	Bonus: $
Savings Plan: Y	Stock Purch. Plan:		Second Exec. Salary: $	Bonus: $

COMPETITIVE ADVANTAGE: Major, diversified communications firm/ Nationwide presence/Will merge with Bell Atlantic.

OTHER THOUGHTS:

Apparent Women Officers or Directors: 4
Apparent Minority Officers or Directors: 3
Hot Spot for Advancement for Women/Minorities: Y

LOCATIONS: ("Y" = Yes)

West:	Southwest:	Midwest:	Southeast:	Northeast:	International:
Y	Y	Y	Y	Y	Y

HEADHUNTER.NET INC   www.headhunter.net

Industry Group Code: 514191
Ranks within this company's industry group: Sales: 35   Profits: 20

BUSINESS ACTIVITIES ("Y" = Yes)

Financial Services:	Information/Publ.:		Technology:	Services:	Retailing:	Telecommunications:
Stock Brokerage	Portal/Hub/News	Y	Computer Manuf.	Payments/Transfers	Retailer	Internet Serv. Provider
Mortgages/Loans	On-Line Community		Networking Equip.	Consulting	Auctions	Web Site Host
Banking	Search Engine		Software Manuf.	Advertising/Marketing	Mall	Server Farm
Insurance	Financial Data Publ.		Specialty Equipment	Outsourcing	Tickets/Travel	Specialty Telecom.
Credit Cards	Broadcasting/Music				Price Comparisons	High Speed Access

TYPES OF BUSINESS:
On-line Career Services

BRANDS/DIVISIONS/AFFILIATES:
HNET, Inc

CONTACTS: *Note: Officers with more than one job title may be intentionally listed here more than once.*
Robert M. Montgomery Jr., CEO
Robert M. Montgomery Jr., Pres.
Mark W. Partin, CFO
James R. Canfield, VP-Sales
C. Eric Presley, VP-Tech.
Mark W. Fouraker, VP-Oper.

Phone: 770-300-9272	Fax: 770-300-9298
Toll-Free: 877-638-4473	
Address: 6410 Atlantic Blvd., Ste. 160, Norcross, GA, 30071	

GROWTH PLANS/SPECIAL FEATURES:

Headhunter.net is one of the largest, high-trafficked sources of information on the Internet for job seekers, employers and recruiters. On average, 90,000 to 110,000 unique users visit Headhunter.net every day. The site currently has over 150,000 job listings, with salary values ranging from entry level to over $500,000, and over 215,000 résumés. Because it offers a $20 basic posting fee, Headhunter.net is a popular job site among companies of all sizes that place value on what they spend to attract high-quality candidates. Many global companies use Headhunter.net as an integral component of their strategic recruiting programs. Jobs on Headhunter.net are all directly posted by registered users. Jobs and résumés are drawn from all areas of the United States and from many foreign countries. Approximately 95% of jobs are based in the U.S., although some positions are for prospective employees who will be working abroad. All industries are represented among Headhunter.net jobs and résumés. The top five industries represented are Information Technology, Engineering, Accounting, Sales and Marketing. The most common salary ranges among Headhunter.net jobs are from $51,000 to $75,000 and from $76,000 to $100,000. The company was recently ranked the number one Internet employment site by recruiters in a Hunt-Scanlon survey. The study also ranked Headhunter.net the number two recruiting site on the web in overall usage by employment decision makers and found the site to be one of the most recognized among employment sites.

FINANCIALS: Sales and profits are in thousands of dollars—add 000 to get the full amount.
Notes regarding 1999: *(1999 sales and profits were not available for all companies at press time.)*

1999 Sales: $9,300	1999 Profits: $-10,300	Stock Ticker: **HHNT**
1998 Sales: $1,100	1998 Profits: $-4,300	Employees: 64
1997 Sales: $ 200	1997 Profits: $- 200	Fiscal Year Ends: 12/31
1996 Sales: $ 200	1996 Profits: $ 100	
1995 Sales: $ 100	1995 Profits: $	

SALARIES/BENEFITS:

Pension Plan:	ESOP Stock Plan:	Profit Sharing:	Top Exec. Salary: $108,157	Bonus: $13,500
Savings Plan:	Stock Purch. Plan:		Second Exec. Salary: $76,564	Bonus: $12,253

COMPETITIVE ADVANTAGE: Attractive fee structure.

OTHER THOUGHTS:
Apparent Women Officers or Directors:
Apparent Minority Officers or Directors:
Hot Spot for Advancement for Women/Minorities:

LOCATIONS: ("Y" = Yes)

West:	Southwest:	Midwest:	Southeast:	Northeast:	International:
			Y		

HEALTHEON/WEBMD CORP www.healtheon.com

Industry Group Code: 51339A
Ranks within this company's industry group: Sales: 3   Profits: 15

BUSINESS ACTIVITIES ("Y" = Yes)

Financial Services:	Information/Publ.:	Technology:		Services:	Retailing:	Telecommunications:
Stock Brokerage	Portal/Hub/News	Computer Manuf.		Payments/Transfers	Retailer	Internet Serv. Provider
Mortgages/Loans	On-Line Community	Networking Equip.		Consulting	Auctions	Web Site Host
Banking	Search Engine	Software Manuf.	Y	Advertising/Marketing	Mall	Server Farm
Insurance	Financial Data Publ.	Specialty Equipment		Outsourcing	Tickets/Travel	Specialty Telecom.
Credit Cards	Broadcasting/Music				Price Comparisons	High Speed Access

TYPES OF BUSINESS:

Software-Health Care
ASP
Practice Management
EDI Transactions
Benefits Processing Solutions

BRANDS/DIVISIONS/AFFILIATES:

WebMD, Inc.
MEDE America Corp.
Medcast
Healtheon/WebMD

CONTACTS: *Note: Officers with more than one job title may be intentionally listed here more than once.*

Jeffrey T. Arnold, CEO
Michael K. Hoover, Pres.
John L. Westermann III, CFO
Debra Machado, Dir. of Human Resources
Mark Bailey, VP-Business Dev.
Matthew Moore, VP-Consumer Internet Services

Phone: 404-479-7600	Fax: 404-479-7651
Toll-Free:	
Address: 400 The Lenox Bldg. 3399 Peachtree Rd. NE, Atlanta, GA, 30326	

GROWTH PLANS/SPECIAL FEATURES:

Healtheon's mission is to leverage advanced Internet technology to connect all healthcare participants and enable them to communicate, exchange information and perform transactions that cut across the healthcare maze. This will simplify healthcare, reduce costs, enhance service and result in higher quality and more accessibility. Healtheon recognizes that the healthcare industry, because of its size, fragmentation and extreme dependence on information exchange, is particularly well suited to benefit from the use of the Internet. Most transactions in healthcare remain duplicative and paper-based, resulting in wasted effort, frustrated users, high labor costs and delays in care. Healtheon Corporation, WebMD, Inc., MEDE America Corporation and Medcast recently merged to form Healtheon/WebMD. Demonstrating the combined strengths and vision behind the new merger, the company recently announced the launch of its robust new healthcare destination, www.webmd.com, to connect consumers and physicians to the entire healthcare industry.

FINANCIALS: Sales and profits are in thousands of dollars—add 000 to get the full amount.

Notes regarding 1999: *(1999 sales and profits were not available for all companies at press time.)*

1999 Sales: $	1999 Profits: $	Stock Ticker: **HLTH**
1998 Sales: $48,800	1998 Profits: $-54,000	Employees: 648
1997 Sales: $13,400	1997 Profits: $-26,300	Fiscal Year Ends: 12/31
1996 Sales: $11,000	1996 Profits: $-22,500	
1995 Sales: $2,200	1995 Profits: $-4,500	

SALARIES/BENEFITS:

Pension Plan:	ESOP Stock Plan: Y	Profit Sharing:	Top Exec. Salary: $458,337	Bonus: $
Savings Plan: Y	Stock Purch. Plan:		Second Exec. Salary: $225,000	Bonus: $

COMPETITIVE ADVANTAGE: Focus on the lucrative health care market/Excellent positioning and strong backers.

OTHER THOUGHTS:

Apparent Women Officers or Directors:
Apparent Minority Officers or Directors:
Hot Spot for Advancement for Women/Minorities:

LOCATIONS: ("Y" = Yes)

West:	Southwest:	Midwest:	Southeast:	Northeast:	International:
			Y		

HEARME.COM   www.hearme.com

Industry Group Code: 514191
Ranks within this company's industry group: Sales: 18   Profits: 31

BUSINESS ACTIVITIES ("Y" = Yes)

Financial Services:		Information/Publ.:		Technology:		Services:	Retailing:	Telecommunications:
Stock Brokerage		Portal/Hub/News		Computer Manuf.		Payments/Transfers	Retailer	Internet Serv. Provider
Mortgages/Loans		On-Line Community	Y	Networking Equip.		Consulting	Auctions	Web Site Host
Banking		Search Engine		Software Manuf.	Y	Advertising/Marketing	Mall	Server Farm
Insurance		Financial Data Publ.		Specialty Equipment		Outsourcing	Tickets/Travel	Specialty Telecom.
Credit Cards		Broadcasting/Music	Y				Price Comparisons	High Speed Access

TYPES OF BUSINESS:

Chat Rooms
On-line Conversation Technology
On-line Customer Support Technology

BRANDS/DIVISIONS/AFFILIATES:

Mplayer.com
HearMe Software Developer Kit
Voice Presence
HearMe Starter Applications

CONTACTS: *Note: Officers with more than one job title may be intentionally listed here more than once.*

Paul Matteucci, CEO/Pres.
Lynn Heublein, COO
Linda Palmor, CFO
Margaret Hughes, VP-Brand Mktg.
Steven Roskowski, Chief Tech. Officer
James Schmidt, VP-Engineering
Kristin Asleson, VP-Business Mktg., Live Communities
Jeremy Verba, Exec. VP-Live Communities
Robert Csongor, VP-HearMe Tech. Products

Phone: 650-429-3900	Fax: 650-429-3911
Toll-Free:	
Address: 665 Clyde Ave., Mountain View, CA, 94043	

GROWTH PLANS/SPECIAL FEATURES:

Hearme.com, formerly Mpath Interactive, Inc., develops, licenses and operates technologies that enable Internet sites to create and manage live communities characterized by real-time interaction among multiple simultaneous users through text, voice and video. The company also operates its own live communities, HearMe.com and Mplayer.com, serving over 2.6 million registered users. HearMe.com provides its business customers with live voice communication capabilities on the Internet. The HearMe Software Developer Kit allows a business to customize the look and feel of Voice Presence, a free program that allows the addition of live voice to web sites. HearMe Starter Applications add live interaction with voice-enabled chat, instant messaging, lobbies and whiteboards with turn-key applications that can be customized to the look and feel of a company's site. Through a partnership with theglobe.com, Voice Presence has been integrated into theglobe's uPublish web site building tools. Voice Presence requires only a few lines of HTML to implement, a minimal one-time download and automatic installation. HearMe technologies can enhance a wide range of Internet applications including e-commerce, live customer support, business-to-business collaboration, distance learning, entertainment and consumer communities. Yahoo!, Excite and AltaVista have incorporated HearMe's technology into their existing chat features. Other customers include MTV Online, StarMedia Network, GTECH Corporation and CSK Sega.

FINANCIALS: Sales and profits are in thousands of dollars—add 000 to get the full amount.

Notes regarding 1999: Through 9 months/Pro forma *(1999 sales and profits were not available for all companies at press time.)*

1999 Sales: $9,500	1999 Profits: $-15,900	Stock Ticker: **HEAR**
1998 Sales: $8,000	1998 Profits: $-12,000	Employees: 111
1997 Sales: $2,700	1997 Profits: $-13,600	Fiscal Year Ends: 12/31
1996 Sales: $ 100	1996 Profits: $-25,000	
1995 Sales: $	1995 Profits: $	

SALARIES/BENEFITS:

Pension Plan:	ESOP Stock Plan: Y	Profit Sharing:	Top Exec. Salary: $206,853	Bonus: $
Savings Plan:	Stock Purch. Plan:		Second Exec. Salary: $187,378	Bonus: $

COMPETITIVE ADVANTAGE: Excellent alliances/Strong technology.

OTHER THOUGHTS:

Apparent Women Officers or Directors: 4
Apparent Minority Officers or Directors: 3
Hot Spot for Advancement for Women/Minorities: Y

LOCATIONS: ("Y" = Yes)

West:	Southwest:	Midwest:	Southeast:	Northeast:	International:
Y					

HEWLETT-PACKARD CO   www.hp.com

Industry Group Code: 3341A
Ranks within this company's industry group: Sales: 2 Profits: 2

BUSINESS ACTIVITIES ("Y" = Yes)

Financial Services:	Information/Publ.:	Technology:		Services:		Retailing:	Telecommunications:
Stock Brokerage	Portal/Hub/News	Computer Manuf.	Y	Payments/Transfers		Retailer	Internet Serv. Provider
Mortgages/Loans	On-Line Community	Networking Equip.	Y	Consulting		Auctions	Web Site Host
Banking	Search Engine	Software Manuf.	Y	Advertising/Marketing		Mall	Server Farm
Insurance	Financial Data Publ.	Specialty Equipment	Y	Outsourcing	Y	Tickets/Travel	Specialty Telecom.
Credit Cards	Broadcasting/Music					Price Comparisons	High Speed Access

TYPES OF BUSINESS:

Computer Hardware Manufacturer
Computer Systems
Integration
Network Systems Management Outsourcing
Electronic Test Equipment and Systems
Medical Electronic Equipment
Ultrasound Equipment
Support and Maintenance Services

BRANDS/DIVISIONS/AFFILIATES:

Convex Computer Corp.
Agilent Technologies
GeneArray Scanner
Rockland Technologies, Inc.
Viridia Patient Care System
Laserjet
ImagePoint
Dazel Corp

CONTACTS: Note: Officers with more than one job title may be intentionally listed here more than once.

Carleton S. Fiorina, CEO
Carleton S. Fiorina, Pres.
Robert P. Wayman, Exec. VP-Finance/CFO
Susan D. Bowick, VP-Human Resources
Raymond W. Cookingham, VP/Controller
Robert P. Wayman, Exec. VP-Admin.
Nick Earle, Head-E-Services.Solutions Group
Carolyn Ticknor, CEO/Pres., LaserJet Imaging Systems
Ann Livermore, CEO/Pres., Enterprise Computing

Phone: 650-857-1501	Fax: 650-857-7299
Toll-Free:	
Address: 3000 Hanover Street, Palo Alto, CA, 94304	

GROWTH PLANS/SPECIAL FEATURES:

Hewlett-Packard designs, manufactures and services equipment and systems for measurement, computation and communications. It provides 36,000 different products, including computer systems, personal computers, printers, hardcopy and imaging products, calculators and personal information products, electronic test equipment and systems, medical electronic equipment, components based on optoelectronic, silicon and compound semiconductor technologies and instrumentation for chemical analysis. HP offers services such as systems integration, selective-outsourcing management, consulting, education, product financing and rentals, as well as customer support and maintenance. The company's 600 sales and support offices and distributorships in 130 countries employ 124,000 technicians. HP's primary customers are retailers, dealers and original equipment manufacturers. HP is ranked thirteenth on the Fortune 500 list and tenth in Fortune Magazine's Best Companies to Work for in America. HP is separating into two companies. The computing and imaging business will retain the HP name. The new company, Agilent Technologies, will consist of HP's industry-leading test-and-measurement, semiconductor products, chemical-analysis and medical businesses. Agilent's initial focus will be on the communications and life sciences industries.

The company has flexible work hours for employees and offers a family resources and referral program and an educational assistance program. The company strives to maintain a no-layoff policy.

FINANCIALS: Sales and profits are in thousands of dollars—add 000 to get the full amount.

Notes regarding 1999: (1999 sales and profits were not available for all companies at press time.)

1999 Sales: $42,370,000	1999 Profits: $3,491,000	Stock Ticker: HWP
1998 Sales: $47,061,000	1998 Profits: $2,945,000	Employees: 124,600
1997 Sales: $42,895,000	1997 Profits: $3,119,000	Fiscal Year Ends: 10/31
1996 Sales: $38,420,000	1996 Profits: $2,586,000	
1995 Sales: $31,519,000	1995 Profits: $2,433,000	

SALARIES/BENEFITS:

Pension Plan: Y	ESOP Stock Plan:	Profit Sharing: Y	Top Exec. Salary: $1,000,000	Bonus: $910,700
Savings Plan: Y	Stock Purch. Plan:		Second Exec. Salary: $997,625	Bonus: $147,804

COMPETITIVE ADVANTAGE: Name recognition/Worldwide offices/Superior technology.

OTHER THOUGHTS:

Apparent Women Officers or Directors: 5
Apparent Minority Officers or Directors: 2
Hot Spot for Advancement for Women/Minorities: Y

LOCATIONS: ("Y" = Yes)

West:	Southwest:	Midwest:	Southeast:	Northeast:	International:
Y	Y	Y	Y	Y	Y

HIGH SPEED ACCESS CORP · www.hsacorp.net

Industry Group Code: 5133C
Ranks within this company's industry group: Sales: 5   Profits: 1

BUSINESS ACTIVITIES ("Y" = Yes)

Financial Services:	Information/Publ.:	Technology:	Services:	Retailing:	Telecommunications:	
Stock Brokerage	Portal/Hub/News	Computer Manuf.	Payments/Transfers	Retailer	Internet Serv. Provider	Y
Mortgages/Loans	On-Line Community	Networking Equip.	Consulting	Auctions	Web Site Host	
Banking	Search Engine	Software Manuf.	Advertising/Marketing	Mall	Server Farm	
Insurance	Financial Data Publ.	Specialty Equipment	Outsourcing	Tickets/Travel	Specialty Telecom.	
Credit Cards	Broadcasting/Music			Price Comparisons	High Speed Access	Y

TYPES OF BUSINESS:

Internet Service Provider
Cable Modem Access

BRANDS/DIVISIONS/AFFILIATES:

GROWTH PLANS/SPECIAL FEATURES:

High Speed Access Corp. is a leading provider of high speed Internet access, via cable modems, to residential and commercial end users. The company provides the most comprehensive turnkey solution available to the cable operator in these markets. Its service enables subscribers to receive Internet access at speeds substantially faster than traditional Internet access at minimal cost to the cable operator. High Speed Access pays its cable partners a portion of the monthly fees it receives from the end users in exchange for the opportunity to access and provide service to the cable partner's subscribers. High Speed Access and NorthPoint Communications recently formed a strategic partnership to deliver broadband data communications services to small- and mid-size businesses nationwide. NorthPoint, a leading competitive local exchange carrier, provides high-speed Internet access over a DSL network currently spanning 28 major U.S. markets. High Speed Access will integrate NorthPoint DSL into its service portfolio, expanding the broadband options its cable operator partners are able to offer their customers. The agreement strengthens High Speed Access' high-speed Internet access services specifically designed for small- and mid-size businesses that are not passed by the cable network and are unable to afford expensive T-1 service.

CONTACTS: Note: Officers with more than one job title may be intentionally listed here more than once.

Kent Oyler, COO
George E. Willett, CFO
Christopher P. Britton, Sr. VP-Commerical Mktg. and Sales
Cheryl Rowles-Stokes, VP-Human Resources
Atul C. Doshi, Chief Tech. Officer
Brenda Fox, Sr. VP-Business Dev.
Andy Holdate, VP-Corp. Comm.

Phone: 303-256-2000	Fax: 303-256-2001
Toll-Free:	
Address: 4100 E. Mississippi Ave., Denver, CO, 80246	

FINANCIALS: Sales and profits are in thousands of dollars—add 000 to get the full amount.

Notes regarding 1999: Through 9 months *(1999 sales and profits were not available for all companies at press time.)*

1999 Sales: $2,000	1999 Profits: $-267,900	Stock Ticker: **HSAC**
1998 Sales: $ 300	1998 Profits: $-10,000	Employees: 156
1997 Sales: $	1997 Profits: $	Fiscal Year Ends: 12/31
1996 Sales: $	1996 Profits: $	
1995 Sales: $	1995 Profits: $	

SALARIES/BENEFITS:

Pension Plan:	ESOP Stock Plan: Y	Profit Sharing: Y	Top Exec. Salary: $112,792	Bonus: $
Savings Plan:	Stock Purch. Plan:		Second Exec. Salary: $64,375	Bonus: $

COMPETITIVE ADVANTAGE: New alliance with Northpoint Communications.

OTHER THOUGHTS:

Apparent Women Officers or Directors: 1
Apparent Minority Officers or Directors:
Hot Spot for Advancement for Women/Minorities:

LOCATIONS: ("Y" = Yes)

West:	Southwest:	Midwest:	Southeast:	Northeast:	International:
		Y			

Note: Financial information, benefits and other data can change quickly and may vary from those stated here.

HOMECOM COMMUNICATIONS INC   www.homecom.com

Industry Group Code: 5112
Ranks within this company's industry group: Sales: 66   Profits: 24

BUSINESS ACTIVITIES ("Y" = Yes)

Financial Services:		Information/Publ.:		Technology:		Services:		Retailing:		Telecommunications:	
Stock Brokerage		Portal/Hub/News		Computer Manuf.		Payments/Transfers		Retailer		Internet Serv. Provider	
Mortgages/Loans		On-Line Community		Networking Equip.		Consulting	Y	Auctions		Web Site Host	
Banking	Y	Search Engine		Software Manuf.	Y	Advertising/Marketing	Y	Mall		Server Farm	
Insurance	Y	Financial Data Publ.	Y	Specialty Equipment		Outsourcing	Y	Tickets/Travel		Specialty Telecom.	
Credit Cards		Broadcasting/Music						Price Comparisons		High Speed Access	

TYPES OF BUSINESS:
Software-Financial Services

BRANDS/DIVISIONS/AFFILIATES:
InsureRate
Harvey
Personal Internet Banker
FirstInsure, Inc.

CONTACTS: *Note: Officers with more than one job title may be intentionally listed here more than once.*
Harvey W. Sax, CEO
Harvey W. Sax, Pres.
Jim Ellsworth, CFO
Ken Bozzi, VP-Sales
Jim Alvihiera, Human Resources
Gia Bokuchava, Chief Tech. Officer
Roger J. Nebel, VP-Security Services

Phone: 404-237-4646	**Fax:** 404-237-3060
Toll-Free: 888-466-3266	
Address: 3535 Piedmont Rd., Bldg. 14, Ste. 100, Atlanta, GA, 30305	

GROWTH PLANS/SPECIAL FEATURES:

HomeCom Communications, Inc. develops and markets specialized software applications, products and services that enable consumers and financial institutions to use the Internet, intranets and extranets to obtain and communicate important business information, conduct commercial transactions and improve business productivity. HomeCom's principal mission is to enable financial institutions to establish an electronic channel for consumers and businesses by providing secure, innovative, Internet-based solutions to the banking, insurance and brokerage industries. HomeCom also provides web development and maintenance, insurance consulting and marketing services. A few of HomeCom's partners include AT&T, Checkpoint, Council of Insurance Agents & Brokers, Compaq, Internet Security Systems, Inuit, Microsoft, Netscape and UNISYS. In recent news, HomeCom announced a marketing alliance with FirstInsure, Inc., an insurance and financial portal that features comprehensive insurance quotes, to be a provider of on-line insurance services through InsureRate, HomeCom's on-line insurance marketplace. InsureRate is one of the nation's leading on-line sources for insurance products including term life, homeowners and automobile policies. The company has recently signed contracts with Summit Bank and National Commercial Bank to provide consulting, Internet security services and web development. National Commercial Bank is Saudi Arabia's oldest and largest bank, and this contract marks HomeCom's first large international client.

FINANCIALS: Sales and profits are in thousands of dollars—add 000 to get the full amount.
Notes regarding 1999: Through 9 months *(1999 sales and profits were not available for all companies at press time.)*

1999 Sales: $5,100	1999 Profits: $-8,200	
1998 Sales: $3,300	1998 Profits: $-1,200	Stock Ticker: **HCOM**
1997 Sales: $2,900	1997 Profits: $-4,900	Employees: 103
1996 Sales: $2,300	1996 Profits: $- 600	Fiscal Year Ends: 12/31
1995 Sales: $ 300	1995 Profits: $	

SALARIES/BENEFITS:

Pension Plan:	ESOP Stock Plan:	Profit Sharing:	Top Exec. Salary: $147,192	Bonus: $
Savings Plan:	Stock Purch. Plan:		Second Exec. Salary: $157,508	Bonus: $

COMPETITIVE ADVANTAGE: Diversified solutions for the financial services industry.

OTHER THOUGHTS:

Apparent Women Officers or Directors:
Apparent Minority Officers or Directors: 2
Hot Spot for Advancement for Women/Minorities: Y

LOCATIONS: ("Y" = Yes)

West:	Southwest:	Midwest:	Southeast:	Northeast:	International:
	Y	Y		Y	Y

Note: Financial information, benefits and other data can change quickly and may vary from those stated here.

HOMESTORE.COM INC   www.homestore.com

Industry Group Code: 514191
Ranks within this company's industry group: Sales: 44   Profits: 5

BUSINESS ACTIVITIES ("Y" = Yes)

Financial Services:	Information/Publ.:		Technology:	Services:	Retailing:	Telecommunications:
Stock Brokerage	Portal/Hub/News	Y	Computer Manuf.	Payments/Transfers	Retailer	Internet Serv. Provider
Mortgages/Loans	On-Line Community		Networking Equip.	Consulting	Auctions	Web Site Host
Banking	Search Engine		Software Manuf.	Advertising/Marketing	Mall	Server Farm
Insurance	Financial Data Publ.		Specialty Equipment	Outsourcing	Tickets/Travel	Specialty Telecom.
Credit Cards	Broadcasting/Music				Price Comparisons	High Speed Access

TYPES OF BUSINESS:

On-line Real Estate Data

BRANDS/DIVISIONS/AFFILIATES:

RealSelect, Inc.
REALTOR.com
CommercialSource.com
Homebuilder.com
HomeFair.com
Remodel.com
SpringStreet.com

CONTACTS: Note: Officers with more than one job title may be intentionally listed here more than once.

Stuart H. Wolff, CEO
Michael A. Buckman, COO/Pres.
John M. Giesecke Jr., CFO
David M. Rosenblatt, VP-Mktg.
Catherine Kwong Giffen, VP-Human Resources
David M. Rosenblatt, VP-General Counsel
Catherine Kwong Giffen, VP-Admin.
Peter B. Taffen, VP-Business Dev.

Phone: 805-557-2300	Fax: 805-557-2680
Toll-Free:	
Address: 225 W. Hillcrest Dr., Ste. 100, Thousand Oaks, CA, 91360	

GROWTH PLANS/SPECIAL FEATURES:

Homestore.com operates a family of web sites including REALTOR.com, Remodel.com, HomeBuilder.com, SpringStreet.com, HomeFair.com and CommercialSource.com that are leading destinations on the Internet for real estate. The sites contain a wide variety of information and tools for real estate industry professionals, advertisers and consumers. The REALTOR.com site contains listings for over 1.3 million homes that are for sale, information on the buying/selling process, detailed information about the homes and their surroundings and pictures of the homes. The Remodel.com site is endorsed by the National Association of Home Builders, Remodelers Council and the National Association of the Remodeling Industry, and offers information for consumers and professionals on all aspects of home improvement and maintenance. SpringStreet.com features detailed information on rental properties in more than 6,000 U.S. cities. Homestore.com serves as a portal site devoted to serving a single content category and is a complete source of home and real estate content on the web for buying, selling, moving, renting, decorating and shopping. Homestore.com recently formed an alliance, through its subsidiary RealSelect, Inc., with LoopNet, Inc. The agreement permits RealSelect to provide Internet distribution, commercial listings and revenue sharing opportunities on commercial products and services while LoopNet, Inc. will operate the CommercialSource.com web site.

FINANCIALS: Sales and profits are in thousands of dollars—add 000 to get the full amount.

Notes regarding 1999: *(1999 sales and profits were not available for all companies at press time.)*

1999 Sales: $73,400	1999 Profits: $-71,100	Stock Ticker: **HOMS**
1998 Sales: $	1998 Profits: $	Employees: 540
1997 Sales: $	1997 Profits: $	Fiscal Year Ends: 12/31
1996 Sales: $1,400	1996 Profits: $- 300	
1995 Sales: $	1995 Profits: $	

SALARIES/BENEFITS:

Pension Plan:	ESOP Stock Plan:	Profit Sharing:	Top Exec. Salary: $	Bonus: $
Savings Plan:	Stock Purch. Plan:		Second Exec. Salary: $	Bonus: $

COMPETITIVE ADVANTAGE: Focus on the real estate industry/Owns REALTOR.com.

OTHER THOUGHTS:

Apparent Women Officers or Directors: 1
Apparent Minority Officers or Directors:
Hot Spot for Advancement for Women/Minorities:

LOCATIONS: ("Y" = Yes)

West:	Southwest:	Midwest:	Southeast:	Northeast:	International:
Y					

HOOVER'S INC   www.hoovers.com

Industry Group Code: 514191
Ranks within this company's industry group: Sales: 22   Profits: 10

BUSINESS ACTIVITIES ("Y" = Yes)

Financial Services:	Information/Publ.:		Technology:	Services:	Retailing:		Telecommunications:
Stock Brokerage	Portal/Hub/News	Y	Computer Manuf.	Payments/Transfers	Retailer	Y	Internet Serv. Provider
Mortgages/Loans	On-Line Community		Networking Equip.	Consulting	Auctions		Web Site Host
Banking	Search Engine		Software Manuf.	Advertising/Marketing	Mall		Server Farm
Insurance	Financial Data Publ.	Y	Specialty Equipment	Outsourcing	Tickets/Travel	Y	Specialty Telecom.
Credit Cards	Broadcasting/Music				Price Comparisons		High Speed Access

TYPES OF BUSINESS:

On-line Corporate Information
Reference Books and CD-ROMs
On-line Business Travel Information
On-line Careers Information
On-line Finance and Investment Data
Business News

BRANDS/DIVISIONS/AFFILIATES:

Hoover's Online
IPO Central
Cyberstocks
Hoover's UK

CONTACTS: *Note: Officers with more than one job title may be intentionally listed here more than once.*

Patrick J. Spain, CEO
Carl G. Sheperd, COO/Exec. VP
Lynn Atchison, CFO/Sr. VP-Finance & Admin.
William R. Cargill, VP-Mktg.
Patti Brower, Dir.-Human Resources
Thomas M. Ballard, CIO & VP-Tech.
Jeffrey A. Cross, Controller
Elisabeth DeMarse, Exec. VP-Content, Strategy/Acquisition
Jani F. Spede, VP-Advertising/E-commerce
Lisa Glass, Publicity Manager
Kathryn Akers, Investor Relations Manager
Jeffrey A. Cross, Treas.
George W. Howe, VP-Sales
Leslie A. Wolke, VP-Web Operations

Phone: 512-374-4500	Fax: 512-374-4501
Toll-Free:	
Address: 1033 La Posada Dr., Suite 250, Austin, TX, 78752-3812	

GROWTH PLANS/SPECIAL FEATURES:

Hoover's Inc. is an Austin-based Internet provider of company and industry information, designed to meet the diverse needs of business organizations, businesspeople, investors and educational institutions worldwide. The company was one of the first to provide high-quality, proprietary business information via the Internet. Users of its web site can use the information for their professional endeavors, including financial and competitive research, as well as for personal activities. Hoover's core asset is its proprietary editorial content which includes in-depth information on 14,000 public and private enterprises and data on 45 industry sectors. Hoover's provides information on initial public offerings through the IPO Central page, feature stories, news, career information, personal finance information, SEC documents, management biographical information, brokerage reports and credit reports. While the firm's primary focus is the Internet, the company also issues reference books and CD-ROMs. Hoover's has distribution agreements with AOL, Bloomberg, Dow Jones Interactive, go.com, LEXIS-NEXIS, Microsoft Investor and Reuters. Recent service innovations include the addition of travel information.

FINANCIALS: Sales and profits are in thousands of dollars—add 000 to get the full amount.

Notes regarding 1999: *(1999 sales and profits were not available for all companies at press time.)*

1999 Sales: $9,200	1999 Profits: $-2,300	Stock Ticker: **HOOV**
1998 Sales: $5,200	1998 Profits: $-1,800	Employees: 173
1997 Sales: $3,400	1997 Profits: $- 900	Fiscal Year Ends: 3/31
1996 Sales: $2,400	1996 Profits: $- 300	
1995 Sales: $1,500	1995 Profits: $- 600	

SALARIES/BENEFITS:

Pension Plan:	ESOP Stock Plan: Y	Profit Sharing:	Top Exec. Salary: $144,236	Bonus: $25,000
Savings Plan: Y	Stock Purch. Plan:		Second Exec. Salary: $97,694	Bonus: $12,000

COMPETITIVE ADVANTAGE:
One of the most active of all the business related sites, with approximately 2.4 million users quarterly and 165,000 paid subscribers/Focus on outstanding content.

OTHER THOUGHTS:

Apparent Women Officers or Directors: 6
Apparent Minority Officers or Directors:
Hot Spot for Advancement for Women/Minorities: Y

LOCATIONS: ("Y" = Yes)

West:	Southwest:	Midwest:	Southeast:	Northeast:	International:
	Y			Y	Y

Note: Financial information, benefits and other data can change quickly and may vary from those stated here.

HOTJOBS.COM LTD   www.hotjobs.com

Industry Group Code: 514191
Ranks within this company's industry group: Sales: 24   Profits: 8

BUSINESS ACTIVITIES ("Y" = Yes)

Financial Services:	Information/Publ.:		Technology:	Services:		Retailing:		Telecommunications:
Stock Brokerage	Portal/Hub/News	Y	Computer Manuf.	Payments/Transfers		Retailer		Internet Serv. Provider
Mortgages/Loans	On-Line Community		Networking Equip.	Consulting	Y	Auctions		Web Site Host
Banking	Search Engine		Software Manuf.	Advertising/Marketing	Y	Mall		Server Farm
Insurance	Financial Data Publ.		Specialty Equipment	Outsourcing		Tickets/Travel		Specialty Telecom.
Credit Cards	Broadcasting/Music					Price Comparisons		High Speed Access

TYPES OF BUSINESS:

Portal-Careers

BRANDS/DIVISIONS/AFFILIATES:

Softshoe recruiting software
WorkWorld job fairs

CONTACTS: Note: Officers with more than one job title may be intentionally listed here more than once.

Richard S. Johnson, CEO
Dimitri J. Boyland, COO
Stephen W. Ellis, CFO
Dean Harris, Sr. VP-Mktg.
David Carvajal, Dir. Staffing
George J. Nassef Jr., Chief Tech. Officer
John Rusak, VP/Controller

Phone: 212-302-0060	Fax: 212-944-8962
Toll-Free: 877-468-5627	
Address: 24 W. 40th St., 14th Fl., New York, NY, 10018	

GROWTH PLANS/SPECIAL FEATURES:

HotJobs.com, Ltd. is a leading supplier of Internet-based recruiting solutions, providing a direct exchange of information between employers and job seekers. HotJobs.com allows employers to more effectively manage recruiting processes, saving time and money. The company offers a real-time environment that provides member employers with the tools to post, track and manage job openings, with access to a database of over 550,000 job seekers. Job seekers have the ability to identify, research, apply for and evaluate job opportunities. Headhunters are prohibited from using the employment exchange, ensuring direct contact between job seekers and employers. Additional recruiting solutions include Softshoe software, WorkWorld job fairs and on-line advertising and consulting services. Softshoe recruiting software is a private label job board and applicant tracking system that enables companies to define, manage and analyze recruiting processes and share relevant information throughout the organization. The WorkWorld job fairs integrate with HotJobs.com to provide on-line interaction and direct physical interaction between employers and job seekers. Revenues are primarily derived from employer memberships with companies such as Coors Brewing Company, Merrill Lynch, Amazon.com, Nike, Hewlett-Packard, The Home Depot, Microsoft, Intel and The Walt Disney Company.

FINANCIALS: Sales and profits are in thousands of dollars—add 000 to get the full amount.

Notes regarding 1999: (1999 sales and profits were not available for all companies at press time.)

1999 Sales: $20,700	1999 Profits: $-17,800	Stock Ticker: **HOTJ**	
1998 Sales: $4,200	1998 Profits: $-1,600	Employees: 89	
1997 Sales: $ 700	1997 Profits: $- 600	Fiscal Year Ends: 12/31	
1996 Sales: $	1996 Profits: $		
1995 Sales: $	1995 Profits: $		

SALARIES/BENEFITS:

Pension Plan:	ESOP Stock Plan: Y	Profit Sharing:	Top Exec. Salary: $182,000	Bonus: $
Savings Plan: Y	Stock Purch. Plan:		Second Exec. Salary: $	Bonus: $

COMPETITIVE ADVANTAGE: Vast database of job seekers.

OTHER THOUGHTS:

Apparent Women Officers or Directors:
Apparent Minority Officers or Directors:
Hot Spot for Advancement for Women/Minorities:

LOCATIONS: ("Y" = Yes)

West:	Southwest:	Midwest:	Southeast:	Northeast:	International:
Y		Y		Y	Y

Note: Financial information, benefits and other data can change quickly and may vary from those stated here.

IDT CORPORATION www.idt.net

Industry Group Code: 5133B
Ranks within this company's industry group: Sales: 6   Profits: 3

BUSINESS ACTIVITIES ("Y" = Yes)

Financial Services:	Information/Publ.:	Technology:	Services:	Retailing:	Telecommunications:	
Stock Brokerage	Portal/Hub/News	Computer Manuf.	Payments/Transfers	Retailer	Internet Serv. Provider	Y
Mortgages/Loans	On-Line Community	Networking Equip.	Consulting	Auctions	Web Site Host	
Banking	Search Engine	Software Manuf.	Advertising/Marketing	Mall	Server Farm	
Insurance	Financial Data Publ.	Specialty Equipment	Outsourcing	Tickets/Travel	Specialty Telecom.	Y
Credit Cards	Broadcasting/Music			Price Comparisons	High Speed Access	Y

TYPES OF BUSINESS:

Long Distance Telephone Service
Internet Long Distance Phone Service
Local Telephone Carrier
Calling Cards
Telecommunications Services
Internet Services

BRANDS/DIVISIONS/AFFILIATES:

Net2Phone, Inc.

CONTACTS: Note: Officers with more than one job title may be intentionally listed here more than once.

Howard S. Jonas, CEO
Hal Brecher, COO
Stephen R. Brown, CFO
Joshua Winkler, Exec. VP-Sales
Howard Millendorf, Dir.-Human Resources
Joyce J. Mason, Sec.
Joyce J. Mason, General Counsel
Hal Brecher, Exec. VP-Oper.
Howard S. Jonas, Treas.

Phone: 201-928-1000	Fax: 201-928-1057
Toll-Free:	
Address: 190 Main St., Hackensack, NJ, 07601	

GROWTH PLANS/SPECIAL FEATURES:

IDT Corporation is a facilities-based multinational carrier that provides a broad range of telecommunications services to wholesale and retail customers worldwide. The company offers integrated and competitively priced international and domestic long distance service and Internet access. IDT's telecommunications services include prepaid calling cards and wholesale carrier, domestic long distance and international retail services. The company provides phone services to more than 50,000 customers in more than 170 countries. It has approximately 125 wholesale customers located in the U.S. and Europe. Within the U.S., IDT provides dedicated and dial-up Internet access services to approximately 65,000 retail customers. The company's Net2Phone, Inc. subsidiary offers a variety of Internet telephony products and services. Net2Phone's web-based Internet telephony services, which allow customers to make telephone calls from a multimedia PC to any telephone, and the Net2Phone Direct service, which enables users to make phone-to-phone calls over the Internet, have been used by a total of more than 1.8 million registered customers. IDT's telecommunications services are delivered over a network of 70 switches in the U.S. and Europe and 16 undersea fiber optic cables. The company obtains additional transmission capacity from other carriers.

FINANCIALS: Sales and profits are in thousands of dollars—add 000 to get the full amount.

Notes regarding 1999: (1999 sales and profits were not available for all companies at press time.)

1999 Sales: $701,500	1999 Profits: $2,900	Stock Ticker: **IDTC**
1998 Sales: $335,400	1998 Profits: $-6,400	Employees: 1,271
1997 Sales: $135,200	1997 Profits: $-3,800	Fiscal Year Ends: 7/31
1996 Sales: $57,700	1996 Profits: $-15,600	
1995 Sales: $11,700	1995 Profits: $2,100	

SALARIES/BENEFITS:

Pension Plan: Y	ESOP Stock Plan:	Profit Sharing:	Top Exec. Salary: $200,000	Bonus: $
Savings Plan: Y	Stock Purch. Plan:		Second Exec. Salary: $167,938	Bonus: $

COMPETITIVE ADVANTAGE: Rapidly growing Internet telephone services.

OTHER THOUGHTS:

Apparent Women Officers or Directors: 1
Apparent Minority Officers or Directors:
Hot Spot for Advancement for Women/Minorities:

LOCATIONS: ("Y" = Yes)

West:	Southwest:	Midwest:	Southeast:	Northeast:	International:
				Y	Y

Note: Financial information, benefits and other data can change quickly and may vary from those stated here.

ILIFE.COM   www.ilife.com

Industry Group Code: 514191
Ranks within this company's industry group: Sales: 26   Profits: 12

BUSINESS ACTIVITIES ("Y" = Yes)

Financial Services:	Information/Publ.:		Technology:	Services:	Retailing:	Telecommunications:
Stock Brokerage	Portal/Hub/News	Y	Computer Manuf.	Payments/Transfers	Retailer	Internet Serv. Provider
Mortgages/Loans	On-Line Community		Networking Equip.	Consulting	Auctions	Web Site Host
Banking	Search Engine		Software Manuf.	Advertising/Marketing	Mall	Server Farm
Insurance	Financial Data Publ.	Y	Specialty Equipment	Outsourcing	Tickets/Travel	Specialty Telecom.
Credit Cards	Broadcasting/Music				Price Comparisons	High Speed Access

TYPES OF BUSINESS:

Portal-Financial Services

BRANDS/DIVISIONS/AFFILIATES:

theWhiz.com
ilife.com
Consejero.com
go2pivot.com
bankrate.com
IntelligentTaxes.com
CPNet.com

CONTACTS: *Note: Officers with more than one job title may be intentionally listed here more than once.*

William P. Anderson III, CEO
William P. Anderson III, Pres.
G. Cotter Cuningham, Sr. VP-Sales and Mktg.
Peter W. Minford, Sr.VP-Admin.
Robert J. DeFranco, VP-Investor Relations
Jim Cerbone, VP-Sales

Phone: 561-627-7330	Fax: 561-627-7335
Toll-Free:	
Address: 11811 US Hwy. 1, Ste. 101, North Palm Beach, FL, 33408	

GROWTH PLANS/SPECIAL FEATURES:

Intelligent Life is a leading provider of independent, objective research regarding consumer banking and credit services, and a significant publisher of original editorial content relating to personal finance matters. The company publishes its data on-line through its principal web site, bankrate.com, and through arrangements with more than 60 distribution partners. Its partners include Yahoo!, Quicken.com, America Online and Money.com. Information provided by Intelligent Life covers a wide variety of categories, including mortgage and home equity loans, credit cards, car loans, checking accounts, ATM fees and yields on savings instruments. Intelligent Life also runs a family of web sites that specialize in offering information on different facets of personal finance, which can all be reached through ilife.com, the company's newly launched portal. TheWhiz.com delivers information on creating budgets for holiday spending, debt management and shopping. Other sites in the family include go2pivot.com, Consejero.com, CPNet.com, greenmagazine.com and IntelligentTaxes.com. TheWhiz.com recently hosted a Get Out and Stay Out of Debt marathon clinic. The clinic was one week long, and participants had the opportunity to communicate with an on-line team of financial writers and money experts to answer credit and debt questions.

FINANCIALS: Sales and profits are in thousands of dollars—add 000 to get the full amount.

Notes regarding 1999: *(1999 sales and profits were not available for all companies at press time.)*

1999 Sales: $12,118	1999 Profits: $-13,037	Stock Ticker: **ILIF**
1998 Sales: $3,500	1998 Profits: $-2,100	Employees: 164
1997 Sales: $3,800	1997 Profits: $-2,800	Fiscal Year Ends: 12/31
1996 Sales: $1,600	1996 Profits: $- 700	
1995 Sales: $1,100	1995 Profits: $-1,000	

SALARIES/BENEFITS:

Pension Plan:	ESOP Stock Plan:	Profit Sharing:	Top Exec. Salary: $	Bonus: $
Savings Plan:	Stock Purch. Plan:		Second Exec. Salary: $	Bonus: $

COMPETITIVE ADVANTAGE:
This company has a special niche that touches the lives of most Americans every day: personal savings, borrowing, checking and credit cards.

OTHER THOUGHTS:

Apparent Women Officers or Directors: 1
Apparent Minority Officers or Directors:
Hot Spot for Advancement for Women/Minorities:

LOCATIONS: ("Y" = Yes)

West:	Southwest:	Midwest:	Southeast:	Northeast:	International:
			Y		

IMAGEX.COM INC   www.imagex.com

Industry Group Code: 51339A
Ranks within this company's Industry group: Sales: 12   Profits: 8

BUSINESS ACTIVITIES ("Y" = Yes)

Financial Services:	Information/Publ.:	Technology:		Services:		Retailing:	Telecommunications:
Stock Brokerage	Portal/Hub/News	Computer Manuf.		Payments/Transfers		Retailer	Internet Serv. Provider
Mortgages/Loans	On-Line Community	Networking Equip.		Consulting		Auctions	Web Site Host
Banking	Search Engine	Software Manuf.		Advertising/Marketing		Mall	Server Farm
Insurance	Financial Data Publ.	Specialty Equipment	Y	Outsourcing	Y	Tickets/Travel	Specialty Telecom.
Credit Cards	Broadcasting/Music					Price Comparisons	High Speed Access

TYPES OF BUSINESS:
On-line Commercial Printing Intermediary

BRANDS/DIVISIONS/AFFILIATES:
Fine Arts Graphics
eCompanystore.com
On-line Printing Center

CONTACTS: *Note: Officers with more than one job title may be intentionally listed here more than once.*
Richard P. Begert, CEO
Richard P. Begert, Pres.
Robin Krueger, CFO
Dana F. Manciagli, VP-Sales and Mktg.
Lori Sunich, Dir.-Human Resources
Cory E. Klatt, Chief Tech. Officer
Cory E. Klatt, Treas.

Phone: 425-452-0011	Fax: 425-452-9266
Toll-Free:	
Address: 10800 NE Eighth St., Ste. 200, Bellevue, WA, 98004	

GROWTH PLANS/SPECIAL FEATURES:

ImageX.com is a leading Internet-based business-to-business intermediary in the U.S. commercial printing industry. The company offers an integrated e-commerce solution that automates the error-prone, time-consuming and labor-intensive traditional commercial printing process. With the ImageX.com solution, businesses access a customized, secure web site, the On-line Printing Center, that contains a digital catalog of its custom-printed business materials, such as marketing brochures, stationery and business cards. ImageX.com's On-line Printing Center enables users to modify, proof, procure and manage all business materials from any Internet-enabled personal computer. This solution almost eliminates the possibility of print errors and greatly reduces procurement time. ImageX.com recently formed a strategic alliance with eCompanyStore.com, a leading provider of logo merchandise for mid- to large-sized businesses. eCompanyStore will provide on-line logo merchandise for both companies' clients. ImageX.com will soon feature logo merchandise such as apparel and uniforms. The company will also have its e-procurement services available on the Commerce One MarketSite portal, a site that links buying and supplying organizations into real-time trading communities and provides the largest, Internet-based business-to-business marketplace for Fortune 1000 companies.

FINANCIALS: Sales and profits are in thousands of dollars—add 000 to get the full amount.
Notes regarding 1999: *(1999 sales and profits were not available for all companies at press time.)*

1999 Sales: $11,500	1999 Profits: $3,000	Stock Ticker: **IMGX**
1998 Sales: $1,000	1998 Profits: $-8,600	Employees: 188
1997 Sales: $ 100	1997 Profits: $-3,600	Fiscal Year Ends: 12/31
1996 Sales: $ 100	1996 Profits: $- 500	
1995 Sales: $	1995 Profits: $	

SALARIES/BENEFITS:

Pension Plan:	ESOP Stock Plan:	Profit Sharing:	Top Exec. Salary: $	Bonus: $
Savings Plan:	Stock Purch. Plan:		Second Exec. Salary: $	Bonus: $

COMPETITIVE ADVANTAGE: Relationships that expand its market reach.

OTHER THOUGHTS:
Apparent Women Officers or Directors: 2
Apparent Minority Officers or Directors: 1
Hot Spot for Advancement for Women/Minorities:

LOCATIONS: ("Y" = Yes)

West:	Southwest:	Midwest:	Southeast:	Northeast:	International:
				Y	

Note: Financial information, benefits and other data can change quickly and may vary from those stated here.

IMALL INC   www.imall.com

Industry Group Code: 4541
Ranks within this company's industry group: Sales: 25 Profits: 2

BUSINESS ACTIVITIES ("Y" = Yes)

Financial Services:	Information/Publ.:		Technology:	Services:	Retailing:		Telecommunications:	
Stock Brokerage	Portal/Hub/News		Computer Manuf.	Payments/Transfers	Retailer		Internet Serv. Provider	
Mortgages/Loans	On-Line Community		Networking Equip.	Consulting	Auctions		Web Site Host	Y
Banking	Search Engine	Y	Software Manuf.	Advertising/Marketing	Mall	Y	Server Farm	
Insurance	Financial Data Publ.		Specialty Equipment	Outsourcing	Tickets/Travel		Specialty Telecom.	
Credit Cards	Broadcasting/Music				Price Comparisons		High Speed Access	

TYPES OF BUSINESS:

On-line Mall
Hosts Retail Web Sites
Operates Stuff.com
Provides Classified Ad Space

BRANDS/DIVISIONS/AFFILIATES:

Stuff.com
Excite@Home

GROWTH PLANS/SPECIAL FEATURES:

Through its one-stop e-shopping Internet site, iMall, Inc. receives around 30 million visitors per month, making it one of the busiest malls on the Internet. The company hosts web sites for over 1,600 merchants and provides space for sellers to post classified ads. Additionally, iMall operates Stuff.com, a product search engine and shopping conduit. The company's revenues are derived from commissions earned on each sale, as well as through site hosting and maintenance fees charged to merchants. E-commerce tools and consulting are also provided by iMall to approximately 200,000 small- to mid-sized companies. In October 1999, Excite@Home acquired iMall.

CONTACTS: *Note: Officers with more than one job title may be intentionally listed here more than once.*

Richard M. Rosenblatt, CEO
Joseph Ruszkiewiczs, COO/Exec. VP
Anthony P. Mazzarella, CFO/Exec. VP
Dan Odette, VP-Mktg.
Phil Windley, Chief Tech. Officer
Stephen W. Fulling, VP-Info. Tech. Services
Anthony P. Mazzarella, Sec.
Anthony P. Mazzarella, Treas.

Phone: 310-309-4000	**Fax:** 310-309-4106
Toll-Free:	
Address: 233 Wilshire Blvd., Suite 820, Santa Monica, CA, 90401	

FINANCIALS: Sales and profits are in thousands of dollars—add 000 to get the full amount.

Notes regarding 1999: *(1999 sales and profits were not available for all companies at press time.)*

1999 Sales: $	1999 Profits: $	Stock Ticker: **IMAL**
1998 Sales: $1,600	1998 Profits: $13,200	Employees: 130
1997 Sales: $16,800	1997 Profits: $-4,700	Fiscal Year Ends: 12/31
1996 Sales: $16,000	1996 Profits: $ 100	
1995 Sales: $	1995 Profits: $	

SALARIES/BENEFITS:

Pension Plan:	ESOP Stock Plan:	Profit Sharing:	Top Exec. Salary: $119,792	Bonus: $
Savings Plan: Y	Stock Purch. Plan:		Second Exec. Salary: $	Bonus: $

COMPETITIVE ADVANTAGE: Operates through the profitable and popular medium of e-commerce.

OTHER THOUGHTS:

	LOCATIONS: ("Y" = Yes)					
Apparent Women Officers or Directors:	West:	Southwest:	Midwest:	Southeast:	Northeast:	International:
Apparent Minority Officers or Directors:	Y					
Hot Spot for Advancement for Women/Minorities:						

INFONAUTICS INC   www.infonautics.com

Industry Group Code: 514191
Ranks within this company's industry group: Sales: 13   Profits: 39

BUSINESS ACTIVITIES ("Y" = Yes)

Financial Services:	Information/Publ.:		Technology:	Services:	Retailing:	Telecommunications:
Stock Brokerage	Portal/Hub/News	Y	Computer Manuf.	Payments/Transfers	Retailer	Internet Serv. Provider
Mortgages/Loans	On-Line Community		Networking Equip.	Consulting	Auctions	Web Site Host
Banking	Search Engine		Software Manuf.	Advertising/Marketing	Mall	Server Farm
Insurance	Financial Data Publ.		Specialty Equipment	Outsourcing	Tickets/Travel	Specialty Telecom.
Credit Cards	Broadcasting/Music				Price Comparisons	High Speed Access

TYPES OF BUSINESS:

On-line Information Services
On-Line Research and Reference

BRANDS/DIVISIONS/AFFILIATES:

Electric Library
Sports Sleuth
Job Sleuth
Company Sleuth
Encyclopedia.com
Researchpaper.com
Bigchalk.com

CONTACTS: *Note: Officers with more than one job title may be intentionally listed here more than once.*

David V. Morris, CEO
David V. Morris, Pres.
Frederica F. O'Brien, CFO/VP-Finance
Alan S. Preston, VP-Human Resources
Cedarampattu Mohan, VP-Tech./Chief Tech. Officer
Joshua M. Kopelman, Exec.VP-Corp. Sec.
Gerard J. Lewis Jr., VP-General Counsel
William R. Burger, VP-Content and Media Services

Phone: 610-971-8840	Fax: 610-971-8859
Toll-Free:	
Address: 900 W. Valley Rd.,Ste. 1000, Wayne, PA, 19087	

GROWTH PLANS/SPECIAL FEATURES:

Infonautics is an Internet information company that specializes in providing on-line research and reference tools to individuals, businesses, colleges, libraries and schools. Infonautics also offers e-commerce on-line publishing services to top publishers and content creators to manage their on-line offerings. Some of the company's web properties include Electric Library, Company Sleuth, Sports Sleuth, Job Sleuth, Encyclopedia.com and Researchpaper.com. Its primary subscription service, Electric Library, is licensed to more than 17,000 schools and libraries all over the U.S. and is the leading paid subscription service on the Internet, with more than 85,000 individual subscribers. Sports Sleuth is the company's newest service and was named Site of the Day by Yahoo! and Hot Site by USA Today. The Electric Library has won numerous awards, such as the Educational Press Association of America's Golden Lamp Award and the WebCrawler Select Best of the Web award. Infonautics recently entered an agreement with Microsoft Corporation to provide the Electric Library service to individual consumers on Microsoft Network's Research & School channel, as well as to Microsoft's Encarta on-line users. Microsoft will place its Encarta service on Encyclopedia.com as part of the agreement.

FINANCIALS: Sales and profits are in thousands of dollars—add 000 to get the full amount.

Notes regarding 1999: Through 9 months *(1999 sales and profits were not available for all companies at press time.)*

1999 Sales: $17,380	1999 Profits: $-7,195	Stock Ticker: **INFO**
1998 Sales: $14,900	1998 Profits: $-17,400	Employees: 175
1997 Sales: $6,800	1997 Profits: $-17,400	Fiscal Year Ends: 12/31
1996 Sales: $1,400	1996 Profits: $-13,800	
1995 Sales: $ 400	1995 Profits: $-7,500	

SALARIES/BENEFITS:

Pension Plan: Y	ESOP Stock Plan:	Profit Sharing:	Top Exec. Salary: $166,667	Bonus: $
Savings Plan:	Stock Purch. Plan:		Second Exec. Salary: $109,000	Bonus: $15,000

COMPETITIVE ADVANTAGE: 85,000 paid subscribers.

OTHER THOUGHTS:

Apparent Women Officers or Directors:
Apparent Minority Officers or Directors: 1
Hot Spot for Advancement for Women/Minorities:

LOCATIONS: ("Y" = Yes)

West:	Southwest:	Midwest:	Southeast:	Northeast:	International:
				Y	

INFOSPACE.COM INC   www.infospace.com

Industry Group Code: 514191
Ranks within this company's industry group: Sales: 15   Profits: 27

BUSINESS ACTIVITIES ("Y" = Yes)

Financial Services:	Information/Publ.:		Technology:	Services:	Retailing:	Telecommunications:	
Stock Brokerage	Portal/Hub/News	Y	Computer Manuf.	Payments/Transfers	Retailer	Internet Serv. Provider	Y
Mortgages/Loans	On-Line Community		Networking Equip.	Consulting	Auctions	Web Site Host	
Banking	Search Engine		Software Manuf.	Advertising/Marketing	Mall	Server Farm	
Insurance	Financial Data Publ.		Specialty Equipment	Outsourcing	Tickets/Travel	Specialty Telecom.	Y
Credit Cards	Broadcasting/Music				Price Comparisons	High Speed Access	

TYPES OF BUSINESS:

Content Provider-Local News and Information
Publisher-Video Press Releases

BRANDS/DIVISIONS/AFFILIATES:

Saraide

CONTACTS: Note: Officers with more than one job title may be intentionally listed here more than once.

Naveen Jain, CEO
Bernee D.L. Strom, Pres./COO
Douglas A. Bevis, VP-CFO
Randy Massengale, VP-Human Resources
Tammy D. Halstead, VP-Chief Acct. Officer
Ellen B. Alben, VP-Corp. Sec.
Ellen B. Alben, VP-Legal and Business Affairs
Chris Matty, VP-Strategic Dev.

Phone: 425-882-1602	Fax: 425-882-0988
Toll-Free:	
Address: 15375 NE 90th St., Redmond, WA, 98052	

GROWTH PLANS/SPECIAL FEATURES:

InfoSpace.com is a leading provider of private label solutions for content and commerce to web sites and Internet appliances. It has an affiliate network that consists of more than 1,500 web sites, including America Online, Netscape Communications, Microsoft Network, Lycos and ABC LocalNet. The company's web site features a variety of information, such as yellow and white pages, maps, classified advertisements, real-time stock quotes, sports news, shopping, public records, local business and events, weather forecasts and horoscopes. The majority of InfoSpace.com's revenues come from national and local advertising, promotions and non-advertising-based private label solutions. The fastest growing segment of the company's business is its wireless services. Major wireless carriers and device manufacturers launched new products and services that featured InfoSpace.com's services. Sprint, the nation's largest personal communications service provider (with more than four million customers), launched its PCS Wireless Web, which uses InfoSpace.com's wireless directory services. The company also provides its services to AT&T, Bell Atlantic, Airtouch, British Telecom Cellnet, Dutchtone and Omnitel. InfoSpace.com has agreed to acquire Saraide, the leading wireless Internet service provider in Europe, Japan and Canada.

FINANCIALS: Sales and profits are in thousands of dollars—add 000 to get the full amount.

Notes regarding 1999: (1999 sales and profits were not available for all companies at press time.)

1999 Sales: $36,800	1999 Profits: $5,800	Stock Ticker: **INSP**
1998 Sales: $9,400	1998 Profits: $-9,100	Employees: 76
1997 Sales: $1,700	1997 Profits: $- 700	Fiscal Year Ends: 12/31
1996 Sales: $ 200	1996 Profits: $- 400	
1995 Sales: $	1995 Profits: $	

SALARIES/BENEFITS:

Pension Plan:	ESOP Stock Plan:	Profit Sharing:	Top Exec. Salary: $	Bonus: $
Savings Plan:	Stock Purch. Plan:		Second Exec. Salary: $	Bonus: $

COMPETITIVE ADVANTAGE: Focus on the hot wireless market.

OTHER THOUGHTS:

Apparent Women Officers or Directors: 2
Apparent Minority Officers or Directors: 1
Hot Spot for Advancement for Women/Minorities:

LOCATIONS: ("Y" = Yes)

West:	Southwest:	Midwest:	Southeast:	Northeast:	International:
				Y	

INKTOMI CORP   www.inktomi.com

Industry Group Code: 5112
Ranks within this company's industry group: Sales: 39   Profits: 72

BUSINESS ACTIVITIES ("Y" = Yes)

Financial Services:	Information/Publ.:	Technology:	Services:	Retailing:	Telecommunications:
Stock Brokerage	Portal/Hub/News	Computer Manuf.	Payments/Transfers	Retailer	Internet Serv. Provider
Mortgages/Loans	On-Line Community	Networking Equip.	Consulting	Auctions	Web Site Host
Banking	Search Engine	Software Manuf. Y	Advertising/Marketing	Mall	Server Farm
Insurance	Financial Data Publ.	Specialty Equipment	Outsourcing	Tickets/Travel	Specialty Telecom.
Credit Cards	Broadcasting/Music			Price Comparisons	High Speed Access

TYPES OF BUSINESS:

Software-Search Engines

BRANDS/DIVISIONS/AFFILIATES:

Traffic Server
Impulse! Buy Network
Content Delivery Suite

CONTACTS: Note: Officers with more than one job title may be intentionally listed here more than once.

David C. Peterschmidt, CEO
David C. Peterschmidt, Pres.
Jerry M. Kennelly, VP-Finance/CFO
Richard B. Pierce, VP-Mktg.
Rita Schueling, Dir.-Human Resources
Paul Gauthier, Chief Tech. Officer
Jerry M. Kennelly, Corp. Sec.
Timothy Stevens, VP-Corp. Affairs/General Counsel
Dennis L. McEvoy, VP-Dev. and Support

Phone: 650-653-2800	Fax: 650-653-2801
Toll-Free:	
Address: 1900 S. Norfolk St., San Mateo, CA, 94403	

GROWTH PLANS/SPECIAL FEATURES:

Inktomi develops and markets high performance network information and infrastructure applications primarily used by Internet service providers and backbone carriers. Inktomi's main products and services are Traffic Server, Content Delivery Suite, search engine, directory engine and shopping engine. The Traffic Server is the industry's first large-scale commercial network cache designed to reduce Internet congestion and increase network efficiency. Inktomi's search engine has received multiple awards, including PC Magazine's Editor's Choice Award, PC Computing's Five Star rating and Internet World's Top Search Engine Award. Some of Inktomi's key customers and partners include America Online, Excite@Home, British Telecom, Cisco, Microsoft Corp., Yahoo! and NBC Snap. Recently, Inktomi formed a strategic alliance with SAP AG, a leading provider of inter-enterprise software solutions, to incorporate Inktomi's search and directory engines into the mySAP.com Marketplace. Inktomi is growing aggressively and has entered into a strategic agreement with Enron Communications to integrate Inktomi's caching software into the Enron Intelligent Network.

FINANCIALS: Sales and profits are in thousands of dollars—add 000 to get the full amount.

Notes regarding 1999: *(1999 sales and profits were not available for all companies at press time.)*

1999 Sales: $71,200	1999 Profits: $-24,200	Stock Ticker: **INKT**
1998 Sales: $20,400	1998 Profits: $-22,400	Employees: 185
1997 Sales: $5,800	1997 Profits: $-8,700	Fiscal Year Ends: 9/30
1996 Sales: $ 500	1996 Profits: $-3,500	
1995 Sales: $	1995 Profits: $	

SALARIES/BENEFITS:

Pension Plan:	ESOP Stock Plan:	Profit Sharing:	Top Exec. Salary: $200,000	Bonus: $73,105
Savings Plan:	Stock Purch. Plan:		Second Exec. Salary: $150,000	Bonus: $125,000

COMPETITIVE ADVANTAGE: Enables faster access through high throughput caching.

OTHER THOUGHTS:

Apparent Women Officers or Directors: 1
Apparent Minority Officers or Directors:
Hot Spot for Advancement for Women/Minorities:

LOCATIONS: ("Y" = Yes)

West:	Southwest:	Midwest:	Southeast:	Northeast:	International:
Y					

INPRISE CORPORATION   www.inprise.com

Industry Group Code: 5112
Ranks within this company's industry group: Sales: 6   Profits: 8

BUSINESS ACTIVITIES ("Y" = Yes)

Financial Services:	Information/Publ.:		Technology:		Services:	Retailing:	Telecommunications:
Stock Brokerage	Portal/Hub/News	Y	Computer Manuf.		Payments/Transfers	Retailer	Internet Serv. Provider
Mortgages/Loans	On-Line Community	Y	Networking Equip.		Consulting	Auctions	Web Site Host
Banking	Search Engine		Software Manuf.	Y	Advertising/Marketing	Mall	Server Farm
Insurance	Financial Data Publ.		Specialty Equipment		Outsourcing	Tickets/Travel	Specialty Telecom.
Credit Cards	Broadcasting/Music					Price Comparisons	High Speed Access

TYPES OF BUSINESS:

Software-Development Tools
On-line Community for Developers
ASP Tools
ASP Suite

BRANDS/DIVISIONS/AFFILIATES:

Inprise AppServices
Borland.com
Inprise Technology, Inc.
Interactive Objects Software GMBH
Apogee Information Systems, Inc.
Borland International Inc.
Visigenic
Starfish Software Inc.

CONTACTS: Note: Officers with more than one job title may be intentionally listed here more than once.

Dale Fullor, CEO/Pres.
John Walshe, COO
Frederick A. Ball, VP/CFO
Stephanie Schwieghofer-Jones, VP-Mktg.
Nancy Hauge, VP-Human Resources
Frank Careccia, VP-Research and Dev.
Hobart Birmingham, Chief Admin. Officer
George Macintyre, Sr. VP/Corp. Sec.
Marilee Adams, VP-Corp. Comm.
David Intersimone, VP-Dev. Relations
John Floisand, Pres.-Borland.com
Jim Weil, Pres.-Inprise Div.

Phone: 831-431-1000	Fax: 831-431-4141
Toll-Free:	
Address: 100 Enterprise Way, Scotts Valley, CA, 95066	

GROWTH PLANS/SPECIAL FEATURES:

Inprise Corporation is a leading provider of cross-platform software, software development tools and services that simplify the complexity of application development, integration, deployment and management. The company markets and distributes its products through its direct sales force, single and two-tier distribution, value-added resellers (VARs), independent software vendors (ISVs) and the Internet. This multiple distribution approach allows customers to select the channel that addresses their particular needs and provides Inprise with broad coverage of worldwide markets. Recently, the company announced the formation of two operating divisions, Inprise and Borland.com. The Inprise division provides integrated enterprise solutions to Global 1000 corporations, and Borland.com is developing a destination web site and an on-line community serving software developers' needs. It also intends to offer a wide range of products, services and technical information, including advanced Internet products and technologies. The company has entered into an alliance with Corel Corporation to accelerate commercial mainstreaming of Linux technology. Inprise recently announced its new business strategy, which is in support of application service providers (ASP). The firm plans to create Inprise AppServices, a new service to integrate software and services from many application service providers into a single, easy-to-use suite.

FINANCIALS: Sales and profits are in thousands of dollars—add 000 to get the full amount.

Notes regarding 1999: *(1999 sales and profits were not available for all companies at press time.)*

1999 Sales: $174,800	1999 Profits: $22,700	Stock Ticker: **INPR**
1998 Sales: $189,100	1998 Profits: $8,300	Employees: 900
1997 Sales: $127,500	1997 Profits: $4,400	Fiscal Year Ends: 12/31
1996 Sales: $151,400	1996 Profits: $-108,000	
1995 Sales: $215,200	1995 Profits: $14,300	

SALARIES/BENEFITS:

Pension Plan:	ESOP Stock Plan:	Profit Sharing: Y	Top Exec. Salary: $399,538	Bonus: $247,600
Savings Plan:	Stock Purch. Plan: Y		Second Exec. Salary: $219,653	Bonus: $53,672

COMPETITIVE ADVANTAGE: Focus on the needs of software developers.

OTHER THOUGHTS:

Apparent Women Officers or Directors: 1
Apparent Minority Officers or Directors:
Hot Spot for Advancement for Women/Minorities:

LOCATIONS: ("Y" = Yes)

West:	Southwest:	Midwest:	Southeast:	Northeast:	International:
Y	Y	Y	Y	Y	Y

Note: Financial information, benefits and other data can change quickly and may vary from those stated here.

INSIGHT ENTERPRISES INC   www.insight.com

Industry Group Code: 4541
Ranks within this company's industry group: Sales: 1   Profits: 1

BUSINESS ACTIVITIES ("Y" = Yes)

Financial Services:	Information/Publ.:	Technology:	Services:	Retailing:		Telecommunications:
Stock Brokerage	Portal/Hub/News	Computer Manuf.	Payments/Transfers	Retailer	Y	Internet Serv. Provider
Mortgages/Loans	On-Line Community	Networking Equip.	Consulting	Auctions		Web Site Host
Banking	Search Engine	Software Manuf.	Advertising/Marketing	Mall		Server Farm
Insurance	Financial Data Publ.	Specialty Equipment	Outsourcing	Tickets/Travel		Specialty Telecom.
Credit Cards	Broadcasting/Music			Price Comparisons		High Speed Access

TYPES OF BUSINESS:

Retail-Computers

BRANDS/DIVISIONS/AFFILIATES:

Direct Alliance Corporation
Insight Direct, Inc.

CONTACTS: Note: Officers with more than one job title may be intentionally listed here more than once.

Eric J. Crown, CEO
Timothy A. Crown, Pres.
Stanley Laybourne, CFO
Dino Farfante, Sr. VP-Sales, Insight Direct
Kaylene Moss, VP-Human Resources
Dennis A. Faggioni, CIO
Gary Franza, Sr.VP-Business Dev. And Product Mgmt.
Stanley Laybourne, Treas.

Phone: 602-902-1001	Fax:
Toll-Free:	
Address: 6820 South Harl Avenue, Tempe, AZ, 85283	

GROWTH PLANS/SPECIAL FEATURES:

Insight Enterprises, Inc. is a leading direct marketer of computers, hardware and software. The company markets primarily to small- and medium-sized businesses comprised of 100 to 1,000 employees through a combination of a strong outbound telemarketing sales force, electronic commerce, targeted direct marketing and advertising in computer magazines. Insight offers a broad line of more than 80,000 brand name products to customers in the United States, Canada, the United Kingdom and Germany. Products are sold via the Internet at www.insight.com and by a staff of customer account executives through outbound telesales. The company's growth strategy is to increase sales and earnings by increasing penetration of its existing customer base, leveraging its existing infrastructure, expanding its product offerings and customer base and utilizing emerging technologies. A large part of the company's strategy is to increase its staff of account executives. The company has done so consistently, increasing the number of executives by 500% over the last five years.

FINANCIALS: Sales and profits are in thousands of dollars—add 000 to get the full amount.

Notes regarding 1999: (1999 sales and profits were not available for all companies at press time.)

1999 Sales: $1,500,000	1999 Profits: $35,000	Stock Ticker: **NSIT**
1998 Sales: $1,002,800	1998 Profits: $20,500	Employees: 2,066
1997 Sales: $627,700	1997 Profits: $13,200	Fiscal Year Ends: 12/31
1996 Sales: $485,400	1996 Profits: $9,900	
1995 Sales: $342,800	1995 Profits: $5,700	

SALARIES/BENEFITS:

Pension Plan:	ESOP Stock Plan:	Profit Sharing:	Top Exec. Salary: $250,000	Bonus: $111,879
Savings Plan:	Stock Purch. Plan:		Second Exec. Salary: $215,000	Bonus: $52,980

COMPETITIVE ADVANTAGE: Strong direct marketing sales force.

OTHER THOUGHTS:

Apparent Women Officers or Directors:
Apparent Minority Officers or Directors:
Hot Spot for Advancement for Women/Minorities:

LOCATIONS: ("Y" = Yes)

West:	Southwest:	Midwest:	Southeast:	Northeast:	International:
	Y				Y

Note: Financial information, benefits and other data can change quickly and may vary from those stated here.

INSWEB CORP   www.insweb.com

Industry Group Code: 52421
Ranks within this company's industry group: Sales: 2   Profits: 2

BUSINESS ACTIVITIES ("Y" = Yes)

Financial Services:		Information/Publ.:		Technology:	Services:	Retailing:	Telecommunications:
Stock Brokerage		Portal/Hub/News	Y	Computer Manuf.	Payments/Transfers	Retailer	Internet Serv. Provider
Mortgages/Loans		On-Line Community		Networking Equip.	Consulting	Auctions	Web Site Host
Banking		Search Engine		Software Manuf.	Advertising/Marketing	Mall	Server Farm
Insurance	Y	Financial Data Publ.		Specialty Equipment	Outsourcing	Tickets/Travel	Specialty Telecom.
Credit Cards		Broadcasting/Music				Price Comparisons	High Speed Access

TYPES OF BUSINESS:
On-line Insurance Broker

BRANDS/DIVISIONS/AFFILIATES:
SOFTBANK

CONTACTS: Note: Officers with more than one job title may be intentionally listed here more than once.
Hussein A. Enan, CEO
Hussein A. Enan, Pres.
Stephen I. Robertson, CFO
Nancy Mills, Sr. VP-Human Resources
Marian C. Taylor, Sec.
Marian C. Taylor, Sr. VP/General Counsel
Mark P.Gutherie, Exec.VP-Oper.
Kevin M. Keegan, Exec.VP/Pres., Insurance Services Group

Phone: 650-298-9100	Fax: 650-298-9101
Toll-Free:	
Address: 901 Marshall St., Redwood City, CA, 94063	

GROWTH PLANS/SPECIAL FEATURES:

InsWeb operates an on-line insurance marketplace that enables consumers to shop on-line for automobile, term life, homeowners, renters and individual health insurance, and obtain insurance company-sponsored quotes for actual coverage. InsWeb's marketplace brings consumers and insurance companies together on-line, providing consumers with the insurance they need and insurance companies with the customers they want. InsWeb's service is free to consumers; its principal source of revenue is transaction fees paid by insurance companies. InsWeb's participating insurance companies pay fees to InsWeb based on qualified leads delivered to them electronically. The company has combined extensive knowledge of the insurance industry, technological expertise and close relationships with more than 35 insurance companies to develop a sophisticated, integrated on-line delivery platform. InsWeb's platform enables consumers to efficiently research insurance-related topics, search for, analyze and compare insurance products and apply for and receive insurance company-sponsored quotes for actual coverage. In addition, InsWeb provides insurance companies with a flow of pre-qualified consumers at substantially lower acquisition costs, as well as the scalable, cost-efficient distribution capabilities of InsWeb's Internet-based model.

FINANCIALS: Sales and profits are in thousands of dollars—add 000 to get the full amount.
Notes regarding 1999: *(1999 sales and profits were not available for all companies at press time.)*

1999 Sales: $21,800	1999 Profits: $-36,200	Stock Ticker: **INSW**
1998 Sales: $4,300	1998 Profits: $-22,500	Employees: 158
1997 Sales: $ 800	1997 Profits: $-9,100	Fiscal Year Ends: 12/31
1996 Sales: $ 200	1996 Profits: $-7,300	
1995 Sales: $	1995 Profits: $-2,000	

SALARIES/BENEFITS:

Pension Plan:	ESOP Stock Plan: Y	Profit Sharing:	Top Exec. Salary: $	Bonus: $
Savings Plan: Y	Stock Purch. Plan:		Second Exec. Salary: $	Bonus: $

COMPETITIVE ADVANTAGE: Excellent backing.

OTHER THOUGHTS:
Apparent Women Officers or Directors: 2
Apparent Minority Officers or Directors: 1
Hot Spot for Advancement for Women/Minorities:

LOCATIONS: ("Y" = Yes)

West:	Southwest:	Midwest:	Southeast:	Northeast:	International:
Y					

Note: Financial information, benefits and other data can change quickly and may vary from those stated here.

INTEL CORP   www.intel.com

Industry Group Code: 3344
Ranks within this company's industry group: Sales: 1   Profits: 1

BUSINESS ACTIVITIES ("Y" = Yes)

Financial Services:	Information/Publ.:	Technology:		Services:	Retailing:	Telecommunications:	
Stock Brokerage	Portal/Hub/News	Computer Manuf.	Y	Payments/Transfers	Retailer	Internet Serv. Provider	Y
Mortgages/Loans	On-Line Community	Networking Equip.	Y	Consulting	Auctions	Web Site Host	Y
Banking	Search Engine	Software Manuf.	Y	Advertising/Marketing	Mall	Server Farm	Y
Insurance	Financial Data Publ.	Specialty Equipment	Y	Outsourcing	Tickets/Travel	Specialty Telecom.	
Credit Cards	Broadcasting/Music				Price Comparisons	High Speed Access	

TYPES OF BUSINESS:

Microprocessors
Mother Boards
Circuit Boards
Server Farms
Internet Service
Home Network Equipment
Internet Appliances
Venture Capital

BRANDS/DIVISIONS/AFFILIATES:

Pentium Series
Chips & Technologies, Inc.
Intel Products Group
Soft-Pak Intel
Intel Supercomputer Systems
Communications Products Group

CONTACTS: *Note: Officers with more than one job title may be intentionally listed here more than once.*

Craig R. Barrett, CEO
Craig R. Barrett, Pres.
Andy D. Bryant, VP/CFO
Sean M. Maloney, Sr.VP/Dir.-Sales and Mktg.
Patricia Murray, VP-Human Resources
Micahel R. Splinter, Sr.VP/General Mgr.-Tech. Group
Jon A. Olson, VP-Finance and Controller
Michael R. Splinter, Sr.VP/General Mgr.-Mfg. Group
Leslie L. Vadasz, Sr.VP/Dir.-Corp. Business Dev.
Michael A. Aymar, VP/Gen. Mgr.-Internet Data Services
Ann Lewnes, VP-Sales and Mktg. Group

Phone: 408-765-8080	**Fax:** 408-765-6284
Toll-Free: 800-547-8806	
Address: 2200 Mission College Blvd., Santa Clara, CA, 95052	

GROWTH PLANS/SPECIAL FEATURES:

Intel Corporation is the world's largest chip-maker and a leading manufacturer of personal computer, networking and communications products. Along with Microsoft, IBM and their peers, Intel is among the most important and successful firms in the technology industry. Intel supplies the computing industry with the chips, boards, systems and software that are necessary for computer architecture. In 1971, Intel developed its 4004 preprocessor. This breakthrough powered the Busicom calculator and paved the way for embedding intelligence in inanimate objects and the development of the personal computer. Since then, Intel has developed continuous upgrades and cutting-edge innovations. One of the most recent processors is Intel Pentium III, which is designed specifically to process video, audio and graphics data efficiently. It contains a high-speed cache memory chip in a Single Edge Contact (S.E.C) cartridge that connects to a motherboard via a single edge connector. Intel's Internet Service Provider Program is also making progress by adding new features and technologies. The company's e-business solution provides web, database, application and co-location hosting services. The company has offices throughout the U.S., with major offices in Arizona, California, New Mexico, Oregon, Washington, Massachusetts, Texas, Utah and Puerto Rico. Intel also has sales offices worldwide, with major facilities in Costa Rica, England, Germany, Hong Kong, India, Ireland, Israel, Japan, Malaysia, the People's Republic of China, the Philippines, Taiwan, Brazil and Russia. Intel employs approximately 65,000 people worldwide.

Intel has special career-training programs, regular performance reviews and a promote-from-within policy. The company also has a tuition reimbursement program and in-house college level courses. Three week vacations are given to all salaried employees. After seven years, employees receive an 8-week paid sabbatical. The entire workforce, including the CEO, works in a cubicle, and there are no reserved parking spaces.

FINANCIALS: Sales and profits are in thousands of dollars—add 000 to get the full amount.

Notes regarding 1999: *(1999 sales and profits were not available for all companies at press time.)*

1999 Sales: $29,400,000	1999 Profits: $7,300,000	Stock Ticker: **INTC**
1998 Sales: $26,273,000	1998 Profits: $6,068,000	Employees: 64,500
1997 Sales: $25,070,000	1997 Profits: $6,945,000	Fiscal Year Ends: 12/31
1996 Sales: $20,847,000	1996 Profits: $5,157,000	
1995 Sales: $16,202,000	1995 Profits: $3,566,000	

SALARIES/BENEFITS:

Pension Plan: Y	ESOP Stock Plan:	Profit Sharing: Y	Top Exec. Salary: $490,000	Bonus: $1,926,800
Savings Plan:	Stock Purch. Plan: Y		Second Exec. Salary: $	Bonus: $

COMPETITIVE ADVANTAGE:
Name recognition/Intel's semiconductors are used in about 80% of PCs/Unsurpassed commitment to research.

OTHER THOUGHTS:

	LOCATIONS: ("Y" = Yes)					
Apparent Women Officers or Directors: 1	West:	Southwest:	Midwest:	Southeast:	Northeast:	International:
Apparent Minority Officers or Directors:	Y	Y	Y	Y	Y	Y
Hot Spot for Advancement for Women/Minorities:						

INTERLIANT INC   www.interliant.com

Industry Group Code: 51339
Ranks within this company's industry group: Sales: 20   Profits: 15

BUSINESS ACTIVITIES ("Y" = Yes)

Financial Services:	Information/Publ.:	Technology:		Services:		Retailing:	Telecommunications:	
Stock Brokerage	Portal/Hub/News	Computer Manuf.		Payments/Transfers		Retailer	Internet Serv. Provider	Y
Mortgages/Loans	On-Line Community	Networking Equip.		Consulting	Y	Auctions	Web Site Host	Y
Banking	Search Engine	Software Manuf.	Y	Advertising/Marketing		Mall	Server Farm	Y
Insurance	Financial Data Publ.	Specialty Equipment		Outsourcing	Y	Tickets/Travel	Specialty Telecom.	
Credit Cards	Broadcasting/Music					Price Comparisons	High Speed Access	

TYPES OF BUSINESS:

Internet Site Hosting and Co-Location
Internet Systems Consulting
High Speed Access
Marketing Consulting

BRANDS/DIVISIONS/AFFILIATES:

Interliant International, Inc.
The Daily-e Corporation
Sales Technology Limited

CONTACTS: Note: Officers with more than one job title may be intentionally listed here more than once.

Stephen W. Maggs, CEO
William A. Wilson, CFO
Lori Knowlton, Dir.-Human Resources
Jennifer J. Lawton, Sr. VP-Tech.
Leonard J. Fassler, Sec.
Edward A. Cavazos, Sr. VP-General Counsel
Paul E. Chollett, Sr. VP-Admin.
Jesse J. Bornfreund, Sr. VP-Business Corp.
Stephen W. Maggs, Treas.

Phone: 617-374-4700	Fax: 617-374-4790
Toll-Free:	
Address: 215 First St., Cambridge, MA, 02142	

GROWTH PLANS/SPECIAL FEATURES:

Interliant, Inc. provides a wide range of Internet hosting and enhanced Internet services that enable customers to deploy and manage their web sites and network-based applications more effectively than they might using internally developed solutions. Interliant's hosting services store customers' web sites, software applications and data on servers typically housed in the company's data centers so that others on the Internet can access and interact with the customer's web sites and network-based applications. The company's consulting services provide Internet-based solutions, internal networking implementations and application development solutions. Interliant recently purchased all of the assets of The Daily-e Corporation, a provider of business process re-engineering and web development services. Through its wholly-owned subsidiary, Interliant International, Inc., the company acquired all of the outstanding stock of Sales Technology Limited, a United Kingdom-based systems integrator of Customer Relationship Management (CRM) software products. Interliant provides web-hosting solutions to more than 37,000 customers, representing over 65,000 active domains. More than 1,300 customers worldwide also rely on Interliant to host over 10,000 customized applications, and the company continues to be the leading provider of Lotus Notes/Domino hosting solutions. Investment firm Charterhouse Group International is a major shareholder of the company.

FINANCIALS: Sales and profits are in thousands of dollars—add 000 to get the full amount.

Notes regarding 1999: *(1999 sales and profits were not available for all companies at press time.)*

1999 Sales: $46,000	1999 Profits: $	**Stock Ticker: INIT**
1998 Sales: $4,900	1998 Profits: $-9,700	Employees: 489
1997 Sales: $	1997 Profits: $- 200	Fiscal Year Ends: 12/31
1996 Sales: $	1996 Profits: $	
1995 Sales: $	1995 Profits: $	

SALARIES/BENEFITS:

Pension Plan:	ESOP Stock Plan:	Profit Sharing:	Top Exec. Salary: $	Bonus: $
Savings Plan: Y	Stock Purch. Plan:		Second Exec. Salary: $	Bonus: $

COMPETITIVE ADVANTAGE:
Interliant is wisely adding complementary services, such as customer support software, to its offerings, differentiating itself from other hosts.

OTHER THOUGHTS:

Apparent Women Officers or Directors: 4
Apparent Minority Officers or Directors: 1
Hot Spot for Advancement for Women/Minorities: Y

LOCATIONS: ("Y" = Yes)

West:	Southwest:	Midwest:	Southeast:	Northeast:	International:
				Y	Y

INTERNATIONAL BUSINESS MACHINES CORP
www.ibm.com
Industry Group Code: 3341A
Ranks within this company's industry group: Sales: 1   Profits: 1

BUSINESS ACTIVITIES ("Y" = Yes)

Financial Services:	Information/Publ.:	Technology:		Services:		Retailing:	Telecommunications:	
Stock Brokerage	Portal/Hub/News	Computer Manuf.	Y	Payments/Transfers		Retailer	Internet Serv. Provider	Y
Mortgages/Loans	On-Line Community	Networking Equip.	Y	Consulting	Y	Auctions	Web Site Host	Y
Banking	Search Engine	Software Manuf.	Y	Advertising/Marketing		Mall	Server Farm	
Insurance	Financial Data Publ.	Specialty Equipment	Y	Outsourcing	Y	Tickets/Travel	Specialty Telecom.	Y
Credit Cards	Broadcasting/Music					Price Comparisons	High Speed Access	Y

TYPES OF BUSINESS:
Computer Hardware and Software Manufacturer
Notebook Computers
Microelectronic Technology
High Speed Internet Access
Networking Systems
Information Technology-related Services
E-commerce Solutions and Support
IT Department Consulting and Outsourcing

BRANDS/DIVISIONS/AFFILIATES:
Unison Software
Advantis
Lotus
Tivoli
NetObjects
System.390 G4
Nefinity PC
ThinkPad

CONTACTS: *Note: Officers with more than one job title may be intentionally listed here more than once.*
Louis V. Gerstner, Jr., CEO
John Joyce, Sr. VP/CFO
Abby F. Kohnstamm, VP-Corp. Mktg.
J. Thomas Bouchard, Sr. VP-Human Resources
Paul M. Horn, Sr. VP-Research
Nicholas M. Donofrio, Sr. VP-Tech. and Mfg.
Lawrence R. Ricciardi, Sr.VP/General Counsel
J. Bruce Harreld, Sr.VP-Strategy
David B. Kalis, VP-Comm.
Douglas L. Maine, VP-TeleWeb
Jeffrey D. Serkes, VP-Global Sales

Phone: 914-499-1900	**Fax:**
Toll-Free: 800-426-3333	
Address: New Orchard Road, Armonk, NY, 10504	

GROWTH PLANS/SPECIAL FEATURES:

International Business Machines Corporation (IBM) develops, manufactures and sells advanced information processing products, including computers and microelectronic technology, software, networking systems and information technology-related services. IBM is a major player in Internet related software and services of all types and has been carefully repositioning itself as an Internet enabler. Recent business acquisitions include Unison Software, a systems management company, and Advantis, the U.S. data network services unit of the IBM Global Network. The firm is also a major stockholder of NetObjects, a web site design software business. IBM's new products include DB2 Universal Database, a reinvigorated server line including the System/390 G4; the IBM ThinkPad, a Notebook PC; Lotus's eSuite, a personal productivity application and the IBM IntelliStation, a Microsoft Windows NT-based workstation. The company's breakthrough in copper microchips increased the capacity and speed of semiconductors. IBM's hard-disk drive capacity has been quadrupled due to its patented giant magnetoresistive (GMR) head technology. The company set a world record in storage density by packing more than 10 billion bits (10 gigabits) per square inch of disk surface. IBM is in the process of expanding its global network of research laboratories into India and other areas.

FINANCIALS: Sales and profits are in thousands of dollars—add 000 to get the full amount.
Notes regarding 1999: *(1999 sales and profits were not available for all companies at press time.)*

1999 Sales: $87,500,000	1999 Profits: $7,700,000	Stock Ticker: **IBM**
1998 Sales: $81,667,000	1998 Profits: $6,328,000	Employees: 291,067
1997 Sales: $78,508,000	1997 Profits: $6,093,000	Fiscal Year Ends: 12/31
1996 Sales: $75,947,000	1996 Profits: $5,429,000	
1995 Sales: $71,940,000	1995 Profits: $4,178,000	

SALARIES/BENEFITS:
Pension Plan: Y	ESOP Stock Plan:	Profit Sharing: Y	Top Exec. Salary: $	Bonus: $
Savings Plan: Y	Stock Purch. Plan: Y		Second Exec. Salary: $	Bonus: $

COMPETITIVE ADVANTAGE:
IBM receives approximately 25% of revenues from Internet-based e-commerce products and services, making it one of the world leaders in this booming field.

OTHER THOUGHTS:
Apparent Women Officers or Directors: 4
Apparent Minority Officers or Directors: 7
Hot Spot for Advancement for Women/Minorities: Y

LOCATIONS: ("Y" = Yes)
West:	Southwest:	Midwest:	Southeast:	Northeast:	International:
Y	Y	Y	Y	Y	Y

Note: Financial information, benefits and other data can change quickly and may vary from those stated here.

INTERNET AMERICA INC   www.airmail.net

Industry Group Code: 51339
Ranks within this company's industry group: Sales: 15   Profits: 2

BUSINESS ACTIVITIES ("Y" = Yes)

Financial Services:	Information/Publ.:	Technology:	Services:	Retailing:	Telecommunications:	
Stock Brokerage	Portal/Hub/News	Computer Manuf.	Payments/Transfers	Retailer	Internet Serv. Provider	Y
Mortgages/Loans	On-Line Community	Networking Equip.	Consulting	Auctions	Web Site Host	Y
Banking	Search Engine	Software Manuf.	Advertising/Marketing	Mall	Server Farm	Y
Insurance	Financial Data Publ.	Specialty Equipment	Outsourcing	Tickets/Travel	Specialty Telecom.	
Credit Cards	Broadcasting/Music			Price Comparisons	High Speed Access	Y

TYPES OF BUSINESS:

Internet Service Provider

BRANDS/DIVISIONS/AFFILIATES:

Neosoft, Inc.
KDi, Inc.
PointeCom, Inc.
PDQ.net

CONTACTS: Note: Officers with more than one job title may be intentionally listed here more than once.

Michael T. Maples, CEO
Douglas L. Davis, COO
James T. Chaney, CFO
Doulglas G. Sheldon, VP-Mktg.
Bobby R.B. Manson, VP-Network Oper.
Elizabeth Palmer Daane, VP/Sec.
Elizabeth Palmer Daane, VP/General Counsel
Douglas L. Davis, Exec.VP-New Product Development
John James Stewart III, VP-Customer Care
James T. Chaney, Treas.
John James Stewart III, VP-Customer Care

Phone: 214-861-2500	Fax: 214-861-2578
Toll-Free:	
Address: One Dallas Centre, 350 N. St. Paul, Suite 3000, Dallas, TX, 75201	

GROWTH PLANS/SPECIAL FEATURES:

Internet America is an Internet service provider in the Southwestern United States, with over 100,000 subscribers. The company provides a wide array of Internet consumer services, such as dial-up Internet access, multiple e-mail and/or personalized e-mail addresses, World Wide Web access, Internet Relay Chat (IRC), Usenet News and personal web sites. Internet America also provides a full range of business services, including dedicated access at a variety of bandwidths, Domain Names Service (DNS) registration and several choices of web services, including server co-location. The company's business model is to create high user density in each geographic area that it serves, allowing it to realize substantial marketing and operating efficiencies. Internet America's highest priority is to rapidly build market share in specific regions instead of deploying an extensive network infrastructure with a substantial number of underutilized points of presence (POPs). The company acquired all the outstanding common stock of NeoSoft, Inc., a Houston-based ISP, the subscribers of KDi, Inc, the Texas dial-up subscribers of PointeCom, Inc. and the outstanding stock of PDQ.net, a Houston-based ISP.

FINANCIALS: Sales and profits are in thousands of dollars—add 000 to get the full amount.

Notes regarding 1999: (1999 sales and profits were not available for all companies at press time.)

1999 Sales: $18,100	1999 Profits: $-2,500	Stock Ticker: **GEEK**
1998 Sales: $10,600	1998 Profits: $1,000	Employees: 190
1997 Sales: $9,400	1997 Profits: $-3,800	Fiscal Year Ends: 6/30
1996 Sales: $3,800	1996 Profits: $-3,400	
1995 Sales: $	1995 Profits: $	

SALARIES/BENEFITS:

Pension Plan:	ESOP Stock Plan: Y	Profit Sharing:	Top Exec. Salary: $110,000	Bonus: $
Savings Plan: Y	Stock Purch. Plan:		Second Exec. Salary: $108,333	Bonus: $

COMPETITIVE ADVANTAGE: Rapid growth through acquisitions.

OTHER THOUGHTS:

Apparent Women Officers or Directors:
Apparent Minority Officers or Directors:
Hot Spot for Advancement for Women/Minorities:

LOCATIONS: ("Y" = Yes)

West:	Southwest:	Midwest:	Southeast:	Northeast:	International:
	Y				

INTERNET CAPITAL GROUP INC
www.internetcapital.com

Industry Group Code: 5511
Ranks within this company's industry group: Sales: 2   Profits: 2

BUSINESS ACTIVITIES ("Y" = Yes)

Financial Services:	Information/Publ.:		Technology:	Services:	Retailing:	Telecommunications:
Stock Brokerage	Portal/Hub/News	Y	Computer Manuf.	Payments/Transfers	Retailer	Internet Serv. Provider
Mortgages/Loans	On-Line Community		Networking Equip.	Consulting	Auctions	Web Site Host
Banking	Search Engine		Software Manuf.	Advertising/Marketing	Mall	Server Farm
Insurance	Financial Data Publ.		Specialty Equipment	Outsourcing	Tickets/Travel	Specialty Telecom.
Credit Cards	Broadcasting/Music				Price Comparisons	High Speed Access

TYPES OF BUSINESS:
Investment Firm-E-Commerce Companies

BRANDS/DIVISIONS/AFFILIATES:
VerticalNet
BidCom
Arbinet

GROWTH PLANS/SPECIAL FEATURES:
Internet Capital Group, Inc. is an Internet holding company engaged in business-to-business e-commerce through a network of partner companies. The company provides operational assistance, capital support, industry expertise and a strategic network of business relationships intended to maximize the long-term market potential of more than 45 business-to-business e-commerce partner companies. Internet Capital Group focuses on two types of business-to-business e-commerce companies: market makers and infrastructure service providers. Market makers bring buyers and sellers in a particular industrial marketplace together to exchange products, services and information via the Internet. Infrastructure service providers assist traditional businesses in one of four ways: providing strategic consulting, systems integration, software or outsourced services. Recently, 26 business-to-business e-commerce companies were added to Internet Capital Group's network.

CONTACTS:
Note: Officers with more than one job title may be intentionally listed here more than once.
Walter W. Buckley III, CEO
Walter W. Buckley III, Pres.
David D. Gathman, CFO
Richard G. Bunker, Chief Tech. Officer
David D. Gathman, Sec.
Henry N. Nassau, General Counsel
Vitor Hwang, VP-Strategic Business Dev.
Sherri Wolf, VP-Investor Relations
David D. Gathman, Treas.
Rick Devine, Managing Dir.-Mgmt. Recruiting

Phone: 610-989-011	**Fax:** 610-989-0112
Toll-Free:	
Address: 435 Devon Park Dr., Bldg. 800, Wayne, PA, 19087	

FINANCIALS:
Sales and profits are in thousands of dollars—add 000 to get the full amount.
Notes regarding 1999: Through 9 months *(1999 sales and profits were not available for all companies at press time.)*

1999 Sales: $14,783	1999 Profits: $-6,405	Stock Ticker: **ICGE**
1998 Sales: $3,100	1998 Profits: $13,900	Employees: 21
1997 Sales: $ 800	1997 Profits: $-6,600	Fiscal Year Ends: 12/31
1996 Sales: $ 300	1996 Profits: $-2,100	
1995 Sales: $	1995 Profits: $	

SALARIES/BENEFITS:

Pension Plan:	ESOP Stock Plan:	Profit Sharing:	Top Exec. Salary: $	Bonus: $
Savings Plan:	Stock Purch. Plan:		Second Exec. Salary: $	Bonus: $

COMPETITIVE ADVANTAGE:
Tremendous success in fostering the growth of startups.

OTHER THOUGHTS:

	LOCATIONS: ("Y" = Yes)					
Apparent Women Officers or Directors:	West:	Southwest:	Midwest:	Southeast:	Northeast:	International:
Apparent Minority Officers or Directors:					Y	
Hot Spot for Advancement for Women/Minorities:						

INTERNET INITIATIVE JAPAN INC   www.iij.ad.jp

Industry Group Code: 51339
Ranks within this company's industry group: Sales: 6   Profits: 7

BUSINESS ACTIVITIES ("Y" = Yes)

Financial Services:	Information/Publ.:	Technology:	Services:		Retailing:	Telecommunications:	
Stock Brokerage	Portal/Hub/News	Computer Manuf.	Payments/Transfers		Retailer	Internet Serv. Provider	Y
Mortgages/Loans	On-Line Community	Networking Equip.	Consulting	Y	Auctions	Web Site Host	Y
Banking	Search Engine	Software Manuf.	Advertising/Marketing		Mall	Server Farm	
Insurance	Financial Data Publ.	Specialty Equipment	Outsourcing	Y	Tickets/Travel	Specialty Telecom.	
Credit Cards	Broadcasting/Music				Price Comparisons	High Speed Access	

TYPES OF BUSINESS:

Internet Service Provider

BRANDS/DIVISIONS/AFFILIATES:

Asia Internet Holding Co., Ltd.
IIJ Media Communications, Inc.
IIJ Technology, Inc.
Crosswave Communications, Inc.

CONTACTS: Note: Officers with more than one job title may be intentionally listed here more than once.

Koichi Suzuki, CEO
Koichi Suzuki, Pres.
Yasuhiro Nishi, CFO/ Chief Acc. Officer
Toshiya Asaba, Co-Chief Tech. Officer
Akio Onishi, Chief Strategic Officer
Junko Higasa, Public Relations
Kazumasa Utashiro, Co-Chief Tech. Officer

Phone: 81-3-5259-6000	Fax: 81-3-5259-6001
Toll-Free:	
Address: Takebashi Yasuda Bldg., 3-13, Kanda Nishiki-cho, Chiyoda-ku Tokyo, Japan, 101-0054	

GROWTH PLANS/SPECIAL FEATURES:

Internet Initiative Japan, IIJ, provides Internet access and service to users in Japan, including corporations and other Internet service providers. The company offers total Internet solutions, including such services as connectivity, security, web design and hosting and systems integration. The company leases networks connecting Japan to the U.S. via one of the largest Internet network backbones in Japan. IIJ's Japan-US lines are connected directly to Internet exchange points in the U.S., and their lines serve as the main backbone for the increasing volume of Internet traffic between the U.S. and all of the Asia Pacific region. IIJ Group companies each apply the company's amassed engineering knowledge to their respective fields of specialty. Asia Internet Holding Co., Ltd. is building Internet infrastructure in Asia. IIJ Media Communications Inc. provides engineering expertise that focuses on media development. IIJ Technology Inc. engineers and implements networks. Crosswave Communications, Inc. is building Japan's first new-generation network infrastructure optimized for data communications.

FINANCIALS: Sales and profits are in thousands of dollars—add 000 to get the full amount.
Notes regarding 1999: (1999 sales and profits were not available for all companies at press time.)

1999 Sales: $124,000	1999 Profits: $-12,000	Stock Ticker: IIJI
1998 Sales: $92,600	1998 Profits: $-2,700	Employees: 266
1997 Sales: $68,900	1997 Profits: $1,600	Fiscal Year Ends: 3/31
1996 Sales: $	1996 Profits: $	
1995 Sales: $	1995 Profits: $	

SALARIES/BENEFITS:

Pension Plan:	ESOP Stock Plan:	Profit Sharing:	Top Exec. Salary: $	Bonus: $
Savings Plan:	Stock Purch. Plan:		Second Exec. Salary: $	Bonus: $

COMPETITIVE ADVANTAGE: Combines several comprehensive Internet delivery-related businesses.

OTHER THOUGHTS:

	LOCATIONS: ("Y" = Yes)					
Apparent Women Officers or Directors:	West:	Southwest:	Midwest:	Southeast:	Northeast:	International:
Apparent Minority Officers or Directors:						Y
Hot Spot for Advancement for Women/Minorities:						

Note: Financial information, benefits and other data can change quickly and may vary from those stated here.

INTERNET PICTURES CORP   www.ipix.com/

Industry Group Code: 5112
Ranks within this company's industry group: Sales: 68   Profits: 63

BUSINESS ACTIVITIES ("Y" = Yes)

Financial Services:	Information/Publ.:	Technology:		Services:	Retailing:	Telecommunications:
Stock Brokerage	Portal/Hub/News	Computer Manuf.		Payments/Transfers	Retailer	Internet Serv. Provider
Mortgages/Loans	On-Line Community	Networking Equip.		Consulting	Auctions	Web Site Host
Banking	Search Engine	Software Manuf.	Y	Advertising/Marketing	Mall	Server Farm
Insurance	Financial Data Publ.	Specialty Equipment		Outsourcing	Tickets/Travel	Specialty Telecom.
Credit Cards	Broadcasting/Music				Price Comparisons	High Speed Access

TYPES OF BUSINESS:

Software-IPIX Technology

BRANDS/DIVISIONS/AFFILIATES:

Wizard

CONTACTS: *Note: Officers with more than one job title may be intentionally listed here more than once.*

James M. Phillips, CEO
Jeffrey D. Peters, Pres.
John J. Kalec, VP/CFO
Edmond B. Lewis, VP-Mktg.
Christy Wilson, VP-Human Resource Admin.
Michael J. Tourville, VP-Product Engineering
Edmond B. Lewis, VP/Corp. Sec.
Joseph M. Viglione, VP-Admin.
Mark R. Searle, COO

Phone: 423-482-3000	Fax: 423-482-5447
Toll-Free:	
Address: 1009 Commerce Park Dr., Oak Ridge, TN, 37830	

GROWTH PLANS/SPECIAL FEATURES:

Internet Pictures Corporation (iPIX), formerly Interactive Pictures Corporation, provides global visual content and infrastructure for leading e-commerce and new media web sites. The company produces interactive imaging for the Internet, allowing users to step inside the picture with iPIX technology. This technology is changing the way real estate is sold, vacations and business trips are planned and the way news is delivered. The company's multi-dimensional, 360-degree environment provides a complete field of vision that can be navigated by the viewer. Companies are using iPIX's technology to create virtual tours and multimedia content to enhance marketing and accelerate e-commerce. iPIX customers include the Hilton Hotels, Disney, Toyota, Intel, Prudential, CNN, MTV, Microsoft and NASA. Discovery Online and the Hawaiian Visitor and Convention Bureau selected iPIX Movies to develop interactive media showcasing the nature, culture and history of the Hawaiian Islands. When watching an iPIX movie, the viewer can control the point-of-view by moving a mouse or other control device to look up, down, left, right, ahead and behind. These images are captured through the use of two opposing fisheye lenses and a standard film or digital video camera. iPIX software corrects for the fisheye distortion and records ground-to-sky images. The company recently premiered this technology at the Sundance Film Festival. With 360-degree images, a film viewer could experience a bank robbery and be able to look anywhere and everywhere in the scene.

FINANCIALS: Sales and profits are in thousands of dollars—add 000 to get the full amount.

Notes regarding 1999: *(1999 sales and profits were not available for all companies at press time.)*

1999 Sales: $12,500	1999 Profits: $-56,900	Stock Ticker: **IPIX**
1998 Sales: $3,000	1998 Profits: $-13,200	Employees: 136
1997 Sales: $2,400	1997 Profits: $-5,600	Fiscal Year Ends: 12/31
1996 Sales: $1,500	1996 Profits: $-1,200	
1995 Sales: $	1995 Profits: $	

SALARIES/BENEFITS:

Pension Plan:	ESOP Stock Plan:	Profit Sharing:	Top Exec. Salary: $	Bonus: $
Savings Plan:	Stock Purch. Plan:		Second Exec. Salary: $	Bonus: $

COMPETITIVE ADVANTAGE: Very successful and innovative multimedia technology for the Internet.

OTHER THOUGHTS:

Apparent Women Officers or Directors: 1
Apparent Minority Officers or Directors:
Hot Spot for Advancement for Women/Minorities:

LOCATIONS: ("Y" = Yes)

West:	Southwest:	Midwest:	Southeast:	Northeast:	International:
			Y		

INTERNET.COM   www.internet.com

Industry Group Code: 514191
Ranks within this company's industry group: Sales: 27   Profits: 16

BUSINESS ACTIVITIES ("Y" = Yes)

Financial Services:	Information/Publ.:		Technology:	Services:	Retailing:	Telecommunications:
Stock Brokerage	Portal/Hub/News	Y	Computer Manuf.	Payments/Transfers	Retailer	Internet Serv. Provider
Mortgages/Loans	On-Line Community	Y	Networking Equip.	Consulting	Auctions	Web Site Host
Banking	Search Engine		Software Manuf.	Advertising/Marketing	Mall	Server Farm
Insurance	Financial Data Publ.	Y	Specialty Equipment	Outsourcing	Tickets/Travel	Specialty Telecom.
Credit Cards	Broadcasting/Music				Price Comparisons	High Speed Access

TYPES OF BUSINESS:

Major Business and Technology News Portal
On-line Publishing

BRANDS/DIVISIONS/AFFILIATES:

Allnetresearch.com
SharkyExtreme.com

CONTACTS:
Note: Officers with more than one job title may be intentionally listed here more than once.

Alan M. Meckler, CEO
Cristopher S. Cardell, COO/Pres.
Christopher J. Baudouin, CFO
Mark J. Berns, Chief Tech. Officer
Mitchell S. Eisenberg, General Counsel
Kirk Holland, VP Business Dev.
Augustine Venditto, Editor in Chief
Christopher S. Elwell, General Mgr.

Phone: 203-662-2800	Fax: 203-655-4686
Toll-Free:	
Address: 23 Old Kings Highway South, Darien, CT, 06820	

GROWTH PLANS/SPECIAL FEATURES:

Internet.com Corporation provides global real-time news and information resources for the Internet industry and Internet technology professionals, web developers and experienced Internet users. The company operates a network of 89 web sites, 71 e-mail newsletters, 101 on-line discussion forums and 75 moderated e-mail discussion lists. The site receives over two million unique visitors that generate more then 90 million page views monthly. The network is divided into nine subject areas. Site visitors are offered real-time Internet industry news, tutorials, training and skills development, market research, buyer's guides and product reviews, discussion forums and software downloads. In recent years, Internet.com has completed 40 acquisitions of Internet media properties consisting of 53 web sites, 40 e-mail newsletters, 74 on-line discussion forums and 61 moderated e-mail discussion lists. The recent acquisition of SharkyExtreme.com added over 10 million monthly page views and the latest hardware and software technology. Internet.com has editions of its web site in multiple locations, including Japan, Israel, the UK, France and Arabia. The company is headquartered in Connecticut and has offices in New York, California, Michigan, Kentucky and Hong Kong. Internet.com has the support of over 850 advertisers, including IBM, Sun Microsystems, Lucent Technologies, Compaq, GoTo.com and uBid, Inc.

FINANCIALS: Sales and profits are in thousands of dollars—add 000 to get the full amount.

Notes regarding 1999: *(1999 sales and profits were not available for all companies at press time.)*

1999 Sales: $	1999 Profits: $-22,000	Stock Ticker: **INTM**
1998 Sales: $3,500	1998 Profits: $-2,700	Employees: 82
1997 Sales: $1,500	1997 Profits: $-2,200	Fiscal Year Ends: 12/31
1996 Sales: $ 500	1996 Profits: $1,275	
1995 Sales: $ 100	1995 Profits: $ 400	

SALARIES/BENEFITS:

Pension Plan:	ESOP Stock Plan: Y	Profit Sharing:	Top Exec. Salary: $185,000	Bonus: $
Savings Plan: Y	Stock Purch. Plan:		Second Exec. Salary: $130,000	Bonus: $

COMPETITIVE ADVANTAGE: Rapid accumulation of excellent news sources.

OTHER THOUGHTS:

	LOCATIONS: ("Y" = Yes)					
	West:	Southwest:	Midwest:	Southeast:	Northeast:	International:
Apparent Women Officers or Directors:	Y		Y	Y	Y	Y
Apparent Minority Officers or Directors:						
Hot Spot for Advancement for Women/Minorities:						

INTERVU INC   www.intervu.com

Industry Group Code: 51311B
Ranks within this company's industry group: Sales: 5   Profits: 6

BUSINESS ACTIVITIES ("Y" = Yes)

Financial Services:	Information/Publ.:		Technology:	Services:		Retailing:	Telecommunications:	
Stock Brokerage	Portal/Hub/News		Computer Manuf.	Payments/Transfers		Retailer	Internet Serv. Provider	
Mortgages/Loans	On-Line Community		Networking Equip.	Consulting		Auctions	Web Site Host	
Banking	Search Engine		Software Manuf.	Advertising/Marketing		Mall	Server Farm	
Insurance	Financial Data Publ.		Specialty Equipment	Outsourcing	Y	Tickets/Travel	Specialty Telecom.	Y
Credit Cards	Broadcasting/Music	Y				Price Comparisons	High Speed Access	

TYPES OF BUSINESS:
Software-On-line Live Content

BRANDS/DIVISIONS/AFFILIATES:
Multimedia Manager

CONTACTS: *Note: Officers with more than one job title may be intentionally listed here more than once.*
Harry E. Gruber, CEO
Edward L. Huguez, COO
Kenneth L. Ruggiero, CFO
Stephen P. Condon, VP-Mktg.
Darlene Shaffer, Dir.-Human Resources
Brian Kenner, Chief Tech. Officer
Larry Behmer, VP-Engineering
Scott Crowder, VP-Oper.
Stephen Klein, VP-Business Dev.

Phone: 858-623-8400	Fax: 858-623-2323
Toll-Free:	
Address: 6815 Flanders Drive, Suite 200, San Diego, CA, 92121	

GROWTH PLANS/SPECIAL FEATURES:

InterVU, Inc. provides its customers with Internet video delivery solutions. InterVU offers web site owners with cost-effective, feature-rich powerful streaming of live and on-demand audio and video content. This content is delivered over the Internet using narrow band and broadband applications. Customers use the company's audio and video distribution services to transmit entertainment, sports, news reporting, corporate communications, investor relations, advertising and distance learning content. InterVU's services automate the publishing, distribution and programming of video and audio content, allowing web site owners to more quickly and efficiently add video and audio content to web sites and to avoid purchasing or developing costly hardware and software that would require hiring employees with audio and video expertise. There are thousands of potential uses for this application. For example, InterVU's Multimedia Manager and Audience technology software allow streaming video service users to view news, sports and other events from around the world, listen to live radio broadcasts, hear a company's quarterly earnings report live with graphical presentation, view a movie trailer, watch music videos and listen to music on demand. InterVU's delivery of products does not require special equipment or personnel. Instead, it is directed through InterVU's nationwide network of over 100 servers that support all major audio and video formats, including Microsoft Windows Media Player and Real Player.

FINANCIALS: Sales and profits are in thousands of dollars—add 000 to get the full amount.
Notes regarding 1999: *(1999 sales and profits were not available for all companies at press time.)*

1999 Sales: $11,800	1999 Profits: $-24,800	**Stock Ticker: ITVU**
1998 Sales: $1,700	1998 Profits: $-15,700	Employees: 100
1997 Sales: $ 100	1997 Profits: $-5,300	Fiscal Year Ends: 12/31
1996 Sales: $ 100	1996 Profits: $-2,300	
1995 Sales: $	1995 Profits: $	

SALARIES/BENEFITS:

Pension Plan:	ESOP Stock Plan: Y	Profit Sharing:	Top Exec. Salary: $180,003	Bonus: $10,000
Savings Plan: Y	Stock Purch. Plan:		Second Exec. Salary: $128,062	Bonus: $

COMPETITIVE ADVANTAGE: Provides technology that enables web sites to rapidly deploy audio and video content.

OTHER THOUGHTS:
Apparent Women Officers or Directors: 1
Apparent Minority Officers or Directors: 1
Hot Spot for Advancement for Women/Minorities:

LOCATIONS: ("Y" = Yes)

West:	Southwest:	Midwest:	Southeast:	Northeast:	International:
Y		Y	Y	Y	

INTRAWARE INC   www.intraware.com

Industry Group Code: 51339A
Ranks within this company's industry group: Sales: 6   Profits: 5

BUSINESS ACTIVITIES ("Y" = Yes)

Financial Services:	Information/Publ.:		Technology:	Services:		Retailing:		Telecommunications:
Stock Brokerage	Portal/Hub/News	Y	Computer Manuf.	Payments/Transfers		Retailer	Y	Internet Serv. Provider
Mortgages/Loans	On-Line Community	Y	Networking Equip.	Consulting	Y	Auctions		Web Site Host
Banking	Search Engine		Software Manuf.	Advertising/Marketing		Mall		Server Farm
Insurance	Financial Data Publ.		Specialty Equipment	Outsourcing		Tickets/Travel		Specialty Telecom.
Credit Cards	Broadcasting/Music					Price Comparisons		High Speed Access

TYPES OF BUSINESS:

Software Evaluation and Procurement Services
Business-to-Business Intermediary

BRANDS/DIVISIONS/AFFILIATES:

Intraware.shop
IT Knowledge Center
Intraware Subscribnet
RadarScope
Compariscope

CONTACTS: *Note: Officers with more than one job title may be intentionally listed here more than once.*

Peter H. Jackson, CEO
Peter H. Jackson, Pres.
Donald M. Freed, Exec. VP/CFO
Terence J. Healey, Sr. VP-Mktg.
Joanie Croger, Dir.of Human Resources
Paul A. Martinelli, Sr. VP/Chief Tech. Officer
David L. Dunlap, VP-Oper.
Joanie Creger, VP-Business Dev.
Terence J. Healey, VP-Sales
Mark Long, VP-Strategic Dev.

Phone: 925-253-4500	Fax: 925-253-4599
Toll-Free: 888 446-8729	
Address: 25 Orinda Way, Orinda, CA, 94563	

GROWTH PLANS/SPECIAL FEATURES:

Intraware, Inc. is a leading provider of business-to-business e-commerce-based services for the corporate IT community. Intraware enables IT professionals worldwide to research, evaluate, purchase, download and update business-class software on-line. As a business-to-business e-commerce company, Intraware provides software through its on-line purchasing service, Intraware.shop, IT information and interactive research services through the Intraware IT Knowledge Center and software update management services through Intraware Subscribnet. Intraware IT Knowledge Center is a web site that provides IT professionals with technical information, resources, interactive services and third party content to help them assess the wide array of business software solutions available in the marketplace. Intraware Subscribnet is an on-line service which enables IT professionals to keep their software updated and manage their software licenses. Subscribnet provides corporate IT subscribers with highly-specific information that is relevant only to their specific account profile, licensed software and enterprise computing platforms. The Intraware.shop service is an on-line purchase and delivery service tailored exclusively for corporate business software buyers. Intraware recently formed an alliance with Business Week Online that provides Business Week Online's 300,000 registered users full access to the company's centralized IT resources that contain technical information, articles and interactive knowledge tools designed exclusively for IT decision makers.

FINANCIALS: Sales and profits are in thousands of dollars—add 000 to get the full amount.

Notes regarding 1999: *(1999 sales and profits were not available for all companies at press time.)*

1999 Sales: $38,400	1999 Profits: $-12,000	Stock Ticker: **ITRA**	
1998 Sales: $10,400	1998 Profits: $-4,000	Employees: 169	
1997 Sales: $	1997 Profits: $- 900	Fiscal Year Ends: 2/28	
1996 Sales: $	1996 Profits: $		
1995 Sales: $	1995 Profits: $		

SALARIES/BENEFITS:

Pension Plan:	ESOP Stock Plan: Y	Profit Sharing:	Top Exec. Salary: $263,990	Bonus: $40,000
Savings Plan: Y	Stock Purch. Plan:		Second Exec. Salary: $181,317	Bonus: $

COMPETITIVE ADVANTAGE: Focus on business software buyers.

OTHER THOUGHTS:

Apparent Women Officers or Directors: 4
Apparent Minority Officers or Directors:
Hot Spot for Advancement for Women/Minorities: Y

LOCATIONS: ("Y" = Yes)

West:	Southwest:	Midwest:	Southeast:	Northeast:	International:
Y					

INTUIT INC   www.intuit.com

Industry Group Code: 5112
Ranks within this company's industry group: Sales: 4   Profits: 60

BUSINESS ACTIVITIES ("Y" = Yes)

Financial Services:		Information/Publ.:		Technology:		Services:	Retailing:	Telecommunications:
Stock Brokerage		Portal/Hub/News	Y	Computer Manuf.		Payments/Transfers	Retailer	Internet Serv. Provider
Mortgages/Loans	Y	On-Line Community		Networking Equip.		Consulting	Auctions	Web Site Host
Banking		Search Engine		Software Manuf.	Y	Advertising/Marketing	Mall	Server Farm
Insurance	Y	Financial Data Publ.		Specialty Equipment		Outsourcing	Tickets/Travel	Specialty Telecom.
Credit Cards		Broadcasting/Music					Price Comparisons	High Speed Access

TYPES OF BUSINESS:

Software-Financial Management
Small Business Accounting Software
Consumer Finance Software
Tax Preparation Software
On-line Financial Services
On-line Mortgages
On-line Insurance

BRANDS/DIVISIONS/AFFILIATES:

Quicken
QuickBooks
TurboTax
MacInTax
QuickenMortgage
QuickenInsurance
Rock Financial

CONTACTS: *Note: Officers with more than one job title may be intentionally listed here more than once.*

William V. Campbell, CEO
Greg J. Santora, VP/CFO/Chief Acc. Officer
Alan A. Gleicher, Sr. VP-Sales
Mari J. Baker, Sr. VP-Human Resources
Eric C. W. Dunn, Sr. VP-Chief Tech. Officer
Catherine L. Valentine, Corp. Sec.
Catherine L. Valentine, VP/General Counsel
David A. Kinser, Sr. VP-Oper.
Kristen Brown, VP-Corp. Business Dev.
Linda Fellows, Dir.-Investor Relations
Linda Fellows, Corp. Treas.

Phone: 650-944-6000	**Fax:** 650-329-6718
Toll-Free: 800-624-8742	
Address: 2535 Garcia Avenue, Mountain View, CA, 94043	

GROWTH PLANS/SPECIAL FEATURES:

Intuit, Inc. is a worldwide leader in consumer and small business financial management software and is an innovative provider of on-line financial services, including mortgages and insurance. The company has introduced popular titles such as Quicken and QuickBooks. Quicken is now the top-selling personal finance software in the United States, the United Kingdom, Australia, Canada, South Africa and Germany. Intuit's QuickBooks became the number-one selling small business accounting application within two months of its introduction in the U.S. and has played a major role in developing and expanding this market. The company also developed TurboTax, which is tax preparation software. The company's mission is to revolutionize the way individuals and small businesses manage their finances. Quicken, its original software product, was the first application to automate the everyday task of balancing a personal checkbook. Recently, the company introduced Open Financial Exchange, a cooperative venture with Microsoft and CheckFree Corporation. Open Financial Exchange creates a single, unified specification that enables financial institutions to exchange financial data over the Internet with web users and users of software such as Quicken. Open Financial Exchange supports a wide range of financial activities (such as consumer and small business banking and bill paying) and investing (including stocks, bonds and mutual funds). The firm intends to acquire Rock Financial.

The company offers its employees a range of child and elder care referral services, as well as discounted gym memberships. The company has a casual dress policy.

FINANCIALS: Sales and profits are in thousands of dollars—add 000 to get the full amount.

Notes regarding 1999: *(1999 sales and profits were not available for all companies at press time.)*

1999 Sales: $847,600	1999 Profits: $376,500	
1998 Sales: $592,700	1998 Profits: $-12,200	**Stock Ticker: INTU**
1997 Sales: $598,900	1997 Profits: $68,300	**Employees:** 4,025
1996 Sales: $538,600	1996 Profits: $-20,700	**Fiscal Year Ends:** 7/31
1995 Sales: $395,700	1995 Profits: $-45,400	

SALARIES/BENEFITS:

Pension Plan:	ESOP Stock Plan:	Profit Sharing:	Top Exec. Salary: $489,981	Bonus: $516,424
Savings Plan: Y	Stock Purch. Plan:		Second Exec. Salary: $386,827	Bonus: $217,803

COMPETITIVE ADVANTAGE: Broad customer base for product upgrades and line extensions/Excellent web-based marketing strategy.

OTHER THOUGHTS:

Apparent Women Officers or Directors: 6
Apparent Minority Officers or Directors:
Hot Spot for Advancement for Women/Minorities: Y

LOCATIONS: ("Y" = Yes)

West:	Southwest:	Midwest:	Southeast:	Northeast:	International:
Y	Y	Y		Y	Y

Note: Financial information, benefits and other data can change quickly and may vary from those stated here.

ISS GROUP INC   www.iss.net

Industry Group Code: 5112
Ranks within this company's industry group: Sales: 26   Profits: 30

BUSINESS ACTIVITIES ("Y" = Yes)

Financial Services:	Information/Publ.:	Technology:		Services:	Retailing:	Telecommunications:
Stock Brokerage	Portal/Hub/News	Computer Manuf.		Payments/Transfers	Retailer	Internet Serv. Provider
Mortgages/Loans	On-Line Community	Networking Equip.		Consulting	Auctions	Web Site Host
Banking	Search Engine	Software Manuf.	Y	Advertising/Marketing	Mall	Server Farm
Insurance	Financial Data Publ.	Specialty Equipment		Outsourcing	Tickets/Travel	Specialty Telecom.
Credit Cards	Broadcasting/Music				Price Comparisons	High Speed Access

TYPES OF BUSINESS:

Software-Security

BRANDS/DIVISIONS/AFFILIATES:

SAFEsuite
ePatrol
Real Secure

CONTACTS: *Note: Officers with more than one job title may be intentionally listed here more than once.*

Thomas E. Noonan, CEO
Thomas E. Noonan, Pres.
Richard Macchia, CFO/VP-Finance
Tim McCormick, VP-Commercial Mktg.
Christopher W. Klaus, Chief Tech. Officer
H. Keith Cooley, VP-Engineering and Support
Richard Macchia, VP-Admin.
Glenn McGonnigle, VP-Business Dev.
Charles Meyers, VP-Business and Corp. Dev.
Patrick J.D. Taylor, VP-Strategic Mktg.

Phone: 678-443-6000	Fax: 678-443-6477
Toll-Free:	

Address: 6600 Peachtree-Dunwoody Rd., Bldg. 300, Ste 500, Atlanta, GA, 30328

GROWTH PLANS/SPECIAL FEATURES:

ISS Group, Inc. provides end-to-end security management solutions. The company is a leading provider of monitoring, detection and response software that protects the security and integrity of enterprise e-business environments. ISS' products use an innovative Adaptive Network Security approach that incorporates continuous security risk monitoring, detection and response to develop and enforce an active network security policy. The SAFEsuite family of products utilizes risk assessment, intrusion detection and enterprise security decision support solutions to protect corporate networks, extranets and the Internet from misuse and security violations. The SAFEsuite products and other products, including Internet Scanner, System Scanner, Database Scanner and Real Secure, coupled with the ePatrol product (which provides around-the-clock remote security monitoring), offers companies a comprehensive network and Internet security solution. ISS has licensed its products to over 3,000 organizations worldwide, including firms in the Global 2,000, United States and international government agencies, major universities and 21 of the 25 largest commercial banks in the United States.

FINANCIALS: Sales and profits are in thousands of dollars—add 000 to get the full amount.

Notes regarding 1999: *(1999 sales and profits were not available for all companies at press time.)*

1999 Sales: $116,487	1999 Profits: $7,490	Stock Ticker: **ISSX**
1998 Sales: $35,900	1998 Profits: $-4,100	Employees: 328
1997 Sales: $13,500	1997 Profits: $-3,900	Fiscal Year Ends: 12/31
1996 Sales: $4,500	1996 Profits: $-1,100	
1995 Sales: $ 300	1995 Profits: $- 100	

SALARIES/BENEFITS:

Pension Plan:	ESOP Stock Plan: Y	Profit Sharing:	Top Exec. Salary: $185,486	Bonus: $95,000
Savings Plan:	Stock Purch. Plan:		Second Exec. Salary: $135,000	Bonus: $35,320

COMPETITIVE ADVANTAGE: Large, global client base.

OTHER THOUGHTS:

	LOCATIONS: ("Y" = Yes)					
	West:	Southwest:	Midwest:	Southeast:	Northeast:	International:
Apparent Women Officers or Directors: 1				Y	Y	Y
Apparent Minority Officers or Directors:						
Hot Spot for Advancement for Women/Minorities:						

ITURF INC   www.iturf.com

Industry Group Code: 514191
Ranks within this company's industry group: Sales: 40   Profits: 6

BUSINESS ACTIVITIES ("Y" = Yes)

Financial Services:	Information/Publ.:		Technology:	Services:	Retailing:	Telecommunications:
Stock Brokerage	Portal/Hub/News	Y	Computer Manuf.	Payments/Transfers	Retailer	Internet Serv. Provider
Mortgages/Loans	On-Line Community	Y	Networking Equip.	Consulting	Auctions	Web Site Host
Banking	Search Engine		Software Manuf.	Advertising/Marketing	Mall	Server Farm
Insurance	Financial Data Publ.		Specialty Equipment	Outsourcing	Tickets/Travel	Specialty Telecom.
Credit Cards	Broadcasting/Music				Price Comparisons	High Speed Access

TYPES OF BUSINESS:

Youth (Ages 10-24) Portal

BRANDS/DIVISIONS/AFFILIATES:

gURL.com
OnTap.com
gURLnet.com
gURLpages.com
gURLmail.com
dotdotdash.com
discountdomain.com

CONTACTS: *Note: Officers with more than one job title may be intentionally listed here more than once.*

Stephen I. Kahn, CEO/Pres.
Alex S. Navarro, COO
Dennis Goldstein, CFO
Renny Gleason, Sr. VP-Mktg.
Tracy Koenig, Dir.-Human Resources
Oliver Sharp, Chief Tech. Officer
Dennis Goldstein, Treas.

Phone: 212-741-7785	Fax: 212-547-7988
Toll-Free:	
Address: 435 Hudson St., New York, NY, 10014	

GROWTH PLANS/SPECIAL FEATURES:

iTurf, Inc. is a leading provider of Internet communities, content and commerce targeted toward Generation Y. Generation Y is comprised of 56 million people between the ages of 10 and 24, and accounts for $278 billion of disposable income. iTurf is a web site where Generation Y members can interact and shop in an environment of their own. iTurf's network of web sites offers interactive magazines, or web zines, with proprietary information, chat rooms, posting boards, personal homepages, e-mail and on-line shopping. iTurf's gURL community is a family of web sites that provide interactive features and articles on topics of interest to Generation Y girls and young women through the web sites gURL.com, gURLnet.com, gURLpages.com and gURLmail.com. The OnTap.com web site is targeted toward college and university students between the ages of 18 and 24. iTurf provides e-commerce opportunities through the web sites dELiAs.cOm, TSISoccer.com, contentsonline.com, discountdomain.com, droog.com, StorybookHeirlooms.com and dotdotdash.com. These sites offer a wide range of apparel, accessories, footwear, athletic gear and home furnishings for Generation Y. iTurf believes that Generation Y is the most important demographic on-line, projecting that by 2002, e-commerce sales from Generation Y will grow to over $3.8 billion. It is iTurf's goal to build its on-line community to become the most heavily trafficked Generation Y destination on the Internet.

FINANCIALS: Sales and profits are in thousands of dollars—add 000 to get the full amount.

Notes regarding 1999: *(1999 sales and profits were not available for all companies at press time.)*

1999 Sales: $4,000	1999 Profits: $ 500	Stock Ticker: **TURF**
1998 Sales: $ 134	1998 Profits: $- 49	Employees: 40
1997 Sales: $	1997 Profits: $	Fiscal Year Ends: 1/31
1996 Sales: $	1996 Profits: $	
1995 Sales: $	1995 Profits: $	

SALARIES/BENEFITS:

Pension Plan:	ESOP Stock Plan: Y	Profit Sharing:	Top Exec. Salary: $	Bonus: $
Savings Plan:	Stock Purch. Plan:		Second Exec. Salary: $	Bonus: $

COMPETITIVE ADVANTAGE: Focus on the younger segment of the market.

OTHER THOUGHTS:

Apparent Women Officers or Directors: 5
Apparent Minority Officers or Directors:
Hot Spot for Advancement for Women/Minorities: Y

LOCATIONS: ("Y" = Yes)

West:	Southwest:	Midwest:	Southeast:	Northeast:	International:
				Y	

Note: Financial information, benefits and other data can change quickly and may vary from those stated here.

IVILLAGE INC   www.ivillage.com

Industry Group Code: 514191
Ranks within this company's industry group: Sales: 12   Profits: 41

BUSINESS ACTIVITIES ("Y" = Yes)

Financial Services:		Information/Publ.:		Technology:	Services:	Retailing:		Telecommunications:
Stock Brokerage		Portal/Hub/News		Computer Manuf.	Payments/Transfers	Retailer	Y	Internet Serv. Provider
Mortgages/Loans		On-Line Community	Y	Networking Equip.	Consulting	Auctions		Web Site Host
Banking	Y	Search Engine		Software Manuf.	Advertising/Marketing	Mall		Server Farm
Insurance		Financial Data Publ.		Specialty Equipment	Outsourcing	Tickets/Travel		Specialty Telecom.
Credit Cards		Broadcasting/Music				Price Comparisons		High Speed Access

TYPES OF BUSINESS:

On-line Women's Network
On-line Banking Services
On-line Shopping

BRANDS/DIVISIONS/AFFILIATES:

iBaby.com
iMaternity.com

CONTACTS:
Note: Officers with more than one job title may be intentionally listed here more than once.

Candice Carpenter, CEO
Allison Abraham, COO
Craig T. Monaghan, CFO
Donna Introcaso, VP-Human Resources
Stephen Lake, VP-Business Dev.
Betty Hudson, Sr. VP-Corp. Comm.
Nancy Evans, Editor in Chief
John Glascott, Sr. VP-Sponsorship

Phone: 212-604-0963	Fax: 212-604-9133
Toll-Free:	
Address: 170 5th Ave., 4th Fl., New York, NY, 10010	

GROWTH PLANS/SPECIAL FEATURES:

iVillage.com: The Women's Network is a web site created specifically for female web surfers aged 25 to 49. More than 80% of the site's revenue is derived from advertising, but it recently created iBaby.com, an on-line baby products retailer that should make the site's e-commerce presence felt. iVillage's more than 1.5 million registered users may take advantage of e-mail, chat rooms and message boards, as well as over 15 different channels that range in topic from astrology to parenting. Recently, iVillage began partnerships with Gap.com, Macys.com, Petopia.com, Nordstrom.com and others to provide their members with exclusive discounts and daily specials. People who enjoy shopping but find they do not have the time may now do much of their purchasing from this one web site. In addition to shopping, iVillage offers many other services. Members may take advantage of banking services offered through PNC Bank Corp., known for its 15-second on-line loan decisions. The site's Town Hall Tuesdays allow members to flex their political muscles. Another of iVillage's offerings Includes taking questions submitted by some of the 7.3 million monthly visitors and delivering them to politicians in on-line chats broadcast live via streaming audio.

FINANCIALS:
Sales and profits are in thousands of dollars—add 000 to get the full amount.
Notes regarding 1999: *(1999 sales and profits were not available for all companies at press time.)*

1999 Sales: $44,600	1999 Profits: $-93,001	Stock Ticker: **IVIL**
1998 Sales: $15,000	1998 Profits: $-43,700	Employees: 200
1997 Sales: $6,000	1997 Profits: $-21,300	Fiscal Year Ends: 12/31
1996 Sales: $ 700	1996 Profits: $-9,700	
1995 Sales: $	1995 Profits: $-1,600	

SALARIES/BENEFITS:

Pension Plan:	ESOP Stock Plan: Y	Profit Sharing:	Top Exec. Salary: $225,000	Bonus: $
Savings Plan:	Stock Purch. Plan: Y		Second Exec. Salary: $195,000	Bonus: $

COMPETITIVE ADVANTAGE: Has received tremendous media coverage.

OTHER THOUGHTS:

Apparent Women Officers or Directors: 4
Apparent Minority Officers or Directors:
Hot Spot for Advancement for Women/Minorities: Y

LOCATIONS: ("Y" = Yes)

West:	Southwest:	Midwest:	Southeast:	Northeast:	International:
				Y	

IXL ENTERPRISES INC   www.ixl.com

Industry Group Code: 54151
Ranks within this company's industry group: Sales: 3   Profits: 15

BUSINESS ACTIVITIES ("Y" = Yes)

Financial Services:		Information/Publ.:	Technology:	Services:		Retailing:	Telecommunications:	
Stock Brokerage		Portal/Hub/News	Computer Manuf.	Payments/Transfers		Retailer	Internet Serv. Provider	Y
Mortgages/Loans	Y	On-Line Community	Networking Equip.	Consulting	Y	Auctions	Web Site Host	Y
Banking		Search Engine	Software Manuf.	Advertising/Marketing		Mall	Server Farm	
Insurance	Y	Financial Data Publ.	Specialty Equipment	Outsourcing	Y	Tickets/Travel	Specialty Telecom.	
Credit Cards	Y	Broadcasting/Music				Price Comparisons	High Speed Access	

TYPES OF BUSINESS:

Consulting-Internet Solutions
Financial Services On-line

BRANDS/DIVISIONS/AFFILIATES:

Consumer Financial Network, Inc.
YouDecide.com

CONTACTS: Note: Officers with more than one job title may be intentionally listed here more than once.

U. Bertram Ellis, Jr., CEO
C. Cathleen Raffaeli, COO/Pres.
M. Wayne Boylston, CFO
David Clauson, Exec. VP-Worldwide Mktg.
Jodie Littlestone, Human Resources
Benjamin Chen, Chief Tech. Officer
Jeff Radcliffe, CIO
William A. Grana Jr., General Counsel
Niraj Shah, Sr.VP-Oper.
Panna Sharma, Sr.VP-Corp. Strategy

Phone: 404-267-3800	Fax: 404-267-3801
Toll-Free: 800-573-5544	
Address: 1900 Emery St., Atlanta, GA, 30318	

GROWTH PLANS/SPECIAL FEATURES:

IXL delivers complex Internet-based business solutions by employing technologies such as Java, XML, Perl and C++. IXL is an Internet services company that provides Internet strategy consulting and comprehensive Internet-based solutions to Fortune 1000 companies and other corporate users of information technology. The company helps businesses identify how the Internet may be used to their competitive advantage and provides creative design and systems engineering for the design, development and deployment of advanced Internet applications and solutions. The company assembles industry practice groups, including professionals with expertise in the business practices and processes of specific industries. Using an engagement methodology called iD5, iXL defines and delineates business procedures and processes. In the last few years, the company has created more than 3,000 Internet projects, with typical engagements ranging from $250,000 to $1 million. Some of the company's clients are Delta Air Lines, Chase Manhattan Bank, General Electric and WebMD. The company has over 20 full-service offices in North America and Europe. IXL has also developed Consumer Financial Network, Inc., which operates YouDecide.com, a sophisticated e-commerce web site for marketing financial services and benefits over corporate intranets and the Internet. The YouDecide.com web site currently offers the following services: automobile, homeowners and personal insurance, home mortgages, auto finance, financial planning and credit cards.

FINANCIALS: Sales and profits are in thousands of dollars—add 000 to get the full amount.
Notes regarding 1999: (1999 sales and profits were not available for all companies at press time.)

1999 Sales: $216,900	1999 Profits: $-91,200	Stock Ticker: IIXL
1998 Sales: $64,800	1998 Profits: $-48,900	Employees: 1,300
1997 Sales: $19,000	1997 Profits: $-17,000	Fiscal Year Ends: 12/31
1996 Sales: $5,400	1996 Profits: $-1,500	
1995 Sales: $	1995 Profits: $	

SALARIES/BENEFITS:

Pension Plan:	ESOP Stock Plan: Y	Profit Sharing:	Top Exec. Salary: $247,000	Bonus: $100,000
Savings Plan:	Stock Purch. Plan:		Second Exec. Salary: $276,000	Bonus: $

COMPETITIVE ADVANTAGE: Large network of offices/Top-notch client roster.

OTHER THOUGHTS:

Apparent Women Officers or Directors: 2
Apparent Minority Officers or Directors: 1
Hot Spot for Advancement for Women/Minorities:

LOCATIONS: ("Y" = Yes)

West:	Southwest:	Midwest:	Southeast:	Northeast:	International:
Y	Y	Y	Y	Y	Y

IXNET INC   www.ixnet.com

Industry Group Code: 5133E
Ranks within this company's industry group: Sales: 2   Profits: 2

BUSINESS ACTIVITIES ("Y" = Yes)

Financial Services:	Information/Publ.:	Technology:	Services:	Retailing:	Telecommunications:	
Stock Brokerage	Portal/Hub/News	Computer Manuf.	Payments/Transfers	Retailer	Internet Serv. Provider	Y
Mortgages/Loans	On-Line Community	Networking Equip.	Consulting	Auctions	Web Site Host	Y
Banking	Search Engine	Software Manuf.	Advertising/Marketing	Mall	Server Farm	
Insurance	Financial Data Publ.	Specialty Equipment	Outsourcing	Tickets/Travel	Specialty Telecom.	
Credit Cards	Broadcasting/Music			Price Comparisons	High Speed Access	

TYPES OF BUSINESS:
Virtual Private Networks/Voice and Data Connectivity

BRANDS/DIVISIONS/AFFILIATES:
Liquidity

CONTACTS: Note: Officers with more than one job title may be intentionally listed here more than once.
David A. Walsh, CEO
Gerald F. Starr, Pres.
James M. Demitrius, Exec. VP/CFO
William E. Walsh, Sr. VP-Mktg.
Deborah Rhymes, VP-Human Resources
Robert D. Woog, Sr.VP-Network Dev.
William E. Walsh, Sr. VP-Strategic Planning
Charles F. Auster, Exec.VP/COO

Phone: 212-412-6400	Fax: 212-344 8161
Toll-Free:	
Address: Wall Street Plaza, 88 Pine St., New York, NY, 10005	

GROWTH PLANS/SPECIAL FEATURES:
IXnet, Inc., a company largely owned by IPC Communications, offers a diversified range of communication services to such well-known corporations as Citibank, Merrill Lynch and Sempra Energy. IXnet's global Extranet operates as a full-service network for clients in the financial services industry. Through connecting markets, trading companies, corporations and the company's clients, IXnet's Extranet is a vital component to the operation of several other businesses. Additional communication-based services offered by the company include voice connectivity, data connectivity and access to several business information content providers. These services can be utilized by clients in over 70 points-of-presence in more than 39 centers throughout the Americas, Asia/Pacific and Europe. The company recently announced the launch of its Liquidity service offering into Europe and the United Kingdom. Delivering a full spectrum of market data and electronic trading links through a single network connection to IXnet's state-of-the-art Liquidity Content Center, this service will enable financial institutions, including brokers, investment banks and clearing organizations, to access content providers, major exchanges, alternative trading systems and settlement organizations. This single connection solution helps institutions reduce or eliminate requirements for on-site hardware, software and IT support resources.

FINANCIALS: Sales and profits are in thousands of dollars—add 000 to get the full amount.
Notes regarding 1999: (1999 sales and profits were not available for all companies at press time.)

1999 Sales: $73,600	1999 Profits: $-20,900	Stock Ticker: **EXNT**
1998 Sales: $35,900	1998 Profits: $-27,600	Employees: 232
1997 Sales: $17,800	1997 Profits: $-15,200	Fiscal Year Ends: 9/30
1996 Sales: $3,500	1996 Profits: $-6,200	
1995 Sales: $	1995 Profits: $- 700	

SALARIES/BENEFITS:

Pension Plan:	ESOP Stock Plan:	Profit Sharing:	Top Exec. Salary: $242,107	Bonus: $206,250
Savings Plan:	Stock Purch. Plan:		Second Exec. Salary: $	Bonus: $

COMPETITIVE ADVANTAGE: Rapid growth through innovation and strategic partnerships.

OTHER THOUGHTS:
Apparent Women Officers or Directors: 1
Apparent Minority Officers or Directors:
Hot Spot for Advancement for Women/Minorities:

LOCATIONS: ("Y" = Yes)

West:	Southwest:	Midwest:	Southeast:	Northeast:	International:
				Y	

JFAX.COM INC   www.jfax.com

Industry Group Code: 5133D
Ranks within this company's industry group: Sales: 4   Profits: 6

BUSINESS ACTIVITIES ("Y" = Yes)

Financial Services:	Information/Publ.:	Technology:	Services:	Retailing:	Telecommunications:
Stock Brokerage	Portal/Hub/News	Computer Manuf.	Payments/Transfers	Retailer	Internet Serv. Provider
Mortgages/Loans	On-Line Community	Networking Equip.	Consulting	Auctions	Web Site Host
Banking	Search Engine	Software Manuf.	Advertising/Marketing	Mall	Server Farm
Insurance	Financial Data Publ.	Specialty Equipment	Outsourcing	Tickets/Travel	Specialty Telecom. Y
Credit Cards	Broadcasting/Music			Price Comparisons	High Speed Access

TYPES OF BUSINESS:
Unified Messaging

BRANDS/DIVISIONS/AFFILIATES:

CONTACTS: Note: Officers with more than one job title may be intentionally listed here more than once.

Richard S. Ressler, CEO
Gary H. Hickox, Pres./COO
Hemi Zucker, CFO
Patty Brunton, VP-Human Resources
Anand Narsimhan, Chief Tech. Officer
Zohar Loshitzer, CIO
Patty Brunton, VP-Admin.
Tiffany Devitt, VP-Business Dev.
Raymond Thu, VP-Finance

Phone: 310-966-1651	Fax:
Toll-Free: 898-438-5329	
Address: 10960 Wilshire Blvd., Suite 500, Los Angeles, CA, 90024	

GROWTH PLANS/SPECIAL FEATURES:

JFAX.COM is an Internet-based messaging and communications service provider. Its mission is to be the leading global provider of high-quality, easy-to-use messaging and communication services, products and information to Internet-enabled e-mail users throughout the world. The company's services deposit all e-mail, fax and voice mail into the user's e-mail inbox. It also permits the user to retrieve e-mails and voice mail messages through e-mail or by phone. Users receive a free private phone number that can handle unlimited incoming faxes and voice messages. The voice messages are converted into e-mail. JFAX.com has the largest paid subscriber base of any unified messaging company in the industry. It offers telephone numbers in more countries than any telecommunications company. The company has users in over 200 countries. JFAX.COM's global network has expanded to more than 80 area codes on four continents representing nearly 2,000 towns and cities. The company's products are promoted through its relationship with high profile Internet and telecommunications firms.

FINANCIALS: Sales and profits are in thousands of dollars—add 000 to get the full amount.
Notes regarding 1999: *(1999 sales and profits were not available for all companies at press time.)*

1999 Sales: $7,643	1999 Profits: $-17,440	Stock Ticker: **JFAX**
1998 Sales: $3,500	1998 Profits: $-17,200	Employees: 80
1997 Sales: $ 700	1997 Profits: $-4,700	Fiscal Year Ends: 12/31
1996 Sales: $ 100	1996 Profits: $- 800	
1995 Sales: $	1995 Profits: $	

SALARIES/BENEFITS:

Pension Plan:	ESOP Stock Plan:	Profit Sharing:	Top Exec. Salary: $	Bonus: $
Savings Plan: Y	Stock Purch. Plan:		Second Exec. Salary: $	Bonus: $

COMPETITIVE ADVANTAGE: True global capabilities in more than 200 nations.

OTHER THOUGHTS:

Apparent Women Officers or Directors: 3
Apparent Minority Officers or Directors: 3
Hot Spot for Advancement for Women/Minorities: Y

LOCATIONS: ("Y" = Yes)

West:	Southwest:	Midwest:	Southeast:	Northeast:	International:
Y					Y

JUNIPER NETWORKS INC   www.juniper.net

Industry Group Code: 3341C
Ranks within this company's industry group: Sales: 8   Profits: 7

BUSINESS ACTIVITIES ("Y" = Yes)

Financial Services:	Information/Publ.:	Technology:		Services:	Retailing:	Telecommunications:
Stock Brokerage	Portal/Hub/News	Computer Manuf.		Payments/Transfers	Retailer	Internet Serv. Provider
Mortgages/Loans	On-Line Community	Networking Equip.	Y	Consulting	Auctions	Web Site Host
Banking	Search Engine	Software Manuf.	Y	Advertising/Marketing	Mall	Server Farm
Insurance	Financial Data Publ.	Specialty Equipment		Outsourcing	Tickets/Travel	Specialty Telecom.
Credit Cards	Broadcasting/Music				Price Comparisons	High Speed Access

TYPES OF BUSINESS:

Computer Networking Products

BRANDS/DIVISIONS/AFFILIATES:

JUNDS Internet Software
M2O Router
M4O Router

CONTACTS: *Note: Officers with more than one job title may be intentionally listed here more than once.*

Scott Kriens, CEO
Scott Kriens, Pres.
Marcel Gani, CFO
Joe Furgerson, VP-Mktg.
Tom Schaeffer, Dir.-Human Resources
Pradeep Sindhu, Chief Tech. Officer
John Jendricks, CIO
Peter L. Wexler, VP-Engineering
Gary Heidenreich, VP-Oper.
Steven Haley, VP-Worldwide Sales and Service

Phone: 650-526-8000	Fax: 650-526-8001
Toll-Free:	
Address: 385 Ravendale Dr., Mountain View, CA, 94043	

GROWTH PLANS/SPECIAL FEATURES:

Juniper Networks provides high-performance IP networking systems that enable service providers to meet the demands of the rapidly growing Internet. To help its customers remain competitive and grow with the new IP infrastructure, Juniper Network developed a family of router platforms that deliver wire-rate performance, solutions that easily scale, market-leading port density, flexible and manageable control over traffic and optimal bandwidth efficiency. This family consists of the M20 and M40 Internet backbone routers with JUNOS Internet software. The flagship product of the company, M40, combines the features of the JUNOS Internet Software, high performance ASIC-based (application specific integrated circuit) packet forwarding technology and Internet optimized architecture into a purpose-built solution for service providers. The company sells its Internet backbone routers primarily through a direct sales force and original equipment manufacturers. The M40 Internet backbone router is currently used by several of the world's leading service providers, such as UUNet, an MCI WorldCom Company, Cable & Wireless USA, AT&T/IBM Global Services, Frontier GlobalCenter Inc., Ericsson and Verio, Inc. The venture capital firm Kleiner Perkins Caufield & Byers owns about 21% of the company.

FINANCIALS: Sales and profits are in thousands of dollars—add 000 to get the full amount.

Notes regarding 1999: *(1999 sales and profits were not available for all companies at press time.)*

1999 Sales: $102,600	1999 Profits: $-9,000	**Stock Ticker: JNPR**
1998 Sales: $3,800	1998 Profits: $-31,000	Employees: 190
1997 Sales: $	1997 Profits: $-10,400	Fiscal Year Ends: 12/31
1996 Sales: $	1996 Profits: $-1,800	
1995 Sales: $	1995 Profits: $	

SALARIES/BENEFITS:

Pension Plan:	ESOP Stock Plan: Y	Profit Sharing:	Top Exec. Salary: $170,000	Bonus: $
Savings Plan: Y	Stock Purch. Plan:		Second Exec. Salary: $150,000	Bonus: $69,039

COMPETITIVE ADVANTAGE: Blue-ribbon backers/Great proprietary technology.

OTHER THOUGHTS:

Apparent Women Officers or Directors:						
Apparent Minority Officers or Directors: 1						
Hot Spot for Advancement for Women/Minorities:						

LOCATIONS: ("Y" = Yes)

West:	Southwest:	Midwest:	Southeast:	Northeast:	International:
Y				Y	Y

Note: Financial information, benefits and other data can change quickly and may vary from those stated here.

JUNO ONLINE SERVICES INC   www.juno.com

Industry Group Code: 51339
Ranks within this company's industry group: Sales: 12   Profits: 18

BUSINESS ACTIVITIES ("Y" = Yes)

Financial Services:	Information/Publ.:	Technology:	Services:	Retailing:	Telecommunications:
Stock Brokerage	Portal/Hub/News	Computer Manuf.	Payments/Transfers	Retailer	Internet Serv. Provider Y
Mortgages/Loans	On-Line Community	Networking Equip.	Consulting	Auctions	Web Site Host
Banking	Search Engine	Software Manuf.	Advertising/Marketing	Mall Y	Server Farm
Insurance	Financial Data Publ.	Specialty Equipment	Outsourcing	Tickets/Travel	Specialty Telecom.
Credit Cards	Broadcasting/Music			Price Comparisons	High Speed Access

TYPES OF BUSINESS:

Internet Service Provider

BRANDS/DIVISIONS/AFFILIATES:

Shop@Juno

GROWTH PLANS/SPECIAL FEATURES:

Juno provides Internet-related services to millions of computer users throughout the United States. The company offers several levels of service, from basic dial-up e-mail, provided free, to full access to the World Wide Web, competitively priced. Since Juno's April 1996 launch date, more than 7.6 million people have taken advantage of the free e-mail offer. Juno's revenues come from subscription fees for its advanced service levels, direct sale of products to consumers and its advertisers, including such companies as American Express, IBM, Allstate and Procter and Gamble. In addition to advertising, Juno has entered into marketing alliances with First USA for financial services, The Hartford for insurance services and Qwest Communications for long distance and other telecommunications services. Shop@Juno is an Internet shopping channel that offers a wide range of products and services through Juno.com. Marketing alliances with e-commerce sites like 1-800-FLOWERS, Crutchfield, Bluefly and Garden.com provide consumers with a rich shopping environment. Juno is also involved in special interest causes, allowing the American Heart Association and the Heritage Forests Campaign to mount nationwide campaigns to Juno's more than one million subscribers in order to urge Congress to pass legislation.

CONTACTS: *Note: Officers with more than one job title may be intentionally listed here more than once.*

Charles E. Ardai, CEO
Charles E. Ardai, Pres.
Richard M. Eaton Jr., CFO
Robert H. Cherins, Exec. VP-Sales and Mktg.
Laura Stauderman, Dir.-Human Resources
Mark A. Moraes, Exec. VP-Tech.
Peter D. Skopp, Sr.VP-Network Dev.
Richard D. Buchband, Sr.VP/General Counsel
Jordan S. Birnbaum, Sr. VP- Business Dev.
Richard M. Eaton Jr., Treas.

Phone: 212-597-9000	Fax: 212-597-9100
Toll-Free:	
Address: 1540 Broadway, New York, NY, 10036	

FINANCIALS: Sales and profits are in thousands of dollars—add 000 to get the full amount.

Notes regarding 1999: *(1999 sales and profits were not available for all companies at press time.)*

1999 Sales: $52,000	1999 Profits: $-55,834	Stock Ticker: **JWEB**
1998 Sales: $21,700	1998 Profits: $-31,600	Employees: 147
1997 Sales: $9,100	1997 Profits: $-33,700	Fiscal Year Ends: 12/31
1996 Sales: $ 100	1996 Profits: $-23,000	
1995 Sales: $	1995 Profits: $-3,800	

SALARIES/BENEFITS:

Pension Plan:	ESOP Stock Plan: Y	Profit Sharing: Y	Top Exec. Salary: $300,000	Bonus: $
Savings Plan:	Stock Purch. Plan:		Second Exec. Salary: $150,000	Bonus: $300,000

COMPETITIVE ADVANTAGE: A very popular, free e-mail service is used to introduce millions of users to Juno's offerings.

OTHER THOUGHTS:

Apparent Women Officers or Directors:
Apparent Minority Officers or Directors:
Hot Spot for Advancement for Women/Minorities:

LOCATIONS: ("Y" = Yes)

West:	Southwest:	Midwest:	Southeast:	Northeast:	International:
				Y	

LAUNCH MEDIA INC   www.launch.com

Industry Group Code: 51311B
Ranks within this company's industry group: Sales: 4   Profits: 5

BUSINESS ACTIVITIES ("Y" = Yes)

Financial Services:	Information/Publ.:		Technology:	Services:	Retailing:		Telecommunications:
Stock Brokerage	Portal/Hub/News	Y	Computer Manuf.	Payments/Transfers	Retailer	Y	Internet Serv. Provider
Mortgages/Loans	On-Line Community	Y	Networking Equip.	Consulting	Auctions		Web Site Host
Banking	Search Engine		Software Manuf.	Advertising/Marketing	Mall		Server Farm
Insurance	Financial Data Publ.		Specialty Equipment	Outsourcing	Tickets/Travel		Specialty Telecom.
Credit Cards	Broadcasting/Music	Y			Price Comparisons		High Speed Access

TYPES OF BUSINESS:
On-line Music Broadcasting

BRANDS/DIVISIONS/AFFILIATES:
Launch.com

CONTACTS: *Note: Officers with more than one job title may be intentionally listed here more than once.*
David B. Goldberg, CEO
Robert D. Roback, Pres.
Jeffrey M. Mickeal, CFO
Paige M. Arnof-Fenn, Sr. VP- Mktg.
Jeffrey M. Mickeal, Sec.
Elisa Maliman, VP-Investor Relations
Spenser A. McClung Jr., Sr. VP-Broadband
James E. Hughes, Sr. VP/General Mgr.

Phone: 310-526-4300	Fax:
Toll-Free:	
Address: 2700 Pennsylvania Avenue, Santa Monica, CA, 90404	

GROWTH PLANS/SPECIAL FEATURES:

Voted one of the top 100 sites by PC Magazine, Launch Media is a destination for new music and music videos, broadcast via multiple broadband and narrow platforms. Launch Media is the exclusive on-line music content provider for NBC.com, providing behind-the-scenes access to musical guests who have appeared on The Tonight Show, Late Night with Conan O'Brien and Saturday Night Live. Launch.com features CD-quality song samples, exclusive video interviews in 3-D environments where users can choose interviews of specific musicians and direct links to the Internet for downloading additional content or chatting with other users. Members can access fan lists, chat rooms and instant messaging to keep in touch with other music fans. Registered members of launch.com may share their tastes and preferences with other members of the community by writing reviews, rating artists and albums and setting up personalized home pages that other members can visit. Launch.com covers all musical genres, other than classical, targeting the 12-34 age group. About 60% of Launch Media's revenue is from advertising sales and the remainder comes from subscription fees and merchandising. Launch offers a compelling music discovery experience for consumers and provides a valuable marketing platform for record labels, artists, advertisers and merchants.

FINANCIALS: Sales and profits are in thousands of dollars—add 000 to get the full amount.
Notes regarding 1999: *(1999 sales and profits were not available for all companies at press time.)*

1999 Sales: $16,600	1999 Profits: $-33,300	Stock Ticker: **LAUN**
1998 Sales: $5,000	1998 Profits: $-13,400	Employees: 73
1997 Sales: $3,100	1997 Profits: $-6,700	Fiscal Year Ends: 12/31
1996 Sales: $1,400	1996 Profits: $-4,500	
1995 Sales: $	1995 Profits: $	

SALARIES/BENEFITS:

Pension Plan:	ESOP Stock Plan: Y	Profit Sharing:	Top Exec. Salary: $1,125,000	Bonus: $
Savings Plan:	Stock Purch. Plan:		Second Exec. Salary: $110,000	Bonus: $15,789

COMPETITIVE ADVANTAGE: Alliance with NBC.com/Very comprehensive site for younger music fans.

OTHER THOUGHTS:

Apparent Women Officers or Directors:
Apparent Minority Officers or Directors:
Hot Spot for Advancement for Women/Minorities:

LOCATIONS: ("Y" = Yes)

West:	Southwest:	Midwest:	Southeast:	Northeast:	International:
Y					

LEAPNET INC   www.leapnet.com

Industry Group Code: 54189A
Ranks within this company's industry group: Sales: 4   Profits: 12

BUSINESS ACTIVITIES ("Y" = Yes)

Financial Services:	Information/Publ.:	Technology:	Services:		Retailing:		Telecommunications:
Stock Brokerage	Portal/Hub/News	Computer Manuf.	Payments/Transfers		Retailer		Internet Serv. Provider
Mortgages/Loans	On-Line Community	Networking Equip.	Consulting	Y	Auctions		Web Site Host
Banking	Search Engine	Software Manuf.	Advertising/Marketing	Y	Mall		Server Farm
Insurance	Financial Data Publ.	Specialty Equipment	Outsourcing		Tickets/Travel		Specialty Telecom.
Credit Cards	Broadcasting/Music				Price Comparisons		High Speed Access

TYPES OF BUSINESS:

Advertising Agency
New Media Development
Systems Integration
Consulting

BRANDS/DIVISIONS/AFFILIATES:

Leap Partnership, Inc., The
Lilypad Services, Inc.
Tadpole Productions, Inc.
Quantum Leap Communications, Inc.
YAR Communications, Inc.
Leap Group, The
Eagle Technology Partners
Nine Dots

CONTACTS: Note: Officers with more than one job title may be intentionally listed here more than once.

Frederick A. Smith, CEO
Thomas R. Sharbaugh, Pres.
Beth Pastor, CFO
George Gier, Exec.VP- Chief Mktg. Officer
Colleen Gorrera, Mgr. Human Resources
George Gier, CIO
Grace Sajdak, Corp. Controller
Robert C. Bramlette, Corp. Sec.
Robert C. Bramlette, Chief Legal and Strategic Officer
Robert C. Bramlette, Chief Strategy Officer
Joseph A. Sciarrotta, Exec.VP/Chief Creative Officer

Phone: 312-494-0300	Fax: 312-494-0120
Toll-Free:	
Address: 22 W. Hubbard St., Chicago, IL, 60610	

GROWTH PLANS/SPECIAL FEATURES:

Leapnet, Inc., formerly The Leap Group, Inc., develops creative Internet solutions by combining experience in Internet advertising and development, global marketing communications and traditional brand advertising. Leapnet works with market-leading companies to develop and improve relationships with their customers, extend their brands into the mass market and increase sales and market share. Leapnet consists of three subsidiaries. Quantum Leap Communications is an Internet development and advertising company that executes solutions primarily for Internet brands. YAR Communications specializes in globalizing communication content for the Internet and traditional media. The Leap Partnership develops large-scale consumer-focused advertising campaigns to reach mass-market consumers. Eagle Technology Partners is an e-business consulting and systems integration firm. Leapnet recently acquired Nine Dots, an interactive marketing services firm specializing in digital branding, on-line advertising and promotion, strategic consulting and web site development. The company's clients include Wal-Mart, American Airlines, Ernst & Young, Microsoft, Anheuser-Busch, Columbia Tri-Star and Johnson & Johnson. Headquartered in Chicago, the company has offices in New York, Los Angeles and San Francisco.

FINANCIALS: Sales and profits are in thousands of dollars—add 000 to get the full amount.

Notes regarding 1999: *(1999 sales and profits were not available for all companies at press time.)*

1999 Sales: $35,920	1999 Profits: $-12,326	Stock Ticker: **LEAP**	
1998 Sales: $30,660	1998 Profits: $-9,390	Employees: 166	
1997 Sales: $16,088	1997 Profits: $1,386	Fiscal Year Ends: 1/31	
1996 Sales: $8,210	1996 Profits: $ 700		
1995 Sales: $	1995 Profits: $		

SALARIES/BENEFITS:

Pension Plan:	ESOP Stock Plan:	Profit Sharing:	Top Exec. Salary: $280,923	Bonus: $
Savings Plan: Y	Stock Purch. Plan: Y		Second Exec. Salary: $242,235	Bonus: $

COMPETITIVE ADVANTAGE: Impressive client list/Internet company clients.

OTHER THOUGHTS:

Apparent Women Officers or Directors: 3
Apparent Minority Officers or Directors:
Hot Spot for Advancement for Women/Minorities: Y

LOCATIONS: ("Y" = Yes)

West:	Southwest:	Midwest:	Southeast:	Northeast:	International:
Y		Y		Y	

Note: Financial information, benefits and other data can change quickly and may vary from those stated here.

LIBERATE TECHNOLOGIES   www.liberate.com

Industry Group Code: 5112
Ranks within this company's industry group: Sales: 47   Profits: 78

BUSINESS ACTIVITIES ("Y" = Yes)

Financial Services:	Information/Publ.:	Technology:		Services:	Retailing:	Telecommunications:
Stock Brokerage	Portal/Hub/News	Computer Manuf.		Payments/Transfers	Retailer	Internet Serv. Provider
Mortgages/Loans	On-Line Community	Networking Equip.		Consulting	Auctions	Web Site Host
Banking	Search Engine	Software Manuf.	Y	Advertising/Marketing	Mall	Server Farm
Insurance	Financial Data Publ.	Specialty Equipment		Outsourcing	Tickets/Travel	Specialty Telecom.
Credit Cards	Broadcasting/Music				Price Comparisons	High Speed Access

TYPES OF BUSINESS:

Software-Web Access

BRANDS/DIVISIONS/AFFILIATES:

Liberate TV Navigator
Liberate Connect

CONTACTS: *Note: Officers with more than one job title may be intentionally listed here more than once.*

Mitchell E. Kertzman, CEO/Pres.
Coleman Sisson, COO
Nancy J. Hilker, CFO
Charles G. Tritschler, VP-Mktg.
Steven Weinstein, Sr. VP-Engineering
Gordon T. Yamate, VP/Sec.
Gordon T. Yamate, VP/General Counsel
David A. Limp, Sr. VP-Corporate Dev.

Phone: 650-701-4000	Fax: 650-701-4999
Toll-Free:	
Address: 2 Circle Star Way, San Carlos, CA, 94070	

GROWTH PLANS/SPECIAL FEATURES:

Liberate Technologies provides software for information appliances, such as televisions, game consoles, cell phones and personal digital assistants. Liberate Technologies' software serves as a platform for the delivery of Internet-enhanced content and applications delivered through network operators, such as telecommunications companies, cable and satellite television operators, Internet service providers and information appliance manufacturers, providing consumers with Internet access from anywhere at anytime. The Liberate Connect product provides the foundation for its customers' information appliance networks, providing the service management platform to deploy applications that support the customers' distinct service and brand identities. Recently, Liberate and U.S. WEST launched U.S. WEST WebVision, the first Internet-based, interactive television product to be offered by a telecommunications company, available to U.S. WEST.net ISP subscribers. This will allow U.S. WEST customers to access broadcast services, telephony and Internet applications through televisions. Liberate is also working on providing interactive television to Hong Kong through Star TV and is working on offering the worlds first interactive digital cable television service based on Internet standards with the Cable & Wireless company.

FINANCIALS: Sales and profits are in thousands of dollars—add 000 to get the full amount.
Notes regarding 1999: *(1999 sales and profits were not available for all companies at press time.)*

1999 Sales: $17,300	1999 Profits: $-33,100	Stock Ticker: **LBRT**
1998 Sales: $10,300	1998 Profits: $-94,400	Employees: 227
1997 Sales: $ 300	1997 Profits: $-19,000	Fiscal Year Ends: 5/31
1996 Sales: $	1996 Profits: $-3,300	
1995 Sales: $	1995 Profits: $	

SALARIES/BENEFITS:

Pension Plan:	ESOP Stock Plan:	Profit Sharing:	Top Exec. Salary: $516,071	Bonus: $
Savings Plan:	Stock Purch. Plan:		Second Exec. Salary: $153,542	Bonus: $

COMPETITIVE ADVANTAGE: The company is well positioned to participate in the coming explosion in the Internet appliances field.

OTHER THOUGHTS:

Apparent Women Officers or Directors: 1
Apparent Minority Officers or Directors:
Hot Spot for Advancement for Women/Minorities:

LOCATIONS: ("Y" = Yes)

West:	Southwest:	Midwest:	Southeast:	Northeast:	International:
Y					Y

Note: Financial information, benefits and other data can change quickly and may vary from those stated here.

LIONBRIDGE TECHNOLOGIES INC   www.lionbridge.com

Industry Group Code: 54151
Ranks within this company's industry group: Sales: 7   Profits: 10

BUSINESS ACTIVITIES ("Y" – Yes)

Financial Services:	Information/Publ.:	Technology:	Services:		Retailing:	Telecommunications:
Stock Brokerage	Portal/Hub/News	Computer Manuf.	Payments/Transfers		Retailer	Internet Serv. Provider
Mortgages/Loans	On-Line Community	Networking Equip.	Consulting		Auctions	Web Site Host
Banking	Search Engine	Software Manuf.	Advertising/Marketing		Mall	Server Farm
Insurance	Financial Data Publ.	Specialty Equipment	Outsourcing	Y	Tickets/Travel	Specialty Telecom.
Credit Cards	Broadcasting/Music				Price Comparisons	High Speed Access

TYPES OF BUSINESS:
Outsourcing-Web Site Translation
Enables English Language Site To Go Global

BRANDS/DIVISIONS/AFFILIATES:
Rapid Globalization Methodology
LionTrack

CONTACTS: Note: Officers with more than one job title may be intentionally listed here more than once.
Rory J. Cowan, CEO
Rory J. Cowan, Pres.
Stephen J. Lifshatz, CFO
Peter H. Wright, VP-Sales
Stephen J. Lifshatz, Sec.
Myriam Martin-Kail, VP-Oper.
Ken Coleman, VP-Corporate Dev.
Paula Shannon, VP-Internet Alliances
Stephen J. Lifshatz, Treas.

Phone: 781-890-6612	Fax: 781-890-3122
Toll-Free:	
Address: 950 Winter St., Suite 4300, Waltham, MA, 02451	

GROWTH PLANS/SPECIAL FEATURES:

Lionbridge Technologies, Inc. is a provider of globalization and multilingual Internet services to technology companies worldwide. Lionbridge creates and maintains multilingual versions of its customers' hardware, software, Internet technical support, training materials and sales and marketing information for worldwide distribution through regular mail and the Internet. The company translates programs, web sites and other materials into a country's spoken language and also provides source code reengineering and logo certification. Lionbridge serves as a globalization partner with its customers throughout the product development and support cycle by providing localization, internationalization and translation services, as well as compliance, compatibility and localization testing of software and hardware and product management. The company's Rapid Globalization Methodology and LionTrack workflow systems help companies achieve operational efficiencies and predictable, measurable results across multiple geographic areas and languages. Lionbridge plans to continue expanding into other markets, such as automotive technology and medical equipment, requiring language translation through its products. With rapid rates of growth in today's cross continental e-commerce, Lionbridge is a front-runner in providing materials to non-English speaking markets for high-tech companies such as Cisco Systems, Microsoft, Oracle, Motorola and Sun Microsystems.

FINANCIALS: Sales and profits are in thousands of dollars—add 000 to get the full amount.
Notes regarding 1999: (1999 sales and profits were not available for all companies at press time.)

1999 Sales: $49,500	1999 Profits: $-18,300	Stock Ticker: **LIOX**
1998 Sales: $38,400	1998 Profits: $-4,300	Employees: 449
1997 Sales: $26,500	1997 Profits: $-8,700	Fiscal Year Ends: 12/31
1996 Sales: $28,100	1996 Profits: $- 200	
1995 Sales: $	1995 Profits: $	

SALARIES/BENEFITS:

Pension Plan:	ESOP Stock Plan:	Profit Sharing:	Top Exec. Salary: $249,144	Bonus: $112,500
Savings Plan:	Stock Purch. Plan:		Second Exec. Salary: $182,750	Bonus: $41,250

COMPETITIVE ADVANTAGE: Internet use is growing at an accelerating rate in non-English speaking nations. Lionbridge is well positioned to assist web sites in establishing new services suitable to foreign languages and customers.

OTHER THOUGHTS:
Apparent Women Officers or Directors: 1
Apparent Minority Officers or Directors:
Hot Spot for Advancement for Women/Minorities:

LOCATIONS: ("Y" = Yes)

West:	Southwest:	Midwest:	Southeast:	Northeast:	International:
Y				Y	Y

LIQUID AUDIO INC   www.liquidaudio.com

Industry Group Code: 5112
Ranks within this company's industry group: Sales: 69   Profits: 47

BUSINESS ACTIVITIES ("Y" = Yes)

Financial Services:	Information/Publ.:	Technology:		Services:		Retailing:	Telecommunications:
Stock Brokerage	Portal/Hub/News	Computer Manuf.		Payments/Transfers		Retailer	Internet Serv. Provider
Mortgages/Loans	On-Line Community	Networking Equip.		Consulting		Auctions	Web Site Host
Banking	Search Engine	Software Manuf.	Y	Advertising/Marketing		Mall	Server Farm
Insurance	Financial Data Publ.	Specialty Equipment		Outsourcing	Y	Tickets/Travel	Specialty Telecom.
Credit Cards	Broadcasting/Music					Price Comparisons	High Speed Access

TYPES OF BUSINESS:

Software-Digital Music

BRANDS/DIVISIONS/AFFILIATES:

CONTACTS: *Note: Officers with more than one job title may be intentionally listed here more than once.*

Gerald W. Kearby, CEO
Gerald W. Kearby, Pres.
Gary J. Iwatani, CFO
Andrea Cook Fleming, VP-Corp. Mktg.
Belina Pirayo, Dir.-Human Resources
Philip R. Wiser, Chief Tech. Officer
Philip R. Wiser, VP-Engineering
Robert G. Flynn, VP-Business Dev.
Kevin M. Malone, VP-Sales
Heather Furmidge, VP-Internet Business

Phone: 650-549-2000	Fax: 650-549-2099
Toll-Free:	
Address: 810 Winslow St., Redwood City, CA, 94063	

GROWTH PLANS/SPECIAL FEATURES:

Liquid Audio is a provider of services and software that enable musicians, music producers and music retailers to digitally deliver professional quality music via the Internet. Formed by veterans of the music industry and professional recording engineers, Liquid Audio is converging music and technology to establish the Internet as a new medium for music distribution. The company's products and services support all leading digital music formats, including Dolby AC3 and MP3. The company has significantly increased the reach of its Internet music distribution network to include content from major and independent record labels, retail presence at brick-and-mortar and on-line retailers and a huge audience of music fans. With the selection of Liquid Audio by CDNOW, the Liquid Music Network now includes more than 300 on-line music retailers and 800 record labels that use Liquid Audio software and services to deliver one million music previews and 40,000 secure song downloads to consumers. Recently, Liquid Audio was selected as one of 14 rising powers by Entertainment Weekly magazine. As an example of Liquid Audio's innovation and power, using extensive consumer awareness on the Internet through Liquid Audio, rock band Creed's Human Clay album rose to the top of the Billboard sales chart.

FINANCIALS: Sales and profits are in thousands of dollars—add 000 to get the full amount.
Notes regarding 1999: *(1999 sales and profits were not available for all companies at press time.)*

1999 Sales: $4,400	1999 Profits: $-24,200	Stock Ticker: **LQID**
1998 Sales: $2,800	1998 Profits: $-8,500	Employees: 76
1997 Sales: $ 300	1997 Profits: $-6,200	Fiscal Year Ends: 12/31
1996 Sales: $	1996 Profits: $-1,300	
1995 Sales: $	1995 Profits: $	

SALARIES/BENEFITS:

Pension Plan:	ESOP Stock Plan: Y	Profit Sharing:	Top Exec. Salary: $158,077	Bonus: $45,000
Savings Plan:	Stock Purch. Plan:		Second Exec. Salary: $160,343	Bonus: $26,250

COMPETITIVE ADVANTAGE: Vital services for firms that want to build audiences for music on the Internet.

OTHER THOUGHTS:

Apparent Women Officers or Directors: 2
Apparent Minority Officers or Directors: 2
Hot Spot for Advancement for Women/Minorities: Y

LOCATIONS: ("Y" = Yes)

West:	Southwest:	Midwest:	Southeast:	Northeast:	International:
Y					

LITRONIC INC   www.litronic.com

Industry Group Code: 5112
Ranks within this company's industry group: Sales: 58   Profits: 18

BUSINESS ACTIVITIES ("Y" = Yes)

Financial Services:	Information/Publ.:	Technology:		Services:	Retailing:	Telecommunications:
Stock Brokerage	Portal/Hub/News	Computer Manuf.		Payments/Transfers	Retailer	Internet Serv. Provider
Mortgages/Loans	On-Line Community	Networking Equip.		Consulting	Auctions	Web Site Host
Banking	Search Engine	Software Manuf.	Y	Advertising/Marketing	Mall	Server Farm
Insurance	Financial Data Publ.	Specialty Equipment		Outsourcing	Tickets/Travel	Specialty Telecom.
Credit Cards	Broadcasting/Music				Price Comparisons	High Speed Access

TYPES OF BUSINESS:
Sofware-Security

BRANDS/DIVISIONS/AFFILIATES:
Smart Card Campus

CONTACTS: *Note: Officers with more than one job title may be intentionally listed here more than once.*
Kris Shah, CEO
William W. Davis, Sr., COO/Pres.
Ray Russomanno, CFO
Robert J. Brich, VP-Government Mktg. and Sales
Robert J. Gray, VP-Product Dev.
Ray Russomanno, Controller
Aleli Dorsi, Corp. Dev. Mgr.
William S. Holmes, VP-Commercial Mktg. and Sales

Phone: 949-851-1085	Fax: 949-851-8588
Toll-Free:	
Address: 2030 Main St., Ste. 1250, Irvine, CA, 92614	

GROWTH PLANS/SPECIAL FEATURES:

Litronic develops and markets software and microprocessor-based products designed to enable secure electronic commerce business transactions and communications over the Internet. The company's primary security products use a computer security technology called public key infrastructure, or PKI, the standard for Internet-based commerce security to digitally sign messages. Digital signatures uniquely identify the sender of an electronic communication. Litronic's security products may be used with different web browsers, including Netscape Communicator and Microsoft Internet Explorer, to facilitate secure e-commerce transactions and secure e-mail. The company's solutions also provide additional security features for file protection, user authentication and remote access capabilities. A partnership between Litronic and Microsoft led to the development of the smart card campus. A smart card, similar in size to a credit card, is embedded with eight-bit microprocessors. A smart card campus is a closed environment where a smart card is used to enter facilities, access data and contain corporate identification. All of Litronic's products are designed with an open architecture to be algorithm, platform, application and token independent to deliver solutions that meet the needs of the individual organization. Litronics customers include the U.S. Department of Defense, Netscape Communication Corporation, Bank of America, Lucent Technologies and the Entertainment Industry Development Corporation.

FINANCIALS: Sales and profits are in thousands of dollars—add 000 to get the full amount.
Notes regarding 1999: *(1999 sales and profits were not available for all companies at press time.)*

1999 Sales: $	1999 Profits: $15,300	**Stock Ticker: LTNX**
1998 Sales: $6,600	1998 Profits: $ 900	Employees: 63
1997 Sales: $10,200	1997 Profits: $ 200	Fiscal Year Ends: 12/31
1996 Sales: $9,400	1996 Profits: $	
1995 Sales: $2,700	1995 Profits: $	

SALARIES/BENEFITS:

Pension Plan:	ESOP Stock Plan: Y	Profit Sharing:	Top Exec. Salary: $231,998	Bonus: $
Savings Plan:	Stock Purch. Plan:		Second Exec. Salary: $95,046	Bonus: $1,850

COMPETITIVE ADVANTAGE: Excellent technology/Alliance with Microsoft.

OTHER THOUGHTS:
Apparent Women Officers or Directors:
Apparent Minority Officers or Directors:
Hot Spot for Advancement for Women/Minorities:

LOCATIONS: ("Y" = Yes)

West:	Southwest:	Midwest:	Southeast:	Northeast:	International:
Y					

Note: Financial information, benefits and other data can change quickly and may vary from those stated here.

LOG ON AMERICA INC   www.loa.com

Industry Group Code: 51339
Ranks within this company's industry group: Sales: 23   Profits: 4

BUSINESS ACTIVITIES ("Y" = Yes)

Financial Services:	Information/Publ.:	Technology:	Services:	Retailing:	Telecommunications:	
Stock Brokerage	Portal/Hub/News	Computer Manuf.	Payments/Transfers	Retailer	Internet Serv. Provider	Y
Mortgages/Loans	On-Line Community	Networking Equip.	Consulting Y	Auctions	Web Site Host	Y
Banking	Search Engine	Software Manuf.	Advertising/Marketing	Mall	Server Farm	
Insurance	Financial Data Publ.	Specialty Equipment	Outsourcing	Tickets/Travel	Specialty Telecom.	
Credit Cards	Broadcasting/Music			Price Comparisons	High Speed Access	Y

TYPES OF BUSINESS:

Internet Service Provider

BRANDS/DIVISIONS/AFFILIATES:

GROWTH PLANS/SPECIAL FEATURES:

Log On America, Inc. is a northeast U.S. regional Internet Service Provider, with more than 30,000 subscribers. The company provides local dial tone, in-state toll and long distance high-speed Internet access and cable programming solutions using Digital Subscriber Line technology to residential and commercial clients throughout the Northeast. The company's bundled communications suite gives residential and commercial clients a lower-cost alternative, with greater convenience and consistency, and their dial-up presence provides users with Internet access anywhere in the United States. Log On America is in the midst of a $100 million smart build-out of its network, positioning itself for long-term growth in the Northeast market. The company's web site offers virtual hosting, domain name registration, real audio and video and web design with professional consultants available 24 hours a day to assist businesses wishing to design a web page. Working in partnership with Digital Equipment Corporation, the company offers high performance Internet AlphaServers with a choice of three operating systems to combine management, security and server software and browsers. Log On America has established alliances with Cisco Systems, Nortel Networks and Bell Atlantic.

CONTACTS: Note: Officers with more than one job title may be intentionally listed here more than once.

David R. Paolo, CEO
David R. Paolo, Pres.
Kenneth M. Cornell, CFO
Michael Murphy, VP-Sales
Peter Fornal, VP-Human Resources
Donald J. Schattele II, VP-Tech.
Shastri Divakaruni, Dir.-Engineering
Donald J. Schattle II, VP-Oper.
Stephen Gilbert, VP-Dial-up Services
Raymond Paolo, Treas.

Phone: 401-459-6298	Fax: 401-459-6222
Toll-Free:	
Address: 3 Regency Plaza, Providence, RI, 02903	

FINANCIALS: Sales and profits are in thousands of dollars—add 000 to get the full amount.

Notes regarding 1999: *(1999 sales and profits were not available for all companies at press time.)*

1999 Sales: $	1999 Profits: $	Stock Ticker: **LOAX**
1998 Sales: $ 800	1998 Profits: $- 400	Employees: 13
1997 Sales: $ 400	1997 Profits: $- 300	Fiscal Year Ends: 12/31
1996 Sales: $ 200	1996 Profits: $- 200	
1995 Sales: $	1995 Profits: $	

SALARIES/BENEFITS:

Pension Plan:	ESOP Stock Plan:	Profit Sharing:	Top Exec. Salary: $90,000	Bonus: $2,500
Savings Plan:	Stock Purch. Plan:		Second Exec. Salary: $	Bonus: $

COMPETITIVE ADVANTAGE: The firm is making a significant investment in upgraded networks.

OTHER THOUGHTS:

	LOCATIONS: ("Y" = Yes)					
Apparent Women Officers or Directors:	West:	Southwest:	Midwest:	Southeast:	Northeast:	International:
Apparent Minority Officers or Directors:					Y	
Hot Spot for Advancement for Women/Minorities:						

LOOKSMART LTD   www.looksmart.com

Industry Group Code: 514191
Ranks within this company's industry group: Sales: 16   Profits: 33

BUSINESS ACTIVITIES ("Y" = Yes)

Financial Services:	Information/Publ.:		Technology:	Services:	Retailing:	Telecommunications:
Stock Brokerage	Portal/Hub/News	Y	Computer Manuf.	Payments/Transfers	Retailer	Internet Serv. Provider
Mortgages/Loans	On-Line Community		Networking Equip.	Consulting	Auctions	Web Site Host
Banking	Search Engine	Y	Software Manuf.	Advertising/Marketing	Mall	Server Farm
Insurance	Financial Data Publ.		Specialty Equipment	Outsourcing	Tickets/Travel	Specialty Telecom.
Credit Cards	Broadcasting/Music				Price Comparisons	High Speed Access

TYPES OF BUSINESS:

Search Portal

BRANDS/DIVISIONS/AFFILIATES:

LookSmart.com
Beseen.com

CONTACTS: *Note: Officers with more than one job title may be intentionally listed here more than once.*

Evan Thornley, CEO
Tracey Ellery, Pres.
Patricia Cole, CFO
Val Landi, Sr. VP-Mktg.
Martha Clark, VP-Human Resources
David Neylon, Sr. VP-Engineering
Ed O'Dea, VP-Corp. Dev.
Ned Brody, VP-e-commerce
Berkeley Belknap, Dir.-Strategic Comm.
Geoffrey Lewis, VP-Software Dev.
Barbara Read, VP-Advertising Sales

Phone: 415-597-4850	Fax: 415-597-4860

Toll-Free:

Address: 487 Bryant Street, San Francisco, CA, 94107

GROWTH PLANS/SPECIAL FEATURES:

LookSmart is a category-driven directory of web sites. Roughly 200 professional web editors create and update its directory of over one million Internet sites in about 70,000 subject categories. The editors search for the best of the Internet, carefully excluding all sites that contain content not suitable for all ages. Concise descriptions of each web site are available. City Guides are available in 70 markets, offering weather, news, movies, family activities and thousands of links to local businesses, services and community groups. LookSmart is attracting the family and, more specifically, women, who account for 60% of LookSmarts' users. LookSmart also offers Beseen.com, which features tools that enable webmasters to access LookSmart's directory on its web site. LookSmart's Internet partners include Microsoft's MSN, Netscape, AltaVista, IBM and 220 Internet service providers. The company's revenues are primarily from advertising, licensing/syndication and e-commerce.

FINANCIALS: Sales and profits are in thousands of dollars—add 000 to get the full amount.

Notes regarding 1999: *(1999 sales and profits were not available for all companies at press time.)*

1999 Sales: $48,900	1999 Profits: $-49,400	
1998 Sales: $8,800	1998 Profits: $-12,900	Stock Ticker: **LOOK**
1997 Sales: $ 900	1997 Profits: $-7,500	Employees: 184
1996 Sales: $	1996 Profits: $-2,900	Fiscal Year Ends: 12/31
1995 Sales: $	1995 Profits: $	

SALARIES/BENEFITS:

Pension Plan:	ESOP Stock Plan:	Profit Sharing:	Top Exec. Salary: $190,000	Bonus: $
Savings Plan:	Stock Purch. Plan:		Second Exec. Salary: $189,557	Bonus: $

COMPETITIVE ADVANTAGE: The company focuses on enabling families to readily discover consumer content suitable for viewers of all ages.

OTHER THOUGHTS:

Apparent Women Officers or Directors: 4
Apparent Minority Officers or Directors:
Hot Spot for Advancement for Women/Minorities: Y

LOCATIONS: ("Y" = Yes)

West:	Southwest:	Midwest:	Southeast:	Northeast:	International:
Y					Y

LUCENT TECHNOLOGIES INC   www.lucent.com

Industry Group Code: 33421
Ranks within this company's industry group: Sales: 1   Profits: 1

BUSINESS ACTIVITIES ("Y" = Yes)

Financial Services:	Information/Publ.:	Technology:		Services:		Retailing:	Telecommunications:	
Stock Brokerage	Portal/Hub/News	Computer Manuf.		Payments/Transfers		Retailer	Internet Serv. Provider	
Mortgages/Loans	On-Line Community	Networking Equip.	Y	Consulting	Y	Auctions	Web Site Host	
Banking	Search Engine	Software Manuf.	Y	Advertising/Marketing		Mall	Server Farm	
Insurance	Financial Data Publ.	Specialty Equipment	Y	Outsourcing	Y	Tickets/Travel	Specialty Telecom.	Y
Credit Cards	Broadcasting/Music					Price Comparisons	High Speed Access	

TYPES OF BUSINESS:

Telecommunications Equipment
Software Manufacturer and Developer
Networking Equipment

BRANDS/DIVISIONS/AFFILIATES:

Bell Laboratories
Service Provider Networks
Enterprise Networks
Microelectronics and Communications Technologies

CONTACTS: *Note: Officers with more than one job title may be intentionally listed here more than once.*

Richard A. McGinn, CEO/Pres.
Ben Verwaayen, COO
Donald K. Peterson, Exec. VP/CFO
Curtis R. Artis, Sr. VP-Human Resources
Arun N. Netravali, Exec. VP-Research-Bell Labs
Richard J. Rawson, Sr.VP/General Counsel
Robert C. Holder, Exec.VP- Staff Oper.
Pat Russo, Exec. VP-Business Dev., Corp. Oper.
Lance B. Boxer, Comm. Software
John DeBono, VP- Investor Relations
Patricia F. Russo, Exec.VP/CEO-Service Provider Networks

Phone: 908-582-8500	Fax: 908-508-2576
Toll-Free: 888-458-2368	
Address: 600 Mountain Avenue, Murray Hill, NJ, 07974	

GROWTH PLANS/SPECIAL FEATURES:

Lucent Technologies, Inc., formerly a part of AT&T, designs, develops and manufactures communications systems, software products and supplying systems to most of the world's largest communications network operators and service providers. The company's research and development activities are conducted through Bell Laboratories. Lucent is divided into three segments. The Service Provider Networks division (SPN) provides public networking systems and software to service providers and public network operators around the world. Enterprise Networks develops, manufactures, markets and services advanced communications products and data networking systems for business customers. The Microelectronics and Communications Technologies segment designs and manufactures high-performance integrated circuits, power systems, optical fiber and fiber cables and components for applications in the communications and computing industries. Recently, Lucent unveiled a chip set for hands-free cellular phone products that helps eliminate the need for manually dialing cellular phone numbers while driving. In 2000, Lucent received a 10-year, $26 million subcontract from IBM Global Services to outsource, manage and maintain voice network, messaging and customer care center hardware and software. Lucent has offices in more than 90 countries and territories around the world. Bell Laboratories operates in 20 countries.

Of the company's officials and managers, 16.6% are minorities, and 22.8% of employees are minorities. Lucent offers a relocation program as well as tution reimbursement from $7,000-$9,000 a year for college or graudate courses. Many of Lucent's employees teach at colleges that produce African-American engineers. Employees receive 40 hours of training each year.

FINANCIALS: Sales and profits are in thousands of dollars—add 000 to get the full amount.

Notes regarding 1999: *(1999 sales and profits were not available for all companies at press time.)*

1999 Sales: $38,303,000	1999 Profits: $4,766,000	Stock Ticker: **LU**
1998 Sales: $30,147,000	1998 Profits: $970,000	Employees: 141,600
1997 Sales: $26,360,000	1997 Profits: $541,000	Fiscal Year Ends: 9/30
1996 Sales: $15,859,000	1996 Profits: $224,000	
1995 Sales: $21,413,000	1995 Profits: $-867,000	

SALARIES/BENEFITS:

Pension Plan:	ESOP Stock Plan:	Profit Sharing:	Top Exec. Salary: $1,100,000	Bonus: $11,861,652
Savings Plan:	Stock Purch. Plan:		Second Exec. Salary: $764,584	Bonus: $2,376,150

COMPETITIVE ADVANTAGE:
Aggressively acquiring other firms/Is well positioned to benefit from the growing demand for advanced telecom equipment for increased bandwidth.

OTHER THOUGHTS:

Apparent Women Officers or Directors: 2
Apparent Minority Officers or Directors: 1
Hot Spot for Advancement for Women/Minorities: Y

LOCATIONS: ("Y" = Yes)

West:	Southwest:	Midwest:	Southeast:	Northeast:	International:
Y	Y	Y	Y	Y	Y

Note: Financial information, benefits and other data can change quickly and may vary from those stated here.

LYCOS INC   www.lycos.com

Industry Group Code: 514191
Ranks within this company's industry group: Sales: 4   Profits: 43

BUSINESS ACTIVITIES ("Y" = Yes)

Financial Services:	Information/Publ.:		Technology:	Services:	Retailing:	Telecommunications:	
Stock Brokerage	Portal/Hub/News	Y	Computer Manuf.	Payments/Transfers	Retailer	Internet Serv. Provider	
Mortgages/Loans	On-Line Community	Y	Networking Equip.	Consulting	Auctions	Web Site Host	Y
Banking	Search Engine	Y	Software Manuf.	Advertising/Marketing	Mall	Server Farm	
Insurance	Financial Data Publ.		Specialty Equipment	Outsourcing	Tickets/Travel	Specialty Telecom.	
Credit Cards	Broadcasting/Music				Price Comparisons	High Speed Access	

TYPES OF BUSINESS:

Search Portal

BRANDS/DIVISIONS/AFFILIATES:

Web Search
Web Guides
Top 5% Sites
Pictures & Sounds Search
Classifieds
Companies Online
People Find
Road Maps

CONTACTS: Note: Officers with more than one job title may be intentionally listed here more than once.

Robert J. Davis, Pres./CEO
Edward M. Philip, COO
Edward M. Philip, CFO
Jan R.Horsefall, VP-Mktg.
Sangam pant, VP-Engineering

Phone: 781-370-2700	Fax: 781-370-2600
Toll-Free:	
Address: 400-2 Totten Pond Rd., Waltham, MA, 02154-2000	

GROWTH PLANS/SPECIAL FEATURES:

Lycos Inc., founded in 1995, is a network of globally branded media properties and aggregated content distributed through the World Wide Web. Under the Lycos Network brand, the company provides aggregated third party content, web search and directory services, community and personalization features, personal web publishing and on-line shopping to over 28 million consumers. The company's web sites advertise several prominent companies, including Coca-Cola, Disney, Dell, The Gap, Intel, Sony and Visa. Lycos has established electronic commerce and sponsor relationships with companies such as Barnes & Noble, First USA Bank, Fleet Bank and WebMD. In addition, Lycos has established strategic licensing and technological alliances with corporations including Fidelity Investments, IBM, Microsoft, Packard Bell/NEC and Viacom. The company is working to expand the international distribution of its services. Lycos recently entered into joint ventures in Europe with Bertelsmann AG, in Japan with Sumitomo Corporation and Internet Initiative Japan, in Korea with Mirae Corporation and in Asia with Singapore Telecom. Most recently, the company announced that it launched localized sites in six South and Central American countries. Lycos currently offers localized versions of its service in Argentina, Belgium, Brazil, Chile, Denmark, France, Germany, Italy, Japan, Korea, Luxembourg, the Netherlands, Norway, Mexico, Peru, Spain, Sweden and Switzerland.

FINANCIALS: Sales and profits are in thousands of dollars—add 000 to get the full amount.

Notes regarding 1999: (1999 sales and profits were not available for all companies at press time.)

1999 Sales: $135,500	1999 Profits: $-52,000	
1998 Sales: $56,100	1998 Profits: $-96,900	Stock Ticker: **LCOS**
1997 Sales: $22,300	1997 Profits: $-6,600	Employees: 785
1996 Sales: $5,300	1996 Profits: $-5,100	Fiscal Year Ends: 7/31
1995 Sales: $ 100	1995 Profits: $- 100	

SALARIES/BENEFITS:

Pension Plan:	ESOP Stock Plan:	Profit Sharing:	Top Exec. Salary: $170,000	Bonus: $80,000
Savings Plan:	Stock Purch. Plan:		Second Exec. Salary: $	Bonus: $

COMPETITIVE ADVANTAGE: One of the top Internet portals/Rapid international expansion.

OTHER THOUGHTS:

Apparent Women Officers or Directors: 1
Apparent Minority Officers or Directors: 2
Hot Spot for Advancement for Women/Minorities: Y

LOCATIONS: ("Y" = Yes)

West:	Southwest:	Midwest:	Southeast:	Northeast:	International:
Y	Y	Y		Y	Y

Note: Financial information, benefits and other data can change quickly and may vary from those stated here.

MACROMEDIA INC   www.macromedia.com

Industry Group Code: 5112
Ranks within this company's industry group: Sales: 9   Profits: 38

BUSINESS ACTIVITIES ("Y" = Yes)

Financial Services:	Information/Publ.:	Technology:		Services:	Retailing:	Telecommunications:
Stock Brokerage	Portal/Hub/News	Computer Manuf.		Payments/Transfers	Retailer	Internet Serv. Provider
Mortgages/Loans	On-Line Community	Networking Equip.		Consulting	Auctions	Web Site Host
Banking	Search Engine	Software Manuf.	Y	Advertising/Marketing	Mall	Server Farm
Insurance	Financial Data Publ.	Specialty Equipment		Outsourcing	Tickets/Travel	Specialty Telecom.
Credit Cards	Broadcasting/Music				Price Comparisons	High Speed Access

TYPES OF BUSINESS:

Software Tools and Services
Internet Publishing Tools

BRANDS/DIVISIONS/AFFILIATES:

Shockwave
Authorware
Director
FreeHand
Fontographer
MacroModel
SoundEdit 16
Altsys Corporation

CONTACTS: Note: Officers with more than one job title may be intentionally listed here more than once.

Robert K. Burgess, CEO
Elizabeth A. Nelson, CFO
David R. Mendels, VP-Mktg./Gen. Mgr.-Web Publishing
Michele C. Murgel, VP-Human Resources
Joseph D. Dunn, Sr. VP-Products and Tech.
Stephen D. Fields, CEO-shockwave.com
Sally P. Harris, VP/Controller
Kevin M. Lynch, Sr. VP-Product Dev.
Paul J. Madar, VP-Engineering, Dreamweaver
Linda L. Grant, VP-Worldwide Mfg. And Distribution
Loren E. Hillberg, VP/General Counsel
Brian J. Allum, Sr. VP-Worldwide Field Oper.
Benjamin J. Dillon, VP-Business Dev.
Stephen A. Elop, Sr. VP-Web
James N. White, Sr. VP-Corp. Dev.

Phone: 415-252-2000	Fax: 415-626-0554
Toll-Free: 800-756-9603	
Address: 600 Townsend Street, San Francisco, CA, 94103	

GROWTH PLANS/SPECIAL FEATURES:

Macromedia, Inc. develops, markets and supports software products and technologies for web publishing, multimedia and graphics to create web sites for e-commerce, entertainment, news and information. The company's Internet publishing products, including Director, FreeHand, Dreamweaver, Flash, Fireworks and the Shockwave Player, are influencing web content. Macromedia's learning solutions, Authorware and CourseBuilder for Dreamweaver, enable large companies and educational institutions to author, deliver and manage learning programs over the Internet and corporate intranets. At the end of 1999, Macromedia and Andromedia formed Macromedia eBusiness Solutions Group. Andromedia was named to Computerworld's list of the Top 100 Emerging Companies to Watch in 2000. Integrating the products of both companies will allow developers to create content that has built-in tracking, profiling, modeling, analysis, personalization and reporting capabilities. Recently, Macromedia's Dreamweaver 2 was chosen as Software Product of the Year by the editors of Macworld. The magazine also picked Dreamweaver 2 and Fireworks 2 as best in their respective categories of Best Web Authoring Software and Best Web Graphics Software. Presentations Magazine gave Flash 4 and Macromedia Director Standing Ovation awards. The company's customers include BMW, the US Postal Service, Lucent, Cinemax and Tektronix. Macromedia has 800 employees, is headquartered in California and has multiple offices in the Asia/Pacific, Europe and South America.

FINANCIALS: Sales and profits are in thousands of dollars—add 000 to get the full amount.

Notes regarding 1999: *(1999 sales and profits were not available for all companies at press time.)*

1999 Sales: $149,900	1999 Profits: $19,800	Stock Ticker: **MACR**
1998 Sales: $113,086	1998 Profits: $-6,200	Employees: 553
1997 Sales: $107,365	1997 Profits: $-5,900	Fiscal Year Ends: 3/31
1996 Sales: $116,691	1996 Profits: $23,000	
1995 Sales: $53,700	1995 Profits: $6,500	

SALARIES/BENEFITS:

Pension Plan:	ESOP Stock Plan: Y	Profit Sharing:	Top Exec. Salary: $300,055	Bonus: $185,195
Savings Plan: Y	Stock Purch. Plan:		Second Exec. Salary: $193,804	Bonus: $163,750

COMPETITIVE ADVANTAGE: Award-winning reputation for products/Developing worldwide recognition.

OTHER THOUGHTS:

Apparent Women Officers or Directors: 5
Apparent Minority Officers or Directors:
Hot Spot for Advancement for Women/Minorities: Y

LOCATIONS: ("Y" = Yes)

West:	Southwest:	Midwest:	Southeast:	Northeast:	International:
Y	Y				Y

Note: Financial information, benefits and other data can change quickly and may vary from those stated here.

MAIL.COM INC   www.mail.com

Industry Group Code: 5133D
Ranks within this company's industry group: Sales: 5   Profits: 5

BUSINESS ACTIVITIES ("Y" = Yes)

Financial Services:	Information/Publ.:		Technology:	Services:		Retailing:	Telecommunications:
Stock Brokerage	Portal/Hub/News	Y	Computer Manuf.	Payments/Transfers		Retailer	Internet Serv. Provider
Mortgages/Loans	On-Line Community		Networking Equip.	Consulting		Auctions	Web Site Host
Banking	Search Engine		Software Manuf.	Advertising/Marketing		Mall	Server Farm
Insurance	Financial Data Publ.		Specialty Equipment	Outsourcing	Y	Tickets/Travel	Specialty Telecom.
Credit Cards	Broadcasting/Music					Price Comparisons	High Speed Access

TYPES OF BUSINESS:

E-mail Services

BRANDS/DIVISIONS/AFFILIATES:

Allegro

CONTACTS: Note: Officers with more than one job title may be intentionally listed here more than once.

Gerald Gorman, CEO
Gary Millin, Pres.
Debra McClister, Exec. VP/CFO
Catherine Billon, VP-Mktg./Partner Dev.
Keith Nagel, Dir.-Human Resources
Charles Walden, Exec. VP-Tech.
Colin Jenkins, VP-Systems
David Ambrosia, Exec.VP/General Counsel
Jason Gorevic, VP-Oper.
Michael Agesen, VP-Business Dev.

Phone: 212-425-4200	**Fax:** 212-425-3487
Toll-Free:	
Address: 11 Broadway, 6th Fl., New York, NY, 10004	

GROWTH PLANS/SPECIAL FEATURES:

Mail.com provides a wide variety of e-mail services and options. Mail.com manages seven million e-mail boxes in collaboration with more than 40 web sites and ISPs, featuring quality, reliable, feature-rich outsourced solutions for high-traffic web sites, ISPs, schools, organizations and corporations. The company offers free lifetime e-mail accounts, subscription e-mail accounts and fax and voice mail services. Mail.com's corporate e-mail management is offered through its Allegro subsidiary. Mail.com's partner sites include CNN, National Hockey League, GTE, Snap and Standard and Poor's. With approximately 300 million e-mails per day being sent in the United States, and that number possibly growing to 600 million by 2002, Mail.com has the solutions to meet the needs of web sites, ISPs, business and educational institutions. Revenues are generated through advertising, direct marketing, e-commerce activities, premium services and member subscriptions.

FINANCIALS: Sales and profits are in thousands of dollars—add 000 to get the full amount.

Notes regarding 1999: *(1999 sales and profits were not available for all companies at press time.)*

1999 Sales: $12,709	1999 Profits: $-47,014	**Stock Ticker: MAIL**
1998 Sales: $1,500	1998 Profits: $-12,500	Employees: 92
1997 Sales: $ 200	1997 Profits: $-3,000	Fiscal Year Ends: 12/31
1996 Sales: $	1996 Profits: $- 500	
1995 Sales: $	1995 Profits: $	

SALARIES/BENEFITS:

Pension Plan:	ESOP Stock Plan:	Profit Sharing:	Top Exec. Salary: $207,017	Bonus: $
Savings Plan:	Stock Purch. Plan:		Second Exec. Salary: $180,000	Bonus: $

COMPETITIVE ADVANTAGE: Focus on premium e-mail services.

OTHER THOUGHTS:

Apparent Women Officers or Directors: 3
Apparent Minority Officers or Directors:
Hot Spot for Advancement for Women/Minorities: Y

LOCATIONS: ("Y" = Yes)

West:	Southwest:	Midwest:	Southeast:	Northeast:	International:
Y				Y	Y

MAPQUEST.COM INC   www.mapquest.com

Industry Group Code: 514191
Ranks within this company's industry group: Sales: 10   Profits: 17

BUSINESS ACTIVITIES ("Y" = Yes)

Financial Services:	Information/Publ.:		Technology:	Services:	Retailing:	Telecommunications:
Stock Brokerage	Portal/Hub/News	Y	Computer Manuf.	Payments/Transfers	Retailer	Internet Serv. Provider
Mortgages/Loans	On-Line Community		Networking Equip.	Consulting	Auctions	Web Site Host
Banking	Search Engine		Software Manuf.	Advertising/Marketing	Mall	Server Farm
Insurance	Financial Data Publ.		Specialty Equipment	Outsourcing	Tickets/Travel	Specialty Telecom.
Credit Cards	Broadcasting/Music				Price Comparisons	High Speed Access

TYPES OF BUSINESS:
On-line Mapping Services

BRANDS/DIVISIONS/AFFILIATES:

GROWTH PLANS/SPECIAL FEATURES:

Mapquest.com is a leader in providing advanced mapping solutions. Mapquest.com has a leading web site that allows consumers to get on-line maps, interactive maps and driving directions. The company has been in the business of cartography, digital mapping, mapping software and, most recently, advertising and Internet services, with over 30 years of experience. Mapquest.com has millions of hits per day on its web site, offering driving directions and customized maps simply by entering an origin and a destination. Mapquest.com also offers restaurant, lodging and city information to help with trip planning, and computer applications for information kiosks and hotel reservation systems. The company also provides state-the-art mapping technology products and services for the information publishing industry, including the creation of breakthrough solutions for map and atlas, book and reference publishing, as well as for the commercial Internet, travel, telecommunications and real estate markets. Mapquest's top customers include Yahoo!, National Geographic Society and AAA.

CONTACTS: Note: Officers with more than one job title may be intentionally listed here more than once.

Michael Mulligan, CEO
James Thomas, COO
James Thomas, CFO
David Ingerman, VP-Mktg.
Dave Bowen, Mgr.-Human Resources
James Hilliard, VP-Digital Mapping Services
Robert Binford, Corp. Controller
William Muenster, Sr. VP-Dev./Production
Michael Nappi, VP-Business Solutions
James Killick, VP-Product Management

Phone: 212-904-0400	Fax: 212-529-8742
Toll-Free:	
Address: 257 Park Ave. South, Ste. 303, New York, NY, 10010	

FINANCIALS: Sales and profits are in thousands of dollars—add 000 to get the full amount.
Notes regarding 1999: *(1999 sales and profits were not available for all companies at press time.)*

1999 Sales: $	1999 Profits: $	Stock Ticker: **MQST**
1998 Sales: $24,700	1998 Profits: $-3,200	Employees: 222
1997 Sales: $21,400	1997 Profits: $-7,600	Fiscal Year Ends: 12/31
1996 Sales: $19,600	1996 Profits: $-1,300	
1995 Sales: $14,100	1995 Profits: $	

SALARIES/BENEFITS:

Pension Plan:	ESOP Stock Plan:	Profit Sharing:	Top Exec. Salary: $194,769	Bonus: $
Savings Plan:	Stock Purch. Plan:		Second Exec. Salary: $177,322	Bonus: $

COMPETITIVE ADVANTAGE: Rapid growth/Focus on in-depth delivery of maps.

OTHER THOUGHTS:

Apparent Women Officers or Directors:
Apparent Minority Officers or Directors:
Hot Spot for Advancement for Women/Minorities:

LOCATIONS: ("Y" = Yes)

West:	Southwest:	Midwest:	Southeast:	Northeast:	International:
Y					Y

Note: Financial information, benefits and other data can change quickly and may vary from those stated here.

MARIMBA INC   www.marimba.com

Industry Group Code: 5112
Ranks within this company's industry group: Sales: 41   Profits: 35

BUSINESS ACTIVITIES ("Y" = Yes)

Financial Services:	Information/Publ.:	Technology:		Services:	Retailing:	Telecommunications:
Stock Brokerage	Portal/Hub/News	Computer Manuf.		Payments/Transfers	Retailer	Internet Serv. Provider
Mortgages/Loans	On-Line Community	Networking Equip.		Consulting	Auctions	Web Site Host
Banking	Search Engine	Software Manuf.	Y	Advertising/Marketing	Mall	Server Farm
Insurance	Financial Data Publ.	Specialty Equipment		Outsourcing	Tickets/Travel	Specialty Telecom.
Credit Cards	Broadcasting/Music				Price Comparisons	High Speed Access

TYPES OF BUSINESS:
Software-E-commerce

BRANDS/DIVISIONS/AFFILIATES:
Castanet
DocService

GROWTH PLANS/SPECIAL FEATURES:

Marimba provides Internet-based software solutions that enable companies to expand market reach, speed up business processes and strenghthen relationships with customers and business partners. Marimba's software allows companies to install, update and maintain software applications within a company's LAN or WAN or over the Internet. The Castanet line provides management infrastructure for organizations to build e-business solutions. Castanet includes built-in security features for secure Internet transactions and methods to manage e-business applications throughout the entire life cycle, from development through installation and routine maintenance. Charles Schwab, Sun Microsystems, the U.S. Air Force, The Home Depot and Nortel Networks all utilize the Castanet advantage. The company is doing well; for the first half of 1999, revenues rose 95% over that of 1998 to $13 million. Increases in licensing and maintenance for the Castanet products account for the increased revenue.

CONTACTS:
Note: Officers with more than one job title may be intentionally listed here more than once.

Kim K. Polese, CEO/Pres.
Steven P. Williams, Exec. VP/COO
Fred M. Gerson, CFO/VP-Finance
Jacqueline Ross, VP-Mktg.
Arthur A. van Hoff, Chief Tech. Officer
Robert E. Currie, VP-Engineering
Thomas E. Banahan, VP-Dev.
Bob Maynard, VP-Worldwide Sales

Phone: 650-930-5282	Fax: 650-930-5600
Toll-Free:	
Address: 440 Clyde Ave., Mountain View, CA, 94043	

FINANCIALS:
Sales and profits are in thousands of dollars—add 000 to get the full amount.
Notes regarding 1999: *(1999 sales and profits were not available for all companies at press time.)*

1999 Sales: $31,400	1999 Profits: $-4,200	**Stock Ticker: MRBA**
1998 Sales: $17,100	1998 Profits: $-5,700	Employees: 145
1997 Sales: $	1997 Profits: $-1,200	Fiscal Year Ends: 12/31
1996 Sales: $	1996 Profits: $	
1995 Sales: $	1995 Profits: $	

SALARIES/BENEFITS:

Pension Plan:	ESOP Stock Plan:	Profit Sharing:	Top Exec. Salary: $250,000	Bonus: $
Savings Plan:	Stock Purch. Plan:		Second Exec. Salary: $225,000	Bonus: $

COMPETITIVE ADVANTAGE: Castanet offers the ablity to install and maintain a wide variety of applications.

OTHER THOUGHTS:

Apparent Women Officers or Directors: 2
Apparent Minority Officers or Directors: 2
Hot Spot for Advancement for Women/Minorities: Y

LOCATIONS: ("Y" = Yes)

West:	Southwest:	Midwest:	Southeast:	Northeast:	International:
Y	Y	Y	Y	Y	Y

MARKETWATCH.COM INC   www.cbs.marketwatch.com

Industry Group Code: 5141
Ranks within this company's industry group: Sales: 2   Profits: 3

BUSINESS ACTIVITIES ("Y" = Yes)

Financial Services:	Information/Publ.:		Technology:	Services:	Retailing:	Telecommunications:
Stock Brokerage	Portal/Hub/News	Y	Computer Manuf.	Payments/Transfers	Retailer	Internet Serv. Provider
Mortgages/Loans	On-Line Community		Networking Equip.	Consulting	Auctions	Web Site Host
Banking	Search Engine		Software Manuf.	Advertising/Marketing	Mall	Server Farm
Insurance	Financial Data Publ.	Y	Specialty Equipment	Outsourcing	Tickets/Travel	Specialty Telecom.
Credit Cards	Broadcasting/Music				Price Comparisons	High Speed Access

TYPES OF BUSINESS:
On-line Financial Information

BRANDS/DIVISIONS/AFFILIATES:
Big Charts, Inc.
CBS
Data Broadcasting Corp.

CONTACTS: *Note: Officers with more than one job title may be intentionally listed here more than once.*
Larry S. Kramer, CEO
Philip D. Hotchkiss, Pres.
John Platt, VP-Finance/CFO
Michele Chaboudy, VP-Mktg.
Jamie Thinglestad, Chief Tech. Officer
Joe Brichler, Controller
William Bishop, VP-Business Dev.
Richard Yang, Dir.-Mktg.
Thom Calandra, Editor-in-Chief/VP-News

Phone: 415-733-0500	Fax: 415-392-1972
Toll-Free:	
Address: 825 Battery St., San Francisco, CA, 94111	

GROWTH PLANS/SPECIAL FEATURES:
MarketWatch.com offers an on-line look into the financial world. Services include real-time business news, IPO reports, mutual fund data, financial programming and personal finance and analytical tools, free of charge. Subscriptions are available that enable such services as real-time financial data (MarketWatch RT) and streaming real-time quotes from all major U.S. exchanges (MarketWatch LIVE). MarketWatch.com is jointly owned by CBS and Data Broadcasting Corp. The company receives approximately 250,000 hits per day, serving nearly two million pages of data per day. The information delivered by MarketWatch.com allows visitors to act early by providing information as it happens. The company offers special reports from leading experts in the financial field and these exclusive stories cannot be found anywhere else. The company provides decision-making tools through multiple personal portfolios, market and company research, interday and technical charting, mutual and money market fund data, direct brokerage access and reliable delayed quotes. A recent increase in revenue reflects sales of advertising on the web site, subscriptions and increased marketing.

FINANCIALS: Sales and profits are in thousands of dollars—add 000 to get the full amount.
Notes regarding 1999: Pro forma *(1999 sales and profits were not available for all companies at press time.)*

1999 Sales: $24,900	1999 Profits: $-30,100	Stock Ticker: **MKTW**
1998 Sales: $7,000	1998 Profits: $-12,400	Employees: 65
1997 Sales: $1,800	1997 Profits: $-1,000	Fiscal Year Ends: 12/31
1996 Sales: $ 600	1996 Profits: $-1,300	
1995 Sales: $	1995 Profits: $	

SALARIES/BENEFITS:

Pension Plan:	ESOP Stock Plan:	Profit Sharing:	Top Exec. Salary: $220,500	Bonus: $
Savings Plan:	Stock Purch. Plan:		Second Exec. Salary: $200,806	Bonus: $

COMPETITIVE ADVANTAGE: Affiliation with CBS.

OTHER THOUGHTS:

Apparent Women Officers or Directors: 1
Apparent Minority Officers or Directors:
Hot Spot for Advancement for Women/Minorities:

LOCATIONS: ("Y" = Yes)

West:	Southwest:	Midwest:	Southeast:	Northeast:	International:
Y				Y	Y

MCI WORLDCOM INC   www.wcom.com

Industry Group Code: 5133B
Ranks within this company's industry group: Sales: 2   Profits: 6

BUSINESS ACTIVITIES ("Y" = Yes)

Financial Services:	Information/Publ.:	Technology:	Services:	Retailing:	Telecommunications:	
Stock Brokerage	Portal/Hub/News	Computer Manuf.	Payments/Transfers	Retailer	Internet Serv. Provider	Y
Mortgages/Loans	On-Line Community	Networking Equip.	Consulting	Auctions	Web Site Host	Y
Banking	Search Engine	Software Manuf.	Advertising/Marketing	Mall	Server Farm	Y
Insurance	Financial Data Publ.	Specialty Equipment	Outsourcing	Tickets/Travel	Specialty Telecom.	Y
Credit Cards	Broadcasting/Music			Price Comparisons	High Speed Access	Y

TYPES OF BUSINESS:

Long Distance Telephone Service

BRANDS/DIVISIONS/AFFILIATES:

UUNET
Sprint
Skytel

CONTACTS: Note: Officers with more than one job title may be intentionally listed here more than once.

Bernard J. Ebbers, CEO
Bernard J. Ebbers, Pres.
Scott Sullivan, CFO
Dennis Sickle, VP-Human Resources
Scott Sullivan, Corp. Sec.

Phone: 601-360-8600	Fax: 601-974-8350
Toll-Free:	
Address: 500 Clinton Center Drive, Clinton, MS, 39060	

GROWTH PLANS/SPECIAL FEATURES:

MCI WorldCom provides local, long distance and Internet telecommunications services. MCI WorldCom is second only to AT&T in the U.S. long distance market. Through MCI WorldCom's fiber optic networks, digital microwave and satellite stations, the company provides local and international telecommunications and Internet services in over 65 countries to businesses, governments and consumers. One of the company's subsidiaries, UUNET, provides Internet communication solutions to businesses with a complete line of Internet, extranet and intranet services in over 114 countries, including Internet access, web hosting, remote access and other value-added options. In recent news, MCI WorldCom acquired rival long distance provider Sprint, a $129 billion deal that added a nationwide PCS network to MCI WorldCom's long list of services. After the close of the merger, which is estimated to be near the end of 2000, the company will be renamed WorldCom. MCI WorldCom also has plans to become a provider of high-speed wireless Internet access in the near future. The company released a new prepaid paging service that eliminates the hassles of an application process, long-term contract commitment and credit check.

FINANCIALS: Sales and profits are in thousands of dollars—add 000 to get the full amount.

Notes regarding 1999: Through 9 months (1999 sales and profits were not available for all companies at press time.)

1999 Sales: $27,130,000	1999 Profits: $2,660,000	Stock Ticker: WCOM
1998 Sales: $17,678,000	1998 Profits: $-2,669,000	Employees: 77,000
1997 Sales: $7,351,400	1997 Profits: $383,700	Fiscal Year Ends: 12/31
1996 Sales: $4,485,100	1996 Profits: $-2,213,300	
1995 Sales: $3,639,900	1995 Profits: $267,700	

SALARIES/BENEFITS:

Pension Plan:	ESOP Stock Plan: Y	Profit Sharing:	Top Exec. Salary: $1,050,000	Bonus: $9,380,950
Savings Plan: Y	Stock Purch. Plan:		Second Exec. Salary: $935,000	Bonus: $7,115,000

COMPETITIVE ADVANTAGE: Extremely aggressive management has used a bold acquisition strategy to build one of the world's largest telecom companies in a short period of time.

OTHER THOUGHTS:

Apparent Women Officers or Directors:
Apparent Minority Officers or Directors:
Hot Spot for Advancement for Women/Minorities:

LOCATIONS: ("Y" = Yes)

West:	Southwest:	Midwest:	Southeast:	Northeast:	International:
Y	Y	Y	Y	Y	Y

MEDIA METRIX INC
www.mediametrix.com

Industry Group Code: 54189A
Ranks within this company's industry group: Sales: 11   Profits: 9

BUSINESS ACTIVITIES ("Y" = Yes)

Financial Services:	Information/Publ.:	Technology:	Services:		Retailing:		Telecommunications:
Stock Brokerage	Portal/Hub/News	Computer Manuf.	Payments/Transfers		Retailer		Internet Serv. Provider
Mortgages/Loans	On-Line Community	Networking Equip.	Consulting		Auctions		Web Site Host
Banking	Search Engine	Software Manuf.	Advertising/Marketing	Y	Mall		Server Farm
Insurance	Financial Data Publ.	Specialty Equipment	Outsourcing		Tickets/Travel		Specialty Telecom.
Credit Cards	Broadcasting/Music				Price Comparisons		High Speed Access

TYPES OF BUSINESS:
Advertising-Web Measurement

BRANDS/DIVISIONS/AFFILIATES:
AdRelevance
The NPD Group
RelevantKnowledge

CONTACTS: *Note: Officers with more than one job title may be intentionally listed here more than once.*
Tod Johnson, CEO
Mary Ann Packo, Pres./COO
Thomas A. Lynch, CFO
Doug McFarland, Sr. VP-Sales
Cynthia Fico, Dir.-Human Resources
Bruce Ryon, Sr. VP/Chief Tech. Analyst
Jim D'Arcangelo, Sr.VP-Mktg. And Business Dev.
Lindsey Draves, VP-Client Info.
Thomas A. Lynch, Treas.

Phone: 212-460-7980	Fax: 212-533-3036
Toll-Free:	
Address: 35 E. 21st St., 3rd Fl., New York, NY, 10010	

GROWTH PLANS/SPECIAL FEATURES:

Media Metrix, Inc. is leading the way in Internet and digital media measurement services to support Internet growth through advertising and e-commerce. Media Metrix tracks Internet audiences for advertisers, advertising agencies, Internet properties, technology companies and financial institutions. The company also measures e-commerce activity. Media Metrix merged with its chief rival RelevantKnowledge to become a leader in the field of Internet media measurement. Customers use the information provided by Media Metrix to understand consumer behavior, develop e-commerce strategies, make investment decisions, plan marketing strategies and gain a competitive edge in market intelligence. Recently, Media Metrix acquired AdRelevance, an innovator and pioneer in Internet advertising measurement and intelligent agent ad tracking technology. This will add depth to Media Metrix by providing customers with a product portfolio that now includes data tracking on ad spending, ad placement and creative and competitive on-line advertising market share. When used together, this data will provide a more complete picture of the digital marketplace for all of Media Metrix's customers.

FINANCIALS: Sales and profits are in thousands of dollars—add 000 to get the full amount.
Notes regarding 1999: *(1999 sales and profits were not available for all companies at press time.)*

1999 Sales: $20,500	1999 Profits: $-21,908	Stock Ticker: **MMXI**
1998 Sales: $6,300	1998 Profits: $-7,200	Employees: 88
1997 Sales: $3,200	1997 Profits: $-4,600	Fiscal Year Ends: 12/31
1996 Sales: $1,000	1996 Profits: $-3,400	
1995 Sales: $	1995 Profits: $	

SALARIES/BENEFITS:

Pension Plan:	ESOP Stock Plan:	Profit Sharing:	Top Exec. Salary: $216,500	Bonus: $
Savings Plan:	Stock Purch. Plan:		Second Exec. Salary: $199,500	Bonus: $

COMPETITIVE ADVANTAGE: Absolute market leader in Internet traffic intelligence.

OTHER THOUGHTS:

Apparent Women Officers or Directors: 2
Apparent Minority Officers or Directors:
Hot Spot for Advancement for Women/Minorities:

LOCATIONS: ("Y" = Yes)

West:	Southwest:	Midwest:	Southeast:	Northeast:	International:
Y			Y	Y	

Note: Financial information, benefits and other data can change quickly and may vary from those stated here.

MEDIUM4.COM INC   www.medium4.com

Industry Group Code: 51311B
Ranks within this company's industry group: Sales: Profits:

BUSINESS ACTIVITIES ("Y" = Yes)

Financial Services:	Information/Publ.:		Technology:	Services:	Retailing:	Telecommunications:
Stock Brokerage	Portal/Hub/News		Computer Manuf.	Payments/Transfers	Retailer	Internet Serv. Provider
Mortgages/Loans	On-Line Community		Networking Equip.	Consulting	Auctions	Web Site Host
Banking	Search Engine		Software Manuf.	Advertising/Marketing	Mall	Server Farm
Insurance	Financial Data Publ.		Specialty Equipment	Outsourcing	Tickets/Travel	Specialty Telecom.
Credit Cards	Broadcasting/Music	Y			Price Comparisons	High Speed Access

TYPES OF BUSINESS:

On-line Foreign Broadcasting

BRANDS/DIVISIONS/AFFILIATES:

The World Music
Worldcast
Medium4.com
ForeignTV.com

CONTACTS: *Note: Officers with more than one job title may be intentionally listed here more than once.*

Jonathan Braun, CEO
Albert T. Primo, Pres.
Graham Cannon, VP-Mktg.
Marc D. Leve, VP-Legal Affairs
Elorian C. Landers, VP-Corp.
Dennis Oppenheimer, VP-Music
Yeon S. Hong, VP-Creative

Phone: 212-206-1121	Fax:
Toll-Free:	
Address: 162 Fifth Ave., Ste. 1005A, New York, NY, 10010	

GROWTH PLANS/SPECIAL FEATURES:

Medium4.com (formerly foreignTV.com) is an Internet broadcaster that produces streaming media content from locations around the world. Users can get information, on-demand and in English, about global news, fashion, arts, culture, travel, adventure, sports and entertainment. The company's content is updated daily, including interviews and web-only features from ForeignTV.com reporters. The usage of streaming video technology allows the viewer to watch live or on-demand programming without having to download content to the user's hard drive. ForeignTV.com is building a series of in-depth location-specific sites, such as ParisTV.com, BeijingTV.com and RomeTV.com, which will immerse users in each area. These sites will provide a sense of what it is like to visit, live and work in a foreign location, as well as feature video news reports and video tours of different destinations. The site's flagship daily newsmagazine, Worldcast, includes special reports and interviews with world leaders. The World Music site lets the user listen to international artists and genres, plus special reports, biographies and interviews. ForeignTV.com's audience includes business and leisure travelers, students and people just interested in interacting with the world. The company generates most of its revenue from advertising.

FINANCIALS: Sales and profits are in thousands of dollars—add 000 to get the full amount.

Notes regarding 1999: *(1999 sales and profits were not available for all companies at press time.)*

1999 Sales: $ 5	1999 Profits: $-2,381	**Stock Ticker: METV**
1998 Sales: $	1998 Profits: $	Employees:
1997 Sales: $	1997 Profits: $	Fiscal Year Ends: 12/31
1996 Sales: $	1996 Profits: $	
1995 Sales: $	1995 Profits: $	

SALARIES/BENEFITS:

Pension Plan:	ESOP Stock Plan:	Profit Sharing:	Top Exec. Salary: $	Bonus: $
Savings Plan:	Stock Purch. Plan:		Second Exec. Salary: $	Bonus: $

COMPETITIVE ADVANTAGE: Unique niche in content and audience.

OTHER THOUGHTS:

Apparent Women Officers or Directors:
Apparent Minority Officers or Directors: 1
Hot Spot for Advancement for Women/Minorities:

LOCATIONS: ("Y" = Yes)

West:	Southwest:	Midwest:	Southeast:	Northeast:	International:
				Y	Y

METACREATIONS CORP   www.metacreations.com

Industry Group Code: 5112
Ranks within this company's industry group: Sales: 22   Profits: 70

BUSINESS ACTIVITIES ("Y" = Yes)

Financial Services:	Information/Publ.:	Technology:		Services:	Retailing:	Telecommunications:
Stock Brokerage	Portal/Hub/News	Computer Manuf.		Payments/Transfers	Retailer	Internet Serv. Provider
Mortgages/Loans	On-Line Community	Networking Equip.		Consulting	Auctions	Web Site Host
Banking	Search Engine	Software Manuf.	Y	Advertising/Marketing	Mall	Server Farm
Insurance	Financial Data Publ.	Specialty Equipment		Outsourcing	Tickets/Travel	Specialty Telecom.
Credit Cards	Broadcasting/Music				Price Comparisons	High Speed Access

TYPES OF BUSINESS:

Software-Professional Graphics

BRANDS/DIVISIONS/AFFILIATES:

MetaStream
MetaFlash
Ray Dream, Inc.
Dive Laboratories
Real Time Geometry

GROWTH PLANS/SPECIAL FEATURES:

MetaCreations designs, develops and supports innovative 2-D and 3-D visualization computing software for the creation and editing of computer graphic images and digital art for the Internet and print and computer applications. Rapid growth in revenues has enabled MetaCreations to become one of the world's largest developers and publishers of graphics software. With offices worldwide (including Ireland, Germany, Japan and the United Kingdom), MetaCreations has over 8,000 distributors in more than 50 countries. MetaCreations' wide variety of products serves customers that include professional developers, graphic artists, web developers and home users.

CONTACTS: Note: Officers with more than one job title may be intentionally listed here more than once.

Gary L. Lauer, CEO
Gary L. Lauer, Pres.
Jay Jennings, CFO/Sr. VP-Finance
John Hartnett, Sr. VP-Mktg.
Kari Zoni, Dir. Human Resources
Mark Zimmer, Chief Tech. Officer
Timothy Immel, VP-Info. Tech.
Pierre Berkaloff, VP-Engineering
John Hartnett, Sr. VP-Oper.
John Leddy, Sr. VP-Product Dev.
Teresa A. Bridwell, VP-Corp. Comm.

Phone: 805-566-6200	Fax: 805-566-6385
Toll-Free:	
Address: 6303 Carpinteria Ave, Carpinteria, CA, 93013	

FINANCIALS: Sales and profits are in thousands of dollars—add 000 to get the full amount.

Notes regarding 1999: *(1999 sales and profits were not available for all companies at press time.)*

1999 Sales: $10,179	1999 Profits: $-40,032	Stock Ticker: **MCRE**
1998 Sales: $42,800	1998 Profits: $-19,800	Employees: 218
1997 Sales: $69,100	1997 Profits: $-8,200	Fiscal Year Ends: 12/31
1996 Sales: $28,000	1996 Profits: $-9,200	
1995 Sales: $16,700	1995 Profits: $- 500	

SALARIES/BENEFITS:

Pension Plan:	ESOP Stock Plan:	Profit Sharing:	Top Exec. Salary: $288,189	Bonus: $
Savings Plan:	Stock Purch. Plan:		Second Exec. Salary: $273,333	Bonus: $

COMPETITIVE ADVANTAGE: Worldwide distributor network includes 8,000 dealers in over 50 nations.

OTHER THOUGHTS:

	LOCATIONS: ("Y" = Yes)					
	West:	Southwest:	Midwest:	Southeast:	Northeast:	International:
Apparent Women Officers or Directors:	Y				Y	Y
Apparent Minority Officers or Directors:						
Hot Spot for Advancement for Women/Minorities:						

METRICOM INC   www.metricom.com

Industry Group Code: 33421
Ranks within this company's industry group: Sales: 3   Profits: 3

BUSINESS ACTIVITIES ("Y" = Yes)

Financial Services:	Information/Publ.:	Technology:		Services:		Retailing:	Telecommunications:	
Stock Brokerage	Portal/Hub/News	Computer Manuf.		Payments/Transfers		Retailer	Internet Serv. Provider	Y
Mortgages/Loans	On-Line Community	Networking Equip.	Y	Consulting		Auctions	Web Site Host	
Banking	Search Engine	Software Manuf.		Advertising/Marketing		Mall	Server Farm	
Insurance	Financial Data Publ.	Specialty Equipment	Y	Outsourcing		Tickets/Travel	Specialty Telecom.	Y
Credit Cards	Broadcasting/Music					Price Comparisons	High Speed Access	

TYPES OF BUSINESS:

Wireless Network Services
On-line Services

BRANDS/DIVISIONS/AFFILIATES:

Ricochet Private Network
UtiliNet Private Network

CONTACTS: Note: Officers with more than one job title may be intentionally listed here more than once.

Timothy A. Dreisbach, Pres./CEO
Gary M. Green, Exec. VP/COO
James Wall, CFO
John Wernke, Sr. VP-Mktg./Sales
Mike Ritter, Chief Tech. Officer
David Kistner, Controller
Ralph B. Muse, Exec. VP-Engineering
Robert Mott, Sr. VP-Mfg.
Ralph B. Muse, Exec. VP-Oper
Jay Kistner, Treas.

Phone: 409-399-8200	Fax: 408-354-1024
Toll-Free: 800-GO-WIRELESS	
Address: 980 University Avenue, Los Gatos, CA, 95030-2375	

GROWTH PLANS/SPECIAL FEATURES:

Metricom, Inc. is a leading provider of wide area wireless data communications solutions. Metricom provides leading edge technology for wireless and mobile data access, with a focus on three key mobile Internet areas: access technology, network design and buildout and network operation. The company designs, develops and markets wireless network products and services that provide low-cost, high-performance, easy-to-use data communications that can be used in a broad range of personal computer and industrial applications. Metricom's subscriber-based Ricochet products and services division provides portable and desk-top computer users with high-performance, cost-effective wireless access to the Internet, private intranets, local area networks, e-mail and other on-line services. Metricom's options for its industrial customers include virtual private networks, the Utilinet Private Network and the new Ricochet Private Network. These options give customers wide varieties of wireless on-line services quickly, securely and with minimal server impact, in addition to being specifically tailored for each customer.   Metricom's coverage areas include Washington D.C., San Francisco, Seattle, select areas in New York and select hotels, airports and universities. Currently, Metricom is preparing for the launch of Ricochet2, the next generation Ricochet modem.

FINANCIALS: Sales and profits are in thousands of dollars—add 000 to get the full amount.

Notes regarding 1999: Through 9 months (1999 sales and profits were not available for all companies at press time.)

1999 Sales: $13,600	1999 Profits: $-48,200	Stock Ticker: **MCOM**
1998 Sales: $15,900	1998 Profits: $-84,200	Employees: 310
1997 Sales: $13,400	1997 Profits: $-59,300	Fiscal Year Ends: 12/31
1996 Sales: $7,200	1996 Profits: $-39,300	
1995 Sales: $5,800	1995 Profits: $-23,500	

SALARIES/BENEFITS:

Pension Plan:	ESOP Stock Plan: Y	Profit Sharing: Y	Top Exec. Salary: $533,750	Bonus: $
Savings Plan: Y	Stock Purch. Plan:		Second Exec. Salary: $287,774	Bonus: $

COMPETITIVE ADVANTAGE: Equipment provides wireless access to the Internet.

OTHER THOUGHTS:

Apparent Women Officers or Directors:
Apparent Minority Officers or Directors:
Hot Spot for Advancement for Women/Minorities:

LOCATIONS: ("Y" = Yes)

West:	Southwest:	Midwest:	Southeast:	Northeast:	International:
Y	Y			Y	

MICROSOFT CORP   www.microsoft.com

Industry Group Code: 5112
Ranks within this company's industry group: Sales: 1   Profits: 1

BUSINESS ACTIVITIES ("Y" = Yes)

Financial Services:	Information/Publ.:		Technology:		Services:	Retailing:		Telecommunications:	
Stock Brokerage	Portal/Hub/News	Y	Computer Manuf.		Payments/Transfers	Retailer		Internet Serv. Provider	Y
Mortgages/Loans	On-Line Community	Y	Networking Equip.		Consulting	Auctions		Web Site Host	Y
Banking	Search Engine.	Y	Software Manuf.	Y	Advertising/Marketing	Mall		Server Farm	
Insurance	Financial Data Publ.	Y	Specialty Equipment	Y	Outsourcing	Tickets/Travel		Specialty Telecom.	
Credit Cards	Broadcasting/Music					Price Comparisons	Y	High Speed Access	

TYPES OF BUSINESS:

Software Manufacturer
Multimedia
On-line Services
Book Publishing
Entertainment and Broadcasting
Computer Peripherals
Internet Access Appliances
Venture Capital

BRANDS/DIVISIONS/AFFILIATES:

MSN.COM
MSNBC
Microsoft Network
Investor
Sidewalk
Comcast
WebTV

CONTACTS: *Note: Officers with more than one job title may be intentionally listed here more than once.*

Steve Ballmer, CEO
Robert J. Herbold, Exec. VP/COO
Greg Maffei, Sr. VP-Finance/CFO
Jeffrey S. Raikes, Group VP-Sales and Support
Chris Williams, Human Resources
Paul Maritz, Group VP Dovolopor Group
Nathan P. Myhrvold, Group VP/Chief Tech. Officer
Brad Chase, Sr. VP-Consumer & Commerce Group
Jim Allchin, Sr. VP-Business & Enterprise Div.
Bob Muglia, Sr. VP-Business Productivity Group
Bill Neukom, Sr. VP-Law and Corporate Affairs
Mike Murray, VP-Admin.
Laura Jennings, VP-Worldwide Strategic Planning
Mich Mathews, VP-Corp. Comm. Group
Jon DeVaan, Sr. VP-Consumer & Commerce Gr.
Richard Belluzzo, Group VP-Consumer & Commerce
William Gates III, Chairman/Chief Software Architect
Orlando Ayala, Sr. VP-South Pacific and Americas Region

Phone: 425-882-8080	Fax: 206-883-8101
Toll-Free: 800-285-7772	
Address: One Microsoft Way, Redmond, WA, 98052-6399	

GROWTH PLANS/SPECIAL FEATURES:

Microsoft, the world's number one software company, develops, manufactures, licenses, sells and supports a wide range of products. The company offers on-line services, computer books and input devices (including operating systems for intelligent devices, personal computers (PCs) and servers), server applications for client/server environments, business and consumer productivity applications, software development tools and Internet and Intranet software and technologies. These products include the Windows and NT operating systems, Excel spreadsheets, word processing programs (MS Word), presentation tools (Power Point) and reference works (Encarta). The company recently purchased WebTV, which gave it an excellent base of technology in cable modems. Microsoft also made an investment in cable operator Comcast. Windows CE software will be one of the operating systems for what may eventually be 25 million cable modems to be purchased by cable operator TCI and its affiliates. Microsoft revamped and upgraded its Microsoft Network on-line service. It also entered into joint ventures with the NBC television network to form MSNBC news programming. Microsoft's web site receives five million hits a day and contains 500,000 pages.

Microsoft provides relocation expenses and offers health club memberships to employees. The company offers benefits such as paid infant care leave and the Counseling Assistance Referral and Educational Services (CARES). Most employees are eligible for stock options. In fact, the company has created more employee-millionaires than any other firm in history. In mid-1999, Microsoft raised its target for base salaries to average in the top one-third of software industry salaries. Nearly 40% of the company's new hires in 1999 came from employee referrals.

FINANCIALS: Sales and profits are in thousands of dollars—add 000 to get the full amount.

Notes regarding 1999: *(1999 sales and profits were not available for all companies at press time.)*

1999 Sales: $19,747,000	1999 Profits: $7,785,000	Stock Ticker: **MSFT**
1998 Sales: $14,484,000	1998 Profits: $4,490,000	Employees: 31,396
1997 Sales: $11,358,000	1997 Profits: $3,454,000	Fiscal Year Ends: 6/30
1996 Sales: $8,671,000	1996 Profits: $2,195,000	
1995 Sales: $5,937,000	1995 Profits: $1,453,000	

SALARIES/BENEFITS:

Pension Plan:	ESOP Stock Plan:	Profit Sharing:	Top Exec. Salary: $536,127	Bonus: $673,096
Savings Plan: Y	Stock Purch. Plan: Y		Second Exec. Salary: $384,088	Bonus: $329,842

COMPETITIVE ADVANTAGE: Owns industry-standard PC operating systems and office applications.

OTHER THOUGHTS:

	LOCATIONS: ("Y" = Yes)					
		West:	Southwest:	Midwest:	Southeast:	Northeast:	International:

Apparent Women Officers or Directors: 4
Apparent Minority Officers or Directors: 1
Hot Spot for Advancement for Women/Minorities: Y

West:	Southwest:	Midwest:	Southeast:	Northeast:	International:
Y	Y	Y	Y	Y	Y

Note: Financial information, benefits and other data can change quickly and may vary from those stated here.

MINDSPRING ENTERPRISES INC
www.mindspring.net

Industry Group Code: 51339
Ranks within this company's industry group: Sales: 5 Profits: 1

BUSINESS ACTIVITIES ("Y" = Yes)

Financial Services:	Information/Publ.:	Technology:	Services:		Retailing:	Telecommunications:	
Stock Brokerage	Portal/Hub/News	Computer Manuf.	Payments/Transfers		Retailer	Internet Serv. Provider	Y
Mortgages/Loans	On-Line Community	Networking Equip.	Consulting		Auctions	Web Site Host	Y
Banking	Search Engine	Software Manuf.	Advertising/Marketing		Mall	Server Farm	Y
Insurance	Financial Data Publ.	Specialty Equipment	Outsourcing	Y	Tickets/Travel	Specialty Telecom.	
Credit Cards	Broadcasting/Music				Price Comparisons	High Speed Access	Y

TYPES OF BUSINESS:

Internet Service Provider
Co-Location

BRANDS/DIVISIONS/AFFILIATES:

SpryNet
Sbnet
Internet Direct
Earthlink

CONTACTS:
Note: Officers with more than one job title may be intentionally listed here more than once.

Charles M. Brewer, CEO
Michael S. McQuary, Pres./COO
Juliet Reising, CFO
Lance Weatherby, Exec. VP- Sales and Mktg.
John Bushfield, VP- Human Resources
Gregory J. Stromberg, Exec.VP- Office of Tech.
Steve Roberts, VP- Info. Tech.
Brad Ferguson, Controller
Drew Hobson, VP- Engineering
Samuel R. DeSimone Jr., Exec.VP/General Counsel
Ed Douglas, VP- Business Dev.
Susan F. Nicholson, VP- Web Design
Dave Baker, VP- Legal and Regulatory Affairs
Carter W. Calle, VP- Call Centers

Phone: 404-815-0770	Fax: 404-815-8805
Toll-Free: 800-719-4664	
Address: 1430 West Peachtree, Suite 400, Atlanta, GA, 30309	

GROWTH PLANS/SPECIAL FEATURES:

MindSpring Enterprises, Inc. is a national Internet service provider that focuses on serving individuals and small businesses, allowing them to communicate, retrieve and publish information on the Internet. The company offers dial-up Internet access, web hosting, high-speed Internet access, web page design, domain name registration, 800 service and customer web server co-location. MindSpring provides easy-to-use access by offering customized software and customer support. The company purchased the subscriber bases of SpryNet, Sbnet and Internet Direct, and recently merged with Earthlink, creating a subscriber base of about 2.5 million people. The company offers local Internet access in more than 890 locations throughout the U.S. PC Computing and PC World magazines recently chose MindSpring as the Best Internet Service Provider. Home Office Computing, SmartMoney Interactive and C-Net have all named MindSpring as a best buy. MindSpring received the highest ranking in overall customer satisfaction among ISPs in an independent J.D. Power and Associates study. The company has partnerships with Patagonia, Sierra On Line, IBM and Guthy-Renker Corporation.

FINANCIALS:
Sales and profits are in thousands of dollars—add 000 to get the full amount.
Notes regarding 1999: *(1999 sales and profits were not available for all companies at press time.)*

1999 Sales: $235,818	1999 Profits: $-78,155	
1998 Sales: $114,700	1998 Profits: $10,500	Stock Ticker: **MSPG**
1997 Sales: $52,600	1997 Profits: $-4,100	Employees: 1,600
1996 Sales: $18,100	1996 Profits: $-7,600	Fiscal Year Ends: 12/31
1995 Sales: $2,200	1995 Profits: $-2,000	

SALARIES/BENEFITS:

Pension Plan:	ESOP Stock Plan: Y	Profit Sharing:	Top Exec. Salary: $163,750	Bonus: $107,032
Savings Plan: Y	Stock Purch. Plan:		Second Exec. Salary: $136,458	Bonus: $125,000

COMPETITIVE ADVANTAGE:
Rapid growth due to one of the largest on-line subscriber bases in th U.S.

OTHER THOUGHTS:

Apparent Women Officers or Directors: 3
Apparent Minority Officers or Directors:
Hot Spot for Advancement for Women/Minorities: Y

LOCATIONS: ("Y" = Yes)

West:	Southwest:	Midwest:	Southeast:	Northeast:	International:
Y	Y	Y	Y	Y	

MODEM MEDIA.POPPE TYSON INC
www.modemmedia.poppetyson.com

Industry Group Code: 54189A
Ranks within this company's industry group: Sales: 3   Profits: 6

BUSINESS ACTIVITIES ("Y" = Yes)

Financial Services:	Information/Publ.:	Technology:	Services:		Retailing:	Telecommunications:	
Stock Brokerage	Portal/Hub/News	Computer Manuf.	Payments/Transfers		Retailer	Internet Serv. Provider	
Mortgages/Loans	On-Line Community	Networking Equip.	Consulting	Y	Auctions	Web Site Host	Y
Banking	Search Engine	Software Manuf.	Advertising/Marketing	Y	Mall	Server Farm	
Insurance	Financial Data Publ.	Specialty Equipment	Outsourcing		Tickets/Travel	Specialty Telecom.	Y
Credit Cards	Broadcasting/Music				Price Comparisons	High Speed Access	

TYPES OF BUSINESS:

Advertising Agency
Marketing Services
E-Commerce Services
Web Site Design

BRANDS/DIVISIONS/AFFILIATES:

Market Growth Resources, Inc.
Wahlstrom & Co.
Communicomp
Foote, Cone & Belding
Graham Gregory Bozell, Inc
O'Connell, Norton & Partners
Bozell Worldwide, Inc.
BSMG Worldwide

CONTACTS: *Note: Officers with more than one job title may be intentionally listed here more than once.*

Gerald M. O'Connell, CEO
Robert C. Allen II, Pres./COO
Steven C. Roberts, CFO
Jonathan Ewert, VP-Mktg.
Rose Zory, Dir.-Human Resources
Sloane Levy, VP/General Counsel
Jonathan Ewert, VP-Corp. Comm.

Phone: 203-299-7000	Fax: 203-299-7060
Toll-Free:	
Address: 230 East Ave., Norwalk, CT, 06855	

GROWTH PLANS/SPECIAL FEATURES:

Modem Media.Poppe Tyson (MMPT) provides interactive ad and marketing campaigns delivered over the Internet, corporate intranets, interactive kiosks and CD-ROMs, which facilitate two-way communication between the company's clients and their customers. This relationship is called digital interactive marketing solutions. MMPT also offers consulting services, web site design and maintenance, data collection and e-commerce services. The company's top customer, Citibank, accounts for 12% of sales. Other MMPT customers are IBM, Intel, Delta Air Lines, 3Com, Compaq, Coors Brewing and General Electric. Modem Media.Poppe Tyson's 10 largest customers account for more than three-fourths of sales. The company would like to become the front-runner in the way open digital communications fundamentally change how companies support and influence their customers by creating interactive solutions that capitalize on the Internet's digital current to build equity in world-class brands.

FINANCIALS: Sales and profits are in thousands of dollars—add 000 to get the full amount.

Notes regarding 1999: *(1999 sales and profits were not available for all companies at press time.)*

1999 Sales: $	1999 Profits: $	Stock Ticker: **MMPT**
1998 Sales: $42,500	1998 Profits: $-3,200	Employees: 400
1997 Sales: $25,500	1997 Profits: $-3,100	Fiscal Year Ends: 12/31
1996 Sales: $2,100	1996 Profits: $- 700	
1995 Sales: $ 400	1995 Profits: $-1,000	

SALARIES/BENEFITS:

Pension Plan:	ESOP Stock Plan: Y	Profit Sharing:	Top Exec. Salary: $300,000	Bonus: $90,000
Savings Plan:	Stock Purch. Plan:		Second Exec. Salary: $300,000	Bonus: $90,000

COMPETITIVE ADVANTAGE: Excellent client base includes such blue ribbon firms as Citibank/Rapid growth through acquisition.

OTHER THOUGHTS:

Apparent Women Officers or Directors: 1
Apparent Minority Officers or Directors:
Hot Spot for Advancement for Women/Minorities:

LOCATIONS: ("Y" = Yes)

West:	Southwest:	Midwest:	Southeast:	Northeast:	International:
Y		Y	Y	Y	Y

Note: Financial information, benefits and other data can change quickly and may vary from those stated here.

MORGAN STANLEY DEAN WITTER DISCOVER & CO
www.msdw.com
Industry Group Code: 5231
Ranks within this company's industry group: Sales: 1   Profits: 1

BUSINESS ACTIVITIES ("Y" = Yes)

Financial Services:		Information/Publ.:		Technology:	Services:	Retailing:	Telecommunications:
Stock Brokerage	Y	Portal/Hub/News		Computer Manuf.	Payments/Transfers	Retailer	Internet Serv. Provider
Mortgages/Loans		On-Line Community		Networking Equip.	Consulting	Auctions	Web Site Host
Banking		Search Engine		Software Manuf.	Advertising/Marketing	Mall	Server Farm
Insurance		Financial Data Publ.	Y	Specialty Equipment	Outsourcing	Tickets/Travel	Specialty Telecom.
Credit Cards	Y	Broadcasting/Music				Price Comparisons	High Speed Access

TYPES OF BUSINESS:

Stock Brokerage/Investment Banking
Credit and Transaction Services
Asset Management
Trading
Investments
Research
Venture Capital
Financial Consulting

BRANDS/DIVISIONS/AFFILIATES:

Dean Witter
Morgan Stanley Venture Capital Fund, II, L.P.
Morgan Stanley Real Estate Fund, L.P.
Morgan Stanley Capital International
Morgan Stanley Asset Management
Miller Anderson & Sherrerd, LLP
Discover Card

CONTACTS: *Note: Officers with more than one job title may be intentionally listed here more than once.*

Philip J. Purcell, CEO
John J. Mack, Pres./COO
Robert G. Scott, Exec. VP/CFO
Eileen K. Murray, Controller & Principle Acct Officer
Christine A. Edwards, Chief Legal Officer
John H. Schaefer, Exec.VP-Chief Admin. Officer
John H. Schaefer, Exec.VP-Chief Strategic Officer
John Beneke, Dir-Investor Relations
Alexander C. Frank, Treas.
Mary Meeker, Managing Dir.

Phone: 212-761-4000	Fax: 212-761-0086
Toll-Free: 800-292-1495	
Address: 1585 Broadway, New York, NY, 10036	

GROWTH PLANS/SPECIAL FEATURES:

Morgan Stanley Dean Witter Discover & Co. (MSDW) is a preeminent global financial services firm that maintains leading market positions in each of its three primary businesses: securities, asset management and credit and transaction services. The company was formed as a result of the 1997 merger of Dean Witter, Discover & Co. and Morgan Stanley Group, Inc. The company combines global strength in investment banking and institutional sales and trading with strength in investment and global asset management products and services, as well as its Discover Card brand consumer credit products. MSDW has the second largest financial advisor sales organization in the U.S., with 11,238 professional advisors and 438 securities branch offices. MSDW also has one of the largest global asset management operations of any full-service securities firm, with total assets under management and supervision of $376 billion. In addition, the company is the nation's third largest credit card issuer as measured by number of accounts, with the largest proprietary merchant and cash access network in the U.S. Overseas, the company operates highly-successful offices from Tokyo to Zurich, London, Hong Kong and beyond. Recently, the firm launched a new offensive in the discounted brokerage fee arena. Now, trades can be made for as little as $29.95 at the MSDW Online site, while fees may be negotiated with brokers for trades that are placed through individual representatives.

Morgan Stanley is the world's premier investment banking operation. Salaries and benefits are the very best. The company hires liberal arts grads and trains them in MIS and other key areas.

FINANCIALS: Sales and profits are in thousands of dollars—add 000 to get the full amount.
Notes regarding 1999: *(1999 sales and profits were not available for all companies at press time.)*

1999 Sales: $22,000,000	1999 Profits: $4,791,000	Stock Ticker: **MWD**
1998 Sales: $31,131,000	1998 Profits: $3,276,000	Employees: 45,712
1997 Sales: $27,132,000	1997 Profits: $2,586,000	Fiscal Year Ends: 11/30
1996 Sales: $9,028,600	1996 Profits: $951,400	
1995 Sales: $7,934,400	1995 Profits: $856,400	

SALARIES/BENEFITS:

Pension Plan: Y	ESOP Stock Plan: Y	Profit Sharing:	Top Exec. Salary: $775,000	Bonus: $8,112,500
Savings Plan: Y	Stock Purch. Plan:		Second Exec. Salary: $775,000	Bonus: $8,112,500

COMPETITIVE ADVANTAGE: Top-notch client list/Exceptional trading technology and systems.

OTHER THOUGHTS:

Apparent Women Officers or Directors: 1
Apparent Minority Officers or Directors:
Hot Spot for Advancement for Women/Minorities: Y

LOCATIONS: ("Y" = Yes)

West:	Southwest:	Midwest:	Southeast:	Northeast:	International:
Y	Y	Y	Y	Y	Y

Note: Financial information, benefits and other data can change quickly and may vary from those stated here.

MORTGAGE.COM INC
www.mortgage.com

Industry Group Code: 52231
Ranks within this company's industry group: Sales: 1   Profits: 1

BUSINESS ACTIVITIES ("Y" = Yes)

Financial Services:		Information/Publ.:	Technology:	Services:	Retailing:	Telecommunications:
Stock Brokerage		Portal/Hub/News	Computer Manuf.	Payments/Transfers	Retailer	Internet Serv. Provider
Mortgages/Loans	Y	On-Line Community	Networking Equip.	Consulting	Auctions	Web Site Host
Banking		Search Engine	Software Manuf.	Advertising/Marketing	Mall	Server Farm
Insurance		Financial Data Publ.	Specialty Equipment	Outsourcing	Tickets/Travel	Specialty Telecom.
Credit Cards		Broadcasting/Music			Price Comparisons	High Speed Access

TYPES OF BUSINESS:
On-line Mortgages

BRANDS/DIVISIONS/AFFILIATES:

CONTACTS:
Note: Officers with more than one job title may be intentionally listed here more than once.
Seth S. Werner, CEO
Seth S. Werner, Pres.
Edwin Johnson, CFO/Sr. VP
Chris Anderson, Dir.-Human Resources
B. Anderson Young, CIO
Michael Brenner, Sr.VP/General Counsel
John Hogan, Pres.-Mortgage Banking Group
Jack Rodgers, Pres.-Consumer Direct Group

Phone: 954-452-0000	Fax: 954-472-0800
Toll-Free:	
Address: 8751 Broward Blvd., Fifth Fl., Plantation, FL, 33324	

GROWTH PLANS/SPECIAL FEATURES:
Through Mortgage.com, customers can shop for rates and services on-line, with access to more than 50 lenders. Mortgage.com is responsible for over $2 billion in loans annually. The Internet has become one of the easiest, fastest and most cost-effective mechanisms for consumers to use to investigate and apply for mortgages, potentially saving consumers an estimated $1,500 or more in application and closing fees over traditional methods. Analysts project that by 2003, 10% of the mortgage market will be conducted on-line. Mortgage.com is an industry leader, giving consumers many advantages through depth of information. At the same time, this availability of information over the Internet gives opportunities to banks, lending institutions, realtors and other institutions to broaden their customer bases by reaching more potential customers and creating a larger competitive market. Recently, Mortgage.com closed deals acquiring three companies that will enable it to increase its vast offering of purchase-money mortgages to home builders, realtors and financial planners. The acquisitions will fit Mortgage.com's key strategy of using the Internet, not just directly with consumers, but also in a business-to-business fashion with all key participants in the home buying process.

FINANCIALS:
Sales and profits are in thousands of dollars—add 000 to get the full amount.
Notes regarding 1999: *(1999 sales and profits were not available for all companies at press time.)*

1999 Sales: $	1999 Profits: $	Stock Ticker: **MDCM**
1998 Sales: $193,400	1998 Profits: $-6,100	Employees: 594
1997 Sales: $81,900	1997 Profits: $-3,500	Fiscal Year Ends: 12/31
1996 Sales: $	1996 Profits: $	
1995 Sales: $	1995 Profits: $	

SALARIES/BENEFITS:

Pension Plan:	ESOP Stock Plan: Y	Profit Sharing:	Top Exec. Salary: $290,000	Bonus: $
Savings Plan: Y	Stock Purch. Plan:		Second Exec. Salary: $290,000	Bonus: $

COMPETITIVE ADVANTAGE:
Very rapid growth in a very promising market.

OTHER THOUGHTS:
Apparent Women Officers or Directors:
Apparent Minority Officers or Directors:
Hot Spot for Advancement for Women/Minorities:

LOCATIONS: ("Y" = Yes)

West:	Southwest:	Midwest:	Southeast:	Northeast:	International:
Y			Y	Y	

Note: Financial information, benefits and other data can change quickly and may vary from those stated here.

MOTHERNATURE.COM INC   www.mothernature.com

Industry Group Code: 4541
Ranks within this company's industry group: Sales: 28   Profits: 15

BUSINESS ACTIVITIES ("Y" = Yes)

Financial Services:	Information/Publ.:	Technology:	Services:	Retailing:		Telecommunications:
Stock Brokerage	Portal/Hub/News	Computer Manuf.	Payments/Transfers	Retailer	Y	Internet Serv. Provider
Mortgages/Loans	On-Line Community	Networking Equip.	Consulting	Auctions		Web Site Host
Banking	Search Engine	Software Manuf.	Advertising/Marketing	Mall		Server Farm
Insurance	Financial Data Publ.	Specialty Equipment	Outsourcing	Tickets/Travel		Specialty Telecom.
Credit Cards	Broadcasting/Music			Price Comparisons		High Speed Access

TYPES OF BUSINESS:
Retail-Health Products

GROWTH PLANS/SPECIAL FEATURES:

MotherNature.com is a leading on-line supplier of health-conscious products to promote healthy living. The company's product line includes vitamins, minerals, supplements, herbs, alternative medicines, bath and body products, cosmetics, books and pet care items. MotherNature.com offers approximately 13,000 products on-line, including roughly 300 private-label products. The company promotes products that may claim to promote slowing the aging process, increased energy, sleeping better and losing weight through the use of natural products and alternative medical points of view. The company offers free on-line research materials about products, medicine and medical issues, including the ability to read best-selling natural health books, consumer guides and a vast article archive on-line. MotherNature.com intends to maximize the on-line shopping experience by providing the easiest, fastest, most aesthetically pleasing and most technically advanced web site on the Internet and create an on-line community dedicated to caring about the health of the planet and the body to live better and live longer.

BRANDS/DIVISIONS/AFFILIATES:

CONTACTS: Note: Officers with more than one job title may be intentionally listed here more than once.
Michael I. Barach, CEO
Michael I. Barach, Pres.
Michael L. Bayer, CFO
Sharon L. Rice, VP-Brand Mktg.
Donald J. Pettini, Chief Tech. Officer
Michael L. Bayer, Sec.
Beverly J. Weich, VP-Site Dev.
Michael L. Bayer, Treas.
Jeffrey A. Steinberg, Chief Mktg. Officer
Beverly J. Weich, VP-Sales

Phone: 978-929-2000	Fax: 978-929-2001
Toll-Free: 1-800-517-9020	
Address: 1 Concord Farms, 490 Virginia Rd., Concord, MA, 01742	

FINANCIALS: Sales and profits are in thousands of dollars—add 000 to get the full amount.
Notes regarding 1999: (1999 sales and profits were not available for all companies at press time.)

1999 Sales: $	1999 Profits: $	Stock Ticker: MTHR
1998 Sales: $ 500	1998 Profits: $-6,600	Employees: 112
1997 Sales: $ 200	1997 Profits: $- 200	Fiscal Year Ends: 12/31
1996 Sales: $	1996 Profits: $- 100	
1995 Sales: $	1995 Profits: $	

SALARIES/BENEFITS:

Pension Plan:	ESOP Stock Plan: Y	Profit Sharing:	Top Exec. Salary: $37,840	Bonus: $
Savings Plan: Y	Stock Purch. Plan:		Second Exec. Salary: $	Bonus: $

COMPETITIVE ADVANTAGE: Good niche/Focus on health products.

OTHER THOUGHTS:
Apparent Women Officers or Directors: 2
Apparent Minority Officers or Directors:
Hot Spot for Advancement for Women/Minorities:

LOCATIONS: ("Y" = Yes)

West:	Southwest:	Midwest:	Southeast:	Northeast: Y	International:

MP3.COM INC   www.mp3.com

Industry Group Code: 51311B
Ranks within this company's industry group: Sales: 6   Profits: 2

BUSINESS ACTIVITIES ("Y" = Yes)

Financial Services:	Information/Publ.:		Technology:	Services:	Retailing:	Telecommunications:
Stock Brokerage	Portal/Hub/News		Computer Manuf.	Payments/Transfers	Retailer	Internet Serv. Provider
Mortgages/Loans	On-Line Community		Networking Equip.	Consulting	Auctions	Web Site Host
Banking	Search Engine		Software Manuf.	Advertising/Marketing	Mall	Server Farm
Insurance	Financial Data Publ.		Specialty Equipment	Outsourcing	Tickets/Travel	Specialty Telecom.
Credit Cards	Broadcasting/Music	Y			Price Comparisons	High Speed Access

TYPES OF BUSINESS:

Portal-Songs

BRANDS/DIVISIONS/AFFILIATES:

GROWTH PLANS/SPECIAL FEATURES:

MP3.com enables users to listen to thousands of songs over the Internet, free-of-charge, using MP3 technology. MP3.com specializes in regional and lesser-known artists. Artists agree to provide the songs at no cost, in exchange for contract-free exposure and wide distribution. Artists also receive a free web page, including disk space and unlimited downloads. In addition, artists can utilize MP3.com's Digital Audio Music program that allows artists to sell and market their music with no startup costs and a 50% share of proceeds. Users have access to the latest in MP3 technology and an extensive archive of software and hardware to enhance the MP3 experience. MP3.com sells albums and custom compilation CDs, but the majority of revenues are from on-line advertising, e-commerce and off-line advertising. MP3.com averages 300,000 or more visits per day to its web site. Recent investments of $10 million from Sequoia Capital Partners and $45 million from Cox Enterprises led to sponsorship deals with leading recording artists and the ability to go public. MP3.com did not create and does not own the MP3 technology.

CONTACTS: Note: Officers with more than one job title may be intentionally listed here more than once.

Michael L. Robertson, CEO
Robin D. Richards, COO/Pres.
Paul L. H. Ouyang, Exec. VP/CFO
Steven G. Sheinor, Exec.VP Sales/Mktg.
Christine Buckley, Dir-Human Resources
Ronald D. Dotson, Exec. VP-Tech.
William P. Dow, Controller
Daniel K. O'Neill, VP-Engineering
John R. Diaz, VP-Industry Relations

Phone: 858-623-7222	Fax: 858-623-7004
Toll-Free:	
Address: 4790 Eastgate Mall, San Diego, CA, 92121	

FINANCIALS: Sales and profits are in thousands of dollars—add 000 to get the full amount.

Notes regarding 1999: Pro forma *(1999 sales and profits were not available for all companies at press time.)*

1999 Sales: $21,899	1999 Profits: $-36,313	Stock Ticker: **MPPP**
1998 Sales: $1,200	1998 Profits: $- 400	Employees: 8
1997 Sales: $	1997 Profits: $	Fiscal Year Ends: 12/31
1996 Sales: $	1996 Profits: $	
1995 Sales: $	1995 Profits: $	

SALARIES/BENEFITS:

Pension Plan:	ESOP Stock Plan:	Profit Sharing:	Top Exec. Salary: $81,333	Bonus: $
Savings Plan:	Stock Purch. Plan:		Second Exec. Salary: $	Bonus: $

COMPETITIVE ADVANTAGE: Pioneer in delivery of Internet-based music.

OTHER THOUGHTS:

Apparent Women Officers or Directors: 1
Apparent Minority Officers or Directors:
Hot Spot for Advancement for Women/Minorities:

LOCATIONS: ("Y" = Yes)

West:	Southwest:	Midwest:	Southeast:	Northeast:	International:
Y					

MULTEX.COM　　　www.multex.com

Industry Group Code: 5141
Ranks within this company's industry group: Sales: 1　Profits: 2

BUSINESS ACTIVITIES ("Y" = Yes)

Financial Services:	Information/Publ.:		Technology:	Services:	Retailing:	Telecommunications:
Stock Brokerage	Portal/Hub/News		Computer Manuf.	Payments/Transfers	Retailer	Internet Serv. Provider
Mortgages/Loans	On-Line Community		Networking Equip.	Consulting	Auctions	Web Site Host
Banking	Search Engine		Software Manuf.	Advertising/Marketing	Mall	Server Farm
Insurance	Financial Data Publ.	Y	Specialty Equipment	Outsourcing	Tickets/Travel	Specialty Telecom.
Credit Cards	Broadcasting/Music				Price Comparisons	High Speed Access

TYPES OF BUSINESS:
On-line Financial Information

BRANDS/DIVISIONS/AFFILIATES:
Market Guide, Inc.

CONTACTS: *Note: Officers with more than one job title may be intentionally listed here more than once.*
Isaak Karaev, CEO
James M. Tousignant, Pres.
John J. McGovern, CFO
Gregg B. Amonette, Sr. VP-Sales/Mktg.
Olympia Romero, Dir.-Human Resources
Eduard Kitain, VP-Software Engineering
Philip Scheps, Controller
Eduard Kitain, VP-Software Engineering
Mikail Akselrod, VP-Oper.
John J. Mahoney, Product Dev.
John J. Mahoney, Sr.VP-Product Dev.
Ron Waksman, Sr.VP-Business-to-Business Services

Phone: 212-859-9800	Fax: 212-859-9810
Toll-Free: 888-268-5839	
Address: 33 Maiden Lane, 5th floor, New York, NY, 10038	

GROWTH PLANS/SPECIAL FEATURES:

Multex.com is a leading investment research network serving the financial and investment community. Multex.com's products and services are designed to meet the needs of institutional investors, investment banks, brokerage firms, corporations and individual investors. Multex.com provides on-line research and information services to investment professionals and individuals worldwide through the application of Internet technology and the assistance of a systems support team. Advanced searching and filtering applications make it easy to find information by ticker symbol, company name, country and many other variables. The company's services enable timely on-line access to over 1,000,000 research reports and other investment information on over 15,000 companies from more than 400 investment banks, brokerage firms and third-party research providers worldwide. Multex.com offers research reports published by brokers and investment banks such as J.P. Morgan, Merrill Lynch and Solomon Smith Barney. In addition to making its services available through its web site, Multex.com's services are available through alliances with Bloomberg, Reuters and America Online. The company sells access to its data on both a subscription and pay-per-view basis. Recently, the company and Market Guide, Inc. signed a definitive agreement for Multex.com to acquire Market Guide, Inc., a leading provider of financial information on the Internet. Multex.com plans to combine Market Guide, Inc.'s database with its own.

FINANCIALS: Sales and profits are in thousands of dollars—add 000 to get the full amount.
Notes regarding 1999: *(1999 sales and profits were not available for all companies at press time.)*

1999 Sales: $40,850	1999 Profits: $-24,979	**Stock Ticker: MLTX**
1998 Sales: $13,200	1998 Profits: $-9,700	Employees:　149
1997 Sales: $6,000	1997 Profits: $-8,000	Fiscal Year Ends: 12/31
1996 Sales: $2,600	1996 Profits: $-6,400	
1995 Sales: $1,000	1995 Profits: $-5,500	

SALARIES/BENEFITS:

Pension Plan:	ESOP Stock Plan: Y	Profit Sharing:	Top Exec. Salary: $	Bonus: $
Savings Plan: Y	Stock Purch. Plan:		Second Exec. Salary: $	Bonus: $

COMPETITIVE ADVANTAGE: Leader in delivery of stock analysts' reports on-line.

OTHER THOUGHTS:
Apparent Women Officers or Directors: 1
Apparent Minority Officers or Directors: 2
Hot Spot for Advancement for Women/Minorities: Y

LOCATIONS: ("Y" = Yes)

West:	Southwest:	Midwest:	Southeast:	Northeast:	International:
Y				Y	Y

MULTIPLE ZONES INTERNATIONAL INC   www.zones.com

Industry Group Code: 4541
Ranks within this company's industry group: Sales: 3   Profits: 20

BUSINESS ACTIVITIES ("Y" = Yes)

Financial Services:	Information/Publ.:	Technology:	Services:	Retailing:		Telecommunications:
Stock Brokerage	Portal/Hub/News	Computer Manuf.	Payments/Transfers	Retailer	Y	Internet Serv. Provider
Mortgages/Loans	On-Line Community	Networking Equip.	Consulting	Auctions		Web Site Host
Banking	Search Engine	Software Manuf.	Advertising/Marketing	Mall		Server Farm
Insurance	Financial Data Publ.	Specialty Equipment	Outsourcing	Tickets/Travel		Specialty Telecom.
Credit Cards	Broadcasting/Music			Price Comparisons		High Speed Access

TYPES OF BUSINESS:

Retail-Computers
Computer Hardware
Computer Software
Computer Peripherals
Computer Accessories

BRANDS/DIVISIONS/AFFILIATES:

The MAC ZONE
The PC ZONE
The HOME COMPUTER CATALOG
The LEARNING ZONE
The Developer's Marketplace
Little Net
Interworld

CONTACTS: *Note: Officers with more than one job title may be intentionally listed here more than once.*

Firoz Lalji, Pres./CEO
Lorne G. Rubis, COO
Peter J. Biere, Sr. VP-Finance/CFO
Marc Benjamin, VP-Mktg.
Annette Gregorich, VP-Human Resources
Chris Hauser, Sr. VP-MIS
Mark Bradley, Sr. VP-Merch.
Chris Hauser, VP-Oper.
Guio Barela, Sr. VP-Corp. Dev.
Ron McFadden, VP-Admin.

Phone: 425-430-3000	Fax: 425-430-3500
Toll-Free:	
Address: 707 South Grady Way, Renton, WA, 98055-3233	

GROWTH PLANS/SPECIAL FEATURES:

Multiple Zones International, Inc. is a leading international direct marketer of brand name microchip-based hardware, software, peripherals and accessories for users of both the PC/Wintel (PC) and Macintosh (MAC) operating systems. The company markets products primarily through its two flagship catalogs, The PC ZONE(R) and The MAC ZONE(R). Multiple Zones was one of the first participants in the direct marketing channel to participate in on-line sales of computer products. It has built and maintains one of the largest electronic commerce sites on the Internet. The firm's subsidiaries and licensees are located in 26 countries worldwide, offering over 18,000 products from over 1,900 manufacturers. The company's international strategy generally has been to enter a country through a relationship with a local entrepreneur with industry experience who can provide local knowledge for the business operations. Multiple Zones' recent business developments include launching a new special edition catalog called The Developer's Marketplace, which focuses on the needs of application developers and offers the latest in development tools and technology. Its first issue focused on Internet/Intranet tools, and offered a broad selection of Rapid Application Development, Client/Server and networking tools. The company recently announced a strategic partnership with Microsoft, LittleNet and Interworld to provide a complete, fully-functional electronic software distribution solution available through its Internet Superstore.

FINANCIALS: Sales and profits are in thousands of dollars—add 000 to get the full amount.

Notes regarding 1999: *(1999 sales and profits were not available for all companies at press time.)*

1999 Sales: $487,410	1999 Profits: $-6,659	Stock Ticker: **MZON**
1998 Sales: $501,400	1998 Profits: $-8,300	Employees: 859
1997 Sales: $490,000	1997 Profits: $-5,400	Fiscal Year Ends: 12/31
1996 Sales: $457,000	1996 Profits: $10,900	
1995 Sales: $242,600	1995 Profits: $3,200	

SALARIES/BENEFITS:

Pension Plan:	ESOP Stock Plan:	Profit Sharing:	Top Exec. Salary: $300,000	Bonus: $
Savings Plan: Y	Stock Purch. Plan: Y		Second Exec. Salary: $225,000	Bonus: $

COMPETITIVE ADVANTAGE: Catalogs are circulated worldwide to more countries than any other catalog retailer of microcomputer products.

OTHER THOUGHTS:

Apparent Women Officers or Directors: 4
Apparent Minority Officers or Directors:
Hot Spot for Advancement for Women/Minorities: Y

LOCATIONS: ("Y" = Yes)

West:	Southwest:	Midwest:	Southeast:	Northeast:	International:
Y		Y			Y

Note: Financial information, benefits and other data can change quickly and may vary from those stated here.

MUSICMAKER.COM   www.musicmaker.com

Industry Group Code: 4541
Ranks within this company's industry group: Sales: 31   Profits: 9

BUSINESS ACTIVITIES ("Y" = Yes)

Financial Services:	Information/Publ.:	Technology:	Services:	Retailing:	Telecommunications:
Stock Brokerage	Portal/Hub/News	Computer Manuf.	Payments/Transfers	Retailer Y	Internet Serv. Provider
Mortgages/Loans	On-Line Community	Networking Equip.	Consulting	Auctions	Web Site Host
Banking	Search Engine	Software Manuf.	Advertising/Marketing	Mall	Server Farm
Insurance	Financial Data Publ.	Specialty Equipment	Outsourcing	Tickets/Travel	Specialty Telecom.
Credit Cards	Broadcasting/Music Y			Price Comparisons	High Speed Access

TYPES OF BUSINESS:
Retail-Customizable Music

BRANDS/DIVISIONS/AFFILIATES:

GROWTH PLANS/SPECIAL FEATURES:

Musicmaker.com is one of the largest custom CD service digital download sites on the Internet. The company's library approaches 200,000 tracks from over 100 labels in a variety of music genres. Search engines find selections by genre, artist, title and label, and Real Audio allows tracks to be sampled before selection. Each CD may include up to 20 tracks or 70 minutes of music and may be personalized with unique labels. Musicmaker.com also tracks each customer's purchase preferences, as well as histories of others who have made similar selections, in order to provide a recommendation service to guide the completion of CDs based upon prior orders. This service may not only help customers select songs from familiar artists, but may also suggest new artists they have not previously heard. The custom compilation manufacturing process enables Musicmaker.com to provide customers with a CD that contains tracks that are an exact reproduction of the original master recordings without the degradation of sound quality that inevitably occurs through CD-to-CD copying. Musicmaker.com was chosen as a Best of the Web music site by U.S. News and World Report just one year after its launch.

CONTACTS: Note: Officers with more than one job title may be intentionally listed here more than once.
Robert P. Bernardi, Co-CEO
Devarajan S. Puthakarai, Pres./Co-CEO/COO
Mark A. Fowler, CFO/Dir.-Finance and Admin.
William Crowley, VP-Mktg. and Sales
Bruce Block, Chief Tech. Officer
Pierre Tager, VP-Engineering
Mark A. Fowler, Dir.-Admin.

Phone: 703-904-4110	Fax: 703-904-4117
Toll-Free:	
Address: 1831 Wiehle Ave., Ste. 128, Reston, VA, 20190	

FINANCIALS: Sales and profits are in thousands of dollars—add 000 to get the full amount.
Notes regarding 1999: *(1999 sales and profits were not available for all companies at press time.)*

1999 Sales: $	1999 Profits: $-4,700	Stock Ticker: **HITS**
1998 Sales: $ 100	1998 Profits: $-2,100	Employees: 15
1997 Sales: $	1997 Profits: $- 400	Fiscal Year Ends: 12/31
1996 Sales: $	1996 Profits: $	
1995 Sales: $	1995 Profits: $	

SALARIES/BENEFITS:

Pension Plan:	ESOP Stock Plan:	Profit Sharing:	Top Exec. Salary: $350,000	Bonus: $
Savings Plan:	Stock Purch. Plan:		Second Exec. Salary: $175,000	Bonus: $

COMPETITIVE ADVANTAGE: Site enables customers to create custom music CDs.

OTHER THOUGHTS:
Apparent Women Officers or Directors:
Apparent Minority Officers or Directors: 2
Hot Spot for Advancement for Women/Minorities: Y

LOCATIONS: ("Y" = Yes)

West:	Southwest:	Midwest:	Southeast:	Northeast:	International:
				Y	

Note: Financial information, benefits and other data can change quickly and may vary from those stated here.

N2H2   www.n2h2.com

Industry Group Code: 514191
Ranks within this company's industry group: Sales: 30   Profits: 15

BUSINESS ACTIVITIES ("Y" = Yes)

Financial Services:	Information/Publ.:		Technology:	Services:	Retailing:	Telecommunications:
Stock Brokerage	Portal/Hub/News	Y	Computer Manuf.	Payments/Transfers	Retailer	Internet Serv. Provider
Mortgages/Loans	On-Line Community		Networking Equip.	Consulting	Auctions	Web Site Host
Banking	Search Engine		Software Manuf.	Advertising/Marketing	Mall	Server Farm
Insurance	Financial Data Publ.		Specialty Equipment	Outsourcing	Tickets/Travel	Specialty Telecom.
Credit Cards	Broadcasting/Music				Price Comparisons	High Speed Access

TYPES OF BUSINESS:

Internet Content Filtering
Portal With Filtered Search Capabilities
Search Portal for Public Education Facilities

BRANDS/DIVISIONS/AFFILIATES:

Bess
Searchopolis

CONTACTS: Note: Officers with more than one job title may be intentionally listed here more than once.

Peter H. Nickerson, CEO
David Arnold, COO
John F. Duncan, CFO
James J. O'Hollaran, VP-Mktg.
Kevin E. Fink, Chief Tech. Officer
John F. Duncan, Sec.
Michael Jay, Dir.-Strategic Product Planning/Education Div.
Frank R. Fulton, Dir.-Customer Oper.
John F. Duncan, Treas.
B. Patrick Murphy, VP-Sales

Phone: 206-336-1501	Fax: 206-336-1556
Toll-Free:	
Address: 900 Fourth Ave., Suite 3400, Seattle, WA, 98164	

GROWTH PLANS/SPECIAL FEATURES:

N2H2, Inc. is a leading provider of Internet content filtering services to schools. It enables schools and homes to eliminate pornographic, violent and other objectionable sites. It also provides these services to corporations and organizations through Internet service providers. The company was the first to offer a server-based Internet filtering solution for a customer's computer network. N2H2's flagship product, Bess, currently provides filtering services to approximately 7.3 million students in approximately 8,000 schools in the United States and Canada. The company's customers include the statewide networks serving most of the public schools in Ohio, Tennessee, Maine, Oklahoma and Wisconsin, as well as school systems in areas such as Los Angeles County, Baltimore, Boston, Calgary, Seattle, Stockton and Tampa. N2H2's database identifies and categorizes hundreds of thousands of inappropriate sites and is updated daily. N2H2 developed the first Internet educational portal with filtered search capabilities, Searchopolis. Searchopolis offers free services to all Internet users. The company's services are sold via a network of sales representatives that cover North America and are available to both public and private organizations. Filtering is also available to Internet service providers for resale to their customers.

FINANCIALS: Sales and profits are in thousands of dollars—add 000 to get the full amount.

Notes regarding 1999: *(1999 sales and profits were not available for all companies at press time.)*

1999 Sales: $6,400	1999 Profits: $-7,700	Stock Ticker: **NTWO**
1998 Sales: $3,100	1998 Profits: $-2,600	Employees: 156
1997 Sales: $1,100	1997 Profits: $- 900	Fiscal Year Ends: 9/30
1996 Sales: $ 100	1996 Profits: $- 800	
1995 Sales: $	1995 Profits: $	

SALARIES/BENEFITS:

Pension Plan:	ESOP Stock Plan:	Profit Sharing:	Top Exec. Salary: $176,563	Bonus: $50,341
Savings Plan:	Stock Purch. Plan:		Second Exec. Salary: $	Bonus: $

COMPETITIVE ADVANTAGE: Serves a vast school market, enabling the delivery of acceptable content.

OTHER THOUGHTS:

	LOCATIONS: ("Y" = Yes)					
	West:	Southwest:	Midwest:	Southeast:	Northeast:	International:
Apparent Women Officers or Directors:	Y					
Apparent Minority Officers or Directors:						
Hot Spot for Advancement for Women/Minorities:						

Note: Financial information, benefits and other data can change quickly and may vary from those stated here.

NATIONAL DISCOUNT BROKERS   www.ndb.com

Industry Group Code: 5231
Ranks within this company's industry group: Sales: 4   Profits: 3

BUSINESS ACTIVITIES ("Y" = Yes)

Financial Services:		Information/Publ.:	Technology:	Services:	Retailing:	Telecommunications:
Stock Brokerage	Y	Portal/Hub/News	Computer Manuf.	Payments/Transfers	Retailer	Internet Serv. Provider
Mortgages/Loans		On-Line Community	Networking Equip.	Consulting	Auctions	Web Site Host
Banking		Search Engine	Software Manuf.	Advertising/Marketing	Mall	Server Farm
Insurance		Financial Data Publ.	Specialty Equipment	Outsourcing	Tickets/Travel	Specialty Telecom.
Credit Cards		Broadcasting/Music			Price Comparisons	High Speed Access

TYPES OF BUSINESS:
On-line Stock Brokerage/Investment Banking

BRANDS/DIVISIONS/AFFILIATES:
Sherwood Securities Corp.
Equitrade Partners
Triak Services
SHD Corporation
www.ndb.com
NDB University

CONTACTS: *Note: Officers with more than one job title may be intentionally listed here more than once.*
Arthur Kontos, CEO
Samir M. Shah, Co-COO
Denise Isaac, CFO
Joseph Wicklow, Sr.VP-Human Resources
Frank E. Lawatsch Jr., Exec.VP-Sec.
Laura R. Singer, Sr. VP/General Counsel
Michael Long, VP-Oper.
Denise Isaac, Treas.
Greg Sharenow, Co-COO
Thomas Neumann, Exec. VP

Phone: 201-946-2200	Fax: 201-946-4510
Toll-Free:	
Address: 10 Exchange Place Center, Jersey City, NJ, 07302	

GROWTH PLANS/SPECIAL FEATURES:

National Discount Brokers Group is a holding company with principal wholly-owned subsidiaries of Sherwood Securities and Triak Services, which do business as National Discount Brokers (NDB). The company and its subsidiary, SHD Corporation, also own limited partnership interests in Equitrade Partners. As interest continues to grow in the Internet, Internet-based products and e-commerce, the presence of an established on-line broker cannot be underestimated. NDBG's primary focus remains fixed on its on-line services. A new advertising campaign and redeveloped web site was recently launched to increase the company's account base and dramatically lower acquisition costs. The new ndb.com placed second and received four-stars (the highest rating) in Barron's Best of Online Brokers survey, winning high marks for trade execution, ease of use, reliability and amenities. Featured on the new web site is the launch of NDB University, the first organized instructional program to be offered by an on-line broker. The company's web site currently handles 50% of the daily trade volume of the company. NDB has over 120,000 accounts with assets in excess of $5.3 billion. Previous investments in technology infrastructure have enabled NDB to achieve a trade mix of 80% automated versus 20% live broker, enabling the company to execute more trades and reduce costs.

FINANCIALS: Sales and profits are in thousands of dollars—add 000 to get the full amount.
Notes regarding 1999: *(1999 sales and profits were not available for all companies at press time.)*

1999 Sales: $207,900	1999 Profits: $21,005	Stock Ticker: **NDB**
1998 Sales: $164,500	1998 Profits: $12,000	Employees: 572
1997 Sales: $181,100	1997 Profits: $9,300	Fiscal Year Ends: 5/31
1996 Sales: $180,200	1996 Profits: $20,100	
1995 Sales: $103,000	1995 Profits: $103,000	

SALARIES/BENEFITS:

Pension Plan:	ESOP Stock Plan:	Profit Sharing:	Top Exec. Salary: $350,000	Bonus: $250,000
Savings Plan: Y	Stock Purch. Plan:		Second Exec. Salary: $300,000	Bonus: $3,479,439

COMPETITIVE ADVANTAGE: Rapidly growing discount broker/Excellent technology.

OTHER THOUGHTS:
Apparent Women Officers or Directors: 2
Apparent Minority Officers or Directors:
Hot Spot for Advancement for Women/Minorities:

LOCATIONS: ("Y" = Yes)

West:	Southwest:	Midwest:	Southeast:	Northeast:	International:
				Y	

NAVIDEC   www.navidec.com

Industry Group Code: 54151
Ranks within this company's industry group: Sales: 12   Profits: 8

BUSINESS ACTIVITIES ("Y" = Yes)

Financial Services:	Information/Publ.:	Technology:	Services:		Retailing:		Telecommunications:	
Stock Brokerage	Portal/Hub/News	Computer Manuf.	Payments/Transfers		Retailer		Internet Serv. Provider	
Mortgages/Loans	On-Line Community	Networking Equip.	Consulting	Y	Auctions		Web Site Host	Y
Banking	Search Engine	Software Manuf.	Advertising/Marketing	Y	Mall		Server Farm	
Insurance	Financial Data Publ.	Specialty Equipment	Outsourcing	Y	Tickets/Travel		Specialty Telecom.	
Credit Cards	Broadcasting/Music				Price Comparisons		High Speed Access	

TYPES OF BUSINESS:

Consulting-E-Commerce Solutions
Web Site Design, Development and Hosting
Application Management
Reselling/Installation of Systems and E-mail Messaging Solutions
Internet Automobile Sales Services
E-business Consulting

BRANDS/DIVISIONS/AFFILIATES:

NetSolutions Division
Driveoff.com
iPlanet
Netegrity
Oblix
ODI
Oracle
Sun Microsystems

CONTACTS: *Note: Officers with more than one job title may be intentionally listed here more than once.*

Ralph Armijo, CEO/Pres.
Ken P. Bero, COO
Patrick R. Mawhinney, CFO
Greg Hanchin, VP-Sales
Eva Miller, VP-Human Resources
Brad Nixon, VP-Tech
Patrick R. Mawhinney, Treas.
Michael Kranitz, Pres.-Automotive Div.
Harold Anderson II, VP-Automotive Div.

Phone: 303-790-7565	Fax: 303-790-8845
Toll-Free:	

Address: 14 Inverness Dr., Bldg. F, Ste. 116, Englewood, CO, 80112

GROWTH PLANS/SPECIAL FEATURES:

Navidec, Inc. is a leading Internet development, applications, management and consulting company that provides Internet solutions and services to over 200 customers, from newly-formed Internet companies to Fortune 1000/5000 corporations. Navidec assists companies in strengthening their Internet presence and improving e-business results through the wide array of services it offers. Services that comprise the company's main business lines include e-business consulting, commercial e-business site development, systems integration, e-mail messaging systems integration and creation, intranet and extranet application design and application management and hosting. Navidec's NetSolutions Division focuses on integrating e-commerce-based technologies into a company's existing business. Driveoff.com, Inc. is Navidec's automotive e-commerce subsidiary that focuses on incorporating e-commerce technology to the auto buying process. It is also the world's first strictly e-commerce auto-buying site. The company recently expanded its office presence, adding locations in Boston, San Francisco and Salt Lake City.

A casual working environment fosters Navidec workers' creativity, enhances their professional growth and maximizes their opportunities for success. The company's corporate culture values hard work and a dedication to excellence, and rewards performance with competitive salaries, comprehensive benefits and a variety of impromptu activities, from barbecues and ice cream socials to golf tournaments and CEO-led trips to the movies.

FINANCIALS: Sales and profits are in thousands of dollars—add 000 to get the full amount.

Notes regarding 1999: Through 9 months *(1999 sales and profits were not available for all companies at press time.)*

1999 Sales: $2,706	1999 Profits: $-4,644	**Stock Ticker: NVDC**
1998 Sales: $8,600	1998 Profits: $-3,900	Employees: 75
1997 Sales: $6,000	1997 Profits: $-4,100	Fiscal Year Ends: 12/31
1996 Sales: $5,500	1996 Profits: $-1,400	
1995 Sales: $4,100	1995 Profits: $	

SALARIES/BENEFITS:

Pension Plan:	ESOP Stock Plan:	Profit Sharing:	Top Exec. Salary: $172,133	Bonus: $
Savings Plan: Y	Stock Purch. Plan:		Second Exec. Salary: $104,706	Bonus: $25,000

COMPETITIVE ADVANTAGE: Very rapid growth/Expanding list of services.

OTHER THOUGHTS:

Apparent Women Officers or Directors:
Apparent Minority Officers or Directors: 1
Hot Spot for Advancement for Women/Minorities:

LOCATIONS: ("Y" = Yes)

West:	Southwest:	Midwest:	Southeast:	Northeast:	International:
Y				Y	

NAVISITE   www.navisite.com
Industry Group Code: 5611
Ranks within this company's industry group: Sales: 2   Profits: 2

BUSINESS ACTIVITIES ("Y" = Yes)

Financial Services:	Information/Publ.:	Technology:	Services:	Retailing:	Telecommunications:
Stock Brokerage	Portal/Hub/News	Computer Manuf.	Payments/Transfers	Retailer	Internet Serv. Provider
Mortgages/Loans	On-Line Community	Networking Equip.	Consulting	Auctions	Web Site Host Y
Banking	Search Engine	Software Manuf.	Advertising/Marketing	Mall	Server Farm Y
Insurance	Financial Data Publ.	Specialty Equipment	Outsourcing Y	Tickets/Travel	Specialty Telecom.
Credit Cards	Broadcasting/Music			Price Comparisons	High Speed Access

TYPES OF BUSINESS:
Outsourcing-Web Site Solutions
Web Hosting
Server and application management
Internet Application Solutions
E-business Services
ASP

BRANDS/DIVISIONS/AFFILIATES:
CMGI
SiteHarbor

CONTACTS: *Note: Officers with more than one job title may be intentionally listed here more than once.*
Joel B. Rosen, CEO
Robert B. Eisenberg, Pres.
Kenneth W. Hale, CFO
Jay S. Seaton, VP-Mktg.
Jeanne Knight, Dir.- Human Resources
Peter C. Kirwan, Jr., Chief Tech. Officer
Kenneth W. Hale, Sec.
Thomas W. Culver, VP-Oper.
Kenneth W. Hale, Treas.
J. Andrew Sherman, VP-Sales
Johnathan Rodin, VP-Product Dev.

Phone: 978-684-3500	Fax: 978-684-3599
Toll-Free: 888-298-8222	
Address: 100 Brickstone Sq., 5th Floor, Andover, MA, 01810	

GROWTH PLANS/SPECIAL FEATURES:

NaviSite, an Application Services Provider (ASP), offers e-business-based Internet outsourcing solutions. Additionally, the company offers several other services, including web hosting, server management, application management and Internet application solutions. NaviSite also serves its corporate customers by helping them change their infastructure from static on-line marketing to one that is more e-business-based. NaviSite's SiteHarbor product line delivers customizable Internet outsourcing solutions to companies ranging in size from Fortune 500 companies to new businesses. The company recently announced that it has entered into a partnership with Akamai Technologies, which operates a global Internet content delivery service that improves the speed and reliability of web performance. This agreement is a key element of NaviSite's content distribution service offering and is designed to provide NaviSite customers with access to an end-to-end content distribution system combined with application and server management services. NaviSite also recently announced an industry relationship with Informative, a leading provider of web-based, real-time information solutions. The companies have partnered through NaviSite's ISV/ASP program, which is designed to help businesses reduce time to market and minimize up-front capital expenditure.

FINANCIALS: Sales and profits are in thousands of dollars—add 000 to get the full amount.
Notes regarding 1999: *(1999 sales and profits were not available for all companies at press time.)*

1999 Sales: $10,500	1999 Profits: $-24,500	Stock Ticker: **NAVI**
1998 Sales: $4,000	1998 Profits: $-9,200	Employees: 201
1997 Sales: $3,400	1997 Profits: $- 900	Fiscal Year Ends: 7/31
1996 Sales: $	1996 Profits: $	
1995 Sales: $	1995 Profits: $	

SALARIES/BENEFITS:

Pension Plan:	ESOP Stock Plan:	Profit Sharing:	Top Exec. Salary: $	Bonus: $
Savings Plan: Y	Stock Purch. Plan:		Second Exec. Salary: $	Bonus: $

COMPETITIVE ADVANTAGE: Focus on the growing ASP market/Ability to deliver a wide variety of services.

OTHER THOUGHTS:
Apparent Women Officers or Directors: 1
Apparent Minority Officers or Directors:
Hot Spot for Advancement for Women/Minorities:

LOCATIONS: ("Y" = Yes)

West:	Southwest:	Midwest:	Southeast:	Northeast:	International:
				Y	

NEON SYSTEMS   www.neonsys.com

Industry Group Code: 5112
Ranks within this company's industry group: Sales: 45   Profits: 17

BUSINESS ACTIVITIES ("Y" = Yes)

Financial Services:	Information/Publ.:	Technology:		Services:	Retailing:	Telecommunications:
Stock Brokerage	Portal/Hub/News	Computer Manuf.		Payments/Transfers	Retailer	Internet Serv. Provider
Mortgages/Loans	On-Line Community	Networking Equip.		Consulting	Auctions	Web Site Host
Banking	Search Engine	Software Manuf.	Y	Advertising/Marketing	Mall	Server Farm
Insurance	Financial Data Publ.	Specialty Equipment		Outsourcing	Tickets/Travel	Specialty Telecom.
Credit Cards	Broadcasting/Music				Price Comparisons	High Speed Access

TYPES OF BUSINESS:

Software-Computer Communication
Security Software
Legacy Data Enhancement Software
Enterprise Access and Connectivity Software

BRANDS/DIVISIONS/AFFILIATES:

Enterprise Access and Integration Products
Enterprise Security Management Products
ShadowDirect
Shadow OS/390 Web Server
Shadow VM Web Server
Web-to-System 390
Shadow Enterprise Direct
Halo Product Family

CONTACTS: Note: Officers with more than one job title may be intentionally listed here more than once.

Joe Backer, CEO
Joe Backer, Pres.
John S. Reiland, CFO
Jonathan J. Reed, VP-Mktg.
Peter Schaeffer, Chief Tech. Officer
Wayne E. Webb, VP/General Counsel
Don Pate, VP-Worldwide Sales

Phone: 281-491-4200	Fax: 281-242-3880
Toll-Free: 800-505-6366	
Address: 14100 Southwest Frwy., Sugar Land, TX, 77478	

GROWTH PLANS/SPECIAL FEATURES:

NEON Systems, founded in 1991, is a leading provider of Enterprise Access and Integration, Security and Subsystem Management software. NEON software products create access to and connectivity between enterprise data, transactions and applications for all industries. The company's offices are located in Texas, Australia, Brazil, Germany, Great Britain, Korea, Sweden and the United States. NEON offices exist throughout a total of 25 countries. The company's wide array of products includes the Shadow Product Family, which revitalizes legacy data and transactions on the mainframe with access from popular web browsers, application servers or personal productivity tools. Products in this family include Shadow Direct for client-to-mainframe, Shadow OS/390 Web Server and Shadow VM Web Server for Web-to-System/390 and Shadow Enterprise Direct. The Halo Product Family guards information with encryption/decryption technology for the Internet and password synchronization for heterogeneous computing environments. The NEON Product Family of IMS and CICS tools increases the performance of mainframe subsystems to allow quick availability to and control of mission-critical data on a constant basis. The company recently acquired Beyond Software, Inc., a similarly-structured corporation.

FINANCIALS: Sales and profits are in thousands of dollars—add 000 to get the full amount.

Notes regarding 1999: *(1999 sales and profits were not available for all companies at press time.)*

1999 Sales: $20,000	1999 Profits: $2,300	**Stock Ticker: NESY**
1998 Sales: $12,000	1998 Profits: $1,100	Employees: 90
1997 Sales: $7,000	1997 Profits: $ 800	Fiscal Year Ends: 3/31
1996 Sales: $2,300	1996 Profits: $- 600	
1995 Sales: $	1995 Profits: $	

SALARIES/BENEFITS:

Pension Plan:	ESOP Stock Plan:	Profit Sharing:	Top Exec. Salary: $	Bonus: $
Savings Plan: Y	Stock Purch. Plan:		Second Exec. Salary: $	Bonus: $

COMPETITIVE ADVANTAGE: Global network of offices/Diversified products.

OTHER THOUGHTS:

	LOCATIONS: ("Y" = Yes)					
	West:	Southwest:	Midwest:	Southeast:	Northeast:	International:
Apparent Women Officers or Directors:	Y	Y	Y	Y	Y	Y
Apparent Minority Officers or Directors:						
Hot Spot for Advancement for Women/Minorities:						

NET PERCEPTIONS
www.netperceptions.com

Industry Group Code: 5112
Ranks within this company's industry group: Sales: 79   Profits: 34

BUSINESS ACTIVITIES ("Y" = Yes)

Financial Services:	Information/Publ.:	Technology:	Services:		Retailing:	Telecommunications:
Stock Brokerage	Portal/Hub/News	Computer Manuf.	Payments/Transfers		Retailer	Internet Serv. Provider
Mortgages/Loans	On-Line Community	Networking Equip.	Consulting		Auctions	Web Site Host
Banking	Search Engine	Software Manuf.	Advertising/Marketing	Y	Mall	Server Farm
Insurance	Financial Data Publ.	Specialty Equipment	Outsourcing		Tickets/Travel	Specialty Telecom.
Credit Cards	Broadcasting/Music				Price Comparisons	High Speed Access

TYPES OF BUSINESS:

Advertising/Marketing Solutions via Interactive Portal
Call Center Technology
Software-Filtering Database
E-commerce Solutions

BRANDS/DIVISIONS/AFFILIATES:

Net Perceptions for Ad Targeting
Net Perceptions for Call Centers
Net Perceptions for E-Commerce
Net Perceptions Recommendation Engine

CONTACTS: Note: Officers with more than one job title may be intentionally listed here more than once.

Steven J. Snyder, CEO
Steven J. Snyder, Pres.
Thomas N. Donnelly, CFO
P. Stephen Larson, VP-Mktg.
Lori Smith, Dir.-Human Resources
Paul Beiganski, Chief Tech. Officer
Thomas M. Donnelly, Sec.
P. Stephen Larson, VP-Bus. Dev.
Nanci Anderson, VP-Customer Solutions
Bradley N. Miller, VP-Product Dev.

Phone: 612-903-9424	Fax: 612-903-9425
Toll-Free: 800-466-0711	
Address: 7901 Flying Cloud, Minneapolis, MN, 55344	

GROWTH PLANS/SPECIAL FEATURES:

Net Perceptions, a Minneapolis-based developer and supplier of real-time recommendation technology, offers its services to customers such as CDnow, E!Online, iVillage, Music Boulevard, Planet Direct and Ticketmaster Online. In addition to real-time recommendation technology services, the company also provides web site personalization and web site ad targeting. Net Perceptions extended its technology to call centers and ad targeting. The company recently announced a partnership with BroadVision, Inc., with which it will collaborate to deliver an integrated e-commerce personalization solution. Other recently-launched collaborations include those with Vignette Corporation, IBM Corp., net.Genesis and DoubleClick Technologies Inc. to offer an adaptive Internet marketing solution to help customers make more informed decisions about on-line marketing campaigns, sales strategies and web content. The company also recently announced the unveiling of its Net Perceptions for E-Commerce 5.0 product at the first Personalization Summit in San Francisco.

FINANCIALS: Sales and profits are in thousands of dollars—add 000 to get the full amount.
Notes regarding 1999: *(1999 sales and profits were not available for all companies at press time.)*

1999 Sales: $15,100	1999 Profits: $-12,000	Stock Ticker: **NETP**
1998 Sales: $ 300	1998 Profits: $-5,000	Employees: 83
1997 Sales: $	1997 Profits: $-4,700	Fiscal Year Ends: 12/31
1996 Sales: $	1996 Profits: $-1,000	
1995 Sales: $	1995 Profits: $	

SALARIES/BENEFITS:

Pension Plan:	ESOP Stock Plan:	Profit Sharing:	Top Exec. Salary: $	Bonus: $
Savings Plan: Y	Stock Purch. Plan:		Second Exec. Salary: $	Bonus: $

COMPETITIVE ADVANTAGE: Growing list of software and alliances for e-commerce.

OTHER THOUGHTS:

Apparent Women Officers or Directors: 2
Apparent Minority Officers or Directors:
Hot Spot for Advancement for Women/Minorities:

LOCATIONS: ("Y" = Yes)

West:	Southwest:	Midwest:	Southeast:	Northeast:	International:
		Y			

NET.B@NK   www.netbank.com

Industry Group Code: 522A
Ranks within this company's industry group: Sales: 1   Profits: 1

BUSINESS ACTIVITIES ("Y" = Yes)

Financial Services:		Information/Publ.:	Technology:	Services:		Retailing:	Telecommunications:
Stock Brokerage	Y	Portal/Hub/News	Computer Manuf.	Payments/Transfers	Y	Retailer	Internet Serv. Provider
Mortgages/Loans	Y	On-Line Community	Networking Equip.	Consulting		Auctions	Web Site Host
Banking	Y	Search Engine	Software Manuf.	Advertising/Marketing		Mall	Server Farm
Insurance		Financial Data Publ.	Specialty Equipment	Outsourcing		Tickets/Travel	Specialty Telecom.
Credit Cards	Y	Broadcasting/Music				Price Comparisons	High Speed Access

TYPES OF BUSINESS:

On-line Banking
Electronic Bill Paying
Mortgages and Loans

BRANDS/DIVISIONS/AFFILIATES:

B@nk.Notes

CONTACTS: Note: Officers with more than one job title may be intentionally listed here more than once.

D.R. Grimes, CEO
Donald S. Shapleigh, Jr., COO/Pres.
Robert E. Bowers, CFO
Lisa Tyler, Dir.-Human Resources, Admin.
Thomas L. Cable, Chief Tech. Officer
Mary E. Johnson, Corp. Sec.
Catherine Storey, Oper. Mgr.
Jeffery B. Watson, Chief Lending Officer

Phone: 770-343-6006	Fax: 770-343-9349
Toll-Free: 888-256-6932	
Address: 950 N. Point Parkway, Ste. 350, Alpharetta, GA, 30005	

GROWTH PLANS/SPECIAL FEATURES:

Net.B@nk, a member of the FDIC, is the nation's largest federal savings bank to operate exclusively through the Internet. Due to its lack of brick-and-mortar branches, the bank experiences overhead savings that allow it to offer more attractive deposit rates and fees. Net.B@nk offers a full line of financial services, including high-interest checking accounts, free, unlimited on-line bill paying, ATM, debit and credit cards, money market accounts, CDs, brokerage services, mortgage loans and 24-hour on-line access to account information. The company's newsletter, B@nk.Notes, offers information about upcoming developments in the bank. The company's Net.B@nk web-based banking services, technology and security systems are supported by several organizations in order to maintain security, including AT&T, BISYS, CheckFree, Edify and NCR. In addition to on-line banking services, Net.B@nk makes adjustable-rate mortgage loans, as well as construction, equipment and consumer loans.

Net.B@nk is a growing company that offers challenging opportunities for its employees. The company offers a comprehensive benefits package, including vacation time, sick/personal leave, group health insurance, paid holidays, checking accounts and banking services.

FINANCIALS: Sales and profits are in thousands of dollars—add 000 to get the full amount.

Notes regarding 1999: *(1999 sales and profits were not available for all companies at press time.)*

1999 Sales: $	1999 Profits: $3,048	Stock Ticker: **NTBK**
1998 Sales: $18,800	1998 Profits: $4,500	Employees: 42
1997 Sales: $2,300	1997 Profits: $-5,600	Fiscal Year Ends: 12/31
1996 Sales: $	1996 Profits: $-3,800	
1995 Sales: $	1995 Profits: $	

SALARIES/BENEFITS:

Pension Plan:	ESOP Stock Plan:	Profit Sharing:	Top Exec. Salary: $	Bonus: $
Savings Plan:	Stock Purch. Plan:		Second Exec. Salary: $	Bonus: $

COMPETITIVE ADVANTAGE: Aggressive management has made this one of the fastest growing financial sites.

OTHER THOUGHTS:

Apparent Women Officers or Directors: 3
Apparent Minority Officers or Directors:
Hot Spot for Advancement for Women/Minorities: Y

LOCATIONS: ("Y" = Yes)

West:	Southwest:	Midwest:	Southeast:	Northeast:	International:
			Y		

NET2PHONE
www.net2phone.com

Industry Group Code: 5133D
Ranks within this company's industry group: Sales: 3   Profits: 2

BUSINESS ACTIVITIES ("Y" = Yes)

Financial Services:	Information/Publ.:	Technology:	Services:	Retailing:	Telecommunications:
Stock Brokerage	Portal/Hub/News	Computer Manuf.	Payments/Transfers	Retailer	Internet Serv. Provider
Mortgages/Loans	On-Line Community	Networking Equip.	Consulting	Auctions	Web Site Host
Banking	Search Engine	Software Manuf.	Advertising/Marketing	Mall	Server Farm
Insurance	Financial Data Publ.	Specialty Equipment	Outsourcing	Tickets/Travel	Specialty Telecom. Y
Credit Cards	Broadcasting/Music			Price Comparisons	High Speed Access

TYPES OF BUSINESS:

Internet Telephony

GROWTH PLANS/SPECIAL FEATURES:

Net2Phone's products allow users to make phone calls through the Internet to anywhere in the world, usually at a much lower cost than wireless or fixed-line calling. A leading Internet telephone carrier, Net2Phone serves 250,000 customers through a number of portals, including Yahoo! and Excite@Home. The company will expand internationally through a networking services deal with AT&T and is combining forces with such giants as America Online and Compaq. In 1997, Net2Phone was formed as a subsidiary of long-distance carrier IDT, which owns 57% of the firm. Net2Phone Direct, Net2Fax, Net2Phone Pro, Click2Talk and Click2CallMe are among the variety of products offered by Net2Phone. Recently, Sprint agreed to offer the company's services for calls to Asia, a partnership that dramatically increased the worth of shares of stock in the company. Net2Phone entered into an agreement with America Online that allows AOL's instant messaging users to make PC-to-phone and phone-to-PC calls, to access PC-to-fax and fax-to-PC calls and to make conference calls.

BRANDS/DIVISIONS/AFFILIATES:

IDT, Inc.
Net2Phone Direct
Net2Fax
Net2Phone Pro
Click2Talk
Click2CallMe

CONTACTS: Note: Officers with more than one job title may be intentionally listed here more than once.

Howard S. Balter, CEO
Jonathan Fram, Pres.
Ilan M. Slatsky, CFO
Jonathan Reich, VP-Mktg.
Susan Burman, Dir.-Human Resources
J. Jeff Goldberg, Chief Tech. Officer
Ira A. Greenstein, Sec.
Ira A. Greenstein, General Counsel
David Greenblatt, COO
Jonathan Reich, VP-Corp. Dev.
Jonathan Rand, EVP-Int'l Sales, Treas.
Martin Rothberg, EVP-Strategic Sales

Phone: 201-928-2990	Fax: 201-692-3361
Toll-Free:	
Address: 171 Main Street, Hackensack, NJ, 07601	

FINANCIALS: Sales and profits are in thousands of dollars—add 000 to get the full amount.
Notes regarding 1999: (1999 sales and profits were not available for all companies at press time.)

1999 Sales: $33,300	1999 Profits: $-24,700	Stock Ticker: NTOP
1998 Sales: $12,000	1998 Profits: $-3,500	Employees: 333
1997 Sales: $2,700	1997 Profits: $-1,700	Fiscal Year Ends: 7/31
1996 Sales: $	1996 Profits: $- 500	
1995 Sales: $	1995 Profits: $	

SALARIES/BENEFITS:

Pension Plan:	ESOP Stock Plan:	Profit Sharing:	Top Exec. Salary: $209,447	Bonus: $
Savings Plan:	Stock Purch. Plan:		Second Exec. Salary: $	Bonus: $

COMPETITIVE ADVANTAGE: Alliances with AOL, AT&T and others.

OTHER THOUGHTS:

Apparent Women Officers or Directors: 2
Apparent Minority Officers or Directors:
Hot Spot for Advancement for Women/Minorities:

LOCATIONS: ("Y" = Yes)

West:	Southwest:	Midwest:	Southeast:	Northeast: Y	International:

NETCENTIVES   www.netcentives.com

Industry Group Code: 54189A
Ranks within this company's industry group: Sales: 19   Profits: 15

BUSINESS ACTIVITIES ("Y" = Yes)

Financial Services:	Information/Publ.:	Technology:	Services:		Retailing:	Telecommunications:	
Stock Brokerage	Portal/Hub/News	Computer Manuf.	Payments/Transfers		Retailer	Internet Serv. Provider	
Mortgages/Loans	On-Line Community	Networking Equip.	Consulting		Auctions	Web Site Host	
Banking	Search Engine	Software Manuf.	Advertising/Marketing	Y	Mall	Server Farm	
Insurance	Financial Data Publ.	Specialty Equipment	Outsourcing	Y	Tickets/Travel	Specialty Telecom.	Y
Credit Cards	Broadcasting/Music				Price Comparisons	High Speed Access	

TYPES OF BUSINESS:

Frequent Customer Marketing Programs
Customer Incentives

BRANDS/DIVISIONS/AFFILIATES:

ClickRewards Network
ClickMiles

CONTACTS: *Note: Officers with more than one job title may be intentionally listed here more than once.*

West Shell III, CEO
John F. Longinotti, Exec. VP-Oper.
John F. Longinotti, CFO
Paul F. Danielsen, VP-Sales
Marina Rekhlis, Dir.- Human Resources
Timothy J.O. Catlin, Sr. VP-Research and Dev.
Jim Panttaja, VP-Systems Architect
Edward Fong Soo Hoo, Sr. VP-Corp. Dev.
William McGee, VP-Corp. Mktg.
Perryman K. Maynard, VP-Relationship Mktg. and Strategic Alliances
Mary Panttaja, VP-Program Mgmt. and Dev.

Phone: 415-538-1888	**Fax:** 415-538-1889
Toll-Free:	
Address: 690 Fifth Street, San Francisco, CA, 94107	

GROWTH PLANS/SPECIAL FEATURES:

Netcentives, Inc., a leading developer of on-line rewards and loyalty programs, constructs one-to-one marketing solutions designed to maximize the consumer-merchant relationship. Operating on the principal that on-line merchants need to distinguish themselves in order to maintain the loyalty of a growing population of savvy on-line shoppers, Netcentives' products allow companies to efficiently target and reward their audiences. The company's ClickRewards Network is one of the nation's leading Internet loyalty programs. Clients are enabled to reward customers with ClickMiles that can then be redeemed for frequent flyer miles and other merchandise. E-commerce customers offering this service include barnesandnoble.com and 1-800-FLOWERS; these organizations purchase the points and award them to on-line shoppers in an effort to build traffic on their web sites. Programs are also offered by the company to web site operators who want to use their own branded incentives, as well as to employers who want to reward employees.

Netcentives is driven by a team of professionals drawn from widely differing backgrounds. The company's executives earned their stripes in marketing, secure systems design, transaction processing and brand management. Netcentives' advisors lend expertise in travel and tourism, technology, e-commerce and finance.

FINANCIALS: Sales and profits are in thousands of dollars—add 000 to get the full amount.

Notes regarding 1999: *(1999 sales and profits were not available for all companies at press time.)*

1999 Sales: $7,841	1999 Profits: $-46,828	**Stock Ticker: NCNT**
1998 Sales: $ 600	1998 Profits: $-14,100	Employees: 149
1997 Sales: $	1997 Profits: $-4,200	Fiscal Year Ends: 12/31
1996 Sales: $	1996 Profits: $- 300	
1995 Sales: $	1995 Profits: $	

SALARIES/BENEFITS:

Pension Plan:	ESOP Stock Plan:	Profit Sharing:	Top Exec. Salary: $266,936	Bonus: $
Savings Plan:	Stock Purch. Plan:		Second Exec. Salary: $182,624	Bonus: $

COMPETITIVE ADVANTAGE: A market leader in incentive programs.

OTHER THOUGHTS:

Apparent Women Officers or Directors: 3
Apparent Minority Officers or Directors: 3
Hot Spot for Advancement for Women/Minorities: Y

LOCATIONS: ("Y" = Yes)

West:	Southwest:	Midwest:	Southeast:	Northeast:	International:
Y					

Note: Financial information, benefits and other data can change quickly and may vary from those stated here.

NETCOM   www.netcom.se

Industry Group Code: 5133B
Ranks within this company's industry group: Sales: 4   Profits: 2

BUSINESS ACTIVITIES ("Y" = Yes)

Financial Services:	Information/Publ.:	Technology:	Services:	Retailing:	Telecommunications:	
Stock Brokerage	Portal/Hub/News	Computer Manuf.	Payments/Transfers	Retailer	Internet Serv. Provider	Y
Mortgages/Loans	On-Line Community	Networking Equip.	Consulting	Auctions	Web Site Host	
Banking	Search Engine	Software Manuf.	Advertising/Marketing	Mall	Server Farm	
Insurance	Financial Data Publ.	Specialty Equipment	Outsourcing	Tickets/Travel	Specialty Telecom.	Y
Credit Cards	Broadcasting/Music			Price Comparisons	High Speed Access	

TYPES OF BUSINESS:

Voice and Data Transmission Services
Cable TV
Systems Integration
Internet Services
Internet Services

BRANDS/DIVISIONS/AFFILIATES:

Tele2
Tele2 Denmark
Tele2 Norway
Comviq GSM
Kabelvision
NetCom ASA
Industriforvaltnings
AB Kinnerik

CONTACTS: *Note: Officers with more than one job title may be intentionally listed here more than once.*

Lars-Johan Jarnheimer, Pres.
Jorgen Latte, Sr.VP/CFO
Fredrik Berglund, VP- Mktg. and Sales
Lars-Erik Svegander, Mgr.-Human Resources
Krister Skalberg, Dir.-Tech.
Robert Hultman, Mgr.- Info.
Krister Skalberg, Dir.-Oper.
Henrik Ringmar, Pres.-Tele2 Norge AS

Phone: +46-8-562-00-40	**Fax:** +46-8-562-000-40

Toll-Free:

Address: Skeppsbron 18, PO Box 2094, SE-103 13, Stockholm, Sweden,

GROWTH PLANS/SPECIAL FEATURES:

NetCom is a leading telecommunications company in Scandinavia. In the areas of public telecommunications, data communication services and Internet services, NetCom operates Tele2 in Sweden, Tele2 A/S in Denmark and Tele2 Norge AS in Norway. Additionally, NetCom operates NätTeknik and Datametrix, companies specializing in systems integration, and Kabelvision, a Swedish cable TV services company. Other brand name telecommunication products are offered through Comviq and Tele2Mobil in Sweden, NetCom ASA in Norway and through subsidiary Ritabell (Q GSM) in Estonia. Tele2 is a leading operator of voice and data transmission in Sweden. Tele2 Denmark and Tele2 Norway both provide telephony services in their respective countries. Comviq GSM provides Sweden with mobile telecommunications services. NetCom's focus changed from holding its telecommunications companies to operating them after splitting from parent company Industriforvaltnings AB Kinnevik.

FINANCIALS: Sales and profits are in thousands of dollars—add 000 to get the full amount.

Notes regarding 1999: *(1999 sales and profits were not available for all companies at press time.)*

1999 Sales: $	1999 Profits: $	**Stock Ticker: NECS**
1998 Sales: $736,600	1998 Profits: $8,200	Employees: 1,052
1997 Sales: $510,600	1997 Profits: $6,100	Fiscal Year Ends: 12/31
1996 Sales: $434,200	1996 Profits: $36,400	
1995 Sales: $299,600	1995 Profits: $-132,500	

SALARIES/BENEFITS:

Pension Plan:	ESOP Stock Plan:	Profit Sharing:	Top Exec. Salary: $	Bonus: $
Savings Plan:	Stock Purch. Plan:		Second Exec. Salary: $	Bonus: $

COMPETITIVE ADVANTAGE: Major share of Scandinavian Internet service market.

OTHER THOUGHTS:

Apparent Women Officers or Directors:
Apparent Minority Officers or Directors:
Hot Spot for Advancement for Women/Minorities:

LOCATIONS: ("Y" = Yes)

West:	Southwest:	Midwest:	Southeast:	Northeast:	International:
					Y

NETCREATIONS   www.netcreations.com

Industry Group Code: 54189A
Ranks within this company's industry group: Sales: 14   Profits: 2

BUSINESS ACTIVITIES ("Y" = Yes)

Financial Services:	Information/Publ.:	Technology:	Services:		Retailing:	Telecommunications:
Stock Brokerage	Portal/Hub/News	Computer Manuf.	Payments/Transfers		Retailer	Internet Serv. Provider
Mortgages/Loans	On-Line Community	Networking Equip.	Consulting		Auctions	Web Site Host
Banking	Search Engine	Software Manuf.	Advertising/Marketing	Y	Mall	Server Farm
Insurance	Financial Data Publ.	Specialty Equipment	Outsourcing	Y	Tickets/Travel	Specialty Telecom.
Credit Cards	Broadcasting/Music				Price Comparisons	High Speed Access

TYPES OF BUSINESS:

Outsourcing-Direct Marketing Services
Opt-in E-mail Lists

BRANDS/DIVISIONS/AFFILIATES:

PostMaster Direct

GROWTH PLANS/SPECIAL FEATURES:

NetCreations, a direct marketing firm, uses an opt-in system to compile e-mail lists to ensure that only interested parties receive its advertising messages. The company also specializes in e-mail address list management, brokerage and delivery. Its PostMaster Direct service offers a collection of millions of names organized into 3,000 interest areas that clients can rent. NetCreations has arrangements with more than 175 web site operators, including CMPnet and NetZero, to sign up users who wish to receive e-mail ads. Lists are owned by the web sites, which share the generated revenue. The company recently reached a benchmark. Its database now holds over 5 million names. NetCreations formed a strategic alliance with AltaVista, in which the company's services will be utilized in an effort to fight spam (unwanted e-mail).

CONTACTS: Note: Officers with more than one job title may be intentionally listed here more than once.

Rosalind B. Resnick, CEO
Rosalind B. Resnick, Pres.
Gary Sindler, CFO
Larry Mahon, VP-Sales
Ryan Scott Druckenmiller, Chief Tech. Officer
Ryan Scott Druckenmiller, Sec.
Daniel Sweeney, VP-Bus. Dev.

Phone: 212-625-1370	Fax: 212-625-1387
Toll-Free:	
Address: 379 W. Broadway, Ste. 202, New York, NY, 10012	

FINANCIALS: Sales and profits are in thousands of dollars—add 000 to get the full amount.

Notes regarding 1999: *(1999 sales and profits were not available for all companies at press time.)*

1999 Sales: $20,700	1999 Profits: $4,500	Stock Ticker: **NTCR**
1998 Sales: $3,400	1998 Profits: $ 600	Employees: 19
1997 Sales: $1,100	1997 Profits: $ 300	Fiscal Year Ends: 12/31
1996 Sales: $ 500	1996 Profits: $	
1995 Sales: $ 100	1995 Profits: $	

SALARIES/BENEFITS:

Pension Plan:	ESOP Stock Plan:	Profit Sharing:	Top Exec. Salary: $	Bonus: $
Savings Plan:	Stock Purch. Plan:		Second Exec. Salary: $	Bonus: $

COMPETITIVE ADVANTAGE: Over 5 million e-mail addresses in database/Affiliate mandating program.

OTHER THOUGHTS:

Apparent Women Officers or Directors: 1
Apparent Minority Officers or Directors:
Hot Spot for Advancement for Women/Minorities:

LOCATIONS: ("Y" = Yes)

West:	Southwest:	Midwest:	Southeast:	Northeast:	International:
				Y	

NETIVATION.COM INC   www.netivation.com

Industry Group Code: 514191
Ranks within this company's industry group: Sales: 43   Profits: 13

BUSINESS ACTIVITIES ("Y" = Yes)

Financial Services:	Information/Publ.:		Technology:	Services:	Retailing:		Telecommunications:
Stock Brokerage	Portal/Hub/News	Y	Computer Manuf.	Payments/Transfers	Retailer		Internet Serv. Provider
Mortgages/Loans	On-Line Community		Networking Equip.	Consulting	Auctions	Y	Web Site Host
Banking	Search Engine		Software Manuf.	Advertising/Marketing	Mall	Y	Server Farm
Insurance	Financial Data Publ.		Specialty Equipment	Outsourcing	Tickets/Travel		Specialty Telecom.
Credit Cards	Broadcasting/Music				Price Comparisons		High Speed Access

TYPES OF BUSINESS:
Portals-Healthcare and Politics

BRANDS/DIVISIONS/AFFILIATES:
Votenet
Medinex
DiscountMed Books
MedMarket.com
MedMarket Auction
MedMarket, Inc.
MedMarket Network
Politicallyblack.com, Inc.

CONTACTS: Note: Officers with more than one job title may be intentionally listed here more than once.
Anthony J. Paquin, CEO
David C. Paquin, COO
Lawrence L. Burch, CFO
Gary S. Paquin, Chief Mktg. Officer
Robert D. Gober, Medical Dir.
Gary S. Paquin, Sec.
Russell D. Reese, Product Dev. Mgr.
Lawrence L Burch, Treas.

Phone: 208-762-2526	Fax: 208-762-3525
Toll-Free:	
Address: 7950 Meadowlark Way, Coeur d' Alene, ID, 83815	

GROWTH PLANS/SPECIAL FEATURES:

Netivation.com, Inc. develops and operates topic-specific Internet portals designed to permit persons and businesses sharing a common interest to access its services, the resources of the Internet and e-commerce. The company currently operates two Internet portals. Votenet, its public policy and political community site, includes content, products and services designed for candidates for political office, voters, political organizations, political action committees and lobbyists. Medinex, its healthcare-focused community, provides content, products and services for primary care physicians, healthcare conscious consumers, patients and their families, pharmaceutical and insurance companies and others involved in the healthcare market. Netivation.com, Inc. plans to develop a sense of loyalty within each community by offering specialized software applications to key participants that encourage their ongoing involvement within the community. The company's site offers e-mail, web site design and hosting, specialized news, discussion forums and search engines. Netivation.com generates revenue from its growing e-commerce division, including DiscountMedBooks, MedMarket.com and MedMarketAuction. It also generates revenue from the sale of its candidate kits, on-line fundraising fees, revenue from services provided by Raintree Communications and FECinfo, as well as the sale of advertising on its site. Netivation.com recently acquired MedMarket, Inc. and politicalllyblack.com, Inc., the first web site dedicated to promoting African American economics, politics and civic participation.

FINANCIALS: Sales and profits are in thousands of dollars—add 000 to get the full amount.
Notes regarding 1999: Through 9 months (1999 sales and profits were not available for all companies at press time.)

1999 Sales: $ 563	1999 Profits: $-5,300	Stock Ticker: **NTVN**
1998 Sales: $ 100	1998 Profits: $-2,300	Employees: 36
1997 Sales: $	1997 Profits: $- 100	Fiscal Year Ends: 12/31
1996 Sales: $	1996 Profits: $	
1995 Sales: $	1995 Profits: $	

SALARIES/BENEFITS:

Pension Plan:	ESOP Stock Plan:	Profit Sharing:	Top Exec. Salary: $	Bonus: $
Savings Plan:	Stock Purch. Plan:		Second Exec. Salary: $	Bonus: $

COMPETITIVE ADVANTAGE: Focus on politics and social content.

OTHER THOUGHTS:
Apparent Women Officers or Directors:
Apparent Minority Officers or Directors:
Hot Spot for Advancement for Women/Minorities:

LOCATIONS: ("Y" = Yes)

West:	Southwest:	Midwest:	Southeast:	Northeast:	International:
Y				Y	

NETMANAGE INC   www.netmanage.com

Industry Group Code: 5112
Ranks within this company's industry group: Sales: 11   Profits: 51

BUSINESS ACTIVITIES ("Y" = Yes)

Financial Services:	Information/Publ.:	Technology:		Services:	Retailing:	Telecommunications:
Stock Brokerage	Portal/Hub/News	Computer Manuf.		Payments/Transfers	Retailer	Internet Serv. Provider
Mortgages/Loans	On-Line Community	Networking Equip.	Y	Consulting	Auctions	Web Site Host
Banking	Search Engine	Software Manuf.	Y	Advertising/Marketing	Mall	Server Farm
Insurance	Financial Data Publ.	Specialty Equipment		Outsourcing	Tickets/Travel	Specialty Telecom.
Credit Cards	Broadcasting/Music				Price Comparisons	High Speed Access

TYPES OF BUSINESS:

Software-Application
Development Tools
Networking Software
E-mail Software

BRANDS/DIVISIONS/AFFILIATES:

Chameleon
NEWT
OpSession
SupportNow
Syzygy Communications, Inc.
Arabesque Software
Maximum Information, Inc.
AGELogic, Inc.

CONTACTS: *Note: Officers with more than one job title may be intentionally listed here more than once.*

Zvi Alon, CEO/Pres.
Kevin Vitale, Exec.VP/COO
Gary Anderson, CFO/Sr.VP-Finance
Patrick Linehan, Sr. VP-Worldwide Mktg.
Judith Somerville, Dir.-Human Resources
Ido Hardonag, VP-Worldwide Engineering
Gary Anderson, Sec.
Peter Havart-Simkin, Sr. VP-Strategic Dev. and New Bus.
Glen Brownlee, Sr.VP/General Mgr.-eSolutions Group
Richard D. French, Sr.VP/General Mgr.-eSupport Group

Phone: 408-973-7171	Fax: 408-257-6405
Toll-Free:	
Address: 10725 North De Anza Boulevard, Cupertino, CA, 95014	

GROWTH PLANS/SPECIAL FEATURES:

NetManage, Inc. develops, markets and supports software applications for connecting personal computers to UNIX (R), AS/400, midrange and corporate mainframe computers and software. These products increase the productivity of corporate call centers and allow real-time application sharing on corporate networks and across the Internet. The company was one of the first to develop and market a Windows-based transmission protocol that has since become the industry standard for the Internet. The company's business is focused on taking advantage of three major industry trends: expansion of the Internet, continued mobilization of personal computer users and broader access to corporate data and information. NetManage has two types of connectivity software products: personal computer (PC) connectivity and visual connectivity. PC connectivity products provide the technology to enable the connection between personal computers and large corporate computers. Significant products for PC connectivity include the Chameleon family of software products. These provide local and remote connectivity and allow the exchange of information between Windows PCs and other computers across different networking environments and operating systems. The company's visual connectivity products add value to its PC connectivity product offerings and also target new market segments. Current company products include SupportNow and OpSession, software tools that help reduce the length of support phone calls from end users. NetManage's products are used in 90% of Fortune 100 organizations and in more than 55 countries.

FINANCIALS: Sales and profits are in thousands of dollars—add 000 to get the full amount.

Notes regarding 1999: *(1999 sales and profits were not available for all companies at press time.)*

1999 Sales: $79,200	1999 Profits: $-27,500	Stock Ticker: **NETM**
1998 Sales: $71,700	1998 Profits: $-10,000	Employees: 455
1997 Sales: $61,500	1997 Profits: $-33,800	Fiscal Year Ends: 12/31
1996 Sales: $104,600	1996 Profits: $-5,700	
1995 Sales: $125,400	1995 Profits: $22,300	

SALARIES/BENEFITS:

Pension Plan:	ESOP Stock Plan:	Profit Sharing:	Top Exec. Salary: $302,500	Bonus: $45,375
Savings Plan: Y	Stock Purch. Plan: Y		Second Exec. Salary: $250,000	Bonus: $31,250

COMPETITIVE ADVANTAGE: First to develop Transmission Control Protocol/Internet Protocol (TCP/IP) applications specifically for Windows/Capitalizes on market trends.

OTHER THOUGHTS:

Apparent Women Officers or Directors: 1
Apparent Minority Officers or Directors: 4
Hot Spot for Advancement for Women/Minorities: Y

LOCATIONS: ("Y" = Yes)

West:	Southwest:	Midwest:	Southeast:	Northeast:	International:
Y				Y	Y

NETOBJECTS INC   www.netobjects.com

Industry Group Code: 5112
Ranks within this company's industry group: Sales: 43   Profits: 6

BUSINESS ACTIVITIES ("Y" = Yes)

Financial Services:	Information/Publ.:	Technology:		Services:	Retailing:	Telecommunications:
Stock Brokerage	Portal/Hub/News	Computer Manuf.		Payments/Transfers	Retailer	Internet Serv. Provider
Mortgages/Loans	On-Line Community	Networking Equip.	Y	Consulting	Auctions	Web Site Host
Banking	Search Engine	Software Manuf.	Y	Advertising/Marketing	Mall	Server Farm
Insurance	Financial Data Publ.	Specialty Equipment		Outsourcing	Tickets/Travel	Specialty Telecom.
Credit Cards	Broadcasting/Music				Price Comparisons	High Speed Access

TYPES OF BUSINESS:

Software-Web Site Design
ASP-Web Site Building

BRANDS/DIVISIONS/AFFILIATES:

NetObjects Fusion
NetObjects Authoring Server Suite
GoBizGo.com
Sitematic Corporation
IBM

CONTACTS: Note: Officers with more than one job title may be intentionally listed here more than once.

Samir Arora, CEO
Russell F. Surmanek, CFO
Mark Patton, Sr. VP-Worldwide Sales/Corp. Mktg.
Gary White, VP-Human Resources
Gagan Arora, Chief Tech. Architect
Gagan Arora, VP-Engineering
Russell F. Surmanek, Exec. VP-Oper.
Clement Mok, Chief Creative Architect

Phone: 650-482-3200	Fax: 650-562-0288
Toll-Free:	
Address: 301 Galveston Dr., Redwood City, CA, 94063	

GROWTH PLANS/SPECIAL FEATURES:

NetObjects, Inc. is a leading provider of software, solutions and services that enable small businesses to build, deploy and maintain web sites and conduct e-business. The firm also enables large enterprises to effectively create and manage corporate intranets. The company's e-business solutions address the growing challenges faced by businesses in utilizing the Internet as an on-line business medium to publish content, run web applications and manage e-business operations. NetObjects created the category of site-oriented web site building products and leads the market with two product lines: NetObjects Fusion and NetObjects Authoring Server Suite. NetObjects Fusion allows small and medium-sized businesses to build e-business web sites quickly and easily. NetObjects Authoring Server Suite enables web teams to work together to develop, manage and update business web sites more efficiently. In addition, NetObjects offers its customers on-line solutions, including content, products and services to help them register, host, build, maintain and promote their web sites. Recently, the company acquired Sitematic Corporation, an application service provider that offers on-line web site building capabilities for small businesses. NetObjects combined its on-line resources and launched GoBizGo.com, a web application service site where small businesses can find the solutions and services needed to build a successful web presence. IBM Owns 54% of NetObjects.

FINANCIALS: Sales and profits are in thousands of dollars—add 000 to get the full amount.

Notes regarding 1999: *(1999 sales and profits were not available for all companies at press time.)*

1999 Sales: $22,200	1999 Profits: $17,200	Stock Ticker: **NETO**
1998 Sales: $15,300	1998 Profits: $20,900	Employees:
1997 Sales: $7,600	1997 Profits: $17,600	Fiscal Year Ends: 9/30
1996 Sales: $	1996 Profits: $	
1995 Sales: $	1995 Profits: $	

SALARIES/BENEFITS:

Pension Plan:	ESOP Stock Plan: Y	Profit Sharing:	Top Exec. Salary: $175,338	Bonus: $47,434
Savings Plan: Y	Stock Purch. Plan:		Second Exec. Salary: $	Bonus: $

COMPETITIVE ADVANTAGE: Provides turn-key solutions in an easy-to-use format suitable for small businesses.

OTHER THOUGHTS:

Apparent Women Officers or Directors:
Apparent Minority Officers or Directors: 2
Hot Spot for Advancement for Women/Minorities: Y

LOCATIONS: ("Y" = Yes)

West:	Southwest:	Midwest:	Southeast:	Northeast:	International:
Y					

NETSCOUT SYSTEMS   www.netscout.com

Industry Group Code: 5112
Ranks within this company's industry group: Sales: 22   Profits: 10

BUSINESS ACTIVITIES ("Y" = Yes)

Financial Services:	Information/Publ.:	Technology:		Services:	Retailing:	Telecommunications:
Stock Brokerage	Portal/Hub/News	Computer Manuf.		Payments/Transfers	Retailer	Internet Serv. Provider
Mortgages/Loans	On-Line Community	Networking Equip.		Consulting	Auctions	Web Site Host
Banking	Search Engine	Software Manuf.	Y	Advertising/Marketing	Mall	Server Farm
Insurance	Financial Data Publ.	Specialty Equipment		Outsourcing	Tickets/Travel	Specialty Telecom.
Credit Cards	Broadcasting/Music				Price Comparisons	High Speed Access

TYPES OF BUSINESS:

Software-Tracking Network Applications
Application Management Solutions

BRANDS/DIVISIONS/AFFILIATES:

Application Flow Management (AFM)
NetScout Server
NetScout Manager Plus

CONTACTS: Note: Officers with more than one job title may be intentionally listed here more than once.

Anil K. Singhal, CEO
Narendra Popat, COO
Charles W. Tillett, VP-Finance/CFO
Michael Szabados, VP-Mktg.
Joyce Poggi-Hager, Dir.-Human Resources
Ashwani Singhal, VP-Engineering
Tracy Steele, VP-Mfg.
Charles W. Tillett, VP-Admin.
Nathan Kalowski, VP-Business Dev.

Phone: 978-614-4000	Fax: 978-614-4004
Toll-Free: 800-357-7666	
Address: 4 Technology Park Dr., Westford, MA, 01886	

GROWTH PLANS/SPECIAL FEATURES:

NetScout Systems designs, develops, manufactures, markets and supports an integrated family of products that enable businesses and service providers to manage the performance of computer networks and important business software applications. The company's objective is to enhance its leadership position in the network and application performance management market. Its Application Flow Management (AFM) solution consists of data collection devices and analysis and presentation software. AFM collects, aggregates and analyzes network and application data from a wide range of network technologies. Using this data, AFM provides real-time information regarding the performance of computer networks and individual software applications, such as e-mail, order entry and web-based applications. The company's software supports switched LANs, frame relays and Ethernet systems and enables users to analyze, manage and troubleshoot trends and problems in network traffic. NetScout Server works with NetScout Manager Plus to mange remote sites. NetScout Manager Plus generates reports for capacity planning, policy administration and security audits. 3M, AT&Tand Toys 'R' US are customers of NetScout Systems. The company sells its products through distributors, OEMs and VARs.

FINANCIALS: Sales and profits are in thousands of dollars—add 000 to get the full amount.
Notes regarding 1999: *(1999 sales and profits were not available for all companies at press time.)*

1999 Sales: $67,600	1999 Profits: $10,300	**Stock Ticker: NTCT**
1998 Sales: $42,800	1998 Profits: $5,400	Employees: 209
1997 Sales: $30,600	1997 Profits: $5,900	Fiscal Year Ends: 3/31
1996 Sales: $15,700	1996 Profits: $2,000	
1995 Sales: $5,900	1995 Profits: $ 600	

SALARIES/BENEFITS:

Pension Plan:	ESOP Stock Plan:	Profit Sharing:	Top Exec. Salary: $	Bonus: $
Savings Plan: Y	Stock Purch. Plan:		Second Exec. Salary: $	Bonus: $

COMPETITIVE ADVANTAGE: Real-time information regarding the performance of networks.

OTHER THOUGHTS:

Apparent Women Officers or Directors: 2
Apparent Minority Officers or Directors: 3
Hot Spot for Advancement for Women/Minorities: Y

LOCATIONS: ("Y" = Yes)

West:	Southwest:	Midwest:	Southeast:	Northeast:	International:
				Y	

NETSPEAK   www.netspeak.com

Industry Group Code: 5112
Ranks within this company's industry group: Sales: 55   Profits: 59

BUSINESS ACTIVITIES ("Y" – Yes)

Financial Services:	Information/Publ.:	Technology:		Services:		Retailing:	Telecommunications:	
Stock Brokerage	Portal/Hub/News	Computer Manuf.		Payments/Transfers		Retailer	Internet Serv. Provider	
Mortgages/Loans	On-Line Community	Networking Equip.		Consulting		Auctions	Web Site Host	
Banking	Search Engine	Software Manuf.	Y	Advertising/Marketing		Mall	Server Farm	
Insurance	Financial Data Publ.	Specialty Equipment		Outsourcing		Tickets/Travel	Specialty Telecom.	Y
Credit Cards	Broadcasting/Music					Price Comparisons	High Speed Access	

TYPES OF BUSINESS:

Software-Telecommunications
Internet Telephony

BRANDS/DIVISIONS/AFFILIATES:

Netspeak Gatekeeper

CONTACTS: *Note: Officers with more than one job title may be intentionally listed here more than once.*

Stephen R. Cohen, CEO
Michael R. Rich, COO/Pres.
John W. Staten, CFO
James C. Kwock, VP-Mktg.
John W. Staten, Sec.
Neville O'Reilly, VP-Strategy and Business Planning
John C. Mitchell, Chief Architect
Lane M. Bess, Sr.VP-Sales

Phone: 561-998-8700	Fax: 561-997-2401
Toll-Free:	
Address: 902 Clint Moore Rd., Suite 104, Boca Raton, FL, 33487	

GROWTH PLANS/SPECIAL FEATURES:

NetSpeak is a developer of Internet telephony software, enabling real-time voice, data and video conversations between computers and telephones. NetSpeak's solutions allow customers to build new voice and video communications networks or to add communication capabilities to existing enterprises. NetSpeak is working towards creating solutions that are easily compatible with other vendors' equipment, with minimal customization, to make the products easier to market and sell. NetSpeak's customers include Internet service providers and telecommunications providers such as Siemens and Motorola. Motorola owns about 30% of NetSpeak. iBasis, a global leader in Internet-based communications services, has selected NetSpeak to be the provider of call management infrastructure products for deployment on its worldwide Cisco powered network. The company has increased spending on research and development to create new applications and extend the features and functionality of current applications.

FINANCIALS: Sales and profits are in thousands of dollars—add 000 to get the full amount.

Notes regarding 1999: *(1999 sales and profits were not available for all companies at press time.)*

1999 Sales: $7,600	1999 Profits: $-12,200	Stock Ticker: **NSPK**
1998 Sales: $7,700	1998 Profits: $-12,100	Employees: 124
1997 Sales: $5,400	1997 Profits: $-5,100	Fiscal Year Ends: 12/31
1996 Sales: $ 900	1996 Profits: $-2,900	
1995 Sales: $	1995 Profits: $	

SALARIES/BENEFITS:

Pension Plan:	ESOP Stock Plan: Y	Profit Sharing:	Top Exec. Salary: $275,000	Bonus: $
Savings Plan: Y	Stock Purch. Plan:		Second Exec. Salary: $250,000	Bonus: $

COMPETITIVE ADVANTAGE: Relationship with communications giant Motorola.

OTHER THOUGHTS:

Apparent Women Officers or Directors:
Apparent Minority Officers or Directors:
Hot Spot for Advancement for Women/Minorities:

LOCATIONS: ("Y" = Yes)

West:	Southwest:	Midwest:	Southeast:	Northeast:	International:
			Y		

Note: Financial information, benefits and other data can change quickly and may vary from those stated here.

NETWORK APPLIANCE INC   www.netapp.com

Industry Group Code: 3341D
Ranks within this company's industry group: Sales: 2   Profits: 2

BUSINESS ACTIVITIES ("Y" = Yes)

Financial Services:	Information/Publ.:	Technology:		Services:	Retailing:	Telecommunications:
Stock Brokerage	Portal/Hub/News	Computer Manuf.		Payments/Transfers	Retailer	Internet Serv. Provider
Mortgages/Loans	On-Line Community	Networking Equip.	Y	Consulting	Auctions	Web Site Host
Banking	Search Engine	Software Manuf.	Y	Advertising/Marketing	Mall	Server Farm
Insurance	Financial Data Publ.	Specialty Equipment		Outsourcing	Tickets/Travel	Specialty Telecom.
Credit Cards	Broadcasting/Music				Price Comparisons	High Speed Access

TYPES OF BUSINESS:

Manufacturer of Network Data Storage Devices
Clustered Data Servers

BRANDS/DIVISIONS/AFFILIATES:

Data ONTAP
NetAPP F
NetCache

CONTACTS: Note: Officers with more than one job title may be intentionally listed here more than once.

Daniel Warmenhoven, CEO
Daniel Warmenhoven, Pres.
Jeffry Allen, CFO/Sr. VP-Finance
Thomas F. Mendoza, Sr. VP- Worldwide Sales and Mktg.
Christabel Carlton, VP-Human Resources
Scott Klimke, VP- Info. Systems/CIO
M. Helen Bradley, Sr.VP- Engineering
Charles E. Simmons, VP- Corp. Dev.

Phone: 408-822-6000	**Fax:** 408-822-4501
Toll-Free:	
Address: 495 E. Java Dr., Sunnyvale, CA, 94089	

GROWTH PLANS/SPECIAL FEATURES:

Network Appliance supplies network-attached data storage and access devices, filers, that provide fast, simple, reliable and cost-effective file service for data-intensive network environments. The company pioneered the concept of the network appliance, an extension of the industry trend towards dedicated, specialized devices that perform a single function in the network. Network Appliance's filer products combine specialized proprietary software and state-of-the-art industry standard hardware to provide a unique solution for NFS, Common Internet File System and HTTP server markets. As a part of the company's ongoing development process, Network Appliance recently introduced a significant software release - Data ONTAP release 4.1. The company also released NetApp F210, NetApp F230, NetApp F520, NetApp F630 and NetCache. In addition, the company has new network file servers under development. The company recently announced the use of advanced features from Tandem Computers' ServerNet Interconnect technology in NetApp's new F6300 clustered data server. The result is an ultra-high availability data server cluster for supporting enterprise-level applications. In the future, Network Appliance will continue to work with customers and other industry leaders in order to develop fast, simple and reliable data access solutions.

FINANCIALS: Sales and profits are in thousands of dollars—add 000 to get the full amount.

Notes regarding 1999: *(1999 sales and profits were not available for all companies at press time.)*

1999 Sales: $289,400	1999 Profits: $35,600	**Stock Ticker: NTAP**
1998 Sales: $166,200	1998 Profits: $21,000	Employees: 816
1997 Sales: $93,300	1997 Profits: $ 300	Fiscal Year Ends: 4/30
1996 Sales: $46,600	1996 Profits: $6,600	
1995 Sales: $14,800	1995 Profits: $-4,800	

SALARIES/BENEFITS:

Pension Plan:	ESOP Stock Plan:	Profit Sharing:	Top Exec. Salary: $292,789	Bonus: $102,000
Savings Plan: Y	Stock Purch. Plan: Y		Second Exec. Salary: $193,077	Bonus: $53,000

COMPETITIVE ADVANTAGE: Focus on the data storage market.

OTHER THOUGHTS:

Apparent Women Officers or Directors: 2
Apparent Minority Officers or Directors:
Hot Spot for Advancement for Women/Minorities: Y

LOCATIONS: ("Y" = Yes)

West:	Southwest:	Midwest:	Southeast:	Northeast:	International:
Y					Y

NETWORK ASSOCIATES INC   www.nai.com

Industry Group Code: 5112
Ranks within this company's industry group: Sales: 3   Profits: 4

BUSINESS ACTIVITIES ("Y" = Yes)

Financial Services:	Information/Publ.:	Technology:		Services:	Retailing:	Telecommunications:
Stock Brokerage	Portal/Hub/News	Computer Manuf.		Payments/Transfers	Retailer	Internet Serv. Provider
Mortgages/Loans	On-Line Community	Networking Equip.		Consulting	Auctions	Web Site Host
Banking	Search Engine	Software Manuf.	Y	Advertising/Marketing	Mall	Server Farm
Insurance	Financial Data Publ.	Specialty Equipment		Outsourcing	Tickets/Travel	Specialty Telecom.
Credit Cards	Broadcasting/Music				Price Comparisons	High Speed Access

TYPES OF BUSINESS:
Software-Security

BRANDS/DIVISIONS/AFFILIATES:
McAfee Total Virus Defense
PGP Total Network Security
Sniffer Total Network Visibility
McAfee Total Service Desk
Gauntlet
Magic Help Desk Applications

CONTACTS: Note: Officers with more than one job title may be intentionally listed here more than once.
William L. Larson, CEO
William L. Larson, Pres.
Prabhat K. Goyal, CFO/VP-Finance
Zachary A. Nelson, Exec. VP-Worldwide Mktg.
Pat Schoof, Dir.-Human Resources
Gerri Martin-Flickinger, VP-CIO
Prabhat K. Goyal, VP-Admin.
Joanne Evans, Exec.VP-Worldwide Field Oper.

Phone: 408-988-3832	Fax: 408-970-9727
Toll-Free:	
Address: 3965 Freedom Circle, Santa Clara, CA, 95054	

GROWTH PLANS/SPECIAL FEATURES:

Network Associates, Inc., is the worldwide leading supplier of network security and management software and the eighth largest independent software company in the U.S.   The company's product offerings include McAfee anti-virus, PGP encryption, Gauntlet firewall Magic Help Desk Applications and Sniffer network analyzers, which are designed to be centrally managed from within the Network Associates' Net Tools unified management environment. Many of the company's network security and management products, including its industry-leading network security products for anti-virus protection and Sniffer software-based fault and performance solutions for managing computer networks, are available as stand-alone products or as part of smaller product suites.   The company is also a leader in electronic software distribution, which is the principal means by which it markets its products and one of the principal ways it distributes its software products to its customers. Revenues have fallen since December 1998, reflecting the decision to limit distributor orders and efforts in developing marketing force and infrastructure. Network Associates plans to continue to enhance its products and expand its product coverage.   One distribution method involves including complimentary software in suite packages. Networks Associates is the first company to provide an anti-virus for Lotus Notes R5.

FINANCIALS: Sales and profits are in thousands of dollars—add 000 to get the full amount.
Notes regarding 1999: Estimated (1999 sales and profits were not available for all companies at press time.)

1999 Sales: $683,700	1999 Profits: $-159,900	Stock Ticker: **NETA**
1998 Sales: $990,000	1998 Profits: $36,400	Employees: 2,700
1997 Sales: $421,794	1997 Profits: $64,110	Fiscal Year Ends: 12/31
1996 Sales: $278,910	1996 Profits: $42,341	
1995 Sales: $	1995 Profits: $	

SALARIES/BENEFITS:

Pension Plan:	ESOP Stock Plan:	Profit Sharing:	Top Exec. Salary: $1,051,921	Bonus: $178,850
Savings Plan: Y	Stock Purch. Plan: Y		Second Exec. Salary: $659,515	Bonus: $41,771

COMPETITIVE ADVANTAGE: Excellent technology/ Extensive investment in R&D.

OTHER THOUGHTS:

Apparent Women Officers or Directors:
Apparent Minority Officers or Directors: 1
Hot Spot for Advancement for Women/Minorities:

LOCATIONS: ("Y" = Yes)

West:	Southwest:	Midwest:	Southeast:	Northeast:	International:
Y	Y	Y		Y	

NETWORK SOLUTIONS INC   www.netsol.com

Industry Group Code: 51339A
Ranks within this company's industry group: Sales: 2   Profits: 2

BUSINESS ACTIVITIES ("Y" = Yes)

Financial Services:	Information/Publ.:	Technology:	Services:		Retailing:	Telecommunications:	
Stock Brokerage	Portal/Hub/News	Computer Manuf.	Payments/Transfers		Retailer	Internet Serv. Provider	
Mortgages/Loans	On-Line Community	Networking Equip.	Consulting	Y	Auctions	Web Site Host	
Banking	Search Engine	Software Manuf.	Advertising/Marketing		Mall	Server Farm	
Insurance	Financial Data Publ.	Specialty Equipment	Outsourcing		Tickets/Travel	Specialty Telecom.	Y
Credit Cards	Broadcasting/Music				Price Comparisons	High Speed Access	

TYPES OF BUSINESS:
Internet Registration Services

BRANDS/DIVISIONS/AFFILIATES:
Science Applications International

CONTACTS: *Note: Officers with more than one job title may be intentionally listed here more than once.*
James P. Rutt, CEO
Robert J. Korzeniewski, CFO
Douglas L. Wolford, Sr. VP-Mktg.
Karla Leavelle, Dir.-Human Resources
David H. Holtzman, Chief Tech. Officer
Rick Walsh, Acting CIO
Jonathan W. Emery, Sec
Jonathan W. Emery, General Counsel
Neil Edwards, VP-Business Dev.
J. Christopher Clough, VP-Corp. Comm.
Michael G. Voslow, Treas.

Phone: 703-742-0400	Fax: 703-742-3386

Toll-Free: 888-642-9675
Address: 505 Huntmar Park Dr., Herndon, VA, 20170

GROWTH PLANS/SPECIAL FEATURES:

Network Solutions, Inc. is a leading Internet domain name registration services provider. The company currently acts as a registrar for second level domain names within the .com, .org, .net and .edu top-level domains, pursuant to a cooperative agreement with the Department of Commerce. The company also facilitates global registration of domain names in other existing top level domains, including country code top level domains. Through its consulting services division, the company provides enterprise network consulting services to large business that desire to establish or enhance their Internet presence or re-engineer legacy network infrastructures to accommodate the integration of both Internet connectivity and intranetwork technology into their information technology base. The company has agreed with the Department of Commerce to a shared or competitive registration system, which allows America Online, France Telecom and several others to assign web addresses during a two-month trial period. As part of the agreement, these companies will have to pay Network Solutions, Inc. $6 annually for each new registration. Research and development company Science Applications International Corp. owns 45 percent of Network Solutions.

FINANCIALS: Sales and profits are in thousands of dollars—add 000 to get the full amount.
Notes regarding 1999: *(1999 sales and profits were not available for all companies at press time.)*

1999 Sales: $220,811	1999 Profits: $26,886	Stock Ticker: **NSOL**	
1998 Sales: $93,700	1998 Profits: $11,200	Employees: 385	
1997 Sales: $45,300	1997 Profits: $4,200	Fiscal Year Ends: 12/31	
1996 Sales: $18,900	1996 Profits: $		
1995 Sales: $6,500	1995 Profits: $		

SALARIES/BENEFITS:

Pension Plan: Y	ESOP Stock Plan:	Profit Sharing:	Top Exec. Salary: $434,281	Bonus: $
Savings Plan:	Stock Purch. Plan: Y		Second Exec. Salary: $188,999	Bonus: $85,000

COMPETITIVE ADVANTAGE:
Has been the domain name registrar since the beginning of the Internet's rapid growth, making it the dominant player.

OTHER THOUGHTS:
Apparent Women Officers or Directors:
Apparent Minority Officers or Directors:
Hot Spot for Advancement for Women/Minorities:

LOCATIONS: ("Y" = Yes)

West:	Southwest:	Midwest:	Southeast:	Northeast:	International:
				Y	Y

NETWORK-1 SECURITY SOLUTIONS   www.network-1.com

Industry Group Code: 5112
Ranks within this company's industry group: Sales: 73   Profits: 36

BUSINESS ACTIVITIES ("Y" = Yes)

Financial Services:	Information/Publ.:	Technology:		Services:	Retailing:	Telecommunications:
Stock Brokerage	Portal/Hub/News	Computer Manuf.		Payments/Transfers	Retailer	Internet Serv. Provider
Mortgages/Loans	On-Line Community	Networking Equip.		Consulting	Auctions	Web Site Host
Banking	Search Engine	Software Manuf.	Y	Advertising/Marketing	Mall	Server Farm
Insurance	Financial Data Publ.	Specialty Equipment		Outsourcing	Tickets/Travel	Specialty Telecom.
Credit Cards	Broadcasting/Music				Price Comparisons	High Speed Access

TYPES OF BUSINESS:
Software-Security

BRANDS/DIVISIONS/AFFILIATES:
CyberwallPLUS

CONTACTS: Note: Officers with more than one job title may be intentionally listed here more than once.
Avi A. Fogel, CEO
Avi A. Fogel, Pres.
Murray P. Fish, CFO
Lance Westbrook, VP-North American Sales
William Hancock, Chief Tech. Officer
Joseph A. Donohue, VP-Engineering
Robert M. Russo, VP-Prof.Services and Sec.
Robert P. Olsen, VP-Product Mgmt.
Joseph D. Harris, VP-Int'l Sales

Phone: 781-522-3400	Fax: 781-522-3450
Toll-Free: 800-638-9751	
Address: 1601 Trapelo Rd., Reservoir Place, Waltham, MA, 02451	

GROWTH PLANS/SPECIAL FEATURES:

Network-1 Security Solutions develops, licenses and supports software products that provide security for computer networks, Internet-based and internal systems and information resources. The security solutions help protect computer networks from external and internal security breaches and secure communication over the Internet. Network-1's feature product line is the CyberwallPLUS line, available in three different packages. CyberwallPLUS for Windows NT is a family of firewalls that provide advanced network access controls and intrusion prevention for networks and NT servers. The CyberwallPlus packages enable system administrators to protect NT servers from unwanted access and intrusion, protect internal high-speed LANs from network intruders and attackers, and for Internet protocols, provide access controls, address translations, traffic logs and intrusion detection. Network Associates and Electronic Data Systems account for 35% of Network-1's sales. Some of the company's other customers include American Airlines, TRW, National Semiconductor, Fairchild Semiconductor, GTE and Continental Airlines.

FINANCIALS: Sales and profits are in thousands of dollars—add 000 to get the full amount.
Notes regarding 1999: Through 9 months *(1999 sales and profits were not available for all companies at press time.)*

1999 Sales: $1,357	1999 Profits: $-5,100	Stock Ticker: **NSSI**
1998 Sales: $1,800	1998 Profits: $-5,800	Employees: 36
1997 Sales: $2,400	1997 Profits: $-2,400	Fiscal Year Ends: 12/31
1996 Sales: $1,000	1996 Profits: $-4,500	
1995 Sales: $	1995 Profits: $	

SALARIES/BENEFITS:

Pension Plan:	ESOP Stock Plan: Y	Profit Sharing: Y	Top Exec. Salary: $160,000	Bonus: $
Savings Plan: Y	Stock Purch. Plan:		Second Exec. Salary: $153,746	Bonus: $5,000

COMPETITIVE ADVANTAGE: Excellent customer list/security products for networks as well as for Internet sites.

OTHER THOUGHTS:

Apparent Women Officers or Directors:
Apparent Minority Officers or Directors:
Hot Spot for Advancement for Women/Minorities:

LOCATIONS: ("Y" = Yes)

West:	Southwest:	Midwest:	Southeast:	Northeast:	International:
				Y	

NETZERO   www.netzero.com

Industry Group Code: 51339
Ranks within this company's industry group: Sales: 25   Profits: 3

BUSINESS ACTIVITIES ("Y" = Yes)

Financial Services:	Information/Publ.:	Technology:	Services:		Retailing:	Telecommunications:	
Stock Brokerage	Portal/Hub/News	Computer Manuf.	Payments/Transfers		Retailer	Internet Serv. Provider	Y
Mortgages/Loans	On-Line Community	Networking Equip.	Consulting		Auctions	Web Site Host	
Banking	Search Engine	Software Manuf.	Advertising/Marketing	Y	Mall	Server Farm	
Insurance	Financial Data Publ.	Specialty Equipment	Outsourcing		Tickets/Travel	Specialty Telecom.	
Credit Cards	Broadcasting/Music				Price Comparisons	High Speed Access	

TYPES OF BUSINESS:

Internet Service Provider-No Fee
Advertising Medium

BRANDS/DIVISIONS/AFFILIATES:

ZeroPort

GROWTH PLANS/SPECIAL FEATURES:

NetZero is the leading Internet service provider that offers Internet access free of charge. To compensate, NetZero offers advertisers an opportunity to target its users. The company also offers e-mail and navigational tools with Internet access. It has over two million registered users. NetZero's service feature is The ZeroPort. The ZeroPort is a small window that is displayed while users are navigating the Internet, regardless of where they go. The ZeroPort may be moved to any position on the screen but cannot be closed or reduced in size. The ZeroPort displays advertisements, and advertiser-sponsored buttons and icons may be linked directly to sites and services. At the time potential users sign up for the service, they must fill out a survey, including information such as age, occupation, salary and on-line behavior, so that demographic information may be transferred to advertisers to track users' on-line activity.

CONTACTS: *Note: Officers with more than one job title may be intentionally listed here more than once.*

Mark R. Goldston, CEO
Ronald T. Burr, Pres.
Charles S. Hilliard, CFO/Sr. VP-Finance
Janet C. Daly, VP-Mktg.
Paul Jordan, VP-Human Resources
Ronald T. Burr, Chief Tech. Officer
Dennis L. Gordon, VP-Info. Systems
David J. Dowling, VP-Business Dev.
Marwan A. Zebian, VP-Comm.

Phone: 805-418-2000	**Fax:** 805-418-2001
Toll-Free:	
Address: 2555 Townsgate Rd., Westlake Village, CA, 91361	

FINANCIALS: Sales and profits are in thousands of dollars—add 000 to get the full amount.

Notes regarding 1999: *(1999 sales and profits were not available for all companies at press time.)*

1999 Sales: $4,600	1999 Profits: $-15,300	Stock Ticker: **NZRO**
1998 Sales: $	1998 Profits: $	Employees: 116
1997 Sales: $	1997 Profits: $	Fiscal Year Ends: 6/30
1996 Sales: $	1996 Profits: $	
1995 Sales: $	1995 Profits: $	

SALARIES/BENEFITS:

Pension Plan:	ESOP Stock Plan: Y	Profit Sharing:	Top Exec. Salary: $140,000	Bonus: $
Savings Plan:	Stock Purch. Plan:		Second Exec. Salary: $135,000	Bonus: $

COMPETITIVE ADVANTAGE: Over 2 million users.

OTHER THOUGHTS:

Apparent Women Officers or Directors: 1
Apparent Minority Officers or Directors: 1
Hot Spot for Advancement for Women/Minorities:

LOCATIONS: ("Y" = Yes)

West:	Southwest:	Midwest:	Southeast:	Northeast:	International:
Y					

NEWSEDGE   www.newsedge.com

Industry Group Code: 51311B
Ranks within this company's industry group: Sales: 1 Profits: 7

BUSINESS ACTIVITIES ("Y" = Yes)

Financial Services:	Information/Publ.:		Technology:	Services:	Retailing:	Telecommunications:
Stock Brokerage	Portal/Hub/News	Y	Computer Manuf.	Payments/Transfers	Retailer	Internet Serv. Provider
Mortgages/Loans	On-Line Community		Networking Equip.	Consulting	Auctions	Web Site Host
Banking	Search Engine		Software Manuf.	Advertising/Marketing	Mall	Server Farm
Insurance	Financial Data Publ.		Specialty Equipment	Outsourcing	Tickets/Travel	Specialty Telecom.
Credit Cards	Broadcasting/Music	Y			Price Comparisons	High Speed Access

TYPES OF BUSINESS:

On-line News Broadcasting

BRANDS/DIVISIONS/AFFILIATES:

Individual.com, Inc.
The Enterprise Unit

CONTACTS: *Note: Officers with more than one job title may be intentionally listed here more than once.*

Donald L. McLagan, CEO
Clifford M. Pollan, COO/Pres.
Ronald Benanto, CFO/VP
Marion Hoyle, VP-Global Mktg.
Al Zink, Dir.-Human Resources
Daniel F. X. O'Rielly Jr., VP/Chief Tech. Officer
Thomas Barone, VP-Controller
John L. Moss, VP-Dev.
John Zahner, VP-Inernet Services

Phone: 781-229-3000	Fax: 781-229-3030
Toll-Free: 800-252-9980	
Address: 80 Blanchard Rd., Burlington, MA, 01803	

GROWTH PLANS/SPECIAL FEATURES:

The NewsEdge Corporation is a leading independent supplier of comprehensive business news and current awareness solutions over the Internet. The company's mission is to make news valuable for business. NewsEdge serves over 1.5 million people around the globe, delivering news on two different levels. The Enterprise Unit provides service to organizations for delivery directly to company intranets, LANs and extranets to make employees more effective and competitive. NewsEdge also offers Individual.com, Inc., a wholly-owned subsidiary providing news to individuals who make their own choices about news and information on the Internet. Some features include customized real-time news, a real-time news scroll, personalized briefings, full searching capabilities and industry-specific, company and general business news. NewsEdge searches through and adds value to news and information from over 2,000 sources, then customizes and filters the information so that users can find the most important, relevant stories from the overwhelming volume of daily news available.

FINANCIALS: Sales and profits are in thousands of dollars—add 000 to get the full amount.

Notes regarding 1999: *(1999 sales and profits were not available for all companies at press time.)*

1999 Sales: $78,400	1999 Profits: $-17,000	**Stock Ticker: NEWZ**
1998 Sales: $79,500	1998 Profits: $-17,200	Employees: 412
1997 Sales: $42,200	1997 Profits: $2,700	Fiscal Year Ends: 12/31
1996 Sales: $33,800	1996 Profits: $4,600	
1995 Sales: $23,200	1995 Profits: $2,100	

SALARIES/BENEFITS:

Pension Plan:	ESOP Stock Plan: Y	Profit Sharing:	Top Exec. Salary: $156,000	Bonus: $19,991
Savings Plan: Y	Stock Purch. Plan:		Second Exec. Salary: $156,000	Bonus: $19,991

COMPETITIVE ADVANTAGE: Well-designed, customizable news filter.

OTHER THOUGHTS:

Apparent Women Officers or Directors: 1
Apparent Minority Officers or Directors:
Hot Spot for Advancement for Women/Minorities:

LOCATIONS: ("Y" = Yes)

West:	Southwest:	Midwest:	Southeast:	Northeast:	International:
Y	Y	Y	Y	Y	Y

NEXTCARD   www.nextcard.com

Industry Group Code: 52221
Ranks within this company's industry group: Sales: 1   Profits: 1

BUSINESS ACTIVITIES ("Y" = Yes)

Financial Services:		Information/Publ.:	Technology:	Services:	Retailing:	Telecommunications:
Stock Brokerage		Portal/Hub/News	Computer Manuf.	Payments/Transfers	Retailer	Internet Serv. Provider
Mortgages/Loans		On-Line Community	Networking Equip.	Consulting	Auctions	Web Site Host
Banking		Search Engine	Software Manuf.	Advertising/Marketing	Mall	Server Farm
Insurance		Financial Data Publ.	Specialty Equipment	Outsourcing	Tickets/Travel	Specialty Telecom.
Credit Cards	Y	Broadcasting/Music			Price Comparisons	High Speed Access

TYPES OF BUSINESS:
On-line Credit Cards

BRANDS/DIVISIONS/AFFILIATES:

GROWTH PLANS/SPECIAL FEATURES:

NextCard unites banking and the Internet by providing the first truly interactive Internet credit card. NextCard wants to pave the way for Internet-based consumer credit services by providing innovative products and personalized services via the Internet. The company wants to provide the one-on-one attention of a small community bank to its customers. NextCard offered the first on-line application and approval service for a Visa card and has added features such as the NextCard rewards program, guaranteed safe on-line shopping, personalized credit card offers, PictureCard, complete on-line access to account management and customer service, a customer service chat area and a collection of powerful on-line shopping tools. NextCard provides on-line credit approval within seconds as well as customized offers based on applicants' credit profiles. The NextCard is good for both on line and off-line purchases. Over two million applications for the NextCard Visa have been received. The company has recently signed marketing agreements with Beyond.com, Travelscape.com and Amazon.com to promote the NextCard. It will make additional agreements with other leading e-commerce companies. The firm may expand into complete banking services.

CONTACTS: *Note: Officers with more than one job title may be intentionally listed here more than once.*
Jeremy R. Lent, CEO/Pres.
Timothy J. Coltrell, COO
John V. Hashman, CFO
Daniel D. Springer, Chief Mktg. Officer
Bernadette Robertson, Dir.-Human Resources
Yinzi Cai, Sr. VP-Decision Analytics
Molly Lent, Chief Corporate Dev. Officer

Phone: 415-836-9700	Fax: 415-836-9790
Toll-Free:	
Address: 595 Market St., Suite 1800, San Francisco, CA, 94105	

FINANCIALS: Sales and profits are in thousands of dollars—add 000 to get the full amount.
Notes regarding 1999: *(1999 sales and profits were not available for all companies at press time.)*

1999 Sales: $	1999 Profits: $	Stock Ticker: **NXCD**
1998 Sales: $1,200	1998 Profits: $-16,100	Employees: 122
1997 Sales: $ 100	1997 Profits: $1,900	Fiscal Year Ends: 12/31
1996 Sales: $	1996 Profits: $	
1995 Sales: $	1995 Profits: $	

SALARIES/BENEFITS:

Pension Plan:	ESOP Stock Plan: Y	Profit Sharing:	Top Exec. Salary: $384,375	Bonus: $
Savings Plan:	Stock Purch. Plan:		Second Exec. Salary: $179,167	Bonus: $

COMPETITIVE ADVANTAGE: The most innovative on-line credit card source.

OTHER THOUGHTS:

Apparent Women Officers or Directors: 1	
Apparent Minority Officers or Directors: 1	
Hot Spot for Advancement for Women/Minorities:	

LOCATIONS: ("Y" = Yes)

West:	Southwest:	Midwest:	Southeast:	Northeast:	International:
Y					

NFRONT.COM   www.nfront.com

Industry Group Code: 5112
Ranks within this company's industry group: Sales: 76   Profits: 21

BUSINESS ACTIVITIES ("Y" = Yes)

Financial Services:	Information/Publ.:	Technology:		Services:	Retailing:	Telecommunications:	
Stock Brokerage	Portal/Hub/News	Computer Manuf.		Payments/Transfers	Retailer	Internet Serv. Provider	
Mortgages/Loans	On-Line Community	Networking Equip.		Consulting	Auctions	Web Site Host	Y
Banking	Search Engine	Software Manuf.	Y	Advertising/Marketing	Mall	Server Farm	
Insurance	Financial Data Publ.	Specialty Equipment		Outsourcing	Tickets/Travel	Specialty Telecom.	
Credit Cards	Broadcasting/Music				Price Comparisons	High Speed Access	

TYPES OF BUSINESS:

Software-Internet Based Banks
Financial Services Enabler

BRANDS/DIVISIONS/AFFILIATES:

nHome
nBusiness
nBranch
Digital Insight

CONTACTS: Note: Officers with more than one job title may be intentionally listed here more than once.

Brady L. Rackley III, CEO
Robert L. Campbell, COO/Pres.
Jeffrey W. Hodges, CFO
Adam M. Naide, VP-Mktg.
Yvette Niles, Dir.-Human Resources
Shyam Dunna, VP-Info. Tech.
Steven S. Neel, Sr.VP-Oper.
W. Derek Porter, VP-Research and Dev.

Phone: 770-209-4460	Fax: 770-209-9093

Toll-Free:

Address: 520 Guthridge Ct. NW, Ste. 100, Norcross, GA, 30092

GROWTH PLANS/SPECIAL FEATURES:

nFront, Inc. provides banking and technology expertise for small- to mid-sized community banking institutions by offering its products and services quickly and affordably over the Internet through Internet-based branches. nFront has over 165 client banks using software that is specifically designed to meet the needs of customers. nFront's software packages allow individual bank customers to open new accounts, access personal financial information, pay bills and transfer funds. The software allows small business clients to debit customer accounts and process stop payment requests, payroll and tax payments. Its product line includes nHome and nBusiness, banking software for retail and small business customers, and nBranch, customized web site services, security, administrative tools and more. The solutions provided by nFront enable clients to utilize the Internet to retain current customers, acquire new customers, offer additional products and services, decrease costs and increase fee income. nFront provides customers with development and implementation services, web site design, maintenance, customer service, training, support and on-line transaction processing. nFront works closely with its clients to design the appearance of its Internet branches, implement and integrate the new software with the existing computer system and train bank employees to market nFront's products. Currently, nFront is completing a merger with Digital Insight to combine two of the leading Internet banking providers.

FINANCIALS: Sales and profits are in thousands of dollars—add 000 to get the full amount.

Notes regarding 1999: (1999 sales and profits were not available for all companies at press time.)

1999 Sales: $5,000	1999 Profits: $-3,400	Stock Ticker: NFNT
1998 Sales: $1,100	1998 Profits: $- 500	Employees: 95
1997 Sales: $ 800	1997 Profits: $	Fiscal Year Ends: 6/30
1996 Sales: $	1996 Profits: $	
1995 Sales: $	1995 Profits: $	

SALARIES/BENEFITS:

Pension Plan:	ESOP Stock Plan: Y	Profit Sharing:	Top Exec. Salary: $175,000	Bonus: $140,000
Savings Plan: Y	Stock Purch. Plan:		Second Exec. Salary: $131,550	Bonus: $94,500

COMPETITIVE ADVANTAGE: Merger with Digital Insight.

OTHER THOUGHTS:

Apparent Women Officers or Directors: 1
Apparent Minority Officers or Directors: 1
Hot Spot for Advancement for Women/Minorities:

LOCATIONS: ("Y" = Yes)

West:	Southwest:	Midwest:	Southeast:	Northeast:	International:
			Y		

NOVELL INC   www.novell.com

Industry Group Code: 3341C
Ranks within this company's industry group: Sales: 3   Profits: 8

BUSINESS ACTIVITIES ("Y" = Yes)

Financial Services:	Information/Publ.:	Technology:		Services:		Retailing:	Telecommunications:
Stock Brokerage	Portal/Hub/News	Computer Manuf.		Payments/Transfers		Retailer	Internet Serv. Provider
Mortgages/Loans	On-Line Community	Networking Equip.	Y	Consulting		Auctions	Web Site Host
Banking	Search Engine	Software Manuf.	Y	Advertising/Marketing		Mall	Server Farm
Insurance	Financial Data Publ.	Specialty Equipment	Y	Outsourcing		Tickets/Travel	Specialty Telecom.
Credit Cards	Broadcasting/Music					Price Comparisons	High Speed Access

TYPES OF BUSINESS:

Networking and Application Software
Distributed Infrastructure
Network Services
Advanced Network Access
Network Applications

BRANDS/DIVISIONS/AFFILIATES:

WordPerfect Corporation
UNIX System Laboratories, Inc.
Quattro Pro product line
NetWare Systems Group
NetWare Products Division
AppWare Division
Novell Applications Group

CONTACTS: Note: Officers with more than one job title may be intentionally listed here more than once.

Eric E. Schmidt, CEO
Dennis R. Raney, Sr. VP/CFO
Ronald E. Heinz Jr., Sr. VP-Worldwide Sales
Jennifer A. Konecny-Costa, Sr. VP-Human Resources
Drew Major, VP-Advanced Dev./Chief Scientist
Sheri Anderson, Sr. VP/CIO
David R. Bradford, Sr. VP/Corp. Sec.
Brian Dudley, VP-Oper.
Stewart G. Nelson, Sr. VP-Product Dev.
Steve L. Adams, VP/General Mgr., In-The-Net Solutions Group

Phone: 801-861-7000	Fax: 801-228-7077
Toll-Free: 800-453-1267	
Address: 122 East 1700 South, Provo, UT, 84606	

GROWTH PLANS/SPECIAL FEATURES:

Novell, Inc. is a leading provider of network software. The company offers a wide range of network solutions, education and support for distributed network, Internet and small-business markets. Novell Directory Services (NDS) is a key part of Novell's strategy for providing infrastructure software for business intranets and the Internet. NDS is a distributed database of users, network equipment, computer systems, applications, files and other network resources. It is a full-service directory that assists companies in managing all facets of its networks and also integrates with the company's NetWare server operating system. NDS is available as a standalone product for single servers that run other leading server operating systems. Novell's In-The-Net Solutions Group was formed to market and distribute free Internet applications and services. The usefulness of the free Internet applications will ultimately lead e-businesses, ASPs (application service providers), ISPs (Internet service providers), portals and retailers to purchase NDS. Novell plans to introduce a wide range of free applications. Instantme, a program that Novell developed with AOL, allows enterprise users to send messages instantly to over 45 million AOL Instant Messenger users, as well as those users in the Digitalmo network. Novell recently launched its newest operating system, NetWare 5.1, that helps customers take greater advantage of open, web-based e-business applications. NetWare 5.1 also delivers improved management, a world leading network directory, reliability, security and greater performance.

The company reimburses employees for certain child care expenses.

FINANCIALS: Sales and profits are in thousands of dollars—add 000 to get the full amount.
Notes regarding 1999: *(1999 sales and profits were not available for all companies at press time.)*

1999 Sales: $1,273,000	1999 Profits: $191,000	Stock Ticker: **NOVL**
1998 Sales: $1,007,311	1998 Profits: $-78,296	Employees:
1997 Sales: $1,374,856	1997 Profits: $125,991	Fiscal Year Ends: 10/31
1996 Sales: $2,041,174	1996 Profits: $338,305	
1995 Sales: $	1995 Profits: $	

SALARIES/BENEFITS:

Pension Plan:	ESOP Stock Plan: Y	Profit Sharing:	Top Exec. Salary: $602,308	Bonus: $619,420
Savings Plan: Y	Stock Purch. Plan:		Second Exec. Salary: $351,345	Bonus: $213,051

COMPETITIVE ADVANTAGE: Novell is one of the best known names in computer networking/New focus on Internet products.

OTHER THOUGHTS:

Apparent Women Officers or Directors: 4
Apparent Minority Officers or Directors:
Hot Spot for Advancement for Women/Minorities: Y

LOCATIONS: ("Y" = Yes)

West:	Southwest:	Midwest:	Southeast:	Northeast:	International:
Y	Y	Y	Y	Y	Y

Note: Financial information, benefits and other data can change quickly and may vary from those stated here.

ONDISPLAY INC   www.ondisplay.com

Industry Group Code: 5112
Ranks within this company's industry group: Sales: 66 Profits: 45

BUSINESS ACTIVITIES ("Y" = Yes)

Financial Services:	Information/Publ.:	Technology:		Services:	Retailing:	Telecommunications:
Stock Brokerage	Portal/Hub/News	Computer Manuf.		Payments/Transfers	Retailer	Internet Serv. Provider
Mortgages/Loans	On-Line Community	Networking Equip.		Consulting	Auctions	Web Site Host
Banking	Search Engine	Software Manuf.	Y	Advertising/Marketing	Mall	Server Farm
Insurance	Financial Data Publ.	Specialty Equipment		Outsourcing	Tickets/Travel	Specialty Telecom.
Credit Cards	Broadcasting/Music				Price Comparisons	High Speed Access

TYPES OF BUSINESS:

Software-Infrastructure
System Design Services
Implementation
Maintenance Services

GROWTH PLANS/SPECIAL FEATURES:

Through an array of cutting-edge content integration software products, OnDisplay, Inc. is making an impressive mark on the e-commerce industry. The company's CenterStage line of software enables users to integrate applications, automate e-commerce transactions, provide personalized product updates and more. Through CenterStage eIntegrate, CenterStage eContent, CenterStage eNotify, CenterStage eBizXchange and CenterStage eSyndicate, OnDisplay's clients are able to accelerate and streamline communications with suppliers, distributors and customers. The installation and maintenance of software systems is an additional facet of the company's operations, as is software system design. OnDisplay provides software training services as well. Recently, the company announced that AltaVista Shopping.com, a web-wide advanced and objective comparison shopping guide, has selected OnDisplay's CenterStage solution to address its information aggregation requirements. The company has also recently acquired Oberon, Inc., a move that is intended to accelerate OnDisplay's development of comprehensive e-business exchange and integration solutions for its broad base of customers. E-business portals such as Travelocity.com and Grainger.com, and e-marketplaces such as PurchasePro.com, FASTXchange, Imetrikus and Harbinger.net utilize the company's products to streamline operations. OnDisplay recently added yet another client, Vignette Corporation, which now licenses the company's CenterStage technology for inclusion in its flagship e-Business applications. Additionally, OrderTrust, a leading provider of integrated order management services for e-commerce, recently selected the same application suite to upgrade components of its OrderTrust Product MarketPlace.

BRANDS/DIVISIONS/AFFILIATES:

CenterStage eIntegrate
CenterStage eContent
CenterStage eNotify
CenterStage eBizXchange
CenterStage eSyndicate

CONTACTS: Note: Officers with more than one job title may be intentionally listed here more than once.

Mark Pine, Pres./CEO
Vankat Mohan, Pres./COO
David F. Larson, CFO
Peter Buzzard, VP-Mktg.
Janet Azevedo, VP-Human Resources
Trung Dung, Chief Tech. Officer
Kevin Cantoni, CIO
Chris Stark, VP-Bus. Dev.
Mark Deppe, VP-Software Dev.

Phone: 925-355-3200	Fax: 925-355-3222
Toll-Free: 800-508-8800	
Address: 12667 Alcosta Blvd., Ste. 300, San Ramon, CA, 94583	

FINANCIALS: Sales and profits are in thousands of dollars—add 000 to get the full amount.

Notes regarding 1999: Through 9 months *(1999 sales and profits were not available for all companies at press time.)*

1999 Sales: $6,600	1999 Profits: $-9,300	Stock Ticker: **ONDS**
1998 Sales: $3,300	1998 Profits: $-8,300	Employees: 80
1997 Sales: $ 300	1997 Profits: $-5,500	Fiscal Year Ends:
1996 Sales: $	1996 Profits: $	
1995 Sales: $	1995 Profits: $	

SALARIES/BENEFITS:

| Pension Plan: | ESOP Stock Plan: | Profit Sharing: | Top Exec. Salary: $ | Bonus: $ |
| Savings Plan: | Stock Purch. Plan: | | Second Exec. Salary: $ | Bonus: $ |

COMPETITIVE ADVANTAGE:
Offers a comprehensive range of cutting-edge products and services, including e-commerce software enabling the consolidation and publishing of data from widely divergent sources.

OTHER THOUGHTS:

Apparent Women Officers or Directors:
Apparent Minority Officers or Directors:
Hot Spot for Advancement for Women/Minorities:

LOCATIONS: ("Y" = Yes)

West:	Southwest:	Midwest:	Southeast:	Northeast:	International:
Y					

Note: Financial information, benefits and other data can change quickly and may vary from those stated here.

ONEMAIN.COM   www.onemain.com

Industry Group Code: 51339
Ranks within this company's industry group: Sales: 8   Profits: 23

BUSINESS ACTIVITIES ("Y" = Yes)

Financial Services:	Information/Publ.:		Technology:		Services:	Retailing:	Telecommunications:	
Stock Brokerage	Portal/Hub/News		Computer Manuf.		Payments/Transfers	Retailer	Internet Serv. Provider	Y
Mortgages/Loans	On-Line Community	Y	Networking Equip.		Consulting	Auctions	Web Site Host	Y
Banking	Search Engine		Software Manuf.		Advertising/Marketing	Mall	Server Farm	
Insurance	Financial Data Publ.		Specialty Equipment		Outsourcing	Tickets/Travel	Specialty Telecom.	
Credit Cards	Broadcasting/Music					Price Comparisons	High Speed Access	Y

TYPES OF BUSINESS:

Internet Service Provider

BRANDS/DIVISIONS/AFFILIATES:

CONTACTS:
Note: Officers with more than one job title may be intentionally listed here more than once.

Stephen E. Smith, CEO
Michael Read, COO/Pres.
Joseph M. Songer, CFO
Scott Hoyt, VP-Mktg.
Joseph M. Songer, Chief Controller
M. Cristina Dolan, Exec.VP-Strategic Alliances Officer
M. Cristina Dolan, Exec.VP-Chief Content Officer

Phone: 703-375-3000	Fax: 703-375-3162
Toll-Free:	
Address: 1860 Michael Faraday Dr., 2nd Floor, Reston, VA, 20190	

GROWTH PLANS/SPECIAL FEATURES:

OneMain.com, Inc. is an Internet service provider with a unique approach to attracting customers. OneMain.com targets individuals and businesses that are located predominantly in secondary, suburban, small town and rural markets throughout the United States. OneMain.com feels that, traditionally, individuals in these markets have been under-served or not served at all by the national ISPs. Many customers in these markets have been forced to pay long distance fees to log on the Internet by national service providers and are given a homepage with no relevance to their communities. OneMain.com offers geographically-based on-line communities with dial-up and high-speed Internet access, web hosting, e-mail and instant messaging. OneMain.com is providing customers with an Internet service based on location, affordable rates and a homepage specific to the customer's region. With over 600,000 current subscribers and revenues totaling $50 million for the first nine months of 1999, OneMain.com is one of the top ten ISPs in the country.

FINANCIALS:
Sales and profits are in thousands of dollars—add 000 to get the full amount.
Notes regarding 1999: Pro forma *(1999 sales and profits were not available for all companies at press time.)*

1999 Sales: $102,300	1999 Profits: $-98,900	**Stock Ticker: ONEM**
1998 Sales: $56,700	1998 Profits: $-67,600	Employees: 696
1997 Sales: $29,100	1997 Profits: $-24,500	Fiscal Year Ends: 12/31
1996 Sales: $	1996 Profits: $	
1995 Sales: $	1995 Profits: $	

SALARIES/BENEFITS:

Pension Plan:	ESOP Stock Plan: Y	Profit Sharing:	Top Exec. Salary: $150,000	Bonus: $50,000
Savings Plan: Y	Stock Purch. Plan:		Second Exec. Salary: $150,000	Bonus: $50,000

COMPETITIVE ADVANTAGE: Focus on smaller community.

OTHER THOUGHTS:

Apparent Women Officers or Directors:
Apparent Minority Officers or Directors:
Hot Spot for Advancement for Women/Minorities:

LOCATIONS: ("Y" = Yes)

West:	Southwest:	Midwest:	Southeast:	Northeast:	International:
				Y	

Note: Financial information, benefits and other data can change quickly and may vary from those stated here.

ONESOURCE INFORMATION SERVICES

www.onesource.com

Industry Group Code: 514101
Ranks within this company's industry group: Sales: 9 Profits: 4

BUSINESS ACTIVITIES ("Y" = Yes)

Financial Services:	Information/Publ.:		Technology:	Services:	Retailing:	Telecommunications:
Stock Brokerage	Portal/Hub/News	Y	Computer Manuf.	Payments/Transfers	Retailer	Internet Serv. Provider
Mortgages/Loans	On-Line Community		Networking Equip.	Consulting	Auctions	Web Site Host
Banking	Search Engine		Software Manuf.	Advertising/Marketing	Mall	Server Farm
Insurance	Financial Data Publ.	Y	Specialty Equipment	Outsourcing	Tickets/Travel	Specialty Telecom.
Credit Cards	Broadcasting/Music				Price Comparisons	High Speed Access

TYPES OF BUSINESS:

Retail-On-line Business Information

BRANDS/DIVISIONS/AFFILIATES:

Business Browser

CONTACTS: Note: Officers with more than one job title may be intentionally listed here more than once.

Daniel J. Schimmel, CEO
Daniel J. Schimmel, Pres.
Roy D. Landon, VP-Finance
Philip J. Garlick, VP-Mktg./Sales
Jennifer Souza, Human Resources
Mark C. VanDine, VP-Engineering
Roy D. Landon, VP-Admin.
Christine Eyre, Dir.-Strategic Mktg.
James A. Becker, VP-Global Strategic Web Applications

Phone: 978-318-4300	Fax: 978-318-4690
Toll-Free:	
Address: 300 Baker Ave, Concord, MA, 01742	

GROWTH PLANS/SPECIAL FEATURES:

OneSource Information Services, Inc. delivers in-depth company and industry information to business individuals and organizations via the Internet. OneSources' Business Browser product line provides reliable, up-to-date, comprehensive business and financial information on over one million companies from over 2,500 sources. The information offers professionals quick access to corporate, industry and market intelligence, with such information as news, trade press, executive biographies, analyst reports, company financial results, stock quotes and industry statistics. Customers access the information over standard web browsers at fixed annual subscription rates. The fixed rate is particularly attractive to large corporations because the cost decreases as the number of company users increases. With the use of standard web technology, end users require minimal training and minimal installation and systems support. Customers have full access to the products anytime from anywhere over the Internet. OneSources' customer line includes American Express, BankAmerica, Boeing, Ernst & Young, Harvard Business School, MCI Worldcom, Merrill Lynch and Oracle.

FINANCIALS: Sales and profits are in thousands of dollars—add 000 to get the full amount.

Notes regarding 1999: (1999 sales and profits were not available for all companies at press time.)

1999 Sales: $35,500	1999 Profits: $-4,400	Stock Ticker: **ONES**
1998 Sales: $30,400	1998 Profits: $5,600	Employees: 166
1997 Sales: $30,400	1997 Profits: $-1,800	Fiscal Year Ends: 12/31
1996 Sales: $30,400	1996 Profits: $-1,900	
1995 Sales: $	1995 Profits: $	

SALARIES/BENEFITS:

Pension Plan:	ESOP Stock Plan: Y	Profit Sharing:	Top Exec. Salary: $222,746	Bonus: $
Savings Plan:	Stock Purch. Plan:		Second Exec. Salary: $191,520	Bonus: $

COMPETITIVE ADVANTAGE: Gathers business data from a wide variety of sources into a single web site.

OTHER THOUGHTS:

Apparent Women Officers or Directors: 2
Apparent Minority Officers or Directors:
Hot Spot for Advancement for Women/Minorities:

LOCATIONS: ("Y" = Yes)

West:	Southwest:	Midwest:	Southeast:	Northeast:	International:
Y		Y		Y	Y

ONLINE RESOURCES & COMMUNICATIONS
www.orcc.com

Industry Group Code: 5112
Ranks within this company's industry group: Sales: 64   Profits: 58

BUSINESS ACTIVITIES ("Y" = Yes)

Financial Services:		Information/Publ.:	Technology:		Services:		Retailing:		Telecommunications:	
Stock Brokerage		Portal/Hub/News	Computer Manuf.		Payments/Transfers	Y	Retailer		Internet Serv. Provider	
Mortgages/Loans		On-Line Community	Networking Equip.		Consulting		Auctions		Web Site Host	Y
Banking	Y	Search Engine	Software Manuf.	Y	Advertising/Marketing		Mall		Server Farm	
Insurance		Financial Data Publ.	Specialty Equipment		Outsourcing	Y	Tickets/Travel		Specialty Telecom.	
Credit Cards		Broadcasting/Music					Price Comparisons		High Speed Access	

TYPES OF BUSINESS:
Software-Electronic Banking
Consulting
Outsourcing
Financial Services Enabler

BRANDS/DIVISIONS/AFFILIATES:
Opus

CONTACTS: Note: Officers with more than one job title may be intentionally listed here more than once.
Matthew P. Lawlor, CEO
Raymond T. Crosier, COO
George E. Northup, CFO
Lori S. Stewart, Sr. VP-Corporate Mktg.
Beth Nettuno, Human Resources Mgr.
Alex J. Seltzer, Exec. VP-Systems and Tech.
Alex J. Seltzer, Chief Info. Officer
Richard A. Martin, Sr. VP-Oper.

Phone: 703-394-5100	Fax: 703-394-5105
Toll-Free:	
Address: 7600 Colshire Drive, McLean, VA, 22102	

GROWTH PLANS/SPECIAL FEATURES:

Online Resources & Communications Corporation provides on-line banking services to banks and credit unions of all sizes. Online Resources delivers a complete single-source solution by integrating Internet, PC, ScreenPhone and telephone access devices with remote banking, bill payment, investment information, trading and other value-added financial services. With estimates of over 25 million households utilizing on-line banking by 2004, and six million currently using on-line banking, the company believes that traditional banking methods can not be solely relied upon. Online Resources delivers a cost-effective solution with the necessary infrastructure, market and support that financial services companies need. The firm's product, Opus, integrates customer and financial data through its access, electronic funds transfer and service gateways. The company internally develops, integrates and controls many critical services, such as bill paying and call center support, whereas many companies in this field rely on third party sources. Online Resources provides low-cost solutions through its patented method of connecting to retail customers through 50 established ATM networks such as Star, Honor, NYCE, EDS and Alltel. Online Resources also offers web site design and hosting services and an Internet portal site that provides access to the services. Revenues are derived from long-term service contracts with clients who pay recurring fees based on the number of enrolled retail customers and transaction volume, along with an up-front implementation fee.

FINANCIALS: Sales and profits are in thousands of dollars—add 000 to get the full amount.
Notes regarding 1999: (1999 sales and profits were not available for all companies at press time.)

1999 Sales: $	1999 Profits: $	Stock Ticker: ORCC
1998 Sales: $4,300	1998 Profits: $-11,600	Employees: 171
1997 Sales: $2,900	1997 Profits: $-11,000	Fiscal Year Ends: 12/31
1996 Sales: $1,100	1996 Profits: $-7,000	
1995 Sales: $	1995 Profits: $	

SALARIES/BENEFITS:

Pension Plan:	ESOP Stock Plan: Y	Profit Sharing:	Top Exec. Salary: $169,594	Bonus: $
Savings Plan: Y	Stock Purch. Plan:		Second Exec. Salary: $157,500	Bonus: $

COMPETITIVE ADVANTAGE: Turn-key services enable a bricks-and-mortar bank to complete on-line services.

OTHER THOUGHTS:

Apparent Women Officers or Directors:
Apparent Minority Officers or Directors:
Hot Spot for Advancement for Women/Minorities:

LOCATIONS: ("Y" = Yes)

West:	Southwest:	Midwest:	Southeast:	Northeast:	International:
				Y	

Note: Financial information, benefits and other data can change quickly and may vary from those stated here.

ONLINETRADINGINC.COM

www.onlinetradinginc.com

Industry Group Code: 5231
Ranks within this company's industry group: Sales: 9　Profits: 6

BUSINESS ACTIVITIES ("Y" = Yes)

Financial Services:		Information/Publ.:	Technology:	Services:	Retailing:	Telecommunications:
Stock Brokerage	Y	Portal/Hub/News	Computer Manuf.	Payments/Transfers	Retailer	Internet Serv. Provider
Mortgages/Loans		On-Line Community	Networking Equip.	Consulting	Auctions	Web Site Host
Banking		Search Engine	Software Manuf.	Advertising/Marketing	Mall	Server Farm
Insurance		Financial Data Publ.	Specialty Equipment	Outsourcing	Tickets/Travel	Specialty Telecom.
Credit Cards		Broadcasting/Music			Price Comparisons	High Speed Access

TYPES OF BUSINESS:

On-line Stock Brokerage

BRANDS/DIVISIONS/AFFILIATES:

GROWTH PLANS/SPECIAL FEATURES:

Onlinetradinginc.com is a leader in next generation professional brokerage services. Onlinetradinginc.com offers financial brokerage services for small-to mid-sized financial institutions and experienced investors through a variety of communication mediums. The company hopes to provide the customer with excellent brokerage service at the lowest possible cost, while giving customers advanced information sources and trading systems. Onlinetradinginc.com offers more than just Internet trading services; the company is a full-service financial services firm providing its brokers with the latest in technology, news information, research capabilities and after hours trading. Onlinetradinginc.com uses its computerized intranet infrastructure to save costs and increase investing efficiency. The company focuses on customer service, with experienced brokers that proactively monitor client portfolios and guide trading and investing decisions with up-to-date information and knowledge of the customer and the customer's investments.

CONTACTS: Note: Officers with more than one job title may be intentionally listed here more than once.

Andrew A. Allen, CEO
E. Steven zum Tobel, Pres.
E. Steven zum Tobel, CFO
Farshid Tafazzoli, CIO
Derek J. Hernquist, VP-Oper.

Phone: 561-995-1010	Fax: 561-995-0606
Toll-Free:	
Address: 2700 N. Military Trail, Ste. 200, Boca Raton, FL, 33431	

FINANCIALS: Sales and profits are in thousands of dollars—add 000 to get the full amount.

Notes regarding 1999: *(1999 sales and profits were not available for all companies at press time.)*

1999 Sales: $	1999 Profits: $ 100	Stock Ticker: **LINE**
1998 Sales: $3,549	1998 Profits: $- 20	Employees:　34
1997 Sales: $	1997 Profits: $	Fiscal Year Ends: 1/31
1996 Sales: $	1996 Profits: $	
1995 Sales: $	1995 Profits: $	

SALARIES/BENEFITS:

Pension Plan:	ESOP Stock Plan: Y	Profit Sharing:	Top Exec. Salary: $74,000	Bonus: $525,000
Savings Plan: Y	Stock Purch. Plan:		Second Exec. Salary: $72,000	Bonus: $300,000

COMPETITIVE ADVANTAGE:　A focus on services for experienced investors and financial institutions.

OTHER THOUGHTS:

Apparent Women Officers or Directors:
Apparent Minority Officers or Directors: 1
Hot Spot for Advancement for Women/Minorities:

LOCATIONS: ("Y" = Yes)

West:	Southwest:	Midwest:	Southeast:	Northeast:	International:
		Y	Y	Y	

Note: Financial information, benefits and other data can change quickly and may vary from those stated here.

ONSALE INC

www.onsale.com

Industry Group Code: 4541
Ranks within this company's industry group: Sales: 6   Profits: 22

BUSINESS ACTIVITIES ("Y" = Yes)

Financial Services:	Information/Publ.:	Technology:	Services:	Retailing:		Telecommunications:	
Stock Brokerage	Portal/Hub/News	Computer Manuf.	Payments/Transfers	Retailer		Internet Serv. Provider	
Mortgages/Loans	On-Line Community	Networking Equip.	Consulting	Auctions	Y	Web Site Host	
Banking	Search Engine	Software Manuf.	Advertising/Marketing	Mall		Server Farm	
Insurance	Financial Data Publ.	Specialty Equipment	Outsourcing	Tickets/Travel	Y	Specialty Telecom.	
Credit Cards	Broadcasting/Music			Price Comparisons		High Speed Access	

TYPES OF BUSINESS:

Retail-Computer and Software Products

BRANDS/DIVISIONS/AFFILIATES:

Onsale.com

CONTACTS: *Note: Officers with more than one job title may be intentionally listed here more than once.*

S. Jerrold Kaplan, Pres./CEO
Jeffery F. Sheahan, Sr. VP/COO
John Labbett, Sr. VP/CFO
Alan S. Fisher, Sr. VP/Chief Tech. Officer
Martha D. Greer, VP-Merch. Mgmt.
Dennis J. Separd, VP-Oper.
Alan S. Fisher, VP-Dev. and Oper.
Merle W. McIntosh, Sr. VP-Merch. Acquisition

Phone: 650-470-2400	Fax: 650-473-6990
Toll-Free:	
Address: 1350 Willow Road, Ste. 202, Menlo Park, CA, 94205	

GROWTH PLANS/SPECIAL FEATURES:

A pioneer of the interactive on-line auction format of retailing, Onsale, Inc. operates onsale.com. The company's auction format serves as an efficient and entertaining marketing channel for products typically unavailable through more conventional distribution means. Specialties of the company include selling excess, refurbished and close-out merchandise over the Internet to businesses, resellers and general consumers. Computers, peripherals, housewares, consumer electronics, sporting goods and vacation packages are sold at online.com, as well as a variety of consumer merchandise. The company believes that the fresh and exciting nature of Internet auctioning as an alternative to traditional retailing offers customers a viable and desirable shopping option. The company additionally believes that the edge Onsale, Inc. is gaining in this emerging market is putting it in a leading place in the world retail market. Onsale, Inc. is currently relocating several of its facilities, including accounting, engineering and web site operation, to a new principal building located in Menlo Park, California. This move should provide smoother operations and better communication for future growth.

FINANCIALS: Sales and profits are in thousands of dollars—add 000 to get the full amount.

Notes regarding 1999: Through 9 months *(1999 sales and profits were not available for all companies at press time.)*

1999 Sales: $242,400	1999 Profits: $-33,600	Stock Ticker: **ONSL**
1998 Sales: $207,751	1998 Profits: $-14,666	Employees: 200
1997 Sales: $88,981	1997 Profits: $-2,472	Fiscal Year Ends: 12/31
1996 Sales: $14,269	1996 Profits: $ 361	
1995 Sales: $	1995 Profits: $	

SALARIES/BENEFITS:

Pension Plan:	ESOP Stock Plan:	Profit Sharing:	Top Exec. Salary: $175,000	Bonus: $
Savings Plan: Y	Stock Purch. Plan: Y		Second Exec. Salary: $	Bonus: $

COMPETITIVE ADVANTAGE: Focus on auctions/Broad variety of merchandise.

OTHER THOUGHTS:

Apparent Women Officers or Directors: 1
Apparent Minority Officers or Directors:
Hot Spot for Advancement for Women/Minorities:

LOCATIONS: ("Y" = Yes)

West:	Southwest:	Midwest:	Southeast:	Northeast:	International:
Y					

Note: Financial information, benefits and other data can change quickly and may vary from those stated here.

OPEN MARKET INC   www.openmarket.com

Industry Group Code: 5112
Ranks within this company's industry group: Sales: 14   Profits: 76

BUSINESS ACTIVITIES ("Y" = Yes)

Financial Services:	Information/Publ.:	Technology:		Services:	Retailing:	Telecommunications:
Stock Brokerage	Portal/Hub/News	Computer Manuf.		Payments/Transfers	Retailer	Internet Serv. Provider
Mortgages/Loans	On-Line Community	Networking Equip.		Consulting	Auctions	Web Site Host
Banking	Search Engine	Software Manuf.	Y	Advertising/Marketing	Mall	Server Farm
Insurance	Financial Data Publ.	Specialty Equipment		Outsourcing	Tickets/Travel	Specialty Telecom.
Credit Cards	Broadcasting/Music				Price Comparisons	High Speed Access

TYPES OF BUSINESS:

Software
E-commerce Solutions

BRANDS/DIVISIONS/AFFILIATES:

SecureLink
IPS
Transact
ShopSite
LiveCommerce

CONTACTS: Note: Officers with more than one job title may be intentionally listed here more than once.

Gary B. Eichhorn, CEO
Ronald Matros, Pres./COO
Regina O. Sommer, VP/CFO
Jeffrey Bussgang, VP-Mktg.
Michael Messier, VP-Human Resources
Kurt L. Freidrich, Chief Tech. Officer
Brad Nelson, CIO
Brad Nelson, VP-Oper.
Paul Esdale, VP-Corp. Dev.
Julie Lorigan, Dir.-Investor Relations

Phone: 781-359-3000	Fax: 781-359-8111
Toll-Free:	
Address: One Wayside Road, Burlington, MA, 01803	

GROWTH PLANS/SPECIAL FEATURES:

Open Market, Inc. develops, markets, licenses and supports enterprise-class, application software products that allow customers to engage in business-to-business and business-to-consumer Internet commerce, information commerce and commercial publishing. The products are complemented by maintenance, support, professional service offerings and training. Open Market's software includes a wide spectrum of functionality required to effectively conduct business on the Internet, allowing companies to attract customers to their web sites, engage them in acting upon an offer, complete a transaction and service them once a transaction has been completed. The company's software is able to manage business transactions and Internet applications from secure, centrally managed sites. The company seeks to offer comprehensive, on-line order management, which usually includes the capability to capture, process and service orders on-line. Open Market's products are based on SecureLink architecture that allows business to take place over the Internet using any software, any web server and virtually any system, allowing purchases to be made and transactions to take place securely. Open Market's product and service offerings are marketplace-driven and reflect the best practices of customers that have been at the forefront of Internet commerce. Some of the company's clients include Disney, Time Warner and AT&T.

FINANCIALS: Sales and profits are in thousands of dollars—add 000 to get the full amount.

Notes regarding 1999: *(1999 sales and profits were not available for all companies at press time.)*

1999 Sales: $	1999 Profits: $	Stock Ticker: **OMKT**
1998 Sales: $62,100	1998 Profits: $-30,500	Employees: 398
1997 Sales: $61,300	1997 Profits: $-58,000	Fiscal Year Ends: 12/31
1996 Sales: $22,500	1996 Profits: $-26,500	
1995 Sales: $1,800	1995 Profits: $-13,900	

SALARIES/BENEFITS:

Pension Plan:	ESOP Stock Plan: Y	Profit Sharing:	Top Exec. Salary: $297,083	Bonus: $101,541
Savings Plan: Y	Stock Purch. Plan:		Second Exec. Salary: $219,186	Bonus: $47,402

COMPETITIVE ADVANTAGE: Growth through acquisitions.

OTHER THOUGHTS:

Apparent Women Officers or Directors: 2
Apparent Minority Officers or Directors: 2
Hot Spot for Advancement for Women/Minorities: Y

LOCATIONS: ("Y" = Yes)

West:	Southwest:	Midwest:	Southeast:	Northeast:	International:
Y	Y	Y	Y	Y	Y

OPEN TEXT www.opentext.com

Industry Group Code: 5112
Ranks within this company's industry group: Sales: 19   Profits: 74

BUSINESS ACTIVITIES ("Y" = Yes)

Financial Services:	Information/Publ.:	Technology:		Services:		Retailing:	Telecommunications:
Stock Brokerage	Portal/Hub/News	Computer Manuf.		Payments/Transfers		Retailer	Internet Serv. Provider
Mortgages/Loans	On-Line Community	Networking Equip.		Consulting		Auctions	Web Site Host
Banking	Search Engine	Software Manuf.	Y	Advertising/Marketing	Y	Mall	Server Farm
Insurance	Financial Data Publ.	Specialty Equipment		Outsourcing	Y	Tickets/Travel	Specialty Telecom.
Credit Cards	Broadcasting/Music					Price Comparisons	High Speed Access

TYPES OF BUSINESS:

Software-Corporate
Intranet Leasing Services
Knowledge and Document Management Software
Enterprise Group Scheduling Software
Search and Retrieval Software

BRANDS/DIVISIONS/AFFILIATES:

BASIS
Livelink
OnTime
RIMS
Techlib
Livelink Online
Livelink Pinstripe

CONTACTS: *Note: Officers with more than one job title may be intentionally listed here more than once.*

P. Thomas Jenkins, CEO
John Shackleton, Pres.
Marc Schnabolk, VP-Sales, North America
Beth Tarter, VP-Human Resources
Daniel Cheifetz, Exec. VP-Software Dev.
Kirk Roberts, Sr. VP-Info. Tech.
Michael Farrell, Exec. VP-Business Dev.

Phone: 519-888-7111	Fax: 519-888-0677
Toll-Free:	
Address: 185 Columbia St. West, Waterloo, Ontario, Canada, N2L 5Z5	

GROWTH PLANS/SPECIAL FEATURES:

Open Text Corporation produces collaborative knowledge management solutions for companies of any size for use on intranets, extranets and the Internet. The flagship product of Open Text is Livelink, a collaborative application for companies that want to leverage information and resources through their intranets. This software allows companies to search intranets, manage documents and workflow and capture, share and reuse corporate knowledge to help the customer achieve success. Livelink is an industry leader in comprehensive enterprise document management, information retrieval, workflow and project collaboration and enterprise group scheduling capabilities. Livelink is complex enough to handle engineering change order systems, ISO 9000 compliance and maintenance of standard operating procedures in government-regulated industries. Other products include BASIS, cataloged information management software; OnTime, group scheduling software; RIMS, web-based records management applications and services and Livelink Pinstripe, an Internet search engine for business users. Open Text products have over 2.5 million users in more than 3,500 corporations, including customers such as Ford Motor Company, Quallcom, AT&T, British Petroleum and Motorola.

FINANCIALS: Sales and profits are in thousands of dollars—add 000 to get the full amount.

Notes regarding 1999: *(1999 sales and profits were not available for all companies at press time.)*

1999 Sales: $92,500	1999 Profits: $20,200	Stock Ticker: **OTEX**
1998 Sales: $45,600	1998 Profits: $-23,500	Employees: 400
1997 Sales: $22,600	1997 Profits: $-28,200	Fiscal Year Ends: 6/30
1996 Sales: $	1996 Profits: $	
1995 Sales: $2,500	1995 Profits: $-1,200	

SALARIES/BENEFITS:

Pension Plan:	ESOP Stock Plan: Y	Profit Sharing:	Top Exec. Salary: $	Bonus: $
Savings Plan:	Stock Purch. Plan:		Second Exec. Salary: $	Bonus: $

COMPETITIVE ADVANTAGE: Software from Open Text opens up the long-term value of a company's proprietary knowledge and internal documents.

OTHER THOUGHTS:

Apparent Women Officers or Directors: 1
Apparent Minority Officers or Directors:
Hot Spot for Advancement for Women/Minorities:

LOCATIONS: ("Y" = Yes)

West:	Southwest:	Midwest:	Southeast:	Northeast:	International:
		Y			Y

ORACLE CORP   www.oracle.com

Industry Group Code: 5112
Ranks within this company's industry group: Sales: 2   Profits: 2

BUSINESS ACTIVITIES ("Y" = Yes)

Financial Services:	Information/Publ.:	Technology:		Services:		Retailing:	Telecommunications:
Stock Brokerage	Portal/Hub/News	Computer Manuf.		Payments/Transfers		Retailer	Internet Serv. Provider
Mortgages/Loans	On-Line Community	Networking Equip.		Consulting	Y	Auctions	Web Site Host
Banking	Search Engine	Software Manuf.	Y	Advertising/Marketing		Mall	Server Farm
Insurance	Financial Data Publ.	Specialty Equipment		Outsourcing	Y	Tickets/Travel	Specialty Telecom.
Credit Cards	Broadcasting/Music					Price Comparisons	High Speed Access

TYPES OF BUSINESS:

Computer Software Products
Database Management and Network Products
Applications Development Productivity Tools
End User Applications
ASPs

BRANDS/DIVISIONS/AFFILIATES:

Oracle
Developer/2000
Designer/2000
Oracle Power Objects
Oracle Media Server

CONTACTS: *Note: Officers with more than one job title may be intentionally listed here more than once.*

Lawrence J. Ellison, CEO
Raymond J. Jane, Pres./COO
Jeffrey O. Henley, Exec. VP/CFO
Carole Goldberg, Human Resources
Jennifer L. Minton, Controller
Daniel Cooperman, Sec.
Daniel Cooperman, General Counsel
Karen White, Sr. VP-Business Dev.
Mark Barrenechea, Sr. VP-Customer Relationship

Phone: 650-506-7000	**Fax:** 650-506-7200

Toll-Free: 800-672-2531
Address: 500 Oracle Parkway, Redwood City, CA, 94065

GROWTH PLANS/SPECIAL FEATURES:

Oracle Corporation is a leading supplier of software for information management and ranks second among the world's independent software specialists behind Microsoft. The company's software products can be categorized into two broad categories: systems software and business applications software. Systems software consists of a complete Internet platform to develop and deploy applications for computing on the Internet and corporate intranets. Business applications software automates the performance of specific business data processing functions for customer relationship management, supply chain management, financial management, procurement, project management and human resources management. The company's principal products allow businesses to engage in commerce electronically and run a broad range of computers, information appliances and over 85 different operating systems. In addition to computer software products, the company offers consulting, education, support and systems integration services in support of customer use of its products. The company has also moved into application hosting, charging fees to users who access Oracle programs off the Internet. Currently, 60% of Oracle's sales are from consulting and other services. The company is using small acquisitions to expand into customer service software and other markets.

Oracle helps integrate computer technology into classrooms for all grade levels. The company recently established its $1 Million Challenge Grant to encourage the creation of new and compelling educational software to combine traditional teaching values with the impact and persuasion of full-motion interactive video. The Oracle Volunteers program enables employees to donate time and skills to a wide variety of needs and opportunities throughout their communities.

FINANCIALS: Sales and profits are in thousands of dollars—add 000 to get the full amount.

Notes regarding 1999: *(1999 sales and profits were not available for all companies at press time.)*

1999 Sales: $8,827,300	1999 Profits: $1,289,800	**Stock Ticker: ORCL**
1998 Sales: $7,143,900	1998 Profits: $813,700	Employees: 43,800
1997 Sales: $5,684,300	1997 Profits: $821,500	Fiscal Year Ends: 5/31
1996 Sales: $4,223,300	1996 Profits: $603,300	
1995 Sales: $2,966,900	1995 Profits: $441,500	

SALARIES/BENEFITS:

Pension Plan:	ESOP Stock Plan:	Profit Sharing:	Top Exec. Salary: $999,987	Bonus: $530,000
Savings Plan: Y	Stock Purch. Plan: Y		Second Exec. Salary: $974,991	Bonus: $206,250

COMPETITIVE ADVANTAGE:
World's largest vendor of database software and information management services/Provides significant software power for financial institutions and Internet companies.

OTHER THOUGHTS:

Apparent Women Officers or Directors: 3
Apparent Minority Officers or Directors: 2
Hot Spot for Advancement for Women/Minorities: Y

LOCATIONS: ("Y" = Yes)

West:	Southwest:	Midwest:	Southeast:	Northeast:	International:
Y	Y	Y	Y	Y	Y

PACIFIC SOFTWORKS　　www.pacificsw.com

Industry Group Code: 5112
Ranks within this company's industry group: Sales: 69　Profits: 21

BUSINESS ACTIVITIES ("Y" = Yes)

Financial Services:	Information/Publ.:	Technology:		Services:	Retailing:	Telecommunications:
Stock Brokerage	Portal/Hub/News	Computer Manuf.		Payments/Transfers	Retailer	Internet Serv. Provider
Mortgages/Loans	On-Line Community	Networking Equip.		Consulting	Auctions	Web Site Host
Banking	Search Engine	Software Manuf.	Y	Advertising/Marketing	Mall	Server Farm
Insurance	Financial Data Publ.	Specialty Equipment		Outsourcing	Tickets/Travel	Specialty Telecom.
Credit Cards	Broadcasting/Music				Price Comparisons	High Speed Access

TYPES OF BUSINESS:

Software-Web

BRANDS/DIVISIONS/AFFILIATES:

FUSION WebPilot Micro Browser

CONTACTS: Note: Officers with more than one job title may be intentionally listed here more than once.

Glenn P. Russell, CEO
Glenn P. Russell, Pres.
William E. Sliney, CFO
Sandra J. Garcia, VP-North American Sales
William E. Sliney, Human Resources
Joseph Lechman, Sec.
Mark Sewell, VP-Business Dev.

Phone: 805-499-7722	Fax: 805-499-5512
Toll-Free: 800-541-9508	
Address: 703 Rancho Conejo Blvd., Newbury Park, CA, 91320	

GROWTH PLANS/SPECIAL FEATURES:

Pacific Softworks develops and licenses Internet and web-related software and software development tools. Pacific Softworks' products are embedded into systems and information appliances such as telephones, televisions, fax machines and other digitally-based devices located in the industries of defense and aerospace, navigation, office automation, medical care and wireless communications, enabling Internet and web-based communications. Some of the company's customers are AT&T, Cisco Systems, Hewlett Packard, Ericsson, Motorola, Siemens, Philips and Intel. The products offered by Pacific Softworks provide significant benefits to customers, including accelerated product development and market entry, portability across multiple hardware and software environments and solutions that enable information appliances to connect with the Internet. Pacific Softworks has developed an Internet browser for use within non-windows-based Information appliances. This browser, FUSION WebPilot Micro Browser, does not require an operating system or large amounts of memory. Pacific Softworks plans to expand its existing relationships and to create new collaborative relationships to capitalize on new browser and other technologies and to maintain research and development of new Internet-based products that enable reliable and secure communication and transportation of data over the Internet.

FINANCIALS: Sales and profits are in thousands of dollars—add 000 to get the full amount.

Notes regarding 1999: Through 9 months *(1999 sales and profits were not available for all companies at press time.)*

1999 Sales: $1,954	1999 Profits: $-1,336	Stock Ticker: **PASW**
1998 Sales: $2,800	1998 Profits: $- 500	Employees:　21
1997 Sales: $3,300	1997 Profits: $- 100	Fiscal Year Ends: 12/31
1996 Sales: $3,700	1996 Profits: $ 400	
1995 Sales: $	1995 Profits: $	

SALARIES/BENEFITS:

Pension Plan:	ESOP Stock Plan:	Profit Sharing:	Top Exec. Salary: $215,384	Bonus: $118,201
Savings Plan:	Stock Purch. Plan:		Second Exec. Salary: $207,962	Bonus: $

COMPETITIVE ADVANTAGE:　　Focus on products for the booming Internet appliance market.

OTHER THOUGHTS:

	LOCATIONS: ("Y" = Yes)					
	West:	Southwest:	Midwest:	Southeast:	Northeast:	International:
Apparent Women Officers or Directors:	Y					Y
Apparent Minority Officers or Directors:						
Hot Spot for Advancement for Women/Minorities:						

Note: Financial information, benefits and other data can change quickly and may vary from those stated here.

PACKETEER
www.packeteer.com

Industry Group Code: 5112
Ranks within this company's industry group: Sales: 56   Profits: 48

BUSINESS ACTIVITIES ("Y" = Yes)

Financial Services:	Information/Publ.:	Technology:		Services:	Retailing:	Telecommunications:
Stock Brokerage	Portal/Hub/News	Computer Manuf.		Payments/Transfers	Retailer	Internet Serv. Provider
Mortgages/Loans	On-Line Community	Networking Equip.		Consulting	Auctions	Web Site Host
Banking	Search Engine	Software Manuf.	Y	Advertising/Marketing	Mall	Server Farm
Insurance	Financial Data Publ.	Specialty Equipment		Outsourcing	Tickets/Travel	Specialty Telecom.
Credit Cards	Broadcasting/Music				Price Comparisons	High Speed Access

TYPES OF BUSINESS:
Software-Bandwidth Management Services

BRANDS/DIVISIONS/AFFILIATES:
PacketShaper bandwidth management devices

CONTACTS: Note: Officers with more than one job title may be intentionally listed here more than once.
Craig W. Elliot, CEO/Pres.
Brett D. Galloway, COO
David C. Yntema, CFO
Todd J. Krautkremer, VP-Mktg
Robert L. Packer, Chief Tech. Officer
Margaret Echerd, Controller
Brett D. Galloway, VP-Engineering
David C. Yntema, Sec.
William E. Klaus, VP-Business Dev.

Phone: 408-873-4400	Fax: 408-873-4410
Toll-Free:	
Address: 10495 N. De Anza Blvd., Cupertino, CA, 95014	

GROWTH PLANS/SPECIAL FEATURES:

Packeteer develops products that address the severe problems related to congested bandwidth resources on enterprise wide area networks and the Internet. The company's bandwidth management products increase the value of a network by lowering application response times, aligning network resources with corporate goals and increasing the ability to quickly adapt to changing business priorities. PacketShaper bandwidth management devices allow network managers and service providers to set and enforce policies to control network traffic, ensuring that networks deliver predictable performance. Packeteer feels that companies struggling with network congestion do not need to purchase more bandwidth, but instead need to have better control of it to fully utilize the bandwidth already available. Packeteer's products require simple installation with no changes to existing network infrastructure. The company's vision for its products is to continue to ensure bandwidth to applications, enable interactive services, increase network efficiency and facilitate e-commerce.

FINANCIALS: Sales and profits are in thousands of dollars—add 000 to get the full amount.
Notes regarding 1999: *(1999 sales and profits were not available for all companies at press time.)*

1999 Sales: $18,400	1999 Profits: $-10,900	Stock Ticker: **PKTR**
1998 Sales: $7,200	1998 Profits: $-8,800	Employees: 76
1997 Sales: $1,400	1997 Profits: $-5,900	Fiscal Year Ends: 12/31
1996 Sales: $	1996 Profits: $-1,200	
1995 Sales: $	1995 Profits: $	

SALARIES/BENEFITS:

Pension Plan:	ESOP Stock Plan:	Profit Sharing:	Top Exec. Salary: $150,033	Bonus: $
Savings Plan:	Stock Purch. Plan:		Second Exec. Salary: $143,783	Bonus: $69,912

COMPETITIVE ADVANTAGE: Answering a critical need for bandwidth management at effective cost.

OTHER THOUGHTS:

	LOCATIONS: ("Y" = Yes)					
	West:	Southwest:	Midwest:	Southeast:	Northeast:	International:
Apparent Women Officers or Directors:	Y					
Apparent Minority Officers or Directors:						
Hot Spot for Advancement for Women/Minorities:						

PCORDER.COM   www.pcorder.com

Industry Group Code: 51339A
Ranks within this company's industry group: Sales: 4   Profits: 9

BUSINESS ACTIVITIES ("Y" = Yes)

Financial Services:	Information/Publ.:	Technology:		Services:	Retailing:	Telecommunications:
Stock Brokerage	Portal/Hub/News	Computer Manuf.		Payments/Transfers	Retailer	Internet Serv. Provider
Mortgages/Loans	On-Line Community	Networking Equip.		Consulting	Auctions	Web Site Host
Banking	Search Engine	Software Manuf.	Y	Advertising/Marketing	Mall	Server Farm
Insurance	Financial Data Publ.	Specialty Equipment		Outsourcing	Tickets/Travel	Specialty Telecom.
Credit Cards	Broadcasting/Music				Price Comparisons	High Speed Access

TYPES OF BUSINESS:

Enabler of On-line PC Products Ordering and Configuration
On-line Database of PC Product Information

BRANDS/DIVISIONS/AFFILIATES:

CONTACTS: *Note: Officers with more than one job title may be intentionally listed here more than once.*

Ross A. Cooley, CEO
Christina C. Jones, COO/Pres.
James J. Luttenbacher, CFO
Raj Shah, VP-Mktg.
Stephanie Derrick, Dir-Human Resources
James L. Luttenbacher, Sec.
Rob Favaron, VP-Business Dev.
Alan Godfrey, VP-Client Services

Phone: 512-684-1100	Fax: 512-684-1200
Toll-Free:	
Address: 5001 Plaza on the Lake, Austin, TX, 78746	

GROWTH PLANS/SPECIAL FEATURES:

pcOrder.com is an independent provider of Internet-based e-commerce solutions for the computer industry. pcOrder.com's business-to-business software applications and related services enable computer industry suppliers, manufacturers, resellers and end users to buy and sell products on-line. The company feels that by taking advantage of the e-commerce market to automate sales and distribution functions (such as product searches), comparisons, configurations, quoting, pricing, financing, ordering and reselling, pcOrder.com's solutions will enable customers to lower the cost of sales and marketing, reduce inventory levels and more efficiently interact with customers and business partners. pcOrder.com's comprehensive e-commerce software contains a database of computer product information and information on more than 600,000 products from over 1,000 manufacturers, including product pricing and availability, compatibility and technical information. pcOrder.com's customers include Compaq, Nortel Networks and Hewlett Packard.

FINANCIALS: Sales and profits are in thousands of dollars—add 000 to get the full amount.

Notes regarding 1999: *(1999 sales and profits were not available for all companies at press time.)*

1999 Sales: $44,000	1999 Profits: $-8,300	Stock Ticker: **PCOR**
1998 Sales: $21,700	1998 Profits: $-9,600	Employees: 194
1997 Sales: $10,600	1997 Profits: $-1,100	Fiscal Year Ends: 12/31
1996 Sales: $5,900	1996 Profits: $- 300	
1995 Sales: $3,700	1995 Profits: $ 400	

SALARIES/BENEFITS:

Pension Plan:	ESOP Stock Plan:	Profit Sharing:	Top Exec. Salary: $150,362	Bonus: $
Savings Plan:	Stock Purch. Plan:		Second Exec. Salary: $101,408	Bonus: $

COMPETITIVE ADVANTAGE: Rapidly growing revenues/Unique on-line database provides a valuable service.

OTHER THOUGHTS:

Apparent Women Officers or Directors: 2
Apparent Minority Officers or Directors: 2
Hot Spot for Advancement for Women/Minorities: Y

LOCATIONS: ("Y" = Yes)

West:	Southwest:	Midwest:	Southeast:	Northeast:	International:
	Y				

PEAPOD INC   www.peapod.com

Industry Group Code: 4541
Ranks within this company's industry group: Sales: 12   Profits: 26

BUSINESS ACTIVITIES ("Y" = Yes)

Financial Services:	Information/Publ.:	Technology:	Services:	Retailing:		Telecommunications:
Stock Brokerage	Portal/Hub/News	Computer Manuf.	Payments/Transfers	Retailer	Y	Internet Serv. Provider
Mortgages/Loans	On-Line Community	Networking Equip.	Consulting	Auctions		Web Site Host
Banking	Search Engine	Software Manuf. Y	Advertising/Marketing	Mall		Server Farm
Insurance	Financial Data Publ.	Specialty Equipment	Outsourcing	Tickets/Travel		Specialty Telecom.
Credit Cards	Broadcasting/Music			Price Comparisons		High Speed Access

TYPES OF BUSINESS:
Retail On-line Grocery Sales
Software Developer

BRANDS/DIVISIONS/AFFILIATES:
Smart Shopping For Busy People
Split Pea Software

CONTACTS: *Note: Officers with more than one job title may be intentionally listed here more than once.*
Andrew B. Parkinson, Pres./CEO
John C. Walden, COO
John P. Miller, Sr. VP/CFO/Chief Admin. Officer
Anthony Priore, VP-Mktg.
Toya Campbell, Human Resources
Thomas L. Parkinson, Exec. VP/Chief Tech.Officer
William J. Christopher, Dir.-Member Services

Phone: 847-583-9400	Fax: 847-583-9494
Toll-Free:	
Address: 9933 Woods Drive, Skokie, IL, 60077-1057	

GROWTH PLANS/SPECIAL FEATURES:

Peapod is a leading interactive on-line grocery shopping and delivery company and a provider of targeted media and research services. The company provides an integrated, comprehensive service designed to address the distinct needs of on-line consumers, grocery retailers and consumer goods companies. Peapod's Smart Shopping for Busy People solution allows consumers to save time through a user-friendly, highly-functional virtual supermarket and through personalized shopping, delivery and customer service. By establishing a relationship with the company, grocery retailers gain access to Peapod's on-line sales channel. This channel is designed to enable the retailer to gain incremental revenues and profits by capturing an increased share of the purchases of existing customers and by attracting new customers. Peapod provides consumer goods companies with a forum for targeted interactive advertising, high-impact electronic couponing and extensive product research by linking together members from multiple markets into a national on-line network and collecting substantial data regarding purchase intentions, purchasing behavior and demographics. The company's consumer software is based upon a three-tiered architecture, which positions Peapod at the forefront of Internet computing. Recently, the company created its Split Pea Software subsidiary, an extension of projects undertaken with Australian retail giant Coles Myer.

FINANCIALS: Sales and profits are in thousands of dollars—add 000 to get the full amount.
Notes regarding 1999: Through 9 months *(1999 sales and profits were not available for all companies at press time.)*

1999 Sales: $51,600	1999 Profits: $-19,300	Stock Ticker: **PPOD**
1998 Sales: $69,300	1998 Profits: $-21,565	Employees: 240
1997 Sales: $59,600	1997 Profits: $-12,979	Fiscal Year Ends: 12/31
1996 Sales: $29,200	1996 Profits: $-9,566	
1995 Sales: $15,900	1995 Profits: $6,600	

SALARIES/BENEFITS:

Pension Plan:	ESOP Stock Plan:	Profit Sharing:	Top Exec. Salary: $173,922	Bonus: $
Savings Plan: Y	Stock Purch. Plan: Y		Second Exec. Salary: $161,315	Bonus: $

COMPETITIVE ADVANTAGE: Very rapid growth/Alliances with leading bricks and mortar grocers in major markets.

OTHER THOUGHTS:
Apparent Women Officers or Directors: 1
Apparent Minority Officers or Directors:
Hot Spot for Advancement for Women/Minorities:

LOCATIONS: ("Y" = Yes)

West:	Southwest:	Midwest:	Southeast:	Northeast:	International:
Y	Y	Y	Y	Y	

Note: Financial information, benefits and other data can change quickly and may vary from those stated here.

PEGASUS SYSTEMS   http://pegasus.thisco.com

Industry Group Code: 52252A
Ranks within this company's industry group: Sales: 2   Profits: 1

BUSINESS ACTIVITIES ("Y" = Yes)

Financial Services:	Information/Publ.:	Technology:	Services:		Retailing:		Telecommunications:
Stock Brokerage	Portal/Hub/News	Computer Manuf.	Payments/Transfers	Y	Retailer		Internet Serv. Provider
Mortgages/Loans	On-Line Community	Networking Equip.	Consulting		Auctions		Web Site Host
Banking	Search Engine	Software Manuf.	Advertising/Marketing		Mall		Server Farm
Insurance	Financial Data Publ.	Specialty Equipment	Outsourcing	Y	Tickets/Travel	Y	Specialty Telecom.
Credit Cards	Broadcasting/Music				Price Comparisons		High Speed Access

TYPES OF BUSINESS:

On-line Travel Services
Transaction and Commission Processing

BRANDS/DIVISIONS/AFFILIATES:

Pegasus Electronic Distribution
Pegasus Commission Processing
Pegasus Business Intellegence
Travel Web
NetBooker
UltraRes
Driving Revenue L.L.C.

CONTACTS: Note: Officers with more than one job title may be intentionally listed here more than once.

John F. Davis, CEO
Joseph W. Nicholson, COO
Jerome L. Galant, CFO
Carolyn Lane, Human Resources
Steve Reynolds, CIO
Gideon Dean, VP-Int'l Oper.
William S. Lush, Business Dev.
Kevin P. Short, Exec.VP-Pegasus Business Intelligence

Phone: 214-528-5656	Fax: 214-528-5675
Toll-Free:	
Address: 3811 Turtle Creek Blvd., Suite 1100, Dallas, TX, 75219	

GROWTH PLANS/SPECIAL FEATURES:

Pegasus Systems, Inc. provides transaction processing services to the hotel industry worldwide. The company's services are divided into three operating segments: Pegasus Electronic Distribution, Pegasus Commission Processing and Pegasus Business Intelligence. Pegasus Electronic Distribution improves the efficiency and effectiveness of the hotel reservation process by enabling travel agents and individual travelers to electronically access hotel room inventory information and conduct reservation transactions. It also allows for travel reservations to be booked through Internet services (Travel Web, NetBooker and UltraRes). Pegasus Commission Processing improves the efficiency and effectiveness of the commission payment process for participating hotels and travel agencies by consolidating payments and providing comprehensive transaction reports. It links nearly 24,000 hotels with 80,000 agencies in more than 200 countries. Pegasus Business Intelligence provides information services to hotel industry participants with transaction specific information on industry trends and guest behavior. Recently, the company supplemented its Business Intelligence services by acquiring all of the equity interest in Driving Revenue L.L.C., a hotel database marketing consulting firm.

FINANCIALS: Sales and profits are in thousands of dollars—add 000 to get the full amount.

Notes regarding 1999: Through 9 months *(1999 sales and profits were not available for all companies at press time.)*

1999 Sales: $27,600	1999 Profits: $5,500	Stock Ticker: **PEGS**
1998 Sales: $29,100	1998 Profits: $5,400	Employees: 137
1997 Sales: $20,900	1997 Profits: $ 600	Fiscal Year Ends: 12/31
1996 Sales: $15,900	1996 Profits: $-3,500	
1995 Sales: $9,300	1995 Profits: $-3,600	

SALARIES/BENEFITS:

Pension Plan:	ESOP Stock Plan:	Profit Sharing:	Top Exec. Salary: $300,000	Bonus: $150,000
Savings Plan: Y	Stock Purch. Plan:		Second Exec. Salary: $195,833	Bonus: $68,548

COMPETITIVE ADVANTAGE: Focus on the hotel industry.

OTHER THOUGHTS:

Apparent Women Officers or Directors: 1
Apparent Minority Officers or Directors:
Hot Spot for Advancement for Women/Minorities:

LOCATIONS: ("Y" = Yes)

West:	Southwest:	Midwest:	Southeast:	Northeast:	International:
	Y				

Note: Financial information, benefits and other data can change quickly and may vary from those stated here.

PERFICIENT   www.perficient.com

Industry Group Code: 54151
Ranks within this company's industry group: Sales: 15   Profits: 5

BUSINESS ACTIVITIES ("Y" – Yes)

Financial Services:	Information/Publ.:	Technology:	Services:		Retailing:		Telecommunications:
Stock Brokerage	Portal/Hub/News	Computer Manuf.	Payments/Transfers		Retailer		Internet Serv. Provider
Mortgages/Loans	On-Line Community	Networking Equip.	Consulting	Y	Auctions		Web Site Host
Banking	Search Engine	Software Manuf.	Advertising/Marketing		Mall		Server Farm
Insurance	Financial Data Publ.	Specialty Equipment	Outsourcing	Y	Tickets/Travel		Specialty Telecom.
Credit Cards	Broadcasting/Music				Price Comparisons		High Speed Access

TYPES OF BUSINESS:

Consulting-On Site Technical Services
Outsourced Implementation

BRANDS/DIVISIONS/AFFILIATES:

Ventix
LoreData

CONTACTS: Note: Officers with more than one job title may be intentionally listed here more than once.

John T. McDonald, CEO
Bryan R. Menell, Pres.
John A. Hinners, CFO
Tammy Baker, Human Resources
Barry Demak, VP- Business Dev.

Phone: 512-306-7337	Fax: 512-306-7331
Toll-Free:	

Address: 7600-B N. Capital of Texas Hwy., Ste. 220, Austin, TX, 78731

GROWTH PLANS/SPECIAL FEATURES:

Perficient provides virtual professional services organizations, V-PSOs, to Internet software companies. V-PSOs are teams of information technology professionals that plan, manage and execute software product implementations, allowing companies to rapidly expand their software deployment capabilities. The companies using this service are then able to focus on the business of improving and selling their software without maintaining a large in-house PSO. The company's first partnership was with Vignette Corporation, an Internet relationship management company. Perficient has since developed relationships with Interwoven, Inc., an enterprise web production company, Motive Communications, Inc., a support chain automation company and Ventix Systems, Inc., a knowledge support company. Perficient and Ventix created a partnership that launched The Ventix System, a knowledge support system for companies to train and support end users of mission-critical enterprise applications. Knowledge support systems address the gap between traditional training and support solutions such as help desks and experts. Based in Austin, the company recently acquired LoreData and opened an East Coast office.

FINANCIALS: Sales and profits are in thousands of dollars—add 000 to get the full amount.

Notes regarding 1999: Through 9 months *(1999 sales and profits were not available for all companies at press time.)*

1999 Sales: $1,916	1999 Profits: $-1,082	
1998 Sales: $ 826	1998 Profits: $ 68	Stock Ticker: **PRFT**
1997 Sales: $	1997 Profits: $	Employees: 19
1996 Sales: $	1996 Profits: $	Fiscal Year Ends: 12/31
1995 Sales: $	1995 Profits: $	

SALARIES/BENEFITS:

Pension Plan:	ESOP Stock Plan: Y	Profit Sharing:	Top Exec. Salary: $80,000	Bonus: $
Savings Plan: Y	Stock Purch. Plan:		Second Exec. Salary: $	Bonus: $

COMPETITIVE ADVANTAGE: Growth through alliances and acquisitions.

OTHER THOUGHTS:

Apparent Women Officers or Directors: 1
Apparent Minority Officers or Directors:
Hot Spot for Advancement for Women/Minorities:

LOCATIONS: ("Y" = Yes)

West:	Southwest:	Midwest:	Southeast:	Northeast:	International:
	Y			Y	

Note: Financial information, benefits and other data can change quickly and may vary from those stated here.

PERSISTENCE SOFTWARE   www.persistence.com

Industry Group Code: 5112
Ranks within this company's industry group: Sales: 48   Profits: 30

BUSINESS ACTIVITIES ("Y" = Yes)

Financial Services:	Information/Publ.:	Technology:		Services:		Retailing:	Telecommunications:
Stock Brokerage	Portal/Hub/News	Computer Manuf.		Payments/Transfers		Retailer	Internet Serv. Provider
Mortgages/Loans	On-Line Community	Networking Equip.		Consulting		Auctions	Web Site Host
Banking	Search Engine	Software Manuf.	Y	Advertising/Marketing		Mall	Server Farm
Insurance	Financial Data Publ.	Specialty Equipment		Outsourcing	Y	Tickets/Travel	Specialty Telecom.
Credit Cards	Broadcasting/Music					Price Comparisons	High Speed Access

TYPES OF BUSINESS:

Software-E-Commerce
Training

BRANDS/DIVISIONS/AFFILIATES:

PowerTier
Fulcrum Innovations

CONTACTS: *Note: Officers with more than one job title may be intentionally listed here more than once.*

Christopher T. Keene, CEO
Larry Hootnick, Pres.
Christine Russell, CFO
Erik Frieberg, VP-Corp. Mktg.
Roma Martwick, Human Resources Mgr.
Mark Douglas, Chief Tech Officer
Derek Henninger, VP-Engineering
Barry Goss, VP-Strategic Mktg.
Alan Cohen, Sr. VP- Sales and Int'l Oper.

Phone: 650-372-3600	Fax: 650-341-8432
Toll-Free:	
Address: 1720 S. Amphlett Blvd., 3rd Fl., San Mateo, CA, 94402	

GROWTH PLANS/SPECIAL FEATURES:

Persistence Software, formerly Fulcrum Innovations, Inc., provides transactional application server software products that comprise the Internet software infrastructure for high volume and high performance e-commerce applications. The company's PowerTier family of products consists of transactional application servers specifically designed to enable high performance e-commerce. PowerTier products offer real-time response times for up to thousands of concurrent users and transactions, scalability and reliability to prevent system crashes and downtime. The company's products also offer dramatic reductions in time-to-market for building and deploying e-commerce applications and capabilities that enable businesses to extend processes across organizational boundaries. Persistence also offers educational services for developers, systems integrators and application administrators. The company's professionals provide hands-on mentoring in architecture and design, product education, rapid prototyping and implementation tuning. The company's over 200 Global 1000 customers include AT&T, Boeing, Cisco, FedEx, IBM, Instinet, Lucent, Morgan Stanley Dean Witter and SuperValu. Recently, Java Developer's Journal picked Persistence's PowerTier EJB 5.0 as an Editor's Choice Best Java Application Server. Java Report magazine's Annual Writers' Choice awards, given by over 60 Java Report writers, also chose PowerTier as one of the top three Hottest and Coolest products for 1999. Intelligent Enterprise magazine chose Persistence software as a Best E-Commerce Application, Business-to-Business.

FINANCIALS: Sales and profits are in thousands of dollars—add 000 to get the full amount.

Notes regarding 1999: *(1999 sales and profits were not available for all companies at press time.)*

1999 Sales: $14,400	1999 Profits: $-3,700	Stock Ticker: **PRSW**
1998 Sales: $10,200	1998 Profits: $-4,100	Employees: 81
1997 Sales: $5,400	1997 Profits: $-4,700	Fiscal Year Ends: 12/31
1996 Sales: $3,800	1996 Profits: $-3,300	
1995 Sales: $	1995 Profits: $	

SALARIES/BENEFITS:

Pension Plan:	ESOP Stock Plan: Y	Profit Sharing:	Top Exec. Salary: $151,670	Bonus: $23,630
Savings Plan:	Stock Purch. Plan:		Second Exec. Salary: $140,004	Bonus: $25,980

COMPETITIVE ADVANTAGE: Very hot application server technology.

OTHER THOUGHTS:

Apparent Women Officers or Directors: 2
Apparent Minority Officers or Directors:
Hot Spot for Advancement for Women/Minorities:

LOCATIONS: ("Y" = Yes)

West:	Southwest:	Midwest:	Southeast:	Northeast:	International:
Y					Y

PHONE.COM   www.phone.com

Industry Group Code: 5112
Ranks within this company's industry group: Sales: 71   Profits: 52

BUSINESS ACTIVITIES ("Y" – Yes)

Financial Services:	Information/Publ.:	Technology:		Services:	Retailing:	Telecommunications:	
Stock Brokerage	Portal/Hub/News	Computer Manuf.		Payments/Transfers	Retailer	Internet Serv. Provider	
Mortgages/Loans	On-Line Community	Networking Equip.	Y	Consulting	Auctions	Web Site Host	
Banking	Search Engine	Software Manuf.	Y	Advertising/Marketing	Mall	Server Farm	
Insurance	Financial Data Publ.	Specialty Equipment		Outsourcing	Tickets/Travel	Specialty Telecom.	Y
Credit Cards	Broadcasting/Music				Price Comparisons	High Speed Access	Y

TYPES OF BUSINESS:

Software-Communications
Wireless Internet Delivery Software

BRANDS/DIVISIONS/AFFILIATES:

MyPhone
@Motion, Inc.
ApiON
Unwired Planet, Inc.

CONTACTS: Note: Officers with more than one job title may be intentionally listed here more than once.

Alain Rossmann, CEO
Alan Black, CFO/VP-Finance and Admin.
Benjamin Linder, VP-Mktg.
Maureen Grandcolas, Dir.-Human Resources
Andrew Laursen, VP-Product Dev. & Engineering
Maurice Jeffery, VP- North American Sales
Malcolm Bird, Managing Dir. - Unwired Planet (Europe) Ltd.

Phone: 650-562-0200	Fax: 650-817-1499
Toll-Free:	
Address: 800 Chesapeake Dr., Redwood City, CA, 94063	

GROWTH PLANS/SPECIAL FEATURES:

Phone.com, formerly Unwired Planet, Inc., is a provider of software that enables the delivery of Internet-based services to mass-market wireless telephones. Using the company's software, network operators can provide Internet-based services to their wireless subscribers and wireless telephone manufacturers can turn their mass-market wireless telephones into mobile Internet appliances. This allows wireless subscribers to have access to Internet and corporate Intranet-based services, including e-mail, news, stocks, weather, travel and sports. Additionally, subscribers have access via their wireless telephones to network operators' intranet-based telephony services, including over-the-air activation, call management, billing history information, pricing plan subscription and voice message management. MyPhone is Phone.com's mobile Internet portal platform that enables network operators to rapidly deploy branded portal sites for their wireless subscribers, allowing subscribers a customized set of information services and applications that are optimized for the mobile user. At the end of 1999, Phone.com acquired @Motion Inc., an emerging provider of Voice Portal technology for the converging telephony and Internet industries and ApiON, a European WAP (wireless application protocol) software supplier. As Unwired Planet, Phone.com was a Red Herring Top 50 Private Company and received the magazine's Best Partnerships award. Phone.com is headquartered in Silicon Valley and has regional offices in Belfast, London and Tokyo.

FINANCIALS: Sales and profits are in thousands of dollars—add 000 to get the full amount.

Notes regarding 1999: (1999 sales and profits were not available for all companies at press time.)

1999 Sales: $13,400	1999 Profits: $-20,800	Stock Ticker: PHCM
1998 Sales: $2,200	1998 Profits: $-10,600	Employees: 233
1997 Sales: $ 300	1997 Profits: $-8,000	Fiscal Year Ends: 06/30
1996 Sales: $	1996 Profits: $-2,500	
1995 Sales: $	1995 Profits: $- 100	

SALARIES/BENEFITS:

Pension Plan:	ESOP Stock Plan: Y	Profit Sharing:	Top Exec. Salary: $167,500	Bonus: $107,352
Savings Plan: Y	Stock Purch. Plan:		Second Exec. Salary: $157,500	Bonus: $

COMPETITIVE ADVANTAGE: An early leader in wireless Internet access technology.

OTHER THOUGHTS:

Apparent Women Officers or Directors: 1
Apparent Minority Officers or Directors:
Hot Spot for Advancement for Women/Minorities:

LOCATIONS: ("Y" = Yes)

West:	Southwest:	Midwest:	Southeast:	Northeast:	International:
Y					Y

Note: Financial information, benefits and other data can change quickly and may vary from those stated here.

PHOTOWORKS INC   www.filmworks.com

Industry Group Code: 4541
Ranks within this company's industry group: Sales: 11   Profits: 5

BUSINESS ACTIVITIES ("Y" = Yes)

Financial Services:	Information/Publ.:	Technology:	Services:	Retailing:		Telecommunications:
Stock Brokerage	Portal/Hub/News	Computer Manuf.	Payments/Transfers	Retailer	Y	Internet Serv. Provider
Mortgages/Loans	On-Line Community	Networking Equip.	Consulting	Auctions		Web Site Host
Banking	Search Engine	Software Manuf.	Advertising/Marketing	Mall		Server Farm
Insurance	Financial Data Publ.	Specialty Equipment	Outsourcing	Tickets/Travel		Specialty Telecom.
Credit Cards	Broadcasting/Music			Price Comparisons		High Speed Access

TYPES OF BUSINESS:

Photofinishing
On-line Delivery of Photos
CD-ROM Delivery of Photos

BRANDS/DIVISIONS/AFFILIATES:

PhotoMail
FilmWorks
Seattle FilmWorks
PhotoWorks Uploader

CONTACTS: Note: Officers with more than one job title may be intentionally listed here more than once.

Gary R. Christophersen, CEO
Gary R. Christophersen, Pres.
Case H. Kuehn, CFO/VP-Finance
Gary T. Tashjian, VP-Mktg.
Annette F. Mack, VP-Human Resources
Loran Cashmore Bond, Corp. Controller
Mich K. Earl, Corp. Sec.
Michael F. Lass, VP-Oper.
Case H. Kuehn, Treas.

Phone: 206-281-1390	Fax: 206-284-5357
Toll-Free: 1-800-345-6967	
Address: 1260 16th Ave. West, Seattle, WA, 98119	

GROWTH PLANS/SPECIAL FEATURES:

PhotoWorks, Inc. (formerly Seattle FilmWorks) is a photofinishing and on-line image management company and a leader in providing digital images over the Internet. The company markets 35mm film, photo processing and photofinishing services and products. The company additionally offers a variety of digital photo services, including PhotoMail, digital photo delivery via an on-line Internet account, PhotoWorks Uploader, service for digital cameras, and Pictures On Disk, digitized photos delivered on disk or CD. PhotoWorks' on-line image processing is an increasingly popular way for people to share photos over the Internet. The company has over 75 million images archived, making it the largest on-line consumer photo archive site on the Internet. The on-line archive expands the way customers can enjoy photos by enabling the growing popularity of photo e-mails and the ability to order photographic reprints without the need for negatives. After registering on-line with PhotoWorks, the customer receives a starter package including free rolls of film, postage paid mailing envelopes for sending the film and order forms. The customer mails the film and is then notified by e-mail that the photos are ready to be viewed and e-mailed on-line through a password-protected account. The company will develop any brand of film, however, PhotoWorks brand film is returned with each order. The PhotoWorks service includes free scanning of every photograph (with normal processing fees), web posting to a private site, new rolls of PhotoWorks film delivered with the customers' pictures (the fee for 1 new roll is included in each processing fee) and lifetime archiving as long as the customer develops at least two rolls per year.

FINANCIALS: Sales and profits are in thousands of dollars—add 000 to get the full amount.
Notes regarding 1999: (1999 sales and profits were not available for all companies at press time.)

1999 Sales: $89,613	1999 Profits: $-10,127	Stock Ticker: FOTO
1998 Sales: $96,700	1998 Profits: $7,600	Employees:
1997 Sales: $1,012	1997 Profits: $ 426	Fiscal Year Ends: 9/30
1996 Sales: $	1996 Profits: $	
1995 Sales: $	1995 Profits: $	

SALARIES/BENEFITS:

Pension Plan:	ESOP Stock Plan: Y	Profit Sharing:	Top Exec. Salary: $150,483	Bonus: $30,588
Savings Plan: Y	Stock Purch. Plan:		Second Exec. Salary: $132,390	Bonus: $14,737

COMPETITIVE ADVANTAGE: The company has successfully made the leap to become a leading Internet-based business.

OTHER THOUGHTS:

Apparent Women Officers or Directors: 3
Apparent Minority Officers or Directors: 2
Hot Spot for Advancement for Women/Minorities:

LOCATIONS: ("Y" = Yes)

West:	Southwest:	Midwest:	Southeast:	Northeast:	International:
Y					

PILOT NETWORK SERVICES   www.pilot.net

Industry Group Code: 51339
Ranks within this company's industry group: Sales: 13   Profits: 10

BUSINESS ACTIVITIES ("Y" = Yes)

Financial Services:	Information/Publ.:	Technology:	Services:	Retailing:	Telecommunications:	
Stock Brokerage	Portal/Hub/News	Computer Manuf.	Payments/Transfers	Retailer	Internet Serv. Provider	Y
Mortgages/Loans	On-Line Community	Networking Equip.	Consulting	Auctions	Web Site Host	Y
Banking	Search Engine	Software Manuf.	Advertising/Marketing	Mall	Server Farm	
Insurance	Financial Data Publ.	Specialty Equipment	Outsourcing	Tickets/Travel	Specialty Telecom.	
Credit Cards	Broadcasting/Music			Price Comparisons	High Speed Access	Y

TYPES OF BUSINESS:

ISP
Web Site Host
Access

BRANDS/DIVISIONS/AFFILIATES:

Pilot Secure Access & Gateway Services

CONTACTS: *Note: Officers with more than one job title may be intentionally listed here more than once.*

M. Marketta Silvera, CEO
M. Marketta Silvera, Pres.
William C. Leetham, CFO
Dana Nelson, Sr. VP-Sales & Mktg.
Julie Cottton, VP-Human Resources
Thomas A. Wadlow, VP-Engineering and Dev.
William C. Leetham, Sec.
Martin Wegenstein, Sr.VP-Oper.
William C. Leetham, Treas.

Phone: 510-433-7800	Fax: 510-433-7809
Toll-Free:	
Address: 1080 Marina Village Pkwy., Alameda, CA, 94501	

GROWTH PLANS/SPECIAL FEATURES:

Pilot Network Services provides a wide range of secure Internet services that incorporate high-bandwidth connectivity and enable secure electronic business over the Internet. The services are offered for a fixed monthly fee on an annual subscription basis. Pilot's services include secure hosting and Internet connectivity services that enable secure connectivity between a corporate network and the Internet. The company also offers secure virtual private networking services that enable remote users and wide-area networks to securely communicate enterprise-wide and over the Internet. The company provides a scalable solution that allows customers to quickly deploy and expand electronic business capabilities by subscribing to Pilot's secure Internet services. Pilot's subscription-based secure services allow customers to avoid the risks associated with traditional approaches to Internet security. Customers can also avoid extensive costs associated with implementing an in-house solution, including set-up costs for security and systems design, hardware, software, Internet access services provided by Internet Service Providers (ISPs) and labor and ongoing costs for telecommunications, staffing, maintenance and upgrades. Commerce One recently chose Pilot to protect the confidentiality of exchanges between trading partners on Commerce One MarketSite. Pilot Secure Access & Gateway Services will provide dedicated and redundant T1 connections to ensure reliability and availability of the e-business portal.

FINANCIALS: Sales and profits are in thousands of dollars—add 000 to get the full amount.

Notes regarding 1999: *(1999 sales and profits were not available for all companies at press time.)*

1999 Sales: $17,500	1999 Profits: $-18,100	Stock Ticker: **PILT**
1998 Sales: $11,300	1998 Profits: $-6,700	Employees: 149
1997 Sales: $6,300	1997 Profits: $-2,700	Fiscal Year Ends: 3/31
1996 Sales: $2,500	1996 Profits: $-1,800	
1995 Sales: $ 800	1995 Profits: $- 400	

SALARIES/BENEFITS:

Pension Plan:	ESOP Stock Plan: Y	Profit Sharing:	Top Exec. Salary: $225,000	Bonus: $10,200
Savings Plan: Y	Stock Purch. Plan:		Second Exec. Salary: $150,150	Bonus: $13,600

COMPETITIVE ADVANTAGE: Focus on corporate clients, rather than consumers/Excellent international capabilities.

OTHER THOUGHTS:

Apparent Women Officers or Directors: 3
Apparent Minority Officers or Directors:
Hot Spot for Advancement for Women/Minorities: Y

LOCATIONS: ("Y" = Yes)

West:	Southwest:	Midwest:	Southeast:	Northeast:	International:
Y		Y		Y	Y

Note: Financial information, benefits and other data can change quickly and may vary from those stated here.

PORTAL SOFTWARE   www.portal.com

Industry Group Code: 5112
Ranks within this company's industry group: Sales: 49   Profits: 42

BUSINESS ACTIVITIES ("Y" = Yes)

Financial Services:	Information/Publ.:	Technology:		Services:	Retailing:	Telecommunications:	
Stock Brokerage	Portal/Hub/News	Computer Manuf.		Payments/Transfers	Retailer	Internet Serv. Provider	
Mortgages/Loans	On-Line Community	Networking Equip.		Consulting	Auctions	Web Site Host	
Banking	Search Engine	Software Manuf.	Y	Advertising/Marketing	Mall	Server Farm	
Insurance	Financial Data Publ.	Specialty Equipment		Outsourcing	Tickets/Travel	Specialty Telecom.	Y
Credit Cards	Broadcasting/Music				Price Comparisons	High Speed Access	

TYPES OF BUSINESS:

Software-Customer Management and Billing

BRANDS/DIVISIONS/AFFILIATES:

Real Time No Limits Infranet Solution
Infranet IPT

CONTACTS: *Note: Officers with more than one job title may be intentionally listed here more than once.*

John E. Little, CEO
John E. Little, Pres.
Jack L. Acosta, CFO/VP-Finance
Kevin P. Mosher, VP-Sales
Annette D. Surtees, VP-Human Resources
David S. Labuda, Chief Tech. Officer
David S. Labuda, VP-Engineering/Chief Tech. Officer
Steven R. Sommer, VP-Mktg. And Business Dev.
Mike Regan, VP-Professional Services Group

Phone: 408-343-4400	Fax: 408-343-4401
Toll-Free:	
Address: 20883 Stevens Creek Blvd., Cupertino, CA, 95014	

GROWTH PLANS/SPECIAL FEATURES:

Portal Software, Inc. develops, markets and supports customer management and billing software (CM&B software) for providers of Internet-based services. The company's Real Time No Limits Infranet solution enables the real-time provisioning and reporting of services, including account creation, user authentication and authorization, activity tracking, pricing and rating, billing and customer service, all on a scale of up to millions of users. The company's targeted markets include providers of dial-up and broadband consumer Internet access, high-speed business Internet access and backbone networking, virtual private networks, IP telephony and fax, web, storefront and application hosting, e-mail and unified messaging, on-line content services and other emerging IP-based consumer and business services. With American headquarters in California and European headquarters in England, Portal recently established operations in Japan, based in Tokyo, to support the specific requirements of the Japanese market. Recently, Internet Telephony magazine selected Portal's Intranet IPT as 1999 Product of the Year in the Billing category. Portal's customers include Juno Online, Qwest Communications, Inktomi, 3Com, BellSouth, France Telcom and U.S. West. The company's technology partners include Cisco, Compaq, Hewlett Packard, Microsoft, Oracle and Sun Microsystems.

FINANCIALS: Sales and profits are in thousands of dollars—add 000 to get the full amount.

Notes regarding 1999: *(1999 sales and profits were not available for all companies at press time.)*

1999 Sales: $26,700	1999 Profits: $-17,400	Stock Ticker: **PRSF**
1998 Sales: $9,400	1998 Profits: $-7,600	Employees: 242
1997 Sales: $5,000	1997 Profits: $-2,300	Fiscal Year Ends: 01/31
1996 Sales: $1,900	1996 Profits: $- 500	
1995 Sales: $1,500	1995 Profits: $- 200	

SALARIES/BENEFITS:

Pension Plan:	ESOP Stock Plan: Y	Profit Sharing:	Top Exec. Salary: $	Bonus: $
Savings Plan:	Stock Purch. Plan: Y		Second Exec. Salary: $	Bonus: $

COMPETITIVE ADVANTAGE: Enables Internet access to account and billing information for a client's customers.

OTHER THOUGHTS:

Apparent Women Officers or Directors: 1
Apparent Minority Officers or Directors:
Hot Spot for Advancement for Women/Minorities:

LOCATIONS: ("Y" = Yes)

West:	Southwest:	Midwest:	Southeast:	Northeast:	International:
Y					Y

PREVIEW TRAVEL INC   www.previewtravel.com

Industry Group Code: 51339A
Ranks within this company's industry group: Sales: 5   Profits: 14

BUSINESS ACTIVITIES ("Y" – Yes)

Financial Services:	Information/Publ.:	Technology:	Services:	Retailing:		Telecommunications:	
Stock Brokerage	Portal/Hub/News	Computer Manuf.	Payments/Transfers	Retailer		Internet Serv. Provider	
Mortgages/Loans	On-Line Community	Networking Equip.	Consulting	Auctions		Web Site Host	
Banking	Search Engine	Software Manuf.	Advertising/Marketing	Mall		Server Farm	
Insurance	Financial Data Publ.	Specialty Equipment	Outsourcing	Tickets/Travel	Y	Specialty Telecom.	Y
Credit Cards	Broadcasting/Music			Price Comparisons		High Speed Access	

TYPES OF BUSINESS:
On-line Travel Services

BRANDS/DIVISIONS/AFFILIATES:
Travelocity

GROWTH PLANS/SPECIAL FEATURES:

Preview Travel, Inc. is a leading provider of on-line travel services for leisure and small business travelers. The company provides travel and reservation services with reliable, real-time access to schedule, pricing and availability information for over 500 airlines, 25,000 hotels and all major car rental companies. In addition to reservation and ticketing services, Preview Travel offers vacation packages, discounted promotional fares, travel news and destination content. The company complements its high-tech, user-friendly content with a high level of customer service. Preview Travel is America Online's primary and preferred provider of on-line travel services. Preview has also linked with Excite, a leading Internet search engine, to become the exclusive provider of travel services on Excite's Travel Channel, City.net. Currently, Preview Travel is merging with Travelocity to increase market share.

CONTACTS: *Note: Officers with more than one job title may be intentionally listed here more than once.*

Chris Clouser, CEO
Chris Clouser, Pres.
Bruce Carmedelle, CFO
Barrie Seidenberg, Exec. VP/Chief Mktg. Officer
Ken Farber, VP-Human Resources
John M. Petrone, Exec. VP-Tech.
Amy Guggenheim, Sr. VP-Business Dev.
Wendy Strickman, VP-Corp. Comm.
Amy Guggenheim, Investor Relations

Phone: 415-439-1200	Fax: 415-421-4982
Toll-Free:	
Address: 747 Front St., San Francisco, CA, 94111	

FINANCIALS: Sales and profits are in thousands of dollars—add 000 to get the full amount.
Notes regarding 1999: *(1999 sales and profits were not available for all companies at press time.)*

1999 Sales: $31,100	1999 Profits: $20,100	**Stock Ticker: PTVL**
1998 Sales: $14,000	1998 Profits: $-27,000	Employees: 224
1997 Sales: $13,600	1997 Profits: $-10,200	Fiscal Year Ends: 12/31
1996 Sales: $12,400	1996 Profits: $-5,600	
1995 Sales: $10,100	1995 Profits: $-4,900	

SALARIES/BENEFITS:

Pension Plan:	ESOP Stock Plan: Y	Profit Sharing:	Top Exec. Salary: $241,905	Bonus: $112,096
Savings Plan: Y	Stock Purch. Plan:		Second Exec. Salary: $195,603	Bonus: $75,782

COMPETITIVE ADVANTAGE: Relationship with AOL.

OTHER THOUGHTS:
Apparent Women Officers or Directors: 5
Apparent Minority Officers or Directors:
Hot Spot for Advancement for Women/Minorities: Y

LOCATIONS: ("Y" = Yes)

West:	Southwest:	Midwest:	Southeast:	Northeast:	International:
Y					

Note: Financial information, benefits and other data can change quickly and may vary from those stated here.

PRICELINE.COM   www.priceline.com

Industry Group Code: 5141B
Ranks within this company's industry group: Sales: 1   Profits: 1

BUSINESS ACTIVITIES ("Y" = Yes)

Financial Services:		Information/Publ.:	Technology:	Services:	Retailing:		Telecommunications:	
Stock Brokerage		Portal/Hub/News	Computer Manuf.	Payments/Transfers	Retailer		Internet Serv. Provider	
Mortgages/Loans	Y	On-Line Community	Networking Equip.	Consulting	Auctions	Y	Web Site Host	
Banking		Search Engine	Software Manuf.	Advertising/Marketing	Mall		Server Farm	
Insurance		Financial Data Publ.	Specialty Equipment	Outsourcing	Tickets/Travel	Y	Specialty Telecom.	
Credit Cards		Broadcasting/Music			Price Comparisons	Y	High Speed Access	Y

TYPES OF BUSINESS:
On-line Travel, Cars and Loans
Auction-Based Purchasing System

BRANDS/DIVISIONS/AFFILIATES:
WebHouse Club

CONTACTS: *Note: Officers with more than one job title may be intentionally listed here more than once.*
Richard S. Braddock, CEO
Daniel H. Shulman, Pres./COO
Paul E. Francis, CFO
Paul Breitenbach, Sr. VP-Mktg.
Jeanne Wisniewski, Exec. VP-Human Resources
Michael Diliberto, Sr. VP-Tech.
Andrew Abowitz, VP-Oper. and Customer Service
Maryann Keller, Pres.-Auto Services

Phone: 203-705-3000	Fax: 203-595-0160
Toll-Free:	
Address: 5 High Ridge Park, Stamford, CT, 06905	

GROWTH PLANS/SPECIAL FEATURES:
Priceline.com is a patented Internet purchasing system that enables consumers to attempt to save money by naming their own prices for goods and services, including airfare, hotel rooms, new and rental cars, home mortgages, refinancing and home equity loans. Using a demand collection system, name-your-own-price, Priceline.com has pioneered a unique type of e-commerce. Consumers are able to save money on a wide range of products, and sellers are able to generate incremental revenue, without disrupting their existing distribution channels or retail pricing structures. Recently, Priceline.com licensed its business model to a privately owned company, Priceline WebHouse Club, offering name-your-own-price retail goods, beginning with groceries in the New York city area. WebHouse Club attracted over 15,000 members in its first week. Beginning the first quarter of 2000, Priceline.com will offer name-your-own-price long distance telephone service, making it possible for U.S. consumers to buy IP-based communications, with no strings attached, to call any city in the world. The company has plans to expand to business-to-business long distance service. Priceline.com was chosen as one of the top three places on the Internet to save money by web shoppers polled in a recent Princeton Opinion Research survey.

FINANCIALS: Sales and profits are in thousands of dollars—add 000 to get the full amount.
Notes regarding 1999: Estimated *(1999 sales and profits were not available for all companies at press time.)*

1999 Sales: $482,409	1999 Profits: $-1,055,100	Stock Ticker: **PCLN**
1998 Sales: $35,200	1998 Profits: $-112,200	Employees: 141
1997 Sales: $	1997 Profits: $-2,500	Fiscal Year Ends: 12/31
1996 Sales: $	1996 Profits: $	
1995 Sales: $	1995 Profits: $	

SALARIES/BENEFITS:
Pension Plan:	ESOP Stock Plan:	Profit Sharing:	Top Exec. Salary: $	Bonus: $
Savings Plan: Y	Stock Purch. Plan:		Second Exec. Salary: $	Bonus: $

COMPETITIVE ADVANTAGE: Early leader in delivering self-pricing and bargains over the Internet.

OTHER THOUGHTS:
Apparent Women Officers or Directors: 2
Apparent Minority Officers or Directors:
Hot Spot for Advancement for Women/Minorities:

LOCATIONS: ("Y" = Yes)
West:	Southwest:	Midwest:	Southeast:	Northeast:	International:
				Y	

Note: Financial information, benefits and other data can change quickly and may vary from those stated here.

PRIMIX SOLUTIONS INC   www.primix.com

Industry Group Code: 54151
Ranks within this company's industry group: Sales: 13   Profits: 9

BUSINESS ACTIVITIES ("Y" = Yes)

Financial Services:	Information/Publ.:	Technology:	Services:		Retailing:	Telecommunications:
Stock Brokerage	Portal/Hub/News	Computer Manuf.	Payments/Transfers		Retailer	Internet Serv. Provider
Mortgages/Loans	On-Line Community	Networking Equip.	Consulting	Y	Auctions	Web Site Host
Banking	Search Engine	Software Manuf.	Advertising/Marketing		Mall	Server Farm
Insurance	Financial Data Publ.	Specialty Equipment	Outsourcing		Tickets/Travel	Specialty Telecom.
Credit Cards	Broadcasting/Music				Price Comparisons	High Speed Access

TYPES OF BUSINESS:

Technology Consulting/Systems Integration
Creative Systems Design

BRANDS/DIVISIONS/AFFILIATES:

Essential e-business

CONTACTS: Note: Officers with more than one job title may be intentionally listed here more than once.

Lennart Mengwall, CEO
David W. Chapman, CFO
Frank Mainero, VP-Mktg.
Sarah H. Gibbs, VP-Human Resources
Timothy J. Dion, VP/Chief Tech. Officer
Joseph W. Seebach, Exec. VP-Business Dev.
David W. Chapman, Treas.
David Buck, VP-Strategic Alliances
Scott Chizzo, VP-Strategic Services

Phone: 617-923-6500	Fax: 617-923-6565
Toll-Free:	
Address: One Arsenal Marketplace, Watertown, MA, 02472	

GROWTH PLANS/SPECIAL FEATURES:

Primix Solutions, Inc. provides solutions for organizations to use information technology in order to solve business problems and capitalize on new business opportunities. Through strategic technology consulting, creative design and systems integration support, Primix Solutions services link a company's existing system hardware and software to the Internet. The linked systems provide an opportunity to build the client's on-line sales, manage order processing and provide customer service. Recently, Primix Solutions moved away from selling software to providing more services in order to help generate more profits. Primix Solutions' product, Essential e-business, is about building Internet-enabled solutions that create business value by increasing revenue, reducing costs, moving faster and optimizing assets. This incorporates teaming strategic, technical and creative people to help define objects, get measured results and manage improvements to become a leader in e-commerce solutions. Primix Solutions' customers include Gillette, PeopleSoft, Apple, MCI Worldcom and Aetna.

FINANCIALS: Sales and profits are in thousands of dollars—add 000 to get the full amount.

Notes regarding 1999: Through 9 months *(1999 sales and profits were not available for all companies at press time.)*

1999 Sales: $8,200	1999 Profits: $-4,449	Stock Ticker: **PMIX**
1998 Sales: $4,800	1998 Profits: $-4,200	Employees: 90
1997 Sales: $5,600	1997 Profits: $-7,600	Fiscal Year Ends: 12/31
1996 Sales: $13,200	1996 Profits: $-12,300	
1995 Sales: $6,100	1995 Profits: $-2,700	

SALARIES/BENEFITS:

Pension Plan:	ESOP Stock Plan: Y	Profit Sharing:	Top Exec. Salary: $194,615	Bonus: $
Savings Plan: Y	Stock Purch. Plan:		Second Exec. Salary: $161,654	Bonus: $62,560

COMPETITIVE ADVANTAGE: A focus on systems integration and installation of applications for e-business firms.

OTHER THOUGHTS:

Apparent Women Officers or Directors: 1
Apparent Minority Officers or Directors: 1
Hot Spot for Advancement for Women/Minorities:

LOCATIONS: ("Y" = Yes)

West:	Southwest:	Midwest:	Southeast:	Northeast:	International:
				Y	

PRIMUS KNOWLEDGE SOLUTIONS   www.primus.com

Industry Group Code: 5112
Ranks within this company's industry group: Sales: 50   Profits: 52

BUSINESS ACTIVITIES ("Y" = Yes)

Financial Services:	Information/Publ.:	Technology:		Services:	Retailing:	Telecommunications:
Stock Brokerage	Portal/Hub/News	Computer Manuf.		Payments/Transfers	Retailer	Internet Serv. Provider
Mortgages/Loans	On-Line Community	Networking Equip.		Consulting	Auctions	Web Site Host
Banking	Search Engine	Software Manuf.	Y	Advertising/Marketing	Mall	Server Farm
Insurance	Financial Data Publ.	Specialty Equipment		Outsourcing	Tickets/Travel	Specialty Telecom.
Credit Cards	Broadcasting/Music				Price Comparisons	High Speed Access

TYPES OF BUSINESS:
Software-Internet Customer Service

BRANDS/DIVISIONS/AFFILIATES:
Primus eService
SolutionSeries

CONTACTS: *Note: Officers with more than one job title may be intentionally listed here more than once.*
Michael A. Brochu, CEO
Michael A. Brochu, Pres.
Elizabeth J. Heubner, CFO/VP-Finance
Kim M. Nelson, VP-Sales
Diana Wong, VP-Human Resources
Edward I. Walter, VP-Product Dev. & Tech.
Elizabeth J. Heubner, Corp. Sec.
Elizabeth J. Heubner, Treas.

Phone: 206-292-1000	Fax: 206-292-1825
Toll-Free:	
Address: 1601 5th Ave., Ste. 1900, Seattle, WA, 98101	

GROWTH PLANS/SPECIAL FEATURES:

Primus Knowledge Solutions, Inc. provides Internet-based problem resolution software for customer service and self-service. Primus' software enables businesses to capture problem resolution information, solve customer problems, reuse solutions stored in the knowledge base and share captured knowledge throughout the extended enterprise. Primus also provides training, maintenance and support services. Primus eService software allows companies to effectively manage all points of contact with customers. Customers can serve themselves or choose from other methods to reach customer service, such as the web, e-mail, voice and chat. Primus also offers SolutionSeries software, which is designed to help customer service organizations compete in today's demanding e-service environment, providing tools to increase operational efficiency and effectiveness to increase customer satisfaction and loyalty. This software also enables users to realize a substantial economic return on investments. Primus believes its software will help organizations reduce the overall time needed to resolve problems, improve first time call resolution rates, increase call deflections to the Internet, reduce escalation of problems to senior analysts, increase solution reuse and reduce training time. Primus provides solutions for all levels of business, regardless of size, and customers include such companies as 3Com, 3M, Starbucks, Xerox, Novell, Microsoft, Motorola, Lucent, Compaq, Ericsson, Amdahl and Nortel Networks.

FINANCIALS: Sales and profits are in thousands of dollars—add 000 to get the full amount.
Notes regarding 1999: *(1999 sales and profits were not available for all companies at press time.)*

1999 Sales: $25,100	1999 Profits: $-13,000	**Stock Ticker: PKSI**
1998 Sales: $8,600	1998 Profits: $-10,600	Employees: 147
1997 Sales: $5,200	1997 Profits: $-6,000	Fiscal Year Ends: 12/31
1996 Sales: $2,400	1996 Profits: $-5,900	
1995 Sales: $	1995 Profits: $	

SALARIES/BENEFITS:

Pension Plan:	ESOP Stock Plan:	Profit Sharing:	Top Exec. Salary: $245,828	Bonus: $
Savings Plan:	Stock Purch. Plan:		Second Exec. Salary: $46,655	Bonus: $

COMPETITIVE ADVANTAGE: Focus on products that enhance vital customer service and retention.

OTHER THOUGHTS:

Apparent Women Officers or Directors: 3
Apparent Minority Officers or Directors: 1
Hot Spot for Advancement for Women/Minorities: Y

LOCATIONS: ("Y" = Yes)

West:	Southwest:	Midwest:	Southeast:	Northeast:	International:
Y	Y	Y	Y	Y	Y

PRODIGY COMMUNICATIONS   www.prodigy.com

Industry Group Code: 51339
Ranks within this company's industry group: Sales: 3 Profits: 21

BUSINESS ACTIVITIES ("Y" = Yes)

Financial Services:	Information/Publ.:	Technology:	Services:	Retailing:	Telecommunications:	
Stock Brokerage	Portal/Hub/News	Computer Manuf.	Payments/Transfers	Retailer	Internet Serv. Provider	Y
Mortgages/Loans	On-Line Community	Networking Equip.	Consulting	Auctions	Web Site Host	Y
Banking	Search Engine	Software Manuf.	Advertising/Marketing	Mall	Server Farm	
Insurance	Financial Data Publ.	Specialty Equipment	Outsourcing	Tickets/Travel	Specialty Telecom.	
Credit Cards	Broadcasting/Music			Price Comparisons	High Speed Access	

TYPES OF BUSINESS:

Internet Service Provider

BRANDS/DIVISIONS/AFFILIATES:

GROWTH PLANS/SPECIAL FEATURES:

Prodigy Communications Corporation is a leading nationwide Internet Service Provider offering fast, reliable Internet access and related services. Prodigy was an early service leader, providing the company with substantial brand name recognition that it believes will offer a significant competitive advantage in attracting new customers. Prodigy's current subscriber base is about 1.2 million Internet users and small- to mid-sized business customers. Prodigy's nationwide network covers all 50 states and over 700 cities, allowing approximately 83% of the United States population to connect to Prodigy through a local phone call. The company is enjoying a recent large increase in its number of subscribers. Currently, Prodigy is expanding its web hosting services and e-commerce activities, while also evaluating and introducing other value-added services such as long distance and cellular phone services, Internet-based telephony, fax services and on-line bill presentment.

CONTACTS: *Note: Officers with more than one job title may be intentionally listed here more than once.*

Samer F. Salameh, CEO
David C. Trachtenberg, COO/Pres.
David R. Henkel, CFO/Exec. VP-Finance
Pat Anderson, Dir.-Human Resources
Bill Kirkner, Chief Tech.Officer
Andrea S. Hirsch, Exec.VP/General Counsel
Andrea S. Hirsch, Exec. VP-Business Dev.

Phone: 914-448-8000	**Fax:** 914-448-3467
Toll-Free:	
Address: 44 S. Broadway, White Plains, NY, 10601	

FINANCIALS: Sales and profits are in thousands of dollars—add 000 to get the full amount.

Notes regarding 1999: Through 9 months *(1999 sales and profits were not available for all companies at press time.)*

1999 Sales: $121,900	1999 Profits: $-50,700	Stock Ticker: **PRGY**
1998 Sales: $136,100	1998 Profits: $-65,100	Employees: 394
1997 Sales: $134,200	1997 Profits: $-129,300	Fiscal Year Ends: 12/31
1996 Sales: $98,900	1996 Profits: $-114,100	
1995 Sales: $	1995 Profits: $-3,100	

SALARIES/BENEFITS:

Pension Plan:	ESOP Stock Plan: Y	Profit Sharing:	Top Exec. Salary: $216,042	Bonus: $
Savings Plan: Y	Stock Purch. Plan:		Second Exec. Salary: $215,000	Bonus: $

COMPETITIVE ADVANTAGE: Name brand recognition.

OTHER THOUGHTS:

Apparent Women Officers or Directors: 1
Apparent Minority Officers or Directors: 1
Hot Spot for Advancement for Women/Minorities:

LOCATIONS: ("Y" = Yes)

West:	Southwest:	Midwest:	Southeast:	Northeast:	International:
				Y	

PROTEAM.COM INC   www.proteam.com

Industry Group Code: 4541
Ranks within this company's industry group: Sales: 10   Profits: 31

BUSINESS ACTIVITIES ("Y" = Yes)

Financial Services:	Information/Publ.:	Technology:	Services:	Retailing:		Telecommunications:
Stock Brokerage	Portal/Hub/News	Computer Manuf.	Payments/Transfers	Retailer	Y	Internet Serv. Provider
Mortgages/Loans	On-Line Community	Networking Equip.	Consulting	Auctions		Web Site Host
Banking	Search Engine	Software Manuf.	Advertising/Marketing	Mall		Server Farm
Insurance	Financial Data Publ.	Specialty Equipment	Outsourcing	Tickets/Travel		Specialty Telecom.
Credit Cards	Broadcasting/Music			Price Comparisons		High Speed Access

TYPES OF BUSINESS:

Retail-Sports On-line

BRANDS/DIVISIONS/AFFILIATES:

Applecreek Catalog
The Edge Company Catalog
1-800-Pro-Team
Carol Wright Gifts
Gensis Direct, Inc.

CONTACTS: Note: Officers with more than one job title may be intentionally listed here more than once.

Warren Struhl, CEO
Hunter Cohen, Exec. VP/COO
Ronald R. Benanto, CFO/VP
David Sable, Chief Mktg. Officer
Kathleen M. Davis, VP-Human Resources
Dominic J. DiMascia, VP-Info. Systems
George J. Mollo, Jr., VP-Merch. Oper.& Inventory Control
Douglas S. Rose, VP-Corp. Dev.
Warren Struhl, Pres.
George A. D'Amico, VP-Customer Service and Sales

Phone: 201-867-2800	Fax: 201-867-1112
Toll-Free:	
Address: 100 Plaza Drive, Secaucus, NJ, 07094	

GROWTH PLANS/SPECIAL FEATURES:

Proteam.com, Inc., formerly Genesis Direct, Inc., is a leading database-driven specialty retailer in the rapidly growing universe of non-store shopping. The company was recently repositioned as an on-line sports equipment store at Proteam.com. With a current portfolio of 33 brands, the company offers products directly to consumers in targeted niche markets primarily through a variety of distinctive, information-rich catalogs, as well as Internet sites and electronic media, including television and radio. Proteam.com offers more than 15,000 products within distinct but interrelated market categories: sports, kids, gifts, collectibles and institutional business-to-business. The firm established strategic relationships in the sports market with the NBA, NHL, Major League Baseball, NASCAR and the NFL Quarterback Club. Some of the company's recent business endeavors include an expansion of Proteam.com's e-commerce business with an e-commerce agreement to bring products to Excite and WebCrawler. An agreement signed with Yahoo! will provide one-click access to ProTeam.com. The company recently acquired The Edge Company Catalog, a specialty catalog featuring distinctive gifts, tools and collectibles and the Carol Wright Gifts unit of Cox Enterprises, Inc., which includes the Applecreek catalog.

FINANCIALS: Sales and profits are in thousands of dollars—add 000 to get the full amount.

Notes regarding 1999: *(1999 sales and profits were not available for all companies at press time.)*

1999 Sales: $252,300	1999 Profits: $-155,800	Stock Ticker: **PRTMQ**
1998 Sales: $107,200	1998 Profits: $-76,200	Employees: 1,255
1997 Sales: $18,500	1997 Profits: $-13,500	Fiscal Year Ends: 3/28
1996 Sales: $	1996 Profits: $-2,700	
1995 Sales: $	1995 Profits: $	

SALARIES/BENEFITS:

Pension Plan:	ESOP Stock Plan:	Profit Sharing:	Top Exec. Salary: $	Bonus: $
Savings Plan: Y	Stock Purch. Plan:		Second Exec. Salary: $	Bonus: $

COMPETITIVE ADVANTAGE: Growth through acquisitions/Strong Internet presence.

OTHER THOUGHTS:

Apparent Women Officers or Directors: 3
Apparent Minority Officers or Directors: 3
Hot Spot for Advancement for Women/Minorities: Y

LOCATIONS: ("Y" = Yes)

West:	Southwest:	Midwest:	Southeast:	Northeast:	International:
Y			Y	Y	Y

Note: Financial information, benefits and other data can change quickly and may vary from those stated here.

PROXICOM INC   www.proxicom.com

Industry Group Code: 54151
Ranks within this company's industry group: Sales: 6   Profits: 13

BUSINESS ACTIVITIES ("Y" = Yes)

Financial Services:	Information/Publ.:	Technology:	Services:		Retailing:	Telecommunications:
Stock Brokerage	Portal/Hub/News	Computer Manuf.	Payments/Transfers		Retailer	Internet Serv. Provider
Mortgages/Loans	On-Line Community	Networking Equip.	Consulting	Y	Auctions	Web Site Host
Banking	Search Engine	Software Manuf.	Advertising/Marketing	Y	Mall	Server Farm
Insurance	Financial Data Publ.	Specialty Equipment	Outsourcing		Tickets/Travel	Specialty Telecom.
Credit Cards	Broadcasting/Music				Price Comparisons	High Speed Access

TYPES OF BUSINESS:

Internet/Intranet Consulting
On-line Site Development
Internet-Focused Advertising/Marketing Services

BRANDS/DIVISIONS/AFFILIATES:

Adhoc Group, Inc.

CONTACTS: Note: Officers with more than one job title may be intentionally listed here more than once.

Raul J. Fernandez, CEO
Raul J. Fernandez, Pres.
Kenneth J. Tarpey, CFO
Mike Pusateri, Sr. VP-Sales and Mktg.
Brenda A. Wagner, Sr. VP-Organizational Strategies (HR)
Betsy Cragon, Dir. Mktg. Comm.
Steve Tempini, Sr. VP-Financial Services
Larry D. Clark, Sr. VP-Services

Phone: 703-262-3200	Fax: 703-262-3201
Toll-Free:	
Address: 11600 Sunrise Valley Dr., Reston, VA, 20191	

GROWTH PLANS/SPECIAL FEATURES:

Proxicom, Inc. is an Internet consulting and e-business development company for Global 1000 businesses in the telecommunications, retail, energy, financial services and manufacturing fields. Since 1994, the company has provided Internet solutions, including business-to-consumer e-commerce Internet sites, business-to-business e-commerce extranets and company-specific intranets. Proxicom recently acquired the Adhoc Group, Inc., a full service interactive marketing and communications agency recognized for its Internet advertising work with America Online, Day Runner, Old Navy and Disney. Along with Giggo.com, Proxicom launched the first on-line auto-financing portal that provides customers with direct financing and customer service from their desktops. Proxicom is featured in a Cisco Systems, Inc. sponsored research study as a prime example of a company that is utilizing the Internet to its full potential. Proxicom also ranked number 44 in a list of the fastest growing private companies in the country by Inc. magazine. The company was chosen by Interactive Week magazine as one of the top 10 companies to work for, and Internet Computing placed Proxicom on its list of top 20 Internet consulting firms.

FINANCIALS: Sales and profits are in thousands of dollars—add 000 to get the full amount.

Notes regarding 1999: *(1999 sales and profits were not available for all companies at press time.)*

1999 Sales: $82,700	1999 Profits: $- 849	Stock Ticker: **PXCM**
1998 Sales: $42,400	1998 Profits: $-20,600	Employees: 380
1997 Sales: $27,400	1997 Profits: $2,700	Fiscal Year Ends: 12/31
1996 Sales: $12,400	1996 Profits: $1,100	
1995 Sales: $6,100	1995 Profits: $ 900	

SALARIES/BENEFITS:

Pension Plan:	ESOP Stock Plan: Y	Profit Sharing:	Top Exec. Salary: $262,990	Bonus: $113,836
Savings Plan:	Stock Purch. Plan:		Second Exec. Salary: $185,742	Bonus: $

COMPETITIVE ADVANTAGE: Growth through acquisition.

OTHER THOUGHTS:

Apparent Women Officers or Directors: 2
Apparent Minority Officers or Directors: 2
Hot Spot for Advancement for Women/Minorities: Y

LOCATIONS: ("Y" = Yes)

West:	Southwest:	Midwest:	Southeast:	Northeast:	International:
Y	Y	Y		Y	Y

Note: Financial information, benefits and other data can change quickly and may vary from those stated here.

PSINET INC   www.psi.net

Industry Group Code: 51339
Ranks within this company's industry group: Sales: 1   Profits: 25

BUSINESS ACTIVITIES ("Y" = Yes)

Financial Services:	Information/Publ.:	Technology:	Services:	Retailing:	Telecommunications:	
Stock Brokerage	Portal/Hub/News	Computer Manuf.	Payments/Transfers	Retailer	Internet Serv. Provider	Y
Mortgages/Loans	On-Line Community	Networking Equip.	Consulting	Auctions	Web Site Host	Y
Banking	Search Engine	Software Manuf.	Advertising/Marketing	Mall	Server Farm	
Insurance	Financial Data Publ.	Specialty Equipment	Outsourcing	Tickets/Travel	Specialty Telecom.	Y
Credit Cards	Broadcasting/Music			Price Comparisons	High Speed Access	Y

TYPES OF BUSINESS:

Internet Service Provider to Businesses
Web Hosting
High Speed Datanets

BRANDS/DIVISIONS/AFFILIATES:

LAN-Dial
InterMAN
InterFrame
PSI IntraNet
PSINet Security Services
PSIWeb
PSIWeb eCommerce
PSINet InterPaper

CONTACTS: Note: Officers with more than one job title may be intentionally listed here more than once.

William L. Schrader, CEO
Harold S. Willis, Pres./COO
Edward D. Postal, VP/CFO
William P. Cripe, VP-Human Resources
James R. Davin, VP/Chief Tech. Officer
Anthony A. Aveta, VP/CIO
Mark S. Fedor, VP-Engineering
Robert D. Leahy, Sr. VP-Corp. Mktg. and Comm.

Phone: 703-904-4100	Fax: 703-904-4200
Toll-Free: 800-827-7482	
Address: 510 Huntmar Park Drive, Herndon, VA, 22070	

GROWTH PLANS/SPECIAL FEATURES:

PSINet is a global provider of Internet access services and related products to businesses. The company provides dedicated and dial-up Internet connections to businesses in 90 of the 100 largest metropolitan statistical areas in the U.S. and in 12 of the 20 largest global telecommunications markets, with operations organized into four geographic operating segments: the U.S., Canada, Europe and Asia. In addition to Internet connectivity services, PSINet also offers services and products to businesses, enabling them to maximize utilization of the Internet in their day-to-day operations in and outside of the workplace. Some of these value-added services include corporate intranets, web hosting services, remote user access services, multi-currency electronic commerce services, security services and Internet telephony services. PSINet also owns and operates a high-speed network that is one of the primary backbones that comprise the Internet. PSINet and Cisco Systems, the worldwide leader in networking for the Internet, recently announced that PSINet has expanded its participation in the Cisco Powered Network program to include full-time, maximum-performance, dedicated and shared network Internet access services. Recently, PSINets' business grade wireless access service was certified by Cisco.

FINANCIALS: Sales and profits are in thousands of dollars—add 000 to get the full amount.

Notes regarding 1999: Through 9 months (1999 sales and profits were not available for all companies at press time.)

1999 Sales: $369,300	1999 Profits: $-197,700	Stock Ticker: **PSIX**	
1998 Sales: $259,600	1998 Profits: $-261,900	Employees: 1,817	
1997 Sales: $121,900	1997 Profits: $-45,600	Fiscal Year Ends: 12/31	
1996 Sales: $84,400	1996 Profits: $-55,100		
1995 Sales: $38,700	1995 Profits: $-53,200		

SALARIES/BENEFITS:

Pension Plan: Y	ESOP Stock Plan: Y	Profit Sharing:	Top Exec. Salary: $360,500	Bonus: $150,000
Savings Plan:	Stock Purch. Plan:		Second Exec. Salary: $334,192	Bonus: $150,000

COMPETITIVE ADVANTAGE: Leading-edge Internet services, focused on business and commercial customers rather than consumers.

OTHER THOUGHTS:

Apparent Women Officers or Directors: 5
Apparent Minority Officers or Directors: 5
Hot Spot for Advancement for Women/Minorities: Y

LOCATIONS: ("Y" = Yes)

West:	Southwest:	Midwest:	Southeast:	Northeast:	International:
Y	Y	Y	Y	Y	Y

QUALCOMM INC   www.qualcomm.com

Industry Group Code: 33421
Ranks within this company's industry group: Sales: 2   Profits: 2

BUSINESS ACTIVITIES ("Y" = Yes)

Financial Services:	Information/Publ.:	Technology:	Services:	Retailing:	Telecommunications:
Stock Brokerage	Portal/Hub/News	Computer Manuf.	Payments/Transfers	Retailer	Internet Serv. Provider
Mortgages/Loans	On-Line Community	Networking Equip.	Consulting	Auctions	Web Site Host
Banking	Search Engine	Software Manuf.	Advertising/Marketing	Mall	Server Farm
Insurance	Financial Data Publ.	Specialty Equipment	Outsourcing	Tickets/Travel	Specialty Telecom. Y
Credit Cards	Broadcasting/Music			Price Comparisons	High Speed Access

TYPES OF BUSINESS:

Internet Connectivity
Digital Wireless Communications Products
Satellite-based, 2-way Mobile Communications
Cellular Technology
Integration Products
Communications Components and Systems
Software

BRANDS/DIVISIONS/AFFILIATES:

Eudora Light
Eudora Pro
Globalstar
OmniTRACS
Globalstar
Personal Communications Services (PCS)
Wireless Local Loop (WLL)

CONTACTS: *Note: Officers with more than one job title may be intentionally listed here more than once.*

Irwin M. Jacobs, CEO
Richard Sulpizio, Exec. VP/COO
Anthony S. Thornley, Exec. VP/CFO
Daniel L. Sullivan, Sr. VP-Human Resources
Franklin P. Antonio, Chief Tech. Officer
Norm Fieldheim, CIO
Steven R. Altman, Asst. Sec.
Steven R. Altman, Exec. VP/General Counsel/General Mgr,
Jeff Jacobs, Sr. VP-Corp. Business Dev.

Phone: 858-587-1121	Fax: 858-658-2100
Toll-Free:	
Address: 6455 Lusk Boulevard, San Diego, CA, 92121-2779	

GROWTH PLANS/SPECIAL FEATURES:

QUALCOMM, Inc. is a leading provider of digital wireless communications products, technologies and services. The company develops, manufactures and markets wireless communications, infrastructure and subscriber products. It also designs application specific integrated circuits (ASICs) based on CDMA technology. QUALCOMM licenses and receives royalty payments on its CDMA technology from major domestic and international telecommunications equipment suppliers. In addition, the company manufactures and operates products and services for the OmniTRACS system. The firm also has contracts with Globalstar L.P. to design and manufacture subscriber products and ground communications systems (gateways) and to provide contract development services (Globalstar System). QUALCOMM's CDMA technology has been adopted as an industry standard for digital cellular, personal communications services (PCS) and wireless local loop (WLL) networks as well as other wireless services. The company is the number two U.S. cellular phone seller behind Nokia. QUALCOMM also produces the e-mail software Eudora. QUALCOMM is allied with Microsoft, Hitachi, Hughes and Nortel Networks. It is focusing on a new wireless data standard called high data rate (HDR), which is expected to bridge the transition between current technologies and third generation products now in development.

QUALCOMM offers an Employee Assistance Program, and a Computer Loan Program to its employees. As an extra added bonus, the company has three fitness centers, tennis courts, swimming pool and a sand volleyball court. The company sifts through approximately 100,000 job applications per year. QUALCOMM boasts on-site fitness centers, basketball, tennis and volleyball courts. The company additionally pays 100% of its employees' insurance premiums. Generally, QUALCOMM employees are trained for 55 hours out of the year.

FINANCIALS: Sales and profits are in thousands of dollars—add 000 to get the full amount.

Notes regarding 1999: *(1999 sales and profits were not available for all companies at press time.)*

1999 Sales: $3,937,300	1999 Profits: $200,900	Stock Ticker: **QCOM**
1998 Sales: $3,347,900	1998 Profits: $108,500	Employees: 9,700
1997 Sales: $2,096,400	1997 Profits: $91,900	Fiscal Year Ends: 9/28
1996 Sales: $813,900	1996 Profits: $21,000	
1995 Sales: $386,600	1995 Profits: $30,200	

SALARIES/BENEFITS:

Pension Plan:	ESOP Stock Plan:	Profit Sharing:	Top Exec. Salary: $660,467	Bonus: $555,000
Savings Plan: Y	Stock Purch. Plan: Y		Second Exec. Salary: $480,373	Bonus: $320,000

COMPETITIVE ADVANTAGE: Owns Eudora e-mail software/ Leading edge cellular phone technology for dual mode operations.

OTHER THOUGHTS:

Apparent Women Officers or Directors: 1
Apparent Minority Officers or Directors: 2
Hot Spot for Advancement for Women/Minorities: Y

LOCATIONS: ("Y" = Yes)

West:	Southwest:	Midwest:	Southeast:	Northeast:	International:
Y	Y	Y	Y	Y	Y

Note: Financial information, benefits and other data can change quickly and may vary from those stated here.

QUEPASA.COM   www.quepasa.com

Industry Group Code: 514191
Ranks within this company's industry group: Sales: 42   Profits: 24

BUSINESS ACTIVITIES ("Y" = Yes)

Financial Services:	Information/Publ.:		Technology:	Services:	Retailing:	Telecommunications:
Stock Brokerage	Portal/Hub/News	Y	Computer Manuf.	Payments/Transfers	Retailer	Internet Serv. Provider
Mortgages/Loans	On-Line Community		Networking Equip.	Consulting	Auctions	Web Site Host
Banking	Search Engine		Software Manuf.	Advertising/Marketing	Mall	Server Farm
Insurance	Financial Data Publ.		Specialty Equipment	Outsourcing	Tickets/Travel	Specialty Telecom.
Credit Cards	Broadcasting/Music				Price Comparisons	High Speed Access

TYPES OF BUSINESS:
Portal-Spanish Speaking Users

BRANDS/DIVISIONS/AFFILIATES:

CONTACTS:
Note: Officers with more than one job title may be intentionally listed here more than once.
Gary L. Trujillo, CEO
Gary L. Trujillo, Pres.
Juan C. Galan, CFO
Bryan L. Ross, VP-Tech.
Robert J. Taylor, VP-Strategy and Oper.
Jose Ronstadt, Sr. VP-Content Dev.
Jeffrey S. Peterson, Chief Tech. Officer

Phone: 602-716-0106	Fax:
Toll-Free:	
Address: 1 Arizona Center, 400 E. Van Buren, 4th Fl., Phoenix, AZ, 85004	

GROWTH PLANS/SPECIAL FEATURES:

Quepasa.com, Inc. is an Internet portal and search engine that provides the rapidly growing U.S. Hispanic market with information and content -- all in Spanish. The site includes a search engine, free e-mail, free web pages, Spanish-language news feeds, worldwide weather information, chat rooms, games, maps and message boards. The site has areas of interest that cover everything from news and technology to entertainment and sports to employment and education. The news channel reports news of the day, economy and business information and sports news. The company has formed alliances with Fox Sports, Telemundo, Reuters NewMedia, AutoNation and 24/7 Media to expand its content and technology. In an agreement with Net2Phone, Quepasa.com provides its users with unified messaging, where users have the ability to send and receive voice mail, faxes, e-mail and telephone calls to any telephone in the world. Revenue is currently generated from advertisers and the site has plans to eventually sell products and services to its clientele. GlobalEnglish provides English language on-line learning to Quepasa.com's members who wish to learn English or enhance English language skills. Quepasa.com also offers content completely written in English, according to the user's preference.

FINANCIALS:
Sales and profits are in thousands of dollars—add 000 to get the full amount.
Notes regarding 1999: *(1999 sales and profits were not available for all companies at press time.)*

1999 Sales: $ 670	1999 Profits: $-27,976	Stock Ticker: **PASA**
1998 Sales: $ 100	1998 Profits: $-6,500	Employees: 34
1997 Sales: $	1997 Profits: $	Fiscal Year Ends: 12/31
1996 Sales: $	1996 Profits: $	
1995 Sales: $	1995 Profits: $	

SALARIES/BENEFITS:

Pension Plan:	ESOP Stock Plan: Y	Profit Sharing:	Top Exec. Salary: $31,500	Bonus: $
Savings Plan:	Stock Purch. Plan:		Second Exec. Salary: $	Bonus: $

COMPETITIVE ADVANTAGE:
Focus on the large and rapidly growing Spanish-speaking consumer base.

OTHER THOUGHTS:
Apparent Women Officers or Directors:
Apparent Minority Officers or Directors: 2
Hot Spot for Advancement for Women/Minorities: Y

LOCATIONS: ("Y" = Yes)

West:	Southwest:	Midwest:	Southeast:	Northeast:	International:
	Y				

Note: Financial information, benefits and other data can change quickly and may vary from those stated here.

QUEST SOFTWARE   www.quest.com

Industry Group Code: 5112
Ranks within this company's industry group: Sales: 27   Profits: 13

BUSINESS ACTIVITIES ("Y" = Yes)

Financial Services:	Information/Publ.:	Technology:		Services:	Retailing:	Telecommunications:
Stock Brokerage	Portal/Hub/News	Computer Manuf.		Payments/Transfers	Retailer	Internet Serv. Provider
Mortgages/Loans	On-Line Community	Networking Equip.		Consulting	Auctions	Web Site Host
Banking	Search Engine	Software Manuf.	Y	Advertising/Marketing	Mall	Server Farm
Insurance	Financial Data Publ.	Specialty Equipment		Outsourcing	Tickets/Travel	Specialty Telecom.
Credit Cards	Broadcasting/Music				Price Comparisons	High Speed Access

TYPES OF BUSINESS:

Software-Corporate Enterprise Efficiency

BRANDS/DIVISIONS/AFFILIATES:

CONTACTS:
Note: Officers with more than one job title may be intentionally listed here more than once.

Vincent C. Smith, CEO
David M. Doyle, Pres.
John J. Laskey, CFO/VP-Finance
Carla S. Fitzgerald, VP-Mktg.
Amada Zapata, Human Resources
Eyal M. Aronoff, VP-Tech.
Eyal M. Aronoff, VP-Engineering
Juli Ackerman, Dir.-Business Dev.

Phone: 949-720-1434	Fax: 949-720-0426
Toll-Free:	
Address: 610 Newport Center Dr., Newport Beach, CA, 92660	

GROWTH PLANS/SPECIAL FEATURES:

Quest Software, Inc. provides information and application availability solutions that enhance the performance and reliability of an organization's e-business. These are packaged and customized applications that enable the delivery of information across extended enterprises. The company is focusing its development on software solutions for companies' corporate computer networks and Internet information management. Quest Software's solutions enable efficient, reliable application development, change management and deployment, on-line backup and load balancing, proactive network monitoring, capacity planning, diagnostics, data replication and resolution of database performance issues. The family of products provides information and application availability for uninterrupted high-performance access to databases under widely varying conditions and allows for distribution of critical business information throughout the extended enterprise. The company delivers its software solutions across a wide range of industries, including technology, financial services, manufacturing, healthcare, energy, insurance and telecommunications.

FINANCIALS:
Sales and profits are in thousands of dollars—add 000 to get the full amount.
Notes regarding 1999: Pro forma *(1999 sales and profits were not available for all companies at press time.)*

1999 Sales: $70,900	1999 Profits: $3,400	**Stock Ticker: QSFT**
1998 Sales: $34,800	1998 Profits: $2,300	Employees: 307
1997 Sales: $18,300	1997 Profits: $ 300	Fiscal Year Ends: 12/31
1996 Sales: $12,900	1996 Profits: $	
1995 Sales: $	1995 Profits: $	

SALARIES/BENEFITS:

Pension Plan:	ESOP Stock Plan: Y	Profit Sharing:	Top Exec. Salary: $200,000	Bonus: $175,000
Savings Plan: Y	Stock Purch. Plan:		Second Exec. Salary: $200,000	Bonus: $

COMPETITIVE ADVANTAGE:
Focus on software that enhances availability and efficiency of enterprise-wide computer operations.

OTHER THOUGHTS:

Apparent Women Officers or Directors: 2
Apparent Minority Officers or Directors: 1
Hot Spot for Advancement for Women/Minorities:

LOCATIONS: ("Y" = Yes)

West:	Southwest:	Midwest:	Southeast:	Northeast:	International:
Y					Y

QUOKKA SPORTS   www.quokka.com

Industry Group Code: 51311B
Ranks within this company's industry group: Sales: 3   Profits: 4

BUSINESS ACTIVITIES ("Y" = Yes)

Financial Services:	Information/Publ.:		Technology:	Services:	Retailing:	Telecommunications:
Stock Brokerage	Portal/Hub/News	Y	Computer Manuf.	Payments/Transfers	Retailer	Internet Serv. Provider
Mortgages/Loans	On-Line Community		Networking Equip.	Consulting	Auctions	Web Site Host
Banking	Search Engine		Software Manuf.	Advertising/Marketing	Mall	Server Farm
Insurance	Financial Data Publ.		Specialty Equipment	Outsourcing	Tickets/Travel	Specialty Telecom.
Credit Cards	Broadcasting/Music	Y			Price Comparisons	High Speed Access

TYPES OF BUSINESS:

On-line Sports Broadcasting
Sports Information and News

BRANDS/DIVISIONS/AFFILIATES:

GROWTH PLANS/SPECIAL FEATURES:

Quokka Sports is a global sports programming Internet site that allows users to experience and view sports from many different perspectives. The web site incorporates a wide range of digital assets including video, text, audio, images, athlete biometrics, telemetry, environmental data, e-mails, results and timing. Leveraging the merger of entertainment and information now available with Internet technology, Quokka Sports brings sports entertainment programming to a global community of enthusiasts. The site reports on sports that have continuous action with multiple activities, such as the Olympics, motor racing, sailing and adventure sports. The company covered all nine legs of the Whitbread around-the-world sailing race live, something the networks and ESPN could not do. Two million unique visitors logged on to Quokka.com during the race. Users of the web site are able to experience events as they happen, something not possible with traditional sports coverage. The company is partnered with NBC to cover the Olympics through August 2004 and with Forsythe Racing, Inc. to cover Championship Auto Racing Team events through 2003. PC magazine listed Quokka.com as one of the Top 100 Web Sites, and the site was nominated for a Webby Award for Best Sports Site of the year.

CONTACTS: Note: Officers with more than one job title may be intentionally listed here more than once.

Alan S. Ramadan, CEO/Pres.
Alvaro J. Saralequi, COO
Les Schmidt, CFO
David A. Riemer, Sr. VP-Mktg.
Pascal Wattiaux, Sr. VP-Tech.
G. Michael Novelly, VP-Finance/Controller
Thomas P. Newell, Sr. VP- Business and Legal Affairs
M. Elizabeth Sandell, VP-Organizational Design and Dev.
Jay Thomas, VP-e-Commerce
Brian J. Terkelsen, VP-Programming and Production
Richard O'Connell, VP-Entertainment Mktg.

Phone: 415-908-3800	Fax: 415-908-1841
Toll-Free:	
Address: 525 Brannan St., Ground Fl., San Francisco, CA, 94107	

FINANCIALS: Sales and profits are in thousands of dollars—add 000 to get the full amount.

Notes regarding 1999: *(1999 sales and profits were not available for all companies at press time.)*

1999 Sales: $13,100	1999 Profits: $-56,900	Stock Ticker: **QKKA**
1998 Sales: $8,600	1998 Profits: $-9,500	Employees: 186
1997 Sales: $4,000	1997 Profits: $-4,900	Fiscal Year Ends: 12/31
1996 Sales: $	1996 Profits: $-1,600	
1995 Sales: $ 100	1995 Profits: $	

SALARIES/BENEFITS:

Pension Plan:	ESOP Stock Plan: Y	Profit Sharing: Y	Top Exec. Salary: $214,583	Bonus: $
Savings Plan: Y	Stock Purch. Plan:		Second Exec. Salary: $172,051	Bonus: $

COMPETITIVE ADVANTAGE: Unique and in-depth coverage and news.

OTHER THOUGHTS:

Apparent Women Officers or Directors: 1
Apparent Minority Officers or Directors: 3
Hot Spot for Advancement for Women/Minorities: Y

LOCATIONS: ("Y" = Yes)

West:	Southwest:	Midwest:	Southeast:	Northeast:	International:
Y					

QUOTESMITH.COM INC

www.quotesmith.com

Industry Group Code: 52421
Ranks within this company's industry group: Sales: 1 Profits: 1

BUSINESS ACTIVITIES ("Y" = Yes)

Financial Services:		Information/Publ.:	Technology:	Services:	Retailing:	Telecommunications:
Stock Brokerage		Portal/Hub/News	Computer Manuf.	Payments/Transfers	Retailer	Internet Serv. Provider
Mortgages/Loans		On-Line Community	Networking Equip.	Consulting	Auctions	Web Site Host
Banking		Search Engine	Software Manuf.	Advertising/Marketing	Mall	Server Farm
Insurance	Y	Financial Data Publ.	Specialty Equipment	Outsourcing	Tickets/Travel	Specialty Telecom.
Credit Cards		Broadcasting/Music			Price Comparisons	High Speed Access

TYPES OF BUSINESS:

On-line Insurance Broker

BRANDS/DIVISIONS/AFFILIATES:

GROWTH PLANS/SPECIAL FEATURES:

Quotesmith.com, Inc. enables consumers and business owners to obtain instant quotes from over 300 insurance companies. The company provides complete, toll-free quote-to-policy delivery service through the use of insurance-experienced, in-house, salaried representatives, without the involvement of any commissioned salespeople. Quotesmith.com provides quotes for several lines of insurance, including workers' compensation, auto, motorcycle, life, individual, family and group medical, dental, Medicare supplement and annuities. A typical Quotesmith.com quote comes with two pages of policy coverage and reference information and shows the latest independent ratings of insurance underwriters from A.M. Best, Duff & Phelps, Moody's, Standard & Poor's and Weiss Ratings, Inc. Quotesmith.com guarantees the accuracy of its quotes and backs that claim up with a $500 cash reward program. Available in all 50 states, the company often processes one quote request every four seconds. Recently, Money magazine named Quotesmith.com a Super Deal, and SmartMoney Interactive called the company the number one site for on-line insurance quotes.

CONTACTS: Note: Officers with more than one job title may be intentionally listed here more than once.

Robert S. Bland, CEO/Pres.
Thomas A. Munro, CFO
Ronald A. Wozniak, VP-Info. Tech.
Burke A. Christensen, General Counsel
Burke A. Christensen, VP-Oper.
Grant F. Kuphall, VP-Business Dev.
Richard W. Graeber, VP-Internet Oper.
Richard C. Claahsen, VP-Regulatory Affairs

Phone: 630-515-0170	Fax: 630-515-0270
Toll-Free:	
Address: 8205 S. Cass Ave., Ste. 102, Darien, IL, 60561	

FINANCIALS: Sales and profits are in thousands of dollars—add 000 to get the full amount.

Notes regarding 1999: (1999 sales and profits were not available for all companies at press time.)

1999 Sales: $8,408	1999 Profits: $-13,820	Stock Ticker: QUOT
1998 Sales: $5,600	1998 Profits: $- 200	Employees: 77
1997 Sales: $4,300	1997 Profits: $- 500	Fiscal Year Ends: 12/31
1996 Sales: $3,800	1996 Profits: $ 200	
1995 Sales: $	1995 Profits: $	

SALARIES/BENEFITS:

Pension Plan:	ESOP Stock Plan:	Profit Sharing:	Top Exec. Salary: $198,077	Bonus: $
Savings Plan:	Stock Purch. Plan:		Second Exec. Salary: $192,308	Bonus: $

COMPETITIVE ADVANTAGE: While the company faces a great deal of competition, it remains one of the best on-line insurance sites.

OTHER THOUGHTS:

Apparent Women Officers or Directors:
Apparent Minority Officers or Directors:
Hot Spot for Advancement for Women/Minorities:

LOCATIONS: ("Y" = Yes)

West:	Southwest:	Midwest:	Southeast:	Northeast:	International:
		Y			

QWEST COMMUNICATIONS INTERNATIONAL INC

www.qwest.net

Industry Group Code: 5133B
Ranks within this company's industry group: Sales: 3   Profits: 5

BUSINESS ACTIVITIES ("Y" = Yes)

Financial Services:	Information/Publ.:	Technology:	Services:	Retailing:	Telecommunications:	
Stock Brokerage	Portal/Hub/News	Computer Manuf.	Payments/Transfers	Retailer	Internet Serv. Provider	Y
Mortgages/Loans	On-Line Community	Networking Equip.	Consulting	Auctions	Web Site Host	
Banking	Search Engine	Software Manuf.	Advertising/Marketing	Mall	Server Farm	
Insurance	Financial Data Publ.	Specialty Equipment	Outsourcing	Tickets/Travel	Specialty Telecom.	Y
Credit Cards	Broadcasting/Music			Price Comparisons	High Speed Access	Y

TYPES OF BUSINESS:

Multimedia Communications Services-Fiber Optics
Long Distance Service
Internet Access
Fiber Optic System Installation
Local Telephone Service
Comprehensive Telecommunications Services
Wholesale Bandwidth

BRANDS/DIVISIONS/AFFILIATES:

Qwest MacroCapacity Network
U.S. West, Inc.

CONTACTS: Note: Officers with more than one job title may be intentionally listed here more than once.

Joseph P. Nacchio, Pres./CEO
Afshin Mohebbi, COO
Robert S. Woodruff, Exec. VP-Finance/CFO
Gregory M. Casey, Sr. VP-Wholesale Mktg.
Brij Khandelwal, CIO
David R. Boast, Acting Exec. VP-Engineering/Planning/Network/Oper.
Drake S. Tempest, Corp. Sec.
Drake S. Tempest, General Counsel
David R. Boast, Acting Exec. VP-Oper./Eng./Planning/Network
Scott A. Baxter, Chief Strategy Officer Strategic Planning
Lewis O. Wilks, Pres.-Internet/Multimedia Markets
Michael P. Tarpey, Sr. VP-Comm.
Lee W. Wolfe, VP-Investor Relations.
Philip F. Anschutz, Chairman

Phone: 303-992-1400	Fax: 303-992-1724
Toll-Free:	
Address: 700 Qwest Tower, 555 17th St., Denver, CO, 80202	

GROWTH PLANS/SPECIAL FEATURES:

Qwest Communications International Inc. is a leading communications services provider with a nationwide, high-capacity fiber optic communications network. The company was founded by legendary business leader Philip Anschutz who later brought in a respected former executive of AT&T to be CEO, Joseph Nacchio. By aggressively building out a major fiber optic network and making major acquisitions, Qwest has rapidly become one of the world's leading telecom firms. Qwest is engaged in two core business segments: communications and construction services. The company's communications services business offers Internet and multimedia services as well as traditional voice communication to business, government agencies and consumers in domestic and international markets. The company also provides wholesale services to other communication providers, including Internet service providers. Qwest's network uses both Internet and traditional telephone communications technology. Qwest's construction services installs fiber-optic systems for itself and other communications providers. The company has completed an 18,800-mile Internet protocol-based fiber-optic network, linking 150 U.S. metro areas, and is connecting Mexico with a 1,400-mile segment. Across the Atlantic, the company is building a 9,100-mile fiber-optic network in a joint venture with Dutch phone company KPN. Recently, the company entered into a definitive merger agreement with U.S. West, Inc., a local phone service provider in 14 states. This will make Qwest a major local service provider in addition to its status as one of the largest long-distance companies. Qwest has announced its intent to launch a second nationwide fiber network that will feature next-generation technologies.

Qwest employs more than 1,500 sales professionals. Many of them focus on offering a comprehensive suite of telecom services to corporate customers.

FINANCIALS: Sales and profits are in thousands of dollars—add 000 to get the full amount.

Notes regarding 1999: Pro forma (1999 sales and profits were not available for all companies at press time.)

1999 Sales: $3,900,000	1999 Profits: $759,200	Stock Ticker: **QWST**
1998 Sales: $2,242,700	1998 Profits: $-844,000	Employees: 8,700
1997 Sales: $696,700	1997 Profits: $14,500	Fiscal Year Ends: 12/31
1996 Sales: $231,000	1996 Profits: $-7,000	
1995 Sales: $125,100	1995 Profits: $-25,100	

SALARIES/BENEFITS:

Pension Plan:	ESOP Stock Plan:	Profit Sharing:	Top Exec. Salary: $630,000	Bonus: $567,128
Savings Plan: Y	Stock Purch. Plan: Y		Second Exec. Salary: $279,875	Bonus: $243,669

COMPETITIVE ADVANTAGE: Focus on high-speed, advanced technology data network spanning the nation.

OTHER THOUGHTS:

Apparent Women Officers or Directors:
Apparent Minority Officers or Directors: 3
Hot Spot for Advancement for Women/Minorities: Y

LOCATIONS: ("Y" = Yes)

West:	Southwest:	Midwest:	Southeast:	Northeast:	International:
Y	Y	Y	Y	Y	Y

Note: Financial information, benefits and other data can change quickly and may vary from those stated here.

RAMP NETWORKS
www.rampnet.com

Industry Group Code: 3341C
Ranks within this company's industry group: Sales: 7   Profits: 3

BUSINESS ACTIVITIES ("Y" = Yes)

Financial Services:	Information/Publ.:	Technology:		Services:	Retailing:	Telecommunications:
Stock Brokerage	Portal/Hub/News	Computer Manuf.		Payments/Transfers	Retailer	Internet Serv. Provider
Mortgages/Loans	On-Line Community	Networking Equip.	Y	Consulting	Auctions	Web Site Host
Banking	Search Engine	Software Manuf.	Y	Advertising/Marketing	Mall	Server Farm
Insurance	Financial Data Publ.	Specialty Equipment		Outsourcing	Tickets/Travel	Specialty Telecom.
Credit Cards	Broadcasting/Music				Price Comparisons	High Speed Access

TYPES OF BUSINESS:

Software-Internet Connections
Networking Hardware
Firewalls

GROWTH PLANS/SPECIAL FEATURES:

Ramp Networks makes cost-effective routers, firewalls and other equipment that provide enterprise-level Internet and web access capabilities to small and branch offices at an affordable cost. The company's WebRamp family of products is designed to satisfy the particular requirements of specific types of customers in the small office market. WebRamp software provides a full range of corporate-level Internet features, such as virtual private networking (VPN), remote access to corporate networks or extranet applications, remote dial-in for telecommuters, Internet faxing, firewall security and Internet content and access control, without the added complexity or cost associated with products designed for large companies with full information technology staffs. Ramp's reseller network includes more than 5,000 distributors, ranging in size from sole proprietors focused exclusively on the small business market to large, multi-site networking resellers that manage nationwide office roll-outs for large corporations. Additionally, Ramp sells its products to original equipment manufacturers, co-markets with industry leaders and sells directly via its web site. The company's WebRamp 315e recently won the prestigious PC Computing Most Valuable Product Award (MVP) in the network hub/router category. This is the second year in a row that Ramp has garnered this award; last time, the WebRamp 300e took top honors. Ramp was also recently chosen by Smart Reseller as one of the channel's Smart 50 Companies.

BRANDS/DIVISIONS/AFFILIATES:

WebRamp
COLT

CONTACTS: Note: Officers with more than one job title may be intentionally listed here more than once.

Mahesh Veerina, CEO
Mahesh Veerina, Pres.
Terry Gibson, CFO
Patty Burke, VP-Mktg.
Rohini Shankar, Dir.-Human Resources
Elie Habib, VP-Engineering
Jerry Jalaba, VP-Worldwide Sales and Support

Phone: 408-988-5353	Fax: 408-988-6363
Toll-Free:	
Address: 3100 De La Cruz Blvd., Santa Clara, CA, 95054	

FINANCIALS: Sales and profits are in thousands of dollars—add 000 to get the full amount.
Notes regarding 1999: (1999 sales and profits were not available for all companies at press time.)

1999 Sales: $18,226	1999 Profits: $-13,219	
1998 Sales: $9,900	1998 Profits: $-13,400	Stock Ticker: **RAMP**
1997 Sales: $5,600	1997 Profits: $-11,500	Employees: 103
1996 Sales: $ 500	1996 Profits: $-6,300	Fiscal Year Ends: 12/31
1995 Sales: $	1995 Profits: $	

SALARIES/BENEFITS:

Pension Plan:	ESOP Stock Plan:	Profit Sharing:	Top Exec. Salary: $	Bonus: $
Savings Plan:	Stock Purch. Plan:		Second Exec. Salary: $	Bonus: $

COMPETITIVE ADVANTAGE: Superb hub and router technology for less than $1,000.

OTHER THOUGHTS:

Apparent Women Officers or Directors: 1
Apparent Minority Officers or Directors: 2
Hot Spot for Advancement for Women/Minorities: Y

LOCATIONS: ("Y" = Yes)

West:	Southwest:	Midwest:	Southeast:	Northeast:	International:
Y					

RAZORFISH   www.razorfish.com

Industry Group Code: 54151
Ranks within this company's industry group: Sales: 10   Profits: 6

BUSINESS ACTIVITIES ("Y" = Yes)

Financial Services:	Information/Publ.:	Technology:	Services:		Retailing:		Telecommunications:
Stock Brokerage	Portal/Hub/News	Computer Manuf.	Payments/Transfers		Retailer		Internet Serv. Provider
Mortgages/Loans	On-Line Community	Networking Equip.	Consulting	Y	Auctions		Web Site Host
Banking	Search Engine	Software Manuf.	Advertising/Marketing		Mall		Server Farm
Insurance	Financial Data Publ.	Specialty Equipment	Outsourcing	Y	Tickets/Travel		Specialty Telecom.
Credit Cards	Broadcasting/Music				Price Comparisons		High Speed Access

TYPES OF BUSINESS:

Consulting-Internet Development

BRANDS/DIVISIONS/AFFILIATES:

CONTACTS: Note: Officers with more than one job title may be intentionally listed here more than once.

Jeffrey A. Dachis, CEO
Jeffrey A. Dachis, Pres.
Susan Black, CFO
Elizabeth Semple, Dir.-Human Resources
Craig M. Kanarick, Chief Scientist
Jean-Philippe Maheu, Exec.VP-North American Oper.
Jonas S. A. Svensson, Exec.VP-Corp. Dev.
Peter Seidler, Chief Creative Officer
Michael S. Simon, Exec.VP-Business Affairs/General Counsel

Phone: 212-966-5960	Fax: 212-966-6915
Toll-Free:	
Address: 107 Grand St., 3rd Fl., New York, NY, 10013	

GROWTH PLANS/SPECIAL FEATURES:

Razorfish provides strategic creative and technological solutions to digital businesses. The company creates partnerships with its clients to plan, design and build Internet based products and services. The company's more than 1,100 employees throughout the U.S. and Europe work across platforms, devices and networks to create Internet-based solutions, wireless technologies, back-end systems integration, broadband solutions and physical devices. The company has a five-part business strategy for conceptualizing, planning and executing solutions to business problems. Razorfish is a member of the Microsoft Site Builders Network and has achieved Level 3 status. The company is also a member of Netscape DevEdge Developer, Vignette's VIP Partners Program, The Palace Developer Program and RealNetworks Developers Program. Razorfish's clients include such firms as Charles Schwab Corp., eBay Inc., theglobe.com and IBM. The company was named to Fortune Magazine's e-50, a guide for tracking the Internet economy.

FINANCIALS: Sales and profits are in thousands of dollars—add 000 to get the full amount.

Notes regarding 1999: *(1999 sales and profits were not available for all companies at press time.)*

1999 Sales: $	1999 Profits: $	Stock Ticker: **RAZF**
1998 Sales: $13,800	1998 Profits: $	Employees: 350
1997 Sales: $3,600	1997 Profits: $ 300	Fiscal Year Ends: 12/31
1996 Sales: $1,200	1996 Profits: $- 300	
1995 Sales: $ 300	1995 Profits: $	

SALARIES/BENEFITS:

Pension Plan:	ESOP Stock Plan:	Profit Sharing:	Top Exec. Salary: $125,000	Bonus: $13,500
Savings Plan:	Stock Purch. Plan:		Second Exec. Salary: $112,500	Bonus: $2,000

COMPETITIVE ADVANTAGE: Very rapid growth and a first class client list.

OTHER THOUGHTS:

Apparent Women Officers or Directors: 2
Apparent Minority Officers or Directors: 3
Hot Spot for Advancement for Women/Minorities: Y

LOCATIONS: ("Y" = Yes)

West:	Southwest:	Midwest:	Southeast:	Northeast:	International:
Y				Y	Y

Note: Financial information, benefits and other data can change quickly and may vary from those stated here.

REALNETWORKS INC   www.real.com

Industry Group Code: 5112
Ranks within this company's industry group: Sales: 13   Profits: 67

BUSINESS ACTIVITIES ("Y" = Yes)

Financial Services:	Information/Publ.:	Technology:	Services:	Retailing:	Telecommunications:
Stock Brokerage	Portal/Hub/News	Computer Manuf.	Payments/Transfers	Retailer	Internet Serv. Provider
Mortgages/Loans	On-Line Community	Networking Equip.	Consulting	Auctions	Web Site Host Y
Banking	Search Engine	Software Manuf. Y	Advertising/Marketing	Mall	Server Farm
Insurance	Financial Data Publ.	Specialty Equipment	Outsourcing	Tickets/Travel	Specialty Telecom.
Credit Cards	Broadcasting/Music Y			Price Comparisons	High Speed Access

TYPES OF BUSINESS:

Software-Audio and Video

BRANDS/DIVISIONS/AFFILIATES:

RealSystem G2
RealAudio
RealVideo
RealPlayer
RealServer Internet Solutions
RealPublisher

CONTACTS: *Note: Officers with more than one job title may be intentionally listed here more than once.*

Robert Glaser, CEO
Thomas Frank, COO
Paul Bialek, Sr. VP/CFO
Shelley Morrison, VP-Advertising and Sales
Karen Schlemmer, Dir.-Human Resources
Philip Rosedale, VP/Chief Tech. Officer
Robert Glaser, Sec.
Kelly Jo MacArthur, General Counsel
Paul Bialek, Sr. VP-Oper.
Mark Klebanoff, VP-Business Oper.
Maria Cantwell, Sr. VP-E-Commerce
Steve Haworth, VP-Comm.

Phone: 206-674-2700	**Fax:** 206-674-2699

Toll-Free: 888-768-3248

Address: 2601 Elliott Ave., Suite 100, Seattle, WA, 98121

GROWTH PLANS/SPECIAL FEATURES:

RealNetworks, Inc. is a leading provider of branded software products and services. These products and services enable the creation, real-time delivery and playback (streaming) of audio, video, text, animation and other media content over the Internet and intranets on both a live and on-demand basis. RealNetworks' products and services include its RealSystem G2, a streaming media solution that includes the company's popular RealAudio and RealVideo technologies and an electronic commerce web site. From the web site, the company distributes, sells and promotes streaming media content and products, services, programming and a network of advertising-supported web sites that RealNetworks hosts. Some 80 million people have downloaded the company's RealPlayer software, free of cost. The company is pursuing alliances with Internet service, satellite and other infrastructure providers. Customers such as ABC, Bloomberg, Turner Broadcasting and Microsoft use RealNetworks' products. Microsoft accounts for 15% of RealNetworks' sales.

FINANCIALS: Sales and profits are in thousands of dollars—add 000 to get the full amount.

Notes regarding 1999: *(1999 sales and profits were not available for all companies at press time.)*

1999 Sales: $87,800	1999 Profits: $6,926	
1998 Sales: $64,800	1998 Profits: $-16,400	**Stock Ticker: RNWK**
1997 Sales: $32,700	1997 Profits: $-11,200	Employees: 434
1996 Sales: $14,000	1996 Profits: $-3,800	Fiscal Year Ends: 12/31
1995 Sales: $1,800	1995 Profits: $-1,500	

SALARIES/BENEFITS:

Pension Plan:	ESOP Stock Plan: Y	Profit Sharing:	Top Exec. Salary: $126,667	Bonus: $40,625
Savings Plan:	Stock Purch. Plan: Y		Second Exec. Salary: $100,000	Bonus: $113,639

COMPETITIVE ADVANTAGE:

Well positioned to grow with the soaring use of the Internet/Aggressive growth of its own sites/Focus on streaming streaming media.

OTHER THOUGHTS:

Apparent Women Officers or Directors: 4
Apparent Minority Officers or Directors: 1
Hot Spot for Advancement for Women/Minorities: Y

LOCATIONS: ("Y" = Yes)

West:	Southwest:	Midwest:	Southeast:	Northeast:	International:
Y	Y				Y

RED HAT · www.redhat.com

Industry Group Code: 5112
Ranks within this company's industry group: Sales: 62 Profits: 20

BUSINESS ACTIVITIES ("Y" = Yes)

Financial Services:	Information/Publ.:	Technology:	Services:	Retailing:	Telecommunications:
Stock Brokerage	Portal/Hub/News	Computer Manuf.	Payments/Transfers	Retailer	Internet Serv. Provider
Mortgages/Loans	On-Line Community	Networking Equip.	Consulting Y	Auctions	Web Site Host
Banking	Search Engine	Software Manuf. Y	Advertising/Marketing	Mall	Server Farm
Insurance	Financial Data Publ.	Specialty Equipment	Outsourcing	Tickets/Travel	Specialty Telecom.
Credit Cards	Broadcasting/Music			Price Comparisons	High Speed Access

TYPES OF BUSINESS:

Software-Linus Operating Systems
Consulting
Training

BRANDS/DIVISIONS/AFFILIATES:

Linux Systems
Cygnus Solutions

CONTACTS: Note: Officers with more than one job title may be intentionally listed here more than once.

Matthew Szulik, CEO/Pres.
Timothy J. Buckley, COO
Manoj K. George, CFO
Thomas V. Butta, Chief Mktg. Officer
Karen Clark, Dir.- Human Resources
Marc Ewing, Exec. VP/Chief Tech. Officer
Manoj K. George, Treas.
Lisa F. Sullivan, Dir.-Mktg.

Phone: 919-547-0012	Fax: 919-547-0024
Toll-Free: 888-733-4281	
Address: 2600 Meridian Pkwy., Durham, NC, 27713	

GROWTH PLANS/SPECIAL FEATURES:

Red Hat Inc. is a developer and provider of open source operating system (OS) software and services, including the Red Hat Linux OS. Open source software allows modification, change or redistribution of the source code to meet a user's unique needs, which is not something that can be done with traditional proprietary software. Red Hat Linux represents approximately 68% of the distribution of Linux systems to U.S. users. The company's recent merger with Cygnus Solutions makes Red Hat one of the largest companies in the world dedicated to providing OS technology, information and services. The company's web site, redhat.com, is one of the largest on-line communities of OS software users and developers. The site also offers software downloads and on-line shopping. Red Hat's professional services include technical support, developer training and education, custom development, on-site consulting and hardware certification programs. The company has partnerships with Compaq, Dell, IBM, Intel, Netscape, Novell, Oracle and SAP. Recently, Red Hat was chosen as one of Red Herring magazine's Top 100 companies of the Electronic Economy. Red Hat Linux OS has been voted InfoWorld magazine's Product of the Year for three years in a row.

FINANCIALS: Sales and profits are in thousands of dollars—add 000 to get the full amount.

Notes regarding 1999: *(1999 sales and profits were not available for all companies at press time.)*

1999 Sales: $10,800	1999 Profits: $- 100	Stock Ticker: **RHAT**
1998 Sales: $5,200	1998 Profits: $	Employees: 127
1997 Sales: $2,600	1997 Profits: $	Fiscal Year Ends: 02/28
1996 Sales: $ 900	1996 Profits: $- 200	
1995 Sales: $ 500	1995 Profits: $- 100	

SALARIES/BENEFITS:

Pension Plan:	ESOP Stock Plan: Y	Profit Sharing:	Top Exec. Salary: $161,458	Bonus: $25,000
Savings Plan: Y	Stock Purch. Plan:		Second Exec. Salary: $145,125	Bonus: $20,000

COMPETITIVE ADVANTAGE:

Red Hat is a leader in the very hot open systems market. It is benefitting from growing user acceptance and an extremely successful IPO.

OTHER THOUGHTS:

Apparent Women Officers or Directors: 2
Apparent Minority Officers or Directors: 2
Hot Spot for Advancement for Women/Minorities: Y

LOCATIONS: ("Y" = Yes)

West:	Southwest:	Midwest:	Southeast:	Northeast:	International:
Y				Y	Y

Note: Financial information, benefits and other data can change quickly and may vary from those stated here.

RHYTHMS NETCONNECTIONS   www.rhythms.net

Industry Group Code: 5133C
Ranks within this company's industry group: Sales: 4   Profits: 4

BUSINESS ACTIVITIES ("Y" = Yes)

Financial Services:	Information/Publ.:	Technology:	Services:	Retailing:	Telecommunications:	
Stock Brokerage	Portal/Hub/News	Computer Manuf.	Payments/Transfers	Retailer	Internet Serv. Provider	Y
Mortgages/Loans	On-Line Community	Networking Equip.	Consulting	Auctions	Web Site Host	
Banking	Search Engine	Software Manuf.	Advertising/Marketing	Mall	Server Farm	
Insurance	Financial Data Publ.	Specialty Equipment	Outsourcing	Tickets/Travel	Specialty Telecom.	
Credit Cards	Broadcasting/Music			Price Comparisons	High Speed Access	Y

TYPES OF BUSINESS:
DSL-based Internet Access Provider

BRANDS/DIVISIONS/AFFILIATES:

GROWTH PLANS/SPECIAL FEATURES:

Rhythms NetConnections is a North American service provider of high-speed local access networking solutions using DSL technology. The company provides a number of DSL technologies ranging from 128 Kbps to 7.1 Mbps. The 7.1 Mbps rate provides faster transfer than frame relay and T-1 circuits, is approximately 125 times the speed of the fastest dial-up modem and is over 55 times the speed of ISDN lines. Rhythms led the fight to force incumbent local exchange carriers to allow line sharing among competitive providers of DSL services over the same telephone lines that already carry voice services. The regulatory decision allows customers to order DSL services from competitors without having to change voice carriers or install a second telephone line. The company currently offers service in 33 markets, including San Francisco, Chicago, Boston, Sacramento, New York and Washington D.C. Rhythms recently entered into separate strategic arrangements with MCI WorldCom, Inc. and Microsoft Corporation. Rhythms customers include QUALCOMM Incorporated, Cisco and Broadcom Corporation. Fortune magazine recently named Rhythms as one of its Cool Companies and Red Herring magazine chose Rhythms as one of its Ten to Watch.

CONTACTS: *Note: Officers with more than one job title may be intentionally listed here more than once.*
Catherine M. Hapka, CEO
Steve Stringer, COO/Pres.
Scott C. Chandler, VP/CFO
B.P. Rick Adams, Jr., Chief Mktg. Officer
David J. Shrimp, Sr. VP-Human Resources
Michael Lanier, CIO
Jeffrey Blumenfeld, VP/General Counsel
Rand A. Kennedy, Sr. VP-Networks
Richard H. Johnston, Chief Sales Officer

Phone: 303-476-4200	**Fax:** 303-476-4201
Toll-Free: 800-749-8467	
Address: 6933 S. Revere Pkwy., Englewood, CO, 80112	

FINANCIALS: Sales and profits are in thousands of dollars—add 000 to get the full amount.
Notes regarding 1999: *(1999 sales and profits were not available for all companies at press time.)*

1999 Sales: $5,600	1999 Profits: $-99,000	Stock Ticker: **RTHM**
1998 Sales: $ 500	1998 Profits: $-36,300	Employees: 220
1997 Sales: $	1997 Profits: $-2,400	Fiscal Year Ends: 12/31
1996 Sales: $	1996 Profits: $	
1995 Sales: $	1995 Profits: $	

SALARIES/BENEFITS:

Pension Plan:	ESOP Stock Plan: Y	Profit Sharing:	Top Exec. Salary: $339,583	Bonus: $134,584
Savings Plan: Y	Stock Purch. Plan:		Second Exec. Salary: $145,000	Bonus: $31,538

COMPETITIVE ADVANTAGE: Focus on service as an alternate DSL provider.

OTHER THOUGHTS:

Apparent Women Officers or Directors: 1
Apparent Minority Officers or Directors:
Hot Spot for Advancement for Women/Minorities:

LOCATIONS: ("Y" = Yes)

West:	Southwest:	Midwest:	Southeast:	Northeast:	International:
Y	Y	Y	Y	Y	

RMI.NET

www.rmi.net

Industry Group Code: 51339
Ranks within this company's industry group: Sales: 16   Profits: 16

BUSINESS ACTIVITIES ("Y" = Yes)

Financial Services:	Information/Publ.:	Technology:	Services:	Retailing:	Telecommunications:	
Stock Brokerage	Portal/Hub/News	Computer Manuf.	Payments/Transfers	Retailer	Internet Serv. Provider	Y
Mortgages/Loans	On-Line Community	Networking Equip.	Consulting	Auctions	Web Site Host	Y
Banking	Search Engine	Software Manuf.	Advertising/Marketing	Mall	Server Farm	
Insurance	Financial Data Publ.	Specialty Equipment	Outsourcing	Tickets/Travel	Specialty Telecom.	
Credit Cards	Broadcasting/Music			Price Comparisons	High Speed Access	

TYPES OF BUSINESS:

Internet Service Provider

BRANDS/DIVISIONS/AFFILIATES:

Rocky Mountain Internet

CONTACTS: *Note: Officers with more than one job title may be intentionally listed here more than once.*

Douglas H. Hanson, CEO
Mary Beth Vitale, COO/Pres.
Peter J. Kushar, CFO
Melinda Schild, VP-Human Resources and Admin.
Ehud Gavron, Chief Tech. Officer
Christopher J. Melcher, VP-Legal and Legislative Affairs/Gen. Coun.
Michael R. Mara, VP-Internet Services
Michael D. Dingman, Jr., Treas.

Phone: 303-672-0700	Fax: 303-672-0711
Toll-Free:	
Address: 999 18th, Ste. 2201, Denver, CO, 80202	

GROWTH PLANS/SPECIAL FEATURES:

RMI.Net, formerly Rocky Mountain Internet, is a full service communications solutions provider of switched and IP-based communications products and services for businesses and residential customers. The company provides small and medium-sized business enterprises with scalable e-business capabilities, customized web page development and hosting, nationwide Internet dial-up and dedicated access. RMI operates 11 points of presence in Colorado and, through agreements with third-party providers, provides Internet access in 90 of the 100 largest metropolitan statistical areas in the U.S. The company uses clever marketing ideas. For example, RMI recently entered into a partnership with Rocky Mountain Public Broadcasting Network, Inc. to further enhance and support Rocky Mountain PBS's commitment to education and lifelong learning. RMI.Net will offer members and viewers of Rocky Mountain PBS a chance to purchase Internet access and related services. Rocky Mountain PBS will then receive a percentage of all RMI.Net sales for those participating in the offer. In recent news, RMI announced a partnership with OnDisplay, Inc., which will provide technology to power RMI.NET's Assemble! Commerce community product and services suite. OnDisplay, a leading provider of e-commerce infrastructure software for building and managing e-business portals and e-marketplaces, provides RMI.NET with its CenterStage product suite. CenterStage is incorporated with Assemble! to integrate publisher content and advertiser product information into a comprehensive e-Business Portal, or commerce community suite.

FINANCIALS: Sales and profits are in thousands of dollars—add 000 to get the full amount.

Notes regarding 1999: Through 9 months *(1999 sales and profits were not available for all companies at press time.)*

1999 Sales: $20,783	1999 Profits: $-7,556	Stock Ticker: **RMII**
1998 Sales: $10,100	1998 Profits: $-10,700	Employees: 235
1997 Sales: $6,100	1997 Profits: $4,200	Fiscal Year Ends: 12/31
1996 Sales: $3,300	1996 Profits: $2,300	
1995 Sales: $1,200	1995 Profits: $- 100	

SALARIES/BENEFITS:

Pension Plan:	ESOP Stock Plan: Y	Profit Sharing:	Top Exec. Salary: $120,000	Bonus: $
Savings Plan: Y	Stock Purch. Plan:		Second Exec. Salary: $96,767	Bonus: $

COMPETITIVE ADVANTAGE: Very good market share in Colorado.

OTHER THOUGHTS:

OTHER THOUGHTS:	LOCATIONS: ("Y" = Yes)					
Apparent Women Officers or Directors: 2	West:	Southwest:	Midwest:	Southeast:	Northeast:	International:
Apparent Minority Officers or Directors:	Y	Y				
Hot Spot for Advancement for Women/Minorities:						

Note: Financial information, benefits and other data can change quickly and may vary from those stated here.

ROGUE WAVE SOFTWARE

www.roguewave.com

Industry Group Code: 5112
Ranks within this company's industry group: Sales: 20　Profits: 15

BUSINESS ACTIVITIES ("Y" = Yes)

Financial Services:	Information/Publ.:	Technology:		Services:	Retailing:	Telecommunications:
Stock Brokerage	Portal/Hub/News	Computer Manuf.		Payments/Transfers	Retailer	Internet Serv. Provider
Mortgages/Loans	On-Line Community	Networking Equip.		Consulting	Auctions	Web Site Host
Banking	Search Engine	Software Manuf.	Y	Advertising/Marketing	Mall	Server Farm
Insurance	Financial Data Publ.	Specialty Equipment		Outsourcing	Tickets/Travel	Specialty Telecom.
Credit Cards	Broadcasting/Music				Price Comparisons	High Speed Access

TYPES OF BUSINESS:

Software-Java Based and C++

BRANDS/DIVISIONS/AFFILIATES:

Sting Ray Software
Studio.J Software

CONTACTS: Note: Officers with more than one job title may be intentionally listed here more than once.

Bruce Coleman, CEO
Bruce Coleman, Pres.
Robert M. Holburn Jr., CFO
Kathy Brush, VP-Mktg.
Mary Kreidler, Mgr.-Human Resources
Robert M. Holburn Jr., Sec.
Michael M. Foreman, VP-Int'l and Domestic Sales

Phone: 303-473-9118	Fax: 303-443-7780
Toll-Free: 800-487-3217	
Address: 5500 Flatiron Pkwy., Boulder, CO, 80301	

GROWTH PLANS/SPECIAL FEATURES:

Rogue Wave Software is a leading provider of software solutions that use object-oriented component technology. The company offers software components for building distributed client-server, intranet and Internet applications that scale to the enterprise, honor legacy investments and are highly customizable. The company's products and Professional Services Group provide organizations worldwide with the business expertise and technology to build, manage and grow scalable enterprise-class systems. Rogue Wave's products are marketed to professional programmers in all industrial segments through multiple distribution channels. The company's products are designed to enable customers to construct robust applications quickly, with higher quality across multiple platforms, while reducing the complexity associated with the development process. Rogue Wave provides customers with proven object-oriented development technology so that they can better apply the principles of software reuse to their own software development efforts. The company's products are designed to be general purpose in nature, supporting a broad range of development environments and methodologies. Rogue Wave recently announced its Studio.J suite of products for Sun Microsystems' Java 2 Platform, Enterprise Edition (J2EE). This edition of the Java 2 platform is a unified platform that simplifies the development, management and deployment of enterprise-class software solutions.

FINANCIALS: Sales and profits are in thousands of dollars—add 000 to get the full amount.

Notes regarding 1999: (1999 sales and profits were not available for all companies at press time.)

1999 Sales: $53,100	1999 Profits: $2,000	Stock Ticker: **RWAV**
1998 Sales: $44,400	1998 Profits: $2,200	Employees:　346
1997 Sales: $30,200	1997 Profits: $2,800	Fiscal Year Ends: 10/30
1996 Sales: $18,800	1996 Profits: $	
1995 Sales: $11,900	1995 Profits: $ 100	

SALARIES/BENEFITS:

Pension Plan:	ESOP Stock Plan:	Profit Sharing:	Top Exec. Salary: $210,000	Bonus: $35,000
Savings Plan: Y	Stock Purch. Plan: Y		Second Exec. Salary: $200,000	Bonus: $37,500

COMPETITIVE ADVANTAGE: Scalable systems that capitalize on object-oriented technologies.

OTHER THOUGHTS:

Apparent Women Officers or Directors: 2
Apparent Minority Officers or Directors:
Hot Spot for Advancement for Women/Minorities:

LOCATIONS: ("Y" = Yes)

West:	Southwest:	Midwest:	Southeast:	Northeast:	International:
Y			Y	Y	

Note: Financial information, benefits and other data can change quickly and may vary from those stated here.

ROWECOM   www.rowe.com

Industry Group Code: 42292
Ranks within this company's industry group: Sales: 1   Profits: 1

BUSINESS ACTIVITIES ("Y" = Yes)

Financial Services:	Information/Publ.:		Technology:	Services:		Retailing:		Telecommunications:
Stock Brokerage	Portal/Hub/News	Y	Computer Manuf.	Payments/Transfers		Retailer		Internet Serv. Provider
Mortgages/Loans	On-Line Community		Networking Equip.	Consulting		Auctions		Web Site Host
Banking	Search Engine		Software Manuf.	Advertising/Marketing		Mall		Server Farm
Insurance	Financial Data Publ.		Specialty Equipment	Outsourcing	Y	Tickets/Travel		Specialty Telecom.
Credit Cards	Broadcasting/Music					Price Comparisons		High Speed Access

TYPES OF BUSINESS:

ASP with On-line Ordering System for Publication Purposes
Intermediary for Publication Ordering
Distribution of Books and Magazines to End Users

BRANDS/DIVISIONS/AFFILIATES:

Knowledge Store
Knowledge Library
Corporate Subscription Services
Dawson Information Services Group
NewsEdge

CONTACTS: Note: Officers with more than one job title may be intentionally listed here more than once.

Richard Rowe, CEO
Richard Rowe, Pres.
Jeffrey Sands, CFO
David Rifkin, Sr.VP-Sales, Mktg. and Client Services
Jeri Cande, Dir.-Human Resources
Walter Crosby, Chief Tech. Officer
Judy Schott, VP-Strategic Initiatives
Adam Klein, Chief Client Officer

Phone: 617-497-5800	Fax: 617-497-6825
Toll-Free: 888-769-3266	
Address: 725 Concord Ave., Cambridge, MA, 02138	

GROWTH PLANS/SPECIAL FEATURES:

RoweCom is a business-to-business provider of e-commerce solutions for the purchasing and managing of magazines, newspapers, journals, books and other knowledge resources. The company offers its clients and their employees easy access to one of the largest catalogs of knowledge resources on the Internet. RoweCom's flagship services, Knowledge Store (kStore) and Knowledge Library (kLibrary), allow companies to order, pay for and manage 240,000 titles on-line. Businesses are allowed to create custom on-line stores where employees can order from a pre-selected choice of titles. These sites also provide access to millions of discounted books via the company's partner barnesandnoble.com. Recently, RoweCom acquired Corporate Subscription Services and UK-based Dawson Information Services Group, both key elements to the company's growth. The recent purchase of NewsEdge will allow RoweCom to provide web-based services for individual business people, giving them customized business, technical and political news from hundreds of sources, organized into thousands of topics of interest. RoweCom's clients range from Fortune 1000 companies to academic libraries, organizations with intensive knowledge requirements and high-volume purchasers, and include Bank of America, Arthur Andersen, Prudential Securities, Bayer and First Union.

FINANCIALS: Sales and profits are in thousands of dollars—add 000 to get the full amount.
Notes regarding 1999: Through 9 months *(1999 sales and profits were not available for all companies at press time.)*

1999 Sales: $13,159	1999 Profits: $-13,453	**Stock Ticker: ROWE**
1998 Sales: $19,100	1998 Profits: $-7,600	Employees: 101
1997 Sales: $12,900	1997 Profits: $-3,300	Fiscal Year Ends: 12/31
1996 Sales: $3,100	1996 Profits: $-1,400	
1995 Sales: $ 300	1995 Profits: $- 600	

SALARIES/BENEFITS:

Pension Plan:	ESOP Stock Plan: Y	Profit Sharing:	Top Exec. Salary: $153,000	Bonus: $
Savings Plan:	Stock Purch. Plan: Y		Second Exec. Salary: $124,000	Bonus: $

COMPETITIVE ADVANTAGE: Has acquired several of the world's leading subscription services.

OTHER THOUGHTS:

Apparent Women Officers or Directors: 2
Apparent Minority Officers or Directors:
Hot Spot for Advancement for Women/Minorities:

LOCATIONS: ("Y" = Yes)

West:	Southwest:	Midwest:	Southeast:	Northeast:	International:
Y		Y		Y	Y

RSA SECURITY INC   www.rsasecurity.com

Industry Group Code: 5112
Ranks within this company's industry group: Sales: 7   Profits: 5

BUSINESS ACTIVITIES ("Y" = Yes)

Financial Services:	Information/Publ.:	Technology:		Services:	Retailing:	Telecommunications:
Stock Brokerage	Portal/Hub/News	Computer Manuf.		Payments/Transfers	Retailer	Internet Serv. Provider
Mortgages/Loans	On-Line Community	Networking Equip.		Consulting	Auctions	Web Site Host
Banking	Search Engine	Software Manuf.	Y	Advertising/Marketing	Mall	Server Farm
Insurance	Financial Data Publ.	Specialty Equipment	Y	Outsourcing	Tickets/Travel	Specialty Telecom.
Credit Cards	Broadcasting/Music				Price Comparisons	High Speed Access

TYPES OF BUSINESS:

Software-Security
Software Development Tools
Security Device Management Software

BRANDS/DIVISIONS/AFFILIATES:

SecurSight
Security Dynamics Technologies, Inc.
RSA Data Security, Inc.
DynaSoft
SecurWorld
SecurID

CONTACTS: *Note: Officers with more than one job title may be intentionally listed here more than once.*

Charles R. Stuckey, Jr., CEO
Arthur W. Coviello, Jr., Pres./COO
John Kennedy, CFO
Scott Schnell, Sr. VP-Mktg.
Vivian Vitale, VP-Human Resources
John Adams, Sr. VP-Engineering
Margaret K. Seif, VP/Sec.
Margaret K. Seif, VP/General Counsel
Roger Nichols, VP-Corp. Dev.

Phone: 781-687-7000	Fax: 781-687-7010
Toll-Free: 800-732-8743	
Address: 36 Crosby Drive, Bedford, MA, 01730	

GROWTH PLANS/SPECIAL FEATURES:

RSA Security, Inc., formerly Security Dynamics Technologies, is a leading provider of enterprise network and data security solutions. The company enables electronic business by providing technologies, products and services that secure access to and protect information in networks, systems, applications and Internet commerce initiatives. It uses its expertise in authentication management, public key encryption and access control to help organizations in a range of industries to conduct business and electronic commerce. Through its family of enterprise security solutions, partnerships and acquisitions, RSA Security intends to expand its addressable market by delivering solutions that provide secure access to information wherever it resides in an enterprise. The company sells its products to Fortune 500 firms and to users in finance, research and government markets. More than 40% of sales come from its flagship product, SecurID. SecurID authorizes entry by personal identification numbers (PINs) and random access codes displayed on cards and tokens. Other company products are data encryption and e-business security tools. Two-thirds of RSA Security's sales are generated in the U.S.

FINANCIALS: Sales and profits are in thousands of dollars—add 000 to get the full amount.

Notes regarding 1999: *(1999 sales and profits were not available for all companies at press time.)*

1999 Sales: $218,100	1999 Profits: $183,800	Stock Ticker: **RSAS**
1998 Sales: $171,300	1998 Profits: $29,400	Employees: 764
1997 Sales: $135,900	1997 Profits: $16,400	Fiscal Year Ends: 12/31
1996 Sales: $76,100	1996 Profits: $13,000	
1995 Sales: $33,800	1995 Profits: $5,800	

SALARIES/BENEFITS:

Pension Plan:	ESOP Stock Plan:	Profit Sharing:	Top Exec. Salary: $231,000	Bonus: $
Savings Plan: Y	Stock Purch. Plan:		Second Exec. Salary: $200,000	Bonus: $

COMPETITIVE ADVANTAGE: Focus on data security products/Very rapid growth/Excellent margins.

OTHER THOUGHTS:

Apparent Women Officers or Directors: 3
Apparent Minority Officers or Directors:
Hot Spot for Advancement for Women/Minorities: Y

LOCATIONS: ("Y" = Yes)

West:	Southwest:	Midwest:	Southeast:	Northeast:	International:
Y	Y	Y	Y	Y	Y

S1 CORPORATION   www.s1.com

Industry Group Code: 5112
Ranks within this company's industry group: Sales: 32   Profits: 77

BUSINESS ACTIVITIES ("Y" = Yes)

Financial Services:	Information/Publ.:	Technology:	Services:	Retailing:	Telecommunications:
Stock Brokerage	Portal/Hub/News	Computer Manuf.	Payments/Transfers	Retailer	Internet Serv. Provider
Mortgages/Loans	On-Line Community	Networking Equip.	Consulting	Auctions	Web Site Host
Banking	Search Engine	Software Manuf. Y	Advertising/Marketing	Mall	Server Farm
Insurance	Financial Data Publ.	Specialty Equipment	Outsourcing Y	Tickets/Travel	Specialty Telecom.
Credit Cards	Broadcasting/Music			Price Comparisons	High Speed Access

TYPES OF BUSINESS:

Software-Financial Services
On-Line Banking Enabler

BRANDS/DIVISIONS/AFFILIATES:

Virtual Financial Manager (VFM)
Broadvision
Anderson Consulting
Hewlett-Packard

GROWTH PLANS/SPECIAL FEATURES:

S1 Corporation develops integrated, brandable Internet applications that enable companies offering financial services to create their own financial portals on the Internet. S1's Virtual Financial Manager (VFM) integrates banking, investment, loan and credit card accounts at an institution with content such as news, weather and sports, each personalized by the end user. VFM also enables clients to offer their customers a complete view of their personal finances with the institution in one consolidated financial statement. The company licenses its VFM software, provides installation and integration services and offers outsourced Internet transaction processing through its data center. S1 targets organizations that view providing their products and services on the Internet as a strategic competitive advantage and an integral component of their businesses. The company's Installation, implementation, outsourced transaction processing and other follow-on services account for 80% of sales. The company has marketing alliances with BroadVision (an e-commerce software maker), Anderson Consulting and Hewlett-Packard.

CONTACTS: Note: Officers with more than one job title may be intentionally listed here more than once.

James S. Mahan III, CEO
Daniel H. Drechsel, COO
Robert F. Stockwell, CFO
Charles W. Ogilvie III, Exec. VP-Mktg. and Sales
Nancy D. Coleman, Exec. VP-Human Resources
Stuart A. Granger, CIO
Robert F. Stockwell, Treas.
Jan Smith, VP-Mktg.

Phone: 404-812-6200	Fax: 404-812-6727

Toll-Free: 888-457-2237
Address: 3390 Peachtree Rd. NE, Suite 1700, Atlanta, GA, 30326

FINANCIALS: Sales and profits are in thousands of dollars—add 000 to get the full amount.

Notes regarding 1999: *(1999 sales and profits were not available for all companies at press time.)*

1999 Sales: $	1999 Profits: $	Stock Ticker: **SONE**
1998 Sales: $24,200	1998 Profits: $-30,800	Employees: 312
1997 Sales: $10,800	1997 Profits: $-28,000	Fiscal Year Ends: 12/31
1996 Sales: $6,500	1996 Profits: $-22,100	
1995 Sales: $4,600	1995 Profits: $-1,500	

SALARIES/BENEFITS:

Pension Plan:	ESOP Stock Plan:	Profit Sharing:	Top Exec. Salary: $200,000	Bonus: $
Savings Plan: Y	Stock Purch. Plan: Y		Second Exec. Salary: $150,000	Bonus: $

COMPETITIVE ADVANTAGE: Unique range of turn-key services/Important strategic alliances.

OTHER THOUGHTS:

Apparent Women Officers or Directors: 2
Apparent Minority Officers or Directors:
Hot Spot for Advancement for Women/Minorities:

LOCATIONS: ("Y" = Yes)

West:	Southwest:	Midwest:	Southeast:	Northeast:	International:
Y	Y		Y	Y	Y

Note: Financial information, benefits and other data can change quickly and may vary from those stated here.

SABRE INC   www.sabre.com

Industry Group Code: 51339A
Ranks within this company's industry group: Sales: 1   Profits: 1

BUSINESS ACTIVITIES ("Y" = Yes)

Financial Services:	Information/Publ.:	Technology:	Services:		Retailing:		Telecommunications:
Stock Brokerage	Portal/Hub/News	Computer Manuf.	Payments/Transfers		Retailer		Internet Serv. Provider
Mortgages/Loans	On-Line Community	Networking Equip.	Consulting		Auctions		Web Site Host
Banking	Search Engine	Software Manuf.	Advertising/Marketing		Mall		Server Farm
Insurance	Financial Data Publ.	Specialty Equipment	Outsourcing	Y	Tickets/Travel	Y	Specialty Telecom.
Credit Cards	Broadcasting/Music				Price Comparisons		High Speed Access

TYPES OF BUSINESS:

Outsourcing-Travel Reservations
On-line Ticket and Travel Sales

BRANDS/DIVISIONS/AFFILIATES:

SABRE Technology Solutions
SABRE Interactive
SABRE Travel Information Network
Planet SABRE
Turbo SABRE
SABRE Business Travel Solutions
Travelocity
easySABRE

CONTACTS: *Note: Officers with more than one job title may be intentionally listed here more than once.*

William J. Hannigan, CEO
William J. Hannigar, Pres.
Jeffery Jackson, CFO
Eric J. Speck, Exec. VP-Mktg. and Sales
Mary Morrse, Dir.-Human Resources
Carol Kelly, CIO
Andrew B. Steinberg, Corp. Sec.
Andrew B. Steinberg, General Counsel
Jeffery Jackson, Treas.

Phone: 817-963-8040	Fax: 817-931-6382
Toll-Free:	
Address: 4255 Amon Carter Boulevard, Fort Worth, TX, 76155	

GROWTH PLANS/SPECIAL FEATURES:

Sabre, Inc. is a world leader in the electronic distribution of travel through its proprietary travel reservation information system, SABRE, and is the largest electronic distributor of travel in North America. In addition, the company is a pioneer in information technology (IT) solutions for the travel and transportation industry, and fulfills substantially all of the data processing, network and distributed systems needs of American Airlines, AMR Corporation and Canadian Airlines International, Ltd. SABRE is one of the few distribution systems that acts as a principal means of air travel distribution in the United States, and the company has a growing presence in international travel means distribution. Through the SABRE system, travel agencies, corporate travel departments and individual consumers who are subscribers can access information on and book reservations with airlines and other providers of travel and travel-related products and services. Planet SABRE and Turbo SABRE platforms are designed to meet the needs of travel agents of any size. SABRE Business Travel Solutions is designed to help companies control travel and entertainment expenses. Travelocity and easySABRE provide air, car, hotel and reservation capabilities for travelers and on-line computer users with interfaces to the SABRE computer reservations system. Individuals can make travel arrangements using the Travelocity web site. Sabre is currently forming an alliance with Priceline.com; Preview Travel is allying with Travelocity.com. Under the alliances, the companies will leverage their combined user base of more than 20 million travelers, offering seamless access to each other's products and services.

FINANCIALS: Sales and profits are in thousands of dollars—add 000 to get the full amount.
Notes regarding 1999: *(1999 sales and profits were not available for all companies at press time.)*

1999 Sales: $2,400,000	1999 Profits: $399,000	Stock Ticker: **TSG**
1998 Sales: $2,306,400	1998 Profits: $231,900	Employees: 10,800
1997 Sales: $1,783,500	1997 Profits: $200,000	Fiscal Year Ends: 12/31
1996 Sales: $1,622,000	1996 Profits: $186,600	
1995 Sales: $1,529,600	1995 Profits: $225,900	

SALARIES/BENEFITS:

Pension Plan: Y	ESOP Stock Plan:	Profit Sharing:	Top Exec. Salary: $543,333	Bonus: $460,697
Savings Plan:	Stock Purch. Plan: Y		Second Exec. Salary: $	Bonus: $

COMPETITIVE ADVANTAGE: World's largest airline reservation system/State-of-the-art technology.

OTHER THOUGHTS:

Apparent Women Officers or Directors: 2
Apparent Minority Officers or Directors:
Hot Spot for Advancement for Women/Minorities:

LOCATIONS: ("Y" = Yes)

West:	Southwest:	Midwest:	Southeast:	Northeast:	International:
Y	Y	Y	Y	Y	Y

Note: Financial information, benefits and other data can change quickly and may vary from those stated here.

SAGENT TECHNOLOGY   www.sagent.com

Industry Group Code: 5112
Ranks within this company's industry group: Sales: 42   Profits: 64

BUSINESS ACTIVITIES ("Y" = Yes)

Financial Services:	Information/Publ.:	Technology:		Services:		Retailing:	Telecommunications:
Stock Brokerage	Portal/Hub/News	Computer Manuf.		Payments/Transfers		Retailer	Internet Serv. Provider
Mortgages/Loans	On-Line Community	Networking Equip.		Consulting		Auctions	Web Site Host
Banking	Search Engine	Software Manuf.	Y	Advertising/Marketing	Y	Mall	Server Farm
Insurance	Financial Data Publ.	Specialty Equipment		Outsourcing		Tickets/Travel	Specialty Telecom.
Credit Cards	Broadcasting/Music					Price Comparisons	High Speed Access

TYPES OF BUSINESS:

Software-Marketing Intelligence

BRANDS/DIVISIONS/AFFILIATES:

Enterprise Intelligence
Data Mart Solution (DMS)
Qualitative Marketing Software, Inc.

CONTACTS: *Note: Officers with more than one job title may be intentionally listed here more than once.*

Kenneth C. Gardner, CEO
Kenneth C. Gardner, Pres.
W. Virginia Walker, Exec. VP-Finance and Admin./CFO
Thomas M. Lounibos, Exec. VP-Sales and Oper.
Greta Bron, Human Resources Specialist
John E. Zicker, Exec. VP-Tech./Chief Tech. Officer
Kenneth C. Holcomb, VP-Oper.
Vincent DeGennaro, Sr. VP-Worldwide Sales
Malcolm Hobbs, VP-Mktg.

Phone: 650-815-3100	Fax: 650-815-3500
Toll-Free:	
Address: 800 W. El Camino Real, Ste. 300, Mountain View, CA, 94040	

GROWTH PLANS/SPECIAL FEATURES:

Sagent Technology develops, markets and supports software products that gather, analyze and deliver information throughout an organization via the Internet. This information helps businesses collect, analyze, understand and act on customer and operational information in real-time. Sagent's software, Enterprise Intelligence, enables organizations to make more informed decisions and to spread that ability across the enterprise. The Sagent Data Mart Solution, or DMS, gathers data from a variety of sources (such as mainframe databases and the Internet), and organizes that data into a repository called a data mart. Once in the data mart, an organization can analyze the data and provide access to the information through web browsers over the Internet. Sagent recently acquired Qualitative Marketing Software, Inc., a company that delivers real-time customer information by hosting data for over 125 million households on the Web. This partnership allows Sagent to provide e-businesses with a multi-layered view of the customer, based on historical transactions and clickstream, demographic, credit and geographic data. Drugstore.com selected Sagent's software to gather and analyze customer purchase data patterns in an effort to improve its product revenue projections from quarter to quarter. Other Sagent clients include Sony Online Entertainment, Mapquest, Barnes & Noble, Ticketmaster and AT&T.

FINANCIALS: Sales and profits are in thousands of dollars—add 000 to get the full amount.

Notes regarding 1999: *(1999 sales and profits were not available for all companies at press time.)*

1999 Sales: $48,000	1999 Profits: $-12,091	Stock Ticker: **SGNT**
1998 Sales: $17,000	1998 Profits: $-13,700	Employees: 152
1997 Sales: $7,100	1997 Profits: $-6,900	Fiscal Year Ends: 12/31
1996 Sales: $ 300	1996 Profits: $-7,000	
1995 Sales: $	1995 Profits: $	

SALARIES/BENEFITS:

Pension Plan:	ESOP Stock Plan: Y	Profit Sharing:	Top Exec. Salary: $225,000	Bonus: $90,000
Savings Plan: Y	Stock Purch. Plan:		Second Exec. Salary: $173,965	Bonus: $69,586

COMPETITIVE ADVANTAGE: Unique technology provides a new view of customer data.

OTHER THOUGHTS:

Apparent Women Officers or Directors: 2
Apparent Minority Officers or Directors:
Hot Spot for Advancement for Women/Minorities:

LOCATIONS: ("Y" = Yes)

West:	Southwest:	Midwest:	Southeast:	Northeast:	International:
Y	Y		Y	Y	Y

SALON.COM   www.salon.com

Industry Group Code: 514191
Ranks within this company's industry group: Sales: 34   Profits: 19

BUSINESS ACTIVITIES ("Y" = Yes)

Financial Services:	Information/Publ.:		Technology:	Services:	Retailing:		Telecommunications:
Stock Brokerage	Portal/Hub/News	Y	Computer Manuf.	Payments/Transfers	Retailer	Y	Internet Serv. Provider
Mortgages/Loans	On-Line Community	Y	Networking Equip.	Consulting	Auctions		Web Site Host
Banking	Search Engine		Software Manuf.	Advertising/Marketing	Mall		Server Farm
Insurance	Financial Data Publ.		Specialty Equipment	Outsourcing	Tickets/Travel		Specialty Telecom.
Credit Cards	Broadcasting/Music	Y			Price Comparisons		High Speed Access

TYPES OF BUSINESS:
Portal-News and Media

GROWTH PLANS/SPECIAL FEATURES:

Salon.com is an Internet media company that produces a network of ten subject-specific, demographically-targeted web sites and a variety of on-line communities. Salon's ten sites provide news, features, interviews and regular columnists writing about specific topics, from arts and entertainment to parenting and health. Salon.com's other media offerings consist of Table Talk, an interactive forum, and The Well, a paid subscription community. The site's on-line communities allow users to interact and discuss salon content with other users and with Salon's editorial staff. Salon Shopping is an e-commerce destination aimed at marketing upscale Salon-branded and third party products to a high-value demographic base. In partnership with theDial, Salon.com features original and syndicated audio content, which will soon include a talk-based channel with on-air essays, commentaries and interviews. Salon.com has won three consecutive Webby Awards for Best Online Magazine. Entertainment Weekly chose Salon.com as Best Web Site two years in a row, and Time Magazine picked Salon.com as the Best Web Site of the Year. Salon's e-commerce partners include Microsoft Expedia, barnesandnoble.com, drkoop.com and 911gifts.com. The site also provides content to America Online, Lycos, Go.com, Netscape, TheStreet.com and Reuters.

BRANDS/DIVISIONS/AFFILIATES:
theDial
Table Talk
The Well
Salon Shopping

CONTACTS: *Note: Officers with more than one job title may be intentionally listed here more than once.*
Michael O'Donnell, CEO
Michael O'Donnell, Pres.
Todd Hagen, CFO/VP-Finance and Admin.
Bruce Roberts, Sr.VP-Sales
Donna DeLuca, Dir.-Finance and Human Resources
Chad Dickerson, VP-Tech.
Andrew Ross, VP-Business and Strategic Dev.
Scott Rosenberg, VP-Site Dev.
Cliff Figallo, Dir.-Community Dev.
David Talbot, Editor in Chief
Gary Kamiya, VP-Content and Exec. Editor

Phone: 415-882-8720	Fax: 415-882-8728
Toll-Free:	
Address: 706 Mission St., San Francisco, CA, 94103	

FINANCIALS: Sales and profits are in thousands of dollars—add 000 to get the full amount.
Notes regarding 1999: *(1999 sales and profits were not available for all companies at press time.)*

1999 Sales: $2,900	1999 Profits: $-6,200	**Stock Ticker: SALN**
1998 Sales: $1,200	1998 Profits: $-3,800	Employees: 99
1997 Sales: $ 300	1997 Profits: $-1,900	Fiscal Year Ends: 03/31
1996 Sales: $ 200	1996 Profits: $- 500	
1995 Sales: $	1995 Profits: $	

SALARIES/BENEFITS:

Pension Plan:	ESOP Stock Plan: Y	Profit Sharing:	Top Exec. Salary: $130,312	Bonus: $
Savings Plan: Y	Stock Purch. Plan:		Second Exec. Salary: $90,040	Bonus: $15,000

COMPETITIVE ADVANTAGE: Unique business model/Trendy topics.

OTHER THOUGHTS:
Apparent Women Officers or Directors: 1
Apparent Minority Officers or Directors:
Hot Spot for Advancement for Women/Minorities:

LOCATIONS: ("Y" = Yes)

West:	Southwest:	Midwest:	Southeast:	Northeast:	International:
Y					

Note: Financial information, benefits and other data can change quickly and may vary from those stated here.

SCIENT CORP   www.scient.com

Industry Group Code: 54151
Ranks within this company's industry group: Sales: 16   Profits: 7

BUSINESS ACTIVITIES ("Y" = Yes)

Financial Services:	Information/Publ.:	Technology:	Services:	Retailing:	Telecommunications:
Stock Brokerage	Portal/Hub/News	Computer Manuf.	Payments/Transfers Y	Retailer	Internet Serv. Provider
Mortgages/Loans	On-Line Community	Networking Equip.	Consulting	Auctions	Web Site Host
Banking	Search Engine	Software Manuf. Y	Advertising/Marketing	Mall	Server Farm
Insurance	Financial Data Publ.	Specialty Equipment	Outsourcing	Tickets/Travel	Specialty Telecom.
Credit Cards	Broadcasting/Music			Price Comparisons	High Speed Access

TYPES OF BUSINESS:

Consulting-Internet and Technology
Software Development
Systems Architecture

BRANDS/DIVISIONS/AFFILIATES:

CONTACTS: *Note: Officers with more than one job title may be intentionally listed here more than once.*

Robert M. Howe, CEO/Pres.
Stephen A. Mucchetti, COO
William H. Kurtz, CFO
Christopher W. Lochhead, Chief Mktg. Officer
Robert N. Beck, VP-People
C. Scott Frisbie, Chief Tech. Officer
William P. Kim, VP-Oper.
Gerry Komlofske, Chief Strategy Officer
Nicholas J. DiGiacomo, VP-Electronic Markets
Andres Gutierrez, Master Architect
Diana L. Brown, VP-Financial Services

Phone: 415-733-8200	Fax: 415-733-8299
Toll-Free:	
Address: 1 Front St., 28th Fl., San Francisco, CA, 94111	

GROWTH PLANS/SPECIAL FEATURES:

Scient Corp. is an electronic commerce software developer. The company integrates business and technology strategy for clients that are creating eBusinesses or are restructuring their existing businesses in order to integrate eBusiness capabilities. Scient offers strategy consulting, customer experience design, systems architecture and application and technology infrastructure development. All new Scient employees participate in an orientation program called SPARK. During training, employees learn why the Internet is changing the way business works. They also improve their public speaking skills and become exposed to Scient's philosophy. CEO Bob Howe was named one of the Top 25 Executives of 1999 by Computer Reseller News. Recently, the company spent $100,000 for a full page ad in The Wall Street Journal that was completely blank except for two things: the statement - This is not our ad - and the company's Internet address. The company's web site contained the advertising message. This was one of the first times a newspaper ad was used for the sole purpose of drawing attention to a web page. Scient's clients include such firms as AIG, Chase Manhattan, eBay, First Union and PlanetRx.

FINANCIALS: Sales and profits are in thousands of dollars—add 000 to get the full amount.

Notes regarding 1999: *(1999 sales and profits were not available for all companies at press time.)*

1999 Sales: $20,700	1999 Profits: $-11,700	Stock Ticker: **SCNT**
1998 Sales: $ 200	1998 Profits: $-1,200	Employees: 260
1997 Sales: $	1997 Profits: $	Fiscal Year Ends: 3/31
1996 Sales: $	1996 Profits: $	
1995 Sales: $	1995 Profits: $	

SALARIES/BENEFITS:

Pension Plan:	ESOP Stock Plan: Y	Profit Sharing:	Top Exec. Salary: $250,000	Bonus: $
Savings Plan:	Stock Purch. Plan: Y		Second Exec. Salary: $239,583	Bonus: $33,333

COMPETITIVE ADVANTAGE: Services cover the full spectrum of a new e-buisness's needs.

OTHER THOUGHTS:

Apparent Women Officers or Directors: 1
Apparent Minority Officers or Directors: 4
Hot Spot for Advancement for Women/Minorities: Y

LOCATIONS: ("Y" = Yes)

West:	Southwest:	Midwest:	Southeast:	Northeast:	International:
Y	Y	Y		Y	Y

SECURE COMPUTING CORP   www.sctc.com

Industry Group Code: 5112
Ranks within this company's industry group: Sales: 15   Profits: 26

BUSINESS ACTIVITIES ("Y" = Yes)

Financial Services:	Information/Publ.:	Technology:		Services:	Retailing:	Telecommunications:
Stock Brokerage	Portal/Hub/News	Computer Manuf.		Payments/Transfers	Retailer	Internet Serv. Provider
Mortgages/Loans	On-Line Community	Networking Equip.		Consulting	Auctions	Web Site Host
Banking	Search Engine	Software Manuf.	Y	Advertising/Marketing	Mall	Server Farm
Insurance	Financial Data Publ.	Specialty Equipment		Outsourcing	Tickets/Travel	Specialty Telecom.
Credit Cards	Broadcasting/Music				Price Comparisons	High Speed Access

TYPES OF BUSINESS:
Software-Security

BRANDS/DIVISIONS/AFFILIATES:
SideWinder firewall
SafeWord
SecureWire
SecureZone

CONTACTS: *Note: Officers with more than one job title may be intentionally listed here more than once.*
John McNulty, CEO
Timothy P. McGurran, CFO
Craig Caudill, Sr. VP-Worldwide Sales
Mary Ann Stoffels, Dir.-Human Resources
J. Thomas Haigh, Chief Tech. Officer
William Bosen, VP-Engineering, Enterprise Security Div.
Mary K. Budge, General Counsel
Timothy P. McGurran, Sr. VP-Oper.
Carr Biggerstaff, Sr. VP-Mktg., Business Dev.,Strategic & Plan.
Joseph Perez, VP-Customer Service Div.

Phone: 408-918-6100   **Fax:** 408-918-6101
Toll-Free: 800-379-4944
Address: One Almaden Blvd., Suite 400, San Jose, CA, 95113

GROWTH PLANS/SPECIAL FEATURES:
Secure Computing Corp. designs, develops, markets and sells a comprehensive offering of interoperable, standards-based products for end-to-end network solutions, including firewalls, web filters, authentication, extranet access control and security-related professional services. The company enables business and government network security through its integrated and interoperable solutions, core technologies, services and partner programs. Secure Computing is the market share leader in providing network perimeter security to the U.S. Federal Government. In the world market, Secure Computing is the leader in web productivity tools and security professional services, the second largest provider of identification and authentication solutions and the third largest provider of firewalls. The company's flagship software, SideWinder, creates firewalls around government and corporate networks. Another product, SecureZone, delivers the first of the next generation of firewalls using role-based access control and policy management. The company's customers include Fortune 500 companies, small branch offices and government agencies. Secure Computing's government contracts are decreasing as the company focuses on marketing its high-end products and services to commercial customers, which account for 70% of sales.

FINANCIALS: Sales and profits are in thousands of dollars—add 000 to get the full amount.
Notes regarding 1999: *(1999 sales and profits were not available for all companies at press time.)*

1999 Sales: $27,113	1999 Profits: $-44,907	**Stock Ticker: SCUR**
1998 Sales: $61,400	1998 Profits: $-3,300	Employees: 321
1997 Sales: $47,000	1997 Profits: $-4,300	Fiscal Year Ends: 12/31
1996 Sales: $40,300	1996 Profits: $-25,100	
1995 Sales: $20,700	1995 Profits: $-1,000	

SALARIES/BENEFITS:
Pension Plan: Y	ESOP Stock Plan:	Profit Sharing:	Top Exec. Salary: $387,500	Bonus: $641,178
Savings Plan: Y	Stock Purch. Plan: Y		Second Exec. Salary: $266,897	Bonus: $65,000

COMPETITIVE ADVANTAGE: Full range of security software services/Steady growth/ Major government contracts.

OTHER THOUGHTS:
Apparent Women Officers or Directors: 3
Apparent Minority Officers or Directors:
Hot Spot for Advancement for Women/Minorities: Y

LOCATIONS: ("Y" = Yes)
West:	Southwest:	Midwest:	Southeast:	Northeast:	International:
Y		Y		Y	Y

Note: Financial information, benefits and other data can change quickly and may vary from those stated here.

SILICON GRAPHICS INC   www.sgi.com

Industry Group Code: 3341A
Ranks within this company's industry group: Sales: 8   Profits: 7

BUSINESS ACTIVITIES ("Y" = Yes)

Financial Services:	Information/Publ.:	Technology:		Services:		Retailing:	Telecommunications:
Stock Brokerage	Portal/Hub/News	Computer Manuf.	Y	Payments/Transfers		Retailer	Internet Serv. Provider
Mortgages/Loans	On-Line Community	Networking Equip.		Consulting		Auctions	Web Site Host
Banking	Search Engine	Software Manuf.	Y	Advertising/Marketing		Mall	Server Farm
Insurance	Financial Data Publ.	Specialty Equipment	Y	Outsourcing		Tickets/Travel	Specialty Telecom.
Credit Cards	Broadcasting/Music					Price Comparisons	High Speed Access

TYPES OF BUSINESS:

Computer Hardware-Advanced Graphics
Software
3-D Computing Solutions
Digital Media
RISC Microprocessors
Symmetric Multiprocessing

BRANDS/DIVISIONS/AFFILIATES:

Cray Research
Octane
Alias/Wavefront
Onyx2
MIPS Group
IRIX
Origin2000
Vector Systems

CONTACTS: *Note: Officers with more than one job title may be intentionally listed here more than once.*

Robert R. Bishop, CEO
Steven J. Gomo, Sr. VP/CFO
Kenneth L. Coleman, Sr. VP-Global Sales, Service and Mktg.
Kirk Froggatt, VP-Human Resources
Kurt B. Akeley, Sr. VP/Chief Tech. Officer
Betsy Rafael, VP/Controller
Phil Uchno, VP-Mfg. Industries
William M. Kelly, Sr. VP/Corp. Sec.
Sandra Escher, General Counsel
William M. Kelly, Sr. VP-Corp. Oper.

Phone: 650-960-1980	Fax: 650-932-0661
Toll-Free:	

Address: 1600 Amphitheatre Pkwy., Mountain View, CA, 94043-1351

GROWTH PLANS/SPECIAL FEATURES:

Silicon Graphics, Inc. is a leader in high-performance computing. The company's broad range of workstations and graphics servers deliver advanced 3-D graphics and computing capabilities for engineering and creative professionals. SGI servers are the market leaders in technical computing applications. The company's highly scalable servers also have a growing presence in strategic business analysis, with a particular emphasis on Internet, large corporate data and telecommunications applications. Silicon Graphics' MIPS Group designs and licenses the RISC microprocessor intellectual property and core technology. The company's Alias\\Wavefront subsidiary markets applications software targeted at engineering and creative professionals in the digital content creation and manufacturing sectors. The firm's computer systems range from desktop workstations to servers and supercomputers. Most of these systems are designed around MIPS. RISC microprocessors are developed by Silicon Graphics MIPS Group and the IRIX operating system, which is the company's enhanced version of the UNIX operating system. Over the next several years, the firm plans to introduce new generations of its products based on Intel microprocessor architecture and the Linux and Windows NT operating systems. The company also intends to diversify its line of NT-based workstations and its supercomputer business by spinning off its streaming media software operations. In addition, Silicon Graphics plans products for hot markets such as media streaming, digital asset management and high-volume Internet traffic.

Silicon Graphics has an employee assistance program which offers counseling and referrals services.

FINANCIALS: Sales and profits are in thousands of dollars—add 000 to get the full amount.

Notes regarding 1999: *(1999 sales and profits were not available for all companies at press time.)*

1999 Sales: $2,749,000	1999 Profits: $53,800	**Stock Ticker: SGI**
1998 Sales: $3,100,600	1998 Profits: $-459,600	Employees: 9,191
1997 Sales: $3,662,600	1997 Profits: $78,600	Fiscal Year Ends: 6/30
1996 Sales: $2,921,300	1996 Profits: $115,000	
1995 Sales: $228,300	1995 Profits: $224,900	

SALARIES/BENEFITS:

Pension Plan:	ESOP Stock Plan:	Profit Sharing:	Top Exec. Salary: $457,945	Bonus: $46,000
Savings Plan: Y	Stock Purch. Plan: Y		Second Exec. Salary: $426,462	Bonus: $1,000,000

COMPETITIVE ADVANTAGE: World's leading supplier of 3-D computing solutions/Continually identifies and invests in key technologies.

OTHER THOUGHTS:

Apparent Women Officers or Directors: 3
Apparent Minority Officers or Directors: 2
Hot Spot for Advancement for Women/Minorities: Y

LOCATIONS: ("Y" = Yes)

West:	Southwest:	Midwest:	Southeast:	Northeast:	International:
Y	Y	Y	Y	Y	Y

Note: Financial information, benefits and other data can change quickly and may vary from those stated here.

SILKNET SOFTWARE

www.silknet.com

Industry Group Code: 5112
Ranks within this company's industry group: Sales: 65   Profits: 37

BUSINESS ACTIVITIES ("Y" = Yes)

Financial Services:	Information/Publ.:	Technology:		Services:	Retailing:	Telecommunications:
Stock Brokerage	Portal/Hub/News	Computer Manuf.		Payments/Transfers	Retailer	Internet Serv. Provider
Mortgages/Loans	On-Line Community	Networking Equip.		Consulting	Auctions	Web Site Host
Banking	Search Engine	Software Manuf.	Y	Advertising/Marketing	Mall	Server Farm
Insurance	Financial Data Publ.	Specialty Equipment		Outsourcing	Tickets/Travel	Specialty Telecom.
Credit Cards	Broadcasting/Music				Price Comparisons	High Speed Access

TYPES OF BUSINESS:

Software-Customer Service

BRANDS/DIVISIONS/AFFILIATES:

Silknet eBusiness System
Silknet eService
Silknet eCommerce

CONTACTS: *Note: Officers with more than one job title may be intentionally listed here more than once.*

James C. Wood, Pres./CEO
Nigel K. Donovan, Sr. VP/COO
Patrick J. Scannell Jr., VP/CFO
David Fowler, VP-Mktg.
Karen Hume, Dir.-Human Resources
Patricia D. Stimpson, VP-Research and Dev.
Eric Carlson, VP/Chief Tech. Officer
James P. Davis, VP-Business Dev.
Patrick J. Scannell Jr., Treas.
Mark H. Green, VP-Sales
V. Anthony Giannelli, VP-Int'l

Phone: 603-625-0070	Fax: 603-625-0428
Toll-Free:	
Address: 50 Phillippe Cote St., Manchester, NH, 03101	

GROWTH PLANS/SPECIAL FEATURES:

Silknet Software provides leading customer-centric e-business applications and systems for Global 2000 and .com companies such as Office Depot, Microsoft, Priceline.com, Sprint, KPMG and Bell Canada. Silknet operates through three segments: eBusiness, eService and eCommerce. The company's belief is that, as the Internet grows in scope and importance, companies must choose between E-business or E-limination. One thing that can set a company apart and propel it to higher levels of profit making is superior customer service. Silknet provides Internet-centric customer relationship management solutions for Internet service providers and the telecommunications, financial services and computer reselling industries. The company's eBusiness System provides a framework for managing interactions, collaborations and transactions with customers, partners and employees. eService is a leading customer service system, dedicated to turning call centers from cost centers into profit makers and is used by Bank of America, Cigna Healthcare, Compaq and Microsoft. eCommerce allows companies one view of customer transactions across departments and functions. In response to rising sales and service demands, Silknet now has offices coast-to-coast and in Canada. The company recently closed on $16 million in new financing from a group of investors headed by CMG@Ventures, the investment arm of CMG Information Services.

FINANCIALS: Sales and profits are in thousands of dollars—add 000 to get the full amount.

Notes regarding 1999: *(1999 sales and profits were not available for all companies at press time.)*

1999 Sales: $13,900	1999 Profits: $-9,400	Stock Ticker: **SILK**
1998 Sales: $3,600	1998 Profits: $-6,000	Employees: 161
1997 Sales: $ 200	1997 Profits: $-2,800	Fiscal Year Ends: 6/30
1996 Sales: $ 300	1996 Profits: $- 500	
1995 Sales: $	1995 Profits: $	

SALARIES/BENEFITS:

Pension Plan:	ESOP Stock Plan:	Profit Sharing:	Top Exec. Salary: $140,881	Bonus: $
Savings Plan: Y	Stock Purch. Plan: Y		Second Exec. Salary: $120,750	Bonus: $

COMPETITIVE ADVANTAGE: Blue ribbon backers/Unique technology for customer service needs.

OTHER THOUGHTS:

Apparent Women Officers or Directors: 2
Apparent Minority Officers or Directors: 1
Hot Spot for Advancement for Women/Minorities:

LOCATIONS: ("Y" = Yes)

West:	Southwest:	Midwest:	Southeast:	Northeast:	International:
Y	Y	Y	Y	Y	Y

SILVERSTREAM SOFTWARE www.silverstream.com

Industry Group Code: 5112
Ranks within this company's industry group: Sales: 57   Profits: 61

BUSINESS ACTIVITIES ("Y" = Yes)

Financial Services:	Information/Publ.:	Technology:	Services:	Retailing:	Telecommunications:
Stock Brokerage	Portal/Hub/News	Computer Manuf.	Payments/Transfers	Retailer	Internet Serv. Provider
Mortgages/Loans	On-Line Community	Networking Equip.	Consulting Y	Auctions	Web Site Host
Banking	Search Engine	Software Manuf. Y	Advertising/Marketing	Mall	Server Farm
Insurance	Financial Data Publ.	Specialty Equipment	Outsourcing Y	Tickets/Travel	Specialty Telecom.
Credit Cards	Broadcasting/Music			Price Comparisons	High Speed Access

TYPES OF BUSINESS:
Software-Internet Applications
Training
Consulting
Implementation

BRANDS/DIVISIONS/AFFILIATES:
SilverStream Application Server

GROWTH PLANS/SPECIAL FEATURES:

SilverStream Software, Inc. is a global provider of application server software and services that enable businesses and other large organizations to create, deploy and manage software applications for intranets, extranets and the Internet. The company markets its software worldwide and has sales offices in the United Kingdom, the Netherlands, Belgium, Germany, Hong Kong, Singapore and Taiwan. The firm's SilverStream Application Server serves more than 500 customers around the world, which include Enron, Siemens and NASA. The server helps customers deploy intranet, extranet and Internet applications for e-commerce, customer service and work flow management that can link employees, customers, suppliers and partners. Silverstream offers training, consulting and technical support services. The company markets its products and services globally through its direct sales force and its network of independent software vendors, value-added resellers and consulting partners. International customers account for approximately 25 percent of the company's sales.

CONTACTS:
Note: Officers with more than one job title may be intentionally listed here more than once.
David A Litwack, CEO
Craig A. Dynes, CFO
Peter E. Brumme, Exec VP-Sales and Mktg.
Ginay Pinzer, Dir.-Human Resources
Arnold S. Epstein, Chief Tech. Officer
Diane Gordon, VP-Customer Services
Craig A. Dynes, Treas.

Phone: 781-238-5400	Fax: 781-238-5499
Toll-Free:	
Address: 1 Burlington Woods, Suite 200, Burlington, MA, 01803	

FINANCIALS:
Sales and profits are in thousands of dollars—add 000 to get the full amount.
Notes regarding 1999: *(1999 sales and profits were not available for all companies at press time.)*

1999 Sales: $23,000	1999 Profits: $-22,300	Stock Ticker: **SSSW**
1998 Sales: $6,800	1998 Profits: $-12,900	Employees: 195
1997 Sales: $ 200	1997 Profits: $-8,300	Fiscal Year Ends: 12/31
1996 Sales: $	1996 Profits: $-1,000	
1995 Sales: $	1995 Profits: $	

SALARIES/BENEFITS:
Pension Plan:	ESOP Stock Plan: Y	Profit Sharing:	Top Exec. Salary: $	Bonus: $
Savings Plan: Y	Stock Purch. Plan:		Second Exec. Salary: $	Bonus: $

COMPETITIVE ADVANTAGE: A full range of outsourced services.

OTHER THOUGHTS:
Apparent Women Officers or Directors: 2
Apparent Minority Officers or Directors:
Hot Spot for Advancement for Women/Minorities:

LOCATIONS: ("Y" = Yes)
West:	Southwest:	Midwest:	Southeast:	Northeast:	International:
Y	Y	Y	Y	Y	Y

SOFTWARE.COM   www.software.com

Industry Group Code: 5112
Ranks within this company's Industry group: Sales: 30   Profits: 41

BUSINESS ACTIVITIES ("Y" = Yes)

Financial Services:	Information/Publ.:	Technology:		Services:		Retailing:	Telecommunications:
Stock Brokerage	Portal/Hub/News	Computer Manuf.		Payments/Transfers		Retailer	Internet Serv. Provider
Mortgages/Loans	On-Line Community	Networking Equip.		Consulting		Auctions	Web Site Host
Banking	Search Engine	Software Manuf.	Y	Advertising/Marketing		Mall	Server Farm
Insurance	Financial Data Publ.	Specialty Equipment		Outsourcing	Y	Tickets/Travel	Specialty Telecom.
Credit Cards	Broadcasting/Music					Price Comparisons	High Speed Access

TYPES OF BUSINESS:

Software-Internet Messaging
Outsourced E-mail Management
Integrated Web-based Mail, Address Book and Calendar

BRANDS/DIVISIONS/AFFILIATES:

InterMail
InterMail Post Office
InterMail Kx
InterMail Mx
Mobility.Net Corp.

CONTACTS: Note: Officers with more than one job title may be intentionally listed here more than once.

John McFarlane, CEO
John S. Ingalls, CFO
Thomas S. Cullen, VP-Sales, Worldwide Service Providers
Michele R. Nivens, Human Resources
Adarbad Master, Chief Tech. Officer
Craig A. Shelburne, Corp. Sec.
Craig A. Shelburne, VP-General Counsel
John F. Poulack, Sr. VP-Oper.
Robert R. Martin, Sr. VP-Strategy

Phone: 805-882-2470	Fax: 805-957-0180
Toll-Free:	
Address: 525 Anacapa St., Santa Barbara, CA, 93101	

GROWTH PLANS/SPECIAL FEATURES:

Software.com is a leading developer and provider of scalable, high-performance messaging software applications for providers of Internet communications and services. The company has developed a software platform utilizing Internet standards-based technologies, enabling its customers to use a variety of messaging services. Software.com has multiple messaging applications based on this platform, including web browser-based e-mail, desktop client-based e-mail and outsourced or managed business messaging. It also includes Internet based voice-mail and fax-mail messaging. The company's service provider customers include telecommunications carriers, Internet service providers and wholesalers, cable-based Internet access providers, competitive local exchange telephone carriers and Internet destination sites or portals. Software.com has licensed over 37 million mailboxes to over 1,000 service providers. The company has established strategic relationships with Cisco Systems, Hewlett-Packard and IBM in order to further develop, market and sell its messaging solutions. Software.com's InterMail family of messaging product packages includes InterMail Post Office (for service providers with up to 25,000 users), InterMail Kx (for service providers with up to 250,000 users) and InterMail Mx (for service providers with more than 250,000 users). Recently, the company completed the acquisition of Silicon Valley-based Mobility.Net Corp., the developer of the Mobility.Net Integrated Web Mail System, a Java-based, high-performance and customizable integrated web mail, address book and calendar product.

FINANCIALS: Sales and profits are in thousands of dollars—add 000 to get the full amount.

Notes regarding 1999: *(1999 sales and profits were not available for all companies at press time.)*

1999 Sales: $44,638	1999 Profits: $-10,533	**Stock Ticker: SWCM**
1998 Sales: $25,600	1998 Profits: $-7,400	Employees: 208
1997 Sales: $10,700	1997 Profits: $-11,500	Fiscal Year Ends: 12/31
1996 Sales: $7,900	1996 Profits: $-3,200	
1995 Sales: $4,700	1995 Profits: $2,000	

SALARIES/BENEFITS:

Pension Plan:	ESOP Stock Plan: Y	Profit Sharing:	Top Exec. Salary: $	Bonus: $
Savings Plan: Y	Stock Purch. Plan:		Second Exec. Salary: $	Bonus: $

COMPETITIVE ADVANTAGE: Has licensed over 37 million mailboxes.

OTHER THOUGHTS:

Apparent Women Officers or Directors: 1
Apparent Minority Officers or Directors: 3
Hot Spot for Advancement for Women/Minorities: Y

LOCATIONS: ("Y" = Yes)

West:	Southwest:	Midwest:	Southeast:	Northeast:	International:
Y				Y	Y

SPLITROCK SERVICES   www.splitrock.com

Industry Group Code: 51339
Ranks within this company's industry group: Sales: 7   Profits: 19

BUSINESS ACTIVITIES ("Y" = Yes)

Financial Services:	Information/Publ.:	Technology:	Services:	Retailing:	Telecommunications:	
Stock Brokerage	Portal/Hub/News	Computer Manuf.	Payments/Transfers	Retailer	Internet Serv. Provider	Y
Mortgages/Loans	On-Line Community	Networking Equip.	Consulting	Auctions	Web Site Host	
Banking	Search Engine	Software Manuf.	Advertising/Marketing	Mall	Server Farm	
Insurance	Financial Data Publ.	Specialty Equipment	Outsourcing	Tickets/Travel	Specialty Telecom.	
Credit Cards	Broadcasting/Music			Price Comparisons	High Speed Access	Y

TYPES OF BUSINESS:

Internet Service Provider

BRANDS/DIVISIONS/AFFILIATES:

GROWTH PLANS/SPECIAL FEATURES:

Splitrock Services, Inc. is a provider of high speed Internet dial access services on a nationwide network. This network is based on Asynchronous Transfer Mode (ATM) switching technology, which is deployed in every point of presence (POP) of the network. The deployment of ATM switches throughout the network enables the company to serve as a broad-based Internet Service Provider (ISP). Through the creation of a multi-service platform, the company efficiently delivers Internet Protocol (IP), frame relay and Internet services. This flexibility allows the company to expand its service offerings to provide fully integrated data, video and voice services and to incorporate future technological innovations into its network architecture with a lower incremental investment than that required by other less flexible networks. In addition, the company currently provides nationwide Internet dial access and related services to Prodigy Communications Corporation. Splitrock is also providing Internet dedicated access (transit), web hosting and virtual private network (VPN) services to other businesses. Recently, the company began constructing and installing its advance nationwide network, designed to have a physical presence in all 50 states and targeting 90% of U.S. businesses and households, which it can reach with V.90 modem access. The company expects to achieve its planned coverage with approximately 370 POPs by the end of 2000.

CONTACTS: Note: Officers with more than one job title may be intentionally listed here more than once.

William R. Wilson, CEO
J. Robert Fugate, CFO
David M. Boatner, Exec. VP/Chief Mktg. Officer
Daryl Krimsky, Head of Human Resources
Larry A. Walberg, Sr.VP-Network Oper.
Todd W. Wilkens, Sr.VP-Engineering
Partrick J. McGettigan Jr., Sr. VP-Sec.
Patrick J. McGettigan Jr., General Counsel

Phone: 281-465-1200	Fax: 281-364-6668
Toll-Free:	
Address: 8665 New Trails Dr., The Woodlands, TX, 77381	

FINANCIALS: Sales and profits are in thousands of dollars—add 000 to get the full amount.
Notes regarding 1999: Through 9 months (1999 sales and profits were not available for all companies at press time.)

1999 Sales: $57,944	1999 Profits: $-77,380	Stock Ticker: **SPLT**
1998 Sales: $63,600	1998 Profits: $-57,800	Employees: 265
1997 Sales: $22,700	1997 Profits: $-10,100	Fiscal Year Ends: 12/31
1996 Sales: $	1996 Profits: $	
1995 Sales: $	1995 Profits: $	

SALARIES/BENEFITS:

Pension Plan:	ESOP Stock Plan:	Profit Sharing:	Top Exec. Salary: $151,440	Bonus: $
Savings Plan:	Stock Purch. Plan:		Second Exec. Salary: $150,833	Bonus: $

COMPETITIVE ADVANTAGE: High speed, flexible and multi-service platform.

OTHER THOUGHTS:

Apparent Women Officers or Directors:
Apparent Minority Officers or Directors: 1
Hot Spot for Advancement for Women/Minorities:

LOCATIONS: ("Y" = Yes)

West:	Southwest:	Midwest:	Southeast:	Northeast:	International:
	Y				

SPORTSLINE USA
www.cbs.sportsline.com

Industry Group Code: 514191
Ranks within this company's industry group: Sales: 8 Profits: 40

BUSINESS ACTIVITIES ("Y" = Yes)

Financial Services:	Information/Publ.:		Technology:	Services:	Retailing:	Telecommunications:
Stock Brokerage	Portal/Hub/News	Y	Computer Manuf.	Payments/Transfers	Retailer	Internet Serv. Provider
Mortgages/Loans	On-Line Community		Networking Equip.	Consulting	Auctions	Web Site Host
Banking	Search Engine		Software Manuf.	Advertising/Marketing	Mall	Server Farm
Insurance	Financial Data Publ.		Specialty Equipment	Outsourcing	Tickets/Travel	Specialty Telecom.
Credit Cards	Broadcasting/Music	Y			Price Comparisons	High Speed Access

TYPES OF BUSINESS:
On-line Sports Information

BRANDS/DIVISIONS/AFFILIATES:
Sportsline Worldwide
cbs.sportsline.com

CONTACTS: Note: Officers with more than one job title may be intentionally listed here more than once.
Michael Levy, CEO
Kenneth W. Sanders, CFO
Lawrence D. Krueger, VP-Mktg.
Randall Hafer, Dir.-Human Resources
James W. Bracken, VP-Engineering
Dan Leichtenshlag, Sr. VP-Oper.
Andrew S. Sturner, Pres.-Corp/Business Dev.
Daniel Head, VP-E-commerce
Lawrence G. Wahl, Dir.-Corp. Comm.
Lawrence G. Wahl, Dir.-Investor Relations

Phone: 954-351-2120	Fax: 954-351-9175
Toll-Free:	
Address: 6340 N.W. 5th Way, Fort Lauderdale, FL, 33309	

GROWTH PLANS/SPECIAL FEATURES:

SportsLine USA is a leading Internet-based sports media company that provides branded, interactive information, programming and merchandise worldwide. The company produces and distributes original, interactive sports content, including editorials and analyses, radio shows, contests, games, fantasy league products and fan clubs. It also distributes a broad range of up-to-date news, scores, player and team statistics and standings, photos, audio clips and video clips obtained from CBS and other leading sports news organizations. Sportsline offers some 400,000 pages of continuously updated coverage on collegiate and professional sports on its flagship web site, cbs.sportsline.com. The company believes that its relationship with CBS will enable it to establish SportsLine as a broadly recognized worldwide consumer brand. SportsLine also has distribution agreements and relationships with American Online, Excite, Netscape, InfoSpace.com, Microsoft and Sports Byline USA. Sportsline generates nearly 60% of sales from advertising. Membership subscriptions, e-commerce and licensing account for the remainder of sales. Recently, the company launched SportsLine WorldWide, a separate web site dedicated to providing comprehensive coverage of international news.

FINANCIALS: Sales and profits are in thousands of dollars—add 000 to get the full amount.
Notes regarding 1999: (1999 sales and profits were not available for all companies at press time.)

1999 Sales: $21,042	1999 Profits: $-17,097	Stock Ticker: **SPLN**
1998 Sales: $30,600	1998 Profits: $-35,500	Employees: 303
1997 Sales: $10,300	1997 Profits: $-26,500	Fiscal Year Ends: 12/31
1996 Sales: $2,400	1996 Profits: $-12,900	
1995 Sales: $ 100	1995 Profits: $-5,300	

SALARIES/BENEFITS:

Pension Plan:	ESOP Stock Plan:	Profit Sharing:	Top Exec. Salary: $306,250	Bonus: $105,000
Savings Plan: Y	Stock Purch. Plan: Y		Second Exec. Salary: $225,000	Bonus: $72,717

COMPETITIVE ADVANTAGE: Alliance with CBS.

OTHER THOUGHTS:
Apparent Women Officers or Directors:
Apparent Minority Officers or Directors:
Hot Spot for Advancement for Women/Minorities:

LOCATIONS: ("Y" = Yes)

West:	Southwest:	Midwest:	Southeast:	Northeast:	International:
Y		Y	Y	Y	Y

Note: Financial information, benefits and other data can change quickly and may vary from those stated here.

SPYGLASS www.spyglass.com

Industry Group Code: 5112
Ranks within this company's industry group: Sales: 37   Profits: 44

BUSINESS ACTIVITIES ("Y" = Yes)

Financial Services:	Information/Publ.:	Technology:		Services:		Retailing:		Telecommunications:
Stock Brokerage	Portal/Hub/News	Computer Manuf.		Payments/Transfers		Retailer		Internet Serv. Provider
Mortgages/Loans	On-Line Community	Networking Equip.		Consulting	Y	Auctions		Web Site Host
Banking	Search Engine	Software Manuf.	Y	Advertising/Marketing		Mall		Server Farm
Insurance	Financial Data Publ.	Specialty Equipment		Outsourcing	Y	Tickets/Travel		Specialty Telecom.
Credit Cards	Broadcasting/Music					Price Comparisons		High Speed Access

TYPES OF BUSINESS:

Software
Custom Application Development

BRANDS/DIVISIONS/AFFILIATES:

Spyglass Mobile Forms Database
Spyglass Device Mail
Spyglass ThinGUI Library
Spyglass Device Mosaic
NetHopper
Prism
Navitel Communications, Inc.
SurfWatch

CONTACTS: Note: Officers with more than one job title may be intentionally listed here more than once.

Douglas P. Colbeth, CEO
Martin Leamy, COO/Pres.
Gary L. Vilchick, CFO
Susan L. Kizman, Dir.-Human Resources
Daryl Dahlberg, VP-Info Systems
Gary L. Vilchick, Exec.VP-Oper. and Admin.
Michael F. Tyrrell, Exec.VP-Business Dev.
Christian T. Nall, VP-Worldwide Business Dev.

Phone: 630-505-1010	Fax: 630-505-4944
Toll-Free:	
Address: 1240 E. Diehl Rd., 4th Fl., Naperville, IL, 605663	

GROWTH PLANS/SPECIAL FEATURES:

Spyglass, Inc. entered the Internet market in 1994 to develop, market and distribute Internet client and server technologies for integration into a variety of Internet-based software products and services. The company provides its customers with expertise, software and professional services that enable them to rapidly develop cost effective Internet-enabled information appliances. Spyglass' professional services include custom engineering for defining, developing and delivering complete, end-to-end project solutions. Recently, the company reorganized its business to integrate its development, professional services and marketing resources, which allowed Spyglass to target its tailored solutions to the needs of the various vertical markets within the Internet information appliance marketplace. The company has increased its focus on Interactive Television and Mobile Data Services vertical markets. Spyglass solutions have been integrated into exciting new categories of products, including television set-top boxes, screen and cellular phones, office equipment, medical devices and industrial controls. Several major corporations, schools and ITV service providers have bought the company's SurfWatch, a leading content filtering software designed to block unwanted material from the Internet. Spyglass and Microsoft Corporation entered into an agreement under which Spyglass licensed technology and will provide services for a three-year period to Microsoft. Spyglass will develop and integrate multiple Windows CE-based applications for Internet information appliance manufacturers that are developing products utilizing the Windows CE operating system. Recently, Spyglass acquired Navitel Communications, Inc.

FINANCIALS: Sales and profits are in thousands of dollars—add 000 to get the full amount.

Notes regarding 1999: (1999 sales and profits were not available for all companies at press time.)

1999 Sales: $29,610	1999 Profits: $-3,279	Stock Ticker: **SPYG**
1998 Sales: $20,500	1998 Profits: $-8,000	Employees: 164
1997 Sales: $21,300	1997 Profits: $-9,700	Fiscal Year Ends: 9/30
1996 Sales: $22,300	1996 Profits: $3,500	
1995 Sales: $12,100	1995 Profits: $2,200	

SALARIES/BENEFITS:

Pension Plan:	ESOP Stock Plan:	Profit Sharing:	Top Exec. Salary: $190,000	Bonus: $
Savings Plan: Y	Stock Purch. Plan:		Second Exec. Salary: $116,250	Bonus: $149,791

COMPETITIVE ADVANTAGE: Focus on emerging markets such as wireless access providers/Alliance with Microsoft.

OTHER THOUGHTS:

Apparent Women Officers or Directors: 2
Apparent Minority Officers or Directors:
Hot Spot for Advancement for Women/Minorities:

LOCATIONS: ("Y" = Yes)

West:	Southwest:	Midwest:	Southeast:	Northeast:	International:
Y				Y	Y

Note: Financial information, benefits and other data can change quickly and may vary from those stated here.

STAMPS.COM   www.stamps.com

Industry Group Code: 51339A
Ranks within this company's industry group: Sales: 13   Profits: 3

BUSINESS ACTIVITIES ("Y" = Yes)

Financial Services:	Information/Publ.:	Technology:		Services:	Retailing:	Telecommunications:
Stock Brokerage	Portal/Hub/News	Computer Manuf.		Payments/Transfers	Retailer	Internet Serv. Provider
Mortgages/Loans	On-Line Community	Networking Equip.		Consulting	Auctions	Web Site Host
Banking	Search Engine	Software Manuf.		Advertising/Marketing	Mall	Server Farm
Insurance	Financial Data Publ.	Specialty Equipment	Y	Outsourcing	Tickets/Travel	Specialty Telecom.
Credit Cards	Broadcasting/Music				Price Comparisons	High Speed Access

TYPES OF BUSINESS:
On-line Postage Stamps

BRANDS/DIVISIONS/AFFILIATES:
EncrypTix Inc.

CONTACTS: *Note: Officers with more than one job title may be intentionally listed here more than once.*
John M. Payne, CEO
Loren Smith, Pres./COO
John W. LaValle, CFO
Jeffrey L. Green, VP-Mktg.
Lanchi Dan, Mgr.-Human Resources
Candelario J. Andalon, Corp. Controller
John W. LaValle, Corp. Sec.
John W. LaValle, Sr.VP-Oper.
Douglas J. Walner, VP-Business Dev.
Ari Engelberg, VP-Web Oper.

Phone: 310-450-1444	Fax: 310-450-3474
Toll-Free:	
Address: 2900 31st St., Ste. 150, Santa Monica, CA, 90405	

GROWTH PLANS/SPECIAL FEATURES:

Stamps.com provides a convenient and cost-effective way to purchase and print postage through the Internet, and the company is a participant in the United States Postal Service's Information-Based Indicia Program. The United States Postal Service provides regulation for financial and security protocols established by Stamps.com. Stamps.com's service can be accessed 24-hours daily, with only an Internet-enabled personal computer and laser or ink-jet printer needed to start printing postage. The service also comes with instant on-line address correction, and the free software integrates with existing address books, including Microsoft Outlook. The company has received numerous outstanding reviews and awards, including a ranking in PC Magazine's Top 100 Websites and PC Computing's MVP Winner for Business Services. The company recently released a new pricing plan, called the Simple Plan, which enhances the company's existing two-tiered pricing structure. In addition to the new plan, Stamps.com has used various marketing techniques, including a free trial offer and $25 in postage for new customers. The company also announced the formation of EncrypTix Inc., a new subsidiary created to serve the needs of the travel and financial industries, which prints tickets, vouchers and certificates securely over the Internet.

FINANCIALS: Sales and profits are in thousands of dollars—add 000 to get the full amount.
Notes regarding 1999: *(1999 sales and profits were not available for all companies at press time.)*

1999 Sales: $ 357	1999 Profits: $-56,487	Stock Ticker: **STMP**
1998 Sales: $ 100	1998 Profits: $4,200	Employees: 77
1997 Sales: $	1997 Profits: $	Fiscal Year Ends: 12/31
1996 Sales: $	1996 Profits: $	
1995 Sales: $	1995 Profits: $	

SALARIES/BENEFITS:

Pension Plan:	ESOP Stock Plan:	Profit Sharing:	Top Exec. Salary: $	Bonus: $
Savings Plan:	Stock Purch. Plan:		Second Exec. Salary: $	Bonus: $

COMPETITIVE ADVANTAGE: This company is going after an enormous market currently dominated by Pitney Bowes.

OTHER THOUGHTS:

Apparent Women Officers or Directors: 1
Apparent Minority Officers or Directors: 2
Hot Spot for Advancement for Women/Minorities: Y

LOCATIONS: ("Y" = Yes)

West:	Southwest:	Midwest:	Southeast:	Northeast:	International:
Y	Y				Y

STARMEDIA NETWORK   www.starmedia.com

Industry Group Code: 514191
Ranks within this company's industry group: Sales: 21   Profits: 42

BUSINESS ACTIVITIES ("Y" = Yes)

Financial Services:	Information/Publ.:		Technology:	Services:	Retailing:	Telecommunications:	
Stock Brokerage	Portal/Hub/News	Y	Computer Manuf.	Payments/Transfers	Retailer	Internet Serv. Provider	Y
Mortgages/Loans	On-Line Community	Y	Networking Equip.	Consulting	Auctions	Web Site Host	Y
Banking	Search Engine	Y	Software Manuf.	Advertising/Marketing	Mall	Server Farm	
Insurance	Financial Data Publ.		Specialty Equipment	Outsourcing	Tickets/Travel	Specialty Telecom.	
Credit Cards	Broadcasting/Music				Price Comparisons	High Speed Access	

TYPES OF BUSINESS:
Portal-Latin

BRANDS/DIVISIONS/AFFILIATES:

GROWTH PLANS/SPECIAL FEATURES:

StarMedia Network, Inc. offers Spanish and Portuguese speaking Internet users the ability to go on-line with Latin America's largest web portal. The company's web site features regionally oriented sites that provide news, free e-mail, home pages and chat rooms to visitors from over 20 countries. The Spanish and Portuguese content is tailored for regional dialects and local cultural norms. StarMedia also provides advertisers and merchants with a demographic user base targeted toward Latin American Internet users. The company's network provides 16 interest-specific channels, extensive community features, sophisticated search capabilities and on-line shopping in Spanish and Portuguese.

CONTACTS:
Note: Officers with more than one job title may be intentionally listed here more than once.

Fernando J. Espuelas, CEO
Tracy J. Leeds, COO
Steven J. Heller, VP-Finance
Gary Bonilla-Latoni, VP-Mktg.
Tyrone Fripp, Human Resources
James D. Granlund, Chief Tech. Officer
Steven J. Heller, VP-Admin.
Gary Bonilla-Lotoni, VP-Strategic Planning
Romi Schutzer, VP-Corporate Relations

Phone: 212-548-9600	**Fax:** 212-631-9100
Toll-Free:	
Address: 29 W. 36th., 5th Fl., New York, NY, 10018	

FINANCIALS:
Sales and profits are in thousands of dollars—add 000 to get the full amount.
Notes regarding 1999: *(1999 sales and profits were not available for all companies at press time.)*

1999 Sales: $20,089	1999 Profits: $-90,673	Stock Ticker: **STRM**
1998 Sales: $5,300	1998 Profits: $-45,900	Employees: 247
1997 Sales: $ 500	1997 Profits: $-3,500	Fiscal Year Ends: 12/31
1996 Sales: $	1996 Profits: $- 100	
1995 Sales: $	1995 Profits: $	

SALARIES/BENEFITS:

Pension Plan:	ESOP Stock Plan: Y	Profit Sharing:	Top Exec. Salary: $152,084	Bonus: $200,000
Savings Plan:	Stock Purch. Plan:		Second Exec. Salary: $152,104	Bonus: $200,000

COMPETITIVE ADVANTAGE: Focus on the immense Latin market.

OTHER THOUGHTS:

Apparent Women Officers or Directors: 4
Apparent Minority Officers or Directors: 5
Hot Spot for Advancement for Women/Minorities: Y

LOCATIONS: ("Y" = Yes)

West:	Southwest:	Midwest:	Southeast:	Northeast:	International:
				Y	

STARTRONIX
www.startronix.com

Industry Group Code: 33421
Ranks within this company's industry group: Sales: Profits:

BUSINESS ACTIVITIES ("Y" = Yes)

Financial Services:	Information/Publ.:	Technology:		Services:	Retailing:	Telecommunications:	
Stock Brokerage	Portal/Hub/News	Computer Manuf.		Payments/Transfers	Retailer	Internet Serv. Provider	
Mortgages/Loans	On-Line Community	Networking Equip.		Consulting	Auctions	Web Site Host	
Banking	Search Engine	Software Manuf.	Y	Advertising/Marketing	Mall	Server Farm	
Insurance	Financial Data Publ.	Specialty Equipment	Y	Outsourcing	Tickets/Travel	Specialty Telecom.	Y
Credit Cards	Broadcasting/Music				Price Comparisons	High Speed Access	

TYPES OF BUSINESS:

Internet Screen Telephone
Internet Appliance

BRANDS/DIVISIONS/AFFILIATES:

StarTronix eSolutions
StarScreen System

CONTACTS: Note: Officers with more than one job title may be intentionally listed here more than once.

Lloyd N. Adams, Co-CEO
Greg Gilbert, Pres.
Kevin Sorenson, Investor Relations

Phone: 949-727-7420	Fax:
Toll-Free:	
Address: 7700 Irvine Center Drive, Ste. 510, Irvine, CA, 92618	

GROWTH PLANS/SPECIAL FEATURES:

StarTronix International markets technological and Internet-related products and services to private label users and the home-based business industry. Through StarTronix eSolutions, the company is responsible for designing, developing and supporting technology for the StarScreen System. Starscreen is a unique telephone set that features a small screen with which to view the Internet. Customers can use StarScreen with the touch of a button for banking, home shopping, video conferencing, Internet phone calling, home automation and emergency response services. The StarScreen system provides small business communications and e-commerce solutions, including the ability to process credit and debit cards on its built-in card reader, the integration of a two-line speakerphone and digital fax software. The system also provides on-line services that include web-site set-up, on-line storefront creation, merchant account set-up and secure payment processing. This fully-fuctional system can be particularly useful to small businesses that do not have extensive technology departments in-house, or to home users who want to access a unique set of services.

FINANCIALS: Sales and profits are in thousands of dollars—add 000 to get the full amount.
Notes regarding 1999: (1999 sales and profits were not available for all companies at press time.)

1999 Sales: $	1999 Profits: $	Stock Ticker: **STNX**
1998 Sales: $	1998 Profits: $	Employees:
1997 Sales: $	1997 Profits: $	Fiscal Year Ends:
1996 Sales: $	1996 Profits: $	
1995 Sales: $	1995 Profits: $	

SALARIES/BENEFITS:

Pension Plan:	ESOP Stock Plan:	Profit Sharing:	Top Exec. Salary: $164,650	Bonus: $
Savings Plan:	Stock Purch. Plan:		Second Exec. Salary: $	Bonus: $

COMPETITIVE ADVANTAGE: Interactive system that appeals to a wide range of customers.

OTHER THOUGHTS:

Apparent Women Officers or Directors:
Apparent Minority Officers or Directors:
Hot Spot for Advancement for Women/Minorities:

LOCATIONS: ("Y" = Yes)

West:	Southwest:	Midwest:	Southeast:	Northeast:	International:
Y			Y		

STUDENT ADVANTAGE   www.studentadvantage.com

Industry Group Code: 514191
Ranks within this company's industry group: Sales: 11   Profits: 22

BUSINESS ACTIVITIES ("Y" = Yes)

Financial Services:	Information/Publ.:		Technology:	Services:	Retailing:	Telecommunications:
Stock Brokerage	Portal/Hub/News	Y	Computer Manuf.	Payments/Transfers	Retailer	Internet Serv. Provider
Mortgages/Loans	On-Line Community		Networking Equip.	Consulting	Auctions	Web Site Host
Banking	Search Engine		Software Manuf.	Advertising/Marketing	Mall	Server Farm
Insurance	Financial Data Publ.		Specialty Equipment	Outsourcing	Tickets/Travel	Specialty Telecom.
Credit Cards	Broadcasting/Music				Price Comparisons	High Speed Access

TYPES OF BUSINESS:

Portal-College Students
News Service

BRANDS/DIVISIONS/AFFILIATES:

U-WIRE

CONTACTS: Note: Officers with more than one job title may be intentionally listed here more than once.

Raymond V. Sozzl Jr., CEO/Pres.
Ronald J. Kos, Pres.
Chistopher B. Andrews, CFO/VP-Finance
Kevin Watters, VP-Mktg.
Jennifer Bowen, Sr. Associate-Human Resources
Mason Myers, VP-Business Dev.
Andrea K. Abegglen, VP-Mktg. Comm.

Phone: 617-912-2011	Fax: 617-912-2019
Toll-Free:	
Address: 280 Summer St., Boston, MA, 02210	

GROWTH PLANS/SPECIAL FEATURES:

Student Advantage is a comprehensive on-line resource for college students that features information on numerous subjects, such as careers, health, money and travel. Student Advantage runs a national fee-based membership program that has a variety of benefits to members, including discounts on products and services offered by 40 national partners like AT&T, Foot Locker, Greyhound, Staples and Tower Records. Members also get other benefits, such as web-based e-mail, a full-feature address book, 15 MB of storage and file sharing. The membership program currently has over one million members. Student Advantage publishes U-WIRE, a daily, on-line, student-written news service that connects members across the county. In recent news, Student Advantage announced a marketing and content agreement with Mascot Network, Inc., a new provider of on-line student centers. Under the agreement, Student Advantage will offer content briefs from its U-WIRE news service, and Mascot Network will feature promotions for the Student Advantage Membership Program. According to Student Monitor LLC, the only nationally syndicated market research study of the college student market, Student Advantage's web site is the most visited web destination for students. The company's publication, Student Advantage Magazine, was also the most frequently read student-focused publication in the college market. CEO Raymond Sozzi was awarded a Young Entrepreneur of the Year award from Ernst and Young.

FINANCIALS: Sales and profits are in thousands of dollars—add 000 to get the full amount.

Notes regarding 1999: *(1999 sales and profits were not available for all companies at press time.)*

1999 Sales: $	1999 Profits: $	Stock Ticker: **STAD**
1998 Sales: $17,400	1998 Profits: $-5,100	Employees: 175
1997 Sales: $3,800	1997 Profits: $-3,200	Fiscal Year Ends: 12/31
1996 Sales: $1,700	1996 Profits: $- 700	
1995 Sales: $ 400	1995 Profits: $	

SALARIES/BENEFITS:

Pension Plan:	ESOP Stock Plan:	Profit Sharing:	Top Exec. Salary: $	Bonus: $
Savings Plan: Y	Stock Purch. Plan:		Second Exec. Salary: $	Bonus: $

COMPETITIVE ADVANTAGE: College students are among the most active groups on the Internet.

OTHER THOUGHTS:

Apparent Women Officers or Directors: 2
Apparent Minority Officers or Directors:
Hot Spot for Advancement for Women/Minorities:

LOCATIONS: ("Y" = Yes)

West:	Southwest:	Midwest:	Southeast:	Northeast:	International:
Y		Y	Y	Y	

SUN MICROSYSTEMS INC   www.sun.com

Industry Group Code: 3341A
Ranks within this company's industry group: Sales: 5   Profits: 4

BUSINESS ACTIVITIES ("Y" = Yes)

Financial Services:	Information/Publ.:	Technology:		Services:	Retailing:	Telecommunications:
Stock Brokerage	Portal/Hub/News	Computer Manuf.	Y	Payments/Transfers	Retailer	Internet Serv. Provider
Mortgages/Loans	On-Line Community	Networking Equip.	Y	Consulting	Auctions	Web Site Host
Banking	Search Engine	Software Manuf.	Y	Advertising/Marketing	Mall	Server Farm
Insurance	Financial Data Publ.	Specialty Equipment		Outsourcing	Tickets/Travel	Specialty Telecom.
Credit Cards	Broadcasting/Music				Price Comparisons	High Speed Access

TYPES OF BUSINESS:

UNIX-based Computer Manufacturer
Workstations
Multiprocessing Servers
Operating System Software
Systems Integration
Office Application Software

BRANDS/DIVISIONS/AFFILIATES:

Sun Microsystems Computer Company
SunService Division
SunSoft, Inc.
Sun Microelectronics
JavaSoft
SPARC Technology
SunSoft, Inc.
Lucent Technologies

CONTACTS: Note: Officers with more than one job title may be intentionally listed here more than once.

Scott G. McNealy, Pres./CEO
Edward J. Zander, COO/Pres.
Michael E. Lehman, VP/CFO
Edward Saliba, VP-Human Resources
Gregory M. Papadopolous, Chief Tech. Officer
H. William Howard, VP/CIO
Michael H. Morris, Sec.
Michael H. Morris, General Counsel

Phone: 650-960-1300	Fax: 650-336-0646
Toll-Free: 800-801-7869	
Address: 901 San Antonio Road, Palo Alto, CA, 94303	

GROWTH PLANS/SPECIAL FEATURES:

Sun Microsystems, Inc. is a worldwide provider of products, services and support solutions for building and maintaining network computing environments. The company sells scalable computer systems, high-speed microprocessors and a complete line of high performance software for operating network computing equipment and storage products. Sun also provides a full range of support, education and professional services. The company's products and services command a significant share of the rapidly growing network computing market, which includes the Internet and corporate intranets. Sun's products are used for many demanding commercial and technical applications in various industries, including telecommunications, manufacturing, financial services, education, retail, government, energy and healthcare. Much of the company's success comes from its adherence to open industry standards, the Solaris Operating Environment, the UNIX platform and the UltraSPARC (Ultra Scalable Processor Architecture) microprocessor architecture. Sun recently allied with Lucent Technologies to create infrastructure to support next-generation Internet business applications that will speed delivery of next-generation electronic business services. Sun's new Star Office software suite runs on a server/thin client network, offering full functionality similar to that of Microsoft Office.

The company offers a variety of wellness programs, and on-site training facilities. Of Sun's officials and managers, 20.6% are minorities, and 28.7% of the employees in the entire work force are minorities. Employees enjoy generous salaries, excellent benefits and spot bonuses averaging $2,300. Two thirds of the work force are younger than 40. Sun, which hires 6,000 people annually, is developing Internet links to schools with which it has strong recruting ties, including three historically black colleges: Florida A&M, Howard and Southern. The company's workforce is trained for about 48 hours out of the year. The company also offers rooms for rest and meditation, table tennis, pinball or trash-can basketball. Dress at the office is casual.

FINANCIALS: Sales and profits are in thousands of dollars—add 000 to get the full amount.

Notes regarding 1999: *(1999 sales and profits were not available for all companies at press time.)*

1999 Sales: $11,726,300	1999 Profits: $1,031,300	Stock Ticker: **SUNW**
1998 Sales: $9,790,800	1998 Profits: $762,900	Employees: 29,000
1997 Sales: $8,598,300	1997 Profits: $762,400	Fiscal Year Ends: 6/30
1996 Sales: $7,094,800	1996 Profits: $476,400	
1995 Sales: $5,901,900	1995 Profits: $355,800	

SALARIES/BENEFITS:

Pension Plan:	ESOP Stock Plan:	Profit Sharing:	Top Exec. Salary: $698,846	Bonus: $998,760
Savings Plan:	Stock Purch. Plan: Y		Second Exec. Salary: $665,192	Bonus: $522,467

COMPETITIVE ADVANTAGE: World class workstations and servers based on superior technology/Exciting new Star Office product line.

OTHER THOUGHTS:

	LOCATIONS: ("Y" = Yes)					
Apparent Women Officers or Directors:	West:	Southwest:	Midwest:	Southeast:	Northeast:	International:
Apparent Minority Officers or Directors: 5	Y	Y	Y	Y	Y	Y
Hot Spot for Advancement for Women/Minorities: Y						

Note: Financial information, benefits and other data can change quickly and may vary from those stated here.

TALK CITY
www.talkcity.com

Industry Group Code: 514191
Ranks within this company's industry group: Sales: 33   Profits: 37

BUSINESS ACTIVITIES ("Y" = Yes)

Financial Services:	Information/Publ.:		Technology:	Services:		Retailing:	Telecommunications:	
Stock Brokerage	Portal/Hub/News	Y	Computer Manuf.	Payments/Transfers		Retailer	Internet Serv. Provider	Y
Mortgages/Loans	On-Line Community	Y	Networking Equip.	Consulting		Auctions	Web Site Host	
Banking	Search Engine		Software Manuf.	Advertising/Marketing		Mall	Server Farm	
Insurance	Financial Data Publ.		Specialty Equipment	Outsourcing	Y	Tickets/Travel	Specialty Telecom.	
Credit Cards	Broadcasting/Music					Price Comparisons	High Speed Access	

TYPES OF BUSINESS:

Diversified Portal
On-line Communities
On-line Events

BRANDS/DIVISIONS/AFFILIATES:

GROWTH PLANS/SPECIAL FEATURES:

Talk City, Inc. is a leading Internet provider of high quality on-line communities and interactive services for businesses and consumers. The company's services offer businesses the ability to develop and expand on-line relationships with customers, suppliers and employees. Services offered to business customers include designing fully integrated, customized communities, producing on-line events, conducting on-line market research and facilitating on-line meetings. Talk City provides consumers with a network of on-line communities that include 20 topical categories, over 50 themed communities, 50 co-branded partner communities and thousands of user-generated communities. These user-generated communities provide home pages, moderated chat, special event production, message boards and on-line event guides. Talk City's community network is family-oriented; the nature of the community is based around a set of published behavior standards, which are maintained by trained City standards advisors who can be called upon at any time to resolve issues relating to standards violations. This provides a clean, attractive environment for businesses, advertisers, partners and consumers.

CONTACTS:
Note: Officers with more than one job title may be intentionally listed here more than once.

Peter H. Friedman, CEO
Peter H. Friedman, Pres.
Jeffrey Snetiker, CFO
Christopher J Escher, VP-Mktg.
Christine Walker, Dir.-Human Resources
Chris N. Christensen, VP-Engineering
Arwyn Bryant, VP-Business Oper.
Daniel Paul, VP-Business Dev.
Jenna Woodul, VP-Community

Phone: 408-871-5200	Fax: 408-871-5303
Toll-Free:	
Address: 307 Orchard City Drive., Ste. 350, Campbell, CA, 95008	

FINANCIALS:
Sales and profits are in thousands of dollars—add 000 to get the full amount.
Notes regarding 1999: *(1999 sales and profits were not available for all companies at press time.)*

1999 Sales: $7,700	1999 Profits: $-40,107	Stock Ticker: **TCTY**
1998 Sales: $1,500	1998 Profits: $-15,700	Employees: 82
1997 Sales: $ 200	1997 Profits: $-6,400	Fiscal Year Ends: 12/31
1996 Sales: $	1996 Profits: $-1,300	
1995 Sales: $	1995 Profits: $	

SALARIES/BENEFITS:

Pension Plan:	ESOP Stock Plan: Y	Profit Sharing:	Top Exec. Salary: $225,000	Bonus: $
Savings Plan: Y	Stock Purch. Plan:		Second Exec. Salary: $150,000	Bonus: $

COMPETITIVE ADVANTAGE:
Enables web site owners to offer complete community environments.

OTHER THOUGHTS:

Apparent Women Officers or Directors: 3
Apparent Minority Officers or Directors:
Hot Spot for Advancement for Women/Minorities: Y

LOCATIONS: ("Y" = Yes)

West:	Southwest:	Midwest:	Southeast:	Northeast:	International:
Y		Y		Y	

TANDY CORP   www.tandy.com

Industry Group Code: 443
Ranks within this company's industry group: Sales: 1   Profits: 1

BUSINESS ACTIVITIES ("Y" = Yes)

Financial Services:	Information/Publ.:	Technology:	Services:	Retailing:		Telecommunications:	
Stock Brokerage	Portal/Hub/News	Computer Manuf.	Payments/Transfers	Retailer	Y	Internet Serv. Provider	
Mortgages/Loans	On-Line Community	Networking Equip.	Consulting	Auctions		Web Site Host	
Banking	Search Engine	Software Manuf.	Advertising/Marketing	Mall		Server Farm	
Insurance	Financial Data Publ.	Specialty Equipment	Outsourcing	Tickets/Travel		Specialty Telecom.	Y
Credit Cards	Broadcasting/Music			Price Comparisons		High Speed Access	Y

TYPES OF BUSINESS:

Retail-Electronics, Audio and Appliance Stores
Cellular Telephone Sales and Retail Distribution (Sprint PCS)
Internet Services Retail Sales and Distribution (Northpoint Comm.)
Audio and Video Equipment Distribution (Sony and Radio Shack)
Personal Computer Sales (Compaq)

BRANDS/DIVISIONS/AFFILIATES:

Radio Shack
Sprint Store at Radio Shack

CONTACTS: Note: Officers with more than one job title may be intentionally listed here more than once.

Leonard H. Roberts, CEO
Leonard H. Roberts, Pres.
Dwain H. Hughes, CFO/Sr. VP
George J. Berger, VP-Human Resources
Evelyn V. Follit, CIO
Marck C. Hill, Corp. Sec.
Ronald L. Parrish, VP-Corp. Dev.

Phone: 817-415-3700	**Fax:** 817-415-2647

Toll-Free:

Address: 100 Throckmorton St., Ste. 1800, Fort Worth, TX, 76102

GROWTH PLANS/SPECIAL FEATURES:

Tandy Corporation is one of the largest retailers of consumer electronics in the United States, selling its products through approximately 7,000 Radio Shack stores nationwide. The firm recently sold its Computer City stores and has closed its Incredible Universe stores. Radio Shack carries a broad assortment of major brand name and private label electronic parts and accessories, audio/video equipment, digital satellite systems, personal computers, cellular and conventional telephones, scanners, electronic toys and hard-to-find batteries. Radio Shack recently expanded its company owned store base to 5,000 locations (many stores are franchised). Radio Shack is also focusing on the introduction of the Sprint Store at RadioShack. The firm's strength today lies in its new strategy of creating strategic alliances with makers of well known and popular brands. In exchange for exclusive nationwide distribution through 7,000 stores, companies like Compaq and Sprint pay Radio Shack handsome fees and royalties. In addition to selling personal computers and cellular phone service through such deals, Radio Shack offers Internet service (through Northpoint Communications Group) as well as television, audio and video equipment made by Sony. Radio Shack's Internet service offerings are, in fact, a current main focus. Through partnerships with Sprint ION and Amerilink, Tandy is dedicated to delivering speedy home connectivity services. Tandy received a $100 million investment from Microsoft Corporation, designed to support RadioShack.com. Through the partnership with Microsoft, consumers will be able to purchase WebTV, pocket PCs and net access in a store-within-a-store format. Radio Shack and Microsoft have plans to combine their marketing forces.

Company employees may use the on-site fitness center at a reduced cost and receive day care center discounts.

FINANCIALS: Sales and profits are in thousands of dollars—add 000 to get the full amount.

Notes regarding 1999: *(1999 sales and profits were not available for all companies at press time.)*

1999 Sales: $	1999 Profits: $	**Stock Ticker: TAN**
1998 Sales: $4,787,900	1998 Profits: $61,300	Employees: 38,200
1997 Sales: $5,372,200	1997 Profits: $-186,900	Fiscal Year Ends: 12/31
1996 Sales: $6,285,500	1996 Profits: $-91,600	
1995 Sales: $	1995 Profits: $	

SALARIES/BENEFITS:

Pension Plan:	ESOP Stock Plan: Y	Profit Sharing:	Top Exec. Salary: $810,000	Bonus: $810,000
Savings Plan: Y	Stock Purch. Plan:		Second Exec. Salary: $610,000	Bonus: $610,000

COMPETITIVE ADVANTAGE: Nationwide chain/Alliances with major name brand manufacturers and service providers.

OTHER THOUGHTS:

Apparent Women Officers or Directors: 3
Apparent Minority Officers or Directors: 1
Hot Spot for Advancement for Women/Minorities: Y

LOCATIONS: ("Y" = Yes)

West:	Southwest:	Midwest:	Southeast:	Northeast:	International:
Y	Y	Y	Y	Y	

TANNING TECHNOLOGY   www.tanning.com

Industry Group Code: 5112
Ranks within this company's industry group: Sales: 28   Profits: 14

BUSINESS ACTIVITIES ("Y" = Yes)

Financial Services:	Information/Publ.:	Technology:	Services:	Retailing:	Telecommunications:
Stock Brokerage	Portal/Hub/News	Computer Manuf.	Payments/Transfers	Retailer	Internet Serv. Provider
Mortgages/Loans	On-Line Community	Networking Equip.	Consulting	Auctions	Web Site Host
Banking	Search Engine	Software Manuf. Y	Advertising/Marketing	Mall	Server Farm
Insurance	Financial Data Publ.	Specialty Equipment	Outsourcing	Tickets/Travel	Specialty Telecom.
Credit Cards	Broadcasting/Music			Price Comparisons	High Speed Access

TYPES OF BUSINESS:

Software-Internet Solutions
Transaction Processing Software

BRANDS/DIVISIONS/AFFILIATES:

CONTACTS: *Note: Officers with more than one job title may be intentionally listed here more than once.*

Larry G. Tanning, CEO
Larry G. Tanning, Pres.
Henry F. Skelsey, CFO
John N. Piccone, VP-Mktg./Sales
Mark W. Tanning, VP-Human Resources
Louis A. D'Alessandro, VP-Tech. Services
Mark S. Whitfield, Corp. Controller
Bipin Agarwal, Sr. VP-Consulting Oper.

Phone: 303-220-9944	Fax: 303-220-9958
Toll-Free:	
Address: 4600 S. Ulster St., Ste. 380, Denver, CO, 80237	

GROWTH PLANS/SPECIAL FEATURES:

Tanning Technology is a leading information technology services provider that designs, builds and deploys enterprise solutions for companies throughout the world. The company specializes in large, complex and integrated solutions that incorporate on-line transaction processing and large databases. Internet technologies are the focus of Tanning Technology's solutions, enabling direct interaction between customers and business partners on the Internet and among employees over company intranets. The company aims toward solutions for the most challenging and critical problems for the information technology industry, including ultra-high transaction rates (up to millions per hour), large databases (including terabytes of information) and business-critical operational requirements (for reliability, scalability, flexibility and availability). The key solutions of Tanning Technology are e-commerce, enterprise customer relationship management and core operations solutions. The company's e-commerce solutions enable businesses to interact with customers, suppliers and business partners directly over the Internet. The core operations solutions improve business processes such as billing system integration and order, claim, trade and credit card transaction processing. Tanning Technology delivers solutions to the communications, financial services, media and entertainment, healthcare and logistics industries, with clients including Blockbuster, E*Trade, Federal Express, MCI Worldcom, Sprint and U.S. West.

FINANCIALS: Sales and profits are in thousands of dollars—add 000 to get the full amount.

Notes regarding 1999: *(1999 sales and profits were not available for all companies at press time.)*

1999 Sales: $58,500	1999 Profits: $2,400	Stock Ticker: **TANN**
1998 Sales: $33,300	1998 Profits: $2,300	Employees: 177
1997 Sales: $26,100	1997 Profits: $ 100	Fiscal Year Ends: 12/31
1996 Sales: $12,800	1996 Profits: $2,800	
1995 Sales: $4,800	1995 Profits: $1,000	

SALARIES/BENEFITS:

Pension Plan:	ESOP Stock Plan:	Profit Sharing:	Top Exec. Salary: $480,000	Bonus: $28,720
Savings Plan:	Stock Purch. Plan:		Second Exec. Salary: $450,000	Bonus: $

COMPETITIVE ADVANTAGE: Focus on very large databases and ultra high transaction rates.

OTHER THOUGHTS:

Apparent Women Officers or Directors: 4
Apparent Minority Officers or Directors: 1
Hot Spot for Advancement for Women/Minorities: Y

LOCATIONS: ("Y" = Yes)

West:	Southwest:	Midwest:	Southeast:	Northeast:	International:
Y	Y			Y	Y

Note: Financial information, benefits and other data can change quickly and may vary from those stated here.

TECH DATA CORP   www.techdata.com

Industry Group Code: 42143
Ranks within this company's industry group: Sales: 1   Profits: 1

BUSINESS ACTIVITIES ("Y" = Yes)

Financial Services:	Information/Publ.:	Technology:	Services:		Retailing:		Telecommunications:
Stock Brokerage	Portal/Hub/News	Computer Manuf.	Payments/Transfers		Retailer	Y	Internet Serv. Provider
Mortgages/Loans	On-Line Community	Networking Equip.	Consulting		Auctions		Web Site Host
Banking	Search Engine	Software Manuf.	Advertising/Marketing		Mall		Server Farm
Insurance	Financial Data Publ.	Specialty Equipment	Outsourcing	Y	Tickets/Travel		Specialty Telecom.
Credit Cards	Broadcasting/Music				Price Comparisons		High Speed Access

TYPES OF BUSINESS:

Computer and Sofware Distributor
Peripherals
Systems
Software

BRANDS/DIVISIONS/AFFILIATES:

Tech Data Education

CONTACTS:
Note: Officers with more than one job title may be intentionally listed here more than once.

Steven A. Raymund, CEO
Jeffery P. Howells, Exec. VP/CFO
Gerald M. Labie, Sr. VP-Mktg.
Lawrence W. Hamilton, Sr. VP-Human Resources
H. John Lochow, Exec. VP-Info.Tech. and Logistics
Arthur W. Singleton, Sec.
Arthur W. Singleton, Treas.

Phone: 727-539-7429	Fax: 727-538-7803
Toll-Free: 800-553-7976	
Address: 5350 Tech Data Dr., Clearwater, FL, 33760	

GROWTH PLANS/SPECIAL FEATURES:

Tech Data Corporation is a leading full-time distributor of computer hardware and software products worldwide. The firm, a Fortune 500 company, and its subsidiaries operate in over 30 countries, serving more than 100,000 resellers in the United States, Canada, the Caribbean, Latin America, Europe and the Middle East. In addition to distributing more than 75,000 products from over 1,000 manufacturers and publishers, Tech Data provides extensive pre- and post-sale training, service and support, as well as high-quality configuration and assembly services and a full range of electronic commerce solutions. Tech Data is becoming a premier provider of products and services to the on-line reseller channel and is also doing business with thousands of resellers via its web site, with $2 million in average daily sales. Using Tech Data's Web Customization toolkit, more than 200 resellers are conducting business electronically with their end users. The company's entire electronic catalog is made available this way and through API connections that streamline orders from reseller web sites directly to Tech Data. Recently, the company announced an industry first: its electronic software distribution (ESD) initiative, which allows resellers and vendors to easily access software titles directly from a secure location on Tech Data's web site.

FINANCIALS: Sales and profits are in thousands of dollars—add 000 to get the full amount.

Notes regarding 1999: *(1999 sales and profits were not available for all companies at press time.)*

1999 Sales: $11,529,000	1999 Profits: $129,000	**Stock Ticker: TECD**
1998 Sales: $7,056,600	1998 Profits: $89,500	Employees: 8,240
1997 Sales: $4,598,900	1997 Profits: $57,000	Fiscal Year Ends: 1/31
1996 Sales: $3,086,600	1996 Profits: $21,500	
1995 Sales: $2,418,400	1995 Profits: $34,900	

SALARIES/BENEFITS:

Pension Plan:	ESOP Stock Plan: Y	Profit Sharing:	Top Exec. Salary: $700,000	Bonus: $853,000
Savings Plan: Y	Stock Purch. Plan: Y		Second Exec. Salary: $430,000	Bonus: $315,000

COMPETITIVE ADVANTAGE: One of the world's largest and most successful full-service distributors of PC products.

OTHER THOUGHTS:

Apparent Women Officers or Directors: 1
Apparent Minority Officers or Directors: 1
Hot Spot for Advancement for Women/Minorities:

LOCATIONS: ("Y" = Yes)

West:	Southwest:	Midwest:	Southeast:	Northeast:	International:
Y	Y	Y	Y	Y	Y

TERAYON COMMUNICATION SYSTEMS
www.terayon.com

Industry Group Code: 3341C
Ranks within this company's industry group: Sales: 4   Profits: 6

BUSINESS ACTIVITIES ("Y" = Yes)

Financial Services:	Information/Publ.:	Technology:	Services:	Retailing:	Telecommunications:
Stock Brokerage	Portal/Hub/News	Computer Manuf.	Payments/Transfers	Retailer	Internet Serv. Provider
Mortgages/Loans	On-Line Community	Networking Equip. Y	Consulting	Auctions	Web Site Host
Banking	Search Engine	Software Manuf.	Advertising/Marketing	Mall	Server Farm
Insurance	Financial Data Publ.	Specialty Equipment	Outsourcing	Tickets/Travel	Specialty Telecom.
Credit Cards	Broadcasting/Music			Price Comparisons	High Speed Access

TYPES OF BUSINESS:
Two Way Data Transmission Systems
Cable Modems

BRANDS/DIVISIONS/AFFILIATES:
TeraComm
Synchronous Code Division Multiple Access (S-CDMA)
TeraLink 1000 Master Controller
TeraLink Gateway
TeraView Element Management
Provisioning Software

CONTACTS: Note: Officers with more than one job title may be intentionally listed here more than once.
Zaki Rakib, CEO
Dennis J. Picker, COO
Ray M. Fritz, CFO
De Moore, Sr. VP-Worldwide Sales
Linda Edwards, Dir.- Human Resources
Shlomo Rakib, Pres./Chief Tech. Officer
Claude Hamou, VP- Engineering
Lee Stalcup, VP- Mfg. Oper.
Gary W. Law, VP- Mktg. And Business Dev.
Gershon Schatzberg, VP- Customer Support and Service
Brain Bentley, VP- Worldwide Sales

Phone: 408-727-4400	Fax: 408-727-6205
Toll-Free:	
Address: 2952 Bunker Hill Ln., Santa Clara, CA, 95054	

GROWTH PLANS/SPECIAL FEATURES:
Terayon Communication Systems provides broadband communication systems for the delivery of advanced data and video services over cable television networks. The cable TV market offers an existing infrastructure that serves millions of homes worldwide. Terayon's advanced digital video management systems give cable, terrestrial and satellite operators flexibility in assembling customized programming line-ups, using programs from multiple sources. This allows operators to deliver a full range of programming services specifically tailored for their subscribers, including Pay-Per-View, Video-On-Demand, local advertising and data services. The company's TeraComm system is designed to enable cable operators to maximize the capacity and reliability of broadband access services over any cable plant. This allows cable operators to minimize time-consuming and costly network infrastructure upgrades, achieve reduced time-to-market and provide a wide range of service levels to residential and commercial end users. The TeraComm system is based on the company's Synchronous Code Division Multiple Access, S-CDMA, technology. The TeraComm system is comprised of the TeraPro cable modem, the TeraLink 1000 Master Controller, the TeraLink Gateway and the TeraView Element Management and Provisioning Software. Terayon's customers include Time Warner, Cox Communications, Jupiter Communications and United Pan-Europe Communications.

FINANCIALS: Sales and profits are in thousands of dollars—add 000 to get the full amount.
Notes regarding 1999: Pro forma (1999 sales and profits were not available for all companies at press time.)

1999 Sales: $97,000	1999 Profits: $-8,200	Stock Ticker: **TERN**
1998 Sales: $31,700	1998 Profits: $-23,200	Employees: 130
1997 Sales: $2,100	1997 Profits: $-22,500	Fiscal Year Ends: 12/31
1996 Sales: $	1996 Profits: $-10,700	
1995 Sales: $	1995 Profits: $-3,700	

SALARIES/BENEFITS:

Pension Plan:	ESOP Stock Plan: Y	Profit Sharing:	Top Exec. Salary: $172,500	Bonus: $
Savings Plan:	Stock Purch. Plan:		Second Exec. Salary: $153,000	Bonus: $

COMPETITIVE ADVANTAGE: Contracts with major cable firms such as Time Warner.

OTHER THOUGHTS:
Apparent Women Officers or Directors: 1
Apparent Minority Officers or Directors: 3
Hot Spot for Advancement for Women/Minorities: Y

LOCATIONS: ("Y" = Yes)

West:	Southwest:	Midwest:	Southeast:	Northeast:	International:
Y					

THEGLOBE.COM
www.theglobe.com

Industry Group Code: 514191
Ranks within this company's industry group: Sales: 20   Profits: 38

BUSINESS ACTIVITIES ("Y" = Yes)

Financial Services:	Information/Publ.:		Technology:	Services:	Retailing:		Telecommunications:
Stock Brokerage	Portal/Hub/News	Y	Computer Manuf.	Payments/Transfers	Retailer	Y	Internet Serv. Provider
Mortgages/Loans	On-Line Community	Y	Networking Equip.	Consulting	Auctions		Web Site Host
Banking	Search Engine		Software Manuf.	Advertising/Marketing	Mall	Y	Server Farm
Insurance	Financial Data Publ.	Y	Specialty Equipment	Outsourcing	Tickets/Travel		Specialty Telecom.
Credit Cards	Broadcasting/Music				Price Comparisons	Y	High Speed Access

TYPES OF BUSINESS:
Diversified Portal

BRANDS/DIVISIONS/AFFILIATES:
Accompany, Inc.
HappyPuppy.com
GamesDomain.com
KidsDomain.com
ConsoleDomain.com

CONTACTS: Note: Officers with more than one job title may be intentionally listed here more than once.
Todd V. Krizelman, Co-Pres./Co-CEO
Stephan J. Paternot, Co-Pres./Co-CEO
Francis T. Joyce, CFO
David Tonkin, Dir.-Human Resources
Edward A. Cespedes, VP-Corp. Dev.
Ronald Diprete, Dir.-Corp. Dev.

Phone: 212-894-3600	Fax: 212-367-8588
Toll-Free:	
Address: 120 Broadway, 22nd, New York, NY, 10027	

GROWTH PLANS/SPECIAL FEATURES:

TheGlobe.com is one of the world's largest on-line communities. Members are able to create a site based around a specific theme of personal interest, such as art, business, entertainment, life, news, romance, metro, sports, technology or travel. Content providers for the theme-based experience include Reuters, E! Online, Thomson Investors Network, SonicNet, UPI and C/NET. Theglobe.com Network is comprised of theglobe.com community and leading on-line game sites HappyPuppy.com, GamesDomain.com, KidsDomain.com and ConsoleDomain.com. Theglobe.com is empowering its users to drive down prices and save money through its group buying club, Accompany, Inc. The customized club lowers prices as more people buy by taking advantage of theglobe.com's interest-based communities. Users save on brand name items from top suppliers through group buys in such product categories as computers, entertainment, home and garden, software and sports and fitness. The company's primary revenue source is the sale of advertising, with additional revenues generated through e-commerce arrangements and the sale of membership subscriptions for enhanced services. The New York Times called theglobe.com an interactive Nightline, and the site has also received coverage from the BBC, CNN, CNBC, Reuters and Dow Jones, as well as dozens of other U.S. publications.

FINANCIALS: Sales and profits are in thousands of dollars—add 000 to get the full amount.
Notes regarding 1999: Pro forma (1999 sales and profits were not available for all companies at press time.)

1999 Sales: $18,600	1999 Profits: $-30,500	
1998 Sales: $5,500	1998 Profits: $-16,000	Stock Ticker: TGLO
1997 Sales: $ 800	1997 Profits: $-3,600	Employees: 210
1996 Sales: $ 200	1996 Profits: $- 800	Fiscal Year Ends: 12/31
1995 Sales: $	1995 Profits: $	

SALARIES/BENEFITS:

Pension Plan: Y	ESOP Stock Plan: Y	Profit Sharing:	Top Exec. Salary: $140,554	Bonus: $
Savings Plan:	Stock Purch. Plan:		Second Exec. Salary: $83,625	Bonus: $

COMPETITIVE ADVANTAGE: A be all things to all people strategy.

OTHER THOUGHTS:
Apparent Women Officers or Directors:
Apparent Minority Officers or Directors: 2
Hot Spot for Advancement for Women/Minorities: Y

LOCATIONS: ("Y" = Yes)

West:	Southwest:	Midwest:	Southeast:	Northeast:	International:
				Y	

THESTREET.COM www.thestreet.com
Industry Group Code: 5141
Ranks within this company's industry group: Sales: 3 Profits: 4

BUSINESS ACTIVITIES ("Y" = Yes)

Financial Services:	Information/Publ.:		Technology:	Services:	Retailing:	Telecommunications:
Stock Brokerage	Portal/Hub/News	Y	Computer Manuf.	Payments/Transfers	Retailer	Internet Serv. Provider
Mortgages/Loans	On-Line Community		Networking Equip.	Consulting	Auctions	Web Site Host
Banking	Search Engine		Software Manuf.	Advertising/Marketing	Mall	Server Farm
Insurance	Financial Data Publ.	Y	Specialty Equipment	Outsourcing	Tickets/Travel	Specialty Telecom.
Credit Cards	Broadcasting/Music				Price Comparisons	High Speed Access

TYPES OF BUSINESS:
On-line Financial Information

BRANDS/DIVISIONS/AFFILIATES:
TheStreet.co.uk

CONTACTS: Note: Officers with more than one job title may be intentionally listed here more than once.
Thomas J. Clarke, CEO
Paul Kothari, CFO
Richard Auletta, VP-Sales
Gerard Conlon, VP-Human Resources
Daniel K. Appelquist, VP-Global Tech.
Michael Smith, Chief Info. Officer
Gautam Guliani, VP-Software Engineering
Abby Marr, VP Consumer Mktg.
Dave Kansas, Editor-In-Chief
Jonathan Krim, Exec. Editor

Phone: 212-271-4004	Fax: 212-271-4005
Toll-Free:	
Address: 2 Rector St., 14th Fl., New York, NY, 10006	

GROWTH PLANS/SPECIAL FEATURES:
TheStreet.com, Inc. is a web-based provider of timely, comprehensive financial news, commentary and information aimed at helping readers make informed investment decisions. As individuals take greater control of their investments, the need for easy access to financial information, once available only to investment professionals, grows. TheStreet.com's editorial team is composed of more than 80 financial journalists publishing approximately 50 original news stories and commentaries each business day, in real-time. TheStreet.com has entered into partnerships with various companies to expand its presence on the web. Together with The New York Times, TheStreet.com recently launched a joint newsroom designed to expand coverage on late-breaking news and stock market coverage. In another venture, TheStreet's partnership with First USA allows the company to tap into an extensive cardholder base to target potential subscribers. Many of TheStreet's editors, reporters and outside contributors are featured on TheStreet.com, a weekly television investing show co-produced and aired on the FOX News Channel. Revenues are derived primarily from sales of subscriptions to the web site and from sales of advertising. TheStreet.co.uk, is a new site intended for UK investors.

FINANCIALS: Sales and profits are in thousands of dollars—add 000 to get the full amount.
Notes regarding 1999: (1999 sales and profits were not available for all companies at press time.)
1999 Sales: $14,300	1999 Profits: $-33,600	Stock Ticker: TSCM
1998 Sales: $4,600	1998 Profits: $-16,400	Employees: 122
1997 Sales: $ 600	1997 Profits: $-5,800	Fiscal Year Ends: 12/31
1996 Sales: $	1996 Profits: $-1,700	
1995 Sales: $	1995 Profits: $	

SALARIES/BENEFITS:
Pension Plan:	ESOP Stock Plan: Y	Profit Sharing:	Top Exec. Salary: $150,000	Bonus: $25,944
Savings Plan:	Stock Purch. Plan:		Second Exec. Salary: $130,000	Bonus: $78,769

COMPETITIVE ADVANTAGE: Rapid growth/High Visibility.

OTHER THOUGHTS:
Apparent Women Officers or Directors: 2
Apparent Minority Officers or Directors: 2
Hot Spot for Advancement for Women/Minorities: Y

LOCATIONS: ("Y" = Yes)
West:	Southwest:	Midwest:	Southeast:	Northeast:	International:
				Y	Y

THINK NEW IDEAS
www.thinkinc.com

Industry Group Code: 54151
Ranks within this company's industry group: Sales: 5   Profits: 14

BUSINESS ACTIVITIES ("Y" = Yes)

Financial Services:	Information/Publ.:	Technology:	Services:		Retailing:		Telecommunications:
Stock Brokerage	Portal/Hub/News	Computer Manuf.	Payments/Transfers		Retailer		Internet Serv. Provider
Mortgages/Loans	On-Line Community	Networking Equip.	Consulting	Y	Auctions		Web Site Host
Banking	Search Engine	Software Manuf.	Advertising/Marketing	Y	Mall		Server Farm
Insurance	Financial Data Publ.	Specialty Equipment	Outsourcing	Y	Tickets/Travel		Specialty Telecom.
Credit Cards	Broadcasting/Music				Price Comparisons		High Speed Access

TYPES OF BUSINESS:

Consulting
Strategic Planning
Marketing Communications
Implementation
Analysis
Custom Applications

BRANDS/DIVISIONS/AFFILIATES:

Answer Think Consulting Group
WebMechanic
THINK Vision Process

CONTACTS: Note: Officers with more than one job title may be intentionally listed here more than once.

Ted Fernandez, CEO
Joseph Nicholson, COO
Dan Nicholas, CFO
Ronald Bloom, Chief Strategic Officer

Phone: 212-629-6800	Fax: 212-629-6850
Toll-Free:	
Address: 45 W. 36th St., 12th Fl., New York, NY, 10018	

GROWTH PLANS/SPECIAL FEATURES:

Think New Ideas, which at the end of 1999 merged with AnswerThink Consulting Group, Inc., is one of the largest end-to-end e-business solutions providers, with over 1,600 associates in 17 offices in the U.S. and Europe. The company provides marketing, communications and technology solutions to Fortune 1000 e-business and .com companies. Utilizing the THINK Vision Process, the company researches a client's entire business to determine the effectiveness of existing communications programs and how such programs may be improved. The process is composed of six phases: assessment, strategy development/specification, concept development, implementation, review/adjustment and maintenance/long-term planning. Think New Ideas incorporates various technologies, including customized interactive applications, e-commerce and e-catalog technology, consumer modeling, response technology and database development. The company begins with strategic planning and consulting and continues through implementation review and maintenance. WebMechanic, an automated web site and Intranet building and management tool, enables real-time generation of customized, dynamically generated web sites, while providing the ability to edit, create and refresh content from any location in a user-friendly process. Think New Ideas was recently hired by eVisa to design a program to make VISA the credit card of choice on the Internet.

FINANCIALS: Sales and profits are in thousands of dollars—add 000 to get the full amount.

Notes regarding 1999: *(1999 sales and profits were not available for all companies at press time.)*

1999 Sales: $49,800	1999 Profits: $-8,300	Stock Ticker: **THNK**
1998 Sales: $42,600	1998 Profits: $-27,600	Employees: 391
1997 Sales: $17,400	1997 Profits: $-7,600	Fiscal Year Ends: 06/30
1996 Sales: $12,100	1996 Profits: $-1,400	
1995 Sales: $10,300	1995 Profits: $ 100	

SALARIES/BENEFITS:

Pension Plan:	ESOP Stock Plan: Y	Profit Sharing:	Top Exec. Salary: $304,166	Bonus: $150,000
Savings Plan:	Stock Purch. Plan:		Second Exec. Salary: $203,330	Bonus: $

COMPETITIVE ADVANTAGE: Merger with Answer Think Consulting Group.

OTHER THOUGHTS:

Apparent Women Officers or Directors:
Apparent Minority Officers or Directors:
Hot Spot for Advancement for Women/Minorities:

LOCATIONS: ("Y" = Yes)

West:	Southwest:	Midwest:	Southeast:	Northeast:	International:
Y	Y	Y	Y	Y	Y

TIBCO SOFTWARE   www.tibco.com

Industry Group Code: 5112
Ranks within this company's industry group: Sales: 16   Profits: 62

BUSINESS ACTIVITIES ("Y" = Yes)

Financial Services:	Information/Publ.:	Technology:		Services:	Retailing:	Telecommunications:
Stock Brokerage	Portal/Hub/News	Computer Manuf.		Payments/Transfers	Retailer	Internet Serv. Provider
Mortgages/Loans	On-Line Community	Networking Equip.		Consulting	Auctions	Web Site Host
Banking	Search Engine	Software Manuf.	Y	Advertising/Marketing	Mall	Server Farm
Insurance	Financial Data Publ.	Specialty Equipment		Outsourcing	Tickets/Travel	Specialty Telecom.
Credit Cards	Broadcasting/Music				Price Comparisons	High Speed Access

TYPES OF BUSINESS:
Software-Internet

BRANDS/DIVISIONS/AFFILIATES:
The Information Bus (TIB)
TIB/Acive Enterprise

CONTACTS: *Note: Officers with more than one job title may be intentionally listed here more than once.*
Vivek Y. Ranadive, CEO
Paul G. Hansen, CFO
Rajesh U. Mashruwala, Exec. VP-Sales/Mktg.
Darby E. Siempelkamp, VP-Human Resources
Thomas Joseph, Chief Tech. Officer
Ginger M. Kelly, Corp. Controller
Richard M. Tavan, Exec. VP-Engineering
Robert P. Stefanski, Sec.
Robert P. Stefanski, Exec. VP/General Counsel
Richard M. Taven, Exec VP-Oper.
Thomas W. Jasek, Sr. VP-Business Dev.

Phone: 650-846-5000	Fax: 650-846-5005
Toll-Free:	
Address: 3165 Porter Dr., Palo Alto, CA, 94304	

GROWTH PLANS/SPECIAL FEATURES:

TIBCO Software, Inc. is a leading provider of real-time infrastructure software for the Internet that enables businesses to dynamically link internal operations, business partners and customer channels. The company's flagship solution, TIB/AciveEnterprise, facilitates this business process integration by connecting applications, web sites, databases and other content sources using patented technology called The Information Bus (TIB). TIB, a publishing and subscribing technology, integrates and delivers market data such as stock quotes, news and other financial information. In the trading rooms of large banks and financial institutions, TIB permitted the integration of disparate information from various data sources and its distribution across a variety of networks and platforms in banks, financial institutions and the world's largest stock exchanges. TIBCO's e-commerce, consulting and support services generate two-thirds of sales. The company's customers include more than 300 telecom, high tech, energy, financial services and Internet companies that license TIBCO's software to integrate, personalize and distribute content from web sites, databases and other sources. Reuters owns 65% of the company.

FINANCIALS: Sales and profits are in thousands of dollars—add 000 to get the full amount.
Notes regarding 1999: *(1999 sales and profits were not available for all companies at press time.)*

1999 Sales: $96,400	1999 Profits: $-6,900	Stock Ticker: **TIBX**
1998 Sales: $52,800	1998 Profits: $-13,000	Employees: 306
1997 Sales: $35,300	1997 Profits: $-4,700	Fiscal Year Ends: 11/30
1996 Sales: $30,300	1996 Profits: $-4,600	
1995 Sales: $	1995 Profits: $	

SALARIES/BENEFITS:

Pension Plan:	ESOP Stock Plan: Y	Profit Sharing:	Top Exec. Salary: $345,833	Bonus: $231,708
Savings Plan:	Stock Purch. Plan:		Second Exec. Salary: $	Bonus: $

COMPETITIVE ADVANTAGE: Patented technology enables connections to disparate data sources.

OTHER THOUGHTS:

Apparent Women Officers or Directors: 1
Apparent Minority Officers or Directors: 4
Hot Spot for Advancement for Women/Minorities: Y

LOCATIONS: ("Y" = Yes)

West:	Southwest:	Midwest:	Southeast:	Northeast:	International:
Y	Y	Y	Y	Y	Y

TICKETMASTER ONLINE-CITYSEARCH INC
www.ticketmaster.com
Industry Group Code: 4541
Ranks within this company's industry group: Sales: 17   Profits: 24

BUSINESS ACTIVITIES ("Y" = Yes)

Financial Services:	Information/Publ.:		Technology:	Services:	Retailing:		Telecommunications:	
Stock Brokerage	Portal/Hub/News	Y	Computer Manuf.	Payments/Transfers	Retailer	Y	Internet Serv. Provider	
Mortgages/Loans	On-Line Community		Networking Equip.	Consulting	Auctions		Web Site Host	Y
Banking	Search Engine		Software Manuf.	Advertising/Marketing	Mall		Server Farm	
Insurance	Financial Data Publ.		Specialty Equipment	Outsourcing	Tickets/Travel		Specialty Telecom.	Y
Credit Cards	Broadcasting/Music				Price Comparisons		High Speed Access	

TYPES OF BUSINESS:
Tickets
City Directories
Entertainment Data

BRANDS/DIVISIONS/AFFILIATES:
Ticketmaster Online
CitySearch
CityAuction
Match.com
One & Only
Ticketmaster Store
USA/Lycos Interactive Networks, Inc.

CONTACTS: Note: Officers with more than one job title may be intentionally listed here more than once.
Charles Conn, CEO
David Hagan, COO
Bradley Ramberg, CFO
Sharon Smith, VP-Human Resources
Bradley Ramberg, Sec.
Douglas McPherson, Chief Legal Officer
Bradley Ramberg, VP-Admin.
Douglas McPherson, VP-Business Dev.
Thomas Layton, Treas.

Phone: 626-405-0050	Fax: 626-405-9929
Toll-Free:	
Address: 790 E. Colorado Blvd., Suite 200, Pasadena, CA, 91101	

GROWTH PLANS/SPECIAL FEATURES:

Ticketmaster Online-CitySearch, Inc. has merged two powerful and popular sites to create a leading provider of local city guides, local advertising and live event ticketing on the Internet. The company offers on-line ticketing, merchandise, electronic coupons and other transactions to a broad audience of consumers and integrates these activities with additional services offered by CityAuction, Match.com and One & Only. The CitySearch city guides provide up-to-date information regarding arts and entertainment events, community activities, recreation, business, shopping, professional services and news/sports/weather to consumers in metropolitan areas. Ticketmaster Online offers consumers up-to-date information on live entertainment events and is a convenient means of purchasing tickets and related merchandise on the web for live events in 44 states, Canada and the United Kingdom. Ticketmaster Online has added new services, such as on-line restaurant reservations, golf tee-time bookings and baby-sitter scheduling. The company has also launched the Ticketmaster Store, a web site that features more than 150,000 products, including CDs, clothes and memorabilia from various artists. Ticketmaster Online-CitySearch, USAi and Lycos, Inc. entered into definitive agreements relating to the combination of the company, Lycos, USAi's Home Shopping Network, Ticketmaster and Internet Shopping Network/First Auction businesses in a new company to be named USA/Lycos Interactive Networks, Inc.

FINANCIALS: Sales and profits are in thousands of dollars—add 000 to get the full amount.
Notes regarding 1999: (1999 sales and profits were not available for all companies at press time.)

		Stock Ticker: TMCS
1999 Sales: $105,303	1999 Profits: $-42,743	
1998 Sales: $27,900	1998 Profits: $-17,200	Employees: 608
1997 Sales: $9,900	1997 Profits: $2,300	Fiscal Year Ends: 12/31
1996 Sales: $1,200	1996 Profits: $- 600	
1995 Sales: $	1995 Profits: $- 300	

SALARIES/BENEFITS:

Pension Plan:	ESOP Stock Plan:	Profit Sharing:	Top Exec. Salary: $	Bonus: $
Savings Plan: Y	Stock Purch. Plan:		Second Exec. Salary: $	Bonus: $

COMPETITIVE ADVANTAGE: Merger with Lycos.

OTHER THOUGHTS:

Apparent Women Officers or Directors: 1
Apparent Minority Officers or Directors:
Hot Spot for Advancement for Women/Minorities:

LOCATIONS: ("Y" = Yes)

West:	Southwest:	Midwest:	Southeast:	Northeast:	International:
Y	Y	Y	Y	Y	Y

Note: Financial information, benefits and other data can change quickly and may vary from those stated here.

TIME WARNER INC   www.timewarner.com

Industry Group Code: 5132
Ranks within this company's industry group: Sales: 1   Profits: 1

BUSINESS ACTIVITIES ("Y" = Yes)

Financial Services:	Information/Publ.:		Technology:	Services:	Retailing:		Telecommunications:	
Stock Brokerage	Portal/Hub/News	Y	Computer Manuf.	Payments/Transfers	Retailer	Y	Internet Serv. Provider	Y
Mortgages/Loans	On-Line Community		Networking Equip.	Consulting	Auctions		Web Site Host	
Banking	Search Engine		Software Manuf.	Advertising/Marketing	Mall		Server Farm	
Insurance	Financial Data Publ.		Specialty Equipment	Outsourcing	Tickets/Travel		Specialty Telecom.	
Credit Cards	Broadcasting/Music	Y			Price Comparisons		High Speed Access	Y

TYPES OF BUSINESS:

Film Entertainment
Television Production
Theme Parks
Cable Programming
Magazine Publishing
Music Production

BRANDS/DIVISIONS/AFFILIATES:

Time, Inc.
Warner Bros.
America Online
Home Box Office
Turner Broadcasting System
Cable News Network
Road Runner
EMI Music

CONTACTS: *Note: Officers with more than one job title may be intentionally listed here more than once.*

Gerald M Levin, CEO
Richard D. Parsons, Pres.
Joseph A. Ripp, Sr. VP/CFO
Carolyn McLandless, VP-Corp. Human Resources
Alan Horn, Pres.-COO-Warner Bros.
Barry Meyer, Chmn.- CEO-Warner Bros.

Phone: 212-484-8000	Fax: 212-956-2847
Toll-Free:	
Address: 75 Rockefeller Plaza, New York, NY, 10019	

GROWTH PLANS/SPECIAL FEATURES:

Time Warner Entertainment, Inc. is the world's leading media and entertainment company. Its principal business objective is to create and distribute branded information and entertainment throughout the world. Time Warner's business classifications consist of: Entertainment, including interests in recorded music and music publishing, filmed entertainment, television production, television broadcasting and theme parks; Cable Networks, including interests in cable television programming and sports franchises; Publishing, including interests in magazine publishing, book publishing and direct marketing and Cable, including interests in cable television systems. The company owns the Looney Tunes, Flintstones and Batman trademarks, a 49% interest in Six Flags, the largest regional theme park operator in the U.S. and Time Magazine, People and other magazines. Time Warner is one of the leading providers of cable television in the nation, and, through its cable systems, it is a major provider of cable modem-based Internet access service. The company plans to be acquired by America Online. Time and EMI Music intend to combine their recorded music businesses in a joint venture that will approximately equal Universal Music Group in size. Universal is currently the world's largest music firm.

Home Box Office, a division of Time Warner, reports these female employees: VPs, 27%; managers and higher officials, 48% and professional staff, 51%. Home Box Office reimburses child care costs for nonroutine business travel, allows up to 24 weeks maternity leave, 1 week paid paternity leave, a phase-back for new mothers and adoption aid benefits of up to $2,500 with 1 week paid leave.

FINANCIALS: Sales and profits are in thousands of dollars—add 000 to get the full amount.

Notes regarding 1999: *(1999 sales and profits were not available for all companies at press time.)*

1999 Sales: $	1999 Profits: $	**Stock Ticker: TWX**
1998 Sales: $14,582,000	1998 Profits: $168,000	Employees: 67,500
1997 Sales: $13,294,000	1997 Profits: $246,000	Fiscal Year Ends: 12/31
1996 Sales: $10,064,000	1996 Profits: $-191,000	
1995 Sales: $8,067,000	1995 Profits: $-166,000	

SALARIES/BENEFITS:

Pension Plan: Y	ESOP Stock Plan:	Profit Sharing:	Top Exec. Salary: $1,000,000	Bonus: $7,800,000
Savings Plan: Y	Stock Purch. Plan:		Second Exec. Salary: $700,000	Bonus: $6,000,000

COMPETITIVE ADVANTAGE:
Plans to merge with America Online/Owns some of the best names in publishing and programming/Major cable television and Internet assets.

OTHER THOUGHTS:

Apparent Women Officers or Directors: 2
Apparent Minority Officers or Directors:
Hot Spot for Advancement for Women/Minorities:

LOCATIONS: ("Y" = Yes)

West:	Southwest:	Midwest:	Southeast:	Northeast:	International:
Y	Y	Y	Y	Y	Y

TMP WORLDWIDE INC
www.tmpw.com

Industry Group Code: 54189
Ranks within this company's industry group: Sales: 1 Profits: 1

BUSINESS ACTIVITIES ("Y" = Yes)

Financial Services:	Information/Publ.:		Technology:	Services:		Retailing:	Telecommunications:
Stock Brokerage	Portal/Hub/News	Y	Computer Manuf.	Payments/Transfers		Retailer	Internet Serv. Provider
Mortgages/Loans	On-Line Community		Networking Equip.	Consulting		Auctions	Web Site Host
Banking	Search Engine		Software Manuf.	Advertising/Marketing	Y	Mall	Server Farm
Insurance	Financial Data Publ.		Specialty Equipment	Outsourcing		Tickets/Travel	Specialty Telecom.
Credit Cards	Broadcasting/Music					Price Comparisons	High Speed Access

TYPES OF BUSINESS:

Advertising-Internet
Yellow Pages Advertising
Full-service Advertising
On-line Careers Sites
Executive Recruiting

BRANDS/DIVISIONS/AFFILIATES:

The Monster Board
Online Career Center
Be the Boss
MedSearch
Dealer Locator
Austin Knight
Morgan & Banks, Ltd.
LAI Worldwide

CONTACTS: Note: Officers with more than one job title may be intentionally listed here more than once.

Anrew J. McKelvey, CEO
James J, Treacy, COO
Bart W. Catalane, CFO
Paul M. Camara, Exec. VP-Creative/Sales/Mktg.
Margaretta Cullen, Dir.-Human Resources
Brian Farrey, Chief Tech. Officer
Jane L. Aboyoun, CIO
Thomas G. Collison, Sec.
James J. Treacy, Strategy

Phone: 212-977-4200	Fax: 212-956-2142
Toll-Free:	
Address: 1633 Broadway, 33rd Fl., New York, NY, 10019	

GROWTH PLANS/SPECIAL FEATURES:

TMP Worldwide, Inc. is a marketing services, communications, executive search and technology company that provides comprehensive and individually-tailored advertising services. This includes development of creative content, media planning, production and placement of corporate advertising and market research, which is conducted through traditional media such as newspapers, yellow page directories and the Internet. The company also provides executive and mid-level search services. TMP's clients include more than 80 of the Fortune 100 and approximately 400 of the Fortune 500 companies. The company has become the world's largest Yellow Pages advertising agency. It places ads in directories all across the United States. With more than 2,500 clients, TMP is also a leader in the recruitment ad business. In addition, the company offers direct marketing and customer relations services such as call center operations and order fulfillment. TMP also owns and runs the Internet career portal, Monster.com. The site has more than 180,000 job ads and a database of more than 2 million resumes. Recently, TMP acquired Morgan & Banks Limited. TMP also acquired LAI Worldwide, one of the top job recruitment companies in the US. TMP plans to acquire UK-based executive headhunter HW Group as part of its global expansion strategy.

FINANCIALS: Sales and profits are in thousands of dollars—add 000 to get the full amount.

Notes regarding 1999: Through 9 months (1999 sales and profits were not available for all companies at press time.)

1999 Sales: $539,500	1999 Profits: $23,600	Stock Ticker: **TMPW**
1998 Sales: $406,800	1998 Profits: $4,300	Employees: 5,200
1997 Sales: $237,400	1997 Profits: $9,600	Fiscal Year Ends: 12/31
1996 Sales: $162,600	1996 Profits: $-52,200	
1995 Sales: $123,900	1995 Profits: $3,200	

SALARIES/BENEFITS:

Pension Plan:	ESOP Stock Plan:	Profit Sharing: Y	Top Exec. Salary: $1,500,000	Bonus: $
Savings Plan: Y	Stock Purch. Plan:		Second Exec. Salary: $401,314	Bonus: $50,000

COMPETITIVE ADVANTAGE: Leadership in recruitment advertising and Internet advertising/World's largest yellow pages ad agency.

OTHER THOUGHTS:

Apparent Women Officers or Directors: 4
Apparent Minority Officers or Directors:
Hot Spot for Advancement for Women/Minorities: Y

LOCATIONS: ("Y" = Yes)

West:	Southwest:	Midwest:	Southeast:	Northeast:	International:
Y	Y	Y	Y	Y	Y

TOWN PAGES NET.COM   www.townpages.co.uk

Industry Group Code: 514191
Ranks within this company's industry group: Sales: 31   Profits: 7

BUSINESS ACTIVITIES ("Y" = Yes)

Financial Services:	Information/Publ.:		Technology:	Services:	Retailing:		Telecommunications:
Stock Brokerage	Portal/Hub/News	Y	Computer Manuf.	Payments/Transfers	Retailer	Y	Internet Serv. Provider
Mortgages/Loans	On-Line Community	Y	Networking Equip.	Consulting	Auctions		Web Site Host
Banking	Search Engine		Software Manuf.	Advertising/Marketing	Mall		Server Farm
Insurance	Financial Data Publ.		Specialty Equipment	Outsourcing	Tickets/Travel		Specialty Telecom.
Credit Cards	Broadcasting/Music				Price Comparisons		High Speed Access

TYPES OF BUSINESS:
Community News Sites-U.K.

BRANDS/DIVISIONS/AFFILIATES:
TownPages

CONTACTS: *Note: Officers with more than one job title may be intentionally listed here more than once.*
Andrew Lyndon-Skeggs, CEO
Andrew Lyndon-Skeggs, Pres.
Richard J. Smith, CFO
Francoise James, Mgr.-Mktg.
James Wilkinson, Head of Tech.
John Holder, Web Editor

Phone: 44-1420-543-468	Fax: 44-1420-541-322
Toll-Free:	
Address: 11 Market Sq., Alton, Hampshire, UK, GU34 1HD	

GROWTH PLANS/SPECIAL FEATURES:

TownPages is an interactive Internet information service in the United Kingdom, providing comprehensive, up-to-date information about each covered town or city. Users can access detailed information about each community, such as its tourist attractions, hotels, restaurants, public transportation schedules, real estate listings, employment opportunities, local news, sports and weather. Interactive Town Diaries, Message Boards and E-commerce allow users to edit information about local events, exchange messages and make purchases. The Go National section provides users with nation-wide information from the Internet in such categories as government, automobiles and employment, allowing users a more broad-based experience. TownPages is not only accessible through its web site, but also through touch-screen kiosks located throughout communities in the UK. The free-to-use touch-screen kiosks are placed in high traffic, high visibility locations and are easily operated by people with little or no Internet or computer experience. Through TownPages, Local businesses are finding a cost-effective means for advertising to specific demographics, interests and geographic locations. The company plans to cover every major town and city in the UK in the next three years.

FINANCIALS: Sales and profits are in thousands of dollars—add 000 to get the full amount.
Notes regarding 1999: *(1999 sales and profits were not available for all companies at press time.)*

1999 Sales: $	1999 Profits: $	Stock Ticker: **TPN**
1998 Sales: $1,900	1998 Profits: $-1,500	Employees: 21
1997 Sales: $	1997 Profits: $- 600	Fiscal Year Ends: 12/31
1996 Sales: $	1996 Profits: $- 300	
1995 Sales: $	1995 Profits: $	

SALARIES/BENEFITS:

Pension Plan: Y	ESOP Stock Plan: Y	Profit Sharing:	Top Exec. Salary: $108,082	Bonus: $
Savings Plan:	Stock Purch. Plan:		Second Exec. Salary: $	Bonus: $

COMPETITIVE ADVANTAGE: An early leader in community portals in the U.K.

OTHER THOUGHTS:

Apparent Women Officers or Directors:
Apparent Minority Officers or Directors:
Hot Spot for Advancement for Women/Minorities:

LOCATIONS: ("Y" = Yes)

West:	Southwest:	Midwest:	Southeast:	Northeast:	International:
					Y

Note: Financial information, benefits and other data can change quickly and may vary from those stated here.

TUMBLEWEED COMMUNICATIONS
www.tumbleweed.com

Industry Group Code: 5112
Ranks within this company's industry group: Sales: 72   Profits: 39

BUSINESS ACTIVITIES ("Y" = Yes)

Financial Services:	Information/Publ.:	Technology:		Services:		Retailing:	Telecommunications:	
Stock Brokerage	Portal/Hub/News	Computer Manuf.		Payments/Transfers		Retailer	Internet Serv. Provider	
Mortgages/Loans	On-Line Community	Networking Equip.		Consulting	Y	Auctions	Web Site Host	
Banking	Search Engine	Software Manuf.	Y	Advertising/Marketing		Mall	Server Farm	
Insurance	Financial Data Publ.	Specialty Equipment		Outsourcing		Tickets/Travel	Specialty Telecom.	Y
Credit Cards	Broadcasting/Music					Price Comparisons	High Speed Access	

TYPES OF BUSINESS:

Software-Secure E-Mail
Professional Services

BRANDS/DIVISIONS/AFFILIATES:

Worldtalk Corp.
Integrated Messaging Exchange

CONTACTS: *Note: Officers with more than one job title may be intentionally listed here more than once.*

Jeffrey C. Smith, CEO
Joseph C. Consul, CFO/VP-Finance
Donald N. Taylor, VP-North America Sales
Jean-Christophe D. Bandini, Chief Tech. Officer
Kerry S. Champion, VP-Engineering
Bernard J. Cassidy, Sec.
Robert A. Krauss, VP-Business Dev.
Mark R. Pastore, VP-Corp. Dev.
Donald R. Gammon, VP-Int'l Sales

Phone: 650-216-2000	Fax: 650-216-2001
Toll-Free:	
Address: 700 Saginaw Dr., Redwood City, CA, 94063	

GROWTH PLANS/SPECIAL FEATURES:

Tumbleweed Communications Corp. provides Internet-based systems that enable businesses to conduct secure on-line communications using e-mails and the Web. The Tumbleweed Integrated Messaging Exchange (IME), Tumbleweed's comprehensive technology solution, powers on-line services from leading application providers throughout the world. Tumbleweed supplies both technology and professional services, providing the foundation for on-line delivery applications. With Tumbleweed Integrated Messaging Exchange, businesses have a secure on-line communication solution that allows them to extend their existing web and e-mail infrastructures to support critical business processes. Recently, Tumbleweed entered into a definitive agreement to acquire Worldtalk Corp. The acquisition is expected to extend Tumbleweed's lead in secure messaging and e-mail content filtering, two of the fastest-growing segments of the messaging market. Worldtalk brings more than 400 customers to Tumbleweed, including Chevron, Nike, Time Warner, U.S. Department of Energy, Blue Cross, Glaxo-Wellcome and GE Capital. Upon completion of the transaction, Worldtalk will become a wholly-owned subsidiary of Tumbleweed. Japanese telecom provider Hikari Tsushin owns 20% of Tumbleweed.

FINANCIALS: Sales and profits are in thousands of dollars—add 000 to get the full amount.

Notes regarding 1999: *(1999 sales and profits were not available for all companies at press time.)*

1999 Sales: $5,780	1999 Profits: $-12,920	Stock Ticker: **TMWD**
1998 Sales: $2,000	1998 Profits: $-6,600	Employees: 60
1997 Sales: $ 700	1997 Profits: $-4,400	Fiscal Year Ends: 12/31
1996 Sales: $ 600	1996 Profits: $-1,200	
1995 Sales: $	1995 Profits: $	

SALARIES/BENEFITS:

Pension Plan:	ESOP Stock Plan:	Profit Sharing: Y	Top Exec. Salary: $	Bonus: $
Savings Plan:	Stock Purch. Plan: Y		Second Exec. Salary: $	Bonus: $

COMPETITIVE ADVANTAGE: Growth through acquisition.

OTHER THOUGHTS:

Apparent Women Officers or Directors:
Apparent Minority Officers or Directors: 2
Hot Spot for Advancement for Women/Minorities: Y

LOCATIONS: ("Y" = Yes)

West:	Southwest:	Midwest:	Southeast:	Northeast:	International:
Y				Y	Y

Note: Financial information, benefits and other data can change quickly and may vary from those stated here.

TUT SYSTEMS   www.tutsys.com

Industry Group Code: 3341C
Ranks within this company's Industry group: Sales: 6   Profits: 5

BUSINESS ACTIVITIES ("Y" = Yes)

Financial Services:	Information/Publ.:	Technology:		Services:	Retailing:	Telecommunications:
Stock Brokerage	Portal/Hub/News	Computer Manuf.		Payments/Transfers	Retailer	Internet Serv. Provider
Mortgages/Loans	On-Line Community	Networking Equip.	Y	Consulting	Auctions	Web Site Host
Banking	Search Engine	Software Manuf.		Advertising/Marketing	Mall	Server Farm
Insurance	Financial Data Publ.	Specialty Equipment	Y	Outsourcing	Tickets/Travel	Specialty Telecom.
Credit Cards	Broadcasting/Music				Price Comparisons	High Speed Access

TYPES OF BUSINESS:

Internet Access Products
Broadband Enhancing Products
Multi-plexers
Routers
Modems
Subscriber Management Systems

BRANDS/DIVISIONS/AFFILIATES:

PublicPort, Inc.
Vintel Communications, Inc.
FastCopper technology
Expresso multiplexers
XL Ethernet products
HomeRun technology

CONTACTS: *Note: Officers with more than one job title may be intentionally listed here more than once.*

Salvatore D'Aurla, CEO
Nelson Cadwell, CFO/VP-Finance
Allen Purdy, VP-Sales
Billie Mowers, Dir.-Human Resources
Matthew Taylor, Chief Tech. Officer
La Monte M. Thompson, Dir.-Info.Services
Thomas Warner, VP-Engineering
Craig Bender, VP/Market Dev.

Phone: 925-682-6510	Fax: 925-682-4125
Toll-Free:	
Address: 2495 Estand Way, Pleasant Hill, CA, 94523-3911	

GROWTH PLANS/SPECIAL FEATURES:

Tut Systems designs, develops and markets advanced communications products that enable high-speed data access over the copper infrastructure of telephone companies, as well as the copper telephone wires in homes, businesses and other buildings. These products incorporate Tut's proprietary FastCopper technology in a cost-effective, scalable and easy-to-deploy solution to exploit the underutilized bandwidth of copper telephone wires. The company's products include Expresso high bandwidth access multiplexers, associated modems and routers, XL Ethernet extension products and integrated network management software. Tut's award-winning HomeRun technology, an in-home application of FastCopper, has been chosen by the Home Phone Line Networking Alliance (HomePNA) as the initial specification for in-home networking over phone lines. To manufacture its products, Tut relies on contractors. Chevron and Lockheed Martin are among the company's clients, and Microsoft and AT&T are among the company's investors. Recently, the company acquired PublicPort, Inc. PublicPort designs and develops subscriber management systems that enable users to access public Internet or private corporate networks without having to reconfigure their laptop's network access software. Tut also acquired an 11% interest in Vintel Communications, Inc., and the company entered into a definitive agreement with Vintel to acquire the remaining 89%. Vintel designs and develops high-performance integrated service routers to allow service providers to offer services like voice-over-IP and high-speed Internet connections over a common IP infrastructure for customers in multi-dwelling unit markets.

FINANCIALS: Sales and profits are in thousands of dollars—add 000 to get the full amount.

Notes regarding 1999: *(1999 sales and profits were not available for all companies at press time.)*

1999 Sales: $27,807	1999 Profits: $-11,969	Stock Ticker: **TUTS**
1998 Sales: $10,600	1998 Profits: $-16,300	Employees: 98
1997 Sales: $6,200	1997 Profits: $-10,800	Fiscal Year Ends: 12/31
1996 Sales: $4,500	1996 Profits: $-5,600	
1995 Sales: $3,400	1995 Profits: $-4,100	

SALARIES/BENEFITS:

Pension Plan:	ESOP Stock Plan:	Profit Sharing:	Top Exec. Salary: $187,500	Bonus: $110,000
Savings Plan:	Stock Purch. Plan:		Second Exec. Salary: $149,808	Bonus: $35,100

COMPETITIVE ADVANTAGE: Growth through acquisitions.

OTHER THOUGHTS:

Apparent Women Officers or Directors:
Apparent Minority Officers or Directors: 1
Hot Spot for Advancement for Women/Minorities:

LOCATIONS: ("Y" = Yes)

West:	Southwest:	Midwest:	Southeast:	Northeast:	International:
Y					

Note: Financial information, benefits and other data can change quickly and may vary from those stated here.

U S INTERACTIVE
www.usinteractive.com

Industry Group Code: 54151
Ranks within this company's industry group: Sales: 11　Profits: 12

BUSINESS ACTIVITIES ("Y" = Yes)

Financial Services:	Information/Publ.:	Technology:	Services:		Retailing:		Telecommunications:
Stock Brokerage	Portal/Hub/News	Computer Manuf.	Payments/Transfers		Retailer		Internet Serv. Provider
Mortgages/Loans	On-Line Community	Networking Equip.	Consulting	Y	Auctions		Web Site Host
Banking	Search Engine	Software Manuf.	Advertising/Marketing	Y	Mall		Server Farm
Insurance	Financial Data Publ.	Specialty Equipment	Outsourcing	Y	Tickets/Travel		Specialty Telecom.
Credit Cards	Broadcasting/Music				Price Comparisons		High Speed Access

TYPES OF BUSINESS:

Consulting-Internet Business
Strategic Planning
Marketing Services
Application Development

BRANDS/DIVISIONS/AFFILIATES:

Digital Evolution, Inc.
InVenGen LLC.
Access, Inc.
Digital Bindery, LLC.
e-Roadmap

CONTACTS: Note: Officers with more than one job title may be intentionally listed here more than once.

Stephen T. Zarrilli, CEO
James Huser, Sr. VP/COO
Philip Calamia, CFO
Michael M, Carter, VP-Mktg.
Anita Masino, Dir.-Human Resources
Eric Pulier, Chief Tech. Officer
James Letts, CIO
Mark Silverman, Exec. VP-Corp. Dev.

Phone: 610-313-9700	Fax: 610-382-8908
Toll-Free:	
Address: 2012 Renaissance Blvd., King of Prussia, PA, 19406	

GROWTH PLANS/SPECIAL FEATURES:

U.S. Interactive, Inc. is a provider of Internet professional services that help companies take advantage of the business opportunities presented by the Internet. The company provides integrated Internet strategy consulting, marketing and technology services that enable clients to align their people, processes and systems to form an electronic enterprise. U.S. Interactive's formula for an electronic enterprise is one that utilizes Internet-based technologies to transact business, communicate information and share knowledge among employees, customers and suppliers. The company delivers its services through its development plan called e-Roadmap, a group of service offerings that can be customized to meet the needs of each client. Through e-Roadmap, the firm focuses on four areas: e-commerce, digital marketing, enterprise relationship management and knowledge management. To facilitate its implementation process, U.S. Interactive employs extranets that provide work plans, project updates, new proposals and other project information. The company recently completed its merger with Digital Evolution, Inc., an Internet professional services firm that provides development services for Internet, intranet and extranet applications. U.S. Interactive acquired certain assets and assumed certain liabilities of InVenGen LLC, a regional Internet professional service firm. Chairman and co-founder Eric Pulier owns 18% of U.S. Interactive.

FINANCIALS: Sales and profits are in thousands of dollars—add 000 to get the full amount.

Notes regarding 1999: (1999 sales and profits were not available for all companies at press time.)

1999 Sales: $35,300	1999 Profits: $-14,389	Stock Ticker: **USIT**
1998 Sales: $13,600	1998 Profits: $-8,400	Employees:　232
1997 Sales: $6,100	1997 Profits: $- 300	Fiscal Year Ends: 12/31
1996 Sales: $1,900	1996 Profits: $- 100	
1995 Sales: $	1995 Profits: $	

SALARIES/BENEFITS:

Pension Plan: Y	ESOP Stock Plan:	Profit Sharing:	Top Exec. Salary: $	Bonus: $
Savings Plan:	Stock Purch. Plan:		Second Exec. Salary: $	Bonus: $

COMPETITIVE ADVANTAGE:　A full array of strategic services.

OTHER THOUGHTS:

Apparent Women Officers or Directors:
Apparent Minority Officers or Directors:
Hot Spot for Advancement for Women/Minorities:

LOCATIONS: ("Y" = Yes)

West:	Southwest:	Midwest:	Southeast:	Northeast:	International:
Y				Y	Y

UBID INC   www.ubid.com

Industry Group Code: 4541B
Ranks within this company's industry group: Sales: 1   Profits: 2

BUSINESS ACTIVITIES ("Y" = Yes)

Financial Services:	Information/Publ.:	Technology:	Services:	Retailing:		Telecommunications:
Stock Brokerage	Portal/Hub/News	Computer Manuf.	Payments/Transfers	Retailer		Internet Serv. Provider
Mortgages/Loans	On-Line Community	Networking Equip.	Consulting	Auctions	Y	Web Site Host
Banking	Search Engine	Software Manuf.	Advertising/Marketing	Mall		Server Farm
Insurance	Financial Data Publ.	Specialty Equipment	Outsourcing	Tickets/Travel		Specialty Telecom.
Credit Cards	Broadcasting/Music			Price Comparisons		High Speed Access

TYPES OF BUSINESS:
Auctions- On-line

BRANDS/DIVISIONS/AFFILIATES:
Creative Computers, Inc.

CONTACTS: Note: Officers with more than one job title may be Intentionally listed here more than once.

Gregory Jones, CEO
Tom Werner, CFO
Kenneth Dotson, Chief Mktg. Officer
Maria Lorello, Human Resources
George Lu, VP-Information Systems
David L. Hirschman, Sr. VP-Oper.
David M. Matthews, Dir.-Applications Dev.
Norm Wesley, Treas.

Phone: 847-860-5000	Fax: 847-616-0318
Toll-Free:	
Address: 2525 Busee Road, Elk Grove Village, IL, 60007	

GROWTH PLANS/SPECIAL FEATURES:

uBid, Inc. is an on-line auction house that offers consumers and small -to medium-sized businesses excess, refurbished, closeout and limited edition merchandise through live-auction bidding. On-line auctioning is one of the fastest-growing segments of e-commerce. The company's Internet auctions feature a rotating selection of brand name computer, consumer electronics, home/leisure and sports/fitness products. uBid is publicly traded, with headquarters in the greater Chicago area, and is a subsidiary of Creative Computers, Inc. The company experienced a tremendous increase in registered users during 1999 and also expanded its auction categories, adding apparel, appliances, art, travel & events, home improvement and off-lease computer equipment. The structure of the web site has recently been redesigned and enhanced in order to provide an increased level of functionality. uBid also offers an e-mail alert system that contacts users when a particular item they are interested in becomes available for bidding. In recent news, uBid subscribed to Ask Jeeves' Corporate Service in order to enhance customer service for its approximately one million registered users. Ask Jeeves is a leading provider of question answering services for consumers and companies on the Web.

FINANCIALS: Sales and profits are in thousands of dollars—add 000 to get the full amount.
Notes regarding 1999: (1999 sales and profits were not available for all companies at press time.)

		Stock Ticker: UBID
1999 Sales: $204,900	1999 Profits: $-25,495	Employees: 74
1998 Sales: $48,200	1998 Profits: $-10,200	Fiscal Year Ends: 12/31
1997 Sales: $ 100	1997 Profits: $- 300	
1996 Sales: $	1996 Profits: $	
1995 Sales: $	1995 Profits: $	

SALARIES/BENEFITS:

Pension Plan:	ESOP Stock Plan:	Profit Sharing:	Top Exec. Salary: $175,000	Bonus: $50,000
Savings Plan:	Stock Purch. Plan:		Second Exec. Salary: $	Bonus: $

COMPETITIVE ADVANTAGE: Offers limited edition, excess, refurbished & closeout merchandise.

OTHER THOUGHTS:

Apparent Women Officers or Directors:
Apparent Minority Officers or Directors:
Hot Spot for Advancement for Women/Minorities:

LOCATIONS: ("Y" = Yes)

West:	Southwest:	Midwest:	Southeast:	Northeast:	International:
		Y			

US SEARCH CORP.COM
www.1800ussearch.com

Industry Group Code: 51339
Ranks within this company's industry group: Sales: 17   Profits: 11

BUSINESS ACTIVITIES ("Y" = Yes)

Financial Services:	Information/Publ.:		Technology:	Services:	Retailing:	Telecommunications:
Stock Brokerage	Portal/Hub/News	Y	Computer Manuf.	Payments/Transfers	Retailer	Internet Serv. Provider
Mortgages/Loans	On-Line Community		Networking Equip.	Consulting	Auctions	Web Site Host
Banking	Search Engine		Software Manuf.	Advertising/Marketing	Mall	Server Farm
Insurance	Financial Data Publ.		Specialty Equipment	Outsourcing	Tickets/Travel	Specialty Telecom.
Credit Cards	Broadcasting/Music				Price Comparisons	High Speed Access

TYPES OF BUSINESS:

People Search Site
Internet-Based Vital Statistics and Personal Records

BRANDS/DIVISIONS/AFFILIATES:

CONTACTS: Note: Officers with more than one job title may be intentionally listed here more than once.

C. Nicholas Keating, Jr., CEO
C. Nicholas Keating, Jr., Pres.
William G. Langley, CFO
Debra Drucker, Dir.-Human Resources
Robert J. Richards, VP-Oper.
Meg Shea-Chiles, VP-Business Dev.
Alan S. Mazurksy, VP-Finance

Phone: 310-553-7000	Fax: 310-786-8349
Toll-Free: 877-327-2410	
Address: 9107 Wilshire Blvd., Ste. 700, Beverly Hills, CA, 90210	

GROWTH PLANS/SPECIAL FEATURES:

US SEARCH Corp.com is a provider of public record information about individuals and companies. Through the Internet at www.1800USSEARCH.com, or toll-free at 1-800-US-SEARCH, clients can access a broad range of information for asset verification, people and business locating, fraud prevention and employment screening. All services are quick, easy and highly-automated for fast response and low cost. Internet-based instant searches are processed on-line, and results are often delivered in a few seconds or minutes through real-time display, or by e-mail, telephone, fax or mail. Clients can obtain addresses, aliases, phone numbers, property ownership, court records, judgments, license verification, corporate affiliations and date of death information. Searches are performed by electronically accessing multiple geographically dispersed public record databases and choosing the most reliable data from each. US SEARCH advertises on the top web properties, integrating text links on thousands of pages, including Yahoo!, MSN, America Online, Lycos Network and GO Network. US SEARCH has ranked in the top 70 most frequented web sites by Nielsen/NetRatings.

FINANCIALS: Sales and profits are in thousands of dollars—add 000 to get the full amount.
Notes regarding 1999: (1999 sales and profits were not available for all companies at press time.)

1999 Sales: $19,541	1999 Profits: $-17,072	Stock Ticker: **SRCH**
1998 Sales: $9,200	1998 Profits: $-6,800	Employees: 118
1997 Sales: $3,000	1997 Profits: $- 400	Fiscal Year Ends: 12/31
1996 Sales: $5,700	1996 Profits: $-1,400	
1995 Sales: $ 900	1995 Profits: $- 400	

SALARIES/BENEFITS:

Pension Plan:	ESOP Stock Plan: Y	Profit Sharing:	Top Exec. Salary: $127,460	Bonus: $
Savings Plan:	Stock Purch. Plan:		Second Exec. Salary: $	Bonus: $

COMPETITIVE ADVANTAGE: Very unique services provided to an interesting niche/High visitor rate.

OTHER THOUGHTS:

Apparent Women Officers or Directors:
Apparent Minority Officers or Directors:
Hot Spot for Advancement for Women/Minorities:

LOCATIONS: ("Y" = Yes)

West:	Southwest:	Midwest:	Southeast:	Northeast:	International:
Y					

Note: Financial information, benefits and other data can change quickly and may vary from those stated here.

USINTERNETWORKING INC   www.usinternetworking.com

Industry Group Code: 5611
Ranks within this company's industry group: Sales: 1   Profits: 1

BUSINESS ACTIVITIES ("Y" = Yes)

Financial Services:	Information/Publ.:	Technology:	Services:		Retailing:	Telecommunications:
Stock Brokerage	Portal/Hub/News	Computer Manuf.	Payments/Transfers		Retailer	Internet Serv. Provider
Mortgages/Loans	On-Line Community	Networking Equip.	Consulting		Auctions	Web Site Host
Banking	Search Engine	Software Manuf.	Advertising/Marketing		Mall	Server Farm
Insurance	Financial Data Publ.	Specialty Equipment	Outsourcing	Y	Tickets/Travel	Specialty Telecom.
Credit Cards	Broadcasting/Music				Price Comparisons	High Speed Access

TYPES OF BUSINESS:

Outsourcing-Internet Accessible Software
ASPs
Sales Force Automation
Human Resources Automation

BRANDS/DIVISIONS/AFFILIATES:

Grotech Capital

CONTACTS: Note: Officers with more than one job title may be intentionally listed here more than once.

Christopher R. McCleary, CEO
Andrew A. Stern, COO
Chuck Teubner, CFO
Michele Perry, VP-Mktg.
Brenda K. Woodsmall, VP-Human Resources
David Goldschlag, Chief Tech. Officer
Ronald Freedman, VP-Info. Assurance
Kurt C. Gastrock, VP-Engineering
Jay W. Robertson, VP-Oper.
Lee Tanner, VP-Business Dev.
John Tomljanovic, VP-Client Care

Phone: 410-897-4400	Fax: 410-573-1906
Toll-Free: 800-839-4874	
Address: 1 Usi Plaza, Annapolis, MD, 21401-7478	

GROWTH PLANS/SPECIAL FEATURES:

Usinternetworking, Inc., the first Internet Managed Application Provider (iMAP), implements, operates and supports packaged software applications that can be accessed and used over the Internet. USI's services enable their clients to use leading business software applications without the cost and burden of owning or managing the underlying technologies, such as computer servers, networking equipment and software licenses. Their clients access these applications through USI's global network of Enterprise Data Centers. USI has established its iMAP offerings as a leading single-source solution for middle market companies implementing distributed business functions. These functions include sales force automation, customer support, e-commerce and human resources and financial systems. The company allows clients to host their own software applications on USI's reliable and secure data centers. USI does not develop application software, but instead implements and manages applications developed by others. To deliver its services, USI has built a network of four Enterprise Data Centers located in Annapolis, Silicon Valley, Amsterdam and Tokyo. USI's client care operation supports client's needs 24-hours daily. Customers include Lattice Semiconductor, Lockheed Martin and NIKE. Investment firm Grotech Capital owns 21% of USI.

FINANCIALS: Sales and profits are in thousands of dollars—add 000 to get the full amount.

Notes regarding 1999: (1999 sales and profits were not available for all companies at press time.)

1999 Sales: $35,500	1999 Profits: $-103,300	Stock Ticker: **USIX**
1998 Sales: $4,100	1998 Profits: $-32,500	Employees: 348
1997 Sales: $	1997 Profits: $	Fiscal Year Ends: 12/31
1996 Sales: $	1996 Profits: $	
1995 Sales: $	1995 Profits: $	

SALARIES/BENEFITS:

Pension Plan:	ESOP Stock Plan:	Profit Sharing:	Top Exec. Salary: $	Bonus: $
Savings Plan:	Stock Purch. Plan:		Second Exec. Salary: $	Bonus: $

COMPETITIVE ADVANTAGE: Excellent assortment of ASP services/International presence.

OTHER THOUGHTS:

Apparent Women Officers or Directors: 2
Apparent Minority Officers or Directors:
Hot Spot for Advancement for Women/Minorities:

LOCATIONS: ("Y" = Yes)

West:	Southwest:	Midwest:	Southeast:	Northeast:	International:
Y				Y	Y

USWEB/CKS   www.uswebcks.com

Industry Group Code: 54189A
Ranks within this company's industry group: Sales: 1   Profits: 20

BUSINESS ACTIVITIES ("Y" = Yes)

Financial Services:	Information/Publ.:	Technology:	Services:		Retailing:	Telecommunications:
Stock Brokerage	Portal/Hub/News	Computer Manuf.	Payments/Transfers		Retailer	Internet Serv. Provider
Mortgages/Loans	On-Line Community	Networking Equip.	Consulting	Y	Auctions	Web Site Host
Banking	Search Engine	Software Manuf.	Advertising/Marketing	Y	Mall	Server Farm
Insurance	Financial Data Publ.	Specialty Equipment	Outsourcing		Tickets/Travel	Specialty Telecom.
Credit Cards	Broadcasting/Music				Price Comparisons	High Speed Access

TYPES OF BUSINESS:

Advertising Services-Internet Business
Strategic Consulting
Implementation
Integration

BRANDS/DIVISIONS/AFFILIATES:

CKS Group Holding
Mitchell Madison Group
Whitman-Hart, Inc.
USWeb Corp

CONTACTS: Note: Officers with more than one job title may be intentionally listed here more than once.

Robert Shaw, CEO
Robert Clarkson, COO
Carolyn Aver, CFO
Lisa McConnell, Human Resources
Sheldon Laube, Chief Tech. Officer
Carolyn Aver, Sec.
Ian Small, Chief Strategist

Phone: 408-987-3200	Fax: 415-284-7090
Toll-Free:	
Address: 2880 Lakeside Drive, Suite 300, Santa Clara, CA, 95054	

GROWTH PLANS/SPECIAL FEATURES:

USWeb Corporation, which is also known as USWeb/CKS, is a professional services firm with expertise in business strategy, marketing communications and Internet technology solutions. The company's clients are typically medium-sized and large companies. USWeb has consulting offices throughout the United States and in several countries abroad. It provides a comprehensive range of intranet, extranet and web site solutions and services, as well as marketing communications programs that use advanced technology and new media. The company has built and implemented strategic branding and advertising, system integration, network design and e-commerce solutions for Fortune 500 companies around the globe. USWeb Internet professional services include strategy consulting, analysis and design, technology development, implementation and integration, audience development and maintenance. Its marketing communications services include strategic corporate and product positioning, corporate identity and product branding, new media, collateral systems, environmental design, packaging, advertising, media placement, direct marketing and consumer and trade promotions. USWeb's mission is to provide clients with the vision, expertise and resources required to help build their businesses using Internet solutions and integrated marketing communications, and its objective is to become the leading global Internet professional services and integrated marketing communications firm. Recently, the firm announced its intention to be acquired by Whitman-Hart, Inc. for $5.9 billion in stock, in a move that will create a mammoth Internet professional services corporation.

FINANCIALS: Sales and profits are in thousands of dollars—add 000 to get the full amount.

Notes regarding 1999: (1999 sales and profits were not available for all companies at press time.)

1999 Sales: $511,000	1999 Profits: $47,000	Stock Ticker: USWB
1998 Sales: $228,600	1998 Profits: $-188,300	Employees: 1,960
1997 Sales: $19,300	1997 Profits: $-58,300	Fiscal Year Ends: 12/31
1996 Sales: $1,800	1996 Profits: $-13,800	
1995 Sales: $	1995 Profits: $	

SALARIES/BENEFITS:

Pension Plan: Y	ESOP Stock Plan: Y	Profit Sharing:	Top Exec. Salary: $259,992	Bonus: $100,000
Savings Plan:	Stock Purch. Plan: Y		Second Exec. Salary: $225,000	Bonus: $65,938

COMPETITIVE ADVANTAGE: Merger with Whitman-Hart, Inc.

OTHER THOUGHTS:

Apparent Women Officers or Directors: 3
Apparent Minority Officers or Directors:
Hot Spot for Advancement for Women/Minorities: Y

LOCATIONS: ("Y" = Yes)

West:	Southwest:	Midwest:	Southeast:	Northeast:	International:
Y	Y	Y	Y	Y	Y

V-ONE   www.v-one.com

Industry Group Code: 5112
Ranks within this company's industry group: Sales: 60   Profits: 50

BUSINESS ACTIVITIES ("Y" = Yes)

Financial Services:	Information/Publ.:	Technology:		Services:	Retailing:	Telecommunications:
Stock Brokerage	Portal/Hub/News	Computer Manuf.		Payments/Transfers	Retailer	Internet Serv. Provider
Mortgages/Loans	On-Line Community	Networking Equip.		Consulting	Auctions	Web Site Host
Banking	Search Engine	Software Manuf.	Y	Advertising/Marketing	Mall	Server Farm
Insurance	Financial Data Publ.	Specialty Equipment	Y	Outsourcing	Tickets/Travel	Specialty Telecom.
Credit Cards	Broadcasting/Music				Price Comparisons	High Speed Access

TYPES OF BUSINESS:
Software-Security

BRANDS/DIVISIONS/AFFILIATES:
SmartGate
SmartWall
Wallet Technology
SmartCAT

CONTACTS: *Note: Officers with more than one job title may be intentionally listed here more than once.*
David D. Dawson, CEO
Margaret E. Grayson, CFO
William Taylor, VP-Mktg.
Dan Davis, Dir.-Human Resources
Jieh-Shan Wang, Chief Tech. Officer
James Boyle, VP-Engineering
Steven D. Mogul, VP-Business Dev.

Phone: 301-515-5200	Fax: 301-515-5280
Toll-Free:	
Address: 20250 Century Blvd., Suite 300, Germantown, MD, 20874	

GROWTH PLANS/SPECIAL FEATURES:

V-ONE Corporation develops, markets and licenses suites of network security products that enable organizations to conduct secured electronic transactions and information exchange using public switched networks such as the Internet. The company's products address network user authentication, perimeter security, access control and data integrity through the use of smart cards, tokens, digital certificates, firewalls and encryption technology. The company's products can be combined to form a complete integrated network security solution or can be used as independent components. In addition, the company's products enable organizations to deploy and scale their solutions from small, single-site networks to large, multi-site environments and can accommodate both wireline and wireless media. The company's software includes SmartGate network security, SmartWall firewall, Wallet Technology (for securing electronic payments) and SmartCAT smart cards. V-ONE has alliances with companies such as Spyglass, Oracle and MCI WorldCom. U.S. government contracts represent more than 60% of sales.

FINANCIALS: Sales and profits are in thousands of dollars—add 000 to get the full amount.
Notes regarding 1999: *(1999 sales and profits were not available for all companies at press time.)*

1999 Sales: $	1999 Profits: $	Stock Ticker: **VONE**
1998 Sales: $6,300	1998 Profits: $-9,200	Employees: 68
1997 Sales: $9,400	1997 Profits: $-9,400	Fiscal Year Ends: 12/31
1996 Sales: $6,300	1996 Profits: $-6,700	
1995 Sales: $1,100	1995 Profits: $-1,000	

SALARIES/BENEFITS:

Pension Plan:	ESOP Stock Plan:	Profit Sharing:	Top Exec. Salary: $200,000	Bonus: $
Savings Plan:	Stock Purch. Plan:		Second Exec. Salary: $120,000	Bonus: $

COMPETITIVE ADVANTAGE: Products can be combined to create multi-purpose security solutions/Very valuable government contracts.

OTHER THOUGHTS:

Apparent Women Officers or Directors:
Apparent Minority Officers or Directors:
Hot Spot for Advancement for Women/Minorities:

LOCATIONS: ("Y" = Yes)

West:	Southwest:	Midwest:	Southeast:	Northeast:	International:
Y	Y	Y	Y	Y	Y

Note: Financial information, benefits and other data can change quickly and may vary from those stated here.

VALUE AMERICA INC   www.valueamerica.com

Industry Group Code: 4541
Ranks within this company's industry group: Sales: 15   Profits: 30

BUSINESS ACTIVITIES ("Y" = Yes)

Financial Services:	Information/Publ.:	Technology:	Services:	Retailing:		Telecommunications:
Stock Brokerage	Portal/Hub/News	Computer Manuf.	Payments/Transfers	Retailer	Y	Internet Serv. Provider
Mortgages/Loans	On-Line Community	Networking Equip.	Consulting	Auctions		Web Site Host
Banking	Search Engine	Software Manuf.	Advertising/Marketing	Mall		Server Farm
Insurance	Financial Data Publ.	Specialty Equipment	Outsourcing	Tickets/Travel		Specialty Telecom.
Credit Cards	Broadcasting/Music			Price Comparisons		High Speed Access

TYPES OF BUSINESS:
On-line Discount Retailer

BRANDS/DIVISIONS/AFFILIATES:

GROWTH PLANS/SPECIAL FEATURES:

Through its retail web site, Value America, Inc. sells over 1,000 brands of discount-priced products. Categories of merchandise sold on the site include technology merchandise (computers, peripherals and software), office merchandise (equipment, furniture and supplies) and consumer merchandise (electronics, housewares, jewelry, books, music, home furnishings, sporting goods, toys, health and beauty products and pet supplies). All merchandise is showcased through multimedia presentations. Value America also offers a personal shopper feature that enables the site to track receipts, warranties, important dates and discounts. The company is currently considering changing the basis of its now free membership to include a fee. Value America also sells through extensive magazine advertising in such publications as The Wall Street Journal. In an effort to control costs and boost profits, the company recently laid-off a large number of employees and restructured operations.

CONTACTS: *Note: Officers with more than one job title may be intentionally listed here more than once.*
Thomas Morgan, CEO
Glenda M. Dorchak, Pres./COO
Dean M. Johnston, Exec. VP/CFO
Melissa M. Monk, VP-Sales
Tana Tornabene, VP-Human Resources
Joseph L. Page, Chief Tech. Officer
Jerry K. Goode, CIO
Sandra T. Watson, VP-Finance/Controller
Kenneth K. Erickson, Jr., VP-Merch.
Jerry K. Goode, VP-Engineering
Steven Tungate, VP-Oper.
Kenneth R. Power, VP-Advertising
Richard L. Gerhardt, Pres.-Consumer Products Div.

Phone: 804-817-7700	Fax: 804-817-7885
Toll-Free:	
Address: 1550 Insurance Ln., Charlottesville, VA, 22911	

FINANCIALS: Sales and profits are in thousands of dollars—add 000 to get the full amount.
Notes regarding 1999: Through 9 months *(1999 sales and profits were not available for all companies at press time.)*

1999 Sales: $121,400	1999 Profits: $-129,800	
1998 Sales: $41,500	1998 Profits: $-53,600	**Stock Ticker: VUSA**
1997 Sales: $ 100	1997 Profits: $- 400	Employees: 227
1996 Sales: $	1996 Profits: $- 400	Fiscal Year Ends: 12/31
1995 Sales: $	1995 Profits: $	

SALARIES/BENEFITS:

Pension Plan:	ESOP Stock Plan:	Profit Sharing:	Top Exec. Salary: $233,718	Bonus: $
Savings Plan: Y	Stock Purch. Plan:		Second Exec. Salary: $177,692	Bonus: $

COMPETITIVE ADVANTAGE: Offers multimedia merchandise presentations as well as discounts and extended selection.

OTHER THOUGHTS:
Apparent Women Officers or Directors: 4
Apparent Minority Officers or Directors:
Hot Spot for Advancement for Women/Minorities: Y

LOCATIONS: ("Y" = Yes)

West:	Southwest:	Midwest:	Southeast:	Northeast:	International:
			Y		

Note: Financial information, benefits and other data can change quickly and may vary from those stated here.

VASCO DATA SECURITY www.vdsi.com

Industry Group Code: 5112
Ranks within this company's industry group: Sales: 46 Profits: 23

BUSINESS ACTIVITIES ("Y" = Yes)

Financial Services:	Information/Publ.:	Technology:		Services:		Retailing:	Telecommunications:
Stock Brokerage	Portal/Hub/News	Computer Manuf.		Payments/Transfers		Retailer	Internet Serv. Provider
Mortgages/Loans	On-Line Community	Networking Equip.		Consulting		Auctions	Web Site Host
Banking	Search Engine	Software Manuf.	Y	Advertising/Marketing		Mall	Server Farm
Insurance	Financial Data Publ.	Specialty Equipment	Y	Outsourcing	Y	Tickets/Travel	Specialty Telecom.
Credit Cards	Broadcasting/Music					Price Comparisons	High Speed Access

TYPES OF BUSINESS:
Software-Security

BRANDS/DIVISIONS/AFFILIATES:
VASCO Corporation Subsidiary
Digipass
VACMan

CONTACTS: Note: Officers with more than one job title may be intentionally listed here more than once.
Mario Houthooft, CEO
Mario Houthooft, Pres.
Gregory T. Apple, VP-Finance and Admin.
Jan Valcke, Sales and Mktg. Mgr
John C. Haggard, Chief Tech. Officer
Chantal Boudaer-Vanderplasschen, Oper. Mgr.
Hyon C. Im, VP- Research and Dev.

Phone: 630-932-8844	**Fax:** 630-932-8852

Toll-Free:

Address: 1901 South Meyers Road, Ste. 210, Oakbrook Terrace, IL, 60181

GROWTH PLANS/SPECIAL FEATURES:

Vasco Data Security, formerly Digipass, provides information security solutions that range from tokens, smart cards and biometric technology to integrated authentication, access control, auditing and accounting. Vasco's products secure, control and monitor access to computer systems, whether remote, local or Internet, ensuring that corporate information assets remain secure. The Vasco Access Control Manager, VACMan, server product line is a software solution that enables security decisions to be centralized and enables clients to utilize state-of-the-art authentification technologies. The company's key markets are banking, telecommunications and corporate networks. Vasco serves over 130 financial institutions in more than 45 countries and has deployed over 2.6 million authentification tokens. Vasco's corporate headquarters are in Illinois and the company is represented in over 20 countries, including France, Germany, Japan, the Netherlands, Thailand and the UK. End users of the company's products include First Union National Bank, Generale Bank, France Telecom and Manitoba Telephone.

FINANCIALS: Sales and profits are in thousands of dollars—add 000 to get the full amount.
Notes regarding 1999: *(1999 sales and profits were not available for all companies at press time.)*

1999 Sales: $13,413	1999 Profits: $ 254	**Stock Ticker: VDSI**
1998 Sales: $10,432	1998 Profits: $- 648	Employees:
1997 Sales: $12,302	1997 Profits: $-3,936	Fiscal Year Ends: 12/30
1996 Sales: $10,193	1996 Profits: $-8,657	
1995 Sales: $	1995 Profits: $	

SALARIES/BENEFITS:

Pension Plan:	ESOP Stock Plan: Y	Profit Sharing:	Top Exec. Salary: $155,000	Bonus: $
Savings Plan:	Stock Purch. Plan:		Second Exec. Salary: $128,333	Bonus: $

COMPETITIVE ADVANTAGE: International network of offices/Excellent technology.

OTHER THOUGHTS:

	LOCATIONS: ("Y" = Yes)					
	West:	Southwest:	Midwest:	Southeast:	Northeast:	International:
Apparent Women Officers or Directors:			Y			Y
Apparent Minority Officers or Directors:						
Hot Spot for Advancement for Women/Minorities:						

Note: Financial information, benefits and other data can change quickly and may vary from those stated here.

VERIO INC
www.verio.com

Industry Group Code: 51339
Ranks within this company's industry group: Sales: 4   Profits: 24

BUSINESS ACTIVITIES ("Y" = Yes)

Financial Services:	Information/Publ.:	Technology:	Services:	Retailing:	Telecommunications:	
Stock Brokerage	Portal/Hub/News	Computer Manuf.	Payments/Transfers	Retailer	Internet Serv. Provider	Y
Mortgages/Loans	On-Line Community	Networking Equip.	Consulting	Auctions	Web Site Host	Y
Banking	Search Engine	Software Manuf.	Advertising/Marketing	Mall	Server Farm	
Insurance	Financial Data Publ.	Specialty Equipment	Outsourcing	Tickets/Travel	Specialty Telecom.	
Credit Cards	Broadcasting/Music			Price Comparisons	High Speed Access	Y

TYPES OF BUSINESS:

Internet Service Provider
DSL Services
Web Site Hosting
Virtual Private Networks
E-Commerce Solutions
ASP-based Oracle8 Solutions

BRANDS/DIVISIONS/AFFILIATES:

iServer
TABNet
Hiway
RAINet, Inc.
CCNet, Inc.
Global Enterprise Services, Inc.
Pioneer Global Telecommunications, Inc.
Web Communications, LLC

CONTACTS: *Note: Officers with more than one job title may be intentionally listed here more than once.*

Justin L. Jaschke, CEO
Herbert R. Hribar, COO
Peter B. Fritzinger, CFO
James E. Cunningham, VP-Mktg.
Deb Mayfield Gahan, VP-Human Resources
Chris J. DeMarche, Chief Tech. Officer
Eric S. Hood, VP-Regional Engineering
Carla Hamre Donelson, Sec.
Carla Hamre Donelson, General Counsel
Sean G. Brophy, VP-Corp. Dev.

Phone: 303-645-1900	Fax: 303-792-5644
Toll-Free:	
Address: 8005 South Chester Street, Suite 200, Englewood, CO, 80112	

GROWTH PLANS/SPECIAL FEATURES:

Verio Inc. is a leading provider of comprehensive Internet services, with an emphasis on serving the small and medium sized business market. The company provides customers with the telecommunications circuits that permit them to make connections to and transmissions over the Internet. Verio Inc. also hosts sites for a broad range of nationwide customers. The company offers an expanding package of enhanced Internet tools, such as electronic commerce, enabling buyers to conduct transactions with their customers and vendors over the Internet. Verio Inc. also offers virtual private networks, permitting customers to engage in private communications with their employees, vendors, customers and suppliers, with whom secure Internet communication capabilities are important. The company markets its enhanced Internet services on AOL's U.S. sites and through a network of resellers in more than 170 countries. Verio also markets through a large, nationwide network of offices selling combined service packages, including high speed access through DSL lines and web site vesting. Verio's growth is largely due to acquisitions, as the company has acquired more than 45 Internet companies since its founding. Japan's Nippon Telegraph and Telephone owns 12% of Verio, and MCI WorldCom owns about 10%.

FINANCIALS: Sales and profits are in thousands of dollars—add 000 to get the full amount.
Notes regarding 1999: *(1999 sales and profits were not available for all companies at press time.)*

1999 Sales: $	1999 Profits: $	**Stock Ticker: VRIO**
1998 Sales: $120,700	1998 Profits: $-122,000	Employees: 1,360
1997 Sales: $35,700	1997 Profits: $-46,100	Fiscal Year Ends: 12/31
1996 Sales: $2,400	1996 Profits: $-5,100	
1995 Sales: $	1995 Profits: $	

SALARIES/BENEFITS:

Pension Plan:	ESOP Stock Plan:	Profit Sharing: Y	Top Exec. Salary: $221,041	Bonus: $
Savings Plan:	Stock Purch. Plan:		Second Exec. Salary: $173,541	Bonus: $

COMPETITIVE ADVANTAGE: Rapid growth through acquisitions/International backers.

OTHER THOUGHTS:

Apparent Women Officers or Directors: 2
Apparent Minority Officers or Directors: 2
Hot Spot for Advancement for Women/Minorities: Y

LOCATIONS: ("Y" = Yes)

West:	Southwest:	Midwest:	Southeast:	Northeast:	International:
Y	Y	Y	Y	Y	Y

VERISIGN   www.verisign.com

Industry Group Code: 5112
Ranks within this company's industry group: Sales: 24   Profits: 69

BUSINESS ACTIVITIES ("Y" = Yes)

Financial Services:	Information/Publ.:	Technology:		Services:	Retailing:	Telecommunications:
Stock Brokerage	Portal/Hub/News	Computer Manuf.		Payments/Transfers	Retailer	Internet Serv. Provider
Mortgages/Loans	On-Line Community	Networking Equip.		Consulting	Auctions	Web Site Host
Banking	Search Engine	Software Manuf.	Y	Advertising/Marketing	Mall	Server Farm
Insurance	Financial Data Publ.	Specialty Equipment		Outsourcing	Tickets/Travel	Specialty Telecom.
Credit Cards	Broadcasting/Music				Price Comparisons	High Speed Access

TYPES OF BUSINESS:
Software-Secure Digital Ids

BRANDS/DIVISIONS/AFFILIATES:
Website Digital Certificate
VeriSign OnSite Service
British Telecommunications
Certplus
VeriSign Japan
HiTrust
SACA
AT&T

CONTACTS: *Note: Officers with more than one job title may be intentionally listed here more than once.*
Stratton D. Sclavos, CEO
Stratton D. Sclavos, Pres.
Dana L. Evan, VP-Finance/CFO
Richard A. Yanowitch, VP-Mktg.
Gary Pohl, Mgr.-Human Resources
Arnold Schaeffer, VP-Engineering
Quentin P. Gallivan, VP-Worldwide Sales

Phone: 650-961-7500	Fax: 650-961-7300
Toll-Free:	
Address: 1390 Shorebird Way, Mountainview, CA, 94043	

GROWTH PLANS/SPECIAL FEATURES:

VeriSign is a provider of Internet-based secure identification services needed by web sites, enterprises and individuals to conduct trusted and secure electronic commerce and communications over the Internet, intranets and extranets. The company has established strategic relationships with industry leaders, including AT&T, Cisco, Microsoft, Netscape, Network Associates and VISA, to enable widespread utilization of its digital certificate services and to assure their interoperability with a wide variety of applications and network equipment. Verisign has used its own secure on-line infrastructure to issue over 100,000 of its Website Digital Certificates and over 3.5 million of its digital certificates for individuals. The company's Website Digital Certificate services are used by over 400 of the Fortune 500 companies and all of the top 25 electronic commerce web sites, as reported by Jupiter Communications. VeriSign also offers the VeriSign OnSite service, which allows an organization to leverage Verisign's trusted service infrastructure to develop and deploy customized digital certificate services for use by its employees, customers and business partners. VeriSign has become increasingly active around the globe, thanks to the efforts of its international affiliates and the addition of new strategic partnerships. The company's global affiliate network was expanded recently to include British Telecommunications, Certplus (France), VeriSign Japan, HiTrust (Taiwan), SACA (South Africa) and AT&T (U.S.).

FINANCIALS: Sales and profits are in thousands of dollars—add 000 to get the full amount.
Notes regarding 1999: *(1999 sales and profits were not available for all companies at press time.)*

1999 Sales: $84,800	1999 Profits: $4,000	Stock Ticker: **VRSN**
1998 Sales: $38,900	1998 Profits: $-19,700	Employees: 315
1997 Sales: $9,400	1997 Profits: $-19,200	Fiscal Year Ends: 12/31
1996 Sales: $1,400	1996 Profits: $-10,200	
1995 Sales: $ 400	1995 Profits: $-2,000	

SALARIES/BENEFITS:

Pension Plan:	ESOP Stock Plan:	Profit Sharing:	Top Exec. Salary: $250,000	Bonus: $130,625
Savings Plan:	Stock Purch. Plan: Y		Second Exec. Salary: $167,708	Bonus: $65,046

COMPETITIVE ADVANTAGE: Client list includes most major e-commerce companies.

OTHER THOUGHTS:
Apparent Women Officers or Directors:
Apparent Minority Officers or Directors:
Hot Spot for Advancement for Women/Minorities:

LOCATIONS: ("Y" = Yes)

West:	Southwest:	Midwest:	Southeast:	Northeast:	International:
Y				Y	

Note: Financial information, benefits and other data can change quickly and may vary from those stated here.

VERITY www.verity.com

Industry Group Code: 5112
Ranks within this company's industry group: Sales: 24 Profits: 68

BUSINESS ACTIVITIES ("Y" = Yes)

Financial Services:	Information/Publ.:	Technology:		Services:		Retailing:	Telecommunications:
Stock Brokerage	Portal/Hub/News	Computer Manuf.		Payments/Transfers		Retailer	Internet Serv. Provider
Mortgages/Loans	On-Line Community	Networking Equip.		Consulting		Auctions	Web Site Host
Banking	Search Engine	Software Manuf.	Y	Advertising/Marketing		Mall	Server Farm
Insurance	Financial Data Publ.	Specialty Equipment		Outsourcing		Tickets/Travel	Specialty Telecom.
Credit Cards	Broadcasting/Music					Price Comparisons	High Speed Access

TYPES OF BUSINESS:

Software-Document Management

BRANDS/DIVISIONS/AFFILIATES:

CONTACTS: Note: Officers with more than one job title may be intentionally listed here more than once.

Gary Sbona, CEO
Anthony J. Bettencourt III, Pres.
James Ticehurst, VP-Finance/CFO
Rena Schaut, Mgr.of Human Resources
Hugh S. Njemanze, Chief Tech.Officer
John Navas, VP-Dev. and Tech. Services
Todd K. Yamami, Corp. Controller
Ronald F. E. Weissman, VP-Strategy and Corporate Dev.

Phone: 408-541-1500	Fax: 408-541-1600
Toll-Free:	
Address: 894 Ross Dr., Sunnyvale, CA, 94089	

GROWTH PLANS/SPECIAL FEATURES:

Verity develops, markets and supports knowledge retrieval software products for corporate intranets and extranets, on-line publishers, e-commerce providers, original equipment manufacturers (OEMs) and independent software vendors. The company's integrated product family enables enterprise-wide document indexing, classification, search and retrieval, organization and navigation, personalized dissemination and hybrid on-line and CD publishing, all from the same underlying Verity information index. Verity's products organize and provide simple, single-point access to business information across the entire enterprise. Verity's software has been licensed directly to over 1,000 corporations, government agencies, software developers, information publishers and e-commerce vendors. The company focuses on three core markets: intranet-based knowledge retrieval applications for large corporate and government organizations, information retrieval solutions for e-commerce and electronic publishers and embedded solutions for OEMs. Verity received the first annual Market Recognition Award for information retrieval, presented by the Delphi Group, a leader in knowledge management research and advisory services. Based on a survey of 600 users and evaluators of information retrieval products, Verity was selected from a field of more than 150 competitors that were perceived to be leading the industry.

FINANCIALS: Sales and profits are in thousands of dollars—add 000 to get the full amount.

Notes regarding 1999: *(1999 sales and profits were not available for all companies at press time.)*

1999 Sales: $64,400	1999 Profits: $12,100	Stock Ticker: **VRTY**
1998 Sales: $38,900	1998 Profits: $-16,500	Employees: 295
1997 Sales: $42,700	1997 Profits: $-17,900	Fiscal Year Ends: 5/31
1996 Sales: $30,700	1996 Profits: $- 300	
1995 Sales: $15,900	1995 Profits: $-5,800	

SALARIES/BENEFITS:

Pension Plan:	ESOP Stock Plan:	Profit Sharing:	Top Exec. Salary: $213,333	Bonus: $42,667
Savings Plan: Y	Stock Purch. Plan: Y		Second Exec. Salary: $200,000	Bonus: $200,000

COMPETITIVE ADVANTAGE: Superior retrieval and indexing of enterprise wide information

OTHER THOUGHTS:

Apparent Women Officers or Directors: 1
Apparent Minority Officers or Directors: 2
Hot Spot for Advancement for Women/Minorities: Y

LOCATIONS: ("Y" = Yes)

West:	Southwest:	Midwest:	Southeast:	Northeast:	International:
Y					Y

VERSANT CORP   www.versant.com

Industry Group Code: 5112
Ranks within this company's industry group: Sales: 33   Profits: 71

BUSINESS ACTIVITIES ("Y" = Yes)

Financial Services:	Information/Publ.:	Technology:		Services:		Retailing:		Telecommunications:
Stock Brokerage	Portal/Hub/News	Computer Manuf.		Payments/Transfers		Retailer		Internet Serv. Provider
Mortgages/Loans	On-Line Community	Networking Equip.		Consulting	Y	Auctions		Web Site Host
Banking	Search Engine	Software Manuf.	Y	Advertising/Marketing		Mall		Server Farm
Insurance	Financial Data Publ.	Specialty Equipment		Outsourcing	Y	Tickets/Travel		Specialty Telecom.
Credit Cards	Broadcasting/Music					Price Comparisons		High Speed Access

TYPES OF BUSINESS:
Software-Database Management

BRANDS/DIVISIONS/AFFILIATES:
Object Database Management System

CONTACTS: *Note: Officers with more than one job title may be intentionally listed here more than once.*
Nick Ordon, CEO
Nick Ordon, Pres.
Gary Rhea, CFO/VP-Finance and Admin.
George C. Franzen, Chief Tech. Officer
Nipun Sehgal, VP-Engineering
Bernhard Woebker, Sr. VP-Worldwide Field Oper.

Phone: 510-789-1500	Fax: 510-789-1515
Toll-Free: 800-837-7268	
Address: 6539 Dumbarton Circle, Fremont, CA, 94555	

GROWTH PLANS/SPECIAL FEATURES:

Versant Corporation provides database management systems that enable businesses to access and manage information from anywhere. The company offers products that reduce the time and cost of creating complex applications and enable the rapid development of next generation applications, including those that are difficult or impossible to build using traditional database management technologies. Solutions created to maximize the use of network resources allow high transaction performance that can integrate up to 65,000 different databases into one network through the Versant Object Database Management System (ODBMS). Versant enables telephony applications, nationwide transportation control and automation systems, follow-the-sun derivative trading systems and international fraud management applications. The system supports multiple languages and processes data in audio, video and alphanumeric forms. The company is in compliance with the ISO 9001 international standard for quality business processes as well as ODMG, OMG, CORBA AND ANSI standards. Versant products are sold worldwide through a direct sales force and distributor network to assure local representation and support. The company's customers include British Airways, Lucent Technologies, Kodak, Nexus and Sun Microsystems. Versant also offers consulting, training and custom development services.

FINANCIALS: Sales and profits are in thousands of dollars—add 000 to get the full amount.
Notes regarding 1999: *(1999 sales and profits were not available for all companies at press time.)*

1999 Sales: $25,900	1999 Profits: $-1,700	**Stock Ticker: VSNT**
1998 Sales: $23,200	1998 Profits: $-19,900	Employees: 173
1997 Sales: $29,200	1997 Profits: $-2,300	Fiscal Year Ends: 12/31
1996 Sales: $18,400	1996 Profits: $1,400	
1995 Sales: $11,900	1995 Profits: $-1,200	

SALARIES/BENEFITS:

Pension Plan:	ESOP Stock Plan: Y	Profit Sharing:	Top Exec. Salary: $198,590	Bonus: $
Savings Plan:	Stock Purch. Plan: Y		Second Exec. Salary: $168,300	Bonus: $82,884

COMPETITIVE ADVANTAGE: Ability to integrate up to 65,000 different databases.

OTHER THOUGHTS:

Apparent Women Officers or Directors:					
Apparent Minority Officers or Directors:					
Hot Spot for Advancement for Women/Minorities:					

LOCATIONS: ("Y" = Yes)

West:	Southwest:	Midwest:	Southeast:	Northeast:	International:
Y					Y

Note: Financial information, benefits and other data can change quickly and may vary from those stated here.

VERTICALNET   www.verticalnet.com

Industry Group Code: 51339A
Ranks within this company's industry group: Sales: 8   Profits: 12

BUSINESS ACTIVITIES ("Y" = Yes)

Financial Services:	Information/Publ.:		Technology:	Services:	Retailing:	Telecommunications:	
Stock Brokerage	Portal/Hub/News	Y	Computer Manuf.	Payments/Transfers	Retailer	Internet Serv. Provider	
Mortgages/Loans	On-Line Community	Y	Networking Equip.	Consulting	Auctions	Web Site Host	Y
Banking	Search Engine	Y	Software Manuf.	Advertising/Marketing	Mall	Server Farm	
Insurance	Financial Data Publ.		Specialty Equipment	Outsourcing	Tickets/Travel	Specialty Telecom.	
Credit Cards	Broadcasting/Music				Price Comparisons	High Speed Access	

TYPES OF BUSINESS:

On-line Vertical Trade Marketplace
Niche Industry Sites
Industrial Data Content
On-line Procurement Nesting

BRANDS/DIVISIONS/AFFILIATES:

Aerospace Online
Auto Central.com
Electronic Engineering.com
Embedded Technology.com
Plant Automation.com
Semiconductor Online
Test and Measurement.com

CONTACTS: Note: Officers with more than one job title may be intentionally listed here more than once.

Mark L. Walsh, CEO
Mark L. Walsh, Pres.
Gene S. Godick, CFO/VP-Finance
Barry Wynkoop, Sr. VP-Sales and Mktg. Dev.
Barbara Caprice, Dir.- Human Resources
C. H. Low, Chief Tech. Officer
Mario V. Shaffer, VP- New Business Dev.
Blaire LaCorte, Sr. VP- Electronic Commerce
Michael J. Hagan, Sr. VP- Mergers and Acquisitions
Michael P. McNulty, Sr. VP- Audience Dev.

Phone: 215-328-6100	Fax: 215-443-3336
Toll-Free:	
Address: 2 Walnut Grove Dr., Ste. 150, Horsham, PA, 19044	

GROWTH PLANS/SPECIAL FEATURES:

VerticalNet operates more than 40 industry-specific vertical trade communities. VerticalNet was a pioneer in industry-specific web sites, recognizing early on the significant advantages that niche web portals can offer to buyers and sellers of industrial goods and services. The company focuses exclusively on the needs of industrial audiences such as engineers, scientists and manufacturers. Focusing on one industrial sector at a time allows VerticalNet to create communities where individuals with similar professional interests can communicate with each other. All VerticalNet sites have an on-line buyer's guide and search engine, allowing customers to search for specific products based on name and supplier. Each of the company's vertical trade communities is built to attract the professionals responsible for selecting and purchasing highly specialized industry-related products and services. The company creates a marketplace for advertisers and includes news and product analysis created by an in-house editorial team. Some VerticalNet sites allow visitors to engage in discussions with industry professionals, while providing access to freeware, demo software, industry guides and virtual trade shows and offering a career center with resumes and job listings. Previously, most access to this information required a trade magazine subscription or a trip to a trade show. VerticalNet also offers web site creation, management and hosting services for companies and trade organizations. Microsoft Corporation recently invested $100 million in the firm.

FINANCIALS: Sales and profits are in thousands of dollars—add 000 to get the full amount.

Notes regarding 1999: *(1999 sales and profits were not available for all companies at press time.)*

1999 Sales: $20,760	1999 Profits: $-15,280	Stock Ticker: **VERT**
1998 Sales: $3,100	1998 Profits: $-13,600	Employees: 220
1997 Sales: $ 800	1997 Profits: $-4,800	Fiscal Year Ends: 12/31
1996 Sales: $ 300	1996 Profits: $- 700	
1995 Sales: $	1995 Profits: $- 200	

SALARIES/BENEFITS:

Pension Plan:	ESOP Stock Plan: Y	Profit Sharing:	Top Exec. Salary: $233,333	Bonus: $100,000
Savings Plan:	Stock Purch. Plan: Y		Second Exec. Salary: $112,916	Bonus: $25,000

COMPETITIVE ADVANTAGE: Leader in this market/Highly successful IPO/Major investment from Microsoft.

OTHER THOUGHTS:

Apparent Women Officers or Directors:
Apparent Minority Officers or Directors:
Hot Spot for Advancement for Women/Minorities:

LOCATIONS: ("Y" = Yes)

West:	Southwest:	Midwest:	Southeast:	Northeast:	International:
				Y	

Note: Financial information, benefits and other data can change quickly and may vary from those stated here.

VIACOM INC   www.viacom.com, www.blockbuster.com

Industry Group Code: 5132
Ranks within this company's industry group: Sales: 2   Profits: 2

BUSINESS ACTIVITIES ("Y" = Yes)

Financial Services:	Information/Publ.:		Technology:	Services:	Retailing:		Telecommunications:
Stock Brokerage	Portal/Hub/News	Y	Computer Manuf.	Payments/Transfers	Retailer	Y	Internet Serv. Provider
Mortgages/Loans	On-Line Community		Networking Equip.	Consulting	Auctions		Web Site Host
Banking	Search Engine		Software Manuf.	Advertising/Marketing	Mall		Server Farm
Insurance	Financial Data Publ.		Specialty Equipment	Outsourcing	Tickets/Travel		Specialty Telecom.
Credit Cards	Broadcasting/Music	Y			Price Comparisons		High Speed Access

TYPES OF BUSINESS:

Networks and Broadcasting
Video Rental Stores
Filmed Entertainment
On-line Retailing
Cable Television Networks
Book Publishing
Radio Broadcasting
Amusement Parks

BRANDS/DIVISIONS/AFFILIATES:

MTV Networks
Showtime Networks, Inc.
Nickelodeon
Paramount Pictures/Paramount Stations Group
Blockbuster Video
CBS
Prentice Hall
Simon & Schuster

CONTACTS: *Note: Officers with more than one job title may be intentionally listed here more than once.*

Sumner M. Redstone, CEO
George S. Smith, Sr. VP/CFO
William A. Roskin, Sr. VP-Human Resources
Paul A. Heimbach, Sr.VP-Chief Tech. Officer
Susan C. Gordon, VP-Controller/Chief Acct. Officer
Michael D. Fricklas, Sr.VP-Corp. Sec.
Michael D. Fricklas, Sr.VP-General Counsel
William A. Roskin, Sr.VP- Admin.
Robert M. Bakish, Sr. VP-Planning, Devel. & Tech.
Russ Pillar, VP CBS Internet
Karen O'Rourke Zatorski, VP-Corp. Relations
Martin M. Shea, Sr.VP-Investor Relations

Phone: 212-258-6000	Fax: 212-258-6464
Toll-Free:	
Address: 1515 Broadway, New York, NY, 10036	

GROWTH PLANS/SPECIAL FEATURES:

Viacom Inc. is a diversified entertainment company with operations in six segments, including networks, entertainment, video, parks, on-line and publishing. Through the networks segment, the company operates MTV: Music Television, Showtime, Nickelodeon/Nick at Nite, VH1 Music First and TV Land. Viacom also operates Paramount Pictures, Paramount Television and Paramount Stations Group. Viacom operates and franchises Blockbuster Video stores worldwide and operates five theme parks. The company's publishing segment includes imprints such as Simon & Schuster, Pocket Books, Scribner and The Free Press. The on-line division of Viacom features MTV, Nickelodeon/Nick at Nite and VH1 Music first. Viacom has enormous presence internationally and domestically. Viacom distributes its films in Europe, Southeast Asia and Africa, and the company distributes its television channels and programming to Asia, Australia, Brazil, Europe, Latin America and Russia. In recent news, TiVo, Inc., the creator of personalized television, and Blockbuster Inc. recently announced an alliance. The companies plan to develop a virtual video-on-demand service that will enable TiVo subscribers to view films through their TiVo receivers. Also, shareholders of Viacom and CBS Corporation approved the merger of the two companies in December 1999. Viacom is ranked 138th in the Fortune 500 list, 159th in Hoover's 500 and is a member of the S&P 500 Index.

FINANCIALS: Sales and profits are in thousands of dollars—add 000 to get the full amount.

Notes regarding 1999: *(1999 sales and profits were not available for all companies at press time.)*

1999 Sales: $	1999 Profits: $	**Stock Ticker: VIA**
1998 Sales: $12,096,100	1998 Profits: $-122,400	Employees: 111,730
1997 Sales: $13,206,100	1997 Profits: $793,600	Fiscal Year Ends: 12/31
1996 Sales: $12,084,200	1996 Profits: $1,247,900	
1995 Sales: $	1995 Profits: $	

SALARIES/BENEFITS:

Pension Plan: Y	ESOP Stock Plan:	Profit Sharing:	Top Exec. Salary: $1,000,000	Bonus: $6,000,000
Savings Plan: Y	Stock Purch. Plan:		Second Exec. Salary: $612,500	Bonus: $475,000

COMPETITIVE ADVANTAGE: Excellent cross-marketing between film production, theaters, television networks and retail video stores.

OTHER THOUGHTS:

Apparent Women Officers or Directors: 4
Apparent Minority Officers or Directors:
Hot Spot for Advancement for Women/Minorities: Y

LOCATIONS: ("Y" = Yes)

West:	Southwest:	Midwest:	Southeast:	Northeast:	International:
Y	Y	Y	Y	Y	Y

VIANT   www.viant.com

Industry Group Code: 54151
Ranks within this company's industry group: Sales: 18   Profits: 11

BUSINESS ACTIVITIES ("Y" = Yes)

Financial Services:	Information/Publ.:	Technology:	Services:		Retailing:		Telecommunications:
Stock Brokerage	Portal/Hub/News	Computer Manuf.	Payments/Transfers		Retailer		Internet Serv. Provider
Mortgages/Loans	On-Line Community	Networking Equip.	Consulting	Y	Auctions		Web Site Host
Banking	Search Engine	Software Manuf.	Advertising/Marketing		Mall		Server Farm
Insurance	Financial Data Publ.	Specialty Equipment	Outsourcing	Y	Tickets/Travel		Specialty Telecom.
Credit Cards	Broadcasting/Music				Price Comparisons		High Speed Access

TYPES OF BUSINESS:

Consulting-Internet
Systems Design and Implementation

BRANDS/DIVISIONS/AFFILIATES:

CONTACTS: Note: Officers with more than one job title may be intentionally listed here more than once.

Robert L. Gett, CEO
Robert L. Gett, Pres.
M. Dwayne Nesmith, CFO
Sherwin A. Uretsky, VP-Worldwide Sales
Diane M. Hall, Chief People Officer (HR)
Timothy A. Andrews, Chief Tech. Officer
Christopher Newell, Chief Knowledge Officer
Edward J. Mello, VP- Strategic Dev.
Michael J. Tubridy, VP- Finance/Treas.

Phone: 617-531-3700	Fax: 617-531-3803
Toll-Free:	
Address: 89 South St., Boston, MA, 02111	

GROWTH PLANS/SPECIAL FEATURES:

Viant is an Internet consulting firm that helps clients from a broad range of industries plan, build and launch digital businesses. The company's approach is a combination of strategic consulting, creative design and technology services, which helps companies capitalize on the opportunities provided by doing business on the Internet. The firm designs and develops strategies that integrate a customer's Internet projects and investments with its broader corporate strategies and business practices. Viant provides e-commerce solutions that enable a company to attract new customers and sell goods and services over a web site. The company's extranets allow clients to share information and communicate effectively with one another, while intranets improve a company's ability to capture, store and distribute helpful information to its employees. Viant focuses on Internet initiatives critical to their clients' businesses. For example, Blue Tape hired Viant to build and launch sputnik7.com, the first real-time, interactive music video experience on the Internet. In addition, Viant redesigned Compaq's entire approach to using the Internet for customer relations. Kinko's hired Viant to build its worldwide intranet, which is now a connection among Kinko's 900+ stores. Other Viant customers include American Express, Deutsche Bank, General Motors, Hewlett-Packard, Lucent Technologies Inc., Polo/Ralph Lauren, Radio Shack, Sears and Sony Pictures Entertainment.

FINANCIALS: Sales and profits are in thousands of dollars—add 000 to get the full amount.
Notes regarding 1999: (1999 sales and profits were not available for all companies at press time.)

1999 Sales: $61,300	1999 Profits: $1,400	Stock Ticker: **VIAN**
1998 Sales: $20,000	1998 Profits: $-6,500	Employees: 246
1997 Sales: $8,800	1997 Profits: $-4,100	Fiscal Year Ends: 12/31
1996 Sales: $ 600	1996 Profits: $-1,700	
1995 Sales: $	1995 Profits: $	

SALARIES/BENEFITS:

Pension Plan: Y	ESOP Stock Plan: Y	Profit Sharing:	Top Exec. Salary: $210,073	Bonus: $51,282
Savings Plan: Y	Stock Purch. Plan: Y		Second Exec. Salary: $195,408	Bonus: $55,576

COMPETITIVE ADVANTAGE: Global, blue ribbon

OTHER THOUGHTS:

Apparent Women Officers or Directors:
Apparent Minority Officers or Directors:
Hot Spot for Advancement for Women/Minorities:

LOCATIONS: ("Y" = Yes)

West:	Southwest:	Midwest:	Southeast:	Northeast:	International:
Y	Y			Y	Y

VISUAL DATA   www.vdat.com

Industry Group Code: 54189A
Ranks within this company's industry group: Sales: 18   Profits: 13

BUSINESS ACTIVITIES ("Y" = Yes)

Financial Services:	Information/Publ.:		Technology:	Services:		Retailing:	Telecommunications:
Stock Brokerage	Portal/Hub/News	Y	Computer Manuf.	Payments/Transfers		Retailer	Internet Serv. Provider
Mortgages/Loans	On-Line Community		Networking Equip.	Consulting		Auctions	Web Site Host
Banking	Search Engine		Software Manuf.	Advertising/Marketing	Y	Mall	Server Farm
Insurance	Financial Data Publ.	Y	Specialty Equipment	Outsourcing		Tickets/Travel	Specialty Telecom.
Credit Cards	Broadcasting/Music	Y				Price Comparisons	High Speed Access

TYPES OF BUSINESS:

Advertising-Video Previews
Multi-Media Content
Medical Information
Travel Information

BRANDS/DIVISIONS/AFFILIATES:

Ednet
TheFirstNews.com (TFN)
MedicalView
VideoNewswire
TalentView
ResortView
HotelView
CareView

CONTACTS: *Note: Officers with more than one job title may be intentionally listed here more than once.*

Randy S. Selman, CEO
Randy S. Selman, Pres.
Pauline Schneider, CFO
Joann Tepper, Human Resources
Alan M. Saperstein, Treas.

Phone: 954-917-6655	Fax: 954-917-6660
Toll-Free:	
Address: 1291 SW 29 Ave., Pompano Beach, FL, 33069	

GROWTH PLANS/SPECIAL FEATURES:

Visual Data Corporation is a creator of original multi-media content for the Internet, ranging from hotel tours to medical information. The company's HotelView is a distributor of on-line travel videos, giving full-motion video and audio tours that provide the prospective traveler with a look at rooms and amenities. A more broad-based guide sponsored by Visual Data is broadcast.com's travel channel, where users will find video tours and previews of hotels, resorts, timeshare properties, golf courses and attractions ideal for planning business trips or vacations. The company's new Internet-based audio information service for the investor and day trader community is TheFirstNews.com (TFN). Subscribers to TFN will receive breaking corporate news releases in streaming audio. The releases broadcast will be based on preferences set by the subscriber, creating faster and more specific news than that provided by traditional news services. TheFirstNews.com player can be set on quiet mode or at a continuous low volume on the user's desktop. When news concerning a company or industry is released, the player automatically raises the volume. Through Visual Data's TalentView, producers, casting agents and professional talent scouts can find performers on-line. The searchable database is available only to industry professionals. MedicalView presents medical procedures, lectures and the latest information for health care professionals, while also offering consumers help with many different medical questions.

FINANCIALS: Sales and profits are in thousands of dollars—add 000 to get the full amount.

Notes regarding 1999: *(1999 sales and profits were not available for all companies at press time.)*

1999 Sales: $4,600	1999 Profits: $-7,200	**Stock Ticker: VDAT**
1998 Sales: $1,900	1998 Profits: $-3,400	Employees: 41
1997 Sales: $ 200	1997 Profits: $-3,600	Fiscal Year Ends: 09/30
1996 Sales: $ 100	1996 Profits: $-1,900	
1995 Sales: $	1995 Profits: $- 500	

SALARIES/BENEFITS:

Pension Plan:	ESOP Stock Plan: Y	Profit Sharing:	Top Exec. Salary: $145,563	Bonus: $
Savings Plan:	Stock Purch. Plan:		Second Exec. Salary: $145,563	Bonus: $

COMPETITIVE ADVANTAGE: Excellent technology delivers niche-specific audio/video.

OTHER THOUGHTS:

Apparent Women Officers or Directors: 1
Apparent Minority Officers or Directors:
Hot Spot for Advancement for Women/Minorities:

LOCATIONS: ("Y" = Yes)

West:	Southwest:	Midwest:	Southeast:	Northeast:	International:
			Y		

VITAMINSHOPPE
www.vitaminshoppe.com

Industry Group Code: 4541
Ranks within this company's industry group: Sales: 23   Profits: 12

BUSINESS ACTIVITIES ("Y" = Yes)

Financial Services:	Information/Publ.:	Technology:	Services:	Retailing:		Telecommunications:
Stock Brokerage	Portal/Hub/News	Computer Manuf.	Payments/Transfers	Retailer	Y	Internet Serv. Provider
Mortgages/Loans	On-Line Community	Networking Equip.	Consulting	Auctions		Web Site Host
Banking	Search Engine	Software Manuf.	Advertising/Marketing	Mall		Server Farm
Insurance	Financial Data Publ.	Specialty Equipment	Outsourcing	Tickets/Travel		Specialty Telecom.
Credit Cards	Broadcasting/Music			Price Comparisons		High Speed Access

TYPES OF BUSINESS:
Retail-Vitamins

BRANDS/DIVISIONS/AFFILIATES:
The Vitamin Shoppe premium brand

CONTACTS: *Note: Officers with more than one job title may be intentionally listed here more than once.*
Jeffrey J. Horowitz, CEO
Ann Sardini, CFO
Eliot D. Russman, Chief Mktg. Officer
Joel Gurzinsky, VP-Oper.
Lisa H. Kern, VP-Business Dev. and Sales

Phone: 212-551-7851	Fax: 949-666-9428
Toll-Free:	
Address: 380 Lexington Ave., Ste. 1700, New York, NY, 10168	

GROWTH PLANS/SPECIAL FEATURES:

VitaminShoppe.com, Inc. is a leading on-line source for products and information related to vitamins, nutritional supplements and minerals. The VitaminShoppe.com web site provides a convenient and informative shopping experience for consumers wishing to purchase products that promote healthy living. The company offers an extensive selection of over 18,000 items representing over 400 brands, including The Vitamin Shoppe premium brand, and a comprehensive line of herbal formulas, homeopathic products, personal care items, body building supplements, healthcare products and books on health and nutrition. The entire line of products is sold year-round at discounts generally ranging from 20% to 40% off suggested retail prices. In addition to product sales, the web site offers specific pages for women, men and seniors, as well as links to other web sites, such as Dr. Raymond Weil's page for mental and physical health advice or vitaminbuzz.com, an alternative health site. Media Metrix ranked VitaminShoppe.com number four in its listing of the Top 10 E-Commerce Sites of 1999, after powerhouses eBay, Amazon and Barnes and Noble.

FINANCIALS: Sales and profits are in thousands of dollars—add 000 to get the full amount.
Notes regarding 1999: Through 9 months *(1999 sales and profits were not available for all companies at press time.)*

1999 Sales: $8,406	1999 Profits: $-10,893	Stock Ticker: **VSHP**
1998 Sales: $2,900	1998 Profits: $-3,200	Employees: 14
1997 Sales: $	1997 Profits: $	Fiscal Year Ends: 12/31
1996 Sales: $	1996 Profits: $	
1995 Sales: $	1995 Profits: $	

SALARIES/BENEFITS:

Pension Plan:	ESOP Stock Plan: Y	Profit Sharing:	Top Exec. Salary: $	Bonus: $
Savings Plan:	Stock Purch. Plan:		Second Exec. Salary: $	Bonus: $

COMPETITIVE ADVANTAGE: Very high viewer base/Extensive line of discount priced products.

OTHER THOUGHTS:

Apparent Women Officers or Directors:
Apparent Minority Officers or Directors:
Hot Spot for Advancement for Women/Minorities:

LOCATIONS: ("Y" = Yes)

West:	Southwest:	Midwest:	Southeast:	Northeast:	International:
				Y	

VOCALTEC   www.vocaltec.com

Industry Group Code: 5112
Ranks within this company's industry group: Sales: 31   Profits: 73

BUSINESS ACTIVITIES ("Y" = Yes)

Financial Services:	Information/Publ.:	Technology:		Services:	Retailing:	Telecommunications:
Stock Brokerage	Portal/Hub/News	Computer Manuf.		Payments/Transfers	Retailer	Internet Serv. Provider
Mortgages/Loans	On-Line Community	Networking Equip.	Y	Consulting	Auctions	Web Site Host
Banking	Search Engine	Software Manuf.	Y	Advertising/Marketing	Mall	Server Farm
Insurance	Financial Data Publ.	Specialty Equipment		Outsourcing	Tickets/Travel	Specialty Telecom.
Credit Cards	Broadcasting/Music				Price Comparisons	High Speed Access

TYPES OF BUSINESS:

Software-Internet Messaging

BRANDS/DIVISIONS/AFFILIATES:

VocalTec Ensemble Architecture
VocalTec Gatekeeper
VocalTec Surf and Call Center
VocalTec Internet Phone Lite
VocalTec Network Manager
SNMP Management
VocalTec Internet Phone

CONTACTS: Note: Officers with more than one job title may be intentionally listed here more than once.

Elon A. Ganor, CEO
Charles Giambalvo, Pres.
Jeffrey Dykan, CFO
Elazar Azi Ronen, VP-Mktg.
Carla Cooper, Mgr.-Human Resources
Ira Palti, VP-Research and Dev.
Jerry W. Lambert, Sr., VP-Application Engineering
Ami Tal, VP-Oper./COO
David Gurle, VP-Business Alliances

Phone: 201-228-7000	Fax: 201-363-8986
Toll-Free:	
Address: One Executive Dr., Suite 320, Fort Lee, NJ, 07024	

GROWTH PLANS/SPECIAL FEATURES:

VocalTec Inc.'s Internet Phone was the first software sold that allowed PC users to transmit voice calls over Internet data channels. The user speaks into the PC's microphone, and VocalTec's software digitizes and compresses the sounds into packets that travel over the Internet, which are then decompressed by the receiving PC with the same software. For the first time, users of PCs with a sound card, microphone and Internet connection could talk to others with similar systems anywhere in the world, with no long-distance charges. VocalTec develops and markets software that combines the power of telephones and networked computers by delivering an Internet dial tone to businesses and consumers for multimedia communications worldwide. The company's Surf and Call is an innovative plug-in enabling web-to-phone call center applications through a standard web page. Internet Phone includes enhanced audio, live-motion video and PC-to-phone calling, enabling users to simultaneously talk and see each other in real-time for the cost of an Internet connection. Network World recently named VocalTec one of the top companies to watch. VocalTec has been profiled on NBC, NBC Dateline, ABC, CBS, CNBC and MSNBC and has been covered in Business Week magazine, Reuters, The Wall Street Journal and Fortune magazine.

FINANCIALS: Sales and profits are in thousands of dollars—add 000 to get the full amount.

Notes regarding 1999: *(1999 sales and profits were not available for all companies at press time.)*

1999 Sales: $26,600	1999 Profits: $-28,400	Stock Ticker: **VOCL**
1998 Sales: $24,700	1998 Profits: $-23,200	Employees: 343
1997 Sales: $15,700	1997 Profits: $-7,700	Fiscal Year Ends: 12/31
1996 Sales: $8,500	1996 Profits: $-7,200	
1995 Sales: $2,500	1995 Profits: $-1,400	

SALARIES/BENEFITS:

Pension Plan:	ESOP Stock Plan:	Profit Sharing:	Top Exec. Salary: $156,000	Bonus: $
Savings Plan:	Stock Purch. Plan:		Second Exec. Salary: $	Bonus: $

COMPETITIVE ADVANTAGE: Superior Internet telephony technology.

OTHER THOUGHTS:

	LOCATIONS: ("Y" = Yes)					
	West:	Southwest:	Midwest:	Southeast:	Northeast:	International:
Apparent Women Officers or Directors:					Y	Y
Apparent Minority Officers or Directors:						
Hot Spot for Advancement for Women/Minorities:						

VOXWARE
www.voxware.com

Industry Group Code: 5112
Ranks within this company's industry group: Sales: 61   Profits: 33

BUSINESS ACTIVITIES ("Y" = Yes)

Financial Services:	Information/Publ.:	Technology:		Services:	Retailing:	Telecommunications:
Stock Brokerage	Portal/Hub/News	Computer Manuf.		Payments/Transfers	Retailer	Internet Serv. Provider
Mortgages/Loans	On-Line Community	Networking Equip.		Consulting	Auctions	Web Site Host
Banking	Search Engine	Software Manuf.	Y	Advertising/Marketing	Mall	Server Farm
Insurance	Financial Data Publ.	Specialty Equipment	Y	Outsourcing	Tickets/Travel	Specialty Telecom.
Credit Cards	Broadcasting/Music				Price Comparisons	High Speed Access

TYPES OF BUSINESS:
Software-Speech Recognition

BRANDS/DIVISIONS/AFFILIATES:
Voxware MVP
MetaVoice

CONTACTS: *Note: Officers with more than one job title may be intentionally listed here more than once.*
Bathsheba J. Malsheen, CEO
Bathsheba J. Malsheen, Pres.
Nicholas Narlis, CFO/VP-Finance
Eric R. Nahm, VP-Sales
J. Gerard Aguilar, VP-Research and Dev.
Sherri Meade, VP-Engineering and Oper.
Ken Finkel, VP-Business Dev.
Jeff Hill, Dir.-Mktg.

Phone: 609-514-4100	Fax: 609-514-4101
Toll-Free:	
Address: 305 College Rd. East, Princeton, NJ, 08540	

GROWTH PLANS/SPECIAL FEATURES:

Voxware, Inc. develops, markets, licenses and supports a comprehensive and integrated set of digital speech processing technologies that provide the ability to compress, model and transform speech. The company's innovative coding technology, MetaVoice, is designed to reproduce high-quality speech while requiring low communications bandwidth and processing power, which is helpful in a bandwidth-constrained environment such as the Internet. Digital speech technologies are being integrated into a variety of applications, including voice-enabled web pages, Internet telephony and conferencing, Internet broadcasting, interactive games, voice messaging, wireless and satellite communications, multimedia computing and voice-enabled devices. Voxware develops and deploys innovative, productivity-enhancing solutions for picking, receiving, inventory/cycle counting, package sorting and manufacturing inspection applications. The company builds portable hardware, called Voxware MVP, that enables warehouse and manufacturing workers to record critical information and receive instructions while keeping their hands and eyes free to do their jobs safely, accurately and quickly. Voxware builds the applications and interface codes necessary to integrate products into its customers' existing warehouse management systems (WMS). The company has licensed its products to such big names as Netscape, America Online, Apple Computers, Lucent Technologies and Microsoft.

FINANCIALS: Sales and profits are in thousands of dollars—add 000 to get the full amount.
Notes regarding 1999: *(1999 sales and profits were not available for all companies at press time.)*

1999 Sales: $2,900	1999 Profits: $-4,300	**Stock Ticker: VOXW**
1998 Sales: $5,900	1998 Profits: $-4,700	Employees: 31
1997 Sales: $7,800	1997 Profits: $-7,000	Fiscal Year Ends: 06/30
1996 Sales: $1,600	1996 Profits: $-2,900	
1995 Sales: $	1995 Profits: $-1,200	

SALARIES/BENEFITS:

Pension Plan:	ESOP Stock Plan: Y	Profit Sharing:	Top Exec. Salary: $198,752	Bonus: $41,875
Savings Plan:	Stock Purch. Plan:		Second Exec. Salary: $133,538	Bonus: $21,675

COMPETITIVE ADVANTAGE: Bandwidth-efficient reproduction of speech with very high quality.

OTHER THOUGHTS:
Apparent Women Officers or Directors: 1
Apparent Minority Officers or Directors: 1
Hot Spot for Advancement for Women/Minorities:

LOCATIONS: ("Y" = Yes)

West:	Southwest:	Midwest:	Southeast:	Northeast:	International:
Y			Y	Y	Y

VOYAGER.NET   www.voyager.net

Industry Group Code: 51339
Ranks within this company's industry group: Sales: 14 Profits: 13

BUSINESS ACTIVITIES ("Y" = Yes)

Financial Services:	Information/Publ.:	Technology:	Services:	Retailing:		Telecommunications:	
Stock Brokerage	Portal/Hub/News	Computer Manuf.	Payments/Transfers	Retailer	Y	Internet Serv. Provider	Y
Mortgages/Loans	On-Line Community	Networking Equip.	Consulting	Auctions		Web Site Host	Y
Banking	Search Engine	Software Manuf.	Advertising/Marketing	Mall		Server Farm	
Insurance	Financial Data Publ.	Specialty Equipment	Outsourcing	Tickets/Travel		Specialty Telecom.	Y
Credit Cards	Broadcasting/Music			Price Comparisons		High Speed Access	Y

TYPES OF BUSINESS:

Internet Service Provider
Long Distance Provider
On-line Shopping
Cable Modem Access

BRANDS/DIVISIONS/AFFILIATES:

ExecPC Internet
Net Link
Freeway
Hoosier Online
Infinite Systems, Ltd.
Exchange Network Services
Voyager.net TV
PC Link

CONTACTS: Note: Officers with more than one job title may be intentionally listed here more than once.

Christopher Torto, CEO/Pres.
Osvaldo deFaria, COO
Dennis Stepaniak, CFO
Tony Paalz, Sr. VP-Mktg.
Joan Holda, VP-Human Resources
Christopher Michaels, Chief Tech. Officer
David Shires, VP-Business Dev.

Phone: 517-324-8940	Fax: 517-324-8965
Toll-Free:	

Address: 4660 S. Hegadorn Rd., Ste. 320, East Lansing, MI, 48823

GROWTH PLANS/SPECIAL FEATURES:

Voyager.net is a provider of Internet connectivity and enhanced Internet services for businesses and individuals in the Midwest. The company operates under such names as ExecPC Internet, Net Link, Freeway, Hoosier Online, EriNet and PC Link. Voyager.net offers customers the resources of a super-regional provider combined with the personal attention and focus of a local ISP (Internet Service Provider), operating the largest dial-up ISP network in the Midwest in terms of geographic coverage, with approximately 150 Voyager.net-owned points of presence. The firm provides a wide range of Internet access solutions and services to customers throughout Illinois, Indiana, Michigan, Minnesota, Ohio and Wisconsin. Specifically targeting the Midwest enables the company to conduct highly targeted sales and marketing programs, cultivate local brand-name recognition and generate a significant number of word-of-mouth referrals. The company offers Voyager.netTV, a system that allows people without a computer, or who need a second Internet terminal, to access the Internet easily and inexpensively through their television sets. The company's VoyagerLink is a low-cost long distance service which may be accessed via the Internet. Together with WizShop.com, Voyager.net offers on-line shopping with links to almost 1,000 of the shopping sites in all of the major e-commerce product categories.

FINANCIALS: Sales and profits are in thousands of dollars—add 000 to get the full amount.

Notes regarding 1999: (1999 sales and profits were not available for all companies at press time.)

1999 Sales: $48,498	1999 Profits: $-16,495	Stock Ticker: VOYN
1998 Sales: $10,700	1998 Profits: $-7,300	Employees: 278
1997 Sales: $3,500	1997 Profits: $- 800	Fiscal Year Ends: 12/31
1996 Sales: $1,700	1996 Profits: $-1,500	
1995 Sales: $ 200	1995 Profits: $- 700	

SALARIES/BENEFITS:

Pension Plan:	ESOP Stock Plan:	Profit Sharing:	Top Exec. Salary: $118,000	Bonus: $23,350
Savings Plan: Y	Stock Purch. Plan:		Second Exec. Salary: $59,900	Bonus: $100,000

COMPETITIVE ADVANTAGE: Aggressive marketing/Built a major regional system through acquisitions.

OTHER THOUGHTS:

Apparent Women Officers or Directors: 1
Apparent Minority Officers or Directors: 1
Hot Spot for Advancement for Women/Minorities:

LOCATIONS: ("Y" = Yes)

West:	Southwest:	Midwest:	Southeast:	Northeast:	International:
		Y			

Note: Financial information, benefits and other data can change quickly and may vary from those stated here.

WALT DISNEY COMPANY (THE)   www.disney.com

Industry Group Code: 7131
Ranks within this company's industry group: Sales: 1   Profits: 1

BUSINESS ACTIVITIES ("Y" = Yes)

Financial Services:	Information/Publ.:		Technology:	Services:		Retailing:	Telecommunications:	
Stock Brokerage	Portal/Hub/News	Y	Computer Manuf.	Payments/Transfers		Retailer	Internet Serv. Provider	Y
Mortgages/Loans	On-Line Community	Y	Networking Equip.	Consulting		Auctions	Web Site Host	
Banking	Search Engine	Y	Software Manuf.	Advertising/Marketing	Y	Mall	Server Farm	
Insurance	Financial Data Publ.	Y	Specialty Equipment	Outsourcing		Tickets/Travel	Specialty Telecom.	
Credit Cards	Broadcasting/Music	Y				Price Comparisons	High Speed Access	

TYPES OF BUSINESS:

Theme Parks and Resorts
Filmed Entertainment
Retail Toy, Game and Book Stores
Cable and Broadcast Television Networks
Music and Book Publishing
On-line Entertainment Programs
On-line Communities
Search Engine Portals

BRANDS/DIVISIONS/AFFILIATES:

The Disney Channel
Disney Consumer Products
Infoseek
Miramax
Go.com
Chilton Publications
ABC Television
Touchstone Pictures

CONTACTS: *Note: Officers with more than one job title may be intentionally listed here more than once.*

Michael D. Eisner, CEO
Robert A. Iger, Pres./COO
Thomas O. Staggs, Sr. Exec. VP/CFO
Oren Aviv, Co-Pres.-Mktg.
Peter Murphy, Strategic Planning Chief
Steven Bornstein, Chairman, Buena Vista Internet Group/Pres., Go.com
John F. Cooke, Exec. VP-Corp. Affairs
Geoffrey Ammer, Co-Pres.-Mktg.
Andrew P. Mooney, Pres., Consumer Products Div.

Phone: 818-560-1000	**Fax:** 818-560-1930
Toll-Free:	
Address: 500 South Buena Vista Street, Burbank, CA, 91521	

GROWTH PLANS/SPECIAL FEATURES:

Walt Disney Company is a diversified international entertainment company with operations in filmed entertainment, theme parks and resorts, television and radio broadcasting, on-line entertainment, retailing, music and book publishing and consumer products. In recent years, Disney acquired television giant Capital Cities/ABC, Inc., operator of the ABC television and radio networks. This pushed Disney's combined entity to over $20 billion in sales, $4.6 billion in cash flow and 100,000 employees. ABC brought 11 company-owned TV stations, 228 affiliated stations and 21 radio stations to the group. The ABC purchase makes Disney one of the most powerful, diversified media firms in the world, ranking with Time-Warner and News Corp. in ability to deliver mass entertainment. Disney has an exceptional ability to create animated, feature-length films and to market these titles on cassette, on its own television network, on-line and in consumer products including books and records. Disney has been investing aggressively in new theme park attractions. The company recently opened its first new theme park in nine years: Animal Kingdom near Orlando, Florida. By the end of 2001, Disney will have spent $4 billion to add two new theme parks, a cruise line and three regional entertainment chains to its stable of companies. Disney purchased a 100% interest in Infoseek and then combined its Internet assets with Infoseek to create a new firm, Go.com, which trades its common stock as a separate company.

This is one of the premier entertainment firms in the world, in virtually every niche: publishing, theme parks, movies, television and multimedia. Job seekers wanting to be on the leading edge of the InfoTech Revolution should apply to Disney's on-line film, television and multimedia units. Watch for a third major U.S. Disney theme park. Some business areas in the company, such as Theme Parks and Resorts, do have specific grooming guidelines for employees. In most other areas of the company, employees dress appropriately for the job function they are performing.

FINANCIALS: Sales and profits are in thousands of dollars—add 000 to get the full amount.

Notes regarding 1999: *(1999 sales and profits were not available for all companies at press time.)*

1999 Sales: $23,402,000	1999 Profits: $1,300,000	
1998 Sales: $22,976,000	1998 Profits: $1,850,000	**Stock Ticker: DIS**
1997 Sales: $22,473,000	1997 Profits: $1,966,000	Employees: 117,000
1996 Sales: $18,739,000	1996 Profits: $1,214,000	Fiscal Year Ends: 9/30
1995 Sales: $12,112,100	1995 Profits: $1,380,100	

SALARIES/BENEFITS:

Pension Plan: Y	ESOP Stock Plan:	Profit Sharing:	Top Exec. Salary: $764,423	Bonus: $5,000,000
Savings Plan: Y	Stock Purch. Plan:		Second Exec. Salary: $509,615	Bonus: $410,000

COMPETITIVE ADVANTAGE: Entertainment products that capitalize on the well-known Disney characters/Has diversified aggressively into nearly all segments of entertainment/Rapidly growing on-line interests.

OTHER THOUGHTS:

Apparent Women Officers or Directors: 2
Apparent Minority Officers or Directors:
Hot Spot for Advancement for Women/Minorities: Y

LOCATIONS: ("Y" = Yes)

West:	Southwest:	Midwest:	Southeast:	Northeast:	International:
Y	Y	Y	Y	Y	Y

Note: Financial information, benefits and other data can change quickly and may vary from those stated here.

WEBB INTERACTIVE   www.webb.net

Industry Group Code: 5112
Ranks within this company's industry group: Sales: 74   Profits: 52

BUSINESS ACTIVITIES ("Y" = Yes)

Financial Services:	Information/Publ.:	Technology:		Services:	Retailing:	Telecommunications:
Stock Brokerage	Portal/Hub/News	Computer Manuf.		Payments/Transfers	Retailer	Internet Serv. Provider
Mortgages/Loans	On-Line Community	Networking Equip.		Consulting	Auctions	Web Site Host
Banking	Search Engine	Software Manuf.	Y	Advertising/Marketing	Mall	Server Farm
Insurance	Financial Data Publ.	Specialty Equipment		Outsourcing	Tickets/Travel	Specialty Telecom.
Credit Cards	Broadcasting/Music				Price Comparisons	High Speed Access

TYPES OF BUSINESS:

Technology Consulting

BRANDS/DIVISIONS/AFFILIATES:

AccelX
CommunityWare/XML
NetIgnite 2, LLC
Durand Communications, Inc.
Online Systems Services

CONTACTS: Note: Officers with more than one job title may be intentionally listed here more than once.

R. Steven Adams, CEO
Perry Evans, Pres.
William Cullen, CFO
Edward Robinson, VP- Mktg.
Kim Castillo, Dir.- Human Services and Office Mgr.
Paul H. Spieker, VP- Tech. Oper.
Chris Fanjoy, Sr.VP- Tech.
Lindley S. Branson, Exec.VP/ General Counsel
Paul Beckelheimer, Sr.VP- Business Dev.
Mike Murphy, Sr.VP- Electronic Banking

Phone: 303-296-9200	Fax: 303-295-3584
Toll-Free:	
Address: 1800 Glenarm Place, Ste. 700, Denver, CO, 80202	

GROWTH PLANS/SPECIAL FEATURES:

Webb Interactive, formerly Online Systems Services, develops, markets and supports products and services that enable individuals and organizations to create and manage their own Internet web presence and on-line communities. Buyers and sellers are able to interact within their local economies more easily. The company's site development tools, AccelX and CommunityWare/XML, enable individuals and organizations to create their own personal/organizational portals. Users can add features such as calendars, e-mail, instant messaging and newsletters. Webb Interactive focuses on different markets: community, consumer, enterprise, education and financial services. With the acquisitions of NetIgnite 2, LLC and Durand Communications, Inc., and partnerships with Microsoft, Verio and Compaq, the company has been able to enhance its products. Recently, CBS.com, Inc. began implementing Webb's CommunityWare to facilitate message board discussions and the News and Entertainment features of its CBS.com web site. Other Webb Interactive customers include Corel, Switchboard, Net Shepherd, the TCI Education Project and RE/MAX.

FINANCIALS: Sales and profits are in thousands of dollars—add 000 to get the full amount.
Notes regarding 1999: Through 9 months *(1999 sales and profits were not available for all companies at press time.)*

1999 Sales: $1,126	1999 Profits: $-15,042	Stock Ticker: **WEBB**
1998 Sales: $1,600	1998 Profits: $-10,600	Employees: 53
1997 Sales: $2,800	1997 Profits: $-3,400	Fiscal Year Ends: 12/31
1996 Sales: $1,400	1996 Profits: $-1,400	
1995 Sales: $ 400	1995 Profits: $- 500	

SALARIES/BENEFITS:

Pension Plan:	ESOP Stock Plan:	Profit Sharing:	Top Exec. Salary: $155,203	Bonus: $
Savings Plan:	Stock Purch. Plan:		Second Exec. Salary: $165,000	Bonus: $

COMPETITIVE ADVANTAGE: Growth through acquisitions/Ability to enable a full-service community quickly and easily.

OTHER THOUGHTS:

Apparent Women Officers or Directors:
Apparent Minority Officers or Directors:
Hot Spot for Advancement for Women/Minorities:

LOCATIONS: ("Y" = Yes)

West:	Southwest:	Midwest:	Southeast:	Northeast:	International:
Y					

Note: Financial information, benefits and other data can change quickly and may vary from those stated here.

WEBTRENDS CORP   www.webtrends.com

Industry Group Code: 5112
Ranks within this company's industry group: Sales: 52   Profits: 19

BUSINESS ACTIVITIES ("Y" = Yes)

Financial Services:	Information/Publ.:	Technology:	Services:	Retailing:	Telecommunications:
Stock Brokerage	Portal/Hub/News Y	Computer Manuf.	Payments/Transfers	Retailer	Internet Serv. Provider
Mortgages/Loans	On-Line Community	Networking Equip.	Consulting	Auctions	Web Site Host
Banking	Search Engine	Software Manuf. Y	Advertising/Marketing	Mall	Server Farm
Insurance	Financial Data Publ.	Specialty Equipment	Outsourcing	Tickets/Travel	Specialty Telecom.
Credit Cards	Broadcasting/Music			Price Comparisons	High Speed Access

TYPES OF BUSINESS:
Software-Web User Information
E-Business Management Solutions
Portal for Internet professionals

BRANDS/DIVISIONS/AFFILIATES:
NetScreen Technologies
WebTrends Commerce Trends
WebTrends Professional Services Group
WebTrends Security Analyzer
WebTrends Enterprise Reporting Server
WebTrends Network
RADWARE

CONTACTS: *Note: Officers with more than one job title may be intentionally listed here more than once.*
Elijahu Shapira, CEO
W. Glen Boyd, Pres.
James T. Richardson, Sr. VP/CFO
Daniel J. Meub, Sr. VP-Mktg. & Sales
Margie Huetter, Mgr.-Human Resources
John D. Teddy, VP-Research & Dev.
W. Glen Boyd, Chief Tech. Officer
James T. Richardson, Sec.

Phone: 503-294-7025   **Fax:** 503-294-7130
Toll-Free:
Address: 851 SW 6th Ave., Ste. 1200, Portland, OR, 97204

GROWTH PLANS/SPECIAL FEATURES:
WebTrends Corporation is a leading provider of enterprise management and reporting solutions for Internet-based systems, which include web servers, intranets and extranets. Its products have been specifically designed to enable organizations to centrally manage and administer multiple Internet-based systems across their enterprises, regardless of the quantity or geographic locations of servers supporting those systems. WebTrends offers organizations a comprehensive set of solutions that are integrated, modular and easy-to-use and that scale to high-volume environments. The company recently produced a trial version of its WebTrends Enterprise Reporting Server for Linux on the upcoming server edition of Red Hat's Linux Applications CD (LACD). This edition, included with the Professional Edition of Red Hat Linux 6.1, extends WebTrends' award-winning solution to a targeted Internet server audience. It also marks the first web traffic analysis product designed for Linux. In addition, WebTrends introduced the industry's first comprehensive portal site for Internet professionals. The company is involved in a few strategic partnerships including one with RADWARE, a leader in load balancing and high availability solutions, to provide best of breed solutions for server farm management. Best of breed solutions are also provided for Firewall/VPN security management through an alliance with NetScreen Technologies, a leading developer of integrated security appliances. Recently, WebTrends released its entire Windows-based product line to be compatible with the newly released Mirosoft Office 2000 suite and Windows 2000 Beta 3 operating systems. Web Trends' strategy is to continue to innovate in an attempt to be the leading provider of enterprise solutions for management.

FINANCIALS: Sales and profits are in thousands of dollars—add 000 to get the full amount.
Notes regarding 1999: *(1999 sales and profits were not available for all companies at press time.)*

1999 Sales: $19,700	1999 Profits: $2,700	**Stock Ticker: WEBT**
1998 Sales: $8,000	1998 Profits: $ 200	Employees: 78
1997 Sales: $4,100	1997 Profits: $ 300	Fiscal Year Ends: 12/31
1996 Sales: $1,900	1996 Profits: $ 400	
1995 Sales: $ 600	1995 Profits: $ 200	

SALARIES/BENEFITS:
| Pension Plan: | ESOP Stock Plan: | Profit Sharing: | Top Exec. Salary: $150,000 | Bonus: $20,000 |
| Savings Plan: Y | Stock Purch. Plan: Y | | Second Exec. Salary: $ | Bonus: $ |

COMPETITIVE ADVANTAGE: Widely distributed and well known line of software.

OTHER THOUGHTS:
Apparent Women Officers or Directors: 1
Apparent Minority Officers or Directors:
Hot Spot for Advancement for Women/Minorities:

LOCATIONS: ("Y" = Yes)
West: Y	Southwest:	Midwest:	Southeast:	Northeast:	International:

WEBVAN GROUP INC   www.webvan.com

Industry Group Code: 4541
Ranks within this company's industry group: Sales: 31   Profits: 21

BUSINESS ACTIVITIES ("Y" = Yes)

Financial Services:	Information/Publ.:	Technology:	Services:	Retailing:	Telecommunications:	
Stock Brokerage	Portal/Hub/News	Computer Manuf.	Payments/Transfers	Retailer	Internet Serv. Provider	Y
Mortgages/Loans	On-Line Community	Networking Equip.	Consulting	Auctions	Web Site Host	
Banking	Search Engine	Software Manuf.	Advertising/Marketing	Mall	Server Farm	
Insurance	Financial Data Publ.	Specialty Equipment	Outsourcing	Tickets/Travel	Specialty Telecom.	
Credit Cards	Broadcasting/Music			Price Comparisons	High Speed Access	

TYPES OF BUSINESS:
Retail-On-line Grocery Store

BRANDS/DIVISIONS/AFFILIATES:
Webvan

CONTACTS: *Note: Officers with more than one job title may be intentionally listed here more than once.*

George T. Shaheen, CEO
George T. Shaheen, Pres.
Kevin R. Czinger, Sr. VP-Finance
Christian T. Mannella, VP-Mktg.
Arvind Peter Relan, Sr. VP-Tech.
Mark J. Holtzman, VP/Controller
S. Coppy Holzman, Sr. VP-Merch.
Kevin R. Czinger, Sr. VP-Corp. Oper.
Mark X. Zaleski, Sr. VP-Area Oper.
Vivek M. Joshi, VP-Program Management

Phone: 650-524-2200	Fax: 650-524-4801
Toll-Free:	

Address: 1241 East Hillsdale Boulevard, Suite 210, Foster City, CA, 94404

GROWTH PLANS/SPECIAL FEATURES:

Webvan Group, Inc. is an Internet retailer providing same-day delivery of consumer products through an innovative proprietary business design that integrates a webstore, distribution center and delivery system. Its current product offerings are principally focused on food, non-prescription drug products and general merchandise. The company offers over 50,000 items that are generally priced at or below everyday supermarket prices. Webvan provides consumers with a convenient grocery shopping center 24-hours daily. Customers can monitor orders and information accuracy, eliminating the need to wait in line through product offerings delivered directly to their homes. The firm opened its first distribution facility in Oakland, California and intends to open other distribution centers in over 20 major cities in the U.S. to capitalize on market opportunities. Its second distribution center, located in Atlanta, Georgia, is scheduled to be launched soon. Webvan's other business endeavors include an agreement with Bechtel Corporation for the construction of up to 26 additional distribution centers over the next three years in various designated locations. Webvan's business strategy includes the strengthening of its brand name and customer loyalty through its public relations programs, advertising campaigns and promotional activities. Webvan was founded by retail bookstore magnate Louis Borders, who previously established the Borders book superstore chain.

FINANCIALS: Sales and profits are in thousands of dollars—add 000 to get the full amount.
Notes regarding 1999: *(1999 sales and profits were not available for all companies at press time.)*

1999 Sales: $13,305	1999 Profits: $-144,569	Stock Ticker: **WBVN**
1998 Sales: $ 100	1998 Profits: $-12,000	Employees:
1997 Sales: $	1997 Profits: $-2,800	Fiscal Year Ends: 12/31
1996 Sales: $	1996 Profits: $	
1995 Sales: $	1995 Profits: $	

SALARIES/BENEFITS:

Pension Plan:	ESOP Stock Plan:	Profit Sharing:	Top Exec. Salary: $219,431	Bonus: $
Savings Plan: Y	Stock Purch. Plan: Y		Second Exec. Salary: $178,600	Bonus: $8,750

COMPETITIVE ADVANTAGE: Aggressive strategy/Extensive financing/Proprietary, state-of-the-art workhouses.

OTHER THOUGHTS:

	LOCATIONS: ("Y" = Yes)					
	West:	Southwest:	Midwest:	Southeast:	Northeast:	International:
Apparent Women Officers or Directors:	Y			Y		
Apparent Minority Officers or Directors:						
Hot Spot for Advancement for Women/Minorities:						

WHITE PINE SOFTWARE　　www.wpine.com

Industry Group Code: 5112
Ranks within this company's industry group: Sales: 54　Profits: 46

BUSINESS ACTIVITIES ("Y" = Yes)

Financial Services:	Information/Publ.:	Technology:	Services:		Retailing:		Telecommunications:
Stock Brokerage	Portal/Hub/News	Computer Manuf.	Payments/Transfers		Retailer		Internet Serv. Provider
Mortgages/Loans	On-Line Community	Networking Equip.	Consulting		Auctions		Web Site Host
Banking	Search Engine	Software Manuf.	Advertising/Marketing	Y	Mall		Server Farm
Insurance	Financial Data Publ.	Specialty Equipment	Outsourcing		Tickets/Travel		Specialty Telecom.
Credit Cards	Broadcasting/Music				Price Comparisons		High Speed Access

TYPES OF BUSINESS:

Software-Multimedia Communication

BRANDS/DIVISIONS/AFFILIATES:

White Pine Software
Advanced Modular Solutions, Inc.
MeetingPoint
Belgacom
CU-SeeMe Web
WebTerm
Class Point
Red Hat, Inc.

CONTACTS: Note: Officers with more than one job title may be intentionally listed here more than once.

Killko A. Caballero, CEO
Killko A. Caballero, Pres.
Christine J. Cox, VP-Finance/CFO
John E. Kelly, VP-Worldwide Sales & Mktg.
Marilyn Condodemetraky, Dir-Human Resources
David O. Bundy, Chief Tech. Officer
Jeff Krampf, VP-Engineering

Phone: 603-886-9050	Fax: 603-886-9051
Toll-Free:	
Address: 542 Amherst St., Nashua, NH, 03063	

GROWTH PLANS/SPECIAL FEATURES:

White Pine Software develops multimedia conferencing applications tailored to business, education and training. The company is focused on providing application-specific solutions that enrich the way people interact, moderate and administer conferences in real-world conference situations. White Pine develops, markets and supports multiplatform browser-based internetworking software that facilitates worldwide video and audio communication and data collaboration across the Internet, intranets, extranets and other networks that use the Internet Protocol. The firm's videoconferencing software products include CU-SeeMe Web and MeetingPoint, which creates a client-server solution that allows users to participate in real-time, multipoint video, audio and data conferences over the Internet and intranets. ClassPoint, based on Cu-SeeMe and MeetingPoint, creates an instructor-led virtual classroom, which facilitates learning for any environment where the instructor and students are in different locations. CU-SeeMe was recently awarded the Best of Show for Internet Client Software at the Fall Internet World. Novell, Inc., the world's leading provider of directory-enabled networking software, announced it will license CU-SeeMe technology for integration into its new digitalme Internet service and its Novell instantme messaging client. Other companies using the technology include the NHL, Belgacom, Canon NetTV, Panasonic and the Bailey Group. White Pine recently formed an alliance with Advanced Modular Solution, Inc., a leading provider of video, streaming media, terabyte storage and fault tolerant solutions, which will integrate the company's video-conferencing technology into its line of complete video offerings and deliver distance learning and business communications solutions.

FINANCIALS: Sales and profits are in thousands of dollars—add 000 to get the full amount.

Notes regarding 1999: (1999 sales and profits were not available for all companies at press time.)

1999 Sales: $12,000	1999 Profits: $-4,800	
1998 Sales: $7,800	1998 Profits: $-8,400	Stock Ticker: WPNE
1997 Sales: $11,100	1997 Profits: $-6,800	Employees: 110
1996 Sales: $11,700	1996 Profits: $-3,600	Fiscal Year Ends: 12/31
1995 Sales: $7,200	1995 Profits: $-3,500	

SALARIES/BENEFITS:

Pension Plan:	ESOP Stock Plan:	Profit Sharing:	Top Exec. Salary: $150,445	Bonus: $
Savings Plan: Y	Stock Purch. Plan: Y		Second Exec. Salary: $132,405	Bonus: $

COMPETITIVE ADVANTAGE: Focus on superior technology for the conferencing market.

OTHER THOUGHTS:

Apparent Women Officers or Directors: 3
Apparent Minority Officers or Directors: 1
Hot Spot for Advancement for Women/Minorities: Y

LOCATIONS: ("Y" = Yes)

West:	Southwest:	Midwest:	Southeast:	Northeast:	International:
Y				Y	Y

WHITTMAN-HART INC   www.whittman-hart.com

Industry Group Code: 54151
Ranks within this company's industry group: Sales: 2   Profits: 2

BUSINESS ACTIVITIES ("Y" = Yes)

Financial Services:	Information/Publ.:	Technology:	Services:		Retailing:		Telecommunications:
Stock Brokerage	Portal/Hub/News	Computer Manuf.	Payments/Transfers		Retailer		Internet Serv. Provider
Mortgages/Loans	On-Line Community	Networking Equip.	Consulting	Y	Auctions		Web Site Host
Banking	Search Engine	Software Manuf.	Advertising/Marketing	Y	Mall		Server Farm
Insurance	Financial Data Publ.	Specialty Equipment	Outsourcing	Y	Tickets/Travel		Specialty Telecom.
Credit Cards	Broadcasting/Music				Price Comparisons		High Speed Access

TYPES OF BUSINESS:

Consulting Services-Computer & Internet
Advertising and Marketing Services
Custom Applications
Implementation
Integration

BRANDS/DIVISIONS/AFFILIATES:

Whittman-Hart Institute for Strategic Education
Axis Consulting International, Inc.
World Consulting Limited
USWEB/CKS

CONTACTS: *Note: Officers with more than one job title may be intentionally listed here more than once.*

Robert F. Bernard, CEO
Michael J. Berent, COO
Bert Young, CFO
Sara Cavin, VP-Mktg.
Mary Sawall, VP-Human Resources
Maureen G. Osborne, CIO
Edward V. Szofer, Pres./Sec.
Susan B. Reardon, Exec. VP-Strategic Education

Phone: 312-922-9200	Fax: 312-913-3020

Toll-Free: 800-426-7767

Address: 311 South Wacker Drive, Suite 3500, Chicago, IL, 60606

GROWTH PLANS/SPECIAL FEATURES:

Whittman-Hart, Inc. provides strategic information technology business solutions designed to improve its clients' productivity and competitive positions. The company offers its clients a single source for a comprehensive range of services required to successfully design, develop and implement integrated solutions in the client/server, open systems and midrange computing environments. Whittman-Hart provides its services through five business units: Solution Strategies, Package Software Solutions, Custom Applications, Network Enabled Solutions and Interactive Solutions. Services offered by the company are systems integration, strategic IT planning, business process improvement, organizational change management, package software evaluation and implementation. The company serves clients in a broad range of industries, including communications, consumer products, distribution, diversified services, financial services and manufacturing. Whittman-Hart sells and delivers its services through a network of 17 branch offices located throughout the United States, as well as one in London. The company uses its acquisitions to boost its portfolio of services and has developed a geographic expansion strategy. It has identified 25 companies that meet its expansion criteria. Recently, the company announced that it signed a definitive agreement to merge with USWeb/CKS, a leader in Internet professional services.

FINANCIALS: Sales and profits are in thousands of dollars—add 000 to get the full amount.

Notes regarding 1999: *(1999 sales and profits were not available for all companies at press time.)*

1999 Sales: $480,900	1999 Profits: $303,000	**Stock Ticker: WHIT**
1998 Sales: $307,600	1998 Profits: $18,800	Employees: 3,500
1997 Sales: $173,500	1997 Profits: $10,300	Fiscal Year Ends: 12/31
1996 Sales: $87,500	1996 Profits: $5,500	
1995 Sales: $49,800	1995 Profits: $1,100	

SALARIES/BENEFITS:

Pension Plan:	ESOP Stock Plan: Y	Profit Sharing:	Top Exec. Salary: $305,769	Bonus: $4,500
Savings Plan: Y	Stock Purch. Plan: Y		Second Exec. Salary: $242,308	Bonus: $

COMPETITIVE ADVANTAGE: Broad network of offices/Rapid growth through acquisitions.

OTHER THOUGHTS:

Apparent Women Officers or Directors: 4
Apparent Minority Officers or Directors:
Hot Spot for Advancement for Women/Minorities: Y

LOCATIONS: ("Y" = Yes)

West:	Southwest:	Midwest:	Southeast:	Northeast:	International:
Y	Y	Y	Y	Y	Y

Note: Financial information, benefits and other data can change quickly and may vary from those stated here.

WINK COMMUNICATIONS   www.wink.com

Industry Group Code: 514191
Ranks within this company's industry group: Sales: 39   Profits: 34

BUSINESS ACTIVITIES ("Y" = Yes)

Financial Services:	Information/Publ.:		Technology:	Services:	Retailing:	Telecommunications:
Stock Brokerage	Portal/Hub/News	Y	Computer Manuf.	Payments/Transfers	Retailer	Internet Serv. Provider
Mortgages/Loans	On-Line Community		Networking Equip.	Consulting	Auctions	Web Site Host
Banking	Search Engine		Software Manuf.	Advertising/Marketing	Mall	Server Farm
Insurance	Financial Data Publ.		Specialty Equipment	Outsourcing	Tickets/Travel	Specialty Telecom.
Credit Cards	Broadcasting/Music	Y			Price Comparisons	High Speed Access

TYPES OF BUSINESS:

Interactive Features for Television
News and Entertainment Enhancement
Advertising and Marketing Features On-line

BRANDS/DIVISIONS/AFFILIATES:

Charter Advertiser Program
Wink Enhanced Broadcasting

CONTACTS: Note: Officers with more than one job title may be intentionally listed here more than once.

Mary Agnes Wilderotter, CEO
Mary Agnes Wilderotter, Pres.
Howard L. Schrott, Sr. VP/CFO
Katherine Sullivan, VP-Mktg.
Rita Dettore, VP-People Dev.
Brian P. Dougherty, Chief Tech. Officer
Patrick Ransil, VP-Engineering
Timothy V. Travaille, Sr. VP-Oper. & Deployment
Allan C. Thygesen, Exec. VP-Sales and Business Dev.
Stephen Carmassi, VP-Strategic Account Management
Shigenori Matsushita, Pres.-Wink Japan

Phone: 510-337-2950	Fax: 510-337-2960
Toll-Free:	
Address: 1001 Marina Village Pkwy., Alameda, CA, 94501	

GROWTH PLANS/SPECIAL FEATURES:

Wink Communications provides a complete end-to-end system for low-cost electronic commerce on television. Wink Enhanced Broadcasting allows advertisers, merchants and broadcast and cable networks to create interactive enhancements to traditional television advertisements and programs. With a click of the remote control during an enhanced program or advertisement, viewers can purchase merchandise or request product samples, coupons or catalogues. Similarly, viewers can use Wink to access program-related information, such as news, sports and weather, participate in votes and polls and play along with various games. The company was only recently launched and is meeting immediate success. The four largest broadcast networks, NBC, ABC, CBS and FOX as well as 16 cable networks, agreed to air Wink-enhanced programming and advertising. Five of the six largest cable operators in the U.S., AT&T/TCI, Time Warner, Comcast Cable, Cox Communications and Charter Communications, have agreed to distribute Wink-enhanced programming and advertising in their local markets. DIRECTV, the largest direct broadcast satellite operator in the U.S., expects to deploy approximately four million Wink-enabled set-top boxes by January 2002. Also, Microsoft Corporation agreed to develop, market and distribute Wink-enhanced programming and advertising on Microsoft's television platforms. Wink's other business endeavors include an alliance with ValueVision, America's largest home shopping network, to be the first home shopping network to use Wink's interactive broadcasting technology. Wink's business strategy is to use television as a mass market medium for sales lead generation and electronic commerce.

FINANCIALS: Sales and profits are in thousands of dollars—add 000 to get the full amount.

Notes regarding 1999: *(1999 sales and profits were not available for all companies at press time.)*

1999 Sales: $1,601	1999 Profits: $-18,224	Stock Ticker: **WINK**
1998 Sales: $ 500	1998 Profits: $-14,000	Employees: 93
1997 Sales: $ 600	1997 Profits: $-9,200	Fiscal Year Ends: 12/31
1996 Sales: $ 300	1996 Profits: $-5,900	
1995 Sales: $ 100	1995 Profits: $-2,100	

SALARIES/BENEFITS:

Pension Plan:	ESOP Stock Plan:	Profit Sharing:	Top Exec. Salary: $208,333	Bonus: $25,000
Savings Plan: Y	Stock Purch. Plan: Y		Second Exec. Salary: $124,583	Bonus: $100,000

COMPETITIVE ADVANTAGE: Aggressive creation of strategic alliances.

OTHER THOUGHTS:

Apparent Women Officers or Directors: 4
Apparent Minority Officers or Directors: 1
Hot Spot for Advancement for Women/Minorities: Y

LOCATIONS: ("Y" = Yes)

West:	Southwest:	Midwest:	Southeast:	Northeast:	International:
Y					Y

Note: Financial information, benefits and other data can change quickly and may vary from those stated here.

WIT CAPITAL GROUP   www.witcapital.com

Industry Group Code: 5231
Ranks within this company's industry group: Sales: 10   Profits: 9

BUSINESS ACTIVITIES ("Y" = Yes)

Financial Services:		Information/Publ.:	Technology:	Services:	Retailing:	Telecommunications:
Stock Brokerage	Y	Portal/Hub/News	Computer Manuf.	Payments/Transfers	Retailer	Internet Serv. Provider
Mortgages/Loans		On-Line Community	Networking Equip.	Consulting	Auctions	Web Site Host
Banking		Search Engine	Software Manuf.	Advertising/Marketing	Mall	Server Farm
Insurance		Financial Data Publ.	Specialty Equipment	Outsourcing	Tickets/Travel	Specialty Telecom.
Credit Cards		Broadcasting/Music			Price Comparisons	High Speed Access

TYPES OF BUSINESS:

On-line Investment Banking
Stock Brokerage
Research

BRANDS/DIVISIONS/AFFILIATES:

Wit Capital Group, Inc.
SoundView Technology Group, Inc.
e-Dealers

CONTACTS: *Note: Officers with more than one job title may be intentionally listed here more than once.*

Robert H. Lessin, Co-CEO
Ronald Readmond, Co-CEO/Pres.
M. Bernard Siegel, Sr. VP/CFO
Susan J. Berkowitz, Sr. VP-Mktg.
Diane Ciccolini, VP-Human Resources
George M. Lieberman, Sr. VP/CIO
Harry Silver, Sr. VP/Chief Admin. Officer
Elizabeth Schimel, Sr. VP/Dir.-Business Dev.
James Fontanetta, VP-Brokerage
William C. Feeley, Dir.-Capital Markets

Phone: 212-253-4400	Fax: 212-253-4428
Toll-Free: 888-294-8227	
Address: 826 Broadway, 6th Floor, New York, NY, 10003	

GROWTH PLANS/SPECIAL FEATURES:

Wit Capital Group, Inc. is an on-line investment banking and brokerage firm that uses electronic mail and the Internet to offer and sell shares in public offerings to individuals. The company produces and electronically distributes investment research to individual investors, directly and through arrangements with 20 discount brokerage firms, including Quick & Reilly, SureTrade, Waterhouse Investor Services and Datek Online. Wit Capital Group recently announced it has signed a definitive agreement to acquire SoundView Technology Group, a Connecticut-based private investment banking firm focused exclusively on technology. The company also announced that it closed its first proprietary fund, Arista Capital Partners LP, a $39.45 million Internet-related private equity fund. This fund will enable Wit Capital to expand its investment banking services to corporate clients, including public underwriting, strategic advisory, private equity placements, investment research and the management of venture capital funding. Wit Capital plans to establish a Japanese Internet investment banking firm, to be known as Wit Capital Japan, with Mitsubishi Corporation and Trans Cosmos Inc. as initial joint venture partners. The company will be based in Tokyo. Using the Internet, Wit Capital Japan will offer Japanese investors opportunities to invest in public offerings and venture capital funds of Japanese companies.

FINANCIALS: Sales and profits are in thousands of dollars—add 000 to get the full amount.
Notes regarding 1999: *(1999 sales and profits were not available for all companies at press time.)*

1999 Sales: $48,617	1999 Profits: $-20,903	**Stock Ticker: WITC**
1998 Sales: $1,900	1998 Profits: $-8,800	Employees: 99
1997 Sales: $ 200	1997 Profits: $-3,000	Fiscal Year Ends: 12/31
1996 Sales: $	1996 Profits: $-1,800	
1995 Sales: $	1995 Profits: $	

SALARIES/BENEFITS:

Pension Plan:	ESOP Stock Plan:	Profit Sharing:	Top Exec. Salary: $146,000	Bonus: $
Savings Plan: Y	Stock Purch. Plan:		Second Exec. Salary: $120,000	Bonus: $

COMPETITIVE ADVANTAGE: Unique positioning as a leading on-line investment house.

OTHER THOUGHTS:

Apparent Women Officers or Directors: 2
Apparent Minority Officers or Directors:
Hot Spot for Advancement for Women/Minorities:

LOCATIONS: ("Y" = Yes)

West:	Southwest:	Midwest:	Southeast:	Northeast:	International:
Y				Y	

Note: Financial information, benefits and other data can change quickly and may vary from those stated here.

WORLDGATE COMMUNICATIONS   www.wgate.com

Industry Group Code: 5133C
Ranks within this company's industry group: Sales: 3   Profits: 3

BUSINESS ACTIVITIES ("Y" = Yes)

Financial Services:	Information/Publ.:	Technology:		Services:	Retailing:	Telecommunications:	
Stock Brokerage	Portal/Hub/News	Computer Manuf.		Payments/Transfers	Retailer	Internet Serv. Provider	Y
Mortgages/Loans	On-Line Community	Networking Equip.		Consulting	Auctions	Web Site Host	
Banking	Search Engine	Software Manuf.	Y	Advertising/Marketing	Mall	Server Farm	
Insurance	Financial Data Publ.	Specialty Equipment		Outsourcing	Tickets/Travel	Specialty Telecom.	
Credit Cards	Broadcasting/Music				Price Comparisons	High Speed Access	Y

TYPES OF BUSINESS:

Internet Service Provider
Cable Modem Access

BRANDS/DIVISIONS/AFFILIATES:

WorldGate Service
Channel Hyperlinking

CONTACTS: *Note: Officers with more than one job title may be intentionally listed here more than once.*

Hal M. Krisbergh, CEO
Gerard K. Kunkel, Sr. VP-Sales & Mktg.
Jamie Press, Human Resources
Joseph E. Augenbraun, VP-Engineering
Randall J. Gort, Sec.
Randall J. Gort, General Counsel
Jae Hea Edward Lee, VP-Oper.
Scott B. Campbell, VP-Business Dev.
Ed Bamford, Mgr.-Oper.
David E. Wachob, VP/General Mgr.

Phone: 215-633-5100	**Fax:** 215-633-9590
Toll-Free:	
Address: 3220 Tillman Dr., Ste. 300, Bensalem, PA, 19020	

GROWTH PLANS/SPECIAL FEATURES:

WorldGate Communications provides a television-based Internet service, the WorldGate Service, which enables cable television subscribers to access the Internet through their televisions. It is designed to operate with cable systems using advanced analog and/or current and future generation digital cable television set-top boxes. There are currently over 10,000 subscribers to the service. The company recently entered into deployment agreements with four additional cable operators, bringing its total number of cable networks to 11, including Comcast Cable Communications, Inc., Bresnan Communications, Inc., Buckeye CableSystem, Inc. and The Hunan Multimedia Communications Bureau in China. WorldGate's technology, Channel Hyperlinking, integrates the dynamics of the Internet with television's proven advertiser-sponsored entertainment model. It enables the viewer watching a television program or advertisement to link within seconds to a related interactive web site. The firm is conducting a major research study with General Motors, Warner Lambert, Kraft, Sprint and Nielsen Media Research to track consumer response and usage of Channel Hyperlinking. WorldGate's new technology, The Ultra Thin-Client architecture, was recently patented and provides a system and method for accessing an information source without the need for a personal computer, and, more importantly, the access of such information through the use of existing television distribution systems. Other business endeavors include a joint marketing agreement with General Instrument Corporation that enables the WorldGate Internet Over TV Application to a be a native application on the SURFview platform, a set-top terminal of General Instrument's. WorldGate's current business strategy entails focusing on expanding its service into international markets.

FINANCIALS: Sales and profits are in thousands of dollars—add 000 to get the full amount.

Notes regarding 1999: *(1999 sales and profits were not available for all companies at press time.)*

1999 Sales: $	1999 Profits: $	**Stock Ticker: WGAT**
1998 Sales: $1,000	1998 Profits: $-27,000	Employees: 131
1997 Sales: $ 100	1997 Profits: $-14,000	Fiscal Year Ends: 12/31
1996 Sales: $	1996 Profits: $-2,900	
1995 Sales: $	1995 Profits: $	

SALARIES/BENEFITS:

Pension Plan:	ESOP Stock Plan:	Profit Sharing:	Top Exec. Salary: $320,250	Bonus: $144,113
Savings Plan:	Stock Purch. Plan:		Second Exec. Salary: $193,218	Bonus: $67,626

COMPETITIVE ADVANTAGE: Concentrating on international markets.

OTHER THOUGHTS:

Apparent Women Officers or Directors: 2
Apparent Minority Officers or Directors:
Hot Spot for Advancement for Women/Minorities:

LOCATIONS: ("Y" = Yes)

West:	Southwest:	Midwest:	Southeast:	Northeast:	International:
				Y	

XOOM.COM   www.xoom.com

Industry Group Code: 514191
Ranks within this company's industry group: Sales: 17   Profits: 29

BUSINESS ACTIVITIES ("Y" = Yes)

Financial Services:	Information/Publ.:	Technology:		Services:	Retailing:		Telecommunications:	
Stock Brokerage	Portal/Hub/News	Computer Manuf.	Y	Payments/Transfers	Retailer	Y	Internet Serv. Provider	
Mortgages/Loans	On-Line Community	Networking Equip.		Consulting	Auctions		Web Site Host	Y
Banking	Search Engine	Software Manuf.		Advertising/Marketing	Mall		Server Farm	
Insurance	Financial Data Publ.	Specialty Equipment		Outsourcing	Tickets/Travel		Specialty Telecom.	
Credit Cards	Broadcasting/Music				Price Comparisons		High Speed Access	

TYPES OF BUSINESS:

Diversified Portal
Electronic Newsletters
Software Libraries
On-line Greeting Cards
E-commerce Shopping Channel

BRANDS/DIVISIONS/AFFILIATES:

NBCi
General Electric
InfoSpace.com
Quintel Communications
Investor Place
Phillips Publishing
ZD Net
Private One, Inc.

CONTACTS: *Note: Officers with more than one job title may be intentionally listed here more than once.*

Laurent Massa, CEO
Laurent Massa, Pres.
John Harbottle, CFO/VP-Finance
Vijay Vaidyanathan, Chief Tech. Officer
John Harbottle, Sec.
Rajesh Aji, General Counsel/Asst. Sec.
Russell S. Hyzen, VP-Bussiness Dev.
Rajesh Aji, VP-Corp. and Legal Affairs
Scott Duffy, VP-Sponsorships and On line Sales Dev.
Janine Popick, VP-E-commerce

Phone: 415-288-2500	Fax: 415-288-2580
Toll-Free:	
Address: 300 Montgomery Street, Suite 300, San Francisco, CA, 94104	

GROWTH PLANS/SPECIAL FEATURES:

Xoom.com is one of the fastest growing direct e-commerce companies on the Internet. It offers a variety of free services, including homepages, e-mail, chat rooms, electronic newsletters, clip art, software libraries, page counters and on-line greeting cards, all used to attract members. Members must agree to receive periodic offers of products and services via e-mail. These competitively priced and continuously updated offers include computer software, computer accessories and peripherals, consumer electronics, clip art on CD-ROM and collectible items. Xoom.com recently partnered with WebNext s.r.l., an Italian corporation, to launch the Italian site Xoom.it. Other targeted countries include the United Kingdom, France and Spain. The company recently entered into several strategic alliances, including a $75 million deal with Snap.com. Xoom.com and HealthGate will offer co-branded direct e-commerce to HealthGate members or those on-line users who sign up specifically for HealthGate content on Snap.com's Health Channel. Recently, Xoom launched XoomPoints, in partnership with MyPoints.com, a leading provider of Internet direct marketing, incentive and loyalty products. XoomPoints is a buyer loyalty program enabling Xoom.com's more than 10.5 million members to earn points by shopping on the Internet with approved merchants and on purchases made from the company's direct e-mail offers. Other business endeavors include the acquisition of Private One, Inc., a developer of secure encryption technology for e-mail. This allows Xoom.com to add enhanced security to its e-mail offerings, which play a significant role within the company's direct e-commerce strategy.

FINANCIALS: Sales and profits are in thousands of dollars—add 000 to get the full amount.

Notes regarding 1999: Through 9 months/Pro forma *(1999 sales and profits were not available for all companies at press time.)*

1999 Sales: $19,903	1999 Profits: $-8,175	Stock Ticker: **XMCM**
1998 Sales: $8,318	1998 Profits: $-10,798	Employees: 71
1997 Sales: $ 841	1997 Profits: $-3,132	Fiscal Year Ends: 12/31
1996 Sales: $	1996 Profits: $	
1995 Sales: $	1995 Profits: $	

SALARIES/BENEFITS:

Pension Plan:	ESOP Stock Plan:	Profit Sharing:	Top Exec. Salary: $216,124	Bonus: $15,593
Savings Plan: Y	Stock Purch. Plan: Y		Second Exec. Salary: $150,085	Bonus: $24,573

COMPETITIVE ADVANTAGE: Over 10 million members/Excellent strategic alliances.

OTHER THOUGHTS:

Apparent Women Officers or Directors: 3
Apparent Minority Officers or Directors: 2
Hot Spot for Advancement for Women/Minorities: Y

LOCATIONS: ("Y" = Yes)

West:	Southwest:	Midwest:	Southeast:	Northeast:	International:
Y				Y	Y

Note: Financial information, benefits and other data can change quickly and may vary from those stated here.

YAHOO! INC　　　www.yahoo.com

Industry Group Code: 514191
Ranks within this company's industry group: Sales: 3　Profits: 2

BUSINESS ACTIVITIES ("Y" = Yes)

Financial Services:	Information/Publ.:		Technology:	Services:		Retailing:		Telecommunications:	
Stock Brokerage	Portal/Hub/News	Y	Computer Manuf.	Payments/Transfers		Retailer	Y	Internet Serv. Provider	Y
Mortgages/Loans	On-Line Community		Networking Equip.	Consulting		Auctions	Y	Web Site Host	Y
Banking	Search Engine		Software Manuf.	Advertising/Marketing	Y	Mall	Y	Server Farm	
Insurance	Financial Data Publ.		Specialty Equipment	Outsourcing		Tickets/Travel		Specialty Telecom.	
Credit Cards	Broadcasting/Music	Y				Price Comparisons		High Speed Access	

TYPES OF BUSINESS:

Search Portal
Broadcast Media

BRANDS/DIVISIONS/AFFILIATES:

Yahooligans!
North Point Communications
Yahoo Online service
Yahoo!
GeoCities

CONTACTS: *Note: Officers with more than one job title may be intentionally listed here more than once.*

Timothy Koogle, CEO
Jeff Mallett, Pres./COO
Gary Valenzuela, Sr. VP-Finance/CFO
Karen Edwards, VP-Brand Mktg.
Beth Haba, Mgr.-Human Resources
Farzad Nazem, Sr. VP-Product Dev./Chief Tech. Officer
David Filo, Chief Yahoo
John Place, Sec.
John Place, General Counsel
Gary Valenzuela, Sr VP-Admin.
Ellen Siminoff, VP-Bussiness Dev. & Planning
Geoff Ralston, VP-Dev. & Comm.

Phone: 408-731-3300	Fax: 408-731-3301
Toll-Free:	

Address: 3420 Central Expressway, Suite 201, Santa Clara, CA, 95051

GROWTH PLANS/SPECIAL FEATURES:

Yahoo! Inc. is a global Internet media company that offers a branded network of comprehensive information, communication and shopping services to millions of users daily. As the first on-line navigational guide to the World Wide Web, www.yahoo.com is a leading guide in terms of traffic, advertising and household and business user reach, and is one of the most recognized brands associated with the Internet. Under the Yahoo! brand, the company provides broadcast media, personal communications and direct services. In order to serve users more effectively and to extend the Yahoo! brand to new media properties, the company entered into strategic relationships with business partners that offer content, technology and distribution capabilities, including Ziff-Davis, SOFTBANK, Reuters, Granite Broadcasting, Sporting News, ESPN SportsTicker, E! Online, Fox Sports, PriMedia, The Wall Street Journal and the Motley Fool, which permit the company to bring Yahoo!-branded, targeted media products to market more quickly. Recent business endeavors include a distribution agreement with North Point Communications, a national digital subscriber line (DSL) Internet access provider, to develop, market and distribute a co-branded My Yahoo! service featuring content and services designed for broadband-enabled businesses and consumers. A co-marketing agreement with Covad Communications, the leading national broadband services provider utilizing DSL, was designed to encourage the adoption of broadband services to residential and business Internet users. Yahoo! and Motorola, Inc. recently announced an agreement to enable access to Yahoo! content and services from Motorola's Internet-connected wireless devices. As part of its business strategy, Yahoo! completed several acquisitions, including a merger with GeoCities, a publicly-traded Internet company.

FINANCIALS: Sales and profits are in thousands of dollars—add 000 to get the full amount.

Notes regarding 1999: Pro forma *(1999 sales and profits were not available for all companies at press time.)*

1999 Sales: $588,608	1999 Profits: $61,133	**Stock Ticker: YHOO**
1998 Sales: $203,300	1998 Profits: $25,600	Employees: 803
1997 Sales: $67,400	1997 Profits: $-22,900	Fiscal Year Ends: 12/31
1996 Sales: $19,100	1996 Profits: $-2,300	
1995 Sales: $1,400	1995 Profits: $- 600	

SALARIES/BENEFITS:

Pension Plan:	ESOP Stock Plan:	Profit Sharing:	Top Exec. Salary: $195,000	Bonus: $
Savings Plan: Y	Stock Purch. Plan: Y		Second Exec. Salary: $185,000	Bonus: $

COMPETITIVE ADVANTAGE:　New joint venture with MCI to provide an Internet access service/The giant among portals.

OTHER THOUGHTS:

Apparent Women Officers or Directors: 1
Apparent Minority Officers or Directors:
Hot Spot for Advancement for Women/Minorities:

LOCATIONS: ("Y" = Yes)

West:	Southwest:	Midwest:	Southeast:	Northeast:	International:
Y	Y	Y	Y	Y	Y

ZDNET GROUP www.zdnet.com

Industry Group Code: 514191
Ranks within this company's industry group: Sales: 5 Profits: 25

BUSINESS ACTIVITIES ("Y" = Yes)

Financial Services:	Information/Publ.:		Technology:	Services:	Retailing:	Telecommunications:
Stock Brokerage	Portal/Hub/News	Y	Computer Manuf.	Payments/Transfers	Retailer	Internet Serv. Provider
Mortgages/Loans	On-Line Community		Networking Equip.	Consulting	Auctions	Web Site Host
Banking	Search Engine		Software Manuf.	Advertising/Marketing	Mall	Server Farm
Insurance	Financial Data Publ.		Specialty Equipment	Outsourcing	Tickets/Travel	Specialty Telecom.
Credit Cards	Broadcasting/Music				Price Comparisons	High Speed Access

TYPES OF BUSINESS:

Portal-Technology
Print Publishing
Tradeshows and Conferences

BRANDS/DIVISIONS/AFFILIATES:

Computer Gaming World
NetWorld+Interop
SOFTBANK
Ziff-Davis, Inc.
PC Week
FamilyPC

GROWTH PLANS/SPECIAL FEATURES:

ZDNet, together with Ziff-Davis, Inc., is a leading media and marketing company that provides information on computing and technology, including the Internet. The company is focused on the businesses of print publishing, trade shows and conferences, Internet, market research, education and television. It also provides technology companies worldwide with marketing strategies for reaching key decision makers. Strategic alliances are important sources of content exchange, revenue, brand visibility and increased user traffic. The company is engaged in many alliances with some of the Internet's leading web sites, including Yahoo!, Excite, MSNBC and Deja News. Consistent with its business strategy, ZDNet recently entered into a strategic alliance with GameSpy Industries to develop co-branded versions of GameSpy's gaming and digital music content and software for ZDNet's domestic and international sites. Other business endeavors include an agreement with the Associated Press Television News (APTN) to provide the world's first global video news feed devoted entirely to technology.

CONTACTS: Note: Officers with more than one job title may be intentionally listed here more than once.

Eric Hippeau, CEO
Timothy C. O'Brien, CFO
Barry D. Briggs, VP-Advertising Sales and Mktg.
Pam Harbidge, Human Resources Associate
Alan Phillips, VP-Internet Oper. and Tech.
Mark D. Moyer, VP/Controller
J. Malcolm Morris, Sr. VP/General Counsel
Massimo De Nadai, VP-Business Oper.
Russell Klein, VP-Corp. Dev.
Thomas L. Wright, VP/Treas.

Phone: 415-551-4800	Fax: 415-551-4605
Toll-Free:	
Address: 650 Townsend St. 650 Townsend St., San Francisco, CA, 94103	

FINANCIALS: Sales and profits are in thousands of dollars—add 000 to get the full amount.

Notes regarding 1999: *(1999 sales and profits were not available for all companies at press time.)*

1999 Sales: $104,178	1999 Profits: $1,939	Stock Ticker: **ZDZ**
1998 Sales: $56,100	1998 Profits: $-7,900	Employees: 316
1997 Sales: $32,200	1997 Profits: $-21,200	Fiscal Year Ends: 12/31
1996 Sales: $16,200	1996 Profits: $-16,900	
1995 Sales: $	1995 Profits: $	

SALARIES/BENEFITS:

Pension Plan:	ESOP Stock Plan:	Profit Sharing:	Top Exec. Salary: $1,050,000	Bonus: $
Savings Plan:	Stock Purch. Plan: Y		Second Exec. Salary: $800,000	Bonus: $288,493

COMPETITIVE ADVANTAGE: Owns the world's largest archive of published computer and Internet news.

OTHER THOUGHTS:

Apparent Women Officers or Directors: 1
Apparent Minority Officers or Directors: 4
Hot Spot for Advancement for Women/Minorities: Y

LOCATIONS: ("Y" = Yes)

West:	Southwest:	Midwest:	Southeast:	Northeast:	International:
Y	Y	Y	Y	Y	Y

ZIPLINK INC   www.ziplink.net

Industry Group Code: 51339
Ranks within this company's industry group: Sales: 18   Profits: 14

BUSINESS ACTIVITIES ("Y" = Yes)

Financial Services:	Information/Publ.:	Technology:	Services:	Retailing:	Telecommunications:	
Stock Brokerage	Portal/Hub/News	Computer Manuf.	Payments/Transfers	Retailer	Internet Serv. Provider	Y
Mortgages/Loans	On-Line Community	Networking Equip.	Consulting	Auctions	Web Site Host	Y
Banking	Search Engine	Software Manuf.	Advertising/Marketing	Mall	Server Farm	
Insurance	Financial Data Publ.	Specialty Equipment	Outsourcing	Tickets/Travel	Specialty Telecom.	
Credit Cards	Broadcasting/Music			Price Comparisons	High Speed Access	Y

TYPES OF BUSINESS:

Internet Service Provider- Wholesale
Wholesale Dial-up Services
Services for Internet-Based Appliances

BRANDS/DIVISIONS/AFFILIATES:

Broadcast.com
ZipDial
Nortel Networks
Williams Communications
Microsoft WebTV Network
Websurfer
WebMachines

CONTACTS: *Note: Officers with more than one job title may be intentionally listed here more than once.*

Henry M. Zachs, CEO
Christopher W. Jenkins, Pres.
Christopher W. Jenkins, CFO
Ronald C. Lipof, Chief Mktg. and Strategic Officer
Karen Johnson Taylor, Dir.-Human Resources
Daniel Rather, Dir.-Networking
Kathleen A. Stillson, Dir.-Oper.
Ronald C. Lipov, Chief Strategic Dev. Officer

Phone: 978-551-8100	Fax: 978-551-2777
Toll-Free:	
Address: 900 Chelmsford St., Tower One, 5th Fl., Lowell, MA, 01851	

GROWTH PLANS/SPECIAL FEATURES:

ZipLink, Inc. acts as an Internet service provider (ISP) for ISPs that serve retail customers. The company has 19 SuperPOPs in 16 major cities throughout the United States, allowing ZipLink to utilize unlimited local access numbers and thus expanding its network. The company's traffic is routed over a network that operates at 45 megabits per second. ZipLink's additional business segments deal in the service of Internet-related appliances, including set-top boxes that route the Internet into televisions instead of computers. Hence, the company's WebTV product utilizes the television as an Internet portal. ZipLink is a rapidly expanding company, and has made several recent acquisitions that increased its market coverage. For instance, the acquisition of Interhop Network Services, Inc. expanded ZipLink's span of coverage to include Canada. Firewall, site hosting and web-to-fax services were added to ZipLink's service offerings following the merger as well. The company recently agreed to provide Spinway.com, a company that operates alongside Kmart's e-commerce segment, with wholesale Internet connectivity. Rhythms NetConnections, HomeAccess, Williams Communications and NetZero are among the long list of prestigious companies that do business with ZipLink.

FINANCIALS: Sales and profits are in thousands of dollars—add 000 to get the full amount.

Notes regarding 1999: Through 9 months *(1999 sales and profits were not available for all companies at press time.)*

1999 Sales: $9,196	1999 Profits: $-5,338	Stock Ticker: ZIPL
1998 Sales: $7,100	1998 Profits: $-8,400	Employees: 54
1997 Sales: $5,200	1997 Profits: $-6,700	Fiscal Year Ends: 12/31
1996 Sales: $ 800	1996 Profits: $-8,800	
1995 Sales: $	1995 Profits: $	

SALARIES/BENEFITS:

Pension Plan:	ESOP Stock Plan:	Profit Sharing:	Top Exec. Salary: $	Bonus: $
Savings Plan:	Stock Purch. Plan:		Second Exec. Salary: $	Bonus: $

COMPETITIVE ADVANTAGE: Focus on selling Internet service at wholesale to resellers.

OTHER THOUGHTS:

Apparent Women Officers or Directors: 2
Apparent Minority Officers or Directors:
Hot Spot for Advancement for Women/Minorities:

LOCATIONS: ("Y" = Yes)

West:	Southwest:	Midwest:	Southeast:	Northeast:	International:
				Y	

Additional Indexes and Information

INDEX OF FIRMS NOTED AS "HOT SPOTS FOR ADVANCEMENT" FOR WOMEN AND MINORITIES

QUALCOMM INC
QUEPASA.COM
QUOKKA SPORTS
QWEST COMMUNICATIONS
INTERNATIONAL INC
RAMP NETWORKS
RAZORFISH
REALNETWORKS INC
RED HAT
RSA SECURITY INC
SCIENT CORP
SECURE COMPUTING CORP
SILICON GRAPHICS INC
SOFTWARE.COM
STAMPS.COM
STARMEDIA NETWORK
SUN MICROSYSTEMS INC
TALK CITY
TANDY CORP
TANNING TECHNOLOGY
TERAYON COMMUNICATION
SYSTEMS
THEGLOBE.COM
THESTREET.COM
TIBCO SOFTWARE
TMP WORLDWIDE INC
TUMBLEWEED COMMUNICATIONS
USWEB/CKS
VALUE AMERICA INC
VERIO INC
VERITY
VIACOM INC
WALT DISNEY COMPANY (THE)
WHITE PINE SOFTWARE
WHITTMAN-HART INC
WINK COMMUNICATIONS
XOOM.COM
ZDNET GROUP

INDEX BY SUBSIDIARIES, BRAND NAMES AND SELECTED AFFILIATIONS

**Brand or subsidiary,
Followed by the name of the related
corporation.**

Banc One Funds Management Company; **BANK ONE**
Banc One Insurance Services Corporation; **BANK ONE**
bankrate.com; **ILIFE.COM**
BankVest; **AMERITRADE HOLDING CORP**
Barnes and Noble, Inc.; **BARNESANDNOBLE.COM**
BASIS; **OPEN TEXT**
Be the Boss; **TMP WORLDWIDE INC**
Belgacom; **WHITE PINE SOFTWARE**
Bell Atlantic; **GTE CORPORATION**
Bell Laboratories; **LUCENT TECHNOLOGIES INC**
Benchmark Capital; **E-LOAN INC**
Beseen.com; **LOOKSMART LTD**
Bess; **N2H2**
Beyond.com; **CYBERSOURCE.COM CORP**
BidCom; **INTERNET CAPITAL GROUP INC**
Big Charts, Inc.; **MARKETWATCH.COM INC**
Big Think; **DATEK ONLINE HOLDING CORP**
BIG/ip Server monitor/request router; **F5 NETWORKS**
bigchalk.com; **INFONAUTICS INC**
Billpoint; **EBAY INC**
Blockbuster Video; **VIACOM INC**
Bloomlink; **1-800-FLOWERS.COM INC**
BloomNet; **1-800-FLOWERS.COM INC**
Books.com; **BARNESANDNOBLE.COM INC**
Borg Internet Service; **BIZNESS ONLINE.COM INC**
Borland International Inc.; **INPRISE CORPORATION**
Borland.com; **INPRISE CORPORATION**
Bozell Worldwide, Inc.; **MODEM MEDIA.POPPE TYSON INC**
Bridge International; **DOW JONES & COMPANY INC**
British Telecommunications; **VERISIGN**
Broadband Interactive Group Inc. (B.I.G.);
BROADCOM
Broadcast.com; **ZIPLINK INC**
Broadvision; **S1 CORPORATION**
BroadVision One-to-One; **BROADVISION INC**
BroadVision One-to-One Application Center;
BROADVISION
BroadVision One-to-One Visual Development Center;
BROADVISION
BroadVision One-to-One Webapps; **BROADVISION**
BSMG Worldwide; **MODEM MEDIA.POPPE TYSON**
Builder.com; **CNET INC**
Business Anywhere; **CAIS INTERNET INC**
Business Browser; **ONESOURCE INFORMATION SERVICES**
BUSINESSOBJECTS; **BUSINESS OBJECTS S A**
Butterfield & Butterfield; **EBAY INC**
BUYCARS.com, Inc.; **BUY.COM INC**
BUYCLEARANCE.com, Inc.; **BUY.COM INC**
BuyDirect; **BEYOND.COM CORP**
BUYGOLF.com, Inc.; **BUY.COM INC**
BuySite; **COMMERCE ONE INC**
C3-Comcast Content & Communications; **COMCAST**
Cable News Network; **TIME WARNER INC**
CablexChange; **BROADCOM CORP**
CAIS Software Solutions; **CAIS INTERNET INC**
Calico Commerce; **CONNECTINC.COM**

Cambridge Enterprise Resource; **CAMBRIDGE TECHNOLOGY PARTNERS INC**
Cambridge Management Consulting; **CAMBRIDGE TECHNOLOGY PARTNERS INC**
Camden Graphics Group;
AMERICANGREETINGS.COM INC
CareView; **VISUAL DATA**
Carlton Cards Retail, Inc.;
AMERICANGREETINGS.COM INC
Carol Wright Gifts; **PROTEAM.COM INC**
CarSmart.com; **AUTOBYTEL.COM INC**
Castanet; **MARIMBA INC**
Catalyst LAN switch; **CISCO SYSTEMS INC**
CBS; **MARKETWATCH.COM INC**
CBS; **VIACOM INC**
CBS Cable; **CBS ENTERPRISES**
CBS Cable Group; **CBS ENTERPRISES**
CBS News Inc.; **CBS ENTERPRISES**
CBS Television Networks Group; **CBS ENTERPRISES**
CBS Television Station Group; **CBS ENTERPRISES**
cbs.sportsline.com; **SPORTSLINE USA**
CCNet, Inc.; **VERIO INC**
CENTERLINQ System;
GENESISINTERMEDIA.COM
CenterStage eBizXchange; **ONDISPLAY INC**
CenterStage eContent; **ONDISPLAY INC**
CenterStage eIntegrate; **ONDISPLAY INC**
CenterStage eNotify; **ONDISPLAY INC**
CenterStage eSyndicate; **ONDISPLAY INC**
Cerent; **CISCO SYSTEMS INC**
Certplus; **VERISIGN**
Chameleon; **NETMANAGE INC**
Champion; **EMC CORP**
Channel Hyperlinking; **WORLDGATE COMMUNICATIONS**
ChanneliShop; **FRONTLINE COMMUNICATIONS**
Charles Schwab & Co.; **CHARLES SCHWAB CORP**
Charles Schwab Investment Management, Inc.;
CHARLES SCHWAB CORP (THE)
Charles Schwab Trust Company; **CHARLES SCHWAB**
Charter Advertiser Program; **WINK COMMUNICATIONS**
CheckFree Corporation; **CHECKFREE HOLDINGS**
CheckFree Investment Corporation; **CHECKFREE HOLDINGS CORP**
Chilton Publications; **WALT DISNEY COMPANY**
China.com; **24/7 MEDIA INC**
Chipcom Corporation; **3COM CORP**
Chips & Technologies, Inc.; **INTEL CORP**
Christian Community Network; **CROSSWALK.COM**
Cisco Service Management; **CISCO SYSTEMS INC**
CityAuction; **TICKETMASTER ONLINE-CITYSEARCH**
CitySearch; **TICKETMASTER ONLINE-CITYSEARCH**
CKS Group Holding; **USWEB/CKS**
Claims.now; **CLAIMSNET.COM INC**
ClarentONE; **CLARENT CORP**

CLASS Data Systems; **CISCO SYSTEMS INC**
Class Point; **WHITE PINE SOFTWARE**
Classifieds; **LYCOS INC**
Click2CallMe; **NET2PHONE**
Click2Talk; **NET2PHONE**
ClickMiles; **NETCENTIVES**
ClickRewards Network; **NETCENTIVES**
CLIQNOW! Sales Group; **24/7 MEDIA INC**
CMGI; **NAVISITE**
CMGI, Inc.; **ENGAGE TECHNOLOGIES INC**
ColdFusion; **ALLAIRE CORP**
COLT; **RAMP NETWORKS**
Comcast; **MICROSOFT CORP**
Comcast Telecommunications; **COMCAST CORP**
Commerce Chain Solution; **COMMERCE ONE INC**
CommerceBid.com; **COMMERCE ONE INC**
CommercialSource.com; **HOMESTORE.COM INC**
Communications Products Group; **INTEL CORP**
Communicomp; **MODEM MEDIA.POPPE TYSON**
CommunityWare/XML; **WEBB INTERACTIVE**
Companies Online; **LYCOS INC**
Company Sleuth; **INFONAUTICS INC**
Compaq Works; **COMPAQ COMPUTER CORP**
Compariscope; **INTRAWARE INC**
CompuServe; **AMERICA ONLINE INC**
Computer Currents Interactive Software Shop; **BEYOND.COM**
Computer Gaming World; **ZDNET GROUP**
Computer Literacy Bookshops, Inc.; **FATBRAIN.COM**
Computers.com; **CNET INC**
Comviq GSM; **NETCOM**
Concentric CustomLink; **CONCENTRIC NETWORK**
Concentric RemoteLink; **CONCENTRIC NETWORK**
Conde Nast Publications; **ADVANCE PUBLICATIONS**
Conde Net; **ADVANCE PUBLICATIONS INC**
Conroy's Flowers; **1-800-FLOWERS.COM INC**
Consejero.com; **ILIFE.COM**
ConsoleDomain.com; **THEGLOBE.COM**
Consumer Financial Network, Inc.; **IXL ENTERPRISES**
Content Delivery Suite; **INKTOMI CORP**
Contour System; **GENESISINTERMEDIA.COM**
Convex Computer Corp.; **HEWLETT-PACKARD CO**
Corporate Subscription Services; **ROWECOM**
CoStar Group; **COMPS.COM INC**
CPNet.com; **ILIFE.COM**
Cray Research; **SILICON GRAPHICS INC**
Creative Computers, Inc.; **UBID INC**
Crescendo Communications, Inc.; **CISCO SYSTEMS**
CrossingGuard; **CROSSWALK.COM INC**
Crosswave Communications, Inc.; **INTERNET INITIATIVE JAPAN INC**
CU-SeeMe Web; **WHITE PINE SOFTWARE**
cww.com; **CHINADOTCOM CORP**
CyberCoin; **CYBERCASH INC**
CyberGuard Firewall; **CYBERGUARD CORP**
Cyberstocks; **HOOVER'S INC**
CyberwallPLUS; **NETWORK-1 SECURITY SOLUTIONS**

Cygnus Solutions; **RED HAT**
Data Broadcasting Corp.; **MARKETWATCH.COM**
Data Mart Solution (DMS); **SAGENT TECHNOLOGY**
Data ONTAP; **NETWORK APPLIANCE INC**
DataCom Mall; **CREATIVE COMPUTERS INC**
Datamation.com; **EARTHWEB INC**
Datek Online Brokerage Services; **DATEK ONLINE HOLDING**
Datek Online Clearing Corp.; **DATEK ONLINE HOLDING**
David Isay; **AUDIBLE INC**
Dawson Information Services Group; **ROWECOM**
Dazel Corp; **HEWLETT-PACKARD CO**
Dealer Locator; **TMP WORLDWIDE INC**
Dealernet; **COBALT GROUP (THE)**
DealPoint; **COMPS.COM INC**
Dean Witter; **MORGAN STANLEY DEAN WITTER DISCOVER & CO**
Designer/2000; **ORACLE CORP**
Deskpro; **COMPAQ COMPUTER CORP**
Developer.com; **EARTHWEB INC**
Developer/2000; **ORACLE CORP**
Dice.com; **EARTHWEB INC**
DIDAX; **CROSSWALK.COM INC**
Digipass; **VASCO DATA SECURITY**
Digital Bindery, LLC.; **U S INTERACTIVE**
Digital DM; **FLYCAST COMMUNICATIONS CORP**
Digital Equipment Corp.; **COMPAQ COMPUTER**
Digital Evolution, Inc.; **U S INTERACTIVE**
Digital Independence; **CITRIX SYSTEMS INC**
Digital Insight; **NFRONT.COM**
Digital Market, Inc.; **AGILE SOFTWARE CORP**
Dimension XPS; **DELL COMPUTER**
Direct Alliance Corporation; **INSIGHT ENTERPRISES**
Director; **MACROMEDIA INC**
discountdomain.com; **ITURF INC**
DiscountMed Books; **NETIVATION.COM INC**
Discover Card; **MORGAN STANLEY DEAN WITTER DISCOVER & CO**
Disney Consumer Products; **WALT DISNEY CO**
Dive Laboratories; **METACREATIONS CORP**
DocService; **MARIMBA INC**
Dogpile; **GO2NET INC**
Donaldson, Lufkin and Jenrette (DLJ); **DLJDIRECT**
dotdotdash.com; **ITURF INC**
DoubleClick; **ACCRUE SOFTWARE INC**
DoubleClick AdServer; **DOUBLECLICK INC**
DoubleClick DART; **DOUBLECLICK INC**
DoubleClick Direct; **DOUBLECLICK INC**
DoubleClick International; **DOUBLECLICK INC**
DoubleClick Local; **DOUBLECLICK INC**
DoubleClick Network; **DOUBLECLICK INC**
Dow Jones Asian Equities Report; **DOW JONES & CO**
Dow Jones Capital Markets Report; **DOW JONES & CO**
Dow Jones News Service; **DOW JONES & COMPANY**
Dow Jones Telerate; **DOW JONES & COMPANY INC**
Download.com; **CNET INC**
Driveoff.com; **NAVIDEC**

Driving Revenue L.L.C.; **PEGASUS SYSTEMS**
Drugstore.com; **AMAZON.COM INC**
Durand Communications, Inc.; **WEBB INTERACTIVE**
Dynamic Command Center; **BROADVISION INC**
Dynamo; **ART TECHNOLOGY GROUP INC**
DynaSoft; **RSA SECURITY INC**
E! Entertainment; **COMCAST CORP**
E*TRADE Capital, Inc.; **E*TRADE GROUP INC**
E*TRADE Online Ventures, Inc.; **E*TRADE GROUP**
E*TRADE Securities, Inc.; **E*TRADE GROUP INC**
Eagle Technology Partners; **LEAPNET INC**
Earthlink; **MINDSPRING ENTERPRISES INC**
easySABRE; **SABRE INC**
eBay Magazine; **EBAY INC**
ebay.com; **EBAY INC**
eCompanystore.com; **IMAGEX.COM INC**
E-COMPS; **COMPS.COM INC**
e-Dealers; **WIT CAPITAL GROUP**
EDGE Consultants; **AGENCY.COM LTD**
eDispatch; **FLYCAST COMMUNICATIONS CORP**
Editors service; **AMAZON.COM INC**
Ednet; **VISUAL DATA**
Electra; **AMERICA ONLINE INC**
Electric Library; **INFONAUTICS INC**
Electronic Engineering.com; **VERTICALNET**
Electronic Press Services Group; **DIGEX INC**
Electronic Workforce; **EDIFY CORP**
electronics.net; **CYBERSHOP.COM INC**
Embedded Technology.com; **VERTICALNET**
EMI Music; **TIME WARNER INC**
EncrypTix Inc.; **STAMPS.COM**
Encyclopedia.com; **INFONAUTICS INC**
Engage AdManager; **ENGAGE TECHNOLOGIES INC**
Engage AudienceNet; **ENGAGE TECHNOLOGIES**
Engage Technologies; **CMGI INC**
ENS Connect; **CONVERGENT COMMUNICATIONS**
Enterprise Access and Integration Products; **NEON SYSTEMS**
Enterprise Intelligence; **SAGENT TECHNOLOGY**
Enterprise Networks; **LUCENT TECHNOLOGIES**
Enterprise Security Management Products; **NEON SYSTEMS**
Enterprise VPN; **CONCENTRIC NETWORK**
Entre Business Technology Group; **CONVERGENT COMMUNICATIONS INC**
Entrust/AutoRA; **ENTRUST TECHNOLOGIES INC**
Entrust/PKI 5.0; **ENTRUST TECHNOLOGIES INC**
Entrust/Roaming; **ENTRUST TECHNOLOGIES INC**
Entrust/Toolkit; **ENTRUST TECHNOLOGIES INC**
ePatrol; **ISS GROUP INC**
Equitrade Partners; **NATIONAL DISCOUNT BROKERS**
e-Roadmap; **U S INTERACTIVE**
E-Series; **GATEWAY INC**
ESPN.com; **GO.COM**
Essential e-business; **PRIMIX SOLUTIONS INC**
Eudora Light; **QUALCOMM INC**
Eudora Pro; **QUALCOMM INC**

eVentures; **E-LOAN INC**
Excell Data Corporation; **CAMBRIDGE TECHNOLOGY PARTNERS INC**
Exchange Network Services; **VOYAGER.NET**
Excite Boards; **EXCITE@HOME**
Excite email; **EXCITE@HOME**
Excite Search; **EXCITE@HOME**
Excite Shopping Channel; **EXCITE@HOME**
Excite, Inc.; **EXCITE@HOME**
Excite, Inc.; **EXCITE@HOME**
Excite@Home; **IMALL INC**
ExecPC Internet; **VOYAGER.NET**
Expresso multiplexers; **TUT SYSTEMS**
Factory Outlet Mall; **CYBER MERCHANTS EXCHANGE**
Family.com; **GO.COM**
FamilyPC; **ZDNET GROUP**
FastCopper technology; **TUT SYSTEMS**
FEDplu$; **FUNDTECH LTD**
FileMaker; **APPLE COMPUTER INC**
FilmWorks; **PHOTOWORKS INC**
Finance Solution 2-1-1; **COBALT GROUP (THE)**
Fine Arts Graphics; **IMAGEX.COM INC**
First Union Complex; **COMCAST CORP**
First USA; **BANK ONE CORP**
FirstInsure, Inc.; **HOMECOM COMMUNICATIONS**
flexemortgage.com; **E-LOAN INC**
Flora Plenty; **1-800-FLOWERS.COM INC**
Floraminder; **1-800-FLOWERS.COM INC**
Flycast Communications; **ENGAGE TECHNOLOGIES**
Fontographer; **MACROMEDIA INC**
Foote, Cone & Belding; **MODEM MEDIA.POPPE TYSON**
ForeignTV.com; **MEDIUM4.COM INC**
FreeEDGAR.com; **EDGAR ONLINE INC**
FreeHand; **MACROMEDIA INC**
Freeway; **VOYAGER.NET**
Frontier Corporation; **GLOBAL CROSSING LTD**
Fulcrum Innovations; **PERSISTENCE SOFTWARE**
FUSION WebPilot Micro Browser; **PACIFIC SOFTWORKS**
Gamecenter.com; **CNET INC**
GamesDomain.com; **THEGLOBE.COM**
GATEWAY 2000; **GATEWAY INC**
Gateway Country Stores; **GATEWAY INC**
Gateway Gear; **GATEWAY INC**
Gateway Partners; **GATEWAY INC**
Gateway Solo; **GATEWAY INC**
Gauntlet; **NETWORK ASSOCIATES INC**
Gear.com; **AMAZON.COM INC**
Gemini 2000; **APPLIEDTHEORY CORP**
GeneArray Scanner; **HEWLETT-PACKARD CO**
General Electric; **XOOM.COM**
General Nutrition Companies (GNC); **DRUGSTORE.COM**
Genesis Media Group; **GENESISINTERMEDIA.COM**
Gensia Direct, Inc.; **PROTEAM.COM INC**
GeoCities; **YAHOO! INC**

Gibson Greetings; **AMERICANGREETINGS.COM**
Global CASHstar; **FUNDTECH LTD**
Global Enterprise Services, Inc.; **VERIO INC**
global/SITE controller; **F5 NETWORKS INC**
Globalstar; **QUALCOMM INC**
Globalstar; **QUALCOMM INC**
Go.com; **WALT DISNEY COMPANY (THE)**
go2pivot.com; **ILIFE.COM**
GoBizGo.com; **NETOBJECTS INC**
GQ; **ADVANCE PUBLICATIONS INC**
Graham Gregory Bozell, Inc; **MODEM MEDIA.POPPE TYSON INC**
Grotech Capital; **USINTERNETWORKING INC**
GTE Card Services; **GTE CORPORATION**
GTE Data Services, Inc.; **GTE CORPORATION**
GTE Internetworking; **GTE CORPORATION**
GTE Long Distance; **GTE CORPORATION**
GTE Service Corporation; **GTE CORPORATION**
GTE Supply; **GTE CORPORATION**
GTE Wireless; **GTE CORPORATION**
GuideSites; **ABOUT.COM INC**
gURL.com; **ITURF INC**
gURLmail.com; **ITURF INC**
gURLnet.com; **ITURF INC**
gURLpages.com; **ITURF INC**
Haggie Online; **GO2NET INC**
Halo Product Family; **NEON SYSTEMS**
Hanson White Ltd.; **AMERICANGREETINGS.COM**
HappyPuppy.com; **THEGLOBE.COM**
Harmonix; **EMC CORP**
Harvey; **HOMECOM COMMUNICATIONS INC**
Healtheon/WebMD; **HEALTHEON/WEBMD CORP**
HearMe Software Developer Kit; **HEARME.COM**
HearMe Starter Applications; **HEARME.COM**
Hebenstreit Communications; **COMCAST CORP**
Hewlett-Packard; **S1 CORPORATION**
HiTrust; **VERISIGN**
Hiway; **VERIO INC**
HNET, Inc; **HEADHUNTER.NET INC**
Home Box Office; **TIME WARNER INC**
Homebuilder.com; **HOMESTORE.COM INC**
HomeFair.com; **HOMESTORE.COM INC**
Homegrocer.com; **AMAZON.COM INC**
HomeRun technology; **TUT SYSTEMS**
HomeSite; **ALLAIRE CORP**
hongkong.com; **CHINADOTCOM CORP**
Hoosier Online; **VOYAGER.NET**
Hoover's Online; **HOOVER'S INC**
Hoover's UK; **HOOVER'S INC**
HotelView; **VISUAL DATA**
HotSend; **EFAX INC**
HTMLGoodies.com; **EARTHWEB INC**
HyperMart; **GO2NET INC**
I/PRO; **ENGAGE TECHNOLOGIES INC**
iBaby.com; **IVILLAGE INC**
IBM; **NETOBJECTS INC**
iCast; **CMGI INC**
ICAST; **FVC.COM INC**

ICONN, L.L.C.; **BIZNESS ONLINE.COM INC**
ICVerify, Inc.; **CYBERCASH INC**
IDT, Inc.; **NET2PHONE**
IIJ Media Communications, Inc.; **INTERNET INITIATIVE JAPAN INC**
IIJ Technology, Inc.; **INTERNET INITIATIVE JAPAN**
ilife.com; **ILIFE.COM**
iMac; **APPLE COMPUTER INC**
ImagePoint; **HEWLETT-PACKARD CO**
ImagiNation Network; **AT&T CORP**
iMall; **EXCITE@HOME**
iMaternity.com; **IVILLAGE INC**
Impulse! Buy Network; **INKTOMI CORP**
iNautix Technologies Inc.; **DLJDIRECT INC**
Independent Computing Architecture; **CITRIX SYSTEMS**
Indepth Data, Inc.; **DOW JONES & COMPANY INC**
Individual.com, Inc.; **NEWSEDGE**
Industriforvaltnings; **NETCOM**
Infinite Systems, Ltd.; **VOYAGER.NET**
Infinity Broadcasting Corporation; **CBS ENTERPRISES**
InfoBeat, Inc.; **EXACTIS.COM INC**
Infoboard, Inc.; **BIZNESS ONLINE.COM INC**
Infoseek; **WALT DISNEY COMPANY (THE)**
Infoseek, Inc.; **GO.COM**
InfoSort; **DIALOG CORPORATION PLC (THE)**
InfoSpace.com; **XOOM.COM**
Infranet IPT; **PORTAL SOFTWARE**
Inprise AppServices; **INPRISE CORPORATION**
Inprise Technology, Inc.; **INPRISE CORPORATION**
Insight Direct, Inc.; **INSIGHT ENTERPRISES INC**
InstaBuy; **CYBERCASH INC**
InsureRate; **HOMECOM COMMUNICATIONS INC**
Integrated Cash Management Services, Inc.; **BOTTOMLINE TECHNOLOGIES INC**
Integrated Messaging Exchange; **TUMBLEWEED COMMUNICATIONS**
Intel Products Group; **INTEL CORP**
Intel Supercomputer Systems; **INTEL CORP**
Intelligent Interacting Corp.; **24/7 MEDIA INC**
IntelligentTaxes.com; **ILIFE.COM**
Interactive Marketing, Inc.; **AMERICANGREETINGS.COM INC**
Interactive Objects Software GMBH; **INPRISE CORP**
Interactive Pictures; **BAMBOO.COM INC**
Interactive Solutions; **AGENCY.COM LTD**
InterAd Holdings, Ltd.; **24/7 MEDIA INC**
InterFrame; **PSINET INC**
Interliant International, Inc.; **INTERLIANT INC**
InterMail; **SOFTWARE.COM**
InterMail Kx; **SOFTWARE.COM**
InterMail Mx; **SOFTWARE.COM**
InterMail Post Office; **SOFTWARE.COM**
InterMAN; **PSINET INC**
Intermedia Communications; **DIGEX INC**
Internet Commerce Solution; **CISCO SYSTEMS INC**
Internet Direct; **MINDSPRING ENTERPRISES INC**

MetaStream; **METACREATIONS CORP**
MetaVoice; **VOXWARE**
Metromedia Fiber Network; **ABOVENET COMMUNICATIONS INC**
Microelectronics and Communications Technologies; **LUCENT TECHNOLOGIES INC**
Microsoft Corporation; **COMCAST CORP**
Microsoft Network; **MICROSOFT CORP**
Microsoft WebTV Network; **ZIPLINK INC**
Miller Anderson & Sherrerd, LLP; **MORGAN STANLEY DEAN WITTER DISCOVER & CO**
MindSpring; **EARTHLINK NETWORK INC**
MiningCo.com; **ABOUT.COM INC**
MIPS Group; **SILICON GRAPHICS INC**
Miramax; **WALT DISNEY COMPANY (THE)**
Mitchell Madison Group; **USWEB/CKS**
Mobility.Net Corp.; **SOFTWARE.COM**
Morgan & Banks, Ltd.; **TMP WORLDWIDE INC**
Morgan Stanley Asset Management; **MORGAN STANLEY DEAN WITTER DISCOVER & CO**
Morgan Stanley Capital International; **MORGAN STANLEY DEAN WITTER DISCOVER & CO**
Morgan Stanley Real Estate Fund, L.P.; **MORGAN STANLEY DEAN WITTER DISCOVER & CO**
Morgan Stanley Venture Capital Fund, II, L.P.; **MORGAN STANLEY DEAN WITTER DISCOVER & CO**
MOSAIC:2000; **EMC CORP**
Mplayer.com; **HEARME.COM**
Mr. Showbiz; **GO.COM**
MSN.COM; **MICROSOFT CORP**
MSNBC; **MICROSOFT CORP**
MTV Networks; **VIACOM INC**
Multimedia Manager; **INTERVU INC**
MyPhone; **PHONE.COM**
MyWay.com; **CMGI INC**
N2K; **CDNOW INC**
National Business Employment Weekly; **DOW JONES & COMPANY INC**
NaviNet; **CMGI INC**
NaviSite; **CMGI INC**
NaviSoft, Inc.; **AMERICA ONLINE INC**
Navitel Communications, Inc.; **SPYGLASS**
NBC Interactive; **CNET INC**
NBCi; **XOOM.COM**
nBranch; **NFRONT.COM**
nBusiness; **NFRONT.COM**
NDB University; **NATIONAL DISCOUNT BROKERS**
Nefinity PC; **INTERNATIONAL BUSINESS MACHINES**
Neosoft, Inc.; **INTERNET AMERICA INC**
Net Link; **VOYAGER.NET**
Net Perceptions for Ad Targeting; **NET PERCEPTIONS**
Net Perceptions for Call Centers; **NET PERCEPTIONS**
Net Perceptions for E-Commerce; **NET PERCEPTIONS**
Net Perceptions Reccommendation Engine; **NET PERCEPTIONS**
Net2Fax; **NET2PHONE**

Net2Phone Direct; **NET2PHONE**
Net2Phone Pro; **NET2PHONE**
Net2Phone, Inc.; **IDT CORPORATION**
NetAPP F; **NETWORK APPLIANCE INC**
NetBooker; **PEGASUS SYSTEMS**
NetCache; **NETWORK APPLIANCE INC**
NetCom ASA; **NETCOM**
Netegrity; **NAVIDEC**
NetGravity; **DOUBLECLICK INC**
NetHopper; **SPYGLASS**
NetIgnite 2, LLC; **WEBB INTERACTIVE**
NetObjects; **INTERNATIONAL BUSINESS MACHINES CORP**
NetObjects Authoring Server Suite; **NETOBJECTS INC**
NetObjects Fusion; **NETOBJECTS INC**
Netscape; **AMERICA ONLINE INC**
NetScout Manager Plus; **NETSCOUT SYSTEMS**
NetScout Server; **NETSCOUT SYSTEMS**
NetScreen Technologies; **WEBTRENDS CORP**
NetSolutions Division; **NAVIDEC**
Netspeak Gatekeeper; **NETSPEAK**
NetSpeed, Inc.; **CISCO SYSTEMS INC**
NetWare Products Division; **NOVELL INC**
NetWare Systems Group; **NOVELL INC**
Network; **FLYCAST COMMUNICATIONS CORP**
Network System Group; **AT&T CORP**
NetWorld+Interop; **ZDNET GROUP**
NewsEdge; **ROWECOM**
NEWT; **NETMANAGE INC**
Next Action Technology; **BUSINESS OBJECTS S A**
nHome; **NFRONT.COM**
NiceCom, Ltd.; **3COM CORP**
Nickelodeon; **VIACOM INC**
Nine Dots; **LEAPNET INC**
Nortel Networks; **ZIPLINK INC**
North Point Communications; **YAHOO! INC**
Novell Applications Group; **NOVELL INC**
NS-Series; **GATEWAY INC**
NYSERNet; **APPLIEDTHEORY CORP**
Obkect Database Management System; **VERSANT**
Oblix; **NAVIDEC**
O'Connell, Norton & Partners; **MODEM MEDIA.POPPE TYSON INC**
Octane; **SILICON GRAPHICS INC**
ODI; **NAVIDEC**
OfficeShopper; **DIALOG CORPORATION PLC**
OmniTRACS; **QUALCOMM INC**
One & Only; **TICKETMASTER ONLINE-CITYSEARCH INC**
Online Career Center; **TMP WORLDWIDE INC**
Online Magic; **AGENCY.COM LTD**
On-line Printing Center; **IMAGEX.COM INC**
Online Systems Services; **WEBB INTERACTIVE**
OnMoney; **AMERITRADE HOLDING CORP**
Onsale.com; **ONSALE INC**
OnTap.com; **ITURF INC**
OnTime; **OPEN TEXT**
Onyx2; **SILICON GRAPHICS INC**

Operating Resource Management System; **ARIBA INC**
OpSession; **NETMANAGE INC**
OptiPlex; **DELL COMPUTER CORPORATION**
Opus; **ONLINE RESOURCES & COMMUNICATIONS**
Oracle; **NAVIDEC**
Oracle; **ORACLE CORP**
Oracle Media Server; **ORACLE CORP**
Oracle Power Objects; **ORACLE CORP**
Origin2000; **SILICON GRAPHICS INC**
Outletmall.com, Inc.; **FASHIONMALL.COM INC**
Outpost.com; **CYBERIAN OUTPOST INC**
OverVoice; **CAIS INTERNET INC**
Pacific Analysis & Computing; **FINE.COM INTERNATIONAL CORP**
Pacific Capital Group; **GLOBAL CROSSING LTD**
PacketShaper bandwidth management devices; **PACKETEER**
Palm Computing; **3COM CORP**
PaperMaster; **EFAX INC**
Paramount Pictures/Paramount Stations Group; **VIACOM**
PartsVoice; **COBALT GROUP (THE)**
Passport Solutions; **GLOBAL CROSSING LTD**
PayNow; **CYBERCASH INC**
PC Link; **VOYAGER.NET**
PC Mall; **CREATIVE COMPUTERS INC**
PC Week; **ZDNET GROUP**
PDQ.net; **INTERNET AMERICA INC**
Pegasus Business Intellegence; **PEGASUS SYSTEMS**
Pegasus Commission Processing; **PEGASUS SYSTEMS**
Pegasus Electronic Distribution; **PEGASUS SYSTEMS**
Pentium Series; **INTEL CORP**
People Find; **LYCOS INC**
Performance Technologies Inc.; **CHARLES SCHWAB**
Personal Communications Services (PCS); **QUALCOMM**
Personal Internet Banker; **HOMECOM COMMUNICATIONS INC**
Pets.com; **AMAZON.COM INC**
PGP Total Network Security; **NETWORK ASSOCIATES INC**
Phillips Publishing; **XOOM.COM**
PhotoDisc; **GETTY IMAGES INC**
PhotoMail; **PHOTOWORKS INC**
PhotoWorks Uploader; **PHOTOWORKS INC**
Pictures & Sounds Search; **LYCOS INC**
Pilot Secure Access & Gateway Services; **PILOT NETWORK SERVICES**
Pioneer Global Telecommunications, Inc.; **VERIO INC**
Pivot Rules; **BLUEFLY INC**
Planet SABRE; **SABRE INC**
Planetall.com; **AMAZON.COM INC**
Plant Automation.com; **VERTICALNET**
PlaySite; **GO2NET INC**
Plus Mark, Inc.; **AMERICANGREETINGS.COM INC**
PointeCom, Inc.; **INTERNET AMERICA INC**
Politicallyblack.com, Inc.; **NETIVATION.COM INC**

PostMaster Direct; **NETCREATIONS**
Power Macintosh G4; **APPLE COMPUTER INC**
PowerBook G3; **APPLE COMPUTER INC**
Powered by Jeeves; **ASK JEEVES INC**
PowerEdge; **DELL COMPUTER CORPORATION**
PowerTier; **PERSISTENCE SOFTWARE**
PowerVault; **DELL COMPUTER CORPORATION**
Precision Workstation; **DELL COMPUTER**
Prentice Hall; **VIACOM INC**
Presario; **COMPAQ COMPUTER CORP**
Primary Access Corporation; **3COM CORP**
Primus eService; **PRIMUS KNOWLEDGE SOLUTIONS**
Prism; **SPYGLASS**
Private One, Inc.; **XOOM.COM**
PrivateWire; **CYLINK CORP**
ProLinea; **COMPAQ COMPUTER CORP**
Provisioning Software; **TERAYON COMMUNICATION SYSTEMS**
PSI IntraNet; **PSINET INC**
PSINet InterPaper; **PSINET INC**
PSINet Security Services; **PSINET INC**
PSIWeb; **PSINET INC**
PSIWeb eCommerce; **PSINET INC**
PublicPort, Inc.; **TUT SYSTEMS**
Quadris; **AGENCY.COM LTD**
Qualitative Marketing Software, Inc.; **SAGENT TECHNOLOGY**
Quantum Leap Communications, Inc.; **LEAPNET INC**
Quattro Pro product line; **NOVELL INC**
QuickBooks; **INTUIT INC**
Quickbridges; **ACCRUE SOFTWARE INC**
Quicken; **INTUIT INC**
QuickenInsurance; **INTUIT INC**
QuickenMortgage; **INTUIT INC**
Quintel Communications; **XOOM.COM**
QVC; **COMCAST CORP**
Qwest MacroCapacity Network; **QWEST COMMUNICATIONS INTERNATIONAL INC**
Rack-Mountable ProLiant; **COMPAQ COMPUTER**
RadarScope; **INTRAWARE INC**
Radio Shack; **TANDY CORP**
RADWARE; **WEBTRENDS CORP**
RAINet, Inc.; **VERIO INC**
Rapid Globalization Methodology; **LIONBRIDGE TECHNOLOGIES INC**
Ray Dream, Inc.; **METACREATIONS CORP**
RCM Systems, Inc.; **CHECKFREE HOLDINGS**
Real Fans Sport Network; **AMERICA ONLINE INC**
Real Secure; **ISS GROUP INC**
Real Time Geometry; **METACREATIONS CORP**
Real Time No Limits Infranet Solution; **PORTAL SOFTWARE**
RealAudio; **REALNETWORKS INC**
ReaLBid; **COMPS.COM INC**
RealPlayer; **REALNETWORKS INC**
RealPublisher; **REALNETWORKS INC**
RealSelect, Inc.; **HOMESTORE.COM INC**

RealServer Internet Solutions; **REALNETWORKS INC**
RealSystem G2; **REALNETWORKS INC**
REALTOR.com; **HOMESTORE.COM INC**
RealVideo; **REALNETWORKS INC**
Red Hat, Inc.; **WHITE PINE SOFTWARE**
RelevantKnowledge; **MEDIA METRIX INC**
Remodel.com; **HOMESTORE.COM INC**
Researchpaper.com; **INFONAUTICS INC**
ResortView; **VISUAL DATA**
Response Point; **FLYCAST COMMUNICATIONS**
Ricochet Private Network; **METRICOM INC**
RIMS; **OPEN TEXT**
Rite Aid; **DRUGSTORE.COM INC**
Road Maps; **LYCOS INC**
Road Runner; **TIME WARNER INC**
Rock Financial; **INTUIT INC**
Rockland Technologies, Inc.; **HEWLETT-PACKARD**
Rocky Mountain Internet; **RMI.NET**
RSA Data Security, Inc.; **RSA SECURITY INC**
RxAmerica; **DRUGSTORE.COM INC**
S1; **EDIFY CORP**
SABRE Business Travel Solutions; **SABRE INC**
SABRE Interactive; **SABRE INC**
SABRE Technology Solutions; **SABRE INC**
SABRE Travel Information Network; **SABRE INC**
SACA; **VERISIGN**
SAFEsuite; **ISS GROUP INC**
SafeWord; **SECURE COMPUTING CORP**
Sales Technology Limited; **INTERLIANT INC**
Salon Shopping; **SALON.COM**
Saraide; **INFOSPACE.COM INC**
SavvySearch.com; **CNET INC**
Sbnet; **MINDSPRING ENTERPRISES INC**
SchwabAlerts; **EXACTIS.COM INC**
SchwabFunds; **CHARLES SCHWAB CORP (THE)**
Science Applications International; **NETWORK SOLUTIONS INC**
Searchopolis; **N2H2**
Seattle FilmWorks; **PHOTOWORKS INC**
Secure Network Consulting, Inc.; **AXENT TECHNOLOGIES INC**
SecureLink; **OPEN MARKET INC**
SecureWire; **SECURE COMPUTING CORP**
SecureZone; **SECURE COMPUTING CORP**
SecurID; **RSA SECURITY INC**
Security Design International Inc.; **CYLINK CORP**
Security Dynamics Technologies, Inc.; **RSA SECURITY**
SecurSight; **RSA SECURITY INC**
SecurWorld; **RSA SECURITY INC**
see/IT Network management console; **F5 NETWORKS**
Semiconductor Online; **VERTICALNET**
Service Metrics, Inc.; **EXODUS COMMUNICATIONS**
Service Provider Networks; **LUCENT TECHNOLOGIES INC**
Shadow Enterprise Direct; **NEON SYSTEMS**
Shadow OS/390 Web Server; **NEON SYSTEMS**
Shadow VM Web Server; **NEON SYSTEMS**
ShadowDirect; **NEON SYSTEMS**

Share Data, Inc.; **E*TRADE GROUP INC**
SharkyExtreme.com; **INTERNET.COM**
SHD Corporation; **NATIONAL DISCOUNT BROKERS**
Sherwood Securities Corp.; **NATIONAL DISCOUNT BROKERS**
Shockwave; **MACROMEDIA INC**
Shop@Juno; **JUNO ONLINE SERVICES INC**
Shopper.com; **CNET INC**
ShopperConnection; **CYBERIAN OUTPOST INC**
ShopSite; **OPEN MARKET INC**
Showtime Networks, Inc.; **VIACOM INC**
Sidewalk; **MICROSOFT CORP**
SideWinder firewall; **SECURE COMPUTING CORP**
Sift, Inc.; **24/7 MEDIA INC**
Silicon Investor; **GO2NET INC**
Silknet eBusiness System; **SILKNET SOFTWARE**
Silknet eCommerce; **SILKNET SOFTWARE**
Silknet eService; **SILKNET SOFTWARE**
SilverStream Application Server; **SILVERSTREAM SOFTWARE**
Simon & Schuster; **VIACOM INC**
SiteHarbor; **NAVISITE**
Sitematic Corporation; **NETOBJECTS INC**
Skytel; **MCI WORLDCOM INC**
Smart Card Campus; **LITRONIC INC**
SMART Options; **EDIFY CORP**
Smart Shopping For Busy People; **PEAPOD INC**
SmartCAT; **V-ONE**
SmartForce; **FOREFRONT DIRECT**
SmartGate; **V-ONE**
SmartStamp; **E-STAMP CORP**
SmartWall; **V-ONE**
Snap.com; **CNET INC**
Sniffer Total Network Visibility; **NETWORK ASSOCIATES INC**
SNMP Management; **VOCALTEC**
SOFTBANK; **INSWEB CORP**
SOFTBANK; **ZDNET GROUP**
Soft-Pak Intel; **INTEL CORP**
Softshoe recruiting software; **HOTJOBS.COM LTD**
SolutionSeries; **PRIMUS KNOWLEDGE SOLUTIONS**
SonicNet; **ALLOY ONLINE INC**
SoundEdit 16; **MACROMEDIA INC**
SoundView Technology Group, Inc.; **WIT CAPITAL GROUP**
SPARC Technology; **SUN MICROSYSTEMS INC**
Spectra; **ALLAIRE CORP**
Spiral Media; **AGENCY.COM LTD**
Split Pea Software; **PEAPOD INC**
Sports Sleuth; **INFONAUTICS INC**
Sportsline Worldwide; **SPORTSLINE USA**
SpringStreet.com; **HOMESTORE.COM INC**
Sprint; **EARTHLINK NETWORK INC**
Sprint; **MCI WORLDCOM INC**
Sprint Store at Radio Shack; **TANDY CORP**
SpryNet; **MINDSPRING ENTERPRISES INC**

Spyglass Device Mail; **SPYGLASS**
Spyglass Device Mosaic; **SPYGLASS**
Spyglass Mobile Forms Database; **SPYGLASS**
Spyglass ThinGUI Library; **SPYGLASS**
Starfish Software Inc.; **INPRISE CORPORATION**
StarScreen System; **STARTRONIX**
StarTronix eSolutions; **STARTRONIX**
Sting Ray Software; **ROGUE WAVE SOFTWARE**
StockSite; **GO2NET INC**
Studio.J Software; **ROGUE WAVE SOFTWARE**
Stuff.com; **IMALL INC**
Sun Microelectronics; **SUN MICROSYSTEMS INC**
Sun Microsystems; **NAVIDEC**
Sun Microsystems Computer Company; **SUN MICROSYSTEMS INC**
SunService Division; **SUN MICROSYSTEMS INC**
SunSoft, Inc.; **SUN MICROSYSTEMS INC**
SunSoft, Inc.; **SUN MICROSYSTEMS INC**
SuperNet; **BIZNESS ONLINE.COM INC**
SupportNow; **NETMANAGE INC**
SurfWatch; **SPYGLASS**
Surplus Software, Inc.; **EGGHEAD.COM INC**
Surplusauction.com; **EGGHEAD.COM INC**
Surplusdirect.com; **EGGHEAD.COM INC**
Symmetrix; **EMC CORP**
Synchronous Code Division Multiple Access (S-CDMA); **TERAYON COMMUNICATION SYSTEMS**
System.390 G4; **INTERNATIONAL BUSINESS MACHINES CORP**
Syzygy Communications, Inc.; **NETMANAGE INC**
Table Talk; **SALON.COM**
TABNet; **VERIO INC**
Tadpole Productions, Inc.; **LEAPNET INC**
taiwan.com; **CHINADOTCOM CORP**
TalentView; **VISUAL DATA**
TCI (Telecommunications, Inc.); **AT&T CORP**
TDI-Transportation Displays; **CBS ENTERPRISES**
Tech Data Education; **TECH DATA CORP**
Techlib; **OPEN TEXT**
TechShopper Software Store; **BEYOND.COM CORP**
TechWave Inc.; **24/7 MEDIA INC**
Tele2; **NETCOM**
Tele2 Denmark; **NETCOM**
Tele2 Norway; **NETCOM**
Teleport Communications Group; **AT&T CORP**
Televest; **AMERITRADE HOLDING CORP**
TENPERCENTOFFWALMART.com, Inc.; **BUY.COM**
TeraComm; **TERAYON COMMUNICATION SYSTEMS**
TeraLink 1000 Master Controller; **TERAYON COMMUNICATION SYSTEMS**
TeraLink Gateway; **TERAYON COMMUNICATION SYSTEMS**
TeraView Element Management; **TERAYON COMMUNICATION SYSTEMS**
Test and Measurement.com; **VERTICALNET**
The Daily-e Corporation; **INTERLIANT INC**

The Developer's Marketplace; **MULTIPLE ZONES INTERNATIONAL INC**
The Disney Channel; **WALT DISNEY COMPANY**
The Edge Company Catalog; **PROTEAM.COM INC**
The Enterprise Unit; **NEWSEDGE**
The ForeFront Group; **FOREFRONT DIRECT**
The HOME COMPUTER CATALOG; **MULTIPLE ZONES INTERNATIONAL INC**
The Information Bus (TIB); **TIBCO SOFTWARE**
The IPO Profiler; **EDGAR ONLINE INC**
The LEARNING ZONE; **MULTIPLE ZONES INTERNATIONAL INC**
The MAC ZONE; **MULTIPLE ZONES INTERNATIONAL INC**
The Mall; **EARTHLINK NETWORK INC**
The Monster Board; **TMP WORLDWIDE INC**
The New Yorker; **ADVANCE PUBLICATIONS INC**
The NPD Group; **MEDIA METRIX INC**
The PC ZONE; **MULTIPLE ZONES INTERNATIONAL INC**
The Sporting News Online; **24/7 MEDIA INC**
The Vitamin Shoppe premium brand; **VITAMINSHOPPE**
The Wall Street Journal; **DOW JONES & COMPANY**
The Web Connection; **CHINADOTCOM CORP**
The Well; **SALON.COM**
The World Music; **MEDIUM4.COM INC**
theDial; **SALON.COM**
TheFirstNews.com (TFN); **VISUAL DATA**
TheStreet.co.uk; **THESTREET.COM**
theWhiz.com; **ILIFE.COM**
THINK Vision Process; **THINK NEW IDEAS**
ThinkPad; **INTERNATIONAL BUSINESS MACHINES CORP**
TIB/Acive Enterprise; **TIBCO SOFTWARE**
Ticketmaster Online; **TICKETMASTER ONLINE-CITYSEARCH INC**
Ticketmaster Store; **TICKETMASTER ONLINE-CITYSEARCH INC**
Time Warner; **AMERICA ONLINE INC**
Time, Inc.; **TIME WARNER INC**
TimeZone.com; **ASHFORD.COM INC**
Tivoli; **INTERNATIONAL BUSINESS MACHINES**
Tony Stone Images; **GETTY IMAGES INC**
Top 5% Sites; **LYCOS INC**
Touchstone Pictures; **WALT DISNEY COMPANY**
TownPages; **TOWN PAGES NET.COM**
Toys.com; **ETOYS INC**
TradeWave; **CYBERGUARD CORP**
Traffic Server; **INKTOMI CORP**
Transact; **OPEN MARKET INC**
Transcend Network Software; **3COM CORP**
Travel Web; **PEGASUS SYSTEMS**
Travelocity; **PREVIEW TRAVEL INC**
Travelocity; **SABRE INC**
TravelReach Paging; **GLOBAL CROSSING LTD**
Triak Services; **NATIONAL DISCOUNT BROKERS**
TrustMark; **CHARLES SCHWAB CORP (THE)**

Turbo SABRE; **SABRE INC**
TurboTax; **INTUIT INC**
Turner Broadcasting System; **TIME WARNER INC**
U S Robotics; **3COM CORP**
U.S. West, Inc.; **QWEST COMMUNICATIONS INTERNATIONAL INC**
uBID; **CREATIVE COMPUTERS INC**
uCommand; **GLOBAL CROSSING LTD**
Ultimate Trader; **A B WATLEY GROUP INC**
UltraRes; **PEGASUS SYSTEMS**
Unison Software; **INTERNATIONAL BUSINESS MACHINES CORP**
UNIX System Laboratories, Inc.; **NOVELL INC**
Unwired Planet, Inc.; **PHONE.COM**
Up4sale; **EBAY INC**
URLe2Market.com; **CONNECTINC.COM**
USA/Lycos Interactive Networks, Inc.; **TICKETMASTER ONLINE-CITYSEARCH INC**
USWeb Corp; **USWEB/CKS**
USWEB/CKS; **WHITTMAN-HART INC**
UtiliNet Private Network; **METRICOM INC**
UUNET; **MCI WORLDCOM INC**
U-WIRE; **STUDENT ADVANTAGE**
VACMan; **VASCO DATA SECURITY**
VASCO Corporation Subsidiary; **VASCO DATA SECURITY**
Vector Systems; **SILICON GRAPHICS INC**
Ventix; **PERFICIENT**
VeriSign Japan; **VERISIGN**
VeriSign OnSite Service; **VERISIGN**
Vertex Partners; **BRAUN CONSULTING INC**
VerticalNet; **INTERNET CAPITAL GROUP INC**
Viacom, Inc.; **CBS ENTERPRISES**
Video Services; **FVC.COM INC**
VideoCapsule; **DIGITAL LAVA INC**
VideoNewswire; **VISUAL DATA**
VideoVisor; **DIGITAL LAVA INC**
VIEWonTV; **DIGITAL ISLAND INC**
Vintel Communications, Inc.; **TUT SYSTEMS**
Viridia Patient Care System; **HEWLETT-PACKARD**
Virtual Financial Manager (VFM); **S1 CORPORATION**
Visigenic; **INPRISE CORPORATION**
VocalTec Ensemble Architecture; **VOCALTEC**
VocalTec Gatekeeper; **VOCALTEC**
VocalTec Internet Phone; **VOCALTEC**
VocalTec Internet Phone Lite; **VOCALTEC**
VocalTec Network Manager; **VOCALTEC**
VocalTec Surf and Call Center; **VOCALTEC**
Voice Presence; **HEARME.COM**
Votenet; **NETIVATION.COM INC**
Voxware MVP; **VOXWARE**
Voyager.net TV; **VOYAGER.NET**
vPrism; **DIGITAL LAVA INC**
Wahlstrom & Co.; **MODEM MEDIA.POPPE TYSON**
Wall of Sound; **GO.COM**
Wallet Technology; **V-ONE**
Walt Disney Co.; **GO.COM**
Warner Bros.; **TIME WARNER INC**

Watley Trader; **A B WATLEY GROUP INC**
Web Communications, LLC; **VERIO INC**
Web Guides; **LYCOS INC**
Web Prime; **FRONTLINE COMMUNICATIONS**
Web Search; **LYCOS INC**
WebHouse Club; **PRICELINE.COM**
WebMachines; **ZIPLINK INC**
WebMD, Inc.; **HEALTHEON/WEBMD CORP**
WebMechanic; **THINK NEW IDEAS**
WebRamp; **RAMP NETWORKS**
Website Digital Certificate; **VERISIGN**
Websurfer; **ZIPLINK INC**
WebTerm; **WHITE PINE SOFTWARE**
WebTop.com; **DIALOG CORPORATION PLC (THE)**
Web-to-System 390; **NEON SYSTEMS**
WebTrends Commerce Trends; **WEBTRENDS CORP**
WebTrends Enterprise Reporting Server; **WEBTRENDS**
WebTrends Network; **WEBTRENDS CORP**
WebTrends Professional Services Group; **WEBTRENDS**
WebTrends Security Analyzer; **WEBTRENDS CORP**
WebTV; **MICROSOFT CORP**
Webvan; **WEBVAN GROUP INC**
WebWay L.L.C.; **BIZNESS ONLINE.COM INC**
White Pine Software; **WHITE PINE SOFTWARE**
Whitman-Hart, Inc.; **USWEB/CKS**
Whittman-Hart Institute for Strategic Education; **WHITTMAN-HART INC**
Wholesale Auction Center; **CYBER MERCHANTS EXCHANGE INC**
Williams Communications; **ZIPLINK INC**
Wingspan.com; **BANK ONE CORP**
Wink Enhanced Broadcasting; **WINK COMMUNICATIONS**
Wireless Local Loop (WLL); **QUALCOMM INC**
Wit Capital Group, Inc.; **WIT CAPITAL GROUP**
Wizard; **INTERNET PICTURES CORP**
WordPerfect Corporation; **NOVELL INC**
WorkWorld job fairs; **HOTJOBS.COM LTD**
World Consulting Limited; **WHITTMAN-HART INC**
World Wide Magic Net; **CYBER MERCHANTS EXCHANGE INC**
Worldcast; **MEDIUM4.COM INC**
WorldGate Service; **WORLDGATE COMMUNICATIONS**
Worldtalk Corp.; **TUMBLEWEED COMMUNICATIONS**
WOWfactor; **FRONTLINE COMMUNICATIONS**
www.digitalriver.com; **DIGITAL RIVER INC**
www.indieaudio.com; **GLOBAL MEDIA**
www.ndb.com; **NATIONAL DISCOUNT BROKERS**
XETI, Inc.; **CRITICAL PATH INC**
XL Ethernet products; **TUT SYSTEMS**
Yahoo Online service; **YAHOO! INC**
Yahoo!; **ALLOY ONLINE INC**
Yahoo!; **YAHOO! INC**
Yahooligans!; **YAHOO! INC**
YAR Communications, Inc.; **LEAPNET INC**
YouDecide.com; **IXL ENTERPRISES INC**

ZD Net; **XOOM.COM**
ZeroPort; **NETZERO**
Ziff-Davis, Inc.; **ZDNET GROUP**
ZipDial; **ZIPLINK INC**

Appendix A
Quick-Start Instructions and End-User License Agreement
for Plunkett's CD-ROM

Note: Graphics used as examples here may be from books other than the book you purchased—nonetheless, these instructions apply to all Plunkett CDs.

Welcome to Plunkett's CD-ROM. This booklet contains information about installing data from the CD, and information about possible errors that may occur during installation. There are two things you should know before you install:

- You must be running Windows 95 or later to use this CD-ROM.

- The database will be installed from the CD-ROM onto the hard drive of your computer. After installation, you will no longer need the CD-ROM to use the database.

To install the database...
1.   Close any and all open applications.
2.   Insert the CD-ROM into your CD-ROM drive.
3.   Click **Start**, and choose **Run...**.Now, you're going to find setup on your CD-ROM drive, which is frequently **d:\setup.exe** or **e:\setup.exe**. You can do this using "Browse".

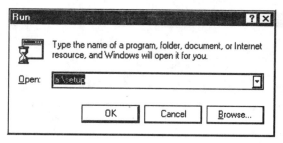

> *Don't worry if your **Run** dialog box doesn't say the same thing as the one shown here. We're going to change what it says in a minute anyway.*

4.   Click **Browse...**.

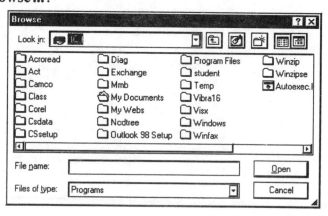

5.   Click the drop-down arrow for **Look in:**.

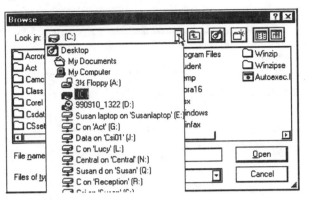

6.   Click the drive for your CD-ROM. (It's probably the D: drive like the one shown here, or perhaps the E: drive.)

7.   Click **setup.exe** and click **Open**. Be sure to click the one that ends with **.exe** (if you don't see an **.exe**, look for a picture next to **setup** that looks like a computer).

8.   Click **OK**. The installation begins, and after displaying a screen telling you that the process has begun, the following dialog box appears:

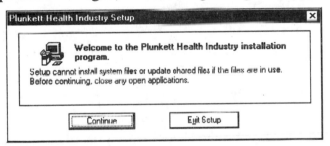

9.   Click **Continue**. The program checks your system for installed components. After a few moments, the next dialog box appears:

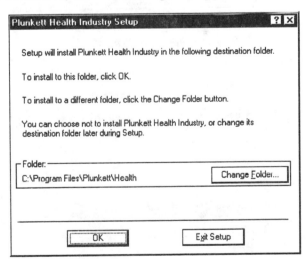

10.   Click **OK**.

*You can change the folder in which the data will be stored by clicking **Change Folder...**, and choosing the name of the folder. For most users, accepting the folder specified works just fine.*

11. Click **Typical** to install the Plunkett data files to their default locations with standard options.

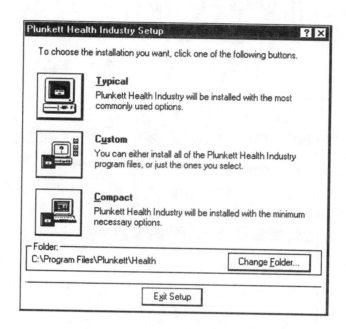

You can also click **Custom** to choose from a list of files to install, or **Compact** to install the minimum number of files necessary to run the program.

 *If you choose **Custom** or **Compact**, you may not have all of the program's options available to you. When in doubt, click **Typical**.*

Once you click an option, the installation program checks for space on your PC and then installs the files to their destinations. The process usually takes several minutes.

12. Click **OK**.

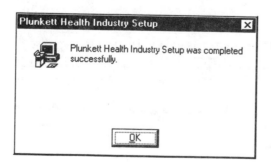

If an error message appears while you are installing...
Some people will see the following error message when installing Plunkett's CD-ROM. Don't panic. There is an easy fix for the problem.

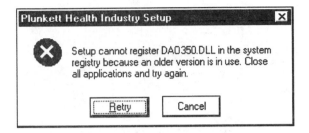

By the way, the reason this error occurs for some people is that there are other programs running in Windows that conflict with the installation. Your job, if you see this error, is to temporarily close those programs.

1. Click **Cancel** to close the error message.
2. Press **[Ctrl+Alt+Delete]**. The Windows Task List appears, listing everything that is currently running on your PC.

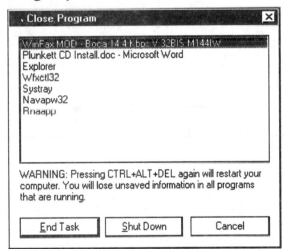

 Don't worry if your list doesn't display the same things as the ones shown here. We're going to change what it says in a minute anyway.

3. If necessary, click the first item in the list (as long as the first item is not **Explorer** or **Systray**). A dark blue highlight appears across an item when it is selected.
4. Click **End Task**. You may see a second window in which you must click **End Task** again.
5. Press **[Ctrl+Alt+Delete]** again to display the list again. Repeat steps 3 and 4 until the only items remaining in the list are **Explorer** and **Systray**.
6. Now begin the Plunkett CD-ROM installation steps again. You should not receive any error messages.

To reinstall the CD-ROM...

If, for some future reason, you find that you need to reinstall the CD-ROM on your computer, you must first <u>uninstall</u> your previous setup and installation. (Otherwise, you will receive error messages.)

1. Click **Start**, point to **Settings**, and choose **Control Panel**.

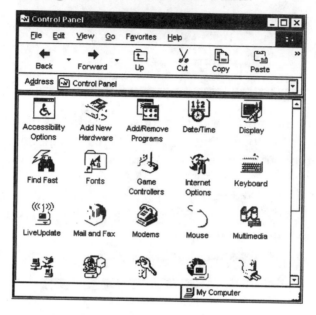

2. Double-click **Add/Remove Programs**.

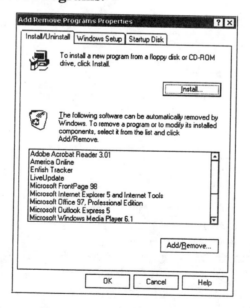

3. You may have to scroll down the list to see the Plunkett CD data you have installed (do this by clicking the down arrow on the scroll bar to the right of the list of programs). When you find it, click it to select it and then click **Add/Remove...**.

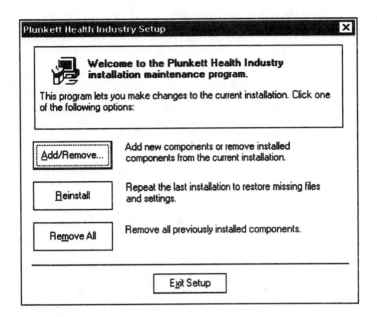

4. A Setup program runs, during which you see the dialog box shown above. Click **Remove All**.
5. Click **Yes** when you are asked if you are sure that you want to remove the program.
6. When the process is complete, close any open windows (such as the Control Panel). Now you are ready to reinstall. Follow the procedures to install on page 452.

To use the CD-ROM Database after Installation...
1. After installation, the database resides on your hard drive. You will not need the CD-ROM to use the program.
2. Click **Start**, point to **Programs**, and click **Plunketts Health Industry** (or the name of the book you have purchased). That's it. The program opens and you're ready to use it. When the program first starts, click **OK** to acknowledge the copyright agreement.

 *The CD-ROM installs an abbreviated version (sometimes called **run-time**) of the powerful Microsoft Access database program at no additional cost to you. If you already have Access, you will have additional features when using Plunkett's data such as the ability to view the entire table underlying the database.*

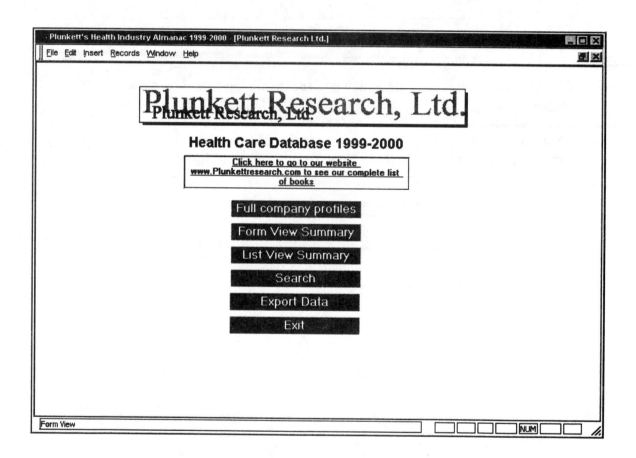

To use a Plunkett database...
1. Click the link at the top of the home page to go directly to the Plunkett Research, Ltd. web site. While there, you can see sample chapters from our entire line of books.
2. The **Full company profiles** button takes you to complete profiles of each of the companies in the database. Navigation arrows at the top enable you to go back and forth or to return to the home page.

3. The **Form View Summary** gives you an abbreviated overview of the entire set of companies in a convenient grid format. Buttons at the top let you sort the list by **Sales, State, Industry Code** and **Number of Employees**. Just click the appropriate button.

4. The **List View Summary** operates similarly to Form View but places the data in long rows rather than a grid format. You can sort here as well by clicking the button you want.

5. Click **Search** to define criteria for the companies that you want to find. You can develop your own set of companies that are, for example, based in California and that operate within the HMO business, *and* that have at least $50 million in yearly sales.

6. **Export Data** gives you two choices. The first button lets you build a set of companies via a custom search and then export it to a Microsoft Excel spreadsheet. The second button lets you build a set of companies and then export it to an ASCII file that can be easily opened by most types of software, including word processors, spreadsheets, contact management software and database software. The export feature enables you to create data that you can use for mail merge letters and other business projects. The data exported includes the selected companies' name, address, phone, fax, web site and executive contact names/titles.

7. Click **Exit** to close the program.

END-USER LICENSE AGREEMENT FOR PLUNKETT DATA DELIVERED ON CD-ROMS AND DISKETTES

Important, read carefully: This agreement is a legal agreement between you (whether as an individual or an organization) and Plunkett Research, Ltd. By installing, copying, downloading, accessing or otherwise using the Plunkett Data, you agree to be bound by the terms of this Agreement. If you do not agree to the terms of this Agreement, do not install or use the Plunkett Data.

Copyright laws and international copyright treaties as well as other intellectual property laws and treaties protect the Plunkett Data.

Plunkett Research, Ltd. grants you as an individual or an organization a non-exclusive license to use and install this data on an individual computer or on a server, provided that the data is not to be distributed in any form beyond a single premises. This is a single-location license, which may be applied to a single user or to multiple users within a single location. Universities, schools, government agencies and businesses operating multiple buildings on one campus may consider the entire campus to be a single location for these purposes.

Entities desiring to distribute the data beyond a single location will need to purchase an additional copy of the CD for each additional location to be served.

Rights under this license may not be sold or transferred.

Customer Remedies: Plunkett Research, Ltd. and its suppliers' entire liability and your exclusive remedy shall be, at Plunkett Research, Ltd.'s option, either (a) return of the price paid, if any, or (b) repair or replacement of the product that does not meet Plunkett Research, Ltd.'s Limited Warranty and that is returned to Plunkett Research, Ltd. with sufficient evidence of or receipt for your original purchase. This Limited Warranty is void if failure of the product has resulted from accident, abuse or misapplication.

Limited Warranty: Plunkett Research, Ltd. makes no warranties, expressed or implied, regarding the accuracy or usability of this product or the data contained herein.

No Other Warranties: To the maximum extent permitted by applicable law, Plunkett Research, Ltd. and its suppliers disclaim all other warranties and conditions, either expressed or implied, including, but not limited to, implied warranties or conditions of merchantability, fitness for a particular purpose, title and non-infringement, with regard to the product, and the provision of or failure to provide support services. This limited warranty gives you specific legal rights. You may have others, which vary from state/jurisdiction to state/jurisdiction.

Limitation of Liability: To the maximum extent permitted by applicable law, in no event shall Plunkett Research, Ltd. or its suppliers be liable for any special, incidental or consequential damages whatsoever (including, without limitation, damages for loss of business profits, business interruption, loss of business information, ability to obtain or retain employment or remuneration, ability to profitably make an investment, or any other pecuniary loss) arising out of the use of or inability to use this product or the failure to provide support services, even if Plunkett Research, Ltd. has been advised of the possibility of such damages. In any case, Plunkett Research, Ltd.'s entire liability under any provision of this End-User License Agreement shall be limited to the greater amount of the amount actually paid by you for the product or U.S.$5.00. Because some states/jurisdictions do not allow the exclusion or limitation of liability, the above limitation may not apply to you.

Plunkett's CD-ROM version 1.0
Copyright © 1999, Plunkett Research, Ltd., all rights reserved